The Liris River near Arpinum, the Birthplace of Cicero

THIRD YEAR LATIN

REVISION OF KELSEY'S CICERO

WITH

ADDED SELECTIONS FROM CICERO, SALLUST,
LIVY, AND PLINY

ARRANGED AND EDITED

WITH EXPLANATORY NOTES, A COMPANION INCLUDING
ESSENTIALS OF GRAMMAR AND SYNTAX,
AND A VOCABULARY

BY

BRUNO MEINECKE, PH.D.
UNIVERSITY OF MICHIGAN

1962

ALLYN AND BACON, INC.

BOSTON   ENGLEWOOD CLIFFS   CHICAGO
ATLANTA   SAN FRANCISCO   DALLAS

PRINTED IN THE UNITED STATES OF AMERICA

TO

MY BELOVED FATHER

THE REVEREND

PETER CHRISTOPHER WILHELM MEINECKE

DOCTOR OF DIVINITY

UNDER WHOSE WISE GUIDANCE

A LOVE FOR THE CLASSICS

WAS EARLY INSTILLED AND NURTURED

Nil me paeniteat sanum patris huius.
— HORACE

PREFACE

The present volume conforms fully to all requirements for a third year Latin course as defined by the College Entrance Examination Board, the Syllabus in Latin of New York State, and the Classical Investigation.

Shortly after the close of the Great War Professor Francis W. Kelsey had recognized the desirability of revising his Cicero and making some additions, but the numerous projects in which he was constantly engaged and his untimely death prevented the execution of this plan. The writer, therefore, considers it a privilege and an honor to have been chosen to do this work, and thereby help to perpetuate the memory of a man whom he greatly loved and esteemed, a man who was both a humanist and a scholar.

This book contains enough material from Cicero's writings alone to occupy the student's time for more than a full year, and these selections have been so chosen and so organized as to present a great variety of style, and at the same time provide a unified view of his life and career reconstructed in the original. There are also the parallel passages from Sallust's Conspiracy of Catiline, the poetic and romantic chapters from Livy, and the fascinating Letters of Pliny. Thus the book comprises a wide range of reading material to suit various tastes and requirements.

The sectional headings are designed to give continuity to the text, and to focus the student's attention and interest. For instance, the first two selections under " Cicero and Caesar " will suggest a natural transition from the second to the third year's work, and so help to create for the student a familiar environment. These and the Catilinarian Orations should be read in the order of presentation.

The Illustrations. — *Third Latin* has been profusely illustrated
by more than two hundred pictures, many of them being originals collected by Professor Kelsey on his expeditions. These
pictures were mostly photographed by Mr. George R. Swain,
Photographer to the University of Michigan, and are designed
to furnish a visual background for interpreting the text as well
as to portray basic aspects of ancient culture. They should
receive fully as much attention as the rest of the text.

The Text. — The Latin text corresponds in general with the
Teubner editions except in a few passages where the editor
exercised his own judgment. The following selections with
their notes, revised, adapted, rearranged, and occasionally
re-written, are from Professor Kelsey's edition of Cicero: The
Oration for Marcellus, The Four Catilinarian Orations, The
Manilian Law, The Looting of Syracuse from the Verres
Oration, The Oration for Archias, The Dē Senectūte, and
The Dē Amīcitiā.

The Companion. — Every effort has been made to produce
a volume that is usable and practical; for that reason all material which is not a component part of the text and notes has
been systematically arranged in the Companion, pages 485ff.
In this way all explanatory matter, including biographies, outlines, the Greek alphabet, and further practical helps and suggestions, may be easily found. Such an arrangement is logical
and natural, and brings related material into juxtaposition.

The Notes. — The notes are at the bottom of the page, where
they should be. They have been written with a view to adopting a *modus in rēbus* between generous doses of "placebo"
and misplaced scholarship. Half-truths, however, have been
religiously avoided, because they fail to offer real help to the
student and seriously interfere with his progress and success in
Latin study. He is given a gentle lift over difficult passages to
avoid complete discouragement, but at the same time it is
realized that a third year high school student has intelligence
capable of being stimulated. This viewpoint explains the use
of simple Latin quotations from other authors, and references

here and there to well-known Latin writers. In the selections from the Dē Senectūte and the Dē Amīcitiā the author has boldly introduced even some Greek words and quotations, but these are always apropos, and are either translated or otherwise explained. Cicero's philosophy can hardly be studied apart from a Greek atmosphere, which the text aims to create in part. Brevity may be "the soul of wit," but Horace is equally right when he says: *Brevis esse labōrō, Obscūrus fīō.* No apology is offered for the use of cross references, for they help to bind the book together into a compact whole. Grammatical references also have been inserted in addition to those to the Companion to throw further light on some points of syntax.

The Vocabulary. — From the student's viewpoint the vocabulary represents the hub of the book. For that reason, every effort has been employed to make it practical and complete. The teacher should direct all Word Study from this as a source, and associate it with sections 74–86 under Essentials of Latin Grammar. Most of the approved etymologies have been indicated in the vocabulary, and all proper names have received more than ordinary attention.

Grammar and Syntax. — This portion of the book is unusually full and complete. The principles and rules have been briefly stated, and in each instance are fortified by illustrations located in the Latin text. An Index at the back of the volume will be found helpful.

English Pronunciation of Proper Names. — Proper names have been Anglicized in the notes on the page where they first occur. In the vocabulary such words also have been frequently provided with accent marks to remind the student. Here, as elsewhere, the trite old saying, *Repetitiō est māter studiōrum,* coupled with infinite patience will insure accuracy. The Key will be found in the Companion, page 709.

Cicero and the Modern World. — Interesting suggestions are offered in the Companion to associate ancient and modern life, and to make the study of Cicero real and tangible. Parallels should be constantly employed in the form of oral discussions and themes. The modern Latin teacher, who keeps up with the times, will find frequent opportunity to impress the student with the modernity of ancient thinking.

To the Teacher. — The first recitation should be used to familiarize the student with the plan and make-up of the book from cover to cover. A special effort should be put forth to orient the student, for experience has shown that, unless this is done, the average student rarely comes to know his text well enough to gain the maximum benefit from its use. No book will succeed in inculcating on the mind and heart of the modern student the spiritual contribution of the great Greek and Roman nations unless the teacher constantly charges the atmosphere of the classroom with love and enthusiasm for excellence and high achievement, and consecrates himself to the ideal so perfectly expressed by Terence: *Homō sum; hūmānī nihil ā mē aliēnum putō.*

The editor wishes to express his indebtedness to Mrs. Francis W. Kelsey for so willingly offering the use of Professor Kelsey's library; to Professor Henry A. Sanders of the University of Michigan for reading a part of the proof and for other valuable suggestions; to Dr. Axel Boethius, Director of the Swedish Archeological Institute in Rome, for the use of photographs from his personal collection; to Malcolm F. McGregor of British Columbia for his work on the Index; to Dr. Orma F. Butler of the University of Michigan for numerous courtesies; and especially to Dr. Eugene S. McCartney, Editor of Scholarly Publications in the Graduate School of the University of Michigan, for invaluable assistance, freely given.

Ann Arbor, Michigan,   Bruno Meinecke
    August 5, 1933.

CONTENTS

TEXT AND NOTES

CONTENTS

LIST OF ILLUSTRATIONS

xv

MAPS AND PLANS

CICERO AND CAESAR

CICERO AND CAESAR

M. TULLĪ CICERŌNIS
DĒ PRŌVINCIĪS CŌNSULĀRIBUS
IN SENĀTŪ ŌRĀTIŌ

Partēs Sēlēctae

*The public interest demands that Caesar continue in Gaul; he has won my
favor by his remarkable achievements.*

8. Quod sī essent illī optimī virī, tamen ego meā
sententiā C. Caesarī succēdendum nōndum putārem.
Quā dē rē dīcam, patrēs cōnscrīptī, quae sentiō, atque

To THE STUDENT: The background for this oration is reconstructed in
the Companion, pages 509 to 511, where the part preceding chapter 8 is
summarized.

Title. M. TULLĪ CICERŌNIS: For
Tullī instead of Tulliī, see the Companion, *8, a.* For the probable derivation of Cicero's name, see the
vocabulary under *Cicerō.*

8. 1. **Quod sī ... virī:** ' But
if Gabinius and Piso (*illī*) were
men of the highest integrity.' *208,
a (1).* Figures in light italic type
like the preceding refer to the Companion at the back of the book.
ego ... putārem: ' I should still
not favor the proposal to supersede
Gaius Caesar '; how literally?

2. **C. Caesarī:** dative with compound verb. *107, a.* **succēdendum:** its subject is impersonal.
239, c.

3. **patrēs cōnscrīptī:** the common translation ' conscript fathers '

CICERO

The bust in the Vatican Museum at
Rome.

(compare Macaulay, in *The Battle of Lake Regillus:* Now hearken, conscript fathers, to that which I advise) is not accurate. Originally, the

illam interpellātiōnem meī familiārissimī, quā paulō ante
5 interrupta est ōrātiō mea, nōn pertimēscam. Negat mē vir
optimus inimīciōrem Gabīniō dēbēre esse quam Caesarī;
omnem illam tempestātem, cui cesserim, Caesare impulsōre
atque adiūtōre, esse excitātam. Cui sī prīmum sīc respondeam, mē commūnis ūtilitātis habēre ratiōnem, nōn dolōris
10 meī, possimne probāre, cum id mē facere dīcam, quod
exemplō fortissimōrum et clārissimōrum cīvium facere
possim?

Bellum in Galliā maximum gestum est; domitae sunt ā
Caesare maximae nātiōnēs, sed nōndum lēgibus, nōndum

---

phrase was *patrēs et cōnscrīptī*, 'patricians and (elected) plebeians,' but it
came to lose all suggestion of social distinction. It should be translated ·
'gentlemen of the senate,' or simply 'senators.'

4. **interpellātiōnem:** by the consul L. Philippus, mentioned in a
subsequent chapter.

5. **vir optimus:** ' the honorable gentleman.'

6. **Gabīniō** (gạ-bin'i̯-ụs) (see Key to Pronunciation, page 709): consul
in 58 B.C. and proconsul of Syria the next year. He led a profligate life,
and had a part in promoting Cicero's exile in 58 B.C. *108, a.*

7. **cui cesserim:** ' to which I have fallen heir.' *214, a.* **Caesare
impulsōre:** *144, a; 211.* Cicero does not deny the truth of this, but
he insists that past animosities are forgotten in the present crisis.

8. **Cui sī:** = *eī sī.* **sī. . . respondeam. . . possim:** type of conditional sentence? *207 (1).*

9. **mē . . . ratiōnem:** ' that I am concerned about the public interest.'

10. **possimne probāre:** ' should I not be able to make good my
case?' While the *-ne* is regularly neutral, it may have its original
negative force if the context so colors it. *179, a (1).*

11. **exemplō:** ' precedent.' The specific illustrations, cited from
Roman history, are here omitted.

13. **domitae sunt . . . maximae nātiōnēs:** Caesar had thus far subdued the Helvetii, Ariovistus, and the Belgians. Since this oration was
delivered approximately in June of 56 B.C. and Caesar had received the
provinces of Gaul for a period of five years, that is, till the end of 54 B.C.,
he still had more than two years left to administer his command.
However, his enemies wished to remove him before that time.

iūre certō, nōndum satis fīrmā pāce dēvinctae. Bellum 15
affectum vidēmus et, vērē ut dīcam, paene cōnfectum, sed
ita, ut, sī īdem extrēma persequitur, quī incohāvit, iam omnia

perfecta videāmus, sī succēditur,
perīculum sit, nē īnstaurātās
maximī bellī reliquiās ac renovā- 20
tās audiāmus. Ergō ego senātor
— inimīcus, sī ita vultis, hominī
— amīcus esse, sīcut semper fuī,
reī pūblicae dēbeō. Quid? sī
ipsās inimīcitiās dēpōnō reī 25
pūblicae causā, quis mē tandem
iūre reprehendet? praesertim
cum ego omnium meōrum cōnsiliōrum atque factōrum exempla
semper ex summōrum hominum 30
factīs mihi cēnsuerim petenda.

---

15. **dēvinctae :** sc. *sunt;* from *dēvincīre,* ' to bind together.'

16. **affectum :** ' has progressed favorably.' See Aulus Gellius, **3,** 16.
cōnfectum : ' successfully finished.' Notice the wordplay, called
' paronomasia '; *239, q.* **sed ita,** etc.: ' but it has been brought to such
a point that, if the same man who began it follows it out to the end, we
shall presently see everything successfully carried out, (but) if he is
superseded, there will be danger lest we may hear that the smoldering
ashes of a mighty conflict have been fully revived.' **dīcam:** *196, b.*

19. **īnstaurātās ac renovātās :** Cicero frequently combines synonyms
for emphasis; in English we prefer an adverb; see translation above.

20. **reliquiās :** refers to the remains or ashes of a deceased person.

22. **hominī :** Caesar; used in place of *is* when a person is to be
emphatically set apart.

24. **Quid :** ' Again '; often used to indicate a transition.

25. **ipsās inimīcitiās :** ' even my personal animosities.' *162, a.* **In**
this sense the Latin noun is regularly in the plural.

27. **praesertim cum . . . cēnsuerim :** causal. *184, b.*

29. **exempla :** ' models,' subject of *petenda (esse).*

Caesar desires to remain in Gaul not because he finds life there attractive,
but because he is impelled by a sense of duty to complete the task
which he has begun.

12. At ego īdem nunc in prōvinciīs dēcernendīs, quī
illās omnīs rēs ēgī silentiō, interpellor, cum in superiōribus
causīs hominis ōrnāmenta fuerint, in hāc mē nihil aliud nisi
ratiō bellī, nisi summa ūtilitās reī pūblicae moveat. Nam
5 ipse Caesar quid est cūr in prōvinciā commorārī velit, nisi
ut ea, quae per eum affecta sunt, perfecta reī pūblicae
trādat? Amoenitās eum, crēdō, locōrum, urbium pulchritūdō, hominum nātiōnumque illārum hūmānitās et lepōs,
victōriae cupiditās, fīnium imperī prōpāgātiō retinet. Quid
10 illīs terrīs asperius, quid incultius oppidīs, quid nātiōnibus
immānius, quid porrō tot victōriīs praestābilius, quid
Ōceanō longius invenīrī potest? An reditus in patriam
habet aliquam offēnsiōnem? Utrum apud populum, ā

---

12. 1. **īdem:** 'also.' **quī . . . silentiō:** 'who have made all of the
foregoing proposals without interruption.' In a previous chapter, here
omitted, Cicero enumerates these proposals, such as a *supplicātiō* of
fifteen days, additional pay for the army, and an increase in Caesar's
military staff.

2. **silentiō:** ablative of manner; one of several stock expressions
used without the preposition. *136, b.* **cum . . . fuerint:** 'although in
the previous suggestions personal honors to Caesar were involved.'

3. **hominis:** see note on page 3, line 22. **in hāc:** '(whereas) in the
present case.' *238, d; 160, a.*

4. **ratiō bellī:** 'a military policy.'

5. **ipse Caesar:** 'as for Caesar himself.'

6. **affecta, perfecta:** see note on page 3, line 16. Paronomasia.
239, q.

7. **Amoenitās locōrum:** 'Attractive surroundings.' **crēdō:** ironical. *239, l.*

8. **hūmānitās et lepōs:** 'culture and charm.'

9. **prōpāgātiō:** 'extension.'

11. **praestābilius:** 'more desirable.'

12. **Ōceanō:** the Atlantic.

13. **habet offēnsiōnem:** 'involve unpopularity.'

quō missus, an apud senātum, ā quō ōrnātus est? An
diēs auget eius dēsīderium, an magis oblīviōnem, ac laurea 15
illa magnīs perīculīs parta āmittit longō intervāllō viridi-
tātem? Quā rē, sī quī hominem nōn dīligunt, nihil est
quod eum dē prōvinciā dēvocent; ad glōriam dēvocant,
ad triumphum, ad grātulātiōnem, ad summum honōrem
senātūs, equestris ōrdinis grātiam, populī cāritātem. Sed 20
sī ille hāc tam eximiā fortūnā propter ūtilitātem reī pūblicae
fruī nōn properat, ut omnia illa cōnficiat, quid ego senātor
facere dēbeō, quem, etiam sī ille aliud vellet, reī pūblicae
cōnsulere oportēret?

Caesar has substituted aggressive warfare against the Gauls
for our defensive policy of old.

13. Bellum Gallicum, patrēs cōnscrīptī, C. Caesare
imperātōre, gestum est, anteā tantummodo repulsum.
Semper illās nātiōnēs nostrī imperātōrēs refūtandās potius

---

14. **ōrnātus**: ' honored,' as suggested above in note to line 2. **An
diēs,** etc.: ' Does time (*diēs*) add to our longing for him, or tend to make
us forget him, and does the glorious (*illa*) laurel, won at great risk, lose
its freshness after a long interval? '

16. **parta**: from *parĕre*.

17. **hominem**: see note on page 3, line 22. **nihil est quod . . . dēvocent**: ' there is no reason why they should call him home.'

18. **dēvocent**: *194, a.*

21. **ille**: ' Caesar.' This pronoun sometimes emphatically indicates a noun just mentioned. In English we prefer to repeat the noun.
tam: omit here; why?

22. **ut omnia illa cōnficiat**: ' in order that he may bring all of his
plans to a successful issue.' *illa* is the demonstrative of the third
person. *160, a.*

23. **quem . . . oportēret**: ' whom it would behoove to consult for
the good of the state.' **etiam sī . . . vellet**: ' even if Caesar wished
otherwise.' Contrary to fact condition. *208, a.*

13. 2. **gestum est**: ' has been waged aggressively.' **repulsum**:
' warded off.'

3. **refūtandās**: ' were to be withstood.' *63.*

bellō quam lacessendās putā-
5 vērunt. Ipse ille C. Marius,
cuius dīvīna atque eximia virtūs
magnīs populī Rōmānī lūctibus
fūneribusque subvēnit, īnfluentīs
in Italiam Gallōrum maximās
10 cōpiās repressit, nōn ipse ad
eōrum urbīs sēdīsque penetrāvit.
Modo ille meōrum labōrum perīculōrum cōnsiliōrum socius,
C. Pomptīnus, fortissimus vir,
15 ortum repente bellum Allobrogum atque hāc scelerātā coniūrātiōne excitātum proeliīs frēgit
eōsque domuit quī lacessīverant,
et eā victōriā contentus, rē

MARIUS

A statue in the Capitoline
Museum at Rome.

5. **Ipse ille C. Marius:** 'Even the famous Gaius Marius.' *160, f.*

7. **lūctibus fūneribusque:** 'sorrows and deaths.' Dative with compounds. *107, a.*

12. **Modo:** 'Just lately.'

14. **C. Pomptīnus** (gā′(y)ụs pom(p)-tī′nụs) : praetor in 63 B.C., who
rendered important service to Cicero in the Catilinarian conspiracy, and
is mentioned, *In Catilīnam,* **3,** 2; 6.

15. **Allobrogum:** Pomptinus arrested the envoys of the Allobroges at
the Mulvian bridge. See *In Catilīnam* **3,** 2; Sallust, *Catilīna* 45.

COIN OF THE ROMAN REPUBLIC

Obverse: Head of the Goddess Roma.   **Reverse:** Marius in a Quadriga.

pūblicā metū līberātā, quiēvit. C. Caesaris longē aliam 20
videō fuisse ratiōnem; nōn enim sibi sōlum cum iīs quōs
iam armātōs contrā populum Rōmānum vidēbat bellandum
esse dūxit, sed tōtam Galliam in nostram diciōnem esse
redigendam. Itaque cum ācerrimīs nātiōnibus et maximīs
Germānōrum et Helvētiōrum proeliīs fēlīcissimē dēcertāvit, 25

SITE OF THE BATTLE WITH THE HELVETIANS

View from the hill where Caesar's army was posted, looking toward the
right. The hill on which Caesar took up his position, and the height to which
the Helvetians retreated, are similar to this hill in formation and appearance.

cēterās conterruit, compulit, domuit, imperiō populī Rōmānī
pārēre assuēfēcit, et quās regiōnēs quāsque gentīs nūllae
nōbīs anteā litterae, nūlla vōx, nūlla fāma nōtās fēcerat,
hās noster imperātor nosterque exercitus et populī Rōmānī
arma peragrārunt. Sēmitam tantum Galliae tenēbāmus 30

20. **līberātā:** *212, a.* **C. Caesaris:** in emphatic position. *211.*
22. **bellandum esse dūxit:** ' considered that war must be waged.'
24. **maximīs:** ' decisive.' *212, n.*
30. **peragrārunt:** contracted form for *peragrāvērunt;* syncope. *238, n.*

anteā, patrēs cōnscrīptī; cēterae partēs ā gentibus aut
inimīcīs huic imperiō aut īnfīdīs aut incognitīs aut certē
immānibus et barbarīs et bellicōsīs tenēbantur; quās
nātiōnēs nēmō umquam fuit quīn frangī domārīque cuperet.
35 Nēmō sapienter dē rē pūblicā nostrā cōgitāvit iam inde ā
prīncipiō huius imperī, quīn Galliam maximē timendam
huic imperiō putāret; sed propter vim ac multitūdinem
gentium illārum numquam est anteā cum omnibus dīmicātum. Restitimus semper lacessītī. Nunc dēnique est
40 perfectum, ut imperī nostrī terrārumque illārum idem esset
extrēmum.

*Even if I still harbored a feeling of resentment against Caesar, it would be
incumbent upon me to forgive and forget. My reconciliation with
Caesar springs from a grateful heart, and I shall vote for him.*

20. Extrēmum illud est. Ego, sī essent inimīcitiae
mihi cum C. Caesare, tamen hōc tempore reī pūblicae
cōnsulere, inimīcitiās in aliud tempus reservāre dēbērem.
Possem etiam summōrum virōrum exemplō inimīcitiās reī

Sēmitam : ' A mere path.' This refers to the southern portion of Gaul
along the Mediterranean, which served as a road to Spain.

33. **quās:** = *et eās. 167.*

34. **nātiōnēs:** subject of *frangī domārīque.* **quīn:** translate as if *quī
nōn.* **cuperet:** subjunctive of characteristic. *194, a; 195.*

35. **iam inde ā prīncipiō:** ' even from the very beginning.'

36. **quīn:** as above, line 32. **Galliam maximē timendam:** this was
literally true; for the Gauls had always been one of Rome's most
formidable enemies, until Caesar took matters in hand.

38. **est dīmicātum:** impersonal. *172, e.*

39. **est perfectum:** its subject is the following *ut*-clause.

40. **extrēmum:** ' border '; an adjective used substantively.

20. 1. **Extrēmum illud est:** ' This is my last word.' **sī:** = *etsī.*

4. **Possem . . . dēpōnere:** ' I might lay aside.' Potential subjunctive. While the imperfect subjunctive of *posse* may represent the
potential of the past (' could have,' ' might have '), it is more often used
of present time. *180, e (3).* **summōrum virōrum exemplō:** the prece-

pūblicae causā dēpōnere. Sed cum inimīcitiae fuerint 5 numquam, opīniō iniūriae beneficiō sit exstīncta, sententiā

CONQUERED GAUL, PER-
SONIFIED

A coin struck to com-
memorate Caesar's con-
quest of Gaul. Behind
the head is a Gallic war-
trumpet.

meā, patrēs cōnscrīptī, sī dignitās agitur Caesaris, hominī tribuam; sī honōs quīdam, senātūs concordiae cōnsulam; sī auctōritās dēcrētōrum 10 vestrōrum, cōnstantiam ōrdinis in eōdem ōrnandō imperātōre servābō; sī perpetua ratiō Gallicī bellī, reī pūblicae prōvidēbō; sī aliquod meum prīvātum officium, mē nōn ingrātum 15 esse praestābō. Atque hōc velim probāre omnibus, patrēs cōnscrīptī; sed levissimē feram, sī forte aut iīs minus probāverō, quī meum

dents referred to on pages 2 and 3; 'on the strength of precedents furnished by the most eminent men.'

5. **cum**: causal. **inimīcitiae fuerint numquam**: the differences between Cicero and Caesar were political rather than personal.

6. **opīniō iniūriae . . . sit exstīncta**: sc. *et;* asyndeton. *238, d;* ' and since the impression of wrong (done me) has been wiped out.'

7. **sī dignitās agitur Caesaris**: ' if Caesar's official position is at stake.'

8. **hominī** is used as on page 3, line 22; see note. **tribuam**: prob-ably an absolute use, ' I shall give him his due by my vote.' **sī honōs quīdam**: sc. *agitur*, as also in the following *sī*-clauses.

14. **meum prīvātum officium**: ' some personal favor of my own.' Note the distinction between *officium* and *beneficiō* in line 6 above; viz. *officium* = a favor or service rendered to one whose claim to it is recog-nized, whereas *beneficium* = a favor or service rendered where there is no claim.

15. **nōn ingrātum**: litotes. *239, m.*

16. **Atque . . . omnibus**: ' And so I should like to make this view acceptable to you all.' **velim**: potential subjunctive. *180, e (1).*

18. **levissimē feram**: ' I shall endure it without great difficulty.'

19. **meum inimīcum**: Clodius, Cicero's most bitter enemy. See Companion, pages 490–493.

20 inimīcum repugnante vestrā auctōritāte tēxērunt, aut iīs,
sī quī meum cum inimīcō suō reditum in grātiam vituperābunt, cum ipsī et cum meō et cum suō inimīcō in grātiam
nōn dubitāverint redīre.

21. sī quī . . . vituperābunt: 'if any will disparage my reconciliation (*reditum in grātiam*) with their enemy,' namely, Caesar.
22. cum meō et suō inimīcō: Clodius. See page 381, line 57, note.

M. TULLĪ CICERŌNIS
PRŌ M. MĀRCELLŌ ŌRĀTIŌ

Partēs Sēlēctae

*Great, Caesar, are your deeds of war, but greater still your
deeds of peace.*

2. Nūllīus tantum flūmen est ingenī, nūllīus dīcendī
aut scrībendī tanta vīs, tanta cōpia, quae nōn dīcam exōrnāre, sed ēnārrāre, C. Caesar, rēs tuās gestās possit. Tamen
affīrmō, et hōc pāce dīcam tuā, nūllam in hīs esse laudem
ampliōrem quam eam, quam hodiernō diē cōnsecūtus es. 5

Soleō saepe ante oculōs pōnere idque libenter crēbrīs
ūsūrpāre sermōnibus, omnēs nostrōrum imperātōrum,
omnēs exterārum gentium potentissimōrumque populōrum,
omnēs clārissimōrum rēgum rēs gestās cum tuīs nec contentiōnum magnitūdine nec numerō proeliōrum nec vari- 10

To the Student: The occasion and circumstances of delivery together
with an outline of the oration will be found on page 511 of the Companion.

2. 1. Nūllīus: the regular genitive of *nēmō;* a predicate genitive of
possession; not to be taken with *ingenī.*   Translate, ' No one has such
a flow of genius.'

2. nōn dīcam: parenthetical. **exōrnāre, ēnārrāre:** ' embellish,'
' fully relate.'   Notice the wordplay. *212, d.*

3. possit: *195;* B. 284, 2; A. & G. 537, 2; G. 631. The letters
before these figures refer to the Latin grammars of Bennett, Allen and
Greenough, and Gildersleeve, respectively.

4. pāce tuā: ' with your permission.' **laudem ampliōrem quam
eam, quam:** notice the effect of the final letter of each word.

6. idque . . . ūsūrpāre: ' to dwell upon this (statement),' namely,
omnēs, etc.

10. numerō proeliōrum: Pliny the Elder (*Historia Nātūrālis,* **7,** 25,
92) says that Caesar fought in fifty pitched battles, being the only

11

etāte regiōnum nec celeritāte cōnficiendī nec dissimilitū-
dine bellōrum posse cōnferrī, nec vērō disiūnctissimās
terrās citius passibus cuiusquam potuisse peragrārī, quam
tuīs nōn dīcam cursibus, sed victōriīs lūstrātae sunt.

To win victories is glorious; to forgive is godlike.

3. Domuistī gentēs immānitāte barbarās, multitūdine
innumerābilēs, locīs īnfīnītās, omnī cōpiārum genere abun-
dantēs; sed tamen ea vīcistī, quae et nātūram et condi-
ciōnem, ut vincī possent, habēbant. Nūlla est enim tanta
5 vīs, quae nōn ferrō et vīribus dēbilitārī frangīque possit.
Animum vincere, īrācundiam cohibēre, victōriam tempe-

---

commander that surpassed the number of Marcus Marcellus, the con-
queror of Syracuse, who fought in thirty-nine. **varietāte regiōnum:**
Gaul, Britain, Germany, Spain, Italy, Epirus, Thessaly, Asia Minor,
Egypt, Africa.

11. **celeritāte cōnficiendī:** speed was Caesar's watchword in his
military campaigns; "*Vēnī, vīdī, vīcī,*" the words with which he
announced his victory over Pharnaces (fär'nạ-sēz) in Pontus, 47 B.C., may
well be suggested by Cicero's alliterative phrase.

12. **disiūnctissimās terrās citius:** in the Civil War, 49–46 B.C.

13. **passibus cuiusquam potuisse peragrārī:** 'could have been
traversed by the footsteps of anyone.'

14. **nōn dīcam:** exactly as in line 2 above. **cursibus:** 'by your
marches.' **lūstrātae sunt:** *237, d.*

3. 1. **gentēs immānitāte barbarās:** 'nations savage in their
cruelty.' He is referring to the Gallic campaigns.

2. **locīs īnfīnītās:** 'unlimited in territory.' **cōpiārum:** 'resources.'

3. **ea vīcistī, quae:** 'you have conquered forces which.'

6. **Animum:** adversative asyndeton, *i.e.* omission of an adversative
conjunction, such as 'but,' 'however,' 'nevertheless,' 'yet,' etc.; here
'but' should be used. *238, d;* B. 346, *b*); A. & G. 323, *b; 601, c;*
G. 473, R; 483, N. **vincere, etc.:** the infinitives have a loose dependence
on *iūdico* (line 12), but are gathered up by *haec,* the form of the sentence
having been changed after it was started; this lack of grammatical
consistency is called anacoluthon. *238, a;* B. 374, 6; A. & G. 640;
G. 697. **īrācundiam cohibēre:** see Proverbs, **16,** 32 : "He that is slow to
anger is better than the mighty; and he that ruleth his spirit than he
that taketh a city."

That Julius Caesar was a famous man;
With what his valour did enrich his wit,
His wit set down to make his valour live:
Death makes no conquest of this conqueror;
For now he lives in fame, though not in life. — RICHARD III.

rāre, adversārium nōbilitāte, ingeniō, virtūte praestantem
nōn modo extollere iacentem, sed etiam amplificāre eius
prīstinam dignitātem, haec quī facit, nōn ego eum cum
summīs virīs comparō, 10
sed simillimum deō
iūdicō.

THE GODDESS OF VICTORY

She bears a Gallic war trumpet, in commemoration of a victory over Gauls. From
a relief at Pompeii.

Itaque, C. Caesar,
bellicae tuae laudēs cele-
brābuntur illae quidem 15
nōn sōlum nostrīs, sed
paene omnium gentium
litterīs atque linguīs,
nec ūlla umquam aetās
dē tuīs laudibus conti- 20
cēscet; sed tamen eius
modī rēs nesciō quō
modō, etiam cum le-
guntur, obstrepī clāmōre
mīlitum videntur et 25
tubārum sonō.

7. **adversārium . . . iacentem:** 'not merely to lift up a prostrate
foe outstanding in birth, ability, and merit.' These words are meant to
reflect credit on Caesar's pardon of Marcellus. How would they apply?

9. **dignitātem:** 'eminence.' **haec:** see note 6 above.

15. **illae quidem:** very emphatic position, supported by *quidem*,
'surely.'

17. **omnium gentium litterīs . . . :** Has this prophecy been fulfilled?

21. **eius modī rēs nesciō quō modō:** 'such praises somehow.'

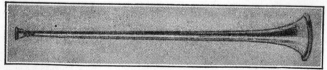

A ROMAN TUBA

24. **obstrepī:** we say, 'to be drowned out.' **clāmōre mīlitum . . .**
tubārum sonō: 'by the cheering of the soldier . . . by the blare of

At vērō cum aliquid clēmenter, mānsuētē, iūstē, moderātē, sapienter factum, in īrācundiā praesertim, quae est
inimīca cōnsiliō, et in victōriā, quae nātūrā īnsolēns et
30 superba est, audīmus aut legimus, quō studiō incendimur,
nōn modo in gestīs rēbus, sed etiam in fictīs, ut eōs saepe,
quōs numquam vīdimus, dīligāmus!
4. Et cēterōs quidem omnēs victōrēs bellōrum cīvīlium
iam ante aequitāte et misericordiā vīcerās: hodiernō vērō
diē tē ipsum vīcistī. Vereor, ut hōc, quod dīcam, perinde
intellegī possit audītum, atque ipse cōgitāns sentiō; ipsam
5 victōriam vīcisse vidēris, cum ea, quae illa erat adepta,

---

trumpets.' Notice the chiastic order. *239, e;* B. 350, 11, *c*); A. &
G. 598, *f* and N.; G. 682 and R. The ancient *tuba* must not be confused
with its modern namesake, for it was a long, straight horn; the ancient
cornū was curved. See illustration, page 13.

28. **in īrācundiā:** ' in the heat of passion.' *145, d.*
29. **in victōriā:** ' in the flush of victory.' **īnsolēns et superba:**
especially in civil war. 'And in one respect particularly,' Cicero wrote
to Sulpicius shortly after this speech was delivered (*Ad Familiārēs,*
4, 4, 2), ' your lot is better than mine, because you can freely write what
gives you pain, but I cannot do even this with safety; and that too
not the fault of our conqueror, — whose self-command is simply wonderful, — but because victory in a civil war is always arrogant.'
30. **quō studiō incendimur:** ' what a thrill we experience.' How
literally?
31. **in gestīs rēbus . . . in fictīs:** ' in real life . . . in fiction.'
in fictīs (rēbus) refers to the drama, the epic, a story, or even a picture.
ut . . . dīligāmus: for the sentiment see Selections from the *Dē
Amīcitiā*, page 302, line 24: ' There is nothing more' attractive than a
noble character, nothing more draws out our affection; we even in a way
conceive an affection for those whom we have never seen, on account
of their lofty character and uprightness.'
4. 1. **victōrēs bellōrum cīvīlium:** such as Sulla and Marius.
3. **ut:** how to be translated after verbs of fearing? Why? *202;*
B. 296, 2; A. & G. 564; G. 550, 2. **perinde . . . atque ipse cōgitāns
sentiō:** ' just as I myself think and feel it.' *211; 228, a.*
4. **audītum:** modifies *hōc,* ' this . . . on being heard.'
5. **illa:** i.e. *victōria.* Note emphasis on ' victory,' in this chapter.

victīs remīsistī. Nam cum ipsīus victōriae condiciōne
omnēs victī occidissēmus, clēmentiae tuae iūdiciō cōnservātī sumus. Rēctē igitur ūnus invictus es, ā quō etiam
ipsīus victōriae condiciō vīsque dēvicta est.

*Throughout the Civil War I constantly agitated for peace. I followed
Pompey as an individual, not as a politician.*

5. Quō quidem in bellō semper dē pāce audiendum putāvī
semperque doluī nōn modo pācem, sed etiam ōrātiōnem

---

6. **cum:** concessive. *187, a.*

7. **omnēs victī:** ' all of us, the vanquished.' Cicero also had a
share in the opposition to Caesar. **occidissēmus:** ' we had been lost.'
Cicero's meaning may be made clear by a passage in a letter to Marcellus
(*Ad Familiārēs*, **4**, 9, 3) : ' All the conditions of civil war are wretched;
. . . but nothing is more wretched than victory itself. Even if this
has come into the hands of the better sort of men, yet it makes them
savage and violent, so that even though they may not be so by nature,
they are forced to become so by necessity. You see, the conqueror is
obliged, even against his will, to do many things at the beck of those
with the help of whom he has conquered.' **iūdiciō:** ' by the deliberate
decision.'

9. **dēvicta est:** in translating, do not overlook the force of *dē;* see
vocabulary.

The effect of Caesar's action with regard to Marcellus is far-reaching,
indeed, for all of us who, having espoused the cause of Pompey, have
been acquitted of crime. He has decided that most of his so-called
enemies undertook war against him because of ignorance or because of
some groundless apprehension; that is, through an error of judgment.

5. 1. **Quō in bellō,** etc.; Cicero improves this first opportunity to
offer a public explanation of his reasons for having gone over to Pompey,
and of his real attitude in the late war. He had previously made similar
explanations to his friends, as indicated by a letter to Marius (*Ad
Familiārēs*, **7**, 3, 6), in which he says : ' I should have preferred to
talk this over with you by ourselves; but as it would be some time
before I could see you, I wanted to lay the matter before you in a letter,
in order that, if you should chance to fall in with any of my critics, you
might know what to say to them. For there are some people who,
though my taking off would have brought no advantage to the state,

cīvium pācem flāgitantium repudiārī. Neque enim ego
illa nec ūlla umquam secūtus sum arma cīvīlia, semperque
5 mea cōnsilia pācis et togae socia, nōn bellī atque armōrum
fuērunt. Hominem sum secūtus prīvātō cōnsiliō, nōn
pūblicō, tantumque apud mē grātī animī fidēlis memoria
valuit, ut nūllā nōn modo cupiditāte, sed nē spē quidem
prūdēns et sciēns tamquam ad interitum ruerem volun-
10 tārium.

yet think it a downright crime that I am alive'; *i.e.* not having laid
down his life at Pharsalus (fär-sa′lus) or Thapsus. **dē pāce audiendum:**
' that the voice of peace should be heard.'

3. **cīvium pācem flāgitantium:** among them Cicero himself, as the
following sentence implies. **Neque enim ego,** etc.: ' For I, for my part,
adopted neither that nor any other
cause in civil strife.' **Neque . . .
semperque:** after a negative -*que* or
et is often translated by ' but.' *234, b.*

5. **mea . . . socia:** ' my intentions were always associated with
peace and the toga,' — the toga as
the garb of peace, typifying the peaceful citizen. *102.*

6. **Hominem:** very emphatic, referring, of course, to Pompey; ' It
was the man whom I followed.' **prīvātō cōnsiliō, non pūblicō:** ' from a
personal, not a political motive.' His
statements are borne out by letters
to Atticus and to Pompey himself in
49 B.C.

7. **tantumque . . . voluntārium:**
' and so swayed was I by the faithful
recollection of a thankful heart, that
not only without any ulterior motive,
but even devoid of hope I rushed

A ROMAN TOGA

From a relief in the Vatican
Museum.

with wide open eyes to voluntary destruction, as it were.' **grātī animī:**
no doubt Cicero especially remembered how zealously Pompey pro-
moted his recall from exile.

9. **prūdēns et sciēns:** a stereotyped phrase, borrowed originally
from the language of law; it is best translated as suggested above.

*Your suspicion of a plot against your life calls for special precautions;
for your safety is our safety. Friend and foe alike cannot but know
that the very existence of the commonwealth depends upon you alone.*

7. Nunc veniō ad gravissimam querellam et atrōcissimam
suspīciōnem tuam, quae nōn tibi ipsī magis quam cum
omnibus cīvibus, tum maximē nōbīs, quī ā tē cōnservātī
sumus, prōvidenda est; quam etsī spērō falsam esse, tamen
numquam extenuābō verbīs. Tua enim cautiō nostra 5
cautiō est, ut, sī in alterutrō peccandum sit, mālim vidērī
nimis timidus quam parum prūdēns.

Sed quisnam est iste tam dēmēns? dē tuīsne — tametsī quī magis sunt tuī, quam quibus tū salūtem īnspēranti-
bus reddidistī? — an ex hōc numerō, quī ūnā tēcum 10
fuērunt? Nōn est crēdibilis tantus in ūllō furor, ut, quō duce
omnia summa sit adeptus, huius vītam nōn antepōnat suae.

An, sī nihil tuī cōgitant sceleris, cavendum est, nē quid

---

7. 1. **querellam, suspīciōnem:** referring to a plot to assassinate
Caesar.

2. **ipsī:** 'personally.' **cum . . . tum maximē:** 'both . . . and
especially.'

3. **nōbīs:** dative of agent, as also *cīvibus* and *tibi* above. *110.*

4. **prōvidenda est:** 'should be guarded against.' **quam:** refers to
suspīciōnem; translate as if *et eam.* Why?

5. **cautiō:** 'safety.' As Drumann aptly remarks (*Geschichte Roms*,
Volume 6, page 264), "So far as human calculations can determine,
if Caesar had not been murdered in 44, Cicero would not have been
killed in 43."

6. **sī . . . peccandum sit:** 'if I must err on one side or the other.'

8. **tam dēmēns:** i.e. *ut tibi īnsidiētur.* **dē tuīsne:** 'is it one of your
friends?' **tametsī:** corrective, 'and yet.'

9. **quam quibus:** *quam eī, quibus.*

10. **ex hōc numerō, quī:** translate as if *ex hōrum numerō, quī.*

11. **quō duce, huius vītam:** 'the life of this man, under whose
leadership.'

12. **omnia summa:** 'all of the greatest blessings.'

13. **nihil cōgitant sceleris:** 'are plotting no crime.' Why is *sceleris*
in the genitive? *97, b.*

inimīcī? Quī? omnēs enim, quī fuērunt, aut suā pertināciā
15 vītam āmīsērunt aut tuā misericordiā retinuērunt, ut aut
nūllī supersint dē inimīcīs aut, quī fuērunt, sint amīcissimī.

Sed tamen cum in animīs hominum tantae latebrae sint
et tantī recessūs, augeāmus sānē suspīciōnem tuam; simul
enim augēbimus dīligentiam. Nam quis est omnium tam
20 ignārus rērum, tam rudis in rē pūblicā, tam nihil umquam
nec dē suā nec dē commūnī salūte cōgitāns, quī nōn intellegat tuā salūte continērī suam et ex ūnīus tuā vītā pendēre
omnium?

Your life-work is not complete while so much remains to be done.

8. Omnia sunt excitanda tibi, C. Caesar, ūnī, quae
iacēre sentīs, bellī ipsīus impetū, quod necesse fuit, per-

14. **fuērunt:** sc. *inimīcī.* **pertināciā:** as in the recent struggle in
Africa.

16. **supersint, sint:** a good illustration of sequence in a result clause.
The perfect subjunctive may be used after a secondary tense to express
the finality of the act (*superfuerint* would mean that there is absolutely
no question that none survived) and the present tense, as here, may be
used after a similar sequence to denote that the action continues into the
present. *177, b;* B. 268, 6 and 7; A. & G. 485, *c;* G. 513. **dē inimīcīs:**
translate as if *inimīcōrum. 97, d;* B. 201, 1, *a;* A. & G. 346, *c;* G. 372, R. 2.

17. **cum:** 'since.' **in animīs hominum:** 'in the heart of man.'
We prefer to use the generic singular in many cases where Latin has the
plural. **latebrae:** 'hidden depths.'

18. **augeāmus sānē:** 'let us by all means exaggerate.'

20. **rudis in rē pūblicā:** 'uninformed in politics.' **nihil . . .
cōgitāns:** 'unreflecting.'

21. **intellegat:** *194, a;* B. 283, 2; A. & G. 535, *a;* G. 631.

22. **continērī:** 'is bound up.' **ex,** etc.: 'and that on your life
alone hang the lives of all.' **ūnīus:** in apposition with the genitive idea
in *tuā. 96, b;* B. 243, 3, *a;* A. & G. 302, *e;* G. 321, R. 2.

23. **omnium:** sc. *vītam;* note its emphatic position.

8. 1. **sunt excitanda:** 'must be lifted up,' in contrast with *iacēre,*
etc. Measures looking toward all the reforms suggested — and many
besides — had already been sanctioned, or were under consideration.

2. **impetū:** 'shock.' **quod necesse fuit:** 'as was inevitable.'
What is the antecedent of *quod?*

culsa atque prōstrāta; cōnstituenda iūdicia, revocanda
fidēs, comprimendae libīdinēs, prōpāganda subolēs, omnia,
quae dīlāpsa iam diffluxērunt, sevērīs lēgibus vincienda 5
sunt.

Itaque illam tuam praeclārissimam et sapientissimam

---

3. **iūdicia:** regulated by a *lēx Iūlia iūdiciāria*, which took away
from the tribunes of the treasury the privilege of sitting on juries.

4. **fidēs:** 'credit.' The *lēx Iūlia dē fēnore* (passed in 49 B.C.)
ordered an assessment of mortgaged property at the valuation held

before the depreciation caused by
the civil wars, and obliged creditors
to accept it at this valuation in
satisfying their claims, without the
payment of any arrears of interest
that might be due. In this way
burdensome debts were canceled,
with a loss to creditors of only
about one fourth their original in-
vestment (Caesar, *Dē Bellō Cīvīlī,*
3, 1; Suetonius, *Iūlius Caesar,* 42).
libīdinēs: 'extravagant pleasures,'
referring particularly to extravagance in living, eating, drinking,
dress, appointments of the house,
etc. Caesar carried the enforce-
ment of sumptuary laws so far as
to place guards about the market
to confiscate forbidden luxuries;
in some cases even dishes were
taken from the table in private
houses (Suetonius, *Iūlius Caesar,*

MARS, GOD OF WAR

A statue in the Capitoline Museum.

43). **prōpāganda subolēs:** 'the
population must be increased.' Caesar " proposed extraordinary rewards for the fathers of numerous families, while he at the same time
as supreme judge of the nation treated divorce and adultery with a rigor
according to Roman ideas unparalleled " (Mommsen, Volume 4,
page 623). **omnia, quae dīlāpsa iam diffluxērunt:** ' all (bonds) which
have now become disorganized and disturbed.' *211; 228, a.*

5. **vincienda:** What does this verb come from? Distinguish carefully between the principal parts of *vincīre, vincere,* and *vīvere.*

vōcem invītus audīvī: "Satis diū vel nātūrae vīxī vel glōriae."

10 Satis, sī ita vīs, fortasse nātūrae, addō etiam, sī placet, glōriae; at, quod maximum est, patriae certē parum. Quā rē omitte istam, quaesō, doctōrum hominum in contemnendā morte prūdentiam ; nōlī nostrō perīculō esse sapiēns.

Saepe enim vēnit ad aurēs meās, tē idem istud nimis 15 crēbrō dīcere, tibi satis tē vīxisse. Crēdō; sed tum id audīrem, sī tibi sōlī vīverēs aut sī tibi etiam sōlī nātus essēs.

---

8. **vōcem:** 'utterance.' **invītus:** 'regretfully.' **Satis diū:** 'Long enough.' According to Suetonius (*Iūlius Caesar*, 86) Caesar declared that he did not wish to live longer, and that his failing health did not worry him; that it was not so much a matter of concern to him as to

COIN OF CAESAR

Obverse: Head of Caesar with inscription, LAUS IULI. Reverse: Bellerophon mounted on Pegasus.

the state that he should continue to live; that he had long ago had his share of power and glory; that if anything untoward happened to him the state would not enjoy peace but would approach an era of civil war under conditions considerably worse.

10. **vīs:** What verb form?

11. **maximum:** 'most important.' **parum:** 'not long enough.'

12. **istam:** remember that *iste* is the demonstrative of the second person. **doctōrum hominum:** translate as if *philosophōrum*.

13. **nōlī . . . sapiēns:** 'do not play the philosopher at our expense.' Note the position of *nostrō*. *157, b.* **perīculō:** *138.*

15. **tum . . . sī:** 'I would listen to this only if.'

16. **audīrem, sī . . . vīverēs aut . . . nātus essēs:** What kind of conditional sentence? *208, a* (*1*); B. 304; A. & G. 517; G. 597.

Omnium salūtem cīvium cūnctamque rem pūblicam rēs
tuae gestae complexae sunt; tantum abes ā perfectiōne
maximōrum operum, ut fundāmenta nōndum, quae cōgitās,
iēcerīs. Hīc tū modum vītae tuae nōn salūte reī pūblicae, 20
sed aequitāte animī dēfīniēs? Quid, sī istud nē glōriae
tuae quidem satis est? cuius tē esse avidissimum, quamvīs
sīs sapiēns, nōn negābis.

Quod sī rērum tuārum immortālium, C. Caesar, hīc exitus
futūrus fuit, ut, dēvictīs adversāriīs, rem pūblicam in eō 25
statū relinquerēs, in quō nunc est, vidē, quaesō, nē tua dīvīna
virtūs admīrātiōnis plūs sit habitūra quam glōriae, sī quidem
glōria est illūstris ac pervagāta magnōrum vel in suōs cīvēs
vel in patriam vel in omne genus hominum fāma meritōrum.

You have a duty to the state, for present needs and future glory.

9. Haec igitur tibi reliqua pars est; hīc restat āctus,
in hōc ēlabōrandum est, ut rem pūblicam cōnstituās, eā-

---

18. **tantum . . . iēceris:** ' so far are you from completing your
greatest works, that you have not yet laid the foundation of those which
you are planning.' The sentence refers not only to the great plans Caesar
had formed for the reorganization of the state, but also to a series of
magnificent public buildings on which work had already been commenced.

20. **Hīc:** ' At this point.' **modum:** ' limit.'

21. **aequitāte animī:** ' by the composure of your mind,' the philo-
sophic calm which even the thought of death cannot disturb. **istud:**
' that boundary (which you have set).'

24. **Quod sī:** ' But if.' *118, d.*

25. **futūrus fuit:** ' was destined to be.' **ut . . . relinquerēs:**
explains *hīc exitus. 203 (2).*

26. **vidē,** etc.: ' see to it, I beg of you, that your godlike character
shall not have more of admiration than of glory, since (*sī quidem*) glory
is the bright and wide-spread fame (arising from) signal services either
towards one's fellow-citizens or towards one's country or towards the
whole race of mankind.' A similar definition of *glōria* may be found
in Cicero's *Philippic* **1,** 12, 29.

9. 1. **pars . . . āctus:** ' part,' ' rôle ' . . . ' act '; implied comparison of life to a drama.

2. **in hōc ēlabōrandum:** ' to this end you must strive,' namely,

que tū in prīmīs summā tranquillitāte et ōtiō perfruāre;
tum tē, sī volēs, cum et patriae, quod dēbēs, solveris et
5 nātūram ipsam explēveris satietāte vīvendī, satis diū vīxisse dīcitō.

Obstipēscent posterī certē imperia, prōvinciās, Rhēnum,
Oceanum, Nīlum, pugnās innumerābilēs, incrēdibilēs victō-
riās, monumenta, mūnera, triumphōs audientēs et legentēs

THE NILE

A statue in the Vatican Museum. Notice the crocodile at the left and the
sphinx at the right. The sixteen little figures symbolize the sixteen cubits
of the Nile's annual overflow.

---

ut, etc. **eā :** ablative with *perfruāre*. *131, c;* B. 218, A. & G. 410;
G. 407.

3. **tū in prīmīs :** ' you above all others.' **summā tranquillitāte et
ōtiō :** ablative of manner. *136, a.*

4. **solveris :** ' you shall have paid.'

6. **dīcitō :** future imperative, ' you shall say.' *181, a* (1).

7. **Obstipēscent :** ' Will stand amazed ' ; note the emphatic position.
imperia, prōvinciās, etc. : objects of *audientēs et legentēs* below (' when
they hear and read of '). **Rhēnum, Oceanum :** Germany, Britain.

8. **Nīlum :** Caesar followed Pompey to Egypt, and became involved
in the Alexandrine War. By April of 47 B.C. Caesar had the country
under complete control. *239, t.*

9. **mūnera :** ' shows,' ' exhibitions,' referring especially to gladiatorial combats. They were called *mūnera* because they were gifts or

tuōs. Sed nisi haec urbs stabilīta tuīs cōnsiliīs et īnsti- 10
tūtīs erit, vagābitur modo tuum nōmen longē atque lātē,
sēdem stabilem et domicilium certum nōn habēbit.

Servī igitur eīs etiam iūdicibus, quī multīs post saeculīs
dē tē iūdicābunt, et quidem haud sciō an incorruptius quam
nōs; nam et sine amōre et sine cupiditāte et rūrsus sine odiō 15
et sine invidiā iūdicābunt. Id autem etiam sī tum ad tē, ut
quīdam putant, nōn pertinēbit, nunc certē pertinet esse tē
tālem, ut tuās laudēs obscūrātūra nūlla umquam sit oblīviō

---

presents from the magistrates, particularly the aediles, to the people.
Caesar entertained with a lavish hand. His biographer (Suetonius,
Iūlius Caesar, 10 and 39) tells us that when he was aedile he exhibited
combats with wild beasts (*vēnātiōnēs*), stage-plays, and a gladiatorial
show (*gladiātōrium mūnus*), and that he had so large a band of gladiators that a bill was passed limiting the number of such men whom
anyone was permitted to have in Rome. Later, during the time of his
triumphs, he gave even more elaborate entertainments, stage-plays
in every district of the city, races, athletic contests, gladiatorial shows,
combats with wild beasts for five successive days, a battle between two
opposing armies, and a sham sea-fight for which an artificial lake had
been dug. These entertainments attracted such throngs of people, that
tents were pitched in the streets to house them, and often the jam was
so great that fatalities occurred. **triumphōs**: Caesar had just celebrated a fourfold triumph for his victories in Gaul, Egypt, Asia Minor,
and over the allies of the Pompeian leaders in Africa.

13. **Servī**: verb, 'Look to.' **multīs post saeculīs**: degree of
difference; *post* is an adverb. *140.*

14. **quidem haud sciō an,** etc.: 'indeed, I am inclined to think that
their judgment will be more impartial than ours.' *haud sciō an* expresses a mild affirmation, and regularly takes the subjunctive; sc.
iūdicent. 180, e (1); B. 300, 5; A. & G. 447, 1; G. 457, 2.

15. **sine amōre et sine cupiditāte**: we should say, 'without fear or
favor.' *212, b.*

17. **quīdam**: Epicureans; Caesar leaned towards Epicureanism,
believing that there was no life beyond the grave. This explains his
argument as reported by Sallust (see Selection, page 139, line 21, etc.)
that a life sentence was a severer punishment for the Catilinarian conspirators than the death penalty.

18. **obscūrātūra sit**: 'will be likely to becloud.'

10. Nisi tē, C. Caesar, salvō et in istā sententiā, quā cum
anteā, tum hodiē vel maximē ūsus es, manente, salvī
esse nōn possumus.

Quā rē omnēs tē, quī haec salva esse volumus, et hortā-
5 mur et obsecrāmus, ut vītae tuae et salūtī cōnsulās, omnēs-
que tibi, — ut prō aliīs etiam loquar, quod dē mē ipse
sentiō, — quoniam subesse aliquid putās, quod cavendum sit, nōn modo excubiās et cūstōdiās, sed etiam laterum
nostrōrum oppositūs et corporum pollicēmur.

---

10. 1. **Nisi tē salvō et manente:** 'Without your being safe and
remaining.' *229, d;* A. & G. 496, N. 3; G. 431, 3. **cum . . . tum:**
'not only . . . but also.'

2. **vel maximē :** 'most of all.'

4. **omnēs:** 'all of us.' **haec:** 'this, our empire,' probably spoken
with a gesture. *Haec* is often a substantive; see *In Catilīnam, 1,* 8, 44;
In Catilīnam, **4,** 4, 7; *Philippic,* **4,** 3, 17.

7. **subesse:** translate as if *latēre*.

8. **excubiās:** 'watches,' stationed outside of a camp or building,
as distinguished from *cūstōdiae,* 'guards,' set to protect a given point
or place, and *vigiliae,* 'patrol-men.' The following year the senate
voted Caesar a select body-guard, but he refused to accept it. **laterum
nostrōrum . . . corporum:** literally, 'the interposition of our chests
and our bodies'; translate, 'to interpose all our physical powers.'
The combination of *laterum* and *corporum* is merely a general expression
to indicate physical strength. See *ex lateribus et lacertīs* ('lungs and
arms') and *laterum et vīrium,* Selections from *Dē Senectūte,* pages 265,
266. Horace also (*Epistulae,* **1,** 7, 26) refers half humorously to his *forte
latus* ('manly chest'). Such physical designations as 'good lungs'
are regularly *bona latera.*

9. **oppositūs:** the plural is due to the limiting genitive, because
there are many interpositions of the many sides and bodies.

Perōrātiō. (See Companion, page 498, for the divisions of a typical
oration.)

Cicero now reverts to the thought expressed in the exordium: We
all express to you, Gaius Caesar, our deepest gratitude for the restoration of Marcus Marcellus to this order, to the Roman people, and to the
state; and while I personally thank you for the countless favors which
you have bestowed upon me, yet your present action in pardoning
Marcellus is a crowning addition to all of them.

CICERO THE ORATOR AND STATESMAN

CICERO THE ORATOR AND STATESMAN

M. TULLĪ CICERŌNIS
IN L. CATILĪNAM ŌRĀTIŌ PRĪMA
HABITA IN SENĀTŪ

Catiline, how long will you tax our endurance?   Your plots are known.

1. Quō ūsque tandem abūtēre, Catilīna, patientiā nostrā? Quam diū etiam furor iste tuus nōs ēlūdet? Quem ad fīnem sēsē effrēnāta iactābit audācia? Nihilne

To THE STUDENT: Read the Companion, pages 514 to 523, to get the setting of this oration, before trying to translate.

Title. IN L. CATILĪNAM: 'against Catiline.' HABITA: 'delivered.'

1. 1. Quō ūsque: strengthened by *tandem*, 'How long, pray'; introduces an abrupt, indignant question, suggested by the appearance of Catiline in the senate. *Quam diū* and *quem ad fīnem* below have a similar meaning. Sallust (*Catilīna*, **20**, 9) puts a similar expression into the mouth of Catiline; *quae* ('and this state of affairs') *quō ūsque tandem patiēminī, ō fortissumī virī?* **abūtēre:** not *abūtĕre.* **patientiā:** *131, c;* B. 218, 1; A. & G. 410; G. 407.

AN ANCIENT MANUSCRIPT OF THE FIRST CATILINARIAN ORATION

2. etiam: temporal, 'still.' **furor iste tuus:** 'that frenzy of yours.' Why is *iste* used? See *160, a;* B. 246, 4; A. & G. 297, *c;* G. 306, N. **ēlūdet:** here in the sense of 'make sport of.'

3. Quem ad fīnem: *i.e.* how far, how long. **effrēnāta:** suggests what comparison? **Nihil:** adverbial accusative, taking the place of an emphatic *nōn.* B. 176, 3; A. & G. 390, *d,* N. 2; G. 442, N. 2. The rhetorical force is heightened by the repetition of *nihil* with each item mentioned, a figure technically known as anaphora. *239, b.*

tē nocturnum praesidium Palātī, nihil urbis vigiliae, nihil
5 timor populī, nihil concursus bonōrum omnium, nihil hīc
mūnītissimus habendī senātūs locus, nihil hōrum ōra
vultūsque mōvērunt? Patēre tua cōnsilia nōn sentīs? Cōnstrīctam iam omnium
hōrum scientiā tenērī coniūrātiōnem tuam nōn vidēs?
10 Quid proximā, quid superiōre nocte ēgerīs, ubi fuerīs, quōs
convocāverīs, quid cōnsilī cēperīs, quem nostrum ignōrāre
arbitrāris?

---

4. **praesidium Palātī:** the situation, shape, and elevation of the
Palatine hill made it one of the strongest military positions in Rome.
At a very early period it was surrounded by a massive wall, extensive
portions of which still remained in Cicero's time.   Consequently in times
of special danger it was occupied by a garrison.   See Middleton's
Remains of Ancient Rome, Volume I, Chapter IV.   **vigiliae:** the senate
had ordered that watchmen be placed on guard throughout the city,
under the charge of the lesser magistrates (aediles, tribunes, and quaestors).   See Sallust, *Catilīna,* **30,** 7, and **31,** 1-3, where the 'terror' of the
Roman populace is vividly described.

5. **bonōrum:** i.e. *bonōrum cīvium,* 'of the patriotic,' who had
assembled in great numbers before the temple where the senate was in
session.   **hīc . . . locus:** the temple of Jupiter Stator (see pages 61,
414, and the notes), on the Palatine, where the senate had met, for the
sake of security, rather than in the senate-house (see vocabulary under
cūria, 1), or in one of the temples about the Forum.   Cicero had taken
the precaution to protect the temple with a company of armed knights.
See Plan facing page 62.

6. **hōrum:** the senators; spoken with a gesture.   **ōra vultūsque:**
'the expression on the faces' (see Selection from Sallust, page 134, *et seq.,*
particularly lines 27 and 28); hendiadys. *238, h;* B. 374, 4; A. & G.
640; G. 698.

8. **Cōnstrīctam . . . tenērī:** 'is held and bound fast,' as a captive
wild beast closely fettered. *228, a;* B. 336, 3; A. & G. 496, N. 2;
G. 664.

10. **proximā** [*nocte*]: November 7.   **superiōre nocte:** November 6;
see Companion, page 526.   **quōs:** for a list of the principal conspirators
see Sallust, *Catilīna,* **17,** 3-4.

11. **quem:** introduces a direct question; the other interrogatives in
this sentence are indirect.

Ō tempora, Ō mōrēs! Senātus haec intellegit, cōnsul
videt; hīc tamen vīvit.

Vīvit? Immō vērō etiam in senātum venit, fit pūblicī 15
cōnsilī particeps, notat et dēsignat oculīs ad caedem ūnum
quemque nostrum. Nōs autem, fortēs virī, satis facere reī
pūblicae vidēmur, sī istīus furōrem ac tēla vītēmus.

CICERO DELIVERING HIS FIRST ORATION AGAINST CATILINE

13. **tempora**: *124, c;* B. 183; A. & G. 397, *d;* G. 343, 1. **cōnsul**:
singular as referring to the office rather than to the consuls as individuals;
so in line 19 also.

15. **Vīvit?** ' " Lives " did I say? ' the argument is strengthened
by first questioning, then supplementing, the previous statement, —
a figure called by the grammarians *corrēctiō. 239, g.* **pūblicī cōnsilī
particeps**: in accordance with the Roman custom, after his praetorship
Catiline had been given a seat in the senate.

16. **notat et dēsignat**: ' singles out and marks.' **ūnum quemque
nostrum**: *i.e.* ' us one by one,' individually. Why not *nostrī? 155;*
B. 242, 2; A. & G. 295, *b;* G. 304, 2 and 3.

17. **fortēs virī**: ironical. **satis facere reī pūblicae vidēmur** [*nōbīs*]:
translate ' we think we are doing our duty by the state '; *satis facere
vidēmur* is stronger than *satis faciāmus,* which would have been more
in accordance with the ordinary construction. *207 (3).*

18. **istīus**: ' of that (wretch).' *160, a.*

The fault is ours that you have not been put to death.

Ad mortem tē, Catilīna, dūcī iussū cōnsulis iam prīdem
20 oportēbat, in tē cōnferrī pestem, quam tū in nōs māchināris.
An vērō vir amplissimus, P. Scīpiō, pontifex maximus, Ti.
Gracchum mediocriter labefactantem statum reī pūblicae
prīvātus interfēcit; Catilīnam, orbem terrae caede atque
incendiīs vāstāre cupientem, nōs cōnsulēs perferēmus?
25 Nam illa nimis antīqua praetereō, quod C. Servīlius
Ahāla Sp. Maelium, novīs rēbus studentem, manū suā

---

19. **Ad mortem tē dūcī . . . iam prīdem oportēbat:** 'You ought
long ago to have been led to execution.' Note the emphasis given to *ad
mortem* by its position. **iussū cōnsulis:** *i.e.* in accordance with the
authority vested in the consuls by the senate's decree of October 21;
see page 519. Whether this authority was
sufficient to warrant putting a Roman citizen
to death without a formal trial is yet an
open question; see page 519 for a discussion of the arguments.

20. **cōnferrī:** sc. *iam prīdem oportēbat.*

21. **An:** introduces a rhetorical double
question, in which (see Quintilian, **8,** 4, 13)
not only wholes but even parts are forcefully
contrasted. In translating, the first member may be made subordinate and introduced
by 'If' or 'While'; or the expression may
be varied, thus: 'What? did not Publius
Scipio . . ., and shall we . . .?' **P. Scipiō** (pub'li̧-u̧s sip'i̧-ō): see
vocabulary under *Scipio* (4), and Mommsen's *History of Rome,*
Volume III. **pontifex maximus . . . prīvātus:** the office of supreme
pontiff, although one of great dignity and influence, was not reckoned
among the magistracies; see Companion, page 571. **Ti. Gracchum**
(ti̧-bē'ri̧-u̧s gra̧k'u̧s): see vocabulary.

AHALA
From a Republican coin.

22. **mediocriter labefactantem:** 'though but slightly impairing';
strongly contrasted with *orbem . . . cupientem.*

24. **cōnsulēs:** contrasted with *prīvātus,* line 23.

25. **illa nimis antīqua:** 'those (precedents) as too remote'; only
one is given. *161, a;* B. 246, 2; A. & G. 297, *b;* G. 307, 3. **praetereō:**
the figure is called *praeteritiō,* a favorite device with Cicero. *239, r.*
quod . . . occīdit: in apposition with *illa. 198. b;* B. 299, 1, *a;* A. & G.

occīdit. Fuit, fuit ista quondam in hāc rē pūblicā virtūs,
ut virī fortēs ācriōribus suppliciīs cīvem perniciōsum quam
acerbissimum hostem coērcērent.

Habēmus senātūs cōnsultum in tē, Catilīna, vehemēns 30
et grave, nōn dēest reī pūblicae cōnsilium neque auctōritās
huius ōrdinis; nōs, nōs, dīcō, apertē, cōnsulēs dēsumus.

Precedent and authority warrant your execution.

2. Dēcrēvit quondam senātus, ut L. Opīmius cōnsul
vidēret, *nē quid rēs pūblica dētrīmentī caperet.* Nox nūlla
intercessit : interfectus est propter quāsdam sēditiōnum

572, and N.; G. 525, 2. **C. Servīlius Ahāla** (gā′(y) ụs sẹr-vil′ị-ụs ạ-hā′lạ) :
master of the horse under the dictator Cincinnatus.

27. **Fuit, fuit :** so in line 32, *nōs, nōs:* such repetitions often indicate
feeling and emotional stress. **ista :** here almost *tālis.*

30. **senātūs cōnsultum :** the decree (*ultimum dēcrētum*) of October
21 ; see page 516.

31. **reī pūblicae :** dative with *deest.* The thought is : the senate
has given the emergency due deliberation, and has conferred the proper
authority upon the consuls; not the deliberative but the executive
branch of the government is at fault. By thus complimenting the
senate and transferring the blame to his colleague and himself, the
orator clearly strengthens his case with the senators.

32. **dēsumus :** i.e. *reī pūblicae dēsumus.*

2. 1. **Dēcrēvit,** etc.: having alluded to remote precedents, the
orator passes to those nearer his own time. Those cited present a sharp
contrast with the dilatoriness of the consuls in dealing with Catiline,
and suggest immediate and decisive action. The intent of the speaker
here is evidently not so much to convince the senate as to frighten
Catiline into leaving the city. **L. Opīmius** (lū′sh(y)ụs ọ-pịm′ị-ụs)
. . . *caperet:* the language of the decree is of interest (see Cicero,
Philippic, **8,** 4, 14) : *quod L. Opīmius cōnsul verba fēcit dē rē pūblicā,
dē eā rē cēnsuērunt, uti L. Opīmius cōnsul rem pūblicam dēfenderet.* The
other consul, Q. Fabius Maximus, was in the southern part of Transalpine Gaul at the time.

2. *quid dētrīmentī:* 'any harm.' *97, b;* B. 201, 2; A. & G. 346,
a, 3 ; G. 369.

3. **propter . . . suspīciōnēs :** a form of expression purposely mild,
to heighten the contrast.

suspīciōnēs C. Gracchus, clārissimō patre, avō, maiōribus; 5 occīsus est cum līberīs M. Fulvius cōnsulāris.

Similī senātūs cōnsultō C. Mariō et L. Valeriō cōn-sulibus est permissa rēs pūblica; num ūnum diem posteā L. Sāturnīnum tribūnum plēbis et C. Servīlium prae-tōrem mors ac reī pūblicae poena remorāta est? At 10 nōs vīcēsimum iam diem patimur hebēscere aciem hōrum auctōritātis.

Habēmus enim huiusce modī senātūs cōnsultum, vērum inclūsum in tabulīs, tamquam in vāgīnā reconditum, quō ex senātūs cōnsultō cōnfestim tē interfectum esse, Catilīna,

---

4. **clārissimō . . .**: 'though a son, grandson, and descendant of very famous men.' *143, a;* B. 224; A. & G. 415; G. 400. The mother of the Gracchi (grąk'ī) was the noblé Cornelia, daughter of the elder Scipio Africanus; their father, Tiberius Sempronius Gracchus, was twice consul, and twice honored with a triumph; and among their ancestors of the same name was that Tiberius Gracchus who in 214 B.C. got together an army composed largely of slaves and conquered Hanno near Beneventum.

5. **līberīs**: two sons; see page 115, lines 13-15, and note. **M. Ful-vius**: see vocabulary under *Flaccus* (1).

6. **C. Mariō et L. Valeriō** (gā'(y)ųs mā'rĭ-ųs, lū'sh(y)ųs vą-lē'rĭ-ųs): dative. See vocabulary under *Flaccus* (2).

8. **L. Sāturnīnum** (lū'sh(y)-ųs sat-ųr-nī'nųs) . . . **C. Servīlium**: see vocabulary under *Glaucia*.

9. **ac**: introduces an explanation of *mors*, 'and (that) as state's penalty.'

9. **remorāta est**: the force of *remorārī* here, as often, is 'to keep' one 'waiting.'   Translate, 'Was the death penalty imposed by the state upon . . . deferred for a single day afterwards?'   Hendiadys. *238, h.*

10. **vīcēsimum**: in round numbers; how many days since October 21? **hōrum**: spoken with a gesture; but the reference is not so much to the authority of the senate as to that which the senate had vested in the consuls.

13. **in tabulīs**: 'in the archives,' among the records of the proceed-ings of the senate. **tamquam**, etc.: carries out the comparison sug-gested by *aciem*, line 10. In English the simile should be completed, viz. 'like a sword hidden in the scabbard.'

convēnit. Vīvis, et vīvis nōn ad dēpōnendam sed ad 15 cōnfīrmandam audāciam.

Cupiō, patrēs cōnscrīptī, mē esse clēmentem, cupiō in tantīs reī pūblicae perīculīs mē nōn dissolūtum vidērī, sed iam mē ipse inertiae nēquitiaeque condemnō.

Castra sunt in Italiā contrā populum Rōmānum in 20 Etrūriae faucibus collocāta, crēscit in diēs singulōs hostium

A COIN OF THE REPUBLIC
Obverse: Jupiter. Reverse: Victory crowning a trophy.

15. **convēnit**: milder than *oportuit;* 'you might well have been put to death.' **et**: put rhetorically for *et quidem.* **ad . . . audāciam**: in what ways may purpose be expressed in Latin?

17. **Cupiō . . . cupiō . . . vidērī**: rhetorical expression for *cupiō mē esse clēmentem neque tamen dissolūtum vidērī. 223, a;* B. 331, IV, *a;* G. 532, R. 2. **patrēs cōnscrīptī**: simply 'senators'; do not translate by such meaningless words as 'conscript fathers,' 'assembled fathers,' etc. The senators as individuals were called *senātōrēs;* sitting as a body they were always addressed as *patrēs cōnscrīptī.* The origin and primitive force of the latter title are not entirely understood, but see Livy's explanation, page 432 and note 35.

18. **dissolūtum**: stronger than *neglegēns.*

19. **inertiae nēquitiaeque**: 'of inactivity and negligence.' *103, b;* B. 208, 2, *a;* A. & G. 352; G. 378.

20. **in Italiā**: not in the provinces, but near home, where rebellion would least be expected. **in Etruriae faucibus**: at Faesulae (fes'yū-lē), a convenient center for military operations because it commanded one of the main routes into Cisalpine Gaul. It was also a good rallying point for the old soldiers of Sulla, being one of Sulla's colonies; see page 70, line 21, and note.

21. **in diēs**: see IDIOMS, page 714.

numerus; eōrum autem castrōrum imperātōrem ducemque
hostium intrā moenia atque adeō in senātū vidēmus, in-
testīnam aliquam cotīdiē perniciem reī pūblicae mōlientem.

Though exposing myself to censure, I defer action; but you will be killed.

25 Sī tē iam, Catilīna, comprehendī, sī interficī iusserō, crēdō,
erit verendum mihi, nē nōn potius hōc omnēs bonī sērius ā
mē quam quisquam crūdēlius factum esse dīcat.   Vērum
ego hōc, quod iam prīdem factum esse oportuit, certā dē
causā nōndum addūcor ut faciam.   Tum dēnique inter-
30 ficiēre, cum iam nēmō tam improbus, tam perditus, tam tuī
similis invenīrī poterit, quī id nōn iūre factum esse fateātur.

Quam diū quisquam erit, quī tē dēfendere audeat, vīvēs; et
vīvēs ita, ut vīvis, multīs meīs et fīrmīs praesidiīs oppressus,
nē commovēre tē contrā rem pūblicam possīs.   Multōrum
35 tē etiam oculī et aurēs nōn sentientem, sīcut adhūc fēcērunt,
speculābuntur atque cūstōdient.

---

23. **adeō:** ' actually.'

24. **reī pūblicae:** *not* genitive.   *109, a.*

25. **iam:** 'at once.'   **crēdō:** ironical, 'I suppose,' or 'of course.'

26. **nē nōn . . . hōc:** i.e. *nē nōn omnēs bonī hōc ā mē sērius factum
esse dīcant potius quam,* etc.   ' I shall have to fear that patriotic men will
say that I have acted too cruelly rather than that,' etc.   The force of
erit verendum is really made negative by the ironical turn, as if the
orator had said *nōn verendum erit.*   From the influence of this negation
the subordinate negative clause *nē nōn . . . (dīcant)* acquires an affirmative force; ' I shall not have to fear that . . . will not say,' ' I shall
have to fear that . . . will say.'   *202; B. 296, 2, a; A. & G. 564.*
bonī: see page 26, line 4, and note.   **sērius, crūdēlius:** *153, a;* B. 240,
1; A. & G. *291, a.*

27. **quisquam:** usually found in negative sentences; here 'any one
at all,' implying that there may be one or two such, but not more.

29. **interficiēre:** the consul avoids the expression *tē interficiam,*
which might have been expected from the preceding argument.

30. **tuī:** why not dative?   *108, b;* B. 204, 3; A. & G. 385, *c,* 2;
G. 359. R. 1.

33. **ita, ut:** 'just as.'   **et:** *152, c.*   **oppressus:** ' overpowered.'

34. **Multōrum:** emphatic.

What have you to hope for, now that your plots are revealed?

3. Etenim quid est, Catilīna, quod iam amplius exspectēs, sī neque nox tenebrīs obscūrāre coetūs nefāriōs nec prīvāta domus pariētibus continēre vōcēs coniūrātiōnis tuae potest, sī illūstrantur, sī ērumpunt omnia?

Mūtā iam istam mentem, mihi crēde; oblīvīscere caedis 5 atque incendiōrum. Tenēris undique. Lūce sunt clāri-ōra nōbīs tua cōnsilia omnia; quae iam mēcum licet recognōscās.

Meministīne mē ante diem XII Kalendās Novembrēs dīcere in senātū, fore in armīs certō diē, quī diēs futūrus 10 esset ante diem VI Kalendās Novembrēs, C. Mānlium, audāciae satellitem atque administrum tuae? Num mē fefellit, Catilīna, nōn modo rēs tanta, tam atrōx tamque incrēdibilis, vērum, id quod multō magis est admīrandum, diēs? 15

Dīxī ego īdem in senātū, caedem tē optimātium con-

---

3. 1. **exspectēs:** *194, a;* B. 283, 2; A. & G. 535, *a;* G. 631.

3. **pariētibus:** how different from *mūrus, moenia?* See vocabulary. **continēre:** i.e. *intus servāre.*

5. **mihi crēde:** see IDIOMS, page 715. **caedis:** *103, a;* B. 206, 2; A. & G. 350; G. 376.

6. **Tenēris:** i.e. *Dēprehēnsus es.*

7. **licet recognōscās:** 'you may recall'; concessive expression instead of the imperative. *200, a;* B. 295, 6, 8; A. & G. 565, N. 2; G. 422, 4; 546.

9. **ante diem XII,** etc.: *ante diem duodecimum;* translate as if *diē duodecimō ante Kalendās Novembrēs,* i.e. October 21. *241, b;* B. 371, 372; A. & G. 424, *g,* and 631, *a;* G. page 491.

11. **ante diem VI:** see pages 516, 526.

12. **satellitem:** implies a lower kind of service than *administrum.*

13. **fefellit:** from *fallere; rēs* and *diēs* are the subjects, but the English idiom prefers a personal subject. Translate, 'Not only was I not mistaken in so great a plot, so revolting and so unbelievable, but, what is much more surprising, not even in the day, was I, Catiline?' It is seldom that *rēs* is translated by 'thing'; it should be colored to suit the context. *211.*

tulisse in ante diem v Kalendās Novembrēs, tum cum
multī prīncipēs cīvitātis Rōmā, nōn tam suī cōnservandī
quam tuōrum cōnsiliōrum reprimendōrum causā, pro-
20 fūgērunt. Num īnfitiārī potes tē, illō ipsō diē meīs praesidiīs, meā dīligentiā circumclūsum, commovēre tē contrā
rem pūblicam nōn potuisse, cum tū discessū cēterōrum
nostrā tamen, quī remānsissēmus, caede tē contentum
esse dīcēbās?

25 Quid? cum tū tē Praeneste Kalendīs ipsīs Novembribus
occupātūrum nocturnō impetū esse cōnfīderēs, sēnsistīne
illam colōniam meō iussū meīs praesidiīs, cūstōdiīs, vigiliīs
esse mūnītam? Nihil agis, nihil mōlīris, nihil cōgitās
quod nōn ego nōn modo audiam, sed etiam videam plā-
30 nēque sentiam.

---

18. **suī cōnservandī** [*causā*]: ' in order to save themselves'; idiomatic use of the gerundive with *suī*. *230, a* (1); B. 339, 5; A. & G.
504, *b* and *c*, G. 428, R. 1.

19. **profūgērunt**: why not subjunctive? *185, b;* B. 288, 1, *A*,
A. & G. 545; G. 580.

20. **diē**: see Companion, page 526.

22. **discessū**, etc.: verbal nouns in the ablative case are often used
to replace the missing perfect active participle of verbs, as here; translate as a concessive clause to balance the following *tamen*, viz. ' when you
said that, although the rest had departed, nevertheless you were satisfied
with the murder of us who should remain.' **cēterōrum**: *96, b.*

23. **nostrā caede**: translate as if *caede nostrī*. B. 251, 2; A. & G.
306, *b*, N. 1.   **remānsissēmus**: what form in direct discourse?

25. **Quid**: accusative; idiomatic use, originating in some such
expression as *Quid dīcam dē hōc?*   This word is often used in rhetorical
writing to indicate a transition to another point or thought; its force
here is that of our ' again,' ' furthermore.' **Praeneste**: from its location, its situation upon an eminence, and its strong fortifications,
Praeneste was an advantageous base for military operations.   In early
times it had been an important member of the Latin League.   When
it became a Roman colony is not known; probably in the time of Sulla.

28. **Nihil . . . cōgitās**: climax, with anaphora. *239, b;* B. 350,
11, *b;* A. & G. 598, *f;* G. 682.

Num negāre audēs? Quid tacēs?

Convincam, si negās; videō enim esse hīc in senātū
quōsdam, quī tēcum ūnā fuērunt.

Ō dī immortālēs! Ubinam gentium sumus? In quā
urbe vīvimus? Quam rem pūblicam habēmus? Hīc,
hīc sunt in nostrō numerō, patrēs cōnscrīptī, in hōc orbis
terrae sānctissimō gravissimōque cōnsiliō, quī dē nostrō
omnium interitū, quī dē huius urbis atque adeō dē orbis
terrārum exitiō cōgitent! Hōs ego videō et dē rē pūblicā
sententiam rogō et, quōs ferrō trucīdārī oportēbat, eōs
nōndum vōce vulnerō!

Finding me a hindrance, you tried to kill me.

Fuistī igitur apud Laecam illā nocte, Catilīna; dis-

---

7. **Quid tacēs:** spoken after a brief pause, — doubtless a dramatic
moment.

8. **in senātū:** defines and strengthens *hīc.*

10. **Ō dī,** etc.: outburst against the treason of Catiline's sympathizers in the senate, suggested by the thought of the preceding sentence. **Ubinam gentium:** see IDIOMS. 97, *b;* B. 201, 3; A. & G. 346,
a, 4; G. 372, N. 3.

11. **Hīc, hīc:** see page 29, line 27, and note.

13. **sānctissimō:** *sānctus,* as often, ' worthy of reverence,' ' worthy
of respect.' **quī:** ' (men) who.' **nostrō omnium:** ' of all of us.'
96, b; B. 243, 2, 3, *a;* A. & G. 348, *a;* G. 304, 2, N. 2, 321, R. 2.

15. **dē rē pūblicā sententiam rogō:** with *hōs,* in the phrase of our
parliamentary law, ' I put the question to them on (matters affecting)
the public welfare.' As consul Cicero presided at meetings of the
senate appointed by him, and called upon the senators in turn for their
votes upon each question. A senator might respond either with his
vote simply or with a speech explaining or defending his position
(*sententia*).

17. **vōce vulnerō:** *i.e.* I do not call them by name. Imitate the
alliteration.

18. **Fuistī igitur:** the orator returns from his digression (lines 10–
17) to the topic in hand; *igitur* refers back to line 7, *Num negāre
audēs? Quid tacēs?* implying that Catiline's silence indicates his
assent. This use of *igitur* is termed " resumptive." Translate, ' well
then (as I was saying).'

Recall with me your plottings at Laeca's house.

4. Recognōsce tandem mēcum noctem illam super
iam intelleges multō mē vigilāre ācrius ad salūtem
tē ad perniciem reī pūblicae. Dīcō tē priōre nocte
inter falcāriōs — nōn agam obscūrē — in M. Laecae do
convēnisse eōdem complūrēs eiusdem āmentiae scele
sociōs.

PRAENESTE
The ancient city crowned the hill; the modern Palestrina lies at the

4. 1. **noctem superiōrem . . . priōre nocte** (line 3): ' night
last,' the night of November 6. **mēcum:** *238, b.*

2. **ad:** ' with a view to,' ' with reference to.'

3. **Dīcō:** emphatic, directing attention to the speaker's int
knowledge of all the plans and acts of the conspirators.

4. **inter falcāriōs:** ' on Scythe-Makers' Street,' or 'in the Sc
Makers' Quarter '; condensed expression to indicate the locatio
Laeca's (lē′ka's) house. **nōn agam obscūrē:** i.e. *apertē dīcam*, men
tng the name. **in M. Laecae domum:** *domum*, with a possessive
noun or limited by a genitive, may mean ' house,' and then ma
used with or without the preposition. *119, b;* B. 182, 1, N.; G. 337,

5. **complūrēs . . . sociōs:** see Sallust, *Catilīna*, **27**, 3–4: *in
pestā nocte* (' in the dead of night ') *coniūrātiōnis prīncipēs convocat
M. Porcium Laecam*, etc.

tribuistī partēs Italiae; statuistī quō quemque proficīscī
placēret; dēlēgistī, quōs Rōmae relinquerēs, quōs tēcum ₂₀
ēdūcerēs; discrīpsistī urbis partēs ad incendia; cōnfīrmāstī tē ipsum iam esse exitūrum; dīxistī paulum
tibi esse etiam nunc morae, quod ego vīverem. Repertī
sunt duo equitēs Rōmānī, quī tē istā cūrā līberārent et
sēsē illā ipsā nocte paulō ante lūcem mē in meō lectulō ₂₅
interfectūrōs esse pollicērentur.

Haec ego omnia, vixdum etiam coetū vestrō dīmissō,
comperī. Domum meam maiōribus praesidiīs mūnīvī
atque fīrmāvī; exclūsī eōs, quōs tū ad mē salūtātum

---

19. **statuistī . . . placēret:** this fullness of expression should not be
imitated in English; translate, ' you decided to which point each man
should proceed ': *statuistī* reters to the process of deliberation, while
placēret (tibi) suggests the decision. *204 (3)*.

21. **ad incendia:** modern anarchists have an advantage over the
ancient in that they understand the use of violent explosives. Had
Catiline and his followers been familiar with dynamite, — the last
resort of the coward and the desperado, — the conspiracy might not so
easily have been suppressed. **cōnfīrmāstī:** *64, a;* B. 116, 1; A. & G.
181, *a;* G. 131, 1.

22. **paulum . . . morae:** in direct discourse, *est mihi etiam nunc
paulum morae* (idiomatically, ' I am even now suffering a little delay ');
hence in the indirect form we find *nunc* instead of *tum*, which might have
been expected from the tense of *dīxistī*. G. 660, 3.

23. **vīvcrcm:** why not indicative?

24. **duo equitēs:** according to Sallust (*Catilīna*, **28,** 1), C. Cor-
neḷius, a knight, and L. Vargunteius (vär-gun-tē'yụs), a senator. **cūrā:**
127, a; B. 214, 1, *a;* A. & G. 401; G. 390, 2. **līberārent:** subjunctive
of characteristic, with *quī* to be translated as if *tālēs, ut. 194, a;* B. 283,
1; A. & G. 535; G. 631.

25. **illā . . . lūcem:** *i.e.* early in the morning of November 7; see
chronology on page 526. **lectulō:** ' on my cozy little couch,' 'as I was
lying cozily on my couch '; the diminutive, suggestive of home life and
retirement, heightens the impression of wickedness associated with the
intended crime.

29. **salūtātum:** ' in order to pay their respects.' *231, a;* B. 340, 1;
A. & G. 509; G. 435. Roman gentlemen received their clients and friends
early in the morning; the earlier the visit, the greater the respect implied.

30 māne mīserās, cum illī ipsī vēnissent, quōs ego iam multīs ac summīs virīs ad mē id temporis ventūrōs esse praedīxeram.

Since you have become a menace and are foiled, leave the city.

5. Quae cum ita sint, Catilīna, perge, quō coepistī. Ēgredere aliquandō ex urbe; patent portae, proficīscere. Nimium diū tē imperātōrem tua illa Mānliāna castra dē-

FAESULAE

This is the modern Fiesole near Florence.　It was here that Manlius had his camp.

30. **cum**: ‘since.’　**iam**: ‘already,’ *i.e.* after the meeting at Laeca’s and before the early morning call of the would-be assassins.　By means of his numerous slaves and special guards (see page 81, lines 32–35), Cicero was able to keep in constant communication with his friends and supporters, day and night.

31. **id temporis:** see IDIOMS.　B. 185, 2; A & G. 346, *a*, 3, and 397 *a;* G. 336, N. 2.

5. 1. **Quae . . . sint:** see IDIOMS.　*167; 184, a;* B. 286, 2; 251, 6; A. & G. 308, *f;* G. 610, R. 1.　For the outline of the following argument, see page 521.

2. **aliquandō:** for *tandem aliquandō*.　**patent portae, proficīscere:** *239, a.*

3. **Mānliāna castra:** the camp at Faesulae.　B. 354, 4; A. & G. 343, *a*.　**dēsīderant:** this present tense must be translated by a progressive perfect, viz. ‘has been yearning for.’　*175, f;* B. 259, 4; A. & G. 466; G. 230.

sīderant. Ēdūc tēcum etiam omnēs tuōs; sī minus,
quam plūrimōs; pūrgā urbem.   5
Magnō mē metū līberābis, dum modo inter mē atque
tē mūrus intersit. Nōbīscum versārī iam diūtius nōn
potes; nōn feram, nōn patiar, nōn sinam.
   Magna dīs immortālibus habenda est atque huic ipsī
Iovī Statōrī, antīquissimō cūstōdī huius urbis, grātia, 10
quod hanc tam taetram, tam horribilem tamque īnfestam
reī pūblicae pestem totiēns iam effūgimus. Nōn est
saepius in ūnō homine summa salūs perīclitanda reī pūblicae.
   Quam diū mihi, cōnsulī dēsignātō, Catilīna, īnsidiātus
es, nōn pūblicō mē praesidiō, sed prīvātā dīligentiā dē- 15
fendī. Cum proximīs comitiīs cōnsulāribus mē cōnsulem

---

   4. **Ēdūc,** etc.: i.e. *Ēdūc etiam omnēs tuōs* ('your associates')
tēcum, sī fierī potest; sī minus (translate as if *sī nōn*), *at tamen ēdūc quam
plūrimōs.*
   5. **quam plūrimōs :** see IDIOMS.
   7. **intersit:** subjunctive of proviso. *190, d;* B. 310, II; A. & G. 528;
G. 573. **versārī:** here 'abide.' **nōn . . . sinam:** another climax,
with anaphora; see page 34, line 28, and note.
   9. **Magna:** i.e. *magna gratia habenda est dīs immortālibus,* etc.
B. 348, 349; A. & G. 598, e; G. 672, 2, a; 674 N. **huic ipsī Iovī Statōrī :**
with a gesture toward the statue of the divinity in whose temple they
were. See illustrations, pages 61, 107, 350, 413.
   10. **antīquissimō cūstōdī:** see note on page 61, line 30.
   12. **pestem :** 'scourge,' abstract for concrete. *92, b.*
   13. **in ūnō homine :** i.e. *in tē ūnō,* as shown by what follows; the
existence of the state ought not too often to be endangered by the
conduct of one man. **summa salūs reī pūblicae :** ' the highest interests
of the state.'
   14. **mihi, cōnsulī dēsignātō :** *i.e.* during the latter part of the year 64.
That Cicero was Catiline's main object of attack is evident from the
statement of Sallust, *Catilīna,* **26,** 1.
   15. **prīvātā dīligentiā :** (*Cicerō*) *circum sē praesidia amīcōrum atque
clientium occultē habēbat.* Sallust, *Catilīna,* **26,** 4.
   16. **proximīs comitiīs :** held for the election of consuls for the year
62; see Companion, pages 515, 516.

in campō et competītōrēs tuōs interficere voluistī, compressī
cōnātūs tuōs nefāriōs amīcōrum praesidiō et cōpiīs, nūllō
tumultū pūblicē concitātō; dēnique, quotiēnscumque mē
20 petistī, per mē tibi obstitī, quamquam vidēbam perniciem
meam cum magnā calamitāte reī pūblicae esse coniūnctam. Nunc iam apertē rem pūblicam ūniversam petis;
templa deōrum immortālium, tēcta urbis, vītam omnium cīvium, Italiam tōtam ad exitium et vāstitātem vocās.
25 Quā rē, quoniam id, quod est prīmum, et quod huius
imperī disciplīnaeque maiōrum proprium est, facere nōndum audeō, faciam id, quod est ad sevēritātem lēnius et
ad commūnem salūtem ūtilius. Nam sī tē interficī iusserō, residēbit in rē pūblicā reliqua coniūrātōrum manus;
30 sīn tū, quod tē iam dūdum hortor, exieris, exhauriētur

---

17. **in campō**: i.e. *in campō Mārtiō*, where the *comitia centuriāta*
(see Companion, page 570) were held. **competītōrēs tuōs**: D. Junius
Silanus (dẹs'i-mụs jūn'yụs sị-lā'nụs) and L. Licinius Murena (lū'sh(y)ụs
lị-sin'ị-ụs mụ-rē'nạ), who received the election, and Servius Sulpicius
(sẹr'vị-ụs (sụl-pish'(y)ụs).

18. **nūllō tumultū pūblicē concitātō**: *i.e.* without calling out the
troops, ' without any official summons to arms.'

19. **mē**: for *mē ūnum.*

20. **per mē**: i.e. *meīs cōpiīs*, instead of *pūblicīs cōpiīs*. **perniciem
meam . . . coniūnctam**: i.e. *sī perīrem, fore ut etiam rēs pūblica magnā
calamitāte afficerētur.*

21. **reī pūblicae**: kind of genitive?

22. **Nunc iam**: ' Now at last.'

25. **Quā rē**: ' And for this reason,' ' Wherefore.' **id**: the putting
of Catiline to death. **prīmum**: ' the first thing ' to be done, as we say.
huius imperī: i.e. *nostrī imperī*, the power given to the consuls by the
senate's decree of October 21; see page 29, lines 30–32. *102; B*. 204, 2;
A. & G. 349; G. 359, R. 1.

26. **disciplīnae maiōrum proprium**: shown by the precedents cited,
pages 28–30.

27. **ad**: ' with respect to.'

30. **quod**: for *id* (referring to the clause *sīn tū exieris*) *quod;* translate, *quod . . . hortor* idiomatically, ' as I have long been urging you.'

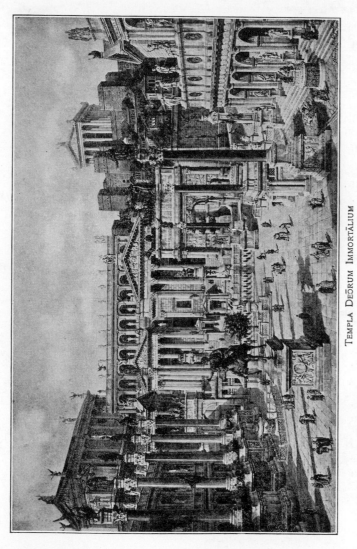

TEMPLA DEŌRUM IMMORTĀLIUM

Looking northwest in the Roman Forum of the Empire. The temple of Jupiter on the Capitoline Hill at the left; the Rostra in the background below.

ex urbe tuōrum comitum magna et perniciōsa sentīna
reī pūblicae.

Quid est, Catilīna? Num dubitās id, mē imperante,
facere, quod iam tuā sponte faciēbās? Exīre ex urbe
iubet cōnsul hostem. Interrogās mē, num in exsilium? 35
Nōn iubeō, sed sī mē cōnsulis, suādeō.

Why do you remain here, branded with crimes committed or attempted?

6. Quid est enim, Catilīna, quod tē iam in hāc urbe
dēlectāre possit? in quā nēmō est, extrā istam coniūrātiōnem perditōrum hominum, quī tē nōn metuat; nēmō,
quī nōn ōderit.

Quae nota domesticae turpitūdinis nōn inūsta vītae 5
tuae est? Quod prīvātārum rērum dēdecus nōn haeret
in fāmā? Quae libīdō ab oculīs, quod facinus ā manibus

---

31. **sentīna reī pūblicae :** treated as expressing one concept, hence
followed by the genitive (*tuōrum*) *comitum*, 'the bilge-water of the
(ship of) state consisting of your associates.' See Sallust, *Catilīna*, **37,**
5 : *Omnēs, quōs flāgitium aut facinus domō expulerat eī Rōmam sīcut
in sentīnam cōnflūxerant,* where *sentīna* by metonymy is used of the
receptacle (' cess-pool ') rather than of the ' sewage.'

33. **Quid est :** like our ' How now? ' ' How is that? ' **mē impe-**
rante : see IDIOMS.

34. **faciēbās :** ' you were on the point of doing.' *175, e;* B. 260, 3 ;
A. & G. 471, *c;* G. 233.

35. **cōnsul hostem :** more dignified and more forcible than *ego tē.*
num : ' still, not ' ; fuller, ' you don't mean into exile, do you? '

6. 1. **Quid est enim :** rhetorical question, much more effective than
the simple form of statement, *Nihil est enim.* The very thought of his
career of crime, and the fear and hatred with which he is regarded, ought
to make Catiline flee the city. *179, b.*

2. **possit :** *194, a.* **coniūrātiōnem :** concrete, ' sworn band.' *92, b.*

5. **domesticae :** arising from his family relations (see line 12, *et seq.*),
while *prīvātārum rērum* (line 6) refers to his private life in general, as
distinguished from his public career. **inūsta :** ' branded upon,' as on
the forehead of a runaway slave.

7. **facinus :** ' wicked deed ' affecting others, while *flāgitium* is a
' burning shame ' touching more directly the agent himself.

umquam tuīs, quod flāgitium ā tōtō corpore āfuit? Cuǐ
tū adulēscentulō, quem corruptēlārum illecebrīs irrētissēs,
10 nōn aut ad audāciam ferrum aut ad libīdinem facem praetulistī?

Quid vērō? nūper, cum morte superiōris uxōris novīs
nūptiīs domum vacuēfēcissēs, nōnne etiam aliō incrēdibilī scelere hōc scelus cumulāstī? quod ego praetermittō
15 et facile patior silērī, nē in hāc cīvitāte tantī facinoris
immānitās aut exstitisse aut nōn vindicāta esse videātur.
Praetermittō ruīnās fortūnārum tuārum, quās omnēs impendēre tibi proximīs Īdibus sentiēs; ad illa veniō, quae nōn

---

10. **facem praetulistī**: as slaves were wont to do for their masters
when going about the streets by night. The fascinating but baneful
influence which Catiline gained over the young is described by Sallust,
Catilīna, **14,** 5-7.

12. **Quid vērō**: introduces still stronger evidence of Catiline's
wickedness. **morte**: for *nece*, could be ablative either of time or of
means, though Cicero intends it for the latter. Both the word and the
case, therefore, are purposely ambiguous. This murder is mentioned
nowhere else.

13. **aliō scelere**: *i.e.* the murder of a son by the first marriage, from
fear that he might become a source of annoyance to the new wife, whose
name was Aurelia Orestilla.

14. **quod**: 'but this.' The relative is freely used in Latin at the
beginning of a sentence, but the English idiom prefers a conjunction and
a demonstrative. *167*. **praetermittō**, etc.: what is the technical name
for this rhetorical device? See page 28, note 25.

16. **nōn vindicāta esse**: 'to have been left unpunished'; sc. *sī
exstiterit*. According to Roman criminal procedure (see Companion,
page 572) a court would take cognizance of a crime only when some one
formally directed attention to it by lodging a complaint. In this instance the fact that no one could be found who would bring so atrocious
and well-known a crime to the notice of the authorities — the orator
implies — bore witness to the shameful degeneracy of the times.

17. **omnēs**: accusative with *quās*. *97, c*. Translate as if *omnium
fortūnārum*, ' the complete downfall of all your fortunes, which.'

18. **proximīs Īdibus**: the Ides and Kalends (to a less extent the
Nones also) were the customary times for the computation of interest
and the payment of debts. Cicero hints that Catiline, hopelessly in

ad prīvātam ignōminiam vitiōrum tuōrum, nōn ad domes-
ticam tuam difficultātem ac turpitūdinem, sed ad summam 20
rem pūblicam atque ad omnium nostrum vītam salūtem-
que pertinent.

Potestne tibi haec lūx, Catilīna, aut huius caelī spīritus
esse iūcundus, cum sciās esse hōrum nēminem, quī nesciat,
tē prīdiē Kalendās Iānuāriās, Lepidō et Tullō cōnsulibus, 25
stetisse in comitiō cum tēlō, manum cōnsulum et prīncipum
cīvitātis interficiendōrum causā parāvisse, scelerī ac furōrī
tuō nōn mentem aliquam aut timōrem tuum, sed fortūnam
populī Rōmānī obstitisse?

Ac iam illa omittō — neque enim sunt aut obscūra 30
aut nōn multa commissa posteā; quotiēns tū mē dē-
signātum, quotiēns cōnsulem interficere cōnātus es! Quot
ego tuās petītiōnēs ita coniectās, ut vītārī posse nōn vidē-

---

debt (see Companion, page 515), is nearing a financial crisis, and will
realize the failure of all his schemes when the next day of settlement
comes, as his creditors are losing confidence in him.

20. **difficultātem**: financial 'straits.' **summam**: see IDIOMS.

24. **cum**: 'seeing that.' *184, a;* B. 286, 2; A. & G. 549; G. 586.
hōrum: see page 26, line 6, and note.

25. **prīdiē Kalendās Iānuāriās**: *i.e.* the last day of December, 66 B.C.;
on the following day it was proposed to murder the incoming consuls,
Cotta and Torquatus; see Companion, page 514. *241 c;* B. 144, 1, 2;
A. & G. 432, *a;* G. page 491.

26. **manum . . . parāvisse**: in preparation for the attempt on
February 5, 65 B.C.

28. **mentem aliquam**: 'any reflection,' 'any (change of) purpose.'
fortūnam: Catiline by accident gave the signal prematurely; see
Companion, page 515.

30. **illa**: 'those (earlier attempts).' **neque . . . posteā**: 'for
they are neither unknown nor few which you perpetrated afterwards';
the negative force of *neque* affects the whole sentence, while that of *nōn*
is confined to *multa*. The litotes makes this a forceful sentence. *239, m.*

33. **petītiōnēs ita coniectās**: 'thrusts so directed'; this phrase, as
well as that in the next line, is borrowed from the speech of fencers or
gladiators. **ut . . . vidērentur**: render idiomatically, 'that it seemed

rentur, parvā quādam dēclīnātiōne et, ut aiunt, corpore
35 effūgī!
Nihil assequeris, neque tamen cōnārī ac velle dēsistis.
Quotiēns tibi iam extorta est sīca ista dē manibus! Quotiēns excidit cāsū aliquō et ēlāpsa est! Quae quidem quibus
abs tē initiāta sacrīs ac dēvōta sit, nesciō, quod eam necesse
40 putās esse in cōnsulis corpore dēfīgere.

The senators and all good men shun you.

7. Nunc vērō quae tua est ista vīta? Sīc enim iam tē
cum loquar, nōn ut odiō permōtus esse videar, quō dēbeō,
sed ut misericordiā, quae tibi nūlla dēbētur.
Vēnistī paulō ante in senātum. Quis tē ex hāc tantā
5 frequentiā, tot ex tuīs amīcīs ac necessāriīs salūtāvit?
Sī hōc post hominum memoriam contigit nēminī, vōcis
exspectās contumēliam, cum sīs gravissimō iūdiciō taci-
turnitātis oppressus?

---

impossible to avoid them.' How literally? In cases like this the Latin
prefers the personal construction, the English the impersonal. *224, a;*
B. 332, *b;* A. & G. 582; G. 528, 1, 2.

34. **dēclīnātiōne et corpore:** hendiadys; 'by a mere twist of the
body.' *238, h.*

36. **neque tamen:** translate as if *et tamen* . . . *nōn.*

37. **tibi:** *109, b;* B. 188, 2, *d;* A. & G. 381; G. 345, R.

38. **excidit:** i.e. *ē manibus tuīs.* **Quae . . . dēfīgere:** i.e. *Et
quidem quibus sacrīs ea* (*sīca*) *abs tē initiāta ac dēvōta sit, quod* (' for the
reason that ') *putās necesse esse eam in corpore cōnsulis dēfīgere, nesciō*
(' I'm sure I don't know,' *i.e.* ' I don't care to say '). A weapon with
which a violent deed had been committed was often consecrated to a
divinity.

7. 2. **odiō:** ' enmity.' **permōtus esse:** why not *permovērī?*

3. **quae tibi nūlla dēbētur:** idiomatically, ' which you do not at
all deserve '; *nūlla* is much stronger here than *nōn.*

4. **hāc tantā frequentiā:** ' this large assembly,' not ' this so large.'
Guard against developing a Latin-English idiom.

6. **contigit:** used often of favorable occurrences. **vōcis, taciturni-
tātis:** explanatory genitives. *96, a.*

Quid, quod adventū tuō ista subsellia vacuēfacta sunt, quod omnēs cōnsulārēs, quī tibi persaepe ad caedem 10 cōnstitūtī fuērunt, simul atque assēdistī, partem istam subselliōrum nūdam atque inānem relīquērunt, quō tandem animō tibi ferendum putās?

Servī mē hercule meī sī mē istō pactō metuerent, ut tē metuunt omnēs cīvēs tuī, domum meam relinquendam 15 putārem; tū tibi urbem nōn arbitrāris? et, sī mē meīs cīvibus iniūriā suspectum tam graviter atque offēnsum vidērem, carēre mē aspectū cīvium, quam īnfestīs omnium oculīs cōnspicī māllem; tū, cum cōnscientiā scelerum tuōrum agnōscās odium omnium iūstum et iam diū tibi 20 dēbitum, dubitās, quōrum mentēs sēnsūsque vulnerās, eōrum aspectum praesentiamque vītāre?

---

9. **Quid, quod:** ' What of this, that '; see note on page 34, line 25. **quod . . . sunt:** explained by the following clause.

10. **tibi:** translate as if *abs tē*. This type of dative is by no means equivalent to an expression of agency, but indicates rather the person who is concerned in the action. *110, b;* B. 189, 2; A. & G. 375; G. 354.

11. **cōnstitūtī fuērunt:** more forcible than *cōnstitūtī sunt*, as implying that Catiline's attempts are all and altogether in the past.

12. **quō animō:** see IDIOMS.

14. **istō pactō, ut:** ' in such a way, as,' = ' as.'

15. **omnēs cīvēs:** Cicero does not regard the followers of Catiline as citizens. **domum . . . arbitrāris:** i.e. *domum meam mihi relinquendam esse putārem; tū tibi urbem relinquendam esse nōn arbitrāris?* Notice the conditional statements in this paragraph, which lead up to a climax (' slaves ' — ' citizens ' — ' parents '), and present the orator's thought far more effectively than the simple direct assertion of the same points.

17. **iniūriā:** ' undeservedly.' **suspectum:** here an adjective, but translate, ' an object of suspicion.'

18. **aspectū:** *127, a.* **omnium:** we should say ' by all.'

19. **cum:** see page 43, line 24, and note. **cōnscientiā:** *not* ' conscience.'

20. **odium:** sc. *esse*.

Your country begs you to depart.

Sī tē parentēs timērent atque ōdissent tuī neque eōs ūllā
ratiōne plācāre possēs, tū, opīnor, ab eōrum oculīs aliquō
25 concēderēs.   Nunc tē patria, quae commūnis est parēns omnium nostrum, ōdit ac metuit et iam diū nihil tē iūdicat nisi
dē parricīdiō suō cōgitāre; huius tū neque auctōritātem
verēbere, nec iūdicium sequēre, nec vim pertimēscēs?
Quae tēcum, Catilīna, sīc agit et quōdam modō tacita
30 loquitur:
   "Nūllum iam aliquot annīs facinus exstitit nisi per tē,
nūllum flāgitium sine tē; tibi ūnī multōrum cīvium necēs,
tibi vexātiō dīreptiōque sociōrum impūnīta fuit ac lībera;
tū nōn sōlum ad neglegendās lēgēs et quaestiōnēs, vērum
35 etiam ad ēvertendās perfringendāsque valuistī.
   "Superiōra illa, quamquam ferenda nōn fuērunt, tamen,

---

23. tuī: *211;* B. 348, 349; A. & G. 598, *e;* G. 672, 2, *a,* 674 N.

25. Nunc: *νῦν δέ,* ' But as it is.'   omnium nostrum: *155.*

26. nihil . . . cōgitāre: *tē cōgitāre nihil* (for *dē nūllā rē*) *nisi dē,* etc.

27. parricīdiō: for *exitiō,* or *interitū,* carrying out the personification
of *patria* as *commūnis parēns.*   Review introductory note, page 520.
huius: ' her.'

28. iūdicium sequēre: i.e. *iūdiciō, quod dē tē facit, obtemperābis.*

29. Quae: ' Now she.'   tacita: ' (though) silent '; oxymóron in
tacita loquitur, the force of which is somewhat lessened by *quōdam
modō,* ' in a way.'   *239, p;* B. *375, 2;* A & G. 641; G. 694.

31. annīs: ablative as indicating the period in which (*not* through
which) the statement in *exstitit* was true.   per tē: why not *abs tē?*

32. necēs: in connection with the proscriptions of Sulla; see
Companion, page 514.   The plural of *nex* is rare.

33. sociōrum: i.e. *prōvinciālium.*   Previous to 89 B.C. only the
inhabitants of the Italian cities in league with Rome were called *sociī;*
but as these were then admitted to the Roman citizenship (page 229,
lines 9–12), the term was afterwards extended to the natives of the
provinces.   The reference here is to Catiline's governorship in Africa,
which was characterized by rapacity and brutality.   See page 514.

34. quaestiōnēs: ' judicial investigations.'   Catiline had been
accused of provincial extortion, but had purchased an acquittal.

36. Superiōra illa: ' Those former acts.'   *211.* ferenda: see IDIOMS.

ut potuī, tulī; nunc vērō mē tōtam esse in metū propter
ūnum tē, quicquid increpuerit, Catilīnam timērī, nūllum
vidērī contrā mē cōnsilium inīrī posse, quod ā tuō scelere
abhorreat, nōn est ferendum.

40

"Quam ob rem discēde atque hunc mihi timōrem ēripe;
sī est vērus, nē opprimar, sīn falsus, ut tandem aliquandō
timēre dēsinam."

8. Haec sī tēcum, ut dīxī, patria loquātur, nōnne impetrāre dēbeat, etiam sī vim adhibēre nōn possit?

Reputable citizens have declined to vouch for you.

Quid, quod tū tē ipse in cūstōdiam dedistī, quod vītandae
suspīciōnis causā ad M'. Lepidum tē habitāre velle dīxistī?

---

37. **tōtam:** *i.e.* not now merely in regard to individuals or provinces,
but as a whole.

38. **quicquid increpuerit:** 'at every sound.' How literally? Subjunctive by attraction. *220.*

39. **vidērī:** forms of this verb are often best translated by adverbs,
such as ' evidently,' ' manifestly.' **quod ā tuō scelere:** translate as if
ā quō tuum scelus.

8. 1. **loquātur, dēbeat:** the condition is in fact impossible; but
consistently with the personification of *patria* it is conceived as possible,
and hence put in the present subjunctive. *218 (2).*

2. **possit:** concessive. *191;* B. 309, 2, *a;* A. & G. 527, *c;* G.
604, and R. 2.

3. **Quid, quod:** see page 45, line 9, and note. **in cūstōdiam:**
i.e. *in cūstōdiam līberam.* In cases in which a Roman citizen was charged
with a crime against the state, if a person of rank, he was not imprisoned
but put under surveillance, either in his own house or in the house
of some magistrate who became responsible for his appearance when
wanted for trial. In this instance Catiline had been accused of inciting
to riot (sedition) by Lucius Paulus; see Companion, page 516. Nothing
better illustrates the audacity of the man than the attempt to get
Lepidus, Metellus, and even Cicero, to take charge of him. Owing to
the rapid culmination of events the trial did not take place.

4. **ad M'. Lepidum:** in the sense of *apud,* 'at the house of M'.
Lepidus (mā'nǐ-ŭs lep'ǐ-dŭs).'

₅Ā quō nōn receptus etiam ad mē venīre ausus es atque, ut domī meae tē asservārem, rogāstī.

Cum ā mē quoque id respōnsum tulissēs, mē nūllō modō posse īsdem parietibus tūtō esse tēcum, quī magnō in perīculō essem, quod īsdem moenibus continērēmur, ₁₀ad Q. Metellum praetōrem vēnistī. Ā quō repudiātus ad sodālem tuum, virum optimum, M. Metellum, dēmigrāstī; quem tū vidēlicet et ad cūstōdiendum dīligentissimum et ad suspicandum sagācissimum et ad vindicandum fortissimum fore putāstī.

₁₅   Sed quam longē vidētur ā carcere atque ā vinculīs abesse dēbēre, quī sē ipse iam dignum cūstōdiā iūdicārit! Quae cum ita sint, Catilīna, dubitās, sī ēmorī aequō animō nōn potes, abīre in aliquās terrās et vītam istam, multīs suppliciīs iūstīs dēbitīsque ēreptam, fugae sōlitūdinīque ₂₀mandāre?

Judgment has silently been passed upon you by the senate.

"Refer," inquis, "ad senātum"; id enim postulās et, sī hīc ōrdō placēre dēcrēverit tē īre in exsilium, obtempe-

---

6. **domī:** *146;* B. 232, 2; A. & G. 427, *a;* G. 411, R. 2.

7. **nūllō modō:** ' by no means.'

8. **parietibus:** ablative of means, but translate by ' within.'

9. **continērēmur:** why not indicative?

10. **Q. Metellum** (kwin′tụs mẹ-tel′ụs). **repudiātus:** *227, a (5).*

11. **virum optimum:** bitter irony.

12. **quem . . .:** be careful of your English. **vidēlicet:** sarcastic.

15. **carcere, vinculīs:** contrasted with *cūstōdiā* in the sense of *cūstōdiā lībera.*

16. **iūdicārit:** *194, b;* B. 283; A. & G. 535; G. 631.   Full form? **Quae . . . sint:** see Idioms.

17. **aequō animō:** ' with resignation.'   You deserve physical death, by your own hand or by that of the executioner; if you cannot be brought to this, at least favor us with your political death by going into exile.

21. **Refer:** sc. *rem,* ' the matter.'   See Idioms.   **postulās:** perhaps referring to previous utterances of Catiline.

rātūrum tē esse dīcis. Nōn referam, id quod abhorret ā
meīs mōribus; et tamen faciam, ut intellegās, quid hī dē
tē sentiant.   25

Egredere ex urbe, Catilīna, līberā rem pūblicam
metū; in exsilium, sī hanc vōcem exspectās, proficīscere.

Quid est, Catilīna? ecquid attendis, ecquid animadvertis
hōrum silentium?   30

Patiuntur, tacent.   Quid exspectās auctōritātem loquen-
tium, quōrum voluntātem tacitōrum perspicis?

At sī hōc idem huic adulēscentī optimō P. Sēstiō, sī
fortissimō virō, M. Mārcellō, dīxissem, iam mihi cōnsulī hōc
ipsō in templō iūre optimō senātus vim et manūs intulisset. 35

Dē tē autem, Catilīna, cum quiēscunt, probant;   cum

---

23. **referam**: i.e. *rem ad senātum*. **id . . . mōribus**: 'a course
inconsistent with my character' as a mild man opposed to severe
measures.   As a matter of fact, however, the right to pronounce a
sentence of exile belonged to the courts alone, and was outside the
jurisdiction of the senate.

24. **hī**: see *hōrum*, page 26, line 6, and note.

26. **Ēgredere . . . proficīscere**: probably spoken with deliberation
and great distinctness.   Review introductory note, page 520.

29. **Quid est**: spoken after a pause, giving opportunity for dissent;
see page 41, line 33, and note.   There were friends of Catiline present
(see page 58, line 14, *et seq.*), but after the orator's vigorous reference to
them (page 36, lines 8–17) they did not dare to come to the rescue of
their leader.

31. **auctōritātem**: 'the express request.'

34. **M. Mārcellō** (mär'kŭs mȧr-sel'ŭs):   see vocabulary under
Mārcellus (2), and pages 511–513. **hōc ipsō in templō**: heightens the
rhetorical effect; a temple was considered a place of refuge, its sacredness being a protection against violence.

35. **iūre optimō**: 'with perfect right.' **vim et manūs**: 'violent
hands'; hendiadys. *238, h.*

36. **cum quiēscunt, probant**: 'by their stillness, they approve';
coincident action, hence indicative with *cum*. *185, a*. Notice the
oxymoron and climax in the three *cum*-clauses. *239, p; 239, f.*

patiuntur, dēcernunt; cum tacent, clāmant; neque hī
sōlum, quōrum tibi auctōritās est vidēlicet cāra, vīta vīlis-
sima, sed etiam illī equitēs Rōmānī, honestissimī atque
40 optimī virī, cēterīque fortissimī cīvēs, quī circumstant
senātum, quōrum tū et frequentiam vidēre et studia perspicere et vōcēs paulō ante exaudīre potuistī. Quōrum
ego vix abs tē iam diū manūs ac tēla contineō, eōsdem facile
addūcam, ut tē haec, quae vāstāre iam prīdem studēs,
45 relinquentem ūsque ad portās prōsequantur.

You are beyond all hope.

9. Quamquam quid loquor? Tē ut ūlla rēs frangat?
tū ut umquam tē corrigās? tū ut ūllam fugam meditēre?
tū ut exsilium cōgitēs? Utinam tibi istam mentem dī
immortālēs duint!

---

37. **neque hī sōlum :** translate as if *et nōn sōlum hī.*

38. **auctōritās,** etc. : refers back to page 48, line 22.

39. **illī :** with a gesture; the knights were gathered in front of the
temple, in view of the speaker. See note on page 26, lines 4-5. **hones··
tissimī :** *not* ' very honest.'

40. **cēterī cīvēs :** below the rank of senator and knight.

42. **paulō ante :** *i.e.* as Catiline was entering the temple to meet
with the senate. **exaudīre :** here ' plainly hear,' ' hear distinctly.'

44. **haec :** ' this country of ours,' *i.e.* the city of Rome and the Roman
power; doubtless spoken with a wide gesture; *haec* is so used in other
passages. **iam prīdem :** see Idioms.

45. **ad portās :** it was customary for the friends and relatives of those
who were going into exile to escort them as far as the city gate ; Catiline
will have a large escort of those eager to see him depart, who will also
protect him.

9. 1. **Quamquam :** ' And yet.' This word is often used in independent clauses with a corrective meaning. **Tē ut,** etc. : idiomatic,
' You . . . anything break your resolution? You . . . ever reform
yourself? ' Note the anaphora and the *staccato* effect produced by the
dental and palatal consonants, as well as the vibrant ring expressed by
an abundance of ' m ' sounds. *179, c;* B. 277, *a;* A. & G. 462, *a;* G. 558.

4. **duint :** *dent;* archaic form, apparently from stem *du-*, with
subjunctive ending same as in *velint, possint;* appropriate in prayers

Tametsī videō, sī meā vōce perterritus īre in exsilium 5
animum indūxeris, quanta tempestās invidiae nōbīs, sī
minus in praesēns tempus, recentī memoriā scelerum tuōrum, at in posteritātem impendeat. Sed est tantī, dum
modo ista sit prīvāta calamitās et ā reī pūblicae perīculīs
sēiungātur.   10

Sed tū ut vitiīs tuīs commoveāre, ut lēgum poenās
pertimēscās, ut temporibus reī pūblicae cēdās, nōn est postulandum. Neque enim is es, Catilīna, ut tē aut pudor umquam ā turpitūdine aut metus ā perīculō aut ratiō ā furōre
revocārit.   15

Depart, and join your associates in crime.

Quam ob rem, ut saepe iam dīxī, proficīscere, ac, sī
mihi inimīcō, ut praedicās, tuō cōnflāre vīs invidiam, rēctā
perge in exsilium.

Vix feram sermōnēs hominum, sī id fēceris; vix mōlem

---

and wishes, just as our so-called " solemn " style, as in English, " Thy
Kingdom *come,* Thy will *be done.*" *180, c;* B. 116, 4, *d,* and 279; A. &
G. 183, 2, and 442; G. 130, 4, and 261.

    6. animum: see IDIOMS. **nōbīs:** refers to Cicero alone, as shown
by the use of *meā* in line 5. *107, a;* B. 187, III; A. & G. 143, *a;* 370;
G. 347, R. 2.

    8. in posteritātem: = *in posterum tempus.* That Cicero's fear was
not groundless, his subsequent persecution and sufferings plainly enough
showed. See Companion, page 491. **est tantī:** ' it is worth while,' i.e.
invidiam istam mihi impendēre. 101; B. 203, 3; A. & G. 417; G. 380, R.

    9. prīvāta: ' personal,' not extending beyond the person of the
speaker.

    11. ut . . . commoveāre . . . pertimēscās . . . cēdās: substantive
clauses of purpose, subjects of *est postulandum. 199, b;* B. 295; A. & G.
566; G. 546.

    12. temporibus: ' to the exigencies,' — that Catiline subordinate
his personal convenience to the good of the state.

    13. is: ' such a man.'

    17. inimīcō, ut praedicās: Catiline interpreted the acts of the consul
as those of a ' personal enemy.' See note on page 39, line 14.

    19. Vix feram: see IDIOMS.

20 istīus invidiae, sī in exsilium iussū cōnsulis ieris, sustinēbō. Sīn autem servīre meae laudī et glōriae māvīs, ēgredere cum importūnā scelerātōrum manū, cōnfer tē ad Mānlium, concitā perditōs cīvēs, sēcerne tē ā bonīs, īnfer patriae bellum, exsultā impiō latrōciniō, ut ā mē nōn ēiectus ad 25 aliēnōs, sed invītātus ad tuōs īsse videāris.

Quamquam quid ego tē in-vītem, ā quō iam sciam esse praemissōs, quī tibi ad Forum 30 Aurēlium praestōlārentur, armātī? cui iam sciam pactam et cōnstitūtam cum Mānliō diem? ā quō etiam aquilam illam argen-team, quam tibi ac tuīs omnibus 35 cōnfīdō perniciōsam ac fūnestam futūram, cui domī tuae sacrārium

A SACRARIUM

This is a family shrine with idols.

24. **impiō latrōciniō:** ' treasonable brigandage,' as against law and order; called *impiō* because against the Father-land — *commūnis parēns.* Review in-troductory note, page 520. **ad aliēnōs:** sc. *īsse.*

27. **Quamquam:** as on page 50, line 1. **quid:** adverbial accusative, ' why.' *118, e.* **invītem:** *179, b* (2); B. 277, and *a;* A. & G. 444; G. 265.

28. **esse praemissōs:** ' (men) have been sent forward,' in the night of November 7.

29. **quī . . . praestōlārentur:** translate by ' to ' with the infinitive. **Forum Aurelium** (fō'rŭm â-rē'lǐ-ŭm). See Key to Pronunciation, page 709.

32. **diem:** why feminine? *21, a.*

33. **aquilam illam argenteam:** in Marius' time a silver eagle with outstretched wings was adopted as the ensign of the legion; later eagles were sometimes of gold. The one mentioned here had been carried in the army of Marius, in the campaign against the Cimbri (sim'brī) (Sallust, *Catilīna,* **59,** 3).

36. **cui:** refers to *aquilam.* **sacrārium:** the eagle of a legion was

scelerum tuōrum cōnstitūtum fuit, sciam esse praemissam?
Tū ut illā carēre diūtius possīs, quam venerārī ad caedem
proficīscēns solēbās, ā cuius altāribus saepe istam impiam
dexteram ad necem cīvium trānstulistī? 4⑤

You will find happiness only in the society of criminals.

10. Ībis tandem aliquandō, quō tē iam prīdem ista tua
cupiditās effrēnāta ac furiōsa rapiēbat; neque enim tibi
haec rēs affert dolōrem, sed quandam incrēdibilem voluptātem. Ad hanc tē āmentiam nātūra peperit, voluntās
exercuit, fortūna servāvit. 5

Numquam tū nōn modo ōtium, sed nē bellum quidem
nisi nefārium concupīstī. Nactus es ex perditīs atque ab
omnī nōn modo fortūnā, vērum etiam spē dērelīctīs
cōnflātam improbōrum manum. Hīc tū quā laetitiā per-
fruēre! quibus gaudiīs exsultābis! quantā in voluptāte 10

considered sacred, and intimately associated with the fortunes of the
host. When in camp it was kept in a consecrated place near the commander's tent. So Catiline is here represented as having the eagle in
a 'sanctuary' or 'shrine' in his house, and as making it an object
of veneration.

37. **scelerum tuōrum :** characterizes *sacrārium;* freely, 'sacred to
your crimes.'

38. **Tū . . . possīs :** see page 50, line 1, and note.

10. 3. **haec rēs :** 'this action,' departure to join Manlius in war
against the state.

4. **voluntās :** 'inclination.'

5. **fortūna servāvit :** Catiline had thus far escaped punishment for
his misdeeds.

6. **nōn modo :** translate as if *nōn modo nōn.* In expressions like
this the Latin omits the negative after *modo,* because a negative is
understood with the verb (in this case *concupīstī*) from the following
clause; but as English idiom requires the verb in the first clause, the
negative must be supplied in translating. *236, e;* B. 343, 2, *a;* A. & G.
217, *e;* G. 482, R. 1.

7. **nefārium :** i.e. *cīvīle.* **ex perditīs :** i.e. *ex (hominibus) perditīs
atque dērelīctīs nōn modo ab omnī fortūnā vērum etiam (ab omnī) spē.*
126, b; B. 216, 1; A. & G. 405, N. 3; G. 214, R. 2.

bacchābere, cum in tantō numerō tuōrum neque audiēs
virum bonum quemquam neque vidēbis!

Ad huius vītae studium meditātī illī sunt, quī feruntur,
labōrēs tuī, iacēre humī nōn sōlum ad obsidendum stuprum,
15 vērum etiam ad facinus obeundum, vigilāre nōn sōlum
īnsidiantem somnō marītōrum, vērum etiam bonīs ōtiōsōrum. Habēs, ubi ostentēs tuam illam praeclāram pati-
entiam famis, frīgoris, inopiae rērum omnium, quibus tē
brevī tempore cōnfectum esse sentiēs. Tantum prōfēcī
20 tum, cum tē ā cōnsulātū reppulī, ut exsul potius temptāre
quam cōnsul vexāre rem pūblicam possēs, atque ut id, quod
esset ā tē scelerātē susceptum, latrōcinium potius quam
bellum nōminārētur.

*I subject myself to the charge of failing to do my duty if I allow you to leave
instead of ordering you put to death.*

11. Nunc, ut ā mē, patrēs cōnscrīptī, quandam prope
iūstam patriae querimōniam dētester ac dēprecer, percipite,

11. **bacchābere:** this word connotes far more than the English
' revel '; it is more realistic and refers to the wild orgies of the frenzied
Bacchanals, the female worshipers of the god Dionysus (dī-ō-nī′sŭs).

13. **Ad huius vītae studium:** ' To pursue this kind of life,' *i.e.* the life
of a bandit. **meditātī sunt:** here passive. **feruntur:** here = *praedi-
cantur*, ' are (so much) talked about,' ' are a matter of current report.'

14. **labōrēs:** ' exertions.' **iacēre, vigilāre:** in apposition with
labōrēs. *222, d.* **obsidendum:** here *speculandum*.

16. **ōtiōsōrum:** peaceably disposed citizens, who would go to bed
with no thought of danger from burglars or brigands.

17. **Habēs, ubi ostentēs:** ' You have an opportunity to display ';
ubi with the sense of *(locum) in quō* is used with the subjunctive of
characteristic. *194, a.*

20. **ā cōnsulātū reppulī:** at the last consular election; see page 39,
lines 16–18, and note. **exsul, cōnsul:** play upon words; so below (lines
11–12), *ēmissus, immissus.*

22. **latrōcinium:** see page 52, line 24, and note.

11. 2. **dētester ac dēprecer:** ' I may completely preclude '; synonymic combination, a mark of Cicero's style. The following justifica-

quaesō, dīligenter, quae dīcam, et ea penitus animīs vestrīs
mentibusque mandāte. Etenim, sī mēcum patria, quae
mihi vītā meā multō est cārior, sī cūncta Italia, sī omnis rēs 5
pūblica loquātur:

"M. Tullī, quid agis? Tūne eum, quem esse hostem com-
peristī, quem ducem bellī futūrum vidēs, quem exspectārī
imperātōrem in castrīs hostium sentīs, auctōrem sceleris,
prīncipem coniūrātiōnis, ēvocātōrem servōrum et cīvium 10
perditōrum, exīre patiēre, ut abs tē nōn ēmissus ex urbe,
sed immissus in urbem esse videātur? Nōnne hunc in

ROMAN REPUBLICAN COIN

Obverse: The Goddess Roma.   Reverse: The Dioscuri, Castor and Pollux.

tion of the orator's course is a kind of *refūtātiō;* it seems too elaborate
to have been altogether extempore, and was very probably inserted, or
at least expanded, when the speech was revised.

5. **est:** why not *sit?* See *214, c;* B. 324, 1; A. & G. 593, *a,* N. 1;
G. 663, 1.

6. **loquātur:** the apodosis is omitted, on account of the length of
the address which follows; for the mood, see page 47, line 1, and note.
Notice the climax in *patria . . . cūncta Italia . . . omnis rēs pūblica.*
Review introductory note, page 520. *238, a; 239, f.*

7. **Tūne . . . patiēre:** see *211;* B. 351, 5; A. & G. 601, *a, b;*
G. 684.

10. **ēvocātōrem servōrum:** according to Sallust (*Catilīna,* **56,** 5),
Catiline refused the help of slaves, thinking that it would be to his
disadvantage if he should appear to have made common cause with
them; yet Lentulus urged their employment, and there were uprisings
of slaves at Capua and in Apulia at this time.

vincula dūcī, nōn ad mortem rapī, nōn summō suppliciō
mactārī imperābis?

15 "Quid tandem tē impedit? Mōsne maiōrum? At persaepe etiam prīvātī in hāc rē pūblicā perniciōsōs cīvēs
morte multārunt.

"An lēgēs, quae dē cīvium Rōmānōrum suppliciō rogātae
sunt? At numquam in hāc urbe, quī ā rē pūblicā dēfēcē-
20 runt, cīvium iūra tenuērunt.

"An invidiam posteritātis timēs? Praeclāram vērō
populō Rōmānō refers grātiam, quī tē, hominem per tē
cognitum, nūllā commendātiōne maiōrum tam mātūrē ad

---

13. **dūcī . . . rapī . . . mactārī imperābis:** while *imperāre* regularly
takes the subjunctive with *ut* or *nē*, Cicero and Caesar sometimes employ
the infinitive when this is passive. *199, c.*

15. **persaepe . . . multārunt:** rhetorical exaggeration; the orator
has cited only one case of the kind (page 28, line 21, *et seq.*).

18. **lēgēs:** the laws guarding the right of appeal to the people from
the decision of a magistrate. The earliest was one of the Valerian Laws
(508 B.C.), which enacted: *nē quis magistrātus cīvem Rōmānum adversus
prōvocātiōnem* (' against an appeal ' to the people assembled in *comitia*)
necāret nēve verberāret. There was also a *Lēx Porcia* (probably of
197 B.C.), which seems to have made it possible for a Roman citizen to
save himself from the death penalty, or from scourging, by voluntarily
going into exile; and the right of appeal, in accordance with which a
Roman could not be put to death or flogged without the assent of the
people, was reaffirmed by one of the laws proposed by Gaius Gracchus
(123 B.C.). Cicero's position is, that citizens who have taken up arms
against the state have forfeited their civil rights, and are no longer
entitled to the protection afforded by the laws. On this question, see
note on page 519, line **11.**

21. **Praeclāram vērō,** etc.: ' 'Tis indeed a fine gratitude which you
show, etc.'

22. **refers:** see IDIOMS. **hominem . . . maiōrum:** Cicero was a
novus homō.

23. **commendātiōne:** *143, a;* B. 224; A. & G. 415; G. 400. **tam
mātūrē . . . extulit:** Cicero was elected to each office *suō annō,* i.e.
as soon as he had reached the age required by law. Usually ' new men '
were not able to secure the consulship till some years after they had
reached the legal age.

summum imperium per omnēs honōrum gradūs extulit, sī propter invidiae aut alicuius perīculī metum salūtem 25 cīvium tuōrum neglegis. Sed, sī quis est invidiae metus, num est vehementius sevēritātis ac fortitūdinis invidia quam inertiae ac nēquitiae pertimēscenda?

"An, cum bellō vāstābitur Italia, vexābuntur urbēs, tēcta ārdēbunt, tum tē nōn exīstimās invidiae incendiō 30 cōnflagrātūrum?"

But it is better, senators, that Catiline be permitted to leave and thus draw his accomplices away from the city.

12. Hīs ego sānctissimīs reī pūblicae vōcibus et eōrum hominum, quī hōc idem sentiunt, mentibus pauca respondēbō.

Ego, sī hōc optimum factū iūdicārem, patrēs cōnscrīptī, Catilīnam morte multārī, ūnīus ūsūram hōrae gladiātōrī 5 istī ad vīvendum nōn dedissem. Etenim, sī summī virī et clārissimī cīvēs Sāturnīnī et Gracchōrum et Flaccī et superiōrum complūrium sanguine nōn modo sē nōn contāminārunt, sed etiam honestārunt, certē verendum mihi nōn

---

24. **honōrum :** ' of public office,' quaestorship, aedileship, praetorship, consulship.

27. **sevēritātis :** ' arising from strictness.'

28. **inertiae :** see page 31, line 19, and note.

29. **vexābuntur urbēs, tēcta ārdēbunt :** chiasmus. *239, e.*

12. 1. **vōcibus :** ' utterances,' as contrasted with the ' thoughts ' (*mentibus*) of those who keep their opinions to themselves.

2. **hōc idem sentiunt :** ' entertain this same view.' **pauca :** ' a few words.'

4. **factū :** *232;* B. 340, 2; A. & G. 510; G. 436. **iūdicārem :** why not pluperfect?

5. **Catilīnam multārī :** in apposition with *hōc.* **gladiātōrī :** ' ruffian,' ' rowdy,' ' rough-neck,' ' bully.'

6. **summī virī :** magistrates, as L. Opimius; while *clārissimī cīvēs* refers to private citizens, as P. Scipio (page 28, line 21, *et seq.*).

7. **Flaccī :** M. Fulvius Flaccus; see page 30, line 5.

10 erat, nē quid, hōc parricīdā cīvium interfectō, invidiae
mihi in posteritātem redundāret. Quod sī ea mihi maximē
impendēret, tamen hōc animō semper fuī, ut invidiam
virtūte partam glōriam, nōn invidiam putārem.

Quamquam nōn nūllī sunt in hōc ōrdine, quī aut ea,
15 quae imminent, nōn videant aut ea, quae vident, dissi-
mulent; quī spem Catilīnae mollibus sententiīs aluērunt
coniūrātiōnemque nāscentem nōn crēdendō corrōborāvē-
runt; quōrum auctōritātem secūtī multī nōn sōlum improbī, vērum etiam imperītī, sī in hunc animadvertissem,
20 crūdēliter et rēgiē factum esse dīcerent.

Nunc intellegō, sī iste, quō intendit, in Mānliāna castra
pervēnerit, nēminem tam stultum fore, quī nōn videat
coniūrātiōnem esse factam, nēminem tam improbum, quī
nōn fateātur. Hōc autem ūnō interfectō, intellegō hanc
25 reī pūblicae pestem paulisper reprimī, nōn in perpetuum
comprimī posse. Quod sī sē ēiēcerit sēcumque suōs ēdūx-

---

10. **quid invidiae :** here ' any enmity.' *97, b.*

11. **in posteritātem :** see page 51, line 8, and note. **redundāret:**
' should overwhelm me,' as a flood which has burst over the banks of a
stream. **Quod :** ' But.' *118, d;* B. 185, 2; 251, 6; A. & G. 397, *a;*
G. 610, R. 2.

14. **Quamquam :** corrective, as on page 50, line 1. **nōn nūllī :**
' some.' **hōc ōrdine :** = *senātū.* **quī :** why with subjunctive, while
quae . . . quae . . . (line 15) are with the indicative?

16. **sententiīs :** ' expressions of opinion.'

18. **multī :** i.e. *multī aliī, extrā hunc ōrdinem.* **improbī :** i.e. *eī quī
ea quae vident, dissimulant;* while *imperītī* refers to those *quī ea, quae
imminent, nōn vident.*

20. **rēgiē :** τυραννικῶς, *tyrannicē,* i.e. more after the manner of
a tyrant than of a Roman magistrate. **factum esse :** '(the deed) had
been done.' **dīcerent :** notice the force of the imperfect, ' would be
saying.' *208, a.*

24. **Hōc autem . . . :** notice the paronomasia, alliteration, and pre-
dominance of ' p ' sounds. *239, a, q.*

26. **ēiēcerit :** i.e. *ex urbe.*

erit et eōdem cēterōs undique collēctōs naufragōs aggre-
gārit, exstinguētur atque dēlēbitur nōn modo haec tam
adulta reī pūblicae pestis, vērum etiam stirps ac sēmen
malōrum omnium. 30

*Crimes have reached a climax; but with Catiline gone, public safety is
assured.*

13. Etenim iam diū, patrēs cōnscrīptī, in hīs perīculīs coniūrātiōnis īnsidiīsque versāmur, sed nesciō quō pactō omnium
scelerum ac veteris furōris et audāciae mātūritās in nostrī
cōnsulātūs tempus ērūpit. Quod sī ex tantō latrōciniō
iste ūnus tollētur, vidēbimur fortasse ad breve quoddam 5
tempus cūrā et metū esse relevātī, perīculum autem residēbit et erit inclūsum penitus in vēnīs atque vīsceribus
reī pūblicae.

Ut saepe hominēs aegrī morbō gravī, cum aestū febrīque iactantur, sī aquam gelidam bibērunt, prīmō relevārī 10
videntur, deinde multō gravius vehementiusque afflīctan-
tur, sīc hīc morbus, quī est in rē pūblicā, relevātus istīus
poenā, vehementius, reliquīs vīvīs, ingravēscet.

---

27. **naufragōs**: implies financial wreck; while *perditus* usually refers
to moral ruin.

28. **exstinguētur atque dēlēbitur**: ' will be completely destroyed,'
another example of synonymic combination. *212, b.* **tam**: should this
word appear in the English translation?

13. 2. **versāmur**: with *iam diū*, ' we have been involved.' *175, f.*
nesciō quō pactō: translate as if *nesciō quō modō*, ' somehow.' *168;*
B. 253, 6; A. & G. 575, *d;* G. 467, R, 1.

4. **latrōciniō**: abstract for concrete, ' band of brigands.' *92, b.*

7. **vēnīs atque vīsceribus**: a parallel to our ' flesh and blood,' the
language of medicine, used also in the next sentence. *212, b.*

9. **Ut**, etc.: *211;* B. 351, 5; A. & G. 601, *b;* G. 684, 687. **aestū
febrīque**: ' in the burning heat of fever.' What figure? *238, h.*

12. **relevātus**: *sī relevātus erit.* *227, a* (*2*); B. 305, 1; A. & G. 521,
a; G. 667.

13. **reliquīs vīvīs**: ablative absolute, ' if the rest remain alive.' *144, b (4).*

Quā rē sēcēdant improbī, sēcernant sē ā bonīs, ūnum
15 in locum congregentur, mūrō dēnique, id quod saepe iam
dīxī, sēcernantur ā nōbīs; dēsinant īnsidiārī domī suae
cōnsulī, circumstāre tribūnal praetōris urbānī, obsidēre
cum gladiīs cūriam, malleolōs et facēs ad īnflammandam
urbem comparāre; sit dēnique īnscrīptum in fronte ūnīus
20 cuiusque, quid dē rē pūblicā sentiat.

Polliceor hōc vōbīs, patrēs cōnscrīptī, tantam in nōbīs
cōnsulibus fore dīligentiam, tantam in vōbīs auctōritātem,
tantam in equitibus Rōmānīs virtūtem, tantam in omnibus
bonīs cōnsēnsiōnem, ut Catilīnae profectiōne omnia pate-
25 facta, illūstrāta, oppressa, vindicāta esse videātis.

Hīsce ōminibus, Catilīna, cum summā reī pūblicae salūte,
cum tuā peste ac perniciē cumque eōrum exitiō, quī sē tēcum
omnī scelere parricīdiōque iūnxērunt, proficīscere ad impium
bellum ac nefārium.

16. **īnsidiārī . . . cōnsulī:** see page 37, lines 22–32.

17. **circumstāre tribūnal:** for the purpose of intimidation, thus
interfering with the administration of justice. The tribunal of the ' city
praetor ' (see Companion, page 571) was in the Comitium.

18. **cum gladiīs:** for *armātī.* **cūriam:** the Curia Hostilia, where the
senate usually met; see vocabulary under *cūria* (1). **malleolōs:** ' fire-
darts,' used principally in siege operations. They were shaped like a
mallet, the head being filled with tow and pitch, which were ignited
before the missile was thrown.

20. **quid dē rē pūblicā sentiat:** ' what his political views are.'   212,*j.*
The indirect question is the subject of *sit īnscrīptum.*

21. **tantam,** *et seq.:* find examples of anaphora, asyndeton, and climax in
this sentence.   *239, b; 238, d; 239, f.*

23. **omnibus bonīs:** ' all patriotic citizens,' exclusive of the senators
and knights just mentioned.

25. **videātis:** ' you shall see.' Why is the present subjunctive in
Latin often used with reference to future time?

26. **Hīsce ōminibus:** 'With these prophetic words.' **cum . . .
exitiō:** in our idiom, ' to the highest welfare of the state, to the plague
and destruction of yourself,' etc.

28. **impium:** see page 52, line 24, and note.

Thou, Jupiter, wilt protect us and wilt impose fitting punishments.

Tū, Iuppiter, quī eīsdem quibus haec urbs auspiciīs ā 30 Rōmulō es cōnstitūtus, quem Statōrem huius urbis atque imperī vērē nōminȧmus, hunc et huius sociōs ā tuīs cēterīs-que templīs, ā tēctīs urbis ac moenibus, ā vītā for-tūnīsque cīvium arcēbis, 35 et hominēs bonōrum in-imīcōs, hostēs patriae, latrōnēs Italiae, scelerum foedere inter sē ac nefāriā societāte coniūnctōs, 40 aeternīs suppliciīs vīvōs mortuōsque mactābis.

JUPITER

The famous bust in the Vatican Museum in Rome.

30. **Tū, Iuppiter:** the orator addresses the statue of Jupiter Stator in the temple, and through it the divinity represented by it. **eīsdem quibus auspiciīs:** = *eīsdem auspiciīs quibus.* The statement is not literally true; for though there was a tradition that Romulus in a battle with the Sabines vowed a temple to Jupiter Stator on this site, the temple was not actually built till 294 B.C. (Livy, **1,** 12, 20, Selection, page 412; **10,** 37, 15).

31. **Statōrem:** here 'Establisher,' 'Protector'; in the vow as given by Livy, the word means rather 'stayer of flight.' See page 413, lines 15–21.

34. **vītā:** we should say 'lives.'

35. **arcēbis:** the future indicative sometimes has the force of a mild command. *181, c.*

41. **aeternīs suppliciīs:** Cicero himself did not believe in future punish-ment; but see note on page 524.

SOUTHEAST END OF THE FORUM

The Colosseum seen through the Arch of Titus. It was in this direction
that the Rostra faced.

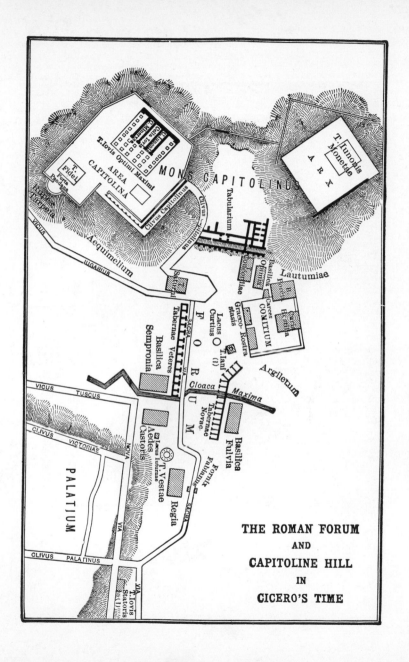

THE ROMAN FORUM
AND
CAPITOLINE HILL
IN
CICERO'S TIME

M. TULLĪ CICERŌNIS
IN L. CATILĪNAM ŌRĀTIŌ SECUNDA
HABITA AD POPULUM

Partēs Sēlēctae

*You see the conspiracy laid bare; the conspirators, fit associates
in Catiline's infamies.*

4. Quod exspectāvī, iam sum assecūtus, ut vōs omnēs
factam esse apertē coniūrātiōnem contrā rem pūblicam
vidērētis; nisi vērō sī quis est, quī Catilīnae similēs cum
Catilīnā sentīre nōn putet. Nōn est iam lēnitātī locus;
sevēritātem rēs ipsa flāgitat.

UPPER END OF THE FORUM TODAY

To the Student: Before translating, read the Companion, pages 517,
522–523, to get the setting of this oration.

Habita ad Populum: 'addressed to the people' in the Forum. The
first part of the oration (**1–3**) may be summed up as follows:

In driving forth Catiline, citizens, we have gloriously conquered him; but
unfortunately some of his gang remain. These men are more to be feared
than Catiline's army, but they can do no harm.

4. 3. **nisi sī**: 'unless perhaps,' *nisi* having an adverbial force. *210, b;*
B. 306, 5; A. & G. 525, 3; G. 591 (*b*) 2, R. 2.

3. **similēs**: accusative; '(men) like Catiline.'

Ūnum etiam nunc concēdam : exeant, proficīscantur,
nē patiantur dēsīderiō suī Catilīnam miserum tābēscere.
Dēmōnstrābō iter, Aurēliā viā profectus est; sī accele-
rāre volent, ad vesperam cōnsequentur.

10 Ō fortūnātam rem pūblicam, sī quidem hanc sentīnam
urbis ēiēcerit ! Ūnō mē hercule Catilīnā exhaustō, levāta
mihi et recreāta rēs pūblica vidētur.

Quid enim malī aut sceleris fingī aut cōgitārī potest,
quod nōn ille concēperit? Quis tōtā Italiā venēficus,
15 quis gladiātor, quis latrō, quis sīcārius, quis parricīda, quis
testāmentōrum subiector, quis circumscrīptor, quis gāneō,
quis nepōs, quis adulter, quae mulier īnfāmis, quis corruptoi
iuventūtis, quis corruptus, quis perditus invenīrī potest,
quī sē cum Catilīnā nōn familiārissimē vīxisse fateātur?
20 Quae caedēs per hōsce annōs sine illō facta est? quod nefārium stuprum nōn per illum?

Iam vērō quae tanta umquam in ūllō homine iuventūtis illecebra fuit, quanta in illō? quī aliōs ipse amābat
turpissimē, aliōrum amōrī flāgitiōsissimē serviēbat, aliīs
25 frūctum libīdinum, aliīs mortem parentum nōn modo impellendō, vērum etiam adiuvandō pollicēbātur.

---

7. **miserum**: ' wretchedly,' ' in wretchedness.' *151;* B. 239; A.
& G. 290; G. 325, R. 6.

8. **viā**: *134 a;* B. 218, 9; A. & G. 429, *a;* G. 389.   The report was
circulated that Catiline was going to Marseilles, into exile.

9. **volent**: future, where our idiom requires the present.

10. **rem pūblicam**: why accusative?   **sentīnam**: see page 41, line
31, and note.

11. **exhaustō**: carries out the idea of *sentīnam.*

14. **Italiā**: *145, c;* B. 228, 1, *b;* A. & G. 429, 2; G. 388.

16. **circumscrīptor**: ' confidence man,' who makes it his business to
defraud the inexperienced, particularly the young.

18. **perditus**: here a substantive, ' reprobate.'

22. **iuventūtis illecebra**: see page 42, line 10, and note.

25. **frūctum**: ' gratification.'   **impellendō, adiuvandō**: almost =
impellēns, adiuvāns.

Nunc vērō quam subitō nōn sōlum ex urbe, vērum etiam
ex agrīs ingentem numerum perditōrum hominum collē-
gerat! Nēmō nōn modo Rōmae, sed nē ūllō 'quidem in angulō
tōtīus Italiae oppressus aere aliēnō fuit, quem nōn ad hōc 30
incrēdibile sceleris foedus ascīverit.

From Catiline we turn to consider the classes of his followers.

8. Sed cūr tam diū dē ūnō hoste loquimur, et dē eō hoste,
quī iam fatētur sē esse hostem, et quem, quia, quod semper

A BIT OF ROMAN HIGHWAY

29. **nōn modo:** i.e. *nōn modo nōn fuit;* see page 53, line 6, and
note.

How great would be our good fortune, if these reprobates would leave
the city! If they remain, I will be your leader against them.

Catiline has left the impression that he was driven into exile; his
plot stands revealed, he went to Faesulae to join Manlius.

8. 1. **Sed:** the orator passes from Catiline's case to that of his
associates. **hoste, hoste, hostem:** why this emphasis? According
to Sallust (see page 136, line 28) Catiline's attempt to justify himself
in the senate meeting of the day before was greeted with cries of " *hostis* "
and " *parricīda.*"

2. **quem . . . timeō:** a fine illustration of the principle of " suspen-
sion " so natural to Latin. *Quem, quia, quod* are the introductory

voluī, mūrus interest, nōn timeō;   dē hīs, quī dissimulant,
quī Rōmae remanent, quī nōbīscum sunt, nihil dīcimus?
5 Quōs quidem ego, sī ūllō modō fierī possit, nōn tam ulcīscī
studeō quam sānāre sibi ipsōs, plācāre reī pūblicae, neque,
id quā rē fīerī nōn possit, sī mē audīre volent, intellegō.

Expōnam enim vōbīs, Quirītēs, ex quibus generibus
hominum istae cōpiae comparentur;   deinde singulīs medi-
10 cīnam cōnsilī atque ōrātiōnis meae, sī quam poterō, afferam:

The first class: men of means who through a revolution wish to clear off
debts.   These are not dangerous.

Ūnum genus est eōrum, quī magnō in aere aliēnō maiōrēs
etiam possessiōnēs habent, quārum amōre adductī dissolvī
nūllō modō possunt.   Hōrum hominum speciēs est hones-
15 tissima; sunt enim locuplētēs; voluntās vērō et causa im-
pudentissima.

---

words of clauses, whose verbs *voluī, interest, timeō* are introduced inversely
in order to postpone the appearance of the important verb, *timeō*, till
the very end of the sentence.   **quod:** see page 40, line 30, and note.

3. **mūrus:** why not *pariēs?* see page 48, lines 7–10.   **dē hīs:** in
contrast with the absent Catiline.   **quī dissimulant:** i.e. *sē hostēs esse.*

5. **ulcīscī:** here = *pūnīre, persequī.*

6. **sānāre sibi ipsōs:** ' to restore (them) to themselves,' *i.e.* ' to
restore them to their right minds '; like our colloquial phrase, ' to bring
him to his senses.'

8. **ex . . . comparentur:** the following characterizations (see
Companion, page 523) seem to have been introduced for two reasons: to
disabuse the people of any apprehensions regarding the extent and
strength of the conspiracy, and to overawe the conspirators themselves
by revealing an intimate acquaintance with the character and condition
of their constituency.

12. **in:** '(although) in.'

13. **possessiōnēs:** particularly lands and buildings.   **dissolvī:** ' to
clear themselves,' by selling out and paying their indebtedness.

14. **speciēs:** ' outward appearance.'

15. **voluntās, causa:** ' inclination ' or ' intentions,' ' attitude '
toward the government.

"Tū agrīs, tū aedificiīs, tū argentō, tū familiā, tū rēbus omnibus ōrnātus et cōpiōsus sīs, et dubitēs dē possessiōne dētrahere, acquīrere ad fidem?

"Quid enim exspectās? Bellum? Quid ergō? in vās- 20 tātiōne omnium tuās possessiōnēs sacrōsānctās futūrās putās?

"An tabulās novās?" Errant, quī istās ā Catilīnā

SILVER PLATE OF THE TIME OF AUGUSTUS

17. **Tū,** etc.: addressed to an imaginary representative of this class, 'You — to be abundantly supplied . . . and (yet) to hesitate . . .' See page 50, line 1, and note. **argentō:** 'with silver ware,' 'with plate,' chased and ornamented with artistic designs. Much beautiful silver ware of the Roman period has been discovered. **familiā:** 'establishment,' comprising slaves and freedmen, particularly the former.

19. **acquīrere ad fidem:** *i.e.* by the cancellation of indebtedness, on the principle that a man's credit is better if he have even a small property free from debt than if he have a great estate mortgaged to nearly or quite its full value.

21. **sacrōsānctās:** *i.e.* exempt from the general destruction.

23. **tabulās novās:** 'new accounts,' following the repudiation of all outstanding debts. This was an important part of Catiline's program: *Tum Catilīna pollicērī tabulās novās, prōscrīptiōnem locuplētium, magis-*

exspectant; meō beneficiō tabulae novae prōferentur,
25 vērum auctiōnāriae; neque enim istī, quī possessiōnēs
habent, aliā ratiōne ūllā salvī esse possunt.

Quod sī mātūrius facere voluissent neque, id quod stultis-
simum est, certāre cum ūsūrīs frūctibus praediōrum, et
locuplētiōribus hīs et meliōribus cīvibus ūterēmur. Sed
30 hōsce hominēs minimē putō pertimēscendōs, quod aut,
dēdūcī dē sententiā possunt aut, sī permanēbunt, magis
mihi videntur vōta factūrī contrā rem pūblicam quam
arma lātūrī.

The second class: men burdened with debt, who desire to obtain power.
These are short-sighted.

9. Alterum genus est eōrum, quī, quamquam premuntur
aere aliēnō, dominātiōnem tamen exspectant, rērum potīrī
volunt, honōrēs, quōs, quiētā rē pūblicā, dēspērant, perturbātā sē cōnsequī posse arbitrantur.

---

*trātūs, sacerdōtia, rapīnās, alia omnia, quae bellum atque libīdō victōrum
fert* (Sallust, *Catilīna*, **21,** 7, page 123).

24. **meō beneficiō:** ' thanks to me.'

25. **auctiōnāriae:** '(those) of the auctioneers '; the consul will interfere, and will clear off these debts by confiscating the mortgaged property
and selling it at auction. It seems that Cicero when consul actually
made an attempt to improve the general credit by drastic measures of
some sort; see Cicero, *Dē Officiīs*, **2,** 24, 84; see *Prō Sullā*, **20,** 56.

26. **salvī:** financially ' sound.'

28. **frūctibus praediōrum:** ' by the income of their estates '; as
this was less than the interest they had to pay, the contest between income and outgo was a losing one.

29. **hīs . . . ūterēmur:** ' we should find them ' (or ' in them ').

30. **minimē:** as compared with the following classes.

9. 1. **premuntur aere aliēnō:** *i.e.* are hopelessly in debt, not having
property to offset their indebtedness, and thus being worse off than those
in the first class.

2. **rērum:** *131, d;* B. 212, 2; 218, 1, *a;* A. & G. 357, *a;* G. 407,
N. 2 (*d*).

3. **honōrēs:** ' the public offices.'   **perturbātā:** sc. *eā.*

Quibus hōc praecipiendum vidētur, ūnum scilicet et idem 5
quod reliquīs omnibus, ut dēspērent sē id, quod cōnantur,
cōnsequī posse; prīmum omnium mē ipsum vigilāre, adesse,
prōvidēre reī pūblicae; deinde magnōs animōs esse in
bonīs virīs, magnam concordiam in maximā multitūdine,
magnās praetereā cōpiās mīlitum; deōs dēnique immortālēs 10
huic invictō populō, clārissimō imperiō, pulcherrimae urbī
contrā tantam vim sceleris praesentīs auxilium esse lātūrōs.

THE IMPERIAL FORUM

At the lower left is the Rostra, beyond which we see the curia, to the right
of which is the Basilica Aemilia. At the front corner of this is the tiny
temple of Janus. The columns commemorate Roman heroes and divinities,
the nearest honoring Diocletian.

5. **ūnum et idem:** much stronger than *idem* alone. **scilicet:** ' that
is to say,' ' as I hardly need say.'

6. **quod reliquīs omnibus:** sc. *praecipiendum vidētur.*

7. **prīmum:** adjective or adverb? **mē . . . lātūrōs:** gives the
ground for *ut dēspērent;* '(from the thought) that I,' etc.

8. **animōs:** ' spirit.' *92, a.*

12. **praesentīs:** ' with immediate presence.'

Quod sī iam sint id, quod summō furōre cupiunt, adeptī,
num illī in cinere urbis et in sanguine cīvium, quae mente
15 cōnscelerātā ac nefāriā concupīvērunt, sē cōnsulēs aut dic-
tātōrēs aut etiam rēgēs spērant futūrōs? Nōn vident id
sē cupere, quod sī adeptī sint, fugitīvō alicui aut gladiātōrī
concēdī sit necesse?

*The third class: aged spendthrifts, who hope for a return of Sulla's
proscriptions.*

Tertium genus est aetāte iam affectum, sed tamen
20 exercitātiōne rōbustum; quō ex genere iste est Mānlius,
cui nunc Catilīna succēdit. Hī sunt hominēs ex eīs colōniīs,
quās Sulla cōnstituit; quās ego ūniversās cīvium esse
optimōrum et fortissimōrum virōrum sentiō, sed tamen
eī sunt colōnī, quī sē in īnspērātīs ac repentīnīs pecūniīs
25 sūmptuōsius īnsolentiusque iactārunt.
Hī dum aedificant tamquam beātī, dum praediīs lēctīs,

---

13. **Quod sī . . . adeptī sint:** ' But supposing they have once
obtained.' *207 (3)*.

17. **fugitīvō alicui:** ' to some runaway (slave)'; an allusion not only
to the fact of human experience that if free reign be given to violence the
most violent and lawless will prevail, but also to the terrible experiences
of the wars with Spartacus and the slaves. See page 55, line 10, and
note.

18. **concēdī:** see IDIOMS.

19. **Tertium genus:** see Companion, page 523, and Sallust, *Catilīna,*
16, 4: *Plerīque Sullānī mīlitēs, largius suō ūsī, rapīnārum et victōriae
veteris memorēs, cīvīle bellum exoptābant.*

21. **eīs colōniīs:** Sulla rewarded 120,000 of his troops (so Appian, *Dē
Bellīs Cīvīlibus,* **1,** 104) with lands, dispossessing the previous owners.
A large number of these ' colonies' were planted in Etruria, the inhabi-
tants of which had been stanch supporters of the party of Marius.

22. **ūniversās:** ' on the whole,' ' in general '; the orator softens his
sweeping statement in order not to give offense.

26. **beātī:** ' well off,' ' well-to-do.' To a soldier who had been
serving for about six cents a day the possession of even a small landed
property naturally seemed great wealth.

familiīs magnīs, convīviīs apparātīs dēlectantur, in tantum aes aliēnum incidērunt, ut, sī salvī esse velint, Sulla sit eīs ab īnferīs excitandus; quī etiam nōn nūllōs agrestēs, hominēs tenuēs atque egentēs, in eandem illam spem rapī- 30 nārum veterum impulē-runt.

Quōs ego utrōsque in eōdem genere praedā-tōrum dīreptōrumque 35 pōnō; sed eōs hōc moneō, dēsinant furere ac prōscrīptiōnēs et dic-tātūrās cōgitāre. Tantus enim illōrum temporum 40 dolor inūstus est cīvitātī, ut iam ista nōn modo hominēs, sed nē pecudēs quidem mihi passūrae esse videantur. 45

SULLA

The bust in the Vatican Museum.

27. **apparātīs:** ' splendid,' in the decoration and furniture of the dining-room, as well as in the table service and viands. **in tantum aes:** see IDIOMS under *aes*.

28. **salvī:** as on page 68, line 26.

29. **agrestēs:** in many cases no doubt the previous possessors of the farms taken by Sulla's soldiers; see Sallust, *Catilīna*, **28**, 4: *Intereā Mānlius in Etrūriā plebem sollicitāre, egestāte simul ac dolōre iniūriae novārum rērum cupidam, quod Sullae dominātiōne agrōs bonaque omnia āmīserat.*

33. **Quōs, etc.:** ' Now I put both of these classes in the same cate-gory.' *167; 97, c.*

36. **eōs hōc:** see IDIOMS under *eōs. 117, a;* B. 178, *d;* A. & G. 390, *c;* G. 333, 1.

40. **illōrum temporum:** of the dictatorship and proscriptions of Sulla.

42. **nōn modo:** see page 53, line 6, and note.

45. **videantur:** for translation see page 43, line 33, and note.

The fourth class: hopeless failures, who have nothing to lose.

10. Quārtum genus est sānē varium et mixtum et tur-
bulentum; quī iam prīdem premuntur, quī numquam
ēmergunt, quī partim inertiā, partim male gerendō negōtiō,
partim etiam sūmptibus in vetere aere aliēnō vacillant;
5 quī vadimōniīs, iūdiciīs, prōscrīptiōne bonōrum dēfatīgātī,
permultī et ex urbe et ex agrīs sē in illa castra cōnferre
dīcuntur. Hōsce ego nōn tam mīlitēs ācrēs quam īnfitiā-
tōrēs lentōs esse arbitror.

Quī hominēs prīmum, sī stāre nōn possunt, corruant;
10 sed ita, ut nōn modo cīvitās, sed nē vīcīnī quidem proximī
sentiant. Nam illud nōn intellegō, quam ob rem, sī
vīvere honestē nōn possunt, perīre turpiter velint, aut cūr
minōre dolōre peritūrōs sē cum multīs, quam sī sōlī pereant,
arbitrentur.

The fifth class: criminals; the last class, vilest of the vile.

15 Quīntum genus est parricīdārum, sīcāriōrum, dēnique
omnium facinerōsōrum. Quōs ego ā Catilīnā nōn revocō;
nam neque ab eō dīvellī possunt et pereant sānē in latrōciniō,
quoniam sunt ita multī, ut eōs carcer capere nōn possit.

Postrēmum autem genus est nōn sōlum numerō, vērum

---

10. 2. **quī:** i.e. *eōrum quī.* **premuntur:** i.e. *aere aliēnō;* see page 68,
line 1, and note.

3. **ēmergunt:** ' get their heads above water,' as we say.

5. **iūdiciīs:** by *vadimōniīs, iūdiciīs,* and *prōscrīptione bonōrum,* the
three steps in an action for debt are indicated: (1) the ' summons,' in
response to which the debtor must give ' bail ' to present himself at the
specified time for trial; (2) the ' trial,' followed by a sentence; (3) the
' execution,' which comprised a taking possession of the property and the
sale of it at auction, in case the judgment was not satisfied in full within
a certain fixed period.

10. **nōn modo cīvitās:** i.e. *nōn sentiat.*

13. **sōlī:** ' by themselves.'

17. **pereant:** '(I pray) they may perish.' *180, b.*

18. **carcer:** see note to page 76, line 15. See illustrations, pages 118, 119.

19. **est:** sc. *postrēmum,* in the sense of both ' last ' and ' lowest.'

etiam genere ipsō atque vītā, quod proprium Catilīnae est, 20
dē eius dīlēctū, immō vērō dē complexū eius ac sinū ; quōs

A Roman Boy

pexō capillō, nitidōs, aut
imberbēs aut bene bar-
bātōs vidētis, manicātīs
et tālāribus tunicīs, vēlīs 25
amictōs, nōn togīs ; quō-
rum omnis industria vītae
et vigilandī labor in ante-
lūcānīs cēnīs exprōmitur.
In hīs gregibus omnēs 30
āleātōrēs, omnēs adulterī,
omnēs impūrī impudīcī-
que versantur.

Hī puerī tam lepidī ac
dēlicātī nōn sōlum amāre 35
et amārī, neque saltāre, et cantāre, sed etiam sīcās vibrāre et
spargere venēna didicērunt. Quī nisi exeunt, nisi pereunt,

20. **proprium Catilīnae . . . sinū:** 'Catiline's own, of his special
choice, — no, rather his dearest bosom friends.'

23. **imberbēs:** *i.e.* with
smooth, womanish faces. **bene
barbātōs :** a sign of dissolute
life ; for in this period it was not
customary to let the beard grow
except in times of mourning.

24. **manicātīs . . . tunicīs :**
at this time it was considered
in good taste to wear the tunic
sleeveless and extending just
below the knees ; sleeved tunics
were looked upon as a badge
of effeminacy.

A Roman Razor

25. **vēlīs :** 'with sails,' spoken contemptuously of the fop's toga.

30. **gregibus :** scornfully, ' gangs.'

36. **amārī:** *159.* **neque :** 'and not (only).'

37. **spargere venēna :** *i.e.* in wine or other drinks.

etiam sī Catilīna perierit, scītōte hōc in rē
pūblica sēminārium Catilīnārum futūrum.

40 Vērum tamen quid sibi istī miserī
volunt? Num suās sēcum mulierculās
sunt in castra ductūrī? Quem ad modum
autem illīs carēre poterunt, hīs praesertim
iam noctibus? Quō autem pactō illī
45 Appennīnum atque illās pruīnās ac nivēs
perferent? nisi idcircō sē facilius hiemem
tolerātūrōs putant, quod nūdī in convīviīs saltāre didicērunt.

A ROMAN LADY

With such forces contrast the forces of the state.

11. Ō bellum magnopere pertimēscendum, cum hanc sit
habitūrus Catilīna scortōrum cohortem praetōriam!

Īnstruite nunc, Quirītēs, contrā hās tam praeclārās
Catilīnae cōpiās vestra praesidia vestrōsque exercitūs.

5 Et prīmum gladiātōrī illī cōnfectō et sauciō cōnsulēs
imperātōrēsque vestrōs oppōnite; deinde contrā illam
naufragōrum ēiectam ac dēbilitātam manum, flōrem tōtīus
Italiae ac rōbur ēdūcite. Iam vērō urbēs colōniārum ac

---

38. **scītōte:** *181, a (3).* **hōc . . . futūrum:** ' that this will be a state
nursery for men like Catiline.' *212, i.*

39. **Catilīnārum:** the plural of proper names regularly means ' men
like.' See page 244, note 38. *92, d.*

41. **mulierculās:** diminutive here to express contempt, ' dear little
women.' *92, e.*

11. 4. **praesidia:** ' garrisons ' of troops stationed in the cities for
defense, as distinguished from *exercitūs,* the ' hosts ' under training in
the field.

5. **cōnfectō et sauciō:** ' worn out and crippled.'

7. **naufragōrum:** see note on page 59, line 27. **ēiectam:** carrying
out the idea of *naufragōrum,* ' stranded.'

8. **colōniārum, mūnicipiōrum:** partitive genitive, dividing the concept *urbēs,* both of these classes of towns possessing fortifications.

mūnicipiōrum respondēbunt Catilīnae tumulīs silvestribus.
Neque ego cēterās cōpiās, ōrnāmenta, praesidia vestra 10
cum illīus latrōnis inopiā atque egestāte cōnferre dēbeō.

Sed sī, omissīs hīs rēbus, quibus nōs suppeditāmur, eget
ille, senātū, equitibus Rōmānīs, urbe, aerāriō, vectīgālibus,
cūnctā Italiā, prōvinciīs omnibus, exterīs nātiōnibus, sī,
hīs rēbus omissīs, causās ipsās, quae inter sē cōnflīgunt, con- 15
tendere velīmus, ex eō ipsō, quam valdē illī iaceant, intellegere possumus.

To Catiline's followers in the city I again give warning.

12. Nunc illōs, quī in urbe remānsērunt, atque adeō quī
contrā urbis salūtem omniumque vestrum in urbe ā Catilīnā
relīctī sunt, quamquam sunt hostēs, tamen, quia sunt cīvēs,
monitōs etiam atque etiam volō.

Mea lēnitās adhūc sī cui solūtior vīsa est, hōc exspectāvit, 5
ut id, quod latēbat, ērumperet.   Quod reliquum est, iam
nōn possum oblīvīscī, meam hanc esse patriam, mē hōrum
esse cōnsulem, mihi aut cum hīs vīvendum aut prō hīs
esse moriendum.

Nūllus est portīs cūstōs, nūllus īnsidiātor viae ;   sī quī 10
exīre volunt, cōnīvēre possum ;   quī vērō sē in urbe com-

---

9. **respondēbunt :** in ordinary prose *parēs erunt.*   **tumulīs silvestribus :** the natural resort of brigands.

11. **inopiā, egestāte :** Catiline had two legions, but according to
Sallust (*Catilīna,* **56,** 3) only about one fourth of his men were properly
armed.

15. **causās :** the parties and the principles.   **contendere :** here =
cōnferre.

16. **intellegere possumus :** instead of *intellegāmus.*   207 (*3*).

Guard your homes ; provision has been made for the public safety.

12. 3. **hostēs :** see note on page 519.

5. **hōc exspectāvit :** ' it has held this in view.'

6. **Quod reliquum :** see IDIOMS.   *212, j.*

10. **portīs :** in our idiom, ' at the gates.'   **quī :** ' if any one.'

mōverit, cuius ego nōn modo factum, sed inceptum ūllum
cōnātumve contrā patriam dēprehenderō, sentiet in hāc
urbe esse cōnsulēs vigilantēs, esse ēgregiōs magistrātūs,
15 esse fortem senātum, esse arma, esse carcerem quem vin-
dicem nefāriōrum ac manifestōrum scelerum maiōrēs nostrī
esse voluērunt.

---

12. **cuius :** almost *sī illīus.*

15. **carcerem :** now known as the Mamertine Prison ; properly called
'an avenger,' because never used as a place of confinement for life sentences, but only for the detention of prisoners who gave no bail pending
trial, or for the execution of those condemned.   In the lower Dungeon,
or *Tulliānum,* many notable men perished, among them Jugurtha,
and the Gallic general Vercingetorix.   See illustrations on pages 118,
119, and note on page 119, line 6.

M. TULLĪ CICERŌNIS
IN L. CATILĪNAM ŌRATIŌ TERTIA
HABITA AD POPULUM

Partēs Sēlēctae

The state, your lives, this city have escaped destruction.

1. Rem pūblicam, Quirītēs, vītamque omnium vestrum,
bona, fortūnās, coniugēs līberōsque vestrōs atque hōc
domicilium clārissimī imperī, fortūnātissimam pulcherri-
mamque urbem, hodiernō diē deōrum immortālium summō
ergā vōs amōre, labōribus, cōnsiliīs, perīculīs meīs ē flammā₅
atque ferrō ac paene ex faucibus fātī ēreptam et vōbīs
cōnservātam ac restitūtam vidētis.

Et sī nōn minus nōbīs iūcundī atque illūstrēs sunt eī diēs,
quibus cōnservāmur, quam illī, quibus nāscimur, quod salūtis
certa laetitia est, nāscendī incerta condiciō, et quod sine₁₀

To THE STUDENT: Before translating, study the conditions under which
this oration was delivered, Companion, page 517.

1. This first chapter is a fine example of Latin periodic sentence
structure. Note the contrasts and parallelism. *211.*

1. **Quirītēs** (kwĭ-rī'tēz) : see note on page 416, line 17. For an outline of the matter, see Companion, pages 523–525. **omnium vestrum :**
compare page 75, line 2. *155.* **vītamque :** ' lives '; see page 61, note 34.

5. **flammā atque ferrō :** compare *faucibus fātī.* Which did Cicero
consider worse, *flamma* or *ferrum? 233, a;* B. 341, 1, *c;* A. & G.,
324, *b;* G. 477.

6. **ex faucibus fātī :** like our expression, ' from the jaws of death.'

7. **restitūtam vidētis :** sc. *esse.* The news of the arrest at the
Mulvian bridge had spread like wildfire, so that many already knew
something at least of what the orator was about to say to them. *228, c.*

10. **nāscendī condiciō :** '(our) lot at birth,' the position or surroundings into which we are born.

sēnsū nāscimur, cum voluptāte servāmur, profectō, quoniam
illum, quī hanc urbem condidit, ad deōs immortālēs benevolentiā fāmāque sustulimus, esse apud vōs posterōsque
vestrōs in honōre dēbēbit is, quī eandem hanc urbem con-
15 ditam amplificātamque servāvit. Nam tōtī urbī, templīs,
dēlūbrīs, tēctīs ac moenibus subiectōs prope iam ignēs cir-
cumdatōsque restīnximus, īdemque gladiōs in rem pūblicam
dēstrīctōs rettudimus mūcrōnēsque eōrum ā iugulīs vestrīs
dēiēcimus.

I shall explain, citizens, what was done in the senate.

20 Quae quoniam in senātū illūstrāta, patefacta, comperta
sunt, per mē, vōbīs iam expōnam breviter, Quirītēs, ut, et

---

11. **sēnsū:** ' consciousness.' **profectō:** adverb, ' truly,' ' assuredly.'
12. **illum:** the belief in the deification of Romulus, under the name
Quirīnus, was kept alive by an annual festival, the Quirinālia. This

ROMAN REPUBLICAN COIN

Obverse: Quirinus.   Reverse: Ceres holding three stalks of wheat.

was held on the 17th of February, in commemoration of the day on
which he was said to have been taken up into heaven. See Livy **1,** 16
(Selection, page 416). **benevolentiā fāmāque:** better taken as hendiadys, ' with thankful recognition.' *238, h.*
16. **dēlūbrīs:** the lesser sanctuaries.
18. **rettudimus:** ' we have struck back.'
20. **Quae quoniam:** ' And since all this.' *167.*
21. **per mē:** '(and that too) through my agency.' *123, a;* A. & G.
405, *b;* G. 401.

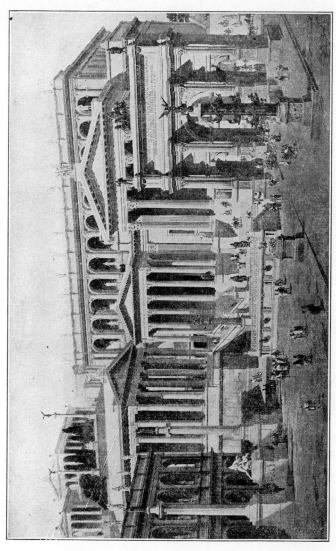

THE FORUM, LOOKING WEST

On the height is the Temple of Jupiter and at the back the Tabularium. From left to right are the Basilica Julia, Temple of Saturn, Temple of Vespasian with the Rostra in front, then the Temple of Concord, the Arch of Septimius Severus and the Column of Duilius. The events of this oration took place in the Temple of Concord, after which Cicero came out upon the Rostra and addressed the people.

quanta et quā ratiōne invēstīgāta et comprehēnsa sint,
vōs, quī et ignōrātis et exspectātis, scīre possītis.

First, I sought to assure your safety, and obtain evidence.

Prīncipiō, ut Catilīna paucīs ante diēbus ērūpit ex urbe,
cum sceleris suī sociōs, huiusce nefāriī bellī ācerrimōs 25
ducēs Rōmae relīquisset, semper vigilāvī et prōvīdī, Quirītēs, quem ad modum in tantīs et tam absconditīs īnsidiīs
salvī esse possēmus.

2. Nam tum, cum ex urbe Catilīnam ēiciēbam — nōn
enim iam vereor huius verbī invidiam, cum illa magis sit
timenda, quod vīvus exierit — sed tum, cum illum exterminārī volēbam, aut reliquam coniūrātōrum manum simul
exitūram aut eōs, quī restitissent, īnfīrmōs sine illō ac dēbi- 5
lēs fore putābam.

Atque ego, ut vīdī, quōs maximō furōre et scelere esse
īnflammātōs sciēbam, eōs nōbīscum esse et Rōmae remān-

---

22. **quanta :** = *quantae rēs.*

23. **exspectātis :** the people had a right to look to the consul for an
official report.

24. **ut :** here ' ever since.' **paucīs ante diēbus :** in fact almost four
weeks before; for Catiline left Rome on the night of November 8 (see
Companion, page 526). The orator makes as little as possible of the interval, in order not to direct attention to the fact that during so long
a time nothing was accomplished in the way of checking the conspiracy.
ērūpit : ' he suddenly rushed out.'

25. **sceleris suī sociōs :** their nefarious plans for the destruction of
the city are given by Sallust, *Catilīna*, 43.

2. 1. **ēiciēbam :** why imperfect indicative? *175, e; 185, b.* **nōn
. . . invidiam :** see page 51, line 5, *et seq.*

2. **huius verbī invidiam :** ' the odium arising from this word.'
illa : sc. *invidia.*

3. **exterminārī :** *not* ' exterminated.' Avoid guessing.

5. **restitissent :** represents the future perfect of direct **discourse.**
177, a. **eōs . . . putābam :** see page 75, line 1, *et seq.*

7. **Atque :** here a particle of transition, ' And so,' ' Now.'

8. **nōbīscum esse et remānsisse :** *238, j.*

sisse, in eō omnēs diēs noctēsque cōnsūmpsī, ut, quid agerent,
10 quid mōlīrentur, sentīrem ac vidērem, ut, quoniam auribus
vestrīs propter incrēdibilem magnitūdinem sceleris minōrem
fidem faceret ōrātiō mea, rem ita comprehenderem, ut tum
dēmum animīs salūtī vestrae prōvidērētis, cum oculīs maleficium ipsum vidērētis.

*I heard that envoys of the Allobroges were leaving with letters of the
conspirators; I had them stopped at the Mulvian bridge.*

15 Itaque, ut comperī lēgātōs Allobrogum, bellī Trāns-
alpīnī et tumultūs Gallicī excitandī causā, ā P. Lentulō
esse sollicitātōs, eōsque in Galliam ad suōs cīvēs eōdemque
itinere cum litterīs mandātīsque ad Catilīnam esse missōs,
comitemque eīs adiūnctum esse T. Volturcium, atque huic
20 ad Catilīnam esse datās litterās, facultātem mihi oblātam
putāvī, ut, quod erat difficillimum, quodque ego semper
optābam ab dīs immortālibus, ut tōta rēs nōn sōlum ā mē,
sed etiam ā senātū et ā vōbīs manifestō dēprehenderētur.

---

9. **in eō**: 'in this purpose,' anticipating the following *ut*-clause.

10. **sentīrem ac vidērem**: synonymic combination, sometimes called
hendiadys of verbs, is a characteristic of Cicero's style; translate, ' perceive fully ' or ' clearly.' *212, b.* **quoniam . . . minōrem fidem faceret
ōrātiō mea**: ' since my words failed to convince.'

12. **fidem faceret**: see IDIOMS. **rem ita comprehenderem**: ' I
might get the matter so in my grasp '; the consul bent all his energies
toward securing tangible and convicting evidence.

15. **ut comperī**: through Quintus Fabius Sanga; see Companion,
page 517.

16. **tumultūs**: when applied to political matters, used only of disturbances in Italy and Cisalpine Gaul; see Cicero's explanation (*Philippic*, **8**, 1, 3): *Quid est enim aliud tumultus nisi perturbātiō tanta, ut
maior timor oriātur? . . . Itaque maiōrēs nostrī tumultum Italicum, quod
erat domesticus* (hence liable to cause a panic on account of its nearness),
*tumultum Gallicum, quod erat Italiae fīnitimus, praetereā nūllum nōminā-
bant.*

17. **eōdem itinere**: their road lay through Etruria.

18. **ad**: '(addressed) to.'

20. **facultātem oblātam**: see IDIOMS.

Itaque hesternō diē L. Flaccum et C. Pomptīnum praetōrēs, fortissimōs atque amantissimōs reī pūblicae virōs, 25
ad mē vocāvī; rem exposuī; quid fierī placēret, ostendī.
Illī autem, quī omnia dē rē pūblicā praeclāra atque ēgregia
sentīrent, sine recūsātiōne ac sine ūllā morā negōtium sus-
cēpērunt et, cum advesperāsceret, occultē ad pontem
Mulvium pervēnērunt atque ibi in proximīs vīllīs ita bi- 30
pertītō fuērunt, ut Tiberis inter eōs et pōns interesset.

Eōdem autem et ipsī sine cuiusquam suspīciōne multōs
fortēs virōs ēdūxerant, et ego ex praefectūrā Reātīnā

THE MULVIAN BRIDGE

24. **hesternō diē**: December 2. **L. Flaccum**: see vocabulary under
Flaccus (3). **C. Pomptīnum** (gā′(y)ụs pọm(p)-tǐ′nụs).

25. **amantissimōs**: see IDIOMS.

26. **rem**: ' the plan ' for intercepting the deputies of the Allobroges.
placēret: see vocabulary.

27. **quī . . . sentīrent**: in our idiom, ' being men of sound and excellent political sentiments in all respects '; subjunctive on account of the
causal force of *quī*. *194, c.* **dē rē pūblicā**: often ' political.' *212, i.*

29. **pontem Mulvium**: the foundations at least still remain in the
Ponte Molle, two Roman miles north of Rome; see illustration above.
Across this bridge ran the *Via Flaminia*, one of the most important of
the roads leading to the north of Italy; and here Constantine defeated
Maxentius in the memorable battle of 312 A.D.

33. **ex praefectūrā Reātīnā**: Cicero was patron of Reate (rē-ā′tē),
i.e. he was the legal representative of the inhabitants of Reate at Rome;
he could therefore count on their loyalty to him.

complūrēs dēlēctōs adulēscentēs, quōrum operā ūtor assi-
35 duē in rē pūblicā, praesidiō cum gladiīs mīseram.

Interim tertiā ferē vigiliā exāctā, cum iam pontem Mulvium magnō comitātū lēgātī Allobrogum ingredī inciperent
ūnāque Volturcius, fit in eōs impetus ; ēdūcuntur et ab
illīs gladiī et ā nostrīs. Rēs praetōribus erat nōta sōlīs,
40 ignōrābātur ā cēterīs.

> The letters were brought to me; I sent for the writers and
> summoned the senate.

3. Tum interventū Pomptīnī atque Flaccī pugna sēdā-
tur. Litterae, quaecumque erant in eō comitātū, integrīs
signīs praetōribus trāduntur ; ipsī comprehēnsī ad mē,
cum iam dīlūcēsceret, dēdūcuntur.

5 Atque hōrum omnium scelerum improbissimum māchinā-

---

35. **in rē pūblicā :** *i.e.* ' for public business.' *212, i.*

36. **tertiā ferē vigiliā exāctā :** about 3 A.M. ; the night was divided up into four watches of equal length. *242, c.* See IDIOMS.

37. **magnō comitātū :** *137, a;* B. 222, 1 ; A. & G. 413, *a; * G. 392. **Allobrogum** (a-lob'rọ-jēz).

38. **Volturcius** (vọl-tur'sh(y)ụs).

39. **Rēs praetōribus . . . sōlīs :** *rēs* ' plan.' The soldiers with the praetors did not know for what purpose they had been sent out ; and the deputies of the Allobroges, though they no doubt understood in a general way that they would be asked to give up the documents received from the conspirators, had apparently not been informed when or how the demand would be made upon them, so that the attack at first surprised them. See Sallust, *Catilīna*, 45.

3. 1. **Tum interventū,** *et seq.: i.e.* the praetors explained that they represented the consul, to whom the documents were to be delivered. Sallust says that the Gauls, as soon as they understood matters, placed themselves in charge of the praetors ; but that Volturcius made a valiant resistance until he saw that he was deserted by the rest, whereupon he surrendered, begging that his life be spared.

2. **integrīs signīs :** ' with the seals unbroken ' ; see Companion, page 559.

3. **ipsī :** the Gallic deputies and Volturcius.

4. **cum iam dīlūcēsceret :** early in the morning of December 3.

tōrem, Cimbrum Gabīnium, statim ad mē, nihil dum suspi-
cantem, vocāvī; deinde item arcessītus est L. Statilius
et post eum C. Cethēgus; tardissimē autem Lentulus
vēnit, crēdō, quod in litterīs dandīs praeter cōnsuētūdinem
proximā nocte vigilārat.   10

Cum summīs et clārissimīs huius cīvitātis virīs, quī,
audītā rē, frequentēs ad mē māne convēnerant, litterās
ā mē prius aperīrī quam ad senātum dēferrī placēret, nē,
sī nihil esset inventum, temerē ā mē tantus tumultus
iniectus cīvitātī vidērētur, negāvī mē esse factūrum, ut 15
dē perīculō pūblicō nōn ad cōnsilium pūblicum rem integram

---

6. **Cimbrum Gabīnium** (gạ-bin'ịụs sim'bẹr).

7. **vocāvī:** as chief executive the consul had the right to summon
citizens into his presence, and even to have them brought by force
if they offered resistance. In this case the deputies and the conspirators
were no doubt kept at the orator's house, which stood on the northwest
slope of the Palatine hill, until they were taken before the senate; see
Plan facing page 62. **L. Statilius** (lū'sh(y)ụs stạ-til'ịụs).

8. **C. Cethēgus** (gā'(y)ụs sẹ-thē'gụs).

9. **crēdō:** scornful, alluding to the 'sleepiness' of Lentulus (see
page 94, lines 6, 7); the letter (see page 90, lines 56–59), in the preparation
of which he is represented as having "burned the midnight oil," contains
less than forty words!

10. **vigilārat:** 'he had been up late.' *64, a.*

11. **Cum . . . placēret:** 'Although most eminent and famous men
of this state of ours favored my opening the letter before reporting it to
the senate.' **virīs:** many of them had no doubt been sent for by the
consul himself, to be his witnesses and advisers. **quī, audītā rē:** 'who
having heard the news'; the ablative absolute is here a substitute for the
missing perfect active participle, and is to be regarded as appositive to *quī*.
Study the reference under *Latin Style* in the Companion. *211; 212, a.*

12. **frequentēs:** 'in great numbers.'

13. **quam dēferrī:** *quam dēferrem* or *quam dēferrentur* might have been
expected. *237, d;* A. & G. 583, *c;* G. 644.

14. **nihil:** *i.e.* nothing incriminating. **temerē:** 'rashly,' without
sufficient reason.

15. **esse factūrum, ut . . . dēferrem:** periphrasis, more emphatic
than the simple *dēlātūrum esse;* with *negāvī (dīxī nōn),* 'I said that in
a matter fraught with danger to the state I could not but lay the

dēferrem. Etenim, Quirītēs, sī ea, quae erant ad mē
dēlāta, reperta nōn essent, tamen ego nōn arbitrābar in
tantīs reī pūblicae perīculīs esse mihi nimiam dīligentiam
20 pertimēscendam.

Senātum frequentem celeriter, ut vīdistis, coēgī. Atque
intereā statim, admonitū Allobrogum, C. Sulpicium praetōrem, fortem virum, mīsī, quī ex aedibus Cethēgī, sī quid
tēlōrum esset, efferret; ex quibus ille maximum sīcārum
25 numerum et gladiōrum extulit.

> *Volturcius, who was taking letters to Catiline, and the Gallic
> envoys gave evidence before the senate.*

4. Intrōdūxī Volturcium sine Gallīs; fidem pūblicam
iussū senātūs dedī; hortātus sum, ut ea, quae scīret, sine
timōre indicāret.

Tum ille dīxit, cum vix sē ex magnō timōre recreāsset,
5 ā P. Lentulō sē habēre ad Catilīnam mandāta et litterās,
ut servōrum praesidiō ūterētur, ut ad urbem quam prīmum cum exercitū accēderet; id autem eō cōnsiliō, ut, cum

---

facts unprejudiced before the state's council.' *203 (3)*; B. 297, 1; A.
& G. 568, N. 1; G. 556.

17. **sī**: translate as if *etiam sī*, ' even if.' See page 8, line 1, note.

18. **in tantīs reī pūblicae perīculīs**: ' in so great a political crisis.'

19. **nimiam dīligentiam**: ' the criticism of being unduly careful.'

21. **frequentem**: ' with full attendance.' The senate met in the
Temple of Concord, in the Forum; see Plan facing page 62. **coēgī**:
the term regularly used of convoking the senate.

22. **C. Sulpicium** (gā′(y)ụs sụl-pish′(y)ụs).

23. **sī quid tēlōrum esset**: ' whatever weapons there were.' *97, a.*
See IDIOMS.

4. 1. **Intrōdūxī**: *i.e.* before the senate. **fidem pūblicam dedī**:
' I gave him a pledge in the name of the state,' *i.e.* a pledge of pardon
if he would turn state's evidence; followed by *iussū senātūs* because the
senate alone had authority to grant or promise amnesty.

5. **ad**: as page 80, line 18.

6. **ut**: ' (to the effect) that.' *199, a.*

7. **id**: i.e. *ut id faceret.*

urbem ex omnibus partibus, quem ad modum dēscrīptum distribūtumque erat, incendissent caedemque īnfīnītam cīvium fēcissent, praestō esset ille, quī et fugientēs exci- 10 peret et sē cum hīs urbānīs ducibus coniungeret.

Intrōductī autem Gallī iūs iūrandum sibi et litterās ab Lentulō, Cethēgō, Statiliō ad suam gentem data esse dīxērunt, atque ita sibi ab hīs et ā L. Cassiō esse prae- scrīptum equitātum in Italiam quam prīmum mitterent. 15

Pedestrēs sibi cōpiās nōn dēfutūrās; Lentulum autem sibi cōnfīrmāsse ex fātīs Sibyllīnīs haruspicumque respōnsīs, sē

---

8. **ex**: in our idiom, ' in.' Latin is fond of expressing source rela- tions with *ā* or *ab*, *ē* or *ex*, where English uses ' at,' ' in,' ' on,' or similar words. **omnibus partibus**: according to Sallust (*Catilīna*, **43**, 2) the city was to be fired in twelve places at once, under the direction of Statilius and Gabinius; but Plutarch (*Cicero*, 18) says in a hundred places. **quem . . . erat**: parenthetical explanation of the speaker; hence with the indicative. *214, c.* See page 37, line 21. **dēscrīptum distribūtum- que**: note the alliteration and hendiadys of verbs. *239, a; 238, h; 212, b.* Compare **1,** 4, 18, and 21.

9. **incendissent**: represents what tense of the direct discourse? *177, a.* **caedem īnfīnītam**: see Plutarch, *Cicero*, 18: ' There was nothing small or mean about the designs of Lentulus; for he had resolved to kill the entire senate, and as many of the other citizens as he could.'

10. **praestō**: not a verb. **ille**: Catiline.

14. **dīxērunt**: followed by indirect discourse in two degrees of sub- ordination, — as a wheel within a wheel, — thus: (1) by *esse prae- scrīptum*, which in turn is followed by *pedestrēs . . . dēfutūrās* in indirect discourse subordinate to itself; (2) by *Lentulum . . . cōnfīrmāsse*, similarly followed by *sē . . . fuisse;* (3) by *eundem dīxisse*, to which *annum . . . vīcēsimus* is subordinate. The reflexive in each case refers to the chief agent or subject of the clause to which its own clause is sub- ordinate; thus *sibi* (line 14) refers to *Gallī* (line 12), but *sibi* (line 16) tc *hīs et L. Cassiō* (line 14). **L. Cassiō** (lṵ'sh(y)ṵs kash'(y)ṵs).

17. **ex fātīs Sibyllīnīs** (sib'ị-līn): ' from the Sibylline prophecies.' The original Sibylline Books, purchased by King Tarquin, perished when the temple of Jupiter on the Capitoline hill was burned, in 83 B.C. After that a new collection of Sibylline prophecies was made with great care at the different places where oracles were given through sibyls, and placed in the new temple (see note to line 22). Here they were guarded

esse tertium illum Cornēlium, ad quem rēgnum huius urbis
atque imperium pervenīre esset necesse; Cinnam ante sē et
20 Sullam fuisse; eundemque dīxisse fātālem hunc annum esse
ad interitum huius urbis atque imperī, quī esset annus
decimus post virginum absolūtiōnem, post Capitōlī autem
incēnsiōnem vīcēsimus.

Hanc autem Cethēgō cum cēterīs contrōversiam fuisse
25 dīxērunt, quod Lentulō et aliīs Sāturnālibus caedem fierī
atque urbem incendī placēret, Cethēgō nimium id longum
vidērētur.

---

by a special college of priests, the quindecimvirī, who consulted them,
however, only upon request of the senate.   In addition to these, there
appear to have been smaller private collections, of a similar character;
and to one of the latter, in the possession of some family of the Cornelian gens, Lentulus probably referred.

19. **necesse:** see IDIOMS.   **Cinnam** (sin'ạ).

20. **fātālem annum:** really no more ' decreed by fate ' than that year
in the famous prophecy of Mother Shipton, —

> "The world unto an end shall come
> In eighteen hundred and eighty-one."

22. **virginum:** for *virginum Vestālium.*   The trial of a Vestal on the
charge of breaking her vows was considered in a high degree portentous,
even though her innocence might be proved and the trial followed by
acquittal.   **Capitōlī incēnsiōnem:** in 83 B.C.; immediately afterwards
Sulla commenced to rebuild the temple on a much grander scale, but the
edifice was not completed till some years later, by Quintus Lutatius
Catulus (kat'ū-lụs, or kat'chu-lụs).   According to Sallust, the soothsayers were quoted as affirming that the twentieth year after the burning
of the Capitol would be one of bloody civil war.

25. **Sāturnālibus** (sat-ụr-nā'lị-ạ) :   December 19, the chief day of the
festival; a favorable time for a bold stroke, on account of the cessation
of business and the merriment and freedom from restraint characteristic
of the festival of Saturn, during which the Romans " kept open house "
to friends and clients.   Parts of our Christmas festivities bear a close
resemblance to the customs that accompanied the celebration of the
Saturnalia.

26. **nimium longum :** ' too far off,' ' too remote (a date).'

The letters of Cethegus and Statilius were opened and read.

5. Ac nē longum sit, Quirītēs, tabellās prōferrī iussimus quae ā quōque dīcēbantur datae.

Prīmum ostendimus Cethēgō; signum cognōvit.

Nōs līnum incīdimus, lēgimus. Erat scrīptum ipsīus manū Allobrogum senātuī et populō, sēsē, quae eōrum 5 lēgātīs cōnfīrmāsset, factūrum esse; ōrāre, ut item illī

facerent, quae sibi eōrum lēgātī recēpissent.

Tum Cethēgus, quī paulō ante aliquid tamen 10 dē gladiīs ac sīcīs, quae apud ipsum erant dēprehēnsa, respondisset dīxissetque sē semper

TABLET AND SEALS

5. Notice the vivid narration in this chapter and its many realistic touches, especially in the last two sentences.

1. **nē longum:** see IDIOMS. **tabellās:** containing the *litterae* of page 85, line 12. See illustration.

2. **datae:** sc. *esse.*

3. **cognōvit:** 'he acknowledged (it)' as his own. For the seal, the thread, and other matters connected with the form of the letters, see Companion, pages 558, 559. Cicero had done well to leave the letters untouched until they could be opened in the presence of the senate.

7. **sibi . . . recēpissent:** 'had undertaken for him,' *i.e.* had promised him.

10. **aliquid:** see vocabulary. Kind of accusative? **tamen:** 'nevertheless,' though appearances were all against him.

11. **quae:** why neuter? *163, c;* B. 250, 2: A. & G. 305, *a;* G. 614, R. 5.

15 bonōrum ferrāmentōrum studiōsum fuisse, recitātīs litteris, dēbilitātus atque abiectus cōnscientiā repente conticuit. Intrōductus est Statilius; cognōvit et signum et manum suam. Recitātae sunt tabellae in eandem ferē sententiam; cōnfessus est.

Letters of Lentulus to the Allobroges and Catiline were read.

20 Tum ostendī tabellās Lentulō et quaesīvī, cognōsceretne signum. Adnuit. "Est vērō," inquam, "nōtum quidem signum, imāgō avī tuī, clārissimī virī, quī amāvit ūnicē patriam et cīvēs suōs; quae quidem tē ā tantō scelere etiam mūta revocāre dēbuit."

25 Leguntur eādem ratiōne ad senātum Allobrogum populumque litterae.

COIN STRUCK BY LUCIUS LENTULUS AS CONSUL
Obverse: Jupiter Pluvius.   Reverse. Diana of Ephesus.

15. **bonōrum ferrāmentōrum studiōsum:** ' a fancier of good tools '; avoiding the use of *tēlōrum* and implying that he was a collector, a connoisseur, of steel implements in general. *239, i.*

16. **cōnscientiā:** ' by his guilty knowledge,' ' by his sense of guilt.'

18. **in eandem sententiam:** i.e. *scrīptae.* See vocabulary.

22. **avī tuī:** see vocabulary under *Lentulus* (1). It was customary to place upon seals the likenesses of distinguished ancestors.

24. **etiam mūta:** ' even though speechless '; with *revocāre*, oxymoron. *239, p.*

25. **eādem ratiōne:** ' of the same tenor,' ' to the same effect.'

Sī quid dē hīs rēbus dīcere vellet, fēcī potestātem.   Atque ille prīmō quidem negāvit;

THE CUMAEAN SIBYL

The painting by Michelangelo in the Sistine Chapel of the Vatican. The Sibyl is said to have sold the Sibylline books to Tarquin the Proud.

post autem aliquantō, tōtō iam indiciō expositō atque ēditō, surrēxit; quaesīvit ā 30 Gallīs, quid sibi esset cum eīs, quam ob rem domum suam vēnissent, itemque ā Volturciō.

Quī cum illī breviter cōn- 35 stanterque respondissent, per quem ad eum quotiēnsque vēnissent, quaesissentque ab eō, nihilne sēcum esset dē fātīs Sibyllīnīs locūtus, tum 40 ille subitō, scelere dēmēns, quanta cōnscientiae vīs esset, ostendit.   Nam, cum id posset īnfitiārī, repente praeter opīniōnem omnium cōnfessus 45 est.   Ita eum nōn modo ingenium illud et dīcendī exercitātiō, quā semper valuit,

27. Sī: ' In case.'   This is not a contrary-to-fact condition; the subjunctive *vellet* is due to implied indirect discourse.   *214, b.*

28. negāvit: ' said, "No," ' *i.e.* that he did not care to say anything.

29. expositō atque ēditō: in our court phrase, ' given and taken down,' *i.e.* taken down in writing by the senators who were keeping the record.

31. quid . . .: see IDIOMS.   ' what business he had with them (which served as a reason) why they had come.'

36. per quem: i.e. *ā quō perductī*, referring to Umbrēnus.

39. nihilne sēcum esset . . . locūtus: ' whether he had said nothing to them.'

41. scelere dēmēns: i.e. *cōnscientiā sceleris dēmēns factus.*

47. exercitātiō: ' readiness.'   Of the oratory of this Lentulus Cicero elsewhere says (*Brūtus*, **66,** 235): ' His slowness of thought and delivery

sed etiam propter vim sceleris manifestī atque dēprehēnsī
50 impudentia, quā superābat omnēs, improbitāsque dēfēcit.

Volturcius vērō subitō litterās prōferrī atque aperīrī
iubet, quās sibi ā Lentulō ad Catilīnam datās esse dīcēbat.
Atque ibi, vehementissimē perturbātus, Lentulus tamen et
signum et manum suam cognōvit. Erant autem sine
55 nōmine sed ita :

"Quis sim, sciēs ex eō, quem ad tē mīsī. Cūrā, ut vir
sīs, et cōgitā, quem in locum sīs prōgressus. Vidē, quid
tibi iam sit necesse, et cūrā, ut omnium tibi auxilia ad-
iungās, etiam īnfimōrum."

Gabinius entered no denial.   The conduct of all showed guilt.

60   Gabīnius deinde intrōductus cum prīmō inpudenter respondēre coepisset, ad extrēmum nihil ex eīs, quae Gallī
īnsimulābant, negāvit.

---

was lost sight of by reason of the impressiveness of his person, his
gesticulation alike skillful and full of grace, and the sweetness and
power of his voice.'

50. **superābat :** ' endeavored to surpass.' *175, e.*

54. **sine nōmine :** without address or signature, we should say.

55. **sed ita :** ' but as follows,' the contents indicating the personality
of sender and receiver.   The same letter is thus given by Sallust (*Catilīna*, **44,** 5 ; text of Eussner) :

*Quī sim, ex eō, quem ad tē mīsī, cognōscēs.   Fac cōgitēs, in quantā
calamitāte sīs, et meminerīs tē virum esse.   Cōnsīderēs, quid tuae ratiōnēs
postulent.   Auxilium petās ab omnibus, etiam ab īnfimīs.*

This version of the letter differs from that given by Cicero only in
greater refinement of expression.   The latter shows traces of the haste
in which the letter was no doubt written, and may be accepted as
unquestionably the original form.

56. **vir :** how do *vir* and *homō* differ?

59. **īnfimōrum :** = *servōrum;* see page 84, line 6, and note on page 55,
line 10.

60. **cum prīmō . . . coepisset :** ' although at first he had begun.' *238, k.*

61. **ex eīs :** *97, a;* B. 201, 1, *a;* A. & G. 346, *c;* G. 372, R. 2.

Ac mihi quidem, Quirītēs, cum illa certissima vīsa sunt argūmenta atque indicia sceleris, tabellae, signa, manūs, dēnique ūnīus cuiusque cōnfessiō, tum multō certiōra illa, 65 color, oculī, vultūs, taciturnitās. Sīc enim obstipuerant, sīc terram intuēbantur, sīc fūrtim nōn numquam inter sēsē aspiciēbant, ut nōn iam ab aliīs indicārī, sed indicāre sē ipsī vidērentur.

The senate passed a vote of thanks to me and others.

6. Indiciīs expositīs atque ēditīs, Quirītēs, senātum cōnsuluī, dē summā rē pūblicā quid fierī placēret.   Dictae sunt ā prīncipibus ācerrimae ac fortissimae sententiae, quās senātus sine ūllā varietāte est secūtus.   Et quoniam nōndum est perscrīptum senātūs cōnsultum, ex memoriā vōbīs, 5 Quirītēs, quid senātus cēnsuerit, expōnam.

Prīmum mihi grātiae verbīs amplissimīs aguntur, quod virtūte, cōnsiliō, prōvidentiā meā rēs pūblica maximīs perīculīs sit līberāta.   Deinde L. Flaccus et C. Pomptīnus praetōrēs, quod eōrum operā fortī fidēlīque ūsus essem, 10

---

63. **Ac mihi quidem :** ' Moreover, to me personally.' The intensive particle *quidem* must be variously translated to suit the context; here it lends emphasis to *mihi*. **certissima :** force of the superlative? See *certiōra* in line 65.

67. **nōn numquam :** *239, m.* **inter sēsē :** ' at one another.' *159.*

6. 1. **expositis atque ēditīs :** see page 89, line 29, and note. Why is *Indiciīs* plural?

2. **dē summā rē pūblicā :** i.e. *dē salūte reī pūblicae.* **Dictae . . . sententiae :** on the method of procedure, see note to page 36, line 15.

3. **ā prīncipibus :** ' by the leaders ' of the senate, comprising the consuls-elect, who voted first; after them the ex-consuls voted. **quās . . . :** ' which the senate adopted without any dissenting opinion.'

7. **grātiae :** see IDIOMS. **verbīs amplissimīs :** ' in elaborate terms.' See IDIOMS. *212, n.* **quod :** ' because (as they said).' *183, a;* B. 285; 286, 1; A. & G. 592, 3; G. 541.

8. **virtūte :** ' by my resolution.'

10. **operā :** we say ' services.'

meritō ac iūre laudantur. Atque etiam virō fortī, collēgae
meō, laus impertītur, quod eōs, quī huius coniūrātiōnis
participēs fuissent, ā suīs et ā reī pūblicae cōnsiliīs remōvisset.

Iṭ then ordered nine conspirators placed under guard.

15 Atque ita cēnsuērunt, ut P. Lentulus, cum sē praetūrā
abdicāsset, in cūstōdiam trāderētur; itemque utī C.
Cethēgus, L. Statilius, P. Gabīnius, quī omnēs praesentēs
erant, in cūstōdiam trāderentur; atque idem hōc dēcrētum
est in L. Cassium, quī sibi prōcūrātiōnem incendendae
20 urbis dēpoposcerat; in M. Cēpārium, cui ad sollicitandōs
pāstōrēs Āpūliam attribūtam esse erat indicātum; in
P. Furium, quī est ex eīs colōnīs, quōs Faesulās L. Sulla
dēdūxit: in Q. Annium Chīlōnem, quī ūnā cum hōc Furiō
semper erat in hāc Allobrogum sollicitātiōne versātus;
25 in P. Umbrēnum, lībertīnum hominem, ā quō prīmum
Gallōs ad Gabīnium perductōs esse cōnstābat.

Atque eā lēnitāte senātus est ūsus, Quirītēs, ut ex tantā
coniūrātiōne tantāque hāc multitūdine domesticōrum
hostium, novem hominum perditissimōrum poenā rē

---

11. **collēgae meō**: in the consulship; *i.e.* Gaius Antonius Hybrida
(hĭ'brĭ-dạ), who had been a supporter of Catiline until Cicero won him
over; see Companion, page 516.

12. **eōs . . . remōvisset**: *i.e.* he had refused to have anything more
to do with them, either as a public officer or as an individual.

15. **cum . . . abdicāsset**: no action could be brought against a
Roman magistrate so long as he remained in office, his person and office
being considered inviolable (*sacrōsānctus*).

18. **in cūstōdiam**: see note on page 47, line 3.

19. **L. Cassium**: Cássius, Fúrius, Ánnius Chilo (kī'lō), and Um-
brénus escaped; Ceparius (sẹ-pā'rĭ-ụs) had left the city, but was
arrested and brought back.

22. **colōnīs**: see note on page 70, line 21.

29. **novem hominum**: of these only five actually suffered the penalty
imposed; see note on page 119, line 6.

pūblicā cōnservātā, reliquōrum mentēs sānārī posse arbitrā- 30
rētur.

It decreed a thanksgiving, and forced Lentulus to resign
his praetorship.

Atque etiam supplicātiō dīs immortālibus prō singulārī
eōrum meritō meō nōmine dēcrēta est, quod mihi prīmum
post hanc urbem conditam togātō contigit, et hīs dēcrēta
verbīs est, *quod urbem incendiīs, caede cīvēs, Italiam bellō* 35
līberāssem. Quae supplicātiō sī cum cēterīs supplicātiō-
nibus cōnferātur, hōc interest, quod cēterae, bene gestā, haec
ūna, cōnservātā rē pūblicā, cōnstitūta est.

Atque illud, quod faciendum prīmum fuit, factum atque
trānsāctum est. Nam P. Lentulus, quamquam pate- 40
factīs indiciīs, cōnfessiōnibus suīs, iūdiciō senātūs nōn modo
praetōris iūs, vērum etiam cīvis āmīserat, tamen magistrātū

---

32. **supplicātiō :** here refers to a period of public thanksgiving, in
this case probably of five days' duration. The chief religious observance
on such occasions was the banquet for the gods (*lectisternium*). Couches
on which images of the gods reclined were placed in front of the temples
and shrines, and offerings of food and wine were set before them.

33. **meō nōmine :** translate as if *honōris meī causā,* ' in my honor.'
quod : '(an experience) which.' **prīmum :** ' for the first time.'

34. **togātō :** *i.e.* as a civil magistrate; in previous cases a thanksgiving had been appointed only in recognition of military successes.

35. *quod:* see page 91, line 7, and note. *Italiam bellō:* rhetorical
exaggeration.

36. **Quae sī :** ' And if this.' *167.*

37. **hōc interest:** ' there is this difference'; more forcible than *hōc*
interesse videātur, the indicative implying that the difference certainly
exists, whether the comparison be made or not. **cēterae, bene gestā :**
i.e. *cēterae supplicātiōnēs bene gestā rē pūblicā cōnstitūtae sunt.*

39. **factum atque trānsāctum est :** originally a legal formula.

42. **magistrātū sē abdicāvit :** of course under compulsion ; but the
form of voluntary resignation must be kept up (see line 18 above).
Plutarch says (*Cicero,* 19) : ' Lentulus, having been convicted, resigned
his office (for he happened to be praetor), and laying aside his purple-

sē abdicāvit, ut, quae religiō C. Mariō, clārissimō virō,
nōn fuerat, quō minus C. Glauciam, dē quō nihil nōminātim
45 erat dēcrētum, praetōrem occīderet, eā nōs religiōne in
prīvātō P. Lentulō pūniendō līberārēmur.

*With the capture of these conspirators the plot has collapsed. If Catiline
had remained, our task would have been more difficult.*

7. Nunc quoniam, Quirītēs, cōnscelerātissimī perīculō-
sissimīque bellī nefāriōs ducēs captōs iam et comprehēnsōs
tenētis, exīstimāre dēbētis omnēs Catilīnae cōpiās, omnēs
spēs atque opēs, hīs dēpulsīs urbis perīculīs, concidisse.
5 Quem quidem ego cum ex urbe pellēbam, hōc prōvidēbam
animō, Quirītēs, remōtō Catilīnā, nōn mihi esse P. Lentulī
somnum nec L. Cassī adipēs nec C. Cethēgī furiōsam temeritātem pertimēscendam.

---

bordered toga in the senate, assumed a garb in keeping with his misfortune.' The last clause may mean that he put on the white toga of
the ordinary citizen (the wool being undyed), but more likely that he
secured one of dark color, as the Romans were wont to do, as a sign of
mourning in times of trouble.

43. ut, . . . : 'that we might be free from religious scruple, . . .
though such scruples had not prevented Gaius Marius from,' etc.;
referring to the sacredness of the person of a magistrate. Marius, however, was only indirectly responsible for the death of Glaucia, who was
pelted to death by a mob. **religiō**: *not* 'religion.' See vocabulary.

44. **C. Glauciam** (gā'(y)ụs glȧ'sh(y)ạ). **quō minus . . . occīderet**: depends upon the idea of preventing in *religiō* above. *201, a.*
nihil: see IDIOMS.

7. 7. **somnum, adipēs**: see note on page 83, line 9. Shakespeare
(following a hint of Plutarch's) represents Caesar as saying:

> "Let me have men about me that are fat;
> Sleek-headed men, and such as sleep o' nights:
> Yond' Cassius has a lean and hungry look;
> He thinks too much; such men are dangerous."

C. Cethēgī furiōsam temeritātem: according to Sallust (*Catilīna*, **43**, 3),
'Cethegus kept making complaint about the inactivity of his associates.
He said that they were losing great opportunities by their hesitation
and procrastination; that at such a critical time they needed action,

Ille erat ūnus timendus ex istīs omnibus, sed tam diū
dum urbis moenibus continēbātur. Omnia nōrat, omnium 10
aditūs tenēbat; appellāre, temptāre, sollicitāre poterat,
audēbat. Erat eī cōnsilium ad facinus aptum, cōnsiliō
autem neque manus neque lingua deerat. Iam ad certās
rēs cōnficiendās certōs hominēs dēlēctōs ac dēscrīptōs
habēbat. Neque vērō, cum aliquid mandārat, cōnfectum 15
putābat; nihil erat, quod nōn ipse obīret, occurreret,
vigilāret, labōrāret; frīgus, sitim, famem ferre poterat.

Hunc ego hominem tam ācrem, tam audācem, tam
parātum, tam callidum, tam in scelere vigilantem, tam in
perditīs rēbus dīligentem nisi ex domesticīs īnsidiīs in 20
castrēnse latrōcinium compulissem — dīcam id, quod sentiō,
Quirītēs, — nōn facile hanc tantam mōlem malī ā cervīcibus vestrīs dēpulissem.

Nōn ille nōbīs Sāturnālia cōnstituisset neque tantō ante
exitī ac fātī diem reī pūblicae dēnūntiāvisset neque com- 25
mīsisset, ut signum, ut litterae suae testēs manifestī sceleris

---

not deliberation; and that if he could get a few to help him, even if the
rest should hang back, he would make an attack on the senate.'

9. **tam diū dum**: '(only) so long as.'   *190, a;* B. 293, II; A. & G.
556, *a;* G. 569, N. 1.

10. **omnium aditūs tenēbat**: 'he understood how to get at every
one.'

12. **cōnsilium . . .**: he could not only plan crime, but also carry out
his wicked plans.

13. **certās, certōs**: 'particular,' 'special.'

14. **dēscrīptōs**: 'assigned' to the part they were to take, 'detailed.'

16. **quod**: properly with *obīret* only; 'which he did not undertake,
did not meet; on which he did not bestow watchfulness, effort.' *194, a.*

19. **parātum**: 'ready (to strike).' **in perditīs**: see vocabulary.

24. **Sāturnālia**: see page 86, line 25, and note. It yet lacked more
than two weeks to the Saturnalia; Catiline would have set the day of
destruction earlier.

25. **neque commīsisset**: 'and would not have made the mistake
of allowing his seal . . . to be secured as,' etc.; *i.e.* if he had remained in
the city.

dēprehenderentur. Quae nunc, illō absente, sīc gesta sunt,
ut nūllum in prīvātā domō fūrtum umquam sit tam palam
inventum, quam haec tanta in rē pūblicā coniūrātiō mani-
30 festō inventa atque dēprehēnsa est.

Quod sī Catilīna in urbe ad hanc diem remānsisset, quamquam, quoad fuit, omnibus eius cōnsiliīs occurrī atque obstitī, tamen, ut levissimē dīcam, dīmicandum nōbīs cum illō
fuisset neque nōs umquam, cum ille in urbe hostis esset,
35 tantīs perīculīs rem pūblicam tantā pāce, tantō ōtiō, tantō
silentiō līberāssēmus.

The gods have been very near to us, warning us by signs and wonders.

8. Quamquam haec omnia, Quirītēs, ita sunt ā mē ad-
ministrāta, ut deōrum immortālium nūtū atque cōnsiliō et
gesta et prōvīsa esse videantur. Idque cum coniectūrā
cōnsequī possumus, quod vix vidētur hūmānī cōnsilī tantā-
5 rum rērum gubernātiō esse potuisse, tum vērō ita praesentēs
hīs temporibus opem et auxilium nōbīs tulērunt, ut eōs paene
oculīs vidēre possēmus.

Nam ut illa omittam, vīsās nocturnō tempore ab occidente facēs ārdōremque caelī, ut fulminum iactūs, ut terrae

---

33. **ut levissimē dīcam :** see vocabulary. *196, b;* B. 282, 4; A. & G.
532; G. 545, R. 3.

8. 1. **Quamquam :** ' And yet.'

3. **cum :** ' not only,' correlative to *tum* below.

4. **vix vidētur . . . esse potuisse :** ' it seems hardly possible that
human wisdom can have directed matters of so great moment.' *94, d;*
B. 203, 5; A. & G. 343, *b;* G. 366.

5. **tum vērō ita praesentēs :** ' but in reality so vividly present.'

8. **illa :** those that had been noticed some time previously; contrasted with *haec* in line 11.   How far Cicero himself believed in portents
is doubtful; but, like other Roman statesmen, he was ready to make the
most of them in dealing with a superstitious populace.   These unusual
phenomena were treated at length in his poem *On his Consulship.*
omittam . . . omittam : an example of *praeteritiō.* *239, r.* **ab occidente :**
' in the west ' a quarter of ill omen.   See vocabulary.

9. **facēs,** etc. : see Dio Cassius, **37,** 25, 2 (referring to this time):

mōtūs relinquam; ut omittam cētera, quae tam multa, 10
nōbīs cōnsulibus, facta sunt, ut haec, quae nunc fīunt,
canere dī immortālēs vidērentur, hōc certē, quod sum dictūrus, neque praetermittendum neque relinquendum est.

Nam profectō memoriā tenētis, Cottā et Torquātō cōnsulibus, complūrēs in Capitōliō rēs dē caelō esse percussās, 15
cum et simulācra deōrum dēpulsa sunt et statuae veterum

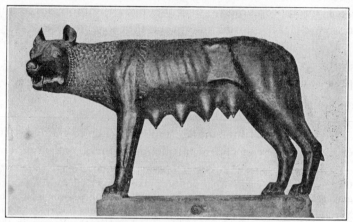

The Wolf in the Capitoline Museum
This is probably the original statue as one of the legs has been scarred
by lightning.

'Many thunderbolts fell from a cloudless sky, and the earth shook
violently; spectral forms also were seen in many places, and torches shot
up into the sky above the sunset.' For the portents preceding the murder
of Caesar, see Kelsey's *Selections from Ovid*, pages 156, 157, and notes.

10. **quae tam multa**: either 'so many of which,' or 'which in so
great number.' *97, c;* B. 201, 1, *b;* A. & G. 346, *e;* G. 370, R. 2.

12. **canere:** 'to predict.'

13. **relinquendum:** 'left out of consideration'; how different from
praetermittendum?

14. **profectō:** adverb, 'doubtless.' **Cottā et Torquātō** (kot'a and
tor-kwā'tus) **cōnsulibus:** the year 65 B.C.

15. **dē caelō:** see vocabulary.

16. **dēpulsa:** from their pedestals. **veterum hominum:** 'of men
of the olden time'; in and about the Capitol stood a host of statues.

hominum dēiectae et lēgum aera liquefacta et tāctus etiam
ille, quī hanc urbem condidit, Rōmulus, quem inaurātum
in Capitōliō, parvum atque lactentem, ūberibus lupīnīs
20 inhiantem, fuisse meministis.

Quō quidem tempore cum haruspicēs ex tōtā Etrūriā
convēnissent, caedēs atque incendia et lēgum interitum et
bellum cīvīle ac domesticum et tōtīus urbis atque imperī
occāsum appropinquāre dīxērunt, nisi dī immortālēs, omnī
25 ratiōne plācātī, suō nūmine prope fāta ipsa flexissent.

Itaque illōrum respōnsīs tum et lūdī per decem diēs factī
sunt, neque rēs ūlla, quae ad plācandōs deōs pertinēret,
praetermissa est.

A great statue of Jupiter was ordered placed on the Capitoline
hill, to overlook the Forum.

Īdemque iussērunt simulācrum Iovis facere maius et in
30 excelsō collocāre et contrā, atque anteā fuerat, ad orientem

17. **aera:** ' the bronzes,' *i.e.* bronze pillars or tablets; see Dio
Cassius, **37,** 9: ' The writing of the pillars, on which the laws were
graven, ran together and became illegible.' Such copies of laws were
set up in and around temples; but this passage does not refer to the
Laws of the Twelve Tables, which were placed in the Forum, in the
earlier period at least on the Rostra.

20. **fuisse:** *i.e.* it was at that time on the Capitoline hill, but has
since been removed. A bronze group similar to that here described (the
twins Romulus and Remus being modern) is now in the museum on the
Capitoline hill at Rome. The wolf, undoubtedly of very ancient workmanship, is perhaps the same as that referred to here, for it shows a fracture
which may possibly have been caused by lightning. Illustration, page 97.

24. **nisi:** *i.e.* and would be upon us ' unless.' *238, f.*

25. **flexissent:** in direct discourse would have been *flexerint;* therefore, what type of condition? *218 (1), b.*

26. **respōnsīs:** why ablative? **lūdī:** all the Roman public games
(including the various spectacles of the circus, amphitheater, and
theater) were religious in their origin.

29. **facere, collocāre, convertere:** these infinitives are mere verbal
nouns, objects of *iussērunt,* and therefore do not require subject-accusa-
tives. **in excelsō:** ' on a high (pedestal).' *211.*

30. **contrā, atque anteā fuerat:** ' opposite to what it had previously

convertere; ac sē spērāre dīxērunt, sī illud signum, quod
vidētis, sōlis ortum et forum cūriamque cōnspiceret, fore
ut ea cōnsilia, quae clam essent inita contrā salūtem urbis
atque imperī, illūstrārentur, ut ā senātū populōque Rōmānō
perspicī possent.   35

Atque illud signum collocandum cōnsulēs illī locāvērunt;
sed tanta fuit operis tarditās, ut, neque superiōribus cōnsulibus neque nōbīs, ante hodiernum diem collocārētur.

*By divine purpose the statue was set up this morning, as the accused were
being conducted to the meeting of the senate. Jupiter has saved us.*

9. Hīc quis potest esse, Quirītēs, tam āversus ā vērō,
tam praeceps, tam mente captus, quī neget haec omnia
quae vidēmus, praecipuēque hanc urbem deōrum immortālium nūtū ac potestāte administrārī? Etenim, cum esset
ita respōnsum, caedēs, incendia, interitum reī pūblicae 5

been.' According to the ancient Roman custom, the worshiper faced
the east, so that statues of divinities would naturally look toward the
west, unless there were some reason to the contrary. *233, c.*

31. **illud signum, quod vidētis:** spoken with a gesture on the right
toward the height of the Capitoline hill, where the new statue on its
column was plainly visible from the Rostra and the Forum; see note
to *Habita ad Populum,* on page 522, and Plan facing page 62.

32. **fore ut . . . illūstrārentur:** a periphrasis (circumlocution) for the
future infinitive passive (*illūstrātum īrī*), which is rarely used. In direct
discourse, *sī cōnspiciet, illūstrābuntur. 225; 218 (1), a.*

36. **collocandum locāvērunt:** ' let the contract for erecting.' *229, b;*
B. 337, 8, *b;* A. & G. 500, 4; G. 430. The charge of such contracts
properly belonged to the censors; but the censors for 65 B.C., Quintus
Lutatius Catulus and Marcus Licinius Crassus, disagreed and resigned,
so that the function in this case devolved upon the consuls.

37. **superiōribus cōnsulibus:** *i.e.* consuls for the two preceding years.
The consuls for 64 were Lucius Julius Caesar and Gaius Figulus.

38. **nōbīs:** sc. *cōnsulibus;* see IDIOMS.

9. 1. **Hīc:** adverb, ' Under these circumstances.'

2. **mente captus:** ' bereft of reason '; *mente* is an ablative of specification. *142, a.* See IDIOMS. **quī neget:** ' as to say that . . . not.' *194, a.*
haec omnia: the visible universe; spoken with a wide gesture.

comparārī, et ea per cīvēs, quae tum propter magnitūdinem
scelerum nōn nūllīs incrēdibilia vidēbantur, ea nōn modo
cōgitāta ā nefāriīs cīvibus, vērum etiam suscepta esse
sēnsistis.

10 Illud vērō nōnne ita praesēns est, ut nūtū Iovis Optimī
Maximī factum esse videātur, ut, cum hodiernō diē māne
per forum meō iussū et coniūrātī et eōrum indicēs in aedem
Concordiae dūcerentur, eō ipsō tempore signum statuerētur?
Quō collocātō atque ad vōs senātumque conversō, omnia,
15 quae erant cōgitāta contrā salūtem omnium, illūstrāta et
patefacta vīdistis.

Quō etiam maiōre sunt istī odiō suppliciōque dignī,
quī nōn sōlum vestrīs domiciliīs atque tēctīs, sed etiam
deōrum templīs atque dēlūbrīs sunt fūnestōs ac nefāriōs
20 ignēs īnferre cōnātī. Quibus ego sī mē restitisse dīcam,
nimium mihi sūmam et nōn sim ferendus ; ille, ille Iuppiter
restitit ; ille Capitōlium, ille haec templa, ille cūnctam
urbem, ille vōs omnēs salvōs esse voluit. Dīs ego immortā-

---

6. et ea : ' and that too.' B. 247, 4 ; A. & G. 298, *a ;* G. 308, R. 2.
quae : '(prophecies) which.'

10. Illud . . . statuerētur : the first *ut* introduces a result clause
depending upon *ita praesēns ;* the second *ut* introduces a substantive
clause explaining *illud.* Translate, ' But is the following fact (*illud*)
not so obvious that it seems to have happened at the nod of Jupiter
Optimus Maximus, namely, that the statue was being set up at that
precise moment (*ipsō tempore*), when, etc.' praesēns : ' immediate,'
' evident.' Optimī Maximī : asyndeton. *238, d.*

12. per forum : as Cicero's house was on the Palatine hill and the
conspirators had come to him there (see page 83, line 7, and note), he
was obliged to conduct them through the Forum in order to reach the
Temple of Concord, where the senate met ; see Plan facing page 62.

17. Quō : ' And on this account.'

21. nōn ferendus : ' intolerable.' *230, b.* ille : with a gesture on the
right toward the statue, the divinity being associated with the image ; see
page 61, line 30, and note. Notice the forceful anaphora, with asyndeta
and climax. Study the pronouns in this paragraph.

22. haec templa : about the Forum ; spoken with a gesture.

THE PALATINE HILL AS SEEN FROM THE FORUM

At the left behind the Arch of Fabian come the Temples of Venus and Rome. Next come the Temple of Julius Cæsar, Temple of Vesta, House of the Vestals, Statue of Vespasian, Temple of Castor and Pollux, and Basilica Julia. On the Palatine is the Palace of the Emperors.

libus ducibus hanc mentem, Quirītēs, voluntātemque suscēpī, atque ad haec tanta indicia pervēnī.   25

Iam vērō ab Lentulō cēterīsque domesticīs hostibus tam dēmenter tantae rēs crēditae et ignōtīs et barbarīs numquam essent profectō, nisi ab dīs immortālibus huic tantae audāciae cōnsilium esset ēreptum.

Quid vērō? ut hominēs Gallī ex cīvitāte male pācātā, 30 quae gēns ūna restat, quae bellum populō Rōmānō facere

CAPITOLIUM AT DOUGGA IN TUNISIA

Such remains show how the Romans encouraged their provincials to copy famous buildings in Rome. This temple was dedicated not only to Jupiter, like the Roman Capitolium, but also to Juno and Minerva.

24. **hanc mentem voluntātemque :** ' this purpose and determination.'

25. **haec tanta indicia :** avoid such meaningless translations as ' these so great proofs,' but translate rather by ' these manifest proofs.'

26. **Iam vērō :** ' Furthermore.'

28. **audāciae :** why dative? abstract for concrete, ' bold men.' *92, b.*

29. **cōnsilium esset ēreptum :** on the theory of the proverb, *quōs deus perdere vult, dēmentat.*

30. **Quid vērō :** denotes a transition and anticipates the following question ; ' But again.' **ut hominēs Gallī,** etc. : ' that men from Gaul, from a state scarcely subdued, the only people remaining, who seem to

et posse et nōn nōlle videātur, spem imperī ac rērum maxi-
mārum ultrō sibi ā patriciīs hominibus oblātam neglege-
rent vestramque salūtem suīs opibus antepōnerent, id nōn,
35 dīvīnitus esse factum putātis, praesertim quī nōs nōn pugnandō, sed tacendō superāre potuerint?

Celebrate the thanksgiving for a deliverance without bloodshed.

10. Quam ob rem, Quirītēs, quoniam ad omnia pulvīnāria supplicātiō dēcrēta est, celebrātōte illōs diēs cum
coniugibus ac līberīs vestrīs. Nam multī saepe honōrēs
dīs immortālibus iūstī habitī sunt ac dēbitī, sed profectō
5 iūstiōrēs numquam. Ēreptī enim estis ex crūdēlissimō ac
miserrimō interitū; sine caede, sine sanguine, sine exercitū,
sine dīmicātiōne; togātī, mē ūnō togātō duce et imperātōre,
vīcistis.

Etenim recordāminī, Quirītēs, omnēs cīvīlēs dissēn-
10 siōnēs, nōn sōlum eās, quās audīstis, sed eās, quās vōsmet
ipsī meministis atque vīdistis.

L. Sulla P. Sulpicium oppressit; C. Marium, cūstōdem

---

be able to make war on the Roman people and not to be unwilling to
do so, that they should disregard the hope of sovereignty and the unusual advantages gratuitously offered them by men of patrician rank
(Catiline, Lentulus, Cethegus), and should prefer your safety to their
own interests, do you think that this did not happen by divine intervention, especially when they might have prevailed over us not by
fighting, but by keeping silent?'

36. **potuerint:** causal subjunctive. *194, c.*

10. 1. **ad omnia pulvīnāria:** i.e. *omnibus dīs quōrum pulvīnāria
Rōmae erant,* referring to the *lectisternium;* see note on page 93, line 32.

2. **celebrātōte:** the tense implies formality and impressiveness.
181, a (2).

7. **togātō:** *i.e.* without appealing to military authority.

10. **sed eās,** *et seq.:* for the events referred to in this paragraph (all
of which had happened within the quarter of a century preceding 63 B.C.),
consult the vocabulary under each name, and the Roman histories.

12. **cūstōdem huius urbis:** so characterized from his victories over
the Teutons and Cimbri.

THIRD CATILINARIAN ORATION

huius urbis, multōsque fortēs virōs partim ēiēcit ex cīvitāte,
partim interēmit. Cn. Octāvius cōnsul armīs expulit ex
urbe collēgam; omnis hīc locus acervīs corporum et 15
cīvium sanguine redundāvit.

Superāvit posteā Cinna cum Mariō; tum vērō, clārissimīs virīs interfectīs lūmina cīvitātis exstīncta sunt. Ultus
est huius victōriae crūdēlitātem posteā Sulla; nē dīcī
quidem opus est, quantā dēminūtiōne cīvium et quantā 20
calamitāte reī pūblicae.

Dissēnsit M. Lepidus ā clārissimō et fortissimō virō,

---

15. **collēgam:** Cornelius Cinna. **hīc locus:** the Forum.

16. **redundāvit:** construed by zeugma (*238, q*) with *acervīs;* translate with *acervīs,* ' was choked '; with *sanguine,* ' overflowed.'

ROMAN REPUBLICAN COIN
Obverse: the goddess Roma. Reverse: Sulla in a quadriga.

17. **Superāvit:** notice the emphatic position of this verb, and also
Ultus est and *Dissēnsit* below; preserve this emphasis in your translation,
viz. ' The upper hand was gained by,' ' Satisfaction was exacted for,' ' A
quarrel arose between.' **Cinna** (sin'a).

18. **lūmina cīvitātis:** members of the aristocratic party, as the consuls
Gnaeus Octavius and Lucius Merula, Quintus Catulus, the orator Marcus
Antonius, the Pontifex Quintus Scaevola, and others. **Ultus est . . .
Sulla:** in 82 B.C.

20. **quantā dēminūtiōne cīvium:** according to Mommsen (*History of
Rome,* Volume III, page 423), the proscription lists of Sulla contained
the names of at least 4,700 citizens, including 40 senators and 1,600 knights.

22. **M. Lepidus** (mär'kŭs lep'ĭ-dŭs).

Q. Catulō; attulit nōn tam ipsīus interitus reī pūblicae
lūctum quam cēterōrum.

25 Atque illae tamen omnēs dissēnsiōnēs erant eius modī,
quae nōn ad dēlendam, sed ad commūtandam rem pūblicam
pertinērent. Nōn illī nūllam esse rem pūblicam, sed in
eā, quae esset, sē esse prīncipēs, neque hanc urbem cōn-
flagrāre, sed sē in hāc urbe flōrēre voluērunt. Atque illae
30 tamen omnēs dissēnsiōnēs, quārum nūlla exitium reī
pūblicae quaesīvit, eius modī fuērunt, ut nōn recon-
ciliātiōne concordiae, sed interneciōne cīvium dīiūdicātae
sint.

In hōc autem ūnō post hominum memoriam maximō
35 crūdēlissimōque bellō, quāle bellum nūlla umquam barbaria cum suā gente gessit, quō in bellō lēx haec fuit ā Lentulō,
Catilīnā, Cethēgō, Cassiō cōnstitūta, ut omnēs, quī, salvā
urbe, salvī esse possent, in hostium numerō dūcerentur, ita
mē gessī, Quirītēs, ut salvī omnēs cōnservārēminī, et, cum
40 hostēs vestrī tantum cīvium superfutūrum putāssent, quantum īnfīnītae caedī restitisset, tantum autem urbis, quantum
flamma obīre nōn potuisset, et urbem et cīvēs integrōs
incolumēsque servāvī.

---

23. **Q. Catulō** (kwin′tŭs kat′ŭ-lŭs).

24. **cēterōrum :** *i.e.* who perished with him.

26. **quae :** translate as if *ut eae.*

34. **ūnō :** strengthens the superlative. **post :** see IDIOMS.

35. **quāle bellum, quō in bellō :** ' a war such as,' ' a war in which.'
barbaria : abstract for concrete, ' horde of savages.' *92, b.*

38. **salvī :** *i.e.* financially ' safe,' who had property enough to make
it worth while to murder them; different force in *salvā* and in *salvī*
of line 38. **in hostium numerō dūcerentur :** ' should be counted as
enemies.'

40. **tantum cīvium :** '(only) so many citizens.' *97, b;* B. 201, 2;
A. & G. 346, *a,* 3. **quantum . . . restitisset :** ' as had remained over
from unlimited slaughter '; *i.e.* ' as had escaped unchecked bloodshed.'

For my services I ask not rewards, but everlasting memory.

11. Quibus prō tantīs rēbus, Quirītēs, nūllum ego ā vōbīs praemium virtūtis, nūllum īnsigne honōris, nūllum monumentum laudis postulō praeterquam huius diēī memoriam sempiternam. In animīs ego vestrīs omnēs triumphōs meōs, omnia ōrnāmenta honōris, monumenta 5 glōriae, laudis īnsignia condī et collocārī volō.

Nihil mē mūtum potest dēlectāre, nihil tacitum, nihil dēnique eius modī, quod etiam minus dignī assequī possint. Memoriā vestrā, Quirītēs, nostrae rēs alentur, sermōnibus crēscent, litterārum monumentīs inveterāscent et corrō- 10 borābuntur; eandemque diem intellegō, quam spērō

A COIN OF THE REPUBLIC

Obverse: Pompey the Great. Reverse: Pompey's son disembarking from a ship.

11. 1. **Quibus prō tantīs rēbus:** ' Now in return for these great services (of mine).' *167.*

4. **In animīs ego vestrīs . . .:** note the position; ' It is in your hearts that I wish all my triumphs, . . . to be deeply enshrined ' (*condī et collocārī*). *211; 212, b.*

5. **ōrnāmenta:** ' distinctions.'

7. **Nihil, nihil, nihil:** what figure? *239, b.*

9. **Memoriā vestrā:** ablative of means; the emphasis should be preserved in your translation. **rēs:** ' achievements.' *211.*

11. **diem:** ' period '; *in eandemque diem prōpāgātam esse et salūtem urbis et memoriam cōnsulātūs meī* might have been expected. Cicero believed that the memory of his consulship would endure as long as Rome's sovereignty, which would last forever. See Bryce's *Holy Roman Empire.*

aeternam fore, prōpāgātam esse et ad salūtem urbis et ad
memoriam cōnsulātūs meī, ūnōque tempore in hāc rē
pūblicā duōs cīvēs exstitisse, quōrum alter fīnēs vestrī im-
15 perī nōn terrae, sed caelī regiōnibus termināret, alter eiusdem imperī domicilium sēdēsque servāret.

It will be your duty to furnish protection to me.

12. Sed quoniam eārum rērum, quās ego gessī, nōn
eadem est fortūna atque condiciō quae illōrum, quī externa
bella gessērunt, quod mihi cum eīs vīvendum est, quōs
vīcī ac subēgī, illī hostēs aut interfectōs aut oppressōs
5 relīquērunt, vestrum est, Quirītēs, sī cēterīs facta suā
rēctē prōsunt, mihi mea nē quandō obsint, prōvidēre.

Mentēs enim hominum audācissimōrum scelerātae ac
nefāriae nē vōbīs nocēre possent, ego prōvīdī; nē mihi
noceant, vestrum est prōvidēre. Quamquam, Quirītēs,
10 mihi quidem ipsī nihil ab istīs iam nocērī potest. Magnum
enim est in bonīs praesidium, quod mihi in perpetuum com-
parātum est, magna in rē pūblicā dignitās, quae mē semper
tacita dēfendet, magna vīs cōnscientiae, quam quī neg-
legunt, cum mē violāre volent, sē ipsī indicābunt.

---

14. **alter . . . termināret:** Pompey; rhetorical exaggeration, yet
not without some basis; for Pompey had fought with Sertorius in the
extreme west, and with Mithridates in the extreme east.

12. 2. **condiciō:** 'lot.' **quae illōrum:** 'as of those.'

5. **vestrum est:** 'it is your (duty).' *94, d;* A. & G. 343, C, N. 2;
G. 366, R. 3.

6. **rēctē:** *meritō,* '(and) deservedly.'

7. **Mentēs:** 'Designs.'

9. **Quamquam:** corrective, not concessive.

10. **nihil:** see IDIOMS. *106;* B. 187, 11, *b;* A. & G. 372; G. 346, R. 1.
Magnum: very emphatic; so also *magna* below.

13. **tacita:** 'though silent,' *i.e.* by silent influence. **cōnscientiae:**
'of inner knowledge' that Cicero had really saved the state. **quam
. . . indicābunt:** i.e. *sī quī, eā (cōnscientiā) neglēctā, mē violāre volent,
sē ipsī indicābunt* ('they will betray themselves' by their very appearance).

Est enim in nōbīs is animus, Quirītēs, ut nōn modo 15 nūllīus audāciae cēdāmus, sed etiam omnēs improbōs ultrō semper lacessāmus.

JUPITER
A statue in the Capitoline Museum.

Quod sī omnis impetus domesticōrum hostium, dēpulsus ā vōbīs, sē in mē 20 ūnum converterit, vōbīs erit videndum, Quirītēs, quā condiciōne posthāc eōs esse velītis, quī sē prō salūte vestrā obtulerint invidiae 25 perīculīsque omnibus; mihi quidem ipsī quid est, quod iam ad vītae frūctum possit acquīrī, cum praesertim neque in honōre vestrō neque 30 in glōriā virtūtis quicquam videam altius, quō mihi libeat ascendere?

Illud profectō perficiam, Quirītēs, ut ea, quae gessī 35 in cōnsulātū, prīvātus tuear atque ōrnem, ut, sī qua est invidia in cōnservandā rē pūblicā suscepta, laedat invidōs, mihi valeat ad glōriam.

---

16. nūllīus: the genitive of *nēmō*. cēdāmus: *203 (2)*.

18. Quod sī, *et seq.*: see page 21, line 24, and note. domesticōrum hostium: *239, p.*

25. obtulerint: *220*.

28. frūctum: 'gains.'

30. in honōre vestrō: *i.e.* 'in the honors you have it in your power to bestow.'

31. virtūtis: 'won by valor.' Kind of genitive? *95.* quicquam altius: 'any greater height.'

34. Illud: anticipates the following *ut*-clause. profectō: 'assuredly.'

37. ōrnem: 'make even more splendid.' *203 (4)*. ut: final. *196, a.*

Dēnique ita mē in rē pūblicā trāctābō, ut meminerím
40 semper, quae gesserim, cūremque, ut ea virtūte, nōn cāsū
gesta esse videantur.

Worship Jupiter, and tonight guard your homes.

Vōs, Quirītēs, quoniam iam est nox, venerātī Iovem
illum, cūstōdem huius urbis ac vestrum, in vestra tēcta
discēdite et ea, quamquam iam est perīculum dēpulsum
45 tamen aequē ac priōre nocte cūstōdiīs vigiliīsque dēfendite.
Id nē vōbīs diūtius faciendum sit, atque ut in perpetuā
pāce esse possītis, prōvidēbō.

---

39. **mē in rē pūblicā trāctābō :** *versābor,* ' I shall conduct myself in
political life.' *212, i.*

42. **quoniam :** used rather than *cum* because the clause expresses an
evident reason. **est nox :** the meeting of the senate preceding this
address lasted till late in the day.

43. **illum :** see page 100, line 21, and note.

45. **aequē ac :** ' just the same as.' *233, c.* **priōre nocte :** after the
second oration.

47. **prōvidēbō :** a hint at the fate of the conspirators in custody.

M. TULLĪ CICERŌNIS
IN L. CATILĪNAM ŌRĀTIŌ QUĀRTA
HABITA IN SENĀTŪ

Partēs Sēlēctae

3. Sed ego īnstituī referre ad vōs, patrēs cōnscrīptī, tamquam integrum, et dē factō quid iūdicētis, et dē poenā quid
cēnseātis. Illa praedīcam, quae sunt cōnsulis.

Ego magnum in rē pūblicā versārī furōrem et nova quaedam miscērī et concitārī mala iam prīdem vidēbam; sed ₅
hanc tantam, tam exitiōsam habērī coniūrātiōnem ā cīvibus
numquam putāvī. Nunc quicquid est, quōcumque vestrae
mentēs inclīnant atque sententiae, statuendum vōbīs ante
noctem est.

Quantum facinus ad vōs dēlātum sit, vidētis. Huic sī ₁₀
paucōs putātis affīnēs esse, vehementer errātis. Lātius

To the Student: The introductory material is in the Companion, pages
518, 525. This oration was delivered in the Temple of Concord.

Though menaced with grave dangers, senators, I am glad to have served
the state. Have regard for the public interest without reference to my
personal safety, for the case with which you have to deal is without a parallel.
You have already accepted the proofs as conclusive.

3. 1. **īnstituī:** here *coepī*. **referre:** object? **tamquam integrum:**
'as still an open question,' notwithstanding the fact that you have
virtually passed a sentence of condemnation already.

3. **cōnsulis:** as chief executive of the state and presiding officer of
the senate; see note to page 27, line 13.

5. **miscērī:** idiomatically, ' were brewing.'

6. **habērī:** stronger than *factam esse; habēre* is used of holding
meetings of political bodies, as the senate.

7. **putāvī:** forcible; so we sometimes say, ' I never thought it of
him,' when we mean, ' I never should have thought it of him.'

8. **statuendum . . . est:** ' you must reach a decision before nightfall';
because a decree of the senate passed after sunset was not valid, and because the emergency was such as to admit of no postponement of action.

11. **vehementer:** see Idioms. **Lātius:** see Idioms.

opīniōne dissēminātum est hōc malum; mānāvit nōn
sōlum per Italiam, vērum etiam trānscendit Alpēs et obscūrē serpēns multās iam prōvinciās occupāvit. Id opprimī
15 sustentandō aut prōlātandō nūllō pactō potest; quācum-
que ratiōne placet, celeriter vōbīs vindicandum est.

It will be easier for me if you adopt Caesar's opinion.

5. Nunc, patrēs cōnscrīptī, ego meā videō quid intersit.
Sī eritis secūtī sententiam C. Caesaris, quoniam hanc is

A VIEW OF THE ALPS

14. **multās prōvinciās occupāvit:** rhetorical exaggeration; yet
Catiline had reckoned on receiving armies from Spain and Mauretania
(Sallust, *Catilīna*, **21,** 3).

There are two opinions: Silanus favors the death penalty; Caesar,
imprisonment for life in the municipal towns.

See Selections from Sallust, page 137, *et seq.;* read the speeches of
Caesar and Silanus.

5. 1. **Nunc:** 'Under these conditions.' **meā . . . quid intersit:** 'what my interest is.' Construction of *meā?* Consult IDIOMS,
103, e; B. 210; 211, 1, *a, 3, c;* A. & G. 355, *a;* G. 381.

in rē pūblicā viam, quae populāris habētur, secūtus est,
fortasse minus erunt, hōc auctōre et cognitōre huiusce
sententiae, mihi populārēs impetūs pertimēscendī; sīn 5
illam alteram, nesciō an amplius mihi negōtī contrahātur.
Sed tamen meōrum perīculōrum ratiōnēs ūtilitās reī pūblicae vincat.

Habēmus enim ā Caesare, sīcut ipsīus dignitās et maiōrum eius amplitūdō postulābat, sententiam tamquam ob- 10
sidem perpetuae in rem pūblicam voluntātis.   Intellēctum
est, quid interesset inter levitātem cōntiōnātōrum et animum vērē populārem, salūtī populī cōnsulentem.

Videō dē istīs, quī sē populārēs habērī volunt, abesse nōn
nēminem, nē dē capite vidēlicet cīvium Rōmānōrum sen- 15

---

3. **in rē pūblicā:** ' political,' a common meaning; see page 108,
note 39. *212, i.* **populāris:** not ' popular,' but ' democratic.'

5. **populārēs impetūs:** ' attacks of the people.'   Caesar was allied
with the popular or democratic party, which was constantly making
efforts to break the power of the senate and the aristocracy.

A COIN OF CAESAR

This represents Aeneas
fleeing from Troy, carry-
ing his aged father. Caesar
claimed descent from
Aeneas.

6. **illam alteram:** of Silanus.   **nesciō
an:** ' I am inclined to think that a larger
measure of difficulty may be in store for me.'
180, e (1); B. 300, 5; A. & G. 447, 1; G. 457, 2.

7. **Sed tamen:** ' But (even if this be
the case), nevertheless.'

9. **enim:** ' then'; the orator enters
upon a closer examination of Caesar's proposition.   **maiōrum:** referring not only to the
prominence of the Caesar family for a century previous to this time, but also to the
alleged descent of the *Iūliī* from *Iūlus*,
Aeneas's son.

10. **obsidem:** ' pledge.'

11. **Intellēctum est, quid interesset:**
' We understood (when Caesar spoke) what
a difference there is.'

14. **nōn nēminem:** ' more than one.'   *239, m.*

15. **dē capite:** ' regarding the life '; they absented themselves with
the pretext that only the people assembled in the comitia had the right to

tentiam ferat; at is et nūdius tertius in cūstōdiam cīvēs
Rōmānōs dedit et supplicātiōnem mihi dēcrēvit et indicēs
hesternō diē maximīs praemiīs affēcit. Iam hōc nēminī

THE ROSTRA AND THE TEMPLE OF CONCORD

pass a sentence of death upon a Roman citizen, and that the senate in
dealing with the conspirators was going beyond its jurisdiction.

16. **is:** refers to *nōn nēmō;* ' but those men.' **nūdius tertius:** *i.e.*
at the meeting of the senate on December 3 ; there these pretended
friends of the people joined with the rest of the senate in acts which virtually condemned the conspirators (see Companion, page 518), thus tacitly
admitting the jurisdiction of the senate in the case. To judge from this
the decrees of the senate on December 3 must have been carried unanimously. See page 113, note 21.

17. **dedit, dēcrēvit, affēcit:** *i.e.* he favored these acts.

18. **maximīs praemiīs affēcit:** ' he favored the bestowing of magnificent gifts'; see IDIOMS. **hōc . . . :** '*hōc, quid (ille), quī . . . dēcrēvit,
dē tōtā rē et causā* ('all the evidence and the law') *iūdicārit, nēminī
dubium est.*

dubium est, quī reō cūstōdiam, quaesitōrī grātulātiōnem, indicī praemium dēcrēvit, quid dē tōtā rē et causā iūdicārit. 20

But the conspirators should be treated as enemies, not as citizens.

At vērō C. Caesar intellegit lēgem Semprōniam esse dē cīvibus Rōmānīs cōnstitūtam; quī autem reī pūblicae sit hostis, eum cīvem esse nūllō modō posse; dēnique ipsum lātōrem Semprōniae lēgis iniussū populī poenās reī pūblicae dēpendisse. Īdem ipsum Lentulum, largītōrem 25 et prōdigum, nōn putat, cum dē perniciē populī Rōmānī, exitiō huius urbis tam acerbē, tam crūdēliter cōgitārit, etiam appellārī posse populārem.

Itaque homō mītissimus atque lēnissimus nōn dubitat P. Lentulum aeternīs tenebrīs vinculīsque mandāre et 30

---

19. **quaesitōrī:** refers to Cicero as having conducted the investigation; the term is technically applied to the presiding officer of a *quaestiō*, or court for criminal cases. **grātulātiōnem:** here = *supplicātiōnem*.

21. **At:** introduces the orator's reply to Caesar's argument. **intellegit:** as shown by Caesar's not refusing to vote on the matters before the senate, December 3; by voting then, as Cicero clearly indicates, he admitted the jurisdiction of the senate in dealing with the conspirators as ' enemies,' not as ' citizens.' **lēgem Semprōniam:** proposed by Gaius Sempronius Gracchus (grak′ŭs) 123 B.C., enacting *nē dē capite cīvium Rōmānōrum iniussū populī iūdicārētur;* see note on page 56, line 18. Cicero cites this enactment particularly because he wishes to point his argument with an allusion to the death of Gracchus without a trial by the people or an appeal, as showing that immediately after the passage of the law it was so construed that those considered enemies of their country were not protected by it.

23. **hostis, eum cīvem nūllō modō:** *i.e.* granted that a Roman citizen may be tried only before a regular court, and may not be put to death without an opportunity to appeal his case to the Roman people gathered in assembly (see note on page 56, line 18); yet if he makes an attempt against his country, by that very act he becomes a ' public enemy,' is no longer entitled to the protection afforded by laws guarding the rights of citizens, and as an enemy may properly be tried and sentenced by the senate. See Companion, page 519.

28. **populārem:** ' a friend of the people.' Note the alliteration. *239, a.*

sancit in posterum, nē quis huius suppliciō levandō sē
iactāre et in perniciem populī Rōmānī posthāc populāris
esse possit. Adiungit etiam pūblicātiōnem bonōrum, ut
omnēs animī cruciātus et corporis etiam egestās ac
35 mendīcitās cōnsequātur.

If we are most severe, we shall seem merciful; if lenient, cruel to our country.

6. Sīc nōs in hīs hominibus, quī nōs, quī coniugēs, quī
līberōs nostrōs trucīdāre voluērunt, quī singulās ūnīus
cuiusque nostrum domōs et hōc ūniversum reī pūblicae
domicilium dēlēre cōnātī sunt, quī id ēgērunt, ut gentem
5 Allobrogum in vēstīgiīs huius urbis atque in cinere
dēflagrātī imperī collocārent, sī vehementissimī fuerimus,
misericordēs habēbimur; sīn remissiōrēs esse voluerimus,
summae nōbīs crūdēlitātis in patriae cīviumque perniciē
fāma subeunda est.
10 Nisi vērō cuipiam L. Caesar, vir fortissimus et amantissimus reī pūblicae, crūdēlior nūdius tertius vīsus est, cum
sorōris suae, fēminae lēctissimae, virum praesentem et

33. **pūblicātiōnem bonōrum:** confiscation of property usually
accompanied severe sentences; still Caesar's attitude in this matter is
difficult to understand. He probably believed that the senate had
no right to condemn the conspirators; yet his motion itself recognized
the senate's jurisdiction. It may be that he proposed the life sentence
simply to save the lives of the prisoners temporarily, trusting to the
future to restore either their freedom or their property, or both, if after
sufficient time the sentence seemed too severe.
6. 1. **in:** 'in the case of.'
5. **vēstīgiīs:** 'remains.'
9. **fāma:** in the sense of *īnfāmia*.
10. **Nisi vērō:** introduces an exception ironically. *210, b;* B. 306,
5; A. & G. 525, *b;* G. 591 (*b*), R. 4. **L. Caesar:** see vocabulary under
Caesar (2). He made these remarks probably at the meeting of the
senate on December 3, when called upon to give his vote.
12. **virum:** 'husband'; the conspirator Lentulus, who had married
Lucius Caesar's sister Julia.

audientem vītā prīvandum esse dīxit, cum avum suum
iussū cōnsulis interfectum filiumque eius impūberem, lēgātum ā patre missum, in carcere necātum esse dīxit. 15
Quōrum quod simile factum, quod initum dēlendae reī
pūblicae cōnsilium?

HOUSE OF THE VESTALS IN THE FORUM

13. **avum:** M. Fulvius Flaccus (mär′kụs ful′vi̯-ụs flak′ụs), put to
death by the consul Opimius; see page 30, line 5. Lucius Caesar
introduced this precedent from his family history in order to justify the
severity of his judgment on Lentulus.

14. **lēgātum:** the boy, eighteen years of age, had been sent by his
father to treat with Opimius, who would listen to no offer of reconciliation. As he was sent a second time, Opimius placed him in custody,
and then suddenly directing a vigorous attack slew among others both
the father and the elder brother. Afterwards the younger son was
killed in prison.

16. **Quōrum:** *Atque hōrum.* *167.* **simile:** *i.e.* to what the Catilinarian conspirators proposed; sc. *fuit.*

Largītiōnis voluntās tum in rē pūblicā versāta est et
partium quaedam contentiō. Atque eō tempore huius
20 avus Lentulī, vir clārissimus, armātus Gracchum est per-
secūtus. Ille etiam grave tum vulnus accēpit, nē quid dē
summā rē pūblicā dēminuerētur; hīc ad ēvertenda reī
pūblicae fundāmenta Gallōs arcessit, servitia concitat, Catilīnam vocat, attribuit nōs trucīdandōs Cethēgō et cēterōs
25 cīvēs interficiendōs Gabīniō, urbem īnflammandam Cassiō,
tōtam Italiam vāstandam dīripiendamque Catilīnae.

Vereāminī, cēnseō, nē in hōc scelere tam immānī ac nefandō nimis aliquid sevēre statuisse videāminī; multō
magis est verendum, nē remissiōne poenae crūdēlēs in
30 patriam, quam nē sevēritāte animadversiōnis nimis vehe-
mentēs in acerbissimōs hostēs fuisse videāmur.

*You have unanimous support; upon your decision rests the future of
the state and all that is dear to us.*

9. Quae cum ita sint, patrēs cōnscrīptī, vōbīs populī
Rōmānī praesidia nōn dēsunt; vōs nē populō Rōmānō
deesse videāminī, prōvidēte. Habētis cōnsulem ex plūrimīs
perīculīs et īnsidiīs atque ex mediā morte nōn ad vītam

---

18. **versāta est:** ' prevailed,' ' was prevalent.'

20. **avus:** see vocabulary under *Lentulus* (1); see page 88, line 22.

21. **quid . . . dēminuerētur:** ' that the welfare of the state might
not suffer in any degree.'

22. **hīc:** i.e. *hīc Lentulus;* but *hīc* does not imply that Lentulus was
now present. Probably the conspirators were kept closely guarded during this meeting of the senate, in the various houses to which they had
been assigned.

23. **servitia:** abstract for concrete. *92, b.* See page 55, line 10, note.

27. **Vereāminī, cēnseō:** ' Of course you may well be afraid ';
ironical; potential subjunctive. *239, l; 180, e.*

The execution of your sentence is assured by the unanimity of feeling
existing between classes. In this crisis the knights, treasury officials,
and secretaries are united; free-born citizens, freedmen, and even
slaves desire the safety of the state.

9. 4. ex mediā morte : see IDIOMS.

suam, sed ad salūtem vestram reservātum. Omnēs ōr- 5
dinēs ad cōnservandam rem pūblicam mente, voluntāte,
studiō, virtūte, vōce cōnsentiunt.

Obsessa facibus et tēlīs impiae coniūrātiōnis vōbīs
supplex manūs tendit patria commūnis, vōbīs sē, vōbīs
vītam omnium cīvium, vōbīs arcem et Capitōlium, vōbīs ārās 10

Penātium, vōbīs illum
ignem Vestae sempi-
ternum, vōbīs omnium
deōrum templa atque
dēlūbra, vōbīs mūrōs 15
atque urbis tēcta com-
mendat.

Praetereā dē vestrā
vītā, dē coniugum ves-
trārum atque līberōrum 20
animā, dē fortūnīs om-
nium, dē sēdibus, dē
focīs vestrīs hodiernō diē
vōbīs iūdicandum est.

A VESTAL

Habētis ducem memorem vestrī, oblītum suī, quae nōn 25
semper facultās datur ; habētis omnēs ōrdinēs, omnēs
hominēs, ūniversum populum Rōmānum, id quod in

10. **arcem :** on the northern summit of the Capitoline hill, while the
Capitōlium occupied the southern ; these elevations were separated at
the middle of the hill by a depression. **ārās Penātium :** i.e. *ārās
Penātium pūblicōrum*, in the Temple of Vesta.

11. **illum :** with a gesture toward the small round Temple of Vesta,
over the center of whose conical roof perhaps a thread of smoke was
seen curling upwards ; see Plan facing page 62. Notice the rhetorical
effect of the anaphora and asyndeta. *239, b; 238, d.*

21. **omnium :** sc. *vestrum. 155.*

23. **hodiernō diē :** see page 109, line 8, and note.

25. **quae . . . facultās :** ' an advantage which.'

26. **habētis :** ' you have (on your side).'

27. **in cīvīlī causā :** ' in a political issue.'

cīvīlī causā hodiernō diē prīmum vidēmus, ūnum atque idem sentientem.

30   Cōgitāte, quantīs labōribus fundātum imperium, quantā virtūte stabilītam lībertātem, quantā deōrum benignitāte auctās exaggerātāsque fortūnās ūna nox paene dēlērit. Id nē umquam posthāc nōn modo nōn cōnficī, sed nē cōgitārī quidem possit ā cīvibus, hodiernō diē prōvidendum est.

THE TULLIANUM

30. **quantīs . . . dēlērit:** condensed for *quantīs labōribus fundātum sit imperium* ('the sovereignty' of our state), *quantā virtūte stabilīta sit lībertās, . . . quae ūna nox paene dēlērit.* Why subjunctive?

32. **ūna nox:** the night of the arrest of the Allobroges, as indicated by a passage in the oration *Prō Flaccō* (**40,** 102): *Ō nox illa, quae paene aeternās huic urbī tenebrās attulistī, cum Gallī ad bellum, Catilīna ad urbem, coniūrātī ad ferrum et flammam vocābantur;* some, however, think that the night of the meeting at Laeca's, or that of the 19th of December, is referred to.

33. **nōn modo nōn:** the second *nōn* is omitted in some of the manuscripts, and may possibly have been inserted by some copyist. See page 53, line 6, and note.

Atque haec, nōn ut vōs, quī mihi studiō paene prae- 35
curritis, excitārem, locūtus sum, sed ut mea vōx, quae
dēbet esse in rē pūblicā prīnceps, officiō fūncta cōnsulārī
vidērētur.

Vote carefully and courageously; your decision shall be carried out.

11. Quāpropter dē summā salūte vestrā populīque Rōmānī, dē vestrīs coniugibus ac līberīs, dē ārīs ac focīs, dē
fānīs atque templīs, dē tōtīus urbis tēctīs ac sēdibus, dē imperiō ac lībertāte, dē salūte Italiae, dē ūniversā rē pūblicā
dēcernite dīligenter, ut īnstituistis, ac fortiter. Habētis eum 5
cōnsulem, quī et pārēre vestrīs dēcrētīs nōn dubitet et ea,

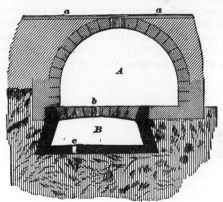

CARCER — MAMERTINE PRISON

A. Upper Dungeon.
B. Lower Dungeon — *Tullianum.*
a a. Lower floor of present church above.

b. Hole through which the condemned were let down into the *Tullianum.*
c. Spring of clear water.
d d. Solid rock.

37. **officiō cōnsulārī:** Cicero felt his responsibility keenly.

11. 6. **quī . . . possit:** Cicero was as good as his word. After
the speech of Marcus Cato (Sallust, *Catilīna,* 52; see page 520), the
senate voted for the execution of the conspirators. The consul thought
it best to carry out the decree before nightfall, as the darkness might
encourage an attempt at rescue (see Sallust, *Catilīna,* 55, on page 148).
Having distributed an armed force about the central parts of the city,

quae statueritis, quoad vīvet, dēfendere et per sē ipsum praestāre possit.

---

he himself conducted Lentulus to the Mamertine Prison; the other conspirators were brought thither by the praetors. ' In the prison,' says Sallust, page 148, ' there is a place called the *Tulliānum* (see illustration on page 149), about twelve feet below the surface of the ground. It is built with strong walls, and above it there is a room constructed with stone vaulting; but it is a disgusting and horrible place, on account of the filth, the darkness, and the stench. After Lentulus had been let down into this dungeon, the executioners broke his neck with a noose; so that patrician, of the most noble line of the Cornelii, a man who had exercised the consular authority at Rome, met an end suited to his character and his deeds. Cethegus, Statilius, Gabinius, and Ceparius suffered the same penalty.' When they were all dead, it is said that Cicero, who had waited at the door of the prison, proclaimed the outcome to the silent and expectant crowd that filled the Forum, with the single word *Vīxērunt*, ' They are no more.' (Plutarch, *Cicero*, 22, " Ἔζησαν," εἶπεν, ' They did live,' he said.) Plutarch tells us that this expression was used for those that are dead, to avoid inauspicious language.

C. SALLUSTĪ CRĪSPĪ
BELLUM CATILĪNAE

Partēs Sēlēctae

Catiline was a man of high birth, great power, and infamous life.

5. L. Catilīna, nōbilī genere nātus, fuit magnā vī et animī et corporis, sed ingeniō malō prāvōque. Huic ab adulēscentiā bella intestīna, caedēs, rapīnae, discordia cīvīlis grāta fuēre, ibique iuventūtem suam exercuit.

Corpus patiēns inediae, algōris, vigiliae suprā quam cui- 5 quam crēdibile est. Animus audāx, subdolus, varius; cuius

---

To the Student. Read the discussion of Sallust in the Companion on page 527.

5. 1. **nōbilī genere:** ablative of source. *128;* B. 215; A. & G. 403, 2, *a;* G. 395, N. 1. Catiline's full name was Lucius Sergius Catilina; the *gēns Sergia* was an old patrician gens, whose descent from Sergestus Virgil recognized in his *Aeneid* (**5,** 121). **magnā vī et animī et corporis:** '(a man) of great mental and physical strength.'

SALLUST

2. **ingeniō:** always refers to an inborn quality, here 'natural bent.'

4. **ibi:** *in iīs rēbus,* i.e. the nouns enumerated above.

5. **Corpus patiēns:** see Cicero, *In Catilīnam,* **1,** 10. *patiēns* does not mean 'patient,' see vocabulary; sc. *fuit.* Sallust often omits forms of *esse* and conjunctions. **suprā quam:** *ultrā quam,* 'more than.'

6. **cuius reī libet, simulātor ac dissimulātor:** 'he could affect the truth or hide it, just as he chose'; a good illustration of the terse, crisp style of our author. *cuius reī libet = reī cuiuslibet,* the separation of *cuiuslibet* being called tmesis, from the Greek word meaning 'a cutting.' *238, p.* Verbal substantives in *-tor* denote a permanent or immanent quality, and in combination with *esse* become a forceful expression. Literally, 'a pretender and dissembler of anything he liked.' What is the difference between *simulāre* and *dissimulāre?* See vocabulary.

reī libet, simulātor ac dissimulātor; aliēnī appetēns, suī
profūsus, ārdēns in cupiditātibus; satis ēloquentiae, sapientiae parum. Vāstus animus immoderāta, incrēdibilia,
10 nimis alta semper cupiēbat.

Hunc post dominātiōnem L. Sullae libīdō maxima invāserat reī pūblicae capiendae, neque, id quibus modīs assequerētur, dum sibi rēgnum parāret, quicquam pēnsī
habēbat. Agitābātur magis magisque in diēs animus ferōx
15 inopiā reī familiāris et cōnscientiā scelerum, quae utraque
eīs artibus auxerat, quās suprā memorāvī. Incitābant,
praetereā, corruptī cīvitātis mōrēs, quōs pessima ac dīversa
inter sē mala, lūxuria atque avāritia, vexābant.

7. aliēnī: neuter, ' of his neighbor's property.' suī: genitive of
suum.

8. satis ēloquentiae: sc. *eī erat.* satis . . . parum: substantives
limited by the partitive genitives. *97, b.* Note the chiasmus. *239, e.*

9. Vāstus animus: ' His insatiable spirit.'

11. Hunc: object of *invāserat.* post dominātiōnem L. Sullae: Sulla's
dictatorship lasted till 79 B.C. libīdō maxima: ' a consuming passion.'

12. reī pūblicae capiendae: with *libīdo,* ' to seize the government.'
id . . . assequerētur: ' by what means he attained this,' indirect
question depending upon *quicquam pēnsī habēbat.*

13. dum: ' provided.' *190, d.* sibi: see page 128, line 5, note.
parāret: *190, d;* B. 310, II; A. & G. 528; G. 573. quicquam pēnsī
habēbat: a favorite phrase of Sallust (chapters 12, 23, 52) ; ' and (*neque*
above) it was immaterial to him '; literally, ' he held it to be nothing
of weight.' *pēnsī* is partitive genitive with *quicquam,* from *pēnsum,* the
substantivized perfect passive participle of *pendere,* ' to weigh.' *97, a*
and *b.*

14. Agitābātur: note its position. in diēs: ' day by day.' animus
ferōx: ' his impetuous spirit.'

15. cōnscientiā: not ' conscience,' but ' consciousness.' quae
utraque: accusative plural neuter; modifiers of two feminine abstract
nouns (*inopiā, cōnscientiā*) are frequently neuter plural. *150, b;* B. 235,
B, 2, a; A. & G. 187, *c;* G. 286, 3.

16. artibus: ' qualities.' Incitābant: see *agitābātur* above; translate by the passive voice to preserve the emphasis.

17. corruptī cīvitātis mōrēs: ' the corruption of public morals,' in
German ' Sittenverderbnis '; a participle in agreement with a noun is

At a secret meeting of the new conspirators Catiline makes lavish promises.

21. Postquam accēpēre ea hominēs, quibus mala abundē omnia erant, sed neque rēs neque spēs bona ūlla, tametsī illīs quiēta movēre magna mercēs vidēbātur, tamen postulāvēre plērīque, ut prōpōneret, quae condiciō bellī foret, quae praemia armīs peterent, quid ubīque opis aut speī 5 habērent.

Tum Catilīna pollicērī tabulās novās, prōscrīptiōnem

---

often equivalent to an abstract noun with a genitive, the participle carrying the main thought. See note to **ab urbe conditā,** page 405. *212, c; 228, b.* **dīversa inter sē mala:** 'evils mutually opposed.'

Then, taking as his theme the *corruptī cīvitātis mōrēs,* Sallust sketches the early history of Roman morals, and pictures the rise of the republic as a golden age, when men's ideals were loyalty, bravery, justice, morality, concord, and liberality. Later, success brought with it lust for power, especially after the conquest of Carthage. Ambition and greed spread like a pestilence. Sulla's régime (82–79 B.C.) also added to the general demoralization, so that riches and power became a means of distinction. In such an atmosphere vice and various forms of dissipation made their appearance, and Catiline found it easy to gather round him bands of broken men and to corrupt the young. Relying on such men and aided by others of rank and influence he planned to overthrow the government. His first conspiracy (66 B.C.) failed owing to excessive haste; but this experience made Catiline all the more furious and determined, with the result that he plotted anew.

21. 2. **rēs:** 'money,' 'possessions.' Note the assonance with *spēs;* Sallust is fond of such combinations. *212, d.*

3. **quiēta movēre:** subject of *vidēbātur;* 'disturbing the public peace.' *222, a; 211.*

4. **condiciō:** 'terms.' **foret:** = *esset.*

5. **ubīque:** 'in any place whatsoever'; to be distinguished from *ubi,* 'where,' with the enclitic *-que,* 'and,' though here the word could be so interpreted. Compare, however, chapter 27, 4, *quem ubīque.* **opis, speī:** partitive genitives.

7. **pollicērī:** historical infinitive; see Selection from Livy, page 415, line 5. *182;* B. 335; A. & G. 463; G. 647. **tabulās novās:** 'cancellation of debts.' The *tabulae* were waxed tablets on which the Romans kept their accounts; 'new tablets,' therefore, means a readjustment of debts, hence, a settlement of debts. See Cicero's promise to the con-

locuplētium, magistrātūs, sacerdōtia, rapīnās, alia omnia,
quae bellum atque libīdō victōrum fert; praetereā, esse in
10 Hispāniā citeriōre Pīsōnem, in Maurētāniā cum exercitū
P. Sittium Nūcerīnum, cōnsiliī suī participēs; petere
cōnsulātum C. Antōnium, quem sibi collēgam fore spērāret,
hominem et familiārem, et omnibus necessitūdinibus circumventum; cum eō sē cōnsulem initium agendī factūrum.
15 Ad hōc maledictīs increpābat omnēs bonōs, suōrum ūnum
quemque nōmināns laudāre; admonēbat alium egestātis,
alium cupiditātis suae, complūrēs perīculī aut ignōminiae,

---

siprators, *In Catilinam*, **1,** 8, 23–26. **prōscrīptiōnem:** Sulla was re-
sponsible for the current meaning of this word, and we may guess that
Catiline had 'proscription lists' in mind. For the original meaning see
Pliny, page 468, line 13.

9. **esse . . . Pīsōnem:** the accusative with the infinitive depends
upon the idea of saying implied in *pollicērī* above. *213, b.*

10. **Pīsōnem** (pī'sō): a profligate young noble, who had dissipated
his fortune and joined Catiline; he was murdered while in Spain as
propraetor.

11. **Sittium Nūcerīnum** (sįt'į-ųs of nū-sē'rį-ą): an opportunist,
whose exact connection with Catiline is not entirely clear. He fought on
Caesar's side during the Civil War in Africa, 46 B.C., and was eventually
slain by Arabio, the son of Masinissa. **petere cōnsulātum:** an idiom used
in the language of politics, viz. 'to be a candidate for the consulship.'

12. **C. Antōnium:** a son of the celebrated orator, M. Antonius, and
Cicero's colleague in the consulship. He was an uncle of Marcus
Antonius, the triumvir, and was in sympathy with the conspiracy at
this time, though later Cicero induced him to desert it. He has been
called "the mean son of a noble father." **quem:** why would it be
incorrect to translate this word by 'whom'?

13. **et . . . et:** 'both . . . and.' **familiārem:** 'his intimate friend.'
omnibus necessitūdinibus circumventum: 'beset by all manner of
distress,' in the form of debts.

15. **Ad hōc:** 'In addition to this,' 'Furthermore.' **bonōs:** 'loyal
subjects.' *211.*

16. **laudāre:** see line 7 above. *182.* **egestātis, cupiditātis, perīculī,
ignōminiae, victōriae:** *103, a;* B. 207; A. & G. 351; G. 376.

17. **suae:** *eius,* since it refers to *alium;* but see *158, a;* B. 244, 4;
A. & G. 301, *c;* G. 309, 2; 521, R. 2.

multōs victōriae Sullānae, quibus ea praedae fuerat. Postquam omnium animōs alacrēs videt, cohortātus, ut petītiōnem suam cūrae habērent, conventum dīmīsit. 20

One of the conspirators, Curius, confides in Fulvia.

23. Sed in eā coniūrātiōne fuit Q. Cūrius, nātus haud
obscūrō locō, flāgitiīs atque facinoribus coopertus, quem
cēnsōrēs senātū, probrī grātiā, mōverant. Huic hominī
nōn minor vānitās inerat quam audācia; neque reticēre,
quae audierat, neque suamet ipse scelera occultāre, prōrsus 5
neque dīcere neque facere quicquam pēnsī habēbat.

Erat eī cum Fulviā, muliere nōbilī, stuprī vetus cōnsuētūdō. Cui cum minus grātus esset, quia inopiā minus

---

18. **quibus ea praedae fuerat :** ' to whom this (victory) had been a
source of plunder.' **quibus, praedae :** *112, b;* B. 191, 2, *a*); A. & G.
382, 1; G. 356, R. 3. **Postquam ... videt :** Sallust prefers the historical
present to the more usual historical perfect with this conjunction.
188, a.

19. **alacrēs :** ' enthusiastic.' **petītiōnem :** see line 11 above.

20. **cūrae habērent :** Cicero would have used *cūrae esse;* see line
18 above.

23. 1. **nātus haud obscūrō locō :** ' a man of no mean birth '; how
literally? **haud obscūrō :** *clārō*, litotes. *239, m.*

2. **locō :** *familiae*, when used with *nātus.*

3. **cēnsōrēs ... mōverant :** idiomatic; ' the censors had removed
from the senate because of a shameful life.' Notice that *grātiā* here
does not denote purpose.

4. **vānitās :** not ' vanity.' See vocabulary. **reticēre ... occultāre :** see chapter 21, line 7.

5. **prōrsus ... habēbat :** ' in short, neither in speaking nor in
doing did he exhibit any concern.' Literally, ' he held neither speaking
nor doing (to be) anything of weight.'

6. **dīcere, facere :** objects of *habēbat;* the infinitive as a verbal
noun may represent the nominative and accusative; the other cases
are supplied by the gerund and the ablative of the supine. **quicquam :**
predicate accusative. *115, a.* **pēnsī :** see page 122, line 13, note.

7. **stuprī vetus cōnsuētūdō :** ' a liaison of long standing.'

8. **minus grātus :** ' less acceptable.'

largīrī poterat, repente glōriāns maria montēsque pollicērī
10 coepit, et minārī interdum ferrō, nī sibi obnoxia foret,
postrēmō ferōcius agitāre quam solitus erat. At Fulvia,
īnsolentiae Curiī causā cognitā, tāle perīculum reī pūblicae
haud occultum habuit, sed, sublātō auctōre dē Catilīnae
coniūrātiōne, quae quōque modō audierat, complūribus
15 narrāvit.

Catiline is not deterred by the election of Cicero and Antonius as consuls.

Ea rēs in prīmīs studia hominum accendit ad cōnsulātum
mandandum M. Tulliō Cicerōnī. Namque anteā plēraque
nōbilitās invidiā aestuābat, et quasi polluī cōnsulātum crēdēbant, sī eum, quamvīs ēgregius, homō novus adeptus

9. **maria montēsque :** proverbial expression like our "the world
and all," " mountains of gold," " oceans of money."

10. **foret :** = *esset*, the subjunctive being due to implied indirect
discourse. *214, b.* What would have been the direct form?

11. **ferōcius agitāre :** ' to behave more wildly,' ' to be more brutish.'
In Sallust *agitāre* is often equivalent to *agere*.

12. **īnsolentiae :** not ' insolence '; the derivation (*in-*, negative,
and *solēre*, ' to be accustomed ') suggests the correct translation, ' his
unwonted behavior.'

13. **sublātō auctōre :** ' without mentioning her authority.' The
English idiom sometimes demands negative translations for affirmative
expressions in Latin. *212, m.*

16. **Ea rēs in prīmīs :** ' It was this rumor especially which . . .';
rēs refers to the information regarding the conspiracy suggested in the
previous sentence and also to the dangerous situation which would
develop should Catiline and Antonius be elected to the consulship. *211.*

17. **plēraque :** Sallust uses this word in the singular with collective
expressions, but in Cicero only the plural occurs.

18. **aestuābat :** ' burned.' **quasi polluī cōnsulātum :** ' that the
consulship was being contaminated, so to speak.' *quasi* is here used
to apologize for *polluī;* a parenthetical purpose clause (*ut ita dīcam*) is
sometimes similarly used. **crēdēbant :** *cōnstrūctiō ad sēnsum*, called
synesis, whereas *aestuābat* is singular to agree grammatically with the
subject, *nōbilitās. 238, o; 173, b.* .

19. **sī . . . adeptus foret** (*esset*) : a present general protasis, representing a perfect indicative (not future perfect indicative) in direct

foret. Sed ubi perīculum advēnit, invidia atque superbia 20
post fuēre.
24. Igitur, comitiīs habitīs, cōnsulēs dēclārantur M.
Tullius et C. Antōnius. Quod factum prīmō populārēs
coniūrātiōnis concusserat. Neque tamen Catilīnae furor
minuēbātur, sed in diēs plūra agitāre; arma per Italiam
locīs opportūnīs parāre, pecūniam, suā aut amīcōrum fidē 5
sūmptam mūtuam, Faesulās ad Mānlium quendam portāre,
quī posteā prīnceps fuit bellī faciendī.

discourse; viz. *sī . . . adeptus est, polluitur* (from *polluī* above), 'if
(ever) he gains, it is contaminated.' The Latin uses a perfect (*adeptus
est*) in the protasis to indicate the antecedent action, whereas English
is less exact. The whole sentence makes known the general belief
(*crēdēbant*) of the nobles, and therefore expresses iterative or repeated
action. *205 (4);* B. 302, 3; A. & G. 518, *b;* G. 567. **homō novus :** ' an
upstart,' ' a parvenu,' a derogatory expression to indicate a man whose
forefathers had never held a curule office, a magistracy which conferred
the privilege of the *sella curūlis,* the official chair of ivory ; such magistracies were the dictatorship, the consulship, the praetorship, the
censorship, the aedileship. Plutarch's definition (*Catō Major,* 1) is
instructive : ' The Romans used to call men who had no family distinction, but became known through their own efforts, " new men." '

21. **post fuēre :** ' were secondary considerations.'

24. 1. **comitiīs habitīs :** ' after the election,' in 64 B.C. **cōnsulēs
dēclārantur :** ' are announced as consuls,' for the ensuing year, 63 B.C.
M. Tullius et C. Antōnius : Cicero was elected by a large majority,
as he himself tells us (*In Pīsōnem,* 1). Antony won over Catiline by
only a narrow margin.

2. **Quod factum :** ' This outcome.' **populārēs coniūrātiōnis :** ' his
associates in the conspiracy.'

3. **concusserat :** the tense must be considered closely with the following verb *minuēbātur.*

4. **plūra agitāre :** ' devised more schemes.' Note the effective use
of the historical infinitive, which portrays the emotional content of *furor.*

5. **suā . . . mūtuam :** ' borrowed on his own security or that of his
friends.'

6. **Faesulās** (fes'yu̯-lē) : see Map following page 6. *119, a.* **ad Mānlium :** we would say ' to Manlius at Faesulae.' Manlius served as centurion under Sulla, and Catiline placed him in charge at Faesulae.

7. **bellī faciendī :** = *bellandī,* colloquial language.

Catiline tries once more for the consulship but fails. His plots against Cicero miscarry.

26. Hīs rēbus comparātīs, Catilīna, nihilō minus in proximum annum cōnsulātum petēbat, spērāns, sī dēsignātus foret, facile sē ex voluntāte Antōniō ūsūrum. Neque intereā quiētus erat, sed omnibus modīs īnsidiās parābat
5 Cicerōnī. Neque illī tamen ad cavendum dolus aut astūtiae deerant. Namque ā prīncipiō cōnsulātūs suī multa pollicendō per Fulviam effēcerat, ut Q. Cūrius, dē quō paulō ante memorāvī, cōnsilia Catilīnae sibi prōderet; ad hōc collēgam suum, Antōnium, pactiōne prōvinciae perpulerat,
10 nē contrā rem pūblicam sentīret; circum sē praesidia amīcōrum atque clientium occultē habēbat.

---

26. 1. **Hīs rēbus comparātīs, Catilīna:** ' Although Catiline had made these preparations.' *212, a.* **in proximum annum:** 62 B.C.

2. **dēsignātus:** ' consul-elect.'

3. **ex voluntāte:** ' according to his will.'

5. **Cicerōnī:** dative of disadvantage. *109, a.* **illī:** Cicero. **dolus, astūtiae:** Sallust is speaking contemptuously.

7. **Fulviam, Cūrius:** page 125, chapter 23.

8. **ad hōc:** see page 124, line 15, note.

9. **pactiōne prōvinciae perpulerat:** ' had constrained by agreeing to resign his province.' Note the alliteration. *239, a.* The senate fixed Cisalpine Gaul and Macedonia as the consular provinces for the year 63 B.C. The assignment of provinces was determined by lot, and Cicero drew Macedonia, the richer province, which, however, he resigned to Antonius. He then surrendered his right to Cisalpine Gaul in favor of Metellus Celer. We may guess his motive in so doing.

10. **nē contrā rem pūblicam:** idiomatic, ' in order that he might not entertain designs against the state.'

After his defeat at the polls Catiline prepares for war, sends Manlius to Faesulae, and other conspirators elsewhere. His plans included the murder of the consuls and the firing of the city. He calls a secret meeting at the house of Laeca (lē′kạ), and plots to assassinate Cicero in his own house, but Cicero frustrates his secret scheme through information received from Curius and Fulvia. In the meantime Manlius stirs up the rabble in Etruria, and receives support from Sulla's veterans,

Cicero, receiving full information, takes drastic measures.

29. Ea cum Cicerōnī nūntiārentur, ancipitī malō permōtus, quod neque urbem ab īnsidiīs prīvātō cōnsiliō longius
tuērī poterat neque, exercitus Mānliī quantus aut quō
cōnsiliō foret, satis compertum habēbat, rem ad senātum
refert, iam anteā vulgī rūmōribus exagitātam. Itaque, 5
quod plērumque in atrōcī negōtiō solet, senātus dēcrēvit,
darent operam cōnsulēs, *nē quid rēs pūblica dētrīmentī
caperet.*

Ea potestās per senātum mōre Rōmānō magistrātuī
maxima permittitur, exercitum parāre, bellum gerere, 10
coercēre omnibus modīs sociōs atque cīvēs, domī mīlitiaeque
imperium atque iūdicium summum habēre ; aliter sine populī iussū nūllīus eārum rērum cōnsulī iūs est.

---

many of whom had settled in and near Faesulae, and had squandered
their wealth.

29. 1. **ancipitī malō :** ' by a twofold danger,' explained by the
quod-clause below.

2. **prīvātō cōnsiliō :** ' by personal precautions.' **longius :** usually
refers to space or distance in Sallust, but here = *diūtius.*

3. **quō cōnsiliō foret :** ' what were its intentions '; ablative of
quality. *143, a.* **neque . . . satis compertum habēbat :** ' and he had
not fully learned.' *229, a.* How literally?

4. **rem ad senātum refert :** the regular idiom for bringing a question
before the senate.

5. **vulgī rūmōribus exagitātam :** ' disturbed by popular rumors.'

6. **quod . . . solet :** ' as is usual in a critical situation.' What
is the antecedent of *quod?* With *solet* understand *fierī* or *dēcernī.*

7. **darent :** *200, a;* B. *295, 8;* A. & G. *565, a;* G. *652.* **darent
operam . . . caperet :** the usual formula for investing the consuls
with supreme authority. See Cicero, *In Catilīnam,* page 30, line 2, note 1.

10. **parāre . . . habēre :** appositives to *potestās. 222, d.*

11. **domī mīlitiaeque :** *146;* B. *232, 2;* A. & G. *427, a;* G. *411, R. 2.*

12. **imperium atque iūdicium :** ' military and judicial authority.'

13. **nūllīus :** objective genitive depending upon *iūs. 102.* **eārum
rērum :** partitive genitive depending upon *nūllīus. 97, a.*

30. Post paucōs diēs L. Saenius, senātor, in senātū litterās recitāvit, quās Faesulīs allātās sibi dīcēbat; in quibus
scrīptum erat C. Mānlium arma cēpisse, cum magnā multitūdine, ante diem VI Kalendās Novembrēs. Simul, id
5 quod in tāli rē solet, aliī portenta atque prōdigia nūntiābant, aliī conventūs fierī, arma portārī, Capuae atque in
Āpūliā servīle bellum movērī.

Igitur senātī dēcrētō Q. Mārcius Rēx Faesulās, Q. Metellus Crēticus in Āpūliam circumque ea loca missī — eī utrī-
10 que ad urbem imperātōrēs erant, impedītī, nē triumphārent,

---

30. 1. **Saenius** (sē′nj̇-ṳs).

2. **recitāvit:** not ' recited '; see vocabulary. **quās . . . dīcēbat:**
' which he said had been brought for him from Faesulae (fes′yṳ-lē).'
allātās: sc. *esse.* **sibi:** not the same as *ad sē;* it denotes the person
interested in the action, hence may be called a dative of advantage.
It is here very closely allied to the dative of indirect object. *109, a.*
See Pliny, page 445, line 22, note.

4. **ante diem VI Kalendās Novembrēs:** ' on the 27th of October.'
Novembrēs is an adjective agreeing with *Kalendās.* See Cicero's statement,
In Catilīnam, **1,** 3, 11. *241, a* and *b;* B. 371; A. & G. 631; G. Appendix,
pages 491–492. **id quod . . . solet:** see chapter 29, line 6 above.

5. **portenta atque prōdigia:** ' signs and wonders,' which Sallust
dismisses lightly, though Livy reports them faithfully.

6. **Capuae atque in Āpūliā servīle bellum:** training schools for
gladiators had been established at Capua, and the population of Apulia
was composed in large measure of a servile class. The army of Spartacus in 73 B.C. had been recruited with slaves and gladiators from
these districts. See illustration, opposite.

7. **servīle bellum:** ' rebellion of slaves.' See Cicero, *In Catilīnam,*
1, line 11, note.

8. **senātī:** = *senātūs,* archaic genitive. **Q. Mārcius** (mär′sh(y)ṳs)
Rēx: consul in 68 B.C., and later as proconsul of Cilicia conducted an
unsuccessful war against the Cilician pirates, who were completely
overpowered by Pompey, his successor in the effort. **Q. Metellus**
(mẹ-tel′ṳs) **Crēticus:** consul in 69 B.C. The title Creticus was given
him for his conquest of Crete while he was proconsul.

9. **missī:** sc. *sunt.*

10. **ad urbem:** ' near the city.' When an *imperātor* entered the
city, he lost the *imperium;* therefore a general remained outside the

calumniā paucōrum, quibus omnia honesta atque inhonesta vēndere mōs erat — sed praetōrēs Q. Pompeius Rūfus Capuam, Q. Metellus Celer in agrum Pīcēnum, eīsque permissum, utī prō tempore atque perīculō exercitum comparārent.   15

GLADIATORS' BARRACKS, POMPEII

city until the senate had voted him his triumph. **impedītī nē triumphārent:** 'prevented from celebrating a triumph.' *201, a.* Pompey objected to the triumph on the ground that they had been merely officers under his command, and therefore were not entitled to a triumph, which was granted only to one who had conquered the enemy *suō auspiciō et imperiō.*

11. **quibus . . . vēndere mōs erat:** 'who made a business of selling.' *222, a;* compare *203 (2)*.

12. **Q. Pompeius Rūfus:** governor of Africa in 61 B.C. Cicero (*Prō Caeliō*) praises his integrity.

13. **Q. Metellus Celer** (sē'lẹr) : served under Pompey in Asia, and was consul in 60 B.C. **in agrum Pīcēnum:** 'to Picenum, (pị-sē'nụm).' See Map following page 6; sc. *missī sunt.*

Ad hōc, sī quis indicāvisset dē coniūrātiōne, quae contrā
rem pūblicam facta erat, praemium servō lībertātem et
sēstertia centum, līberō impūnitātem eius reī et sēstertia
ducenta; itemque dēcrēvēre, utī gladiātōriae familiae
20 Capuam et in cētera mūnicipia distribuerentur prō cuiusque
opibus, Rōmae per tōtam urbem vigiliae habērentur eīsque
minōrēs magistrātūs praeessent.

There is great excitement in Rome.

31. Quibus rēbus permōta cīvitas atque immūtāta
urbis faciēs erat. Ex summā laetitiā atque lascīviā, quae
diūturna quiēs pepererat, repente omnēs trīstitia invāsit:

---

16. **sī indicāvisset:** subjunctive in implied indirect discourse, representing a future perfect of the direct discourse, *sī indicāverit.* *214, c.*

17. **praemium:** in apposition with *lībertātem*, etc., and *impūnitātem*,
etc. Supply *dēcrēvēre* from the next clause.

18. **sēstertia centum:** approximately $4300.

19. **gladiātōriae familiae:** ' the gladiatorial schools.' They were
instructed by a professional coach or trainer called *lanista*, and since
the gladiators were derived mostly from the slave population, they
often became desperate and dangerous, as had been demonstrated in the
Servile War of 73–71 B.C., which had its inception in a gladiatorial
school at Capua under Spartacus, the celebrated Thracian gladiator.
See illustration, page 131.

20. **mūnicipia:** not ' municipalities,' but ' free towns,' ' boroughs.'
prō cuiusque (*mūnicipī*) **opibus:** ' in proportion to the resources of
each.'

22. **minōrēs magistrātūs:** ' the lesser magistrates,' such as aediles,
quaestors, and the *triumvirī capitālēs*, the last named having certain
police duties among which were the custody and execution of the convicted; they were assigned to strangle the fellow-conspirators of Catiline.
See chapter 55.

31. 1. **Quibus rēbus:** ' By these enactments.'

2. **laetitiā atque lascīviā:** ' joy and jollity.' Notice the alliteration
and assonance. *239, a; 212, d.* **quae:** neuter accusative plural; why?
See page 122, line 15, note.

3. **pepererat:** ' had engendered,' from *parĕre.*

festīnāre, trepidāre, neque locō neque hominī cuiquam satis crēdere, neque bellum gerere neque pācem habēre, suō 5 quisque metū perīcula metīrī.

Ad hōc mulierēs, quibus reī pūblicae magnitūdine bellī timor īnsolitus incesserat, afflīctāre sēsē, manūs supplicēs ad caelum tendere, miserārī parvōs līberōs; rogitāre, omnia pavēre; superbiā atque dēliciīs omissīs, sibi patriaeque 10 diffīdere.

At Catilīnae crūdēlis animus eadem illa movēbat, tametsī praesidia parābantur et ipse lēge Plautiā interrogātus erat ab L. Paulō. Postrēmō, dissimulandī causā, aut suī expūrgandī, sīcut iūrgiō lacessītus foret, in senātum vēnit. 15

---

4. **festīnāre, trepidāre, crēdere, gerere, habēre, metīrī**: historical infinitives; what effect is produced by their use? **cuiquam**: modifies both *locō* and *hominī*. **satis crēdere**: ' trusted fully.'

7. **magnitūdine**: ablative of cause, to be taken with *īnsolitus*.

8. **afflīctāre sēsē**: ' would beat their breasts.' The historical infinitive is oftenest equivalent to an imperfect indicative, hence the English ' would.'

9. **rogitāre, omnia pavēre**: ' they kept asking questions, and were terrified at everything.'

10. **superbiā atque dēliciīs omissīs**: ' laying aside pride and frivolity.'

12. **At . . . movēbat**: ' But Catiline's pitiless mind continued to promote the same machinations.'

13. **lēge Plautiā interrogātus erat**: ' had been accused under the Plautian (plâ′sh(y)ạn) law.' This law sponsored by the tribune Plautius in 78 B.C. provided penalties for those who disturbed the public peace.

14. **dissimulandī causā aut suī expūrgandī**: ' in order to mislead or to clear himself.'

15. **sīcut iūrgiō lacessītus foret**: ' just as if he had been irritated by a quarrel.' **sīcut**: here = *quasi*, a usage practically confined to Sallust. **in senātum vēnit**: the meeting was held in the temple of Jupiter Stator (see Selection from Livy, page 412, *et seq.*, and note 20) on November 8. See Cicero, *In Catilīnam*, **1**, 1, 5; **1**, 13, 30. See illustration, page 413.

Cicero arraigns Catiline in the senate — 'First Oration against Catiline.'

Tum M. Tullius cōnsul, sīve praesentiam eius timēns sīve īrā commōtus, ōrātiōnem habuit lūculentam atque ūtilem reī pūblicae, quam, posteā scrīptam, ēdidit. Sed ubi ille assēdit, Catilīna, ut erat parātus ad dissimulanda omnia, 20 dēmissō vultū, vōce supplicī, postulāre ā patribus coepit, nē quid dē sē temerē crēderent ; eā familiā ortum, ita sē ab adulēscentia vītam īnstituisse, ut omnia bona in spē habēret ; nē exīstimārent sibi, patriciō hominī, cuius ipsīus atque

---

17. **ōrātiōnem . . . reī pūblicae :** ' delivered a speech, brilliant and serviceable to the state,' a most interesting criticism by a fellow country-man, who was not a partisan of Cicero but of Caesar.

18. **quam, posteā scrīptam, ēdidit :** Cicero delivered his *First Oration against Catiline* extempore, but, since the Romans had a system of shorthand, it is quite likely that the words of public speakers were taken down and preserved. No doubt Cicero made some alterations in the

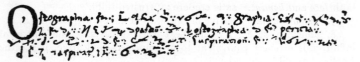

ROMAN SHORTHAND

speech as published, but the content must have been substantially the same, for he was clever enough to know that the legality of the course he was pursuing would be called in question, and that an accurate record of what he had said and had done was imperative to avoid future mis-representation. The traditional name for shorthand is *notae Tīrōniānae,* which suggests the name of Tiro, Cicero's freedman, as the inventor, or perfector, a view supported by some evidence in Cicero and later writers.

19. **ut erat parātus :** ' being ready.'

20. **dēmissō vultū :** ' with downcast countenance,' to give the impression of a man who had been treated unfairly. *144, b* (7). **postulāre ā patribus :** ' to beg the senators.' **patribus :** see Selection from Livy, pages 408 and 429.

21. **ortum :** sc. *esse*, indirect discourse implied in *postulāre* above : ' that such was his birth, such was the conduct of his life that he had everything good in prospect.' *213, b.*

23. **nē exīstimārent, . . . :** ' that they should not think that he, a patrician, whose personal benefits as well as those of his ancestors to

maiōrum plūrima beneficia in plēbem Rōmānam essent
perditā rē pūblicā opus esse, cum eam servāret M. Tullius, 25
inquilīnus cīvis urbis Rōmae.

PUBLIC SQUARE AT ARPINUM

This was Cicero's birthplace.   The busts are of Cicero, Marius, and Agrippa.

the common people of Rome were very many, needed the ruin of the
state, while Marcus Tullius, an immigrating citizen of Rome, was
attempting to save it'; command in indirect discourse, representing
nōlīte exīstimāre of the direct statement.   *216;* B. 316; A. & G. 588, *a,*
note *2;* G. 652.   **sibi . . . perditā rē pūblicā:** *132, a;* B. 218, 2; A. &
G. 411; G. 406.

24. **in plēbem Rōmānam:** contrasted with *patriciō hominī.*   Catiline
means to say that he desired to destroy neither patricians, because he
belonged to their number, nor plebeians, because he and his ancestors
had been their benefactors; the conclusion is obvious.

25. **perditā rē pūblicā:** see page 122, line 17, note.   **cum:** adversative.
187, a; B. 309, 3; A. & G. 549; G. 587.

26. **inquilīnus** (*incolīnus*): a noun used as an adjective, literally,
'a lodger,' living in a place not his own.   The word was spoken with
a sneer, and its use is purposely overdrawn.   It refers, of course, to
Cicero's birthplace, Arpinum.

Ad hōc male dicta alia cum adderet, obstrepere omnēs "hostem" atque "parricīdam" vocāre. Tum ille, furibundus, "Quoniam quidem circumventus," inquit, "ab 30 inimīcīs praeceps agor, incendium meum ruīnā restinguam."

32. Deinde sē ex cūriā domum prōripuit. Ibi multa ipse sēcum volvēns, quod neque īnsidiae cōnsulī prōcēdēbant, et ab incendiō intellegēbat urbem vigiliīs mūnītam, optimum factū crēdens, exercitum augēre ac, priusquam 5 legiōnēs scrīberentur, multa antecapere, quae bello ūsuī forent, nocte intempestā cum paucīs in Mānliāna castra profectus est.

Sed Cethēgō atque Lentulō cēterīsque, quōrum cognōverat prōmptam audāciam, mandat, quibus rēbus possent,

---

27. **obstrepere :** ' howled him down.'

29. **Quoniam quidem circumventus, praeceps agor :** ' Seeing plainly (*quoniam quidem*) that I have been entrapped, and am being driven headlong.' *Quoniam* expresses an evident reason. *183, a.*

30. **incendium meum ruīnā restinguam :** ' I shall extinguish my own burning by a general destruction,' meaning the overthrow of the government.

32. 1. **cūriā :** strictly the meeting-place of the senate was the Curia Hostilia, but at this time the temple of Jupiter Stator.

2. **quod . . . prōcēdēbant :** ' because his plots against the consul were not making progress.' *183, a.* **cōnsulī :** dative of disadvantage. *109, a.*

4. **optimum . . . augēre :** ' believing that the best thing to do was to enlarge the army.' **factū :** *232;* B. 340, 2; A. & G. 510; G. 436. **priusquam . . . scrīberentur :** the clause denotes an ideal limit, design or purpose being implied. *189, b.*

5. **multa antecapere, quae :** ' to take prior possession of many places which.'

6. **nocte intempestā :** ' in the dead of night,' between November 8 and 9. Cicero's *Second Oration against Catiline* was delivered on November 9.

8. **Cethēgō, Lentulō** (sę-thē'gųs, len'tų-lųs or len'chu-lųs).

9. **prōmptam :** ' ready.' **possent, cōnfirment,** etc. : an illustration of *repraesentātiō,* i.e. there may be a choice of sequence regulated by the point of view of the reporter, or that of the speaker. The his-

opēs factiōnis cōnfīrment, īnsidiās cōnsulī mātūrent, caedem 10
incendia aliaque bellī facinora parent; sēsē prope diem
cum magnō exercitū ad urbem accessūrum.

Caesar speaks against the death penalty.
Our decision should be uninfluenced by feelings, and consistent with the
prestige of the senate.

51. "Omnēs hominēs, patrēs cōnscrīptī, quī dē rēbus
dubiīs cōnsultant, ab odiō, amīcitiā, īrā atque misericordiā

---

torical present (here *mandat*) commonly permits this construction,
though examples may be found with the historical perfect. *177, c;* B. 318;
A. & G. 585, *b*, note; G. 654.

    10. **cōnfīrment, mātūrent, parent:** see page 134, line 23, note. *216.*

    11. **prope diem:** ' shortly.'

In the meantime Catiline announces that he is retiring into exile at
Marseilles, but in reality he joins Manlius. Antonius proceeds against
him with an army. The city rabble favors Catiline, largely for social
and economic reasons, and many people leave Rome and join his army.
The conspirators who had been left behind in the city continue their
secret plots, and Lentulus tries to gain the support of the Allobroges,
who had come to Rome at this time to make some complaint regarding
the government of their province. They reveal everything to Cicero,
who instructs them to continue their negotiations with the conspirators.
The Allobroges, after obtaining a signed and sealed agreement from the
conspirators, are intercepted at the Mulvian bridge, the entire party is
arrested, and the documents which they are carrying are seized. On
the strength of written evidence Cicero apprehends the leading conspirators, and examines them before the senate. Five of the conspirators, not including Catiline, are committed to custody; the fickle
rabble veer round, cursing Catiline and praising Cicero. Crassus and
Caesar are implicated in the conspiracy, but Cicero refuses to cast
suspicion on Caesar, who had been threatened with violence as he was
leaving the senate.

The followers of Lentulus and Cethegus, two of the conspirators,
make efforts to rescue them, but their attempts are foiled. Cicero
then convenes the senate to decide the fate of the conspirators. D.
Junius Silanus, consul-elect, moves the death penalty; Caesar speaks
in opposition.

    51. 1. **patrēs cōnscrīptī:** ' senators.' See Selection from Livy,
page 429, and note to line 35. **rēbus:** ' questions.' *211.*

vacuōs esse decet. Haud facile animus vērum prōvidet,
ubi illa officiunt, neque quisquam omnium libīdinī simul et
5 ūsuī pāruit. Ubi intenderīs ingenium, valet; sī libīdō
possidet, ea dominātur, animus nihil valet. Magna mihi
cōpia est memorandī, patrēs cōnscrīptī, quī rēgēs atque
populī, īrā aut misericordiā impulsī, male cōnsuluerint.

"Sed ea mālō dīcere, quae maiōres nostrī contrā libīdi-
10 nem animī suī rēctē atque ōrdine fēcēre.

*The penalty proposed by Silanus does not err on the side of cruelty, but
violates precedent.*

"D. Sīlānum, virum fortem atque strēnuum, certō
sciō, quae dīxerit, studiō reī pūblicae dīxisse, neque illum in

4. **ubi illa officiunt:** ' when those passions obstruct the view.'
neque quisquam omnium: ' no man in all the world.'

5. **intenderīs:** the subjunctive is due to the ideal second person.
180, e (2); B. 356, 3; A. & G. 520, 1; G. 567 below. **libīdō:** ' passion.'

6. **dominātur:** ' overmasters (us).' **Magna . . . memorandī:** ' I
have ample material for reminding you.'

8. **īrā aut misericordiā impulsī:** ' under the influence of anger or
compassion.' **cōnsuluerint:** indirect question. *204 (3)*.

9. **libīdinem animī suī:** ' their impulses.' *animī* and *rērum* are
sometimes used as qualifying genitives either to particularize or to
generalize the noun which they limit; they should ordinarily be omitted
in the English translation. Thus, the poem of Lucretius, entitled *Dē
Rērum Natūrā*, should be translated ' On Nature,' and not ' On the Nature of Things.' *212, e.*

Rome has pursued a policy of restraint and forbearance even
toward her enemies; this traditional principle of conduct should be
employed in the present situation. Let not the emotional utterances
of previous speakers engender psychic contagion in your midst. Although any form of punishment would prove inadequate to the crimes
of these prisoners, you must guard against the charge of severity, because
the manner of punishment of criminals is remembered longer than their
misdeeds.

11. **D. Sīlānum:** ' As for Decimus Silanus (des'ĭ-mŭs sĭ-lā'nŭs).'
Preserve the emphasis in your translation.

12. **studiō reī pūblicae:** ' patriotism.'

tantā rē grātiam aut inimīcitiās exercēre ; eōs mōrēs eamque
modestiam virī cognōvī. Vērum sententia eius mihi nōn
crūdēlis — quid enim in tālēs hominēs crūdēle fierī potest? 15
— sed aliēna ā rē pūblicā nostrā vidētur. Nam profectō
aut metus aut iniūria tē subēgit, Sīlāne, cōnsulem dēsignā-
tum, genus poenae novum dēcernere.

"Dē timōre supervacāneum est disserere, cum praesertim
dīligentiā clārissimī virī cōnsulis tanta praesidia sint in 20

COIN OF CAESAR
Obverse : Head of Pietas, wearing a wreath of oak leaves.
Reverse : Symbols of victories in Gaul.

armīs.   Dē poenā possum equidem dīcere, id quod rēs habet,
in lūctū atque miseriīs mortem aerumnārum requiem, nōn
cruciātum esse ; eam cūncta mortālium mala dissolvere ;
ultrā neque cūrae neque gaudiō locum esse.

" Sed, per deōs immortālēs, quam ob rem in sententiam 25

13. **in tantā rē :** ' in so serious a crisis.' **eōs mōrēs . . . cognōvī :**
' such is the character and such the self-restraint of the gentleman, I
am well aware.'

14. **sententia :** ' motion.'

15. **in :** ' toward.'

16. **aliēna ā rē pūblicā nostrā :** ' inconsistent with our national
policy.' **profectō :** adverb, ' surely.'

21. **equidem :** sc. *ego* from *possum*, ' I for my part.' **id quod rēs
habet :** ' what is the fact.'

22. **aerumnārum requiem :** ' a surcease of woe.' *aerumna* is an
archaic word. *238, c.*

25. **sententiam :** as in line 14 above.

nōn addidistī, utī prius verberibus in eōs animadverterētur?
An quia lēx Porcia vetat? at aliae lēgēs item condemnātīs
cīvibus nōn animam ēripī, sed exsilium permittī iubent.

"An quia gravius est verberārī quam necārī? quid autem
30 acerbum aut nimis grave est in hominēs tantī facinoris con-
victōs? Sīn quia levius est, quī convenit in minōre negōtiō
lēgem timēre, cum eam in maiōre neglēgerīs?

Seemingly good precedents have opened the way to deplorable excesses.

"At enim quis reprehendet, quod in parricīdās reī pūblicae
dēcrētum erit? tempus, diēs, fortūna, cuius libīdō gentibus

---

26. **in eōs animadverterētur :** Latin uses the impersonal subject ;
we should say : ' they be punished.'

27. **An quia :** ' Was it because.' *204 (1);* B. 162, 4 *a;* A. & G.
335, *b;* G. 457, 1. **lēx Porcia :** Livy (**10**, 9) tells us that this law,
under a heavy penalty, forbade the scourging or executing of a Roman
citizen. It was passed *circa* 199 B.C., having been sponsored by
P. Porcius Laeca (pǫr'sh(y)ụs lē'kạ), a tribune of the people. **aliae
lēgēs :** such as the *lēgēs Valeriae* and *lēgēs Semprōniae,* whereby a
magistrate was forbidden to sentence a Roman citizen to death without
the approval of the people.

28. **cīvibus :** dative, to be taken with both *ēripī (109, b;* B. 188,
2, *d;* A. & G. 381 ; G. 345) and *permittī.* **exsilium :** the convicted
man had the alternative of voluntary exile.

29. **An quia :** see line 27 and note.

30. **tantī facinoris :** genitive of the charge with a verb of convicting.
103, b; B. 208 ; A. & G. 352 ; G. 378.

31. **Sīn quia levius est :** supply as follows : *sīn (nōn addidistī) quia
(verberārī quam necārī) levius est.* **quī :** interrogative adverb, an old
form of the ablative, ' how.' **convenit :** ' is it consistent.' **in minōre
negōtiō :** ' in a less important problem.'

32. **neglēgerīs :** = *neglēxerīs.*

33. **At enim :** anticipates an objection, *At* introducing the objection
(' But,' someone will say, ' you are mistaken, Caesar '), and *enim* stating
the reason (' for who, etc.'). Translate, ' But someone will urge.'

34. **Tempus, diēs, fortūna :** Caesar's answer to the objection, ' Time,
the passing day, fortune,' sc. *reprehendent.* **libīdō :** ' caprice.' **gentibus :** *105;* B. 187, II ; A. & G. 367 ; G. 346, R. 2 and N. 2.

moderātur. Illīs meritō accidet, quicquid ēvēnerit; cēte- 35
rum vōs, patrēs cōnscrīptī, quid in aliōs statuātis, cōnsīderāte. Omnia mala exempla ex rēbus bonīs orta sunt.
Sed ubi imperium ad ignārōs eius aut minus bonōs
pervenit, novum illud exemplum ab dignīs et idōneīs ad
indignōs et nōn idōneōs 40
trānsfertur.

"Atque ego haec nōn
in M. Tulliō, neque hīs
temporibus, vereor, sed
in magnā cīvitāte multa 45
et varia ingenia sunt.
Potest aliō tempore, aliō
cōnsule, cui item exer-
citus in manū sit, falsum
aliquid prō vērō crēdī; 50
ubi hōc exemplō per
senātūs dēcrētum cōnsul
gladium ēdūxerit, quis
illī fīnem statuet, aut
quis moderābitur? 55

JULIUS CAESAR

---

35. **accidet, ēvēnerit**: both are used of unfortunate occurrences,
but *accidere* more often refers to the unexpected and *ēvenīre* to the
expected.

37. **exempla**: 'precedents.'

The régime of the Thirty Tyrants at Athens and Sulla's recent
proscriptions were made possible by bad precedents.

42. **Atque . . .**: 'Now, while I do not fear such actions in the
case of Marcus Tullius nor in the present situation, yet in a large state
there are many diverse individualities.'

48. **cui . . . sit**: 'who, like Cicero (*item*), has an army at his
disposal.'

49. **sit**: why subjunctive? *194, a;* B. 283; A. & G. 535; G. 631.

51. **hōc exemplō**: 'in accordance with this precedent.' *136, c.*

I propose imprisonment for life in the municipal towns, without right of appeal or hope of release.

"Placet igitur eōs dīmittī et augērī exercitum Catilīnae? Minimē. Sed ita cēnseō, pūblicandās eōrum pecūniās, ipsōs in vinculīs habendōs per mūnicipia, quae maximē opibus valent; neu quis dē eīs posteā ad senātum referat 60 nēve cum populō agat; quī aliter fēcerit, senātum exīstimāre eum contrā rem pūblicam et salūtem omnium factūrum."

Others spoke, after Caesar; finally, Cato.
I wholly disagree with those who have spoken; our liberty, our lives are at stake.

52. Postquam Caesar dīcendī fīnem fēcit, cēterī verbō alius aliī variē assentiēbantur. At M. Porcius Catō, rogātus sententiam, huiusce modī ōrātiōnem habuit: —

Senators, our ancestors wisely passed laws by which convicted persons were permitted to retire into voluntary exile; this is my strongest argument against adopting any resolution for which there is no precedent.

56. **Placet igitur eōs dīmittī:** 'Is it my opinion then that they (the prisoners) should be discharged?'

57. **ita cēnseō:** 'I make this motion.' **pecūniās:** 'their property.' What is the etymology of this word? See vocabulary.

59. **neu quis,** etc.: 'and that no one hereafter should make a motion regarding them before the senate or propose a measure to the people.' *ad senātum referre* and *agere cum populō* are technical expressions for proposing a question for discussion, the first before the senate and the other before the people in the Comitia.

61. **contrā rem pūblicam et salūtem omnium:** 'contrary to the interests of the state and the general welfare.'

At this juncture Cicero delivered his *Fourth Oration against Catiline*, but Sallust makes no report of this. We may infer from a letter of Cicero to Atticus (**12,** 21) that Cicero moved the death penalty, but that the resolution was passed as Cato worded it, because *verbīs lūculentiōribus* (more lucid) *et plūribus eandem rem comprehenderat* (had expressed).

52. 1. **cēterī . . . assentiēbantur:** 'the rest by a single word signified their assent to one or another of the different motions.' **verbō:** ablative of means; that is, they did not make speeches, as did Caesar and Cato.

2. **aliī:** dative with *assentiēbantur.* *107, a.* **variē:** gives added

"Longē mihi alia mēns est, patrēs cōnscrīptī, cum rēs atque perīcula nostra cōnsīderō, et cum sententiās nōn 5 nūllōrum ipse mēcum reputō.   Illī mihi disseruisse videntur dē poenā eōrum, quī patriae, parentibus, ārīs atque focīs suīs bellum parāvēre; rēs autem monet, cavēre ab illīs magis quam, quid in illōs statuāmus, cōnsultāre.

"Nam cētera maleficia tum persequāre, ubi facta sunt; 10

CATO AND HIS WIFE PORCIA

emphasis to *alius alii*. **M. Porcius Catō** (mär′kṵs pọr′sh(y)ṵs kā-tō): grandson of Cato the Censor; he was thirty-two years of age at this time. Subsequently he was known as Cato Uticensis, because he committed suicide at Utica.   Plutarch recounts his life.   See illustration above.

4. **Longē alia**: ' Far different.'   **rēs atque perīcula nostra**: ' our dangerous situation,' hendiadys.

7. **patriae, parentibus, ārīs atque focīs**: note the spiritual content of these words. *211.*

8. **rēs**: ' the situation.'   **monet**: ' suggests.'   **cavēre**: Cicero would have said, *ut caveāmus*.   Why? *199, a* and *c*.   **illīs**: ' the conspirators '; so also *illōs*.

10. **persequāre**: potential subjunctive, with the indefinite second person, sometimes referred to as the ideal " you." *180, e (2).*

hōc nisi prōvīderīs nē accidat, ubi ēvēnit, frūstrā iūdicia
implōrēs; captā urbe, nihil fit reliquī victīs. Sed, per deōs
immortālēs, vōs ego appellō, quī semper domōs, vīllās, signa,
tabulās vestrās plūris quam rem pūblicam fēcistis; sī ista,
15 cuiuscumque modī sunt, quae amplexāminī, retinēre, sī
voluptātibus vestrīs ōtium praebēre vultis, expergīsciminī
aliquandō et capessite rem pūblicam. Non agitur dē vectīgālibus neque dē sociōrum iniūriīs; lībertās et anima nostra
in dubiō est.

By permitting these leaders to live, as Caesar proposes, you will lend
support to Catiline's army and to all conspirators.

20 "Bene et compositē C. Caesar paulō ante in hōc ōrdine
dē vītā et morte disseruit, crēdō falsa exīstimāns ea, quae
dē īnferīs memorantur, dīversō itinere malōs ā bonīs loca

---

11. **accidat, ēvēnit:** see page 141, note 35.

12. **captā . . . victīs:** a good illustration of Sallust's terse, epigrammatic style. **fit reliquī:** a paraphrase for *relinquitur; reliquī* is
partitive genitive with *nihil. 97, a.*

14. **plūris:** genitive of indefinite value. *101;* B. 203, 3; A. & G.
417; G. 380. **ista:** ' those possessions (of yours).' *211.*

15. **quae amplexāminī:** ' to which your heart clings '; how literally?
Cato was a follower of Stoicism, while Caesar betrays the views of Epicureanism in his speech. See Companion, pages 547, 548.

16. **expergīsciminī aliquandō:** ' bestir yourselves at last.'

17. **capessite rem pūblicam:** ' apply yourselves to the problems
of your government.' **Nōn agitur dē vectīgālibus:** ' It is not a question
that concerns revenue.' The subject of *agitur* is impersonal. *172, e.*

19. **in dubiō:** ' at stake,' ' in jeopardy.' **est:** *173, a.*

Corruption reigns; the question now at stake is not whether our
lives shall be moral or immoral or how great the empire of the Roman
people is to be, but whether this empire, which we now have, shall
remain our own or become the booty of our enemies.

20. **Bene et compositē:** ' In a well-ordered speech.'

21. **crēdō:** ' presumably.'

22. **dīversō itinere malōs . . . habēre:** in apposition with *ea . . .*
memorantur· ' that the wicked, (traveling) by a different road from the
good, etc.'

taetra, inculta, foeda atque formīdulōsa habēre. Itaque
cēnsuit pecūniās eōrum pūblicandās, ipsōs per mūnicipia
in cūstōdiīs habendōs, vidēlicet timēns, nē, sī Rōmae sint, 25
aut ā populāribus coniūrātiōnis aut ā multitūdine conductā
per vim ēripiantur; quasi vērō malī atque scelestī tantum
modo in urbe et nōn per tōtam Italiam sint, aut nōn ibi
plūs possit audācia, ubi ad dēfendendum opēs minōrēs sunt.

" Quā rē vānum equidem hōc cōnsilium est, sī perīculum 30
ex illīs metuit; sī in tantō omnium metū sōlus nōn timet, eō
magis rēfert, mē mihi atque vōbīs timēre. Quā rē, cum dē
P. Lentulō cēterīsque statuētis, prō certō habētōte, vōs simul
dē exercitū Catilīnae et dē omnibus coniūrātīs dēcernere.
Quantō vōs attentius ea agētis, tantō illīs animus īnfīrmior 35
erit; sī paululum modo vōs languēre vīderint, iam omnēs
ferōcēs aderunt.

---

23. **habēre**: translate as if *habitāre*.

25. **vidēlicet** (*licet* + *vidēre*): ' evidently.'

26. **conductā**: ' hired.'

27. **quasi ... sint ... possit**: ' just as if there were ... or
boldness were not more powerful there, etc.' *210,a;* B. 307, 1 and 2;
A. & G. 524, N. 2; G. 602.

30. **equidem**: ' surely.'

31. **in tantō omnium metū**: ' amid such universal alarm.' **sōlus
nōn timet**: an indirect hint that Caesar was implicated in the conspiracy.

32. **rēfert**: ' it is important.'

33. **prō certō habētōte**: ' be assured.' *habēre* in the sense of *scīre*
has its imperative regularly in the future. *181, a (3)*.

35. **Quantō attentius ... tantō īnfīrmior**: ' The more energetically
... the weaker.' Construction of *quantō, tantō? 140.*

36. **paululum modo**: ' but for a moment.' **iam omnēs ferōcēs
aderunt**: ' presently all will be upon you with untamed fury.'

37. **ferōcēs**: belongs with the predicate.

Not arms, but virtues built the Roman state. Unless we unite to
repress pervading evils, the state will be defenseless. Citizens of the
highest rank have conspired against the government; the enemy are
upon us and among us. Do you delay to punish?

I vote for the death penalty!

"Quā rē ego ita cēnseō, cum nefāriō cōnsiliō sceleratōrum
cīvium rēs pūblica in maxima perīcula vēnerit, eīque indiciō
40 T. Volturciī et lēgātōrum Allobrogum convictī cōnfessīque
sint, caedem, incendia, aliaque sē foeda atque crūdēlia facinora in cīvēs patriamque parāvisse, dē cōnfessīs, sīcutī dē
manifestīs rērum capitālium, mōre maiōrum supplicium
sūmendum."

The senate followed Cato in its decree.

53. Postquam Catō assēdit, cōnsulārēs omnēs itemque
senātūs magna pars sententiam eius laudant, virtūtem
animī ad caelum ferunt; aliī aliōs increpantēs timidōs
vocant. Catō clārus atque magnus habētur; senātī
5 dēcrētum fit, sīcutī ille cēnsuerat.

Two outstanding men, of contrasting characters, were Cato and Caesar.

54. Igitur eīs genus, aetās, ēloquentia prope aequālia
fuēre, magnitūdō animī pār, item glōria; sed alia aliī.

38. **ita cēnseō:** see page 142, line 57, note.   **cum:** ' inasmuch as.'

39. **in maxima perīcula vēnerit:** this idiom serves as a passive of
the deponent verb *perīclitārī;* ' has been very greatly endangered.'

42. **dē cōnfessīs . . . supplicium sūmendum:** ' that punishment
be inflicted upon those who have confessed.' *supplicium sūmere dē
aliquō* = ' to exact punishment from someone,' ' to inflict punishment
upon someone.'   **sīcutī dē manifestīs rērum capitālium:** ' just as upon
persons caught in the act (of committing) capital crimes.'

43. **rērum capitālium:** genitive of the charge depending upon *manifestīs = convictīs.*   **mōre maiōrum:** *i.e.* by strangling.

53. 2. **virtūtem animī:** ' his moral courage.'

4. **senātī:** *senātūs;* see page 130, line 8, note.

Caesar had appealed to law, but Cato to ancient precedent, whereby
a criminal could be summarily executed without a trial.

Our country's early success has been due to a few outstanding men;
in our own day Caesar and Cato are men of preëminent merit.

54. 1. **Igitur:** introduces the specific points, which, in the foregoing
sentence, had been referred to in general terms: ' And so.'

2. **magnitūdō animī:** ' spiritual greatness.'   **glōria:** ' fame.'
alia aliī: sc. *erat.*   ' but it (*glōria*) differed in kind.'   How literally?

Caesar beneficiīs ac mūnificentiā magnus habēbātur, integritāte vītae Catō. Ille mānsuētūdine et misericordiā clārus factus, huic sevēritās dignitātem addiderat. Caesar 5 dandō, sublevandō, ignōscendō, Catō nihil largiendō, glōriam adeptus est. In alterō miserīs perfugium erat; in alterō malīs perniciēs. Illīus facilitās, huius cōnstantia laudābātur.

Postrēmō, Caesar in animum indūxerat labōrāre, vigilāre; 10 negōtiīs amīcōrum intentus, sua neglegere; nihil dēnegāre, quod dōnō dignum esset; sibi magnum imperium, exercitum, bellum novum exoptābat, ubi virtūs ēnitēscere posset. At Catōnī studium modestiae, decoris, sed maximē sevēritātis erat; nōn dīvitiīs cum dīvite, neque factiōne cum 15 factiōsō, sed cum strēnuō virtūte, cum modestō pudōre, cum innocente abstinentiā certābat; esse, quam vidērī,

---

4. Ille . . . huic: ' Caesar . . . Cato.' Avoid the translation, ' The former . . . the latter '; it is best to repeat the nouns referred to in translating these demonstratives.

7. glōriam: as above in line 2. miserīs perfugium . . . malīs perniciēs: Notice the effective use of alliteration, ' a source of refuge to the wretched . . . a source of ruin to the wicked.' *239, a; 239, c.*

8. facilitās: ' affability.' cōnstantia: ' firmness.'

10. in animum indūxerat labōrāre: ' had determined upon work (*labōrāre*) and vigilance (*vigilāre*).' How literally? Cicero would have said *animum indūxerat*, etc.

11. neglegere, dēnegāre: probably to be taken as historical infinitives. *182.*

12. dōnō dignum: ' worth the giving.' *142, b;* B. 226, 2; A. & G. 418, *b;* G. 397, N. 2. magnum imperium: ' high authority.'

13. exoptābat: *ex* intensifies the meaning, ' eagerly desired.' virtūs: ' prowess.' posset: subjunctive of purpose.

14. decŏris: ' propriety.' sevēritātis: ' austerity.'

15. nōn dīvitiīs . . . abstinentiā: note the chiastic arrangement. *239, e.*

16. cum strēnuō virtūte: ' with the energetic in worth.'

17. cum innocente abstinentiā: ' with the blameless in self-restraint.' certābat: ' vied.'

bonus mālēbat. Ita, quō minus petēbat glōriam, eō magis illum assequēbātur.

Before nightfall Lentulus and his four associates were executed in the Tullianum.

55. Postquam, ut dīxī, senātus in Catōnis sententiam discessit, cōnsul optimum factū ratus noctem, quae īnstābat, antecapere, nē quid eō spatiō novārētur, triumvirōs, quae supplicium postulābat, parāre iubet. Ipse, praesidiīs 5 dispositīs, Lentulum in carcerem dēdūcit; idem fit cēterīs per praetōrēs.

Est in carcere locus, quod Tulliānum appellātur, ubi paululum ascenderīs ad laevam, circiter duodecim pedēs humī dēpressus; eum mūniunt undique parietēs atque

---

19. **assequēbātur :** sc. *glōria* as subject.

55. 1. **in Catōnis sententiam discessit :** ' voted for Cato's motion.' Another idiom with the same technical meaning is *pedibus īre in alicuius sententiam,* ' to go on foot into the opinion of someone,' hence, ' to vote for someone's motion.' The senators actually moved over to the speaker whose motion they favored.

3. **nē quid eō spatiō novārētur :** ' lest any disturbance should break out during this interval.'

4. **Ipse :** ' The consul personally,' *i.e.* Cicero. Lentulus was still treated as a praetor, although he had abdicated.

5. **in carcerem :** the Mamertine prison, at the foot of the Capitoline hill. See Plan, facing page 62. **cēterīs :** either dative or ablative.

7. **Tulliānum** (tul-ị-ā'nụm) : the underground dungeon of the prison, supposedly built by Servius Tullius, the sixth king of Rome, and named after him. It is more likely, however, that it received its name from *tullius* or *tullus,* the old Latin word for ' well,' and that the name originally meant ' well-house.' Jugurtha (jụ̄-gẹr'thạ) was killed here by starvation, and tradition has it that St. Peter was a prisoner in this place. For a full description of the Mamertine prison and the *Tulliānum* see illustration, page 119. **ubi paululum ascenderīs ad laevam** (sc. *manum*) : ' after a short climb to the left.'

8. **ascenderīs :** the subjunctive is due to the ideal second person. *180, e (2).*

9. **humī dēpressus :** ' sunk in the ground.' *146.*

īnsuper camera lapideīs fornicibus iūncta; sed incultū, 10 tenebrīs, odōre foeda atque terribilis eius faciēs est.

In eum locum postquam dēmissus est Lentulus, vindicēs rěrum capitālium, quibus praeceptum erat, laqueō gulam frēgēre. Ita ille patricius ex gente clārissimā Cornēliōrum, quī cōnsulāre imperium Rōmae habuerat, dignum mōribus 15 factīsque suīs exitium vītae invēnit. Dē Cethēgō, Statiliō, Gabīniō, Caepāriō eōdem modō supplicium sūmptum est.

10. **camera:** ' an arched ceiling.' Compare the French *chambre*, the German *Kammer*, the English *chamber*. **lapideīs fornicibus iūncta:** ' formed by arches of stone.' How literally? **incultū:** ' filth.'

11. **odōre:** ' stench.'

12. **vindicēs . . . frēgēre:** ' the properly appointed executioners strangled him.'

14. **Cornēliōrum** (kǫr-nē'lǐ-ǐ).

16. **Dē Cethēgō . . . supplicium sūmptum est:** the idiom was explained in note, page 146, line 42. **Statiliō, Caepāriō** (stạ-til'ǐ-ụs, sẹ-pā'rǐ-ụs).

The battle begins; Catiline's smaller force fights with desperation, but is utterly defeated; Catiline is slain.

60. Sed ubi, omnibus rēbus explōrātīs, Petreius tubā signum dat, cohortēs paulātim incēdere iubet; idem facit hostium exercitus. Postquam eō ventum est, unde ā feren-tāriīs proelium committī posset, maximō clāmōre cum īn-
5 festīs signīs concurrunt; pīla omittunt, gladiīs rēs geritur. Veterānī, prīstinae virtūtis memorēs, comminus ācriter īnstāre, illī haud timidī resistunt; maximā vī certātur.

The drama rapidly approaches its inevitable end. Catiline, on hearing of the execution, decides to risk an engagement with the Roman forces under Antonius. Before the battle, which was fought in the neighborhood of Pistoria or Pistorium (see Map, back cover), he addresses his soldiers thus: " Soldiers, I know full well that words do not inspire courage. A man is inspirited in proportion to his natural endowment. Our position admits of no choice; we must fight. When you enter battle, remember that you are carrying in your hands not only wealth, honor, and glory, but also your country, your liberty, your lives, while the enemy is fighting for the power of a few. I am confident that you will acquit yourselves courageously; but if fortune should be averse, see to it that you die like men."

60. 1. **rēbus:** ' details.' **Petreius** (pẹ-trē'yụs): Antonius was stricken with an attack of gout, and so intrusted the command to his lieutenant, Marcus Petreius.

3. **Postquam . . . posset:** ' After they reached a point at which the light-armed troops could engage battle.' **ventum est:** Latin may use intransitive verbs in the passive voice with an impersonal subject. *172, e.*

4. **posset:** subjunctive of characteristic. *194, a; 193, a.* **cum īnfestīs signīs:** ' in bitter combat.'

5. **pīla omittunt:** ' they cast aside their javelins.' The legionary soldier carried both a *pīlum*, about six feet long, and a sword. He threw his javelin first, and then drew his sword. Here they fight only with the sword. **rēs:** ' the battle.' *211.*

6. **comminus ācriter īnstāre:** ' pressed on fiercely in a hand-to-hand encounter.' *īnstāre* is an historical infinitive.

7. **illī:** ' their enemies,' Catiline's men. **haud timidī:** ' bravely '; what figure? *239, m.* **certātur:** its subject is impersonal; ' the conflict rages.' *172, e.*

Intereā Catilīna cum expedītīs in prīmā aciē versārī,
labōrantibus succurrere, integrōs prō sauciīs arcessere,
omnia prōvidēre; multum ipse pugnāre, saepe hostem 10
ferīre; strēnuī mīlitis et bonī imperātōris officia simul
exsequēbātur. Petreius ubi videt Catilīnam, contrā ac
ratus erat, magnā vī tendere, cohortem praetōriam in mediōs
hostīs indūcit eōsque perturbātōs atque aliōs alibī resis-
tentēs interficit.   15

Deinde utrimque ex lateribus cēterōs aggreditur. Mānlius et Faesulānus, in prīmīs pugnantēs, cadunt. Catilīna
postquam fūsās cōpiās sēque cum paucīs relīctum videt,
memor generis atque prīstinae suae dignitātis, in cōnfertissimōs hostīs incurrit, ibique pugnāns cōnfoditur.   20

*Catiline's soldiers had died at their posts; he himself is found still breathing.
The victorious army is variously affected.*

61. Sed, cōnfectō proeliō, tum vērō cernerēs, quanta
audācia quantaque animī vīs fuisset in exercitū Catilīnae.
Nam ferē quem quisque vīvus pugnandō locum cēperat,
eum, āmissā animā, corpore tegēbat.

Paucī autem, quōs mediōs cohors praetōria disiēcerat, 5
paulō dīversius, sed omnēs tamen adversīs vulneribus con-
ciderant.

Catilīna vērō, longē ā suīs, inter hostium cadāvera reper-

---

12. **contrā ac ratus erat:** ' contrary to his expectation.'

13. **magnā vī tendere:** Catiline was determined to sell his life dearly.

17. **Faesulānus:** Sallust evidently did not know his name.

19. **generis atque prīstinae suae dignitātis:** ' his birth and his former
rank.' See page 121, chapter 5. **in cōnfertissimōs hostīs:** ' into the
thickest of the enemy.'

61. 1. **cernerēs:** ' you might have seen,' potential of the past with
the ideal " you." *180, e (2).*

6. **adversīs vulneribus:** ' with wounds in front,' indicating that
they had been inflicted in the act of fighting.

tus est, paululum etiam spīrāns ferōciamque animī, quam
10 habuerat vīvus, in vultū retinēns.

Postrēmō, ex omnī cōpiā neque in proeliō neque in fugā
quisquam cīvis ingenuus captus est; ita cūnctī suae hos-
tiumque vītae iūxtā pepercerant. Neque tamen exercitus
populī Rōmānī laetam aut incruentam victōriam adeptus
15 erat. Nam strēnuissimus quisque aut occiderat in proeliō
aut graviter vulnerātus discesserat. Multī autem, quī
ē castrīs vīsendī aut spoliandī grātiā prōcesserant, volventēs
hostīlia cadāvera amīcum aliī, pars hospitem aut cognātum
reperiēbant; fuēre item quī inimīcōs suōs cognōscerent.
20 Ita variē per omnem exercitum laetitia, maeror, lūctus atque
gaudia agitābantur.

---

9. **ferōciamque animī :** do not translate *animī;* see note, page 138,
line 9. *212, e.*

11. **cōpiā :** ' host.'

12. **ita cūnctī . . . pepercerant :** ' so unsparing all had been of their
own lives and those of the enemy alike.'

18. **pars :** = *aliī.*

20. **laetitia maeror . . . lūctus gaudia :** chiasmus. *239, e.*

21. **gaudia :** the plural means ' manifestations of joy.'   *92, c.*
agitābantur : ' prevailed.'

CICERO THE PLEADER AND PROSECUTOR

CICERO THE PLEADER AND PROSECUTOR

M. TULLĪ CICERŌNIS
DĒ IMPERIŌ GNAEĪ POMPEĪ ŌRĀTIŌ
AD QUIRĪTĒS

Partēs Sēlēctae

Citizens, I have not ventured heretofore to address you from the Rostra.

1. Quamquam mihi semper frequēns cōnspectus **vester** multō iūcundissimus, hīc autem locus ad agendum amplis-

POMPEY

A bust in Copenhagen.

Title: IMPERIŌ: here referring to a military command of a special character (see Companion, page 532); = 'Commission.' In the best manuscripts the title is given as *De Imperiō Cn. Pompeī;* in some others, as *Prō Lēge Mānīliā.*

To THE STUDENT: Turn to the Companion, pages 529–535, for an explanation and a complete outline of this speech.

1. 1. **frequēns cōnspectus vester:** refers to the sea of upturned faces over which the orator looked as he came forward on the Rostra; 'your assembled presence,' 'your thronging presence.'

2. **hīc locus:** see note on *Habita ad Populum,* on page 522. **ad agendum:** i.e. *ad agendum cum populō,* 'for addressing the people,' an expression used only of a magistrate,

simus, ad dīcendum ōrnātissimus est vīsus, Quirītēs, tamen
hōc aditū laudis, quī semper optimō cuique maximē patuit,
5 nōn mea mē voluntās adhūc, sed vītae meae ratiōnēs ab
ineunte aetāte susceptae prohibuērunt. Nam cum anteā
per aetātem nōndum huius auctōritātem locī attingere
audērem statueremque nihil hūc nisi perfectum ingeniō,
ēlabōrātum industriā afferrī oportēre, omne meum tempus
10 amīcōrum temporibus trānsmittendum putāvī.

Ita neque hīc locus vacuus umquam fuit ab eīs, quī
vestram causam dēfenderent, et meus labor, in prīvātōrum

---

and applicable to Cicero as praetor; but *ad dīcendum* (sc. *apud
populum*), 'for public speaking,' has reference to any one not a magistrate who may have been permitted to speak from the Rostra.   The
same distinction is carried out in the adjectives; for what was ' most
dignified' for a magistrate was 'most honorable,' 'most full of honor'
for a private citizen.

4. **aditū laudis**: 'pathway to fame.'   Kind of genitive? **quī . . .
patuit**: ' which is always wide open to a man in proportion to his merit.'
Quisque with two superlatives implies a comparison and is a condensed
form of expression for *ut quisque optimus est, ita maximē patuit.   170, a;
A. & G.* 313, *b*, N. 1; G. 318, 2; 642, R. 2 (*a*) and (*b*).   Outside of the
magistrates only the most eminent men of the state were allowed to
speak from the Rostra.

5. **mea mē**: juxtaposition of related words.   **ratiōnēs**: ' plan.'
ab ineunte aetāte: refers to the beginning of life as a citizen, when the
boy put on the *toga virīlis*, the garb of manhood; 'from my entrance
upon civil life,' ' when I became of age.'

7. **per aetātem**: ' by reason of my years.'   **huius auctōritātem locī**:
' this place of dignity.'   *239, k;* B. 350, 11, *a;* A. & G. 641; G. 696.

8. **perfectum ingeniō**: *i.e.* finished with maturity of intellectual
powers; referring to the thought, while *ēlabōrātum* has reference to the
form.

10. **temporibus**: ' demands.'

11. **Ita**: belongs with the clause *meus labor . . . cōnsecūtus*.   In
translating make the first clause subordinate; ' So while this place,
. . . my efforts,' etc.   The coördinate construction was preferred by the
orator for the sake of the rhetorical antithesis.

12. **vestram causam**: i.e. *causam reī pūblicae.*

perīculīs castē integrēque versātus, ex vestrō iūdiciō frūctum est amplissimum cōnsecūtus. Nam cum propter
dīlātiōnem comitiōrum ter praetor prīmus centuriīs cūnc- 15
tīs renūntiātus sum, facile intellēxī, Quirītēs, et quid dē
mē iūdicārētis et quid aliīs praescrīberētis.

Encouraged by evidence of your approval, and by practice in pleading,
I am now glad to speak upon a fruitful theme, the singular merits of
Gnaeus Pompey.

Nunc, cum et auctōritātis in mē tantum sit, quantum
vōs honōribus mandandīs esse voluistis, et ad agendum
facultātis tantum, quantum hominī vigilantī ex forēnsī 20
ūsū prope cotīdiāna dīcendī exercitātiō potuit afferre, certē
et, sī quid auctōritātis in mē est, apud eōs ūtar, quī eam

13. **perīculīs:** often used of criminal trials; here a synonym of *temporibus* above. **castē integrēque:** ' irreproachably,' as not having accepted presents contrary to the Cincian Law, passed in 204 B.C., which made it unlawful for an advocate to receive fees; ' and incorruptibly,' as never having taken a bribe to handle his side of the case poorly so as to allow an opponent to win the suit over his client.

15. **dīlātiōnem comitiōrum:** many circumstances were considered of enough significance to warrant the interruption and postponement of an election. Such was the occurrence of lightning, thunder, or rain, which was supposed to indicate the disapproval of the gods; the setting of the sun before the voting was all done; and the outbreak of a disturbance in the city. The reasons for a postponement in this case are not known. **prīmus ... renūntiātus sum:** ' I had been the first to be announced.' There were eight praetorships to be filled (see Companion, page 571). Cicero each time received the first choice of all the centuries; but on the first two occasions the comitia were adjourned before the other seven praetors had all been elected, and the election had to be held over again as if nothing had been done.

17. **quid aliīs praescrīberētis:** i.e. *ut ipsī quoque castē integrēque in aliōrum perīculīs versārentur.*

18. **auctōritātis:** ' personal influence.'

19. **honōribus mandandīs:** ' by intrusting official positions ' to me.

20. **vigilantī:** ' energetic '; so we speak of a ' wide-awake ' man. **forēnsī:** ' in the courts '; the law courts were about the Forum.

22. **ūtar:** ' I shall make use (of it).'

mihi dedērunt, et, sī quid in dīcendō cōnsequī possum, eīs ostendam potissimum, quī eī quoque reī frūctum suō
25 iūdiciō tribuendum esse dūxērunt.

Atque illud in prīmīs mihi laetandum iūre esse videō, quod in hāc īnsolitā mihi ex hōc locō ratiōne dīcendī causa tālis oblāta est, in quā ōrātiō deesse nēminī possit. Dīcendum est enim dē Cn. Pompeī singulārī eximiāque virtūte;
30 huius autem ōrātiōnis difficilius est exitum quam prīncipium invenīre. Ita mihi nōn tam cōpia quam modus in dīcendō quaerendus est.

In Asia Minor two kings are waging war against us; allies and citizens request the appointment of a certain commander.

2. Atque ut inde ōrātiō mea proficīscātur, unde haec omnis causa dūcitur, bellum grave et perīculōsum vestrīs vectīgālibus ac sociīs ā duōbus potentissimīs rēgibus īnfertur, Mithridāte et Tigrāne, quōrum alter relictus, alter

---

23. **in dīcendō:** ' as an orator.'

24. **eī reī:** ' that accomplishment.' **frūctum:** in the way of a longer opportunity to speak, and that too with the prestige of an official position.

26. **Atque:** ' And further.'

27. **in . . . dīcendī:** ' while I have not had practice in speaking from this place.'

28. **ōrātiō:** ' speech,' ' language.'

29. **Cn.:** Why not *Gn.?* *19, a;* A. & G. 1, *a;* G. 1, R. 1. **virtūte:** i.e. *virtūte imperātōriā*, ' military character,' the combination of qualities found in a perfect general.

30. **ōrātiōnis:** here ' matter.'

2. 1. **Atque:** ' And so.' The *narrātiō* is brief, because the people were already familiar with the facts. **inde . . . unde . . . dūcitur:** ' with that in which this entire state of affairs originates.'

3. **vectīgālibus:** ' payers of tribute,' ' tributaries,' the inhabitants of the provinces Asia and Bithynia; while *sociīs* includes not only the provincials (see note on page 46, line 33), but also the rulers and inhabitants of associated states, as Cappadocia and Galatia.

4. **Mithridāte** (mith-rĭ-dā′tēz) : the original form of the word was *Mithradātes*. **Tigrāne** (tĭ-grā′nēz). **relictus:** ' let slip ' by Lucullus before Cabī′ra; see Companion, page 531.

TIGRANES OF ARMENIA
From a Syrian coin.

lacessītus occāsiōnem sibi ad occupan- 5
dam Asiam oblātam esse arbitrātur.

Equitibus Rōmānīs, honestissimīs
virīs, afferuntur ex Asiā cotīdiē
litterae, quōrum magnae rēs aguntur
in vestrīs vectīgālibus exercendīs 10
occupātae; quī ad me prō necessitūdine, quae mihi est cum illō
ōrdine, causam reī pūblicae perīcu-
laque rērum suārum dētulērunt.

Bīthȳniae, quae nunc vestra prōvincia est, *vīcōs exūstōs* 15
esse complūrēs; rēgnum Ariobarzānis, quod fīnītimum est

SILVER COIN OF BITHYNIA
Obverse: Head of Prusias II. Reverse: Zeus crowning the name
of the king.

---

5. **lacessītus:** 'provoked' by the haughty demand of the Roman
ambassador Appius Claudius for the surrender of Mithridates.

7. **Equitibus:** the capitalists; their agents were in every province.

8. **Asiā:** the Roman province, comprising Mysia, Lydia, Caria,
Lycia, and Phrygia; see Map following page 172.

9. **magnae . . . occupātae:** 'great fortunes are at stake, invested
in farming your revenues'; see note on page 572.

11. **necessitūdine,** etc.: Cicero's family belonged to the order of
knights; see page 485.

15. **Bīthȳniae . . . nēminem:** in indirect discourse as representing
the contents of the letters. **nunc:** Bithynia had been left by will to the
Roman people by Nicomedes III in 75 B.C., and organized as a province
the following year.

16. **rēgnum Ariobarzānis** (ā′rĭ-ọ-bạr-zā′nēz): Cappadocia.

vestrīs vectīgālibus, *tōtum esse in hostium potestāte; L.
Lūcullum, magnīs rēbus gestīs, ab eō bellō discēdere; huic qui
successerit, nōn satis esse parātum ad tantum bellum admi-*
20 *nistrandum.*

*Ūnum ab omnibus sociīs et cīvibus ad id bellum imperā-
tōrem dēposcī atque expetī, eundem hunc ūnum ab hostibus
metuī, praetereā nēminem.*

What is to be done?   I speak first of the c h a r a c t e r of the war.

Causa quae sit, vidētis; nunc, quid agendum sit,
25 cōnsīderāte.   Prīmum mihi vidētur dē genere bellī, deinde
dē magnitūdine, tum dē imperātōre dēligendō esse dīcendum.

Genus est enim bellī eius modī, quod maximē vestrōs
animōs excitāre atque īnflammāre ad persequendī studium
30 dēbeat; in quō agitur populī Rōmānī glōria, quae vōbīs
ā maiōribus cum magna in omnibus rēbus, tum summa in

---

17. **vestrīs vectīgālibus:** ‘ the lands tributary to you,’ ‘ your tithe-
yielding lands,’ the taxes being put by metonymy for the regions in
which they were raised.   *239, n.*
18. **ab eō bellō:** we should say ‘ from the seat of war.’   **huic quī
successerit:** Glabrio.
19. **nōn esse parātum:** sc. *eum;* a hint at the notorious incompetency
of Glabrio.
21. **Ūnum:** *i.e.* Pompey.   **cīvibus:** Roman citizens in Asia Minor,
as indicated by the position after *sociīs.*
24. **Causa,** *et seq.:* a short but clear and appropriate transition to the
treatment of the subject.   A statement of the theme, as that in *quid
agendum sit, cōnsīderāte,* was called by the rhetoricians *prōpositiō.*
28. **quod:** grammatically refers back to *genus,* logically to *bellī;* in our
idiom, ‘ The war is of such a character (*i.e.* being defensive) that it ought.’
29. **ad persequendī studium:** = *ad id (bellum) studiōsē persequendum.*
30. **agitur:** ‘ is at stake.’   In the enumeration with *agitur, aguntur*
(notice the forceful anaphora), an outline of the subsequent argument of
this division is given; first come the considerations involving the national
honor, then those based upon expediency.   *239, b.*

rē mīlitārī trādita est; agitur salūs sociōrum atque amīcōrum, prō quā multa maiōrēs vestrī magna et gravia bella
gessērunt; aguntur certissima populī Rōmānī vectīgālia
et maxima, quibus āmissīs, et pācis ōrnāmenta et subsidia 35
bellī requīrētis; aguntur bona multōrum cīvium, quibus
est ā vōbīs, et ipsōrum et reī pūblicae causā, cōnsulendum.

Our allies, in peril, seek the appointment of Pompey.

5. Quid? quod salūs sociōrum summum in perīculum
ac discrīmen vocātur, quō tandem animō ferre dēbētis?

COIN OF CAPPADOCIA

Obverse: Head of Ariobarzanes I. Reverse: Athena, armed, holding Nike
with wreath. Inscribed: King Ariobarzanes.

32. **amīcōrum**: the title 'friend of the Roman people' was often
conferred upon allied princes.

34. **certissima**: the wealth and fertility of the province Asia were
proverbial.

35. **pācis ōrnāmenta, subsidia bellī**: chiastic order. *239, e.* The
former refers particularly to the sums lavished on the erection of temples
and public buildings, and on the maintenance of public worship.

37. **ā vōbīs**: not dative, to avoid confusion with the dative *quibus;*
'for whose interests you must make provision.'

The disgrace incurred in the first war with Mithridates must be wiped
out. The war is of a kind that involves the reputation of the Roman people,
who have suffered at the hands of Mithridates more flagrant causes of
grievance than those for which our ancestors inflicted summary vengeance.

5. 1. **Quid, quod**: see page 34, line 25, and note. **summum perīculum ac discrīmen**: rhetorical amplification, as if we should say 'the
greatest and extreme danger.' *238, k.* See page 481, note 55.

2. **animō**: see IDIOMS.

Rēgnō est expulsus Ariobarzānēs rēx, socius populī
Rōmānī atque amīcus; imminent duo rēgēs tōtī Asiae
5 nōn sōlum vōbīs inimīcissimī, sed etiam vestrīs sociīs atque
amīcīs; cīvitātēs autem omnēs cūnctā Asiā atque Graeciā
vestrum auxilium exspectāre propter perīculī magnitūdinem
cōguntur; imperātōrem ā vōbīs certum dēposcere, cum
praesertim vōs alium mīserītis, neque audent neque sē id
10 facere sine summō perīculō posse arbitrantur.

Vident et sentiunt hōc idem, quod vōs, ūnum virum esse,
in quō summa sint omnia, et eum propter esse, quō etiam
carent aegrius; cuius adventū ipsō atque nōmine, tametsī
ille ad maritimum bellum vēnerit, tamen impetūs hostium
15 repressōs esse intellegunt ac retardātōs.

Hī vōs, quoniam līberē loquī nōn licet, tacitē rogant, ut
sē quoque, sīcut cēterārum prōvinciārum sociōs, dignōs

---

3. **Ariobarzānēs:** see vocabulary.

4. **amīcus:** see note on page 159, line 32.   **duo rēgēs:** see page 156,
lines 1–6.

6. **cūnctā Asiā:** without *in;* when *tōtus, cūnctus, omnis,* and *medius*
modify the noun, the preposition is often omitted.   *145, c.*

9. **id facere,** etc.: Glabrio or Lucullus might make life a burden for
them if they should present such a request.

11. **quod vōs:** i.e. *vidētis et sentītis.*

12. **summa sint omnia:** ' all qualities exist in the highest degree.'
propter: ' close at hand,' in Cilicia, settling the affairs of that region
after the campaign against the pirates.   **quō:** ' wherefore.'

13. **carent aegrius:** we might say, ' feel all the worse ' not to have
his help.   **ipsō:** ' merely.'   *162, a.*

14. **maritimum bellum:** see Companion, page 531.   **impetūs hostium
repressōs:** it was thought that Mithridates refrained from following up
his victory over Triarius and pushing again to the west of Asia on account of the nearness of Pompey, who might come up from the south
coast and attack him in the rear.

15. **repressōs . . . ac retardātōs:** *212, b.*

16. **tacitē rogant:** *239, p.*

17. **dignōs,** *et seq.:* ' to consider them worthy of having their welfare
intrusted to such a man.'   *194, a;* B. 282, 3; A. & G. 535, *f;* G. 631, I.

exīstimētis, quōrum salūtem tālī virō commendētis, atque
hōc etiam magis, quod cēterōs in prōvinciam eius modī
hominēs cum imperiō mittimus, ut, etiam sī ab hoste dē- 20
fendant, tamen ipsōrum adventūs in urbēs sociōrum nōn
multum ab hostīlī expugnātiōne differant; hunc audiēbant anteā, nunc praesentem vident tantā temperantiā,
tantā mānsuētūdine, tantā hūmānitāte, ut eī beātissimī
esse videantur, apud quōs ille diūtissimē commorātur. 25

VIEW ACROSS THE BOSPORUS
This comparatively small stream separates Europe and Asia.

19. **hōc:** why ablative? **cēterōs:** here ' in other cases.'
20. **dēfendant:** sc. *eam* (i.e. *prōvinciam*).
21. **adventūs:** plural because more than one instance is thought of.
92, c.
22. **hostīlī expugnātiōne:** almost *hostium expugnātiōne;* see page 179,
line 25, *et seq.*
23. **praesentem:** see page 160, line 12, and note.
25. **commorātur:** the indicative shows that here the orator is presenting the thought as his own, rather than that of the provincials.

The investments and commercial interests of many Roman citizens are jeopardized.

7. Ac nē illud quidem vōbīs neglegendum est, quod mihi ego extrēmum prōposueram, cum essem dē bellī genere dictūrus, quod ad multōrum bona cīvium Rōmānō-rum pertinet; quōrum vōbīs prō vestrā sapientiā, Quirītēs, 5 habenda est ratiō dīligenter.

Nam et pūblicānī, hominēs honestissimī atque ōrnā-tissimī, suās ratiōnēs et cōpiās in illam prōvinciam contulē-runt, quōrum ipsōrum per sē rēs et fortūnae vōbīs cūrae esse dēbent. Etenim, sī vectīgālia nervōs esse reī pūblicae 10 semper dūximus, eum certē ōrdinem, quī exercet illa, fīr-māmentum cēterōrum ōrdinum rēctē esse dīcēmus. De-inde ex cēterīs ōrdinibus hominēs gnāvī atque industriī partim ipsī in Asiā negōtiantur, quibus vōs absentibus

---

7. 1. **Ac nē illud quidem:** ' And that too — not.'

2. **cum essem . . . dictūrus:** ' as I set out to speak.'

3. **ad . . . pertinet:** ' it (i.e. *bellum*) affects.'

6. **et:** expects a corresponding *et*, the place of which is taken by *Deinde* in line 11. *238, a.* **ōrnātissimī:** from a financial point of view.

7. **ratiōnēs et cōpiās:** ' enterprises and capital.'

8. **ipsōrum per sē:** ' in and of themselves ' as a class, leaving other interests out of consideration.

9. **nervōs reī pūblicae:** not ' nerves,' but like our ' sinews of war.' See page 444, note 7.

10. **eum ōrdinem:** i.e. *pūblicānōrum.* **fīrmāmentum,** etc.: *i.e.* because holding the purse-strings; Roman citizens at this time paid no taxes anywhere.

11. **cēterōrum ōrdinum:** comprising (*a*) the senatorial order; (*b*) those members of the equestrian order not members of the revenue corporations, i.e. *ōrdō equestris* so far as this was not included in the *ōrdō* (*pūblicānōrum*) of line 10; and (*c*) the third estate, or commons, — all those not belonging to the senatorial or equestrian orders.

13. **ipsī:** ' in person,' referring to the men of the commons who were in the provinces, especially as traders. **absentibus:** ' in their absence ' from Italy; see Companion, page 570, under " citizens."

cōnsulere dēbētis, partim eōrum in eā prōvinciā pecūniās
magnās collocātās habent. 15

Est igitur hūmānitātis vestrae magnum numerum eōrum cīvium calamitāte prohibēre, sapientiae vidēre multōrum cīvium calamitātem ā rē pūblicā sēiūnctam esse nōn
posse. Etenim prīmum illud parvī rēfert, nōs, pūblica,
hīs omissīs, vectīgālia posteā victōriā recuperāre; neque 20
enim īsdem redimendī facultās erit propter calamitātem
neque aliīs voluntās propter timōrem.

*I speak next of the i m p o r t a n c e of the war; it is urgent, but not
to be feared.*

8. Quoniam dē genere bellī dīxī, nunc dē magnitūdine
pauca dīcam. Potest enim hōc dīcī, bellī genus esse ita
necessārium, ut sit gerendum, nōn esse ita magnum, ut

---

14. **cōnsulere:** see IDIOMS. **partim eōrum:** '(while) part of them'
(*97, b;* B. 201, 2; A. & G. 346, *a,* 4; G. 372, N. 3), i.e. *ex cēterīs ōrdinibus,* having especial reference to members of the senate. It was considered inconsistent with the standing of senators to engage openly in
commercial enterprises; hence they often made investments as silent
partners with those engaged in business in the provinces. **pecūniās:**
' sums of money '; hence *magnās* and not *multās.*

15. **collocātās habent:** ' have placed ' in a financial sense, ' have
invested.' *229, a;* B. 337, 6; A. & G. 497, *b;* G. 238.

16. **Est:** subject?

18. **ā rē pūblicā:** i.e. *ā calamitāte reī pūblicae.*

19. **parvī rēfert:** in reply to a possible objection, ' there is little
in the consideration that.' *103, d;* B. 203, 3; A. & G. 417; G. 380, 1;
382, 1.

20. **hīs:** sc. *vectīgālibus.*

21. **īsdem,** etc.: the present revenue farmers, ruined, will not have
the ' means,' others will not dare, to undertake the farming of revenues
in these regions hereafter. **redimendī:** sc. *vectīgālia;* the regular term
used of bidding off the right to collect the revenues of a particular
province or district.

8. 2. **enim:** ' now really.'

3. **ita magnum:** used instead of *tantum,* to correspond with *ita
necessārium.*

sit pertimēscendum. In quō maximē labōrandum est,
5 nē forte ea vōbīs, quae dīligentissimē prōvidenda sunt.
contemnenda esse videantur.

The military operations of Lucullus were at first successful.

Atque ut omnēs intellegant mē L. Lūcullō tantum impertīre laudis, quantum fortī virō et sapientī hominī et
magnō imperātōrī dēbeātur, dīcō eius adventū maximās
10 Mithridātī cōpiās omnibus rēbus ōrnātās atque īnstrūctās
fuisse, urbemque Asiae clārissimam nōbīsque amīcissimam,

SILVER COIN OF PONTUS AND BOSPORUS

Obverse : Head of King Mithridates the Great.   Reverse : Stag feeding.
In field, star and crescent.   Inscribed : King Mithridates Eupator.

4. **In quō :** ' And in this regard.'

7. **L. Lūcullō,** *et seq.*: the laudation of Lucullus is introduced opportunely at this point.   The orator thereby forestalls the possible
charge of slighting the services of this general, arouses the interest of
his audience by suggesting the inquiry how, if Lucullus accomplished
so much, the war can now be so urgent, and prepares the way for the
commendation of Pompey, who is to be made out so much greater.

9. **dīcō :** emphatic, ' I affirm.'   **eius adventū :** ' at (the time of)
his arrival.'

10. **Mithridātī :** *109, a;* B. 188, 1, N.; A. & G. 377; G. 352.   **cōpiās :**
see Companion, page 530.   **īnstrūctās fuisse . . . obsessam esse :** in direct
discourse, *īnstrūctae erant . . . obsidēbātur.*   Why?

11. **urbem,** *et seq.*: after withdrawing from Chalcedon (kal′sẹ-dọn)
(see Map following page 172) Mithridates besieged Cyzicus (siz′ị-kụs),
which held out against him obstinately.   Subsequently Lucullus cut off
his supplies and forced him to give up the siege and to retreat.

Cyzicēnōrum, obsessam esse ab ipsō rēge maximā multitūdine et oppugnātam vehementissimē; quam L. Lūcullus
virtūte, assiduitāte, cōnsiliō, summīs obsidiōnis perīculīs
līberāvit; ab eōdem imperātōre classem magnam et ōrnā- 15
tam, quae ducibus Sertōriānīs ad Italiam studiō atque
odiō īnflammāta raperētur, superātam esse atque dēpressam;
magnās hostium praetereā cōpiās multīs proeliīs esse dēlētās patefactumque nostrīs legiōnibus esse Pontum, quī
anteā populō Rōmānō ex omnī aditū clausus fuisset; Sinō- 20

VIEW ACROSS THE BOSPORUS
Compare this with the picture on page 161.

12. **Cyzicēnōrum** (siz-i̯-sē′nī).

15. **līberāvit**: parenthetical statement, hence not *līberātam esse*.
classem: consisting of fifty ships and conveying ten thousand men;
it was defeated near the island of Lemnos in the Aegean Sea. See note
on page 244, line 30.

16. **studiō**: 'with party feeling.'

17. **raperētur**: 'was being hurried along'; appropriately spoken of
a fleet of warships driven by oars.

19. **Pontum**: see Companion, page 529, and Map. **quī**: concessive,
= *cum is. 194, d.*

20. **ex omnī aditū**: i.e. *ex omnī parte, ubi aditus est.* See page 243,
line 21, *et seq.* **Sinōpēn** (si̯-nō′pę).

pēn atque Amīsum, quibus in oppidīs erant domicilia rēgis,
omnibus rēbus ōrnātās ac refertās, cēterāsque urbēs Pontī
et Cappadociae permultās ūnō aditū adventūque esse
captās; rēgem, spoliātum rēgnō patriō atque avītō, ad
25 aliōs sē rēgēs atque ad aliās gentēs supplicem contulisse;
atque haec omnia, salvīs populī Rōmānī sociīs atque integrīs vectīgālibus, esse gesta.

Our army mutinied, and Mithridates inflicted a crowning disaster.
Lucullus was recalled.

9. Noster autem exercitus, tametsī urbem ex Tigrānis
rēgnō cēperat et proeliīs ūsus erat secundīs, tamen nimiā
longinquitāte locōrum ac dēsīderiō suōrum commovēbātur.
Hīc iam plūra nōn dīcam; fuit enim illud extrēmum, ut
5 ex eīs locīs ā mīlitibus nostrīs reditus magis mātūrus quam
prōcessiō longior quaererētur.

Mithridātēs autem et suam manum iam cōnfīrmārat,
et magnīs adventīciīs auxiliīs multōrum rēgum et nātiōnum

---

21. **Amīsum** (ạ-mī'sụs). **domicilia rēgis :** i.e. βασίλεια, 'royal resi-
dences.'

23. **Cappadociae** (kap-ạ-dō'sh(y)ạ). **permultās :** 'in very great
number.' **ūnō aditū :** rhetorical exaggeration; several of the cities
offered vigorous resistance, and were finally taken only after a siege.

25. **aliōs rēgēs :** Tigranes, king of Armenia; Machares (mak'ạ-rēz),
a son of Mithridates, who ruled the regions about the Cimmerian
Bosporus, and Arsaces (är'sạ-sēz), king of the Parthians.

26. **salvīs :** in a financial sense, as often; freely, ' without taxing
the allies of the Roman people, and without drawing on your revenues,'
the booty amòunting to more than enough to pay the expenses of the
war.

9. 1. **urbem :** Tigranocerta (tig-ran-ọ-sẹr'tạ); see Map. **ex
rēgnō :** instead of *rēgnī;* lends prominence to the fact that but one city
was taken, and indirectly detracts from the credit of Lucullus.

2. **proeliīs :** see IDIOMS. **tamen . . . commovēbātur :** a euphe-
mistic way of alluding to the mutiny, which was the real cause of the
retreat. *239, i.* For the facts see Companion, page 531.

4. **Hīc :** ' On this point.' **illud extrēmum :** ' the final outcome.'

iuvābātur. Nam hōc ferē sīc fierī solēre accēpimus, ut
rēgum afflīctae fortūnae facile multōrum opēs alliciant ad 10
misericordiam, maximēque eōrum, quī aut rēgēs sunt aut
vīvunt in rēgnō, ut eīs nōmen rēgāle magnum et sānctum
esse videātur.

*Finally, I speak of the c h o i c e   o f   a   c o m m a n d e r.   In point
of fitness, Pompey stands alone.*

10. Satis mihi multa verba fēcisse videor, quā rē esset
hōc bellum genere ipsō necessārium, magnitūdine perīculōsum; restat, ut dē imperātōre ad id bellum dēligendō
ac tantīs rēbus praeficiendō dīcendum esse videātur.

Utinam, Quirītēs, virōrum fortium atque innocentium 5
cōpiam tantam habērētis, ut haec vōbīs dēlīberātiō difficilis
esset, quemnam potissimum tantīs rēbus ac tantō bellō
praeficiendum pntārētis! Nunc vērō cum sit ūnus Cn.
Pompeius, quī nōn modo eōrum hominum, quī nunc sunt,
glōriam, sed etiam antīquitātis memoriam virtūte superārit, 10

10. **fortūnae:** plural because referring to more than one instance.
92, c. **multōrum opēs:** i.e. *multōs potentēs;* we should say ' many men of
resources.'

10. 1. **Satis . . . videor:** ' I think I have said enough (to show) ';
followed by a summary of the preceding parts. **esset:** translate as if
present; why not *sit? 177, d;* B. 268, 2; A. & G. 485, *j;* G. 518.

3. **restat, ut . . . dīcendum esse videātur:** ' there remains only
the apparent necessity of speaking,' ' I have yet to speak only of ';
restat ut, like *reliquum est ut,* is used to introduce the last point in a
series; here, the last of the three main divisions of the speech. *203 (1).*

4. **videātur:** used to lend an air of modesty to the expression and
round out the sentence.

5. **innocentium:** opposed to *avārōrum;* see page 178, line 7, *et seq.*

6. **habērētis:** why not *habeātis? 180, d;* B. 279, 2; A. & G. 441,
442; G. 260.

7. **potissimum:** ' above all others.'

8. **ūnus:** '(only) one.'

9. **eōrum . . . sunt:** ' of the present generation.' **sunt:** why not *sint?*

10. **antīquitātis:** abstract for concrete; ' the men of the past cherished in memory.' *92, b.* **virtūte:** see page 156, line 29, and note.

quae rēs est, quae cuiusquam animum in hāc causā dubium
facere possit?

Ego enim sīc exīstimō, in summō imperātōre quattuor
hās rēs inesse oportēre, scientiam reī mīlitāris, virtūtem,
15 auctōritātem, fēlīcitātem.

First, he is a master of the art of war.

Quis igitur hōc homine scientior umquam aut fuit aut
esse dēbuit? quī ē lūdō atque pueritiae disciplīnīs, bellō
maximō atque ācerrimīs hostibus, ad patris exercitum atque
in mīlitiae disciplīnam profectus est; quī extrēmā pueritiā
20 mīles in exercitū fuit summī imperātōris, ineunte adulēscentiā maximī ipse exercitūs imperātor; quī saepius cum
hoste cōnflīxit, quam quisquam cum inimīcō concertāvit,
plūra bella gessit quam cēterī lēgērunt, plūrēs prōvinciās
cōnfēcit quam aliī concupīvērunt; cuius adulēscentia ad

---

13. **summō**: ' of the first rank.'

14. **rēs**: ' qualities.' **scientiam reī mīlitāris**: ' mastery of the art
of war.' An enumeration such as the following was called by the rhetoricians ' a thesis.' **virtūtem**: here ' power as a general.'

16. **scientior**: sc. *reī mīlitāris*.

17. **pueritiae disciplīnīs**: ' the training of childhood.' **bellō maximō**: the Social War. In 89 B.C. Pompey's father, then consul, took
Asculum and conquered the people of Picenum. The next year as
proconsul he reduced the Vestīnī and Paelīgnī. In 87, at the
request of the senate, he went to Rome to prevent Cinna from entering
the city; and at this time young Pompey rendered him important
service in repressing mutiny and thwarting plots to take his life.

20. **ineunte**: see IDIOMS. In 83 B.C., as Sulla came back from the
East, Pompey raised three legions in the Picene country, where his
father had great estates, and set out to join that champion of the aristocracy. On the way he gained three victories over detachments of
the Marian party. When he finally joined Sulla, greeting his commander with the salutation ' Imperator,' the latter, pleased with his troops
and his victories, hailed him ' Imperator ' in return.

22. **hoste, inimīcō**: distinction?

24. **cōnfēcit**: ' has completely reduced.'

scientiam reī mīlitāris nōn aliēnīs praeceptīs, sed suīs 25
imperiīs, nōn offēnsiōnibus bellī, sed victōriīs, nōn stīpendiīs, sed triumphīs est ērudīta.

Quod dēnique genus esse bellī potest, in quō illum nōn
exercuerit fortūna reī pūblicae?   Cīvīle, Āfricānum, Trānsalpīnum, Hispāniēnse, servīle, nāvāle bellum, varia et 30

---

25. **aliēnīs . . . triumphīs**: an elaborate but forceful climax of
antitheses. *239, f.*

29. **Cīvīle** [*bellum*]: between Marius and Sulla; reference in particular to Pompey's brief and victorious campaign in 82 B.C. against

GOLD COIN OF POMPEY

Struck after the African war. Obverse: Head of Africa. Reverse: Pompey
in a quadriga, crowned by Victory and holding a laurel branch.

Carbo in Sicily, and that in 77 against M. Aemilius Lepidus, who endeavored to overthrow the constitution as established by Sulla, but was
driven out of Italy, then out of Cisalpine Gaul.   **Āfricānum**: this campaign, also in 82 B.C., was against Gnaeus Domitius Ahenobarbus, of
the Marian party, and Hiarbas, king of Numidia, who had entered into
an alliance with him.   With six legions Pompey destroyed the forces of
both commanders at Utica, and captured their camp.   Domitius was
killed.   Hiarbas escaped to his own kingdom, where he was shortly
afterwards murdered, being succeeded by Hiempsal.   **Trānsalpīnum**: a
series of engagements with tribes of Transalpine Gaul that had been
induced by emissaries of Sertorius to oppose Pompey on his march to
Spain, in 76 B.C.

30. **Hispāniēnse**: with Sertorius and the remnants of the Sertorian
party in Spain; this war came to an end shortly after the death of
Sertorius in 72 B.C.   Between *Hispāniēnse* and *servīle* the manuscripts
insert *mixtum ex cīvitātibus atque ex bellicōsissimīs nātiōnibus*   The

dīversa genera et bellōrum et hostium, nōn sōlum gesta
ab hōc ūnō, sed etiam cōnfecta, nūllam rem esse dēclārant
in ūsū positam mīlitārī, quae huius virī scientiam fugere
possit.

*Then, he has the qualities of a great military leader, as many lands
bear witness.*

11. Iam vērō virtūtī Cn. Pompeī quae potest ōrātiō
pār invenīrī? Quid est, quod quisquam aut illō dignum aut
vōbīs novum aut cuiquam inaudītum possit afferre?
Neque enim illae sunt sōlae virtūtēs imperātōriae, quae
5 vulgō exīstimantur, labor in negōtiīs, fortitūdō in perīculīs,
industria in agendō, celeritās in cōnficiendō, cōnsilium in
prōvidendō; quae tanta sunt in hōc ūnō, quanta in omnibus

---

thought of the inserted clause is not inappropriate in the connection;
yet it is not good Latin, and interrupts the movement of the sentence,
so that it may safely be rejected as not Ciceronian, at least in its present
form.   **servīle:** on his way from Spain in 71 Pompey accidentally fell
in with a troop of five thousand slaves from the army of Spartacus, and
easily defeated and slew them.   They had escaped the fate of their
associates in the battle with Crassus in Lucania, and were trying to cut
their way through into Gaul.   Elated with the victory, Pompey sent
word to the senate that Crassus had beaten the slaves in battle, but
that he had plucked up the war by the roots.   **nāvāle:** with the pirates;
see Companion, page 531, and chapter 12.   **varia . . . hostium:** *i.e.* ' different kinds of wars with enemies in far different places.'

32.   **nūllam . . . mīlitāri:** ' that there is no point arising in military
experience.'

11.   1.   **virtūtī:** here ' character,' as the sum of the traits mentioned
below.

4.   **illae sunt,** etc.: *illae virtūtēs imperātōriae* (' qualities befitting a
commander '), *quae vulgō exīstimantur* (' are generally so regarded ')
nōn sunt sōlae virtūtēs imperātōriae.   The ' other qualities ' are not discussed till chapter 13 (page 178, line 2, *et seq.*).

5.   **labor in negōtiīs:** *i.e.* ' power of application in matters of
routine.'

6.   **industria in agendō:** ' energy in action.'   **cōnsilium in prōvidendō:** ' resource in calculation.'   *230, a (4).*

7.   **quae:** ' and these qualities.'   *211.*

relĭquīs imperātōribus, quōs aut vīdimus aut audīvimus, nōn fuērunt.

Testis est Italia, quam ille ipse victor L. Sulla huius 10 virtūte et subsidiō cōnfessus est līberātam; testis est Sicilia, quam multīs undique cīnctam perīculīs nōn terrōre bellī, sed cōnsilī celeritāte explicāvit; testis est Āfrica, quae, magnīs oppressa hostium cōpiīs, eōrum ipsōrum

ROMAN GOLD COIN
Obverse: The Goddess Roma.   Reverse: Sulla on horseback.

sanguine redundāvit; testis est Gallia, per quam legiō- 15 nibus nostrīs iter in Hispāniam Gallōrum interneciōne patefactum est; testis est Hispānia, quae saepissimē plūrimōs hostēs ab hōc superātōs prōstrātōsque cōnspexit; testis est iterum et saepius Italia, quae cum servīlī bellō taetrō perīculōsōque premerētur, ab hōc auxilium absente 20 expetīvit, quod bellum exspectātiōne eius attenuātum atque imminūtum est, adventū sublātum ac sepultum;

10. **Italia . . .:** see note on page 168, line 20 above. The orator touches lightly on this point; for Pompey's service under Sulla was against the leaders of that party, to representatives of which he was speaking.

12. **Sicilia, Āfrica:** see note on page 169, line 29 above.

15. **Gallia, Hispānia, Italia:** see note on page 169, lines 29 and 30.

20. **absente:** in Spain. Crassus requested the senate to recall Pompey from Spain and Marcus Lucullus from Thrace to help in putting down the war with Spartacus, then made haste to finish the war himself in order to get the full credit.

testēs nunc vērō iam omnēs sunt ōrae atque omnēs exterae
gentēs ac nātiōnēs, dēnique maria omnia cum ūniversa,
25 tum in singulīs ōrīs omnēs sinūs atque portūs.

*His extraordinary generalship was revealed also in the campaign
against the pirates.*

Quis enim tōtō marī locus per hōs annōs aut tam fīrmum
habuit praesidium, ut tūtus esset, aut tam fuit abditus,
ut latēret? Quis nāvigāvit, quī nōn sē aut mortis aut
servitūtis perīculō committeret, cum aut hieme aut refertō
30 praedōnum marī nāvigāret?

Hōc tantum bellum, tam turpe, tam vetus, tam lātē
dīvīsum atque dispersum, quis umquam arbitrārētur aut
ab omnibus imperātōribus ūnō annō, aut omnibus annīs
ab ūnō imperātōre, cōnficī posse? Quam prōvinciam
35 tenuistis ā praedōnibus līberam per hōsce annōs? Quod
vectīgal vōbīs tūtum fuit? Quem socium dēfendistis?
Cui praesidiō classibus vestrīs fuistis? Quam multās
exīstimātis īnsulās esse dēsertās, quam multās aut metū
relīctās aut ā praedōnibus captās urbēs esse sociōrum?
12. Sed quid ego longinqua commemorō? Fuit hōc

---

23. **iam :** ' further.'

24. **ūniversa :** ' throughout their extent.'

26. **Quis locus,** etc. : the boldness and success of the pirates at the
time referred to almost transcend belief. See Companion, page 531, for
story of the pirates as told by Mommsen.

29. **hieme :** *i.e.* exposed to winter storms; yet even these (see Dio
Cassius, **36,** 4) were not a protection against the freebooters. Navigation on the Mediterranean ordinarily ceased from about the middle of
November to the earlier part of March; see Acts **27,** 9, 12. **refertō :**
followed by the genitive after the analogy of *plēnus.* *102.*

33. **omnibus imperātōribus :** *i.e.* living at that time. Notice the
chiastic order in *ab omnibus ūnō annō — omnibus annīs ab ūnō imperātōre.*
239, e. **omnibus annīs :** *i.e.* of his life.

12. 1. **Fuit :** not *erat*, as implying that what has been no longer is;
see page 29, line 27, and note. *239, b.*

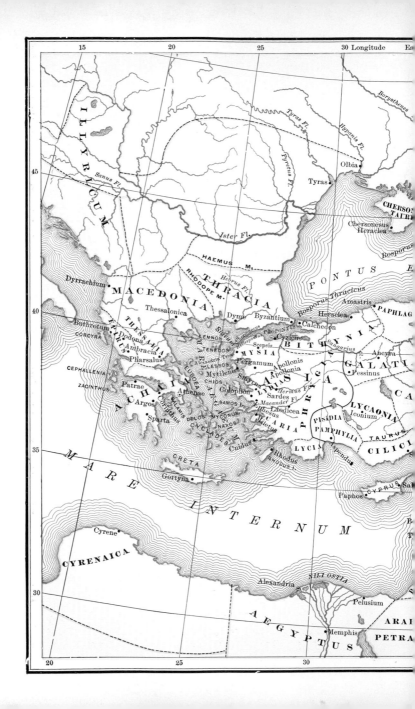

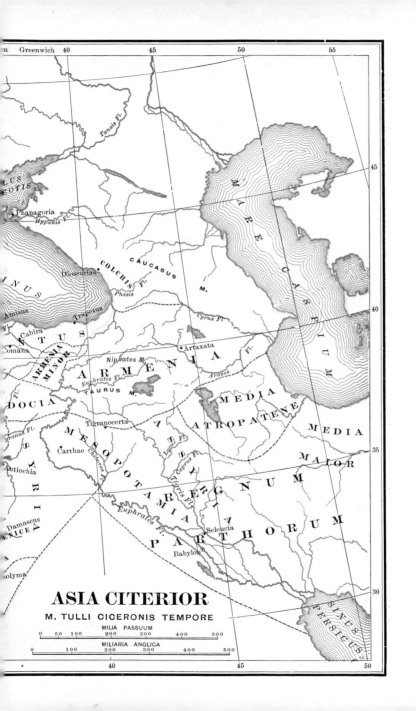

ASIA CITERIOR

M. TULLI CICERONIS TEMPORE

MILIA PASSUUM

0   50   100   200   300   400   500

MILIARIA ANGLICA

0   100   200   300   400   500

quondam, fuit proprium populī Rōmānī, longē ā domō
bellāre et prōpugnāculīs imperī sociōrum fortūnās, nōn
sua tēcta dēfendere. Sociīs ego nostrīs mare per hōs
annōs clausum fuisse dīcam, cum exercitūs vestrī numquam 5
ā Brundisiō nisi hieme summā trānsmīserint?

Quī ad vōs ab exterīs nātiōnibus venīrent, captōs querar,
cum lēgātī populī Rōmānī redēmptī sint? Mercātōribus
tūtum mare nōn fuisse dīcam, cum duodecim secūrēs in
praedōnum potestātem pervēnerint? 10

Cnidum aut Colophōnem aut Samum, nōbilissimās
urbēs, innumerābilēsque aliās captās esse commemorem,
cum vestrōs portūs atque eōs portūs, quibus vītam ac
spīritum dūcitis, in praedōnum fuisse potestāte sciātis?

---

2. **proprium :** ' characteristic.' *102.*

3. **prōpugnāculīs :** armies and fleets.

5. **dīcam :** why subjunctive? *179, b (?).* **vestrī :** emphatic, ' your
own.' According to Plutarch (*Pompey*, 24), the pirates had more
than a thousand ships, and had captured over four hundred towns.

6. **Brundisiō** (brŭn-dizh′(y)-ŭm). **hieme :** see IDIOMS.

7. **venīrent :** to Rome, as ambassadors.

8. **redēmptī sint :** ' were ransomed.' There is a story that a certain
Roman ambassador was ransomed by his wife; as no other instance of
the kind has come down to us, possibly the plural here is rhetorical.

9. **duodecim secūrēs :** *i.e.* two praetors; for outside of Rome a
praetor was allowed to have six lictors. See Plutarch, *Pompey*, 24:
' On one occasion (the pirates) seized two praetors, Sextilius and Belli-
nus, in their purple-bordered robes of office, together with their attendants and lictors, and carried them all off.'

11. **Cnidum** (nī′dŭs), **Colophōnem** (kol′ọ-fọn), **Samum** (sā′mọs) : all
formerly great commercial centers. See Map following page 172.

13. **eōs portūs, quibus,** etc.: Caieta, Misenum, Ostia. Owing to
the decline of Italian farming and the enormous increase of population
at Rome, the city depended for its subsistence on the supplies of grain
which were imported from Sicily, Sardinia, Egypt, and Africa, through
the harbors nearest the city. If the importation of grain was interfered
with, there was immediate alarm; if it was stopped, distress was soon
felt. See illustration, page 531.

He freed the harbors of Italy from danger of piratic raids.

15 An vērō ignōrātis portum Caiētae celeberrimum ac
plēnissimum nāvium, īnspectante praetōre, ā praedōnibus
esse dīreptum, ex Mīsēnō autem eius ipsīus līberōs, quī
cum praedōnibus anteā ibi bellum gesserat, ā praedōnibus
esse sublātōs?

20 Nam quid ego Ōstiēnse incommodum atque illam lābem
atque ignōminiam reī pūblicae querar, cum, prope īnspectantibus vōbīs, classis ea, cui cōnsul populī Rōmānī praepositus esset, ā praedōnibus capta atque oppressa est?

Prō dī immortālēs! tantamne ūnīus hominis incrēdǐ-
25 bilis ac dīvīna virtūs tam brevī tempore lūcem afferre reī
pūblicae potuit, ut vōs, quī modo ante ōstium Tiberīnum classem hostium vidēbātis, eī nunc nūllam intrā
Ōceanī ōstium praedōnum nāvem esse audiātis?

---

15. **An vērō ignōrātis**: in ordinary prose, *Nam profectō nōn ignōrātis.*
Caiētae (ką-yē′tą). **celeberrimum**: not ' most celebrated,' but ' much
frequented.'

16. **īnspectante praetōre**: ' under the eyes of the praetor ' who,
presumably, had been sent to protect the harbor.

17. **Mīsēnō** (mį-sē′nųm). **līberōs**: rhetorical plural; the daughter
of Marcus Antonius the orator was taken, and was ' ransomed for a
great sum of money ' (Plutarch, *Pompey*, 24). For the efforts of this
Antonius against the pirates in 102 B.C., see Mommsen, Volume III,
page 171.

21. **cum**: i.e. *quae tum accepta est, cum.* **prope īnspectantibus vōbīs**:
Ostia, at the mouth of the Tiber, was only sixteen miles from Rome;
yet there the pirates sailed into the harbor ' and burned the ships and
plundered everything ' (Dio Cassius, **36,** 5).

22. **cōnsul**: his name, omitted by Cicero no doubt to spare the disgrace, is not known.

25. **lūcem**: *i.e.* hope of safety. **afferre**: ' shed.'

27. **eī**: saves the repetition of *vōs;* in our idiom, ' even you.'
How literally?

28. **Ōceanī ōstium**: i.e. *fretum Gādītānum*, the Straits of Gibraltar;
contrasted — also with chiastic arrangement — with *ōstium Tiberīnum.*
239, e. The contrast was more forceful to the ancient than to the

This campaign he conducted with amazing rapidity.

Atque haec quā celeritāte gesta sint, quamquam vidētis, tamen ā mē in dīcendō praetereunda nōn sunt. Quis 30
enim umquam aut obeundī negōtī aut cōnsequendī quaes-
tūs studiō tam brevī tempore tot loca adīre, tantōs cursūs
cōnficere potuit, quam celeriter, Cn. Pompeiō duce, tantī
bellī impetus nāvigāvit? Quī, nōndum tempestīvō ad

FOUNDATION OF THE IMPERIAL PALACE AT OSTIA

modern mind, because of the primitive but current conception of the
ocean as a stream flowing about the earth.

29. **Atque :** ' And then.'

30. **praetereunda nōn sunt :** for *praetereundum nōn est;* attracted to
agree with *haec,* which belongs with *gesta sint.*

32. **tam brevī tempore :** repeated in *celeriter;* for *tam brevī tempore
quam celeriter* is simply a fuller expression for *tam celeriter quam,* making
prominent the great rapidity of movement.

33. **tantī bellī impetus :** *i.e.* ' an attacking fleet of so great force '; a
striking metaphor, perhaps chosen to provide a subject parallel with
quis; in simple prose, *quam Cn. Pompeius dux cum tantā classe tantō
impetū nāvigāvit.*

35 nāvigandum marī, Siciliam adiit, Āfricam explōrāvit, in
Sardiniam cum classe vēnit atque haec tria frūmentāria
subsidia reī pūblicae fīrmissimīs praesidiīs classibusque
mūnīvit.

Inde cum sē in Italiam recēpisset, duābus Hispāniīs
40 et Galliā Trānsalpīnā praesidiīs ac nāvibus cōnfīrmātā,
missīs item in ōram Īllyricī maris et in Achaiam omnemque
Graeciam nāvibus, Italiae duo maria maximīs classibus
fīrmissimīsque praesidiīs adōrnāvit, ipse autem, ut Brundisiō profectus est, ūndēquīnquāgēsimō diē tōtam ad impe-
45 rium populī Rōmānī Ciliciam adiūnxit; omnēs, quī ubīque
praedōnēs fuērunt, partim captī interfectīque sunt, partim
ūnīus huius sē imperiō ac potestātī dēdidērunt. Īdem
Crētēnsibus, cum ad eum ūsque in Pamphȳliam lēgātōs

---

35. **adiit, explōrāvit, vēnit:** simultaneously, through his lieutenants.

36. **frūmentāria subsidia:** see note to line 13 above.

39. **duābus Hispāniīs:** *Citeriōre et Ulteriōre;* see page 572.

40. **Galliā Trānsalpīnā:** i.e. *Galliā Narbōnēnsis,* along the southern coast.

41. **Achaiam** (ạ-kā'(y)ạ): when coupled with *Graecia* refers to the Peloponnesus only; the province of *Achaia* was not organized till many years after the subjugation of Greece, in 146 B.C.

42. **Italiae duo maria:** the Tuscan and the Adriatic.

43. **ut:** 'after.' *188, a.*

45. **Ciliciam** (sị-lish'(y)ạ): the stronghold of piracy.

47. **imperiō ac potestātī:** *i.e.* they not only surrendered, but surrendered unconditionally. According to Strabo (**14,** 3, paragraph 665), Pompey burned more than thirteen hundred ships of the pirates (see note on page 173, line 5), 'and utterly destroyed their settlements. Of those who survived the battles he carried some off to Soli (in Cilicia; see Map), to which he gave the name Pompeiopolis, and others to Dyme (in Thrace), which was losing its population, but is now a Roman colony.'

48. **Crētēnsibus,** etc.: the task of subduing the Cretans had been assigned in 68 B.C. to Quintus Metellus, who was carrying it out with the greatest cruelty. Nominally Crete came under the provisions of the Gabinian bill; and Pompey, in the face of all requirements of mili-

dēprecātōrēsque mīsissent, spem dēditiōnis nōn adēmit
obsidēsque imperāvit. 50

Ita tantum bellum, tam diūturnum, tam longē lātēque
dispersum, quō bellō omnēs gentēs ac nātiōnēs premēban-
tur, Cn. Pompeius extrēmā hieme apparāvit, ineunte
vēre suscēpit, mediā aestāte cōnfēcit.

A View in Cilicia

This was the headquarters for the pirate bands.

tary courtesy, encouraged the inhabitants to make terms with him,
from whom they would no doubt receive better treatment than from
Metellus. The latter, however, strenuously resisted this interference
with his prerogatives, and Pompey wisely let the matter drop. **ūsque
in Pamphȳliam** (pạm-fil′ĭ-ạ): strong expression, appropriate for one
going from Rome; but it was only a short distance from Crete to Pam-
phylia. Cicero's hearers were not well posted on nice points in the
geography of the Orient. **lēgātōs dēprecātōrēsque:** i.e. *lēgātōs ad
dēprecandum.*

49. **nōn adēmit**; ' he did not withhold.'

50. **-que**: ' but,' as often after a negative. *234, b.*

52. **quō bellō**: ' a war in which.'

13. Est haec dīvīna atque incrēdibilis virtūs imperātōris.

He possesses the other qualities of a perfect commander: he is
incorruptible, and above avarice.

Quid cēterae, quās paulō ante commemorāre coeperam,
quantae atque quam multae sunt! Nōn enim bellandī
virtūs sōlum in summō ac perfectō imperātōre quaerenda
5 est, sed multae sunt artēs eximiae huius administrae
comitēsque virtūtis.

Ac prīmum, quantā innocentiā dēbent esse imperātōrēs,
quantā deinde in omnibus rēbus temperantiā, quantā
fidē, quantā facilitāte, quantō ingeniō, quantā hūmānitāte!
10 Quae breviter quālia sint in Cn. Pompeiō cōnsīderēmus.
Summa enim omnia sunt, Quirītēs, sed ea magis ex aliōrum
contentiōne quam ipsa per sēsē cognōscī atque intellegī
possunt.

Quem enim imperātōrem possumus ūllō in numerō
15 putāre, cuius in exercitū centuriātūs vēneant atque vēni-
erint? Quid hunc hominem magnum aut amplum dē rē
pūblicā cōgitāre, quī pecūniam ex aerāriō dēprōmptam ad

---

13. 1. **Est haec:** ' Such is.'

2. **Quid:** ' But further.' **quās paulō ante,** etc.: implied rather
than mentioned, page 170, lines 4–5.

3. **bellandī virtūs:** not merely ' fighting quality,' as shown by what
follows; rather ' military character.'

5. **artēs:** not ' arts '; used as a synonym of *virtūtēs.* **huius . . .**
virtūtis: ' which attend and wait upon this trait '; see Companion,
page 534, *b.*

10. **Quae:** ' Now — these.' Why neuter?

11. **Summa,** etc.: see page 160, line 12, and note. **aliōrum:** ' with
others,' we should say.

14. **ūllō in numerō:** i.e. *imperātōrum;* ' of any standing.'

16. **Quid,** etc.: sc. *putāre possumus;* ' What exalted or worthy
thought for the welfare of the state can we suppose that this man has,
who.' *117, a;* B. 176, 2; A. & G. 390, *c;* G. 333, 1. It is not known
to whom reference is made.

bellum administrandum aut propter cupiditātem prōvinciae
magistrātibus dīvīserit aut propter avāritiam Rōmae in
quaestū relīquerit? 20

Vestra admurmurātiō facit, Quirītēs, ut agnōscere videāminī, quī haec fēcerint; ego autem nōminō nēminem;
quā rē īrāscī mihi nēmō poterit, nisi quī ante dē sē voluerit
cōnfitērī.

Itaque propter hanc avāritiam imperātōrum quantās 25
calamitātēs, quōcumque ventum sit, nostrī exercitūs ferant, quis ignōrat? Itinera, quae per hōsce annōs in
Italiā per agrōs atque oppida cīvium Rōmānōrum nostrī
imperātōrēs fēcerint, recordāminī; tum facilius statuētis,
quid apud exterās nātiōnēs fierī exīstimētis. Utrum 30
plūrēs arbitrāminī per hōsce annōs mīlitum vestrōrum
armīs hostium urbēs an hībernīs sociōrum cīvitātēs esse
dēlētās?

---

18. **cupiditātem prōvinciae**: i.e. *cupiditātem prōvinciae retinendae;*
the commander mentioned by way of illustration was supposed to be
already in charge.

19. **in quaestū**: *i.e.* on interest. So Cicero charges Piso (*In Pīsōnem,*
35, 86), among other dishonorable transactions, with having placed
18,000,000 sesterces (more than $725,000) of government money at
interest in Rome.

21. **facit**: ' shows.'

23. **nisi quī**: ' unless (some one) who '; on the principle expressed in
our proverb, " Whom the cap fits, let him put it on."

26. **ventum sit**: *172, e.* **ferant**: ' bring ' with them.

28. **cīvium Rōmānōrum**: free inhabitants of Italy who had become
Roman citizens after 89 B.C.; see page 229, lines 8–12, and note.

29. **fēcerint**: why not *fēcērunt? 194, a.*

31. **plūrēs**, etc.: *plūrēs urbēs hostium armīs mīlitum vestrōrum esse
dēlētās.* Reason for the order of words? *211.*

32. **hībernīs**: provincial cities (with the exception of the *līberae
cīvitātēs*) were required to furnish winter-quarters for the Roman forces;
but they frequently purchased exemption from the intolerable burden
with great sums of money.

*Holding himself under restraint, he restrains his army, and is ready
to listen to the complaints of civilians.*

Neque enim potest exercitum is continēre imperātor,
35 quī sē ipse nōn continet, neque sevērus esse in iūdicandō,
quī aliōs in sē sevērōs esse iūdicēs nōn vult. Hīc mīrāmur
hunc hominem tantum excellere cēterīs, cuius legiōnēs
sīc in Asiam pervēnerint, ut nōn modo manus tantī exercitūs, sed nē vēstīgium quidem cuiquam pācātō nocuisse
40 dīcātur?

Iam vērō quem ad modum mīlitēs hībernent, cotīdiē
sermōnēs ac litterae perferuntur; nōn modo ut sūmptum
faciat in mīlitem, nēminī vīs affertur, sed nē cupientī quidem cuiquam permittitur. Hiemis enim, nōn avāritiae
45 perfugium maiōrēs nostrī in sociōrum atque amīcōrum
tēctīs esse voluērunt.

14. Age vērō, cēterīs in rēbus quā sit temperantiā, cōnsīderāte.

Unde illam tantam celeritātem et tam incrēdibilem cursum inventum putātis? Nōn enim illum eximia vīs

---

34. **Neque enim :** ' And (with good reason), for . . . not.'

35. **quī . . . continet :** perhaps a hint at the self-indulgence of the
luxury-loving Lucullus.

36. **Hīc :** ' Under these conditions.'

38. **nōn modo :** translate as if *nōn modo nōn;* see page 53, line 6,
and note. **manus, vēstīgium :** the former, as free from robbery and
extortion ; the latter, as doing no damage to fields and crops along the
line of march.

39. **cuiquam pācātō :** freely, ' a single friendly native.'

42. **sermōnēs ac litterae :** we should say, ' oral and written reports.'

43. **mīlitem :** collective, ' soldiery.'

44. **Hiemis :** ' From the winter,' objective genitive. *102.* But
avāritiae, ' for avarice,' is subjective. *95.*

14. 1. **Age vērō :** ' But come,' like *Age nunc,* ' Come now,' a mark
of vivid transition ; used in the singular even when the following verb, as
here, is a plural imperative. **temperantiā :** one of the four cardinal virtues.

3. **incrēdibilem cursum :** ' inconceivable (rapidity of) movement.'

4. **inventum :** sc. *esse,* ' was acquired,' ' was made possible.'

rēmigum aut ars inaudīta quaedam gubernandī aut ventī 5
aliquī novī tam celeriter in ultimās terrās pertulērunt, sed
eae rēs, quae cēterōs remorārī solent, nōn retardārunt; nōn

avāritia ab īnstitūtō
cursū ad praedam
aliquam dēvocāvit, 10
nōn libīdō ad volup-
tātem, nōn amoeni-
tās ad dēlectātiōnem,
nōn nōbilitās urbis
ad cognitiōnem, nōn 15
dēnique labor ipse ad
quiētem; postrēmō
signa et tabulās cē-
teraque ōrnāmenta
Graecōrum oppidō- 20
rum, quae cēterī tol-
lenda arbitrantur, ea
sibi ille nē vīsenda
quidem exīstimāvit.

THE TEMPLE OF APOLLO AT CORINTH

Itaque omnēs 25
nunc in eīs locīs Cn.
Pompeium sīcut aliquem nōn ex hāc urbe missum, sed dē
caelō dēlāpsum intuentur; nunc dēnique incipiunt crēdere,
fuisse hominēs Rōmānōs hāc quondam continentiā, quod

---

12. **amoenitās:** i.e. *amoenitās locōrum,* 'the charm of natural
scenery.' See *Dē Prōvinciīs Cōnsulāribus,* **12,** 7, and note, page 4.

15. **ad cognitiōnem:** 'to make its acquaintance,' 'to visit it.'

18. **signa et tabulās:** 'statues and paintings,' which Roman generals
systematically appropriated and carried off, as Mummius had done at the
sacking of Corinth.

28. **dēlāpsum:** we should say, 'sent down,' as having a divinely
appointed mission.

29. **fuisse . . . quod:** *i.e.* 'that there really were men of Rome in the

30 iam nātiōnibus exterīs incrēdibile ac falsō memoriae prōditum
vidēbātur; nunc imperī vestrī splendor illīs gentibus lūcem
afferre coepit; nunc intellegunt nōn sine causā maiōrēs
suōs tum, cum eā temperantiā magistrātūs habēbāmus, servīre populō Rōmānō quam imperāre aliīs māluisse. Iam
35 vērō ita facilēs aditūs ad eum prīvātōrum, ita līberae
querimōniae dē aliōrum iniūriīs esse dīcuntur, ut is, quī
dignitāte prīncipibus excellit, facilitāte īnfimīs pār esse
videātur.

*Remarkable also his wisdom in counsel, his power as a speaker, his
good faith, his humaneness.*

Iam quantum cōnsiliō, quantum dīcendī gravitāte et
40 cōpiā valeat, in quō ipsō inest quaedam dignitās imperātōria, vōs, Quirītēs, hōc ipsō ex locō saepe cognōvistis.

Fidem vērō eius quantam inter sociōs exīstimārī putātis,
quam hostēs omnēs omnium generum sānctissimam iūdi-
cārint?

---

olden time who possessed such self-mastery as this (which we see in
Pompey), a fact which.'

30. **falsō memoriae prōditum:** we should say, ' based upon unfounded tradition.'

32. **afferre:** see page 174, line 25.

33. **eā:** for *tantā*.

35. **aditūs ad:** in our idiom, ' audiences with.' The order in which
the remaining *artēs eximiae* are treated is somewhat different from that
given at the beginning (page 178, lines 8–9), and is as follows: *facilitās*
(lines 3–6); *ingenium* (lines 8–10); *fidēs* (lines 10–12); *hūmānitās*
(line 12, *et seq.*). **līberae:** i.e. *nōn impedītae.*

37. **pār:** ' on a level with.'

39. **quantum . . . valeat:** ' how great power he possesses.' **cōnsiliō:**
' insight.'

40. **in quō ipsō:** '(a talent) in which of itself.' **imperātōria:** ' befitting
a commander.'

41. **hōc ipsō ex locō:** put briefly for *hōc ipsō ex locō* (*i.e.* the Rostra)
verba faceret. For Cicero's estimate of Pompey's oratory, see *Brūtus*, **48,**
239.

Hūmānitāte iam tantā est, ut difficile dictū sit, utrum 45 hostēs magis virtūtem eius pugnantēs timuerint an mānsuētūdinem victī dīlēxerint. Et quisquam dubitābit, quīn huic hōc tantum bellum trānsmittendum sit, quī ad omnia nostrae memoriae bella cōnficienda dīvīnō quōdam cōnsiliō nātus esse videātur? 50

He is highly esteemed at home, and is feared by our enemies.

15. Itaque, ut plūra nōn dīcam neque aliōrum exemplīs cōnfīrmem, quantum auctōritās valeat in bellō, ab eōdem Cn. Pompeiō omnium rērum ēgregiārum exempla sūmantur; quī quō diē ā vōbīs maritimō bellō praepositus est imperātor, tanta repente vīlitās annōnae ex summā inopiā 5 et cāritāte reī frūmentāriae cōnsecūta est, ūnīus hominis spē ac nōmine, quantam vix ex summā ūbertāte agrōrum diūturna pāx efficere potuisset.

---

47. **Et:** 'Then'; *Et quisquam* introduces the conclusion of the preceding line of argument. Notwithstanding the orator's high praise, Pompey's career as a whole shows that he was a cold-blooded and extremely selfish man, with whom his own advancement was ever the ruling motive. His humaneness is praised also by Dio Cassius (**36**, 20); but the fact remains that he could be cruel, and even treacherous, when his own interests seemed to demand it.

48. **trānsmittendum:** *i.e.* from the hands of Glabrio; hence not *dēferendum*.

49. **nostrae memoriae:** i.e. *nostrī temporis; eius temporis cuius meminimus.*

15. 1. **ut plūra nōn dīcam neque:** *i.e.* ' to leave more unsaid and not to '; stronger than *nē plūra dīcam. 196, b.*

4. **quī quō diē:** *nam eō diē quō is,* ' for on the day on which he.'

5. **vīlitās annōnae:** Plutarch says (*Pompey,* 26) that ' the immediate fall in the prices of market goods (τῶν ὠνίων) caused the delighted people to remark that the very name of Pompey had ended the war.' **ex summā inopiā:** temporal, while *ex summā ūbertāte* is causal.

6. **hominis:** objective genitive with *spē* (' in such a man ') and subjective with *nōmine* (' his '). *102; 95.*

8. **potuisset:** why subjunctive? *208, b; B. 304, 3, a,* N.; A. & G. 517, *c,* N. 1; G. 597, R. 3, *b.*

Iam acceptā in Pontō calamitāte ex eō proeliō, dē quō
10 vōs paulō ante invītus admonuī, cum sociī pertimuissent,
hostium opēs animīque crēvissent, satis fīrmum praesidium
prōvincia nōn habēret, āmīsissētis Asiam, Quirītēs, nisi
ad ipsum discrīmen eius temporis dīvīnitus Cn. Pompeium
ad eās regiōnēs fortūna populī Rōmānī attulisset.   Huius

COIN OF MITHRIDATES
Obverse: Head of the King.   Reverse: Pegasus drinking.
Inscribed: King Mithridates Eupator.

15 adventus et Mithridātem, īnsolitā īnflammātum victōriā,
continuit et Tigrānem, magnīs cōpiīs minitantem Asiae,
retardāvit.

Et quisquam dubitābit, quid virtūte perfectūrus sit, quī
tantum auctōritāte perfēcerit?   aut quam facile imperiō
20 atque exercitū sociōs et vectīgālia cōnservātūrus sit, quī
ipsō nōmine ac rūmōre dēfenderit?

---

10. **invītus**: translate as if an adverb.   *151;* B. 239; A. & G. 290;
G. 325, R. 6.

13. **ad ipsum discrīmen eius temporis**: ' at the decisive moment of
that crisis.'

14. **ad**: not *in*, because Pompey did not enter the regions mentioned;
translate, ' into the vicinity of.'

18. **Et**: as on page 183, line 47.   **perfectūrus sit**: ' he is going to
accomplish'; stronger than *perficiat.   204; 201, b;* B. 269, 3; A. &
G. 575, *a,* G. 514 (*b*).

21. **rūmōre**: i.e. *eius adventūs.*

16. Age vērō illa rēs quantam dēclārat eiusdem hominis apud hostēs populī Rōmānī auctōritātem, quod ex locīs tam longinquīs tamque dīversīs tam brevī tempore omnēs huic sē ūnī dēdidērunt! quod Crētēnsium lēgātī, cum in eōrum īnsulā noster imperātor exercitusque esset, ad Cn. 5 Pompeium in ultimās prope terrās vēnērunt eīque sē omnēs Crētēnsium civitātēs dēdere velle dīxērunt!

Quid? Īdem iste Mithridātēs nōnne ad eundem Cn. Pompeium lēgātum ūsque in Hispāniam mīsit? eum, quem Pompeius lēgātum semper iūdicāvit, eī, quibus erat moles- 10 tum ad eum potissimum esse missum, speculātōrem quam lēgātum iūdicārī maluērunt.

Potestis igitur iam cōnstituere, Quirītēs, hanc auctōritātem, multīs posteā rēbus gestīs magnīsque vestrīs iūdiciīs amplificātam, quantum apud illōs rēgēs, quantum apud 15 exterās nātiōnēs valitūram esse exīstimētis.

---

16. 1. **Age vērō:** see page 180, line 1, and note.

5. **noster imperātor:** ' a commander of ours,' *i.e.* Quintus Metellus. The orator makes the most of a proceeding not at all creditable to Pompey; see note on page 176, line 48. **esset:** *185, c;* B. 309, 3; A. & G. 546; G. 585.

6. **in ultimās prope terrās:** rhetorical exaggeration; see page 176, line 48, and note.

8. **Quid:** see page 35, line 25, and note. **Mithridātēs, etc.:** Mithridates conducted negotiations with Sertorius in Spain; but of this incident nothing is known beyond what is said — or intimated — here. The construction of *eum . . . iūdicāvit* is awkward and un-Ciceronian; Eberhard bracketed the words *eum . . . Pompeius lēgātum semper iūdicāvit* as spurious, so that the sentence would read *quem eī, quibus erat molestum,* etc.

10. **quibus erat molestum:** 'who were vexed'; the reference is probably to Metellus Pius, the other commander in the war with Sertorius.

11. **potissimum:** *i.e.* rather than to anyone else. See page 167, line 7, and note.

13. **hanc auctōritātem:** why placed here rather than in the clause *quantum . . . valitūram esse?*

14. **iūdiciīs:** 'formal recognitions (of service).'

Lastly, luck has always been in Pompey's favor.

Reliquum est, ut dē fēlīcitāte, quam praestāre dē sē ipsō nēmō potest, meminisse et commemorāre dē alterō possumus, sīcut aequum est hominēs dē potestāte deōrum, 20 timidē et pauca dīcāmus.

Ego enim sīc exīstimō, Maximō, Mārcellō, Scīpiōnī, Mariō et cēterīs magnīs imperātōribus nōn sōlum propter virtūtem, sed etiam propter fortūnam saepius imperia mandāta atque exercitūs esse commissōs. Fuit enim pro-25 fectō quibusdam summīs virīs quaedam ad amplitūdinem et ad glōriam et ad rēs magnās bene gerendās dīvīnitus adiūncta fortūna.

Dē huius autem hominis fēlīcitāte, dē quō nunc agimus, hāc ūtar moderātiōne dīcendī, nōn ut in illīus potestāte 30 fortūnam positam esse dīcam, sed ut praeterita meminisse, reliqua spērāre videāmur, nē aut invīsa dīs immortālibus ōrātiō nostra aut ingrāta esse videātur.

---

17. **Reliquum est, ut:** ' It only remains to '; introduces a transition to the fourth and last consideration in the argument concerning Pompey's military character. See page 167, line 3, and note. *203 (1).* **praestāre dē:** ' guarantee for.'

18. **meminisse,** etc.: asyndeton; in our idiom, '(but which) we,' etc. *238, d.*

19. **sīcut . . . deōrum:** sc. *dīcere;* ' as men ought to speak of (that which lies within) the power of the gods.'

20. **timidē et pauca:** ' reverently and (with only) a few words.'

21. **sīc exīstimō:** ' hold this opinion.'

24. **Fuit enim profectō . . . adiūncta:** ' For there has certainly been at the side of.'

26. **ad glōriam:** i.e. *ad amplitūdinem augendam et ad glōriam adipīscendam.*

31. **videāmur:** translate, ' that we (I) may be seen.' Why? **invīsa:** ' offensive ' on account of arrogance and presumption, the manifestation of which on the part of mortal man was thought to call down the jealous vengeance and retribution of the gods. The story of Niobe illustrates this belief.

32. **ingrāta:** ' thankless,' as not recognizing in past blessings the hope and promise of future gifts.

Itaque nōn sum praedicātūrus, quantās ille rēs domī
mīlitiae, terrā marīque, quantāque fēlīcitāte gesserit;
ut eius semper voluntātibus nōn modo cīvēs assēnserint, 35
sociī obtemperārint, hostēs oboedierint, sed etiam ventī
tempestātēsque obsecundārint: hōc brevissimē dīcam,
nēminem umquam tam impudentem fuisse, quī ab dīs
immortālibus tot et tantās rēs tacitus audēret optāre, quot
et quantās dī immortālēs ad Cn. Pompeium dētulērunt. 40

Quod ut illī proprium ac perpetuum sit, Quirītēs, cum
commūnis salūtis atque imperī, tum ipsīus hominis causā,
sīcutī facitis, velle et optāre dēbētis.

ANOTHER COIN OF POMPEY

Obverse: Head of Goddess Roma with plumed helmet. Reverse:
Pompey with his foot on the prow of a ship presents a palm branch to a
barbarous tribe.

33. **nōn sum praedicātūrus:** it would be difficult to present the
good luck of Pompey more strongly than in this paragraph, where the
orator professes to refrain from treating the topic, — a fine example
of the rhetorical figure called by the ancient grammarians *praeteritiō.*
239, r.

36. **ventī tempestātēsque:** in our phrase, ' wind and weather.'

37. **hōc:** '(only) this.'

39. **tacitus:** '(even) in silence,' — the unuttered prayers of the heart.
quot et quantās: in our idiom simply ' as '; the Latin expression is
more forcible than the English. *211.*

41. **Quod . . . sit:** ' And that this (favor of fortune) may be his sure
and lasting possession.'

43. **facitis:** ' you are (actually) doing.'

*On all grounds Pompey should be chosen commander; but he has also
the advantage of being near the theater of war.*

Quā rē cum et bellum sit ita necessārium, ut neglegī nōn
45 possit, ita magnum, ut accūrātissimē sit administrandum,
et cum eī imperātōrem praeficere possītis, in quō sit eximia
bellī scientia, singulāris virtūs, clārissima auctōritās, ēgregia
fortūna, dubitātis, Quirītēs, quīn hōc tantum bonī, quod
vōbīs ab dīs immortālibus oblātum et datum est, in rem
50 pūblicam cōnservandam atque amplificandam cōnferātis?

17. Quod sī Rōmae Cn. Pompeius prīvātus esset hōc
tempore, tamen ad tantum bellum is erat dēligendus atque
mittendus; nunc, cum ad cēterās summās ūtilitātēs
haec quoque opportūnitās adiungātur, ut in eīs ipsīs locīs
5 adsit, ut habeat exercitum, ut ab eīs, quī habent, accipere
statim possit, quid exspectāmus? aut cūr nōn, ducibus
dīs immortālibus, eīdem, cui cētera summā cum salūte
reī pūblicae commissa sunt, hōc quoque bellum rēgium
committāmus?

---

44. **Quā rē:** introduces a summary of all the preceding argument
as a preparation for that which is to follow.   See note on page 40, line 25.

48. **dubitātis:** ' do you (still) hesitate '; followed by *quīn . . . cōnferātis* (' to,' etc.) instead of *cōnferre*, because the interrogation gives the
principal clause a negative force.   *201, c;* B. 298, *b;* A & G. 558;
G. 555, R. 3.   **hōc tantum bonī:** 'this great blessing,' 'this great advantage.'   *97, b.*

17. 1. **Quod sī:** *118, d;* B. 185, 2; A. & G. 397, *a;* G. 610, R. 2.
prīvātus: ' a private citizen.'

2. **is erat dēligendus:** ' he would be the one to be chosen.'   *208, b;*
B. 304, 3, *b;* A. & G. 517, *c;* G. 597, R. 3 (*a*).

3. **nunc:** see page 46, line 25, and note.

4. **haec opportūnitās:** explained by the following *ut*-clauses.

5. **quī habent:** for *quī exercitūs habent;* i.e. Lucullus, who with the
remnants of his forces was on the upper Halys (see Map) near Pontus;
Glabrio, who was lingering in the west of Asia; and Marcius Rex, who
had three legions in Cilicia.

7. **cētera summā cum salūte:** ' other (trusts) — to the highest
welfare.'   See page 60, line 26, and note.

The influence of Catulus and Hortensius should not dissuade you from sending to Asia Minor the man best fitted for the task.

22. Quā rē videant, nē sit periniquum et nōn ferendum, illōrum auctōritātem dē Cn. Pompeī dignitāte ā vōbīs comprobātam semper esse, vestrum ab illīs dē eōdem homine iūdicium populīque Rōmānī auctōritātem impro-bārī, praesertim cum iam suō iūre populus Rōmānus in 5 hōc homine suam auctōritātem vel contrā omnēs, quī dissentiunt, possit dēfendere, proptereā quod, īsdem istīs reclāmantibus, vōs ūnum illum ex omnibus dēlēgistis, quem bellō praedōnum praepōnerētis.

Hōc sī vōs temerē fēcistis et reī pūblicae parum cōn- 10 suluistis, rēctē istī studia vestra suīs cōnsiliīs regere cō-nantur; sīn autem vōs plūs tum in rē pūblicā vīdistis, vōs eīs repugnantibus per vōsmet ipsōs dignitātem huic imperiō salūtem orbī terrārum attulistis, aliquandō istī prīncipēs et sibi et cēterīs populī Rōmānī ūniversī auctōritātī pā- 15 rendum esse fateantur.

Atque in hōc bellō Asiāticō et rēgiō nōn sōlum mīlitāris

The objection is urged that all authority ought not to be vested in one person. Hortensius, you urged the same objection to the command of Pompey against the pirates. Under desperate conditions the Roman peo-ple voted against your view, and through a complete victory reëstablished its sovereignty.

Catulus urges that nothing be done contrary to precedent. But precedent has been set aside in conferring absolute military authority in the past; precedent has been disregarded in conferring military powers on Pompey himself.

22. 1. **nōn ferendum :** = *intolerābile. 212, h.*

5. **cum :** 'now that.'

12. **plūs . . . vīdistis :** 'have had a deeper insight in regard to public interests.'

14. **aliquandō :** for *tandem aliquandō.* **istī prīncipēs :** Catulus and Hortensius as leaders of the aristocracy.

17. **Atque,** etc. : application of the more general statement in chap-ters 13 and 14 to the case in hand. **Asiāticō et rēgiō :** the epithets sug-

illa virtūs, quae est in Cn. Pompeiō singulāris, sed aliae
quoque virtūtēs animī magnae et multae requīruntur.
20 Difficile est in Asiā, Ciliciā, Syriā, rēgnīsque interiōrum
nātiōnum ita versārī nostrum imperātōrem, ut nihil aliud
nisi dē hoste ac dē laude cōgitet.   Deinde, etiam sī quī sunt
pudōre ac temperantiā moderātiōrēs, tamen eōs esse tālēs
propter multitūdinem cupidōrum hominum nēmō arbitrā-
25 tur.

Difficile est dictū, Quirītēs, quantō in odiō sīmus apud
exterās nātiōnēs propter eōrum, quōs ad eās per hōs annōs
cum imperiō mīsimus, libīdinēs et iniūriās.   Quod enim
fānum putātis in illīs terrīs nostrīs magistrātibus religiō-
30 sum, quam cīvitātem sānctam, quam domum satis clausam
ac mūnītam fuisse?   Urbēs iam locuplētēs et cōpiōsae

SILVER COIN OF SYRIA[1]
Obverse: Head of Antiochus the Great, King of Syria.   Reverse: An
elephant.   Inscribed: King Antiochus.

gest the luxury of surroundings and wealth of plunder against the seduc-
tions of which few Roman officers were proof.

20. **interiōrum**: 'further inland.'

21. **nostrum imperātōrem**: 'a general of ours.'   **nihil aliud**: i.e. *dē
aliā rē*.   Kind of accusative?   *117, a.*

23. **pudōre ac temperantiā moderātiōrēs**: 'possessed of more than
ordinary conscientiousness and self-mastery.'

24. **cupidōrum**: i.e. *pecūniae;* for *avārōrum*.

28. **libīdinēs**: 'acts of lawlessness.'   Pluralizing abstract nouns
often makes them concrete.   *92, c.*

QUINTUS HORTENSIUS

requīruntur, quibus causa bellī propter dīripiendī cupiditātem īnferātur. 35

Libenter haec cōram cum Q. Catulō et Q. Hortēnsiō, summīs et clārissimīs virīs, disputārem; nōvērunt enim 40 sociōrum vulnera, vident eōrum calamitātēs, querimōniās audiunt. Prō sociīs vōs contrā hostēs exercitum mittere 45 putātis, an hostium simulātiōne contrā sociōs atque amīcōs? Quae cīvitās est in Asiā, quae nōn modo imperātōris 50 aut lēgātī, sed ūnīus tribūnī mīlitum animōs ac spīritūs capere possit?

The standing of those who oppose this measure is offset by that of the men who favor it.

23. Quod sī auctōritātibus hanc causam, Quirītēs, cōnfīrmandam putātis, est vōbīs auctor vir bellōrum omnium

32. **quibus causa bellī . . . īnferātur:** ' against which a pretext for war can be devised.'

36. **cōram:** as we say, ' between ourselves,' where we can talk over men and deeds freely.

46. **hostium simulātiōne:** ' making the enemy a pretext (merely).'

50. **nōn modo:** may be translated as if *nōn dīcam*, ' I will not say '; the following *sed* is for *sed etiam*.

51. **animōs ac spīritūs capere:** ' satisfy the arrogance and insolence.'

23. 2. **est vōbīs auctor:** ' you have as a supporter ' of the bill.

maximārumque rērum perītissimus, P. Servīlius, cuius tantae rēs gestae terrā marīque exstitērunt, ut, cum dē 5 bellō dēlīberētis, auctor vōbīs gravior esse nēmō dēbeat; est C. Cūriō, summīs vestrīs beneficiīs maximīsque rēbus gestīs, summō ingeniō et prūdentiā praeditus; est Cn. Lentulus, in quō omnēs prō amplissimīs vestrīs honōribus summum cōnsilium, summam gravitātem esse cognōvistis; 10 est C. Cassius, integritāte, virtūte, cōnstantiā singulārī.

Quā rē vidēte, ut hōrum auctōritātibus illōrum ōrātiōnī, quī dissentiunt, respondēre posse videāmur.

Stand firm, Manilius, in support of your measure; my advocacy is solely on patriotic grounds.

24. Quae cum ita sint, C. Mānīlī, prīmum istam tuam et lēgem et voluntātem et sententiam laudō vehementissimē- que comprobō; deinde tē hortor, ut, auctōre populō Rōmānō, maneās in sententiā nēve cuiusquam vim aut 5 minās pertimēscās. Prīmum in tē satis esse animī per- sevērantiaeque arbitror; deinde, cum tantam multitūdinem

---

3. **P. Servīlius :** see vocabulary under *Vatia.*

6. **Cūriō :** see vocabulary under *Cūriō.*

7. **ingeniō :** here, as often, refers particularly to oratorical talent.

8. **prō :** ' consistently with.'

9. **gravitātem :** when censor in 70 B.C. with Lucius Gellius, this Lentulus (number 3 in vocabulary) removed from the senate no fewer than sixty-four members, not far from an eighth of the whole number.

11. **ut :** here ' how,' ' whether.' *204 (3).*

24. 1. **Quae . . . sint :** here used to introduce the conclusion of the entire speech; see Companion, page 535.

2. **voluntātem et sententiam :** ' feeling and expressed opinion,' amplifying *lēgem.*

3. **auctōre populō Rōmānō :** as we should say ' backed by the Roman people,' ' with the Roman people behind you.'

4. **vim aut minās :** perhaps a hint at the unhappy experience of Gabinius the year before when he nearly lost his life.

cum tantō studiō adesse videāmus, quantam iterum nunc
in eōdem homine praeficiendō vidēmus, quid est, quod aut
dē rē aut dē perficiendī facultāte dubitēmus?

Ego autem, quicquid est in mē studī, cōnsilī, labōris, 10
ingenī, quicquid hōc beneficiō populī Rōmānī atque hāc
potestāte praetōriā, quicquid auctōritāte, fidē, cōnstantiā
possum, id omne ad hanc rem cōnficiendam tibi et populō
Rōmānō polliceor ac dēferō; testorque omnēs deōs, et eōs
maximē, quī huic locō templōque praesident, quī omnium 15
mentēs eōrum, quī ad rem pūblicam adeunt, maximē per-
spiciunt, mē hōc neque rogātū facere cuiusquam, neque
quō Cn. Pompeī gratiam mihi per hanc causam conciliārī
putem, neque quō mihi ex cuiusquam amplitūdine aut
praesidia perīculīs aut adiūmenta honōribus quaeram, 20
proptereā quod perīcula facile, ut hominem praestāre
oportet, innocentiā tēctī repellēmus, honōrem autem neque
ab ūnō neque ex hōc locō, sed cādcm illā nostrā labōriō-
sissimā ratiōne vītae, sī vestra voluntās feret. cōn-
sequēmur.   25

---

7. **studiō**: 'enthusiasm.' **iterum nunc**: counting the passing of
Gabinius's bill as the first time.

8. **quid est, quod**: 'what reason is there, that.' *194, a.*

9. **dē rē**: i.e. *dē praeficiendō Pompeiō.*

10. **quicquid**: see vocabulary.

11. **hōc beneficiō**: 'by reason of this preferment,' the honor of the
praetorship, as explained and amplified by the following clause.

15. **huic locō templōque**: 'this place and consecrated spot.' The
original idea of *templum* was a place set aside for worship; after that
either a place or a building that had been consecrated by certain religious acts. The Rostra belonged to the latter category.

18. **quō**: = *quia*, 'because.' *183, b, c.*

19. **quō**: = *ut eō*, 'in order that by this means.'

23. **ab ūnō**: for *ab* ('at the hands of') *ūnō homine*, referring to
Pompey.

24. **ratiōne**: 'calling,' 'profession,' of advocate.

Citizens, I have sought only to serve the public interest.

Quam ob rem, quicquid in hāc causā mihi susceptum est, Quirītēs, id ego omne mē reī pūblicae causā suscēpisse cōnfīrmō, tantumque abest, ut aliquam mihi bonam grātiam quaesīsse videar, ut multās mē etiam simultātēs 30 partim obscūrās, partim apertās intellegam, mihi nōn necessāriās, vōbīs nōn inūtilēs suscēpisse. Sed ego mē hōc honōre praeditum, tantīs vestrīs beneficiīs affectum statuī, Quirītēs, vestram voluntātem et reī pūblicae dignitātem et salūtem prōvinciārum atque sociōrum meīs omni-35 bus commodīs et ratiōnibus praeferre oportēre.

---

26. **mihi :** translate as if *ā mē;* see note to page 45, line 10.

28. **tantum, etc.:** see vocabulary under *absum. 197, d;* B. 284, **1;** A. & G. 571, *b;* G. 552, R. 1; 2. Compare note, page 100, line 10.

31. **nōn inūtilēs :** litotes. *239, m.*

32. **beneficiīs :** praetorship, curule aedileship, quaestorship.

35. **ratiōnibus :** 'interests.'

M. TULLĪ CICERŌNIS
ĀCTIŌNIS IN C. VERREM SECUNDAE
LIBRĪ IV CAPITA LII–LX

DĪREPTIŌ SYRĀCŪSĀRUM

For Sight Translation

Marcellus captured Syracuse in war and treated it as if in peace. Verres governed Syracuse in peace as if he had captured it in war.

52. Ūnīus etiam urbis omnium pulcherrimae atque ōrnā-tissimae, Syrācūsārum, dīreptiōnem commemorābō et in medium prōferam, iūdicēs, ut aliquandō tōtam huius generis ōrātiōnem conclūdam atque dēfīniam. 5

Nēmō ferē vestrum est quīn, quem ad modum captae sint ā

To the Student: The necessary background for this oration is to be found in the Companion, page 535, *et seq.*

Title: ĀCTIŌNIS SECUNDAE: 'of the Second Argument.'

VERREM (ve'rēz).

Syrācūsārum: 'Syracuse.'

52. 1. **omnium:** sc. *urbium*, partitive genitive. *97, a.*

2. **in medium prōferam:** 'I shall plainly set forth.' How literally?

3. **iūdicēs:** twelve or more. **aliquandō:** 'at length.' **huius generis ōrātiōnem:** '(my) discussion of this charge,' that Verres systematically robbed Sicilian cities of their works of art.

4. **conclūdam:** 'close up,' 'end,' 'conclude.'

6. **quīn:** translate as if *quī nōn,* 'who has not heard.' *195.*

M. Mārcellō Syrācūsae, saepe audierit, nōn numquam
etiam in annālibus lēgerit. Cōnferte hanc pācem cum illō
10 bellō, huius praetōris adventum cum illīus imperātōris victōriā, huius cohortem impūram cum illīus exercitū invictō,
huius libīdinēs cum illīus continentiā : ab illō, quī cēpit,
conditās, ab hōc, quī cōnstitūtās accēpit, captās dīcētis
Syrācūsās.

15 Ac iam illa omittō, quae dispersē ā mē multīs in locīs
dīcentur ac dicta sunt : forum Syrācūsānōrum, quod
introitū Mārcellī pūrum ā caede servātum esset, id adventū
Verris Siculōrum innocentium sanguine redundāsse ; portum Syrācūsānōrum, quī tum et nostrīs classibus et Kar-
20 thāginiēnsium clausus fuisset, eum, istō praetōre, Cilicum
myoparōnī praedōnibusque patuisse ; mittō adhibitam

---

8. **M. Mārcellō** : Marcus Claudius Marcellus was the most famous
of the Marcelli. After his death his victories in Sicily, which culminated
in the capture of Syracuse in 212 B.C., were commemorated on coins
struck by members of the family connected with the Roman mint. See
illustrations, page 195. **nōn numquam** : ' sometimes.'

9. **annālibus**: sc. *librīs;* ' annals,' records of events year by year.
To what works Cicero here refers is not known. **hanc pācem** : ' this
(condition of) peace,' under Verres.

10. **praetōris** : Verres governed Sicily as propraetor.

11. **cohortem impūram** : ' licentious retinue.'

13. **conditās, captās** : sc. *esse ;* ' that Syracuse was founded by the
man who captured it,' etc. **cōnstitūtās** : i.e. *bene cōnstitūtās.*

15. **dispersē** : ' here and there.' **locīs** : ' passages,' in the fifth book
of the Second Argument.

16. **Syrācūsānōrum** : ' people of Syracuse,' ' Syracusans.'

17. **introitū** : ' an entering,' ' entrance.' **pūrum** : ' clean,' ' free from.'

18. **Siculōrum** : ' inhabitants of Sicily,' ' Sicilians.' **portum** : the
Great Harbor.

20. **clausus fuisset** : Marcellus had blockaded Syracuse both by
land and by sea. **eum** : i.e. *portum;* emphatic. **istō** : ' when that (marauder).' **Cilicum** : ' Cilicians '; inhabitants of Cilicia, a province in
southeastern Asia Minor, notorious for its pirates.

21. **myoparōnī** : ' light vessel.' The Cilician pirates used light,
swift galleys, and were the terror of the Mediterranean. That a

vim ingenuīs, mātrēs familiās violātās, quae tum in urbe
captā commissa nōn sunt neque odiō hostīlī neque licentiā
mīlitārī neque mōre bellī neque iūre victōriae; mittō,
inquam, haec omnia, quae ab istō per triennium perfecta 25
sunt; ea, quae coniūncta cum illīs rēbus sunt, dē quibus
anteā dīxī, cognōscite.

Syracuse, the largest and most beautiful of Greek cities; its four divisions.

Urbem Syrācūsās maximam esse Graecārum, pulcher-
rimam omnium saepe audīstis. Est, iūdicēs, ita ut dīcitur.
Nam et situ est cum mūnītō tum ex omnī aditū, vel terrā 30
vel marī, praeclārō ad aspectum, et portūs habet prope in
aedificātiōne amplexūque urbis inclūsōs; quī cum dīversōs
inter sē aditūs habeant, in exitū coniunguntur et cōnfluunt.
Eōrum coniūnctiōne pars oppidī, quae appellātur Īnsula,

---

pirate ship should have been permitted to enter and leave the harbor
unmolested was a serious charge. The circumstance is more fully related in Book 5, chapter 37. **mittō:** repeats the thought of *omittō* in
line 15; 'I pass over the fact that.'

22. **ingenuīs:** 'the freeborn'; in Cicero's time slaves, and even freedmen, might expect harsh treatment. The Roman slave system necessarily
reacted badly upon the slave-owning class itself. **quae:** '(atrocities) which.'

23. **odiō:** ablative of cause. *135, a.* **licentiā:** 'license,' 'insolence.'

25. **triennium:** 'period of three years,' 73–71 B.C.

26. **ea:** '(only) the depredations.'

28. **Graecārum, omnium:** sc. *urbium.*

30. **situ est:** ablative of quality with *mūnītō* and *praeclārō;* 'it has
a location.' *143, a.*

31. **portūs:** the Great Harbor and the Small Harbor.

32. **aedificātiōne:** 'building'; here 'building area.' **amplexū:**
'embrace'; here 'confines,' 'limits.'

33. **aditūs:** on the side of the sea. It seems that in Cicero's time the
entrance of the Small Harbor was narrower; the waves have washed
away part of the shore. **exitū:** at the inner end of each harbor; the
channel connecting the two harbors separated the Island from the mainland. **cōnfluunt:** 'flow together.'

34. **Īnsula:** translation of the Greek word (Νᾶσος, Doric for Νῆσος),
meaning 'Island.'

35 marī disiūncta angustō, ponte rūrsus adiungitur et continētur.

53. Ea tanta est urbs, ut ex quattuor urbibus maximīs cōnstāre dīcātur. Quārum ūna est ea, quam dīxī, Īnsula, quae duōbus portubus cīncta, in utrīusque portūs ōstium aditumque prōiecta est;
5 in quā domus est, quae Hierōnis rēgis fuit, quā praetōrēs ūtī solent. In eā sunt aedēs sacrae complūrēs, sed duae quae
10 longē cēterīs antecellant : Diānae, et altera, quae fuit ante istīus adventum ōrnātissima,   Minervae.

THE SPRING OF ARETHUSA

The plants in the spring are papyrus, from which paper used to be made. They were probably introduced from Egypt by Hiero II, mentioned in line 6.

35. marī : ' (arm of) the sea.' angustō: 'narrow.' ponte : no bridge is now needed; part of the channel connecting the harbors has been filled in, so that the island is joined with the mainland by an isthmus.

53. 2. Quārum : 'Of these.'
4. prōiecta est : ' has been thrown forward.'   A glance at the Map will make the meaning plain.

5. in quā : ' and in it.'

6. Hierōnis (hī'e̱-rō) : the second ruler of that name ; tyrant of Syracuse 270–216 B.C.

8. sacrae : ' sacred.'

11. Diānae (dī-ā'na̱) : the goddess Diana was identified with the Greek Artemis. The location of this temple is uncertain.

12. istīus : refers to Verres.

13. Minervae (mi̱-ner'va̱) : goddess of wisdom and the arts, identified with the Greek Athene. Her temple was on the highest point of the island, where the Cathedral now stands ; massive stone columns

In hāc īnsulā extrēmā est fōns aquae dulcis, cui nōmen
Arethūsa est, incrēdibilī magnitūdine, plēnissimus piscium, 15
quī fluctū tōtus operīrētur, nisi mūnītiōne ac mōle lapidum
dīiūnctus esset ā marī.

Altera autem est urbs Syrācūsīs, cui nōmen Achradīna
est; in quā forum maximum, pulcherrimae porticūs, ōrnā-

ACHRADINA

This view looks across the lower part of that quarter toward the sea. In the
foreground is one of the large quarries for which Syracuse is famed.

of an ancient temple more than 180 feet in length are built into the
walls of the Cathedral.

14. **In . . . extrēmā:** 'At the end of the Island.'

15. **Arethūsa** (ar-ẹ-thū′sạ) : see illustration, page 198. **piscium:** ' fish.'
The spring of Arethusa is still well stocked with fish.

16. **fluctū:** 'wave'; here 'sea-water.' **operīrētur:** ' cover over,'
'overwhelm.' **mūnītiōne:** 'a fortifying,' 'rampart.' **lapidum:** 'stone.'

17. **dīiūnctus esset:** ' it had been separated.'

18. **Achradīna** (ak-rạ-dī′nạ) : see Map, and illustration above.

19. **porticūs:** ' colonnade,' a walk covered by a roof which is sup-

20 tissimum prytanēum, amplissima est cūria templumque
ēgregium Iovis Olympiī cēteraeque urbis partēs, quae, ūnā
viā lātā perpetuā multīsque trānsversīs dīvīsae, prīvātīs
aedificiīs continentur.

Tertia est urbs, quae, quod in eā parte Fortūnae fānum
25 antīquum fuit, Tycha nōmināta est, in quā gymnasium
amplissimum est et complūrēs aedēs sacrae; coliturque
ea pars et habitātur frequentissimē.   Quārta autem est,
quae, quia postrēma coaedificāta est, Neāpolis nōminātur;
quam ad summam theātrum maximum, praetereā duo
30 templa sunt ēgregia, Cereris ūnum, alterum Līberae; sig-

---

ported by a row of columns on one side and a wall on the other, or by
two parallel rows of columns.

20. **prytanēum:** 'city hall.'   **cūria:** 'senate-house.'   See illustration, page 69.

21. **Olympiī:** 'Olympian,' 'of Olympia,' where there was a great
temple of Zeus (Latin Iuppiter) containing a famous statue of the god
by Phidias.   The statue of the god in the temple at Syracuse probably
resembled that at Olympia.

22. **lātā:** 'broad.'   **perpetuā:** 'continuous.'   **trānsversīs:** 'cross-
wise,' 'by cross streets.'

23. **continentur:** 'are taken up with.'

25. **Tycha** (tī′ka): see Map.   **gymnasium:** 'gymnasium.'   In Greek
cities the gymnasium included an athletic field with a running track
and facilities for outdoor sports as well as buildings for various purposes.

27. **frequentissimē:** 'frequently,' 'in great numbers'; here 'most
thickly.'   **Quārta:** sc. *urbs.*

28. **coaedificāta est:** 'built up.'   **Neāpolis** (nē-a′pọ-lis): the name
of this "new" quarter of Syracuse was the same as that of the ancient
city in Italy which is now called Naples.

29. **quam ad summam:** sc. *urbem;* 'in the highest part of this city.'
theātrum: 'theater.'   This was hewn in the solid rock, and without a
roof.

30. **Cereris** (sē′rēz): goddess of grain, identified with the Greek
Demē′ter.   **Līberae** (lib′ẹ-ra): goddess of the vine, sometimes identified
with the Greek Perseph′one (Latin Proser′pina), the daughter of
Demeter.

numque Apollinis, quī Temenītēs vocātur, pulcherrimum
et maximum; quod iste sī portāre potuisset, nōn dubitāsset
auferre.

*Marcellus thought it inconsistent with the glory of the Roman people to
plunder and destroy.*

54. Nunc ad Mārcellum revertar, nē haec ā mē sine
causā commemorāta esse videantur. Quī cum tam praeclāram urbem vī cōpiīsque cēpisset, nōn putāvit ad laudem
populī Rōmānī hōc pertinēre, hanc pulchritūdinem, ex quā
praesertim perīculī nihil ostenderētur, dēlēre et exstinguere. 5
Itaque aedificiīs omnibus, pūblicīs prīvātīs, sacrīs profānīs,
sīc pepercit, quasi ad ea dēfendenda cum exercitū, nōn

COIN OF THE REPUBLIC

Obverse: Honor with a wreath, and Valor with a helmet. Reverse: Italy
with a horn of plenty, and Rome with her foot on the globe.

31. **Apollinis** (a-pol'ō): worshiped by both Greeks and Romans.
Temenītēs: adjective, ' of the sacred precinct '; the shrine and statue
of Apollo stood in an inclosed area consecrated to him.

32. **quod**: translate as if *et id*. **portāre**: ' carry.'

54. 2. **Quī cum**: translate as if *Cum is*. *167.*

3. **vī . . . cēpisset**: Companion, page 539. **nōn . . . pertinēre**: ' he
thought that it would not contribute,' etc.

4. **pulchritūdinem**: ' beauty '; here abstract for concrete, where
we should say ' this beautiful city.' *92, b.* **ex quā praesertim**: translate as if *praesertim cum ex eā*.

6. **profānīs**: (' before the shrine,' *i.e.* outside it), ' not sacred,'
' profane.'

oppugnanda vēnisset. In ōrnātū urbis habuit victōriae ratiōnem, habuit hūmānitātis; victōriae putābat esse 10 multa Rōmam dēportāre, quae ōrnāmentō urbī esse possent, hūmānitātis nōn plānē exspoliāre urbem, praesertim quam cōnservāre voluisset.

In hāc partītiōne ōrnātūs nōn plūs victōria Mārcellī populō Rōmānō appetīvit quam hūmānitās Syrācūsānīs 15 reservāvit. Rōmam quae apportāta sunt, ad aedem Honōris et Virtūtis itemque aliīs in locīs vidēmus. Nihil in aedibus, nihil in hortīs posuit, nihil in suburbānō; putāvit, sī urbis ōrnāmenta domum suam nōn contulisset, domum suam ōrnāmentō urbī futūram. Syrācūsīs autem 20 permulta atque ēgregia relīquit; deum vērō nūllum violāvit, nūllum attigit.

---

8. **In**: ' In (regard to).' **ōrnātū**: ' adornment '; here abstract for concrete, ' the ornaments,' such as works of art in public places and buildings. *92, b.*

9. **ratiōnem**: ' consideration '; Marcellus recognized the claims not only of victory but also of humanity.

11. **hūmānitātis**: *putābat esse hūmānitātis*. **exspoliāre**: ' despoil.'

13. **partītiōne**: ' division.' **victōria, hūmānitās**: personified. We might express the idea differently: ' Marcellus as a conqueror,' ' as a humane man.'

15. **apportāta sunt**: ' carry to.' **ad**: ' near.'

16. **Honōris et Virtūtis**: a temple to Honor had been built in the southern part of Rome in 234 B.C. Marcellus had made a vow to Honor and Valor at the battle of Clastidium, in Cisalpine Gaul, in 222 B.C.; he was victorious, and, in fulfillment of his vow, in 208 B.C. he restored the temple of Honor already standing and joined with it a shrine for the worship of Valor. **Nihil**: ' None (of the spoil).'

17. **aedibus**: ' (his) house' in Rome. **hortīs**: ' garden,' ' pleasure garden.' **suburbānō**: ' suburban estate.'

19. **domum . . . futūram**: Romans of Cicero's time and later were wont to emphasize the virtues of simplicity and frugality in the life of public men of earlier generations.

20. **violāvit**: *i.e.* by carrying off the god's statue; but see Companion, page 540. Compare page 204, line 16, note.

Verres looted even the temple of Minerva.

Cōnferte Verrem, nōn ut hominem cum homine com-
parētis, nē qua tālī virō mortuō fīat iniūria, sed ut pācem
cum bellō, lēgēs cum vī, forum et iūris dictiōnem cum
ferrō et armīs, adventum et 25
comitātum cum exercitū et
victōriā cōnferātis.

MINERVA
A statue in the National Museum at
Naples.

55. Aedis Minervae est
in Īnsulā, dē quā ante dīxī;
quam Mārcellus nōn attigit,
quam plēnam atque ōrnātam
relīquit; quae ab istō sīc 5
spoliāta atque dīrepta est,
nōn ut ab hoste aliquō, quī
tamen in bellō religiōnem et
cōnsuētūdinis iūra retinēret,
sed ut ā barbarīs praedōnibus 10
vexāta esse videātur. Pugna
erat equestris Agathoclī rēgis

---

23. **tālī virō mortuō :** Marcellus; the thought is, ' to so upright a
man even after death.' **pācem cum bellō :** *pācem quam Syrācūsānī,
Verre praetōre, habērent, cum bellō, Mārcellō victōre.*

24. **forum :** as the place where the propraetor conducted trials, ' tribunal.' **dictiōnem :** ' speaking,' ' delivery '; *iūris dictiō*, ' the administration of justice.'

25. **adventum et comitātum :** more disastrous than the hostile entry
of the victorious army of Marcellus.

55. 1. **Aedis Minervae :** see note on chapter 53, line 13.

2. **dīxī :** see chapter 53, line 3.

8. **tamen :** i.e. *quamvīs hostis erat, tamen.* **religiōnem :** ' religious
scruple.'

11. **Pugna,** etc.: paintings on wood adorned the walls of temples,
and were hung also on walls in houses.

12. **Agathoclī** (ạ-gath′ọ-clēz): tyrant of Syracuse 317 to 289 B.C.
He waged war with Carthage and brought the other Greek cities of
Sicily under his rule.

in tabulīs picta ; hīs autem tabulīs interiōrēs templī parietēs
vestiēbantur.　Nihil erat eā pictūrā nōbilius, nihil Syrācūsīs
15 quod magis vīsendum putārētur.　Hās tabulās M. Mārcellus cum omnia victōriā illā suā profāna fēcisset, tamen,
religiōne impedītus, nōn attigit ; iste, cum illa iam propter
diūturnam pācem fidēlitātemque populī Syrācūsānī sacra
religiōsaque accēpisset, omnēs eās tabulās abstulit ; parietēs,
20 quōrum ōrnātūs tot saecula mānserant, tot bella effūgerant,
nūdōs āc dēformātōs relīquit.

*Marcellus paid his vows to the gods ; Verres turned to base use his thefts
from the temple of Minerva.*

Et Mārcellus, quī, sī Syrācūsās cēpisset, duo templa
sē Rōmae dēdicātūrum vōverat, is id, quod erat aedifi-

13.　**picta** : ' painted.'　**hīs tabulīs** : the painting may have contained
a large number of figures of men and of horses, and may for that reason have been extended over a series of panels on the walls of the principal room of the temple (*cella*), where the statue of Minerva (Athena)
was.　It was very probably painted in fulfillment of a vow made to
the goddess by Agathocles at some critical time.　For Agathocles lived
an even more restless and turbulent life than most tyrants ; and at
the time of his death, though he was more than seventy years old, it is
said that he was planning another attack upon Carthage.

14.　**vestiēbantur** : ' clothed,' ' covered.'　**pictūrā** : ' painting.'

15.　**magis vīsendum** : ' more worth going to see,' on the part of tour-
ists and visitors.

16.　**cum** : ' although.'　**suā** : ' of his,' *i.e.* won by him.　**profāna
fēcisset** : the Romans thought that by the use of certain invocations —
parts of which have been preserved — they could induce the tutelary
gods of a captured city to abandon it ; in this way they could secularize
places of worship so as not to incur the anger of the gods if they should
wish to remove anything that had been consecrated.

19.　**religiōsa** : ' worthy of reverence.'

20.　**ōrnātūs** : see chapter 54, line 8, and note.

21.　**dēformātōs** : ' defaced.'

22.　**duo templa** : of Honor and of Valor.

23.　**Rōmae** : locative.　*146.* **vōverat** : ' vow.'　Marcellus may have
repeated the vow which he had made at the battle of Clastidium (note to

 catūrus, eīs rēbus ōrnāre, quās cēperat, nōluit; Verrēs, quī
nōn Honōrī neque Virtūtī, quem ad modum ille, sed Venerī 25
et Cupīdinī vōta dēbēret, is Minervae templum spoliāre

VENUS

A statue in the Vatican said to
be by Praxiteles.

cōnātus est. Ille deōs deōrum
spoliīs ōrnārī nōluit; hīc ōrnāmenta Minervae virginis in
meretrīciam domum trānstulit. 30
Vīgintī et septem praetereā
tabulās, pulcherrimē pictās, ex
eādem aede sustulit; in quibus
erant imāginēs Siciliae rēgum
ac tyrannōrum, quae nōn sōlum 35
pictōrum artificiō dēlectābant,
sed etiam commemorātiōne
hominum et cognitiōne formārum. Ac vidēte, quantō taetrior
hīc tyrannus Syrācūsānus fuerit 40
quam quisquam superiōrum;

cum illī tamen ōrnārint templa deōrum immortālium, hīc
etiam illōrum monumenta atque ōrnāmenta sustulerit.

---

chapter 54, line 15), or Cicero may have transferred it to the siege of
Syracuse.

25. **Venerī:** (vē′nǔs), goddess of love.

26. **Cupīdinī:** Cupid, god of love, son of Venus. **dēbēret:** subjunctive of characteristic, in bitter sarcasm; excessive attentions to
women on the part of Verres are hinted.

30. **meretrīciam:** ' of a courtesan.'

32. **pulcherrimē:** ' beautifully.'

33. **aede:** of Minerva.

34. **imāginēs:** ' portraits.'

36. **pictōrum:** ' painter.' **artificiō:** ' skill.'

38. **formārum:** ' form,' ' appearance.'

40. **hīc tyrannus:** the Roman governor is put in a class with the
Greek tyrants.

42. **cum:** ' since.' **illī:** refers to *superiōrum*.

43. **sustulerit:** what verb controls its sequence?

Verres stole the gold and ivory ornaments from the temple doors.

56. Iam vērō quid ego dē valvīs illīus templī commemorem? Vereor nē, haec quī nōn vīderint, omnia mē
nimis augēre atque ōrnāre arbitrentur; quod tamen nēmō
suspicārī dēbet, tam esse mē cupidum, ut tot virōs prīmāriōs
5 velim, praesertim ex iūdicum numerō, quī Syrācūsīs fuerint,
quī haec vīderint, esse temeritātī et mendāciō meō cōnsciōs.
Cōnfīrmāre hōc liquidō, iūdicēs, possum, valvās magnificentiōrēs, ex aurō atque ebore perfectiōrēs, nūllās umquam
ūllō in templō fuisse.

10   Incrēdibile dictū est quam multī Graecī dē hārum val-
vārum pulchritūdine scrīptum relīquerint. Nimium forsitan haec illī mīrentur atque efferant. Estō; vērum
tamen honestius est reī pūblicae nostrae, iūdicēs, ea, quae
illīs pulchra esse videantur, imperātōrem nostrum in bellō
15 relīquisse, quam praetōrem in pāce abstulisse. Ex ebore
dīligentissimē perfecta argūmenta erant in valvīs; ea

---

56. 1. **valvīs:** 'doors,' always referring to a double door; each of
the two leaves was called *valva*.

3. **augēre atque ōrnāre:** 'exaggerate and embellish.'   **quod:** 'in
regard to this.'

4. **cupidum:** 'carried away by (my) eagerness.'   **prīmāriōs:** 'of
first rank,' ' of the highest standing.'

6. **mendāciō:** 'lying,' 'falsehood.'   **cōnsciōs:** literally, 'knowing
with' another; 'cognizant of,' with dative.

7. **liquidō:** 'clearly,' 'certainly.'   **magnificentiōrēs:** 'more splendid.'

8. **ebore:** 'ivory.'   The ivory carvings were fastened to the surface
of the panels of the doors.

11. **pulchritūdine:** see note to chapter 54, line 4.   **scrīptum:** 'something written,' in books of travel, and guide books, of which there
were many in the Roman period.

12. **illī:** the Greeks, who were more devoted to art than the matter-
of-fact Romans.   **mīrentur:** *180, e (1)*.   **vērum:** adverb.

13. **honestius est:** 'it is more honorable.'

16. **argūmenta:** here 'subjects' of the designs that 'had been
wrought.'

dētrahenda cūrāvit omnia. Gorgonis ōs pulcherrimum, cīnctum anguibus, revellit atque abstulit, et tamen indicāvit sē nōn sōlum artificiō, sed etiam pretiō quaestūque dūcī; nam 20 bullās aureās omnēs ex eīs valvīs, quae erant multae et gravēs, nōn dubitāvit auferre; quārum iste nōn opere dēlectābātur, sed pondere. Itaque eius modī 25 valvās relīquit, ut quae ōlim ad ōrnandum templum erant maximē, nunc tantum ad claudendum factae esse videantur.

Etiamne grāmineās hastās — 30 vīdī enim vōs in hōc nōmine, cum testis dīceret, commovērī, quod erat eius modī, ut semel

GORGON

A statue by Bernini in the Palace of the Conservatori at Rome.

17. **Gorgonis:** Gorgon, one of the three daughters of Phorcus. The Gorgon referred to here was Medusa. It was said that her hair consisted of snakes, and whatever she looked upon was turned to stone. She was slain by Perseus.

18. **anguibus:** 'snakes.' **revellit:** 'pull off.' The Gorgon's head must have projected from the surface of the door in high relief, or as a knob.

19. **artificiō:** 'by the artistic quality'; see note to chapter 55, line 36.

21. **bullās:** 'stud,' 'boss,' a rounded ornament, such as were fastened in rows on heavy doors as if to cover the ends of large nails. **aureās:** 'of gold.'

22. **quae:** the antecedent is *bullās*.

24. **opere:** 'workmanship.'

25. **pondere:** 'weight.' **eius modī:** 'in such a condition'; literally, 'of that character.'

30. **grāmineās** 'of grass.' The 'poles of grass' were probably sections of bamboo which were much larger than those ordinarily seen. They may have been brought by some traveler from the East, where some species of bamboo grow to the height of trees; they were probably exhibited in the temple either as a votive offering or as a curiosity.

31. **in hōc nōmine:** 'in regard to this item.'

vīdisse satis esset (in quibus neque manū factum quicquam
35 neque pulchritūdō erat ūlla, sed tantum magnitūdō incrēdibilis, dē quā vel audīre satis esset, nimium vidēre
plūs quam semel) — etiam id concupīstī?

He carried off the statue of Sappho that stood in the city hall.

57. Nam Sapphō, quae sublāta dē prytanēō est, dat
tibi iūstam excūsātiōnem, prope ut concēdendum atque
ignōscendum esse videātur. Silaniōnis opus tam perfectum
tam ēlegāns, tam ēlabōrātum quisquam nōn modo prīvātus,
5 sed populus potius habēret quam homō ēlegantissimus atque
ērudītissimus, Verrēs?

Nīmīrum contrā dīcī nihil potest. Nostrum enim ūnus
quisque (quī tam beātī quam iste est nōn sumus, tam
dēlicātī esse nōn possumus) sī quandō aliquid istīus modī
10 vidēre volet, eat ad aedem Fēlīcitātis, ad monumentum

---

34. **vīdisse:** sc. *id.* **quibus:** *in eīs,* i.e. *grāmineīs hastīs.*

36. **nimium:** sc. *esset.*

37. **etiam id:** ' even that (stuff).' **concupīstī:** contraction for
concupīvistī; written as if addressing Verres.

57. 1. **Nam:** (You would not expect him to carry off mere curios)
' for ' he manifested exquisite taste in stealing the Sappho; sarcastic.
Sapphō (saf′o): a famous Greek poetess, who was born on the island
of Mytilene (mit-i-lē′nē) and flourished at the end of the seventh century
B.C.; here ' the Sappho,' referring to a bronze statue (illustration, page
209). **sublāta est:** from *tollō.* **prytanēō:** see note to chapter 53, line 20.

2. **tibi:** as if Verres were present. **concēdendum atque ignōscendum:** ' that allowance ought to be made and pardon granted.'

3. **Silaniōnis** (sị-lā′nị-ō): a noted Greek sculptor, who lived in the
fourth century B.C. **opus:** object of *habēret,* referring to the statue of
Sappho.

4. **ēlegāns:** ' refined.' **ēlabōrātum:** of a work of art, ' finished.'

5. **potius:** ' more deservedly.' **habēret:** deliberative subjunctive.
179, b (2). The question is ironical.

9. **dēlicātī:** ' fastidious '; sc. *quam iste.*

10. **aedem Fēlīcitātis:** this ' Temple of Good Fortune ' was built in
Rome near the Tiber by Lucius Licinius Lucullus, about 150 B.C.;

Catulī, in porticum Metellī; det operam ut admittātur in alicuius istōrum Tusculānum; spectet forum ōrnātum, sī quid iste suōrum aedīlibus commodārit: Verrēs haec habeat domī, Verrēs ōrnāmen⁺ōrum fānōrum atque oppidōrum habeat plēnam domum, vīllās refertās.

15

in front of it stood statues brought from Greece by Mummius, the destroyer of Corinth.

11. **Catulī** (kat'ū-lǔs): Quintus Lutatius Catulus, the conqueror of the Cimbrians. At the decisive battle of Vercellae in Cisalpine Gaul in 101 B.C., Catulus vowed a temple to Fortūna Huiusce Diēī,

SAPPHO

A bust in the National Museum at Naples.

'Fortune (as goddess) of This Day' The temple was built and adorned with statuary; it is here referred to as a 'memorial,' *monumentum*. **porticum:** see note to chapter 53, line 19. **Metellī** (mē-tel'ǔs): Quintus Caecilius Metellus, called Macedonicus on account of his victories in Macedonia. In 147 B.C. he erected two temples in the Campus Martius, one dedicated to Jupiter, the other to Juno. He surrounded the temples with a colonnade, and in front of them, within the colonnade, he placed Greek statues. **det operam:** 'let him make the effort'; it was not easy for one not of their class to gain admission to the villas or town mansions of the aristocracy.

12. **istōrum:** 'of those men,' associated with Verres. **Tusculānum:** 'Tusculan villa.' The town of Tusculum was picturesquely situated on a slope of the Alban Mountains, seventeen miles southeast of Rome. In the vicinity were country houses of wealthy Romans; one of them was owned by Hortensius, Verres' lawyer, who is probably referred to here. See illustration facing page 396. **ōrnātum:** 'in festal array.'

13. **quid suōrum:** 'any of his' art treasures, loaned for a special occasion. **Verrēs . . . refertās:** in contrast with the great Romans of the past, who lived in modest homes but adorned the city with works of art brought from Greek lands.

Etiamne huius operāriī studia ac dēliciās, iūdicēs, per-
ferētis? quī ita nātus, ita ēducātus est, ita factus et animō
et corpore, ut multō appositior ad ferenda quam ad auferenda signa esse videātur. Atque haec Sapphō sublāta
20 quantum dēsīderium suī relīquerit, dīcī vix potest. Nam
cum ipsa fuit ēgregiē facta, tum epigramma Graecum
pernōbile incīsum est in basī; quod iste ērudītus homō et
Graeculus, quī haec subtīliter iūdicat, quī sōlus intellegit,
sī ūnam litteram Graecam scīsset, certē nōn sustulisset.
25 Nunc enim, quod scrīptum est inānī in basī, dēclārat quid
fuerit, et id ablātum indicat.

He carried off statues of gods, even the most sacred image of Jupiter.

Quid? signum Paeānis ex aede Aesculāpī praeclārē
factum, sacrum ac religiōsum, nōn sustulistī? quod omnēs
propter pulchritūdinem vīsere, propter religiōnem colere
30 solēbant. Quid? ex aede Līberī simulācrum Aristaeī nōn
tuō imperiō palam ablātum est?

16. **operāriī:** 'day-laborer'; contemptuous reference to Verres as
a man lacking in cultivated taste. **studia ac dēliciās:** ironical, 'hob-
bies and exquisite pleasures.'

18. **appositior:** 'better adapted,' 'better fitted.' **ferenda, auferenda:**
pun, suggested by Verres' coarse and heavy build; 'to carry' on his back
as a porter, 'to carry away' as a lover of art who had fallen under the
spell of a masterpiece.

21. **ēgregiē:** 'finely.'

22. **pernōbile:** 'very famous.' Such inscriptions on pedestals were
frequently in verse, and were sometimes copied and incorporated in
literary works. **basī:** 'pedestal,' 'base.' **quod:** 'in regard to that.'

23. **Graeculus:** contemptuous, 'Greekling.' **subtīliter:** 'acutely.'

24. **sustulisset:** from *tollō;* sc. *eam statuam.*

25. **quod:** sc. *id* as subject of *dēclārat, indicat.*

27. **Paeānis:** 'Apollo' as god of healing; because he was so considered, a statue of Apollo was placed in the temple of Aesculapius.
Aesculāpī (es-ku̯-lā′pi̯-us̱): son of Apollo and god of medicine.

28. **sacrum:** see note to chapter 53, line 8.

29. **pulchritūdinem:** see note to chapter 54, line 4.

30. **Līberī** (lī′ber): an ancient Italian divinity, identified with

Quid? ex aede Iovis religiōsissimum simulācrum Iovis
Imperātōris, quem Graecī Ūrion nōminant, pulcherrimē
factum, nōnne abstulistī?   Quid? ex aede Līberae, aprī- 35
num caput illud pulcherrimum, quod vīsere solēbāmus, num
dubitāstī tollere?   Atque ille Paeān sacrificiīs anniversāriīs

AESCULAPIUS
A statue in the Capitoline Museum.

simul cum Aesculāpiō apud
illōs colēbātur; Aristaeus,
quī inventor oleī esse dīcitur,
ūnā cum Līberō patre apud 40
illōs eōdem erat in templō
cōnsecrātus.

58. Iovem autcm Impe-
rātōrem quantō honōre in suō
templō fuisse arbitrāminī?
Conicere potestis, sī recordārī
volueritis quantā religiōne 5
fuerit eādem speciē ac formā

the Greek Bacchus, god of wine.
Aristaeī (ar-is-tē'(y)us): a son of
Apollo, said to have taught mankind the management of bees and
the cultivation of the olive. ▾

33. **Imperātōris:** 'Rulcr.'
Ūrion: god ' of Fair Winds.'
34. **Līberae :** note to chapter 53,
line 30. **aprīnum:** 'of a wild boar.'
The ancient sculptors were very
successful in their representation of animals (illustration, page 215).   It
is not certain, however, that a boar is referred to here; the text is not sure.

36. **sacrificiīs:** 'sacrifices.'   **anniversāriīs:** 'yearly.'
37. **apud illōs :** ' among these people.'
39. **inventor:** 'discoverer.'   **oleī:** 'olive-oil.'
40. **Līberō patre :** 'Father Bacchus.'
58. 2. **suō:** ' his own '; not shared with another divinity, as were
the temples just mentioned.
5. **religiōne :** ' sacredness.'
6. **fuerit:** the tense implies that the statue was no longer in existence

signum illud, quod, ex Macedoniā captum, in Capitōliō
posuerat T. Flāminīnus.   Etenim tria ferēbantur in orbe
terrārum signa Iovis Imperātōris ūnō in genere pulcherrimē
10 facta : ūnum illud Macedonicum, quod in Capitōliō vīdimus; alterum in Pontī ōre et angustiīs; tertium, quod
Syrācūsīs ante Verrem praetōrem fuit.

Illud Flāminīnus ita ex aede suā sustulit, ut in Capitōliō,
hōc est, in terrestrī domiciliō Iovis, pōneret.   Quod autem
15 est ad introitum Pontī, id, cum tam multa ex illō marī bella
ēmerserint, tam multa porrō in Pontum invecta sint, ūsque
ad hanc diem integrum inviolātumque servātum est.   Hōc
tertium, quod erat Syrācūsīs, quod M. Mārcellus armātus
et victor vīderat, quod religiōnī concesserat, quod cīvēs

---

at the time of the trial; it had doubtless perished in the burning of the
Capitol thirteen years before, in 83 B.C.

8. **Flāminīnus** (flam-i̯-nī'nu̯s) : Titus Quintius Flamininus, who conquered Philip V of Macedonia in the battle of Cynoscephalae (si̯n-
o̯-sef'a̯-lē), 197 B.C.   **ferēbantur :** in the sense of *dīcēbantur;* sc. *esse.*

9. **ūnō in genere :** ' of the same type,' we should say; for the
same divinity was represented in different ways and with different
attributes.

11. **Pontī :** ' the Black Sea.'   **ōre et angustiīs :** hendiadys ; translate
as if *angustō ōre.*   *238, h.*   This temple of Zeus Urios, who was identified
with Jupiter Imperator, stood on the Asiatic side of the Bosporus, a short
distance below the mouth into which the Black Sea flows.

13. **Illud :** the first of the three statues mentioned.   **ita :** ' with
(only) this in view.'   **Capitōliō :** in this temple there were statues
representing Jupiter under several appellations besides that of Optimus
Maximus.   See illustration, page 350.

14. **terrestrī :** ' of earth '; here ' on earth,' a contrast with *caelestis*
(understood) being implied.   **domiciliō :** the Romans considered that
the temple of Jupiter, Juno, and Minerva on the Capitoline hill was the
center of worship for the whole earth.   **Quod :** *id* (*signum*) *quod.*

15. **introitum :** ' entrance.'

16. **porrō :** ' again,' ' furthermore.'   **invecta sint :** ' bring in'; the
reference is to hostile fleets sailing through the Bosporus into the Black
Sea.

17. **inviolātum :** ' undisturbed,' ' inviolate.'

atque incolae Syrācūsānī colere, advenae nōn sōlum vīsere, 20
vērum etiam venerārī solēbant, id C. Verrēs ex templō
Iovis sustulit.

The Syracusans lost more gods in the thefts of Verres than men in the cap-
ture of the city by Marcellus; yet Verres took also other objects of value.

Ut saepius ad Mārcellum revertar, iūdicēs, sīc habētōte,
plūrēs esse ā Syrācūsānīs istīus adventū deōs, quam victōriā Mārcellī hominēs, dēsīderātōs. Etenim ille requīsīsse 25
etiam dīcitur Archimēdem illum, summō ingeniō hominem

RUINED TOMB AT SYRACUSE
This tomb is pointed out by guides as the tomb of Archimedes, but is
probably of the Roman period.

20. **incolae:** 'inhabitant,' 'resident.' **advenae:** 'strangers,' 'visitors.'

26. **Archimēdem** (är-kị̆-mē′dēz): a great mathematician and inventor, who was born in Syracuse in 287 B.C. and was killed by a Roman soldier when the city was captured by Marcellus in 212 B.C.
Among his inventions was a screw-like machine for raising water; he

ac disciplīnā, quem cum audīsset interfectum, permolestē tulisse; iste omnia, quae requīsīvit, nōn ut cōnservāret, vērum ut asportāret, requīsīvit.

59. Iam illa, quae leviōra vidēbuntur, ideō praeterībō, quod mēnsās Delphicās ē marmore, crātēras ex aere pulcherrimās, vim maximam vāsōrum Corinthiōrum ex omnibus aedibus sacrīs abstulit Syrācūsīs. Itaque, iūdicēs, eī, 5 quī hospitēs ad ea, quae vīsenda sunt, solent dūcere, et ūnum quidque ostendere (quōs illī mystagōgōs vocant) conversam iam habent dēmōnstrātiōnem suam. Nam, ut ante dēmōnstrābant, quid ubīque esset, item nunc quid undique ablātum sit, ostendunt.

He wounded the feelings of the Syracusans and added insult to injury by pretending to purchase what he took.

10 Quid tum? mediocrīne tandem dolōre eōs affectōs esse arbitrāminī? Nōn ita est, iūdicēs, prīmum, quod

---

is said also to have made a concave mirror which would reflect sunlight so as to set wood on fire. Marcellus ordered that an honorable burial should be given to Archimedes (illustration above), and made provision for his relatives.

27. **quem . . . interfectum:** *et cum audīsset eum interfectum esse.* **permolestē:** 'with intense chagrin.'

28. **tulisse:** 'he bore (the loss).'

29. **asportāret:** 'carry away.'

59. 2. **mēnsās:** 'table.' **Delphicās:** 'of Delphi,' 'Delphic.' The " Delphic tables " were round, and were supported by three legs. They were so named from resemblance to the tripod of the priestess of Apollo at Delphi; this, as the name implies, had three feet. **crātēras:** 'mixing-bowls,' large vases with two handles used for mixing water with wine.

3. **vāsōrum:** 'vase.' **Corinthiōrum:** 'of Corinth,' 'Corinthian.' ' Corinthian vases' were made of bronze in which the precious metals, gold and silver, were blended. They were rare and costly. See page 443, Selection 5.

5. **hospitēs:** object of *dūcere.* **vīsenda:** see chapter 55, line 15, and note.

6. **ūnum quidque:** 'every individual thing.' **mystagōgos:** 'guide,' especially for sacred places, like the guides in European cathedrals today.

7. **dēmōnstrātiōnem:** 'a pointing out,' 'description.'

omnēs religiōne moventur, et deōs patriōs, quōs ā maiōribus accēpērunt, colendōs sibi dīligenter et retinendōs esse arbitrantur; deinde hīc ōrnātus, haec opera atque artificia, signa, tabulae pictae, Graecōs hominēs nimiō opere dēlec- 15 tant. Itaque ex illōrum querimōniīs intellegere possumus, haec illīs acerbissima vidērī, quae forsitan nōbīs levia et contemnenda esse videantur. Mihi crēdite, iūdicēs — tametsī vōsmet ipsōs haec eadem audīre certō sciō, — cum multās accēperint per hōsce annōs sociī atque exterae nātiōnēs 20 calamitātēs et iniūriās, nūllās Graecī hominēs gravius ferunt

BRONZE RAM FROM SYRACUSE

Now in Palermo.   This illustrates the exquisite workmanship of the art
treasures stolen by Verres.

14. ōrnātus : see note to chapter 54, line 8.   haec opera atque artificia : ' these works of art and craftsmanship.'

15. tabulae : see note to chapter 55, line 13.   nimiō opere : ' too much.' How literally?   See note to chapter 56, line 12.

19. multās : made emphatic by separation from its noun.

21. nūllās : sc. *calamitātēs et iniūriās.*

ac tulērunt, quam huiusce modī spoliātiōnēs fānōrum atque oppidōrum.

Licet iste dīcat ēmisse sē, sīcutī solet dīcere, crēdite
25 hōc mihi, iūdicēs: nūlla umquam cīvitās tōtā Asiā et Graeciā signum ūllum, tabulam pictam, ūllum dēnique ōrnāmentum urbis, suā voluntāte cuiquam vēndidit, nisi forte exīstimātis, posteā quam iūdicia sevēra Rōmae fierī dēsiērunt, Graecōs hominēs haec vēnditāre coepisse, quae
30 tum nōn modo nōn vēnditābant, cum iūdicia fīēbant, vērum etiam coëmēbant; aut nisi arbitrāminī L. Crassō, Q. Scaevolae, C. Claudiō, potentissimīs hominibus, quōrum aedīlitātēs ōrnātissimās vīdimus, commercium istārum rērum cum Graecīs hominibus nōn fuisse, eīs, quī post
35 iūdiciōrum dissolūtiōnem aedīlēs factī sunt, fuisse.

---

22. **spoliātiōnes:** 'plundering,' 'looting.' Why plural? *92, c.*

24. **ēmisse sē:** *sē ēmisse haec (signa, etc.).*

27. **nisi forte:** introduces an ironical supposition.

28. **iūdicia:** 'courts.' **fierī dēsiērunt:** *i.e.* when the trials of provincial officials for extortion ceased to be conducted before a court in which senators were not permitted to serve as *iūdicēs.* The thought is that before this change, which in 81 B.C. placed such courts under the control of senators, severe judgments held provincial governors in check; now that the administration of justice in such cases has degener- ated, corrupt officials can force the Greeks to give up their art treasures, and claim that these were sold by them.

31. **coëmēbant:** 'bought up.' **L. Crassō, Q. Scaevolae:** dative, with *fuisse.* When Lucius Licinius Crassus and Quintus Mucius Scaevola were curule aediles, in 103 B.C., they gave splendid games, in which fights with lions were introduced.

32. **Claudiō** (clȧ'dį-ụs): Gaius Claudius Pulcher, who as curule aedile gave notable games in 99 B.C. At these games for the first time ele- phants were exhibited in the Circus in Rome, and scene-painting was introduced among the decorations. The implication is that in either aedileship, lavish as the expenditure of funds was, works of Greek art were not shown, for the reason that they could not be bought.

33. **commercium:** 'traffic.'

35. **dissolūtiōnem:** 'abolition' of the earlier courts, in 81 B.C. **fuisse:** sc. *commercium istārum rērum.*

60. Acerbiōrem etiam scītōte esse cīvitātibus falsam
istam et simulātam ēmptiōnem, quam sī quī clam surripiat
aut ēripiat palam atque auferat. Nam turpitūdinem
summam esse arbitrantur referrī in tabulās pūblicās, pretiō
adductam cīvitātem — et pretiō parvō — ea, quae accē- 5
pisset ā maiōribus, vēndidisse atque abaliēnāsse.

The high regard of the Greeks for their works of art.

Etenim mīrandum in modum Graecī rēbus istīs, quās nōs
contemnimus, dēlectantur. Itaque maiōrēs nostrī facile
patiēbantur, haec esse apud illōs quam plūrima : apud sociōs, ut imperiō nostrō quam ōrnātissimī flōrentissimīque 10
essent; apud eōs autem, quōs vectīgālēs aut stīpendiāriōs
fēcerant, tamen haec relinquēbant, ut illī, quibus haec
iūcunda sunt, quae nōbīs levia videntur, habērent haec
oblectāmenta et sōlācia servitūtis.

Quid arbitrāminī Rēgīnōs, quī iam cīvēs Rōmānī sunt, 15
merēre velle, ut ab eīs marmorea Venus illa auferātur?
quid Tarentīnōs, ut Eurōpam in taurō āmittant? ut

---

60. 2. **ēmptiōnem** : ' purchase.' **surripiat** : ' filch,' ' purloin.'

4. **referrī**, etc. : ' that it should be entered in the public records that
a state.'

6. **abaliēnāsse** : ' transfer ownership of,' ' transfer.'

8. **contemnimus** : Cicero expresses a feeling common enough among
the Romans, as among many people today. There were many Romans,
nevertheless, who, like Cicero himself, had a refined appreciation of art.

11. **stīpendiāriōs** : ' subject to tribute.'

14. **oblectāmenta** : ' sources of pleasure.'

15. **Rēgīnōs** : 'the people of Regium' (rē'jǐ-ŭm), a city of Lower
Italy, on the strait separating Italy from Sicily. See Map.

16. **merēre** : ' deserve,' ' earn,' ' obtain '; *merēre velle*, ' would be
willing to take.'

17. **Tarentīnōs** : sc. *merēre velle*. **Eurōpam** (ū-rō'pả) : daughter of
Agenor (ả-jē'nor), king of Phoenicia, and sister of Cadmus. The
story is that Jupiter in the form of a bull bore her on his back across the
sea to Crete. The subject was represented in both sculpture and painting. **taurō** : ' bull.'

Satyrum, quī apud illōs in aede Vestae est, ut cētera?
quid Thespiēnsēs, ut Cupīdinis signum, propter quod ūnum
20 vīsuntur Thespiae? quid Cnidiōs, ut Venerem marmoream?
quid, ut pictam, Coōs? quid Ephesiōs, ut Alexandrum?
quid Cȳzicēnōs, ut Āiācem aut Mēdēam? quid Rhodiōs, ut

---

18. **Satyrum:** one of a class of divinities with goat's feet, the special
attendants of the god Dionysus or Bacchus.   Satyrs were a favorite subject
of painters and sculptors.
ut cētera: sc. *āmittant.*

19. **quid,** etc.: *quid arbitrāminī Thespiēnsēs merēre
velle, ut.* **Thespiēnsēs:** 'the
people of Thespiae (thes'pĭ-ē).'
Cupīdinis: see note to chapter 55, line 26. One of the
most famous representations
of Cupid was the small statue
by Praxiteles (prak-sit'ĕ-lēz).
See illustration.

20. **Thespiae:** a town in
Greece near the foot of Mt.
Helicon (hel'ĭ-kon), in Boeotia
(bē-ō'sh(y)ạ). **Cnidiōs:** 'the
people of Cnidus (nī'dus),' a
city in southwestern Asia
Minor. **Venerem:** by the
sculptor Praxiteles; the type
is known from copies which
are still extant.

21. **quid,** etc.: *quid arbitrāminī Coōs merēre velle,
ut Venerem pictam amittant.*
pictam: note to chapter 55,
line 13. **Coōs:** 'the people of

SO-CALLED CUPID

This was formerly thought to be a copy
of the Cupid of Praxiteles at Thespiae.
Recent authorities deny its Praxitelean
origin, and identify the statue, which is in
the Vatican in Rome, as Thanatos, 'Death.'

Cos,' an island in the Aegean Sea west of Asia Minor.   This painting
of Venus was by the great Apelles (ạ-pel'ēz).   **Ephesiōs:** ' the people
of Ephesus.'   **Alexandrum:** sc. *pictum;* also a painting by Apelles.

22. **Cyzicēnōs:** 'the people of Cyzicus (siz'ĭ-kụs),' a city of western
Asia Minor, on the south shore of what is now called the sea of Mar-
mora. **Āiācem** (ā'jax): a hero of the Trojan war, who became insane

Iālysum? quid Athēniēnsēs, ut ex marmore Iacchum aut Paralum pictum aut ex aere Myrōnis būculam? Longum est, et nōn necessārium, commemorāre, quae apud quōsque 25 vīsenda sunt tōtā Asiā et Graeciā; vērum illud est, quam ob rem haec commemorem, quod exīstimāre vōs hōc volō, mīrum quendam dolōrem accipere eōs, ex quōrum urbibus haec auferantur.

---

and killed himself. **Mēdēam** (mẹ-dē'ạ) : sc. *pictam.* Both paintings are thought to have been by Timo'machus.

23. **Iālysum** (ī-al'ị-sụs) : a descendant of the sun-god. The painting referred to was by Protogenes (prō-toj'ẹ-nēz). **Iacchum** (ī-ak'ụs) : another name for Bacchus.

24. **Paralum** (par'ạ-lụs) : an ancient Athenian hero. **Myrōnis** (mī'-ron) : a Greek sculptor who flourished in the latter part of the fifth century B.C. **būculam :** ' young cow (heifer).'

26. **illud est :** ' that is (the reason)'.

CICERO THE ADVOCATE OF
LITERATURE AND LEARNING

CICERO THE ADVOCATE OF LITERATURE AND LEARNING

M. TULLĪ CICERŌNIS
PRŌ A. LICINIŌ ARCHIĀ POĒTĀ
ŌRĀTIŌ

Judges, a sense of profound obligation leads me to defend Archias.

1. Sī quid est in mē ingenī, iūdicēs, quod sentiō quam sit exiguum, aut sī qua exercitātiō dīcendī, in quā mē nōn īnfitior mediocriter esse versātum, aut sī huiusce rcī ratiō aliqua ab optimārum artium studiīs ac disciplīnā profecta,

---

To THE STUDENT: Consult first the introductory remarks on page 543, *et seq.* of the Companion.

Title: ŌRĀTIŌ: delivered before a court (*quaestiō*), over which the orator's brother, Quintus Cicero, presided, being then praetor.

1. 1. **Sī quid,** etc.: 'Whatever talent (*i.e.* for public speaking; see note on page 192, line 7), . . . whatever readiness of speech, . . . whatever (acquaintance with the) theory of this art (of public speaking), . . . reside in me, jurors.' The orator mentions the first two essentials of success in oratory (natural ability and the readiness acquired by practice) as leading up to the third, in which lay the basis of his obligation to Archias. **ingenī:** why not *ingeniī?* **quod:** subject of *sit;* translate as if *et id.* Self-depreciatory beginnings were common in speeches of this kind, being intended to win the favorable attention of the jurors.

2. **aut . . . aut:** for *et . . . et,* as more modest. **nōn īnfitior:** litotes. *239, m;* B. 375, 1; A. & G. 326, *c;* G. 700. Note the increase in positiveness, *sentiō — nōn īnfitiōr — cōnfiteor.*

4. **optimārum . . . disciplīnā:** 'the pursuit and training of the most liberal studies' (see page 225, line 10), *i.e.* philology, or grammar in the broad sense, rhetoric, music, and philosophy. Cicero was a firm believer in general culture as a foundation for oratory.

5 ā quā ego nūllum cōnfiteor aetātis meae tempus abhorruisse,
eārum rērum omnium vel in prīmīs hīc A. Licinius frūctum ā mē repetere prope suō iūre dēbet.   Nam, quoad
longissimē potest mēns mea respicere spatium praeteritī
temporis et pueritiae memoriam recordārī ultimam, inde
10 ūsque repetēns, hunc videō mihi prīncipem et ad suscipiendam et ad ingrediendam ratiōnem hōrum studiōrum
exstitisse.

Quod sī haec vōx, huius hortātū praeceptīsque cōnfōr-
māta, nōn nūllīs aliquandō salūtī fuit, ā quō id accēpimus,
15 quō cēterīs opitulārī et aliōs servāre possumus, huic pro-

---

5. **ā quā . . . abhorruisse :** ' to which . . . has been inattentive,'
or ' of which . . . has been neglectful '; the antecedent of *quā* is *ratiō*.
Cicero, as a practical lawyer, in a way apologizes to a jury of practical
men for having given attention to the theory of oratory. **aetātis :**
= *vītae*.

6. **vel :** ' even.'   **hīc :** ' my client '; a common use of this pronoun.
A. Licinius : the orator cleverly assumes the citizenship of Archias by
using his Latin name.

7. **suō iūre :** ' by an inalienable right '; stronger than *iūre* alone
as implying that the right is fully admitted by the speaker.   The possessive sometimes has the meaning of ' proper,' ' perfect,' ' characteristic,' ' peculiar,' ' appropriate,' ' favorable,' and related words.   *157, e.*
quoad longissimē : ' just so far as.'   *190, c.*

9. **memoriam ultimam :** ' the earliest recollection.'   **inde ūsque
repetēns :** ' going back even to that time.'   How literally?

10. **hunc :** see note to line 6 above.   **suscipiendam :** ' choosing.'

11. **ratiōnem :** ' course.'

13. **Quod :** ' Now.'   *118, d;* B. 185, 2 ; A. & G. 397, *a;* G. 610, R. 2.
praeceptīs : not *īnstitūtiōne,* ' instruction,' because Archias was only
an intimate adviser, not a teacher, of Cicero.

14. **nōn nūllīs aliquandō :** modest expression.   **ā quō :** the apodosis
begins here.

15. **cēterīs :** ' the rest ' of my clients in general, who have availed
themselves of my services.   **aliōs :** ' (many) others ' than Archias, who
have been brought to trial before a criminal court.   Both *cēterīs* and
aliōs are proleptic, and should be introduced in translation after *huic
ipsī,* ' to this particular man.'   *238, m; 162, a.*

fectō ipsī, quantum est situm in nōbīs, et opem et salūtem ferre dēbēmus.

Ac nē quis ā nōbīs hōc ita dīcī forte mīrētur, quod alia quaedam in hōc facultās sit ingenī neque haec dīcendī ratiō aut disciplīna, nē nōs quidem huic ūnī studiō penitus 20 umquam dēditī fuimus. Etenim omnēs artēs, quae ad hūmānitātem pertinent, habent quoddam commūne vinculum et quasi cognātiōne quādam inter sē continentur.

I crave your indulgence for the use of a kind of argument foreign to the courts.

2. Sed nē cui vestrum mīrum esse videātur, mē in quaestiōne lēgitimā et in iūdiciō pūblicō, cum rēs agātur apud praetōrem populī Rōmānī, rēctissimum virum, et apud sevērissimōs iūdicēs, tantō conventū hominum ac frequen-

16. **quantum,** etc.: see IDIOMS.

18. **ita:** ' so (strongly).' **alia,** etc.: strange that an orator should confess obligation to a poet.

19. **sit:** what different force would *est* have here? **neque:** ' and not.'

20. **aut:** instead of *ac*, on account of the preceding negative. **huic ūnī studiō:** of oratory. **penitus:** ' exclusively.'

21. **dēditī fuimus:** ' have been devoted '; *fuimus* is often preferred to *sumus* when the accompanying perfect passive participle, as here, has more of an adjective than a participial force.

23. **inter sē continentur:** ' stand related to one another.' See Cicero, *Dē Ōrātōre,* **3,** 6, 21. *Est etiam illa Platōnis vēra . . . vōx* (' saying ') *omnem doctrīnam hārum ingenuārum et hūmānārum artium ūnō quōdam societātis vinculō continērī.*

2. 2. **in . . . pūblicō:** in our phrase, ' before a statute commission and state's court '; *quaestiō lēgitima*, as established under a statute (*lēx*) and not as a special commission (*quaestiō extraōrdināria*), such as were sometimes raised for criminal cases; *iūdicium pūblicum*, as a court for cases affecting the state, not for the trial of contentions between individuals. **rēs agātur:** ' the case is being tried.'

3. **praetōrem:** see note to *Ōrātiō*, on page 221.

4. **conventū hominum ac frequentiā:** ablative absolute denoting attendant circumstance. In phrases like this Cicero usually puts the genitive after the first noun. *144, b (2).*

5 tiā, hōc ūtī genere dīcendī, quod nōn modo ā cōnsuētūdine
iūdiciōrum, vērum etiam ā forēnsī sermōne abhorreat,
quaesō ā vōbīs, ut in hāc causā mihi dētis hanc veniam,
accommodātam huic reō, vōbīs, quem ad modum spērō,
nōn molestam, ut mē, prō summō poētā atque ērudītissimō
10 homine dīcentem, hōc concursū hominum litterātissimō-
rum, hāc vestrā hūmānitāte, hōc dēnique praetōre exercente
iūdicium, patiāminī dē studiīs hūmānitātis ac litterārum
paulō loquī līberius et in eius modī persōnā, quae propter
ōtium ac studium minimē in iūdiciīs perīculīsque trāctāta
15 est, utī prope novō quōdam et inūsitātō genere dīcendi.

Quod sī mihi ā vōbīs tribuī concēdīque sentiam, perficiam
profectō, ut hunc A. Licinium nōn modo nōn sēgregandum,
cum sit cīvis, ā numerō cīvium, vērum etiam, sī nōn esset,
putētis ascīscendum fuisse.

---

7. **ut . . . dētis veniam, ut patiāminī:** forceful pleonasm. *238, k.*

8. **accommodātam . . . molestam:** adversative asyndeton and
chiasmus. *238, d; 239, e.* **huic reō:** ' to this (my) client.'

10. **hōc:** ' such.'

11. **hōc praetōre:** the commentators interpret this as a complimentary reference to the taste and achievements of Quintus Cicero as a
literary man and poet. His poems have all perished with the exception
of a few verses, among which are a couple of cynical epigrams.

13. **līberius:** i.e. *līberius quam patitur cōnsuētūdō iūdiciōrum et forī*,
as Cicero himself says elsewhere (*Brūtus*, **31**, 120). **in eius modī
persōnā:** ' in (the case of) a character such as this ' of Archias.

14. **ōtium ac studium:** ' retirement and devotion to study.' **in
. . . tractāta est:** we say ' has been drawn into.' **perīculīs:** ' legal
actions,' referring to criminal cases.

16. **Quod sī:** here = *et sī id.* *167.* **tribuī:** implies that a request is
granted freely; *concēdī*, not without opposition. **perficiam profectō
ut . . . putētis:** ' I shall undoubtedly cause you to think.' *203 (3);*
B. 297, *i;* A. & G. 568; G. 553, *i.*

17. **sēgregandum:** sc. *esse.*

19. **ascīscendum fuisse:** sc. *in numerum cīvium;* the direct form
would have been *ascīscendus erat* or *fuit.* *208, b; 218 (3);* B. 304, 3, *b;*
A. & G. 517, *c;* G. 597, R. 3. Note the skillful word-order in this sentence.

Archias, born at Antioch, early rose to fame. He came to Italy and formed firm friendships at Rome.

3. Nam, ut prīmum ex puerīs excessit Archiās atque ab eīs artibus, quibus aetās puerīlis ad hūmānitātem īnfōrmārī solet, sē ad scrībendī studium contulit, prīmum Antiochīae 5 — nam ibi nātus est locō nōbilī—celebrī quondam urbe et cōpiōsā atque ērudītissimīs hominibus līberālissimīsque studiīs 10 affluentī, celeriter antecellere omnibus ingenī glōriā contigit.

ANTIOCH PERSONIFIED
A statue in the Vatican.

3. 1. **ut prīmum:** see *188, c.* **ex puerīs excessit:** 'outgrew his boyhood'; concrete for abstract; = *ā pueritiā.* *92, f.*

2. **ad:** 'with a view to.'

5. **Antiochīae:** at this time second in importance only to Alexandria among the cities of the East, notwithstanding the fact that it had been greatly disturbed by the dynastic quarrels which had rent the kingdom of Syria, and by the inroads of the Parthians.

6. **locō:** 'station,' 'rank.'

7. **celebrī:** not 'celebrated,' but 'populous.'

8. **urbe:** *146.* **atque . . . affluentī:** 'and especially brimming over with scholarship and liberal education.'

10. **studiīs:** see note on page 221, line 4.

11. **affluentī:** = *abundantī.*

13. **contigit:** sc. *eī,* 'he had the good fortune.'

Post in cēterīs Asiae partibus cūnctāque Graeciā sīc eius
15 adventūs celebrābantur, ut fāmam ingenī exspectātiō
hominis, exspectātiōnem ipsīus adventus admīrātiōque
superāret.

Erat Italia tum plēna Graecārum artium ac disciplīnā-
rum, studiaque haec et in Latiō vehementius tum colēban-
20 tur quam nunc eīsdem in oppidīs et hīc Rōmae propter
tranquillitātem reī pūblicae nōn neglegēbantur. Itaque
hunc et Tarentīnī et Rēgīnī et Neāpolitānī cīvitāte cēterīsque praemiīs dōnārunt, et omnēs, quī aliquid dē ingeniīs
poterant iūdicāre, cognitiōne atque hospitiō dignum ex-
25 īstimārunt.

Hāc tantā celebritāte fāmae cum esset iam absentibus

---

14. **cūnctā Graeciā:** see page 160, line 6, and note. *145, c.*

15. **celebrābantur:** not ' were celebrated,' but ' were widely heralded.'

16. **ipsīus:** subjective with *adventus*, objective with *admīrātiō*; ' his
coming (in each case) and the admiration for him.' It was nothing
uncommon for poets, particularly such as extemporized, to wander from
place to place. See Companion, page 543.

18. **Italia . . . in Latiō . . . Rōmae:** notice the skillful geographical arrangement — a gradual reduction in physical dimensions with a
proportionate enlargement in literary scope. **Italia:** contrasted with
Latiō, but referring particularly to southern Italy, the region of the
Greek cities.

19. **Latiō:** in a broad sense, meaning all that part of Italy where Latin
was spoken ; see page 245, line 8, and note. **tum:** before the Social War.

21. **tranquillitātem:** between the death of Gaius Gracchus (121 B.C.)
and the outbreak of the Social War (91 B.C.) only the disturbance caused
by Saturninus and Glaucia (100 B.C.) broke the ' calm ' of the city.

22. **et Tarentīnī et Rēgīnī et Neāpolitānī:** use of the people of the
country, a natural Latin idiom, but translate ' Tarentum, Regium, and
Neapolis.' *212, f.* The *et* is correlative with *et* before *omnēs*, line 23. A
man might be a citizen of several of these Greek cities at the same time ;
but the citizenship of Rome was exclusive.

23. **praemiīs:** garlands, gifts, banquets, etc.

24. **dignum:** sc. *esse.*

26. **Hāc tantā celebritāte fāmae:** ' As a result of this widespread
publicity (given) his fame.' **absentibus:** ' to men at a distance.'

nōtus, Rōmam vēnit, Mariō cōnsule et Catulō. Nactus
est prīmum cōnsulēs eōs, quōrum alter rēs ad scrībendum
maximās, alter cum rēs gestās tum etiam studium atque
aurēs adhibēre posset. 30

Statim Lūcullī, cum praetextātus etiam tum Archiās
esset, eum domum suam recēpērunt. Et erat hōc nōn
sōlum ingenī ac litterārum, vērum etiam nātūrae atque
virtūtis, ut domus, quae huius adulēscentiae prīma fāvit,
eadem esset familiārissima senectūtī. 35

Erat temporibus illīs iūcundus Q. Metellō illī Numidicō
et eius Piō fīliō, audiēbātur ā M. Aemiliō, vīvēbat cum Q.
Catulō et patre et fīliō, ā L. Crassō colēbātur; Lūcullōs
vērō et Drūsum et Octāviōs et Catōnem et tōtam Hortēn-

---

27. **Mariō cōnsule et Catulō :** 102 B.C.; perhaps instead of the usual
order, *Mariō et Catulō cōnsulibus*, because Marius was much the more
prominent of the two.

28. **rēs maximās, rēs gestās:** sc. *suppeditāre* from *adhibēre*, which
governs them loosely by zeugma. *238, q.*

29. **studium atque aurēs:** ' literary interest and taste.' *aurēs* is
concrete for abstract, since the ear is the medium of appreciation. *92, f.*
Catulus was a man of unusual culture.

31. **praetextātus:** = *adulēscentulus; i.e.* when he was still young.
The orator speaks of Archias as if he had always been a Roman. It is
not easy to understand how the Greek cities could have granted their
franchise so readily to a lad of sixteen or eighteen years; perhaps
Cicero's words are not to be taken literally in regard to the age of the
poet.

32. **erat hōc :** ' this was (an evidence),' explained by the following
ut-clause. *203 (4).*

33. **nātūrae atque virtūtis :** ' of (his) disposition and character.'

34. **quae,** etc.: ' which was the first to appreciate him in his youth,
should also be on most intimate terms with him during his old age.'

36. **temporibus illīs:** following the year 102 B.C. **Q. Metellō
Numidicō** (kwin′t*u*s mẹ-tel′*u*s nū-mid′ĭ-k*u*s).

37. **Piō** (pī′*u*s). **M. Aemiliō** (mar′k*u*s ẹ-mĭl′ĭ-*u*s). **vīvēbat cum:**
' he was on intimate terms with.'

39. **Hortēnsiōrum** (họr-ten′(shy)ī).

40 siōrum domum dēvinctam cōnsuētūdine cum tenēret,
afficiēbātur summō honōre, quod eum nōn sōlum colēbant,
quī aliquid percipere atque audīre studēbant, vērum etiam
sī quī forte simulābant.

He was enrolled a citizen of Heraclea, later a Roman citizen, in
accordance with the terms of the law.

4. Interim satis longō intervāllō, cum esset cum M.
Lūcullō in Siciliam profectus et cum ex eā prōvinciā cum
eōdem Lūcullō dēcēderet, vēnit Hēraclīam.

Quae cum esset cīvitās aequissimō iūre ac foedere, ascrībī
5 sē in eam cīvitātem voluit, idque, cum ipse per sē dignus
putārētur, tum auctōritāte et grātiā Lūcullī, ab Hēra-
cliēnsibus impetrāvit.

---

40. **dēvinctam . . . tenēret:** 'since he held closely bound (to him)
by intimate association.'

41. **afficiēbātur summō honōre :** ' he was most highly honored,' not
only by those mentioned, but by others also.

43. **sī quī :** ' whoever,' ' any who.' A taste for Greek was considered
the proper thing; and many joined in lionizing Archias merely because
it was the fashion. **simulābant :** sc. *sē studēre*, etc.

4. 1. Interim : Rome being still his place of residence. **satis :**
' fairly.' **intervāllō :** probably not far from ten years. Why ablative?
144, a. **esset . . . profectus :** the arrangement of the compound tense
gives strong emphasis to *esset;* viz. Lucullus did not meet Archias in
Sicily by accident, but had actually gone there with him. **M. Lūcullō :**
he appears to have gone to Sicily on private business.

2. **ex eā prōvinciā dēcēderet :** the ordinary expression used of a
provincial officer leaving his province; employed here apparently to
lend an air of dignity and formality to the journey of Archias.

3. **Hēraclīam :** here probably the father of Marcus and Lucius
Lucullus was living in exile.

4. **Quae . . . foedere :** ' Since this state enjoyed most favorable
rights and treaty relations ' with Rome. Heracléa had been connected
with Rome since 278 B.C. by a treaty, the terms of which were unusually favorable.

5. **per sē :** here ' for his own sake,' ' on his own account.'

6. **auctōritāte :** influence arising from high standing, as distinguished from *grātiā,* influence due to private acquaintance.

Data est cīvitās Silvānī lēge et Carbōnis:

Sī quī FOEDERĀTĪS CĪVITĀTIBUS ASCRĪPTĪ FUISSENT,
Sī tum, cum lēx ferēbātur, in Italiā domicilium 10
HABUISSENT ET Sī SEXĀGINTĀ DIĒBUS APUD PRAETŌREM
ESSENT PROFESSĪ.

Cum hīc domicilium Rōmae multōs iam annōs habēret,

COIN OF HERACLEA

Heraclea, the city of Heracles, or Hercules, was founded about 432 B.C.
Obverse: Athena in a helmet on which is carved Scylla, whom Hercules is
said to have killed. Athena was the protectress of heroes such as Hercules,
Perseus, and Achilles. Reverse: Hercules with his club strangling the
Nemean lion.

---

8. **cīvitās:** *cīvitās Rōmāna.* **Silvānī lēge et Carbōnis:** known as
the *lēx Plautia Papīria,* passed 89 B.C.; see Companion, page 544.

9. **Sī quī:** translate as if *eīs, quī.* The provisions of the law are
stated in indirect discourse. **ascrīptī fuissent:** as citizens. *218 (1), b.*

10. **sī . . . sī:** introduce the conditions subordinate to the clause
sī quī . . . fuissent. **ferēbātur:** *185, b; 214, c;* B. 288, 1; 314, 3;
A. & G. 545; 593, *a;* G. 580; 628, R. *(a).* **domicilium:** 'a (legal)
residence.'

11. **sexāgintā diēbus:** 'within sixty days.' Why ablative? **praetōrem:** in 89 B.C. there were six praetors (the number was raised to
eight by Sulla), before any one of whom the acknowledgment con-
templated by the law could be made; see line 32. Three of the six
are mentioned in this speech, Metellus Pius (number 2 in vocabulary),
Appius Claudius Pulcher (chapter 5, line 1), and Lucius Lentulus.

12. **essent professī:** sc. *nōmina,* 'should enter their names.'

13. **habēret:** not *habuisset,* in order to emphasize the fact that
Archias continued to reside at Rome. *175, d.*

professus est apud praetōrem Q. Metellum, familiārissimum
15 suum.

Sī nihil aliud nisi dē cīvitāte ac lēge dīcimus, nihil dīcō
amplius : causa dicta est. Quid enim hōrum īnfīrmārī,
Grātī, potest? Hēraclīaene esse eum ascrīptum negābis?
Adest vir summā auctōritāte et religiōne et fidē, M. Lūcullus :
20 quī sē nōn opīnārī, sed scīre, nōn audīvisse, sed vīdisse,
nōn interfuisse, sed ēgisse dīcit. Adsunt Hēraclīēnsēs
lēgātī, nōbilissimī hominēs, huius iūdicī causā cum man-
dātīs et cum pūblicō testimōniō, quī hunc ascrīptum
Hēraclīēnsem dīcunt.

25   Hīc tū tabulās dēsīderās Hēraclīēnsium pūblicās, quās
Italicō bellō, incēnsō tabulāriō, interīsse scīmus omnēs?

---

14. **familiārissimum :** used as substantive = *familiārissimum amīcum,* ' bosom friend.'

A. Proof that Archias is a Roman citizen. **4** (line 16)–**5**

16. **dē cīvitāte ac lēge :** i.e. *dē cīvitāte Rōmānā lēge Plautiā Papiriā
datā.*

17. **causa dicta est :** ' our case is stated,' in that it has been shown
that my client fulfilled the three conditions, enrollment as a citizen
in an allied state, a legal residence in Italy, and proper acknowledgment
before a praetor.

18. **Grātī** (grā'sh(y)ụs) : curtly addressed without his forename ;
see also *Catilīna* (page 25, line 1, *et al.*), but compare *C. Caesar* (page 11,
line 3, *et al.*) ; *C. Mānīlī* (page 192, line 1) ; *P. Servīlī* (page 347, line 18) ;
C. Laelī (page 288, line 4). **Hēraclīae :** *146;* B. 232, 1 ; A. & G. 427, 3 ;
G. 411.

19. **Adest :** as witness and supporter ; sc. *nōbīs.* **auctōritāte!**
here ' weight,' ' reliability ' ; but *religiōne,* ' scrupulousness.'

20. **opīnārī :** i.e. *hunc Hēraclīae ascrīptum esse.*

21. **ēgisse :** ' was instrumental ' in bringing it about.

23. **pūblicō :** on behalf of the corporation of Heraclea.

25. **Hīc :** ' At this point.' **tabulās :** ' registers,' ' records ' containing the names of the citizens.

26. **Italicō bellō :** probably some sacking of the city in the Social
War caused the conflagration referred to.

Est rīdiculum ad ea, quae habēmus, nihil dīcere; quaerere, quae habēre nōn possumus, et dē hominum memoriā
tacēre, litterārum memoriam flāgitāre; et, cum habeās
amplissimī virī religiōnem, integerrimī mūnicipī iūs iūran- 30
dum fidemque, ea, quae dēprāvārī nūllō modō possunt,
repudiāre; tabulās, quās īdem dīcis solēre corrumpī,
dēsīderāre.

An domicilium Rōmae nōn habuit is, quī tot annīs ante
cīvitātem datam sēdem omnium rērum ac fortūnārum 35
suārum Rōmae collocāvit?

His acknowledgment before the praetor Metellus is on record.

An nōn est professus? Immō vērō eīs tabulīs professus,
quae sōlae ex illā professiōne collēgiōque praetōrum ob-
tinent pūblicārum tabulārum auctōritātem.

5. Nam, cum Appī tabulae neglegentius asservātae
dīcerentur, Gabīnī quam diū incolumis fuit, levitās, post

---

27. **ad :** ' in relation to,' ' in reply to.' **quaerere : =** *requīrere.*

28. **hominum memoriā, litterārum memoriam :** repetition of
memoria in order to heighten the contrast between the depositions of
the witnesses and the missing documentary evidence.

29. **tacēre :** ' to remain silent '; like our phrase ' to keep still,'
implying the suppression of that which might be spoken.

30. **amplissimī virī religiōnem :** ' the word of honor of a noble
gentleman.'

34. **Rōmae :** consistent with line 13 above; stronger than *in Italiā,*
which might have been expected from the wording of the statute
(line 10). **ante cīvitātem datam :** *i.e.* to inhabitants of allied cities.
See IDIOMS. *212, c; 228, b; B. 337, 5;* A. & G. 497; G. 360, R. 2.
See page 122, line 17, and note.

38. **illā professiōne collēgiōque praetōrum : =** *professiōne* (registration) *apud illud collēgium* (board) *praetōrum factā,* covering the registration of the six praetors of 89 B.C.; see note to line 11.

39. **pūblicārum :** not ' public,' but ' official,' ' state.'

5. 1. **Appī :** thought to have been the father of the dissolute
Clodius, Cicero's enemy, for whom see Companion, pages 490–493.

2. **Gabīnī :** asyndeton; we should say ' and of Gabinius.' *238, d.*

damnātiōnem calamitās omnem tabulārum fidem resignāsset, Metellus, homō sānctissimus modestissimusque
5 omnium, tantā dīligentiā fuit, ut ad L. Lentulum praetōrem
et ad iūdicēs vēnerit et ūnīus nōminis litūrā sē commōtum
esse dīxerit.

Hīs igitur in tabulīs nūllam litūram in nōmine A. Licinī
vidētis. Quae cum ita sint, quid est, quod dē eius cīvitāte
10 dubitētis, praesertim cum aliīs quoque in cīvitātibus fuerit
ascrīptus? Etenim, cum mediocribus multīs et aut nūllā
aut humilī aliquā arte praeditīs grātuītō cīvitātem in
Graeciā hominēs impertiēbant, Rēgīnōs crēdō aut Locrēnsēs
aut Neāpolitānōs aut Tarentīnōs, quod scaenicīs artificibus

---

3. **calamitās:** mild expression for the loss of civil rights; Gabinius
Capito had been condemned for provincial extortion in his governorship
of Achaia. **omnem tabulārum fidem resignāsset:** 'had destroyed all
confidence in his records.' For the force of *re-signāre*, literally, 'to
break open the seal of,' see Companion, page 559.

4. **sānctissimus modestissimusque:** 'the most conscientious and
law-observing.'

5. **dīligentiā:** 'painstaking.' **praetōrem, iūdicēs:** Metellus was
probably giving testimony in a case concerning citizenship.

6. **vēnerit, dīxerit:** in result clauses the perfect subjunctive may be
used after a secondary tense to imply final result. See note, page 18,
line 16. *177, b;* B. 268, 6; A. & G. 485, *c,* and N. 1; G. 513.

8. **Hīs in tabulīs:** of Metellus. **A. Licinī:** not *A. Licinī Archiae,*
because the poet would be registered only by his Latin name.

9. **quid est, quod:** 'what reason is there to.' **eius:** instead of
huius, because referring to Archias as registered, as A. Licinius, rather
than as present. **cīvitāte:** at Heraclea.

10. **fuerit:** not *sit,* because the registration of citizens in these places
had ceased after 89 B.C., when the inhabitants became Roman citizens.

11. **Etenim,** etc.: a *reductiō ad absurdum. 239, s.*

13. **Graeciā:** = *Magnā Graeciā.* **Rēgīnōs, Locrēnsēs, Neāpolitānōs,**
Tarentīnōs: translate as on page 226, line 22; viz. ' Regium (rē′ji-ụm),
Locri (lō′krī), Naples, Taren′tum.' **crēdō:** see page 144, line 21, and
note. **Locrēnsēs:** the people of *Locrī Epizephyriī,* on the eastern side
of the extreme southwestern part, the toe, of Italy.

14. **scaenicīs artificibus:** actors in Rome were generally slaves or
freedmen, and therefore acting was held in low esteem.

largīrī solēbant, id huic, summā ingenī praeditō, glōriā 15
nōluisse!

No entry in the census lists is needed.

Quid? cum cēterī nōn modo post cīvitātem datam, sed
etiam post lēgem Pāpiam aliquō modō in eōrum mūnicipiōrum tabulās irrēpsērunt; hīc, quī nē ūtitur quidem illīs,
in quibus est scrīptus, quod semper sē Hēracliēnsem esse 20
voluit, rēicietur?

Cēnsūs nostrōs requīris. Scīlicet; est enim obscūrum
proximīs cēnsōribus hunc cum clārissimō imperātōre,
L. Lūcullō, apud exercitum fuisse, superiōribus cum eōdem
quaestōre fuisse in Asiā, prīmīs, Iūliō et Crassō, nūllam 25
populī partem esse cēnsam. Sed, quoniam cēnsus nōn
iūs cīvitātis cōnfīrmat ac tantum modo indicat eum, quī
sit cēnsus, sē iam tum gessisse prō cīve, eīs temporibus is,

---

17. **Quid:** see page 34, line 25, and note. **post:** see IDIOMS and
page 231, line 34.

18. **lēgem Pāpiam:** passed in 65 B.C., enacting that all persons not
possessing a legal residence in Italy must leave Rome. It was probably
under this law that Archias was brought to trial.

19. **illīs** [*tabulīs*]: the records of Regium, Locri, Naples, Tarentum.

22. **Cēnsūs:** including each census taken between 89 and 65 B.C.
Scīlicet: 'Certainly'; sarcastic. **obscūrum** [*tibi*]: = *tibi nōn nōtum.*

23. **proximīs cēnsōribus:** 'at the last taking of the census,' in
70 B.C., by Lucius Gellius Publicola and Gnaeus Lentulus Clodianus.
Censors had been chosen for 65 and for 64 B.C., but they had resigned
without taking the census.

24. **apud exercitum:** not *in exercitū*, for Archias went merely as a
companion, or *attaché*, of the commander. **superiōribus** [*cēnsōribus*]:
'at the next to the last census,' taken by Lucius Marcius Philippus and
Marcus Perperna, in 86 B.C. **eōdem quaestōre:** 'the same' Lucullus
who was then 'quaestor' under Sulla.

25. **prīmīs** [*cēnsōribus*]: 'the first' after Archias had become a
citizen, in 89; Julius Caesar Strabo and Publicus Licinius Crassus, the
censors for that year, resigned without undertaking the work.

28. **prō:** 'as.' **eīs temporibus:** the apodosis begins here.

quem tū crīmināris nē ipsīus quidem iūdiciō in cīvium Rō-
30 mānōrum iūre esse versātum, et testāmentum saepe fēcit
nostrīs lēgibus et adiit hērēditātēs cīvium Rōmānōrum et in
beneficiīs ad aerārium dēlātus est ā L. Lūcullō prō cōnsule.

Quaere argūmenta, sī quae potes; numquam enim hīc
neque suō neque amīcōrum iūdiciō revincētur.

Literary pursuits, exemplified in Archias, are my recreation.

6. Quaerēs ā nōbīs, Grātī, cūr tantō opere hōc homine
dēlectēmur.

Quia suppeditat nōbīs, ubi et animus ex hōc forēnsī
strepitū reficiātur et aurēs, convīciō dēfessae, conquiēscant.

---

29. **nē ipsīus quidem iūdiciō:** because he did not have his name placed on the census registers.   **in . . . esse versātum:** 'had (any) share in.'

30. **saepe:** perhaps in times of special danger, in his travels with Lucullus.   The Roman law recognized only the wills of Roman citizens as valid.

31. **hērēditātēs cīvium Rōmānōrum:** in general only Roman citizens could inherit from Roman citizens.

32. **dēlātus est:** ' he was reported,' instead of *nōmen dēlātum est.* Proconsuls and propraetors were obliged to deliver their accounts to the Treasury within thirty days after they had come back to Rome.   In connection with these it was customary to hand in a list of those men on the staff or in the retinue of the provincial governor whose services were deemed worthy of compensation from the state.

33. **hīc . . . revincētur:** *i.e.* Archias and his friends have always acted on the assumption that he was a citizen.   With this point the orator closes the technical side of his case.   See Companion, page 545.

34. **neque . . . neque:** ' either . . . or.'   *233, e;* B. 347, 2; A. & G. 327, 2; G. 445.

B. Proof that Archias ought to be a citizen. **6–12** (line 15)

6. 1. **Quaerēs,** etc.: introduces the remarks on literature anticipated in chapter 2; technically they are *extrā causam.*   See Companion, page 544.

3. **ubi:** ' (that) with which'; with the subjunctive of characteristic. *194, a.*   **ex:** 'after.'   **forēnsī:** see page 155, line 20, and note.

4. **convīciō:** i.e. *convīciō lītigantium,* ' din ' of voices in the court.

An tū exīstimās aut suppetere nōbīs posse, quod cotīdiē 5 dīcāmus in tantā varietāte rērum, nisi animōs nostrōs doctrīnā excolāmus, aut ferre animōs tantam posse contentiōnem, nisi eōs doctrīnā eādem relaxēmus?

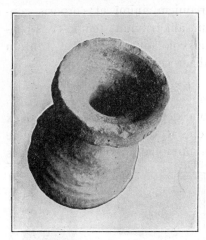

A ROMAN DICE BOX

Ego vērō fateor mē 10 hīs studiīs esse dēditum. Cēterōs pudeat, sī quī ita sē litterīs abdidērunt, ut nihil possint ex eīs neque ad commūnem afferre 15 frūctum neque in aspectum lūcemque prōferre; mē autem quid pudeat, quī tot annōs ita vīvō, iūdicēs, ut ā nūllīus um- 20 quam mē tempore aut commodō aut ōtium meum abstrāxerit aut voluptās āvocārit aut dēnique somnus retardārit?

---

5. **suppetere :** = *suppeditārī.* **nōbīs :** ' us ' advocates and orators as a class. Quintilian (**10**, 1, 27) recommends to orators the reading of poetry, and alludes to this passage.

6. **varietāte rērum :** ' variety of subjects.'

11. **hīs studiīs :** see page 221, line 4, and note. **esse dēditum :** see page 223, line 21, and note.

13. **litterīs :** perhaps originally written *in litterīs;* if not, must be construed as an instrumental ablative.

14. **neque . . . neque :** as in line 35 above; *ad . . . frūctum (ūtilitātem)* refers to the public services of a man of literary culture, *in . . . prōferre* to authorship.

16. **aspectum lūcemque :** ' the light of publicity.'

18. **quid :** as on page 52, line 27. **pudeat,** etc.: another apology to the Roman jury of practical men ; see note on page 222, line 5.

21. **tempore :** for *perīculō;* see page 224, line 14, and note ; contrasted with *commodō,* referring to civil cases.

25 Quā rē quis tandem mē reprehendat, aut quis mihi iūre suscēnseat, sī quantum cēterīs ad suās rēs obeundās, quantum ad fēstōs diēs lūdōrum celebrandōs, quantum ad aliās voluptātēs et ad ipsam requiem animī et corporis concēditur temporum, quantum aliī tribuunt tempestīvīs con-

30 vīviīs, quantum dēnique alveolō, quantum pilae, tantum mihi egomet ad haec studia recolenda sūmpserō?

Such pursuits contribute also preparation for public speaking, and inspire the highest ideals of public service.

Atque hōc ideō mihi concēdendum est magis, quod ex hīs studiīs haec quoque crēscit ōrātiō et facultās, quae quantacumque in mē est, numquam amīcōrum perīculīs

25. **Quā rē :** see page 40, line 25, and note.

26. **quantum . . . temporum :** why so far separated?

27. **lūdōrum :** celebrated in connection with the religious festivals.

28. **ipsam:** 'simply,' 'merely.' *162, a.*

29. **temporum :** plural as referring to the portions of time given to each kind of recreation. **tempestīvīs :** 'early,' commencing before 3 P.M.; hence 'protracted.'

30. **alveolō :** the Romans were addicted to gambling. **pilae :** why put after *convīviīs* and *alveolō* is not clear; for ball-playing was considered an entirely respectable form of amusement.

33. **ōrātiō et facultās :** hendiadys for *facultās ōrātōria*, 'oratorical power.' *238, h.*

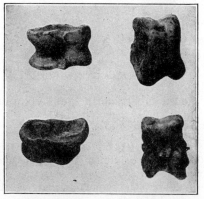

ROMAN DICE

34. **quantacumque in mē est :** 'so far as it resides in me,' 'so far as in me lies.' **amīcōrum perīculīs :** 'my friends in their need.'

dēfuit. Quae sī cui levior vidētur, illa quidem certē, 35 quae summa sunt, ex quō fonte hauriam, sentiō.

Nam, nisi multōrum praeceptīs multīsque litterīs mihi ab adulēscentiā suāsissem, nihil esse in vītā magnō opere expetendum nisi laudem atque honestātem, in eā autem persequendā omnēs cruciātūs corporis, omnia perīcula 40 mortis atque exsilī parvī esse dūcenda, numquam mē prō salūte vestrā in tot ac tantās dīmicātiōnēs atque in hōs prōflīgātōrum hominum cōtīdiānōs impetūs obiēcissem. Sed plēnī omnēs sunt librī, plēnae sapientium vōcēs, plēna exemplōrum vetustās; quae iacērent in tenebrīs omnia, 45 nisi litterārum lūmen accēderet.

Quam multās nōbīs imāginēs nōn sōlum ad intuendum, vērum etiam ad imitandum fortissimōrum virōrum expressās scrīptōrēs et Graecī et Latīnī relīquērunt! Quās ego mihi semper in administrandā rē pūblicā prōpōnēns animum 50 et mentem meam ipsā cōgitātiōne hominum excellentium cōnfōrmābam.

---

35. **illa**: the moral principles set forth in the following paragraph.

37. **praeceptīs**: the teachings of the philosophers. **multīs litterīs**: in our phrase, ' by wide reading.'

39. **laudem atque honestātem**: *i.e.* ' glory gained by merit,' hendiadys; hence the singular *eā* in line 39. *238, h.*

41. **mortis atque exsilī**: by using *atque* the orator indicates that he considers exile worse than death. **parvī**: *101;* B. 203, 3; A. & G. 417; G. 380.

43. **prōflīgātōrum hominum**: sympathizers with the Catilinarian conspirators; they finally brought about the exile of Cicero.

44. **plēnī**: i.e. *tālium praeceptōrum.* **sapientium vōcēs**: the utterances of the philosophers.

45. **quae omnia**: ' all of which,' ' and (yet) they all.' *97, c;* B. 201, 1, *b;* A. & G, 346, *e;* G. 370, R. 2.

47. **imāginēs . . . expressās**: ' forms,' ' ideals ' . . . ' finely portrayed '; *exprimere* is used to denote the sharp, clear presentation of details by the art of the sculptor or painter.

51. **hominum excellentium**: i.e. *dē hominibus excellentibus.*

*Our greatest men owe their eminence to the disciplining and refining
of natural ability through literary studies.*

7. Quaeret quispiam: 'Quid? illī ipsī summī virī,
quōrum virtūtēs litterīs prōditae sunt, istāne doctrīnā,
quam tū effers laudibus, ērudītī fuērunt?'

Difficile est hōc dē omnibus cōnfīrmāre, sed tamen est
5 certum, quid respondeam. Ego multōs hominēs excellentī
animō ac virtūte fuisse sine doctrīnā, et nātūrae ipsīus
habitū prope dīvīnō per sē ipsōs et moderātōs et gravēs
exstitisse, fateor; etiam illud adiungō, saepius ad laudem
atque virtūtem nātūram sine doctrīnā quam sine nātūrā
10 valuisse doctrīnam.

Atque īdem ego contendō, cum ad nātūram eximiam et
illūstrem accesserit ratiō quaedam cōnfōrmātiōque doctrīnae, tum illud nesciō quid praeclārum ac singulāre
solēre exsistere. Ex hōc esse hunc numerō, quem patrēs
15 nostrī vīdērunt, dīvīnum hominem, Āfricānum, ex hōc
C. Laelium, L. Furium, moderātissimōs hominēs et continentissimōs, ex hōc fortissimum virum et illīs temporibus
doctissimum, M. Catōnem, illum senem; quī profectō,

---

7. 1. **Quaeret quispiam:** introduces an objection, which the
orator wishes to meet; see Companion, page 546.

4. **est certum:** sc. *mihi;* 'I am decided what answer to give.' *217, b.*

9. **nātūram sine doctrīnā . . . sine nātūrā doctrīnam:** forceful
chiasmus. *239, e.*

11. **Atque īdem ego contendō:** 'And I maintain (this) also.'

12. **ratiō quaedam cōnfōrmātiōque doctrīnae:** *quīdam* is often
inserted by Cicero to indicate that he is employing a word in an unusual
sense, or is not altogether satisfied with it; 'what I may call the
systematic training and culture afforded by learning.'

13. **illud . . . singulāre:** 'some noble and unique excellence.'

14. **hunc . . . Āfricānum:** the younger Scipio; *hīc* is used to denote
that which is nearer in time. *160, a.*

16. **moderātissimōs et continentissimōs:** 'men of the greatest
self-command and even temper.'

18. **quī:** 'and these men.' *167.*

sī nihil ad percipiendam colendamque virtūtem litterīs adiuvārentur, numquam sē ad eārum studium contulissent. 20

No other resource so enriches life.

Quod sī nōn hīc tantus frūctus ostenderētur, et sī ex hīs studiīs dēlectātiō sōla peterētur, tamen, ut opīnor, hanc animī remissiōnem hūmānissimam ac līberālissimam iūdicārētis. Nam cēterae neque temporum sunt neque aetātum omnium neque locōrum; at haec studia adulēscentiam 25 alunt, senectūtem oblectant, secundās rēs ōrnant, adversīs perfugium ac sōlācium praebent, dēlectant domī, nōn impediunt forīs, pernoctant nōbīscum, peregrīnantur, rūsticantur.

8. Quod sī ipsī haec neque attingere neque sēnsū nostrō gustāre possēmus, tamen ea mīrārī dēbērēmus, etiam cum in aliīs vidērēmus. Quis nostrum tam animō agrestī ac dūrō fuit, ut Rōscī morte nūper nōn commovērētur? Quī cum esset senex mortuus, tamen propter excellentem 5 artem ac venustātem vidēbātur omnīnō morī nōn dēbuisse. Ergō ille corporis mōtū tantum amōrem sibi conciliārat ā nōbīs omnibus; nōs animōrum incrēdibilēs mōtūs celeritātemque ingeniōrum neglegēmus?

---

19. **nihil**: as on page 25, line 3.

20. **adiuvārentur**: ' were (continually) aided,' so long as they lived; more forcible than the pluperfect. *208, c.*

21. **nōn . . . ostenderētur**: ' were not shown (clearly),' *i.e.* ' were not assured.'

24. **cēterae**: sc. *animī remissiōnēs.*

25. **omnium**: with *temporum, aetātum, locōrum.*

26. **alunt**: ' strengthen.' **adversīs**: i.e. *eīs quī in adversīs rēbus sunt.*

8. 2. **etiam cum . . . vidērēmus**: i.e. *etiam videntēs.*

4. **Rōscī**: his chief characteristic as an actor was gracefulness. **commovērētur**: ' was deeply moved.'

7. **Ergō**, etc.: argument from less to greater. **mōtū**: ' (simply) by the movement.'

8. **mōtūs**: the Latin often uses the plural where we prefer a singular abstract noun; here the number is regulated by *animōrum,* because there

Archias deserves consideration because he is a poet.

10 Quotiēns ego hunc Archiam vīdī, iūdicēs, — ūtar enim vestrā benignitāte, quoniam mē in hōc novō genere dīcendī tam dīligenter attenditis, — quotiēns ego hunc vīdī, cum litteram scrīpsisset nūllam, magnum numerum optimōrum versuum dē eīs ipsīs rēbus, quae tum agerentur, dīcere ex 15 tempore! quotiēns revocātum eandem rem dīcere commū-tātīs verbīs atque sententiīs! Quae vērō accūrātē cōgi-tāteque scrīpsisset, ea sīc vīdī probārī, ut ad veterum scrīptōrum laudem pervenīret.

Hunc ego nōn dīligam, nōn admīrer, nōn omnī ratiōne 20 dēfendendum putem? Atque sīc ā summīs hominibus ērudītissimīsque accēpimus, cēterārum rērum studia ex doctrīnā et praeceptīs et arte cōnstāre; poētam nātūrā

---

were several minds. *mōtūs animōrum,* ' mental activity,' developed by training, as distinguished from *celeritātem ingenuōrum,* ' natural quick-ness.' *92, c.*

10. **ūtar :** ' I shall take advantage of.'

13. **nūllam :** emphatic, ' not a.'

14. **agerentur :** *220;* B. 324, 2 ; A. & G. 593 ; G. 629.

15. **revocātum :** for an encore. **eandem rem :** for *dē eādem rē.*

17. **veterum scrīptōrum :** i.e. *Graecōrum.* All the writings of Archias have perished with the exception of eighteen epigrams (see Reinach, *Dē Archiā,* page 28, *et seq.*), which are assigned to him with a strong probability that they are genuine. To judge from these, his success as an extemporizer consisted chiefly in the ability to patch together, on the spur of the moment, phrases, lines, and passages from the older poets which had previously been committed to memory. The same explanation would account also for the resemblance of his more elaborate productions to the writings of the classic Greek writers. By having a memory stored with original and selected passages appropriate to many subjects and occasions, a good ear for metres, and by constant practice, a professional extemporizer was able to perform feats that appeared little short of the marvelous, — and that, too, without being a great poet.

21. **ex . . . cōnstāre :** ' are based on.'

22. **nātūrā ipsā valēre :** ' derives his power from nature herself.'

ipsā valēre et mentis vīribus excitārī et quasi dīvīnō quōdam
spīritū īnflārī. Quā rē suō iūre noster ille Ennius "sānc-

HOMER

A bust in the Vatican.

tōs" appellat poētās, quod 25
quasi deōrum aliquō dōnō
atque mūnere commendātī
nōbīs esse videantur.

Sit igitur, iūdicēs, sānctum apud vōs, hūmānis- 30
simōs hominēs, hōc poētae
nōmen, quod nūlla umquam
barbaria violāvit. Saxa et
sōlitūdinēs vōcī respondent,
bēstiae saepe immānēs cantū 35
flectuntur atque cōnsistunt;
nōs īnstitūtī rēbus optimīs
nōn poētārum vōce move-
āmur?

Homērum Colophōniī 40
cīvem esse dīcunt suum, Chiī
suum vindicant, Salamīniī

23. **mentis vīribus excitārī:** *i.e.* independently of outside influences,
or of education.

24. **suō iūre:** see page 222, line 7, and note. **noster:** 'of ours' as
a Latin poet, in contrast with the Greek poets just referred to.

33. **barbaria,** etc.: there was never a people so sunk in savagery
that it did not respect the poet. **Saxa . . . cōnsistunt:** a reference to
the mythical musicians, as Amphion (am-fī′on), Arion (a-rī′on), and
Orpheus.

37. **rēbus:** for *artibus.*

40. **Homērum:** according to the well-known Greek couplet, **seven**
cities claimed to be the birthplace of Homer:

Ἑπτὰ πόλεις διερίζουσιν περὶ ῥίζαν Ὁμήρου,
Σμύρνα, Ῥόδος, Κολοφών, Σαλαμίς, Χίος, Ἄργος, Ἀθῆναι.

In a Latin hexameter line the cities are as follows:

Smyrna, Rhodos, Colophōn, Salamis, Chios, Argos, Athēnae.

42. **Salamīniī:** the inhabitants of Salamis in Cyprus.

repetunt, Smyrnaeī vērō suum esse cōnfīrmant, itaque etiam dēlūbrum eius in oppidō dēdicāvērunt; permultī
45 aliī praetereā pugnant inter sē atque contendunt.

Further, Archias in his verse is celebrating Roman victories.

9. Ergō illī aliēnum, quia poēta fuit, post mortem etiam expetunt; nōs hunc vīvum, quī et voluntāte et lēgibus noster est, repudiābimus, praesertim cum omne ōlim studium atque omne ingenium contulerit Archiās ad
5 populī Rōmānī glōriam laudemque celebrandam? Nam et Cimbricās rēs adulēscēns attigit et ipsī illī C. Mariō, quī dūrior ad haec studia vidēbātur, iūcundus fuit.

Neque enim quisquam est tam āversus ā Mūsīs, quī nōn mandārī versibus aeternum suōrum labōrum facile prae-
10 cōnium patiātur. Themistoclem illum, summum Athēnīs virum, dīxisse aiunt, cum ex eō quaererētur, quod acroāma aut cuius vōcem libentissimē audīret: *Eius, ā quō sua virtūs optimē praedicārētur.*

---

44. **dēlūbrum:** at Smyrna there was a square portico with a temple and statue of Homer (Strabo, **14,** 1).

45. **pugnant:** over the same thing. For the nativity of the Homeric poems, see Miss Clerke's *Familiar Studies in Homer,* page 10, *et seq.*

9. 1. **aliēnum:** *i.e.* Homer was a 'foreigner' to all the cities excepting the one in which he was born. What would they have said to the assertion that Homer never lived?

3. **omne ōlim studium:** 'all of his erstwhile zeal.'

6. **Cimbricās rēs:** 'the war with the Cimbri (sim′brī),' of which Marius was naturally the hero. **attigit:** implies that the poem was not completed.

7. **dūrior ad haec:** 'too rough for such.'

8. **Neque enim quisquam est:** 'And (yet not strange), for there is no one.' **āversus ā:** 'unfriendly to'; difference between the Latin and the English point of view?

9. **aeternum . . . praecōnium:** i.e. *praecōnium quod aeternum sit.*

10. **Themistoclem** (thẹ-mis′tọ-klēz).

11. **ex eō:** see IDIOMS.

12. **cuius vōcem:** i.e. *cuius cantantis vōcem.*

Itaque ille Marius item eximiē L. Plōtium dīlēxit, cuius ingeniō putābat ea, quae gesserat, posse celebrārī. 15

Mithridāticum vērō bellum, magnum atque difficile et in multā varietāte terrā marīque versātum, tōtum ab hōc expressum est; quī librī nōn modo L. Lūcullum, fortissimum et clārissimum virum, vērum etiam populī Rōmānī nōmen illūstrant. 20

Populus enim Rōmānus aperuit, Lūcullō imperante, Pontum, et rēgiīs quondam opibus et ipsā nātūrā et regiōne vāllātum; populī Rōmānī exercitus, eōdem duce, nōn maximā manū innumerābilēs Armeniōrum cōpiās fūdit; populī Rōmānī laus est, urbem amīcissimam Cyzicēnōrum 25 eiusdem cōnsiliō ex omnī impetū rēgiō atque ē tōtīus bellī ōre ac faucibus ēreptam esse atque servātam; nostra semper

---

14. **L. Plōtium** (lū'sh(y)ụs plō'sh(y)us).

15. **ea, quae gesserat:** *rēs ā sē gestās.*

16. **Mithridāticum bellum:** no doubt chiefly that part of the war with Mithridates (mith-rị-dā'tēz) which reflected most credit on the name of Lucullus, whom the poet accompanied in the Asiatic campaigns. Reinach (*Dē Archiā*, pages 46–54) has made it appear at least probable that this poem consisted of four books, and that it was freely used by Plutarch in writing the life of Lucullus.

18. **expressum est:** ' has been treated.'

21. **aperuit Pontum:** see a similar statement, *Dē Imperiō Cn. Pompeī,* page 165, lines 18–20.

22. **rēgiīs opibus:** including strongholds, troops, financial resources, etc. **regiōne:** ' by its situation.'

24. **innumerābilēs Armeniōrum cōpiās:** at the battle near Tigranocerta, in 69 B.C. (see Companion, page 531 and Map). According to the figures given by Plutarch (*Lucullus*, 26, 27), the Armenians outnumbered the Romans twenty to one, mustering more than 200,000 men, of whom 150,000 were infantry, against a Roman force of only 11,000.

25. **urbem Cyzicēnōrum** (sịz-ị-sē'nī) **. . . servātam:** in 73 B.C.; see page 164, lines 11–15, and note. In enumerating the victories of Lucullus, Cicero does not confine himself to the chronological order.

27. **ōre ac faucibus:** we might say ' the open jaws.' See page 77, line 6, and note.

ferētur et praedicābitur, L. Lūcullō dīmicante, cum, interfectīs ducibus, dēpressa hostium classis est, incrēdibilis
30 apud Tenedum pugna illa nāvālis ; nostra sunt tropaea,
nostra monumenta, nostrī triumphī. Quae quōrum ingeniīs
efferuntur, ab eīs populī Rōmānī fāma celebrātur.

Cārus fuit Āfricānō superiōrī noster Ennius, itaque etiam
in sepulcrō Scīpiōnum putātur is esse cōnstitūtus ex mar-
35 more ; at eīs laudibus certē nōn sōlum ipse, quī laudātur,
sed etiam populī Rōmānī nōmen ōrnātur. In caelum huius
proavus Catō tollitur ; magnus honōs populī Rōmānī
rēbus adiungitur. Omnēs dēnique illī Maximī, Mārcellī,
Fulviī nōn sine commūnī omnium nostrum laude
40 decorantur.

---

28. **interfectīs ducibus :** translate as if *ducēs interfectī sunt et.*

30. **apud Tenedum pugna illa nāvālis :** in 73 B.C. The Roman fleet
sank a part of the enemy's ships between the Trojan coast and Tenedos
(ten'ẹ-dọs). See Map; but the main engagement took place near the
island of Lemnos. The two victories are here spoken of as one. See
page 165, lines 15–17.

33. **noster :** see page 241, line 24, and note.

34. **in sepulcrō Scīpiōnum :** the disposition of the dead by burial was
kept up in the Scipio family long after cremation became the prevalent
method at Rome. The tomb of the Scipios was opened in 1780. It
lies on the left side of the Appian Way, a short distance outside the
Servian wall. It consists of a number of narrow, winding passages
excavated in the soft rock, in the sides of which places were cut out for
the bodies of the dead. At the entrance in Cicero's time (see Livy,
38, 56, 4), there were three statues, of which one was thought to be that
of Ennius. See Platner, *Topography of Ancient Rome*, pages 435–436.

35. **eīs laudibus :** ' by such praises ' as those which Ennius bestowed
on Scipio.

36. **huius :** *huius Catōnis,* ' the present Cato,' *i.e.* Cato Uticensis;
see *hunc Āfricānum,* page 238, line 14, and note. Cato the Censor
found Ennius in Sardinia, serving in the Roman army, and brought him
to Rome.

38. **Omnēs illī Maximī, Mārcellī, Fulviī :** ' All the famous men like
Maximus, Marcellus, and Fulvius.' Proper names of persons in the
plural regularly mean ' men like.' *92, d.*

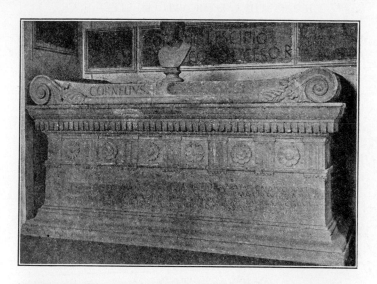

ABOVE: THE SARCOPHAGUS OF SCIPIO AFRICANUS
In the Vatican.

BELOW: A MODERN IMITATION

10. Ergō illum, quī haec fēcerat, Rudīnum hominem, maiōrēs nostrī in cīvitātem recēpērunt; nōs hunc Hēracliēnsem, multīs cīvitātibus expetītum, in hāc autem lēgibus cōnstitūtum, dē nostrā cīvitāte ēiciēmus?

It is no disadvantage that Archias writes Greek verse; Greek is more widely read than Latin.

Nam, sī quis minōrem glōriae frūctum putat ex Graecīs 5 versibus percipī quam ex Latīnīs, vehementer errat, proptereā quod Graeca leguntur in omnibus ferē gentibus, Latīna suīs fīnibus, exiguīs sānē, continentur.

Quā rē, sī rēs eae, quās gessimus, orbis terrae regiōnibus dēfīniuntur, cupere dēbēmus, quō manuum nostrārum tēla 10 pervēnerint, eōdem glōriam fāmamque penetrāre, quod cum ipsīs populīs, dē quōrum rēbus scrībitur, haec ampla

---

10. 1. **haec fēcerat:** i.e. *haec carmina fēcerat* ('had composed'); original meaning of "poet," *poēta*, ποιητής? **Rudīnum:** 'of Rudiae' (rū'dḭ-ē).

2. **in cīvitātem recēpērunt:** the Roman franchise was bestowed on Ennius by the son of Marcus Fulvius Nobilior (see page 249, line 15), in 184 B.C. The poet says of himself (Cicero, *Dē Ōrātōre*, **3**, 42, 168):

Nōs sumus Rōmānī, quī fūimus ante Rudīnī.

Hēracliēnsem: sharply contrasted with *Rudīnum*, because Heraclea was so much more important a place than Rudiae and possessed special treaty relations with Rome. See page 228, lines 4–7, and note.

5. **Nam:** introduces an answer to an assumed, or suppressed, objection; the ellipsis may be supplied thus, ' (But Archias writes in Greek. That is no objection), for ' . . .

6. **vehementer:** see IDIOMS.

7. **Graeca:** neuter plural; we say ' Greek,' with a singular verb.

8. **suīs fīnibus:** even in Cicero's time Latin was spoken very little outside Latium and the Roman and Latin colonies. The Greek language had been carried by Greek commerce and settlements — in the East also by the conquests and colonies of Alexander — over the whole ancient world. Latin made little progress in superseding the native dialects of western Europe till the time of the Empire.

9. **regiōnibus:** = *termin īs*. See page 106, lines 14, 15.

12. **ampla:** ' full of honor,' ' glorious.' It was an honor to any nation to be conquered by Rome!

sunt tum eīs certē, quī dē vītā glōriae causā dīmicant, hōc
maximum et perīculōrum incitāmentum est et labōrum.

The greatest leaders have wished poets to immortalize their deeds.

15   Quam multōs scrīptōrēs rērum suārum magnus ille Alexander sēcum habuisse
dīcitur! Atque is tamen,
cum in Sīgēō ad Achillis
tumulum astitisset, " Ō
20 fortūnāte," inquit, "adulēscēns, quī tuae virtūtis
Homērum praecōnem
invēnerīs!"

Et vērē. Nam, nisi
25 Īlias illa exstitisset, īdem
tumulus, quī corpus eius
contēxerat, nōmen etiam
obruisset.

ALEXANDER

A bust in the Capitoline Museum.

13. **dē vītā:** ' at the risk
of life.'

14. **perīculōrum:** i.e. *ad
perīcula subeunda.* Kind of
genitive? *102.*

15. **scrīptōrēs rērum
suārum:** among them are
mentioned Anaximenes, Aris-
tobulus, Callisthenes, the poet
Choerilus, Onesicritus, and
Ptolemaeus.

18. **Sīgēō** (sĭ-jē'ŭm). **Achillis tumulum:** in the Troad, near the
entrance of the Hellespont, there are several great prehistoric mounds,
or tumuli, to which the names of heroes of the Trojan war were given
at a very early date. At the mound said to mark the burial-place of
Achilles there was a temple erected in his honor (Strabo, **13,** 1, 32).
See illustration, page 247.

24. **Et vērē:** sc. *dīxit.*

Quid? noster hīc Magnus, quī cum virtūte fortūnam adaequāvit, nōnne Theophanem Mytilēnaeum, scrīptōrem 30 rērum suārum, in cōntiōne mīlitum cīvitāte dōnāvit, et nostrī illī fortēs virī, sed rūsticī ac mīlitēs, dulcēdine quādam glōriae commōtī, quasi participēs eiusdem laudis, magnō illud clāmōre approbāvērunt?

Itaque, crēdō, sī cīvis Rōmānus Archiās lēgibus nōn 35 esset, ut ab aliquō imperātōre cīvitāte dōnārētur, perficere nōn potuit. Sulla cum Hispānōs et Gallōs dōnāret, crēdō, hunc petentem repudiāsset; quem nōs in cōntiōne

THE SO-CALLED TOMB OF ACHILLES NEAR TROY

29. **noster hīc Magnus:** Pompey was no doubt pleased at this implied comparison of himself with Alexander.

30. **Theophanem Mytilēnaeum** (thẹ-of′ạ-nēz of mit-ị-lē′nē).

31. **cīvitāte dōnāvit:** after the war with Sertorius a special enactment confirmed the grants of citizenship previously made by Pompey (Cicero, *Prō Balbō*, **8,** 19).

33. **eiusdem laudis:** as that which Theophanes had bestowed on Pompey.

38. **petentem:** = *sī petīsset.* **quem:** 'and (yet) we saw him,' Sulla. **in cōntiōne:** here *in cōntiōne cīvium* (see line 31), in the Forum, where he was superintending the sale of the possessions of the proscribed at auction.

vīdimus, cum eī libellum malus poēta dē populō subiēcisset,
40 quod epigramma in eum fēcisset, tantum modo alternīs
versibus longiusculīs, statim ex eīs rēbus, quās tum vēndē-·
bat, iubēre eī praemium tribuī, sed eā condiciōne, nē quid
posteā scrīberet. Quī sēdulitātem malī poētae dūxerit
aliquō tamen praemiō dignam, huius ingenium et virtūtem
45 in scrībendō et cōpiam nōn expetīsset?

Quid? ā Q. Metellō Piō, familiārissimō suō, quī cīvitāte
multōs dōnāvit, neque per sē neque per Lūcullōs impetrāvisset? quī praesertim ūsque eō dē suīs rēbus scrībī
cuperet, ut etiam Cordubae nātīs poētīs, pingue quiddam
50 sonantibus atque peregrīnum, tamen aurēs suās dēderet.

*All men desire praise; and Archias has commenced a poem on the
events of my consulship.*

11. Neque enim est hōc dissimulandum, quod obscūrārī
nōn potest, sed prae nōbīs ferendum: trahimur omnēs
studiō laudis, et optimus quisque maximē glōriā dūcitur.

---

39. **eī subiēcisset:** 'had thrust up to him (from below)' as he sat
on the tribunal. **libellum:** we should say 'a manuscript.' **dē populō:**
i.e. common, vulgar.

40. **quod epigramma:** explains *libellum,* 'an epigram which.' *165, b;*
B. 324, 1; A. & G. 593; G. 629. **tantum . . . longiusculīs:** *i.e.* it had
no merit except that every other line was longer than its mate, being
written apparently in elegiac stanzas, or distichs. See B. 369, 1, 2;
A. & G. 616; G. 785.

43. **sēdulitātem:** 'persistency,' 'officiousness.'

47. **dōnāvit:** when proconsul in Spain, engaged in the war with
Sertorius. **per Lūcullōs:** Lucius and Marcus Lucullus were kinsmen of
Metellus Pius, perhaps cousins. **impetrāvisset:** sc. *cīvitātem.*

48. **quī:** 'since he,' Metellus Pius. *194, c.*

49. **Cordubae** (kor′dŭ-bặ): a number of Roman veterans had been
settled about Corduba, which was one of the first provincial cities to
become Romanized. **pingue:** see IDIOMS.

11. 3. **optimus quisque,** etc.: not 'all the best men,' but 'the more
noble a man, the more is he attracted by fame.' *quisque* with a superlative degree is often an abridged equivalent of *quō — eō* with a com-

Ipsī illī philosophī etiam in eīs libellīs, quōs dē contemnendā glōriā scrībunt, nōmen suum īnscrībunt; in eō ipsō, in quō praedicātiōnem nōbilitātemque dēspiciunt, praedicārī dē sē ac nōminārī volunt.

Decimus quidem Brūtus, summus vir et imperātor, Accī, amīcissimī suī, carminibus templōrum ac monumentōrum aditūs exōrnāvit suōrum. Iam vērō ille, quī cum Aetōlīs Enniō comite bellāvit, Fulvius, nōn dubitāvit Mārtis manubiās Mūsīs cōnsecrāre. Quā rē, in quā urbe imperātōrēs prope armātī poētārum

APOLLO, LEADER OF THE MUSES

The Greeks ascribe the invention of the cithara to Apollo and that of the lyre to Hermes.

parative degree expressing proportion. *170, a;* A. & G. 313, *b,* N. 1; G. 642, R. 2; 318, 2.

4. **illī philosophī:** the Stoics and Epicureans especially claimed to be indifferent to fame. Cicero wrote a treatise *Dē Glōriā,* which is now lost.

5. **in eō ipsō:** 'in regard to that very matter.'

7. **nōminārī:** for *sē nōminārī,* in the sense of *nōbilitārī.*

11. **amīcissimī suī:** 'of his most intimate friend.' See page 230, line 14, and note. **templōrum, monumentōrum:** built with the proceeds from the sale of booty secured in the conquest of Further Spain. One of the temples was dedicated to Mars, and contained a colossal statue of the god by Scopas (Pliny, *Historia Nātūrālis,* **36,** 5, 26).

15. **Fulvius:** see *Nōbilior* in vocabulary. He was severely censured by Cato the Censor for taking Ennius with him.

16. **Mūsīs:** Fulvius built a temple in honor of Hercules and the Muses, and adorned it richly with works of art taken from Ambracia in Epirus; see note to page 181, line 18.

18. **prope armātī:** 'almost in military attire'; *i.e.* before they had assumed the garb suitable to the city and to civil life.

nōmen et Mūsārum dēlūbra coluērunt, in eā nōn dēbent
20 togātī iūdicēs ā Mūsārum honōre et ā poētārum salūte
abhorrēre.

Atque ut id libentius faciātis, iam mē vōbīs, iūdicēs,
indicābō et dē meō quōdam amōre glōriae nimis acrī
fortasse, vērum tamen honestō, vōbīs cōnfitēbor. Nam,
25 quās rēs nōs in cōnsulātū nostrō vōbīscum simul prō
salūte urbis atque huius imperī et prō vītā cīvium
prōque ūniversā rē pūblicā gessimus, attigit hīc versibus
atque incohāvit. Quibus audītīs, quod mihi magna rēs et
iūcunda vīsa est, hunc ad perficiendum adhortātus sum.

*What incentive has the patriot to devote himself to the public interest
except the prospect of meriting the undying praise of his fellowmen?*

30   Nūllam enim virtūs aliam mercēdem labōrum perīculōrumque dēsīderat praeter hanc laudis et glōriae; quā
quidem dētrāctā, iūdicēs, quid est, quod in hōc tam exiguō
vītae curriculō tantīs nōs in labōribus exerceāmus?

Certē, sī nihil animus praesentīret in posterum, et sī,
35 quibus regiōnibus vītae spatium circumscrīptum est,
eīsdem omnēs cōgitātiōnēs termināret suās, nec tantīs

---

20. ā . . . abhorrēre : ' be insensible to,' ' be inattentive to.'

22. vōbīs : i.e. *vōbīs iūdicibus*, taken as representatives of your
respective classes ; for the jurors at this time were drawn from the ranks
of the senators, knights, and tribunes of the treasury. These classes
as a whole had supported Cicero heartily in the suppression of the
Catilinarian conspiracy.

28. incohāvit : a year later the poem was not yet finished, greatly to
the disappointment of Cicero (see *Ad Atticum*, **1**, 16, 15) ; probably it
was never completed.   Quibus audītīs : *Dē eīs (versibus) cum audīssem.*
rēs : ' the theme.'

31. hanc : *hanc mercēdem.* laudis : explanatory genitive, ' which
consists in praise.'   *96, a.*

32. quid est, quod : see page 232, line 9, and note.

34. nihil . . . praesentīret : ' cherished no anticipation.'

35. regiōnibus : as on page 245, line 9.

sē labōribus frangeret neque tot cūrīs vigiliīsque angerētur nec totiēns dē ipsā vītā dīmicāret. Nunc īnsidet quaedam in optimō quōque virtūs, quae noctēs ac diēs animum glōriae stimulīs concitat atque admonet, nōn cum vītae 40 tempore esse dīmittendam commemorātiōnem nōminis nostrī, sed cum omnī posteritāte adaequandam.

12. An vērō tam parvī animī videāmur esse omnēs, quī in rē pūblicā atque in hīs vītae perīculīs labōribusque versāmur, ut, cum ūsque ad extrēmum spatium nūllum tranquillum atque ōtiōsum spīritum dūxerimus, nōbīscum simul moritūra omnia arbitrēmur? An statuās et imāginēs, 5 nōn animōrum simulācra, sed corporum, studiōsē multī summī hominēs relīquērunt; cōnsiliōrum relinquere ac virtūtum nostrārum effigiem nōnne multō mālle dēbēmus, summīs ingeniīs expressam et polītam?

Ego vērō omnia, quae gerēbam, iam tum in gerendō 10 spargere mē ac dissēmināre arbitrābar in orbis terrae memo‑

---

37. **angerētur:** ' would torment itself.' *174;* B. 256, 1; A. & G. 156, *a;* G. 218.

38. **dē ipsā vītā :** = *etiam dē vītā.* **Nunc :** ' But as it is.'

39. **quōque:** not *quŏque.* **virtūs :** ' noble impulse,' ' noble instinct.'

40. **nōn,** etc.: well expressed by Reid, ' that the story of our fame must not be given up to oblivion when the term of life ends, but that it must be made coextensive with all future time.'

12. 1. **videāmur:** ' are we to let ourselves appear.' Deliberative subjunctive. *179, b (2).*

5. **statuās:** ' statues '; *imāginēs,* ' portraits ' molded or carved in any material; *simulācra,* ' likenesses ' whether carved, drawn, or painted; contrasted with *effigiem,* ' representation,' here used of the ideal.

6. **animōrum, corporum:** we say ' of the soul,' ' of the body,' preferring to use the generic singular in many cases where the Latin has the plural. See note on page 239, line 8.

9. **summīs ingeniīs:** i.e. *ā virīs summō ingeniō.* **expressam:** see note on page 237, line 47.

10. **Ego vērō:** ' I for my part.'

riam sempiternam. Haec vērō sīve ā meō sēnsū post mortem āfutūra est, sīve, ut sapientissimī hominēs putāvērunt,
ad aliquam animī meī partem pertinēbit, nunc quidem certē
15 cōgitātiōne quādam spēque dēlector.

The proof in the case is sufficient; and as a poet of gifts Archias
deserves sympathetic treatment.

Quā rē cōnservāte, iūdicēs, hominem pudōre eō, quem
amīcōrum vidētis comprobārī cum dignitāte tum etiam
vetustāte, ingeniō autem tantō, quantum id convenit
exīstimārī, quod summōrum hominum ingeniīs expetītum
20 esse videātis, causā vērō eius modī, quae beneficiō lēgis,
auctōritāte mūnicipī, testimōniō Lūcullī, tabulīs Metellī
comprobētur.

Quae cum ita sint, petimus ā vōbīs, iūdicēs, sī qua nōn
modo hūmāna, verum etiam dīvīna in tantīs ingeniīs
25 commendātiō dēbet esse, ut eum, quī vōs, quī vestrōs
imperātōrēs, quī populī Rōmānī rēs gestās semper ōrnāvit,
quī etiam hīs recentibus nostrīs vestrīsque domesticīs
perīculīs aeternum sē testimōnium laudis datūrum esse
profitētur, estque ex eō numerō, quī semper apud omnēs
30 sānctī sunt habitī itaque dictī, sīc in vestram accipiātis

---

13. **sapientissimī hominēs:** philosophers who taught the immortality of the soul, as Pythagoras, Socrates.   See Companion, page 547.
14. **ad . . . pertinēbit:** ' it shall continue in relation to some part
of my soul,' *i.e.* ' my soul shall remain conscious of it.'
15. **spē:** *i.e* of an immortality of fame.
16. **pudōre eō:** ' of so fine a sense of honor.'   Ablative of quality
143, a.
17. **dignitāte:** ' high position.'
20. **eius modī:** = *tālī.*
21. **testimōniō mūnicipī:** see page 230, lines 21–24.
27. **domesticīs perīculīs:** the conspiracy of Catiline.
29. **ex eō numerō, quī:** = *ex illōrum numerō, quī.*
30. **sānctī:** see page 241, line 24. **itaque:** = *et ita.*

fidem, ut hūmānitāte vestrā levātus potius quam acerbitāte violātus esse videātur.

Quae dē causā prō meā cōnsuētūdine breviter simpliciterque dīxī, iūdicēs, ea cōnfīdō probāta esse omnibus; quae autem remōta ā meā iūdiciālīque cōnsuētūdine et 35 dē hominis ingeniō et commūniter dē ipsīus studiō locūtus sum, ea, iūdicēs, ā vōbīs spērō esse in bonam partem accepta; ab eō, quī iūdicium exercet, certō sciō.

---

31. **hūmānitāte levātus, acerbitāte violātus:** notice the assonance. *212, d.*

33. **dē causā:** 'in regard to the case,' referring to the earlier, technical portion of the speech.

38. **quī iūdicium exercet:** see page 224, line 11.

CICERO THE PHILOSOPHER

THE ACROPOLIS AT ATHENS

CICERO THE PHILOSOPHER

M. TULLĪ CICERŌNIS CATŌ MAIOR DĒ SENECTŪTE

Partēs Sēlēctae

There are four charges brought against old age.

5. Etenim, cum complector animō, quattuor reperiō

TO THE STUDENT: Consult the Companion, pages 546–553, for the origin and scope of this essay.

After a brief introductory conversation, in which Cato consents to talk about old age, the dialogue becomes really a monologue, since Cato continues to express his views without interruption to the end. This is the Aristotelian form of dialogue, in which there is less discussion but more of exposition; whereas in the Platonic form there is more of debate, and often a quick interchange of question and answer. (Who were Plato and Aristotle?) Cato maintains that right character alone can make old age tolerable, and that the ills usually charged against it are due not to age, but to defects of character.

TERRA COTTA HEAD OF AN AGED ROMAN

5. 1. **Etenim:** this word generally introduces either an explanation or a proof of a preceding statement. Here the words are elliptic, and the real connection with what precedes can be made clear only by a paraphrase. 'Ennius seemed to delight in old age. And no wonder,

causās, cūr senectūs misera videātur: ūnam, quod āvocet
ā rēbus gerendīs; alteram, quod corpus faciat īnfīrmius;
tertiam, quod prīvet omnibus ferē voluptātibus; quārtam,
5 quod haud procul absit ā morte. Eārum, sī placet, causā-
rum quanta, quamque sit iūsta, ūna quaeque videāmus.

First charge: Old age withdraws men from active life.
But old age has compensating activities of its own.

6. Ā rēbus gerendīs senectūs abstrahit.

Quibus? An eīs, quae iuventūte geruntur et vīribus?
Nūllaene igitur rēs sunt·senīlēs, quae, vel īnfīrmīs corpori-
bus, animō tamen administrentur? Nihil ergō agēbat Q.

since there are four causes which make men think old age wretched, and
no one of these will bear examination.' *Etenim* may generally be
translated 'indeed' or 'in fact.' **cum complector animō:** 'when I
grasp them in my thoughts.' The object of *complector* is to be supplied
from *causās*.

2. **āvocet:** sc. *senēs*. The subjunctives denote that these are the
thoughts not of the speaker, but of the persons who do think old age a
wretched thing. *183, a.*

3. **alteram . . . tertiam:** in enumerations of more than two things
ūnus and *alter* generally take the place of *prīmus* and *secundus;* in Cicero
the last two words rarely occur under such circumstances. **īnfīrmius:** sc.
quam anteā erat.

6. **quam sit iūsta:** Cicero generally separates from. the words they
qualify *quam, tam, ita, tantus, quantus,* often, as here, by one small
word. See page 273, line 17, *tam esse inimīcum.*

6. 2. **Quibus:** the preposition *ā* is often omitted. Even when
relative and antecedent are in the same sentence the preposition is not
often repeated. **An eīs:** *an* always introduces a question which is not
independent, but follows upon a previous question either expressed or
implied. Here *quibus* implies *omnibusne.* *204 (1);* B. 162, 4 *a;* A. & G.
335, *b;* G. 457. **iuventūte et vīribus:** commonly explained as hendiadys, *i.e.* as put for *iuventūtis vīribus;* but Cicero no more meant this
than we mean 'the strength of youth' when we speak of 'youth and
strength.' Real instances of hendiadys are much rarer than is generally
supposed. *238, h.*

3. **quae:** = *tālēs ut.* *194, b; 195.*

4. **Q. Maximus:** the famous Quintus Fabius Maximus Verrucosus
Ovicula Cunctator, hero of the Second Punic War, whose dilatory tactics

Maximus, nihil L. Paulus, pater tuus, socer optimī virī, 5
fīlī meī? Cēterī senēs, Fābriciī, Cūriī, Coruncāniī, cum
rem pūblicam cōnsiliō et auctōritāte dēfendēbant, nihil
agēbant?

A ROMAN BRIDGE

The inscription tells that it was built by one of the Fabricii.

against Hannibal were proverbially referred to as the " Fabian policy,"
an expression still used.

5. **L. Paulus:** this is L. Aemilius Paulus Macedonicus, consul in
182 B.C., and again in 168, when he finished the Third Macedonian War
by utterly defeating Perseus at Pydna. He was the father of Scipio
Africanus Minor. **pater tuus:** i.e. *Scīpiō*.

6. **fīlī:** M. Porcius Cato, who married the daughter of Paulus.
Fābriciī, etc.: generic plurals meaning 'men like Fabricius, etc.'
See note on page 244, line 38. *92, d*. C. Fabricius Luscinus (gā'(y)ụs
fạ-brị'sh(y)ụs lus'sị-nụs), consul in 282, 278, and 273 B.C., censor in 275,
held the command against Pyrrhus. The Roman writers, Cicero
especially, are never tired of eulogizing him as a pattern of old-fashioned
Roman virtue. Manius Curius Dentatus (mā'nị-ụs kū'rị-ụs den-tā'tụs),
consul in 290, 275, and 274, practically, if not formally, ended the Third
Samnite War, and also commanded against Pyrrhus. He was famed
for his sturdy Roman simplicity and frugality. Tiberius Coruncanius
(tị-bē'rị-ụs cọr-ụn-cā'nị-ụs) as consul in 280 crushed an Etruscan insurrection. In 252 he became the first plebeian pontifex maximus.
These three men are very frequently mentioned together by Cicero.

7. **nihil agēbant:** observe that *nihil agēbat* is put at the beginning

Nihil igitur afferunt, quī in rē gerendā versārī senectūtem
10 negant; similēsque sunt ut sī quī gubernātōrem in nāvi-
gandō nihil agere dīcant, cum aliī mālōs scandant, aliī per
forōs cursent, aliī sentīnam exhauriant, ille, clāvum tenēns,
quiētus sedeat in puppī, nōn faciat ea, quae iuvenēs. At
vērō multō maiōra et meliōra facit.

15 Nōn vīribus aut vēlōcitāte aut celeritāte corporum rēs
magnae geruntur, sed cōnsiliō, auctōritāte, sententiā;
quibus nōn modo nōn orbārī, sed etiam augērī senectūs
solet.

*Memory fails only if you neglect to exercise it, or if it was defective
in earlier life.*

7. At memoria minuitur. Crēdō, nisi eam exerceās,

---

of the first sentence, *nihil agēbant* at the end of the second; chiasmus.
239, e.

9. **Nihil afferunt:** 'They bring forward nothing,' *i.e.* what they
bring forward is worthless.

10. **similēs ut sī:** a very rare construction. In the English Bible
there are expressions like *similēs sunt ut sī quī dīcant,* ' they are like as
if some men should say.'

11. **scandant:** ' *cum* is used with the subjunctive when it expresses
a kind of comparison, and especially a contrast, between the contents
of a leading proposition and a subordinate ("whereas," etc.).' Madvig,
358, Obs. 3. The underlying idea in this use is generally cause, sometimes concession. **per forōs:** ' over the deck.'

12. **ille:** for the omission of *sed* or *autem (asyndeton adversātīvum)*
see *238, d.* **clāvum:** ' tiller.'

15. **vēlōcitāte:** *vēlōcitās* and *celeritās* differ very slightly; the former
means speed of movement in one line, the latter power of rapid motion
with frequent change of direction. The emphatic word in this clause
is *corporum.*

16. **cōnsiliō . . . sententiā:** *cōnsiliō,* ' advice '; *auctōritāte,* ' weight
of influence '; *sententiā,* ' an opinion ' or ' vote,' formally given.

17. **quibus:** in twofold relation; with *orbārī,* ablative of separation,
with *augērī,* of specification.

7. 1. **At:** = ἀλλὰ γάρ; used to introduce the supposed objection
of an opponent. **Crēdō:** ' Of course.' **exerceās:** the subject is the
indefinite ' you ' equivalent to ' one,' τὶς: ' unless one were to practice

aut etiam sī sīs nātūrā tardior. Themistoclēs omnium cīvium percēperat nōmina; (num igitur cēnsētis eum, cum aetāte prōcessisset, quī Aristī- dēs esset, Lysimachum salūtāre 5 solitum?)

Many men have retained their faculties and interests to extreme age.

Manent ingenia senibus, modo permaneat studium et industria, neque ea sōlum clārīs et honō- rātīs virīs, sed in vītā etiam 10 prīvātā et quiētā. Sophoclēs

THEMISTOCLES

A bust in the Vatican.

it.' For the mood see *180, e (2)*; B. 303, 356, 3; A. & G. 518, *a;* G. 596, 595, R. 3.

2. **tardior**: ' unusually dull.' **The- mistoclēs** (thẹ-mis'tọ-klēz): famed for his memory.

3. **cīvium**: ' fellow-countrymen.' **percēperat**: ' had grasped ' or ' mas- tered.'

4. **quī . . . solitum**: ' that he often addressed as Lysimachus someone who for all that was Aristídes.' The direct object of *salūtāre* is omitted. **quī**: = *tametsī is.* **Aristī'dēs**: surnamed " the Just," for his integrity; a rival of Themistocles.

5. **esset**: *220;* B. 324; A. & G. 593; G. 629. **Lysimachum** (lị-sim'ạ-kụs): for *ut Lysimachum* or *prō Lysimachō.* Lysimachus was the father of Aristides.

7. **ingenia**: = *suum cuique ingenium;* ' old men retain their wits.'

8. **permaneat**: *190, d;* B. 310; A. & G. 528; G. 573. **studium et industria**: ' earnestness and activity '; not a case of hendiadys, as some editors make it. See note on page 256, line 2, *iuventūte et vīribus.*

9. **neque ea sōlum**: ' and that not only.' **honōrātīs**: this does not correspond to our ' honored,' but implies that the persons have held high offices (*honōrēs*). Here translate ' statesmen.'

10. **in vītā . . . quiētā**: ' in an unofficial and retired life.' There is chiasmus here, since *prīvātā* is contrasted with *honōrātīs* and *quiētā* with *clārīs. 239, e.*

ad summam senectūtem tragoediās fēcit; quod propter
studium cum rem neglegere familiārem vidērētur, ā fīliīs
in iūdicium vōcātus est, ut, quem ad modum nostrō mōre
15 male rem gerentibus patribus bonīs interdīcī solet, sīc
illum, quasi dēsipientem, ā rē familiārī removērent iūdicēs.
Tum senex dīcitur eam fābulam, quam in manibus habēbat
et proximē scrīpserat, Oedipum Colōnēum, recitāsse iūdicibus, quaesisseque, num illud carmen dēsipientis vidērētur;
20 quō recitātō, sententiīs iūdicum est līberātus.
    Num igitur hunc, num Homērum, Hēsiodum, Simōnidēn,

---

12. **summam senectūtem:** Sophocles died at the age of 90 in 405 B.C.
quod propter studium: 'from his devotion to this occupation.'

13. **fīliīs:** except Plutarch, who probably follows Cicero's words,
all the authorities tell the story of the poet's eldest son Iophon only.
The tale is full of improbabilities.

15. **rem:** = *rem familiārem*. **patribus bonīs interdīcī solet:** 'fathers
are often prevented from managing their property.' For the interpretation see the expression *interdīcere alicui aquā et ignī*, page 491, and footnote: *interdīcī* is here used impersonally with *patribus* in the dative;
bonīs is ablative of separation (deprivation). *109, c.* The fragment of
the Twelve Tables here referred to is thus given in Dirksen's edition:
*sei fouriōsōs aut prōdicōs (prōdigus) escit (erit) adenātōrum centiliomque
(gentiliumque) eius potestās estod,* i.e. the agnates (male relatives whose
kinship with the *furiōsus* is derived through males) and members of his
gēns are to administer his property.

16. **quasi dēsipientem:** 'on the grounds that he is mentally irre-
sponsible.' ὡς παραφρονοῦντα, says the author of the anonymous life
of Sophocles. *238, g.*

17. **in manibus habēbat:** 'had on hand,' *i.e.* in preparation.

18. **scrīpserat:** he had written it but not finally corrected it. **recitāsse:** the common version of the story states that only the fine chorus
beginning εὔιππου, ξένε, τᾶσδε χώρας (line 668) was read.

19. **vidērētur:** sc. *esse;* the infinitive is often omitted thus after verbs
of desiring, thinking, etc., also verbs of speaking and hearing.

21. **Homērum:** the author of the *Iliad* and the *Odyssey*, who may
have lived between 1000 B.C. and 800 B.C. See *Prō Archiā*, page 241,
line 40. **Hēsiodum** (hē'sĭ-ŏd): the oldest Greek poet after Homer;
flourished 750 B.C. **Simōnidēn** (sĭ-mŏn'ĭ-dēz): Simonides of Ceos (not

Stēsichorum, num, quōs ante dīxī, Īsocratēn, Gorgiān, num
philosophōrum prīncipēs, Pȳthagorān, Dēmocritum, num
Platōnem, Xenocratēn, num posteā Zēnōnem, Cleanthēn,
aut eum, quem vōs etiam vīdistis Rōmae, Diogenēn Stoicum, 25
coēgit in suīs studiīs obmūtēscere senectūs? An in omnibus
studiōrum agitātiō vītae aequālis fuit?

*Old age has new experiences and associations with youth, and may keep
on learning.*

8. Iūcundum potius quam odiōsum! Ut enim adulēscen-

Simonides of Amorgos), one of the greatest Greek lyric poets, lived from
556 to about 469 B.C.

22. Stēsichorum (stē-sik′ǫ-rŭs) : of Himera (him′ę-rą) in Sicily, also
a lyric poet, lived from about 630 to about 556 B.C.   **Īsocratēn** (ī-sok′rą-
tēz), **Gorgiān** (gǫr′ji-ąs): Isocrates (436 B.C.–338 B.C.) was the greatest
Greek teacher of rhetoric of his time.   He died by voluntary starvation
owing to his grief at the loss of Greek freedom.   Gorgias (*circā* 485 B.C.–
380 B.C.) was the greatest of the sophists, and a teacher of Isocrates.

23. philosophōrum prīncipēs : ' in the first rank of philosophers.'
Pȳthagorān (pį-thag′ǫ-rąs) : neither the date of his birth nor that of
his death can be determined; he " flourished " about 530 B.C.   He lived
mostly in the Greek settlements of lower Italy, where his school existed
for some centuries after his death.   **Dēmocritum** (dę-mok′rį-tŭs) :
of Abdē′ra, one of the originators of the theory of atoms; said to have
lived from 460 to 361 or 357 B.C.

24. Xenocratēn (zę-nok′rą-tēz) : after Plato, Speusippus was the first
head of the Academic School; Xenocrates succeeded him.   He lived
from 397 to 315 or 313 B.C.   **Zēnōnem** (zē′nō) : of Citium (sį′sh(y)ŭm)
in Cyprus, founder of Stoicism, born about 357 B.C., is said to have lived
to the age of 98.   **Cleanthēn** (klē-ąn′thēz) : he followed Zeno in the
presidency of the Stoic school.   His age at death is variously given as
80 and as 99 years.

25. quem vīdistis : It is rather curious that Cicero should make Cato
speak with admiration of Diogenes, to whom he had shown great
hostility.   **Diogenēn** (dī-ǫj′ę-nēz) : Cicero probably wrote in -*ān*, -*ēn*,
not in -*am*, -*em*, the accusatives of Greek proper names in -*ās*, -*ēs*.
Stoicum : to distinguish him from Diogenes the Cynic.

27. **agitātiō :** Cicero uses *agitātiō* and *āctiō* almost interchangeably.
Āctus in this sense occurs only in Silver Latin.   See Companion, page 707.

8. 1. Iūcundum . . . odiōsum : elliptic, = ' *iūcundum* ' *potius
quam* ' *odiōsum* ' *senem esse dīcendum est.   238, f.*

tibus, bonā indole praeditīs, sapientēs senēs dēlectantur, leviorque fit senectūs eōrum, quī ā iuventūte coluntur et dīliguntur, sīc adulēscentēs senum praeceptīs gaudent, qui-5 bus ad virtūtum studia dūcuntur; nec minus intellegō mē vōbīs, quam mihi vōs, esse iūcundōs. Sed vidētis, ut senectūs nōn modo languida atque iners nōn sit, vērum etiam sit operōsa et semper agēns aliquid et mōliēns, tāle scīlicet, quāle cuiusque studium in superiōre vītā fuit.

10 Quid, quī etiam addiscunt aliquid? Ut et Solōnem versibus glōriantem vidēmus, quī sē cotīdiē aliquid addiscentem dīcit senem fierī, et ego fēcī, quī litterās Graecās senex didicī; quās quidem sīc avidē arripuī quasi diūturnam

---

2. **sapientēs senēs:** neither of these words is used as an adjective here; the whole expression = *sapientēs, cum factī sunt senēs.*

3. **coluntur et dīliguntur:** *colere* rather implies the external marks of respect, *dīligere* the inner feeling of affection.

5. **mē . . . iūcundōs:** put for *mē iūcundum esse quam vōs mihi estis iūcundī.* The attraction of a finite verb into the infinitive after *quam* is not uncommon. *Minus,* be it observed, does not qualify *intellegō,* but *iūcundōs.*

6. **Sed:** here resumptive, *i.e.* it introduces a return to the subject proper after a digression. **vidētis, ut . . . sit:** here *ut = quō modō,* 'how.' **senectūs . . . cuiusque:** the abstract *senectūs* is put for *senēs,* hence *cuiusque,* sc. *senis. 92, b.*

8. **agēns aliquid:** this phrase differs from *agat* in that while the subjunctive would express the *fact* of action, the participial phrase expresses rather the constant *tendency* to act. *Agēns aliquid* forms a sort of attribute to *senectūs,* parallel with *operōsa. Mōlīrī* differs from *agere* in that it implies the bringing into existence of some object.

10. **Quid . . . aliquid:** *quid* introduces a new point; translate, ' Again, are there not some who, etc.' *Addiscunt* = 'learn on and on,' 'go on learning.' **Ut . . . vidēmus:** put for *Ut Solon fēcit, quem vidēmus.* **Solōnem:** great Athenian statesman of the seventh century B.C., whose age at his death is variously given as 80 or 100 years.

11. **vidēmus:** the Latins frequently use ' we see ' for ' we read.'

12. **senex:** i.e. *cum senex essem.* Plutarch (*Catō,* 2) gives an account of Cato's study of Greek in his old age.

13. **sīc:** this word does not qualify *avidē,* but refers on to *quasi,* so

sitim explēre cupiēns, ut ea ipsa mihi nōta essent, quibus
mē nunc exemplīs ūtī vidētis. Quod cum fēcisse Sōcratēn 15
in fidibus audīrem, vellem equidem etiam illud, discēbant
enim fidibus antīquī, sed in litterīs certē ēlabōrāvī.

A ROMAN LADY PLAYING A LYRE (FIDES)

that *sīc . . . quasi cupiēns* = ' thus, viz. like one desiring.' *Quasi*
serves to soften the metaphor in *sitim.*

14. **cupiēns:** after *quasi* a finite verb (*cuperem*) would have been
more usual. **ea ipsa mihi:** juxtaposition of pronouns, which is rather
sought after in Latin. *212, g; 162, c.*

15. **exemplīs:** = *prō exemplīs*, or *exemplōrum locō.* Editors are
wrong who say that we have here an example of the antecedent thrust
into the relative clause, as though *ea ipsa quibus exemplīs* were put for
ea ipsa exempla quibus.

16. **in fidibus:** ' in the case of the lyre.' **vellem:** sc. *sī possem.*

Second charge: Old age weakens the physical powers.
But old age does not desire or need the strength of youth.

9. Nē nunc quidem vīrēs dēsīderō adulēscentis — is
enim erat locus alter dē vitiīs senectūtis — nōn plūs quam,
adulēscens, taurī aut elephantī dēsīderābam. Quod est,
eō decet ūtī et, quidquid agās, agere prō vīribus.

discēbant . . . fidibus: the
verb *canere*, which means ‘to
play’ as well as ‘to sing,’
must be supplied; *fidibus* is
then an ablative of the means
or instrument. See illustrations, pages 263 and 452.

9. 1. Nē . . . quidem:
these two words together
correspond to the Greek οὐδέ
(οὐ = *nē*, δέ = *quidem*), and
are best translated here by
‘nor’ rather than by ‘not
even.’ The rendering ‘not
even,’ though required by
some passages, often misrep-
resents the Latin.

2. locus: *locus* is a rhetorical term with a technical
meaning. The pleader is to
anticipate the arguments he
may find it necessary to use
in different cases, and arrange
them under certain heads;
each head is called a *locus*,

SOCRATES
A bust in the Vatican.

meaning literally the *place* where a pleader is to look for an argument
when wanted. Hence *locus* came to mean ‘a cut-and-dried argument’
or, as here, a ‘commonplace.’ It is often found in Cicero’s rhetorical
writings. **nōn plūs quam:** ‘any more than.’ After the negative *nē* in
line 1 it is incorrect to translate *nōn* by a negative in English, though
the repetition of the negative is common enough in Latin, as in some
English dialects. *Plūs* here = *magis*.

3. Quod est: sc. *tibi*, ‘What you have.’

4. agās: *quisquis* is generally accompanied by the indicative.
The subjunctive is here used, with the imaginary second person, to

Quae enim vōx potest esse contemptior quam Milōnis 5
Crotōniātae? Quī cum iam senex esset āthlētāsque sē
exercentēs in curriculō vidēret, aspexisse lacertōs suōs
dīcitur illacrimānsque dīxisse, "At hī quidem mortuī iam
sunt." Nōn vērō tam istī, quam tū ipse, nūgātor! Neque
enim ex tē umquam es nōbilitātus, sed ex lateribus et lacertīs 10
tuīs. Nihil Sex. Aelius tāle, nihil, multīs annīs ante, Ti.
Coruncānius, nihil modo P. Crassus, ā quibus iūra cīvibus

---

render prominent the hypothetical and indefinite character of the
verb statement. *180, e (2).*

5. **vōx:** ' utterance '; the word is used only of speeches in some
way specially remarkable. **contemptior:** ' more despicable.' The
passive participle of *contemnō* has the sense of an adjective in *-bilis*,
like *invictus* and many others. *212, h.* **Milōnis:** the most famous of the
Greek athletes. He lived at the end of the sixth century B.C., and the
praises of his victories were sung by Simonides. It was under his leadership that his native city Croton, in Magna Graecia (Southern Italy),
attacked and destroyed Sýbaris. Many stories are told by the ancients
about his feats of strength, and about his power of consuming food. He
is said to have been a prominent disciple of Pythagoras.

8. **dīxisse:** combinations like *dīcitur dīxisse* are exceedingly rare
in good Latin. Cicero nearly always uses two different verbs; *i.e.*
he says *aiunt dīcere* and the like. **At:** there is an ellipsis here such as
' those young men's muscles are powerful but. . . .' This elliptic use
of *at* is common in sudden exclamations of grief, annoyance, surprise,
etc. *238, f.*

9. **vērō:** this is common in emphatic replies, whether the reply
convey assent, or, as here, a retort. **tam:** sc. *mortuī sunt.* **nūgātor:**
nūgārī = ' to trifle.'

10. **ex tē:** Cato here identifies a man's person with his soul and
intellect, the body being regarded as a mere dress. *Ex tē*, literally,
' out of yourself,' *i.e.* ' from your real self's resources.' **lateribus:**
' lungs.' Cicero and the best writers rarely use *pulmōnēs* for ' lungs ';
' good lungs ' is always *bona latera*, never *pulmōnēs*. See page 24,
line 8, and note.

11. **Aelius:** his *cognōmen* was Paetus; he was consul in 198, and
censor in 194 B.C. He was one of the earliest and most famous writers
on Roman law. His great commentary on the Twelve Tables is often
referred to by Cicero. **tāle:** sc. *dīxit.*

12. **Coruncānius:** see note on page 257, line 6. **P. Crassus:**

praescrībēbantur; quōrum ūsque ad extrēmum spīritum
est prōvecta prūdentia.

15 Ōrātor metuō nē languēscat senectūte; est enim mūnus
eius nōn ingenī sōlum, sed laterum etiam et vīrium.　Omnīnō canōrum illud in vōce splendēscit etiam nesciō quō
pactō in senectūte, quod equidem adhūc nōn āmīsī, et
vidētis annōs.　Sed tamen est decōrus senī sermō quiētus

---

consul in 205 B.C. with the elder Africanus; pontifex maximus from 212 to
his death in 183.　He was famous both as a lawyer and as a statesman.
Modo therefore covers a space of at least 33 years, so that it cannot well
be translated by our 'lately'; say rather 'nearer our time.'　The amount
of time implied by *modo* and *nūper* depends entirely on the context.

13. **praescrībēbantur:** the meaning is that these lawyers practiced
in old age as jurisconsults; *i.e.* according to old Roman custom, they
gave audience in the early hours of the day to all who chose to consult
them about legal difficulties.

14. **est prōvecta:** literally, ' was carried forward,' *i.e.* ' continued,'
' remained.'　Some wrongly take the phrase to mean ' made progress,'
' increased,' a sense which would require the imperfect, *prōvehēbātur.*
prūdentia: here, as often, ' legal skill.'

15. **Ōrātor:** emphatic position; translate accordingly.　**senectūte:**
causal ablative; not ' in age,' but ' owing to age.'

16. **Omnīnō . . . sed tamen:** ' No doubt . . . but still.'　*Omnīnō*
(literally, ' altogether ') has two almost exactly opposite uses: (1) the
affirmative; (2) the concessive, which we have here.　The circumstance
which is contrasted with the admitted circumstance is usually introduced
by *sed tamen* or *sed.*

17. **canōrum . . . senectūte:** *canōrum* implies the combination of
power with clearness in a voice.　There is a mixture of metaphors in
canōrum splendēscit.　**nesciō quō pactō:** literally, ' I know not on what
terms '; quite interchangeable with *nesciō quō modō.*

18. **adhūc nōn:** purposely put for *nōndum*, because more emphasis
is thus thrown both on the time-word and on the negation.　The common view that *nōndum* was avoided because it would have implied that
Cato expected to lose the *canōrum* is certainly wrong.　**et vidētis:**
' though you see my years.'　The adversative use of *et* for *autem* or
tamen after the negative is not very uncommon in Cicero, but there are
few examples of the usage in the speeches.　*234, b.*

19. **senī:** in *Dē Lēgibus*, **1**, 11, allusion is made to the great change
which advancing years had wrought in Cicero's own impassioned

et remissus, facitque persaepe ipsa sibi audientiam diserti 10
senis composita et mītis ōrātiō; quam sī ipse exsequī
nequeās, possīs tamen Scīpiōnī praecipere et Laeliō. Quid
enim est iūcundius senectūte stīpātā studiīs iuventūtis?

*Old age accomplishes results chiefly through wisdom, though men may also
retain strength by right living.*

10. Vidētisne, ut apud Homērum saepissimē Nestor dē
virtūtibus suīs praedicet? Tertiam enim aetātem hominum
vidēbat, nec erat eī verendum nē, vēra praedicāns dē sē,

oratory. He was no doubt thinking of that change when he wrote the
words we have here. **sermō:** ' style of speaking '; a word of wider
meaning than *ōrātiō*, which denotes only public speaking. **quiētus
et remissus :** ' subdued and gentle.' The metaphor in *remissus* refers
to the loosening of a tight-stretched string.

20. **facit audientiam :** ' procures of itself a hearing for it.' In the
words *per sē ipsa* there is no doubt an allusion to the custom at large
meetings in ancient times whereby the *praecō* or κῆρυξ called on the
people to listen to the speakers. Note that this is the only classical
use of the word *audientia;* it has not the meaning of our "audience"
either in the sense of a body of listeners or as used in the expression "to
give audience."

21. **composita et mītis :** ' unimpassioned and smooth.' **quam . . .
nequeās:** ' and if you cannot practice oratory yourself.' Evidently
quam refers to *ōrātiō* in the widest sense, not to the special style of
oratory mentioned in the last sentence.

22. **Scīpiōnī et Laeliō :** ' *a* Scipio and *a* Laelius '; *i.e.* ' young friends
such as Scipio and Laelius are to me.' **praecipere :** here absolute, =
praecepta dare; usually an accusative follows.

23. **studiīs iuventūtis :** ' the zeal of youth.' *Studiīs* does not imply
here the deference of youth to age; the *studia* meant are the *virtūtum
studia* of page 262, line 5.

10. 1. **Vidētisne, ut:** here *ne* is the equivalent of *nōnne*, as it often
is in the Latin of Plautus and Terence and in the colloquial Latin of
the classical period. *179, a.* For *ut* after *vidētis* see note on page 262,
line 6. **Nestor:** famous among the Trojan heroes for his wisdom and
eloquence; *Iliad*, **1**, 260, *et seq.*; **11**, 668, *et seq.*

2. **Tertiam aetātem :** he is said to have lived through three generations of men. See *Iliad*, **1**, 250; *Odyssey*, **3**, 245.

3. **vēra . . . sē:** ' if he told the truth about himself.'

nimis vidērētur aut īnsolēns aut loquāx. Etenim, ut ait
5 Homērus, "Ex eius linguā melle dulcior fluēbat ōrātiō";
quam ad suāvitātem nūllīs egēbat corporis vīribus. Et

A GREEK WRESTLING MATCH
From a cast at the University of Michigan.

tamen dux ille Graeciae nūsquam optat, ut Āiācis similēs
habeat decem, sed ut Nestoris; quod sī sibi acciderit, nōn
dubitat, quīn brevī sit Trōia peritūra.

*Physical strength is not required of old age; and weakness is characteristic
of ill-health at all periods of life.*

11. Nē sint in senectūte vīrēs; nē postulantur quidem
vīrēs ā senectūte. Ergō et lēgibus et īnstitūtīs vacat aetās

4. nimis: ' to any great extent.' *Īnsolēns* does not correspond
to our ' insolent '; it is almost the equivalent of *ineptus*, ' tasteless,' and
has no harsher meaning than ' odd,' ' strange,' ' in bad taste.'

5. Ex ōrātiō: a translation of the passage from Homer, *Iliad*, **1**, 249,
τοῦ καὶ ἀπὸ γλώσσης μέλιτος γλυκίων ῥέεν αὐδή.

6. suāvitātem: notice the change from *dulcior*, which seems to be
made for the mere sake of variety, since elsewhere Cicero (*Dē Ōrātōre*,
3, 161) writes *dulcitūdō ōrātiōnis.*

7. dux ille: Agamemnon; see *Iliad*, **2**, 370, *et seq.* **nūsquam:**
i.e. nowhere in Homer. **Āiācis:** *i.e.* Aiax Telamonius, who was the
greatest Greek warrior while Achilles sulked (*Iliad*, **2**, 768). The
genitive after *similis* is the rule in Cicero, though many examples of
the dative are found even with names of persons. *108, b.*

11. 1. Nē sint: ' Grant that old age has no strength.' This formula of concession for argument's sake is frequent in Cicero. *180, f.*

2. senectūte: = *senibus;* see page 262, line 6, note. **lēgibus et
īnstitūtīs:** ' by statute and precedent.'

nostra mūneribus eīs, quae nōn possunt sine vīribus sustinērī. Itaque nōn modo quod nōn possumus, sed nē quantum possumus quidem, cōgimur. 5

At multī ita sunt imbēcillī senēs, ut nūllum officī aut omnīnō vītae mūnus exsequī possint. At id quidem nōn proprium senectūtis vitium est, sed commūne valētūdinis. Quid mīrum igitur in senibus, sī īnfīrmī sunt aliquandō, cum id nē adulēscentēs quidem effugere possint? Resis- 10 tendum, Laelī et Scīpiō, senectūtī est, eiusque vitia dīligentiā compēnsanda sunt; pugnandum, tamquam contrā morbum, sīc contrā senectūtem, habenda ratiō valētūdinis,

---

3. **mūneribus eīs**, etc.: chiefly military service.

4. **nōn modo . . . sed nē quidem:** when a negative follows *nōn modo* these words have the force of *nōn modo nōn*, a negative being borrowed from the negative in the subsequent clause. But often *nōn modo nōn* is written; the negative after *modo* is then more emphatic, being independent. Here *nōn modo nōn quod nōn* would have had a harsh sound. **quod**: its antecedent is *id* understood, cognate accusative with *cogimur*. *117, a;* B. 176, 2, *b;* A. & G. 390, *c;* G. 333, 1.

6. **At:** see page 258, line 1, note. In his reply Cato adopts the same form as that in which the objection is urged, *at id quidem*, etc. So on page 286, line 21, and note. *At senex . . . At est . . .*

8. **commūne valētūdinis:** 'common to weak health,' *i.e.* to all in a weak state of health. *Valētūdō* means in itself neither good nor bad health; the word takes its coloring from the context.

11. **vitia:** 'defects.' **dīligentia:** scarcely corresponds to our 'diligence'; it rather implies minute, patient attention; 'painstaking.'

13. **habenda . . . valētūdinis:** 'attention must be paid to health.' Preventive medicine as a principle is by no means new, for both the Greeks and Romans practiced it. The preservation of health is fully discussed by Celsus (see illustration on page 455) in his *Dē Medicīnā*, Book 1, and elsewhere. Here he lays down sensible and practical rules of conduct both for those who are in good health and for those who have a weak constitution; and it is interesting to note that Cicero's ideas fully coincide with those of Celsus. In another passage (*Dē Medicīnā*, Introduction 5) the author declares that the art of medicine though consisting of many branches 'scarcely brings any of us to the threshold of old age.' If it be true in modern medical practice that less than one per cent of the population dies of "old age," we may safely conclude that in Cicero's time the percentage

ūtendum exercitātiōnibus modicīs, tantum cibī et pōtiōnis
15 adhibendum, ut reficiantur vīrēs, nōn opprimantur.

Nec vērō corporī sōlum subveniendum est, sed mentī
atque animō multō magis. Nam haec quoque, nisi tamquam lūminī oleum īnstillēs, exstinguuntur senectūte.
Et corpora quidem exercitātiōnum dēfatīgātiōne ingravēs-
20 cunt, animī autem exercitandō levantur. Nam quōs ait

was much lower; we may assume then with Cato that physical frailties and
infirmities which are commonly attributed to "old age," ought really to be
charged to ill-health.

14. **tantum**: restrictive, 'only so much'; it is often so used.
pōtiōnis: *cibus et pōtiō* is the regular Latin equivalent for our 'food
and drink.' Roman medicine at this time consisted of three general
branches (see Celsus, *Dē Medicīnā*, Introduction 9): dietetics, pharmaceu-
tics, and surgery. Intelligent Romans like Cicero, Pliny, and Horace show
a remarkable familiarity with a proper regimen of living, a field to which
Roman physicians devoted much attention. Celsus (*Dē Medicīnā*, Books 1
and 2) discusses the proper use of exercise, food and drink according to
their nutritive value and digestibility, the dietetic and therapeutic value of
water for promoting health (hydrotherapy), massage and friction, various
kinds of baths, among them even warm oil-baths, and recommends a
vegetarian diet. Cicero's acquaintance with the theory and practice of
medicine is also proved by a remarkable anatomical survey of the human
body (*Dē Nātūrā Deōrum* 2, 54, *et seq.*), exhibiting a grasp of things medical
the like of which is rarely found among laymen even today. See page 269,
lines 11 to 13, and note; page 394, note 4; page 455, note 16.

15. **adhibendum**: *adhibēre* has here merely the sense of 'to employ'
or 'to use.' **nōn**: we should say 'and not' or 'but not'; the Latins,
however, are fond of *asyndeton*, called *adversātīvum* when two clauses
are contrasted. *238, d.*

16. **mentī . . . animō**: properly *mēns* is the intellect, strictly so
called, *animus* intellect and feeling combined, but the words are often
very loosely used. They frequently occur together in Latin; Lucretius
has even *mēns animī*.

18. **īnstillēs**: ideal "you." *180, e (2).*

19. **Et**: 'Moreover.'

20. **exercitandō**: in good Latin the verb *exercitāre* is rare except
in *exercitātus*, which stands as participle to *exerceō*, *exercitus* being unused. The word seems to have been chosen here as suiting *exercitātiōnibus* better than *exercendō* would. So on page 274, line 2, *dēsī-*

Caecilius "Cōmicōs stultōs senēs," hōs significat crēdulōs, oblīviōsōs, dissolūtōs, quae vitia sunt nōn senectūtis, sed inertis, ignāvae, somniculōsae senectūtis. Ut petulantia, ut libīdō magis est adulēscentium quam senum, nec tamen omnium adulēscentium, sed nōn probōrum, sīc ista senīlis 25 stultitia, quae dēlīrātiō appellārī solet, senum levium est, nōn omnium.

Third charge: Old age deprives of pleasures.
But old age confers a benefit in dulling the zest for sensuous pleasures.

12. Sequitur tertia vituperātiō senectūtis, quod eam carēre dīcunt voluptātibus. O praeclārum mūnus aetātis,

---

derātiō is chosen rather than *dēsīderium*, to correspond with the neighboring *tītillātiō*. **ait:** sc. *esse;* the omission with *aiō* is rare, though common with *di͞o, appellō*, etc.

OLD MEN REPRESENTED IN COMEDY
A headpiece to a manuscript of Terence's
Eunuchus.

21. **Cōmicōs:** not 'comic' in our sense, but = *in cōmoediīs*, 'represented in comedy.' The passage of Caecilius is more fully quoted in *Laelius*, 26. **crēdulōs:** in almost every Latin comedy there is some old man who is cheated by a cunning slave.

23. **somniculōsae:** the adjective contains a diminutive noun stem (*somniculō-*). **petulantia:** 'waywardness.'

25. **nōn probōrum:** Cicero avoids *improbōrum* as being too harsh. **ista:** implying contempt.

26. **dēlīrātiō:** 'dotage'; a rare word, used by Cicero only here and in *Dē Dīvīnātiōne*, **2**, 43, 90. What is its literal meaning? See vocabulary.

12. 1. **quod . . . dīcunt:** not strictly logical, being put for *quod careat, ut dīcunt.* In cases like this the verb of saying is usually in the subjunctive. The indicative here is more vivid and forcible.

2. **mūnus . . . aufert:** to say that a gift robs one of anything is of course an oxymoron. **239**, *p.* **aetātis:** almost = *senectūtis.*

sī quidem id aufert ā nōbīs, quod est in adulēscentia vitiōsissimum!

5 Accipite enim, optimī adulēscentēs, veterem ōrātiōnem Archȳtae Tarentīrī, magnī in prīmīs et praeclārī virī, quae mihi trādita est, cum essem adulēscens Tarentī cum Q. Maximō. *Nūllam capitāliōrem pestem quam voluptātem corporis hominibus dīcēbat ā nātūrā datam, cuius voluptātis* 10 *avidae libīdinēs temerē et effrēnātē ad potiendum incitārentur.*

Hinc patriae prōditiōnēs, hinc rērum pūblicārum ēversiōnēs, hinc cum hostibus clandestīna colloquia nāscī; nūllum dēnique scelus, nūllum malum facinus esse, ad quod suscipiendum nōn libīdō voluptātis impelleret; stupra vērō et adulteria et 15 *omne tāle flāgi*......*num nūllīs excitārī aliīs illecebrīs nisi volup-*

---

3. **id quod est**, etc.: ' the greatest fault of youth'; *i.e.* the love of pleasure. In this passage *voluptās* indicates pleasure of a sensual kind, its ordinary sense, *dēlectātiō, oblectātiō*, etc., being used of the higher pleasures.

5. **Accipite:** ' Hear '; so *dare* often means ' to tell.'

6. **Archȳtae** (är-kī'tạs): Archytas (the subject of Horace's well-known *Ode*, **1**, 28) was a contemporary and friend of Plato, and a follower of the Pythagorean philosophy. He wrote philosophical works, and was also famous as a mathematician and astronomer, besides being the leading statesman and general of the commonwealth of Tarentum. For another saying of Archytas see *Laelius*, page 324, line 33.

7. **trādita est:** ' was imparted to me,' *i.e.*, by word of mouth. **cum . . . Tarentī:** ' when as a young man I stayed at Tarentum.'

8. **capitāliōrem:** ' more deadly '; *caput* was often equivalent to *vīta*, so that *capitālis* comes to mean ' affecting the life.'

11. **Hinc,** etc.: observe the singular *patriae* followed by the plural *rērum pūblicārum;* the plural of *patria* is rare. On the significance of this passage see Lecky, *History of European Morals*, I, page 211, note (American edition).

12. **cum hostibus**, etc.: attributive phrase with *colloquia*.

13. **scelus:** this word looks chiefly to the criminal intention, whether it be carried into action or not, *malum, facinus* to the completed crime; *flāgitium* is iniquity rather than crime. *Facinus* in sense is often rather narrower and lighter than *scelus*.

14. **impelleret:** sc. *hominēs*.

15. **excitārī:** ' stirred up.'

tātis; cumque hominī sīve nātūra sīve quis deus nihil mente praestābilius dedisset, huic dīvīnō mūnerī ac dōnō nihil tam esse inimīcum quam voluptātem; nec enim, libīdine dominante, temperantiae locum esse, neque omnīnō in voluptātis rēgnō virtūtem posse cōnsistere. 20

Quōrsus hōc? Ut intellegerētis, sī voluptātem aspernārī ratiōne et sapientiā nōn possēmus, magnam esse habendam senectūtī grātiam, quae efficeret, ut id nōn līberēt, quod nōn oportēret. Impedit enim cōnsilium voluptās, ratiōnī inimīca est, mentis, ut ita dīcam, praestringit oculōs, nec 25 habet ūllum cum virtūte commercium.

13. Quōrsum igitur tam multa dē voluptāte? Quia nōn modo vituperātiō nūlla, sed etiam summa laus senectūtis est, quod ea voluptātēs nūllās magnō opere dēsīderat. Caret epulīs exstrūctīsque mēnsīs et frequentibus pōculīs; caret ergō etiam vīnulentiā et crūditāte et insomniīs; 5

16. **hominī . . . dedisset:** notice *hominī*, 'man,' in the same sense as *hominibus*, above.

17. **mūnerī ac dōnō:** the two words *mūnus* and *dōnum* are often found together; the difference in meaning is hardly perceptible. *Dōnum* implies the fact of giving, *mūnus* the generosity of the giver. **tam . . . inimīcum:** notice the separation of *tam* from *inimīcum*.

18. **libīdine:** = ἐπιθυμία; *temperantia* = σωφροσύνη. *Dominārī* is a very strong word, 'to tyrannize'; *dominātiō* = τυραννίς.

20. **cōnsistere:** 'find a foothold.'

23. **efficeret:** *efficeret, līberet,* and *oportēret* can be properly rendered in English only by the present tense. Although these verbs express circumstances which *continue*, since the *general* effect of old age is being described, they are thrown into the past to suit the past tense *dīcēbam* or *dīxī* which, though not expressed, is really the principal verb.

24. **cōnsilium:** 'deliberation.'

25. **ut ita dīcam:** this softens the metaphor, as *quasi* or *quasi quīdam* often does, and as οἷον, ὥσπερ do in Greek, but not ὡς ἔπος εἰπεῖν, which is often wrongly said to be the equivalent of *ut ita dīcam.* *196, b.* **nec habet,** etc.: 'and has no relations with virtue.'

13. 5. **crūditāte:** 'indigestion.' **insomniīs:** 'sleeplessness'; the singular *insomnium* occurs only once in prose (Tacitus, *Annālēs*, **11,** 4). *Insomnia, -ae* is found only in poetry and late prose.

14. At nōn est voluptātum tanta quasi tītillātiō in senibus. Crēdō, sed nē dēsīderātiō quidem; nihil autem est molestum, quod nōn dēsīderēs. Cupidīs enim rērum tālium odiōsum fortasse et molestum est carēre; satiātīs vērō et explētīs, iūcundius est carēre quam fruī. Quamquam nōn caret is, quī nōn dēsīderat; ergō hōc nōn dēsīderāre dīcō esse iūcundius.

NEAR ARPINUM

View across land that probably belonged to Cicero's father.

14. 1. **At:** used to introduce the supposed objection of an opponent; see page 258, line 1, note. **quasi tītillātiō:** the *quasi*, as often in Cicero's writings, marks a translation from the Greek. Here the Epicurean word γαργαλισμός is referred to; it is often in Cicero represented by *tītillātiō*.

3. **dēsīderēs:** *194, f.*

5. **Quamquam . . . ergō:** these words may be scanned as a hexameter line, but the pause before *ergō* would prevent them from being taken as a verse.

6. **hōc nōn dēsīderāre:** 'this absence of regret'; the words form the subject of *esse*. *Nōn* is sometimes combined with verbs, substantives, adjectives, and adverbs to take the place of negative *in-* or *ne-*.

And old age has leisure for scientific and literary interests.

At illa quantī sunt, animum, tamquam ēmeritīs stīpendiīs
libīdinis, ambitiōnis, contentiōnum, inimīcitiārum, cupiditātum omnium sēcum esse, sēcumque, ut dīcitur, vīvere! 10
Sī vērō habet aliquod tamquam pābulum studī atque
doctrīnae, nihil est ōtiōsā senectūte iūcundius. Vidēbāmus
in studiō dīmētiendī paene caelī atque terrae Gallum,
familiārem patris tuī, Scīpiō. Quotiēns illum lūx noctū
aliquid dēscrībere ingressum, quotiēns nox oppressit, cum 15
māne coepisset! Quam dēlectābat eum, dēfectiōnēs sōlis
et lūnae multō ante nōbīs praedīcere!
Quid in leviōribus studiīs, sed tamen acūtīs? Quam

---

8. **illa :** put for *illud,* as in Greek ταῦτα and τάδε are often used
for τοῦτο and τόδε. The words from *animum* to the end of the sentence are explanatory of *illa.* **quantī :** ' how valuable! ' but the word
may have exactly the opposite meaning if the context require it. **stīpendiīs :** ' campaigns.' The four words from *libīdinis* to *inimīcitiārum*
are to be taken in pairs, while *cupiditātum* sums them up and is in
apposition to all.

11. **Sī . . . aliquod :** the sense is scarcely different from that of
sī . . . quod; the distinction is as slight as that in English between
' if ' followed by ' some,' and ' if ' followed by ' any.' **pābulum :**
the metaphorical sense is rendered less harsh by *tamquam.* **studī :** an
explanatory genitive dependent on *pābulum. 96, a.*

12. **ōtiōsā senectūte :** ' leisured age '; *ōtium* in the Latin of Cicero
does not imply idleness, but freedom from public business and opportunity for the indulgence of literary and scientific tastes. See
page 293, line 2, note. **Vidēbāmus :** ' We saw over a considerable
period.'

13. **in studiō,** etc. : ' busied with the task of almost measuring bit
by bit (*dī-mētiendī*) the heavens and the earth.' For the sense see
Horace, *Odes,* **1,** 28 (of Archytas). **Gallum :** consul in 157 B.C., famous
as an astronomer and as the first Roman who predicted an eclipse, which
he did before the battle of Pydna. See Livy, **44,** 37.

15. **dēscrībere :** technically used of the drawing of mathematical
figures. *Ingredior* often has an infinitive dependent on it even in the
best Latin.

18. **acūtīs :** requiring keenness of intellect.

gaudēbat Bellō suō Pūnicō Naevius, quam Truculentō
20 Plautus, quam Pseudolō! Vīdī etiam senem Līvium; quī
cum, sex annīs ante quam ego nātus sum, fābulam docuisset, Centōne Tuditānōque cōnsulibus, ūsque ad adulēscentiam meam prōcessit aetāte. Quid dē P. Licinī Crassī
et pontificī et cīvīlis iūris studiō loquar, aut dē huius

---

19. **Naevius** (nē'vi̯-u̯s): Naevius lived about 264–194 B.C. His
great work was a history of the First Punic War. He wrote also
tragedies and comedies. **Truculentō . . . Pseudolō** (tru̯-cu̯-len'tu̯s
. . . sū'do̯-lu̯s): these plays of Plautus (lived from 254 to 184 B.C.) we
still possess. The *Truculentus* is so named from one of the characters,
a slave of savage disposition who is wheedled; the *Pseudolus* from a
cheating slave. The latter name is commonly supposed to be a tran-
scription from a Greek word ψεύδυλος, which however nowhere occurs;
and as the change from Greek υ to Latin ο is not found before l, Corssen
assumes ψεύδ-αλος as the original word. The form *Pseudulus* of the
name is probably later than *Pseudolus*.

20. **Līvium:** Livius Andronī'cus, the founder of Latin literature
(lived from about 285 to 204 B.C.), who translated the *Odyssey*, also
many Greek tragedies. See *Outline of History of Latin Literature*, Companion, page 707. Livius was a Greek captured by Livius Salīnā'tor
at Tarentum in 275 B.C.; for a time he was the slave of Livius, and, according to custom, took his name when set free. For an account of his
writings see Cruttwell's *History of Roman Literature*, Chapter 3; Sellar,
Roman Poets of the Republic, Chapter 3.

21. **docuisset:** 'had brought on to the stage.' *Docēre* (like διδάσκειν
in Greek, which has the same use) meant originally to instruct the
performers in the play.

22. **Centōne Tuditānōque** (sen'tō, tū-di̯-tā'nu̯s) **cōnsulibus:** *i.e.* in
240 B.C. The use of *-que* here is noticeable; when a date is given by
reference to the consuls of the year it is usual to insert *et* (not *-que* or
atque, which rarely occur) between the two names, if only the *cognōmina*
(as here) be given. If the full names be given, then they are put side
by side without *et*.

23. **Crassī** (pub'li̯-u̯s li̯-sin'i̯-u̯s kras'su̯s): see page 265, line 12,
note.

24. **pontificī et cīvīlis iūris:** the *iūs pontificium* regarded mainly
the proper modes of conducting religious ceremonial. *Iūs cīvīle*, which
is often used to denote the whole body of Roman law, here includes only
the secular portion of that law. **huius P. Scīpiōnis** (sip'i̯-ō): 'the

P. Scīpiōnis, quī hīs paucīs diēbus pontifex maximus factus est? 25

Atque eōs omnēs, quōs commemorāvī, hīs studiīs flā-grantēs senēs vīdimus. M. vērō Cethēgum, quem rēctē suādae medullam dīxit Ennius, quantō studiō exercērī in dīcendō vidēbāmus etiam senem! 30

Old age, too, may enjoy the pleasures of country life.

15. Veniō nunc ad voluptātēs agricolārum, quibus ego incrēdibiliter dēlector; quae nec ūlla impediuntur senectūte

AN OLIVE GROVE

present P. Scipio.' The P. Scipio who is meant here is not Africanus, but Nasī'ca Córcŭlum ('dear little heart').

25. **hīs paucīs diēbus:** 'within the last few days.' *147 a.*

27. **flāgrantis:** 'all aglow.'

28. **senēs:** = *cum senēs essent;* so *senem* below. **Cethēgum** (sę-thē'gŭs): this Cethegus was consul in 204 and in 203 defeated Mago in the north of Italy.

29. **suādae medullam:** 'the essence (literally, marrow) of persuasive-ness.' *Suāda* is a translation of πειθώ, which the Greek rhetoricians declared to be the end and aim of oratory. **exercērī:** here reflexive in meaning like the Greek middle.

30. **vidēbāmus:** see page 275, line 12, note.

et mihi ad sapientis vītam proximē videntur accēdere. Habent enim ratiōnem cum terrā, quae numquam recūsat 5 imperium nec umquam sine ūsūrā reddit, quod accēpit, sed aliās minōre, plērumque maiōre cum faenore; quamquam mē quidem nōn frūctus modo, sed etiam ipsīus terrae vīs ac nātūra dēlectat.

Great men in their old age have had enjoyment in farming.

16. Possum persequī permulta oblectāmenta rērum rūsticārum, sed ea ipsa, quae dīxī, sentiō fuisse longiōra. Ignōscētis autem; nam et studiō rērum rūsticārum prōvectus sum, et senectūs est nātūrā loquācior, nē ab omnibus 5 eam vitiīs videar vindicāre.

Sed veniō ad agricolās, nē ā mē ipsō recēdam. In agrīs erant tum senātōrēs, id est senēs, sī quidem arantī L. Quīnctiō Cincinnātō nūntiātum est, eum dictātōrem esse fac-

---

15. 4. **Habent ratiōnem cum**: 'They have their reckonings with,' 'their dealings with'; a phrase of bookkeeping.

5. **imperium**: so Virgil, *Georgics*, **1,** 99, *exercetque frequēns tellūrem atque imperat agrīs; ibid.* **2,** 369, *dūra exercē imperia et rāmōs compesce fluentēs;* Tacitus, *Germānia,* 26, *sōla terrae segēs imperātur.*

6. **sed aliās . . . faenore**: put for *sed semper cum faenore, aliās minōre, plērumque maiōre.*

8. **vīs ac nātūra**: hendiadys, 'natural power.' *238, h.*

16. 1. **Possum persequī**: 'I am able to follow up,' more idiomatically, 'I might follow up.' Latin occasionally uses also a hypothetical form like English, where *possim* or *possem* stands in the apodosis of a conditional sentence, the protasis of which is not expressed, but is generally easily supplied. In translating such expressions from English into Latin it is far safer to use the indicative. B. 271, 1, *a;* A. & G. page 73, footnote 2; G. 254, R. 1.

3. **Ignōscētis**: 'You will excuse (me).' **prōvectus sum**: 'I have been carried away.' Cicero often uses *prōlābī* in the same sense.

6. **Sed veniō ad**: *Redeō ad* might have been expected here. **In agrīs erant**: 'lived on their farms.'

7. **id est senēs**: *senātus* means, literally, 'assembly of elders.' See Selection from Livy, page 409, lines 12–16.

8. **Cincinnātō**: L. Quinctius Cincinna′tus is said to have been dic-

tum; cuius dictātōris iussū magister equitum, C. Servīlius
Ahāla, Sp. Maelium, rēgnum appetentem, occupātum 10
interēmit.

Ā vīllā in senātum arcessēbātur et Cūrius et cēterī senēs;

A ROMAN VINEYARD

Vines are still trained on elm trees in Italy, just as they were in
Cicero's time.

tator twice: In 458 B.C., when he saved the Roman army, which was surrounded by the Aequī, and ended the war in sixteen days from his
appointment; in 439, when Maelius was killed and he himself was
eighty years old. In our passage Cicero seems to assume only one
dictatorship. The story of Cincinnatus at the plow is told in Livy,
3, 26. **factum:** the technical term was *dīcere dictātōrem*, since he was
nominated by the consul on the advice of the senate.

9. **dictātōris:** in apposition with *cuius*.

10. **Sp. Maelium** (spū′ri̯-ŭs mē′li̯-ŭs): a rich plebeian, who distributed corn in time of famine and was charged with courting the
people in order to make himself a king. Ahāla summoned him before
the dictator, and because he did not immediately obey, killed him with
his own hand. For this, Ahala became one of the heroes of his nation.
See Livy, **4**, 13. Cicero often mentions him with praise. See
page 28, line 26. **appetentem:** = *quia appetēbat;* so *occupātum* = *cum
occupāsset.* **227**, *a* (*1*).

ex quō, quī eōs arcessēbant, viātōrēs nōminātī sunt. Num
igitur hōrum senectūs miserābilis fuit, quī sē agrī cultiōne
15 oblectābant? Meā quidem sententiā haud sciō an nūlla
beātior possit esse, neque sōlum officiō, quod hominum
generī ūniversō cultūra agrōrum est salūtāris, sed et dēlec-
tātiōne, quam dīxī, et saturitāte cōpiāque rērum omnium,
quae ad vīctum hominum, ad cultum etiam deōrum perti-
20 nent, ut, quoniam haec quīdam dēsīderant, in grātiam iam
cum voluptāte redeāmus.

Semper enim bonī assiduīque dominī referta cella vīnāria, oleāria, etiam penāria est; vīllaque tōta locuplēs
est, abundat porcō, haedō, agnō, gallīnā, lacte, cāseō, melle.
25 Iam hortum ipsī agricolae succīdiam alteram appellant.
Condītiōra facit haec supervacāneīs etiam operīs aucupium
atque vēnātiō.

---

13. **viātōrēs:** literally, ' travelers,' so ' messengers.' They formed
a regularly organized corporation at Rome and were in attendance on
many of the magistrates. Those officers who had the *fascēs* had also
lictors, who, however, generally remained in close attendance and were
not dispatched on distant errands.

14. **miserābilis:** ' to be pitied.' The word does not quite answer
to our " miserable." **agrī cultiōne:** a rare expression, found elsewhere
only in *Verrēs*, **3**, 226; then not again till the Church Fathers.

15. **haud sciō an nūlla:** ' I am inclined to think none.' Since *haud
sciō an* is affirmative in Cicero, not negative as in some later writers,
nūlla must be read here, not *ūlla*. *180, e (1)*.

18. **quam dīxī:** = *dē quā dīxī*. **saturitāte:** the word is said to
occur nowhere else in Latin.

24. **porcō . . . gallīnā:** these words are used collectively, as *rosa*
often is. *92. g*.

25. **Iam:** ' Further.' **succīdiam alteram:** ' a second meat-supply.'
The word seems to be connected with *caedō*, and probably originally
meant ' slaughter.' In a fragment of Cato preserved by Gellius, **13**, 24,
12 (in some editions **13**, 25, 12) we find *succīdiās hūmānās facere*. Varro,
Dē Rē Rūsticā, **2**, 14, has the word in the sense of ' meat.'

26. **Condītiōra facit:** ' Adds a zest to.' **supervacāneīs operīs:** ' by
the use of spare time '; literally, ' by means of toils that are left over,'
i.e. after completing the ordinary work of the farm.

*The old age that crowns a well-spent life has the enjoyment of influence
and respect far outweighing the pleasures of youth.*

18. Sed in omnī ōrātiōne mementōte, eam mē senectūtem laudāre, quae fundāmentīs adulēscentiae cōnstitūta
sit. Ex quō efficitur id, quod ego magnō quondam cum
assēnsū omnium dīxī, miseram esse senectūtem, quae sē
ōrātiōne dēfenderet. Nōn cānī nec rūgae repente auctōri- 5
tātem arripere possunt, sed honestē ācta superior aetās
frūctūs capit auctōritātis extrēmōs. Haec enim ipsa sunt
honōrābilia, quae videntur levia atque commūnia, salūtārī,
appetī, dēcēdī, assurgī, dēdūcī, redūcī, cōnsulī; quae, et
apud nōs et in aliīs cīvitātibus, ut quaeque optimē mōrāta 10
est, ita dīligentissimē observantur.

Lysandrum Lacedaemonium, cuius modo fēcī mentiōnem,
dīcere aiunt solitum, Lacedaemonem esse honestissimum
domicilium senectūtis: nūsquam enim tantum tribuitur

---

18. 1. **in omnī ōrātiōne:** 'everywhere throughout my speech.'
Tōtā ōrātiōne would have meant 'my speech viewed as a whole.'

5. **dēfenderet:** the tense is accommodated to that of *dīxī*, according
to Latin custom; see note on page 273, line 23, *efficeret.* **cānī:** sc. *capillī;*
the same ellipsis is found in Ovid, *Metamorphoses* **3,** 275, and elsewhere.

7. **frūctūs . . . extrēmōs:** 'receives the reward of influence at
the last.'

9. **appetī:** 'to be courted.' **dēcēdī:** 'to be given precedence,' literally, 'that there should be a yielding of the way.' **assurgī:** 'the
honor shown by rising.' **dēdūcī, redūcī:** 'the escort from home and
the attendance homeward.' The difference between these two words,
which has often been misunderstood, is shown by Valerius Maximus,
2, 1, 9, *iuvenēs senātūs diē utique aliquem ex patribus cōnscrīptīs ad cūriam
dēdūcēbant, affīxīque valvīs exspectābant dōnec redūcendī etiam officiō
fungerentur.* **cōnsulī:** probably refers to private legal consultations
as well as to the deliberations of the senate.

10. **ut quaeque optimē:** Cicero often uses *ut quisque* with superlatives, *ita* following; translate *ut . . . ita* 'in proportion as . . . so.'
170, a. **mōrāta:** from *mōs.*

12. **modo:** 'just now.'

¹⁵ aetātī, nūsquam est senectūs honōrātior. Quīn etiam memoriae prōditum est:

Cum Athēnīs lūdīs quīdam in theātrum grandis nātū vēnisset, magnō cōnsessū locum nūsquam eī datum ā suīs cīvibus; cum autem ad Lacedaemoniōs accessisset, quī, lēgātī cum ²⁰ essent, certō in locō cōnsēderant, cōnsurrēxisse omnēs illī dīcuntur et senem sessum recēpisse; quibus cum ā cūnctō cōnsessū plausus esset multiplex datus, dīxisse ex eīs quendam, Athēniēnsēs scīre, quae rēcta essent, sed facere nōlle.

Multa in nostrō collēgiō praeclāra, sed hōc, dē quō agimus, ²⁵ in prīmīs, quod, ut quisque aetāte antecēdit, ita sententiae prīncipātum tenet, neque sōlum honōre antecēdentibus, sed eīs etiam, quī cum imperiō sunt, maiōrēs nātū augurēs

---

16. **memoriae prōditum est:** in Verrēs, **5,** 36, Cicero uses ad memoriam instead of the dative. The best writers have memoriae prōdere and prōdī, 'for the recollection of posterity,' memoriā prōdī, 'to be handed down by tradition'; but not memoriā prōdere.

17. **lūdīs:** sc. Panathēnāicīs, ablative of time. The Panathenaea was the greatest of the Athenian festivals and was celebrated in honor of Athena, patron goddess of the city, once in four years. The story that follows is told in almost the same words by Valerius Maximus, **4,** 5, ext. 2.

19. **quī:** at this point the ōrātiō oblīqua is broken off, but it is resumed in the next sentence, dīxīsse being dependent on prōditum est. **lēgātī cum essent:** 'being ambassadors.'

20. **certō in locō cōnsēderant:** 'had reserved seats.' **illī:** 'in his honor.'

21. **sessum recēpisse:** 'had admitted to a seat'; but sessum is a supine, recēpisse being regarded as a verb of motion. 231, a.

22. **plausus multiplex:** see Virgil, Aeneid, **1,** 747, ingeminant plausū. Cicero generally says plausus maximus.

24. **collēgiō:** the college or board of augurs to which Cato belonged. In his time there were nine members; later the number was increased.

25. **antecēdit:** sc. aliōs. **sententiae prīncipātum:** 'precedence in debate.'

26. **honōre:** i.e. as regards office, past or present.

27. **quī . . . sunt:** actual praetors or consuls.

anteponuntur. Quae sunt igitur voluptātēs corporis cum
auctōritātis praemiīs comparandae? Quibus quī splendidē
ūsī sunt, eī mihi videntur fābulam aetātis perēgisse nec, tam- 30
quam inexercitātī histriōnēs, in extrēmō āctū corruisse.

A bad disposition in an old man is the fault of character, not of age.

At sunt mōrōsī et anxiī et īrācundī et difficilēs senēs.
Sī quaerimus, etiam avārī; sed haec mōrum vitia sunt,
nōn senectūtis. Ac mōrōsitās tamen et ea vitia, quae
dīxī, habent aliquid excūsātiōnis, nōn illīus quidem iūstae, 35
sed quae probārī posse videātur: contemnī sē putant,
dēspicī, illūdī; praetereā, in fragilī corpore odiōsa omnis
offēnsiō est; quae tamen omnia dulciōra fīunt et mōribus
bonīs et artibus, idque cum in vītā, tum in scaenā, intellegī
potest ex eīs frātribus quī in Adelphīs sunt. Quanta in 40
alterō dīritās, in alterō cōmitās!

---

29. **comparandae:** 'comparable.' *230, b.*

30. **fābulam aetātis:** the comparison of life to a play, and mankind
to the players, is common in all literature; *e.g.* "All the world's a stage,
etc." When Augustus was on his deathbed he asked his friends *ecquid
eīs vidērētur mīmum vītae commodē trānsēgisse* (Suetonius, *Augustus*, 99)
'whether it seemed to them that he had played the farce of life
properly'; compare Gay's epitaph, "Life's a jest, etc."

31. **corruisse:** *i.e.* through fatigue.

32. **At:** as on page 258, line 1. **et . . . et . . . et:** *234, a.*

35. **nōn . . . videātur:** 'not well grounded indeed, but such as
it may seem possible to allow.' *Ille* is often used with *quidem* in making
concessions where the English idiom requires no pronoun.

39. **in vītā:** 'in everyday life.'

40. **Adelphīs:** *Adelphī* = ἀδελφοί, *The Brothers;* this play of Terence is still extant.

41. **dīritās:** 'harshness of temper.' Both *dīrus* and *dīritās* are rare
in Cicero; the former word does not once occur in the whole range of
the speeches, the latter scarcely excepting here and in *In Vatīnium*, 9;
Tusculānae Disputātiōnēs **3,** 29, Cicero uses it in translating from
Euripides.

Fourth charge: Old age implies the approach of death.
But life at the best is uncertain, and brief.   Men ought so to live that
they will be content with the span of life allotted to them.

19. Quārta restat causa, quae maximē angere atque
sollicitam habēre nostram aetātem vidētur, appropinquātiō mortis, quae certē ā senectūte nōn potest esse longē.

Ō miserum senem, quī mortem contemnendam esse, in
5 tam longā aetāte, nōn vīderit ! Quae aut plānē neglegenda est, sī omnīnō exstinguit animum, aut etiam optanda,
sī aliquō eum dēdūcit, ubi sit futūrus aeternus.   Atquī
tertium certē nihil invenīrī potest.

Quid igitur timeam, sī aut nōn miser post mortem, aut
10 beātus etiam futūrus sum?   Quamquam quis est tam

---

19. 2. **sollicitam habēre :** ' to keep in trouble.'   *Sollicitus* is,
literally, ' wholly in motion,' from *sollus*, which has the same root with
ὅλος, ' whole,' and *citus*.   The perfect participle with *habeō* emphasizes
the continuance of the effect produced.   *229, a.*

3. **esse longē :** more usually *abesse*.

4. **Ō miserum :** ' Oh, wretched is that old man.'   Cicero oftener
joins *Ō* with the accusative than with the nominative : he rarely, if
ever, uses the interjection with the vocative in direct address to
persons.

6. **exstinguit animum :** the doctrine of the annihilation of the soul
after death was held by many of Cicero's contemporaries, professedly
by the Epicureans (*e.g.* Lucretius, *Dē Rērum Nātūrā*, **3,** 417, *et seq.;*
see also Caesar's argument at the trial of the Catilinarian conspirators,
Sallust, *Catilīna*, 51; Cicero, *In Catilīnam*, **3,** 4), practically by the
Stoics, who taught that there is a future existence of limited though
indefinite length.   See Companion, page 547.

7. **dēdūcit :** see page 281, line 9, note.

8. **tertium . . . potest :** ' nothing can be found as a third possibility.'

9. **Quid timeam :** deliberative subjunctive.   *179, b (2).*   **aut nōn
miser . . . aut beātus :** a dilemma, but unsound and not conclusive :
for *nōn miser* is used with reference to annihilation, and the soul may
exist after death in a state of unhappiness.

10. **futūrus sum :** ' I am going to be '; *erō* would have implied
much less certainty.

stultus, quamvīs sit adulēscens, cui sit explōrātum, sē ad
vesperum esse vīctūrum? Quīn etiam aetās illa multō
plūrēs, quam nostra, cāsūs mortis habet; facilius in morbōs
incidunt adulēscentēs, gravius aegrōtant, trīstius cūrantur.
Itaque paucī veniunt ad senectūtem; quod nī ita accideret, 15
melius et prūdentius vīverētur. Mēns enim et ratiō et
cōnsilium in senibus est; quī sī nūllī fuissent, nūllae
omnīnō cīvitātēs fuissent.

At spērat adulēscens diū sē vīctūrum, quod spērāre idem
senex nōn potest. Īnsipienter spērat; quid enim stultius 20

---

11. **quamvīs sit:** prose writers of the Republican period use *quamvīs*
with the subjunctive only. **cui sit explōrātum:** ' as to feel certain '; *cui*

is a dative of reference = *ut eī.* *109, a.*
The subjunctive denotes result. *195.*
ad vesperum esse vīctūrum: ' that he
will be alive when evening comes,' *not*
' that he will live till the evening.'
With the prepositions *ad, sub, in* the
form *vesper* is generally used, not
vespera.

12. **aetās illa . . . adulēscentēs:**
some suppose that this sentence was
borrowed from Hippocrates, the "Father
of Medicine," who flourished in the
fifth century, B.C.

14. **trīstius:** ' *sevēriōribus remediīs.*'
So *Dē Officiīs,* **1,** 83, *leviter aegrōtantīs
lēniter cūrant, graviōribus autem morbīs
perīculōsās cūrātiōnēs et ancipitēs adhibēre*

HIPPOCRATES
From the Villa Albani, Rome.

coguntur, ' light cases of illness they
treat gently, whereas to more serious
diseases they are compelled to apply hazardous and risky treat-
ments.'

16. **Mēns . . . ratiō . . . cōnsilium:** ' Thought . . . reason . . .
wisdom.'

17. **quī . . . nūllī:** *nūllī* here almost = *nōn.* **nūllae . . . fuissent:** *i.e.* the young men would have brought every country to ruin.

20. **Īnsipienter:** adversative asyndeton. *238, d.*

quam incerta prō certīs habēre, falsa prō vērīs? At senex
nē quod spēret quidem habet. At est eō meliōre condiciōne
quam adulēscēns, quoniam id, quod ille spērat, hīc cōnsecūtus est : ille vult diū vīvere, hīc diū vīxit.

25 Hōrae quidem cēdunt et diēs et mēnsēs et annī, nec
praeteritum tempus umquam revertitur, nec, quid sequātur, scīrī potest. Quod cuique temporis ad vīvendum
datur, eō dēbet esse contentus. Neque enim histriōnī, ut
placeat, peragenda fābula est, modo, in quōcumque fuerit
30 āctū, probētur; neque sapientibus ūsque ad "Plaudite"
veniendum est.

Breve enim tempus aetātis satis longum est ad bene
honestēque vīvendum; sīn prōcesserit longius, nōn magis
dolendum est, quam agricolae dolent, praeteritā vērnī
35 temporis suāvitāte, aestātem autumnumque vēnisse. Vēr
enim, tamquam adulēscentia, significat ostenditque frūctūs

---

21. **incerta . . . vērīs**: chiasmus avoided. **At . . . at**: the objection and its answer are both introduced by *at*.

22. **At . . . adulēscēns**: these words look back to the preceding
sentence, to which they are an answer.

23. **ille . . . hīc**: usually *ille* refers to the former and *hīc* to the
latter; but here *hīc* denotes the person who is more important, *ille* the
person who is less important for the matter in hand; the first may
therefore be regarded as nearer to the speaker, the second as more
remote. *161, b;* A. & G. 297, *a, b;* G. 307, R. 1, *a, b.*

26. **quid sequātur**: ' the future.'

28. **ut placeat**: ' in order to secure approval.'

30. **" Plaudite "**: the Latin plays nearly always ended with this
word, addressed by the actor to the audience; see Horace, *Ars Poētica,*
153, *sī plausōris egēs aulaea manentis et ūsque sessūrī donec cantor ' vōs
plaudite' dīcat,* ' if you want an applauder who waits for the curtain
and will remain in his seat until the singer exclaims, "Applaud ye."'

32. **Breve tempus,** etc.: one of the poets has said that "in small
measures lives may perfect be."

33. **prōcesserit**: probably the subject is *sapiēns,* in which case *aetāte*
must also be supplied from *aetātis;* the subject may, however, be *aetās.*

36. **ostendit**: ' gives promise of.'

futūrōs; reliqua autem tempora dēmetendīs frūctibus et percipiendīs accommodāta sunt. Frūctus autem senectūtis est, ut saepe dīxī, ante partōrum bonōrum memoria et cōpia.

Whatever is in accord with nature is good; it is in accord with nature that old men die.

Omnia autem, quae secundum nātūram fīunt, sunt ha-40 benda in bonīs; quid est autem tam secundum nātūram quam senibus ēmorī? Quod idem contingit adulēscentibus adversante et repugnante nātūrā. Itaque adulēscentēs mihi morī 45 sīc videntur, ut cum aquae multitūdine flammae vīs opprimitur; senēs autem sīc, ut cum suā sponte, nūllā adhibitā vī, cōnsūmptus ignis exstinguitur; et 50 quasi pōma ex arboribus, crūda sī sunt, vix ēvelluntur, sī mātūra et cocta, dēcidunt, sīc vītam adulēscentibus vīs aufert, senibus

THE VOYAGE OF LIFE

The transport is just entering the harbor, gliding into still water. The helmsman sits at the stern, and one of the two steering-paddles is plainly seen; the sailors are furling the large sail. From a relief on a tomb at Pompeii, symbolizing entrance into a haven of rest, after the stormy voyage of life.

40. **secundum nātūram :** = κατὰ φύσιν, a Stoic phrase. See Companion, page 547.

42. **senibus :** dative of reference. *109, a.* *ēmorī* stands as subject of an implied *est*.

43. **contingit :** 'falls to the lot of'; this verb is not, as is often assumed, used merely of *good* fortune; it implies in itself nothing concerning the *character* of events, whether they be good or bad, but simply that the events take place *naturally*, and were to be expected.

51. **quasi . . . ēvelluntur :** it is rare to find in Cicero or the other prose writers of the best period a verb in the indicative mood immediately dependent on *quasi*, in the sense of *sīcut* or *quem ad modum*. When two things are compared by *quasi . . . ita*, the indicative verb is nearly always put in the second clause, and may be supplied in the clause with *quasi;* very rarely are there two different verbs for the two clauses. **sī . . . sī :** for the more usual *sī . . . sīn.*

55 mātūritās; quae quidem mihi tam iūcunda est, ut, quō
propius ad mortem accēdam, quasi terram vidēre videar
aliquandōque in portum ex longā nāvigātiōne esse ventūrus.

Death leads to a blessed immortality.

21. Nōn enim videō, cūr, quid ipse sentiam dē morte,
nōn audeam vōbīs dīcere, quod eō cernere mihi melius
videor, quō ab eā propius absum.

Ego vestrōs patrēs, P. Scīpiō tūque, C. Laelī, virōs clāris-
5 simōs mihique amīcissimōs, vīvere arbitror, et eam quidem
vītam, quae est sōla vīta nōminanda. Nam, dum sumus
inclūsī in hīs compāgibus corporis, mūnere quōdam necessitātis et gravī opere perfungimur; est enim animus caelestis
ex altissimō domiciliō dēpressus et quasi dēmersus in
10 terram, locum dīvīnae nātūrae aeternitātīque contrārium.
Sed crēdō deōs immortālēs sparsisse animōs in corpora
hūmāna, ut essent, quī terrās tuērentur, quīque, caelestium

---

55. **quō propius:** 'the nearer'; construction of *quō?* *140.*
56. **accēdam:** the subjunctive by attraction is due to *videar.* *220.*
21. 1. **quid . . . morte:** 'my own sentiments on death.'
2. **quod:** its antecedent is *quid . . . morte.* **cernere:** 'to visual-
ize.'
4. **vestrōs patrēs:** the elder Laelius was prominent both as general
and as statesman. He commanded the fleet which coöperated with
Scipio Africanus in Spain and afterwards served with honor in Africa.
He was an intimate friend of Cato. See Livy, **26,** 42, *et seq.*
6. **Nam dum sumus,** etc.: the whole of this doctrine is Platonic.
7. **mūnere necessitātis et . . . opere:** 'function and task allotted
us by fate.'
11. **immortālēs:** Cicero rarely mentions the gods without this
epithet. **sparsisse:** Horace calls the soul *dīvīnae particulam aurae.*
12. **tuērentur:** 'rule,' or 'guard,' or 'care for.' Most editors
wrongly take *tuērentur* to be for *intuērentur,* 'to look upon,' and regard
it as an intentional archaism. But see *Dē Rē Pūblicā,* **6,** 15 (where no
archaism can be intended): *hominēs sunt hāc lēge generātī, quī tuērentur
illum globum quae terra vocātur.*

THE TEMPLE OF APOLLO AT DELPHI

ōrdinem contemplantēs, imitārentur eum vītae modō atque cōnstantiā. Nec mē sōlum ratiō ac disputātiō impulit, ut ita crēderem, sed nōbilitās etiam summōrum philosophōrum 15 et auctōritās.

I am eager to see those whom I have known and loved, and those of whom I have heard, but, above all, my son, who passed on before.

23. Equidem efferor studiō patrēs vestrōs, quōs coluī et dīlēxī, videndī, neque vērō eōs sōlum convenīre aveō, quōs ipse cognōvī, sed illōs etiam, dē quibus audīvī et lēgī et ipse conscrīpsī; quō quidem mē, proficīscentem, haud sānē quid facile retrāxerit, nec tamquam Peliān recoxerit. Et sī 5 quis deus mihi largiātur, ut ex hāc aetāte repuerāscam et in cūnīs vāgiam, valdē recūsem, nec vērō velim, quasi dēcursō spatiō, ad carcerēs ā calce revocārī.

---

13. **contemplantēs imitārentur:** perhaps more Stoic than Platonic; the Stoics laid great stress on the ethical value of a contemplation and imitation of the order of the universe. **modō:** here *modus* seems to be the Platonic τὸ μέτριον, or perhaps a reminiscence of the Aristotelian doctrine of the mean. Translate, 'in moderation and consistency of life'; and see *Dē Officiīs,* **1,** 93, *rērum modus,* 'moderation in all things.'

23. 1. **coluī et dīlēxī:** see page 262, note 3.

2. **videndī:** Cicero for the most part avoids the genitive plural of the gerundive in agreement with a noun, and uses the gerund as here. Meissner notes that Latin has no verb with the sense 'to see again,' which a modern would use here.

4. **cōnscrīpsī:** in the *Orīginēs.* **quō:** = *ad quōs.*

5. **Peliān** (pē'li̯-ạs): a mistake of Cicero's. It was not Pelias but his half-brother Aeson, father of Iason, whom Medea made young again by cutting him to pieces and boiling him in her enchanted cauldron. She, however, induced the daughters of Pelias to try the same experiment with their father; the issue, of course, was very different. Plautus, *Pseudolus,* **3,** 2, 80, seems to make the same mistake. **sī quis deus largiātur:** the present subjunctive is noteworthy; strictly, an impossible condition should require the past tense, but in vivid passages an impossible condition is momentarily treated as possible. So Cicero generally says *sī revīvīscat aliquis,* not *revīvīsceret.*

8. **dēcursō spatiō:** 'when I have run my race.' **ad carcerēs ā calce:** *carcerēs* were the barriers behind which the horses and cars stood

Quid habet enim vīta commodī? Quid nōn potius
10 labōris? Sed habeat sānē; habet certē tamen aut satie-
tātem aut modum.   Nōn libet enim mihi dēplōrāre vītam,
quod multī, et eī doctī, saepe fēcērunt, neque mē vīxisse
paenitet, quoniam ita vīxī, ut nōn frūstrā mē nātum exīsti-
mem, et ex vītā ita discēdō tamquam ex hospitiō, nōn tam-
15 quam ē domō; commorandī enim nātūra dīversōrium
nōbīs, nōn habitandī dedit.

SITE OF THE STADIUM AT OLYMPIA

waiting for the race; *calx* (γραμμή), literally, ' a chalked line,' was what
we should call ' the winning post.'

10. **habeat**: concessive. *180, f;* B. 278; A. & G. 440; G. 264.

12. **multī et eī doctī**: Cicero always uses this phrase and not *multī
doctī*.

15. **commorandī . . . dīversōrium**: ' a hostelry wherein to sojourn.'
The idea has been expressed in literature in a thousand ways. See
Lucretius, **3,** 938, *cūr nōn ut plēnus vītae convīva recēdis;* Horace, *Satires,*

Ō praeclārum diem, cum in illud dīvīnum animōrum concilium coetumque proficīscar, cumque ex hāc turbā et colluviōne discēdam !

Proficīscar enim nōn ad eōs sōlum virōs, dē quibus ante 20 dīxī, vērum etiam ad Catōnem meum, quō nēmō vir melior nātus est, nēmō pietāte praestantior; cuius ā mē corpus est cremātum, quod contrā decuit ab illō meum, animus vērō nōn mē dēserēns, sed respectāns, in ea profectō loca discessit, quō mihi ipsī cernēbat esse veniendum. Quem 25 ego meum cāsum fortiter ferre vīsus sum, nōn quō aequō animō ferrem, sed mē ipse cōnsōlābar, exīstimāns nōn longinquum inter nōs dīgressum et discessum fore.

For these reasons old age is agreeable to me. And if there be no life after death, dead philosophers will not then ridicule me on account of my fond belief in immortality.

Hīs mihi rēbus, Scīpiō — id enim tē cum Laeliō admīrārī solēre dīxistī — levis est senectūs, nec sōlum nōn molesta, 30 sed etiam iūcunda.

1, 1, 118, *vīta cēdat utī convīva satur.* Cicero often insists that heaven is the *vēra aeternaque domus* of the soul (see *Tusculānae Disputātiōnēs* **1,** 118). See Epistle to the Hebrews, **13,** 14, " Here have we no continuing city, but we seek one to come."

17. **concilium coetumque :** so in *Dē Rē Pūblicā* **6,** 13, *concilia coetūsque hominum quae cīvitātēs vocantur.* The words here seem to imply that the real *cīvitās* is above; what seems to men a *cīvitās* is merely a disorganized crowd.

21. **Catōnem meum :** Cicero in his letters often calls his own son *Cicerō meus.* See page 378, line 22. **nēmō vir :** *vir* is added for emphasis.

23. **quod contrā :** ' whereas on the contrary.' **meum :** sc. *corpus cremārī.*

25. **quō :** put for *ad quae,* as often.

26. **vīsus sum :** ' people thought I bore up bravely.' **nōn quō . . . sed :** a relative clause parallel with a categorically affirmative clause. The usage is not uncommon, though Cicero often has *nōn quō . . . sed quia.* For mood of *ferrem* see *183, c;* B. 286, *b;* A. & G. 540, 2, N. 3: G. 541, N. 2.

Quod sī in hōc errō, quī animōs hominum immortālēs
esse crēdam, libenter errō, nec mihi hunc errōrem, quō
dēlector, dum vīvō, extorquērī volō; sīn mortuus, ut quī-
35 dam minūtī philosophī cēnsent, nihil sentiam, nōn vereor,
nē hunc errōrem meum philosophī mortuī irrīdeant.

Quod sī nōn sumus immortālēs futūrī, tamen exstinguī
hominī suō tempore optābile est.   Nam habet nātūra, ut
aliārum omnium rērum, sīc vīvendī modum.   Senectūs
40 autem aetātis est perāctiō tamquam fābulae, cuius dēfa-
tīgātiōnem fugere dēbēmus, praesertim adiūnctā satietāte.

Haec habuī dē senectūte quae dīcerem; ad quam utinam veniātis, ut ea, quae ex mē audīstis, rē expertī probāre possītis!

---

32. **quī:** here = *cum ego*, 'since I . . .' *194, c.*

34. **extorquērī volō:** the best Latin writers frequently use the
passive infinitive with verbs expressing desire, where moderns would
incline to the active.

35. **minūtī philosophī:** 'insignificant philosophers.'   **sentiam:** future indicative.

40. **perāctiō:** the noun is said to occur only here in Cicero.

42. **Haec . . . dīcerem:** the same words occur at the end of the
Laelius, page 329; for *habeō quod dīcam* Cicero often says *habeō dīcere*,
as in *Prō Balbō*, 34.

M. TULLĪ CICERŌNIS LAELIUS DĒ AMĪCITIĀ

Partēs Sēlēctae

Fannius and Scaevola request Laelius to discourse on friendship.

4. *Fannius.* Istūc quidem, Laelī, ita necesse est. Sed quoniam amīcitiae mentiōnem fēcistī et sumus ōtiōsī, pergrātum mihi fēceris, spērō item Scaevolae, sī, quem ad modum solēs dē cēterīs rēbus, cum ex tē quaeruntur, sīc dē amīcitiā disputāris, quid sentiās, quālem exīstimēs, 5 quae praecepta dēs.

To THE STUDENT: Read the introductory note to the *Laelius dē Amīcitiā* on page 553, where also an outline may be found.

4. 1. Istūc quidem, Laelī, ita necesse est: ' It must be as you say, Laelius.' He had just ventured the opinion that out of all generations scarcely three or four friendships are mentioned, and had expressed the hope that the friendship between him and Scipio (sip'ĭ-ō) would be put in the same class by future generations. The *ita* is not pleonastic in phrases of this sort, though often so regarded. The sense here is *istūc necesse est, et eō modō quō tū dīcis necesse esse.*

2. sumus ōtiōsī: according to Roman feeling it was not considered proper for statesmen to discuss philosophical questions except as a relaxation from more serious business.

4. solēs: sc. *respondēre.* **cēterīs rēbus:** ' all of the other questions.' *97, c.*

5. quālem exīstimēs, quae . . . dēs: these two clauses are explanatory of *quid.* Taking with them the words *dē amīcitiā quid sentiās* the whole may be freely rendered, ' your opinion concerning the theory and practice of friendship.' In chapters 5-7, which correspond to *quālem exīstimēs,* Laelius gives his view of the nature and value of friendship; in chapters 11-26 he lays down practical rules and maxims concerning true friendship.

Scaevola. Mihi vērō erit grātum; atque id ipsum cum tēcum agere cōnārer, Fannius antevertit. Quam ob rem utrīque nostrum grātum admodum fēceris.

Friendship is a complete unanimity in all things, human and divine, coupled with mutual affection. Its essential condition is virtue, and its advantages are manifold.

6. Est enim amīcitia nihil aliud nisi omnium dīvīnārum hūmānārumque rērum cum benevolentiā et cāritāte cōnsēnsiō; quā quidem haud sciō an exceptā sapientiā nihil melius hominī sit ā dīs immortālibus datum. Dīvitiās aliī 5 praepōnunt, bonam aliī valētūdinem, aliī potentiam, aliī honōrēs, multī etiam voluptātēs. (Bēluārum hōc quidem

---

7. **Mihi vērō:** ' To me certainly '; this form of emphatic assent is common in Cicero's dialogues.

8. **antevertit:** literally, 'turned in front,' or 'thrust in front,' *i.e.* his request or his speech. Here translate, ' anticipated me.'

9. **grātum admodum:** = *pergrātum.*

6. 1. **enim:** the conditions of *amīcitia* here given are so difficult of fulfillment that they account for the rarity of *cāritās* (as above *inter duōs aut paucōs*), which is the kernel of friendship. **omnium . . . cōnsēnsiō:** in the omitted passage the statement is made that the whole pith (*omnis vīs*) of friendship lies in the *cōnsēnsiō voluntātum studiōrum sententiārum.* In the present passage the objects towards which the *voluntātēs, studia,* and *sententiae* are to be directed are so described as to include all things in heaven and earth. The division of all things into *rēs dīvīnae* and *rēs hūmānae* belonged to everyday talk and had no reference to any philosophical system. Compare the title of Varro's greatest work, *Antīquitātēs Rērum Hūmānārum et Dīvīnārum;* also Iustiniānus, *Īnstitūtiōnēs,* **1,** 1, 1, definition of *iūris prūdentia, dīvīnārum atque hūmānārum rērum nōtitia, iūstī atque iniūstī scientia.* Sallust, *Catilīna,* 20, *idem velle atque idem nōlle, ea dēmum firma amīcitia est.*

2. **benevolentiā et cāritāte:** ' kindliness and affection.' These words are often thus joined in Cicero. *212, b. Cum benevolentiā et cāritāte* qualify *cōnsēnsiō.*

3. **haud sciō an:** in Cicero and the best writers this phrase is affirmative, meaning, ' I am inclined to think,' ' probably.' *180, e (1).* In later writers negative, with the sense ' probably not.'

6. **Bēluārum:** emphatic; sc. *est.*

extrēmum, illa autem superiōra cadūca et incerta, posita
nōn tam in cōnsiliīs nostrīs quam in fortūnae temeritāte.
Quī autem in virtūte summum bonum pōnunt, praeclārē
illī quidem, sed haec ipsa virtūs amīcitiam et gignit et 10
continet, nec sine virtūte amīcitia esse ūllō pactō potest.
Iam virtūtem ex cōnsuētūdine vītae sermōnisque nostrī
interpretēmur nec eam, ut quīdam doctī, verbōrum magnificentiā mētiāmur virōsque bonōs eōs, quī habentur, nume-

VIEW ON THE PALATINE TODAY

7. **extrēmum:** *extrēmum* here = *fīnis*, in the sense of *fīnis bonōrum*
or *summum bonum*. **cadūca et incerta:** ' fleeting and unstable.'

10. **illī:** sc. *faciunt*. *Illī*, the Stoics and Peripatetics. See page 547.

11. **esse:** emphatic; ' exist.'

12. **Iam:** ' To proceed,' as often. **cōnsuētūdine vītae sermōnisque:**
'its use in daily life and ordinary conversation.' See *Verrēs*, **4,** 109,
cotīdiānā dīcendī cōnsuētūdine.

13. **nec . . . mētiāmur:** not intended to contrast strongly with the
first part of the sentence, otherwise *nōn* would have been written for
nec and *eam* omitted. The clause is really explanatory = *nōn mētientēs.*
verbōrum magnificentiā: ' the grandiloquence of language.'

14. **virōsque:** " If a negative proposition is followed by an affirmative, in which the same thought is expressed or continued, *que*, *et*, or *ac*

15 rēmus, Paulōs, Catōnēs, Gallōs, Scīpiōnēs, Philōs; hīs
commūnis vīta contenta est; eōs autem omittāmus, quī
omnīnō nūsquam reperiuntur. Tālis igitur inter virōs
amīcitia tantās opportūnitātēs habet, quantās vix queō
dīcere. Prīncipiō quī potest esse vīta "vītālis," ut aït
20 Ennius, quae nōn in amīcī mūtuā benevolentiā conquiēscit?
Quid dulcius quam habēre, quīcum omnia audeās sīc loquī
ut tēcum? Quī esset tantus frūctus in prōsperīs rēbus, nisi

---

is employed in Latin where in English we use 'but.'" Madvig, 433,
Obs. 2. *234, b. virōs bonōs* is predicate accusative, *eōs* being the object.

15. **Paulōs**, etc.: the generic plural in the sense of 'men like P.,' etc.
Lucius Aemilius Paulus (lū'sh(y)ŭs e-mil'ĭ-ŭs pâ'lŭs) was the conqueror of Perseus, king of Macedonia, at Pydna in 168 B.C. **Gallōs:**
Gaius Sulpicius Gallus (gā'(y)ŭs sŭl-pish'(y)ŭs gal'ŭs) served under Paulus
in his campaign against Perseus, and as a famous astronomer was the
first Roman who predicted an eclipse (Livy, **44,** 87). **Philōs:** L. Furius
Philus (fūr'ĭ-ŭs fī'lŭs), consul of the year 136 B.C., was a distinguished
scholar, a friend and patron of Greek culture. He was a member of the
famous Scipionic circle, composed of such Greek scholars as the historian
Polybius, the Stoic philosopher Panaetius, and many Latin writers of distinction, including Terence, the most polished author of Latin comedies,
Hemina and Piso, annalists, and among others Lucilius, the father of Roman
satire. See Companion, page 707.

18. **opportūnitātēs**: the word *opportūnitās* is 'opportuneness' rather
than 'opportunity.' To say that friendship has 'opportunenesses'
is equivalent to saying that it shows the characteristic of 'opportuneness' on many occasions. Cicero uses the plural of abstract nouns in
this way more frequently than any other author. *92, c.* **vix queō:** Cicero
always says *nōn queō* or *vix queō*, never *nequeō*, though he uses other parts
of the verb *nequīre.*

19. **quī:** 'how.' **vīta esse vītālis:** 'a life be true life'; it is not known
to what work of Ennius the quotation belongs. The words are an imitation of βίος βιωτός. In his own style, Cicero would have written *vīta
potest esse ūlla.*

20. **quae . . . conquiēscit:** 'which does not find peace in an interchange of kindness with a friend.'

21. **Quid dulcius:** the omission of both *enim* and *est* gives an abrupt
emphasis to the question. **quīcum:** used when the statement is general,
while *quōcum* is used when some particular person is meant.

22. **Quī:** literally, 'What sort of?' *Quis* would have meant merely

habērēs, quī illīs aequē ac tū ipse gaudēret? Adversās
vērō ferre difficile esset sine eō, quī illās grāvius etiam quam
tū ferret. Dēnique cēterae rēs, quae expetuntur, oppor- 25
tūnae sunt singulae rēbus ferē singulīs, dīvitiae, ut ūtāre,
opēs, ut colāre, honōrēs, ut laudēre, voluptātēs, ut gaudeās,
valētūdō, ut dolōre careās et mūneribus fungāre corporis;
amīcitia rēs plūrimās continet; quōquō tē verteris, praestō
est, nūllō locō exclūditur, numquam intempestīva, num- 30
quam molesta est; itaque nōn aquā, nōn ignī, ut aiunt, locīs
plūribus ūtimur quam amīcitiā. Neque ego nunc dē
vulgārī aut dē mediocrī, quae tamen ipsa et dēlectat et
prōdest, sed dē vērā et perfectā loquor, quālis eōrum, quī
paucī nōminantur, fuit. Nam et secundās rēs splendidiōrēs 35
facit amīcitia et adversās partiēns commūnicānsque leviōrēs.

'what?' *Tantus* is here only a rhetorical variation for *magnus*, and as
tantus implies *quantus* there is really an ellipsis. *238, f.* **frūctus:** 'enjoyment.'

23. **aequē ac tū:** 'equally with you.' Adverbs as well as adjectives
of likeness and their opposite may take *ac* or *atque* = 'as.' *233, c.*

24. **sine eō:** takes the place of a conditional clause.

25. **quae expetuntur:** 'which are objects of desire.'

26. **rēbus ferē singulīs:** 'usually for special ends.'

28. **valētūdō:** here the *bona valētūdo*.

29. **amīcitia:** adversative asyndeton. *238, d.*

30. **locō:** perhaps ablative of separation with *exclūditur.* *Nūllō
locō* may, however, have an adverbial sense equivalent to that of *nūsquam.* The adverb *praestō* in the preceding clause makes this probable,
and the probability is increased by *plūribus locīs* below.

31. **ut aiunt:** 'as the saying goes.' Fire and water were fixed upon
as the first necessaries of life in the *aquā et ignī interdictiō*, which was
equivalent to a sentence of exile. See page 260, line 15, note.

33. **quae . . . prōdest:** a sidelong protest against the theory that
only the σοφοί (the wise) are capable of friendship. **dēlectat et prōdest:**
so Horace, *Ars Poētica*, 333, *aut prōdesse volunt aut dēlectāre poētae.*

34. **vērā et perfectā:** 'pure and faultless.' **eōrum . . . nōminantur:**
'the few who are mentioned.'

36. **partiēns commūnicānsque:** the two participles differ very little
in meaning — no more widely than 'dividing' and 'sharing' in Eng-

Friendship serves to unite the family, the state, and the universe.

7. Cumque plūrimās et maximās commoditātēs amīcitia contineat, tum illā nīmīrum praestat omnibus, quod bonam spem praelūcet in posterum nec dēbilitārī animōs aut cadere patitur. Vērum enim amīcum quī intuētur, tamquam 5 exemplar aliquod intuētur suī. Quōcircā et absentēs adsunt et egentēs abundant et imbēcillī valent et, quod difficilius

---

lish. In *partiēns* the notion of mere division is more prominent, in *commūnicāns* the notion of comradeship or partnership. Synonymic combination. *212, b.*

7. 1. **commoditātēs:** very little different in sense from *opportūnitās* above. *Opportūnitās* expresses rather the idea of exceptional appropriateness, *commoditās* rather the characteristic of usefulness as an ordinary fact. **Cum . . . contineat — tum . . . praestat:** the normal construction with *cum . . . tum* is for both clauses to have the same verb, or for the verbs (if different) in both clauses to be in the same mood and tense. The reason for the variation here is the desire to point out that the fact contained in the clause *cum . . . contineat* is one which has already been mentioned and disposed of. ' Seeing that friendship furnishes very many and important advantages. . . .' *Continet* would have been appropriate had the fact now been mentioned for the first time.

2. **illā . . . omnibus:** *illā*, ablative, sc. *commoditāte; omnibus = omnibus rēbus*, the verbs *praestat* and *praelūcet* having the same subject, *amīcitia.* Many editors, in order to avoid the exceptional *omnibus = omnibus rēbus*, make *illa* (sc. *commoditās*) subject to *praestat* so that *omnibus = omnibus commoditātibus*, while *praelūcet* has for its subject *amīcitia.* The neuter *omnibus* used as substantive, though rare, is well attested.

3. **spem praelūcet:** the verb *praelūcēre* is rare even in poetry and very rare in prose. The transitive use (' holds up the light of hope ') may perhaps be allowed here, though the only passages quoted for it by the editors and dictionaries are Ausonius, *Idyllia*, **4**, 95, *praelūceō lūmen*, and Plautus, *Casina*, **1**, 30, *lūcēbis facem.* Pliny, *Historia Nātūrālis*, **32**, 141, has *adeō ut praelūceat baculum*, i.e. ' sets on fire.'

4. **Vērum amīcum:** the word *vērus* is to be taken in a less strict sense than *vērā amīcitiā* above in line 34.

5. **absentēs adsunt**, etc.: intended contradiction in terms, oxymoron. *239, p.*

6. **egentēs abundant**, etc.: St. Paul, Corinthians, **2**, 6, 10, " As having

dictū est, mortuī vīvunt; tantus eōs honor, memoria, dēsīderium prōsequitur amīcōrum. Ex quō illōrum beāta mors vidētur, hōrum vīta laudābilis. Quod sī exēmeris ex rērum nātūrā benevolentiae coniūnctiōnem, nec domus ūlla 10 nec urbs stāre poterit, nē agrī quidem cultus permanēbit. Id sī minus intellegitur, quanta vīs amīcitiae concordiaeque sit, ex dissēnsiōnibus atque ex discordiīs perspicī potest. Quae enim domus tam stabilis, quae tam fīrma cīvitās est, quae nōn odiīs et discidiīs funditus possit ēvertī? Ex 15 quō, quantum bonī sit in amīcitiā, iūdicārī potest.

---

nothing, and yet possessing all things "; *ibid.*, **6**, 9, " As dying and behold, we live." See previous note. **difficilius dictū**: ' a harder saying.' The Latin like the English phrase is inaccurate, since the statement is not hard to make, but hard to believe. Compare Mark, **2**, 9, " Whether is it *easier to say* to the sick of the palsy . . ." Cicero often has *incredibile dictū;* see Livy, **3**, 5, 12, *difficile ad fidem est affīrmāre.*

7. **tantus eōs honor:** the separation of *tantus* from *honor* is a figure called hyper'baton or trajection (*trāiectiō*). *239, k.* See page 256, line 6, and note.

8. **Ex quō:** the antecedent of *quō* is not *dēsīderium*, but the whole preceding clause; thus *ex quō = ex quā rē.* **beāta . . . laudābilis:** chiasmus. *239, e.*

9. **laudābilis:** because the survivors do well in remembering their friends.

10. **rērum nātūrā:** *i.e.* the universe. *212, e.* **benevolentiae coniūnctiōnem:** ' the bond of good will '; *benevolentia*, the more diffused and weaker form of affection, is here contrasted with *amīcitia*, its more concentrated and intense form. *Benevolentia* here is Aristotle's ὁμόνοια in *Ēthica Nīcomachēa*, 9, Chapter 6.

11. **nē . . . quidem:** ' no, nor '; simply a stronger *nec.*

12. **Id:** explained by the clause *quanta . . . sit.* **minus:** here, and often, scarcely different in sense from *nōn.* **vīs amīcitiae:** ' the essence of friendship.'

13. **perspicī:** a stronger word than *intellegitur* just before.

15. **discidiīs:** ' divisions,' so rightly written, not *dissidiīs*, a reading found in some editions. Most scholars now agree with Madvig in denying *dissidium* to be a Latin word.

The origin of friendship is to be found not in expediency or some ulterior motive, but in love. This kindred impulse of love in its elemental form may be recognized in the instincts of lower animals, but it finds its highest expression in man.

8. Saepissimē igitur mihi dē amīcitiā cōgitantī maximē illud cōnsīderandum vidērī solet, utrum propter imbēcillitātem atque inopiam dēsīderāta sit amīcitia, ut dandīs recipiendīsque meritīs quod quisque minus per sē ipse
5 posset, id acciperet ab aliō vicissimque redderet, an esset hōc quidem proprium amīcitiae, sed antīquior et pulchrior et magis ā nātūrā ipsā profecta alia causa. Amor enim, ex quō amīcitia nōmināta est, prīnceps est ad benevolentiam coniungendam. Nam ūtilitātēs quidem etiam ab iīs percipi-
10 untur saepe, quī simulātiōne amīcitiae coluntur et observantur temporis causā, in amīcitiā autem nihil fictum est, nihil simulātum et, quidquid est, id est vērum et voluntārium.

---

8. 1. mihi . . . cōgitantī: so the *Dē Ōrātōre* begins — *cōgitantī mihi saepenumerō et memoriā vetera repetentī perbeātī fuisse, Quīnte frāter, illī vidērī solent.* . . . So the second book of the *Dē Dīvīnātiōne* — *quaerentī mihi multumque et diū cōgitantī . . . occurrēbat.*

4. **meritīs:** = *officiīs, beneficiīs.* **quisque:** " when a relative and a demonstrative proposition are combined, *quisque* almost always stands in the relative proposition, commonly (without emphasis) immediately after the relative, so that even *sē* and *suus* stand after *quisque.*" *170, b;* B. 252, 5; A. & G. 313, *a;* G. 318, 3, and notes.

5. **posset:** sc. *habēre,* to be supplied from *acciperet.* **esset:** ' was,' *i.e.* from the beginning.

6. **proprium amīcitiae:** *amīcitiae* is genitive, not dative; it is doubtful whether Cicero uses the dative after *proprius* at all. *102.*

7. **alia causa:** sc. *amīcitiae;* emphatic position. **Amor:** emphatic, ' For it is love,' etc.

8. **prīnceps . . . ad:** ' leads to '; so Archias, *hunc videō mihi prīncipem ad suscipiendam ratiōnem hōrum studiōrum exstitisse.*

9. **ab iīs:** ' from those,' not ' by those.'

11. **temporis causā:** ' to suit the occasion.' **fictum:** opposed to *vērum* below, as *simulātum* is to *voluntārium.*

12. **et:** ' but,' in English. *234, h.*

Quāpropter ā nātūrā mihi vidētur potius quam ab indigentiā
orta amīcitia, applicātiōne magis animī cum quōdam sēnsū
amandī quam cōgitātiōne, quantum illa rēs ūtilitātis esset 15
habitūra. Quod quidem quāle sit, etiam in bēstiīs quibusdam animadvertī potest, quae ex sē nātōs ita amant ad
quoddam tempus et ab eīs ita amantur, ut facile eārum
sēnsus appāreat. Quod in homine multō est ēvidentius,

SAN PIETRO, A MOUNTAIN TOWN IN CICERO'S COUNTRY

13. **potius . . . magis:** the difference in sense between these two
words is in use frequently obliterated, but *potius* strictly means ' better,'
and therefore ought to indicate that of alternatives one is preferred by
some individual to the other, while *magis* strictly means ' more,' and
ought to have no direct reference to choice. **ab indigentiā orta:** Cicero
probably never used *ortus* with the ablative without the preposition.

14. **applicātiōne . . . cōgitātiōne:** ablative of means or instrument.

15. **illa rēs:** ' the act of friendship.'

16. **Quod,** etc.: ' The nature of this principle.' **quibusdam:** the limitation is perhaps due to the fact that many creatures abandon their
eggs when laid.

17. **ex sē nātōs:** ' their young.' **ad quoddam tempus:** *Dē Nātūrā
Deōrum,* **2,** 129, *ūsque ad eum fīnem dum possint sē ipsa dēfendere.*

19. **sēnsus:** ' feeling,' or ' impulse,' *i.e.* as opposed to the calculation
of advantages mentioned above.

20 prīmum ex eā cāritāte, quae est inter nātōs et parentēs, quae dirimī nisi dētestābilī scelere nōn potest; deinde cum similis sēnsus exstitit amōris, sī aliquem nactī sumus, cuius cum mōribus et nātūrā congruāmus, quod in eō quasi lūmen aliquod probitātis et virtūtis perspicere videāmur. Nihil 25 est enim virtūte amābilius, nihil quod magis alliciat ad dīligendum: quippe cum propter virtūtem et probitātem etiam eōs, quōs numquam vīdimus, quōdam modō dīligāmus.

It is a basic law of friendship that we should ask nothing dishonorable of a friend and grant nothing dishonorable. History supports this view.

12. Haec igitur lēx in amīcitiā sanciātur, ut neque rogēmus rēs turpēs nec faciāmus rogātī. Turpis enim excūsātiō est et minimē accipienda cum in cēterīs peccātīs, tum sī quis contrā rem pūblicam sē amīcī causā fēcisse 5 fateātur. Etenim eō locō, Fannī et Scaevola, locātī sumus, ut nōs longē prōspicere oporteat futūrōs cāsūs reī pūblicae. Dēflexit iam aliquantum dē spatiō curriculōque cōnsuētūdō maiōrum. Tib. Gracchus rēgnum occupāre cōnātus est,

---

20. **quae . . . potest:** this is contrasted with *ad quoddam tempus* above.

22. **similis sēnsus amōris:** i.e. *sēnsus amōris cāritātī parentum similis;* such brevity is common in comparisons. **sī aliquem:** *sī* has almost the same sense as *cum* here, and was perhaps used because the repetition of *cum* would have been awkward. *Aliquem* after *sī* is perhaps more vivid than *quem:* ' some actual person.'

23. **mōribus et nātūrā:** the collocation *nātūrā et mōribus* is more natural and common. **congruāmus:** subjunctive of characteristic. **quasi:** serves, as usual, to soften the metaphor, which however is a very common one.

26. **quippe cum:** ' inasmuch as.'

12. 1. **neque . . . nec:** common in Cicero for *nec . . . nec; nec . . . neque,* however, is rare (*Prō Archiā*, 29).

3. **minimē accipienda:** ' not to be allowed.'

6. **nōs:** = *Rōmānī*, not simply Laelius and his sons-in-law.

8. **maiōrum:** depends on *spatiō curriculōque.* Metaphors from

THE FALLS OF THE LIRIS RIVER

This beautiful stream flows past Cicero's birthplace, Arpinum, and it is more than probable that Marcus and his brother Quintus often played together on its banks.

vel rēgnāvit is quidem paucōs mēnsēs. Num quid simile populus Rōmānus audierat aut vīderat? Hunc etiam post 10 mortem secūtī amīcī et propinquī quid in P. Scīpiōne effēcerint, sine lacrimīs nōn queō dīcere. Nam Carbōnem, quōcumque modō potuimus, propter recentem poenam Tib. Gracchī sustinuimus; dē C. Gracchī autem tribūnātū quid

---

racing are common in Cicero. There is little difference in meaning between *spatium* and *curriculum* (here perhaps ' course and career '). *Spatium* refers rather to the whole ground of the race-course; *curriculum*, to the track or portion passed over in running. **rēgnum occupāre:** ' to establish a monarchy.'

9. **vel:** = *vel potius*. **is quidem:** in Greek = ἐκεῖνός γε, or ὅ γε as in Homer; not needed for the sense, but added in order to point attention more closely to the subject of the verb.

10. **audierat:** the modern equivalent for *hearing* of such a matter would be *reading about it in history*.

11. **P. Scīpiōne:** P. Cornelius Scipio Nasica Serapio (pub'lị-ụs kọr-nē'lyụs sip'ị-ō nā-sī'cạ sẹ-rā'pị-ō), the murderer of Ti. Gracchus (tị bē'rị-ụs grak'ụs). He is sometimes called *pontifex* (*In Catilīnam*, **1,** 1) to distinguish him from Africanus, but in other passages merely P. Scipio as here. Nasica Serapio was a son of a daughter of the elder Africanus, therefore a cousin of the Gracchi. The senate gave him a *lēgātiō* to Pergamum, a form of honorable exile, in order to withdraw him from the fury of the democratic party. He committed suicide in Pergamum.

12. **effēcerint:** Seyffert rightly points out that the reading *fēcerint* could not stand here, since the democratic party had not itself done anything to Nasica, but had forced the senate to punish him. **Nam:** this is elliptic, as often; so γάρ in Greek. The full sense would be, ' I need hardly mention Carbo, for, etc.' *238, f.*

13. **quōcumque modō potuimus:** ' we ' here = the aristocratic party. **propter poenam:** *i.e.* it would have excited the populace too much to attempt to punish Carbo so soon after Ti. Gracchus's death.

14. **sustinuimus:** ' we have borne with.' **C. Gracchī autem:** but in chapter **19,** 69, *Q. vērō Maximum.* The latter collocation is regular: here *autem* is put after in order to make the contrast between *Ti. Gracchī* and *C. Gracchī* more striking. **tribūnātū:** still in the future at the time when Laelius is supposed to be speaking; Scipio died in 129 B.C. and C. Gracchus did not become tribune till 123 B.C.

15 exspectem, nōn libet augurārī. Serpit deinde rēs, quae prōclīvis ad perniciem, cum semel coepit, lābitur. Vidētis, in tabellā iam ante quanta sit facta lābēs, prīmō Gabīniā lēge, bienniō autem post Cassiā. Vidēre iam videor populum ā senātū disiūnctum, multitūdinis arbitriō rēs maximās 20 agī. Plūrēs enim discent, quem ad modum haec fīant, quam quem ad modum eīs resistātur. Quōrsum haec? Quia sine sociīs nēmō quicquam tāle cōnātur. Praecipiendum est igitur bonīs, ut, sī in eius modī amīcitiās ignārī

---

15. **Serpit:** *serpere* means here ' to make progress imperceptibly or insinuatingly.' **Serpit . . . lābitur:** general in scope, and intended to give the reason why Laelius dreaded to think of the future course of Gaius Gracchus. *Deinde* here is used proleptically, *i.e.* it presupposes *semel* which comes after. *238, m.* The sentence *vidētis . . . Cassiā* simply gives an actual example of this general principle.

16. **coepit:** sc. *lābī.* The omission of the infinitive is exceedingly common with both *coepī* and *dēbeō.* See *In Catilīnam,* **1,** 1, *perge quō coepistī.* Observe that Cicero and Caesar do not, as Sallust, Livy, and later writers, use *coepī* absolutely; *i.e.* an infinitive is always either expressed or implied.

17. **in tabellā:** 'in the matter of voting'; literally, 'of the voting ticket.' **iam ante:** *i.e.* before the time of C. Gracchus. **lābēs:** ' corruption,' *i.e.* of old institutions. **Gabīniā lēge:** this law, entitled *dē magistrātibus mandandīs* (*Dē Lēgibus,* **3,** 35) was carried by A. Gabinius, tribune in 139 B.C., and introduced into elections voting by ballot, *i.e.* by writing the name of the candidate on a ticket or tablet.

18. **Cassiā:** this law was carried by L. Cassius Longinus (lǫn-jī'nǔs) Ravil'la, tribune in 137 B.C., and extended the ballot to the juries in the criminal courts. Cassius was afterwards a judge and for his severity was called *scopulus reōrum;* he was the author of the saying, ' *cui bonō?* ' (*i.e.* who gains by it? viz. the offense). The *lēx tabellāria* of Carbo introduced the ballot for voting on laws proposed to the *comitia.* His law is commonly placed in 131 B.C., but there is no direct evidence for the date and it may have been several years later. **populum . . . multitūdinis:** the change seems made merely for the sake of variety.

21. **Quōrsum haec:** sc. *disputō.*

23. **igitur:** note its position as third word in the sentence. **ignārī cāsū aliquō:** note the two reasons, *ignārī* and *cāsū aliquō,* placed side by side unconnected by a conjunction.

cāsū aliquō inciderint, nē exīstiment ita sē alligātōs, ut ab amīcīs in magnā aliquā rē pūblicā peccantibus nōn discē-25 dant; improbīs autem poena statuenda est, nec vērō minor eīs, quī secūtī erunt alterum, quam eīs, quī ipsī fuerint impietātis ducēs. Quis clārior in Graeciā Themistocle, quis potentior? quī cum imperātor bellō Persicō servitūte Graeciam līberāvisset propterque invidiam in 30 exsilium expulsus esset, ingrātae patriae iniūriam nōn tulit, quam ferre dēbuit, fēcit īdem, quod xx annīs ante apud nōs fēcerat Coriolānus. Hīs adiūtor contrā patriam inventus est nēmō; itaque mortem sibi uterque cōnscīvit.

---

24. **nē:** in final clauses where a negative is needed, as here, *nē* and *ut nē* are used indifferently by Cicero; in consecutive negative clauses *ut nōn* generally stands, as below, but sometimes *ut nē* is found " when precaution, forethought, or restriction is to be indicated, especially with *ita* preceding." Madvig, 456, Obs. 4.

25. **in . . . peccantibus:** ' when transgressing in some public matter of importance.'

26. **nec vērō:** this phrase corresponds to the affirmative expression *et . . . quidem*, the phrase *nec . . . quidem* being rarely used by good writers.

28. **Themistocle** (thę-mis'tǫ-klēz): so *Acadēmicae Quaestiōnēs*, **2,** 2, *Themistocle quem facile Graeciae prīncipem pōnimus.*

29. **imperātor:** = στρατηγός of the Athenians. The whole Grecian fleet at Salamis was commanded not by Themistocles but by Eurybiades (yū-ry-bi'ą-dēz) the Spartan.

30. **invidiam:** = διαβολήν, ' unpopularity.'

32. **xx annīs ante:** the ostracism of Themistocles happened in 471 B.C., whereas the banishment of Coriolanus from Rome is assigned to the year 491. On the banishment of Themistocles, his relation with the king of Persia and death, see Curtius, *History of Greece*, Book 3, Chapter 2; Smith, *History of Greece*, Chapter 22.

33. **Coriolā'nus:** he is compared with Themistocles in *Brūtus,* 42; *Ad Atticum,* **9,** 10, 3. Varying accounts were current concerning the death of both these men, as Cicero himself states in *Brūtus,* 42 and 43, where he refers to Thucydides, **1,** 138. In *Ad Atticum,* **9,** 10, 3 he assumes that Coriolanus died a natural death.

34. **nēmō:** the inference intended is ' so much worse are the Romans now than their forefathers, and than the Greeks of Themistocles' time.'

35 Quā rē tālis improbōrum cōnsēnsiō nōn modo excūsātiōne
amīcitiae tegenda nōn est, sed potius suppliciō omnī vindi-
canda est, ut nē quis concessum putet amīcum vel bellum
patriae īnferentem sequī; quod quidem, ut rēs īre coepit,
haud sciō an aliquandō futūrum sit. Mihi autem nōn
40 minōrī cūrae est, quālis rēs pūblica post mortem meam
futūra, quam quālis hodiē sit.

True friends should counsel frankly and criticize constructively, if necessary.

13. Haec igitur prīma lēx amīcitiae sanciātur, ut ab
amīcīs honesta petāmus, amīcōrum causā honesta faciāmus,
nē exspectēmus quidem, dum rogēmur; studium semper
adsit, cunctātiō absit; cōnsilium vērō dare audeāmus
5 līberē. Plūrimum in amīcitiā amīcōrum bene suādentium
valeat auctōritās, eaque et adhibeātur ad monendum nōn
modo apertē, sed etiam ācriter, sī rēs postulābit, et adhibitae
pāreātur.

Friendships are generated spontaneously; like attracts like. Expediency
and the hope of advantage do not bring about friendship.

14. Cum autem contrahat amīcitiam, ut suprā dīxī, sī
qua significātiō virtūtis ēlūceat, ad quam sē similis animus

---

36. **suppliciō:** a stronger word than *poena* above in line 26; in its
strict sense *supplicium* means 'summary execution.' For *suppliciō
omnī = summō* see *Prō Imperiō Gnaeī Pompeī,* 11.

37. **concessum:** sc. *esse.*

39. **haud sciō an:** see page 294, note 3. *180, e (1).*

13. 1. **Haec . . . faciāmus:** these words almost exactly repeat the
first sentence of chapter 12, page 302. Notice that the clauses are put
side by side without connecting particles.

3. **rogēmur:** *190, b;* B. 292; A. & G. 553; G. 572.

5. **līberē:** = μετὰ παρρησίας, of the Greek, 'with all freedom of
speech.'

7. **apertē:** 'frankly.' **sī rēs postulābit:** 'if the situation demands
it.' **adhibitae:** sc. *auctōritātī.*

14. 1. **contrahat:** the subject is probably *quis* indefinite, omitted
as in *Dē Ōrātōre,* **1,** 30, *quō velit = quō quis velit.* It may be, however, as
Seyffert and Nauck make it, the whole clause *sī . . . ēlūceat.* The sub-

applicet et adiungat, id cum contigit, amor exoriātur necesse
est. Quid enim tam absurdum quam dēlectārī multīs
inanimīs rēbus, ut honōre, ut glōriā, ut aedificiō, ut vestītū 5
cultūque corporis, animante virtūte praeditō, eō quī vel
amāre vel, ut ita dīcam, redamāre possit, nōn admodum
dēlectārī? Nihil est enim remūnerātiōne benevolentiae,
nihil vicissitūdine studiōrum officiōrumque iūcundius.
Quid? sī illud etiam addimus, quod rēctē addī potest, nihil 10
esse, quod ad sē rem ūllam tam alliciat et attrahat quam
ad amīcitiam similitūdō? concēdētur profectō vērum esse,

---

junctive is causal.   **suprā**: an expression inadvertently used by Cicero,
for it implies writing and is inapplicable to a speech.

3. **id cum contigit**: *cum* here simply = *quotiēns*.   The verb *contingere* is not, as is often assumed, used merely of good fortune, it implies in
itself nothing concerning the character of events, whether they be good or
bad, but simply that the events take place naturally and were to be expected.

5. **aedificiō**: see note for page 280, line 24.   *92, g.*

6. **corporis . . . animante**: adversative asyndeton. *238, d.* **praeditō**: as *animāns* is exceptionally used of man it is here made masculine, but when it is applied to the lower animals it is generally feminine.

7. **redamāre**: coined by Cicero here to express ἀντιφιλεῖν (' to love
in return ') and used by him nowhere else: it does not occur again in
Latin literature till very late.   *Ut ita dīcam* is used to soften the harshness of this new word. *196, b; 238, g.*

8. **remūnerātiōne**: this applies to *redamāre* only, while *vicissitūdine*
applies to both *amāre* and *redamāre*.

10. **Quid?**   This little anticipatory question, like τί δέ, in Greek,
serves to draw special attention to what follows.   Its meaning really
is, ' What do you think of this that I am going to say? '   **nihil esse,** etc.:
it will be seen that the comparison is not quite perfect, there being two
members in the first branch (*nihil . . . rem ūllam*) and three in the second
(*amīcitiam . . . [hominēs] . . . similitūdō*).

12. **similitūdō**: properly this should be *similitūdinem* in the same
construction as *nihil*, but it is attracted into the same case with *quod*.
Such attractions of case are common.   **vērum esse, ut**: when the clause
after *vērum est* is an infinitive clause, it is regarded as embodying a fact,
when an *ut*-clause, a consequence or result.   The meaning here may be
represented thus: ' this result will be granted as true, so as to lead to
the fact that the good love the good.' *203 (1).*

ut bonōs bonī dīligant ascīscantque sibi quasi propinquitāte
coniūnctōs atque nātūrā. Nihil est enim appetentius
15 similium suī nec rapācius quam nātūra. Quam ob rem
hōc quidem, Fannī et Scaevola, cōnstet, ut opīnor, bonīs
inter bonōs quasi necessāriam benevolentiam, quī est
amīcitiae fōns ā nātūrā cōnstitūtus. Sed eadem bonitās
etiam ad multitūdinem pertinet. Nōn enim est inhūmāna
20 virtūs neque immūnis neque superba, quae etiam populōs
ūniversōs tuērī eīsque optimē cōnsulere soleat; quod nōn
faceret profectō, sī ā cāritāte vulgī abhorrēret. Atque
etiam mihi quidem videntur, quī ūtilitātum causā fingunt
amīcitiās, amābilissimum nōdum amīcitiae tollere. Nōn
25 enim tam ūtilitās parta per amīcum quam amīcī amor
ipse dēlectat, tumque illud fit, quod ab amīcō est profectum,
iūcundum, sī cum studiō est profectum; tantumque abest,

13. **quasi propinquitāte:** ' a sort of relationship '; opposed to actual
propinquitās.

14. **nātūrā:** ' natural affinity.' **appetentius:** when present participles lose the notion of time and become adjectives they may take a
genitive case.

15. **similium:** the neuter plural of the adjective in the genitive case
used as substantive is rare.

16. **bonīs inter bonōs:** more emphatic than *bonīs inter sē,* the more
ūsual idiom.

17. **necessāriam:** sc. *esse.* **quī:** the attraction of the relative in
sentences like this is almost regular in Cicero, and indeed in most other
writers of the best period. *164, c.*

19. **inhūmāna:** ' unkindly.'

20. **immūnis,** ' unserviceable ' (literally, free from *mūnia* or duties
towards the state). **superba:** ' egotistic.' The last word is difficult to
translate, as it combines the notions ' oppressive,' ' proud,' ' difficult of
approach.' **quae:** = *cum ea. 194, c.*

26. **tum . . . sī:** = *ita . . . sī,* ' then only . . . if.' **ab amīcō est
profectum:** the word *proficīscī* is often thus used in Cicero's letters
of services passing between friends; see *Ad Familiārēs, 2, 19, 2,
quaecumque ā mē ōrnāmenta in tē profiscīscentur;* and *ibid., 3, 1, 1.*

27. **tantumque abest, ut . . . ut:** this clumsy construction is a
favorite one with Cicero. Note that with all good writers the verb in

ut amīcītiae propter indigentiam colantur, ut eī, quī opibus
et cōpiīs maximēque virtūte, in quā plūrimum est praesidī,
minimē alterius indigeant, līberālissimī sint et beneficen- 30
tissimī. Atque haud sciam an nē opus sit quidem nihil
umquam omnīnō deesse amīcīs. Ubi enim studia nostra
viguissent, sī numquam cōnsiliō, numquam operā nostrā
nec domī nec mīlitiae Scīpiō eguisset? Nōn igitur ūtilitātem amīcitia, sed ūtilitās amīcitiam secūta est. 35

*We owe a friend our support in weal or woe. The end may justify the
means when a friend's life or reputation is at stake, but there are limits
to the indulgence which may be granted to a friend.*

17. Hīs igitur fīnibus ūtendum arbitror, ut, cum ēmen-
dātī mōrēs amīcōrum sint, tum sit inter eōs omnium rērum,
cōnsiliōrum, voluntātum sine ūllā exceptiōne commūnitās,
ut, etiam sī quā fortūnā acciderit ut minus iūstae amīcōrum
voluntātēs adiuvandae sint, in quibus eōrum aut caput 5

such phrases (*abest, afuit,* etc.) is impersonal. *197, d;* A. & G. 571, *b;*
G. 552, R. I.

28. **indigentiam :** a rare word, scarcely occurring out of Cicero.

30. **alterius :** Cicero uses *indigēre* far oftener with a genitive than
with an ablative, though the latter is commoner in Silver Latin.

31. **Atque :** here corrective = the Greek καίτοι, ' And yet.' **haud
sciam an :** a well-attested though rare variant for *haud sciō an;* see note
on page 294, 3. *Sciam* is potential subjunctive. 180, *e.* Translate,
' And yet I should be inclined to think that self-sufficiency (*nihil . . .
deesse*) is not even an advantage (*opus*).' **nihil . . . deesse :** Cicero is
here striving to represent the Greek αὐτάρκης = self-sufficient, for which
there was no one word in Latin.

32. **Ubi :** here = *quā in rē* (' wherein ') rather than *quō in locō.* **studia nostra :** ' the ardor of my affection.'

34. **domī, mīlitiae :** locatives. *146.*

17. 1. **Hīs . . . arbitror :** attack the sentence properly : ' These,
therefore, are the limits which I think ought to be adopted.' The
subject of *ūtendum* is impersonal. *172, e.* **ut . . . sit :** explains *fīnibus.*

2. **sint :** subjunctive by attraction. *220.* **sit :** *199, a; 203 (2).*

3. **sine ūllā exceptiōne :** attributive to *commūnitās.*

5. **aut caput agātur aut fāma :** *caput* is *status,* or condition regard-

agātur aut fāma, dēclīnandum dē viā sit, modo nē summa turpitūdō sequātur; est enim, quātenus amīcitiae darī venia possit. Nec vērō neglegenda est fāma, nec mediocre tēlum ad rēs gerendās exīstimāre oportet benevolentiam 10 cīvium; quam blanditiīs et assentandō colligere turpe est; virtūs, quam sequitur cāritās, minimē repudianda est. Sed — saepe enim redeō ad Scīpiōnem, cuius omnis sermō erat dē amīcitiā — querēbātur, quod omnibus in rēbus

ing civil rights, which in the Roman law was viewed with reference to liberty (*status lībertātis*), citizenship (*status cīvitātis*), and domestic position (*status familiae*). See Hadley's, or Hunter's, *Introduction to Roman Law*. The cases alluded to are those which might lead to *dēminūtiō capitis*, the loss of civil rights. In *fāma* the reference is to trials involving *īnfāmia* as part of the punishment which may result from them.

6. **dēclīnandum dē viā sit**: on the nice question of casuistry, how far one is to condone the wrong doings of a friend, Laelius is conveniently vague, as Gellius in his criticism of this passage (*Noctēs Atticae*, **1**, 3, 14) complains. The passage becomes the more unsatisfactory when we go back to Laelius's first principle, *nisi in bonīs amīcitiam esse nōn posse*. Aristotle's discussion of the matter (*Ēthica Nīcomachēa*, **9**, 4, 3) is more careful though still vague. Roman popular morality required a man to go to much greater lengths in assisting a friend than would be allowed even by the popular morality of our time; this is expressed in the words *modo nē summa turpitūdō sequātur*.

7. **sequātur**: subjunctive of proviso. *190, d;* B. 310; A. & G. 528; G. 573.

8. **possit**: subjunctive of characteristic. *194, a*. *Quātenus* is here a relative adverb. **Nec . . . fāma**: i.e. *propter amīcum*.

9. **tēlum**: for the metaphorical use see the old line quoted by Cicero in *Ad Familiārēs*, **7**, 16, 1: *ūsquequāque sapere oportet: id erit tēlum ācerrimum*, ' it behooves us constantly to be wise: this is the sharpest weapon.' **rēs**: here = *pūblicās rēs*.

10. **blanditiīs et assentandō**: it is not often that Cicero makes the gerund thus range with a noun, though the usage is exceedingly common in Tacitus and his contemporaries.

12. **cuius . . . dē amīcitiā**: ' from whom entirely proceeded the discourse concerning friendship '; *not* ' whose whole discourse was of friendship.'

hominēs dīligentiōrēs essent; caprās et ovēs quot quisque habēret, dīcere posse, amīcōs quot habēret, nōn posse 15 dīcere, et in illīs quidem parandīs adhibēre cūram, in amīcīs ēligendīs neglegentīs esse nec habēre quasi signa quaedam et

ANOTHER VIEW OF THE LIRIS
Near Cicero's birthplace.

notās, quibus eōs quī ad amīcitiās essent idōneī, iūdicārent 20 Sunt igitur fīrmī et stabilēs et cōnstantēs ēligendī; cuius generis est magna pēnūria. Et iūdicāre 25 difficile est sānē nisi expertum; experiendum autem est in ipsā amīcitiā. Ita praecurrit amīcitia 30 iūdicium tollitque ex-

14. dīligentiōrēs: 'more painstaking,' i.e. 'than in friendship.' caprās et ovēs quot: imitated from Xenophon, Memorābilia, 2, 4, 4; 2, 4, 1. Note the emphatic position of nouns.

16. in amīcīs: asyndeton; 238, d.

17. quasi signa quaedam et notās: a tentative translation of the Greek σημεῖον or κριτήριον, which Cicero elsewhere renders by iūdicium (Acadēmicae Quaestiōnēs, passim) or nota merely (ibid. 2, 84); in Xenophon, Memorābilia, 2, 6, Socrates describes the marks that should lead to the choosing of a friend.

21. fīrmī, etc.: these adjectives describe the vir gravis, gravitās being the chief part of the ideal Roman character.

27. expertum: accusative masculine; almost equals expertus sīs.

30. praecurrit: like the Greek φθάνει, ' outstrips.'

periendī potestātem. Est igitur prūdentis sustinēre ut
cursum, sīc impetum benevolentiae, quō ūtāmur quasi equīs
temptātīs, sīc amīcitiā ex aliquā parte perīclitātīs mōribus
35 amīcōrum. Quīdam saepe in parvā pecūniā perspiciuntur
quam sint levēs, quīdam autem, quōs parva movēre nōn
potuit, cognōscuntur in magnā. Sīn erunt aliquī repertī,
quī pecūniam praeferre amīcitiae sordidum exīstiment, ubi
eōs inveniēmus, quī honōrēs, magistrātūs, imperia, potes-
40 tātēs, opēs amīcitiae nōn antepōnant, ut, cum ex alterā
parte prōposita haec sint, ex alterā iūs amīcitiae, nōn multō
illa mālint? Imbēcilla enim est nātūra ad contemnendam
potentiam; quam etiam sī neglēctā amīcitiā cōnsecūtī sint,
obscūrātum īrī arbitrantur, quia nōn sine magnā causā
45 sit neglēcta amīcitia. Itaque vērae amīcitiae difficillimē
reperiuntur in iīs, quī in honōribus rēque pūblicā versantur;
ubi enim istum inveniās, quī honōrem amīcī antepōnat

---

32. **sustinēre:** ' to check.'

34. **ex aliquā parte:** ' in some measure.' **perīclitātīs:** used in a
passive sense like *meditātus* and a large number of other deponent participles, the usage being quite common in Cicero. *226, d.*

36. **quam sint levēs:** ' how untrustworthy they are.' **movēre nōn
potuit:** ' could not have changed.' Originally *potestās* at Rome had
a very wide meaning, denoting all power exercised by public authority
and so including *imperium*. Then as certain officers (consul, praetor,
dictator) had *imperium*, while others (censor, aedile, etc.) had not,
the word *potestās* came to be particularly used in connection with the
latter class of officers.

39. **honōrēs, magistrātūs:** not essentially different from *imperia,
potestātēs*.

44. **obscūrātum īrī:** ' they think their fault will be forgotten ' (*i.e.*
in the blaze of their prosperity). Cicero is the only writer who uses the
future infinitive passive with any degree of frequency; the common
periphrasis is *fore* or *futūrum esse ut* and the subjunctive. *225.*

45. **amīcitia:** the repetition is made for the sake of emphasis.

47. **ubi inveniās:** i.e. *sī quaerās;* but above, *ubi inveniēmus;* with
the future the search is looked on as likely to take place, with the subjunctive, as not likely.

suō? Quid? haec ut omittam, quam gravēs, quam difficilēs
plērīsque videntur calamitātum societātēs! ad quās nōn
est facile inventū quī dēscendant. Quamquam Ennius rēctē : 50

"Amī'cus certus ín rē incertā cérnitur,"

tamen haec duo levitātis et īnfīrmitātis plērōsque con-
vincunt, aut sī in bonīs rēbus contemnunt aut in malīs
dēserunt. Quī igitur utrāque in rē gravem, cōnstantem,
stabilem sē in amīcitiā praestiterit, hunc ex maximē rārō 55
genere hominum iūdicāre dēbēmus et paene dīvīnō.

The requisite qualities of friendship are: loyalty, constancy, sympathy,
sincerity, implicit faith, affability of speech and manner, tolerance,
generosity, magnanimity. Friendship based on these qualities is best
made in manhood, not in early life.

18. Fīrmāmentum autem stabilitātis cōnstantiaeque est
eius, quam in amīcitiā quaerimus, fidēs; nihil est enim

---

48. **Quid:** 'Again.' See page 307, note 10. **haec ut omittam:**
observe the fondness of Cicero for placing *ut* as second word in the clause
or sentence. He nearly always says *nihil ut, nōn ut, sīc ut,* and the
like, and not *vice versā. 196, b.*

50. **dēscendant:** see *dēscendere in certāmen,* also *in causam* (Cicero,
Philippic, **8,** 4), and the similar uses with *dēcurrere, dēvenīre.* **Ennius**
(en'ĭ-ŭs): 239–169 B.C., was the father of Roman epic poetry. He
wrote the *Annālēs,* an epic poem in hexameter verse, celebrating
Rome's achievements from the time of Aeneas to the poet's own days.
rēctē: the omission of a *verbum dīcendī* is particularly common in
quotations.

51. **Amīcus,** etc.: compare the English: "A friend in need is a friend
indeed." The line is known only from this passage. It appears to be
imitated from Euripides, *Hecuba,* 1226, ἐν τοῖς κακοῖς γὰρ ἀγαθοὶ σαφέστατοι
φίλοι, 'for 'tis in adversity that friends are most clearly (proved) good.'

53. **aut sī . . . aut:** the omission of the second *sī* is awkward; possibly *cum* has fallen out after the second *aut;* see *Dē Fīnibus* **2,** 15, *sī*
aut . . . aut cum. **in bonīs rēbus:** sc. *suīs,* 'in their own prosperity.'
contemnunt: sc. *amīcōs.* **in malīs:** sc. *amīcōrum.*

54. **utrāque in rē:** 'in either case.'

55. **ex . . . genere:** sc. *esse.*

18. 2. **eius:** goes with *cōnstantiae.*

stabile, quod īnfīdum est. Simplicem praetereā et commūnem et cōnsentientem, id est quī rēbus īsdem moveātur,
5 ēligī pār est, quae omnia pertinent ad fidēlitātem; neque
enim fīdum potest esse multiplex ingenium et tortuōsum,
neque vērō, qui nōn īsdem rēbus movētur nātūrāque
cōnsentit, aut fīdus aut stabilis potest esse. Addendum
eōdem est, ut nē crīminibus aut īnferendīs dēlectētur aut
10 crēdat oblātīs, quae pertinent omnia ad eam, quam iam
dūdum trāctō, cōnstantiam. Ita fit vērum illud, quod
initiō dīxī, amīcitiam nisi inter bonōs esse nōn posse.
Est enim bonī virī, quem eundem sapientem licet dīcere,
haec duo tenēre in amīcitiā: prīmum nē quid fictum sit
15 nēve simulātum; apertē enim vel ōdisse magis ingenuī
est quam fronte occultāre sententiam; deinde nōn sōlum
ab aliquō allātās crīminātiōnēs repellere, sed nē ipsum
quidem esse suspīciōsum semper aliquid exīstimantem ab

---

3. **Simplicem:** 'Frank,' 'Open.' **commūnem:** 'sociable'; compare Nepos, *Miltiadēs*, **8,** 4, *summa hūmānitās mīra commūnitās;* so κοινός
in Greek.

4. **cōnsentientem,** etc.: 'sympathetic.'

5. **pār est:** = *aequum est.* **fidēlitātem:** = *fidēs* above.

6. **multiplex:** here 'deceitful,' but often a word of praise, as in
Acadēmicae Quaestiōnēs, **1,** 17, *Platōnis, quī varius et multiplex* ('many-
sided') *et cōpiōsus fuit.* **tortuōsum:** 'wily'; compare English colloquial
word, 'crooked.' This word is generally used of complicated logical arguments, as in *Acadēmicae Quaestiōnēs* **2,** 98; compare *Tusculānae Disputātiōnēs,* **3,** 22, *contortius.*

7. **neque vērō:** see page 305, note 26.

9. **īnferendīs . . . oblātīs:** chiasmus. *239, e.*

11. **fit:** 'is shown to be.'

15. **apertē vel ōdisse:** 'to go openly the length of hatred.' **ingenuī:**
here in the same sense as in Virgil's line *ingenuī vultūs puer ingenuīque
pudōris* — 'frank.'

16. **occultāre:** stronger than *cēlāre;* implies deliberate and habitual
concealment.

18. **semper . . . violātum:** the clause is an explanation of the one
word *suspīciōsum.*

amīcō esse violātum. Accēdat hūc suāvitās quaedam oportet sermōnum atque mōrum, haudquāquam mediocre 20 condimentum amīcitiae. Trīstitia autem et in omnī rē sevēritās habet illa quidem gravitātem, sed amīcitia remissior esse dēbet et līberior et dulcior et ad omnem comitātem facilitātemque prōclīvior.

20. Ut igitur iī, quī sunt in amīcitiae coniūnctiōnisque necessitūdine superiōrēs, exaequāre sē cum īnferiōribus dēbent, sīc īnferiōrēs nōn dolēre sē ā suīs aut ingeniō aut fortūnā aut dignitāte superārī. Quōrum plērīque aut queruntur semper aliquid aut etiam exprobrant, eōque 5 magis, sī habēre sē putant, quod officiōsē et amīcē et cum labōre aliquō suō factum queant dīcere. Odiōsum sānē genus hominum officia exprobrantium; quae meminisse dēbet is, in quem collāta sunt, nōn commemorāre, quī contulit. Quam ob rem, ut iī, quī superiōrēs sunt, sum- 10

---

19. **hūc:** ' to this.'

20. **haudquāquam mediocre:** = *maximum,* litotes. *239, m.*

21. **condimentum:** ' the seasoning.' **in omnī rē:** attributive to *sevēritās.*

22. **illa quidem:** see note 9 on *is quidem,* page 303.

20. 1. **coniūnctiōnisque:** the *coniūnctio* is the natural association produced by kinship and the like, mentioned in an omitted passage.

2. **superiōrēs:** for the construction *superior esse in aliquā rē* see *Prō Balbō,* 35: *in foedere īnferior.*

3. **nōn dolēre:** the true friendships, Aristotle says, are ' free from offense' (ἀδιάβλητοι, *Ēthica Nīcomachēa,* **8,** 6, 7; ἀνέγκλητοι, *ibid.,* **9,** 2, 7).

7. **queant:** *queō* is rarely used in affirmative sentences by good writers, but the usage is well attested within narrow limits; see *Tusculānae Disputātiōnēs,* **5,** 108; *Catō Maior,* **10,** 32; *Dē Rēpūblicā,* **2,** 6; also found in Sallust and Columella. **Odiōsum genus:** in apposition with *plērīque* above.

8. **officia exprobrantium:** ' who throw up to you their own acts of kindness.' *§2, c.*

9. **commemorāre:** sc. *dēbet;* ' call to mind.'

10. **summittere:** *i.e.* ' to be modest.'

mittere sē dēbent in amīcitiā, sīc quōdam modō īnferiōrēs
extollere. Sunt enim quīdam, quī molestās amīcitiās
faciunt, cum ipsī sē contemnī putant; quod nōn ferē contingit nisi iīs, quī etiam contemnendōs sē arbitrantur;
15 quī hāc opīniōne nōn modo verbīs, sed etiam opere levandī
sunt. Tantum autem cuique tribuendum, prīmum quantum ipse efficere possīs, deinde etiam quantum ille, quem
dīligās atque adiuvēs, sustinēre. Nōn enim neque tū
possīs, quamvīs excellās, omnēs tuōs ad honōrēs amplis-
20 simōs perdūcere, ut Scīpiō P. Rupilium potuit cōnsulem
efficere, frātrem eius Lūcium nōn potuit. Quod sī etiam
possīs quidvīs dēferre ad alterum, videndum est tamen,
quid ille possit sustinēre.

Omnīnō amīcitiae corrōborātīs iam cōnfīrmātīsque et

---

11. **sīc,** etc.: i.e. *sīc dēbent eī quī superiōrēs sunt extollere eōs quī
sunt īnferiōrēs.*

13. **contemnī:** 'slighted' or 'neglected.' *Contemnere* is hardly
ever so strong in meaning as our word 'despise,' which is commonly
used to translate it.

14. **quī:** 'and they.'

17. **ille:** sc. *possit.*

18. **Nōn . . . neque:** there is a slight anacoluthon (*238, a*), the form
of the sentence being changed; for the proper clause introduced by a
second *neque* the clauses introduced by *ut* are substituted. The unemphatic *tū* should be noticed; it is our English ' you ' for ' one.'

20. **perdūcere:** *i.e.* through all the various grades. *Prōdūcere*
(which some editions have) is simply ' to advance,' without the notion
of gradation. **potuit . . . nōn potuit:** Latin idiom requires the repetition of *posse* in the negative clause, where English idiom would omit it.
In *Tusculānae Disputātiōnēs*, **4**, 40, Rupilius is said to have taken his
brother's defeat greatly to heart; and Pliny, *Historia Nātūrālis* **7**, 122,
enlarges the story by making him die immediately on hearing the result
of the election.

21. **efficere:** *facere* would not do here, since *facere aliquem cōnsulem*
means ' to vote for someone's election as consul.'

24. **corrōborātīs . . . aetātibus:** the *cōnfīrmāta* or *corrōborāta aetās*
is the time of life immediately succeeding youth, the καθεστηκυῖα ἡλικία

ingeniīs et aetātibus iūdicandae sunt, nec, sī quī ineunte 25
aetāte vēnandī aut pīlae studiōsī fuērunt, eōs habēre
necessāriōs, quōs tum eōdem studiō praeditōs dīlēxērunt.
Istō enim modō nūtrīcēs et paedagōgī iūre vetustātis
plūrimum benevolentiae postulābunt; quī neglegendī

A BALL GAME
The player at the left is about to throw the ball.

quidem nōn sunt, sed aliō quōdam modō aestimandī. 30
Aliter amīcitiae stabilēs permanēre nōn possunt. Disparēs
enim mōrēs disparia studia sequuntur, quōrum dissimilitūdō
dissociat amīcitiās; nec ob aliam causam ūllam bonī
improbīs, improbī bonīs amīcī esse nōn possunt, nisi quod

---

of Thucydides (thū-sid'ĭ-dēs); the opposite expression is *īnfirmissimum
tempus aetātis* in *Acadēmicae Quaestiōnēs*, **2**, 9; *Prō Flaccō*, 5.

26. **habēre**: the construction is carried on as though *oportet iūdicāre
dē amīcitiīs* or something similar had preceded.

28. **Istō modō**: 'On that principle.' **nūtrīcēs et paedagōgī**: in
Rome these were generally slaves. **vetustātis**: 'of long intimacy.'

30. **quidem**: here concessive, 'I admit.' **aliō quōdam modō**: 'in
a somewhat different way.'

32. **mōrēs**, etc.: *mōrēs* is probably in the accusative. Compare the
popular notion that lasting friendships are better formed among
opposite types. **studia**: 'interests.'

34. **nisi quod**: used after negative statements to introduce a limitation or exception.

35 tanta est inter eōs, quanta maxima potest esse, mōrum
studiōrumque distantia.

Misplaced good will may be a positive hindrance to a friend.
A temporary separation is sometimes necessary.

Rēctē etiam praecipī potest in amīcitiīs, nē intemperāta
quaedam benevolentia, quod persaepe fit, impediat magnās
ūtilitātēs amīcōrum. Nec enim, ut ad fābulās redeam,
40 Trōiam Neoptolemus capere potuisset, sī Lycomēdēn, apud
quem erat ēdūcātus, multīs cum lacrimīs iter suum impedientem audīre voluisset. Et saepe incidunt magnae rēs, ut
discēdendum sit ab amīcīs; quās quī impedīre vult, quod
dēsīderium nōn facile ferat, is et īnfīrmus est mollisque
45 nātūra et ob eam ipsam causam in amīcitiā parum iūstus.

---

35. **tanta,** etc.: ' so great as can possibly exist.'

36. **distantia :** a *vōx Cicerōniāna.* In good Latin the word is never
used of distance in space. Aristotle several times discusses the question
of how great a difference in character or other circumstances is required
to render friendships impossible.

38. **quaedam :** *quīdam* is often used to indicate that the word to
which it is attached does not actually represent the writer's meaning.
Cicero cannot find adequate terms, and his expression is only a make-
shift. Translate, 'kindness which I may call untempered.'

39. **Nec enim :** followed by *et saepe* instead of *nec.* **fābulās :**
'legends '; see *Dē Officiīs,* **3,** 94, *ut redeāmus ad fābulās.*

40. **Neoptolemus** (nē-ǫp-tǫl′ę-mụs) : or Pyrrhus, son of Achilles by
Deidamia (dē-id-ạ-mī′ạ), daughter of Lycomedes (lў̆c-ǫ-mē′dēz), king
of Scyros (sī′rǫs). He appears in the *Philoctetes* (fil-ǫk-tē′tēz) as an
ambassador to that hero, without whose bow it was fated Troy should
not fall.

41. **impedientem :** ' when he tried to hinder '; the participle is here
equivalent to a temporal *cum.* *227, a (5).*

44. **mollisque :** the *-que* merely connects *īnfīrmus* with *mollis* and
does not correspond with the first *et.* In Cicero and the best writers
et and *-que* are not correlative. Translate, ' is not only weak and effeminate, but also . . .'

45. **parum iūstus :** ' far from reasonable '; *parum* almost = *nōn,* like
minus on page 299, line 12, note.

Atque in omnī rē cōnsīderandum est, et quid postulēs ab amīcō et quid patiāre ā tē impetrārī.

We must not exact from our friends virtues which we do not possess ourselves. We must practice self-control.

22. Sed plērīque perversē, nē dīcam impudenter, habēre tālem amīcum volunt, quālēs ipsī esse nōn possunt, quaeque ipsī nōn tribuunt amīcīs, haec ab iīs dēsīderant. Pār est autem prīmum ipsum esse virum bonum, tum alterum similem suī quaerere. In tālibus ea, quam iam dūdum 5 trāctāmus, stabilitās amīcitiae cōnfīrmārī potest, cum hominēs benevolentiā coniūnctī prīmum cupiditātibus iīs, quibus cēterī serviunt, imperābunt, deinde aequitāte iūstitiāque gaudēbunt, omniaque alter prō alterō suscipiet, neque quicquam umquam nisi honestum et rēctum alter ab 10 alterō postulābit, neque sōlum colent inter sē ac dīligent, sed etiam verēbuntur. Nam maximum ōrnāmentum amīcitiae tollit, quī ex eā tollit verēcundiam. Itaque in iīs perniciōsus est error, quī exīstimant libīdinum peccātōrumque omnium

---

46. **Atque . . . impetrārī:** this is a little summary of chapter 20 Such summaries are often introduced by *atque* = ' now,' as in *Acadēmicae Quaestiōnēs*, **1**, 42.

22. 1. **nē dīcam:** the phrase is elliptic − *hōc dīcō nē dīcam*, and *impudenter*, which may be regarded as in quotation marks, stands as object of *dīcam*. *238, f*. **habēre tālem amīcum**, etc.: the theory that friendship is based on want of resemblance and not on resemblance is found in Plato's *Lysis*, 215 c, *et seq.* Aristotle, *Ēthica Nīcomachēa*, **8**, 8, 6, *et seq.*, decides that it is almost entirely the lower kind of friendship which is based on lack of resemblance.

3. **Pār est . . . quaerere:** ' It is fair . . . to seek.'

4. **ipsum:** in agreement with *aliquem*, the unexpressed subject of *esse*.

5. **quam . . . trāctāmus:** ' which we have now been treating for some time.' *175, f*.

7. **cupiditātibus:** ' passions.'

8. **aequitāte iūstitiāque:** *aequitās* is the view of justice taken by a man of high principle and honor, *iūstitia* the legal or technical view.

11. **inter sē:** = *alter alterum*, reciprocal relation. *159*.

¹⁵patēre in amīcitiā licentiam; virtūtum amīcitia adiūtrix ā
nātūrā data est, nōn vitiōrum comes, ut, quoniam sōlitāria
nōn posset virtūs ad ea, quae summa sunt, pervenīre,
coniūncta et cōnsociāta cum alterā pervenīret. Quae sī
quōs inter societās aut est aut fuit aut futūra est, eōrum
²⁰est habendus ad summum nātūrae bonum optimus beātissi-
musque comitātus. Haec est, inquam, societās, in quā
omnia īnsunt, quae putant hominēs expetenda, honestās,
glōria, tranquillitās animī atque iūcunditās, ut et, cum
haec adsint, beāta vīta sit et sine hīs esse nōn possit. Quod

15. **virtūtum . . . comes:** the translation should preserve the emphasis: '' 'tis for virtue that nature has granted friendship to be a help,
not to be associated in guilt.' **ā nātūrā data est:** in Cicero *ā nātūrā* and
nātūrā darī both frequently occur. In the former phrase *nātūrā* is
personified, while in the latter *nātūrā* is used adverbially (= φύσει in
Greek).

17. **ea, quae summa sunt:** ' the highest moral views '; see *Prō
Archiā*, 14.

18. **coniūncta et cōnsociāta:** synonymic combination, a mark of
Cicero's style; translate,' closely joined.' *212, b.* **alterā :** as *virtūs* above =
homō virtūte praeditus, so *alterā* here = *alterius hominis virtūte.* **Quae
. . . est:** ' And if this fellowship exists among any.' *167.*

19. **quōs inter:** anastrophe. *238, b.* As a rule, only dissyllabic
prepositions follow the cases to which they are attached, except when
some attribute precedes the noun or pronoun; see *multīs in rēbus,* line 32.
eōrum . . . comitātus: ' theirs must be held to be the finest and most
blessed comradeship towards attaining to (*ad*) the *summum bonum* of life.'

22. **honestās . . . iūcunditās:** the enumeration consists of three
branches, the last of these being subdivided (*tranquillitās atque iūcunditās*). Had *iūcunditās* and *tranquillitās* occupied in the enumeration
the same place as the two other qualities mentioned, Cicero must have
left out *atque.* **expetenda :** ' objects of desire.'

23. **ut et . . . possit:** this clause seems to contain a tacit protest
against the Stoic ethics which made *honestās* (τὸ καλόν = virtue) everything; Laelius asserts that perfect happiness contains other things as
well, and that the perfection of friendship and the perfection of happiness are inextricably connected. See Companion, page 547.

24. **adsint:** subjunctive by attraction. *220.* **Quod:** ' This end,'
referring back to the last sentence and not forward to *id.*

cum optimum maximumque sit, sī id volumus adipīscī, 25
virtūtī opera danda est, sine quā nec amīcitiam neque
ūllam rem expetendam cōnsequī possumus; eā vērō
neglēctā quī sē amīcōs habēre arbitrantur, tum sē dēnique
errāsse sentiunt, cum eōs gravis aliquis cāsus experīrī
cōgit. Quōcircā (dīcendum est enim saepius), cum iūdi- 30
cāris, dīligere oportet, nōn, cum dīlēxeris, iūdicāre. Sed
cum multīs in rēbus neglegentiā plectimur, tum maximē
in amīcīs et dīligendīs et colendīs; praeposterīs enim
ūtimur cōnsiliīs et ācta agimus, quod vetāmur vetere
prōverbiō. Nam implicātī ultrō et citrō vel ūsū diūturnō 35
vel etiam officiīs repente in mediō cursū amīcitiās exortā
aliquā offēnsiōne dīrumpimus.

*Since virtue is the basis of friendship, we should appraise a prospective
friend before we bestow our affection upon him.*

23. Quō etiam magis vituperanda est reī maximē ne-
cessāriae tanta incūria. Ūna est enim amīcitia in rēbus
hūmānīs, dē cuius ūtilitāte omnēs ūnō ōre cōnsentiunt.
Quamquam ā multīs virtūs ipsa contemnitur et vēnditātiō

---

27. **ūllam rem expetendam:** ' any other desirable object.' *212, h.*
29. **experīrī:** ' to apply the test '; used absolutely.
32. **cum . . . tum maximē:** ' not only . . . but especially.' **multīs
in rēbus:** ' in many other relations.'
34. **ācta agimus:** ' we plead a case that is already settled,' an oxymoron (so ' to slay the slain ') for which Seyffert compares Plautus,
Mīles Glōriōsus, **3,** 1, 41, *nōta nōscere; Poenulus,* **4,** 2, 48, *doctum docēre;*
Cicero, *Ad Familiārēs,* **14,** 1, 5, *puerum perditum perdere.* As to the proverb, Dona'tus on Terence, *Adelphī,* **2,** 2, 24, not improbably conjec-
tures that it originated in the law courts, *ubi quod semel iūdicātum est
frūstrā iterum agitur.* See page 298, note 5, *absentēs adsunt. 239, p.*
vetāmur : sc. *facere.*
35. **ultrō et citrō :** here = ' mutually,' as in the common phrase *datā
ultrō citrōque fide* (Livy, **29,** 23, 5). **ūsū, officiīs :** ' by intimacy,' ' by
obligations.'
23. 2. **Ūna :** by attraction for *ūnum,* ' The one thing.'
4. **Quamquam :** elliptic, the full sense being ' Most men agree

5 quaedam atque ostentātiō esse dīcitur; multī dīvitiās
dēspiciunt, quōs parvō contentōs tenuis victus cultusque
dēlectat; honōrēs vērō, quōrum cupiditāte quīdam īnflam-
mantur, quam multī ita contemnunt, ut nihil inānius, nihil
esse levius exīstiment! itemque cētera, quae quibusdam
10 admīrābilia videntur, permultī sunt quī prō nihilō putent;
dē amīcitiā omnēs ad ūnum idem sentiunt, et iī, quī ad rem
pūblicam sē contulērunt, et iī, quī rērum cognitiōne doctrī-
nāque dēlectantur, et iī, quī suum negōtium gerunt ōtiōsī,
postrēmō iī, quī sē tōtōs trādidērunt voluptātibus, sine
15 amīcitiā vītam esse nūllam, sī modo velint aliquā ex parte
līberāliter vīvere. Serpit enim nesciō quō modō per omnium vītās amīcitia nec ūllam aetātis dēgendae ratiōnem
patitur esse expertem suī. Quīn etiam sī quis asperitāte
eā est et immānitāte nātūrae, congressūs ut hominum fugiat
20 atque ōderit, quālem fuisse Athēnīs Tīmōnem nesciō quem

---

about virtue yet,' etc. *238, f.* **multīs:** chiefly the Epicureans. See
Companion, page 547. **ipsa:** 'even.' *162, a.*
   7. **honōrēs:** 'office.'
   8. **quam multī:** no good writers use *quot* as a substantive. Cicero,
however, often prefers to use *quam multī, tam multī* where *quot, tot* would
be permissible.
   11. **ad ūnum:** 'to a man.' **et iī . . . et iī:** those who follow the
πολιτικὸς βίος (political, *i.e.* practical life) and those who follow the
θεωρητικὸς βίος (contemplative or speculative life). One of the main
questions which divided the later Greek philosophers was that of the
comparative value of these two lives.
   13. **ōtiōsī:** here, as often, implies merely the freedom from public
duties.
   15. **vītam esse nūllam:** 'life is no life.'
   16. **līberāliter:** 'properly'; literally, 'in a manner befitting a freeman,' *i.e.* a gentleman. **Serpit:** 'penetrates.' **nesciō quō modō:**
'somehow or other.'
   17. **ratiōnem:** 'method.'
   18. **expertem suī:** 'free from its influence.' For *suī* see *102.*
   20. **Tīmōnem** (tī'mōn): the misanthrope (μισάνθρωπος), a contemporary of Socrates, the subject of Shakespeare's well-known play. **He is**

accēpimus, tamen is patī nōn possit, ut nōn anquīrat aliquem, apud quem ēvomat vīrus acerbitātis suae. Atque hōc maximē iūdicārētur, sī quid tāle posset contingere, ut aliquis nōs deus ex hāc hominum frequentiā tolleret et in sōlitūdine ūspiam collocāret atque ibi suppeditāns omnium 25 rērum, quās nātūra dēsīderat, abundantiam et cōpiam hominis omnīnō aspiciendī potestātem ēriperet.

ATHENS TODAY
With a view of the Acropolis in the background.

also the subject of one of Lucian's (second century A.D.) most famous dialogues. **nesciō quem :** Cicero often inserts *quīdam, nesciō quis* and the like, when it is necessary, in mentioning some Greek, to avoid the appearance of too great a familiarity with Greek literature. The Roman statesmen of the dialogue could not be presumed to know Timon except by vague report. In telling a story of Xenocrates (zę-nǫk′rạ-tēz) to a Roman jury (who objected to Greek learning in an advocate), Cicero calls him *quīdam (Prō Balbō,* 12) ; so of the Stoics, *nōn nūllī litterīs ac studiīs doctrīnae deditī (Prō Balbō,* 1). *Nesciō quem* here has the same purpose as *ut opīnor* below.

21. **is . . . aliquem :** ' he would not be able to refrain from seeking someone.'

22. **apud quem,** etc. : ' before whom he may disgorge the venom of his sour disposition.' **ēvomat :** the metaphorical use is common.

Friendship meets a natural need; even heaven would be lonely without it.

Quis tam esset ferreus, quī eam vītam ferre posset, cui-
30 que nōn auferret frūctum voluptātum omnium sōlitūdō?
Vērum ergō illud est, quod ā Tarentīnō Archȳtā, ut opīnor,
dīcī solitum nostrōs senēs commemorāre audīvī ab aliīs
senibus audītum: "Sī quis in caelum ascendisset nātūramque mundī et pulchritūdinem sīderum perspēxisset, īn-
35 suāvem illam admīrātiōnem eī fore; quae iūcundissima
fuisset, sī aliquem, cui nārrāret, habuisset." Sīc nātūra
sōlitārium nihil amat semperque ad aliquod tamquam
adminiculum annītitur; quod in amīcissimō quōque
dulcissimum est.

Friends must be frank and truthful; flattery is the enemy of friendship.

24. Sed cum tot signīs eadem nātūra dēclāret, quid
velit, anquīrat, dēsīderet, tamen obsurdēscimus nesciō
quō modō nec ea, quae ab eā monēmur, audīmus. Est
enim varius et multiplex ūsus amīcitiae, multaeque causae
5 suspīciōnum offēnsiōnumque dantur, quās tum ēvītāre, tum
ēlevāre, tum ferre sapientis est; ūna illa sublevanda

---

29. **ferreus, ferre, auferret:** notice the wordplay; paronomasia.
239, q. **posset:** why subjunctive? *195.* **cuique:** 'and from whom.'
109, b; B. 188, 2, *d;* A. & G. 381; G. 345, R. 1.

31. **illud:** refers to what follows. *161, a.* **Archȳtā** (är-kī′tạs):
Archytas of Taren′tum was a famous philosopher, general, statesman,
and mathematician who lived about 400 B.C. **ut opīnor:** 'I think.'

35. **illam:** = *eius reī.* **quae ... fuisset:** Nauck takes these words as
being those of Laelius, and not part of his report of Archy′tas; otherwise,
he says, Cicero would have written *quam fore.*

37. **aliquod tamquam adminiculum:** 'some prop, as it were,' in the
language of the vine-dresser. See illustration, page 279.

38. **quod,** etc.: 'and this is the more delightful, the dearer the
friend is'; *quisque,* when used with two superlatives, often implies a
comparison. *170, a;* A. & G. 313, *b,* N. 1; G. 642, R. 2.

24. 1. **cum:** concessive.

5. **tum ... tum ... tum:** 'now ... now ... now.'

6. **ūna illa,** etc.: 'there is one grievance to which we are to submit.

offēnsiō est, ut et ūtilitās in amīcitiā et fidēs retineātur :
nam et monendī amīcī saepe sunt et obiūrgandī, et haec
accipienda amīcē, cum benevolē fīunt. Sed nesciō quō
modō vērum est, quod in Andriā familiāris meus dīcit :   10
"Obséquium amīcōs, vē'ritās odiúm parit."

RUINS OF THE TEMPLE OF ZEUS AT OLYMPIA

Molesta vēritās, sīquidem ex eā nāscitur odium, quod est
venēnum amīcitiae, sed obsequium multō molestius, quod
peccātīs indulgēns praecipitem amīcum ferrī sinit ; maxima
autem culpa in eō, quī et vēritātem āspernātur et in fraudem 15

10. **An'driā :** ' The Woman of Andros,' a comedy of Terence, who lived
from 185 to 159 B.C. See illustration, page 271. **familiāris meus :** Terence.

11. **Obsequium,** etc. : Terence, *Andria*, **1,** 1, 41 (line 68). *Obsequium*
here in a bad sense = ' flattery ' ; often however used in the good sense
of ' deference,' as below. The meter is iambic trimeter.

12. **sīquidem :** ' inasmuch as.'

15. **fraudem :** often means, as here, ' harm,' ' injury.' On the sense,
see *Dē Officiis,* **1,** 91.

obsequiō impellitur. Omnī igitur hāc in rē habenda ratiō et dīligentia est, prīmum ut monitiō acerbitāte, deinde ut obiūrgātiō contumēliā careat; in obsequiō autem, quoniam Terentiānō verbō libenter ūtimur, comitās adsit, assentātiō,
20 vitiōrum adiūtrīx, procul āmoveātur, quae nōn modo amīcō, sed nē līberō quidem digna est; aliter enim cum tyrannō, aliter cum amīcō vīvitur. Cuius autem aurēs clausae vēritātī sunt, ut ab amīcō vērum audīre nequeat, huius salūs dēspēranda est. Scītum est enim illud Catōnis, ut multa :
25 "Melius dē quibusdam acerbōs inimīcōs merērī quam eōs amīcōs, quī dulcēs videantur; illōs vērum saepe dīcere, hōs numquam." Atque illud absurdum, quod iī, quī monentur, eam molestiam, quam dēbent capere, nōn capiunt, eam capiunt, quā dēbent vacāre; peccāsse enim

---

16. **habenda,** etc.: Cicero says both *habēre ratiōnem* and *adhibēre ratiōnem* (*Dē Lēge Agrāriā*, **2**, 2), but only *adhibēre dīligentiam*, so that there is here a slight zeugma (unless *adhibenda* is to be substituted for *habenda*). *238, q.*

17. **monitiō:** said to occur only here in Cicero, who commonly uses *admonitiō.*

18. **in obsequiō:** ' in the payment of deference.'

20. **adiūtrīx:** Cicero is fond of these feminine nouns in *-trīx,* many of which he manufactured himself. **nōn modo . . . sed nē quidem:** when a negative follows *nōn modo* these words have the force of *nōn modo nōn,* a negative being borrowed from the negative in the subsequent clause. *236, e.*

21. **līberō:** ' a gentleman,' adjective for substantive. **aliter . . . vīvitur:** ' for we live in one way with a tyrant, in another way with a friend.'

22. **vīvitur:** its subject is impersonal. *172, e.* **Cuius:** its antecedent is *huius* below.

24. **Scītum . . . Catōnis:** ' A clever saying of Cato is the following.' **ut multa:** ' as many of his sayings are.'

26. **vērum:** ' the truth.'

28. **nōn capiunt . . . capiunt:** Latin idiom requires the repetition of the verb.

29. **peccāsse:** preserve the emphasis in translating.

sē nōn anguntur, obiūrgārī molestē ferunt; quod contrā 30
oportēbat, dēlīctō dolēre, corrēctiōne gaudēre.

Recapitulation and conclusion.   *Laelius bestows a lofty tribute upon*
the character of Scipio.

27. Virtūs, virtūs, inquam, C. Fannī, et tū, Q. Mūcī,
et conciliat amīcitiās et cōnservat. In eā est enim convenientia rērum, in eā stabilitās, in eā cōnstantia; quae
cum sē extulit et ostendit suum lūmen et idem aspexit
agnōvitque in aliō, ad id sē admovet vicissimque accipit 5
illud, quod in alterō est; ex quō exardēscit sīve amor sīve
amīcitia; utrumque enim dictum est ab amandō; amāre
autem nihil est aliud nisi eum ipsum dīligere, quem amēs,
nūllā indigentiā, nūllā ūtilitāte quaesītā; quae tamen ipsa
efflōrēscit ex amīcitiā, etiam sī tū eam minus sccūtus sīs. 10

---

30. **quod contrā :** ' whereas, on the other hand.' *quod* is merely a
connecting link between the clauses, like the ' which ' in vulgar English
and the Greek δ sometimes in Thucydides and Plato at the beginning of
sentences or clauses; the use is the same as that in *quod sī* at the beginning of a clause or sentence. *118, d.*

27. 1. **Virtūs, virtūs :** ' It is virtue, virtue, which '; the repetition
expresses deep conviction. **Mūcī** (mū'sh(y)ụs).

2. **conciliat . . . cōnservat:** ' unites and preserves.' **convenientia**
rērum : ' complete harmony.' *212, e.*

3. **quae :** *virtūs,* not *cōnstantia;* ' and when virtue has lifted up her
head.'

6. **sīve amor sīve amīcitia :** ' either love or friendship, whatever
name you give it.' Aristotle distinguishes φίλησις (' feeling of affection ') and φιλία (' friendship ') (*Ethica Nīcomachēa*, **8,** 5, 5, and elsewhere),
but his φιλία includes both *amīcitia* and *amor,* his φίλησις being that lower
degree of affection which may be felt for the brute creation or for things
inanimate. *235, a.*

9. **nūllā indigentiā :** ' without any feeling of need,' ablative
absolute. *144, a.* **quaesītā :** goes only with *ūtilitāte.* **ipsa :** ' spontaneously.' *162, a.*

10. **efflōrēscit :** a favorite metaphor with Cicero, as in *Dē Ōrātōre,* **1,**
20, *ex rērum cognitiōne efflōrēscat et redundet oportet ōrātiō;* also *ibid.,* **2,**
319; *Dē Fīnibus,* **1,** 69. **minus :** = *nōn.* as often.

Sed quoniam rēs hūmānae fragilēs cadūcaeque sunt, semper
aliquī anquīrendī sunt, quōs dīligāmus et ā quibus dīligā-
mur; (cāritāte enim benevolentiāque sublātā omnis est ē
vītā sublāta iūcunditās.) Mihi quidem Scīpiō, quamquam
15 est subitō ēreptus, vīvit tamen semperque vīvet; virtūtem
enim amāvī illīus virī, quae exstīncta nōn est; (nec mihi
sōlī versātur ante oculōs, quī illam semper in manibus habuī,
sed etiam posterīs erit clāra et īnsignis.) Nēmō umquam
animō aut spē maiōra suscipiet, quī sibi nōn illīus memoriam
20 atque imāginem prōpōnendam putet. Equidem ex omnibus
rēbus, quās mihi aut fortūna aut nātūra tribuit, nihil habeō,
quod cum amīcitiā Scīpiōnis possim comparāre. In hāc
mihi dē rē pūblicā cōnsēnsus, in hāc rērum prīvātārum
cōnsilium, in eādem requiēs plēna oblectātiōnis fuit. Num-
25 quam illum nē minimā quidem rē offendī, quod quidem
sēnserim, nihil audīvī ex eō ipse, quod nōllem; ūna domus
erat, īdem vīctus, isque commūnis, neque sōlum mīlitiā,
sed etiam peregrīnātiōnēs rūsticātiōnēsque commūnēs.

---

11. **rēs hūmānae:** 'human possessions.' **fragilēs cadūcaeque:**
'frail and fleeting.'

14. **Mihi:** 'For me,' 'In my view'; dative of advantage (*datīvus commodī*), a variety of the dative of reference. *109, a.*

17. **in manibus habuī:** 'had at hand.' See Caesar, *Dē Bellō Gallicō,*
2, 19, 7, *in manibus nostrīs hostēs vidērentur.*

21. **fortūna aut nātūra:** note the assonance, *212, d.* The distinction
between good things given by fortune and good things given by nature
is involved in chapter 6, page 294.

23. **dē rē pūblicā:** 'in politics'; but in chapter 6, page 294, *cōnsēnsiō* is followed by the genitive instead of the ablative with *dē.* So
here *rērum cōnsilium = dē rēbus.*

24. **plēna:** Cicero generally uses *plēnus* with the genitive, not with the
ablative.

25. **quod quidem sēnserim:** the subjunctive is used to express a
limitation or restriction; 'at least (*quidem*) as far as I have noticed.'
194, f; B. 283, 5; A. & G. 535, *d;* G. 627, R. 1.

28. **peregrīnātiōnēs:** we hear much of Scipio's travels (*Dē Rē Pūblicā,*
6, 11; *Acadēmicae Quaestiōnēs,* 2, 5), but it is only here mentioned that

Nam quid ego dē studiīs dīcam cognōscendī semper aliquid atque discendī? in quibus rēmōtī ab oculīs populī omne 30 ōtiōsum tempus contrīvimus. Quārum rērum recordātiō et memoria sī ūnā cum illō occidisset, dēsīderium coniūnctissimī atque amantissimī virī ferre nūllō modō possem. Sed nec illa exstīncta sunt alunturque potius et augentur cōgitātiōne et memoriā meā, et, sī illīs plānē orbātus essem, 35 magnum tamen affert mihi aetās ipsa sōlācium. Diūtius enim iam in hōc dēsīderiō esse nōn possum. Omnia autem brevia tolerābilia esse dēbent, etiam sī magna sunt.

Haec habuī dē amīcitiā quae dīcerem. Vōs autem hortor, ut ita virtūtem locētis, sine quā amīcitia esse nōn potest, ut 40 eā exceptā nihil amīcitiā praestābilius putētis.

Laelius accompanied him. **rūsticātiōnĕs:** see *Dē Ōrātōre,* **2,** 22, *Laelium semper ferĕ cum Scīpiōne solitum rūsticārī eōsque incrēdibiliter repuerāscere esse solitōs cum rūs ex urbe tamquam ē vinclīs ēvolāvissent,* ' that Laelius was almost always accustomed to sojourn in the country with Scipio, and that they were wont to become extremely boyish again when they had hurried forth out of the city, as if from a prison, to the country.' For the playful effect of this word compare Cicero, *Epistulae,* page 396, line 8, and note.

31. **recordātiō et memoria:** ' vivid recollection.' *212, b.* These two words frequently come together thus, as in *Tusculānae Disputātiōnēs,* **5,** 88; *Brūtus,* 9; *Dē Ōrātōre,* **1,** 228; Tacitus, *Dialogus dē Ōrātōribus,* **1** and in *Dē Ōrātōre,* **1,** 4, even *memoriae recordātiō. Memoria* indicates the fact that a past event is present to the mind; *recordātiō* properly means the act or process of summoning back past impressions; *cōgitātiō* is substituted for it below — *cōgitātiōne et memoriā.*

33. **possem:** the imperfect gives the sense ' I should now be able.'

34. **nec . . . et:** correlative to *et* below. **alunturque potius:** the *-que* is corrective as in the common phrase *potiusque,* ' or rather.' *aluntur,* ' are strengthened.'

35. **essem . . . affert:** the indicative is sometimes used in the apodosis, though the subjunctive is in the protasis, to state the conclusion as a fact; translate, ' yet the mere fact of my age affords,' etc.

39. **Haec habuī,** etc.: so Cicero makes Cato conclude in the *Catō Maior;* see page 292, line 42.

40. **ita . . . locētis:** ' you rank it so important.'

CICERO THE LOYALIST AND PATRIOT

DEMOSTHENES

A statue in the Vatican. Cicero's speeches against Antony are called Philippics from the famous speeches of Demosthenes against Philip of Macedon.

CICERO THE LOYALIST AND PATRIOT

M. TULLĪ CICERŌNIS
IN M. ANTŌNIUM ŌRĀTIŌ PHILIPPICA
QUĀRTA DECIMA

To assume the garb of peace before we have an official report that Decimus Brutus has been extricated from Mutina would be premature; the war is not yet finished.

1. Sī, ut ex litterīs, quac recitătae sunt, patrēs cōnscrīptī, scelerātissimōrum hostium exercitum caesum fūsumque cognōvī, sīc id, quod et omnēs maximē optāmus et ex eā victōriā, quae parta est, cōnsecūtum arbitrāmur, D. Brūtum ēgressum iam Mutinā esse cognōvissem, propter 5 cuius perīculum ad saga īssēmus, propter eiusdem salūtem redeundum ad prīstinum vestītum sine ūllā dubitātiōne cēnsērem. Ante vērō quam sit ea rēs, quam avidissimē

To the Student: Study the Companion, pages 556, 557.

1. 1. **Sī, ut ex litterīs,** etc.: 'If, just as from the letter which has been read, senators, I have learned that the army of our accursed enemies has been completely routed, so I had learned what we all particularly desire and think has followed from the victory which has been won, namely, that Decimus Brutus had already emerged from Mutina, I should without any hesitation move that we return to our former dress on account of the safety of the same man, on account of whose danger we had resorted to the military cloak.' **patrēs cōnscrīptī:** see note on page 432, line 35.

5. **Mutinā** (mū'tị-nạ).

6. **īssēmus** (*iissēmus*): why subjunctive?

8. **sit allāta:** the subjunctive is prospective, and represents an ideal

331

cīvitās exspectat, allāta, laetitiā fruī satis est maximae
10 praeclārissimaeque pugnae ; reditum ad vestītum cōnfectae
victōriae reservāte. Cōnfectiō autem huius bellī est D.
Brūtī salūs.

When we once return to the garb of peace, let it be final. Some senators
are opposed to this plan, because they wish to withhold signal honor
from Brutus.

Quae autem est ista sententia, ut in hodiernum diem
vestītus mūtētur, deinde crās sagātī prōdeāmus? Nōs
15 vērō cum semel ad eum, quem cupimus optāmusque,
vestītum redierimus, id agāmus, ut eum in perpetuum
retineāmus. Nam hōc quidem cum turpe est, tum nē dīs
quidem inmortālibus grātum, ab eōrum ārīs, ad quās togātī
adierimus, ad saga sūmenda discēdere.
20 Atque animadvertō, patrēs cōnscrīptī, quōsdam huic
favēre sententiae ; quōrum ea mēns idque cōnsilium est,
ut, cum videant glōriōsissimum illum D. Brūtō futūrum
diem, quō diē propter eius salūtem redierimus ad vestītum,
hunc eī frūctum ēripere cupiant, nē memoriae posteritā-
25 tīque prōdātur propter ūnīus cīvis perīculum populum
Rōmānum ad saga īsse, propter eiusdem salūtem redīsse
ad togās. Tollite hanc ; nūllam tam prāvae sententiae
causam reperiētis. Vōs vērō, patrēs cōnscrīptī, cōnservāte
auctōritātem vestram, manēte in sententiā, tenēte vestrā
30 memoriā, quod saepe ostendistis, huius tōtīus bellī in ūnīus
virī fortissimī et maximī vītā positum esse discrīmen.

---

limit. *189, b;* B. 292, 1 ; A. & G. 551, *b,* N. 2 : G. 577, N. 2.

16. **id agāmus, ut:** idiomatic; 'let us resolve to.' **ut . . . re-**
tineāmus: purpose clause. *196, a;* B. 295, 5 ; A. & G. 563, *d;* G
546, N. I.

24. **eī:** the so-called dative of separation. *109, b;* B. 188, 2, *d;*
A. & G. 381 ; G. 345, R.

27. **hanc:** sc. *sententiam.*

31. **positum esse:** 'depends upon.'

*The deliverance of Brutus is the issue involved in this war, and all rejoicing
should be postponed until that end has been attained.*

2. Ad D. Brūtum līberandum lēgātī missī prīncipēs cīvitātis, quī illī hostī ac parricīdae dēnūntiārent, ut ā Mutinā
discēderet; eiusdem D.

Brūtī cōnservandī grātiā
cōnsul sortītū ad bellum 5
profectus A. Hīrtius,
cuius imbēcillitātem va-
lētūdinis animī virtūs et
spēs victōriae cōnfīrmā-
vit; Caesar cum exer- 10
citū per sē comparātō,
cum prīmīs pestibus
rem pūblicam līberāssct,
nē quid posteā sceleris
orerētur, profectus est 15
ad eundem Brūtum
līberandum vīcitque do-
lōrem aliquem domesti-
cum patriae cāritāte.

A ROMAN ORATOR IN THE GARB OF PEACE

---

2. 6. **A. Hīrtius** (â'lŭs hẹr'sh(y)ŭs).

8. **animī virtūs et spēs victōriae**: what figure of speech? *239, e.*

10. **cum . . . comparātō**: take with *profectus est*, line 15: 'Caesar
(Octavianus) with an army organized on his own responsibility.'

11. **per sē**: emphatic, meaning that he had no official authority from the
senate; for, according to Roman law, an army could be recruited only by virtue of the *imperium*, which the senate had not yet bestowed upon Octavian.

12. **cum . . . līberāsset**: this refers to Octavian's persistence in
trying to intimidate Antony and his followers in Rome by declaring
that he had taken up arms to protect his country. **prīmīs pestibus:**
'from the first signs of danger.' *92, c; 127, a.*

15. **orerētur**: the more usual form of this verb in the imperfect
subjunctive.

17. **dolōrem aliquem domesticum:** 'some personal grief.' Decimus
Brutus was one of the conspirators against Julius Caesar, Octavian's

20   Quid C. Pānsa ēgit aliud dīlēctibus habendīs, pecūniā
comparandā, senātūs cōnsultīs faciendīs gravissimīs in
Antōnium, nōbīs cohortandīs, populō Rōmānō ad causam
lībertātis vocandō, nisi ut D. Brūtus līberārētur? Ā quō
populus Rōmānus frequēns ita salūtem D. Brūtī ūnā vōce
25 dēpoposcit, ut eam nōn sōlum commodīs suīs, sed etiam
necessitātī vīctūs anteferret. Quod spērāre nōs quidem
dēbēmus, patrēs cōnscrīptī, aut inibi esse aut iam esse
cōnfectum; sed speī frūctum reī convenit et ēventō reser-
vārī, nē aut deōrum inmortālium beneficium festīnātiōne
30 praeripuisse aut vim fortūnae stultitiā contempsisse videāmur.

Sed quoniam significātiō vestra satis dēclārat, quid hāc
dē rē sentiātis, ad litterās veniam, quae sunt ā cōnsulibus
et ā prōpraetōre missae, sī pauca ante, quae ad ipsās litterās
35 pertineant, dīxerō.

*Antony is guilty of warfare against his country, and yet the senate hesitates
to call him a public enemy. He is guilty of other enormities, and a
decree of thanksgiving for his defeat is not enough.*

3. Imbūtī gladiī sunt, patrēs cōnscrīptī, legiōnum exerci-
tuumque nostrōrum vel madefactī potius duōbus duōrum

---

adoptive father. See Cicero, *Epistulae*, 25, page 402. Cicero means
that Octavian is the type of man who suppresses personal animosities
for the good of the state.

20. **Quid C. Pānsa ēgit aliud . . . nisi ut:** ' What else did Gaius
Pansa strive for if not for the release of Decimus Brutus? '

24. **frequēns:** ' in great numbers.' **ita:** color this word with a
suitable adverb.

25. **commodīs suīs . . . necessitātī vīctūs:** the first expression refers
to the well-to-do, the second to the poor.

26. **anteferret:** sc. *populus Rōmānus* as subject.

27. **inibi esse:** idiom; ' is near at hand.'

28. **et:** connects *reī* and *ēventō*. Translate, ' for the real issue.'

32. **significātiō:** ' behavior.'

34. **prōpraetōre:** Octavian.

3. 2. **duōbus:** sc. *proeliīs*.

cōnsulum, tertiō Caesaris proeliō. Sī hostium fuit ille
sanguis, summa mīlitum pietās; nefārium scelus, sī cīvium.
Quō ūsque igitur is, quī omnēs hostēs scelere superāvit, 5
nōmine hostis carēbit? nisi mūcrōnēs etiam nostrōrum

MARK ANTONY

A statue in the Uffizzi Gallery
in Florence.

mīlitum tremere vultis dubi-
tantīs, utrum in cīve an in
hoste fīgantur. Supplicā-
tiōnem dēcernitis, hostem 10
nōn appellātis. Grātae vērō
nostrae dīs immortālibus
grātulātiōnēs erunt, grātae
victimae, cum interfecta sit
cīvium multitūdō! "Dē 15
improbīs," inquit, "et
audācibus." Nam sīc eōs
appellat clārissimus vir;
quae sunt urbānārum male-
dicta lītium, nōn inūstae 20
bellī internecīvī notae. Testāmenta, crēdō, subiciunt
aut ēiciunt vīcīnōs aut adu-

lēscentulōs circumscrībunt; hīs enim vitiīs affectōs et
tālibus malōs aut audācēs appellāre cōnsuētūdō solet. 25

---

3. **tertiō proeliō :** the three battles were fought on April 15, 43 B.C.,
as described by Servius Galba in a letter to Cicero (*Ad Familiārēs*, **10,**
30). In the first battle Antony was successful against Pansa, who
was mortally wounded. On returning to Forum Gallōrum Antony met
Hirtius, who completely routed his forces in a second engagement. In
the meantime, Octavian successfully defended the Roman camp from
an attack by Antony's brother Lucius. **Sī . . . cīvium :** observe the
arrangement of clauses; what figure? *239, e.*

15. **" Dē improbīs et audācibus ":** the important part of the motion
made by P. Servilius; with these words sc. *supplicātiōnem dēcernendam
cēnseō.* Translate *dē*, 'for victory over.'

Bellum inexpiābile īnfert quattuor cōnsulibus ūnus
omnium latrōnum taeterrimus; gerit īdem bellum cum
senātū populōque Rōmānō; omnibus, — quamquam ruit
ipse suīs clādibus — pestem, vāstitātem, cruciātum, tor-
30 menta dēnūntiat. Dolābellae ferum et immāne facinus,
quod nūlla barbaria posset agnōscere, id suō cōnsiliō factum
esse testātur; quaeque esset factūrus in hāc urbe, nisi
eum hīc ipse Iuppiter ab hōc templō atque moenibus
reppulisset, dēclārāvit in Parmēnsium calamitāte, quōs
35 optimōs virōs honestissimōsque hominēs maximē cum
auctōritāte huius ōrdinis populīque Rōmānī dignitāte

---

26. quattuor cōnsulibus: Pansa and Hirtius, the consuls of 43 B.C.,
have already been mentioned; in addition, D. Brutus and L. Munatius
Plancus, who were designated by Julius Caesar for the consulship of
42 B.C. Of course, Cicero indulges in a clever exaggeration, especially
since Plancus had not even taken part in the opposition to Antony, but
had merely promised his support.

29. suīs clādibus: ablative of attendant circumstance, ' at the risk
of personal ruin.' *138.*

30. Dolābellae . . . facinus: P. Cornelius Dolabella had married
Cicero's daughter, Tullia, in 50 B.C., but the two were divorced in 46 B.C.
He had always been a profligate and a spendthrift, guilty of recklessness
and licentiousness; but his most dastardly deed, here referred to, was
the torture and murder of C. Trebonius, proconsul of Asia and one of
the murderers of Caesar. Though heretofore Cicero had always treated
his son-in-law with patience and forbearance, this crime and the support
he gave Antony aroused his scorn and contempt. See page *387*, *Epistulae*, 14, line 2, and note.

31. suō cōnsiliō . . . testātur: sc. *Antōnius;* of course, a willful
exaggeration. The evidence shows that, although Antony approved of
the murder, he had no hand in it.

32. esset factūrus: although this is the apodosis of a contrary-to-
fact condition, the subjunctive is due to an indirect question depending
on *dēclārāvit;* in the direct form it would normally have been *erat
factūrus.* Why? *208, b; 219;* B. *322;* A. & G. *517, b* and *d;* G. *597, 3
(a)* and *5 (a).*

34. in Parmēnsium calamitāte: the town of Parma was seized and
plundered because it favored the senatorial party. It occupied a
strategic position.

coniūnctōs crūdēlissimīs exemplīs interēmit propudium illud et portentum, L. Antōnius, īnsigne odium omnium hominum vel, sī etiam dī ōdērunt, quōs oportet, deōrum. Refugit animus, patrēs cōnscrīptī, eaque dīcere reformīdat, 40 quae L. Antōnius in Parmēnsium līberīs et coniugibus effēcerit. Quās enim turpitūdinēs Antōniī libenter cum dēdecore subiērunt, eāsdem per vim laetantur aliīs se intulisse. Sed vīs calamitōsa est, quam illīs obtulērunt, libīdō flāgitiōsa, quā Antōniōrum oblita est vīta. 45

4. Est igitur quisquam, quī hostīs appellāre nōn audeat, quōrum scelere crūdēlitātem Karthāginiēnsium victam esse fateātur?

Not even Hannibal was so savage as Antony; 'hostis' is after all but a mild term for him.

Quā enim in urbe tam immānis Hannibal captā quam in Parmā surreptā Antōnius? nisi forte huius colōniae 5 et cēterārum, in quās eōdem est animō, nōn est hostis putandus. Sī vērō colōniārum et mūnicipiōrum sine ūllā dubitātiōne hostis est, quid tandem huius cēnsētis urbis, quam ille ad explendās egestātēs latrōcinī suī concupīvit, quam iam perītus mētātor et callidus decempedā suā Saxa 10

37. **propudium illud et portentum :** ' that degenerate monster.'
38. **L. Antōnius :** brother of Mark Antony.
4. 4. **Hannibal :** frequently cited as the embodiment of cruelty and faithlessness. See Livy, page 436, line 25, and note.
5. **surreptā :** ' seized by stealth '; the word implies questionable methods.
6. **in :** ' toward.'
8. **quid . . . urbis :** ' pray, what relation, think you, is he to this city? ' *quid* is parallel to *hostis*, and *urbis* to *colōniārum*.
9. **egestātēs :** abstract plurals are more freely used in Latin than in English, and deserve careful study. Here the plural is due to the following genitive, *latrōcinī*, which is equivalent to a concrete plural, there being as many cases of indigence as there are brigands. *92, c.*
10. **Saxa :** formerly a *mētātor castrōrum* under Caesar, now a member of Antony's staff.

dīvīserat? Recordāmini, per deōs inmortālēs, patrēs cōnscrīptī, quid hōc biduō timuerimus ā domesticīs hostibus
rūmōribus improbissimīs dissipātīs. Quis līberōs, quis
coniugem aspicere poterat sine flētū, quis domum, quis
15 tēcta, quis larem familiārem? Aut foedissimam mortem
omnēs aut miserābilem fugam cōgitābant. Haec ā quibus
timēbantur, eōs hostēs appellāre dubitāmus? Gravius sī
quis attulerit nōmen, libenter assentiar; hōc vulgārī contentus vix sum, leviōre nōn ūtar.

*I support the proposal of Servilius to decree a 'thanksgiving' but I would
emend it by extending its duration and by conferring the title of
'Imperātor' upon the generals.*

20 Itaque, cum supplicātiōnēs iūstissimās ex iīs litterīs,
quae recitātae sunt, dēcernere dēbeāmus Servīliusque
dēcrēverit, augēbō omnīnō numerum diērum, praesertim
cum nōn ūnī, sed tribus ducibus sint dēcernendae. Sed
hōc prīmum faciam, ut imperātōrēs appellem eōs, quōrum
25 virtūte, cōnsiliō, fēlīcitāte, maximīs perīculīs servitūtis
atque interitūs līberātī sumus. Etenim cui vīgintī hīs
annīs supplicātiō dēcrēta est, ut nōn imperātor appellārētur
aut minimīs rēbus gestīs aut plērumque nūllīs? Quam ob
rem aut supplicātiō ab eō, quī ante dīxit, dēcernenda nōn

---

13. **dissipātīs**: rumors had been noised abroad that Antony had
defeated Hirtius. Naturally, the enemies of Antony were somewhat
apprehensive.

18. **vulgārī**: ' ordinary.'

21. **Servīlius** (sẹr-vil'ị-ụs).

22. **dēcrēverit**: ' has voted for it.' **omnīnō**: ' in all.'

24. **imperātōrēs**: originally the title of ' Imperator' was conferred
upon a victorious general by his soldiers; in Cicero's time it was also
conferred formally by a vote of the senate and was usually followed by
a triumph.

27. **ut nōn appellārētur**: ' without his being called.' *Quin-* and *ut
nōn*-clauses are often so translated, especially after negative sentences or
questions implying a negative.

fuit aut ūsitātus honōs pervulgātusque tribuendus iīs, 30
quibus etiam novī singulārēsque dēbentur.

CARTHAGE TODAY

*The generals fully deserve this honor.   The Roman people tendered me also
an informal triumph yesterday, and their action was a testimony to
loyal service.*

5. An, sī quis Hispānōrum aut Gallōrum aut Thrēcum
mīlle aut duo mīlia occīdisset, eum hāc cōnsuetūdine, quae
incrēbuit, imperātōrem appellāret senātus; tot legiōnibus
caesīs tantā multitūdine hostium interfectā — hostium
dīco? ita, inquam, hostium, quamvīs hōc istī hostēs 5
domesticī nōlint — clārissimīs ducibus supplicātiōnum
honōrem tribuēmus, imperātōrium nōmen adimēmus?

---

5. 1. **An**: another instance of the rhetorical *an* in argumentation,
employing the *argūmentum ā minōre ad maius*. In this use *an* must
not be translated by ' or,' for it has no special equivalent in English;
translate, ' Is it not true?   If anyone, etc.'   See *In Catilīnam*, 1,
page 28, line 21, and note.

3. **tot legiōnibus caesīs**: '(whereas now), when so many legions
have been slain.' **appellāret**: *205.*

Quantō enim honōre, laetitiā, grātulātiōne in hōc templum
ingredī dēbent illī ipsī huius urbis līberātōrēs, cum hesternō
10 diē propter eōrum rēs gestās mē ovantem et prope trium-
phantem populus Rōmānus in Capitōlium domō tulerit,
domum inde redūxerit? Is enim dēmum est meā quidem
sententiā iūstus triumphus ac vērus, cum bene dē rē pūblicā
meritīs testimōnium ā cōnsēnsū cīvitātis datur. Nam sīve
15 in commūnī gaudiō populī Rōmānī ūnī grātulābantur,
magnum iūdicium, sive ūnī grātiās agēbant, eō maius,
sīve utrumque, nihil magnificentius cōgitārī potest.

*It has been rumored abroad that I am aiming at sovereign power; is it
possible that anyone is so bereft of reason as to believe that I, who
crushed Catiline, should on a sudden become a Catiline?*

"Tū igitur ipse dē tē?" dīxerit quispiam. Equidem
invītus, sed iniūriae dolor facit mē praeter cōnsuētūdinem
20 glōriōsum. Nōnne satis est ab hominibus virtūtis ignārīs
grātiam bene merentibus nōn referrī? Etiam in eōs, quī
omnēs suās cūrās in reī pūblicae salūte dēfīgunt, impietātis crīmine invidia quaerētur? Scītis enim per hōs diēs
crēberrimum fuisse sermōnem mē Parīlibus, quī diēs hodiē

---

8. **templum:** the temple of Jupiter on the Capitoline, where this
meeting of the senate was being held. See page 556.

10. **mē ovantem:** ' me in an ovation,' a modified triumph. An
ovation was usually granted for a victory without bloodshed, and the
general entered the city either on horseback or on foot, whereas in the
triumph proper he rode in a chariot. The two differed also in some
other respects. See Smith, *Dictionary of Greek and Roman Antiquities.*
Observe the clever manner in which Cicero contrives to introduce his
own name.

14. **ā cōnsēnsū:** the preposition shows that *cōnsēnsū* has a concrete
signification, and so is personified. *126, b.*

18. **dīxerit:** *180, e;* B. 280, 1; A. & G. 446; G. 257. The perfect
subjunctive as well as the more regular present is used for the potential of the present or future.

24. **Parīlibus:** the feast of *Parīlia* or *Palīlia* was celebrated on
April 21, the anniversary of the founding of Rome. Properly it was the

est, cum fascibus dēscēnsūrum. In aliquem crēdō hōc 25
gladiātōrem aut latrōnem aut Catilīnam esse collātum, nōn
in eum, quī, nē quid tāle in rē pūblicā fierī posset, effēcerit.
An ut ego, quī Catilīnam haec mōlientem sustulerim, ēverterim, afflīxerim, ipse exsisterem repente Catilīna? Quibus

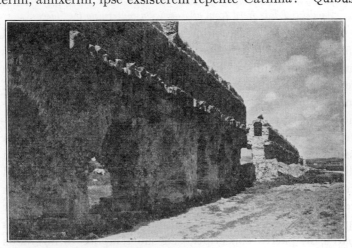

ROMAN AQUEDUCT AT CARTHAGE

The great Roman aqueducts which supplied the ancients with millions of
gallons of pure water daily are one of the finest examples of engineering skill
and indicate the care bestowed on public health. Some are still in use today.

festival of Pales, the tutelary deity of shepherds. Ovid gives a graphic
description in his *Fastī*, **4,** 721, *et seq.*

25. **cum fascibus dēscēnsūrum:** into the forum as dictator. **hōc
. . . esse collātum:** remember to give the neuter *hōc* its proper color,
i.e. ' this story was made up.'

26. **Catilīnam:** ' a Catiline,' announcing the real Catiline in the next
sentence.

27. **nē:** the negative after verbs of effecting is either *ut nōn* or *nē*,
according as either result or purpose predominates. *203 (3)*, footnote.

28. **An ut exsisterem:** sc. *id effēcī* with *an;* translate, ' Or think
you that (*an*) I should myself on a sudden strive to become a Catiline? '
sustulerim, ēverterim, afflīxerim: primary sequence because Cicero is
thinking of present time, even though *exsisterem*, the governing verb,
is imperfect.

30 auspiciīs istōs fascīs augur acciperem, quatenus habērem,
cui traderem? Quemquamne fuisse tam scelerātum, quī
hōc fingeret, tam furiōsum, quī crēderet!

6. Unde igitur ista suspīciō vel potius unde iste sermō?

*The plot to kill me and all of you was foiled, and with the help of Publius
Apuleius I was freed from all suspicion concerning the 'fascēs.'*

Cum, ut scītis, hōc trīduō vel quadrīduō trīstis ā Mutinā
fāma mānāret, īnflātī laetitiā atque īnsolentiā impiī cīvēs
ūnum sē in locum ad illam cūriam furiīs potius suīs quam
5 reī pūblicae īnfēlīcem congregābant. Ibi cum cōnsilia
inīrent dē caede nostrā partīrenturque inter sē, quī Capitōlium, quī rōstra, quī urbis portās occupārent, ad mē concursum futūrum cīvitātis putābant. Quod ut cum invidiā
meā fieret et cum vītae etiam perīculō, fāmam istam fascium
10 dissipāvērunt, fascīs ipsī ad mē dēlātūrī fuērunt. Quod
cum esset quasi meā voluntāte factum, tum in mē impetus
conductōrum hominum quasi in tyrannum parābātur, ex
quō caedēs esset vestrum omnium cōnsecūta. Quae rēs
patefēcit, patrēs cōnscrīptī, sed suō tempore tōtīus huius
15 sceleris fōns aperiētur.

Itaque P. Apuleius, tribūnus pl., meōrum omnium
cōnsiliōrum perīculōrumque iam inde ā cōnsulātū meō
testis, cōnscius, adiūtor, dolōrem ferre nōn potuit dolōris
meī. Cōntiōnem habuit maximam populō Rōmānō ūnum
20 atque idem sentiente. In quā cōntiōne cum mē prō summā

31. **Quemquamne fuisse :** ' To think that anyone should have been ';
exclamatory question. *224, c;* B. 334; A. & G. 462; G. 534.

6. 12. **ex quō :** ' after which.'

13. **esset cōnsecūta :** ' would have followed.' Why subjunctive?
The protasis is disguised. *209.*

13. **Quae :** neuter accusative. **rēs :** ' the order of events.'

14. **suō tempore :** ' at the right time.' *157, e.*

16. **Apuleius** (ap-ū-lē'(y)ụs).

17. **iam inde ā cōnsulātū :** ' ever since my consulship.'

20. **prō :** ' in view of.'

nostrā coniūnctiōne et familiāritāte līberāre suspīciōne fascium vellet, ūnā vōce cūncta cōntiō dēclārāvit nihil esse ā mē umquam dē rē pūblicā nisi optimē cōgitātum. Post hanc habitam cōntiōnem duābus tribusve hōrīs optātissimī nūntiī et litterae vēnērunt, ut īdem diēs nōn modo inīquis- 25 simā mē invidiā līberārit, sed etiam celeberrimā populī Rōmānī grātulātiōne auxerit.

THE FORUM AND THE CAPITOLINE HILL AS SEEN FROM THE PALATINE

Haec interposuī, patrēs cōnscrīptī, nōn tam ut prō mē dīcerem — male enim mēcum agerētur, sī parum vōbīs essem sine dēfēnsiōne pūrgātus, — quam ut quōsdam 30 nimis iēiūnō animō et angustō monērem, id quod semper ipse fēcissem, utī excellentium cīvium virtūtem imitātiōne

23. **optimē :** ' in a loyal manner.'

26. **celeberrimā grātulātiōne :** ' universal rejoicing.'

29. **male enim mēcum agerētur :** ' for I should fare hard.'

30. **vōbīs :** ' in your eyes.'

32. **fēcissem :** a part of the indirect discourse implied in *monērem*, and not a parenthetic explanation, in which case it would have been *fēcī*. *213, b.*

dignam, nōn invidiā putārent. Magnus est in rē pūblicā campus, ut sapienter dīcere Crassus solēbat, multīs apertus 35 cursus ad laudem.

In my efforts to guide the affairs of the state both my motives and methods have been honorable. Leadership can be won in no other way.

7. Utinam quidem illī prīncipēs vīverent, quī mē post meum cōnsulātum, cum iīs ipse cēderem, prīncipem nōn invītī vidēbant! Hōc vērō tempore in tantā inopiā cōnstantium et fortium cōnsulārium quō mē dolōre afficī 5 crēditis, cum aliōs male sentīre, aliōs nihil omnīnō cūrāre videam, aliōs parum cōnstanter in susceptā causā permanēre sententiamque suam nōn semper ūtilitāte reī pūblicae, sed tum spē, tum timōre moderārī?

Quod sī quis dē contentiōne prīncipātūs labōrat, quae 10 nūlla esse dēbet, stultissimē facit, sī vitiīs cum virtūte contendit; ut enim cursū cursus, sīc in virīs fortibus virtūs virtūte superātur. Tū, sī ego dē rē pūblicā optimē sentiam, ut mē vincās, ipse pessimē sentiēs aut, sī ad mē bonōrum concursum fierī vidēbis, ad tē improbōs invītābis?

---

33. **dignam**: what case does this word govern? *142, b;* B. 226, 2; A. & G. 418, *b;* G. 397, N. 2. **in rē pūblicā:** 'political,' as often. *212, i.*

34. **Crassus:** consul 95 B.C., regarded by Cicero as an outstanding orator, in the same category with M. Antonius, with whom he appears as one of the speakers in Cicero's *Dē Ōrātōre.* See page 497.

7. 3. **Hōc:** 'present.' **cōnstantium:** 'steadfast.'

5. **male sentīre:** 'to harbor ill feelings' toward the state. **nihil omnīnō cūrāre:** 'to be entirely indifferent.'

6. **parum . . . permanēre:** 'to persevere with too little steadfast-ness in the cause which they have undertaken.'

9. **Quod sī . . . labōrat:** 'But if anyone is struggling after leader-ship with anxious toil.'

11. **cursus:** 'speed.'

12. **sī optimē sentiam:** 'if I harbor most loyal feelings.'

13. **pessimē sentiēs:** contrasted with *optimē sentiam.*

Nōllem prīmum reī pūblicae causā, deinde etiam dignitātis 15
tuae. Sed sī prīncipātus agerētur, quem numquam expetīvī, quid tandem mihi esset optātius? Ego enim malīs
sententiīs vincī nōn possum, bonīs forsitan possim et
libenter.

The welfare of the state has been my chief concern. It was necessary to urge
war against Antony to avoid a dishonorable peace.

Haec populum Rōmānum vidēre, animadvertere, iūdicāre 20
quīdam molestē ferunt. Poteratne fierī, ut nōn proinde
hominēs dē quōque, ut quisque merērētur, iūdicārent?
Ut enim dē ūniversō senātū populus Rōmānus vērissimē
iūdicat nūllīs reī pūblicae temporibus hunc ōrdinem fīrmi-
ōrem aut fortiōrem fuisse, sīc dē ūnō quōque nostrum et 25
maximē, quī hōc locō sententiās dīcimus, scīscitantur
omnēs, avent audīre, quid quisque sēnserit; ita dē quōque,
ut quemque meritum arbitrantur, exīstimant. Memoriā
tenent mē ante diem XIII Kalendās Iānuāriās prīncipem
revocandae lībertātis fuisse, mē ex Kalendīs Iānuāriīs ad 30
hanc hōram invigilāsse reī pūblicae, meam domum meāsque
aurēs diēs noctēsque omnium praeceptīs monitīsque patuisse, meīs litterīs, meīs nūntiīs, meīs cohortātiōnibus omnēs,
quī ubīque essent, ad patriae praesidium excitātōs, meīs

---

15. **Nōllem:** sc. *tē id facere; 180, e (4)*; B. 280, 4; A. & G. 447, I, N.;
G. 258, N. I. **dignitātis tuae :** ' your personal honor.'

16. **agerētur :** ' were at stake.'

18. **forsitan possim :** ' perhaps I might be '; *180, e* (1); B. 280;
A. & G. 447, 3, *a;* G. 457, 2, N.

21. **proinde . . . ut :** ' according as.'

22. **ut :** ' as,' correlative with *sīc.*

29. **ante diem XIII Kalendās Iānuāriās :** December 20, the date
of the Third and Fourth Philippics. For the Roman calendar see *240,*
241.

30. **ex Kalendīs Iānuāriīs :** the date of the Fifth Philippic.

33. **litterīs :** here with a plural meaning.

35 sententiīs ā Kalendīs Iānuāriīs numquam lēgātōs ad Antōnium, semper illum hostem, semper hōc bellum, ut ego,
quī omnī tempore vērae pācis auctor fuissem, huic essem
nōminī pestiferae pācis inimīcus. Hās in sententiās meās
sī cōnsulēs discessiōnem facere voluissent, omnibus istīs
40 latrōnibus auctōritāte ipsā senātūs iam prīdem dē manibus
arma cecidissent.

*I have always used the terms 'enemy' and 'war' in connection with Antony
and now the proposed thanksgiving supports my view.*

8. Sed, quod tum nōn licuit, patrēs cōnscrīptī, id hōc
tempore nōn sōlum licet, vērum etiam necesse est, eōs, quī
rē sunt hostēs, verbīs notārī, sententiīs nostrīs hostēs
iūdicārī. Anteā cum hostem ac bellum nōmināssem, semel
5 et saepius sententiam meam dē numerō sententiārum
sustulērunt, quod in hāc causā iam fierī nōn potest. Ex
litterīs enim C. Pānsae A. Hīrtī cōnsulum, C. Caesaris prō
praetōre dē honōre dīs immortālibus habendō sententiās
dīcimus. Supplicātiōnem modo quī decrēvit, īdem imprū-
10 dēns hostēs iūdicāvit ; numquam enim in cīvīlī bellō suppli-

---

35. **lēgātōs :** sc. *missōs esse.*
36. **illum, hōc :** sc. *appellātum esse; hostem* and *bellum* are the
predicate nouns.
38. **Hās in sententiās meās discessiōnem facere :** a technical expression referring to the method of taking votes in the Roman senate.
Those who favored the proposal of a certain speaker would formally
group themselves around him, and this was called *discessiō* or *pedibus
īre in sententiam.* See page 148, line 1, and note. Translate, ' If the
consuls had been willing to put these proposals of mine to a vote.'
8. 3. **sententiīs :** ' votes.'
5. **sententiam. . . sustulērunt :** *i.e.* they refused to put the question
to the senate.
6. **Ex litterīs . . . dīcimus :** ' For in accordance with the letters of
Gaius Pansa and Aulus Hirtius and of the propraetor Gaius Caesar we
are giving our votes on the question of paying honor to the gods.'
⁊. **Pānsae** (pan'zą).
9. **modo :** ' just now.' **imprūdēns :** ' unconsciously.' *151.*

cātĭō dēcrēta est. Dēcrētam dīco? nē victōris quidem litterīs postulāta est.

Furthermore, no thanksgiving has ever been decreed in civil war, as Roman history clearly shows. Such a decree implies that Antony is a public enemy.

Cīvīle bellum cōnsul Sulla gessit, legiōnibus in urbem adductīs, quōs voluit, expulit, quōs potuit, occīdit; supplicātiōnis mentiō nūlla. Grave bellum Octāviānum īn-15 secūtum est; supplicātiō Cinnae nūlla victōrī. Cinnae victōriam imperātor ultus est Sulla; nūlla supplicātiō dēcrēta ā senātū. Ad tē ipsum, P. Servīlī, num mīsit ūllās collēga litterās dē illā calamitōsissimā pugnā Pharsāliā, num tē dē supplicātiōne voluit referre? Profectō nōluit. 20 At mīsit posteā dē Alexandrīā, dē Phārnace; Pharsāliae

13. **Cīvīle bellum :** 88–82 B.C., between the optimates under Sulla and the democrats under Marius and Cinna. Sulla eventually made himself master of Rome and Italy, put to death all of his enemies by proscription, and assumed the dictatorship.

15. **Octāviānum** (ok-tā-vĭ-ā'nŭs) : Cn. Octāvius, the colleague of Cinna in the consulship of 87 B. C. and a partisan of Sulla.

16. **Cinnae** (sin'ą).

19. **collēga :** Julius Caesar, consul with Servilius in 48 B.C. **pugnā Pharsāliā** (fär-sā'lĭ-ą) : Caesar's victory over Pompey near the city of Pharsęlus, Thessaly, in 48 B.C.

20. **Profectō nōluit :** ' Certainly not.'

21. **Alexandrīā :** whither Pompey had fled after his defeat at Pharsalus. He was treacherously murdered a few days before Caesar reached Alexandria. On learning that King Ptolemy was plotting against himself also, he attacked the city and reduced it in 47 B.C. **dē Phārnace** (fär'ną-sēz) : Suetonius describes this victory as follows: ' From Alexandria he crossed into Syria, and thence to Pontus, being impelled by messages relating to Pharnaces, who was the son of Mithridates the Great, and, taking advantage of the favorable situation existing at the time, was making war; although he was in a very warlike mood by reason of various successes, Caesar routed him in one battle, within five days after his arrival and four hours after catching sight of him.' This was the battle of Zeła, reported to Rome in the famous dispatch, " *vēnī, vīdī, vīcī.*" See page 12. note 11.

vērō pugnae nē triumphum quidem ēgit. Eōs enim cīvēs pugna illa sustulerat, quibus nōn modo vīvīs, sed etiam victōribus incolumis et flōrēns cīvitās esse posset. Quod 25 idem contigerat superiōribus bellīs cīvīlibus. Nam mihi cōnsulī supplicātiō nūllīs armīs sūmptīs nōn ob caedem hostium, sed ob cōnservātiōnem cīvium novō et inaudītō genere dēcrēta est.

Quam ob rem aut supplicātiō rē pūblicā pulcherrimē 30 gestā postulantibus nostrīs imperātōribus dēneganda est, quod praeter Gabīnium contigit nēminī, aut supplicātiōne dēcernendā hostēs eōs, dē quibus dēcernitis, iūdicētis necesse est.

The three victors — Pansa, Hirtius, Octavian — all richly deserve the title of 'Imperātor.'

9. Quod ergō ille rē, id ego etiam verbō, cum imperātōrēs eōs appellō; hōc ipsō nōmine et eōs, quī iam dēvictī sunt, et eōs, quī supersunt, hostēs iūdicō, cum victōrēs appellō imperātōrēs. Quō modō enim potius Pānsam appellem, 5 etsī habet honōris nōmen amplissimī, quō Hīrtium? Est ille quidem cōnsul, sed alterum nōmen beneficī populī Rōmānī est, alterum virtūtis atque victōriae. Quid? Caesarem deōrum beneficiō reī pūblicae prōcreātum dubitemne appellāre imperātōrem? quī prīmus Antōnī in- 10 mānem et foedam crūdēlitātem nōn sōlum ā iugulīs nostrīs, sed etiam ā membrīs et vīsceribus āvertit.

---

22. **Eōs enim cīvēs :** it is quite likely that this is the true reason why Caesar failed to claim a triumph.

27. **novō et inaudītō genere :** review *In Catilīnam*, **3**, 6, page 91.

31. **Gabīnium** (gạ-bịn′i-ụs): during his proconsulship of Syria in 57 B.C. he engaged in illegal practices, and on returning to Rome was convicted on a charge of misgovernment. A triumph, which he had demanded for unimportant successes in the East, was refused him.

9. 1. **ille :** Servilius. **cum . . . appellō :** explicative *cum. 185, a;* B. 290, 1; A. & G. 545, *a;* G. 582.

5. **nōmen :** i.e. *cōnsul.*

Ūnīus autem diēī quot et quantae virtūtēs, dī immortālēs, fuērunt! Prīnceps enim omnium Pānsa proelī faciendī et cum Antōniō cōnflīgendī fuit, dignus imperātor legiōne Mārtiā, digna legiō imperātōre. Cuius sī ācerrimum 15 impetum cohibēre Pānsa potuisset, ūnō proeliō cōnfecta rēs esset. Sed cum lībertātis avida legiō effrēnātius in aciem hostium irrūpisset ipseque in prīmīs Pānsa pugnāret, duōbus perīculōsīs vulneribus acceptīs sublātus ē proeliō reī pūblicae vītam reservāvit. Ego vērō hunc nōn sōlum 20 imperātōrem, sed etiam clārissimum imperātōrem iūdicō, quī cum aut morte aut victōriā sē satis factūrum reī pūblicae spopondisset, alterum fēcit, alterius dī immortālēs ōmen āvertant!

Hirtius and Octavian performed successful exploits against Antony.

10. Quid, dīcam dē Hīrtiō? quī rē audītā, ē castrīs duās legiōnēs ēdūxit incrēdibilī studiō atque virtūtc, quārtam illam, quae, relīctō Antōniō, sē ōlim cum Mārtiā legiōne coniūnxit, et septimam, quae cōnstitūta ex veterānīs docuit hōc proeliō mīlitibus iīs, quī Caesaris beneficia servāssent, 5 senātūs populīque Rōmānī cārum nōmen esse. Hīs vīgintī cohortibus nūllō equitātū Hīrtius ipse aquilam quārtae legiōnis cum īnferret, quā nūllīus pulchriōrem speciem

---

12. **virtūtēs**: 'acts of bravery.' *92, c.*

14. **legiōne Mārtiā** (mar'sh(y)ạn): this and the fourth legion had deserted Antony, and had joined Octavianus.

23. **alterum fēcit**: 'has achieved the one aim.' victory. **alterius**: death.

10. 1. **rē audītā**: another example of an ablative absolute appositive to the subject (here, *quī*) used as a substitute for the missing perfect active participle. So also *relīctō Antōniō* in line 13. See page 83, note 11. *212, a.*

5. **quī . . . servāssent**: Cicero means to say that the more desirable soldiers had allied themselves with the cause of the state, while Antony's men were revolutionists.

8. **pulchriōrem speciem**: notice the sudden burst of oratory and

imperātōris accēpimus, cum tribus Antōnī legiōnibus equi-
10 tātūque cōnflīxit hostēsque nefāriōs huic Iovis Optimī
Maximī cēterīsque deōrum immortālium templīs, urbis

THE TEMPLE OF JUPITER OPTIMUS MAXIMUS
A reconstruction.

Cicero's appeal to the emotions by a succession of mental pictures, both
pleasant and unpleasant. Study the language and figures of this
passage.

10. **huic:** demonstrative of the first person; translate accordingly.
160, a.

tēctīs, lībertātī populī Rōmānī, nostrae vītae sanguinīque imminentēs prōstrāvit, fūdit, occīdit, ut cum admodum paucīs nocte tēctus, metū perterritus prīnceps latrōnum duxque fūgerit. Ō sōlem ipsum beātissimum, quī, ante-15 quam sē abderet, strātīs cadāveribus parricīdārum cum paucīs fugientem vīdit Antōnium!

An vērō quisquam dubitābit appellāre Caesarem imperātōrem? Aetās eius certē ab hāc sententiā nēminem dēterrēbit, quandō quidem virtūte superāvit aetātem. Ac mihi 20 semper eō maiōra beneficia C. Caesaris vīsa sunt, quō minus erant ab aetāte illā postulanda; cui cum imperium dabāmus, eōdem tempore etiam spem eius nōminis dēferēbāmus; quod cum est cōnsecūtus, auctōritātem dēcrētī nostrī rēbus gestīs suīs comprobāvit. Hīc ergō adulēscēns 25 maximī animī, ut vērissimē scrībit Hīrtius, castra multārum legiōnum paucīs cohortibus tūtātus est secundumque proelium fēcit. Ita trium imperātōrum populī Rōmānī virtūte, cōnsiliō, fēlīcitāte ūnō diē locīs plūribus rēs pūblica est cōnservāta. 30

I propose a thanksgiving of fifty days in honor of these three men.

11. Dēcernō igitur eōrum trium nōmine quīnquagintā diērum supplicātiōnēs; causās, ut honōrificentissimīs verbīs cōnsequī potuerō, complectar ipsā sententiā.

---

18. **An vērō :** often used in questions to introduce an argument which refutes possible objections. Translate, ' On the other hand, is it possible that.'

21. **eō . . . quō :** degree of difference. *140.*

22. **illā :** demonstrative of the third person. *160, a.*

23. **eius nōminis :** i.e. *imperātor.*

11. 2. **ut . . . potuerō :** the highest possible degree is sometimes expressed by *ut* with some form of *possum* together with a superlative; translate, ' the reasons I shall embrace in the motion itself, employing the most honorable terms available.' *153, c.*

Est autem fideī pietātisque nostrae dēclārāre fortissimīs
5 mīlitibus, quam memorēs sīmus quamque grātī. Quam
ob rem prōmissa nostra atque ea, quae legiōnibus bellō
cōnfectō tribūtūrōs nōs spopondimus, hodiernō senātūs
cōnsultō renovanda cēnseō; aequum est enim mīlitum,
tālium praesertim, honōrem coniungī. Atque utinam,
10 patrēs cōnscrīptī, cīvibus omnibus solvere nōbīs praemia
licēret! Quamquam nōs ea, quae prōmīsimus, studiōsē
cumulāta reddēmus. Sed id quidem restat, ut spērō,
victōribus, quibus senātūs fidēs praestābitur; quam
quoniam difficillimō reī pūblicae tempore secūtī sunt, eōs
15 numquam oportēbit cōnsilī suī paenitēre.

*The valor of the soldiers — both the living and the dead — should be
duly recognized.*

Sed facile est bene agere cum iīs, ā quibus etiam tacentibus
flāgitārī vidēmur; illud admīrābilius et maius maximēque
proprium senātūs sapientis est, grātā eōrum virtūtem
memoriā prōsequī, quī prō patriā vītam profūdērunt.
20 Quōrum dē honōre utinam mihi plūra in mentem venīrent!
Duo certē nōn praeterībō, quae maximē occurrunt, quōrum
alterum pertinet ad virōrum fortissimōrum glōriam sempiternam, alterum ad lēniendum maerōrem et lūctum proxi-
mōrum.

---

4. **Est fideī :** ' It is a part of our good faith.' *Fideī* and *pietātis* are
predicate genitives of possession. *94, d.*

9. **coniungī :** ' be associated with that of the generals.'

12. **cumulāta :** ' with interest.'

13. **fidēs :** ' plighted faith.'

14. **difficillimō reī pūblicae tempore :** ' in a most difficult political
situation.' *212, i.*

15. **cōnsilī :** ' decision.'

17. **flāgitārī vidēmur :** ' our support seems to be solicited.' **illud :**
anticipates the following *prōsequī.*

20. **plūra :** ' more thoughts.' *154, a; 211.*

*I favor a public monument as a memorial to the soldiers of the
Martian legion.*

12. Placet igitur mihi, patrēs cōnscrīptī, legiōnis Mārtiae
mīlitibus et eīs, quī ūnā pugnantēs occiderint, monumentum
fierī quam amplissimum.

Magna atque incrēdibilia sunt in rem pūblicam huius
merita legiōnis. Haec sē prīma latrōciniō abrūpit Antōnī, 5

A ROMAN MONUMENT

The tomb of the Plautii near Tivoli, the hill of which is seen in the distance.
In the foreground is a bridge over the Anio.

haec tenuit Albam, haec sē ad Caesarem contulit, hanc
imitāta quārta legiō parem virtūtis glōriam cōnsecūta
est. Quārta victrīx dēsīderat nēminem; ex Mārtiā nōn
nūllī in ipsā victōriā concidērunt. Ō fortūnāta mors, quae
nātūrae dēbita prō patriā est potissimum reddita! Vōs 10

---

12. 1. **Placet mihi:** ' It is my opinion.'   The oration is concluded
with an eloquent eulogy of the dead.

2. **ūnā:** ' by their side.'

9. **in ipsā victōriā:** ' in the very midst of,' ' in the very moment of
victory.' *162, a.*

vērō patriae nātōs iūdicō, quōrum etiam nōmen ā Mārte
est, ut īdem deus urbem hanc gentibus, vōs huic urbī
genuisse videātur. In fugā foeda mors est, in victōriā
glōriōsa. Etenim Mārs ipse ex aciē fortissimum quemque
15 pigaerārī solet. Illī igitur impiī, quōs cecīdistis, etiam ad
īnferōs poenās parricīdī luent, vōs vērō, quī extrēmum
spīritum in victōriā effūdistis, piōrum estis sēdem et locum
cōnsecūtī. Brevis ā nātūrā vīta nōbīs data est, at memoria
bene redditae vītae sempiterna. Quae sī nōn esset longior
20 quam haec vīta, quis esset tam āmēns, quī maximīs labōribus
et perīculīs ad summam laudem glōriamque contenderet?

*The memory of your life, O soldiers, which you have nobly sacrificed, is
everlasting and eternal.*

Āctum igitur praeclārē vōbīscum, fortissimī, dum vīxistis,
nunc vērō etiam sānctissimī mīlitēs, quod vestra virtūs
neque oblīviōne eōrum, quī nunc sunt, nec reticentiā poste-
25 rōrum sepulta esse poterit, cum vōbīs immortāle monumentum suīs paene manibus senātus populusque Rōmānus
exstrūxerit. Multī saepe exercitūs Pūnicīs, Gallicīs, Italicīs
bellīs clārī et magnī fuērunt, nec tamen ūllīs tāle genus
honōris tribūtum est. Atque utinam maiōra possēmus,
30 quandō quidem ā vōbīs maxima accēpimus! Vōs ab urbe
furentem Antōnium āvertistis, vōs redīre mōlientem rep-

---

11. **vērō :** ' truly.'

12. **gentibus :** ' for the world.'

14. **fortissimum quemque pignerāri :** ' to claim as his pledge each
man according as he is most brave.' *quisque* with a superlative is often
used to imply a comparison. *170, a.* For the general sentiment compare the Valkyries, " choosers of the slain," handmaidens of Odin,
immortalized by Wagner in his great music-drama.

15. **ad :** ' among.'

22. **Āctum praeclārē vōbīscum :** ' You have fared splendidly.'

24. **eōrum, quī nunc sunt :** ' of the present generation.' *212, j.*

30. **Vōs :** preserve the emphasis by translating, ' It was you who.'

pulistis. Erit igitur exstrūcta mōlēs opere magnificō
incīsaeque litterae dīvīnae virtūtis testēs sempiternae,
numquamque dē vōbīs eōrum, quī aut vidēbunt vestrum
monumentum aut audient, grātissimus sermō conticēscet.₃₅
Ita prō mortālī condiciōne vītae immortālitātem estis·
cōnsecūtī.

Cicero comforts the surviving relatives, and proposes rewards.

13. Sed quoniam, patrēs cōnscrīptī, glōriae mūnus
optimīs et fortissimīs cīvibus monumentī honōre per-
solvitur, cōnsōlēmur eōrum proximōs, quibus optima est
haec quidem cōnsōlātiō, parentibus, quod tanta reī -pūbli-
cae praesidia genuērunt, līberīs, quod habēbunt domestica ₅
exempla virtūtis, coniugibus, quod iīs virīs carēbunt, quōs
laudāre quam lūgēre praestābit, frātribus, quod in sē ut
corporum, sīc virtūtis similitūdinem esse cōnfīdent. Atque
utinam hīs omnibus abstergēre flētum sententiīs nostrīs
cōnsultīsque possēmus vel aliqua tālis iīs adhibērī pūblicē ₁₀
posset ōrātiō, quā dēpōnerent maerōrem atque lūctum
gaudērentque potius, cum multa et varia impendērent
hominibus genera mortis, id genus, quod esset pulcherrimum, suīs obtigisse eōsque nec inhumātōs esse nec dēsertōs,
quod tamen ipsum prō patriā nōn miserandum putātur, ₁₅
nec dispersīs būstīs humilī sepultūrā cremātōs, sed con-

---

32. **mōlēs opere magnificō :** ' a structure of costly workmanship.'

33. **incīsaeque litterae :** ' an inscription shall be engraved.'

13. 5. **domestica exempla virtūtis :** ' models of manliness in the family.'

7. **quod . . . cōnfīdent:** ' because they will feel assured that just as they resemble them in body so they resemble them in manliness.'

10. **pūblicē :** ' by the state.'

12. **cum :** ' while,' ' whereas.'

15. **quod tamen ipsum :** ' though even this lot.' *162, a.*

16. **contēctōs pūblicīs operibus atque mūneribus :** ' entombed with ceremonies by the state.' *operibus* refers to the sepulcher, *mūneribus* to the funeral rites.

tēctōs pūblicīs operibus atque mūneribus eāque exstrūc-
tiōne, quae sit ad memoriam aeternitātis āra Virtūtis.
Quam ob rem maximum quidem sōlācium erit propin-
20 quōrum eōdem monumentō dēclārārī et virtūtem suōrum
et populī Rōmānī pietātem et senātūs fidem et crūdēlissimī
memoriam bellī; in quō nisi tanta mīlitum virtūs exstitisset,
parricīdiō M. Antōnī nōmen populī Rōmānī occidisset.

Atque etiam cēnseō, patrēs cōnscrīptī, quae praemia
25 mīlitibus prōmīsimus nōs rē pūblicā recuperātā tribūtūrōs,
ea vīvīs victōribusque cumulātē, cum tempus vēnerit,
persolvenda; quī autem ex iīs, quibus illa prōmissa sunt,
prō patriā occidērunt, eōrum parentibus, līberīs, coniugibus,
frātribus eadem tribuenda cēnseō.

*Cicero sums up his proposal in a formal motion: that a public thanks-
giving of fifty days' duration should be voted to the three generals, that
rewards promised to the soldiers should be confirmed, that a monument
should be raised for the dead, and that the appointed rewards should be
paid to the surviving relatives.*

14. Sed ut aliquandō sententiā complectar, ita cēnseō:
"Cum C. Pānsa cōnsul, imperātor, initium cum hostibus
cōnflīgendī fēcerit, quō proeliō legiō Mārtia admīrābilī
incrēdibilīque virtūte lībertātem populī Rōmānī dēfenderit,
5 quod idem legiōnēs tīrōnum fēcerint, ipseque C. Pānsa
cōnsul, imperātor, cum inter media hostium tēla versārētur,
vulnera accēperit, cumque A. Hīrtius cōnsul, imperātor,
proeliō audītō, rē cognitā, fortissimō praestantissimōque
animō exercitum castrīs ēdūxerit impetumque in M. Antō-
10 nium exercitumque hostium fēcerit eiusque cōpiās occīdiōne
occīderit suō exercitū ita incolumī, ut nē ūnum quidem
mīlitem dēsīderārit, cumque C. Caesar prō praetōre, im-

---

14. 1. **ut . . . cēnseō**: 'that I may finally sum it up in a formal
motion, I propose as follows.'
2. **Cum**: 'Whereas.' *187, a.*
8. **rē**: 'the news.'

perātor, cōnsiliō dīligentiāque suā castra fēlīciter dēfenderit cōpiāsque hostium, quae ad castra accesserant,
prōflīgārit, occīderit; ob eās rēs senātum exīstimāre et 15
iūdicāre eōrum trium imperātōrum virtūte, imperiō, cōnsiliō, gravitāte, cōnstantiā, magnitūdine animī, fēlīcitāte

TEMPLES OF THE IMMORTAL GODS

The Temple of Neptune and the Basilica at Paestum. Note the Roman
road in the foreground. In ancient times the region was healthy and famed
for its flowers; now it is malarial and deserted.

populum Rōmānum foedissimā crūdēlissimāque servitūte
līberātum. Cumque rem pūblicam, urbem, templa deōrum
immortālium, bona fortūnāsque omnium līberōsque cōn- 20
servārint dīmicātiōne et perīculō vītae suae, utī ob eās rēs

<hr>

15. **exīstimāre:** indirect discourse after *cēnseō*, line 1.

21. **vītae suae:** to be taken with both *dīmicātiōne* and *perīculō*.
utī . . . cōnstituat: depends on *cēnseō*, which is used here as a verb of
will and desire with a purpose clause (complementary final sentence),
but above (see lines 15 and 16) it governs the indirect discourse construction, because it is used as a verb of saying or thinking. Of

bene, fortiter fēlīciterque gestās C. Pānsa A. Hīrtius
cōnsulēs, imperātōres, alter ambōve, aut, sī aberunt, M.
Cornūtus, praetor urbānus, supplicātiōnēs per diēs quīn-
25 quāgintā ad omnia pulvīnāria cōnstituat.

" Cumque virtūs legiōnum digna clārissimīs imperātōrībus
exstiterit, senātum, quae sit anteā pollicitus legiōnibus
exercitibusque nostrīs, ea summō studiō, rē pūblicā recuperātā, resolūtūrum. Cumque legiō Mārtia prīnceps cum
30 hostibus cōnflīxerit atque ita cum maiōre numerō hostium
contenderit, ut, cum plūrimōs caederent, caderent nōn
nūllī, cumque sine ūllā retrāctātiōne prō patriā vītam
profūderint; cumque similī virtūte reliquārum legiōnum
mīlitēs prō salūte et lībertāte populī Rōmānī mortem
35 oppetīverint : senātuī placēre, ut C. Pānsa A. Hīrtius
cōnsulēs, imperātōrēs, alter ambōve, sī iīs videātur, iīs, quī
sanguinem prō vītā, lībertāte, fortūnīs populī Rōmānī, prō
urbe, templīs deōrum immortālium profūdissent, monumentum quam amplissimum locandum faciendumque
40 cūrent quaestōrēsque urbānōs ad eam rem pecūniam dare,
attribuere, solvere iubeant, ut exstet ad memoriam posteritātis sempiternam scelus crūdēlissimōrum hostium mīli-
tumque dīvīna virtūs, utīque, quae praemia senātus mīliti-

---

course, the English translation must correspond. *199, c.* **rēs :** ' noble
deeds.'

23. **M. Cornūtus, praetor urbānus :** the praetor took the place of the
consuls when they were absent from the city.

25. **pulvīnāria :** see page 93, line 32, and note.

27. **senātum . . . resolūtūrum :** see note to line 21 above.

31. **ut . . . nōn nūllī :** ' so that, while they slew most of them, some
fell into their hands,' *i.e.* were taken prisoners. Cicero uses *caderent*
for the more regular *incidere in manūs* in order to make the paronomasia
(see *239, q*) with *caederent* possible, thus setting the contrasted ideas in
marked opposition.

39. **locandum faciendumque cūrent :** see page 99, line 36, and note.
229, b.

bus ante cōnstituit, ea solvantur eōrum, quī hōc bellō prō
patriā occidērunt, parentibus, līberīs, coniugibus, frātribus 45
iīsque tribuantur, quae mīlitibus ipsīs tribuī oportēret, sī
vīvī vīcissent, quī morte vīcērunt."

---

44. **cōnstituit**: why in the indicative? Compare *vīcērunt* in line 47
below. *214, c;* B. 314, 3; A. & G. 583; G. 655, 2.

This glowing eulogy is a fine illustration of Cicero's ability to sway
his listeners, for the senate not only adopted the motion in detail,
but also declared Antony to be a ' *hostis.*' Cicero had reached the zenith
of his career.

Whether this was his last public utterance or whether there were
other Philippics it is impossible to decide; but two fragments, quoted
by a grammarian of the fourth century A.D., Arusianus Messius, are
assigned to a sixteenth Philippic.

CICERO THE MAN

CICERO THE MAN

M. TULLĪ CICERŌNIS
EPISTULAE SĒLĒCTAE

1. TO ATTICUS (Ad Att. 1, 2)

Written at Rome to Atticus in Athens, in July, 65 B.C.

CICERŌ ATTICŌ SAL.

A son has been born to us. I think of defending Catiline.
You will be needed here.

L. Iūliō Caesare, C. Mārciō Figulō cōnsulibus, fīliolō mē
aucium scītō, salvā Terentiā.

---

1. Cicerō Atticō sal.: the usual heading of the letters to Titus
Pomponius Atticus. **sal.:** = *salūtem;* sc. *dīcit.* For the form and
address of Roman letters see pages 558 to 560. Atticus owed his last
name to a residence of some twenty years at Athens. He was Cicero's
intimate friend, but took no part in politics. He died by voluntary
starvation because he was suffering from an incurable disease. Atticus
was a man of cultivated tastes and much learning, and was fortunate
in possessing great wealth to satisfy his love of books, for the publishing
of which he set up his own establishment. Indeed, his most important
contribution to Roman literature was his edition of Cicero's letters,
which were thus preserved to us. The years of his life are 109–32 B.C.

1. **L. Iūliō Caesare:** not the Caesar of the *Commentaries,* but a
distant relative, who voted for the death of the Catilinarian conspirators, although one of them, P. Lentulus Sura (see Selection from
Sallust, page 136), was his brother-in-law. **C. Mārciō Figulō** (gā'(y)ŭs
mär'sh(y)ŭs fig'yŭ-lŭs): he also favored the death penalty for the
conspirators. **fīliolō:** diminutive of *fīlius,* ' baby boy.'

2. **auctum:** sc. *esse.* **scītō:** this verb has no present imperative, the
future form being used regularly in its stead. Translate, ' learn,' ' be
informed.' *181, a (3).* **salvā Terentiā** (tĕ-ren'sh(y)ą), ablative absolute;
translate, 'Terentia is doing well.' For Terentia see Companion, page 494

Abs tē tam diū nihil litterārum! Ego dē meīs ad tē
ratiōnibus scrīpsī anteā dīligenter.

5 Hōc tempore Catilīnam, competītōrem nostrum, dē-

3. **Abs tē . . . litterārum:** some verb like *vēnisse* may be supplied,
'To think that no letter has come from you for so long!' Exclamatory
sentences are commonly expressed by the infinitive with the subject-
accusative. *224, c;* B. 334; A. & G. 462; G. 534. **litterārum:** partitive
genitive. Distinguish between *epistula, litterae,* and *tabellae.*

5. **Catilīnam competītōrem nostrum:** Catiline's plans for election
to the consulship had already been twice frustrated, and now he was
making his third effort.
It is not definitely known
just what charge had been
lodged against him at
this time, but it may have
been concerned either
with his conduct during
the régime of Sulla or
with extortion during his
governorship of Africa.
dēfendere cōgitāmus: although there is no proof
that Cicero ever carried

A ROMAN TOY

Such as Cicero might have given his little son.

out this intention, his mere statement has provoked much unfavorable
comment. The propriety of such a move on the part of the great orator
may be viewed as follows: Politicians have ever employed every available
means to insure their success, and the Romans were traditionally addicted
to certain practices which were readily adopted by those who aimed to
get into the limelight. Cicero, a *novus homō,* could achieve political
distinction only by the bar, and he was now playing for the highest
stake, the consular office. Impulsively, without much reflection, the
orator aims to improve his prospects by doing a rival candidate a
favor in the hope " that if he is acquitted, he will be more closely united
with me in the conduct of my campaign." Then, too, Catiline, though
a man of unsavory reputation, still had a large following among the
better class of citizens; moreover, he had not yet been declared a *hostis,*
and, publicly at least, had not yet shown his true colors. The Catiline
of the orations was still in the making. Therefore, in accordance with
the Roman viewpoint, it would not have been unprofessional for Cicero
to defend Catiline. But later, when the facts came to light, Cicero never
for a moment compromised with Catiline, the traitor.

fendere cōgitāmus. Iūdicēs habēmus, quōs voluimus,
summā accūsātōris voluntāte. Spērō, sī absolūtus erit,
coniūnctiōrem illum nōbīs fore in ratiōne petītiōnis; sīn
aliter acciderit, hūmāniter ferēmus.

Tuō adventū nōbīs opus est mātūrō; nam prōrsus summa 10
hominum est opīniō tuōs familiārēs, nōbilēs hominēs, adver-
sāriōs honōrī nostrō fore. Ad eōrum voluntātem mihi
conciliandam maximō tē mihi ūsuī fore videō. Quā rē
Iānuāriō mēnse, ut cōnstituistī, cūrā ut Rōmae sīs.

2. TO POMPEY THE GREAT (Ad Fam. 5, 7)

Written at Rome to Pompey, who was in Asia Minor; date, probably June
or July, 62 B.C.

M. TULLIUS M. F. CICERŌ S. D. CN. POMPEIŌ CN. F.

MAGNŌ IMPERĀTŌRĪ

Your official letter is gratifying, your letter to me welcome.

S. T. E. Q. V. B. E.   Ex litteris tuīs, quās pūblicē mīsistī,
cēpī ūnā cum omnibus incrēdibilem voluptātem; tantam

---

6. **Iūdicēs:** 'Jurors,' not 'judges.'
7. **summā accūsātōris voluntāte:** 'with the full approval of the
prosecutor,' P. Clodius. **absolūtus erit:** why future perfect?
10. **Tuō adventū . . . mātūrō:** 'I have need of your return —
and that, too, soon.' *132, a;* B. 218, 2; A. & G. 411; G. 406. **prōrsus
summa:** 'very strong.'
11. **nōbilēs:** 'of high birth.' Cicero was a *novus homō*, a man with
no family prestige.
12. **honōrī:** 'to my election to office.' **Ad eōrum voluntātem mihi
conciliandam:** 'to gain their good will for myself.'
13. **maximō mihi ūsuī:** *112, b;* B. 191, 2; A. & G. 382; G. 356.
14. **Iānuāriō mēnse:** because Cicero planned to begin his campaign
at that time. **ut:** what does it mean with the indicative?
2. **M. Tullius,** etc.: i.e. *Mārcus Tullius Cicerō, Mārcī fīlius,
salūtem dīcit Gnaeō Pompeiō, Gnaeī fīliō, Magnō Imperātōrī.* In less
formal correspondence forenames and titles were usually omitted.
1. **S . . . E.:** a stately greeting, appropriate to a commander with
his army: not common. See vocabulary. **litteris tuīs:** dispatches to

enim spem ōtī ostendistī, quantam ego semper omnibus,
tē ūnō frētus, pollicēbar. Sed hōc scītō, tuōs veterēs hostēs,
5 novōs amīcōs vehementer litterīs perculsōs atque ex magnā
spē dēturbātōs iacēre.

Ad mē autem litterās, quās mīsistī, quamquam exiguam
significātiōnem tuae ergā mē voluntātis habēbant, tamen
mihi scītō iūcundās fuisse; nūllā enim rē tam laetārī soleō
10 quam meōrum officiōrum cōnscientiā, quibus sī quandō nōn
mūtuē respondētur, apud mē plūs officī residēre facillimē
patior. Illud nōn dubitō, quīn, sī tē mea summa ergā tē

---

the senate announcing the finishing of the Mithridatic war. **pūblicē**:
'officially.'

3. **otī**: for *pācis*.

4. **tē ūnō**: *131, c;* B. 218, 3; A. & G. 431, *a;* G. 401, N. 6. **pollicēbar**: particularly in the speech 'On Pompey's Commission,' four years
before. See page 153. **scītō**: *Epistulae*, **1,** 2. **veterēs hostēs, novōs
amīcōs**: a reference to certain persons who were then wishing to be on
good terms with Pompey; perhaps Caesar and other members of the
popular party are meant.

5. **ex magnā spē**, etc.: because Pompey's unparalleled successes
would render him less disposed to effect a reconciliation with former
enemies, and because the finishing of the war would make it possible for
him to come back to Rome in the near future.

6. **dēturbātōs**: 'deprived of.'

7. **Ad mē litterās**: in answer to a letter of Cicero giving a full
account of his consulship and of his services to the state in the suppression of the Catilinarian conspiracy. Pompey's letter in reply was cold
and formal, containing slight evidence of any appreciation of the
orator's achievements.

10. **meōrum officiōrum**: 'of my services' to others, particularly to
you. **quibus . . . patior**: 'and if no adequate return is made to
these, I am entirely satisfied to let the balance of service rendered remain
on my side.'

12. **mea . . . studia**: 'my most enthusiastic efforts on your
behalf.' Cicero not only had urged the passing of the bill of Manilius,
giving Pompey the command under which he was still exercising
authority as *imperātor*, but had also as consul in the latter part of 63
B.C. proposed a ten days' *supplicātiō* in recognition of his public services
in the Mithridatic war.

studia parum mihi adiūnxerint, rēs pūblica nōs inter nōs conciliātūra coniūnctūraque sit.

Yet in your letter I do miss a reference to my public services.

Ac, nē ignōrēs, quid ego in tuīs litterīs dēsīderārim, scrībam apertē, sīcut et mea nātūra et nostra amīcitia postulat. Rēs eās gessī, quārum aliquam in tuīs litterīs et nostrae necessitūdinis et reī pūblicae causā grātulātiōnem exspectāvī; quam ego abs tē praetermissam esse arbitror, quod verērēre, nē cuius animum offenderēs.

Sed scītō ea, quae nōs prō salūte patriae gessimus, orbis terrae iūdiciō ac testimōniō comprobārī; quae, cum vēneris, tantō cōnsiliō tantāque animī magnitūdine ā mē gesta esse cognōscēs, ut tibi multō maiōrī, quam Āfricānus fuit, mē

13. **inter nōs :** 'to each other,' expressing reciprocal relation. *159.*

16. **postulat :** for the number see *172, b;* B. 255, 2; A. & G. 317, *c;* G. 285, 3.

17. **Rēs eās,** etc. : *i.e.* the crushing of the Catilinarian conspiracy; Cicero had supposed that Pompey would make reference to this in his dispatches to the senate.

ROMAN INKPOT, PEN, AND STILUS

20. **verērēre :** for the mood see *214, a;* B. 314, 1; A. & G. 580; G. 650. **cuius :** 'of anyone,' some of Pompey's supporters, who happened to be ill disposed toward Cicero at that time. *168.*

21. **quae :** = *et ea.* *167.*

22. **quae, cum vēneris,** etc. : 'and when you come home, you will learn that I have acted with such discretion and such nobleness of spirit that you will be well pleased that I, a man not much inferior to Laelius, have been associated with you, a man much greater than Africanus, both in politics and in friendship.'

23. **cōnsiliō :** 'discretion.'

24. **Āfricānus :** the intimacy of the younger Scipio with Laelius was proverbial; Cicero afterwards made it the text of his treatise 'On Friendship.' It is not improbable that the ex-consul had looked forward

₂₅ nōn multō minōrem quam Laelium, facile, et in rē pūblicā et in amīcitiā, adiūnctum esse patiāre.

3. TO ATTICUS (Ad Att. 1, 18)

Written at Rome to Atticus in Epirus, January 20, 60 B.C.

CICERŌ ATTICŌ SAL.

I long for you here as an intimate friend in whom I can confide; surrounded by hosts of friends, I find here no true friendship.

Nihil mihi nunc scītō tam deesse quam hominem eum, quōcum omnia, quae mē cūrā aliquā afficiunt, ūnō commūnicem; quī mē amet, quī sapiat, quīcum ego ita loquar ut nihil fingam, nihil dissimulem, nihil obtegam. Abest
⁵ enim frāter ἀφελέστατος et amantissimus. Metellus nōn homō sed

   Lītus atque āēr et sōlitūdō mera!

Tū autem, quī saepissimē cūram et angōrem animī meī sermōne et cōnsiliō levāstī tuō, quī mihi et in pūblicā rē

---

to a kind of partnership in public esteem and influence between himself and Pompey.

25. **Laelium** (lē'lǐ-ụs).

3. 1. **scītō**: 'be assured.' *181*, a (*3*). **hominem eum**: 'the sort of man.'

2. **quōcum** . . . **ūnō commūnicem**: 'with whom alone I may share.' **commūnicem, amet, sapiat, loquar**: *194*, a; B. 283; A. & G. 535; G. 631.

3. **quī sapiat**: 'a man of good sense.' **quīcum**: 'with whom,' *quī* being an old ablative; in Cicero this form is more common than *quōcum* above.

5. **ἀφελέστατος**: a Greek superlative, 'most open-hearted.' **Metellus**: Quintus Caecilius Metellus Celer, consul in 60 B.C., the date of this letter. He had rendered valuable service to Cicero in suppressing the conspiracy of Catiline.

7. **Lītus atque āēr et sōlitūdō mera**: 'Nothing but (*mera*) seashore and air and lonely wilderness.' The quotation cannot be identified.

9. **in pūblicā rē**: 'in my political life,' a common meaning.

socius et in prīvātīs omnibus cōnscius et omnium meōrum 10
sermōnum et cōnsiliōrum particeps esse solēs, ubinam es?

Ita sum ab omnibus dēstitūtus, ut tantum requiētis
habeam, quantum cum uxōre et fīliolā et mellītō Cicerōne
cōnsūmitur. Nam illae ambitiōsae nostrae fūcōsaeque
amīcitiae sunt in quōdam splendōre forēnsī, frūctum 15

A Mountain Town in Epirus

domesticum nōn habent; itaque, cum bene complēta domus
est tempore mātūtīnō, cum ad forum stīpātī gregibus amīcōrum dēscendimus, reperīre ex magnā turbā nēminem possumus, quōcum aut iocārī līberē aut suspīrāre familiāriter
possīmus. 20

11. **sermōnum et cōnsiliōrum:** *102;* B. 204, 1; A. & G. 349, *a;* G. 374.

12. **Ita:** ' So completely.' **requiētis:** partitive genitive. *97, a.*

13. **quantum:** correlative to *tantum.* **mellītō:** ' sweet little,'
' honey sweet.'

14. **ambitiōsae fūcōsaeque:** ' grand and colorful.'

15. **splendōre forēnsī:** ' public glamour.' **frūctum domesticum:**
' personal satisfaction.'

20. **possīmus:** explain the subjunctive.

Quā rē tē exspectāmus, tē dēsīderāmus, tē iam etiam arcessimus. Multa sunt enim, quae mē sollicitant anguntque, quae mihi videor aurēs nactus tuās ūnīus ambulātiōnis sermōne exhaurīre posse.

4. TO ATTICUS (Ad Att. 2, 23)

Written at Rome to Atticus in Epirus, in August or September, 59 B.C.

CICERŌ ATTICŌ SAL.

Dictated while walking. Pompey and his backers are losing ground.

Numquam ante arbitror tē epistulam meam lēgisse, nisi meā manū scrīptam. Ex eō colligere poteris, quantā occupātiōne distinear; nam, cum vacuī temporis nihil habērem, et cum recreandae vōculae causā necesse esset 5 mihi ambulāre, haec dictāvī ambulāns.

Prīmum, igitur, illud tē scīre volō, Sampsiceramum, nostrum amīcum, vehementer suī statūs paenitēre, resti-

---

23. **quae . . . posse:** ' which, I think (*mihi videor*), if I (once) gained your attention, I could unload in the conversation of a single walk.'

4. 1. **meam:** ' of mine.'

3. **cum . . . habērem:** ' as I have no leisure.' *175, g;* B. 265; A. & G. 479; G. 252.

4. **recreandae vōculae:** ' of strengthening my poor voice,' worn out with speaking in the courts.

5. **mihi:** *102;* B. 192; A. & G. 455, 1, 2; G. 535, R. 2. *mē ambulāre* would merely have expressed the necessity of the *act*, whereas *mihi ambulāre* throws the emphasis on the *person*.

6. **Sampsiceramum:** ' the Emir ' (ē-mēr' *or* ē'mer), *i.e.* Pompey. Sampsiceramus was an obscure Syrian prince, conquered by Pompey, whose boastful references to eastern victories led to the application of several sonorous Oriental names to himself. Cicero calls him also *Arabarches,* ' the Sheikh ' (*Ad Atticum,* **2,** 17, 3), and *Hierosolymārius,* ' the Jerusalemite ' (*Ad Atticum,* **2,** 9, 1).

7. **suī statūs paenitēre:** ' is dissatisfied with his position,' *i.e.* his relation with Caesar and Crassus, and his loss of popularity.

tuīque in eum locum cupere, ex quō dēcidit, dolōremque
suum impertīre nōbīs et medicīnam interdum apertē
quaerere, quam ego posse invenīre nūllam putō; deinde, 10
omnēs illīus partis auctōrēs ac sociōs, nūllō adversāriō, cōn-
senēscere; cōnsēnsiōnem ūniversōrum nec voluntātis nec
sermōnis maiōrem umquam fuisse.

I am busy with legal practice but the brother of 'Cow-eyes' is threatening.
Do hurry up and come.

Nōs autem — nam id tē scīre cupere certō sciō — pūblicīs
cōnsiliīs nūllīs intersumus, tōtōsque nōs ad forēnsem 15
operam labōremque contulimus; ex quō, quod facile intellegī
possit, in multā commemorātiōne eārum rērum, quās gessimus, dēsīderiōque versāmur. Sed βοώπιδος nostrae cōnsanguineus nōn mediocrēs terrōrēs iacit atque dēnūntiat,
et Sampsiceramō negat, cēterīs prae sē fert et ostentat. 20

Quam ob rem, sī mē amās tantum, quantum profectō
amās — sī dormīs, expergīscere; sī stās, ingredere; sī

---

10. **deinde:** ' in the second place,' corresponding to *prīmum* above.

11. **illīus partis:** the party of the triumvirate, which Cicero represents as losing all influence, with no one to come to the rescue. In this
he did not read aright the signs of the times, and was sadly mistaken.
nūllō adversāriō: ablative absolute, ' although no one opposes them.'
141, b (5).

13. **maiōrem:** ' greater ' against any party.

14. **Nōs autem:** 'As for me.'

15. **tōtōs nōs:** ' myself wholly.' **forēnsem operam:** ' law practice.'

17. **in . . . versāmur:** freely, ' I live amid frequent recounting of
my former deeds, and am aware of a sense of loss ' which others feel.
eārum rērum, quās gessimus: ' of my past achievements.'

18. **βοώπιδος nostrae:** ' of our dear Cow-eyes '; ironical reference to
Clodia, sister of Cicero's bitter enemy Clodius. The Greek word is
appropriated from Homer, who applies it to Juno. **cōnsanguineus:**
Clodius.

19. **terrōrēs:** ' threats ' against me.

20. **Sampsiceramō . . . ostentat:** ' he denies (all hostile intentions
regarding me) to the Emir, (but) he makes open assertion of them
and displays them to others.'

ingrederis, curre; sī curris, advolā. Crēdibile nōn est, quantum ego in cōnsiliīs et prūdentiā tuā, quodque maxi-
25 mum est, quantum in amōre et fidē, pōnam.

Magnitūdō reī longam ōrātiōnem fortasse dēsīderat, coniūnctiō vērō nostrōrum animōrum brevitāte contenta est. Permagnī nostrā interest tē, sī comitiīs nōn potueris, at, dēclārātō illō, esse Rōmae.
30 Cūrā, ut valeās.

5. TO ATTICUS (Ad Att. 3, 3)
Written at Vibo to Atticus in Rome, in April, 58 B.C.

CICERŌ ATTICŌ SAL.

I am sorry that you forced me to continue to live. Do come to Vibo at once.

Utinam illum diem videam, cum tibi agam grātiās, quod mē vīvere coēgistī! Adhūc quidem valdē mē paenitet.

---

24. **in . . . pōnam:** 'I rely on.'

28. **Permagnī nostrā interest:** 'It is of very great importance to me.' *103, e;* B. 210; 211, 1, *a*, 3, *a;* A. & G. 355, *a;* G. 381. **comitiīs:** for the election of tribunes for 58. **potueris:** sc. *esse Rōmae.*

29. **dēclārātō illō:** 'when he (*i.e.* Clodius) is declared elected'; for Cicero looks upon the election of Clodius as settled. The tribunes were chosen in July, but did not qualify till the following December.

Letters 4, 5, 7, and 8 were written by Cicero during his banishment, which extended from April, 58 B.C., to September, 57 B.C. The immediate cause of his exile was a bill brought in by Clodius, Cicero's deadly enemy, to the effect that fire and water be forbidden to Cicero, the usual formula for punishment by exile. Another bill had preceded this, forbidding fire and water to any man who had put a Roman citizen to death without due course of law. The indirect cause of Cicero's banishment, therefore, was the execution of the Catilinarian conspirators. It is interesting to note that while Caesar condemned Cicero's conduct in executing the conspirators as illegal, he was opposed to Clodius's plan for the punishment of Cicero by exile.

During this period Cicero wrote several letters to Atticus and to his family which give us a fine insight into the human qualities of the great orator.

5. 1. **Utinam . . . videam:** 'May I live to see.' *180, c;* B. 279, 1; A. & G. 441; G. 261. Cicero had fled from Rome, and was on his **way**

Sed tē ōrō, ut ad mē Vibōnem statim veniās, quō ego
multīs dē causīs convertī iter meum.   Sed eō sī vēneris, dē
tōtō itinere ac fugā meā cōnsilium capere poterō. Sī id ₅
nōn fēceris, mīrābor, — sed cōnfīdō tē esse factūrum.

6. TO ATTICUS (Ad Att. 3, 4)

Written on the way from Vibo to Brundisium about April 13, 58 B.C.

CICERŌ ATTICŌ SAL.

The terms of the bill aimed at my destruction obliged me to move on.

Miseriae nostrae potius velim quam incōnstantiae
tribuās, quod ā Vibōne, quō tē arcessēbāmus, subitō dis-
cessimus.   Allāta est enim nōbīs rogātiō dē perniciē meā,
in quā quod corrēctum esse audierāmus, erat eius modī, ut
mihi ultrā quadringenta mīlia licēret esse.   Illō cum per- ₅
venīre nōn licēret, statim iter Brundisium versus contulī ante

---

into exile.   He writes as if only the exhortation of Atticus had kept
him from making away with himself.

3. **Vibōnem** (vī'bō).

4. **multīs dē causīs**: his friend Sicca would entertain him at Vibo,
from which he thought of crossing over into Sicily.

5. **fugā**: ' exile.'

6. 1. **velim . . . tribuās**: ' I should like you to attribute.' *200, c;*
B. 280, 2, *a;* A. & G. 442, *b;* G. 546, 2. **incōnstantiae**: ' fickleness.'

2. **ā Vibōne**: for the preposition see *130, b;* B. 229, 2; A. & G.
428, *a;* G. 391, R.

3. **rogātiō**: the second bill sponsored by Clodius.   See note above.

4. **quod corrēctum esse audierāmus**: ' the amendment, as I had
heard it.'   How literally?   The antecedent of *quod* is *id* understood,
which is also the subject of *erat*.

5. **Illō**: adverb ' to that place,' probably Vibo.

6. **Brundisium versus** (brŭn-dizh'(y)ŭm): ' towards Brundisium.'
versus means, literally, ' turned towards.' *238, b.* **ante diem rogātiōnis**:
' before the passage of the bill.'

diem rogātiōnis, nē et Sicca, apud quem eram, perīret, et quod Melitae esse nōn licēbat.

Nunc tū properā, ut nōs cōnsequāre, sī modo recipiēmur; 10 adhūc invitāmur benignē, sed, quod superest, timēmus.

Mē, mī Pompōnī, valdē paenitet vīvere, quā in rē apud mē tū plūrimum valuistī. Sed haec cōram; fac modo, ut veniās.

7. TO ATTICUS (Ad Att. 3, 26)

Written at Dyrrachium to Atticus, who was probably in Epirus, in January 57 B.C.

CICERŌ ATTICŌ SAL.

I have the resolution about my recall; I await further action.

Litterae mihi ā Q. frātre cum senātūs cōnsultō, quod dē mē est factum, allātae sunt.

Mihi in animō est lēgum lātiōnem exspectāre; et, sī obtrectābitur, ūtar auctōritāte senātūs et potius vītā quam 5 patriā carēbō.

Tū, quaesō, festīnā ad nōs venīre.

---

7. **nē et Sicca perīret:** the bill of Clodius contained a provision making it unlawful for any person to harbor Cicero within the four-hundred-mile limit.

8. **quod Melitae** (mel′i-tạ) **esse nōn licēbat:** why not? See vocabulary. This island was a favorite resort for exiles.

9. **sī modo recipiēmur:** in Epirus, where Atticus was residing.

10. **quod superest:** ' the future.'

12. **haec cōram:** sc. some verb like *dīcēmus.*

7. 1. **senātūs cōnsultō:** a resolution for Cicero's recall was introduced into the senate on January 1, 57 B.C., but it did not pass till August 5 because of the violent opposition of Clodius.

2. **est factum:** ' was passed '; the senate decreed that Cicero had been banished illegally.

3. **lēgum lātiōnem:** ' the presentation of the bill,' for the vote of the people, without which the legislation would be invalid.

4. **vītā carēbō:** Cicero has made up his mind to return at any cost.

8. TO ATTICUS (Ad Att. 3, 27)

Written at Dyrrachium to Atticus, who seems now to be in Rome; date, end of January, 57 B.C.

CICERŌ ATTICŌ SAL.

I am irretrievably ruined; safeguard my family.

Ex tuīs litterīs et ex rē ipsā nōs funditus perīsse videō. Tē ōrō, ut, quibus in rēbus tuī meī indigēbunt, nostrīs miseriīs nē dēsīs. Ego tē, ut scrībis, cito vidēbō.

9. TO ATTICUS (Ad Att. 4, 4b)

Written at Antium, where Cicero had a villa, to Atticus, who was returning from Epirus and was already in Italy on his way to Rome; April or May, 56 B.C.

CICERŌ ATTICŌ SAL.

Please send me a couple of library slaves to help Tyrannio in my library; be sure to come yourself, and bring Pilia along also.

Perbellē fēceris, sī ad nōs vēneris. Offendēs dēsignā-tiōnem Tyranniōnis mīrificam in librōrum meōrum biblio-thēca, quōrum reliquiae multō meliōrēs sunt, quam putāram. Et velim mihi mittās dē tuīs librāriolīs duōs aliquōs,

---

8. 1. **ex rē ipsā:** 'from the actual fact.' *162, a.* Atticus had reported to Cicero that the popular assembly, which had met on January 25 to decide on Cicero's recall, had been broken up by the rowdyism of Clodius and his band of slaves and gladiators. It was this report which led Cicero to exclaim *nōs funditus perīsse videō.*

2. **tuī:** genitive with *indigēbunt; meī,* 'my family,' is the subject. ɪ27, *d;* B. 212, 1, *a;* A. & G. 356, N.; G. 383, 1.

9. 1. **Perbellē fēceris:** 'You will perform a gracious act.' **Of-fendēs:** 'You will find.'

2. **Tyranniōnis:** Tyrannio (tị-ran'ị-ō) was a Greek grammarian, who had come to Rome as a slave, in 72 B.C., but was later manumitted. He was both a teacher and a librarian.

4. **dē tuīs librāriolīs duōs aliquōs:** 'any two of your library slaves.' Atticus not only was a writer and a scholar, but also conducted a publishing business. See page 361, introductory note.

₅quibus Tyranniō ūtātur glūtinātōribus, ad cētera administrīs, eīsque imperēs, ut sūmant membrānulam, ex quā
indicēs fīant, quōs vōs Graecī, ut opīnor, σιλλύβους appellātis.
Sed haec, sī tibi erit commodum. Ipse vērō utique fac
veniās, sī potes in hīs locīs adhaerēscere, et Piliam ad-
₁₀dūcere; ita enim et aequum est, et cupit Tullia.

AN AMPHITHEATER IN TUNISIA
Gladiatorial games were held here.

---

5. **glūtinātōribus**: we should say, 'bookbinders.' The *glūtinātōres*
glued together the papyrus strips to make separate leaves, which in turn
were glued together at the sides, and finally rolled around a stick called
umbilīcus. The book was kept tightly rolled up, hence the name
volūmen. See description, page 559, and illustrations, page 558. **ad
cētera administrīs**: ' as general assistants.'

6. **membrānulam**: 'small pieces of parchment.'

7. **indicēs**: 'labels for titles.' **σιλλύβους**: accusative plural of the
Greek word for Latin *titulōs* or *indicēs*.

8. **utique**: 'at any rate.'

9. **veniās**: *200, a;* B. 295, 5, 8; A. & G. 565; G. 271. **potes in
hīs locīs adhaerēscere**: implying that Atticus might find suburban life
somewhat tedious. **Piliam** (pil′ĭ-ạ): the wife of Atticus, who had just
been married in February.

Mē dīus Fidius, nē tū ēmistī λόχον praeclārum! gla-
diātōrēs audiō pugnāre mīrificē. Sī locāre voluissēs, duōbus
hīs mūneribus līberāssēs.

Sed haec posterius. Tū fac veniās, et dē librāriīs, sī mē
amās, dīligenter. 15

10. TO TREBATIUS TESTA (Ad Fam. 7, 7)

Written in Rome to Trebatius Testa, who was with Julius Caesar in Gaul;
dated probably in May, 54 B.C., some months before Caesar's First
Expedition to Britain.

CICERŌ TREBĀTIŌ

*I am recommending you. Whether you accomplish anything in Britain
or not, get next to Caesar. It is up to you to make good.*

Ego tē commendāre nōn dēsistō ; sed, quid prōficiam, ex
tē scīre cupiō. Spem maximam habeō in Balbō, ad quem

---

11. **Mē dīus Fidius :** sc. *adiuvet;* an asseveration, ' My gracious,'
' On my faith.' **nē :** an interjection, ' really.' **λόχον :** accusative
singular of the Greek word meaning ' troop,' *i.e.* of gladiators. Well-to-
do Romans sometimes made a business of buying and training gladiators, renting and selling them for the forthcoming games.

12. **pugnāre :** while in training. See illustration, page 131. **locāre :**
' to let them out.' **duōbus hīs mūneribus līberāssēs :** ' you would
have cleared your expenses (*liberāsses,* sc. *tē*) on the two shows recently
held (*hīs*).'

13. **mūneribus :** *mūnus* was the term for a public show, especially
a gladiatorial exhibition, which was given to the people by the magistrates, usually by the aediles.

15. **dīligenter :** a suitable verb is easily supplied.

10. C. TREBATIUS TESTA (gā'(y)ụs trẹ-bā'sh(y)ụs tes'tạ) was an
eminent jurist, a friend of Cicero and Caesar. His writings on legal
subjects have perished. The poet Horace addressed one of his satires
(**2,** 1) to him, and Cicero dedicated his *Topica* to the same man. Cicero
had recommended Trebatius to Caesar during his governorship of Gaul,
but Trebatius had little taste for camp life, and Caesar's reception of
him seemed to have been none too enthusiastic. Trebatius was constantly complaining that his friends failed to recommend him warmly
enough, while Cicero tries to encourage him.

2. **in Balbō :** L. Cornelius Balbus (lụ'sh(y)ụs kọr-nē'lyụs bal'bụs}

dē tē dīligentissimē et saepissimē scrībō.   Illud soleō mīrārī, nōn mē totiēns accipere tuās litterās, quotiēns ā Quīntō mihi
5 frātre afferuntur.

In Britanniā nihil esse audiō neque aurī neque argentī. Id sī ita est, essedum aliquod capiās, suādeō, et ad nōs quam prīmum recurrās.

A ROMAN VILLA

This was the type common in Britain, France, Germany, and Belgium.

who, though a native of Gades, received Roman citizenship. He ingratiated himself into Caesar's favor, and during the Gallic campaign was one of his most intimate friends.   On this occasion Cicero seems to enlist his support for Trebatius because of his great influence with Caesar.

3. **Illud:** ' Only this.'

4. **Quīntō:** Cicero's brother Quintus was serving as lieutenant under Caesar in Gaul at this time.   See Caesar's well-known account of his bravery, *Dē Bellō Gallicō,* **5,** 38-42.

6. **In Britanniā:** probably Trebatius was intending soon to go to Britain with Caesar's army; see Caesar, *Dē Bellō Gallicō,* **4,** 20–36. **nihil neque aurī neque argentī:** the Romans believed Britain to be a land of plenty, and Caesar's attempts to subjugate it were no doubt inspired by this belief.   However, these precious metals were actually found there later, as Tacitus (*Agricola,* 12) tells us.

7. **essedum . . . suādeō:** ' seize some chariot, is my advice.' **essedum:** humorous, for this is the only kind of plunder to be found there.   **capiās, recurrās:** *200, a;* B. 295, 8; A. & G. 565, *a;* G. 546, 2.

Sīn autem sine Britanniā tamen assequī, quod volumus, possumus, perfice, ut sīs in familiāribus Caesaris. Multum te in eō frāter adiuvābit meus, multum Balbus, sed, mihi crēde, tuus pudor et labor plūrimum. Imperātōrem līberālissimum, aetātem opportūnissimam, commendātiōnem certē singulārem habēs, ut tibi ūnum timendum sit, nē ipse tibi dēfuisse videāre.

11. TO HIS BROTHER QUINTUS (Ad Q. Fr. 3, 8)

Written in Rome to Quintus Cicero, who was in winter quarters in the country of the Nervii, in Gaul (line 26); dated near the end of November, 54 B.C., before Quintus Cicero's heroic defense of his camp (*Gallic War*, 5, 38–45), or in any case before news of the uprising in Belgic Gaul had reached Rome.

MĀRCUS QUĪNTŌ FRĀTRĪ SALŪTEM

Do not allow yourself to be irritated by untoward conditions in Gaul; rather recall the object for which you are serving under Caesar: what we sought was security for maintaining our political position by winning Caesar's protection for the future.

Superiōrī epistulae quod respondeam, nihil est, quae plēna stomachī et querellārum est, quō in genere alteram quoque tē scrībis prīdiē Labiēnō dedisse, quī adhūc nōn vēnerat.

Dēlēvit enim mihi omnem molestiam recentior epistula. Tantum tē et moneō et rogō, ut in istīs molestiīs et labōribus et dēsīderiīs recordēre, cōnsilium nostrum quod fuerit pro-

---

10. **in familiāribus :** ' among the intimates.'

12. **pudor :.** ' modesty.' His conceit is referred to by Cicero in another letter.

13. **aetātem :** Trebatius was now thirty-five years old.

11. 3. **Labiēnō :** Caesar's lieutenant in Gaul, who later, in the Civil War, joined Pompey and was killed in the battle of Munda, 45 B.C.

5. **molestiam :** ' vexation.'

7. **profectiōnis tuae :** to Caesar's camp.

fectiōnis tuae; nōn enim commoda quaedam sequēbāmur parva ac mediocria. Quid enim erat quod discessū nostrō
10 emendum putārēmus? Praesidium fīrmissimum petēbāmus, ex optimī et potentissimī virī benevolentiā, ad omnem statum nostrae dignitātis. Plūra pōnuntur in spē quam in pecūniīs; reliqua ad iactūram struentur.

Quā rē sī crēbrō referēs animum tuum ad ratiōnem et
15 veteris cōnsilī nostrī et speī, facilius istōs mīlitiae labōrēs cēteraque, quae tē offendunt, ferēs; et tamen, cum volēs, dēpōnēs. Sed eius reī mātūritās nequedum vēnit, et tamen iam appropinquat.

Etiam illud tē admoneō, nē quid ūllīs litterīs committās,
20 quod, sī prōlātum sit, molestē ferāmus; multa sunt, quae ego nescīre mālō quam cum aliquō perīculō fierī certior.

Plūra ad tē vacuō animō scrībam, cum, ut spērō, sē Cicerō meus bellē habēbit. Tū velim cūrēs, ut sciam, quibus nōs dare oporteat eās, quās ad tē deinde litterās mittēmus,
25 Caesarisne tabellāriīs, ut is ad tē prōtinus mittat, an Labiēnī; ubi enim istī sint Nerviī, et quam longē absint, nesciō.

---

10. **emendum:** ' worth the cost.' **putārēmus:** *194, a;* B. 283, 2; A. & G. 535, *a;* G. 631. **Praesidium:** ' Security.'

11. **ad omnem statum nostrae dignitātis:** ' to preserve the integrity of our official position.'

12. **Plūra . . . struentur:** ' More depends on hope than on riches; all other (treasures) are heaped up to be thrown away.' Cicero means that Quintus should not fret over any immediate material rewards to be gained from his present connection with Caesar, but should constantly keep before him his own ambition and future prospects.

14. **ratiōnem:** ' the motive.'

17. **eius reī mātūritās:** ' the right moment for this course.' **nequedum:** = *necdum.*

22. **vacuō:** ' free from care.' **Cicerō meus:** ' my boy Cicero.'

23. **bellē habēbit:** ' will be in good health.' **cūrēs:** *200, c.*

26. **istī Nerviī:** ' those Nervii of yours.' *160. a.*

Dē virtūte et gravitāte Caesaris, quam in summō dolōre adhibuisset, magnam ex epistulā tuā accēpī voluptātem.

Quod mē īnstitūtum ad illum poēma iubēs perficere, etsī 30 distentus cum operā, tum animō sum multō magis, tamen,

quoniam ex epistulā, quam ad tē mīseram, cognōvit Caesar, mē aliquid esse exōrsum, revertar ad īnstitūtum, idque perficiam 35 hīs supplicātiōnum ōtiōsis diēbus, quibus Messallam iam

A COIN OF THE NERVII

nostrum reliquōsque molestiā levātōs vehementer gaudeō; eumque quod certum cōnsulem cum Domitiō numerātis, nihil ā nostrā opīniōne dissentītis. 40

The general political situation is bad; a rumor persists that Pompey is to be appointed dictator. Milo and Pompey are estranged.

Ego Messallam Caesarī praestābō. Sed Memmius in adventū Caesaris habet spem, in quō illum putō errāre; hīc

---

28. **gravitāte:** 'dignity.' **in summō dolōre:** Julia, Caesar's beautiful and talented daughter and the wife of Pompey, had recently died in September.

29. **adhibuisset:** 'he exhibited (as you say).' Why subjunctive?

30. **poēma:** in a subsequent letter (*Ad Quīntum Frātrem*, **3,** 9) we are told that Cicero actually finished a poem in honor of Caesar. The loss of Cicero's poems need not disturb us, however.

31. **cum . . . tum:** 'not only . . . but also.' **animō:** 'feelings.'

36. **hīs supplicātiōnum ōtiōsīs diēbus:** decreed in honor of Caesar's success of 55 B.C.; judicial and political business was suspended at this time.

37. **Messallam:** M. Valerius Messalla, consul in 53 B.C.

39. **Domitiō:** Cn. Domitius Calvinus, elected consul in 53 B.C. In the Civil War he fought for Caesar.

41. **Messallam Caesarī praestābō:** 'I shall guarantee Messal'la to Caesar,' *i.e.* his conduct. **Mem'mius:** a tribune of this year; he hopes to win Caesar's support at the election.

42. **hīc quidem frīget:** 'here, at least, (Memmius) is coldly received.'

quidem frīget. Scaurum autem iam prīdem Pompeius
abiēcit.
45 Rēs prōlātae; ad interrēgnum comitia adducta. Rūmor
dictātōris iniūcundus bonīs — mihi etiam magis, quae
loquuntur. Sed tōta rēs et timētur et refrīgēscit. Pompeius plānē se
negat velle; anteā mihi ipse nōn negābat. Hirrus auctor
50 fore vidētur — Ō dī, quam ineptus! quam sē ipse amāns
sine rīvālī! Caelium Viniciānum, hominem mihi dēditum,
per mē dēterruit: velit, nōlit, scīre difficile est. Hirrō
tamen agente, nōlle sē nōn probābit. Aliud hōc tempore dē
rē pūblicā nihil loquēbantur; agēbātur quidem certē nihil.

43. **Scaurum . . . abiēcit**: 'Scaurus (skȧ'rŭs), on the other hand,
a long time ago was thrown down by Pompey.' He had been praetor
in 56 B.C., but his attempts to win the consulship this year (54 B.C.)
were frustrated by his competitors, who charged him with extortion
in Sardinia. His defense was carried on by six prominent Romans,
among them Hortensius and Cicero, whose oration *Prō Scaurō* is extant.
His acquittal was due in large measure to Cicero's skill. As aedile
Scaurus is especially remembered for the lavish splendor with which
he celebrated the public games. During his trial Pompey testified in
his favor by a deposition in writing.
45. **Rēs prōlātae** (sc. *sunt*) : ' The elections have been put off.'
46. **bonīs** : = *optimātibus.*
48. **rēs** : ' proposal.'
49. **Hirrus** : tribune in 53 B.C. He continued as a partisan of
Pompey in the Civil War. **auctor** : ' the leader,' in the movement to
make Pompey dictator.
51. **Caelium Viniciānum** (sē'lĭ-ŭs vĭn-ĭ-sh(y)-ā'nŭs) : tribune of
53 B.C. In the Civil War he espoused the cause of Caesar.
52. **dēterruit** : ' he (Pompey) discouraged,' *i.e.* prevented him from
moving for his dictatorship. **velit, nōlit, scīre difficile est** : ' it is difficult to tell whether he (Pompey) wishes it or not.' **Hirrō agente** :
' If it is Hirrus who proposes the dictatorship.' *144, b (4).*
53. **nōn probābit** : ' he will not convince (the people).' **Aliud . . .
loquēbantur** : ' There is no other political (*dē rē pūblicā*) gossip at this
time.' *212, i.*
54. **loquēbantur, agēbātur** : epistolary imperfects. *175, g;* B. 265;
A. & G. *479;* G. *252.*

Serrānī Domesticī fīlī fūnus perlūctuōsum fuit a.d. VIII. 55
Kalend. Decembr. Laudāvit pater scrīptō meō.

Nunc dē Milōne. Pompeius eī nihil tribuit, et omnia
Cottae dīcitque sē perfectūrum, ut illō Caesar incumbat;
hōc horret Milō, nec iniūriā, et, sī ille dictātor factus sit,
paene diffīdit. Intercessōrem dictātūrae sī iūverit manū 60
et praesidiō suō, Pompeium metuit inimīcum; sī nōn
iūverit, timet nē per vim perferātur. Lūdōs apparat mag-
nificentissimōs; sīc, inquam, ut nēmō sumptuōsiōrēs —
stultē bis terque, nōn postulātōs, vel quia mūnus magnificum dederat, vel quia facultātēs nōn erant, vel quia potuerat 65
magistrum sē, nōn aedīlem, putāre. Omnia ferē scrīpsī.

Cūrā, mī cārissime frāter, ut valeās.

---

55. **Serrānī Domesticī** (sẹ-rā′nụs dọ-mẹs′tǐ-kus): his identity has
not been established. **a.d. VIII Kalend. Decembr.:** review the rules
for turning Roman dates into English: *241;* B. 371; A. & G. 631; G.
pages 491–492.

56. **Laudāvit scrīptō meō:** ' Delivered the funeral oration in a
speech composed by me.'

57. **Milōne:** Titus Annius Milo Papinianus (tī′tụs an′ǐ-ụs mī′lō pạ-pǐ-
nǐ-ā′nụs), tribune in 57 B.C., the enemy of Clodius and friend of Cicero.
Both Milo and Clodius had large bands of gladiators, whom they
pressed into service when they were campaigning for office in 53 B.C.,
Milo for the consulship and Clodius for the praetorship. Frequent
combats took place between their bands, which reached a climax in
52 B.C. when Clodius was slain. In the ensuing trial Milo was defended
by Cicero (see the oration *Prō Milōne*), but was condemned and went
into exile at Marseilles. **eī nihil tribuit:** ' gives him no preference.'

58. **Cottae:** probably M. Aurelius Cotta, who according to both
Caesar (*Dē Bellō Gallicō*, **1,** 30) and Cicero (*Ad Atticum*, **10,** 16) held Sardinia
for Pompey in the Civil War. He may have had aspirations for the
consulship at this time. **illō:** adverb, ' thither,' ' in that direction.'

60. **Intercessōrem dictātūrae:** ' (the tribune) who vetoes the
dictatorship.' **manū:** ' band.'

62. **Lūdōs:** these were funeral games which Milo as executor gave in
honor of a friend.

64. **mūnus magnificum:** ' a grand spectacle.' See page 375, note 11.

66. **non aedīlem:** an aedile was expected to give great spectacles,
but not an executor, especially if he was a man of limited means.

12. TO ATTICUS (Ad Att. 5, 16)

Written in Asia Minor, on the road between Synnada and Philomelium,
in the second week of August, 51 B.C.

CICERŌ ATTICŌ SAL.

I entered my province July 31. I find it ruined by extortion.

Etsī in ipsō itinere et viā discēdēbant pūblicānōrum tabellāriī et erāmus in cursū, tamen surripiendum aliquid putāvī
spatī, nē mē immemorem mandātī tuī putārēs; itaque
subsēdī in ipsā viā, dum haec, quae longiōrem dēsīderant
5 ōrātiōnem, summātim tibi perscrīberem.

Maximā exspectātiōne in perditam, et plānē ēversam in

---

12. In consequence of a law sponsored by Pompey, the senate
decreed that properly qualified ex-magistrates, who had not yet governed a province, should assume this responsibility, and so Cicero
obtained Cilicia by lot.   He seemed to look upon this appointment as
somewhat of a hardship, and regarded it as an annoying interruption of
his life.   He reached his province late in July of this year, and found
it practically ruined by the rapacious methods employed by his prede-
cessor, Appius Claudius, brother of Cicero's deadly enemy, P. Clodius.
The letter is most illuminating in portraying a vivid picture of the
practices of Roman governors in replenishing a worn-out pocketbook
'full of cobwebs,' as Catullus humorously suggests.

1. **in ipsō itinere et viā:** 'on their journey and actually (*ipsō*) on
the road.'   For the meaning of *ipsō* see *162, a.*   **discēdēbant . . . erāmus:**
remember that these are epistolary tenses, for which we use the present
in English.   See note on page 380, line 54.   **pūblicānōrum tabellāriī:**
'the letter-carriers of the tax-gatherers.'   On their way to Rome they
carried some of Cicero's letters as an accommodation.   He might have
used his own official carriers, called *statōrēs.*   The *tabellāriī* averaged from
forty to fifty miles a day.

2. **erāmus in cursū:** 'I am *en route.*'

3. **mandātī tuī:** *i.e.* to write often.

4. **in ipsā viā:** 'right on the highway.'   *162, a.*   See *in ipsō itinere*
above.   **dum . . . perscrīberem:** the purpose here expressed may be
translated by the infinitive.   *190, b;* B. 293, III, 2; A. & G. 553;
G. 572.

perpetuum, prōvinciam nōs vēnisse scītō prīdiē Kal. Sextīlēs,
morātōs trīduum Lāodicēae, triduum Apamēae totidem diēs
Synnade. Audīvimus nihil aliud nisi imperāta ἐπικεφάλια
solvere nōn posse, ὠνὰς omnium vēnditās, cīvitātum gemitūs, 10
plōrātūs — mōnstra quaedam nōn hominis, sed ferae nesciō
cuius immānis. Quid quaeris? taedet omnīnō eōs vītae.

*I permit no levies upon the wretched towns, not even for the things authorized
by law. My coming inspires new hope.*

Levantur tamen miserae cīvitātēs, quod nūllus fit sūmptus
in nōs neque in lēgātōs neque in quaestōrem neque in quem-

VIEW FROM ICONIUM
In Cicero's province.

7. **nōs**: Cicero is quite fond of the so-called "editorial we."
prīdiē Kal. Sextīlēs: *Sextīlis* (sc. *mēnsis*) was the sixth month (August),
counting from March, with which the old Roman year began; therefore
this date is July 31. Not till 153 B.C. did the consular year begin with
January 1, whereas *Sextīlis* was not changed to *Augustus* till 8 B.C.

8. **Lāodicē′ae, Apamē′ae, Syn′nade**: in Phrygia; see Map.

9. **imperāta ἐπικεφάλια**: 'the required head tax'; a poll tax on
servants and houses. ἐπικεφάλια is neuter plural, object of *solvere*.

10. **solvere nōn posse**: 'the inability (of the people) to pay.' **ὠνὰς
omnium**: 'the holdings of everyone.' ὠνὰς is feminine accusative
plural, subject of *vēnditās* (*esse*).

11. **mōnstra . . . immānis**: 'the barbarities, if I may say so
(*quaedam*), not of a human being, but of some monstrous creature.'
quaedam is here used to soften the metaphor suggested by *mōnstra*.

12. **Quid quaeris**: an idiomatic expression meaning 'in short,' 'in
a word.'

15 quam. Scītō nōn modo nōs faenum aut quod lēge Iūliā darī
solet nōn accipere, sed nē ligna quidem, nec praeter quattuor
lectōs et tēctum quemquam accipere quicquam, multīs locīs
nē tēctum quidem, et in tabernāculō manēre plērumque.

Itaque incrēdibilem in modum concursūs fīunt ex agrīs,
20 ex vīcīs, ex oppidīs omnibus. Mē hercule iam adventū
nostrō revīvīscunt; iūstitia, abstinentia, clēmentia tuī
Cicerōnis opīniōnēs omnium superāvit.

*Appius, hearing of my arrival, went off to Tarsus. No authentic news
about the Parthians. I am hastening to the camp, two days distant.*

Appius, ut audīvit nōs venīre, in ultimam prōvinciam sē
coniēcit Tarsum ūsque; ibi forum agit.

25 Dē Parthō silentium est, sed tamen concīsōs equitēs
nostrōs ā barbarīs nūntiābant eī, quī veniēbant.

Bibulus nē cōgitābat quidem etiam nunc in prōvinciam

---

15. **faenum :** ' hay.'   The *lēx Iūlia* was passed by Caesar in 59 B.C.,
and was directed against extortionate practices in the provinces; it
confined the supplies which the governor could exact to fixed quantities
of corn, hay, wood, and salt, and also restated certain other restrictions
found in former laws.

18. **et :** after a negative best translated by ' but.'   *234, b.*

19. **in modum :** = *ad modum.*   **concursūs fīunt :** ' throngs of people
are gathering.'

20. **Mē hercule :** sc. *adiuvet*, and see page 375, line 11, note.

22. **opīniōnēs :** ' the suspicions.'

23. **Appius :** see introductory note, page 382.

24. **forum agit :** ' he is holding assize,' *i.e.* he is holding court,
although he no longer had any right to do so after Cicero's arrival.

25. **Dē Parthō :** = *Dē Parthīs.*   After the memorable destruction
of Crassus and his army at Carrhae in 53 B.C. the Parthians continued
to be a source of anxiety to the Romans for many years.

26. **nūntiābant, veniēbant :** epistolary imperfects, as also the
others below.   *175, g.*

27. **Bibulus :** he was appointed proconsul of Syria in this same
year, but aimed to put off the end of his governorship by delaying his
entry.   He was consul with Caesar in 59 B.C., and his name was so
eclipsed by the genius of his colleague that it became a sort of standing
joke to write not *Caesare et Bibulō*, but *Iūliō et Caesare cōnsulibus āctum.*

ʒuam accēdere; id autem facere ob eam causam dīcēbant, quod tardius vellet dēcēdere.

Nōs in castra properābāmus, quae aberant bīduī. **30**

THE SITE OF TARSUS
Cicero's administrative office was probably here.

13. CICERO AND HIS SON MARCUS TO TIRO
(Ad Fam. 16, 7)

Written on the island of Corfu to Tiro, who was sick at Patras; November 16, 50 B.C.

TULLIUS ET CICERŌ S. D. TĪRŌNĪ SUŌ.

We are very anxious. Take the best care of yourself and come when you can come safely. Our love to you.

Septimum iam diem Corcȳrae tenēbāmur; Quīntus autem pater et fīlius Būthrōtī.

---

30. bīduī: genitive; sc. *spatium* or *iter*.

13. See introductory note, page 560. Tīrōnī (tī´rō): Cicero's freedman, trusted secretary, and intimate friend. He was manumitted in 54 B.C. Tiro had a cultivated intellect, and was himself an author. The *notae Tīrōniānae*, a species of shorthand writing traditionally associated with Tiro's name, have already been referred to (see vocabulary, and illustration, page 134). It is also generally believed that Tiro preserved the correspondence of his former master, at least in part.

1. Corcȳrae (kọr-sī´rạ).
2. Būthrōtī (bụ-thrō´tụm): locative.

Sollicitī erāmus dē tuā valētūdine mīrum in modum, nec mīrābāmur nihil ā tē litterārum; eīs enim ventīs istim 5 nāvigātur, quī sī essent, nōs Corcȳrae nōn sedērēmus.

Cūrā igitur tē, et cōnfīrmā et, cum commodē et per valētūdinem et per annī tempus nāvigāre poteris, ad nōs aman-

THE WATER FRONT AT PATRAS

tissimōs tuī vēnī. Nēmō nōs amat, quī tē nōn dīligat; cārus omnibus exspectātusque veniēs.
10 Cūrā ut valeās. Etiam atque etiam, Tīrō noster, valē. xv Kal. Dec., Corcȳrā.

---

4. **nihil litterārum:** ' no letter.' For *litterārum* see page 362, line 3, and note. **eīs ... sedērēmus:** ' for if there were any winds whereby a sailing can be effected from where you are, we should not be delaying at Corcyra.'

5. **nāvigātur:** its subject is impersonal. *172, e.* **quī sī essent:** this use of the relative should not be imitated in English.

8. **quī tē nōn dīligat:** ' without regarding you.' **dīligat:** explain the Latin subjunctive. **cārus ... veniēs:** do not translate such a sentence literally; ' your coming will be greeted with an affectionate welcome from everyone.'

14. CICERO AND HIS SON MARCUS TO TERENTIA AND TULLIA (Ad Fam. 14, 18)

Written at Formiae, where Cicero had a villa, to Terentia and Tullia in Rome; date January 27, 49 B.C.

TULLIUS TERENTIAE SUAE ET PATER SUĀVISSIMAE FĪLIAE, CICERŌ MĀTRĪ ET SORŌRĪ S. D. PLŪR.

Please decide whether it is better for you to stay in Rome or join us.

Cōnsīderandum vōbīs etiam atque etiam, animae meae, dīligenter putō, quid faciātis, Rōmaene sītis an mēcum in aliquō tūtō locō; id nōn sōlum meum cōnsilium est, sed etiam vestrum.

Mihi veniunt in mentem haec: Rōmae vōs esse tūtō 5 posse per Dolābellam, eamque rem posse nōbīs adiūmentō esse, sī quae vīs aut sī quae rapīnae fierī coeperint; sed

---

14. This letter was written at the very beginning of the Civil War, between Caesar and Pompey. Cicero had journeyed southward, reaching his villa at Formiae about the twentieth. He was still undecided whether to join Caesar or Pompey, though he feared Caesar and had a lukewarm attitude towards Pompey. He preferred to remain neutral, and hoped that some kind of peace might yet be patched up between the two great leaders. The thought of his family, too, made him hesitate to join either party, and prompted him to address this letter to his wife and daughter.

S. D. Plūr.: i.e. *salūtem dīcit plūrimam,* 'sends heartiest greetings.'

1. **etiam atque etiam:** 'again and again.' **animae meae:** 'my dear ones.'

2. **Rōmaene sītis,** etc.: Cicero was becoming more and more committed to the side of Pompey. But he was not blind to the weakness of that leader, and was in the gravest quandary what course to recommend to his wife and daughter. If they remained in Rome, they would be under the protection of Dolabella, Cicero's son-in-law, who had joined the party of Caesar. See Companion, page 509.

3. **cōnsilium:** 'problem.'

5. **Mihi veniunt in mentem:** 'occur to me.'

6. **Dolābellam** (dol-a-bel'a). **rem:** 'circumstance.'

rūrsus illud mē movet, quod videō omnēs bonōs abesse
Rōmā et eōs mulierēs suās sēcum habēre. Haec autem
10 regiō, in quā ego sum, nostrōrum est cum oppidōrum, tum
etiam praediōrum, ut et multum esse mēcum et, cum abieri-
tis, commodē in nostrīs praediīs esse possītis.
Mihi plānē nōn satis cōnstat adhūc, utrum sit melius.
Vōs vidēte, quid aliae faciant istō locō fēminae, et nē, cum
15 velītis, exīre nōn liceat. Id velim dīligenter etiam atque
etiam vōbīscum et cum amīcīs cōnsīderētis.

Have the house made secure by barricades. Please send letters every day.

Domus ut prōpugnācula et praesidium habeat, Philotīmō
dīcētis. Et velim tabellāriōs īnstituātis certōs, ut cotīdiē
aliquās ā vōbīs litterās accipiam; maximē autem date
20 operam, ut valeātis, sī nōs vultis valēre.
   VIIII Kal. Formiīs.

---

8. **rūrsus:** ' on the other hand.' **illud:** anticipates the following
substantive clause, *quod*, etc. **bonōs:** ' the patriotic,' of course, from
Pompey's standpoint.
   9. **autem:** ' again.'
   10. **nostrōrum . . . praediōrum:** ' consists (*est*) not only (*cum*)
of towns under my patronage, but also (*tum*) of estates which I
own.'
   13. **utrum:** ' which of the two courses.'
   14. **istō locō:** ' in the same position as you.'
   17. **prōpugnācula et praesidium:** against robbers, who would take
advantage of times of political disturbance to commit depredations.
Philotīmō (fil-ọ-tī′mụs): Terentia's steward, whose dishonesty Cicero
refers to in other letters.
   18. **dīcētis:** the future indicative is sometimes used for the imperative. *181, c.* **īnstituātis:** ' organize.' *180, e (1).* **certōs:** ' special.'
   21. **VIIII Kal.:** probably IX *Kalendās Iānuāriās*, for Terentia and
Tullia joined Cicero early in February; but the month is uncertain.
There is much doubt about the month and even the year in which a
number of Cicero's letters were written.

15. POMPEY THE GREAT TO CICERO
(Ad Fam. 8, 11c)

Written at Canusium to Cicero, who was in his villa at Formiae; February 20, 49 B.C

CN. MAGNUS PRŌCOS S. D. M. CICERŌNĪ IMP.

I was glad to have your letter.   Come to Brundisium.

S. V. B. E.   Tuās litterās libenter lēgī; recognōvī enim tuam prīstinam virtūtem etiam in salūte commūnī.

Cōnsulēs ad eum exercitum, quem in Apuliā habuī, vēnērunt.   Magnō opere tē hortor, prō tuō singulārī perpetuōque studiō in rem pūblicam, ut tē ad nōs cōnferās, ut com- 5 mūnī cōnsiliō reī pūblicae afflīctae opem atque auxilium ferāmus.

Cēnseō, viā Appiā iter faciās et celeriter Brundisium veniās.

---

15. Cicero was still torn by conflicting motives — whether he should give Pompey unqualified indorsement or should remain neutral so far as possible.   Caesar he both feared and admired.   His chief motive for following Pompey was a feeling of personal obligation accentuated by a friendly intimacy with him, yet at times he feared Pompey as well as Caesar, and inclined towards the belief that both were aiming at tyranny. Pompey, naturally, was greatly interested in the orator's support, as this letter clearly suggests.   Compare page 509.

The superscription *Imp.* (*Imperātor*) is probably used by Pompey in order to flatter Cicero with an unimportant military success in his province, on the strength of which he had been hailed *Imperātor* by his soldiers.   However, the title might be conceded to any governor of a province who possessed military authority (*imperium*).

1. **S. V. B. E. :** i.e. *sī valēs, bene est.*

3. **Cōnsulēs :** C. Claudius Marcellus and L. Cornelius Lentulus Crus.

8. **Cēnseō :** ' I am of the opinion.'   **faciās, veniās :** *200, a;* B. 295, 8; A. & G. 565, *a;* G. 546, R. 2.

THE APPIAN WAY

16. CAESAR TO CICERO (Ad Att. 10, 8b)

Written by Julius Caesar, who was on the way to Spain, to Cicero at Formiae; April 16, B.C. 49.

CAESAR IMP. SAL. D. CICERŌNĪ IMP.

I beg you not to take sides, but to remain neutral.

Etsī tē nihil temerē, nihil imprūdenter factūrum iūdicāram, tamen, permōtus hominum fāmā, scrībendum ad tē

---

16. This is one of three letters of Caesar's addressed to Cicero, and shows that Caesar also, as well as Pompey, was making a bid for the orator's support. The Caesarians at least hoped that Cicero would remain neutral or refrain from taking sides with their adversaries. The style and language of this letter are quite typical and betray the writer, who avoids needless circumlocution, though he expresses himself with his usual courtesy. However, his meaning is never in doubt. What conclusions may be drawn from this and the previous letter regarding Cicero's character?

   2. **hominum fāmā:** ' by popular rumor.'

exīstimāvī et prō nostrā benevolentiā petendum, nē quō
prōgrederēris, prōclīnātā iam rē, quō, integrā, etiam prō-
grediendum tibi nōn exīstimāssēs. 5

Namque et amīcitiae graviōrem iniūriam fēceris et tibi
minus commodē cōnsulueris, sī nōn fortūnae obsecūtus
vidēberis (omnia enim secundissima nōbīs, adversissima
illīs accidisse videntur), nec causam secūtus (eadem enim
tum fuit, cum ab eōrum cōnsiliīs abesse iūdicāstī), sed 10
meum aliquod factum condemnāvisse, quō mihi gravius
abs tē nihil accidere potest; quod nē faciās, prō iūre
nostrae amīcitiae ā tē petō.

Postrēmō, quid virō bonō, et quiētō et bonō cīvī, magis
convenit quam abesse ā cīvīlibus contrōversiīs? Quod 15
nōn nūllī cum probārent, perīculī causā sequī nōn potuērunt.
Tū, explōrātō et vītae meae testimōniō et amīcitiae iūdiciō,
neque tūtius neque honestius reperiēs quicquam, quam ab
omnī contentiōne abesse.

xv Kal. Maiās, ex itinere. 20

---

3. **quō:** ' anywhere.'

4. **prōclīnātā iam rē :** ' since the fortune (of Pompey) is now wavering.' **integrā :** sc. *rē :* ' unimpaired.'

8. **nōbīs . . . illīs:** ' to my party . . . to Pompey's party.'

9. **causam:** ' the (right) cause.'

10. **iūdicāstī:** why indicative? **sed . . . condemnāvisse:** Caesar
means to say that if Cicero takes sides with Pompey now, it will
appear as if the orator were thereby protesting against some act of
Caesar.

12. **quod:** = *id autem.* **prō iūre nostrae amīcitiae :** ' in the name of
our friendship.'

15. **abesse ā cīvīlibus contrōversiīs :** *i.e.* to remain neutral. **Quod:**
' This course.'

17. **amīcitiae iūdiciō:** ' judgment pronounced by friendship.'
amīcitae is a subjective genitive. *95;* B. 199; A. & G. 343, N. 1;
G. 363, 1.

20. xv **Kal. Maiās, ex itinere :** ' the 16th of April, on the march.'

17. TO TERENTIA (Ad Fam. 14, 21)

Written in Pompey's camp, near Dyrrachium, to Terentia in Rome; **date,**
probably in June, 48 B.C.

TULLIUS TERENTIAE SUAE S. D.

*Do your best to get well. Manage as best you can, and write me about
everything.*

S. V. B. E. V. Dā operam, ut convalēscās; quod opus
erit, ut rēs tempusque postulat, prōvideās atque adminis-
trēs, et ad mē dē omnibus rēbus quam saepissimē litterās
mittās. Valē.

18. TO TERENTIA (Ad Fam. 14, 11)

Written at Brundisium to Terentia in Rome, June 14, 47 B.C.

TULLIUS S. D. TERENTIAE SUAE

*Tullia is here. Her devotion increases my pain that I cannot do for her as
she deserves. I think of sending our son and Gnaeus Sallust to Caesar.*

S. V. B. E. V. Tullia nostra vēnit ad me prīdiē Īdūs
Iūniās; cuius summā virtūte et singulārī hūmānitāte

---

17. 1. **S. V. B. E. V.:** = *sī valēs, bene est; valeō.* **convalēscās:**
Terentia had been ill with fever. See page 562. **quod opus erit:** i.e.
id, quod tibi erit, ' whatever you will need.'

2. **rēs:** ' the situation.'

18. Cicero had spent the first part of 48 B.C. in Pompey's camp or
at Dyrrachium, where Pompey's strategy against Caesar was momentarily successful. Then came the battle of Pharsalia, and shortly afterwards, on the 29th of September, the murder of Pompey in Egypt.
Pompey's cause was now in a bad way, and Cicero was plainly worried
as to how Caesar would treat him. Financial and private difficulties
also added to his anxiety. He had returned to Italy in October of
48 B.C., and remained at Brundisium till September of the next year
in a wretched state of mind and body. During this period of despair
his beloved daughter Tullia came to stay with him, whereas the breach
between Cicero and Terentia was widening, as may be felt from the
formal and cold tenor of this letter.

2. **hūmānitāte:** ' tenderness.'

graviōre etiam sum dolōre affectus, nostrā factum esse neglegentiā, ut longē aliā in fortūnā esset, atque eius pietās ac
dignitās postulābat.   5

Nōbīs erat in animō Cicerōnem ad Caesarem mittere et
cum eō Cn. Sallustium; sī profectus erit, faciam tē certiōrem.

Valētūdinem tuam cūrā dīligenter. Valē.
XVII K. Quīnctīlēs.   10

19. TO TERENTIA (Ad Fam. 14, 23)

Written at Brundisium to Terentia in Rome, August 11, 47 B.C.

TULLIUS TERENTIAE SUAE S. D.

*A gentlemanly letter from Caesar; will let you know when I decide
what to do.*

S. V. B. E. V. Redditae mihi tandem sunt ā Caesare
litterae satis līberālēs, et ipse opīniōne celerius ventūrus

---

4. **aliā in fortūnā**, etc.: a reference to her unhappy marriage with
Dolabella, to whom Tullia had been betrothed during Cicero's governorship in Cilicia. **atque**: ' than.' **pietās ac dignitās**: ' her filial devotion and her position.'

6. **erat**: = *est*; an epistolary imperfect. **Cicerōnem**: his son;
the orator wishes to make terms with Caesar.

7. **Cn. Sallustium** (nē'(y)ụs sạ-lụs'tị-ụs): either a client or a
friend of Cicero, and a man of some literary taste.

10. **Quīnctīlēs**: the fifth month counting from March, later called
July in honor of Julius Caesar.

19. Cicero's letters to his wife continue to be cold and surprisingly
brief, though they are still courteous. The two were divorced early in
46 B.C.

2. **litterae satis līberālēs**: this letter is lost. Caesar treated those
who had joined Pompey with unexpected clemency, and outwardly, at
least, ignored the part Cicero had taken in the Civil War. According
to Plutarch (*Cicero*, 39), the two were completely reconciled. **opīniōne
celerius**: ' more quickly than was expected.'

esse dīcitur; cui utrum obviam prōcēdam, an hīc **eum**
exspectem, cum cōnstituerō, faciam tē certiōrem.
; Tabellāriōs mihi velim quam prīmum remittās.
Valētūdinem tuam cūrā dīligenter. Valē.
D. pr. Īd. Sext.

20. TO LUCIUS PAPIRIUS PAETUS (Ad Fam. 9, 23)

Written at his villa near Cumae to Paetus in Naples, about nine miles distant; November 17, 46 B.C.

CICERŌ PAETŌ

*I hear you have gout, but I plan to come to see you and dine with you; for
I judge your cook hasn't gout too.*

Herī vēnī in Cūmānum; crās ad tē fortasse, sed, cum
certum sciam, faciam tē paulō ante certiōrem. Etsī M.
Caepārius, cum mihi in silvā Gallīnāriā obviam vēnisset
quaesissemque, quid agerēs, dīxit tē in lectō esse, quod ex
5 pedibus labōrārēs.

3. **cui utrum obviam prōcēdam:** ' and whether I shall go to meet
him.' Caesar landed at Tarentum.

5. **Tabellāriōs:** see page 382, line 1, note. **quam prīmum:** 'as
soon as possible.' It took more than two weeks to effect an exchange
of letters between Rome and Brundisium.

7. **D.:** i.e. *Data est epistula*, etc. The word is appropriate, since
the letter was actually *given* to a messenger for delivery. Compare also
the English word " date."

20. **Paetōs** (pē′tŭs): Cicero addressed several letters to L. Papirius
Paetus, who was a man of learning and great taste. He seems to have
been an expert in gastronomy and Cicero cannot refrain from indulging
in a witticism at his expense.

1. **in Cūmānum:** Cicero's estate near Cumae (kū′mē).

2. **certum sciam:** ' know for a certainty.' **Etsī:** = *Quamquam* in
the corrective sense, ' And yet,' ' However.' **M. Caepārius** (sẹ-pā′
rĭ-ŭs): his identity cannot be established.

3. **silvā Gallīnāriā:** a forest of pine trees on the coast of Campania—
a favorite resort of robbers.

4. **quid agerēs:** ' how you were.' **ex pedibus labōrārēs:** ' you
were suffering from gout.' Gout, a form of arthritis, was very

Tulī scīlicet molestē, ut dēbuī, sed tamen cōnstituī ad
tē venīre, ut et vidērem tē et vīserem et cēnārem etiam;
nōn enim arbitror coquum etiam tē arthrīticum habēre.
Exspectā igitur hospitem cum minimē edācem, tum inimīcum cēnīs sūmptuōsīs.   10

21. TO ATTICUS (Ad Att. 12, 1)

Written at Arpinum to Atticus, whom Cicero expects soon to visit, in Atticus' villa near Rome; November 24, 46 B.C.

CICERŌ ATTICŌ SAL.

*I am longing to see my Tullia and to hear all about your Attica. You may
be right in saying that to want a fire in the morning is a sign of approaching old age; I reply that to forget one's appointments is still
more so.*

Undecimō diē, postquam ā tē discesseram, hōc litterulārum exarāvī ēgrediēns ē vīllā ante lūcem, atque eō diē cōgitā-

---

common among the ancients, who were well aware that a luxurious
mode of living, habitual over-indulgence in rich dishes, and the excessive use of alcoholic beverages were among the predisposing factors.
For this reason Celsus (see illustration, page 455), the Roman medical
author (*Dē Medicīnā*, **4**, 24), includes in his treatment restrictions in the
quantity of food and in the use of wine. It is very likely that Paetus
was afflicted with gout for the reasons suggested above, and that
Cicero, knowing his friend's weakness, is making fun of him.

9. **minimē edācem:** ' not in the least gluttonous.'

21. The charm of this letter consists in its informality and the careless ease to which Cicero often resigns himself in his correspondence
with Atticus. It creates an atmosphere of relaxation by both its style
and its trifling prattle, and portrays an element of friendship which is
all too rare.

1. **discesseram:** the pluperfect is used with *postquam* when a definite interval of time is signified; otherwise the perfect is the rule. *188, d.*
hōc litterulārum exarāvī: ' I scrawled this little note.' The partitive
genitive, the diminutive, and the verb all help to emphasize the casual
unconcern of the writer.

2. **ē vīllā:** in Arpī'num. **cōgitābam:** 'I am thinking'; why not
a past tense in English?

bam in Anagnīnō, posterō autem in Tusculānō, ibí ūnum
diem; v Kalend. igitur ad cōnstitūtum.

5 Atque utinam continuō ad complexum meae Tulliae, ad
osculum Atticae possim currere! Quod quidem ipsun,
scrībe, quaesō, ad mē, ut, dum cōnsistō in Tusculānō, sciam,
quid garriat; sīn rūsticātur, quid scrībat ad tē; eīque
intereā aut scrībēs salūtem aut nūntiābis, itemque Piliae.
10 Et tamen, etsī continuō congressūrī sumus, scrībēs ad mē,
sī quid habēbis.

Cum complicārem hanc epistulam, noctuābundus ad mē
vēnit cum epistulā tuā tabellārius; quā lēctā, dē Atticae
febriculā scīlicet valdē doluī.

15 Reliqua, quae exspectābam, ex tuīs litterīs cognōvī omnia.
Sed quod scrībis "igniculum mātūtīnum γεροντικόν," γεροντι-

---

3. **in Anagnīnō**: sc. *esse*, ' on my estate near Anag'nia,' a town
in Latium.

4. **ad cōnstitūtum**: sc. *locum*.

6. **Atticae**: the little seven- or eight-year-old daughter of Atticus.
possim: *180, c;* B. 279, 1; A. & G. 441, 442; G. 260, 261. **Quod
ipsum**: object of *scrībe*.

8. **garriat**: ' she babbles.' **rūsticātur**: the word produces a playful
effect.

9. **Piliae**: the wife of Atticus.

12. **complicārem**: ' I was folding up.' **noctuābundus**: adjectives
in *-bundus*, accentuated present participles in meaning, are regularly
formed only from verbs, so that this adjective presupposes the verb
noctuāre, but we have no record of such a word. However, it is quite
likely that Cicero coined the word for its humorous effect, *i.e.* ' playing
the night owl,' suggesting that the letter-carrier traveled all night.

14. **febriculā**: another diminutive, ' slight fever.'

15. **Reliqua . . . omnia**: keep the emphasis by translating this
sentence in the Latin order.

16. **quod scrībis . . . γεροντικόν**: ' as to your writing that a small
fire in the morning (is) a sign of old age '; the Greek adjective means
' old-mannish.' **γεροντικώτερον . . . vacillāre**: ' it is a surer sign of
old age for one's poor old memory to falter.' The Greek adjective is
now in the comparative degree. The two diminutives are in keeping
with the good-natured banter.

ABOVE: VIEW OF ARPINUM

BELOW: TUSCULUM
View over the site of Cicero's villa.

κώτερον est memoriolā vacillāre; ego enim IIII Kal. Axiō dederam, tibi III, Quīntō, quō diē vēnissem, id est II Kal. Hōc igitur habēbis, novī nihil.

Quid ergō opus erat epistulā? Quid, cum cōram sumus 20 et garrīmus, quicquid in buccam? Est profectō quiddam λέσχη, quae habet, etiam sī nihil subest, collocūtiōne ipsā suāvitātem. 25

ROMAN ROAD LEADING TO TUSCULUM

17. **Axiō** (ax′i-ŭs) : an intimate friend of Cicero.

19. **Hōc habēbis :** appropriated from the arena, *hōc habet* being applied to the wounded gladiator with the meaning 'he is hit.' The future *habēbis* has the force of an imperative, 'take that.' **novī nihil :** 'I have no news.' *97, a.*

20. **Quid . . . epistulā?** Atticus is supposed to put this question. **Quid,** etc.: Cicero's reply.

21. **quicquid in buccam :** 'whatever comes uppermost.' *Bucca* is the colloquial word for the regular *ōs.* Compare French *bouche.* **Est . . .**

λέσχη: 'Without doubt (*profectō*) talk (λέσχη) is something.'

23. **etiam . . . subest:** 'even if there is nothing underneath.'

24. **collocūtiōne ipsā :** 'by reason of the mere act of our talking familiarly.' *162, a.*

25. **suāvitātem:** the keynote of the letter, and for that reason accorded the emphatic position at the very end. The Germans would call it "Liebenswürdigkeit."

22. TO ATTICUS (Ad Att. 12, 16)

Written at Astura, where Cicero had a villa, to Atticus in Rome, March 10, 45 B.C., soon after the death of Tullia.

CICERŌ ATTICŌ SAL.

Come to me if you can without neglecting your business. I cannot be without you. To meet in Rome was out of the question; this solitude is more suitable.

Tē tuīs negōtiīs relīctīs nōlō ad mē venīre. Ego potius accēdam, sī diūtius impediēre; etsī nē discessissem quidem ē cōnspectū tuō, nisi mē plānē nihil ūlla rēs adiuvāret. Quod sī esset aliquod levāmen, id esset in tē ūnō, et, cum 5 prīmum ab aliquō poterit esse, ā tē erit; nunc tamen ipsum sine tē esse nōn possum.

Sed nec tuae domī probābātur, nec meae poteram; nec, sī propius essem ūspiam, tēcum tamen essem; idem enim tē impedīret, quō minus mēcum essēs, quod nunc etiam 10 impedit.

---

22. Tullia's death in February, 45 B.C., was a great blow to Cicero, who was overwhelmed with grief at the loss of his sympathetic companion. He sought refuge in solitude and found much consolation in literature. His *Dē Cōnsōlātiōne*, now lost, was written to mitigate his grief.

1. **tuīs negōtiīs relīctīs venīre :** translate as if *relinquere tua negōtia et venīre;* English prefers coördination, Latin subordination. *211.*

2. **accēdam :** sc. *ad tē.* **etsī :** corrective, 'and yet.' See page 394, line 2, and note.

3. **nihil :** adverbial accusative, equivalent to an emphatic *nōn.*

4. **Quod sī :** ' But if.' *118, d.*

5. **nunc ipsum :** ' at this very moment '; *ipse* is sometimes used with an adverb of time for emphasis.

7. **probābātur :** impersonal; sc. *esse.* Translate, ' it was deemed inadvisable to stay.' Cicero could not stay at Atticus' because of the bustle and publicity, which would be unendurable to him in the midst of his grief; nor at his own home, because of the number of those who would come to offer consolation which he could not accept.

Mihi adhūc nihil aptius fuit hāc sōlitūdine, quam vereor
nē Philippus tollat; herī enim vesperī vēnerat.
Mē scrīptiō et litterae nōn lēniunt, sed obturbant.

23. TO LUCIUS MINUCIUS BASILUS
(Aα Fam. 6, 15)

Written in Rome to Basilus, who was also in Rome, congratulating him on
his part in the assassination of Caesar; date, the same day as the
assassination, March 15, 44 B.C.

CICERŌ BASILŌ SAL.

I congratulate you. I rejoice, I am eager for news.

Tibi grātulor, mihi gaudeō. Tē amō, tua tueor. Ā tē
amārī et, quid agās quidque agātur, certior fierī volō.

---

12. **Philippus:** stepfather of Augustus; he was Cicero's neighbor.
vēnerat: epistolary tense = *vēnit. 175, g;* B. 265; A. & G. 479; G. 252.

COIN COMMEMORATING THE
ASSASSINATION OF CAESAR

Struck by an officer of
Marcus Junius Brutus. A
"cap of liberty" appears
between two daggers. In-
scription: EID · MAR, for
EIDIBUS MARTIIS, 'On the
Ides of March.'

23. This impulsive little note was probably written immediately after the assassination of Caesar, and while we must regret
Cicero's spirit of exultation, it should not
be forgotten that Cicero had come to look
upon Caesar as a tyrant, and as such he felt
that the assassination was an act of duty
in the interests of the state. The familiar
tone of the letter would seem to indicate
that Cicero maintained close connections
with the conspirators. **Basilō:** L. Minucius
Basilus (bas'ĭ-lŭs) had served under Caesar
in Gaul, but afterwards became one of his
assassins. The year after Caesar's death
Basilus was himself murdered by his slaves
because he had inflicted inhuman punishment upon them.

1. **mihi:** 'as for myself.' **tua tueor:**
'I am looking after your interests.'

24. TO ATTICUS (Ad Att. 16, 9)

Written in his villa at Puteoli to Atticus in Rome; November, 44 B.C.

CICERŌ ATTICŌ SAL.

Octavian wants me to come to Rome. I fear Antony will succeed. I see war close at hand.

Bīnae ūnō diē mihi litterae ab Octāviānō; nunc quidem, ut Rōmam statim veniam, velle sē rem agere per senātum.
Cui ego nōn posse senā-
tum ante K. Iānuār.,
5 quod quidem ita crēdō.
Ille autem addit, "Cōn-
siliō tuō." Quid multa?
Ille urget, ego autem
σκήπτομαι. Nōn cōnfīdō
10 aetātī; ignōrō, quō
animō; nihil sine Pānsā
tuō volō.

ARPINUM
Prehistoric gateway to the citadel.

24. 1. **Bīnae:** why the distributive? *37, e;* B. 81, 4, *b;* A. & G. 137, *b;* G. 97, 3. **nunc quidem:** sc. *rogat.*

2. **velle:** depends on the idea of saying in *rogat* understood. *213, b.* **rem agere:** ' to act.'

3. **Cui ego:** sc. *respondī.*

5. **quidem:** ' really.'

6. **Cōnsiliō tuō:** he declared that he would follow Cicero's advice.

7. **Quid multa:** 'Why say more?,' 'In short.' See page 383, note 12.

9. **σκήπτομαι:** present tense, ' I temporize.'

10. **aetātī:** he was in his twentieth year. **quō animō:** sc. *sit.*

11. **nihil . . . volō:** ' I am consenting to nothing without your friend Pansa.' Pansa and Hirtius were consuls in 43 B.C., who fought against Antony in the battle of Mutina. See Companion, page 556.

Vereor, nē valeat Antōnius; nec ā marī discēdere libet, et metuō, nē quae ἀριστεία mē absente. Varrōnī quidem displicet cōnsilium puerī, mihi nōn. Sī firmās cōpiās habet, 15 Brūtum habēre potest, et rem gerit palam; centuriat Capuae, dīnumerat.

Iam iamque videō bellum.

Ad haec rescrībe. Tabellārium meum Kalend. Rōmā profectum sine tuīs litterīs mīror. 20

---

13. **valeat:** 'may succeed.' **Antōnius:** Marcus, the Triumvir, whom Cicero attacked in his Philippic Orations and who included him in his proscriptions in November, 43 B.C., and had him murdered a few weeks later. **nec ... libet:** 'and I do not like to.'

14. **nē quae ἀριστεία:** sc. *sit;* 'lest some great prowess be exhibited.' The Greek word refers to some of the titles of various books of the *Iliad*, in which the prowess of Diomede, Agamemnon, and Menelaus is described.

15. **puerī:** Octavianus. See vocabulary.

16. **Brūtum:** Decimus Brutus, who could hold Cisalpine Gaul against Antony. **centuriat, dīnumerat:** 'he is organizing his troops in companies, he is paying out their bounty-money.' See *Philippic*, pages 331–334.

18. **Iam iamque:** here 'More and more clearly.'

HEAD OF ITALIA
From a coin of the Roman Republic.

25. TO DECIMUS JUNIUS BRUTUS
(Ad Fam. 11, 25)

Written at Rome to Decimus Brutus in Transalpine Gaul, probably at Calaro,
modern Grenoble; June 10, 43 B.C., less than six months before the
new Triumvirate, formed by the now victorious Antony, decreed
Cicero's death.

M. CICERŌ S. D. D. BRŪTŌ.

I imitate your brevity. All our hope is in you and your colleague (Plan-
    cus). No news from Marcus Brutus.

Exspectantī mihi tuās cotīdiē litterās Lupus noster subitō
dēnūntiāvit, ut ad tē scrīberem, sī quid vellem. Ego autem,
etsī quid scrīberem nōn habēbam — ācta enim ad tē mittī
sciēbam, inānem autem sermōnem litterārum tibi iniūcun-
5 dum esse audiēbam — brevitātem secūtus sum, tē magistrō.

---

25. Decimus Junius Brutus must not be confused with M. Junius
Brutus, one of the murderers of Caesar. However, Decimus played a
more reprehensible rôle in the assassination, for it was he who, as an
agent of the conspirators, urged Caesar to attend the senate meeting
on the fatal day, and thereby betrayed the confidence and trust of one
who had many times befriended him. When Caesar's will was read,
Brutus was found to be one of the heirs. After Caesar's death he
assumed the governorship of Cisalpine Gaul, a grant due to the dictator's influence, and when Antony by a decree of the people claimed this
same province, Brutus refused to surrender it. This was the direct
cause of the battle of Mutina (a city of Cisalpine Gaul), April 27,
43 B.C., in which Antony was defeated. The consuls Hirtius and Pansa
both fell in this battle, and so the command of the army passed to Brutus,
who followed Antony into Transalpine Gaul. Brutus had just joined
forces with Plancus, the governor of Transalpine Gaul, early in June,
when Cicero wrote this letter.

1. **Lupus:** a common friend of Cicero and Brutus.

2. **vellem:** sc. *scrībere.*

3. **ācta:** ' proceedings ' of the senate, and also of the popular
assemblies, which at this time were published at the close of each session
or meeting.

4. **inānem sermōnem litterārum:** ' the small talk of letters.'

5. **brevitātem, tē magistrō:** Cicero complains of this shortness
elsewhere.

Scītō igitur in tē et in collēgā spem omnem esse. Dē Brūtō autem nihil adhūc certī; quem ego, quem ad modum praecipis, prīvātīs litterīs ad bellum commūne vocāre nōn dēsinō. Quī utinam iam adesset! Intestīnum urbis malum, quod est nōn mediocre, minus timērēmus. Sed quid agō? 10 Nōn imitor λακωνισμὸν tuum; altera iam pagella prōcēdit. Vince et valē.

XIIII K. Quīnctīl.

---

6. **collēgā :** Plancus. He and Brutus were *cōnsulēs dēsignātī* for 42 B.C.

7. **Brūtō :** Marcus Brutus.

9. **Intestīnum urbis malum :** intrigues were on foot to win the consulship for Octavianus, although he was far from the legal age, and had not held the earlier offices.

10. **minus timērēmus :** i.e. *sī adesset.*

11. **λακωνισμὸν tuum :** 'your laconic style.' **pagella :** the letter was written on a small tablet. Illustration, page 87. See also page 559.

12. **Vince et valē :** a mere formula, ' Success and health (to you).'

LIVY, THE GRAPHIC HISTORIAN
OF ROME

LIVY, THE GRAPHIC HISTORIAN OF ROME

TITĪ LĪVĪ
AB URBE CONDITĀ
LIBER I

Partēs Sēlēctae

The founding of Rome; Romulus and Remus receive an augury, and Remus is slain.

6. Ita Numitōrī Albānā rē permissā Rōmulum Remumque cupīdō cēpit in iīs locīs, ubi expositī ubīque ēducātī erant, urbis condendae. Et supererat multitūdō Albānōrum Latīnōrumque; ad id pāstōrēs quoque accesserant,

To the Student : Consult first the introductory remarks on pages 562–564 of the Companion.

Ab Urbe Conditā : 'from the founding of the city.' A participle in agreement with a noun is often equivalent to an abstract expression in English. *212, c; 228, b.*

6. 1. **Ita Numitōrī Albānā rē permissā:** 'After the Alban state had thus been turned over to Nu'mitor.' Numitor and his brother Amu'lius were the two sons of one of the last kings of Alba Longa, the mother city of Rome, founded by Asca'nius or Iulus (ī-ū'lus), the son of Aeneas (ē-nē'ạs). Amulius, the younger brother, had usurped the throne which rightfully belonged to Numitor. Subsequently Rhea (rē'ạ) Sil'via, the daughter of Numitor, gave birth to the twins Romulus and Remus, whom Amulius ordered thrown into the Tiber, so that there might be no claimants to his throne. The basket containing the infants was found by Faus'tulus (Favorer, Helper), the king's shepherd, who reared them as his own. When grown they slew Amulius and made Numitor king.

3. **urbis condendae:** with *cupīdō* in the previous line. **Et:** 'And in fact.' **supererat multitūdō:** 'the population was excessive.'

4. **ad id . . . accesserant:** 'thereto . . . had been added.'

₅ quī omnēs facile spem facerent, parvam Albam, parvum
Lāvīnium prae eā urbe quae conderētur fore. Intervēnit
deinde hīs cōgitātiōnibus avītum malum, rēgnī cupīdō,
atque inde foedum certāmen coortum ā satis mītī prīncipiō.
Quoniam geminī essent nec aetātis
₁₀ verēcundia discrīmen facere posset, ut
diī, quōrum tūtēlae ea loca essent, auguriīs legerent quī nōmen novae urbī
daret, quī conditam imperiō regeret,
Palātium Rōmulus, Remus Aventīnum
₁₅ ad inaugurandum templa capiunt.

ROMULUS QUIRINUS

---

6. **Lāvī′nium:** a city of Latium founded by Aeneas in honor of his
wife Lavinia; it was about fourteen miles south of Rome. **prae:** ' in
comparison with.' **conderētur:** subordinate clause in indirect discourse. What would be the tense in direct discourse? **Intervēnit:**
' Interrupted.'

7. **hīs cōgitātiōnibus:** ' with this project '; Latin uses abstract
nouns in the plural more freely than does English to denote different instances of the abstract idea, or, as here, because the abstract idea belongs
to more than one person. *92, c.* **avītum malum:** ' the trouble between
their grandfathers.'

8. **inde . . . prīncipiō:** ' as a result of this (*rēgnī cupīdō*) an ugly
quarrel arising from a fairly (*satis*) innocent source.'

9. **Quoniam:** usually indicates an evident reason. *183, a.* **essent
. . . posset:** subordinate clauses in implied indirect discourse. *213, b.*
aetātis verēcundia: ' respect for priority.' What kind of genitive is
aetātis?

10. **ut . . . legerent:** expresses the purpose of *capiunt.*

11. **quōrum tūtēlae:** ' under whose protection'; *tūtēlae* is genitive.
94, c; B. 198, 2; A. & G. 343, *b;* G. 366. **auguriīs:** every official act at
Rome had to be sanctioned by the gods; Cicero (*Dē Nātūrā Deōrum,* **3,**
2) regarded Romulus as the founder of this system.

12. **quī:** here equivalent to *quis* or, better, *uter,* introducing an indirect question.

15. **ad inaugurandum:** ' for taking the omens,' from the flight of
birds. **templa:** not temples. Varro, " most learned of the Romans,"
contemporary of Cicero, says (*Dē Linguā Latīnā,* 7) that a *templum* is
a space marked out to receive augury. The word has this primary
meaning here, and is in apposition with *Palātium* and *Aventīnum.*

7. Priōrī Remō augurium vēnisse fertur sex vulturēs, iamque nūntiātō auguriō cum duplex numerus Rōmulō sēsē ostendisset, utrumque rēgem sua multitūdō cōnsalūtāverat. Tempore illī praeceptō, at hī numerō avium rēgnum trahēbant. Inde cum altercātiōne congressī cer- ₅ tāmine īrārum ad caedem vertuntur. Ibi in turbā ictus

THE PREHISTORIC ALBAN CRATER
At the right is the Alban Mountain. The crater is eleven miles across.
Cicero's villa overlooked it.

capiunt: this sentence is a fair illustration of the periodic sentence-structure so peculiar to Livy. See Companion, *211*.

7. 1. **Priōrī Remō:** a dative of interest or advantage. *109, a.* **vulturēs:** in apposition with *augurium.*

3. **utrumque rēgem . . . cōnsalūtāverat:** 'each was hailed as king by his respective followers.' The awkwardness of *sua* in the English translation is best relieved by using the passive voice. Note the emphasis on *sua*, which refers to *utrumque.*

4. **Tempore illī praeceptō, at hī numerō avium:** 'The one party by priority of time, whereas the other by the number of birds.' *Tempore praeceptō* has the accessory notion of cause or means.

5. **trahēbant:** 'claimed.' **Inde cum altercātiōne congressī:** 'As a result they engaged in a dispute.' Translate *congressī* as a finite verb and join to *vertuntur* by 'and.' **certāmine . . . vertuntur:** 'in the heat of passion resorted to bloodshed.'

6. **īrārum:** another abstract noun in the plural to suggest various angry manifestations in the crowd. *92, c.* **Ibi:** 'Thereupon.'

Remus cecidit. Vulgātior fāma est lūdibriō frātris Remum
novōs trānsiluisse mūrōs, inde ab īrātō Rōmulō, cum verbīs
quoque increpitāns adiēcisset, "Sīc deinde quīcumque alius
10 trānsiliet moenia mea!", interfectum. Ita sōlus potītus
imperiō Rōmulus; condita urbs conditōris nōmine appel-
lāta.

*Romulus increases the population of the city. He opens a sanctuary on
the Capitoline, and thus attracts a miscellaneous rabble of shepherds
and vagrants. He organizes a senate, whose members are called
' patrēs.'*

8. Crēscēbat interim urbs mūnītiōnibus alia atque alia
appetendō loca, cum in spem magis futūrae multitūdinis
quam ad id quod tum hominum erat mūnīrent. Deinde
nē vāna urbis magnitūdō esset, adiciendae multitūdinis
causā vetere cōnsiliō condentium urbēs, quī obscūram

---

7. **Vulgātior fāma:** ' The more usual report is.' **lūdibriō:** dative
of purpose; translate, ' in mockery.' *112, a.*

8. **trānsiluisse mūrōs:** a sacrilegious act because the walls were
being built in accordance with the omens. **ab īrātō Rōmulō:** with
interfectum below. **cum verbīs . . . adiēcisset:** ' when he amid loud
rebukes had added '; *verbīs* is ablative of means.

9. **Sīc:** sc. *interficiātur* or, better, *pereat.*

11. **imperiō:** *131 c;* B. 218, 1; A. & G. 410; G. 407.

Study this selection together with that on page 429.

8. 1. Crēscēbat . . . loca: ' In the meantime the city grew by
extending its fortifications, one place after another being annexed.'
mūnītiōnibus: ablative of means, with *crēscēbat.*

2. **appetendō:** in Livy and later writers the ablative of the gerund
or gerundive may be equivalent to the present participle, i.e. *appetēns.*
This usage became regular in Mediaeval Latin, from which came the
Spanish and Italian forms of the present participle. **cum:** ' since.'
in spem: ' in anticipation.'

3. **ad id quod tum hominum erat:** ' for the existing population.'
hominum: partitive genitive with *quod.* See page 424, line 3, note.
mūnīrent: ' they were building their structures.'

4. **vāna:** ' to no purpose,' ' for naught.'

5. **vetere cōnsiliō condentium urbēs:** ' by an old scheme of the

atque humilem conciendō ad sē multitūdinem nātam ē
terrā sibi prōlem ēmentiēbantur, locum, quī nunc saeptus
dēscendentibus inter duōs lūcōs est, asȳlum aperit. Eō
ex fīnitimīs populīs turba omnis sine discrīmine, līber an
servus esset, avida novārum rērum perfūgit, idque prīmum 10
ad coeptam magnitūdinem rōboris fuit.
Cum iam vīrium haud paenitēret, cōnsilium deinde
vīribus parat : centum creat senātōrēs, sīve quia is numerus
satis erat, sīve quia sōlī centum erant quī creārī patrēs
possent. Patrēs certē ab honōre patriciīque prōgeniēs 15
eōrum appellātī.

---

founders of cities.'   Compare Ovid's story of Cadmus and the dragon's
teeth, *Metamorphoses*, **3**, 105, *et seq.*

6. **conciendō**: as *appetendō* above in line 2; here best translated
as a verb, ' attracted.'   **nātam . . . ēmentiēbantur** : ' feigned that the
earth had produced offspring for them.'   How literally?

7. **locum** : object of *aperit* below.   **quī . . . est**: ' which is now
inclosed between the two groves as you go down the hill.'

8. **dēscendentibus** : sc. *eīs*, dative of local standpoint or reference.
109, d; B. 188, 2, *a*) ; A. & G. 378, 2 ; G. 353.   **asȳlum** : a Latinized Greek
word meaning ' a place of refuge.'   See page 430, line 12.   For the
supposed location in the depression between the two summits of the
Capitoline see Plan of Rome, Frontispiece.

9. **turba omnis** : ' riffraff of every description.'

10. **esset**: indirect question depending upon *sine discrīmine*.
avida novārum rērum : ' eager for a change of fortune.'   **idque . . .**
fuit: ' and this was the beginning of power towards the objective of
greatness which (Romulus) had entered upon.'

11. **rōboris** : partitive genitive with *prīmum*.   *97, b.* This word means
real power as possessed from within.

12. **Cum . . . paenitēret**: ' When he was no longer dissatisfied with
his strength.'   **vīrium** : *103, c;* B. 209, 1 ; A. & G. 354, *b;* G. 377.
paenitēret: sc. *eum*.   This verb often has a negative meaning, ' to be
dissatisfied with.'   *212, m.*   **cōnsilium . . . parat**: ' he provided wisdom for (the city's) strength.'

13. **vīribus**: dative of advantage or reference.   *109, a;* B. 188, 1 ;
A. & G. 376 ; G. 350, 2.

14. **quī . . . possent**: *194, a;* B. 283, 2 ; A. & G. 535, *b;* G. 631, 1.

War with the Sabines; the story of Tarpeia.

11. Novissimum ab Sabīnīs bellum ortum, multōque id maximum fuit; nihil enim per īram aut cupiditātem āctum est, nec ostendērunt bellum prius quam intulērunt. Cōnsiliō etiam additus dolus. Spurius Tarpeius Rōmānae 5 praeerat arcī; huius fīliam virginem aurō corrumpit Tatius, ut armātōs in arcem accipiat, — aquam forte ea tum sacrīs extrā moenia petītum ierat; acceptī obrutam armīs necāvēre, seu ut vī capta potius arx vidērētur seu prōdendī exemplī causā, nē quid ūsquam fīdum prōditōrī 10 esset. Additur fābulae, quod vulgō Sabīnī aureās armillās

---

11. 1. **ortum:** sc. *est.* Livy does not hesitate to omit forms of *esse* in compound indicative tenses.

3. **ostendērunt:** 'parade.' Compare modern use of " advertise."

4. **Cōnsiliō:** ' To wisdom.' **Spu′rius Tarpeius** (tär-pē′yu̯s): the father of Tarpe′ia, the maid referred to below. *Mōns Tarpeius* was the old name of the Capitoline hill. See illustration, page 412, and Plan.

TITUS TATIUS   TARPEIA OVERPOWERED BY THE SHIELDS

5. **fīliam virginem:** ' maiden daughter,' Tarpeia. *Virgō* and a few other nouns are sometimes used as adjectives. According to the usual legend she was a vestal. See illustration, pages 115 and 117.

7. **sacrīs:** what kind of dative? *112, a;* B. 191; A. & G. 382; G. 356. **petītum:** supine. *231.* **obrutam armīs necāvēre:** sc. *eam;* ' they overwhelmed her with their shields and killed her.' *211.*

8. **seu ut . . . seu:** ' whether (they did this) in order that . . . or.'

9. **prōdendī exemplī:** ' setting an example.' **nē quid ūsquam fīdum:** ' that nowhere any faith.' Note carefully the different negative expressions in purpose and result clauses: *197, e;* A. & G. 538; G. 543, 4.

10. **Additur fābulae, quod:** ' There is a further legend that because.'

magnī ponderis bracchiō laevō gemmātōsque magnā speciē
ānulōs habuerint, pepigisse eam quod in sinistrīs manibus
habērent; eō scūta illī prō aureīs dōnīs congesta. Sunt
quī eam ex pactō trādendī quod in sinistrīs manibus habē-

THE ANIO RIVER AND SABINE MOUNTAINS

The subject of *additur* is *pepigisse eam* below. *222, a.* **Sabīnī**: who were
they? See vocabulary and Map, following page 6.

11. **magnī ponderis**: compare with *magnā speciē* below. The genitive of quality is less common than the ablative, but it is the regular
construction with expressions of weight, number, measure, time, and
space. *100, a;* B. 203; A. & G. 345; G. 365. **bracchiō**: Livy sometimes
omits *in* with ablative of place where after the manner of poetry. Poetic
words and phrases are a marked characteristic of his pictorial style.
See Companion, page 563. **magnā speciē**: see *magnī ponderis* above.
External or physical qualities are more often expressed by the ablative;
143, a; B. 224; A. & G. 415, *a;* G. 400, R. 1.

12. **habuerint**: whose reason is this? *183, a;* B. 286, 1; A. & G.
540; G. 541. **pepigisse**: from *pangere*, 'had stipulated for.' **quod**: a
relative. What is its antecedent? *164, a;* B. 251; A. & G. 307; G. 616.

13. **eō**: 'therefore.' **illī**: dative for the more regular *in illam,*
another poetical usage.

14. **ex pactō**: 'in accordance with the agreement.' *136, c.*

15 rent dērēctō arma petīsse dīcant et fraude vīsam agere suā
ipsam perēmptam mercēde.

*Romulus saves the day by vowing a temple to Jupiter; the origin of
'Juppiter Stator.'*

12. Tenuēre tamen arcem Sabīnī atque inde posterō
diē, cum Rōmānus exercitus īnstrūctus quod inter Palātīnum Capitōlīnumque collem campī est complēsset, nōn
prius dēscendērunt in
5 aequum quam īrā et
cupiditāte reciperandae
arcis stimulante animōs
in adversum Rōmānī

THE TARPEIAN ROCK

15. **dīcant:** *194, a;* B. 283,
2; A. & G. 535, *a;* G. 631, 2.
fraude . . . mercēde: ' appearing to act treacherously
she was slain of her own choice
by the reward she specified.'
The literal translations for *ipse*
and *suus* are often inadequate.
See illustration, page 410.
fraude: ablative of manner
without the preposition, used
in several stereotyped expressions. *136, b;* B. 220, 2; A.
& G. 412, *b;* G. 399, note 1.
For a full discussion of this
myth see University of Michigan Studies, Humanistic Series, Volume I,
pages 1–47.

12. 1. **Tenuēre tamen:** ' Be this as it may, they did hold.' Note the
emphatic position of the verb and the resumptive meaning of *tamen*, which
resumes the thought after the brief digression in the last sentence above.

2. **cum:** ' although.' **Rōmānus exercitus:** *Rōmānus* and *Latīnus*
regularly follow their noun: why not here? **quod . . . campī:** ' all
the level ground which '; *campī* is partitive genitive. *97, b.* **Palātīnum
Capitōlīnumque:** see Plan of Rome, Frontispiece.

4. **prius:** with *quam* below = *priusquam*, ' until,' tmesis. *238, p.*

8. **in adversum:** sc. *montem*, ' up the hill '; which one?

subiēre. Prīncipēs utrimque pugnam ciēbant, ab Sabīnīs
Mettius Curtius, ab Rōmānīs Hostius Hostilius. Hīc rem 10
Rōmānam inīquō locō ad prīma signa animō atque audāciā
sustinēbat. Ut Hostius cecidit, cōnfestim Rōmāna inclīnātur aciēs fūsaque est ad veterem portam Palātiī. Rōmulus et ipse turbā fugientium āctus, arma ad caelum tollēns,
"Iuppiter, tuīs," inquit, "iussus avibus hīc in Palātiō prīma 15
urbī fundāmenta iēcī. Arcem iam scelere ēmptam Sabīnī
habent, inde hūc armātī superātā mediā valle tendunt.
At tū, pater deum hominumque, hinc saltem arcē hostēs,
dēme terrōrem Rōmānīs fugamque foedam siste. Hīc

---

9. **pugnam ciēbant:** ' began the fight.' **ab Sabīnīs:** ' on the side of.' Compare *ā latere, ā tergō,* and similar expressions. *126, c.*

10. **Mettius Curtius** (met′ĭ-ŭs kur′sh(y)ŭs). **Hīc:** ' The latter ' = *Hostius* (hŏs′tĭ ŭs) *Hostilius.* **rem:** how should this word be translated? See Companion under *211.*

TEMPLE OF JUPITER STATOR
From an old relief.

11. **ad prīma signa . . . sustinēbat:** ' he kept under control.' How literally? *signa,* ' standards,' is used idiomatically as a part of several military phrases, since standards represent the distinctive mark of the army.

12. **inclīnātur:** ' gave way.'

13. **fūsaque est:** ' was driven in confusion.'

14. **et:** = *etiam.* **turbā fugientium āctus:** ' being carried along in the crowd of fugitives.' *āctus,* though a perfect participle, is here used as a substitute for the missing present participle passive. *212, k.*

16. **iēcī:** ' I laid.'

17. **tendunt:** ' they are bending their course.'

18. **deum:** old genitive, = *deōrum.* **hinc saltem:** ' from this place at least.' **arcē:** imperative. The ablative of *arx* would require a short *e.*

19. **Rōmānīs:** some grammars call this a dative of separation; it is more correctly a dative of interest or advantage. *109, b;* B. 188, 2, *d;* A. & G. 381, N.; G. 345, R. **siste:** ' stay.'

20 ego tibi templum Statōrī Iovī, quod monumentum sit posterīs tuā praesentī ope servātam urbem esse, voveō." Haec precātus, velut sī sēnsisset audītās precēs, "Hinc," inquit, "Rōmānī, Iuppiter optimus maximus resistere atque iterāre pugnam iubet." Restitēre Rōmānī tamquam cae-
15 lestī vōce iussī, ipse ad prīmōrēs Rōmulus prōvolat.

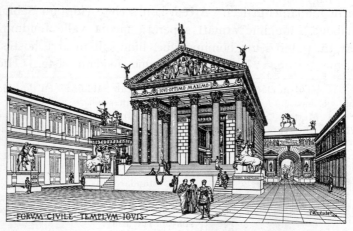

TEMPLE OF JUPITER OPTIMUS MAXIMUS IN POMPEII
A restoration.

---

20. **Statōrī** (stā′tor) **Iovī**: ' Jupiter, the Stayer (of flight).' This temple, however, was not built till 294 B.C., and its remains have been uncovered. See illustration, page 413. In it Cicero delivered his *First Oration against Catiline*. **quod . . . sit**: relative clause of purpose. **monumentum**: ' memorial.'

21. **servātam esse**: indirect discourse caused by the idea of saying in *monumentum sit*. *214, b.*

22. **Haec**: cognate accusative to *precātus;* how to be translated? *117, a;* B. 176, 2, *a;* A. & G. 390, *c;* G. 333. Compare English colloquial expression, " to foot it." **Hinc**: ' Here '; how literally?

24. **Restitēre**: very emphatic. *211.*

25. **ad prīmōrēs**: ' to the front of the battle.' **prōvolat**: ' (fairly) flew.'

The Sabine women act as peacemakers; the origin of 'Quirītēs.'

13. Tum Sabīnae mulierēs, quārum ex iniūriā bellum ortum erat, crīnibus passīs scissāque veste, victō malīs muliebrī pavōre, ausae sē inter tēla volantia īnferre, ex trānsversō impetū factō dirimere īnfestās aciēs, dirimere īrās, hinc patrēs hinc virōs ōrantēs, nē sē sanguine nefandō 5 socerī generīque respergerent, nē parricīdiō maculārent partūs suōs, nepōtum illī, hī līberum prōgeniem. "Sī affīnitātis inter vōs, sī cōnūbiī piget, in nōs vertite īrās, nōs causa bellī, nōs vulnerum ac caedium virīs ac parentibus sumus; melius perībimus quam sine alterīs vestrum viduae 10 aut orbae vīvēmus."

---

13. 2. **crīnibus . . . veste**: note the arrangement. *239, e;* B. 350, 11, *c*); A. & G. 598, *f;* G. 682, and R. **passīs**: from *pandere.* **scissā**: from *scindere.* **victō . . . pavōre**: ' their feminine fear overcome by their misfortunes.'

3. **ex trānsversō impetū factō**: ' rushing in sideways.'

4. **dirimere**: historical infinitive, as is shown from *Sabīnae mulierēs* above. *182.* The repetition of *dirimere* adds vividness to the scene.

5. **īrās**: abstract for concrete, a poetical usage. Translate as if *īrātōs. 92, b.*

7. **suōs**: refers to the Sabine women. **nepōtum . . . līberum**: appositional genitives to *prōgeniem. 96, a.* **illī, hī**: *illī* refers to the fathers, *i.e.* the Sabines; *hī* to the husbands, *i.e.* Romans. Translate, ' the Sabines their (the women's) offspring of grandchildren, the Romans their offspring of children.' **līberum**: = *līberōrum.* For the word order see line 2 above. **Sī**, etc.: what effect does Livy secure by this change to direct discourse? Livy's Latinity is on the whole Ciceronian, but his manner of employing it is far different from that of Cicero. Read this paragraph once more in the Latin, and compare it with a passage from Cicero's orations.

8. **affīnitātis, conūbiī**: *103, c;* B. 209; A. & G. 354, *b;* G. 377. **inter vōs**: ' with one another,' expressing the reciprocal relation. *159.* **piget**: sc. *vōs,* the accusative of the person affected.

10. **melius perībimus**: ' 'twill be better for us to perish,' a concentrated form of expression called brachylogy. *238, e.* **sine alterīs vestrum**: ' without the one or the other of you.'

Movet rēs tum multitūdinem tum ducēs; silentium et repentīna fit quiēs, inde ad foedus faciendum ducēs prōdeunt, nec pācem modo sed cīvitātem ūnam ex duābus

15 faciunt, rēgnum cōnsociant, imperium omne cōnferunt Rōmam. Ita gemināta urbe, ut Sabīnīs tamen aliquid darētur, Quirītēs ā Curibus appellātī.

While a military review is in progress on the Campus Martius Romulus is apotheosized, and declares that Rome will become the capital of the world.

16. Hīs immortālibus ēditīs operibus cum ad exercitum recēnsendum cōntiōnem in campō ad Caprae Palūdem habēret, subitō coorta tempestās cum magnō fragōre tonitribusque tam dēnsō rēgem operuit nimbō ut cōn-

---

12. **rēs:** ' their appeal.'

13. **fit:** ' ensued.'

15. **imperium:** ' the government.'   **cōnferunt:** ' transfer.'

16. **aliquid darētur:** ' some concession might be made.'

17. **Quirītēs** (quĭ-rī'tēz) **ā Curibus** (kū'rēz) **appellātī** (sc. *sunt*): ' they (the citizens) were called Quirites from Cures,' the chief town of the Sabines some twenty-five miles from Rome. This etymology of the word Quirites, interesting though it may be, has not been readily accepted among scholars, who, however, are quite uncertain regarding its correct derivation.

16. 1. **immortālibus operibus:** the achievements of Romulus won for him immortality. See Livy, **1,** 7, 15: ' . . . furthering already then the immortality acquired by worth to which his own destiny was guiding him.' Their history was given by Livy in the chapters here omitted. **ad exercitum recēnsendum:** ' military review,' ' dress parade.'

2. **cōntiōnem:** ' muster.'   **in campō ad Caprae Palūdem:** ' in the Campus Martius near the Goat Swamp.' For the location of the Campus Martius (mär'sh(y)ụs) see Plan of Rome, Frontispiece. It was consecrated to Mars, and was especially adapted to military maneuvers. Nothing definite is known regarding the Goat Swamp in the Campus Martius, but Ovid (*Fastī*, **2,** 491) also describes the mysterious disappearance of Romulus from this place during a thunderstorm.

3. **cum magnō fragōre tonitribusque:** ' with loud peals of thunder,' hendiadys.   Note the onomatopoetic (*239, o*) effect — broad vowels, liquids, gutturals, dentals. *238, h;* B. 374, 4; A. & G. 640; G. 698.

spectum eius cōntiōnī abstulerit; nec deinde in terrīs 5
Rōmulus fuit. Rōmāna pūbes sēdātō tandem pavōre,
postquam ex tam turbidō diē serēna et tranquilla lūx rediit,
ubi vacuam sēdem rēgiam vīdit, etsī satis crēdēbat patribus,
quī proximī steterant, sublīmem raptum procellā, tamen
velut orbitātis metū icta maestum aliquamdiū silentium 10
obtinuit. Deinde, ā paucīs initiō factō, deum deō nātum,
rēgem parentemque urbis Rōmānae salvēre ūniversī Rōmulum iubent, pācem precibus exposcunt, utī volēns propitius suam semper sospitet prōgeniem. Fuisse crēdō tum
quoque aliquōs quī discerptum rēgem patrum manibus 15

---

5. **eius:** = *Rōmulī*. **cōntiōnī:** see page 41○, line 9, and note. **ab-stulerit:** from *auferre*. The perfect subjunctive is often used in a result clause after a secondary tense to emphasize the result, *i.e.* to indicate that it is absolute and final. See page 18, note 16. *177, b.*

6. **Rōmāna pūbēs,** etc. . this sentence is a good illustration of Livy's period, and should not be translated literally. It may be rendered as follows : ' The Roman youth (soldiers) finally repressed their fright, as soon as this period (*diē*) of confusion was again followed by the fair and calm light of day ; yet when they saw the throne unoccupied, although they readily believed the senators who had been standing near by, that he had been seized aloft by a blast, they continued for some time in sorrowful silence, smitten, as it were, by the fear of orphanage.' The longer sentences of Livy are best subdivided as above. Notice again the technique of poetry as exemplified in the choice of words, alliteration and the *staccato* effect of the dentals in *tam turbidō diē*, the *legato* in *serēna et tranquilla lūx*, the imagery in *sublīmem raptum procellā*, and the effective comparison in *orbitātis*.

9. **raptum:** sc. *eum* as subject. *215.* The indirect discourse is due to the idea of saying suggested by *crēdēbat*.

11. **ā paucīs initiō factō:** ' after a few had made the start.' **deum deō nātum, rēgem parentemque:** in apposition with *Rōmulum* below.

12. **salvēre ūniversī Rōmulum iubent:** ' they all offered greetings to Romulus '; they cried, *salvē, Rōmule*, etc.

13. **pācem precibus exposcunt:** ' they implored his grace.' *pācem* is explained by the *utī*-clause. **volēns propitius:** in certain formal phrases *et* is omitted, asyndeton ; see *patrēs cōnscrīptī*, page 432, line 35, note, *optimus maximus*, page 100, line 10, note. *238, d.*

14. **tum quoque:** ' even then.'

tacitī arguerent: mānāvit enim haec quoque, sed perob-
scūra fāma; illam alteram admīrātiō virī et pavor praesēns
nōbilitāvit.

Et cōnsiliō etiam unīus hominis addita reī dīcitur fidēs.
20 Namque Proculus Iūlius, sollicitā cīvitāte dēsīderiō rēgis
et īnfēnsā patribus, gravis, ut trāditur, quamvīs magnae
reī auctor in cōntiōnem prōdit. " Rōmulus," inquit, " Quirītēs, parēns urbis huius, prīmā hodiernā lūce caelō repente
dēlāpsus sē mihi obvium dedit. Cum perfūsus horrōre
25 venerābundus astitissem, petēns precibus ut contrā intuērī fās esset, 'Abī, nūntiā,' inquit, 'Rōmānīs, caelestēs
ita velle, ut mea Rōma caput orbis terrārum sit; proinde,
rem mīlitārem colant sciantque et ita posterīs trādant,

16. **tacitī arguerent:** ' secretly charged.' **mānāvit:** ' leaked out ';
the underlying metaphor suggests the trickling of water through the soil.

17. **illam alteram . . . nōbilitāvit:** ' their admiration for the hero
and the awe inspired by the occasion dignified the former version.'

19. **addita:** sc. *esse.* **reī:** ' to the story,' given above. **fidēs:**
' corroboration.'

20. **Iūlius** (jūl'yus): the Julian family, then, seemed to have been
established as early as the city itself.

21. **gravis . . . auctor:** ' a weighty authority, according to tradition,
on any question, however important '; literally, ' a weighty authority
for however great a thing.'

22. **inquit:** notice that this word is used only for direct discourse.
Quirītes: the accepted etymology of this name among the Romans is
given by Livy in **13,** 17, page 416; see note.

23. **huius:** notice the emphatic position of this pronoun. **prīmā
hodiernā lūce:** ' early this morning.'

24. **dēlāpsus . . . dedit:** ' presented himself to my presence.' **perfūsus . . . astitissem:** ' I, filled with religious awe, stood reverently
before him.'

25. **contrā intuērī:** ' to look upon him face to face.'

26. **caelestēs ita velle, ut:** ' the will of heaven that '; how literally?
The infinitive is the regular construction after *velle,* but here *ita* calls
for an *ut*-clause. *223 (a) 1.*

27. **proinde:** ' accordingly.' *237, a.*

28. **ita posterīs trādant:** ' let them transmit this to their descend-

nūllās opēs hūmānās armīs Rōmānīs resistere posse.'"
"Haec," inquit, "locūtus sublīmis abiit." Mīrum quan- 30
tum illī virō nūntiantī haec fidēs fuerit, quamque dēsīderium Rōmulī apud plēbem exercitumque factā fidē immortālitātis lēnītum sit.

Numa builds the temple of Janus, and arranges the calendar.

19. Quī rēgnō ita potītus urbem novam, conditam vī
et armīs, iūre eam lēgibusque ac mōribus dē integrō condere
parat. Quibus cum inter bella assuēscere vidēret nōn
posse, quippe efferārī mīlitiā animōs, mītigandum ferōcem
populum armōrum dēsuētūdine ratus, Iānum ad īnfimum 5

---

ants.' *ita = hōc* here, and anticipates the substantive idea expressed
by the following indirect discourse.

30. **Mīrum:** sc. *est;* ' It is wonderful to what extent credence was
placed in the report of that man.' *quantum* is an adverbial accusative
limiting *fidēs fuerit.*

31. **fuerit:** indirect question; but the indicative is the usual mood
with *mīrum quantum,* which is ordinarily equivalent to an adverb,
' wonderfully,' ' extraordinarily,' etc. *204 (6)*; A. & G. 575, *d;* G. 467, N.
The exceptional usage here is probably due to Livy's desire to preserve
a proper balance with the following indirect ques-
tion. **quamque:** ' and how.'

32. **factā fidē immortālitātis:** ' when his immortality had been assured.'

19. 1. **Quī:** Numa Pompi'lius, of Sabine descent, who had just been chosen king. **rēgnō:**
' throne.' **vī et armīs:** hendiadys. *238, h.*

2. **iūre . . . lēgibusque ac mōribus:** Numa
was famed for his legal wisdom and his religious
devotion, and was regarded by the Romans as
the founder of their whole religious system. Romulus was essentially
a warlike king.

NUMA POMPILIUS

3. **Quibus:** dative with *assuēscere,* referring to *iūre, lēgibus, mōribus*
above. **assuēscere:** sc. *hominēs.*

4. **quippe** (= *nam*) **efferārī mīlitiā animōs:** ' for (he realized that)
men's hearts are made savage by warfare.'

5. **armōrum dēsuētūdine:** ' by the disuse of arms.' **Iānum:** ' a
temple of Janus (jā'nu̞s),' an old Italian deity, whose worship occupied

Argilētum indicem pācis bellīque fēcit, apertus ut in armīs
esse cīvitātem, clausus pācātōs circā omnēs populōs sig-
nificāret. Bis deinde post Numae rēgnum clausus fuit,
semel T. Mānliō cōnsule post Pūnicum prīmum perfectum
10 bellum, iterum, quod nostrae aetātī diī dedērunt ut vidērēmus, post bellum Actiacum ab imperātōre Caesare
Augustō pāce terrā marīque partā.

Clausō eō cum omnium circā fīnitimōrum societāte ac

an important place in Roman religion.   Numa's so-called temple was
merely a covered passage or arch.   The god Janus had various func-
tions: he presided over the beginning of everything, opened the year
and the seasons; hence the first month of the year was named after
him; he was also the porter of heaven, and
the guardian deity of gates, and so is represented in art with two heads to typify the
two sides of a door (*iānus bifrōns*).   Compare
the Latin word for "door" and the English
word "janitor."   See illustration, page 421.

THE GOD JANUS

īnfimum Argilētum: 'the lowest part of the
Argiletum (är-jĭ-lē'tŭm),' a street at the north-
east end of the Forum.   See Plan of Rome,
Frontispiece.

    6. **apertus:** placed before *ut* to balance
clausus. 211.

    8. **clausus fuit:** not equivalent to *clausus est;* but indicates that
the temple has been in a closed state, 'it has been shut.'

    9. **semel:** 235 B.C.   **post Pūnicum prīmum perfectum:** note the
alliteration. *239, a.*

    10. **iterum:** 29 B.C.   **quod:** object of *vidērēmus.*

    11. **Caesare Augustō:** Octavianus did not receive the title of Augus-
tus before 27 B.C., and, since Livy does not mention the third closing of
the temple of Janus in 25 B.C., it is obvious that Livy began his history
between 27 and 25 B.C.

    12. **partā:** from *parĕre.*

    13. **Clausō eō cum . . . ratus est:** 'After Numa had closed the
temple, he secured the good will of all his neighbors by an alliance and
treaties; and, in order that the national temper, which had been curbed
by fear of the enemy and military training, might not run riot when his
people had laid aside their anxiety concerning foreign dangers, he
thought that first of all fear of the gods ought to be instilled (as being)

foederibus iūnxisset animōs, positīs externōrum perīculōrum cūrīs nē lūxuriārent ōtiō animī, quōs metus hostium disci- 15 plīnaque mīlitāris continuerat, omnium prīmum rem ad multitūdinem imperītam et illīs saeculīs rudem efficācissimam, deōrum metum iniciendum ratus est. Quī cum

THE TEMPLE OF JANUS

In the background is the Basilica Aemilia.
A restoration.

dēscendere ad animōs sine aliquō commentō 20 mīrāculī nōn posset, simulat sibi cum deā Ēgeriā congressūs nocturnōs esse, eius sē monitū, quae acceptissima diīs essent, 25 sacra īnstituere, sacerdōtēs suōs cuique deōrum praeficere.

Atque omnium prīmum ad cursūs lūnae in duo- 30 decim mēnsēs discrībit annum, quem, quia trīcēnōs diēs singulīs mēnsibus lūna nōn explet

the most effective check (*rem*) for a populace which was ignorant and for those times uncultivated.'

18. **Quī cum . . . posset:** ' And since this could not penetrate into their hearts without the intervention of some wonderful occurrence.' *Quī* refers to *deōrum metum*.

22. **sibi:** dative of possession. **Ēge′riā:** Roman goddess of fountains, one of the *Camēnae*, or Muses. She was the wife and teacher of Numa.

24. **eius sē monitū:** very emphatic; ' that it was by her (*eius*) advice that he (*sē*).' **quae:** the antecedent is *sacra* below.

27. **suōs:** ' special.' *157, e.* **cuique deōrum:** = *sacrīs cuiusque deōrum*, brachylogy. *238, e.*

30. **ad cursūs lūnae:** ' according to the revolutions of the moon.'

32. **quem:** object of *dispēnsāvit* below. **quia trīcēnōs diēs . . . nōn explet:** since the lunar month had approximately 29½ days, the lunar year was about 11 days shorter than the solar year.

dēsuntque diēs solidō annō, qui sōlstitiālī circumagitur
35 orbe, intercalāriīs mēnsibus interpōnendīs ita dispēnsāvit
ut vīcēsimō annō ad mētam eandem sōlis, unde ōrsī
essent, plēnīs omnium annōrum spatiīs diēs congruerent.
Īdem nefāstōs diēs fāstōsque fēcit, quia aliquandō nihil
cum populō agī ūtile futūrum erat.

The combat between the Horatii and Curatii.

24. Forte in duōbus tum exercitibus erant trigeminī frātrēs nec aetāte nec vīribus disparēs : Horātiōs Curiātiōsque

---

34. **dēsuntque diēs:** the manuscripts have no numeral; we may
either supply *undecim*, or assume that Livy intentionally avoided a
definite statement. **quī sōlstitiālī circumagitur orbe :** ' which elapses
in a solar revolution.' *114, b.*

35. **orbe:** ablative of way by which. *134, b;* B. 218, 9; A. &. G.
429, *a;* G. 389. **intercalāriīs mēnsibus interpōnendīs :** in order to rectify
the difference between the lunar and the solar year. **dispēnsāvit :**
' regulated.' See note 24 above.

36. **ut vīcēsimō annō . . . congruerent:** ' so that in the twentieth
year the days corresponded to the same position of the sun from which
they had started, all annual intervals being completed.'

37. **plēnīs . . . spatiīs:** ablative absolute.

38. **Īdem :** ' He also.' **nefāstōs diēs fāstōsque :** ' holidays and
workdays.' More specifically, *nefāstī* refers to those days on which
court could not be convened nor popular assemblies be held, whereas
fāstī diēs were those on which it was lawful (*fās*) to transact civil and
judicial business. The list of *diēs fāstī*, usually called only *Fāstī*, was the
origin of the Roman calendar, and is the title of a very important poem of
Ovid on the Roman festivals of the first six months of the year. The
calendar is discussed in the Companion, page 697.

39. **nihil cum populō agī :** ' that nothing should be submitted to the
people.'

This and the following chapters are a good illustration of Livy's
pictorial style, his wealth of imagination, his attractive poetical diction,
his clear and concise narration, his dramatic power. The excellence
of Livy's First Book has been aptly summed up in the descriptive
phrase, " a prose poem." In the final analysis Livy's art does not
differ very widely from that of Virgil.

24. 1. **in duōbus :** ' in each of the two,' the Alban and the Roman.

2. **Horātiōs Curiātiōsque** (hǫ-rā′shў̆-ī and kū-ri-ā′shў̆-ī).

fuisse satis cōnstat, nec fermē rēs antīqua alia est nōbilior;
tamen in rē tam clārā nōminum error manet, utrīus populī
Horātiī, utrīus Curiātiī fuerint. Auctōrēs utrōque tra- 5
hunt: plūrēs tamen inveniō quī Rōmānōs Horātiōs vocent;
hōs ut sequar inclīnat animus.

Cum trigeminīs agunt rēgēs ut prō suā quisque patriā
dīmicent ferrō: ibi imperium fore unde victōria fuerit.
Nihil recūsātur, tempus et locus convenit. Priusquam dīmi- 10
cārent, foedus ictum inter Rōmānōs et Albānōs est hīs

THE ALBAN LAKE

3. **satis cōnstat:** ' it is well known.' **rēs:** ' event.' **nōbilior:**
' more famous.'

4. **in rē tam clārā nōminum error:** ' notwithstanding its great fame,
uncertainty (*error*) regarding the names.' **utrīus populī:** predicative
genitive of possession. *94, d;* B. 198, *w;* A. & G. 343, *b;* G. 366.

5. **fuerint:** why perfect subjunctive? *177, a.* **utrōque trahunt:**
literally, ' pull in both directions,' *i.e.,* ' are divided.'

6. **plūrēs:** ' the majority.' Is this a sound method for an historian? **vocent:** clause of characteristic. *194, a.*

7. **inclīnat animus:** ' I am disposed to.'

8. **agunt:** ' negotiate.' **quisque:** in apposition with the subject.

9. **ibi . . . unde:** relative adverbs in Latin frequently refer to
persons: ' with that people . . . on whose side.'

10. **convenit:** ' were agreed upon.' The verb is in the singular
because the two subjects are thought of as constituting a whole. B. 255,
3; A. & G. 317, *b;* G. 285, Exception 2. Compare also the singular verb
with *senātus populusque Rōmānus.* **dīmicārent:** *189, b;* B. 292; A. & G.
551. b; G. 577. The limit is ideal and not real.

lēgibus, ut, cuius populī cīvēs eō certāmine vīcissent, is
alterī populō cum bonā pāce imperitāret.

25. Foedere ictō trigeminī sīcut convēnerat arma
capiunt. Cum suī utrōsque adhortārentur, deōs patriōs,
patriam ac parentēs, quidquid cīvium domī, quidquid in
exercitū sit, illōrum tunc arma, illōrum intuērī manūs,
5 ferōcēs et suōpte ingeniō et plēnī adhortantium vōcibus
in medium inter duās aciēs prōcēdunt. Cōnsēderant
utrimque prō castrīs duo exercitūs, perīculī magis praesentis
quam cūrae expertēs; quippe imperium agēbātur in tam

---

12. **lēgibus:** 'conditions.' **populī:** *165, c;* B. 251, 4, *a;* A. & G. 307,
b, and N.; G. 616. **vīcissent:** subordinate clause in implied indirect
discourse; the pluperfect tense represents a future perfect of direct
discourse. *177, a; 214, b.* **is:** sc. *populus.*

13. **cum bonā pāce:** 'in peace and quiet.' **imperitāret:** how does
this verb differ from *imperāre?*

25. 2. **Cum . . . adhortārentur:** best translated as an independent
clause.

3. **quidquid cīvium:** ' all the citizens.' *97, b.* The partitive genitive
with *quidquid* referring to persons is poetical and a feature of Livy's style.
This use of the neuter in personal designations imparts an atmosphere
of completeness to the expression.

4. **sit:** subordinate clause in indirect discourse, governed by the
idea of saying implied in *adhortārentur* above, which Livy here treats as
a primary tense to make the discourse more vivid and picturesque.
This is called *repraesentātio,* whereby the time may shift between
speaker and reporter. *177, c;* B. 318; A. & G. 585, *b,* N.; G. 517, 2; 654.
illōrum: in direct discourse this would be *vestra.* **intuērī:** its subjects
are *deōs patriōs, patriam,* etc., above; main clause in indirect discourse
governed by *adhortārentur,* as explained previously.

5. **ferōcēs . . . vōcibus:** ' eager to fight both because of their
natural disposition and because they were inspired by the shouts of
encouragement.' **suōpte:** the enclitic *-pte* is added for the sake of
emphasis. B. 86, 3; A. & G. 145, *a;* G. 102, N. 3.

6. **Cōnsēderant:** note the emphatic position and the tense.

7. **perīculī:** with *expertēs: 102;* B. 204; A. & G. 349, *a;* G. 374,
N. 2. **praesentis:** ' immediate.'

8. **cūrae:** ' anxiety.' The outcome of the contest might greatly
affect their future. **quippe:** = *nam.* **imperium agēbātur:** ' dominion
was at stake.'

ABOVE: THE ALBAN MOUNTAIN

BELOW: THE LAKE AND TOWN OF NEMI

paucōrum virtūte atque fortūnā positum. Itaque ergō
ērēctī suspēnsīque in minimē grātum spectāculum animō 10
intenduntur.

Datur signum īnfēstīsque armīs, velut aciēs, ternī iuvenēs,
magnōrum exercituum animōs gerentēs, concurrunt. Nec
hīs nec illīs perīculum suum, pūblicum imperium servitiumque obversātur animō futūraque ea deinde patriae 15
fortūna quam ipsī fēcissent. Ut prīmō statim concursū
increpuēre arma micantēsque fulsēre gladiī, horror ingēns

---

9. **positum :** ' dependent upon.' **Itaque ergō :** pleonasm, ' Accordingly, therefore.' *238, k; 237, a.*

10. **ērēcti :** ' tense.' **minimē :** an emphatic negative. **spectāculum :** ' exhibition.' **animō intenduntur :** ' their attention was directed '; literally, ' they are put on the stretch by their attention.'

12. **ternī :** why not *trēs?*

13. **gerentēs :** ' exhibiting.'

14. **hīs, illīs :** datives of reference : *109, a;* B. 188, 1, N.; A. &
G. 377; G. 350, 1. **perīculum suum . . . animō :** 'it was not their own
danger which hovered before the mind of either side, (but) their nation's
dominion.' **imperium servitiumque :** we should use ' or ' instead of
' and.'

15. **futūraque ea . . . fortūna :** another subject of *obversātur.* Latin
often uses a noun with a participle where in English some abstract expression would be employed. *212, c.* Here *futūra* may be translated by
a relative clause, viz., ' and the fate of their fatherland, which henceforth would be such (*ea*) as (*quam*) they themselves should determine.'

16. **quam :** relative. **fēcissent :** subordinate clause in indirect discourse implied in *obversātur animō* above. Their direct thought would
have required the future perfect indicative, which in indirect discourse,
dependent upon a secondary verb (*obversātur* is historical present),
becomes a pluperfect subjunctive. *177, a;* B. 269, 1 (*b*); A. & G.
484, *c;* G. 516. **Ut :** 'As soon as.' *188, a.* **prīmō statim concursū :** 'the
moment they charged.' Livy frequently uses adverbs with the force
of adjectives; a Grecism. *238, g.*

17. **increpuēre :** ' clashed,' an onomatopoetic word; *239, o.* It is
best to translate *increpuēre* as an independent verb. **horror . . . perstringit :** ' a deep shudder thrilled (through the veins of) the onlookers.'
The Latin words vividly suggest an overpowering emotional experience, by both their sound and their meaning.

spectantīs perstringit, et neutrō inclīnātā spē torpēbat vōx
spīritusque. Cōnsertīs deinde manibus, cum iam nōn
20 mōtūs tantum corporum agitātiōque anceps tēlōrum
armōrumque sed vulnera quoque et sanguis spectāculō
essent, duo Rōmānī super alium alius, vulnerātīs tribus
Albānīs, exspīrantēs corruērunt. Ad quōrum cāsum cum
conclāmāsset gaudiō Albānus exercitus, Rōmānās legiōnēs
25 iam spēs tōta, nōndum tamen cūra dēseruerat, exanimēs
vice ūnīus, quem trēs Curiātiī circumsteterant. Forte is
integer fuit, ut ūniversīs sōlus nēquāquam pār, sīc adversus
singulōs ferōx. Ergō ut sēgregāret pugnam eōrum, capessit
fugam, ita ratus secūtūrōs ut quemque vulnere affectum
30 corpus sineret. Iam aliquantum spatiī ex eō locō, ubi
pugnātum est, aufūgerat, cum respiciēns videt magnīs
intervallīs sequentēs, ūnum haud procul ab sēsē abesse.
In eum magnō impetū rediit, et dum Albānus exercitus

---

18. **neutrō . . . spīritusque:** literally, ' their hope having been made
to turn in neither direction, their speech and breath were paralyzed.'
Translate it into good English.

19. **Cōnsertīs manibus:** ' In a hand to hand encounter.'

20. **mōtūs corporum agitātiōque anceps tēlōrum armōrumque:** 'their
physical movements and the twofold swinging of swords and shields.'

21. **spectāculō:** dative of purpose. *112, a.*

23. **exspīrantēs:** ' breathing their last,' *i.e.* mortally wounded. **Ad
quōrum cāsum:** ' At the fall of the Romans.'

25. **exanimēs vice ūnīus:** ' breathless on account of the predicament
of the single combatant.'

26. **Forte:** ' Fortunately.'

27. **ut . . . sīc:** ' while . . . yet.' **ūniversīs:** ' all together.'

28. **ferōx:** ' intrepid.'

29. **secūtūrōs:** sc. *esse* and *eōs* as subject. **ut:** ' as.' Correlate
with *ita* above.

30. **sineret:** why subjunctive? **spatiī:** partitive genitive. *97, b.*

31. **cum . . . videt:** called *cum-inversum: 185, d;* B. 288, 2; A. & G.
546, *a;* G. 581. The purpose of this construction is to introduce the
element of astonishment or unexpectedness.

33. **impetū:** ' fierceness.'

inclāmat Curiātiīs utī opem ferant frātrī, iam Horātius,
caesō hoste victor, secundam pugnam petēbat.   35
    Tunc clāmōre, quālis ex īnspērātō faventium solet,
Rōmānī adiuvant mīlitem suum et ille dēfungī proeliō
festīnat. Prius itaque quam alter, quī nec procul aberat,
cōnsequī posset, et alterum Curiātium cōnficit. Iamque
aequātō Mārte singulī supererant, sed nec spē nec vīribus 40
parēs. Alterum intāctum ferrō corpus et gemināta victōria
ferōcem in certāmen tertium dabat; alter, fessum vulnere,
fessum cursū trahēns corpus victusque frātrum ante sē
strāge, victōrī obicitur hostī. Nec illud proelium fuit.
Rōmānus exsultāns "Duōs," inquit, "frātrum Mānibus 45
dedī; tertium causae bellī huiusce, ut Rōmānus Albānō

---

    36. clāmōre: ' with a cheer.' quālis . . . solet: ' such as is wont
to burst forth from the partisans at an unexpected success.' ex īnspērātō: ' unexpectedly,' adverbial phrase. faventium: predicate
genitive of possession. *94, d.* solet: sc. *esse.*

    37. proeliō: *131, c;* B. 218, 1; A. & G. 410, G. 407.

    38. nec: = *nōn*, an archaic usage. *238, c.*

    39. posset: subjunctive, because the limit is ideal., *i.e.* it does not
actually take place. *189, b;* B. 292; A. & G. 551, *b;* G. 577.

    40. aequātō Mārte: ' on even terms.' Mārte: = *pugna* by me-
tonymy. *239, n.* singulī: ' one on each side.'

    41. Alterum: *i.e.* the Roman; accusative case. intāctum corpus et
gemināta victōria: nominative case, subjects of *dabat.* For the singular
verb, see page 423, note 10.

    42. ferōcem: modifies *alterum* above. dabat: ' made.'

    43. ante sē: ' before his eyes.' Livy's use of a prepositional phrase
as an attributive modifier of a noun is a Grecism. *238, g.*

    44. strāge: this word is vividly suggestive. obicitur: ' was pitted
against.' Nec illud proelium fuit: ' But what followed was not a
combat.'

    45. frātrum Mānibus dedī: ' I have given to the Shades of my
brothers.' The *Mānēs* were the deified souls of the departed, to whom
various sacrifices were made regularly.

    46. huiusce: -ce is a demonstrative particle appended for emphasis,
possibly indicating a gesture.

imperet, dabō." Male sustinentī arma gladium supernē
iugulō dēfīgit, iacentem spoliat.

Rōmānī ovantēs ac grātulantēs Horātium accipiunt
50 eō maiōre cum gaudiō, quō prope metum rēs fuerat. Ad
sepultūram inde suōrum nēquāquam paribus animīs vertuntur, quippe imperiō alterī auctī, alterī diciōnis aliēnae
factī. Sepulchra exstant
quō quisque locō cecidit,
55 duo Rōmāna ūnō locō
propius Albam, tria
Albāna Rōmam versus,
sed distantia locīs, ut et
pugnātum est.

THE TOMB OF THE HORATII AND CURIATII

47. **Male:** 'Scarcely.'
sustinentī: sc. *eī;* translate
as if genitive case limiting
iugulō. See page 425, note
14. **supernē:** 'over the top
of his shield.'

48. **iugulō:** sc. *in.* The omission of the preposition is a poetical
usage. In a later passage (chapter 58) Livy says, *cultrum* (knife) *eum
in corde dēfīgit.* **dēfīgit:** 'thrust.' **iacentem:** 'the stricken enemy.'

50. **eō . . . quō:** ablatives of degree of difference; we should expect
another comparative like *magis* with *quō. 140.* **quō prope metum rēs
fuerat:** 'in proportion as their cause (*rēs*) had aroused apprehension.'
prope: used as preposition governing *metum.*

51. **nēquāquam paribus animīs:** 'with very different feelings.'
Litotes. *239, m.*

52. **quippe:** as on page 424, line 8; see note. **imperiō alterī auctī:**
'the one party was exalted with supreme power.' **diciōnis aliēnae factī:**
'was made subject to foreign sway.' *diciōnis* is a predicative genitive
of possession, a common construction in Livy. *94, d.*

56. **propius Albam:** see note 50 above. *122, a.*

57. **Rōmam versus:** 'towards Rome;' *versus* regularly follows its
noun. *238, b.*

58. **distantia locīs:** 'in different places'; literally, 'standing apart
by places.' *locīs* is an ablative of degree of difference. *140;* B. *223;*
A. & G. *414;* G. *403,* N. 1. **et:** 'also.'

LIBER II

Rome becomes a republic (509 B.C.), *and enjoys a new liberty.   The origin
and meaning of 'patrēs cōnscrīptī.'*

1. Līberī iam hinc populī Rōmānī rēs pāce bellōque
gestās, annuōs magistrātūs, imperiaque lēgum potentiōra
quam hominum peragam.   Quae lībertās ut laetior esset,
proximī rēgis superbia fēcerat.| Nam priōrēs ita rēgnā-
runt ut haud immeritō|omnēs deinceps conditōrēs partium 5
certē urbis, quās novās ipsī sēdēs ab sē auctae multitūdinis
addidērunt, numerentur. ◢ Neque ambigitur quīn Brūtus
īdem, quī tantum glōriae Superbō exāctō rēge meruit,
pessimō pūblicō id factūrus fuerit, sī lībertātis immātūrae

---

1.   1. Līberī . . . peragam: do not overlook the emphatic position
accorded to *Līberī;* Livy has now finished the history of the regal period,
and is embarking upon that of the Republic.   Translate, ' Henceforward
(*iam hinc*) it will be a free Roman people whose achievements in peace
and war I shall detail; the annual magistracies, and the sovereignty of
laws mightier than that of men I shall discuss.'

3. **Quae lībertās ut . . . fēcerat:** ' And that this freedom was the
more gladsome, was due to the arrogance of the last king.'   **esset:**
explain the subjunctive.   *203 (3);* B. 297, 1; A. & G. 569, 1 , G. 553, 1.

4. **priōrēs:** sc. *rēgēs.*

5. **omnēs deinceps conditōrēs . . . numerentur:** ' all are counted
as successive founders.'   **deinceps:** Livy's fondness for adverbs and
adverbial expressions as attributes to nouns has already been noted.
See page 425, note 16.

6. **novās sēdēs:** ' as new abodes,' in apposition to *quās.   165, c.*
ipsī: ' as individuals,' ' severally.'   *162, a.*

7. **numerentur:** the present subjunctive in a result clause depending upon a secondary tense (*rēgnārunt = rēgnāvērunt*) denotes that the
action is continuing into the present.   *177, b;* B. 268, 7, *a*); A. & G.
485, *c;* G. 513.   See page 18, line 16. **Neque ambigitur quīn Brūtus
īdem . . . id factūrus fuerit:** ' And there is no doubt that the same
Brutus . . . would have done this.'   For the periphrastic perfect subjunctive see the following note and references.

9. **pessimō pūblicō:** *pessimō* is used substantively, and is modified
by *pūblicō,* ' with the greatest detriment to the state.'   The English
word ' public ' is in most cases an incorrect translation of the Latin

10 cupīdine priōrum rēgum alicui rēgnum extorsisset. Quid
enim futūrum fuit, sī illa pāstōrum convenārumque plēbs,
trānsfuga ex suīs populīs, sub tūtēlā inviolātī templī aut
lībertātem aut certē impūnitātem adepta, solūta rēgiō
metū, agitārī coepta esset tribūniciīs procellīs et in aliēnā
15 urbe cum patribus serere certāmina, priusquam pignora
coniugum ac līberōrum cāritāsque ipsīus solī, cui longō

---

pūblicus; see vocabulary. **factūrus fuerit:** a past active contrary-to-
fact apodosis, when made to depend upon a construction that requires
the subjunctive (here *quīn*), regularly becomes a periphrastic perfect
subjunctive. Independently, *factūrus fuerit* would be *factūrus fuit;*
why? *219;* B. 304, 3, *b*); 322; A. & G. 517, *c* and *d;* G. 597, 3 (*a*)
and 5 (*a*). See *futūrum fuit* in line 11 below. **lībertātis:** compare the
emphatic position with that of *Līberī* in line 1 above.

10. **alicui:** the so-called dative of separation. *109, b;* B. 188, 2,
d; A. & G. 381; G. 345, R. 1. See page 413, line 19, note.

11. **futūrum fuit:** see note to line 9 above. **illa pāstōrum convenārumque plēbs:** 'that rabble of shepherds and vagabonds.' Cicero
(*Dē Ōrātōre,* **1,** 9, 37) says: *Rōmulus ille pāstōrēs et convenās congregāsse
. . . vidētur.* Compare chapter 8, page 408.

12. **trānsfuga:** in apposition with *plēbs.* **sub tūtēlā . . . adepta:**
'who under the protection of an inviolable sanctuary obtained either
freedom or at least exemption from punishment.' See chapter 8, page 408.
inviolātī: the perfect passive participle is sometimes equivalent to an
adjective in *-bilis;* what is the meaning of this suffix? *74, f; 212, h;*
B. 150, 4; A. & G. 252; G. 187, 4. **templī:** on the Capitoline, as told in
chapter 8, page 409, line 8.

13. **lībertātem aut impūnitātem adepta:** see chapter 8, page 409, lines
9 and 10. **solūta rēgiō metū:** 'free from the fear of a king.' *solūta*
modifies *plēbs* above.

14. **agitārī . . . procellīs:** 'had begun to be stirred by storms
aroused by the tribunes.' **coepta esset:** the passive voice of *coepisse*
usually accompanies a passive infinitive (*agitārī*). **in aliēnā urbe . . .
certāmina:** 'in a strange city had begun (*coepisset* to be supplied from
coepta esset above) to sow the seeds of strife with the patricians.'

16. **cui longō tempore assuēscitur:** 'to which men habituate themselves (only) after a long time.' *assuēscitur* has an impersonal subject
in accordance with the Latin idiom for intransitive verbs in the passive
voice. *172, e.*

tempore assuēscitur, animōs eōrum cōnsociāsset? Dis-
sipātae rēs nōndum adultae discordiā forent; quās fovit
tranquilla moderātiō imperiī eōque nūtriendō perdūxit, ut
bonam frūgem lībertātis mātūrīs iam vīribus ferre possent. 20
    Lībertātis autem orīginem inde magis, quia annuum
imperium cōnsulāre factum est, quam quod dēminūtum
quicquam sit ex rēgiā potestāte, numerēs. Omnia iūra,
omnia īnsignia prīmī cōnsulēs tenuēre; id modo cautum
est, nē, sī ambō fascēs habērent, duplicātus terror vidērētur. 25
Brūtus prior, concēdente collēgā, fascēs habuit, quī nōn
ācrior vindex lībertātis fuerat, quam deinde cūstōs fuit.
Omnium prīmum avidum novae lībertātis populum, nē

---

17. **cōnsociāsset:** why subjunctive? See page 427, note 39. **Dissi-
pātae . . . forent** (*essent*): attack the translation properly, viz., ' Dis-
organization and dissension would have come to the state before it had
reached its growth.' *211.* How literally?

18. **quās:** the antecedent is *rēs* = ' state,' ' nation,' ' government.'
fovit: continues the metaphor suggested in *adultae.*

19. **tranquilla moderātiō imperiī:** ' the calm restraint of the government.'

20. **lībertātis:** why does Livy give this word and its cognates such a
prominent place in this selection? How many times is this thought repeated?

21. **Lībertātis autem:** doubly emphasized by position and *autem.*
inde: ' from this.' **annuum:** predicate adjective.

22. **factum est:** ' was fixed.' **quam . . . potestāte:** ' than because
there was any diminution in power from that of the kings.' **dēminūtum
sit:** subjunctive, because it expresses the hypothetical reason, whereas
factum est above states the real reason. *183, c;* B. 286, 1, *b*); A. & G.
540, 2, N. 3; G. 541, N. 2.

23. **numerēs:** its subject is the ideal " you," hence potential subjunctive. *180, e* (2).

24. **id modo cautum est:** ' this precaution only was taken.'

25. **fascēs:** the bundle of rods with the ax. **duplicātus:** sc. *esse.*

26. **Brūtus prior:** ' Brutus was the first to.' **concēdente collēga:**
' with the consent of his colleague,' L. Tarqui'nius Collatī'nus, husband
of the famed Lucrē'tia. See classical dictionary.

27. **ācrior vindex:** ' a more ardent champion.'

28. **Omnium prīmum:** ' First of all.' See *Deinde* below, line 30.
avidum: ' still jealous.'

postmodum flectī precibus aut dōnīs rēgiīs posset, iūre
30 iūrandō adēgit nēminem Rōmae passūrōs rēgnāre. Deinde,
quō plūs vīrium in senātū frequentia etiam ōrdinis faceret,
caedibus rēgis dēminūtum patrum numerum prīmōribus
equestris gradūs lēctīs ad trecentōrum summam explēvit;
trāditumque inde fertur, ut in senātum vocārentur quī
35 patrēs quīque cōnscrīptī essent; cōnscrīptōs vidēlicet
novum in senātum appellābant lēctōs. Id mīrum quantum
prōfuit ad concordiam cīvitātis iungendōsque patribus
plēbis animōs.

---

29. iūre iūrandō adēgit : ' he had them swear.'

30. passūrōs (sc. *esse*) : sc. *sē* as subject. Deinde : see *Omnium*
prīmum above.

31. quō . . . faceret : ' in order that a large attendance of the order
also (as well as power) might produce added strength in the senate.'
quō : *193, b;* B. 282, 1, *a*) ; A. & G. 531, *a; G. 545*, 2. frequentia :
nominative, subject of *faceret*.

32. caedibus rēgis dēminūtum patrum numerum . . . explēvit : ' he
filled up the list of fathers, which had been reduced by the king's murders.'

34. trāditumque . . . vocārentur : ' and thenceforth the practice
of summoning to the senate is said to have been handed down.' trāditum : sc. *esse*. ut . . . vocārentur : substantive clause of result,
subject of *traditum (esse) fertur*. *203 (1)* ; B. 297, 2 ; A. & G. 569, 2 ;
G. 553, 4.

35. cōnscrīptōs . . . lēctōs : ' cōnscrīptī, of course, was the name
applied to those who were elected into the new senate.' *patrēs*, then,
was the original term for senators (see page 409, lines 14 and 15), and
cōnscrīptī designated the new members recently added to the senate.
According to line 35 the senate as a whole was designated by *patrēs et*
cōnscrīptī. In time the distinction lost significance and then the *et*
dropped out, *patrēs cōnscrīptī* being the accepted expression for ' senators.'
In fact Horace (*Ars Poëtica*, 314) uses *cōnscrīptus* without *pater* for
' senator,' and Cicero (*Philippics*, **13**, 23, 28) refers to one senator by
the term *pater cōnscrīptus*. The words *patrēs cōnscrīptī*, occurring so
often in Cicero's orations and elsewhere, should therefore be rendered
simply as ' senators,' and not by such meaningless words as ' conscript
fathers.' See note, Cicero, *In Catilīnam*, 1, page 31, line 17.

36. mīrum quantum : equivalent to an adverb, ' wonderfully.' See
page 419, line 30, and note 31. *204 (6)*.

LIBER XXI

A character delineation of Hannibal.

4. Missus Hannibal in Hispāniam prīmō statim adventū omnem exercitum in sē convertit: Hamilcarem iuvenem redditum sibi veterēs mīlitēs crēdere; eundem vigōrem in vultū vimque in oculīs, habitum ōris līneāmentaque intuērī. Dein brevī effēcit ut pater in sē minimum mōmen- 5 tum ad favōrem conciliandum esset. Numquam ingenium idem ad rēs dīversissimās, pārendum atque imperandum,

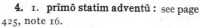

This excellent character delineation deserves careful study, and may be profitably compared with similar sketches of Catiline, Caesar, and Cato in Sallust. A comparative study of other great generals like Alexander, Caesar, Napoleon, would prove interesting also.

HANNIBAL

4. 1. **prīmō statim adventū**: see page 425, note 16.

2. **omnem exercitum**: 'the attention of the whole army'; Latin is exceedingly fond of concrete expressions. **convertit**: notice how effectively this first sentence introduces Han'nibal's personality. **Hamil'carem**: the father of Hannibal, surnamed *Barca* (Lightning), whose death had occurred eight years before, 229 B.C. **iuvenem**: 'as a youth.'

3. **redditum**: sc. *esse*. **crēdere**: historical infinitive, so also *intuērī, mālle, cōnfīdere, audēre* below. This construction expresses rapidity of movement. The effect is lively and dramatic. *182;* B. 335; A. & G. 463; G. 647. **vigōrem . . . vim, habitum . . . līneā-menta**: these four phrases are arranged in pairs, the first two suggesting personality, the last two physical features. *212, b.*

5. **pater in sē**: 'his resemblance to his father.' *sē* is an ablative. See page 427, note 43. **minimum mōmentum**: 'the least important factor.'

7. **rēs**: 'duties.' **pārendum atque imperandum**: the gerund as a noun in apposition is not common before Livy.

habilius fuit.　Itaque haud facile discernerēs utrum imperātōrī an exercituī cārior esset : neque Hasdrubal alium
10 quemquam praeficere mālle ubi quid fortiter ac strēnuē
agendum esset, neque mīlitēs aliō duce plūs cōnfīdere aut
audēre.　Plūrimum audāciae ad perīcula capessenda, plūrimum cōnsiliī inter ipsa perīcula erat.　Nūllo labōre aut
corpus fatīgārī aut animus vincī poterat.　Calōris ac
15 frīgoris patientia pār ; cibī pōtiōnisque dēsīderiō nātūrālī,
nōn voluptāte modus fīnītus ; vigiliārum somnīque nec diē
nec nocte discrīmināta tempora : id quod gerendīs rēbus
superesset quiētī datum ; ea neque mollī strātō neque silen-

---

8. **discernerēs** : a potential subjunctive with the ideal " you."　*180*,
e (*2*).

9. **Has'drubal** : the son-in-law of Hamilcar, who commanded the
army at the time.　Such names as Hamilcar, Hasdrubal, Hannibal were
common among the Carthaginians.

10. **ubi . . . agendum esset** : ' whenever some act was to be performed with bravery and energy.'　**quid** : = *aliquid.*

11. **agendum esset** : iterative subjunctive, common in Livy, but
rare in Cicero and earlier writers.　*186, a;* B. 288, 3, *a;* A. & G. 518, *c;*
G. 567, N.　**aliō duce** : ablative absolute.　*144, a.*　**plūs cōnfīdere aut
audēre** : ' they exhibited more confidence or more daring.'　**plūs** :
117, a; B. 176, 2, *b*) ; A. & G. 390, *c;* G. 333, 1.

14. **Calōris ac frīgoris patientia** : ' As to heat and cold, his power of
endurance.'　Note the assonance.　*212, d.*

15. **pār** : sc. *erat.*　**cibī pōtiōnisque** : note that here, as in the previous and also the following sentences, the genitives which embody the
leading thought stand first ; translate accordingly.　**dēsīderiō nātūrālī** :
a later writer (Iustī'nus, **32,** 4, 10) tells us that Hannibal limited himself
to a pint of wine.　See page 270, line 14, note.

16. **modus fīnītus** (sc. *est*) : ' the quantity was determined.'

17. **discrīmināta tempora** : ' the periods were apportioned.'　*dis-
crīmināre* is a rare word in Latin.　**id** (sc. *temporis*) **quod gerendīs rēbus
superesset** : ' whatever time remained after the performance of duties.'
What is the construction of *temporis?*　*97, b;* B. 201, 1 ; A. & G.
346, 3 ; G. 369.　**gerendīs rēbus** : dative ; why?

18. **superesset** : another instance of iterative subjunctive ; see note
11 above.　**ea** : sc. *quiēs.*　**strātō, silentiō** : ablatives of means or cause.

tiō accersīta; multī saepe mīlitārī sagulō opertum humī
iacentem inter cūstōdiās statiōnēsque mīlitum cōnspexē- 20
runt. Vestītus nihil inter aequālēs excellēns; arma atque
equī cōnspiciēbantur. Equitum peditumque īdem longē
prīmus erat; prīnceps in proelium ībat, ultimus cōnsertō
proeliō excēdēbat. Hās tantās virī virtūtēs ingentia vitia

CARTHAGE TODAY

19. **sagulō**: diminutive of *sagum*, the dress of the common soldier;
to be taken with *opertum* (sc. *Hannibalem*).

20. **cūstōdiās statiōnēsque**: ' sentries and outposts.'

21. **Vestītus**: ' The style of his dress.' **nihil**: adverbial, ' in no respect.' *118, c.* **inter aequālēs**: = *inter aequālium vestītum*, brachylogy.
238, e; B. 374, 2; A. & G. 640; G. 689. **arma atque equī cōnspiciēbantur**: ' it was his arms and his horses that attracted attention.'
The contrast with *vestītus*, etc. is greatly emphasized by the omission of
the adversative conjunction; what is the technical name for this figure
of rhetoric? *238, d.*

22. **īdem**: modifies the subject of *erat*, but is here best translated
adverbally, viz. ' at the same time.'

23. **prīmus**: see *prīnceps* below; *prīmus* is the first considered
locally and temporally, whereas *prīnceps* is the first in rank or fame, and
refers to the action. **cōnsertō proeliō**: ' from a hand-to-hand fight.'

24. **Hās . . . aequābant**: ' These fine manly qualities of our hero
were offset by exceedingly bad qualities ' **virī virtūtēs vitia**: *virī* is

25 aequābant: inhūmāna crūdēlitās, perfidia plūs quam Pūnica, nihil vērī, nihil sanctī, nūllus deum metus, nūllum iūs
iūrandum, nūlla religiō.   Cum hāc indole virtūtum atque
vitiōrum trienniō sub Hasdrubale imperātōre meruit, nūllā
rē, quae agenda videndaque magnō futūrō ducī esset, prae-
30 termissā.

---

used not only to provide effective alliteration, but also to emphasize the
basic composition of *vir-tūs*.

25. **inhūmāna crūdēlitās**: of course, a gross exaggeration. **perfidia
Pūnica**: a proverbial expression among the Romans, suggesting the
last word in faithlessness.   Modern critics more fairly have pronounced Hannibal one of the greatest generals of all times, and
Mommsen states that Hannibal's actions accorded with the interna-
tional law of the times.   It would be interesting to read a history of
the Punic Wars written by a Carthaginian.   One wonders how the
fidēs Rōmāna would have fared.

26. **nihil vērī . . . nūlla religiō**: ' untruthfulness, irreverence, no
fear of the gods (*deum = deōrum*), perjury, no conscientious scruples.'
These negative enumerations serve as a good illustration of Latin
idiom, for Latin lacks negative abstract nouns and regularly replaces
them by the use of *nihil* with the partitive genitive of a substantivized
adjective or the adjective *nūllus* combined with a positive noun.   In
English we use the prefixes *un-*, *ir-*, *in-*, *non-*, and the suffix *-less*. *211.*

27. **indole**: ' heritage.'

28. **nūllā rē . . . praetermissā**: ' without neglecting anything which
was to be done and seen by a man who was destined to become a great
general.'

29. **agenda videndaque esset**: explain the subjunctive. **ducī**:
Livy tells us that Hannibal was eighteen years of age at his father's
death, and that Hasdrubal, the latter's successor, held the command
for eight years; accordingly, Hannibal must have been twenty-six when
he assumed command.

PLINY, ROME'S FOREMOST GENTLEMAN

PLINY, ROME'S FOREMOST GENTLEMAN

C. PLĪNĪ CAECILĪ SECUNDĪ EPISTULAE SĒLĒCTAE

1 (I, I)

C. Plīnius Septiciō Suō S.

Pliny announces that he has made a collection of his letters.

Frequenter hortātus es, ut epistulās, quās paulō cūrātius scrīpsissem, colligerem pūblicāremque.   Collēgī nōn servātō temporis ōrdine (neque enim historiam compōnēbam), sed ut quaeque in manūs vēnerat.   Superest, ut nec tē cōnsiliī nec mē paeniteat obsequiī.   Ita enim fīet, ut eās quae adhūc 5

To the Student: First consult page 558 of the Companion, on Roman Correspondence; then turn to page 564.

1. A dedicatory letter to Pliny's friend, C. Septicius Clarus (gā'(y)u̯s sep-ti'sh(y)u̯s klā'ru̯s), to whom the Roman historian, Suetonius, also a friend of Pliny, may have dedicated his " Lives of the Twelve Caesars." That Pliny had friendly relations with the entire family of Septicius appears from other letters addressed to this same man. (*Epistulae*, **1,** 15; **7,** 28; **8,** 1.)

1. quās . . . scrīpsissem: ' which I had written somewhat more carefully,' *i.e.* composed for publication.   In this respect Pliny's letters stand in direct contrast to those of Cicero.

2. scrīpsissem: *194, a;* B. 283; A. & G. 535; G. 631, 1.   **colligerem . . . Collēgī:** such repetition, called *epanalepsis*, is a mark of Pliny's style. *239, h.* pūblicārem: ' publish '; in Classical Latin this word usually signifies legal confiscation.

4. tē cōnsiliī: *103, c;* B. 209, 1;   A. & G. 354, *b, c;* G. 377.

5. Ita: ' In that case.'

neglēctae iacent requīram et, sī quās addiderō, nōn supprimam. Valē.

2 (1, 6)

C. Plīnius Cornēliō Tacitō Suō S.

Pliny kills two birds with one stone.

Rīdēbis, et licet rīdeās.   Ego ille quem nōstī aprōs ᴜᴜᴇˢ
et quidem pulcherrimōs cēpī.   "Ipse?" inquis.   Ipse;
nōn tamen ut omnīnō ab inertiā meā et quiēte discēderem.
Ad rētia sedēbam: erat in
5 proximō nōn vēnābulum
aut lancea, sed stilus et
pugillārēs: meditābar ali-

ROMAN BAKERY AT POMPEII

6. **addiderō**: why future perfect? Study this tense more
closely. *176, c;* B. 264; A. & G.
478; G. 244. **supprimam**: in
parallel construction to *requīram*.
Note the assonance. *212, d.*

2. Addressed to the historian,
P. Cornelius Tacitus, to whom
Pliny wrote ten other letters.
They were intimate friends. See
page 461 and the note.

1. **et licet rīdeās**: 'and laugh
you may,' *i.e.* you are welcome
to do so. **rīdeas**: *200, a;* B. 295,
6, 8; A. & G. 565, N. 2. **Ego
ille quem nōstī**: 'I, that fellow
whom you know.'

2. **et quidem pulcherrimōs**: 'and that, too, very fine (specimens).'

3. **ut . . . discēderem**: result clause. *197, a.* **inertiā**: here more
nearly approaches the meaning of *ōtium*. Literary pursuits among the
Romans were not regarded as work, but as a form of leisure.

4. **rētia**: hunting nets were stretched around a section of the wood into
which the game was driven by beaters and dogs. **in proximō**: 'close by.'

6. **stilus et pugillārēs**: 'pencil and tablets'; see illustration, page 87.

7. **meditābar aliquid ēnotābamque**: the imperfects express repeated
action; 'I would muse over something and jot it down.'

quid ēnotābamque, ut, sī manūs vacuās, plēnās tamen cērās reportārem. Nōn est quod contemnās hōc studendī genus. Mīrum est ut animus agitātiōne mōtūque corporis excitētur. 10 Iam undique silvae et sōlitūdō ipsumque illud silentium, quod vēnātiōnī datur, magna cōgitātiōnis incitāmenta sunt. Proinde, cum vēnābere, licēbit, auctōre mē, ut pānārium et lagunculam sīc etiam pugillārēs ferās. Experiēris nōn Diānam magis montibus quam Minervam inerrāre. Valē. 15

3 (1, 9)

C. Plīnius Miniciō Fundānō Suō S.

City and country are contrasted.

Mīrum est, quam singulīs diēbus in urbe ratiō aut cōnstet aut cōnstāre videātur, plūribus iūnctīsque nōn cōnstet.

---

9. **Nōn est quod :** ' There is no reason why '; see *nihil est quod*, *quid est quod*, Cicero, *In Catilīnam*, 1, page 41, line 1. **studendī :** what is the fundamental idea of this verb? See vocabulary.

10. **ut . . . excitētur :** ' how the mind is stimulated by physical movement and exercise.' *204 (3)*.

11. **Iam :** ' Furthermore,' ' Moreover,' denotes here a transition to an added point. **ipsumque illud silentium :** ' that characteristic silence.' *162, a*.

13. **Proinde :** ' Accordingly.' **licēbit, auctōre mē,** etc. : ' you will be permitted, after my example, to carry not only bread-basket and wine-flask, but also your notebook.' **auctōre mē :** ablative absolute. *144, a*. How literally? **ut . . . sīc :** correlatives, here almost = *nōn sōlum, sed etiam*.

14. **ferās :** same construction as *rideās* in line 1 above, *i.e.* subjunctive without *ut*, depending upon *licēbit*.

15. **montibus :** dative; why? *107, a*.

3. **Miniciō Fundānō** (mį-ni'sh(y)ųs fun-dā'nųs). The Fundanus to whom this letter is addressed was a statesman of some importance, who appears to have been proconsul of Asia under the Emperor Hadrian. Pliny also addressed three other letters to him, in one of which (*Epistulae*, **5**, 16, Selection 9, page 453) he delineates the character of his daughter, who had just died, in very touching words. Read this selection aloud several times, and observe the rhythmic movement of words, phrases, and clauses.

1. **Mīrum est,** etc. : ' It is surprising how for each separate day

Nam, sī quem interrogēs: "Hodiē quid ēgistī?" respon-
deat: "Officiō togae virīlis interfuī, spōnsālia aut nūptiās
5 frequentāvī, ille mē ad signandum testāmentum, ille in
advocātiōnem, ille in cōnsilium rogāvit." Haec quō diē
fēceris, necessāria, eadem, sī cotīdiē fēcisse tē reputēs,
inānia videntur, multō magis cum sēcesseris. Tunc enim
subit recordātiō: "Quot diēs quam frīgidīs rēbus ab-
10 sūmpsī!" Quod ēvenit mihi, postquam in Laurentīnō meō

---

spent in the city the account either balances or seems to balance,
whereas for several consecutive days it fails to do so.' **ratiō . . .
cōnstet**: a phrase borrowed from the language of bookkeeping, meaning
that profit and loss are equal. For *cōnstet* see *204 (3)*.

4. **Officiō**: ' Ceremony.' **togae virīlis**: a Roman youth formally
celebrated his arrival at majority by assuming the garb of manhood,
the plain white toga, usually between his fourteenth and seventeenth
years. The ceremony was more or less elaborate, and its importance
is shown here by ranking it with betrothals and weddings.

5. **ille, ille, ille**: translate, ' one, another, a third.' **ad signandum
testāmentum**: ' to sign and seal his will '; the Romans had a passion
for making wills, which, in order to be valid, had to be signed by the
testator before seven witnesses, whose names and seals also were required by law. See illustration, page 87. This occasion was sometimes made a social function, as may be seen from *Epistulae*, **2**, 20, where
Aurelia dressed herself in a most beautiful gown, which Regulus had the
effrontery to request as a legacy. **in advocātiōnem**: ' for legal support '; either as a witness or for the moral effect produced by being
present in court, and thereby showing sympathy for a litigant.

6. **in cōnsilium**: ' for advice,' in assisting a judge in his judicial
decisions. A *cōnsilium* was a body of associates to a presiding magistrate, designed to help him render a legal decision.

8. **cum sēcesseris**: ' when you have withdrawn to the country.'
This is a common meaning of *sēcēdere* in Silver Latin (14 A.D.–138 A.D.).
See *Outline of Latin Literature*, Companion, page 707.

9. **subit recordātiō**: ' the thought suggests itself.' **Quot . . .
quam**: Latin not infrequently combines two interrogative words in the
same sentence; translate, ' How many days in pursuits how trivial.'

10. **postquam . . . legō**: ' after I have been reading '; *postquam*
with the historical present is comparatively rare. *188, a.* **in Laurentīnō
meō**: ' at my country home near Laurentum,' Pliny's suburban residence about sixteen miles from Rome, described in *Epistulae*, **2**, 17.

aut legō aliquid aut scrībō aut etiam corporī vacō, cuius
fultūrīs animus sustinētur. Nihil audiō, quod audīsse,
nihil dīcō, quod dīxisse paeniteat; nēmō apud mē quemquam sinistrīs sermōnibus carpit, nēminem ipse reprehendō,
nisi tamen mē, cum parum commodē scrībō; nūllā spē, 15
nūllō timōre sollicitor, nūllīs rūmōribus inquiētor: mēcum
tantum et cum libellīs loquor. Ō rēctam sincēramque
vītam, ō dulce ōtium honestumque ac paene omnī negōtiō
pulchrius! Ō mare, ō lītus, vērum sēcrētumque μουσεῖον,
quam multa invenītis, quam multa dictātis! Proinde, 20
tū quoque strepitum istum inānemque discursum et multum
ineptōs labōrēs, ut prīmum fuerit occāsiō, relinque tēque
studiīs vel ōtiō trāde. Satius est enim, ut Atilius noster
ērudītissimē simul et facētissimē dīxit, ōtiōsum esse quam
nihil agere. Valē. 25

---

11. **corporī vacō:** ' I am free to attend to my physical needs,' similar
in meaning to the more common *corpus cūrāre*, page 269, note 13.

12. **Nihil . . . dīxisse:** observe the contrasted pairs, their arrangement, the assonance, and the rhythm.

13. **paeniteat:** why in subjunctive? *194, a;* B. 283, 2; A. & G.
535, *a;* G.`631, 2. **quemquam . . . carpit:** ' makes insinuating remarks
about anyone.'

15. **nisi tamen:** = *nisi forte.* **parum commodē:** ' not well,' *i.e.*
' badly.' **scrībō . . . sollicitor:** chiasmus. *239, e.*

16. **inquiētor:** not found in the Ciceronian Age (81 B.C.–42 B.C.).

17. **sincēram:** not ' sincere ' but ' genuine.'

18. **honestum:** never translate by ' honest.' See vocabulary. **negōtiō:** = *nec+ōtiō,* therefore the opposite of *ōtium.* See Seneca's idea of
the true *ōtium* in *Dē Brevitāte Vītae,* 14, *et seq.*

19. **μουσεῖον:** the Greek word for ' haunt of the Muses,' *i.e.* an ideal
place for study. Compare our word ' museum.'

20. **quam . . . dictātis:** ' how many ideas do you create, how many
do you compose? ' Do not translate such neuter plurals as *multa* by
' many things,' but color them to suit the context. *211.*

21. **istum:** why not *illum?* **multum:** ' very,' adverb.

23. **Atilius noster:** an intimate friend of Pliny, known for his wit.

24. **ōtiōsum . . . agere:** ' to be at leisure than to be doing nothing.'
The expression *nihil agere* is not to be interpreted in the sense of com-

4 (2, 18)

C. Plīnius Mauricō Suō S.

Pliny is glad to find a teacher for the children of a friend, though the selection may bring upon him the displeasure of the other teachers.

Quid ā tē mihi iūcundius potuit iniungī, quam ut praeceptōrem frātris tuī līberīs quaererem? Nam beneficiō tuō in scholam redeō et illam dulcissimam aetātem quasi resūmō: sedeō inter iuvenēs, ut solēbam, atque etiam 5 experior quantum apud illōs auctōritātis ex studiīs habeam. Nam proximē frequentī auditōriō inter sē cōram multīs ōrdinis nostrī clārē iocābantur; intrāvī, conticuērunt; quod nōn referrem, nisi ad illōrum magis laudem quam ad meam pertinēret, ac nisi spērāre tē vellem posse frātris 10 tuī fīliōs probē discere. Quod superest, cum omnēs quī profitentur audierō, quid dē quōque sentiam scrībam efficiamque, quantum tamen epistulā cōnsequī poterō, ut

plete idleness, but rather refers to the useless trivialities of city life, as Pliny has suggested them in this letter.

4. Mauricō: Junius Mauricus (jūn'yụs mâ'rị-cụs), an intimate friend of Pliny, whom he addressed in two other letters, mentioned also by Tacitus, *Agricola*, 45.

1. **Quid . . . iniungī:** ' What more pleasant charge could you have intrusted to me?' **quam ut:** *197, c.*

2. **frātris tuī:** Aurulēnus Rústicus, a Stoic, eminent for his ability and character, put to death by Domitian (dọ-mị'sh(y)an) for writing a biography. See Tacitus, *Agricola*, **2,** 45. **beneficiō tuō:** ' thanks to you.'

5. **auctōritātis:** partitive genitive with *quantum. 97, b.* **ex:** ' by reason of,' ' in consequence of,' indicating the cause or reason.

6. **Nam . . . iocābantur:** ' For but lately in a large audience they (*iuvenēs*) were loudly jesting among one another in the presence of many men of my rank '; *auditōriō* refers to the audience as well as to the place of meeting.

10. **probē:** ' amid wholesome influences.' **Quod superest:** ' As for the rest.' *212, j.* **omnēs quī profitentur:** ' all who teach,' *i.e.* the professors.

12. **quantum . . . poterō:** ' so far, however, as I shall be able to attain this result by letter.'

ipse omnēs audīsse videāris. Dēbeō enim tibi, dēbeō
memoriae frātris tuī hanc fidem, hōc studium, praesertim
super tantā rē. Nam quid magis interest vestrā quam 15
ut līberī — dīcerem tuī, nisi nunc illōs magis amārēs — dignī
illō patre, tē patruō reperiantur? quam cūram mihi, etiam
sī nōn mandāssēs, vindicāssem. Nec ignōrō suscipiendās
offēnsās in ēligendō praeceptōre, sed oportet mē nōn modo
offēnsās vērum etiam simultātēs prō frātris tuī fīliīs tam 20
aequō animō subīre quam parentēs prō suīs. Valē.

5 (3, 6)

C. Plīnius Anniō Sevērō Suō S.

Pliny describes a valuable antique, a statue of Corinthian bronze.

Ex hērēditāte quae mihi obvēnit ēmī proximē Corinthium
signum, modicum quidem sed fēstīvum et expressum,

---

13. **ipse :** ' personally.' **Dēbeō, dēbeō :** the repetition expresses
emotion.

14. **fidem :** ' promise.' **studium :** ' interest.'

15. **super :** = *dē.* **vestrā :** instead of the genitive of the personal
pronoun *vestrī. 103, e;* B. 211, 1, *a;* A. & G. 355, *a;* G. 381.

16. **nisi. . . amārēs :** *i.e.* ' if you did not love them more than if they
were your own '; Pliny seems to be overdoing the matter.

17. **patre, patruō :** in apposition with *illō* and *tē* respectively.

18. **Nec ignōrō :** ' I know full well '; what figure? *239, m; 212, m.*
suscipiendās offēnsās : sc. *mihi;* ' that I am to incur displeasure.'

5. Anniō Sevērō (an'ị-ụs sẹ-vē'rụs) : nothing further is known
about him, excepting that Pliny addressed one other letter to him,
Epistulae, **5,** 34.

1. **Corinthium signum :** ' a statue of Corinthian bronze '; Pliny
the Elder, *Historia Nātūrālis,* **34,** 7, 8, tells us that the process of manu-
facturing such bronzes was accidentally discovered in the burning of
Corinth in 146 B.C., and that it was also used for dishes, lamps, and
basins. It was a rare alloy, and the secret of its manufacture was
thought to have been lost.

2. **fēstīvum et expressum :** ' handsome and realistic.'

quantum ego sapiō, quī fortasse in omnī rē, in hāc certē
perquam exiguum sapiō: hōc tamen signum ego quoque
5 intellegō. Est enim nūdum nec aut vitia, sī qua sunt, cēlat
aut laudēs parum ostentat: effingit senem stantem; ossa,
mūsculī, nervī, vēnae, rūgae etiam ut spīrantis appārent,
rārī et cēdentēs capillī, lāta frōns, contrācta faciēs, exīle
collum, pendent lacertī, papillae iacent, venter recessit.
10 Ā tergō quoque eadem aetās ut ā tergō. Aes ipsum,
quantum vērus color indicat, vetus et antīquum. Tālia
dēnique omnia ut possint artificum oculōs tenēre, dēlēctāre,
imperitōrum. Quod mē quamquam tīrunculum sollici-

---

3. **quantum . . . sapiō:** ' so far as my taste goes, which perchance
is very poor in all of the arts, and especially in this particular field ';
the antecedent of *quī* is, of course, *ego*.

5. **intellegō:** 'appreciate.' **nec:** = *et nōn*.
vitia: 'bad points.'

6. **laudēs:** ' good points.'

7. **nervī:** 'tendons,' 'sinews'; the word does
not mean ' nerves' in the ordinary sense. Though
Celsus in his *Dē Medicīnā* uses the word with
various meanings, it regularly refers to the sinews
or tendons of the body, and sometimes is equivalent to our word ' muscles.' In only one passage
does it even approximate the meaning of our
word ' nerves,' i.e. *iūncta est vēnae artēria, hīs
nervī*, ' the artery lies close to the vein, close to
these two lie the nerves.'

A GREEK BRONZE
This was found in the
bay of Marathon.

8. **rārī et cēdentēs:** ' thin and receding from the forehead.' **lāta
frōns:** its counterpart, *angusta frōns*, as a mark of beauty has been
immortalized by Horace, *Epistulae*, **1**, 7, 26. **contrācta:** ' drawn.'

9. **papillae iacent:** ' flat-chested.' How literally?

10. **eadem aetās ut ā tergō:** ' the same signs of age so far as can be
determined from behind.'

11. **vērus color:** the reference is to oxidation. **vetus et antīquum:**
' very old,' synonymic combination for emphasis. *212, b*. **Tālia dēnique
omnia:** ' In short, such are all of its characteristics '; sc. *sunt*.

13. **imperitōrum:** ' dilettante.' **Quod:** ' And this fact.' **quamquam tīrunculum:** ' although a mere beginner '; in Pliny's time *quamquam, quamvīs*, and *etsī* were often combined with a participle.

tāvit ad emendum. Ēmī autem, nōn ut habērem domī — neque enim ūllum adhūc Corinthium domī habeō —, verum ut in patriā nostrā celebrī locō pōnerem, ac potissimum in Iovis templō : vidētur enim dignum templō, dignum deō dōnum. Tū ergō, ut solēs omnia quae ā mē tibi iniunguntur, suscipe hanc cūram et iam nunc iubē basim fierī, ex quō volēs marmore, quae nōmen meum honōrēsque capiat, sī hōs quoque putābis addendōs. Ego signum ipsum, ut prīmum invēnerō aliquem quī nōn gravētur, mittam tibi, vel ipse, quod māvīs, afferam mēcum. Dēstinō enim, sī tamen officiī ratiō permīserit, excurrere istō. Gaudēs quod mē ventūrum esse polliceor, sed contrahēs frontem, cum adiēcerō ad paucōs diēs : neque enim diūtius abesse mē eadem haec quae nōndum exīre patiuntur. Valē.

16. **patriā nostrā :** Comum (now called Como). **celebrī :** ' much frequented,' not ' celebrated.'

18. **omnia :** sc. *suscipere*.

19. **iam nunc :** ' straightway,' ' directly.'

20. **honōrēs :** ' official titles.'

22. **tibi :** dative of indirect object denoting the person interested; not equivalent to *ad tē*. A. & G. 363, 2 ; G. 345, R. 2.

24. **officiī ratiō :** ' the requirements of my office.' **istō :** adverb, ' to your place.'

26. **ad paucōs diēs :** ' for only a few days,' an exception to the rule that temporal expressions with *ad* usually refer to the future.

27. **eadem haec :** sc. *officia*, ' obligations.'

SILVER COIN OF BRUTTIUM, EXPRESSING THE LOYALTY OF THE CITY TO ROME
Obverse : Zeus. Reverse : Roma, crowned by Faith.

6 (3, 12)

C. Plīnius Catiliō Sevērō Suō S.

Pliny accepts an invitation to dinner, but stipulates certain conditions.

Veniam ad cēnam, sed iam nunc pacīscor sit expedīta, sit parca, Sōcraticīs tantum sermōnibus abundet, in hīs quoque teneat modum. Erunt officia antelūcāna, in quae incidere impūnē nē Catōnī quidem licuit, quem tamen 5 C. Caesar ita reprehendit ut laudet. Dēscrībit enim eōs quibus obvius fuerit cum caput ēbriī retēxissent, ērubuisse:

6. **Catiliō** (kạ-tíl'ị-ụs) **Sevērō**: he was addressed also in *Epistulae*, **1**, 22, and was proconsul of Asia and governor of Syria under Hadrian (117 A.D.–138 A.D.), to whom, however, he made himself obnoxious by seeking to gain the empire for himself. The emperor Marcus Aurelius (161 A.D.–180 A.D.) was his great-grandson.

1. **iam nunc pacīscor**: 'right now I stipulate.' **sit**: *200, a;* B. 295, 8; A. & G. 565, *a* and N.; G. 546, 2, R. 2. **expedīta**: 'plain and informal.'

2. **parca**: 'inexpensive.' **Sōcraticīs sermōnibus**: on serious themes, such as are found in Plato's *Dialogues*, which may include ethical and political discussions, questions relating to the *summum bonum*, the soul, its immortality, and the like. That the cultured Roman was fond of such discussions and conversations is suggested by Horace (*Satires*, **2**, 6, 70, *et seq.*): "Then (after dinner) a conversation ensues, not about the country homes or houses of others, nor whether Lepos is a good or a bad dancer; but we discuss that which is more a matter of our personal concern and which it is bad not to know: whether wealth or virtue makes men happy; or what it is that attracts us to friendship, whether it is self-interest or integrity; and what is the nature of the good and what is its most perfect form."

3. **Erunt officia antelūcāna**, etc.: 'There will be social calls before daylight upon which not even Cato might safely stumble, although Gaius Caesar so reproaches him as to praise him.' Pliny humorously suggests that if Catilius makes his party too elaborate and prolongs it into the wee hours of the morning, the same fate may befall him, when he returns home, as befell Cato Uticensis, who is said to have been discovered in a drunken condition on the street early in the morning.

5. **C. Caesar**: Julius Caesar, who wrote invectives, entitled *Anticatònēs*, in reply to Cicero's eulogy of Cato.

deinde adicit "putārēs nōn ab illīs Catōnem, sed illōs ā
Catōne dēprehēnsōs." Potuitne plūs auctōritātis tribuī
Catōnī quam sī ēbrius quoque tam venerābilis erat? Nostrae tamen cēnae ut apparātūs et impendiī sīc temporis 10
modus cōnstet. Neque enim eī sumus quōs vituperāre nē
inimīcī quidem possint nisi ut simul laudent. Valē.

7 (4, 13)

C. Plīnius Tacitō Suō S.

*Pliny offers to help endow a school at Comum, and requests Tacitus for
practical assistance.*

Salvum tē in urbem vēnisse gaudeō; vēnistī autem, sī
quandō aliās, nunc maximē mihi dēsīderātus. Ipse pauculīs adhūc diēbus in Tusculānō commorābor, ut opusculum
quod est in manibus absolvam. Vereor enim nē, sī hanc
intentiōnem iam in fīne laxāverō, aegrē resūmam. Interim 5
nē quid festīnātiōnī meae pereat, quod sum praesēns

---

7. **putārēs:** 'you would have thought.' The quotation is from
the work cited above.

9. **Nostrae tamen cēnae:** 'However, as for our dinner.'

10. **ut . . . sīc:** correlatives.

11. **modus cōnstet:** 'let a limit be set.'

12. **possint:** subjunctive of characteristic. *194, a.*

7. On Cornelius Tacitus see note to Selection 2, page 438. This
letter presents an interesting picture of education in the provinces.

2. **pauculīs adhūc diēbus:** 'a few days yet.' An ablative of
extent of time, a construction which Pliny uses often. *147, c.*

3. **in Tusculānō:** sc. *praediō.* Pliny's country home near Tusculum. See illustration, page 449. Cicero also had a *Tusculānum* there,
hence *Tusculānae Disputātiōnēs,* the title of his philosophical work, which
he wrote at that place.

5. **intentiōnem:** 'mental tension.' **iam in fīne:** 'when the end
is already in view.'

6. **nē . . . pereat:** 'in order that my impatience may not suffer any
loss.'

petītūrus hāc quasi praecursōriā epistulā rogō. Sed prius
accipe causās rogandī. Proximē cum in patriā meā fuī,
vēnit ad mē salūtandum mūnicipis meī fīlius praetextā-
10 tus. Huic ego "studēs?" inquam. Respondit "etiam."
"Ubi?" "Mediōlānī." "Cūr nōn hīc?" Et pater eius —
erat enim ūnā atque etiam ipse addūxerat puerum —"quia
nūllōs hīc praeceptōrēs habēmus." "Quā rē nūllōs? nam
vehementer intererat vestrā, quī patrēs estis," et oppor-
15 tūnē complūrēs patrēs audiēbant, "līberōs vestrōs hīc potissimum discere. Ubi enim aut iūcundius morārentur
quam in patriā aut pudicius continērentur quam sub oculīs
parentum aut minōre sūmptū quam domī? Quantulum
est ergō, collātā pecūniā, condūcere praeceptōrēs, quodque
20 nunc in habitātiōnēs, in viātica, in ea quae peregrē emuntur

---

7. **quasi praecursōriā :** ' to act as a precursor, so to speak.' *quasi*
apologizes for the word, which is post-Augustan, *i.e.* used after 14 A.D.

8. **rogandī :** ' request.' Gerunds are often idiomatically translated
by abstract nouns. **patriā :** ' native town,' *i.e.* Novum Comum.

9. **salūtandum :** the usual morning call, when every Roman of
position received his clients and friends in the atrium of his home. See
illustration, page 469. **praetextātus :** not yet old enough to assume the
toga virīlis, but still wearing the toga of boyhood.

10. **studēs :** ' do you go to school? ' **etiam :** ' yes.'

11. **Mediōlānī :** ' at Milan,' about 30 miles south of Comum. It
was already making a bid for honors as a *mētropolis et rēgia urbs*. **pater
eius :** sc. *respondit*.

12. **ūnā :** adverb, ' with him.' **ipse :** ' personally.'

13. **praeceptōrēs :** ' professors of rhetoric.'

14. **vehementer intererat vestrā :** ' it would be greatly to your advantage '; the imperfect, perfect, or pluperfect indicative is used in
expressions signifying propriety, necessity, and the like in the apodosis of
a contrary-to-fact condition, the protasis often being implied in an infinitive, as here, i.e. *discere*. **vestrā :** *103, e.* See note on page 443, line 15.

16. **morārentur . . . continērentur :** potential subjunctive. *179, b (2).*

19. **collātā pecūniā condūcere praeceptōrēs :** ' to contribute money
and hire teachers.' **quod :** its antecedent is *id* understood, object of
adicere.

20. **habitātiōnēs :** ' rooms.'

impenditis adicere mercēdibus! Atque adeō ego, quī
nōndum līberōs habeō, parātus sum prō rē pūblicā nostrā,
quasi prō fīliā vel parente, tertiam partem eius quod cōnferre
vōbīs placēbit dare. Tōtum etiam pollicērer, nisi timērem
nē hōc mūnus meum quandōque ambitū corrumperētur, 25
ut accidere multīs in locīs videō, in quibus praeceptōrēs
pūblicē condūcuntur. Huic vitiō occurrī ūnō remediō
potest, sī parentibus sōlīs iūs condūcendī relinquātur
īsdemque religiō rēctē iūdicandī necessitāte collātiōnis
addātur. Nam quī fortasse dē aliēnō neglegentēs, certē 30

PLINY'S TUSCAN VILLA
A reconstruction.

21. **impenditis:** verb of the clause introduced by *quod* above.
mercēdibus: ' the teacher's salary.'

24. **dare:** with *parātus sum* above.

25. **ambitū corrumperētur:** ' might be misused with ulterior motives.'

27. **pūblicē:** ' by the state,' not ' publicly.' **vitiō:** ' evil.' *107. a.*

29. **religiō rēctē iūdicandī:** ' the sacred obligation of deciding
aright.'

30. **addātur:** ' should fall to.' **dē aliēnō . . . dē suō:** ' with regard
to another's property . . . with regard to their own.'

dē suō dīligentēs erunt dabuntque operam nē ā mē pecūniam
nisi dignus accipiat, sī acceptūrus et ab ipsīs erit. Proinde,
cōnsentīte, cōnspīrāte maiōremque animum ex meō sūmite,
quī cupiō esse quam plūrimum quod dēbeam cōnferre.
35 Nihil honestius praestāre līberīs vestrīs, nihil grātius patriae
potestis. Ēducentur hīc quī hīc nāscuntur statimque ab
īnfantiā nātāle solum amāre, frequentāre cōnsuēscant.
Atque utinam tam clārōs praeceptōrēs indūcātis ut fīnitimīs
oppidīs studia hinc petantur, utque nunc līberī vestrī aliēna
40 in loca, ita mox aliēnī in hunc locum cōnfluant!" Haec
putāvī altius et quasi ā fonte repetenda, quō magis scīrēs
quam grātum mihi foret, sī susciperēs quod iniungō. Iniungō autem et prō reī magnitūdine rogō ut ex cōpiā studiō-
sōrum, quae ad tē ex admīrātiōne ingeniī tuī convenit,
45 circumspiciās praeceptōrēs quōs sollicitāre possīmus, sub eā
tamen condiciōne nē cui fidem meam obstringam. Omnia
enim lībera parentibus servō. Illī iūdicent, illī ēligant:
ego mihi cūram tantum et impendium vindicō. Proinde,
sī quis fuerit repertus quī ingeniō suō fīdat, eat illūc eā
50 lēge ut hinc nihil aliud certum quam fīdūciam suam ferat.
Valē.

31. **nē . . . nisi dignus :** ' that no one but a worthy man.'
32. **Proinde, cōnsentīte, cōnspīrāte :** ' Therefore unite wholeheartedly '; synonyms are often used in Latin to emphasize their common
meaning. *212, b.*
36. **Ēducentur :** jussive subjunctive, therefore not from *ēdūcere. 180,b.*
39. **oppidīs :** dative of agent. *110,b.* **studia :** ' learning.' **ut :** ' as.'
40. **Haec . . . repetenda :** ' I thought that these particulars ought
to be recounted more in detail, and, as it were, from their very source.'
42. **quam grātum :** ' how pleasing.' **iniungō :** ' require.'
43. **prō :** ' in view of.' **reī :** ' undertaking.'
45. **sollicitāre :** ' interest.'
46. **fidem meam obstringam :** ' bind myself.'
48. **vindicō :** ' claim.'
50. **lēge :** ' condition.' **ut . . . nihil :** a final or purpose clause, and
so an irregular use for *nē . . . quid. 197, e.* **hinc :** from Rome.

8 (4, 19)

C. Plīnius Calpurniae Hispullae Suae S.

Pliny praises his wife Calpurnia to the aunt who had trained her.

Cum sīs pietātis exemplum frātremque optimum et amantissimum tuī parī cāritāte dīlēxerīs fīliamque eius ut tuam dīligās nec tantum amitae eī affectum, vērum etiam patris āmissī repraesentēs, nōn dubitō maximō tibi gaudiō fore, cum cognōveris dignam patre, dignam tē, dignam avō 5 ēvādere. Summum est acūmen, summa frūgālitās; amat mē, quod castitātis indicium est. Accēdit hīs studium litterārum, quod ex meī cāritāte concēpit. Meōs libellōs habet, lēctitat, ēdiscit etiam. Quā illā sollicitūdine, cum videor āctūrus, quantō, cum ēgī, gaudiō afficitur! Dis- 10 pōnit, quī nūntient sibi, quem assēnsum, quōs clāmōrēs

8. **Calpurniae Hispullae:** the aunt of Pliny's wife, Calpur'nia. We may conclude from the fact that Hispul'la assumed the responsibility of rearing Pliny's wife that her parents died when she was very young.

1. **exemplum:** 'model.' **frātrem:** the father of Pliny's wife.

2. **dīlēxerīs:** the tense implies that the father is dead. **ut tuam:** 'as your own child.'

3. **affectum:** 'affection,' a post-classical meaning.

4. **repraesentēs:** 'show.'

5. **fore:** the infinitive instead of the usual *quīn*-clause is found in Nepos and Livy, and becomes more common in the period when Pliny wrote. Cicero would probably have written *nōn dubitō quīn futūrum sit.*

6. **ēvādere:** sc. *eam;* 'that she is turning out.' **est:** sc. the dative of possession. **acūmen:** 'understanding.' **summa frūgālitās:** in modern terms, 'she is an excellent housekeeper.'

7. **Accēdit hīs studium litterārum:** 'In addition to this she shows an interest in literature.'

8. **quod ex meī cāritāte concēpit:** 'which is the outgrowth of her affection for me.'

9. **lēctitat, ēdiscit etiam:** 'she constantly reads them, she even memorizes them.'

10. **āctūrus:** 'about to plead a case'; sc. *rem* or *causam.* **Dispōnit:** sc. *cursōrēs;* 'She stations couriers.'

11. **clāmōrēs:** 'applause.'

excitārim, quem ēventum iūdiciī tulerim. Eadem, sī
quandō recitō, in proximō discrēta vēlō sedet laudēsque
nostrās avidissimīs auribus excipit. Versūs quidem meōs
15 cantat etiam fōrmatque citharā, nōn artifice aliquō docente,
sed amōre, quī magister est optimus. Hīs ex causīs in spem
certissimam addūcor perpetuam nōbīs maiōremque in diēs
futūram esse concordiam. Nōn enim aetātem meam aut
corpus. quae paulātim occidunt ac senēscunt, sed glōriam
20 dīligit. Nec aliud decet tuīs manibus ēducātam, tuīs
praeceptīs īnstitūtam, quae nihil in contuberniō tuō vīderit

12. **quem . . . tulerim :** ' what verdict I gained.' **sī quandō recitō :**
' whenever I give a public recital '; the practice of reading one's own
writings before an audience of in-
vited guests was very common in
Pliny's time, though earlier writers
also refer to the custom.

13. **in proximō discrēta vēlō :** ' she
sits near by behind a curtain.' How
literally? It would be improper for
a woman to appear in person, but
Calpurnia might station herself in
the next room, the curtain covering
the doorway between the rooms.

14. **excipit :** ' catches up.'

15. **fōrmatque citharā :** ' and accompanies them on the cithara.'
citharā is an ablative of means. It
should not be translated by ' lyre,'
since the *lyra* and the *cithara*, though
belonging to the same family of
stringed instruments, were quite
different. According to Pausa'nias

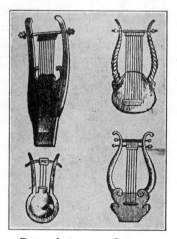

ROMAN LYRAE AND CITHARAE

(**5,** 14, 8), the *cithara* was invented by Apollo, hence Apollo *Citharoedus;*
and the lyre by Hermes. References in Plato and Aristotle also emphasize the difference. See illustrations above.

18. **aetātem aut corpus :** ' youth or physique.' Pliny was about
forty years old.

20. **Nec aliud decet :** ' And nothing else befits her.' **ēducātam :**
modifies *eam* understood with *decet.*

21. **contuberniō :** ' companionship.'

nisi sānctum honestumque, quae dēnique amāre mē ex tuā praedicātiōne cōnsuēverit. Nam, cum mātrem meam parentis locō verērēre, mē ā pueritiā statim fōrmāre, laudāre tālemque, quālis nunc uxōrī meae videor, ōminārī 25 solēbās. Certātim ergō tibi grātiās agimus, ego, quod illam mihi, illa, quod mē sibi dederīs, quasi invicem ēlēgerīs. Valē.

9 (5, 16)

C. Plīnius Mārcellīnō Suō S.

Fundanus has lost his charming daughter on the eve of her marriage.

Trīstissimus haec tibi scrībō, Fundānī nostrī fīlia minōre

---

22. **ex tuā praedicātiōne :** ' as a result of your commendation.'

24. **ā pueritiā statim fōrmāre :** ' to train me from my early years.'

25. **ōminārī :** sc. *mē;* ' to predict that I should be.'

26. **Certātim . . . agimus :** ' We vie with each other in thanking you.' How literally?

27. **sibi :** why not *eī?* **quasi invicem ēlēgerīs :** ' just as if you had picked us out for each other.' In Pliny's time *invicem* was sometimes used to express the reciprocal relation.

9. Mārcellīnō (mär-sẹ-lī'nỵs) : the mutual friend of Pliny and C. Minícius Fundánus, father of the girl, who is the subject of this letter.

The simple humanism of this fine letter is made even more real to the reader by the actual discovery of the maid's tomb, described by Lanciani, *Ancient Rome in the Light of Recent Discoveries*, page 281. The sepulcher, which belonged to the family of the Minicii, was found on Monte Mario, a short distance from Rome, in 1880. A cinerary urn with an inscription to Stato'ria Marcel'la probably contained the ashes of the mother. The following inscription was found engraved upon a marble tombstone :

D · M · MINICIAE · MARCELLAE · FUNDANI · F ·
VIX · A · XII · M · XI · D · VII

i.e. *dīs manibus Miniciae Marcellae, Fundānī fīliae. vīxit annīs XII., mēnsibus XI., diēbus VII.* ' To the spirit of Minicia Marcella, the daughter of Fundanus. She lived for 12 years, 11 months, and 7 days.' See illustration, page 454.

1. **Fundānī :** C. Minicius Fundanus, mentioned above, father of the girl. He belonged to an aristocratic family, held public office, and

dēfunctā, quā puellā nihil umquam fēstīvius, amābilius,
nec modo longiōre vītā sed prope immortālitāte dignius
vīdī. Nōndum annōs quattuordecim implēverat, et iam
5 illī anīlis prūdentia, mātrōnālis gravitās erat, et tamen
suāvitās puellāris cum virginālī verēcundiā. Ut illa
patris cervīcibus inhaerēbat! ut nōs
amīcōs paternōs et amanter et modestē complectēbātur! ut nūtrīcēs,
10 ut paedagōgōs, ut praeceptōrēs prō
suō quemque officiō dīligēbat! quam
studiōsē, quam intellegenter lectītā-
bat! ut parcē cūstōdītēque lūdēbat!
Quā illa temperantiā, quā patientiā,
15 quā etiam cōnstantiā novissimam
valētūdinem tulit! Medicīs obsequē-

CIPPUS OF MINICIA MAR-
CELLA, DAUGHTER OF
FUNDANUS

was a cultured gentleman, as is shown by
other letters of Pliny addressed to him
(*Epistulae*, **1**, 9; **4**, 15; **4**, 6).

2. **nihil:** sometimes used in sweeping
generalizations instead of *nēmō.* **fēstīvius:** ' more gay,' ' more vivacious.'

4. **Nōndum annōs quattuordecim implēverat:** not to be taken
literally, for Pliny has in mind the more usual age at which the Roman
girl was married, namely, after the fourteenth year, though she was
marriageable after her twelfth year.

5. **anīlis prūdentia . . . cum virginālī verēcundiā:** she was the
embodiment of the Roman ideal of womanhood; these two lines are
worthy of intimate study. **gravitās:** ' dignity.'

6. **verēcundiā:** ' modesty.' **Ut:** ' How.'

7. **inhaerēbat:** translate the tense correctly, as well as the subsequent imperfects.

10. **paedagōgōs:** these were special slaves whose duty it was to
accompany children to and from school. **prō suō quemque officiō:**
' each according to his position.'

13. **cūstōdītē:** ' cautiously,' a rare word.

16. **Medicīs obsequēbātur:** ' She always followed the directions of
her physicians.'　Roman laymen of education and discernment esteemed
the art of medicine most highly, and regularly sought the advice of

bātur, sorōrem, patrem adhortābātur, ipsamque sē dēstitūtam corporis vīribus vigōre animī sustinēbat. Dūrāvit hīc illī ūsque ad extrēmum nec aut spatiō valētūdinis aut metū mortis īnfrāctus est, quō plūrēs graviōrēsque 20 nōbīs causās relinqueret et dēsīderiī et dolōris. Ō trīste

---

reputable specialists and general practitioners both as a preventive measure and for proper treatment.

AULUS CORNELIUS CELSUS

Author of a medical work dated about 30 A.D.

Greek and Roman physicians recognized the basic rules of health which are concerned with food and drink, fresh air and sunlight, physical exercise, warmth, cleanliness, mental and physical relaxation and rest, and sought to interpret them to their patients. Not only such references as this in Pliny, but many similar statements in Cicero, Vitruvius, and especially in Horace, bear witness to the skill and high ideals of *bonā fide* physicians. The Romans had no medical colleges; the novice attached himself to a master physician, under whom he studied and with whom he visited patients in order to learn the art. Among such physicians professional ideals were of the highest, and the student may well remember that, notwithstanding the antiquity of the healing art, the Greeks and Romans were the real founders of the art and science of medicine. Hippocrates, Celsus, and Galen are its leading ancient exponents.

17. **sorōrem, patrem:** evidently her mother was no longer living. **ipsamque . . . sustinēbat:** ' and even her own person, when deprived of its physical vigor, she was wont to sustain by her mental power.'

19. **hīc:** i.e. *vigor animī*. **illī:** dative of reference, called also in Latin *datī'vus com'modī aut incom'modī*. *109, a;* B. 188; A. & G. 376; G. 350, 2. **spatiō valētūdinis:** a lingering illness, such as malarial fever or tuberculosis, two diseases very common in antiquity.

20. **quō . . . relinqueret:** relative clause of result; *quō = ut eō*. *195;* B. 284, 2; A. & G. 537, 2; G. 631.

plānē acerbumque fūnus ! ō morte ipsā mortis tempus
indignius ! iam dēstināta erat ēgregiō iuvenī, iam ēlēctus
nūptiārum diēs, iam nōs vocātī.   Quod gaudium quō
25 maerōre mūtātum est ! Nōn possum exprimere verbīs
quantum animō vulnus accēperim, cum audīvī Fundānum
ipsum, ut multa lūctuōsa dolor invenit, praecipientem, quod
in vestēs margarīta gemmās fuerat ērogātūrus, hōc in tūs et
unguenta et odōrēs impenderētur.   Est quidem ille ērudītus
30 et sapiēns, ut quī sē ab ineunte aetāte altiōribus studiīs
artibusque dēdiderit, sed nunc omnia quae audiit saepe,

---

22. **plānē acerbum fūnus:** ' very untimely death '; *acerbus* refers
primarily to the sour taste of unripe fruit, and so becomes a synonym
for *immātūrus*. **ō morte . . . indignius:** ' oh, the time of her death
more cruel than death
itself ! '

23. **dēstināta:** ' be-
trothed.'

27. **ut . . . invenit:**
' as grief finds many
mournful duties.' *188,b.*

28. **vestēs:** ' trous-
seau.' **in tūs et unguenta
et odōrēs:** among the
well-to-do, extravagant
sums were spent on funer-
als; spices and perfumery
of great variety and cost
were often thrown upon
the funeral pyre (*rogus*).

ROMAN GIRLS

29. **impenderētur:** depends upon *praecipientem* above, the *ut* being
frequently omitted in such clauses in Pliny. Remember that the
sequence after *praecipientem* is determined by *audīvī*. Why? **quidem
ille:** ' to be sure, Fundanus.' *Quidem* is often combined with the
pronoun *ille* to concede what is expected as a matter of course, and is
then often followed by a contrasting clause introduced by *sed*. Compare
use of German *ja*.

30. **ut quī . . . dēdiderit:** ' since he has devoted.' What is the force
of *ut*? *194, c;* B. 283, 3, *a;* A. & G. 535, *e*, N. 1; G. 626, N. 1. **ab
ineunte aetāte:** ' from his earliest years.'

quae dīxit aspernātur expulsīsque virtūtibus aliīs pietātis
est tōtus. Ignōscēs, laudābis etiam, sī cōgitāveris quid
āmīserit. Āmīsit enim fīliam quae nōn minus mōrēs eius
quam ōs vultumque referēbat tōtumque patrem mīrā 35
similitūdine exscrīpserat. Proinde, sī quās ad eum dē
dolōre tam iūstō litterās mittēs, mementō adhibēre sōlācium,
nōn quasi castīgātōrium et nimis forte, sed molle et hūmā-
num. Quod ut facilius admittat multum faciet mediī
temporis spatium. Ut enim crūdum adhūc vulnus meden- 40

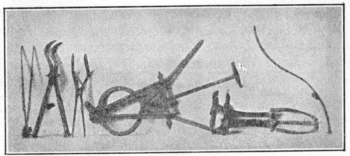

SURGICAL INSTRUMENTS FROM POMPEII

32. **expulsīsque . . . tōtus:** ' and having repudiated other virtues
he is wholly absorbed in parental devotion.' **pietātis:** genitive depending on *tōtus;* the more usual construction is *in* with the ablative; the
genitive being a Grecism. *238, g.*

33. **cōgitāveris:** why future perfect?

34. **Āmīsit:** notice the feeling and emotion portrayed by repeating
the verb, a figure of rhetoric called epanalepsis. *239, h.*

35. **referēbat:** ' reproduced.'

36. **exscrīpserat:** ' had represented.'

37. **tam iūstō:** ' so reasonable.' **mementō:** *181, a (3).* **adhibēre
sōlācium:** ' to employ the treatment of comforting words '; *adhibēre*
suggests the language of medicine.

38. **nōn quasi castīgātōrium et nimis forte:** ' not, as it were, implying
reproof and excessively strenuous.' *quasi* apologizes for Pliny's new
word *castīgātōrium.*

39. **Quod . . . spatium:** ' But a long interval of time will make him
more ready to accept this consolation.'

40. **medentium:** = *medicōrum,* here ' of the surgeon.' See illustra-

tium manūs reformīdat, deinde patitur atque ultrō requīrit,
sīc recēns animī dolor cōnsōlātiōnēs reicit ac refugit, mox
dēsīderat et clementer admōtīs acquiēscit.   Valē.

10 (6, 3)

C. Plīnius Vērō Suō S.

*Pliny has given a little farm to his old nurse, and desires that it should be
made as productive as possible.*

Grātiās agō quod agellum quem nūtrīcī meae dōnāveram
colendum suscēpistī.   Erat, cum dōnārem, centum mīlium
nummum : posteā dēcrēscente reditū etiam pretium minuit,
quod nunc tē cūrante reparābit.   Tū modo memineris
5 commendārī tibi ā mē nōn arborēs et terram, quamquam

----

tion, page 457.   The substantive use of the present participle becomes
more general during Pliny's time, though the genitive plural as a substitute for a noun is fairly common at all periods of the language.   See
note on page 480, line 52.

42. animī dolor: do not translate *animī* here ; this word and *rērum*
are often added as limiting genitives for the purpose of closer definition,
but are frequently superfluous in English.   *212, e.*   See page 138, line 9,
and note.

43. clementer admōtīs acquiēscit: ' is lulled to rest by their gentle
application.' *admōtīs* modifies *cōnsōlātiōnibus* understood, a dative
depending upon *acquiēscit*.   This sentence further amplifies the reference to medicine in line 37 above.   See also note to line 16.

10. Vērō : nothing is known about him.

1. agellum . . . colendum suscēpistī : the accusative of the gerundive as object is used only after verbs of giving, taking, sending, leaving,
letting, and undertaking.   *229, b.*   nūtrīcī : both Greeks and Romans
esteemed their nurses most highly.

2. mīlium : genitive of quality.   *100, a.*

3. nummum : archaic genitive for *nummōrum*.   *8, d; 238, c.*   In
our money the farm was worth approximately $4500.

4. tē cūrante : ' under your management.'   *144, a.*   Tū modo
memineris : ' Do you but remember.'   *memineris* is jussive subjunctive.
180, b.

haec quoque, sed mūnusculum meum; quod esse quam frūctuōsissimum nōn illīus magis interest quae accēpit quam meā quī dedī. Valē.

ROMAN FARM LAND
The ancient Roman bridge is still in use today.

11 (6, 4)

C. Plīnius Calpurniae Suae S.

Pliny expresses an affectionate solicitude for his wife, who has gone to Campania for her health. He begs her to write at least once a day.

Numquam sum magis dē occupātiōnibus meīs questus, quae mē nōn sunt passae aut proficīscentem tē valētūdinis

6. **quam frūctuōsissimum :** ' as productive as possible '; absolute superlative. *153, c.*

7. **illīus, meā :** both are to be construed with *interest. 103, e;* B. 211, 1, *a;* A. & G. 222, *a;* G. 331.

11. Calpurniae : see Selection 8 (**4,** 19). Calpurnia seems to have been Pliny's third wife, for whom he entertained the deepest affection. The tender letters to her indicate that their union was happy and the family relations were harmonious.

1. **occupātiōnibus :** ' business obligations.'

causā in Campāniam prosequī aut profectam ē vēstīgiō
subsequī. Nunc enim praecipuē simul esse cupiēbam, ut
5 oculīs meīs crēderem quid vīribus, quid corpusculō ap-
parārēs, ecquid dēnique sēcessūs voluptātēs regiōnisque
abundantiam inoffēnsa trānsmitterēs. Equidem etiam fortem tē nōn sine cūrā dēsīderārem ; est enim suspēnsum
et anxium dē eō quem ārdentissimē dīligās interdum nihil
10 scīre : nunc vērō mē cum absentiae tum īnfīrmitātis tuae
ratiō incertā et variā sollicitūdine exterret. Vereor omnia,
imāginor omnia, quaeque nātūrā metuentum est, ea maximē
mihi quae maximē abōminor fingō. Quō impēnsius rogō ut
timōrī meō cotīdiē singulīs vel etiam bīnīs epistulīs cōnsulās.
15 Erō enim sēcūrior, dum legō, statimque timēbō, cum legerō.
Valē.

---

3. **in Campāniam :** famous for its health resorts. **prōsequī :**
' escort.' **ē vēstīgiō subsequī :** ' to follow immediately in your tracks.'

4. **cupiēbam :** the so-called epistolary imperfect, which views
the action as of the time when the letter is received. *175, g.* The
English translation requires the present.

5. **corpusculō :** the diminutive expresses affection. *92, e.*

6. **ecquid . . . trānsmitterēs :** ' in short, whether you are bearing
without harm the pleasures of the retreat and the plenty of the district.'
ecquid: = num here ; *sēcessūs* is a genitive.

7. **Equidem etiam fortem :** ' Indeed, even if you were perfectly
well.'

8. **est enim suspēnsum et anxium :** ' for it causes suspense and
anxiety.'

11. **ratiō :** ' thought.'

12. **metuentum : =** *metuentium.*

13. **Quō impēnsius :** ' Wherefore the more earnestly.' *Quō* is an
ablative of degree of difference, which often approaches an ablative of
cause. *140.*

15. **statimque :** *-que* has an adversative force here, ' but.'

12 (6, 16)

C. Plīnius Tacitō Suō S.

A Martyr to Science

Pliny describes the great eruption of Vesuvius in 79 A.D. and the death of his uncle, Pliny the Elder, whose scientific zeal was responsible for his death.

I appreciate the opportunity to tell you about my uncle's death.

Petis ut tibi avunculī meī exitum scrībam, quō vērius trādere posterīs possīs. Grātiās agō; nam videō mortī

---

12. Tacitō : The historian has already been referred to in a previous introductory note (page 438, Selection 2). In the following letter Pliny furnishes information to Tacitus on one of the greatest volcanic outbursts in all history, which completely overwhelmed the two cities of Pompeii and Herculaneum. Though this catastrophe is mentioned by other writers, notably Dio Cassius, Pliny's letters are the recollection of an eye witness ; it is this personal touch which makes the graphic descriptions so valuable. Indeed, none other than Pliny's uncle, a great Roman scientist and scholar, was among the victims.

Tacitus asked Pliny for the story of the eruption in order that he might incorporate it in his *Histories*, for which he was collecting materials at the time. Unfortunately this portion of the historian's work has not survived, a fact which makes these letters all the more valuable.

Vesuvius was not generally regarded as dangerous. Its summit had been crowned with verdure for so long a time that only vague traditions remained to testify to its volcanic character. Naturally the people were unprepared, and their terror only added to the destruction.

Paradoxical though it may seem, the destructive forces of nature have unwittingly bequeathed to us a rich heritage in the excavations of Pompeii and Herculaneum, whereby historians have been able to reconstruct a large portion of Roman and Greco-Roman civilization. Small wonder, then, that these letters appeal to our love of romance! Various difficulties in the Latin text make a complete translation desirable. This will be found on page 567 of the Companion.

In another letter (**6,** 20), equally interesting, Pliny gives a graphic account of his personal experiences in the great eruption. See illustrations, pages 462, 463, 465, 466 (facing).

An Italian excavator, Engineer Don Gennaro Matrone, published in 1903 a pamphlet in French, in which he ventures the assertion that a

eius, sī celebrētur ā tē, immortālem glōriam esse prōpositam.
Quamvīs enim pulcherrimārum clāde terrārum, ut populī,
ut urbēs, memorābilī cāsū quasi semper vīctūrus occiderit,
quamvīs ipse plūrima opera et mānsūra condiderit, multum
tamen perpetuitātī eius scrīptōrum tuōrum aeternitās addet.
Equidem beātōs putō quibus deōrum mūnere datum est

CAPO MISENO NEAR CUMAE

Misenum was the headquarters of the Roman fleet, as those who have read
Ben Hur will recall.

aut facere scrībenda aut scrībere legenda, beātissimōs vērō
10 quibus utrumque.   Hōrum in numerō avunculus meus et
suīs librīs et tuīs erit.   Quō libentius suscipiō, dēposcō etiam
quod iniungis.

---

sumptuous villa discovered by him may be the home of Rectina situated at
the foot of Vesuvius from which she sent an appeal for rescue, and that
the skeleton of an old man found near by is Pliny the Elder.   A résumé
of the pamphlet may be found in *Art and Archaeology*, Volume XXIX,
Number 2, page 52, *et seq.*

My uncle observes a strange phenomenon.

Erat Mīsēnī classemque imperiō praesēns regēbat.
Nōnum Kal. Septembrēs, hōrā ferē septimā, māter mea
indicat eī appārēre nūbem inūsitātā et magnitūdine et 15
speciē. Ūsus ille sōle, mox frīgidā, gustāverat iacēns
studēbatque: poscit soleās, ascendit locum ex quō maximē

VESUVIUS IN ERUPTION

Although this shows a more recent eruption, it illustrates exactly the conditions so well described by Pliny.

mīrāculum illud cōnspicī poterat. Nūbēs, incertum procul
intuentibus ex quō monte — Vesuvium fuisse posteā cognitum est — oriēbātur, cuius similitūdinem et fōrmam nōn 20
alia magis arbor quam pīnus expresserit. Nam longis-
simō velut truncō ēlāta in altum quibusdam rāmīs diffun-
dēbātur, crēdō, quia recentī spīritū ēvecta, dein senēscente
eō dēstitūta aut etiam pondere suō victa in lātitūdinem
vānēscēbat; candida interdum, interdum sordida et macu- 25

lōsa, prout terram cineremve sustulerat. Magnum pro-
piusque nōscendum, ut ērudītissimō virō, vīsum.

*His scientific zeal impels him to investigate; he sets sail intent on offering
assistance wherever needed.*

Iubet Liburnicam aptārī; mihi, sī venīre ūnā vellem, facit
cōpiam: respondī studēre mē mālle, et forte ipse quod
30 scrīberem dederat. Ēgrediēbātur domō: accipit cōdicillōs
Rēctīnae Tascī imminentī perīculō exterritae — nam vīlla
eius subiacēbat, nec ūlla nisi nāvibus fuga —; ut sē tantō
discrīminī ēriperet ōrābat. Vertit ille cōnsilium et quod
studiōsō animō incohāverat obit maximō. Dēdūcit quad-
35 rirēmēs, ascendit ipse, nōn Rēctīnae modo sed multīs — erat
enim frequēns amoenitās ōrae—lātūrus auxilium. Properat
illūc unde aliī fugiunt, rēctumque cursum, rēcta gubernācula in perīculum tenet, adeō solūtus metū ut omnīs
illīus malī mōtūs, omnīs figūrās, ut dēprehenderat oculīs,
40 dictāret ēnotāretque.

*He pushes on in the face of great dangers, and reaches the home of his friend
Pomponianus at Stabiae, whose apprehensions he seeks to allay by
preserving a calm demeanor, even indulging in sleep while the others
remain awake.*

Iam nāvibus cinis incidēbat, quō propius accēderent,
calidior et dēnsior; iam pūmicēs etiam nigrīque et ambūstī
et frāctī igne lapidēs; iam vadum subitum ruīnāque
montis litora obstantia. Cunctātus paulum an retrō
45 flecteret, mox gubernātōrī ut ita faceret monentī. "Fortēs,"
inquit, "fortūna iuvat; Pompōniānum pete." Stabiīs
erat, dirēmptus sinū mediō; nam sēnsim circumāctīs
curvātīsque lītoribus mare īnfunditur. Ibi, quamquam
nōndum perīculō appropinquante, cōnspicuō tamen, et cum
50 crēsceret, proximō, sarcinās contulerat in nāvēs, certus
fugae, sī contrārius ventus resēdisset; quō tunc avunculus
meus secundissimō invectus complectitur trepidantem,

cōnsōlātur, hortātur, utque timōrem eius suā sēcūritāte
lēnīret, dēferrī in balineum iubet; lōtus accubat, cēnat aut
hilaris aut, quod est aequē magnum, similis hilarī. Interim 55
ē Vesuviō monte plūribus in locīs lātissimae flammae
altaque incendia relūcēbant, quōrum fulgor et clāritās
tenebrīs noctis excitābātur. Ille agrestium trepidātiōne

STABIAN STREET IN POMPEII
Vesuvius in the background.

ignēs relīctōs dēsertāsque vīllās per sōlitūdinem ārdēre in
remedium formīdinis dictitābat. Tum sē quiētī dedit, et 60
quiēvit vērissimō quidem somnō. Nam meātus animae,
quī illī propter amplitūdinem corporis gravior et sonantior
erat, ab iīs quī līminī obversābantur audiēbātur.

*Finally, when their lives are imperiled, the entire party decide to leave
the house.*

Sed ārea ex quā diaeta adībātur ita iam cinere mixtīsque
pūmicibus opplēta surrēxerat ut, sī longior in cubiculō mora, 65

exitus negārētur. Excitātus prōcēdit, sēque Pompōniānō
cēterīsque quī pervigilāverant reddit. In commūne cōnsultant, intrā tēcta subsistant an in apertō vagentur.
Nam crēbrīs vāstīsque tremōribus tēcta nūtābant et quasi
70 ēmōta sēdibus suīs nunc hūc nunc illūc abīre aut referrī
vidēbantur. Sub diō rūrsus quamquam levium exēsō-
rumque pūmicum cāsus
metuēbātur; quod tamen
perīculōrum collātiō
75 ēlēgit. Et apud illum
quidem ratiō ratiōnem,
apud aliōs timōrem
timor vīcit. Cervīcālia
capitibus imposita linteīs
80 cōnstringunt; id mūnī-
mentum adversus inci-
dentia fuit. Iam diēs
alibī, illīc nox omnibus
noctibus nigrior dēnsior-
85 que; quam tamen facēs
multae variaque lūmina
sōlābantur. Placuit
ēgredī in lītus et ex
proximō aspicere ecquid
90 iam mare admitteret;

quod adhūc vāstum et adversum permanēbat. Ibi super
abiectum linteum recubāns semel atque iterum frīgidam
aquam poposcit hausitque. Deinde flammae flammārum-
que praenūntius odor sulpuris aliōs in fugam vertunt,
95 excitant illum.

My uncle is suffocated by the gases.

Innītēns servulīs duōbus assurrēxit, et statim concidit,
ut ego colligō, crassiōre cālīgine spīritū obstrūctō clausōque

Two Views of Vesuvius

ABOVE: Across the Bay of Naples from Stabiae.

BELOW: From the Forum at Pompeii.

stomachō, quī illī nātūrā invalidus et angustus et frequenter
aestuāns erat. Ubi diēs redditus — is ab eō quem novissimē
vīderat tertius — corpus inventum integrum, illaesum 100
opertumque ut fuerat indūtus; habitus corporis quiēscentī
quam dēfūnctō similior. Interim Mīsēnī ego et māter.
Sed nihil ad historiam, nec tū aliud quam dē exitū eius
scīre voluistī. Fīnem ergō faciam. Ūnum adiciam omnia
mē quibus interfueram quaeque statim, cum maximē vēra 105
memorantur, audieram persecūtum. Tū potissima ex-
cerpēs; aliud est enim epistulam, aliud historiam, aliud
amīcō, aliud omnibus scrībere. Valē.

13 (7, 27)

C. Plīnius Surae Suō S.

The haunted house

Erat Athēnīs spatiōsa et capāx domus, sed īnfāmis et
pestilēns. Per silentium noctis sonus ferrī, et sī attenderēs ācrius, strepitus vinculōrum longius prīmō, deinde ē
proximō reddēbātur: mox appārēbat īdōlon, senex maciē
et squālōre cōnfectus, prōmissā barbā, horrentī capillō; 5
crūribus compedēs, manibus catēnās gerēbat quatiēbatque.

---

13. Surae: L. Licinius Sura was a native of Spain, a scientist, confidential friend of Trajan, and a statesman.

2. **pestilēns:** ' unhealthful.' **attenderēs:** the so-called iterative
subjunctive, expressing a repeated or customary action. In Cicero's
time the imperfect indicative would have been regular. In this clause
the subjunctive may also be due to the ideal " you." *205 (2); 180, e (2);*
B. 302, 3, *a;* 356, 3; A. & G. 518, *a;* G. 566, 567 and N.

3. **ācrius:** ' more attentively.' **strepitus:** ' rattling.'

4. **reddēbātur:** ' was produced,' ' was heard.' Note the tense.
īdōlon: Pliny Latinizes this Greek word meaning ' ghost.'

5. **cōnfectus:** ' consumed.'

6. **gerēbat quatiēbatque:** translate the tense accurately here and
elsewhere.

Inde inhabitantibus trīstēs dīraeque noctēs per metum
vigilābantur; vigiliam morbus et crēscente formīdine
mors sequēbātur. Nam interdiū quoque, quamquam
10 abscesserat imāgō, memoria imāginis oculīs inerrābat,
longiorque causīs timōris timor erat. Dēserta inde et
damnāta sōlitūdine domus tōtaque illī mōnstrō relīcta;
prōscrībēbātur tamen, seu quis emere, seu quis condūcere
ignārus tantī malī vellet. Vēnit Athēnās philosophus
15 Athēnodōrus, lēgit titulum, audītōque pretiō, quia suspecta
vīlitās, percunctātus, omnia docētur, ac nihilō minus, immō
tantō magis condūcit. Ubi coepit advesperāscere, iubet
sternī sibi prīmā domūs parte, poscit pugillārēs, stilum,
lūmen; suōs omnēs in interiōra dīmittit, ipse ad scrībendum

---

7. **inhabitantibus:** = *incolīs;* dative of agent. *110, a.*

8. **vigilābantur:** ' were spent in sleeplessness.' **vigiliam morbus:**
notice the position to heighten the contrast.

10. **abscesserat:** ' had disappeared '; iterative action completed
before the time of the main verb. *186, a; 205.* **oculīs inerrābat:**
' kept hovering before their mind's eye.'

11. **timōris timor:** such repetition is intentional. See page 437, note
2. *239, h.* **inde:** ' thereupon.'

12. **illī . . . relīcta:** ' was abandoned to the ill-famed portent.'

13. **prōscrībēbātur . . . vellet:** ' nevertheless it was advertised for
sale, in case anyone wished to buy it or, ignorant of the alarming phenomenon, wished to rent it.' *vellet* is subjunctive in a subordinate clause
in implied indirect discourse. *214, a; 213, b.*

15. **Athēnodō'rus:** his identity has not been definitely established, but
he may have been a Stoic philosopher from Tarsus. **titulum:** ' placard.'

16. **omnia docētur:** ' he is told all the details '; since *doceō* takes two
accusatives in the active voice, the accusative of the thing — here
omnia — is retained in the passive. *116, c.* **nihilō minus, immō tantō
magis:** ' not one whit less eagerly, nay rather the more so.'

18. **sternī:** ' his bed made.' **prīmā domūs parte:** ' in the front part
of the house.' For the omission of *in* see *145, c;* B. 228, 1, *b);* A. & G.
429, 1; G. 385, N. 1. **pugillārēs, stilum, lūmen:** ' his writing-tablets,
his pencil, and a lamp.' See illustrations, pages 87, 365, 566.

19. **suōs omnēs . . . dīmittit:** ' he had all his household retire to
the inner part of the house.' See illustration, page 470.

animum, oculōs, manum intendit, nē vacua mēns audīta 20
simulācra et inānēs sibi metūs fingeret. Initiō, quāle
ubīque, silentium noctis, dein concutī ferrum, vincula
movērī; ille nōn tollere oculōs, nōn remittere stilum, sed
offīrmāre animum auribusque praetendere. Tum crēbrēscere fragor, adventāre, et iam ut in līmine, iam ut intrā 25

līmen audīrī. Respicit,
videt, agnōscitque nārrā-
tam sibi effigiem. Stābat
innuēbatque digitō, simi-
lis vocantī. Hīc contrā 30

A ROMAN HOUSE

This shows the atrium and impluvium.

20. **audīta**: 'which he had heard of'; modifies *simulācra*.

21. **sibi**: 'for its own un-doing,' dative of disadvantage. *109, a.*

22. **concutī . . . audīrī**: note how Pliny warms up to his tale by the use of historical infinitives which portray feeling and emotion. *182.* **concutī ferrum, vincula movērī**: 'the clanking of iron resounded and the rattling noise of chains.' Chiasmus. *239, e.*

24. **offīrmāre animum . . . praetendere**: 'he concentrated his attention and (thereby) closed his ears.' *animum* is the object of both verbs, and *auribus* is dative with compound verb. **crēbrēscere fragor**: 'the din kept increasing'; the Latin expression is poetical, and helps to add an artistic touch to the whole passage.

25. **iam . . . audīrī**: 'at one time it sounded as if at the door, at another time as if inside.'

26. **Respicit, videt agnōscitque**: the return to the historical present has the effect of relieving the tenseness of the situation.

28. **Stābat**: note position and tense; an effective and vivid realism is cleverly portrayed.

29. **innuēbatque**: 'and it was beckoning.'

30. **Hīc**: 'Athenodo'rus.'

ut paulum exspectāret manū significat rūrsusque cērīs
et stilō incumbit. Illa scrībentis capitī catēnīs īnsonābat.
Respicit rūrsus idem quod prius innuentem, nec morātus
tollit lūmen et sequitur. Ībat illa lentō gradū, quasi
35 gravis vinculīs. Postquam dēflexit in āream domūs,
repente dīlāpsa dēserit comitem; dēsertus herbās et folia

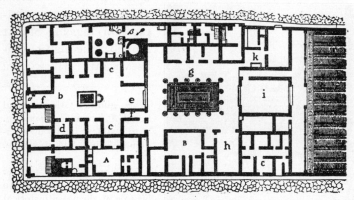

PLAN OF A ROMAN HOUSE

a. Vestibulum	*f.* Fauces	*A B C.* Suites and shops
b. Atrium	*g.* Peristylium	for renting
c. Alae	*h.* Triclinium	*β.* Bake Shop and
d. Cubiculum	*ı.* Oecus	Mill
e. Tablinum	*k.* Culina	

31. **cērīs:** 'his writing-tablets (covered with wax).' See illustration,
page 87.

32. **Illa . . . īnsonābat:** 'The ghost (sc. *effigiēs*) kept clanking the
chains over his head as he wrote.' What is the construction of *scrībentis?*
catēnīs is an ablative of means. *īnsonābat* is commonly poetical.

33. **Respicit:** 'He looked around and saw,' a good illustration of concentrated idiom very natural to Latin. *212, l.* **idem . . . innuentem:**
'beckoning as before.' How literally? **nec morātus:** 'without delay.'

35. **āream:** 'courtyard.' See illustration above.

36. **dīlāpsa dēserit:** 'it faded away and left.' **dēsertus, etc.:**
'(Athenodorus) left alone plucked some grass and leaves and marked the
spot.'

concerpta signum locō pōnit. Posterō diē adit magistrātūs, monet ut illum locum effodī iubeant. Inveniuntur ossa īnserta catēnīs et implicita, quae corpus, aevō terrāque putrefactum, nūda et exēsa relīquerat vinculīs; collēcta 40 pūblicē sepeliuntur. Domus posteā rīte conditīs mānibus caruit. Valē.

14 (8, 16)

C. Plīnius Paternō Suō S.

Pliny's attitude of kindness towards his slaves.

Cōnfēcērunt mē īnfīrmitātēs meōrum, mortēs etiam, et quidem iuvenum. Sōlācia duo, nēquāquam paria tantō dolōrī, sōlācia tamen: ūnum facilitās manūmittendī; videor enim nōn omnīnō immātūrōs perdidisse quōs iam

---

37. locō: best taken as an idiomatic dative closely attached to the noun *signum.*

40. exēsa: ' eaten away,' from *exedere.*

41. pūblicē: ' at public expense.' Domus . . . caruit: ' Thereafter, when the ghost had been duly laid, the house was haunted no more.' The Romans believed that the souls of the dead whose bodies had not received formal burial were condemned to wander.

14. Paternō: Pliny addressed three other letters to him, but he is otherwise unknown.

1. Cōnfēcērunt . . . meōrum: ' The illnesses of my slaves have greatly worried me.' Note the position of the verb. Why does Pliny not use *servōrum?* et quidem iuvenum: ' and that, too, of young men.' We may suspect tuberculosis, a disease which exacted great toll from the youthful population of Rome. Celsus says (*Dē Medicīnā,* **2,** 1, 21): *Adolescentia . . . tābī maximē obiecta est; ferēque iuvenēs sunt quī sanguinem exspuunt:* ' Youth is especially liable to consumption, and it is usually the young men who eject blood.' *Adolēscentia* and *iuvenēs* suggest the period from fifteen to forty years, and it is these very years which represent the prevalence of tuberculosis even today.

3. ūnum: sc. *sōlācium.* facilitās manūmittendī: because manumission could be easily brought about.

4. immātūrōs: ' prematurely.' *151.*

5 līberōs perdidī; alterum, quod permittō servīs quoque
quasi testāmenta facere eaque ut lēgitima cūstōdiō. Man-
dant rogantque quod vīsum; pāreō ut iussus. Dīvidunt,
dōnant, relincunt, dumtaxat intrā domum. Nam servīs
rēs pūblica quaedam et quasi cīvitās domus est. Sed
10 quamquam hīs sōlāciīs acquiēscam, dēbilitor et frangor
eādem illā hūmānitāte quae mē ut hōc ipsum permitterem
indūxit. Nōn ideō tamen velim dūrior fierī. Nec ignōrō
aliōs eiusmodī cāsūs nihil amplius vocāre quam damnum
eōque sibi magnōs hominēs et sapientēs vidērī. Quī an
15 magnī sapientēsque sint nesciō, hominēs nōn sunt. Homi-

---

5. **quod:** ' the fact that.' **servīs:** Pliny cannot avoid the word
here because he is referring to slaves formally, *i.e.* from a legal standpoint.

6. **quasi testāmenta:** slaves had no legal privileges among the
Romans; a slave's will acquired validity only by the favor of his master.
ut lēgitima: ' as if they were legal.'

7. **vīsum:** sc. *est sibi;* ' as they determine.' How literally?

8. **relincunt:** the spelling of Latin words varied greatly in different
periods, as may be seen from Latin inscriptions. During the Archaic
Period (240–81 B.C.) this form was spelled as *relinquont*, and continued
so even through Cicero's time. At the close of the Ciceronian Age
(42 B.C.) the spelling in our text was adopted, while the form *relinquunt*
was not in general use till after Pliny's time. **dumtaxat intrā domum:**
' provided they do so within the household.'

9. **rēs pūblica quaedam:** ' a sort of state.' **quasi cīvitās:** ' body-
politic, so to speak.' The subject is *domus*.

10. **acquiēscam:** ' I try to resign myself.' B. 259, 2; A. & G. 467;
G. 227, N. 2. In the Silver Age (14–138 A.D.) the subjunctive is often
used with *quamquam.* *187, b.*

11. **hūmānitāte:** ' tender sympathy.' **ut hōc ipsum permitterem:**
' to allow them this special privilege.'

12. **velim:** potential subjunctive. *180, e.* **Nec ignōrō:** ' I am fully
aware '; litotes. *239, m.*

13. **damnum:** ' a financial loss.'

14. **an nesciō:** ' perhaps.' *180, e (1);* B. 300, 5; A. & G. 575, *d;*
G. 457, 2.

15. **Hominis est:** ' It is the part of a real man.' *94, d.*

nis est enim afficī dolōre, sentīre, resistere tamen et sōlācia
admittere, nōn sōlāciīs nōn egēre. Vērum dē hīs plūra
fortasse quam debuī, sed pauciōra quam voluī. Est enim
quaedam etiam dolendī voluptās, praesertim sī in amīcī
sinū dēfleās, apud quam lacrimīs tuīs vel laus sit parāta vel 20
venia. Valē.

15 (9, 6)

C. Plīnius Calvisiō Suō S.

Pliny's indifference to the games of the Circus.

Omne hōc tempus inter pugillārēs ac libellōs iūcundissimā
quiēte trānsmīsī. "Quemadmodum," inquis, "in urbe
potuistī?" Circēnsēs erant, quō genere spectāculī nē
levissimē quidem teneor. Nihil novum, nihil varium, nihil
quod nōn semel spectāsse sufficiat. Quō magis mīror tot
mīlia virōrum tam puerīliter identidem cupere currentēs

---

17. **sōlāciīs:** *127, a;* B. 214, 1, *c;* A. & G. 356, N.; G. 405 and note.
dē hīs: ' on this subject.' **plūra:** sc. *scrīpsī.*

19. **dolendī voluptās:** ' pleasure in grieving.'

20. **dēfleās:** the ideal " you," potential subjunctive. *180, e (2)*;
B. 280, 3; A. & G. 447, 2; G. 258. **sit:** subjunctive of characteristic.
194, a.

15. Calvisiō: Calvis'ius was a member of the municipal senate in
Comum, Pliny's birthplace, and one of his intimate friends.

1. **Omne hōc tempus:** when the games were in progress.

3. **potuistī:** sc. *trānsmittere.* **Circēnsēs:** sc. *lūdī,* especially
chariot races. The Romans had a passion for this sport, so much so
that Juvenal (**10**, 81), a contemporary of Pliny, summed up the ideal
of the common people in the famous words, *pānem et circēnsēs.* **nē . . .
teneor:** ' I am attracted not even in the slightest degree.'

4. **Nihil novum, nihil varium:** ' No novelty, no variety.' **nihil
. . . sufficiat:** ' nothing which is worth seeing more than once.' Why
is *sufficiat* in the subjunctive? *194, a;* B. 283, 2; A. & G. 535, *a;*
G. 631, 2.

6. **mīlia virōrum:** the seating capacity of the Circus Maximus is
variously estimated by ancient authorities from *150,000* to *250,000.*
Compare our football stadia.

equōs, īnsistentēs curribus hominēs vidēre. Sī tamen aut
vēlōcitāte equōrum aut hominum arte traherentur, esset
ratiō nōn nūlla : nunc favent pannō, pannum amant, et
10 sī in ipsō cursū mediōque certāmine hīc color illūc, ille hūc
trānsferātur, studium favorque trānsībit, et repente agitā-
tōrēs illōs, equōs illōs, quōs procul nōscitant, quōrum
clāmitant nōmina, relinquent. Tanta grātia, tanta auctōritās in ūnā vīlissimā tunicā, mittō apud vulgus, quod vīlius
15 tunicā, sed apud quōsdam gravēs hominēs ; quōs ego cum
recordor in rē inānī frīgidā assiduā tam īnsatiābiliter dēsi-

---

7. curribus : ' in chariots,' dative with compound verb. *107, a.*

9. nunc : ' as a matter of fact.' pannō, pannum : ' rag ' ; note
the repetition and chiastic arrangement to emphasize Pliny's disgust.
239, h; 239, e.

10. in ipsō cursū : ' in the race proper.' *162, a.* color : rival companies, called *factiōnēs*, provided drivers, horses, and all necessary para-
phernalia for the races. At this time there were four such corporations,
each of which was distinguished by its particular color, worn by the
jockeys. The people naturally became devoted adherents of the different factions, which were designated by their respective colors. These
were green, red, white, and blue. Excitement ran high on such occasions, comparable in some respects to a Kentucky Derby or the major
football games of our great universities.

11. trānsferātur, trānsībit, relinquent : this type of mixed condition,
in which the future indicative displaces the present subjunctive of an
ideal apodosis (*207*) is not infrequently found in Latin. *trānsībit* and
relinquent should be translated as if *trānseat* and *relinquant*. The indicative in the Latin sentence emphasizes the reality. studium : 'enthusiasm.'

12. quōrum clāmitant nōmina : among the names of jockeys and
horses that have been preserved, none is more famous than the horse
Incitā'tus (' Flyer '), the favorite of the Emperor Caligula (37 A.D.–
41 A.D.), who intended to honor it with the consulship, as Suetonius
reports (*Caligula, 55*).

13. grātia : ' influence.'

14. mittō : ' I am not saying.' Affirmative verbs in Latin are sometimes more idiomatically translated by a negative expression. *212, m.*

15. gravēs : ' sedate.'

16. in rē inānī frīgidā assiduā : ' on an empty, insipid, commonplace
amusement.' dēsidēre : ' waste their time.'

(handwritten: Bruno Hills – semi retired) Walter Buck Downtown

dēre, capiō aliquam voluptātem, quod hāc voluptāte nōn
capior. Ac per hōs diēs libentissimē ōtium meum in litterīs collocō, quōs aliī ōtiōsissimīs occupātiōnibus perdunt.
Valē.   20

16 (10, 96)

C. Plīnius Traiānō Imperātōrī

Chrīstus et Chrīstiānī

*Pliny, perplexed about the Christians in his province, writes to the Em-
peror Trajan for advice.*

Sollemne est mihi, domine, omnia dē quibus dubitō
ad tē referre. Quis enim potest melius vel cunctātiōnem

TRAJAN

19. **ōtiōsissimīs occupātiōnibus:** an oxymoron.
239, p.

16. Pliny's letter to the
Emperor Trajan and the cita-
tions below from Tacitus and
Suetonius are the *locī classicī*
in ancient Roman literature
for the historicity of Christ
and the early Christians. By
64 A.D. the Christians were
numerous enough to attract the
attention of the Romans, who,
however, did not understand
the simplicity and humility of
the converts. Pliny wrote this
letter some forty-five to fifty
years after the death of St.
Paul, who according to tradition suffered martyrdom on
the Via Ostia some three miles
from Rome during the Nero-
nian persecution. See illustrations, pages 477–481.

1. **Sollemne est mihi: 'It
is customary for me.'**

meam regere vel ignōrantiam īnstruere? Cognitiōnibus
dē Chrīstiānīs interfuī numquam; ideō nesciō quid et
5 quātenus aut pūnīrī soleat aut quaerī. Nec mediocriter
haesitāvī sitne aliquod discrīmen aetātum an quamlibet
tenerī nihil ā rōbustiōribus differant, dētur paenitentiae
venia an eī quī omnīnō Chrīstiānus fuit dēsīsse nōn prōsit;
nōmen ipsum, sī flāgitiīs careat, an flāgitia cohaerentia
10 nōminī pūniantur. Interim in iīs quī ad mē tamquam
Chrīstiānī dēferēbantur hunc sum secūtus modum. Interrogāvī ipsōs an essent Chrīstiānī. Cōnfitentēs iterum ac
tertiō interrogāvī, supplicium minātus; perseverantēs
dūcī iussī. Neque enim dubitābam, quālecumque esset
15 quod fatērentur, pertināciam certē et īnflexibilem obsti-
nātiōnem dēbēre pūnīrī. Fuērunt aliī similis āmentiae
quōs, quia cīvēs Rōmānī erant, annotāvī in urbem remit-

3. **Cognitiōnibus:** ' Trials,' probably at Rome.
5. **Nec mediocriter haesitāvī:** ' I have been greatly puzzled,'
litotes. *239, m.*
6. **sitne:** the primary sequence is used because the writer is thinking of present time in connection with *haesitāvī.* **quamlibet tenĕrī:** ' the
exceedingly young.'
7. **nihil:** ' not at all.'
8. **omnīnō:** 'constantly.' **dēsīsse:** ' to have ceased to be one.'
9. **nōmen ipsum:** ' whether the mere name,' the indirect question
continues. *162, a.*
10. **in:** ' in the case of.' **quī. . . dēferēbantur:** ' who were charged
before me as being Christians.'
11. **modum:** ' method.' **Interrogāvī ipsōs:** ' I asked them personally '; he did not merely accept the statement of some informer.
12. **Cōnfitentēs:** sc. *eōs = Chrīstiānōs.*
14. **dūcī:** ' to be led to execution.' **Neque enim dubitābam:** ' I
was fully convinced.' The accusative and infinitive with *dubitāre* is
mostly post-Augustan (used after 14 A.D.).
16. **similis āmentiae:** genitive of quality. *100, a.*
17. **annotāvī. . . remittendōs:** ' I designated to be recommitted in
Rome.' Although a provincial governor had full jurisdiction over his
province, he could not punish a Roman citizen, but had to accord him

tendōs. Mox ipsō trāctātu, ut fierī solet, diffundente sē
crīmine, plūrēs speciēs incidērunt. Prōpositus est libellus
sine auctōre multōrum nōmina continēns. Quī negābant 20
esse sē Chrīstiānōs aut fuisse, cum, praeeunte mē, deōs
appellārent et imāginī tuae, quam propter hōc iusseram

St. Paul's Gate at Tarsus

the right of a trial in Rome, as was done in the case of St. Paul under
Nero (Acts, **25**, 11).

18. **ipsō trāctātū . . . crīmine**: ' when, as usually happens, the
charges increased in number from the mere (*ipsō*) act of investigating
them.'

19. **plūrēs speciēs incidērunt**: ' a variety of charges fell under my
notice.' **Prōpositus est . . . sine auctōre**: ' There was placed before
me an anonymous complaint.'

20. **Quī**: ' But these persons who.' sc. *eōs*.

21. **praeeunte mē**: ' at my dictation.' *144, a.* They repeated the
formula as he recited it. See illustration, page 481.

22. **imāginī tuae**: dative with *supplicārent* below. *105;* B. 187, II;
A. & G. 367; G. 346, R. 2. To the Romans such an act was merely an

cum simulācrīs nūminum afferrī, tūre ac vīnō supplicārent,
praetereā maledīcerent Chrīstō, quōrum nihil posse cōgī
25 dīcuntur quī sunt rē vērā Chrīstiānī, dīmittendōs esse putāvī. Aliī ab indice nōminātī esse sē Chrīstiānōs dīxērunt
et mox negāvērunt; fuisse quidem, sed dēsīsse, quīdam ante
triennium, quīdam ante
plūrēs annōs, nōn nēmō
30 etiam ante vīgintī. Hī
quoque omnēs et imāgi-
nem tuam deōrumque
simulācra venerātī sunt
et Chrīstō maledīxērunt.
35 Affīrmābant autem hanc
fuisse summam vel
culpae suae vel errōris,
quod essent solitī statō
diē ante lūcem convenīre

AN ANCIENT MONUMENT

expression of patriotism; to
the Christians it was an act
of idolatry. **propter hōc:** 'for
this purpose.'

This is perhaps the earliest Christian
tombstone showing the cross in its original
form. The two birds on either side are
intended for doves, and the inscription
may be restored as follows:

24. **praetereā... Chrīstō:**
'furthermore, (when) they
cursed Christ.' **Chrīstō:** for
the dative see note on line 22
above.

IN PACE · QUI · VIX[IT]
[ANN]IS · VI · DIES · III

25. **rē vērā:** 'really.' **dīmittendōs esse:** 'they ought to be
released.'

27. **fuisse quidem:** '(they said) that they had, of course (*quidem*),
been (Christians).' **ante:** adverb.

29. **nōn nēmō:** 'one or another.' *239, m.*

36. **summam:** 'the sum total,' explained by the *quod*-clause below.

38. **essent:** *214, a.* **statō diē:** probably Sunday.

39. **ante lūcem:** for two reasons: first, because these early Christians were for the most part slaves or working people, who had their
daily duties to perform; second, because the early hour insured greater
secrecy, and therefore was safer. Meetings held at irregular hours, and

carmenque Chrīstō quasi deō dīcere sēcum invicem, sēque 40
sacrāmentō nōn in scelus aliquod obstringere, sed nē fūrta,
nē latrōcinia, nē adulteria committerent, nē fidem fallerent, nē dēpositum appellātī abnegārent; quibus perāctīs,
mōrem sibi discēdendī fuisse, rūrsusque coeundī ad capiendum cibum, prōmiscuum tamen et innoxium; quod ipsum 45

particularly by night, had always aroused the suspicion of patriotic
Romans, who could not forget such machinations as Catiline and his
followers were guilty of. For their nightly meetings see Cicero, *In Catilīnam* **1**, 1, 10. *Sallust*, **32**, 6.

40. **carmen Chrīstō. . . invicem:** not 'hymn' in the modern sense, but rather 'antiphon.' See English dictionary. **quasi deō:** this would not appear unusual to Pliny, who was quite familiar with the apotheosis of Roman emperors.

41. **sacrāmentō:** Pliny, no doubt, interprets the word in the sense of 'oath,' but it is quite possible that the Christians were using the word with the meaning of 'sacrament,' something which our author could hardly understand. This, then, may be the earliest use of the word *sacrāmentum* as referring to the Lord's Supper. **nē . . . committe-rent, fallerent, abnegārent:** clauses of purpose, balancing *in scelus ali-quod,* and depending upon *sacrāmentō obstringere. 199, a.*

ROMAN REPRESENTATION OF CHRIST
The bearded Christ is of oriental origin.

43. **nē . . . abnegārent:** 'that they would not repudiate a trust when called upon (to return it).' The ancients had no banking system, and therefore found it necessary on occasion to deposit their money and valuables with neighbors and friends.

44. **ad capiendum cibum:** not the Lord's Supper, but the 'love-feast,' called in Greek ἀγάπη.

45. **prōmiscuum tamen et innoxium:** 'but ordinary and harmless,' said to offset the common charge that the Christians ate human flesh

facere dēsīsse post ēdictum meum, quō secundum mandāta tua hetaeriās esse vetueram. Quō magis necessārium crēdidī ex duābus ancillīs, quae ministrae dīcēbantur, quid esset vērī et per tormenta quaerere. Nihil aliud invēnī quam superstitiōnem prāvam, immodicam. Ideō, dīlātā cognitiōne, ad cōnsulendum tē dēcucurrī. Vīsa est enim mihi rēs digna cōnsultātiōne, maximē propter perīclitan-

---

and drank the blood of children, absurdities which probably arose from misunderstanding the language of the Eucharist. **quod ipsum facere dēsīsse:** 'but that they ceased doing even (*ipsum*) this.'

47. **hetaeriās:** a Latinized Greek word meaning 'fraternities,' 'clubs.' Such organizations were regarded as hostile to the government. **Quō . . . crēdidī:** 'Wherefore I believed it the more necessary.' For *quō* see *140;* A. & G. 414, *a*, note.

48. **ministrae:** 'deaconesses.' According to Romans, **16,** 8, this order was already a component part of the early church.

49. **et:** adverb. **per tormenta:** the Romans regularly examined slaves in this way.

50. **superstitiōnem prāvam, immodicam:** the noun connotes excessive fear of the gods due to an unreasonable religious belief, whereas *religiō* indicates a reasonable reverence for the gods. See the expressions of Tacitus and Suetonius below.

A CARICATURE

This drawing, scratched on a wall of the imperial palace on the Palatine by some pagan soldier, is probably the earliest representation of the crucifixion. The Greek inscription means: Alexamenos is worshiping his god.

Ideō . . . dēcucurrī: 'For this reason I suspended court, and came to you for advice.'

52. **rēs:** 'the problem.' **perīclitantium:** 'of defendants.' The genitive plural as well as certain other cases of the present participle may be used substantively. See page 457, note 40.

tium numerum. Multī enim
omnis aetātis, omnis ōrdinis,
utrīusque sexūs etiam, vocantur 55
in perīculum et vocābuntur.
Neque cīvitātēs tantum, sed
vīcōs etiam atque agrōs superstitiōnis istīus contāgiō perva-

---

55. **vocantur in perīculum et vocābuntur :** ' are and will be imperiled.'
in perīculum vocārī is a substitute for
the missing passive of the deponent
verb *perīclitārī*.

57. **cīvitātēs :** = *urbēs*, a meaning
which gradually became more common, and is regular in Mediaeval
Latin.

58. **agrōs :** ' rural districts.'

In this certificate (libellus) the writer
declares his pagan religious loyalty to
the Roman state in order to avoid persecution in accordance with the edict of the
Roman Emperor Decius, 250 A.D. The
Greek text may be translated as follows:

First Hand

"To the Superintendents of Sacrifices,
from Inarous, son of Akis, from the village of Theoxenis, with his children Aian
and Heras, all being of the village of
Theadelphia :

A CERTIFICATE

"It was always our practice to sacrifice to the gods, and now, in your pres-
ence, in accordance with the order, we have sacrificed, have offered liba-
tions, and have tasted the offerings; and we request you to certify this.
Farewell."

Second Hand

"We, Aurelius Serenus and Hermas, saw you sacrificing."

First Hand

"The first year of the Emperor Caesar Gaius Messius Quintus Trajanus
Decius Pius Felix Augustus, Pauni 23 (June 17, 250) "

60 gāta est; quae vidētur sistī et corrigī posse. Certē satis
cōnstat prope iam dēsōlāta templa coepisse celebrārī et
sacra sollemnia diū intermissa repetī pāstumque venīre
victimārum, cuius adhūc rārissimus ēmptor inveniēbātur.
Ex quō facile est opīnārī quae turba hominum ēmendārī
65 possit, sī sit paenitentiae locus.

17 (10, 97)

Traiānus Plīniō S.

Trajan's answer

Āctum, quem dēbuistī, mī Secunde, in excutiendīs causīs
eōrum quī Chrīstiānī ad tē dēlātī fuerant, secūtus es.
Neque enim in ūniversum aliquid, quod quasi certam fōrmam
habeat, cōnstituī potest. Conquīrendī nōn sunt; sī dēferan-
5 tur et arguantur, pūniendī sunt, ita tamen ut quī negāverit

---

60. **quae,** etc.: 'but I think that it (*contāgiō*) can be arrested and
cured.' He is using the language of medicine.

61. **dēsōlāta templa:** Christianity spread with great rapidity.
celebrārī: 'to be frequented,' its primary meaning.

62. **repetī:** 'to be revived.' **pāstumque venīre victimārum:** 'and
that fodder for sacrificial victims is finding a sale.' *venīre* comes from
veneō, used as the passive of *vēndō.* This interference with business
conditions may well have been the cause for charges against the Christians.

65. **locus:** 'opportunity.'

17. 1. **Āctum:** 'Method of procedure.' **excutiendīs:** 'sifting.'
excutere, means literally, 'to shake out.'

3. **Neque,** *et seq.:* 'For nothing can be set up generally, which
represents a definite pattern, as it were.' **in ūniversum:** 'in general,'
'generally.' **quasi:** softens the use of *fōrmam.*

4. **habeat:** *194, a.* **sī ... arguantur, pūniendī sunt:** the indicative
is sometimes used in the apodosis of a less vivid future or ideal conditional sentence to give a vivid effect; any expression implying future
time may be so used instead of the regular present subjunctive. *207 (3)*

5. **ita:** 'with this reservation.'

sē Chrīstiānum esse, idque rē ipsā manifestum fēcerit, id est
supplicandō dīs nostrīs, quamvīs suspectus in praeteritum,
veniam ex paenitentiā impetret. Sine auctōre vērō prō-
positī libellī in nūllō crīmine locum habēre dēbent. Nam
et pessimī exemplī nec nostrī saeculī est.   10

---

6. **rē ipsā :** ' actually.'

7. **quamvīs suspectus :** see page 444, note 13.

9. **in nūllō crīmine . . . dēbent:** ' ought to have no place in a
criminal accusation.' **Nam . . . saeculī est:** this construction takes
various idioms in English; translate, ' For such action sets a very
bad precedent and is not in accord with the spirit of our age.'

10. **exemplī, saeculī :** predicate genitives of possession. *94, d.*

Tacitus, Roman historian who flourished under Trajan and whose
friendship with Pliny has already been noted (page 438, Selection 2;
page 461, Selection 12), in discussing the burning of Rome under Nero,
writes as follows (*Annālēs* **15,** 44) :

*Ergō abolendō rūmōrī Nerō subdidit reōs et quaesītissimīs poenīs affēcit,
quōs per flāgitia invīsōs vulgus* **Chrīstiānōs** *appellābat. Auctor nōminis
eius* **Chrīstus** *Tiberiō imperitante per prōcūrātōrem Pontium Pīlātum suppliciō affectus erat; repressaque in praesēns* **exitiābilis superstitiō** *(see line
50 above) rūrsum ērumpēbat, nōn modo per Iūdaeam, orīginem eius malī, sed
per urbem etiam, quō cūncta undique atrōcia aut pudenda cōnfluunt cele-
branturque.*

' Therefore, to neutralize the rumor (that he had set fire to Rome)
Nero falsely accused and punished with most unusual tortures a group
of men, popularly called Christians, detested on account of their shameful acts. This name originated from Christ, who was put to death by
the governor Pontius Pilate in the reign of Tiberius; and though the
destructive superstition was momentarily checked, it kept breaking
out anew, not only throughout Judaea, where the evil originated, but
even throughout our city, whither everything hideous and shameful,
from all parts of the world, streams and wins approval.'

Suetonius, another Roman historian and friend of Pliny, says (*Nerō, 16*) :
afflīctī suppliciīs **Chrīstiānī,** *genus hominum* **superstitiōnis novae ac male-
ficae.**

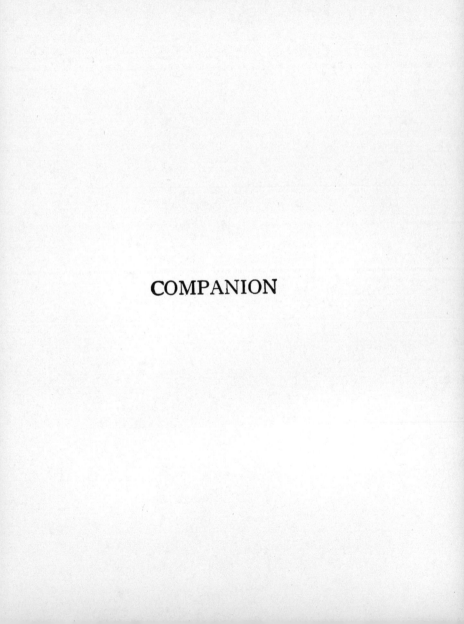

COMPANION

COMPANION

MARCUS TULLIUS CICERO

LIFE OF CICERO

Parentage. — The Cicero family was of plebeian stock. From time immemorial it had been settled near Arpinum, an ancient town in the Volscian territory, about sixty miles southeast of Rome. The ancestral estate of the Ciceros lay in the valley of the Liris, near its junction with the Fibrenus, just below the hill on which the city stood.

THE VALLEY OF THE LIRIS NEAR ARPINUM

Here Marcus Tullius Cicero was born, January 3, 106 B.C. His grandfather had been prominent in the local affairs of Arpinum; his father was a member of the equestrian order, and enjoyed the friendship of prominent men at Rome, — being withal a man of literary tastes. So when Marcus and his younger brother Quintus were old enough to profit by the educational advantages of the metropolis, their father bought a house in Rome and removed thither.

Early Education. — For a time at least, the brothers studied under teachers recommended by the orator Crassus.[1] Among the intimate advisers of Marcus was the gifted Archias, who aroused in him a decided bent for poetry. In his sixteenth year, 91 B.C., Marcus assumed the *toga virīlis*,[2] and became a constant attendant at the Forum; for at this time the Forum was an important means of liberal education. Here were the Rostra, from which orators addressed the people; the courts, where the most distinguished men of the time could be seen and heard; places of business, also, where the financial

REMAINS OF SHOPS ALONG THE VIA SACRA
This view looks into the Forum.

interests of the Roman world centered. In the Forum, too, one might hear the latest news from all quarters, and meet representatives of every nation; and young Cicero was no idle listener. At the same time he pursued regular studies with the greatest industry.

Advanced Study. — In 89 B.C. these pursuits were interrupted for a time by a campaign under the father of Pompey, who was successfully prosecuting the Social War. But on his return to Rome Cicero laid aside all hope of distinction in a military career, and for six years devoted himself to the study of logic, rhetoric, philosophy, and declamation, under the most eminent instructors. One of them —

---

[1] See vocabulary, under *Crassus* (2).
[2] See note on page 227, line 31, *praetexta*.

Diodotus the Stoic — afterwards lived in his house and died there. Every day, Cicero informs us, he practiced speaking, — sometimes in Latin, oftener in Greek. He also made translations from Greek authors, wrote verses, and composed a treatise on rhetoric. Absorbed in these studies, he passed unscathed through the terrible period of strife between Sulla and the party of Marius.

First Public Appearance; Travel and Study Abroad. — At the age of twenty-five (81 B.C.) Cicero entered the courts as a pleader. But the strain of professional life soon began to wear upon his health. Desirous of a change, in 79 B.C. he went to Athens, where he attended lectures on rhetoric and philosophy. Afterwards he traveled in Asia Minor, and spent some time at Rhodes with Molo, the famous rhetorician, under whom he had previously studied at Rome. After an absence of two years he returned home, not only recovered in health but greatly improved in his style of speaking. His abilities as a pleader quickly gained for him a wide reputation.

Beginning of Public Career. — Having now reached the age at which Roman citizens were permitted to enter upon the course of advancement in the public offices, Cicero presented himself as a candidate for the quaestorship, and was elected with flattering evidences of his popularity. The year of office (75 B.C.) he spent in Sicily as quaestor. He discharged the duties assigned him with strict justice and impartiality, — virtues most rare among Roman provincial officers of that period.

Prosecution of Verres. — Five years later he was called upon to plead the cause of the Sicilians against Verres, who had been governor of the island in the years 73–71, and had robbed, scourged, and in other ways maltreated the inhabitants with unprecedented brutality. Many of the most prominent men at Rome found it to their interest to sustain Verres, who was defended by Hortensius, at that time the most famous pleader in the law courts. Every obstacle that bribery or influence could raise was thrown in the way of the prosecution. But with indomitable persistency, Cicero surmounted every difficulty. He collected evidence, and opened the case. Before the evidence was all presented, Hortensius abandoned his client, and Verres fled from Rome, preferring voluntary exile to certain condemnation.

Aedileship and Growing Popularity. — Cicero now rose rapidly to the zenith of his popularity and influence. In 69 B.C. he was aedile. It was customary for aediles to celebrate the public games with lavish expenditure of their own money as a bid for popular favor. Cicero, not possessing the means to rival the display of wealthier predecessors, conducted the celebrations without extravagance, but with so good taste that he lost nothing in general estimation. Striking proof of his standing with the people appeared at the time of his election to the office of praetor, 67 B.C.

THE GREEK THEATER AT SYRACUSE IN SICILY

Praetorship; Defense of Cluentius. — The year of his praetorship (66) was marked by extraordinary activity. His office required him to serve as the highest magistrate for the administration of justice in civil matters, and also to preside at the trial of such criminal cases as might be assigned him. Nevertheless, as the Roman custom permitted, he kept up his practice at the bar, and successfully conducted the defense of Cluentius, who had been accused of poisoning, with one of the most adroit and effective pleas ever made.

The Manilian Law. — This year, also, he mounted the Rostra for the first time, and addressed the people in behalf of the bill of Manilius. The significance of this event was not limited to the fact that it was his first appearance as a political speaker. His attitude regarding the measure proposed sorely offended the aristocratic and senatorial party, with whose principles he was really more in sympathy than with those of the opposition; but it secured for him the friendship of Pompey, who might at any time prove to be the successor of Sulla as master of Rome, and it won the enthusiastic support of the populace, with whom Pompey was then the hero of the hour.

Consulship. — On the expiration of his term as praetor, Cicero declined the governorship of a province, which naturally fell to his lot, and directed all his energies toward securing the consulship, the last and highest of the offices in the order of civil preferment. He had six competitors, among whom were Gaius Antonius, an uncle of Mark Antony, and Catiline. These two united to secure the office. They received the powerful support of Marcus Crassus,[1] who had great influence on account of his wealth, and of Julius Caesar, who was coming to the front as a political organizer. Nevertheless, Cicero was elected by an overwhelming majority. Antonius was chosen as his colleague, having received a few more votes than Catiline. The new consuls entered upon their official duties January 1, 63 B.C.

A Question of Policy. — The consulship of Cicero and Antonius was one of the most memorable in the annals of Rome. At the outset an important question of public policy demanded attention. In December of the preceding year, one of the tribunes of the people, P. Servilius Rullus, had proposed an extravagant scheme for the purchase of lands in Italy for apportionment among the poorer citizens. Cicero's attitude toward the measure in any case could not fail to be one of extreme delicacy. If he opposed it he would jeopardize his standing with the popular party, to which in so great measure he owed his elevation to power; but if he favored it he would alienate the party of the senate, with whose leaders he appeared now to have come to an understanding.

Tact and Persuasiveness. — Yet his position was such that he must commit himself to one side or the other. He spoke against the bill, first in the senate, afterwards before the people, but with so great tact and persuasiveness that he seems to have suffered no loss of influence. A short time afterwards his power over the masses was shown by the ease with which he quelled a popular movement against

---

[1] See vocabulary under *Crassus* (3).

L. Roscius Otho, who had incurred the displeasure of the populace by means of a measure providing separate reserved seats at public spectacles for members of the equestrian order.

The Catilinarian Conspiracy. — While consul he defended Gaius Rabirius, one of the few surviving senators who had been present at the murder of Saturninus, thirty-seven years before, and who was now, for political effect, charged with the crime. He also spoke in opposition to a bill proposing the restoration of political rights to the children of those proscribed by Sulla, on the ground that the harmony of the commonwealth would thereby be endangered. But during the latter part of the year all other interests were lost sight of in the excitement attending the discovery of the Catilinarian conspiracy, which for a time threatened to overwhelm the existing order of things in riot and bloodshed. The prompt and efficient action of Cicero averted the catastrophe. He well deserved the honors which were heaped upon him as savior of the state.

CAESAR. THE NAPLES BUST

The Poet Archias. — After his consulship Cicero again declined the governorship of a province. Since the expiration of his term as quaestor he had been entitled to a seat in the senate, in which he now became an active member, at the same time continuing his practice as an advocate. Among other noteworthy cases, in 62 B.C. he defended P. Cornelius Sulla, who had been accused of complicity in the Catilinarian conspiracy, and made his memorable plea for the poet Archias.

Clodius. — In the same year the mysteries of Bona Dea,[1] from which men were rigorously excluded, were celebrated at the house of Julius Caesar, then pontifex maximus. P. Clodius Pulcher, a dissolute young patrician, disguised himself as a female musician, and thus gained admission. He was discovered, but made his escape. The offense, on account of its impiety, was brought before the senate.

[1] See vocabulary.

It was referred to the board of pontifices, who decided that sacrilege had been committed. At the trial which followed, Clodius tried to prove that he was away from the city on the day of the festival; but Cicero testified to having been with him in Rome only three hours before the discovery at Caesar's house. By means of the most shameful bribery and intimidation, Clodius secured an acquittal, and was afterward bitterly attacked by Cicero in the senate. He thenceforth became an avowed enemy of the orator, all the more dangerous because utterly lacking in principle.

The First Triumvirate. — Furthermore, Pompey, who had returned from the East loaded with spoils, was led to give up in large measure the advantage he had gained over the other public men, and was drawn into the coalition known as the first triumvirate. As the triumvirs proposed to keep the control of public affairs in their own hands, it was clear that Cicero, through his influence, might work mischief to their plans. Pompey was well disposed toward him; but Caesar, the ruling spirit of the coalition, finally resolved to humiliate the orator, and found in Clodius a suitable instrument.

Retaliatory Measures. — With Caesar's help Clodius secured an adoption into a plebeian family, that he might become eligible to the office of tribune; and was chosen to this magistracy for the year 58. Early in the year he brought forward a bill to the effect that any one who should be found to have put Roman citizens to death without a trial should be interdicted from the use of fire and water.[1] This was aimed at Cicero, and had reference to the execution of the Catilinarian conspirators. If he had ignored the attack, assuming his own innocence as a matter of course, he might perhaps have gained the advantage. But instead, thoroughly frightened, he put on mourning, and appeared in public as a suppliant. Many citizens, particularly of the equestrian order, put on mourning also, as a mark of their support. For a time the hostile movement was checked; but the persistency of the tribune availed more than the passing sympathy of the populace.

Banishment. — Foreseeing the success of Clodius, in the latter part of March Cicero fled from Rome. He went first to Vibo,[2] then by way of Tarentum to Brundisium, whence he proceeded through Greece to Thessalonica, — a voluntary exile. Immediately after his

---

[1] That is, *ut ei aquā et igni interdicerētur*, — the usual formula of banishment.
[2] See vocabulary.

departure a formal decree of banishment was passed, forbidding him
to live within four hundred miles of the city. It was enacted also
that any person who should take measures to secure his recall should
be pronounced a public enemy.

Recall. — The spirit of the orator was completely broken. For a
time he lost all courage, all hope. Yet within three months after he
had gone his friends began to agitate the subject of his return. The
consuls and tribunes of the year 57 were well disposed toward him.
The triumvirs had accomplished their purposes, and viewed with
disapprobation the increasing turbulence of Clodius, whose armed
band engaged in frequent riots in the city. Caesar was now in Gaul;

Coin of Dyrrhachium, Illyria

but Pompey joined the movement in Cicero's favor. At length the
senate sanctioned a proposal that voters from all parts of Italy should
be invited to come to Rome and unite in passing a bill for his recall.
The proposed measure was submitted to the comitia centuriata on the
4th of August, and carried by a large majority. Cicero had come
back as far as Dyrrachium the previous November. On the very day
of the assembly he crossed over to Brundisium, where his daughter
met him. He proceeded with her slowly to Rome, being received with
congratulations and distinguished honors in the towns along the way.
At Rome he was welcomed with extravagant demonstrations of joy.
His house on the Palatine and his villas were ordered rebuilt at public
expense.

Disappointment; Augur. — Yet the city was no longer to him what
it had been. The triumvirs were all-powerful. They did not deem it
necessary to take Cicero into their confidence, and he dared not offer
any opposition. In all outward appearances he was friendly to them.
He felt obliged to yield to their wishes on many occasions. In their

interest, as he himself informs us,[1] he even defended men to whom
he had previously been unfriendly. Intervals of leisure in his professional work he devoted to writing. In 53 B.C. he was chosen augur.

Defense of Milo. — On January 20, 52 B.C., the collision between
the armed bands of Clodius and Milo occurred at Bovillae, resulting
in the death of the former. Cicero undertook the defense of Milo.
At the trial, in April, the adherents of Clodius created great disturbance, and Pompey filled the Forum with soldiers. Cicero was afraid
to deliver his speech, but afterward wrote it out and sent it to Milo,

THE FORUM LOOKING WEST

who had gone into exile at Massilia. In the same year a law was
passed that a consul or praetor should not be eligible to the governorship of a province until five years after the expiration of his term of
office. In the meantime provinces were to be assigned to ex-consuls
and ex-praetors who had not yet had such an appointment. To
Cicero was allotted the province of Cilicia, with the surrounding
region.

Proconsul of Cilicia. — He entered upon his duties in Cilicia on the
last day of July, 51 B.C. He administered the affairs of the province
with great uprightness, but found the position, as he had expected,
not at all to his liking. With the help of his brother Quintus, an
experienced officer, he subdued certain mountain tribes along the

[1] See *Ad Familiārēs,* **7,** 1, *Ad Atticum* **4,** 5, 6.

Syrian frontier, and was weak enough to desire a triumph. As soon as the year of his appointment had expired he set out for Rome, reaching the city on the fourth of January, 49 B.C.

Civil War. — In the beginning of the year 49, hostilities commenced between Caesar and Pompey. Cicero, having vainly attempted to bring about a reconciliation between them, hesitated with which to cast in his lot. He finally decided to join the side of Pompey. In June he passed over to Greece, and appears to have been with Pompey till the battle of Pharsalus, which was fought on the 9th of August, 48 B.C. In November he returned to Brundisium. Here he remained unmolested till the following August, when he received a letter from Caesar which relieved him of all apprehensions regarding his personal safety. He now devoted himself to the composition of treatises on subjects connected with rhetoric and philosophy, dividing his time between his different villas.

Domestic Trouble. — In 46 he divorced his wife Terentia, whom he had married about the year 79. She appears to have been a high-spirited woman, having withal a large property, regarding the management of which she and her husband did not agree. Being financially embarrassed, he married Publilia, a wealthy young lady, for whom he had been acting as guardian; but this marriage was soon dissolved. The most crushing blow to his domestic happiness was the death, early in 45 B.C., of his daughter Tullia,[1] to whom he had been devotedly attached. For a time he retired to his secluded villa at Astura, and gave himself up to grief.[2] Her death left a deep impress upon his writings, which were now more than ever undertaken as a means of consolation.

The Ides of March; Philippics. — Cicero was fully in sympathy with the assassination of Caesar (March 15, 44 B.C.).[3] In the reaction against the conspirators he thought it unsafe for him to remain in Italy, and started for Greece. As the ship touched at Regium he learned that there was a prospect of reconciliation between Antony and the party of the senate, and returned to Rome. All hope of a peaceful solution of the existing complications was soon lost. Antony left the city, where Octavianus gradually acquired control. Cicero was once more in a position of influence, the favorite of the people. He assailed Antony before the senate and from the Rostra, in the

---

[1] See vocabulary. [2] See *Epistulae Sēlēctae*, 22, page 398.
[3] *Ibid.*, 23, page 399.

so-called Philippic orations.[1] But the coalition of Antony with Lepidus, and of these two later with Octavianus, was fatal to all hopes of the supporters of constitutional liberty.

Cicero's Assassination. — In the latter part of November, 43 B.C., the new triumvirs made out their proscription list. On it were placed the names of seventeen men who were to be put out of the way at once. That of Cicero was among them. The news reached him at Tusculum. He fled to Antium and took ship. Adverse winds prevented escape. He landed at Formiae and remained in his villa there,

THE ROSTRA

resolved to meet his fate. When the soldiers of the triumvirs came (December 7), his slaves placed him in a litter and started with him through the woods to the seashore, a mile away. They were overtaken, and prepared for defense. Cicero bade them be quiet, and put his head forth from the litter. The executioners struck off both his head and his hands, took them to Rome, and, by order of Antony, nailed them to the Rostra, — the scene of so many of his triumphs.

CICERO THE ORATOR

Importance of Oratory in Greece and Rome. — In the life of Greece and Rome oratory played a much more important part than in that of modern times. In antiquity those who possessed the rights of citizenship, the voters, lived in cities. The number of voters in

[1] See pages 331–359.

ancient states formed a small minority of the whole population. Civic life was concentrated. An orator, speaking in the central part of a city, might gather the whole body of citizens within the sound of his voice.

In those states where a democratic form of government prevailed, oratory naturally reached its highest perfection; for in the ancient democracies, unlike those of the modern era, questions were submitted, not to representatives of the people, but directly to the people themselves, with whom lay the decision of the most important matters.

COIN OF RHODES, CARIA

The easiest way to reach and mold opinion was through public address. Wide opportunity for public speaking was afforded also by the larger governmental bodies, as the Council at Athens and the Senate at Rome. Finally, the constitution of the tribunals, referring the decision of cases generally to a much greater number of individuals than the modern courts, was favorable to the development of oratory.

Greek Oratory. — The golden age of Greek oratory lasted from the end of the fifth to the latter part of the fourth century B.C. Among the numerous orators of this period later criticism reckoned ten as preëminent : Aeschines, Andocides, Antiphon, Deinarchus, Demosthenes, Hyperides, Isaeus, Isocrates, Lycurgus, and Lysias. Demosthenes was recognized both by his own and by succeeding ages as the greatest of them all. After his death, 322 B.C., with the extinction of Greek liberties, Greek eloquence rapidly declined. A new type of oratory came into vogue soon afterwards in the Greek cities of the western part of Asia Minor, known as the Asiatic style (*genus Asiāticum*). It was more ornate and artificial than that of Athens. which by way of distinction was known as the Attic style (*genus Atticum*). Midway between these two stood the Rhodian style (*genus Rhodium*), developed on the island of Rhodes.

Roman Oratory. — At Rome public speaking was extensively practiced from an early time. The flourishing period of Roman oratory lay between the end of the second Punic war (201 B.C.) and the establishment of the Empire (31 B.C.) This period of almost two hundred years may be conveniently viewed in three epochs.

Cato the Censor and Gaius Laelius. — In the first, the most prominent figure was that of Cato the Censor (see page 546), whose unpolished

THE BOSPORUS. THE ROCKS OF THE SYMPLEGADES

but effective oratory reflected his uncompromising sturdiness of character. Among the younger contemporaries of Cato was Gaius Laelius (see page 553), whose speaking showed more refinement. At this time Greek culture was exerting more and more influence upon Roman life, but in oratory apparently there was no study of Greek models.

The Gracchi, Antonius, and Crassus. — The second epoch extends from the time of the Gracchi to that of the eminent orators Marcus Antonius, grandfather of Mark Antony, and L. Licinius Crassus, who died 91 B.C. The Greek orators were now studied, and Greek teachers of rhetoric were freely employed; but there was as yet little open acknowledgment of indebtedness to them.

Hortensius, Cicero, and Caesar. — The three eminent names of the third period are Hortensius, Cicero, and Caesar. In oratory, as in other fields of literature and art, Greek models were now supreme, being taken as standards of excellence. The question was no longer whether Greece should be the instructor of Rome in eloquence; it was rather, which style of Greek oratory should be followed, the Attic, the Asiatic, or the Rhodian. This question each Roman settled for himself, some going so far as to confine their study to a single Greek orator as model. Greek teachers of rhetoric abounded everywhere. Hortensius preferred the florid exuberance of the Asiatic style; Caesar's taste inclined rather to the compact simplicity of the Attic, while Cicero followed a happy medium as represented by the Rhodian style.

Divisions of Oratory. — In Cicero's time the theory of oratory had long since been worked out with so great completeness that modern literary criticism has added nothing of importance to it. The matter of oratory was reckoned of three kinds: *demonstrative*, employed in praising or censuring some one; *deliberative*, used with reference to some measure, or proposal, either in the way of advocacy or of opposition; and *juridical*, employed in the courts, in accusation or defense. Five qualities were considered essential to an orator. These were: *invention,* the power to gather facts and arguments; *disposition*, the ability to arrange matter in the proper or most effective order; *expression*, a choice of words suitable to the thought; *memory*, a firm grasp of matter, words, and arrangement; and *delivery*, a perfect command of the voice, features, and gesticulation.

Parts of an Oration. — A typical oration was said to comprise six parts, as follows: —

I. INTRODUCTION (*exōrdium*), designed to win the favorable attention of the audience; often considered of two kinds: —
   a. The Opening (*prīncipium*), preliminary remarks.
   b. The Ingratiating (*īnsinuātiō*), intended by a skillful use of language to remove prejudices and put the audience into a receptive mood.

II. STATEMENT OF THE CASE (*nārrātiō*), a summary of the facts leading up to the point at issue.

III. DIVISION (*partītiō*, or *dīvīsiō*), indicating the treatment of the theme proposed, or the point to be proved.

IV. PROOF, or affirmative argument (*cōnfīrmātiō*), setting forth the arguments on the speaker's side of the case.

V. REBUTTAL (*refūtātiō*, or *reprehēnsiō*), refuting the arguments of the opposite side.

VI. PERORATION, or CONCLUSION (*perōrātiō*, or *conclūsiō*), bringing the address to an impressive close; frequently divided into three parts: —

    a. Summary (*ēnumerātiō*), a brief recapitulation of the speaker's points.

    b. Outburst (*indignātiō*), a burst of anger, designed to excite the indignation of the audience against the opposite side.

    c. Appeal (*conquestiō*), an appeal to the sympathies of the audience.

According to modern ideas of literary analysis, these six divisions may generally be more conveniently grouped in three, thus: —

    I. INTRODUCTION: —
        Exōrdium.
        Nārrātiō.
        Partītiō.

    II. DISCUSSION: —
        Cōnfīrmātiō.
        Refūtātiō.

    III. CONCLUSION: —
        Perōrātiō or *conclūsiō.*

This arrangement will be followed in presenting the outline of the orations in this edition.

Deviation from the Norm. — Careful rules were laid down by rhetoricians for the handling of each of the divisions. We are not to suppose that orators held rigidly to the outline given; yet it was regarded as the norm, or type, from which wide deviation was exceptional. The subjects most likely to lead away from it were those which inspired invective. Thus, the orations against Catiline show marked divergence from the typical structure. On the other hand, speeches of a more quiet tone, like that for Pompey's commission, and the majority of those made at the bar, were in this respect more nearly regular.

Cicero's Characteristics. — Cicero possessed all the qualities characteristic of a true orator. He was endowed with great activity and versatility of mind, breadth of view, ready sympathy, and intense feelings, — with a marvelous command of language, nice sense of literary form, and excellent memory; with attractive face and figure, great vivacity of manner, and keen power of repartee. From early youth he cultivated his natural gifts with unflagging industry; fired with the ambition to become the leading public speaker of his day, he set before himself the highest ideals. He realized his ambition; and the verdict of the ages has placed his name, with that of Demosthenes, high above all other ancient orators.

THE GREEK ORATOR, AESCHINES
He and Demosthenes were bitter rivals.

Cicero and Demosthenes. — His orations lack the conciseness and nervous force, the unabating earnestness of the Greek orator; but in richness and fullness of expression, in beauty of language, he is superior. His words gush forth like a torrent. He is broader in the range of thought and feeling to which he appeals. He is equally at home in the dignified tone suitable to the tragic, and in the stinging jest; in savage invective, and in the graceful language of compliment. Yet no comparison between the two men would be fair which did not take into account the difference in the character of the audiences before which they spoke. The polished, critical, cool-headed Athenian could best be influenced through the reason; the less critical Roman could be more easily swayed by an appeal to the feelings. Cicero was a consummate master of the art of putting things, of saying what he had to say in a way to carry the greatest weight. His points follow one another so naturally that one almost forgets that there is another side of the case. What the other side was, in most instances we do not clearly know; but Cicero always makes his own appear plausible.

On the whole, Demosthenes was stronger in thought, Cicero in literary form. But here, where the greatest power of the Roman orator lay, was also his greatest weakness; for now and then copiousness and charm of expression conceal a paucity of ideas. We are also at times conscious of a lack of sharpness in the statement of points. Yet the orations today, though in an ancient and difficult tongue, though read and not heard, continue to please and move us as they have pleased and moved men for two thousand years. How much more must they have stirred those to whom they were addressed! No other Roman ever moved an audience as Cicero did. Witness his speech for Roscius Otho, which transformed a hostile mob, against their will, into an assemblage of well-disposed citizens. He was equally successful as a pleader; his contemporaries declared, says Quintilian, that he reigned in the law courts. For these reasons alone, apart from the overwhelming verdict of posterity regarding the power of his speeches, he would worthily be ranked as the greatest of Roman orators, one of the greatest of the world.

CICERO THE WRITER

Rhetoric and Philosophy. — At Rome, both in his lifetime and afterward, Cicero was noted hardly less as a writer than as an orator. In his youth he devoted himself to the study of rhetoric and philosophy as a means of training for public speaking; and he retained an interest

COIN OF CORINTH, STRUCK UNDER JULIUS CAESAR

in both branches, but more particularly in the latter, which appeared to deepen as years passed by. When driven from his customary pursuits by untoward circumstances, he found diversion and consolation in literary composition. Most of his works were written in the two seasons of enforced retirement from political affairs, — the first after his return from exile, 57 B.C., and the second between his reconciliation with Caesar, 47 B.C., and the autumn after the dictator's death, 44 B.C.

Not including orations, poems, or correspondence, Cicero left not far from thirty different works. Fifteen of these works are still extant, and others are known from considerable sections which have been preserved; a few have entirely perished. His extant rhetorical writings comprise several treatises dealing with the theory of oratory and a sketch of the history of oratory down to Cicero's own time. His philosophical works treat a great variety of topics in morals, theology, and political philosophy.

Poetry and Correspondence. — His poems consisted in part of translations from the Greek, in part of verses upon Roman themes. Two at least were autobiographical; their titles were, " On the Events of my Consulship," and " On my Times." Only a few hundred lines of the poems are extant, most of which are from his translation of Aratus. His correspondence was collected and published after his death. The portion extant comprises eight hundred and sixty-four letters, of which ninety, however, are addressed to Cicero.

Contribution to the Latin Language. — As a poet Cicero was not successful. His verses were metrically correct, but lacked poetic inspiration. His prose writings, however, are characterized by a finish and charm that have called forth universal admiration. His services to the Latin language and literature cannot be overestimated. Previous to his time Latin prose had been crude, awkward. and labored; he developed a flowing and graceful style, which set before later writers a model of refined yet forceful expression.

Value of Philosophical Writings. — Very little had been written in Latin on the subject of philosophy; so he formed the design of presenting to his countrymen the gist of the Greek speculation in their own tongue. He was admirably fitted for this task by his extended intercourse with teachers of philosophy, his wide reading in the subject, and his own philosophical position, which was eclectic and negative, rather than dogmatic, so that he was able to present the views of the different schools on the whole fairly. He followed Greek models closely, and made few original contributions to the matter which he borrowed. But he coined new Latin terms, introduced illustrations of his own, and gave to the often dry and technical discussions of the Greeks a living and attractive form. In a word, he popularized philosophy, and his writings in this field are of all the greater value now because in many cases the Greek originals have perished.

Most of his works, after the example of the Greeks, were cast in the form of a dialogue. The philosophical vocabulary which he developed prepared the way not only for later pagan writers, but also for a Latin literature of Christian theology. The orderly development of thought, the graceful transitions, the happy perspective observed in the elaboration of points, the balance, yet variety, in the structure of sentences, the harmonious arrangement of words, the faultless phrasing, — these are some of the qualities that have caused several of his works to be accepted as literary masterpieces of the first rank. As a stylist Cicero has had no superior and few equals.

Worth of His Correspondence. — The tone of the correspondence is naturally less formal than that of the treatises. When chatting with intimate friends, as Atticus, he is frank and artless, — too much so for his reputation; he is more reserved when writing to others. His

GOLD COIN OF AETOLIA

Obverse: Head of Pallas.
Reverse: Aetolia holding a spear and a wreath-bearing Nike.

letters reflect the mood of the moment, — now sparkling with humor, or overflowing with pleasantries; now burdened with trouble, or altogether in despair. Nowhere else do we find so vivid a picture of Roman life in his time; nowhere else, perhaps, except in the autobiography of Benvenuto Cellini, do we have the inmost privacy of a strong mind so unreservedly revealed. The style is matchless for simplicity, clearness, and grace. If the world today were to be forced to choose whether it would more willingly part with Cicero's orations, his prose works, or his correspondence, it is doubtful which would be given up with the greatest regret.

CICERO THE MAN

Various Opinions. — The character of Cicero presents a singular combination of opposite qualities. Modern writers, who have studiously examined the facts of his career, have held the most diverse opinions concerning it. The biographers of Cicero have generally read into his life the lofty ideals of his moral treatises, and have either ignored or tried to explain away his many inconsistencies. A fairer view may be gained by emphasizing neither aspect of his character unduly, but by subjecting his political activities, his moral ideals, and his daily life to the same impartial scrutiny.

Self-Revelation in the Letters. — Although there are various ancient sources which help us to evaluate Cicero's character, by far the greater number of facts about him are gleaned from his own writings, particularly the letters. It is safe to say that if his correspondence had not been preserved, his name would have been spared most of the unfriendly criticism that has gathered about it. He was indiscreet enough to think on paper; his passing fancies or suggestions, to most of which he may have given no second thought, are today before us, subject to cool critical analysis and comparison. The letters of Cicero charm and enlighten us, yet show us many things unworthy of a great man; but, after all, deeds are greater than thoughts, more than words. Granted that a high-minded man, whose prominent position brought him many enemies and numberless trials, may have shown himself, in the privacy of friendly intercourse, at times weak and inconsistent with his professed ideals, — should that make us blind to his nobler traits, or to the greatness of his life work for humanity?

His Achievements. — The age of Cicero abounded in eminent men who from childhood had had the advantages of wealth and family prestige in their favor. Cicero entered the lists a " new man " (*novus homō*), without great wealth, without a long line of distinguished ancestry to bring him favorable recognition, apparently without anything in his favor, excepting a limited acquaintance with public men, a fair education, and an ambition to make the most of himself.

He practiced law, and generally won his cases. He came forward as a candidate, and received from the people unprecedented favor, for a man without powerful connections, in the rapid promotion to public offices. He accomplished all these things by the sheer force of personal effort, in that period of Roman history when the influence of military leaders was rapidly becoming paramount. Surely this betokens no ordinary power.

An Orator by Nature. — The natural gifts of Cicero fitted him to be an orator and writer rather than a statesman. His nice sense of

PART OF THE OLD WALL OF ARPINUM

balance, and his philosophical habit of looking at all sides of a case, sometimes made it impossible for him to decide quickly where a prompt decision was necessary. His mind was rather of the contemplative than the executive type. His tastes drew him toward the ideal; but an irresistible impulse drove him into practical affairs. He did not escape the contagious passion for political power characteristic of his generation; yet he lacked the steadiness of view, the singleness of aim, the persistency — perhaps also the courage — needful for one who would be more than temporarily great as a political leader. He was possessed also of a naïve and thoroughly good-natured egotism, which asserted itself on all occasions

His High-Mindedness. — Yet in an age of bribery, he was never convicted of giving or receiving a bribe. In a period of mad dissipation and debauchery, he remained untainted with vice, and in his affection for his daughter has left us one of the most beautiful pictures of ancient home life. At a time of broils and violence, he was a man of peace, hating strife, — a man of honor in all the relations of life. That was no unfitting tribute paid him by the historian Livy :[1] "Sixty-three years he lived, so that his death, except that it was violent, cannot be considered untimely. . . . After both his faults and his virtues have been taken into account, he remains a great, spirited, and distinguished man, to whose praises only the eloquence of a Cicero could do justice."

[1] Seneca, *Suāsōriae*, 7.

THE ORATIONS OF CICERO

Cicero left more than a hundred speeches. Of these, fifty-seven **are** still extant. Fragments of twenty others remain, and the titles **of** thirty more are known. The themes and general character of **the** extant orations may be learned from the following summary: —

1. *Speeches in Legal Cases.*
      a. In civil cases.

      For Quinctius, delivered 81 B.C.; in connection with a suit for debt.

      For Roscius the Comedian, 76; in a case concerning payment of damages for the death of a slave.

      For Tullius, 72 or 71; in a suit for damages on account of the destruction of property.

      For Caecina, 69; in a suit concerning an inheritance.

   b. In criminal cases.

      For Roscius of Ameria, 80 B.C.

      Against Caecilius, 70; a prelude to the action against Verres.

      Against Verres, 70; six speeches in all, of which only the first was actually delivered. See page 487.

      For Fonteius, 69; against a charge of provincial extortion.

      For Cluentius, 66. See page 488.

      For Rabirius, 63. See page 490.

      For Murena, 63; against a charge of corrupt canvassing for votes.

      For Cornelius Sulla, 62. See page 490.

      For Archias, 62. See page 543.

      For Valerius Flaccus, 59; against a charge of provincial extortion.

      For Sestius, 56; against a charge of violence.

      Against Vatinius, 56; for the impeachment of a witness **for** the prosecution of Sestius.

For Caelius, 56; in a suit arising from an intrigue.

For Cornelius Balbus, 56; against the charge of having illegally assumed the rights of citizenship.

For Plancius, 54; against a charge of bribery.

For Rabirius Postumus, 54; against a charge of extortion.

A CORNER OF THE PALATINE HILL

For Milo, 52.   See page 493.

For Marcellus, 46.   See page 511.

For Ligarius, 46; in favor of a former partisan of Pompey, then in exile.

For Deiotarus, King of Galatia, 45; against a charge of complicity in a plot to murder Caesar.

2. *Political Speeches.*

On Pompey's Commission, 66. See page 529.

On the Agrarian Measure of Rullus, 63; three speeches, the first addressed to the senate, the second and third to the people. There was a fourth speech, now lost. See page 489.

Against Catiline, 63; four speeches. See page 514.

After return from exile, four speeches: the first giving thanks to the senate, 57; the second thanking the people, 57; the third, ' On his House,' showing that his house on the Palatine, destroyed by Clodius, should be restored at public expense, 57; the fourth, ' On the Answers of the Soothsayers,' against objections to the rebuilding of his house on a site that had been consecrated, 56.

On the Consular Provinces, 56; urging the retention of Caesar in Gaul; before the senate. See page 510.

Against Piso, 55; an abusive attack upon a personal enemy; before the senate.

Against Antony, 44–43; fourteen orations. See page 556.

CICERO AND CAESAR

It is somewhat of a coincidence that two of the foremost Romans were coeval. (See *Outline of History of Latin Literature*, page 707.) Their characters and personal relationships present various interesting contrasts. Caesar's birthright qualified him for aristocratic standing; Cicero came from plebeian stock. Cicero himself tells us (Dē Prō-vinciīs Cōnsulāribus, 17) that they were friends in early life, and we may conclude that this relation was based on a kinship in disposition and character. Both had a keen sense of humor, an abundance of natural talent coupled with a genuine enthusiasm for study and literary achievement. These and other similar qualities, such as their oratorical gifts — Caesar ranking only second to Cicero — tended towards a mutual admiration.

As to their political faith, we may say that here their aims did not coincide. Although both men agreed in their opposition to the senatorial oligarchy whenever its conduct was prompted by selfish and arbitrary aims, it was their divergent political outlook which in the final analysis estranged the two, notwithstanding their affinities of taste and temperament. Cicero was, heart and soul, a patriot of the

old school, who believed in the traditional republic with its aristocratic leadership, whereas Caesar, mainly to promote his personal ambitions, championed the democratic party. Caesar was by nature stable, well poised, a man of great executive ability; Cicero was temperamental and idealistic, sensitive, easily disappointed and discouraged.

The Catilinarian Conspiracy (see page 514) was directly responsible for the first break between them. In this crisis Caesar preserved a negative attitude which helped to develop a feeling of distrust and suspicion on the part of Cicero (read Caesar's speech, page 137). In their future relations many a gesture was made by either the one or the other to preserve their natural friendship, and on many occasions Cicero paid glowing tribute to Caesar's ability. There need be no doubt that momentarily, at least, the orator was entirely sincere in these expressions of appreciation and good will. Eventually, however, when Cicero became convinced that Caesar had no intentions of restoring the republic, he could think of him only in terms of tyranny; and so intense did this feeling become that in

BRONZE BALL SUPPOSED TO CONTAIN THE ASHES OF JULIUS CAESAR

After the murder of Julius Caesar his body was taken to the Forum, and there burned. In the Middle Ages his ashes were supposed to be preserved in the large round ball on the top of the obelisk which, till 1586, stood at the side of St. Peter's church in Rome, and now stands in the Piazza in front of St. Peter's. (Illustration from an engraving made in 1569.)

the end he could even congratulate Basilus (see Selection 23, page 399) on his part in the assassination of Caesar.

THE SPEECH ON THE CONSULAR PROVINCES

This speech, delivered in June of 56 B.C., is a fine example of Cicero's eloquence. It is a panegyric of Caesar, praising his success in Gaul and urging his retention there. The occasion was a spirited debate on the floor of the senate in which, in accordance with the Sempronian law, the discussion turned on the selection of the provinces to be governed by the new consuls after they had served their year of office in 55 B.C. Various proposals had been made before Cicero spoke, and among them that the two Gauls, Transalpine and Cisalpine, should be assigned to the new consuls. This legislation was, of course, aimed directly against Caesar, but Cicero's brilliant speech brought about the defeat of the proposal with the result that Caesar's command in Gaul was continued.

The speech has many fine human touches which reveal the more intimate aspirations of the great orator, his sincere lovable nature, and his nobility of character. This is especially true in several passages in which he sums up his relations with Caesar, their early friendship, a slight estrangement, and the subsequent reconciliation (chapter 20, page 8). Cicero's love of peace, his frankness and sincerity, his tolerance and forbearance are qualities especially apparent in this eulogy of Caesar's work in Gaul.

Below is a brief summary of the part of the speech preceding chapter 8.

We are to decide upon the governors of four provinces, Syria and Macedonia, and the two Gauls. Regarding Syria and Macedonia there can be no hesitation; Gabinius and Piso, the present governors, not only have proved themselves incompetent but have been guilty of extortion and other unlawful practices. These men should be superseded by the praetors for the coming year and by the consuls for the year after. With regard to the Gauls a proposal has been made to assign them to the consuls-elect; I am opposed to this motion because it is aimed directly against Caesar, and would deprive him of both his provinces; likewise, it would still leave Gabinius and Piso in command.

THE ADDRESS OF THANKS FOR THE PARDON OF MARCELLUS

Occasion and Circumstances of Delivery. — Marcus Claudius Marcellus belonged to the most distinguished of the plebeian branches of the great Claudian gens. Nothing is known of his early life except that from boyhood he was a warm friend of Cicero. During his consulship (51 B.C.), being an ardent partisan of Pompey, he manifested the most bitter hatred toward Caesar. As the relations

between Pompey and Caesar became more and more strained,
Marcellus was less vehement, and tried to delay the inevitable outbreak of hostilities; failing in this attempt, he lent a half-hearted
support to the side of Pompey, whom he joined in Epirus.

After Caesar had gained the supreme power, his leniency toward his
former enemies was a matter of surprise to all. In accordance with his

usual policy he paid no attention to Marcellus, who resisted the urgent advice of
Cicero to ask the dictator's pardon. Meanwhile Marcellus' friends were active in his
behalf. At length in the summer of 46, at a
meeting of the senate, Gaius Marcellus, a
brother of Marcus, threw himself at Caesar's
feet and implored the forgiveness of the
exile, being joined in his supplication by
many of the senators. Caesar, having com-
mented on the hatred Marcellus had borne
him, and on the danger to himself in freely

COIN OF CAESAR SHOW-
ING GALLIC TROPHIES

allowing his enemies to return, declared that he would leave the decision of the matter to the senate, which was apparently unanimous
in the desire to have Marcellus restored to civil rights. Cicero was
touched by the magnanimity of the dictator, and also thought he saw
in this deference to the opinion of the senate an entering wedge to
the restoration of the authority of that body, and promise of a return to
the old constitutional forms. Inspired by the occasion, he arose and
expressed the feeling of the moment in an impassioned address of thanks
to Caesar, the speech known by the inaccurate title of *Prō Mārcellō*.

PRŌ M. MĀRCELLŌ ŌRĀTIŌ : i.e. *ōrātiō in quā Caesarī ēgit prō M. Mārcellī
restitūtiōnc*, "the speech in which he thanked Caesar for the pardon (literally,
restoration) of Marcus Marcéllus." In the Civil War between Caesar and
Pompey (49–48 B.C.) Marcellus had espoused the cause of Pompey, but
Caesar with his characteristic magnanimity, which he had shown also
towards Cicero, yielded to the entreaties of the senate and pardoned him.
The speech was delivered in the course of a meeting of the senate, in the
senate-house; but it was addressed to Caesar, who as consul presided.
After Caesar declared that he would pardon Marcellus, the senators gave
their votes in the usual order, nearly all expressing their thanks also; when
it came to Cicero's turn to speak, he responded with this address (*Ad Familiārēs*, **4**, 4, 4 : *plūribus verbīs ēgī Caesarī*).

Two other speeches of Cicero, that for Ligarius and another for Deiotarus, were grouped with this by the early grammarians under the title *ōrātiōnēs Caesariānae*. In view of the circumstances of delivery, as well as the character of the subject matter, the *Prō Mārcellō* is seen to lie on the border line between the political speeches and those in criminal cases; but on the whole it may more appropriately be classed — as also the other *Caesariānae* — with the latter. Rhetorically, it is an example of the demonstrative order (see page 498).

The oration possesses a peculiar interest for the modern reader on account of the temporary reconciliation of the orator with the dictator which it pictures, even though the enthusiasm of the moment led to an overstatement of Caesar's virtues. Yet such exaggeration, considering the circumstances and the temperament of the speaker, is far from unnatural; and in fact it lends a poetic coloring to the style.

Outline of the Marcellus

INTRODUCTION

Exōrdium. The unprecedented clemency of Caesar, shown by the pardon of Marcellus, forces me to speak. CHAPTER I.

DISCUSSION

A. *The deeds of Caesar*

Cōnfirmātiō. 1. Great beyond description are Caesar's deeds, especially in war. 2.

2. But greater is his clemency. 3, 4.

3. The pardon of Marcellus augurs well for the peace and welfare of the state. 5, 6.

B. *Caesar's danger*

1. Danger to Caesar is peril to the state. 7.

2. His work is not finished so long as so much remains to be done, not only for the present but also for the future. 8, 9.

5. Caesar's safety is our safety. 10.

CONCLUSION

Conclūsiō. For this gracious pardon we all return our heartfelt thanks. 11.

The Speeches against Catiline

Catiline's Early Life. — LUCIUS SERGIUS CATILINA was born about 108 B.C.   He was descended from an old patrician family which had lost its prestige and was in straitened circumstances.   From early youth he indulged in all forms of vice with seeming recklessness; yet he was a man of great courage, strong personal magnetism, and unusual abilities as a leader.   He gained the office of praetor for the year 68 B.C., and served as governor of Africa in 67.   The following year he returned to Rome to present himself as a candidate for the consulship for 65; but he had scarcely entered the city when he was charged with provincial extortion, and thus disqualified for the proposed candidacy.

His First Conspiracy. — The consuls-elect for 65, P. Autronius Paetus and P. Cornelius Sulla, soon after their election (July, 66) were

THE HILL OF JUNO AT CARTHAGE
Below, remains of a Roman villa; above, modern buildings and church.

impeached for bribery, their office being conferred on L. Aurelius Cotta and L. Manlius Torquatus.   Autronius, Catiline, and Cn. Calpurnius Piso now formed a plot to murder the new consuls on the day of their entry into office (January 1, 65 B.C.), and seize the authority.   As the arrangements were then not complete, the execution of the project was deferred till the 5th of the following February, and it was extended to compass the destruction of many of the leading men of the state.   On the appointed day, however, Catiline gave the signal for attack before the armed helpers had assembled in sufficient numbers, and the plot miscarried.   This is known as the first conspiracy of Catiline; the details of it are obscure and uncertain.

A Candidate for the Consulship of 63 B.C. — Nothing daunted, Catiline presented himself as a candidate for the consulship for the year 63, having meanwhile freed himself from the charges against him by wholesale bribery.   He set before his associates a program which included the division of the offices of state among themselves, the cancellation of all debts, and the murdering of the wealthiest citizens, with the confiscation of their property.   As he failed to receive an election,[1] he now rapidly furthered his preparations for a revolution by force of arms.   He borrowed great sums of money on his own credit and that of his friends, collected military stores, and gave to C. Manlius, who had been an officer under Sulla, a commission to enroll and train an army.   The center of operations was the neighborhood of Faesulae (now *Fiesole*), a few miles north of the city of Florence.   As Pompey was in the East, Italy contained no Roman army and no great general, and the time seemed favorable for a sudden stroke.

A Second Attempt to Win the Consulship. — In the midst of these preparations, early in 63, Catiline offered himself as a candidate for the consulship for 62.   His plan was, if elected, to put Cicero out of the way; then, as consul-elect, to enter into coalition with the consul Antonius, who to some extent at least was committed to his plans, and thus gain the supreme power.   It happened that one of the conspirators, Q. Curius, had made a confidant of Fulvia, a high-born but dissolute woman, in regard to the projects of Catiline; she, becoming disturbed at the prospect of a revolution which threatened the security of all, had allowed information regarding the matter to reach the ears of Cicero, and afterwards entered into communication with him. Through her influence, and the offer of large rewards, Cicero succeeded in inducing Curius to act as a secret agent, or detective, and to report every movement of the conspirators at once to himself.

His Defeat at the Polls; Failure of His Plot. — As the time for the consular election (July) drew near, he threw out hints about the danger to be apprehended from Catiline, and secured a postponement

[1] See page 489.

that there might be opportunity for investigation. He detached his colleague, Antonius, from the revolutionary party by the promise of the governorship of the rich province of Macedonia, after the expiration of the consular term. When the election was finally held (the date is uncertain), Catiline was again rejected, and a plot he had formed for the murder of several magistrates was rendered incapable of execution by the elaborate preparations of Cicero.

His Machinations Renewed. — Driven now to desperation, Catiline fixed upon October 27 (63 B.C.) as the date for raising the standard of open rebellion, and the following day for the massacre of

A ROMAN REPUBLICAN COIN
Obverse: Head of Jupiter. Reverse: Victory crowning a trophy.

his opponents and the pillaging of Rome. But on October 21 Cicero attacked him openly in the senate, which, immediately afterwards, passed a decree vesting supreme authority in the consuls for the protection of the state. Some days later word came that Manlius had actually taken up arms on the 27th, as expected, and that slaves were arming in Capua and in Apulia. Thereupon the senate authorized the drafting of troops, and ordered all precautions for the defense of the city. Catiline was charged with sedition by a young patrician, L. Aemilius Paulus; protesting his innocence, he offered to place himself in free custody.[1]

The First Oration. — On the night of November 6 he met his followers at the house of Marcus Laeca, where arrangements were perfected for the firing and plundering of Rome. He said that Cicero stood in the way of accomplishing his designs; whereupon L. Vargunteius, a senator, and C. Cornelius, a knight, volunteered to murder the consul at daybreak in his own house. A report of the

[1] See note on page 47, line 3

meeting was brought to Cicero in the night; when the would-be assassins went to call on him in the morning, they found the house closed against them.

On the 8th of November Cicero called a meeting of the senate in the temple of Jupiter Stator; finding Catiline present, he assailed the arch-conspirator in the bitter invective known as the **First Oration** against Catiline. Catiline attempted to justify himself, emphasizing the public services and respectability of his family; but being greeted with cries of " enemy " and " traitor " he left the senate. The same night he set out for Etruria, causing the report to be circulated that he was going to live in exile at Marseilles.

The Second Oration. — On the following day (November 9) Cicero addressed the people from the Rostra in the **Second Oration,** congratulating them on the departure of Catiline, and endeavoring to frighten the remaining conspirators into leaving the city. But though Lentulus, Cethegus, and their associates kept actively at work in Rome, three weeks passed before the consul could secure evidence against them sufficient to warrant making any arrests. The 19th of December was the date finally set for murdering the officers of state and plundering the city. Meanwhile news came that Catiline had assumed command of the insurgent forces at Faesulae. The senate promptly pronounced both him and Manlius public enemies, and sent the consul Antonius against them with an army.

The Third Oration. — A delegation from the Allobroges happened to be in Rome at this time, seeking relief from certain abuses. Having received no satisfaction from the senate, they readily listened to a proposal to interest their people in the conspiracy. Impressed with the seriousness of the matter, however, they laid it before their patron, Q. Fabius Sanga, who immediately reported the facts to Cicero.

The consul saw here a golden opportunity for obtaining the evidence he so much needed. Acting in accordance with his instructions, the deputies of the Allobroges professed the warmest interest in the conspiracy, and asked for written pledges to take to their people. These were freely given. They promised furthermore that on their way back to Gaul they would turn aside to confer with Catiline in Etruria; and Lentulus designated a certain T. Volturcius to accompany them, with a letter and messages for Catiline. Late in the night of December 2 the deputies, accompanied by Volturcius, set out from Rome. At the Mulvian bridge, two miles north of the city, they were stopped by two praetors and a company of soldiers sent to intercept them in accordance with a previous understanding with Cicero. After a show of resistance, they yielded up the documents which they had received from the conspirators, and returned to Rome.

Early in the morning of December 3, before news of the affair had spread, Cicero sent for Lentulus, Cethegus, Statilius, and Gabinius, and brought them before the senate, which met in the temple of Concord, in the Forum. Here Volturcius, having turned state's evidence, gave important testimony; the letters delivered to the deputies of the Allobroges, after the seals had been acknowledged by

A ROMAN BRIDGE OVER THE TIBER
This bridge was in use in Cicero's time.

the writers, were read, and the guilt of the conspirators was conclusively established. The meeting of the senate lasted till late in the day. At the close Cicero appeared before the people and delivered the **Third Oration,** which gave an account of the day's proceedings and, like the second, answered the purpose of an official bulletin of information.

The Fourth Oration; Catiline's End. — The day after the arrest of the conspirators, the report was spread abroad that an attempt would be made to rescue them by force; but stringent measures prevented any outbreak. The next day (December 5) the senate met to decide what should be done with the prisoners. Silanus, the consul-elect, declared himself in favor of putting them to death, and was supported in this by the other senators present till the question came to Julius Caesar. He proposed that the conspirators in custody be distributed under life-sentence among the municipal towns. As the senate now wavered in opinion, Cicero arose and delivered the **Fourth Oration,** in which, after reviewing the propositions of both Silanus and Caesar, he clearly revealed his own feeling in favor of the extreme penalty.

Cicero argued that if a man makes an attempt against his country, he thereby becomes a ' public enemy ' (*hostis*), and disqualifies himself for further protection under the laws guarding the rights of citizens, and so, as an enemy, may be properly tried and sentenced by the senate.

To us the argument here seems like begging the question. For, first of all, the question whether a man is a ' public enemy ' or not is one of fact, which can properly be determined only after due deliberation by a judicial body having jurisdiction in such matters; and at Rome there were two courts for two different kinds of crimes against the state, the *quaestiō perpetua* for cases of treason (*dē maiestāte*), and that for cases of violence or riot (*dē vī*). But even in cases of treason the precedents at least of the earlier time guarded sacredly the right of appeal to the people. Certainly according to the letter of the Roman constitution, the senate had not the jurisdiction to try and condemn the conspirators, at any rate without an opportunity to appeal from its decision.

Again, in the first oration Cicero had earnestly maintained the position that the supreme power vested in the consuls by the senate (*ultimum dēcrētum*) was sufficient to warrant putting a disturber of the peace to death at once, without the formality of a trial or appeal; but when the Catilinarian conspirators were actually in his power, he shifted the responsibility by referring their fate to the senate. As a matter of fact this right of the consul, when invested with the supreme power, had been conceded by the aristocracy, but never admitted by the popular party; only this year the aged Rabirius had been called to account for his part in the killing of Saturninus (see page 490).

But if there was no warrant on strictly constitutional grounds for the attitude of the consul or of the senate in this case, and for the execution of the conspirators without a formal trial, on other grounds there was justification most ample. Throughout the speeches the orator is constantly reminding his hearers of the peril which is threatening the state, the city of Rome, their own lives. Human society as an organism, as represented by states and communities, has a right to protect itself to maintain its own existence. At Rome the constitution had literally broken down; it had shown itself incapable of adjustment to the wide expansion of political boundaries and to the rapid development of new conditions in the last centuries of the republic. This plot of Catiline was anarchistic, contemplating not merely a redistribution of political emoluments, but the overthrow of existing institutions amid riot and bloodshed. Where the orator urges the public safety as ground for decisive action against the enemies of society, his argument must stand as long as society itself shall endure; it is just as applicable now as it was then. If it is ever justifiable for a governmental body to violate the letter of a constitution in obedience to the higher law of the self-preservation of society itself, the Roman senate was fully justified in taking cognizance of the case of the Catilinarian conspirators, and dealing with them summarily.

The decisive turn to the debate, however, was given by Marcus Cato, who spoke so earnestly in favor of the immediate execution of the prisoners that he carried the great majority of the senate with him. That evening Lentulus, Cethegus, Gabinius, Statilius, and Ceparius, who had been captured just outside the city, were strangled in the Tullianum, a loathsome subterranean dungeon on the slope of the Capitoline Hill, northwest of the Forum. Early in January (62) the forces of Catiline, comprising not far from 5,000 men, were annihilated near Pistoria (modern *Pistoja*), about twenty miles northwest of Florence, and he himself, while fighting with the courage of despair, was slain. (See Sallust, 60, page 150).

The Catilinarian orations were written out after their delivery, and no doubt carefully revised before publication. As might be expected from the nature of the theme and the occasion, their structure is less symmetrical than that of Cicero's more carefully prepared addresses. The following outlines may be of assistance in following the thought.

The First Oration against Catiline

IN L. CATILĪNAM: this title, though used of the four Catilinarian speeches, is, strictly speaking, applicable only to the first; see the outlines below. Cicero himself, in naming his ten 'consular' orations, characterizes those against Catiline as follows (*Ad Atticum*, **2**, 1, 3): *septima* (*ōrātiō*, the first Catilinarian), *quā Catilīnam ēmīsī ; octāva, quam habuī ad populum postrīdiē quam Catilīna profūgit ; nōna in cōntiōne, quō diē Allobrogēs indicārunt ; decima in senātū, Nōnīs Decembribus.*

HABITA: 'delivered'; an idiomatic use of *habēre*, like that of the German *halten* in *rede halten*.

This oration is intensely dramatic and thrilling, and no other speech of Cicero shows this element in such a marked degree. In this connection the student should remember that Cicero derived a share of his training from the actor Roscius, the orator's friend and teacher (Macrobius, *Sāturnālia*, **3,** 14, 12). It is quite likely, too, that in his boyhood days Cicero imbibed much from the dramatic style of the aged Accius (flourished 135 B.C.). Let the student therefore attempt to reconstruct the dramatic setting — the temple of Jupiter Stator being the theater, the *dramatis persōnae* being Cicero as chief actor, Catiline, for the most part silent though none the less actively present (see Selections from Sallust, page 134 and note 18), the state personified (page 55), and finally the god Jupiter himself, a sort of *deus ex māchinā* (see vocabulary), whose curse the orator invokes upon Catiline and the conspirators. No finer example of dynamic utterance can be found anywhere; the oration is replete with clash and dash, storm and struggle, and pulsates with a rhythm that is the very essence of drama. Let the student read it so.

Outline of the First Oration against Catiline

INTRODUCTION

Exōrdium. Abrupt outburst against Catiline's effrontery, and the degeneracy of the time. CHAPTER 1, lines 1–18.

Nārrātiō. Precedent and authority warrant putting Catiline to death. The danger is great, but he is foiled. 1, line 19 to end; 2.

DISCUSSION

A. *Addressed to Catiline*

Cōnfirmātiō. 1. Your plans are clearly revealed to us. 3, 4.

2. It is best for you to leave Rome and take your followers with you; for

a. Your plots against my life have failed. 5.

b. Here you are hated and feared on account of your crimes, as shown today in the senate. 6, 7.

c. No good man will be security for you. 8, to line 20.

d. The senate wants you to go. 8, line 21 to end.

e. You are altogether hopeless; the life of a freebooter will suit you. 9, 10.

B. *Addressed to the Senate*

1. Why do I not have Catiline put to death, as precedent and public interest demand? Because it is better for him to leave Rome and so lure forth his associates. 11, 12.

2. We are at a climax of wickedness; but I pledge the victory of the good. 13, to line 25.

CONCLUSION

Conclūsiō. Final exhortation to Catiline to depart. Prayer to Jupiter Stator for protection. 13, end.

The Second Oration against Catiline

IN L. CATILĪNAM: see note on page 520. In some of the oldest manuscripts the following argument of this oration is found: *Superiōre librō* (here = *ōrātiōne) Catilīna circumventus ēloquentiā Cicerōnis spontāneum ēlēgit exsilium, unde ōrātōrī maxima vēnisse vidēbātur invidia. Sed posterō diē timōre dissimulātō prōcessit ad populum fingēns sē timēre quod ēmīserit Catilīnam, ut minus sit invidiōsum, quod eum in exsilium expulerit. Prooemium sūmptum ab exsultātiōne dīcentis verbīs paene triumphantibus, quī sine damnō reī pūblicae superāre bellum potuerit.*

HABITA AD POPULUM: speeches addressed 'to the people' were delivered from the Rostra, an elevated speaker's platform, to the front of which were fastened the bronze beaks of the ships captured in the famous sea-fight off Antium, in 338 B.C.; hence the name. The original location of the Rostra was in the Comitium, at the edge of the Forum; see Plan opposite page 62. The speaker faced the people assembled in the Forum; directly behind them were the Old Shops (*Tabernae Veterēs*), low stores or booths along the southwestern side. If he glanced to the left he saw the Temple of Castor and Pollux and perhaps the round Temple of Vesta, behind which rose the northern slope of the Palatine Hill; if he turned toward the right, his eye fell on the Temple of Saturn, or the Temple of Concord, or, high above these, the southern part of the Capitoline Hill crowned with the splendid and imposing Temple of Jupiter Optimus Maximus.

From the old Rostra were delivered many of the greatest speeches of ancient Rome; among them that of Cicero for the Bill of Manilius (page 153), and the Second and Third against Catiline. Probably here Julius Caesar refused the crown offered him by Antony; here also his bleeding form was exposed to public gaze, and Antony's funeral address stirred the populace to fury. Here Cicero delivered several of the *Philippics;* and to the Rostra above the beaks his head and hands were nailed (Plutarch, *Cicero,* 49; see page 495). Julius Caesar planned to move the Rostra into the Forum, bringing thither the beaks and many statues from the old Rostra, but according to present evidence it is doubtful whether the project was carried out in his lifetime. The foundations of the later structure have been discovered. It was about seventy feet long and ten feet high. On the front apparently were thirty-nine beaks, arranged in two tiers. For a description of the remains, with restorations, see Platner's *Topography and Monuments of Ancient Rome*, pages 214–216, with references there cited.

Outline of the Second Oration

INTRODUCTION

Exōrdium. Congratulations on Catiline's departure. CHAPTER 1, lines 1–8. See Kelsey's *Cicero*.

Nārrātiō. He is conquered and undone. 1, line 9 to end.

Partītiō. It was better to drive him forth than to put him to death, on account of his associates. 2.

DISCUSSION

Cōnfirmātiō. 1. Catiline's associates, hopelessly depraved, should leave the city. 3, 4, 5.

2. Catiline himself, reprobate that he is, has not been driven into exile, but has joined Manlius. 6, 7.

3. Catiline's forces are recruited from six classes, each of which needs a special warning :

   a. Rich but extravagant men, in financial embarrassment. 8.

   b. Bankrupts, desirous of power. 9, to line 18.

   c. Veterans of Sulla, who long for a renewal of the seasons of violence. 9, line 19 to end.

   d. Hopeless but restless debtors. 10, to line 14.

   e. Professional criminals. 10, lines 15–18.

   f. Profligates. 10, line 19 to end.

4. Such forces bear no comparison with ours. 11.

CONCLUSION

Conclūsiō. The orator reminds the citizens of their duty, and assures them of safety, warns the conspirators. 12; promises a complete but bloodless victory, with the help of the gods. 13.

The Third Oration against Catiline

This speech stands in direct contrast to the *First Oration against Catiline* (note, page 520). Whereas the latter is highly dramatic, full of impassioned oratory, this oration is more quiet, though delivered in a tone of lofty solemnity. It is couched in a narrative style, characterized by full, well-rounded periods, well suited to the moral and religious reflection with which it abounds. The tension has been relaxed, the conspirators have been caught, Jupiter has saved the city.

The question of Cicero's religious sincerity need not especially concern us; for, while the orator as a thinker could not and did not accept the current opinions and popular superstitions regarding the gods and omens, he was nevertheless a devout believer in a divine power operative in the universe and guiding the affairs of men and nations. Then, too, the philosophical nomenclature of Cicero's gods was unintelligible to the people whom he was now addressing, and consequently he wisely employed the religious terms of popular faith to direct and stabilize popular emotion. In such a momentous crisis he could ill afford to engage in hair-splitting theological discussions such as he fostered in the *Dē Nātūrā Deōrum*, but common sense suggested simple, understandable terms.

Outline of the Third Oration

INTRODUCTION

Exōrdium et Nārrātiō. The state, your lives, this city have narrowly escaped destruction. CHAPTER 1, lines 1–19.

Partītiō. I shall explain how the conspiracy has been traced out and checked. 1, line 20 to end of paragraph.

DISCUSSION

Cōnfirmātiō. 1. My efforts to secure evidence for conviction were crowned with success through the interception of the deputies of the Allobroges and the arrest of leading conspirators. 1, end; 2, 3.

2. This evidence was today presented to the senate : —

a. The testimony of Volturcius, and of the Gauls. 4.

b. Reading of the letters, — their seals acknowledged by the prisoners. 5.

c. Action of the senate after hearing the evidence; rewards to officers, decrees against nine conspirators, appointment of special thanksgiving. 6.

3. The conspiracy is now checked once for all. 7.

4. This result has been achieved through the immediate help of the gods.

5. The present disturbance differs from all preceding disturbances in this state in its deadly character, and in the fact that it has been put down without bloodshed. 10.

SILVER COIN OF EGYPT

Obverse : Head of Ptolemy, King of Egypt.   Reverse : Eagle on thunderbolt.

CONCLUSION

Conclūsiō. For my services I ask only the undying recollection of this day, and your protection, present and future. Guard your homes; I will guard the city. 11, 12.

The Fourth Oration against Catiline

IN L. CATILINAM: see note on page 520.

HABITA IN SENATU: December 5, 63 B. C., the senate being assembled in the Temple of Concord; see Plan facing page 62.

Outline of the Fourth Oration

INTRODUCTION

Exōrdium. My own safety; its relation to the safety of all. CHAPTER I; 2 to line 31.   See Kelsey's *Cicero.*

Nārrātiō. The present state of conspiracy. 2, end; 3 to line 26.

Partītiō. The question of penalty before the senate. 3, line 1 to end.

DISCUSSION

Cōnfīrmātiō. 1. The two proposals regarding punishment, the one of Silanus, that the conspirators be put to death ; the other of Caesar, that they be guarded under life-sentence in the municipalities. 4.

2. The character of Caesar's proposal. 5 to line 20.

Refūtātiō. 3. Caesar's objections to the proposal of Silanus met : —

a. The conspirators should be treated as enemies, not as citizens. 5, end.

b. Apparent cruelty may in reality be kindness and mercy. 6.

4. Well-considered and decisive action demanded,

a. On account of the patriotic feeling of all classes. 7, 8.

b. On account of the magnitude and sacredness of the interests at stake. 9.

5. Digression on the orator's peril, and services. 10, 11, first part.

Conclusion

Conclūsiō. Vote as the importance of the case demands; at no matter how great cost to myself, I will carry out your decision. 11, last paragraph.

Chronology of the Speeches against Catiline

A.U.C. 691 = 63 B.C.

Assembly for the election of consuls for 62	September?	September?
Cicero lays information about the conspiracy before the senate, which confers extraordinary authority on the consuls	a. d. xii. Kal. Nov. =	October 21.
Manlius takes up arms at Faesulae	a. d. vi. Kal. Nov. =	October 27.
Day set by Catiline for the massacre of the nobles . .	a. d. v. Kal. Nov. =	October 28.
Unsuccessful attempt on Praeneste		Kal. Nov. = November 1.
Meeting of the conspirators at Laeca's, night of	a. d. viii. Id. Nov. =	November 6.
Miscarrying of the plan to murder Cicero, morning of .	a. d. vii. Id. Nov. =	November 7.
First Oration, before the senate	a. d. vi. Id. Nov. =	November 8.
The following night Catiline left Rome.		

Second Oration, to the people .	a. d. v. Id. Nov. = November 9.
Antonius sent north with an army	about the middle of November.
Interception of the deputies of the Allobroges, night of . .	a. d. iv. Non. Dec. = December 2.
Arrest of conspirators; laying of evidence before the senate;	

A DENARIUS OF THE ITALIAN CONFEDERACY
Obverse: Head of Italia. Reverse: Warrior with spear and helmet.

Third Oration, to the people.	a. d. iii. Non. Dec. = December 3.
Rumors of a proposed attempt to rescue the conspirators .	pr. Non. Dec. = December 4.
Trial of the conspirators before the senate; **Fourth Oration**	Non. Dec. = December 5.
The following night the five conspirators in custody were executed.	
Catiline falls in battle, beginning of	A.U.C. 692 = 62 B.C.

SALLUST'S VERSION OF THE CATILINARIAN CONSPIRACY

Sallust's Life. — GAÏUS SALLUSTIUS CRISPUS was born in 86 B.C. at Amiternum, a town in the Sabine Hills. He sprang from a plebeian family, and passed his early youth in a period of stress and strife, when Rome was involved in constant difficulties both at home and abroad. This succession of striking events undoubtedly made a deep impression on the youthful mind, which experienced the disorders leading up to the death of Marius, the tyranny of Sulla, the Servile War, and the

Catilinarian conspiracy all before he was scarcely twenty-three years old.

At the age of twenty-seven he became quaestor, and in 52 B.C. he was made *tribūnus plebis*. His expulsion from the senate two years later is generally attributed to profligacy, but, in some measure at least, may have been due to politics. Since Sallust was a partisan of Caesar, and Pompey's supporters had brought about the removal of several friends of Caesar from the senate, we may conclude that politics played some part in Sallust's ejection.

During the Civil War he fought on Caesar's side with some show of military capacity, so that after the battle of Thapsus (46 B.C.) the governorship of Africa was bestowed upon him. His administration seems to have been a typical one, for he returned to Rome a rich man and was immediately assailed by charges of bribery and extortion. These, however, were never proved.

Sallust then retired to private life, and devoted himself to the composition of historical monographs. He himself tells us that already in early life the field of history had engaged his attention. How he managed to avoid the troublesome times after Caesar's assassination is a mystery. There is a story in Jerome that Sallust married Terentia, whom Cicero divorced in 46 B.C. Since Terentia is said to have reached the age of one hundred and three, she might well have had another husband; but the authority of Jerome can hardly be accepted as final without corroborative evidence. Sallust died at the age of fifty-two, and has the distinction of being called the first Roman historian.

His Works. — The extant works of Sallust are the *Catilīna*, a history of Catiline's conspiracy (see page 121), and the *Iugurtha*, a history of the war with Jugurtha. Portions of his *Historiārum Librī Quīnque*, five books of Roman History, have been transmitted to us from the quotations of other authors.

The *Catilīna* is by far his best known work. This monograph, apart from its literary interest, is valuable because it gives the impression of an eye-witness who was well acquainted with most of the principals involved in the conspiracy. He had access to the public records and resolutions of the senate, and must have known Cicero, whose orations may also have supplied him with material. The *Catilīna* seems to have been published soon after Caesar's death.

Notwithstanding Sallust's intimate connection with Caesar the

Catilīna is surprisingly impartial, there being evidence neither of opposition to Cicero — whom he even calls *optimus cōnsul* — nor of partisanship for Caesar.

His Style. — As a writer Sallust is vigorous and original. His sentences are characterized by epigrammatic brevity and antithesis. By the frequent use of archaic and colloquial words, of chiasmus, of anaphora, of asyndeton, and of other devices he avoids monotony in spite of his unusual conciseness. He is especially fond of the historical infinitive, which he employs most effectively. His terse phraseology stands in marked contrast to Cicero's sonorous periods with their smooth musical flow. The difference may be nicely expressed by employing two terms in music, *legato* to describe Cicero's usual style, and *staccato* to suggest that of Sallust.

Speeches in Works of Roman Historians. —

Speeches play a most important rôle in ancient history, and particularly so in Livy and Sallust, who were the first Roman historians to use them extensively. Such speeches help to enliven the narrative and to dramatize situations and personalities; the ancient Roman preferred to present the facts of history concretely. Sallust gives these speeches in his own words, but it is not at all unlikely that shorthand notes (see page 134) and other sources were consulted to make the tenor of the several addresses agree substantially with the arguments of each speaker. Although the phraseology is that of the author, the sentiments conform quite closely to the speaker in question.

THE SPEECH ON POMPEY'S COMMISSION

IMPERIŌ : here referring to a military command of a special character (see page 532) = 'Commission.' In the best manuscripts the title is given as *Dē Imperiō Cn. Pompeī;* in some others, as *Prō Lēge Mānīliā.*

Occasion and Circumstances of Delivery. — One of Rome's most troublesome enemies was Mithridates VI, king of Pontus in Asia Minor, who came to the throne about 120 B.C. At this time the Romans were developing extensive interests in the East, which Mithridates viewed with jealous eye and genuine hatred. And so a collision between these two aggressive powers was inevitable; but the first provocation came from the Romans. It resulted in the first Mithridatic War which lasted from 88 to 84 B.C. The jealous, cruel, and implacable nature of this typical Oriental despot was shown by his decree that on a given day all the Italians in the cities of Asia Minor, without distinction of rank, sex, or age, should be put to death;

COIN OF BITHYNIA

Obverse: Head of Prusias II.   Reverse: Zeus with scepter and thunderbolt.

in one day 80,000 Italians, some say 150,000, perished.   But in the rest of this war Mithridates was less fortunate, for he was decisively defeated by Sulla with the result that the king was forced to pay a huge indemnity.

In the second Mithridatic War (83–81 B.C.) Murena, Sulla's successor, was soon defeated by Mithridates. The results were unimportant.

Early in 74 B.C. Mithridates commenced another war, and prosecuted it vigorously. At first the king was successful, but at length

COIN OF SMYRNA

Obverse: Head of Mithridates Eupator.   Reverse: Nike with wreath and palm.

Lucius Licinius Lucullus, the Roman commander, advanced into Pontus, and forced Mithridates to retreat. A panic ensued; the Romans took advantage of the situation and cut his army to pieces.

The king himself would have fallen into their hands had his pursuers not stopped to plunder a mule laden with gold. Mithridates fled to Armenia, where his son-in-law, Tigranes, received him into his protection. He eventually made common cause with the deposed monarch. The kings both raised armies; but in 69 B.C., before their forces had united, Tigranes engaged in battle with Lucullus at Tigranocerta, and suffered a disastrous defeat. Mutiny among the Roman troops made it possible for Mithridates to return to Pontus and deal the Romans a crushing defeat, so that at the end of the year 67 B.C. the king was once more in power over Pontus and the adjoining regions; he was also in alliance with Tigranes, and liable at any moment to make a descent on the province of Asia.

A ROMAN GRAIN SHIP

From a recent excavation at Ostia.

But the war with Mithridates and Tigranes was not the only cause of disturbance in Roman foreign relations at this time. For some years pirates had gradually become more and more numerous and powerful in all parts of the Mediterranean. They rendered navigation perilous. They cut off the supplies of grain which Rome was wont to receive by sea. They made raids upon cities along the coast, and even carried men of distinction away from Italy to be held for ransom.

In the words of Mommsen (Volume IV, page 99): " Almost under the eyes of the fleet of Lucullus, the pirate Athenodorus surprised in 685 (= 69 B.C.) the island of Delos, destroyed its far-famed shrines and temples, and carried off the whole population into slavery. The island Lipara, near Sicily, paid to the pirates a fixed tribute annually to remain exempt from like attacks. Another pirate chief, Heracleon, destroyed in 682 (72 B.C.) the squadron equipped in Sicily against him, and ventured with no more than four open boats to sail into the open harbor of Syracuse. . . . But even the sacred soil of Italy was no longer respected by the shameless transgressors: from Croton they carried off with them the temple treasures of the Lacinian Hera; they landed in Brundisium, Misenum, and Caieta, in the Etruscan ports, and even in Ostia itself; they seized the most eminent Roman officers as captives, among others the admiral of the Cilician army, and two praetors with their whole retinue, with the dreaded *fascēs* themselves and all the insignia of their dignity; . . . they destroyed in the port of Ostia the Roman war fleet equipped against them and commanded by a consul. The Latin husbandman, the traveler on the Appian highway, the genteel visitor at the terrestrial paradise of Baiae, were no longer secure of their property or their life for a single moment; all traffic and all intercourse were suspended; the most dreadful scarcity prevailed in Italy, and especially in the capital, which subsisted on transmarine grain."

The evil had grown to such intolerable proportions that in 67 B.C. A. Gabinius proposed a bill giving Pompey absolute jurisdiction for three years over all the Mediterranean coast for fifty miles inland. The bill was passed, though contrary to precedent both in the powers it conferred and in the manner of conferring them; for the people in passing the measure assumed a function supposed to belong to the senate. But Pompey more than sustained the reputation he already enjoyed as a commander. In three months he cleared the sea of pirates from the Pillars of Hercules to the Hellespont. While Mithridates was making fruitless the victories of Lucullus, Pompey was capturing the strongholds of the pirates in Cilicia, which was immediately organized into a Roman province.

Under these circumstances, early in 66 B.C., Manilius proposed to the people that the government of Bithynia, which had been given to the incompetent Glabrio, as well as of Cilicia and Asia, and the absolute command of the war with Mithridates, be intrusted to Pompey. The bill was opposed by the leaders of the aristocratic party, particularly Catulus and Hortensius, on constitutional grounds. Cicero's speech was addressed to the people, and served to intensify the popular feeling in favor of Pompey. It is not difficult to see what motives probably influenced him in thus breaking with the party whose principles he favored. The aristocrats were indeed glad to have Cicero on their side; but in the interest of patrician traditions they would never countenance the election of a ' new man ' to the consulship, which was the goal of the orator's ambition. It appeared necessary for him to win the favor of the people; in what way could he do this better than by praising the people's hero? He might at the same time also assure himself of that hero's favor.

The speech for the bill of Manilius, or ' On Pompey's Commission,' as it is more commonly called, shows rather the adroitness of the special pleader than the depth of a true statesman. It belongs to the *deliberative* class, though the part referring to Pompey is properly *demonstrative*. From whatever point it is viewed, it is a masterly effort. The orderly and effective arrangement of the matter is matched by the rich, yet forceful and pleasing, manner of expression.

Whether the objections to Manilius' proposal were valid or not, it was carried. By the end of 66 Pompey had forced Mithridates to

A VIEW ACROSS THE BOSPORUS

take refuge in Dioscurias, a Greek city on the northeast side of the Euxine Sea, and had made terms with Tigranes. The king of Pontus raised another army; but becoming involved in disaffection and treachery, he put an end to his own life in the year 63. Part of his kingdom was annexed to the province of Bithynia; the rest, left for over a century under native princes, in 63 A.D. became a Roman province under the name of Pontus Polemoniacus.

Outline of the Speech on Pompey's Commission

INTRODUCTION

Exōrdium. Reasons for not having come forward previously as a public speaker. Your favor, my practice in speaking, and the happy nature of the theme, the singular merit of Gnaeus Pompey, make it a duty and a pleasure to speak on this occasion. CHAPTER I.

Nārrātiō. A war, destructive to our revenues, fraught with danger to our allies, is being waged against us by two very powerful kings. The voice of all demands the appointment of a certain commander. 2, first paragraph.

Partītiō. What ought to be done? Three points are to be considered: the character of the war, the greatness of the war, and the choice of a commander. 2, second paragraph.

DISCUSSION

Cōnfīrmātiō. A. The character of the war. 2, last paragraph. The war is of a kind that involves: —

1. The reputation of the Roman people, who have suffered at the hands of Mithridates more flagrant causes of grievance than those for which our ancestors inflicted summary vengeance. 3, 4, 5, first paragraph.

2. The safety of our allies, who are threatened by the enemy, and are pleading for the appointment of Pompey. 5, last part.

3. Our most important revenues, which are imperiled, not simply by war, but by the mere rumor of war. 6.

4. The property of many Roman citizens engaged in business in Asia, whom expediency and humanity alike require us to protect. 7.

B. The greatness of the war: so urgent as to demand active measures, yet not so formidable that there need be apprehension regarding the final issue. 8, first paragraph.

1. The efforts of Lucullus against the enemy were at first successful. 8, second paragraph.

2. But reverses followed, and the war is now more urgent than ever. 9.

C. The choice of a commander.

A. Affirmative argument: Pompey the best man.

1. He possesses all the requisite qualifications, namely: —

a. Mastery of the art of war. 10.

b. Traits characteristic of a great general and of a great man: —

On the one hand, power of persistent effort, bravery, activity, rapidity of movement, forethought. 11, 12.

On the other, incorruptibility, self-restraint, good-faith, courtesy, talent, humaneness. 13, 14.

  c. Standing, witnessed by the general demand for his services, the influence of his name, the confidence reposed in him by our enemies. 15, 16, first paragraph.

  d. Good luck. 16, latter part.

  2. He is more favorably situated than anyone else for prosecuting the war. 17, first paragraph.

Refūtātiō. B. Refutation. Objections to the choice of Pompey considered.

  1. Answer to particular objections:

  a. To that of Hortensius, that absolute authority ought not to be vested in one person; met by reference to the success of the war against the pirates. Brief answer also to an objection raised against the lieutenancy of Gabinius. 17, last part; 18, 19.

  b. To those of Catulus, based upon the risk of placing all hope in one person, and upon respect for precedent; shown to be without just grounds, by the citation of examples from the cases of others and of Pompey himself. 20, 21.

  2. Answer to the objections in general:

  a. The influence of opponents of high standing ought not to outweigh the true interests of the Roman people. 22, first paragraph.

  b. This war demands a peculiar combination of military power and irreproachable character, such as only Pompey possesses. 22, last part; 23, first part.

  c. The standing of the opponents of this measure is offset by that of the eminent men who favor it. 23, last paragraph.

Conclusion

Perōrātiō. The orator urges Manilius to stand firm, relying upon the support of the people; calls the gods to witness to the purity of his motives in advocating the measure; assures the people of his loyalty to the interests of the state and to their own wishes. 24.

The Looting of Syracuse

The Site of the City. — The city of Syracuse was situated on the east side of the island of Sicily. It was founded by a colony of Greeks from Corinth in 734 B.C. The colonists, led by Archias, established themselves on a small island, which was named Ortygia, or 'Quail' island; it was, however, often called simply 'The Island,' and it is referred to by Cicero as Insula (see Map below).

The development of commerce was favored by the position of the island between two harbors, one on the west, called the Great Harbor, and the other, the Small Harbor, on the north.

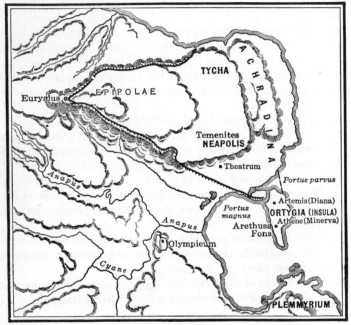

MAP OF ANCIENT SYRACUSE

In course of time the city was extended to the mainland, and at first spread over the east end of a low triangular plateau of limestone. The short side of the triangle ran along the sea north of the Small Harbor, where the quarter of Achradina was built up; the other two sides met at a point west, where on the Map (see above) a fortress called Euryalus is shown. Fort Euryalus, and the strong walls indicated on the Map as leading southeast and northeast from it, were built by the tyrant Dionysius, in the earlier part of the fourth century B.C.

The Importance of Syracuse. -- The rising power of Syracuse aroused antagonisms and led to a succession of wars which threatened its very existence. The most famous of these was the war with Athens, which in 415 B.C. sent a great fleet to conquer Syracuse first, then the rest of Sicily. The Athenian forces besieged the city, and for a time made progress; but finally, in 413 B.C., the Syracusans gained a complete victory. Some 7,000 Athenian prisoners were shut up in a huge quarry which had been excavated for building-stone; and after eight months those that had not perished from exposure and disease were sold as slaves, only a few escaping. (Illustration, page 538.)

In Cicero's time Syracuse was much larger than Athens. It was considered, as he himself says, the largest Greek city in the world. In respect to size, however, ancient cities were relatively small compared with those of our day, and the number of inhabitants within the limits of ancient Syracuse probably at no time exceeded 500,000.

In Cicero's opinion, each of the four main parts of Syracuse might well have been considered a separate city: the Island, Ortygia; Achradina, ' Wild Pear ' quarter, the east part of the limestone hill, which was the first part to be settled after the island; and west of Achradina, Tycha, quarter of ' Fortune,' and Neapolis, ' Newtown.' The west corner of the triangle on the hill, known as Epipolae, ' Flat Height,' is not mentioned by Cicero. The circuit of the portion of the city on the mainland was about twelve English miles.

The Treasures of the City. — On the island were the venerable temples of Athene, mentioned by Cicero under the Latin name Minerva, and of Artemis, or Diana. Here, too, close to the sea, was the fountain of Arethusa (illustration, page 198), about which the Syracusans told a wonderful story.

Arethusa, they said, was a nymph dwelling in Elis in the western part of Greece. The god of the river Alpheus fell in love with her, and pursued her. As her strength failed in flight, she prayed to Artemis for help. The goddess changed her into a spring, and conducted the waters under the sea to Ortygia, where they came up again to the light. But the waters of Alpheus, mingling, flowed with them; and should you throw a cup or other object into the Alpheus in Elis, it would come up in the spring of Arethusa.

There were temples and other important public buildings on the mainland, such as the city hall and a great open-air theater.

As a center of commerce and of political administration, Syracuse, like other Greek cities, became a repository of works of art. A considerable list of masterpieces of sculpture and painting, which were carried off by Verres, is given by Cicero. It would be interesting if these could be positively identified in copies of famous ancient works of art existing today; but such identification is in most cases too doubtful to warrant discussion here. For example, the head of Sappho in Rome (illustration, page 209) has been accepted by many as surely representing the poetess; but some now believe that it may represent a goddess instead. Even the tomb which is pointed out

PARADISE QUARRY AT SYRACUSE

today as that of Archimedes (illustration, page 213) belongs to a later period; and it does not correspond with the description of the real tomb, which was visited by Cicero and identified by him because it had on it a representation of a sphere inscribed in a cylinder. For Archimedes considered that the determining of the mathematical relation of a sphere to a circumscribing cylinder was his most noteworthy achievement.

At the present time, there are few ruins to be seen on the Island; the remains are under modern buildings. But on the mainland there are massive walls and remnants of once imposing structures which bear witness to ancient grandeur. Nothing, however, gives a more vivid impression of the greatness of ancient Syracuse than the vast quarries in the limestone rock which in places are more than 100 feet deep, and today remain much as they were in the time of Cicero (illustrations, pages 199, 538).

SYRACUSE UNDER THE ROMANS

Its History. — At the close of the first Punic War, in 241 B.C., Carthage was obliged to yield to Rome the western part of Sicily, which became the first Roman province. Nevertheless Hiero II, ruler of Syracuse, who had been in alliance with the Romans, was

VIEW ACROSS THE HARBOR AT CARTHAGE

permitted to retain his authority not only over Syracuse but over other Greek cities in southeastern Sicily. Hiero died in 216 B.C., and two years later the Syracusans, becoming favorable to Carthaginian interests, revolted against Rome.

The result was disastrous for Syracuse. Marcus Claudius Marcellus (illustration, page 195), now consul for the third time, laid siege to the city, which was heroically defended by the inhabitants. Though the defense was greatly aided by the ingenuity of Archimedes, who devised appliances that made useless the siege engines of the Romans, in 212 B.C. Syracuse fell into his hands. Notwithstanding the laudatory statements of Cicero (page 196, chapter 52, and elsewhere), in regard to his beneficent treatment of the inhabitants and his safe-guarding of the city's art treasures, there is evidence to indicate that Marcellus gave Syracuse over to plunder and that he carried off so many works of art that he was subjected to censure at Rome : Cicero is speaking as an advocate.

In 210 B.C. Syracuse with the adjacent territory was added to the Province of Sicily, which had been organized thirty-one years before. The administration of the whole island was now vested in a governor sent from Rome. This official at first had the rank of praetor; after 122 B.C. the governor was a propraetor, who had completed his year as praetor in Rome.

THE TRIAL OF ROMAN GOVERNORS FOR EXTORTION

The Governors' Powers. — Roman provincial governors had large powers, and the temptation was great to abuse their power for personal ends. The evils of the system of provincial administration were early recognized by the Romans, who tried to check abuses by making the misconduct of a governor subject to judicial inquiry after the expiration of his term of office; and aggrieved provincials were in a position to present charges of extortion through an advocate who had espoused their cause, and to bring suit against an ex-governor for the recovery of property unjustly taken.

In trials of provincial ex-governors for extortion before 123 B.C. the jurors (*iūdicēs*) were members of the senate. But the interests of the senators as a class were so interwoven with the fortunes of provincial governors that the miscarriage of justice in such cases became a scandal. In consequence, in 123 B.C. a law was passed which limited the choice of such jurors to the equestrian order (*equitēs*). But this arrangement also worked badly, because the knights had pecuniary interests in the operations of provincial tax-collectors. So in 81 B.C. the choice of jurors was again limited to members of the senate; and senators formed the jury in the trial of Verres, in 70 B.C.

References in the speeches of Cicero warrant the inference that at this trial the number of jurors was at least twelve, but probably not much above that number; for the number of jurors was not so closely limited as with us. The 'Court for Cases of Extortion' (*Quaestiō Repetundārum*) in the trial of Verres was presided over by the city praetor, Manius Acilius Glabrio.

THE CASE OF VERRES

Verres' Propraetorship. — Our knowledge of Gaius Verres is derived from Cicero's speeches. Since Cicero was prosecuting Verres for criminal acts while governor of Sicily, and Roman court practice permitted wide indulgence in personalities, the orator's statements must be taken with considerable allowance. Yet Cicero was too astute a lawyer not to understand that a case is always weakened by a misstatement of known facts; and it is safe to believe that Verres was an outstanding representative of the worst type of Roman provincial governor — that is, of the worst type of unscrupulous and rapacious public official of all ages.

The public career of Verres commenced in 80 B.C., when he went out to Asia Minor as quaestor on the staff of Gnaeus Cornelius Dolabella, who was governor of Cilicia. Dolabella and Verres together plundered the province, and on their return to Rome, two years later, both officials were charged with extortion. Verres turned state's evidence and so got off scot-free, while Dolabella, as a result of his testimony, was convicted.

In 74 B.C. by resorting to wholesale bribery Verres secured election as praetor. This opened the way for him to go to Sicily as propraetor in the following year. Here his unbridled greed and rapacity in three years impoverished the island.

His Trial. — On his return to Rome, in 70 B.C., Verres was charged with extortion, and at the request of the Sicilians Cicero undertook the prosecution. Verres and his attorney, Hortensius, who at the time was the most eminent lawyer of Rome, resorted to every possible expedient to prevent the case from coming to trial. However, Cicero proceeded to Sicily and in fifty days accumulated an overwhelming mass of evidence with which he returned to Rome, and forced the prosecution.

Cicero's handling of the case may be briefly outlined under three heads.

1. First, Cicero delivered a preliminary speech (*Dīvīnātiō in Q. Caecilium*) in which he successfully combated the claim of Caecilius to conduct the prosecution of Verres; for Caecilius, who was a Sicilian by birth but secretly a tool of Verres, had come forward with the bold claim that he alone was the proper person to represent the Sicilians.

2. The trial proper was opened with the 'First Argument against

Verres' (*In C. Verrem Āctiō Prīma*), fully supported by evidence.
For the opening of such a case nine days were allowed by law to the
prosecution.   The First Argument, however, was crushing, and Hortensius made no reply.   Before the nine days were over, on the advice
of Hortensius, Verres had left Rome to go into exile at Marseilles.

3. Although Verres had gone, Cicero thought it best to complete
the presentation of his case. He therefore committed to writing his
'Second Argument against Verres' (*In C. Verrem Āctiō Secunda*),

ANCIENT THEATER IN SYRACUSE

which, on account of the amount and variety of the matter, he divided
into five books.

In the first book Cicero discusses the misconduct of Verres before
he went to Sicily, particularly when he was city praetor.

In Books II–V the misconduct of Verres in Sicily is examined.   The
second book is general, dealing with maladministration.   The third
book presents the iniquities of which Verres was guilty in connection
with the forced collection of grain.   The fourth book, from which the
present selection is taken, deals with the thefts of statues and other
works of art, while the fifth book rehearses the unlawful punishments
and other measures with which Verres terrorized the inhabitants.

The Second Argument reads throughout as if it had actually been
delivered before the court and in the presence of Verres.   The vividness of presentation is no doubt due to Cicero's habit of dictation,
which made it easy for him to imagine himself as actually in court.

THE ORATION FOR ARCHIAS

A. LICINIŌ ARCHIĀ (ā′lŭs lĭ-sin′ĭ-ŭs är′kĭ-ạs) : the name *Archias* (Ἀρχίας)
was not an uncommon one, particularly among the Dorian Greeks. The
Latin *nōmen* and *praenōmen* were assumed when the poet became a Roman
citizen, *Licinius* being the gens name of his chief patrons, the Lucul′lī; but
why he chose the forename *Aulus* instead of one of those common in the
family of the Luculli is not clear.

Occasion and Circumstances of Delivery. — The poet Archias was a
Greek by nationality, born at Antioch, then the chief city of Syria,
about 119 B.C. He received what was considered a liberal education,
and early developed a remarkable facility in poetic composition. He

COIN OF SYRIA

Obverse : Head of Antiochus III (the Great), King of Syria.
Reverse : Apollo seated on the Omphalos.

was especially gifted as an improviser, being able to compose and
recite verses offhand with great skill. As the unsettled state of
affairs in his native city gave little encouragement to the arts, while
yet a youth he started out to visit the Greek towns in Asia Minor
and Greece. Everywhere his talents received enthusiastic recognition. After a time he crossed over to Southern Italy, where public
honors were conferred upon him by the citizens of Tarentum, Regium,
Neapolis, and perhaps Locri.

In 102 B.C. Archias came to Rome. Here he was soon on terms of
intimacy with many prominent men ; for the educated Romans of this
period as a rule cultivated a taste for Greek literature. But his chief
patrons were the Luculli.[1] After he had been at Rome for some time
he accompanied M. Lucullus on a journey to Sicily ; on the way back

[1] See vocabulary.

he was honored with the citizenship of Heraclea. See illustration, page 229.

In 89 B.C. a law (*Lēx Plautia Papīria*) was passed which conferred Roman citizenship on the citizens of such Italian towns as possessed formal treaty relations with Rome. In order to become Roman citizens under this act, the inhabitants of the favored cities must be able to fulfill two conditions : they must possess a settled place of residence in Italy, and within sixty days must give their names to one of the Roman praetors holding office at the time. Archias complied with these conditions, and for twenty-seven years his standing as a Roman citizen was unquestioned.

At this time a common way of annoying public men was to attack their friends. Lucius Lucullus, who had taken Archias with him on his Asiatic campaigns, was still a man of influence, but had bitter enemies. It was apparently rather to vex him than to disturb Archias that in 62 B.C. a man named Gratius attempted to invalidate the poet's claim of Roman citizenship. Cicero undertook the defense of the case partly no doubt to accommodate Lucullus, partly to discharge an obligation he felt under to Archias. At the trial Quintus Cicero, the orator's brother, presided, being praetor.

The case for the prosecution was extremely weak. It rested mainly on the assumption that the poet's citizenship of Heraclea could not be established, because the records of that city had perished; and on the fact that his name did not appear on the lists of the Roman census, where it would naturally be registered. But the orator brought forward witnesses whose testimony took the place of the missing records of Heraclea, and easily explained the omission of the poet's name from the census lists. The argument for the defense was irrefutable.

The Speech. — As a piece of legal argument, the speech for Archias is less to the point than would be tolerated in a plea before a modern court. Very likely when Cicero wrote it out for publication he cut down the technical portion, dealing with the facts, eliminating such details as would detract from the interest of the reader, but did not reduce the more attractive matter of the latter part, concerning the relation of literary pursuits to the public welfare, and the services of Archias in extending the glory of Rome. A Roman court allowed the presentation of a wider range of matter in sustaining a point than would now be considered in place; and certainly the orator strengthened his case by showing that the interests of his client were in a measure the interests of the state, whose duty it should always be to favor those who promote literature. The singular charm of this oration lies in its expression of universal sentiment regarding literature, particularly poetry, in a well-nigh faultless style, which at times approaches the manner of the essay.

Outline of the Oration for Archias

INTRODUCTION

Exōrdium. Obligation of the orator to undertake the defense of Archias. The character of the case, requiring treatment out of the ordinary. CHAPTER 1; 2, first part.

Partītiō. It will be proved that Archias is a Roman citizen; that if he were not, he ought to be. 2, end.

Nārrātiō. Birth, fame, travels of Archias; his reception at Rome; his enrollment as a citizen at Heraclea, then at Rome. 3, 4, first part.

DISCUSSION

A. *Proof that Archias is a Roman citizen*

Cōnfirmātiō. 1. Proof of enrollment as a citizen at Heraclea by witnesses. 4, middle.

COIN OF SMYRNA, ONE OF THE CITIES CLAIMING TO BE THE
BIRTHPLACE OF HOMER

Obverse: Head of Apollo. Reverse: Homer.

2. Proof of residence and registration at Rome by the concentration of his interests there, by the presence of his name on a praetor's register, and by the recognition of his standing as a citizen in various transactions. 4, end; 5.

B. *Proof that Archias ought in any case to be a Roman citizen*

1. The promotion of literature a matter of general interest : —
a. Indebtedness of the orator to literature for both ideals and inspiration. 6.
Refūtātiō. b. Refutation of the objection that there have been great men who were not versed in letters. 7, first part.
c. Universal appreciation of literature. 7, latter part; 8, first part.
2. The special claims of Archias as a poet : —
a. Veneration due to poetic genius. 8, latter part.
b. His treatment of national themes. 9, first part.
c. Precedents from the cases of Ennius and Theophanes. 9, end; 10.
d. Fame an incentive and reward of deeds; future services of Archias in magnifying the Roman name. 11, 12; first part.

CONCLUSION

Conclūsiō. a. Summary of evidence. 12, middle.
b. Appeal for a sympathetic consideration of the case. 12, latter part.

THE ESSAY ON OLD AGE

The CATŌ MAIOR DĒ SENECTŪTE and the LAELIUS DĒ AMĪCITIĀ (page 293), two charming colloquies on *Old Age* and *Friendship*, both dedicated to Cicero's friend Atticus, are popular essays in ethics cast in the form of a dialogue, the usual rhetorical device in antiquity for the presentation of abstruse subjects. In the *Catō Maior*, composed in the spring of 44 B.C., the conversation is supposed to take place between Cato, Scipio Africanus the Younger, and Laelius, in the year before Cato's death, *i.e.* 150 B.C., when he was in his eighty-fourth year, Scipio being about thirty-five and Laelius a few years older. M. Porcius Cato, known as Cato the Elder or Cato the Censor, was an eminent general, statesman, orator, and writer in the Archaic Period (240 B.C.–81 B.C.); he was a great nationalist, and in Cicero's time and later was considered the ideal of Roman character. See vocabulary for other personages.

Purpose. — The *Catō Maior* seeks to apply the principles of philosophy to the alleviation of one of life's chief burdens, old age and death. In ancient times philosophy represented the real and only religion of the educated class, and such essays as this formed the only substitute the ancients had for our sermons.

Then, too, the treatise afforded comfort and consolation to Cicero himself; first, because he was keenly disappointed at the downfall of the old constitution, and secondly, because his daughter's death had inflicted a deep wound which was still unhealed.

Furthermore, there was, as in many of Cicero's works, a distinct political purpose in the composition of the *Cato Maior*, for Cicero desired to stimulate in his readers an admiration for what he regarded as the golden age of Roman politics, the era of the Punic Wars, and to contrast this period with that of his own time. This is the reason why he selected Marcus Porcius Cato the Censor as the principal speaker.

Ancient Viewpoints of Life. — Among the many schools of philosophy in ancient times four were especially prominent: namely, the New Academic, the Peripatetic, the Stoic, and the Epicurean.

ZENO

The New Academy was an adaptation of the Academic philosophy of Plato, and had some points in common with modern agnosticism. It was the outgrowth of an age when religion was losing its hold on some of the foremost thinkers, and proclaimed the view that there could be no certain criterion of truth, and that all the inquirer can do is to balance probabilities one against the other. Its founder was Carneades (215 B.C.–130 B.C.). Cicero claimed to be an adherent of this school.

The Peripatetics were followers of Aristotle, and derived their name from his habit of strolling about with his disciples in the Lyceum. They held that the end of human activity was virtue which was dependent on nature, habit, and reason. They believed that external goods are more or less necessary conditions in promoting the perfect life.

The Stoics (so named from the painted stoa or portico in Athens, where Zeno, their founder, lectured) on the other hand held that in

comparison with virtue all other things sink into absolute insignifi-
cance. The morality of the Stoics was a stern one, guided by the
principle that we must live in accordance with nature, which they
considered God. They taught that in man's quest for virtue poverty
and wealth, pain and pleasure, health and sickness were immaterial.
They believed in the immortality of the soul, and in this respect were
diametrically opposed to the teaching of the Epicureans. The Stoics
said that in order to be good, a man must perform his function well.
The important thing in life is not to hold a good hand, but to play a
bad hand well. Stoicism had many points of contact with Christianity, particularly in that it was a religion for the oppressed.

The Epicureans (named after their founder Epicurus) held that it is
man's duty to enlarge his pleasures and to diminish his pains, though
in all fairness we must admit that Epicurus had reference to pleasures
and pains of the mind and soul. " Let us eat, drink, and be merry,"
therefore, is hardly a correct definition of Epicureanism. The highest
pleasure is peace of mind. Their religious views were atheistic, for
they believed in the complete inactivity of the gods, and in the dis-
solution of the soul at death. A man need have no fear of death,
because " where we are, death is not ; and where death is, we are not."
Cicero had no patience with Epicureanism.

The student should bear in mind that most of the later viewpoints
of life were adaptations of the modes of conduct formulated by such
great minds as those of Socrates, Plato, and Aristotle, and that Cicero
played no small part in bequeathing this knowledge to us. An evalu-
ation of Cicero's service in philosophy will be found on page 502.

The Philosophical Writings of Cicero

During the whole of an exceptionally busy public life Cicero devoted
his spare moments to reading and to the society of the learned. After
his exile in 58 and 57 B.C. his political career, except for a brief period
just before his death, was over, and it is at this time that his period of
great literary activity begins. In 55 B.C. he produced the work *Dē
Ōrātōre*, in 54 B.C. the *Dē Rē Pūblicā*, and in 52 B.C. the *Dē Lēgibus*, all
three works, according to ancient ideas, entitled to rank as philosophical. Almost every branch of learning was ranked under the
head of philosophy. Strabo even claimed that one branch of philosophy was geography.

From 51 to 46 B.C., owing first to his absence in Cilicia, then to the civil troubles, Cicero almost ceased to write. But in the latter year he was reconciled with Caesar, and as the senate and law courts were closed against him on his refusal to compromise his political principles, he betook himself with greater devotion than ever to literature. The first work written in 46 B.C. was the *Hortēnsius*, or *Dē Philosophiā*, now lost. It was founded on a lost dialogue of Aristotle, and set forth the advantages of studying philosophy. During the same year Cicero completed several oratorical works, the *Partītiōnēs Ōrātōriae*, the *Brūtus*, or *Dē Clārīs Ōrātōribus*, and the *Ōrātor*, all of which are extant.

Early in 45 B.C. Cicero lost his beloved daughter Tullia. He passed the whole year in retirement, trying to soothe his grief by incessant writing. In quick succession appeared :

EPICURUS

Dē Cōnsōlātiōne, an attempt to apply philosophy to the mitigation of his own sorrow and that of others ;

Acadēmica, an exposition of the New Academic philosophy, advocating probability rather than certainty as the foundation of philosophy ;

Dē Fīnibus Bonōrum et Malōrum, a work criticizing the most prominent views entertained concerning ethics ;

Disputātiōnēs Tusculānae, treating of certain conditions essential to morality and happiness ;

Dē Nātūrā Deōrum, an examination of the principal theories regarding the nature and power of the gods ;

Catō Maior, on old age ; *Laelius*, on friendship ;

Dē Fātō, discussing fate and free will ;

Paradoxa, a book setting forth certain remarkable views of the Stoics ;

Dē Officiīs, a treatise on practical ethics, the application of moral principles to the questions and difficulties of ordinary life.

These works, written mostly in 45 B.C. and 44 B.C., are, except the *Dē Cōnsōlātiōne*, still extant. To the list may be added also other works of a rhetorical nature, such as the *Topica* and *Dē Optimō Genere Dīcendī*, and some lost philosophical books, such as *Dē Glōriā*.

Even though allowance be made for the fact that Cicero was giving in Latin the substance of Greek books with which he had been familiar from boyhood, the mental vigor and literary power exhibited by this series of works appear prodigious when we consider their great compass and variety and the generally high finish of their style.

The following outline is a complete survey of the full essay : —

Subject-Matter

General View

The *Cato Maior* falls naturally into three parts : —

> **Preliminary,** dedication to Atticus, CHAPTER 1.
> **Introductory Conversation,** CHAPTERS 2 and 3.
> **Cato's Defense of Old Age,** CHAPTERS 4 to 23.

After chapter 3 Cato continues to express his views on old age without interruption to the end, and the dialogue thus becomes really a monologue.

Analysis

Preliminary . . . . CHAPTER 1.

Cicero, addressing Atticus, states his purpose in writing the book and the effect of the work on himself, the reasons for putting the sentiments on old age into the mouth of Cato, and the circumstances of the supposed conversation.

Introductory Conversation . . . . CHAPTERS 2 and 3.

Scipio declares his admiration of Cato's vigorous and happy old age. Cato replies that the secret lies in following the guidance of nature. Laelius then asks Cato to point out the road to such an old age as his own. This the old man promises to do, but first remarks that the faults charged against old age are generally due to defects of character. Laelius suggests that prosperity makes Cato's declining years pleasant. Cato admits that there may be some truth in this, but maintains that right character alone can make old age tolerable.

A. Introductory argument from fact. Account of celebrated old men whose lives till death were useful and happy.

    (a) Fabius Maximus

    (b) Plato; (c) Isocrates; (d) Gorgias

    (e) Ennius

B. Refutation of charges made against old age. CHAPTERS 6–23. *Statement of the four charges commonly made against old age:* it withdraws men from active life, it weakens the physical powers, it takes away capacity for enjoyment, and it involves the anticipation of death.

  1. Refutation of the first charge, that old age withdraws men from active life.

    a. There are employments suited to old age which are as necessary to the well-being of society as those which require greater physical powers.

    b. The special objection that old men have weak memories is answered by showing that this is due either to an original defect or to insufficient exercise.

    c. Argument from fact : instances of old men in public and in private life who till death were actively at work.

  2. Rebuttal of the second charge, that old age weakens the physical powers.

    a. Old age does not desire nor require the strength of youth, because it may exert influence through other means. Instances cited to show this.

    b. Temperate habits will retain a good measure of strength till old age; many instances of weakness in old age may be attributed to ill-health, which is common to all periods of life; proper care will greatly retard decay.

  3. Refutation of the third charge, that old age takes away the capacity for enjoyment.

    a. The pleasures in which youth finds its keenest enjoyment are in themselves bad, and old age is beneficent in freeing men from their allurements.

    b. Old age has pleasures far more refined and satisfying than those of sense.

Such as, those of conversation and literature; especially those of agriculture; and lastly, the exercise of influence, which old age will always possess if a rightly spent youth has preceded.

 c. The special objection that old men's tempers spoil their enjoyments is met by the statement that this is the fault of character, not of age.

4. Refutation of the fourth charge, that old age is unhappy because it involves the anticipation of death.

TOMBSTONES IN A ROMAN VAULT AT CARTHAGE

 a. Since the right aim of life is to live not long but well, death ought not to be dreaded at any age.

 b. Old men, especially those of learning and culture, ought not to fear death.

Because, that which is according to nature is good, and it is natural for old men to die; the process of dying is brief and almost painless; even young men and those without learning often set the example of despising death; and old age, just as the other periods of life, has finally its season of ripeness and satiety.

 c. Death is probably the gateway to a happy immortality. Tending towards proof of this are the arguments stated in

Plato; viz. the rapidity of the mind's action, its powers of memory and invention, its self-activity, indivisible nature and preëxistence; also the arguments, attributed to Cyrus, based upon the soul's immateriality, the posthumous fame of great men and the likeness of death to sleep; the instinctive belief in immortality, so strong as even to form an incentive for action; and, finally, the speaker's own longing after immortality and hope of union with those whom he once knew and loved.

THE ESSAY ON FRIENDSHIP

DATE AND CIRCUMSTANCES OF COMPOSITION

The conversation of the *Laelius dē Amīcitiā*, composed in June of 44 B.C., is supposed to take place at the house of Laelius in 129 B.C., between Laelius (lā'lị-ụs) and his sons-in-law, Scaevola (sev'ọ-lạ) and Fannius. Laelius was distinguished as statesman, soldier, and man of letters. Scaevola, born about 157 B.C., belonged to a family of lawyers. Fannius, a soldier and writer, was the first to mount the walls of Carthage at the time of its capture in 146 B.C.

The friendship of Laelius and Scipio was one of the most famous in antiquity. Laelius, says Cicero, reverenced Scipio as a god; Scipio looked up to Laelius, his senior, as a parent. The views of friendship which Laelius gives in the dialogue are said by him to be mainly those of Scipio.

Scope. — The Laelius belongs to the ethical works of Cicero, and is interwoven with Stoicism (see page 547). The subject of friendship to which Laelius is devoted, though very little elaborated by modern philosophers, held an important place in the moral systems of the ancients. Cicero uses *amicītia* in a sense which is almost exactly that of the English ' friendship.' His treatise is indeed a kind of popular essay, dealing with those aspects of the subject which could be best made interesting to readers in general.

SUBJECT-MATTER

General View

The *Laelius*, like the *Catō Maior*, consists of three parts: —

Preliminary, dedication to Atticus, CHAPTER I.
Introductory Conversation, CHAPTERS 2 to 5.
The Discourse of Laelius on Friendship, CHAPTERS 5 to 27.

Analysis

Preliminary, dedication to Atticus . . . . CHAPTER I.

Cicero gives an account of his acquaintance with the Scaevolae, and explains how Scaevola, the augur, happening one day to speak of a quarrel between P. Sulpicius and Q. Pompeius, formerly friends, came to report a conversation between Laelius, himself, and Fannius on friendship. This conversation Cicero has freely rendered. He states why he has dedicated the work to Atticus, his reasons for making Laelius the most prominent character in the dialogue, and the circumstances of the supposed conversation.

Introductory Conversation . . . . . CHAPTERS 2 to 5.

Fannius opens the conversation with an allusion to Scipio Africanus, and remarks that people are wondering how Laelius, whom they call ' wise,' bears the death of his friend. Scaevola speaks to the same effect. Laelius, although alleging ill-health as the cause of temporary retirement, acknowledges that he has been deeply moved by the loss of Scipio. He finds consolation, however, in the reflection that Scipio is better off than he, because, after having enjoyed the highest esteem and honors, Scipio has passed away by a painless death, and no doubt to a happy immortality, while he, older in years, is left behind. But still the greatest solace is the remembrance of the close friendship between himself and Scipio. The subject of friendship having thus been touched upon, Fannius and Scaevola unite in asking Laelius to express his views upon it.

The Discourse of Laelius on Friendship . CHAPTERS 5 to 27.

This discourse of Laelius comprises five distinct portions. In two instances the transitions are gracefully made through remarks by Fannius and Scaevola.

(1) Remarks upon the nature and value of friendship.

Friendship is to be prized above all other things, but can exist only among the good, — good not in the Stoic, but in the ordinary sense, — and is something deeper and stronger than natural association. Friendship is defined, with the statement that virtue is its essential condition, and its advantages and importance are briefly pointed out. Remarks by Fannius and Scaevola.

- (2) The basis of true friendship — love.

  Not expediency, but affection, which, foreshadowed in the instincts of the lower animals, finds its purest and highest outcome among characters of exalted virtue, must be assumed as the source of true friendship. Friendship, therefore, though

COIN OF EGYPT

Obverse : Head of Cleopatra. Reverse : Eagle on thunderbolt.

  strengthened by reciprocal services, cannot originate in them, nor in hope of reward, nor in utility founded upon desire for pleasure.

- (3) Duration of friendship and the dangers to which it is exposed.

  Friendship rarely lasts till death, owing to changes in circumstances, opinions, or character. Especially harmful to it is the struggling after political preferment and after wealth, though frequently disagreements arise from wrong or unreasonable requests on the part of friends.

- (4) Discussion of practical questions connected with friendship.
  - A. Friendships of the wise.
    - a. How far one ought to go in helping a friend.
    - b. Refutation of wrong views, namely, that too close friendships are to be avoided, and that friendships ought to be sought after only for the sake of assistance and freedom from care.
    - c. The proper limits of friendly feeling.
    - d. The choosing and testing of friends.
    - e. Old friends and new.
    - f. The necessity of equality in friendship.

   B. Friendships of common people.
      a. The severing of friendships — when and why necessary.
      b. The choice of friends; need for care, practical rules.
      c. Friendship a necessity of life.
      d. The importance of frankness and truthfulness.
      e. The evil of flattery.

(5) Conclusion.

Virtue is the origin and bond of friendship. Next to virtue true friendship is to be prized above all other things on earth.

THE FOURTEENTH SPEECH AGAINST ANTONY

Occasion and Circumstances of Delivery. — This, the last public speech of Cicero which is extant, belongs to a group called *Philippics* from their similarity to the celebrated *Philippics* of Demosthenes, directed against Philip of Macedon. Plutarch (*Cicero*, 24) says that Cicero himself gave the orations this title, and a reference in one of his letters (*Brūtus*, 2, 3) seems to verify this. At any rate by the time of Juvenal (55?–135? A.D.) this title was in current use.

After the assassination of Caesar in 44 B.C. his colleague in the consulship, Mark Antony, came forward as his avenger, with the result that the leaders of the conspiracy fled from the city. We may safely assume (Cicero, *Epistulae*, 23, and note, page 399) that while Cicero was not a party to Caesar's murder, he approved of it on the grounds that the Dictator was headed for tyranny. Now Antony seemed to be assuming Caesar's powers, and Cicero became deeply apprehensive of the state's welfare. The Philippic orations bear witness to the inevitable collision which followed.

Cicero spoke this oration soon after more or less imperfect reports had reached the city regarding the victory of the consuls Pansa and Hirtius over Antony before Mutina. This success was gained while the consuls were marching up to relieve Decimus Brutus (see Cicero, *Epistulae*, 25, page 402), who was being besieged at Mutina by Antony's superior force. The people in the city of Rome became wild with excitement, assembled about Cicero's house, and carried him in triumph to the Capitol and back again to his home. On the next day, April 21, 43 B.C., a meeting of the senate was called, and Publius Servilius moved that the citizens should lay aside the military garb and that a public thanksgiving should be decreed in honor of the victory. Cicero objected to the first proposition, but supported the second.

Subject-Matter. — The immediate occasion of the Fourteenth Philippic was a formal proposal sponsored by P. Servilius to the effect that the citizens should lay aside the garb of war, and that a *sup-*

plicātiō should be celebrated in honor of Hirtius and Pansa for their victory over Antony. Cicero, being dissatisfied with the resolution mainly because it failed to declare Antony a *hostis*, proposed an amendment which was carried.

In content the speech deviates somewhat from that of a typical oration in that it embodies as a part of an argumentative discourse a noble eulogy of the soldiers fallen in battle, although this laudatory portion is a natural consequence of the argument, and, in fact, quite necessary to it.

Outline of the Fourteenth Philippic

INTRODUCTION

Exōrdium. It would be premature to assume the garb of peace before we are officially informed that Brutus is safe; his deliverance is the issue involved in this war. CHAPTERS 1 and 2.

Nārrātiō. Antony is guilty of warfare against his country, and therefore is a public enemy (*hostis*). He is also guilty of other crimes. 3 and 4 to line 20.

Partītiō. Therefore I support the proposal of a thanksgiving; but I favor amending it by extending the duration and by conferring the title of *Imperātor* upon the generals. 4, from line 20 to 5, line 18.

DISCUSSION

Cōnfirmātiō. Cicero begins with a refutation of the charge that he was aiming at sovereign power: The informal triumph which the people tendered me was merely a testimony to loyal service; the people rate men in proportion to their merits. I have always felt that Antony should be declared a public enemy, and now the proposal of a public thanksgiving implies this. Furthermore, the exploits of Pansa and Hirtius, and Octavianus against Antony fully deserve this honor. I also favor a memorial to the soldiers of the Martian legion. 5, line 18 to 12, line 22.

CONCLUSION

Perōrātiō. The memory of your life, O soldiers, which you have so nobly sacrificed is everlasting and eternal. 12, line 22 to end of oration.

THE LETTERS OF CICERO

Roman Correspondence. — As the relations of Rome with the rest of the ancient world became more and more intimate, and men passed easily from the City to the provinces, while the provincials flocked to Rome, letter-writing increased proportionately in extent and importance. In Cicero's time the Roman of standing frequently carried on a voluminous correspondence. There was, however, no postal

ROMAN WRITING MATERIALS

Inkstand, pen, and roll.

system like that of today; and letters were carried to their destination, if not at too great distance, by special messengers. Letters to persons in distant parts were sent by sea-captains, by the carriers of despatches for certain classes of government officers (particularly the collectors of revenue), and in general by anyone going that way who could be induced to take charge of them. Letters of a confidential nature were often written in cipher, of which the correspondent had been furnished the key, and were sometimes sent in duplicate by different conveyances. In good weather letters conveyed by land traveled about fifty miles a day; but it took three weeks to send from Rome to Athens.

The form of letters varied at different periods and according to circumstances. In the earlier days writing-tablets (*tabulae,* or *pugillārēs*) were exclusively employed. These consisted of two or more thin slips of wood or ivory, usually oblong, and fastened at the back with wires so that they would open as our books. The average size was probably not much smaller than this page. The inside pages or leaves were provided with a slight raised rim about the margin, so that the inclosed surfaces, which were coated with a thin layer of wax, would not rub. On these surfaces the writing was done with the pointed end of a *stilus* of metal or bone; the other end of the *stilus* was flattened, so that it could be used to rub the wax back over a word or line in which there was an error. The wax was usually black, and the writing showed the color of the underlying wood or ivory, which was white, or at least of a light tint. The size of tablets ranged from two to five leaves, eight pages being available for writing in the last named.

When the letter was finished, strong thread was passed through one or more perforations in the margin or even at the center, then wound closely around the tablets and tied. Over the knot the seal of the sender was stamped in wax or in fine clay. As the handwriting within was often that of an amanuensis, who in most cases was a slave, the seal was of very great importance as a means of identification. For this reason when a letter was opened the thread was cut in such a way as to leave the seal undisturbed. These writing-tablets were so convenient that they continued in use to modern times. At Florence there is a waxen tablet of the year 1301.

In the time of Cicero writing-tablets were used for short letters; but longer communications were often written with a reed pen and ink upon paper prepared from the papyrus. Usually before they were written on, but sometimes afterwards, the pages of paper were pasted together at the sides, forming a long sheet, or roll. The writing was in columns, which were parallel to the ends of the sheet, so that the lines ran in the direction of the length. The letter thus prepared was rolled up, in much the same manner as books (*librī*) were at that time, and was then tied about the middle, a seal being placed over the knot.

At the head of a letter stood the name of the sender in the nominative case, with the name of the person to whom it was addressed in the dative, usually accompanied also by the abbreviation S. D. (= *salūtem dīcit*, 'sends greeting'), or S. P. D., S. PLŪR. D. (= *salūtem plūrimam dīcit*, 'sends most cordial greeting'). In more formal correspondence pains was taken to give forenames and titles. At the beginning of the letter, S. V. B. E. V. (= *sī valēs, bene est; valeō*), or a similar formula was often placed. The close was frequently abrupt; sometimes *valē* or a like expression was added, with the date; the place of writing was given in the ablative. The outside address was of the simplest character, containing the name of the person to whom the letter was sent, in the dative case.

Cicero's Correspondence. — Cicero did not publish his letters. They were given to the world probably by Tiro (see vocabulary, and page 502), arranged in several collections. Those extant comprise only a portion of the number once known. Of the letters which have been preserved, the first was written in the year 68 B.C.; the latest in 43, some months before Cicero's death. They vary in length from a few lines to several pages. They are grouped as follows: —

'To his Friends' (*Ad Familiārēs*, abbreviated *Ad Fam.*); sixteen books. The title is inaccurate, because some of the letters were written to persons not included within the orator's circle of friends, and also because a number of them are not from Cicero, but addressed to him.

'To his brother Quintus' (*Ad Quīntum Frātrem, Ad Q. Fr.*); three books. The first letter is a rather formal discussion of the duties of a provincial magistrate, in sixteen chapters.

'To Atticus' (*Ad Atticum, Ad Att.*); sixteen books.

'To Marcus Brutus' (*Ad M. Brūtum, Ad Brūt.*); two books. At least two of the letters to Brutus appear to be forgeries.

The literary value of the letters, and their bearing on our knowledge of Cicero, have been alluded to in another connection (pages 503–504). Among noteworthy characteristics of the style are the common yet delicate use of colloquial expressions and the employment of language akin to that of comedy; the frequent introduction of Greek words and phrases, just as we often give a turn to a sentence with French or German; the coining of new words on the spur of the moment to suit a passing need; and the free use of superlatives and diminutives.

As might be expected of a correspondent at once so sensitive, sympathetic, and vivacious as Cicero, the letters are varied with an ever-surprising richness of feeling and thought; and the variety of the matter is hardly greater than that of the manner of expression. They are pervaded by a breezy freshness that makes the surroundings and emotions of the writer as real to us as our own experiences. Hence it must always be that the more they are read the more they will be appreciated. But they are not simply entertaining or of general human interest; the light they throw on the inner political movements and social life of the time gives them a value as historical documents second to that of no other writings of the period.

Introduction to Letter 13. — When Cicero and his party were homeward bound from Cilicia, Tiro was stricken with a severe attack of malarial fever, and had to be left behind. At every stopping-place Cicero wrote letters to him, and this is one of the series. They are filled with solicitude for Tiro's health, and abound with expressions of love and

AN AGE-OLD PROBLEM

Above : Lake Avernus, whose pestilential surroundings led the Romans to associate it with the entrance to the lower world.

Below : Mussolini outdoing Caesar in setting the unemployed to work at draining the Pontine marshes, since ancient times the favorite breeding grounds of mosquitoes, the source of malaria.

affection. No expense is to be spared in administering to Tiro's comfort; the most skilled physician is to be engaged, and a faithful slave is
to wait upon him. When he finally returns to Italy, a horse and mule
are to be placed at his disposal. That Cicero gives Marcus a share in
the letter is merely another indication of the great esteem in which the
Cicero family held Tiro. This letter together with the others of the
same group reveal the great orator to us as a man possessed of the finest
human traits — a man of soul and feeling.

The accurate descriptions of fever given by Hippocrates, Celsus, and
Galen prove conclusively that malaria was one of the most common afflic-
tions among the ancient Greeks and Romans. Cicero mentions tertian and
quartan fevers, and Varro (see *Outline of Latin Literature*, Companion,
page 707), *Dē Rē Rusticā* 1, 12, 2, states that in marshy districts certain
small creatures are propagated, which enter the body by the mouth and
nostrils, and *efficiunt difficilēs morbōs*. No doubt he was referring to the
mosquito, a species of which, belonging to the *anopheles* group, modern
scientists have definitely linked with the disease. In ancient Rome the
malarial season seems to have extended from July to November, for Horace
in one passage (*Satires*, 2, 6, 18, *et seq.*) refers to the oppressive autumn as a
source of gain for the goddess Libitîna, the goddess of death, and in another
passage (*Epistles*, 1, 7, 5, *et seq.*) as the time of the year when every father and
fond mother feel anxiety for the welfare of their children. The Pomptine
marshes were especially malarial, and even in modern times this district is
infested with mosquitoes which swoop down upon Rome. See illustrations,
page 561. The Romans had even a goddess called *Febris*.

LIVY, THE GRAPHIC HISTORIAN OF ROME

His Life. — Even during his lifetime Livy had already won such
great reknown that a certain man came all the way from Gades, Spain,
merely for the purpose of seeing him, and having satisfied his curiosity
immediately returned home. Notwithstanding Livy's great fame
our present knowledge about him is extremely scanty.

He was born in 59 B.C. at Patavium, modern Padua, a city said to
have been founded by Antênor of Trojan fame, whose inhabitants
prided themselves on their ancient virtue and strict morals. In this
atmosphere Livy spent his early life. Possibly in 30 or 31 B.C. he
went to Rome, where he soon became a member of the great literary
circle of the emperor Augustus, to whose personal interest, no doubt,
it was largely due that Livy interpreted the glory of Rome in prose,
just as Virgil did in poetry. The friendly relations between the

emperor and Livy were so genuine that they were strained not even by the republican tendencies of the historian, whom Augustus humorously dubbed a Pompeian because of his pronounced admiration for Pompey and his party. However, Livy had the good sense to accept the imperial rule without complaint, but his sympathies were with the well-tempered freedom which he associated with the counsels of the state's aristocracy in the good old days. As to Julius Caesar, although he fully recognized his genius, as far as the welfare of the state was concerned he considered it unfortunate that this great leader had ever been born.

His education was the best available, comprehending a thorough training in rhetoric, oratory, and philosophy. He did not enter the political arena, but devoted himself exclusively to literature and writing. About his private life we know practically nothing; he had a son, and a daughter who married a rhetorician. His last years were spent in his native town, where death intervened in 17 A.D.

His Works. — Livy's earliest writings, which have not been preserved, were on rhetoric and philosophy. His greatest achievement, however, was the History of Rome, usually entitled *Librī ab Urbe Conditā*, though Livy refers to it as *Annālēs*. Originally this work consisted of 142 books, closing with the death of Drusus, the stepson of Augustus, in 9 B.C. Only an aggregate of thirty-five books is extant, but we have meager summaries, *periochae*, of most of the others. This immense work was begun when Livy was about thirty-three years of age, and he continued it through the rest of his life over a period of more than forty years. It begins with the story of Aeneas, his landing in Latium, and includes the legendary material associated with early Rome, told in a most fascinating narrative. The story of the death struggle between Rome and Carthage is truly a masterpiece which only a consummate artist could paint. He identifies his very being with the great drama, and when he finally disposes of the conflict, he says: " I, too, feel as much relief in having reached the end of the Punic War as if I had taken a personal part in its toils and dangers."

His Style. — Livy's history reads like an " epic in prose." His style conforms in spirit to the ideal laid down by Cicero, but in actual practice Livy's manner of writing is far more flexible and artistic. He is essentially a pictorial writer, endowed with a vivid imagination and a keen dramatic instinct. In close relation stand two other characteristics of his style, namely, *varietās* and *color poēticus* Livy's syntax was greatly influenced by the language of poetry, and this, coupled with his rhetorical brilliance, imparted to his style a grace and artistic finish which are the trade-marks of a great writer. Livy's language is rich, harmonious, eloquent, and romantic. He had a high ethical purpose which was tempered by a conservative disposition; indeed, nature had richly endowed him to become one of the world's

EXCAVATING CARTHAGE
The expedition of the University of Michigan at work.

greatest stylists. Niebuhr, the German historian, rightly says: " He enriched the literature of his countrymen with a colossal master-piece, with which the Greeks have nothing to compare, nor can any modern people place a similar work by its side. Of all the losses that have befallen us in Roman literature the greatest is that which has left us his history imperfect."

PLINY, ROME'S FOREMOST GENTLEMAN

His Life. — The private correspondence of the Romans has already been discussed on page 558. Letter-writing as a branch of literature was assiduously cultivated by the Romans, who greatly excelled the Greeks in this field as they did also in satire. Horace, Ovid, Cicero,

Seneca, and Pliny are the outstanding representatives of epistolary Latin, — Horace and Ovid of the poetical epistle and the other three of epistolary prose. Cicero wrote true letters, more than eight hundred in number, which reveal the innermost feelings of the great orator; Seneca, the Stoic philosopher, wrote moral essays in the form of letters; Pliny, however, developed the literary and artistic aspect of the letter, and wrote with a view to publication.

As Varro was Rome's greatest scholar, so Pliny may well merit the title of Rome's foremost gentleman. He was born in the Cisalpine town of Comum, in the year 62 A.D., and sprang from a wealthy family of some consequence, in which studious habits and literary appreciation seem to have been fostered as a matter of tradition. Pliny's full name was Gaius Plinius Caecilius Secundus, but he is commonly referred to as Pliny the Younger — in Latin, *Plīnius Minor* or *Iūnior*, to distinguish him from his learned uncle, Pliny the Elder, in Latin, *Plīnius Maior*, whose death in the great eruption of Vesuvius, 79 A.D., is described by his nephew (see pages 461–467). Pliny the Younger lost his father when he was very young, and was adopted by his wealthy uncle, who saw to his education and introduced him into a circle of the best people in Rome.

The Elder Pliny, a man of equestrian rank, was a prodigious reader and a true scientist, whose monumental work was the *Historia Nātūrālis*, an encyclopedia comprising thirty-seven books, which fortunately has been preserved to us. He also held various important offices, being admiral of the fleet (*praefectus classis*) at Misenum (near Cumae; see map following page 6) when the eruption of Vesuvius occurred. At this time his nephew was eighteen years old.

The young Pliny was very precocious and studious, having written a Greek tragedy at the early age of fourteen; but we need hardly regret the loss of this work. His unusual ability, his social and educational advantages all combined to make him very successful at a comparatively early age. He completed the *cursus honōrum*, being consul at thirty-eight. Quintilian, the first professor of rhetoric and author of the *Īnstitūtiō Ōrātōria*, was one of Pliny's teachers, and the historian Tacitus (see outline on page 707) was a life-long friend of his. Pliny's social graces won for him a wide acquaintance, so that he numbered among his friends most of the prominent people of his day. He received the education of a gentleman, studied law and oratory, and had a successful career as a pleader in the courts of Rome. The emperor Trajan, who was one of Pliny's best friends, finally appointed him as governor of Bithynia where his most perplexing problem seems to have been concerned with the Christians, regarding whom he sent his famous letter of inquiry to Trajan (see Selection on page 475).

Pliny was married twice, and possibly a third time, though he had no children. He tells us often about Calpurnia, his last wife, and his letters about her indicate that their union was most happy. Whether Pliny died in Bithynia or in Rome, we do not know; he certainly did not live beyond the year 115 A.D.

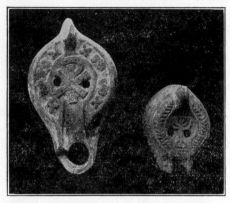

LAMPS SHOWING CHRISTIAN SYMBOLS

The letters reveal Pliny as a man of many virtues, in short, as a typical Roman gentleman. He had a lovable disposition, was amiable, kind, and easygoing. His filial devotion is apparent from his conduct towards his mother and his uncle. He was tolerant and generous towards others. With his money and other possessions he was extremely liberal; he endowed schools and made large bequests to individuals. He was always industrious and studious, spending his time profitably in reading, writing, or traveling. His fondness for the country and his appreciation for the beauties of nature are everywhere evident. He had country villas at Tusculum, Tibur, Praeneste, and an elaborate estate at Laurentum. His faults were such that they are easily overlooked; his vanity and artificiality we may readily forgive him. Posterity willingly grants him his longing for enduring fame as a man of letters.

Pliny's Works. — Pliny has left us a collection of 368 letters in ten books, the last book comprising a correspondence between himself and Trajan. Besides this we have the *Panegyricus*, a eulogy of Trajan, delivered in the senate in 100 A.D. Pliny's enthusiasm for literature knew no bounds; he wrote lyric, epigrammatic, epic, and elegiac poetry, and his youthful drama has already been mentioned. Pliny was too formal to be a good poet.

The letters are especially valuable because they portray the life of the early imperial period, for Pliny lived under the reigns of nine emperors, from Nero to Trajan.

Pliny's Style. — Many of the features of Pliny's style are mentioned in the notes. We may add that he was an imitator of Cicero, whom he greatly admired, although his diction and syntax conform quite closely to the standards of the Silver Age (see outline on page 707). To be sure, his language was influenced by his environment, so that we

COIN OF BITHYNIA

Obverse: Head of Prusias II.   Reverse: Herakles, with club and lion skin.

meet with neologisms, strained figures of speech, excessive word play, and poetic phraseology. On the whole, however, Pliny writes in a good style, which sometimes reaches great heights of beauty.

Below is a translation of Pliny's letter to Tacitus. (Latin on page 461.)

' You request that I depict for you the death of my uncle, in order that you may be able to transmit a more authentic account to posterity. I thank you; for I realize that an undying fame awaits him, if you proclaim his death. For, although he perished in a catastrophe involving the fairest country, and is ever destined to live, as it were, because of a memorable disaster, just as nations and as cities do; although he himself composed very many lasting works, nevertheless the enduring nature of your writings will contribute much to his abiding existence. Personally, I account those men happy to whom by divine dispensation has been granted the ability either to perform deeds worthy of record or to record deeds worthy of being read; but most happy do I account those upon whom both talents have been bestowed. Among these my uncle will appear by reason of both his works and yours as well. The more willingly do I consent; I even solicit the task which you are enjoining upon me.

' He was stationed at Misenum, and was personally in charge of the fleet. On the 24th of August, at about midday, my mother informed him that a cloud of unusual size and shape was visible. My uncle, who had had his sun-bath and a cold plunge, had taken a bite to eat, and was studying on his couch. He called for his slippers, and mounted a place from which that strange phenomenon could be best viewed. A cloud was rising up, from what mountain was uncertain to distant onlookers — though, afterwards, it was found to have been Vesuvius —, whose shape most resembled a pine-tree. For it raised itself on high, so to speak, with a very tall trunk, and was spreading itself out with a branchlike effect, I suppose, because it was carried upwards by a fresh gust of air; then, as its energy spent itself, the cloud, being without support or overcome even by its own weight, dissipated itself laterally; sometimes it was bright, sometimes it was dingy and spotted, according as it had taken up earth or cinders. This phenomenon seemed to so scholarly a man as my uncle unusual and worthy of closer acquaintance.

He ordered a small yacht to be made ready; he gave me the opportunity of going with him, if I wished; I replied that I preferred to pursue my studies, and, as it happened, he had personally given me some writing to do. He was just leaving the house, when he received a note from Recti'na, the wife of Tascus, who had been thoroughly frightened by the impending danger — for her villa lay at the foot of the mountain, and there was no means of escape except by ship — ; she begged him to rescue her from so great a danger. My uncle changed his plan, and what he had begun in the spirit of a scientist, he carried out in the spirit of a hero. He launched vessels with four banks of oars, and went on board himself, intending to bear aid not only to Rectina but to many others — for the delightful shore attracted people in great numbers —. He hastened to a point from which others were fleeing, and steered straight into danger, and so unapprehensive was he that he dictated and noted down all of the variations, and all of the phases of that great disaster.

' Now the cinders were falling upon the ships, and these became hotter and thicker, the nearer they approached; now pumice stones were falling also, together with pieces of black rock, scorched and cracked by the heat; now there was a sudden shoaling, and the shores obstructed navigation owing to the downpour from the mountain. After hesitating a little whether he should turn back, he said to the pilot on advising this course, " Fortune favors the bold; make for the house of Pomponia'nus." He lived at Stabiae, separated (cut off) by the intervening bay; for the sea beats upon shores which it has gradually bent and curved. Although the danger was not yet drawing near, nevertheless, because it was in sight and would be imminent whenever it should advance, Pomponianus had collected his baggage on boats there, being intent on flight if the unfavorable wind should abate; with this wind, most favorable to my uncle at this time, he sailed to Pomponianus, whom he found in a state of anxiety; he embraced and cheered him, urging him by his own unconcern to calm his fear, and ordered the bath to be made ready; after the bath he reclined at the table, and dined in a cheerful frame of mind or, what is equally brave, with the semblance of it. In the meantime from Mt. Vesuvius in many places very broad flames and high fires shone forth, whose bright splendor was accentuated by the darkness of the night. My uncle, to allay his friend's apprehensions, maintained that the hearth-fires had been left burning on account of the panic of the peasants, and that their abandoned houses were burning up amid their loneliness. Then he resigned himself to rest, and enjoyed a very real sleep, I assure you. For his breathing, which on account of his corpulence was rather heavy and noisy, was heard by his attendants before the door.

'But the court, from which his apartment was entered, had already been filled up and raised so high from the cinders mixed with pumice stones that a means of escape would have been denied if he had lingered longer in the bedchamber. Having been aroused from sleep, he went forth and returned to Pomponianus and to the rest who had remained awake. They took counsel together whether they should remain indoors or wander out in the open. For the houses were tottering with frequent violent shocks, and, just as if shaken from their very foundations, seemed to be swaying now this way, now that way. On the other hand, in the open air danger was feared from the pumice stones, light and porous though they were; however, a comparison of dangers led them to make this choice. Whereas with my uncle reason prevailed over reason, with the rest fear overcame fear. They placed pillows upon their heads, and tied them with napkins: this served as a protection against falling objects. It was now daylight elsewhere, but there night prevailed, completely black and pitch-dark; this, however, was relieved by numerous torches and lights of various kinds. They decided to go down to the shore and to see from near-by whether the sea now permitted any sailing; but it still remained stormy and forbidding. There my uncle lay down upon a discarded piece of cloth, asked for a drink of cold water once and again, and drank it. Then flames and the smell of sulphur preceding them put the rest to flight, and aroused my uncle.

'He rose up, leaning upon two of his servants, but immediately collapsed, his breath, as I infer, having been impeded by the rather dense fumes which closed his windpipe, for this in his case was naturally weak and narrow, and often inflamed. As soon as daylight returned — and this was the third day from the last which he had seen —, his body was found intact, uninjured, and dressed just as he had clad himself: his physical posture resembled more that of a sleeping rather than that of a dead man.   In the meantime my mother and I were at Misenum — but this has no connection with your history, and you wished to know only of my uncle's death.   Accordingly I shall conclude.   I shall merely add that I have related everything to which I was an eyewitness and which I had heard at the very time when accounts are most reliable. You will pick out the principal points ; for it is one thing to write a letter, another thing to write a history ; one thing to write a friend, another to write for everybody.   Farewell.'

THE ROMAN GOVERNMENT IN CICERO'S TIME

The speeches and letters of Cicero are full of references to the organization and administration of the Roman state in his time.   The following outline may be found helpful in grouping the scattered information which the reader of them will naturally acquire.   It applies to the constitution after the time of Sulla.   For the literature of the subject see page 702, and Kelsey's " Fifty Topics in Roman Antiquities," pages 35–37, 17, 18.

CITIZENS

Who they were
- Free inhabitants of Rome.
- Free inhabitants of Italy, who must go to Rome if they wished to vote.

Division: — 35 tribes, each tribe subdivided into 5 classes, each class into 2 centuries, = 350 centuries, and 18 centuries of equites.

Registration: — In the lists of the censors, by whom a citizen was assigned to his tribe, class, and century.

ASSEMBLIES

Of the People
- *Comitia Centuriāta*, an assembly by centuries, to elect consuls, praetors, censors.
- *Comitia Tribūta*, an assembly by tribes, to elect the lesser magistrates and enact laws, known as *plēbiscīta*.

Of Counselors designated by appointment: — *Senātus*, containing about 600 members ; charged with legislation upon foreign affairs.

OFFICERS	Magistrates	Ordinary	2 Consuls 8 Praetors (16 under Caesar) 2 Censors 10 Tribunes 4 Aediles (6 under Caesar) 20 Quaestors (40 under Caesar)
		Extraordinary	Dictator Magister Equitum Interrex
	Subordinate Officials		Secretaries — *scrībae* Criers — *praecōnēs* Lictors — *lictōrēs* Summoners — *viātōrēs* Minor magistrates — *vigintīsexvirī*
STATE PRIESTS	The Great Collegia		15 Pontifices (16 under Caesar), including the Pontifex Maximus 15 Augurs (16 under Caesar) 15 Quindecimviri sacris faciundis; in charge of the Sibylline books 7 Epulones (10 under Caesar); provided the banquets for the gods
	Special Priesthoods		15 Flamens; most important, those of Jupiter, Mars, Quirinus 6 Vestal Virgins; in charge of the fire of Vesta Rex Sacrorum; charged with certain rites and ceremonies
	The Lesser Collegia		Fetiales; performed rites in connection with the making of treaties and declaration of war Salii; guardians of the sacred shields Luperci; conducted the rites of the *Lupercālia* Fratres Arvales; priests of Dea Dia

LEGAL JU-RISDICTION	*In Civil Procedure*	For cases between citizens, Praetor Urbanus For cases one or both parties to which were foreigners, Praetor Peregrinus For cases touching the treasury, the Censors For cases arising in the markets, the Aediles
	In Criminal Procedure	For certain crimes against religion, Pontifex Maximus For other crimes, permanent juries or courts — *quaestiōnēs perpetuae* — at least eight in number; of which six were presided over by praetors, the rest by foremen (*iūdicēs quaestiōnis*)
PROVIN-CIAL AD-MINISTRA-TION	*Provinces (64–30 B.C.)*	*Western:* — Sicily, Sardinia (with Corsica), Hither Spain, Farther Spain, Illyricum, Africa, Narbonese Gaul, Cisalpine Gaul *Eastern:* — Achaia, Macedonia, Asia, Bithynia, Cyrene (with Crete), Cilicia, Syria
	Provincial Officers	Governor — either an ex-consul or an ex-praetor Quaestor — primarily a financial officer and second in command Subordinate officers — lieutenants (*lēgātī*), etc.

The revenues of a province were sold to the highest bidder, who would agree to collect and pay over the largest sum to the state treasury each year for a specified term, keeping all that might be collected above that sum for profit. In the case of Asia and other large provinces, the amounts involved were so great that the revenues were farmed by huge stock companies who kept their headquarters at Rome. So wealthy and powerful were these revenue corporations, which were composed of members of the equestrian order, the knights, that in a measure they took the place of government banking institutions.

ESSENTIALS OF LATIN GRAMMAR

INFLECTIONS

NOUNS

1. The Latin language has no article. In translating into English, the definite article *the,* or the indefinite article *a,* should be supplied with nouns in the different cases as the sense may require.

FIRST DECLENSION

2. *a.* The nominative singular of nouns of the first declension ends in -ă.

b. Nouns of the first declension are nearly all of the feminine gender; a few nouns referring to males are masculine, as **nauta,** *sailor;* **Catilīna,** a man's name.

3. An example of the first declension is: **via** (stem **viā-**), F., *way:*

SINGULAR

CASE		MEANING	TERMINATION
Nom.	via	*a way, the way*	-ă
Gen.	viae	*of a way, of the way*	-ae
Dat.	viae	*to* or *for a way,* or *the way*	-ae
Acc.	viam	*a way, the way*	-am
Voc.	via	*O way!*	-ă
Abl.	viā	*from, by, in a way* or *the way*	-ā

PLURAL

Nom.	viae	*ways, the ways*	-ae
Gen.	viārum	*of ways, of the ways*	-ārum
Dat.	viīs	*to* or *for ways,* or *the ways*	-īs
Acc.	viās	*ways, the ways*	-ās
Voc.	viae	*O ways!*	-ae
Abl.	viīs	*from, by, in ways,* or *the ways*	-īs

4. *a.* Besides the six cases of the first declension there is a rare locative case, of which the singular is exactly like the genitive, as **Rōmae,** *at Rome.*

b. The Greek name **Archiās, M.**, is of the first declension, and is declined as follows: *Nom.* **Archiās,** *Gen.* **Archiae,** *Dat.* **Archiae,** *Acc.* **Archiam,** *Voc.* **Archiā** or **Archia,** *Abl.* **Archiā.**

c. The Greek name **Sinōpē, F.**, is of the first declension, and is declined thus: **Sinōpē, Sinōpēs, Sinōpae, Sinōpēn, Sinōpē, Sinōpē.**

SECOND DECLENSION

5. *a.* The nominative singular of the second declension ends in **-um** for neuter nouns and **-us, -er, -ir** for all others.

b. Nouns of the second declension in **-us, -er,** and **-ir** are generally masculine. Most names of trees and plants are feminine, as **fāgus,** *beech,* and most names of countries, islands, and cities, as **Dēlos,** *Delos,* **Corinthus,** *Corinth.*

6. *a.* Examples of nouns of the second declension in **-us** and **-um** are **lēgātus** and **bellum:**

    lēgātus (stem **lēgāto-**), M.,   **bellum** (stem **bello-**), N., *war*
       envoy, lieutenant

SINGULAR

		TERMINATION		TERMINATION
Nom.	lēgātus	-us	bellum	-um
Gen.	lēgātī	-ī	bellī	-ī
Dat.	lēgātō	-ō	bellō	-ō
Acc.	lēgātum	-um	bellum	-um
Voc.	lēgāte	-e	bellum	-um
Abl.	lēgātō	-ō	bellō	-ō

PLURAL

Nom.	lēgātī	-ī	bella	-a
Gen.	lēgātōrum	-ōrum	bellōrum	-ōrum
Dat.	lēgātīs	-īs	bellīs	-īs
Acc.	lēgātōs	-ōs	bella	-a
Voc.	lēgātī	-ī	bella	-a
Abl.	lēgātīs	-īs	bellīs	-īs

b. The neuter **vulgus** is declined thus: *Nom.* **vulgus,** *Gen.* **vulgī,** *Dat.* **vulgō,** *Acc.* **vulgus,** *Abl.* **vulgō.**

c. Cicero uses **locus,** -ī, M., *place,* with a neuter plural **loca,** declined thus : *Nom.* **loca,** *Gen.* **locōrum,** *Dat.* **locīs,** *Acc.* **loca,** *Abl.* **locīs.**

d. The second declension has a rare locative case, of which the singular is like the genitive ; as **Ephesī,** *at Ephesus.*

e. **Dēlos,** F., a Greek name, is declined thus : **Dēlos, Dēlī, Dēlō, Dēlon, Dēle, Dēlō.**

7. *a.* Examples of nouns of the second declension in -er and -ir are **puer,** *boy,* **ager,** *field,* and **vir,** *man:*

puer (stem **puero-**),   **ager** (stem **agro-**),   **vir** (stem **viro-**),
     M., *boy*   M., *field*   M., *man*

	SINGULAR			TERMINATION
Nom.	puer	ager	vir	———
Gen.	puerī	agrī	virī	-ī
Dat.	puerō	agrō	virō	-ō
Acc.	puerum	agrum	virum	-um
Voc.	puer	ager	vir	———
Abl.	puerō	agrō	virō	-ō

	PLURAL			TERMINATION
Nom.	puerī	agrī	virī	-ī
Gen.	puerōrum	agrōrum	virōrum	-ōrum
Dat.	puerīs	agrīs	virīs	-īs
Acc.	puerōs	agrōs	virōs	-ōs
Voc.	puerī	agrī	virī	-ī
Abl.	puerīs	agrīs	virīs	-īs

b. Declined like **puer** are **gener,** -ī, M., *son-in-law,* **vesper,** -ī, M., *evening,* **līberī,** -ōrum, M., plural only, *children,* and in the singular only, **Līber, Līberī,** M., *Liber,* god of wine.

c. Like **ager** is **adulter,** -trī, M., *adulterer;* also, **administer,** -trī, M., *helper,* **liber,** -brī, M., *book,* and **Cimber,** -brī, M., *Cimber,* **Alexander,** -drī, M., *Alexander.*

8. *a.* In Cicero's time nouns of the second declension in -ius and -ium formed the genitive singular in -ī (not -iī), retaining the accent on the penult of words of more than two syllables even when this was short ; thus, **fīlī, Valē'rī, negō'tī, impe'rī.** Afterwards common nouns in -ius, and many proper names in -ius, were written with the genitive in -iī, and for the sake of consistency such genitives are frequently printed with -iī to-day, as **cōnsiliī Gabīniī.** In the vocabulary both forms of the genitive are given.

b. The genitive of **Pompeius** is written with -ī, **Pompe′ī**, as are also the genitives of some other proper names in -ius.

c. The vocative of **fīlius** and of proper names in -ius ends in -ī (not -ie), the accent remaining on the penult of vocatives containing more than two syllables even when the penult is short ; thus : **Grātī, Mānílī**, **Vale′ri**.

d. The declension of **deus**, M., *god*, is irregular :

SINGULAR		PLURAL
Nom.	deus	dī, deī, diī
Gen.	deī	deōrum, deum
Dat.	deō	dīs, deīs, diīs
Acc.	deum	deōs
Voc.	deus	dī, deī, diī
Abl.	deō	dīs, deīs, diīs

THIRD DECLENSION

9. In the third declension are comprised nouns with stems ending in a consonant (mute stems, liquid stems, nasal stems, and -s stems), nouns with stems ending in -i, nouns with mixed stems, and nouns of irregular declension. The stem rarely appears unchanged in the nominative, but may usually be recognized in the genitive.

10. *a.* Mute stems may end in a labial, **p, b** ; in a guttural, **c, g** ; or in a dental, **t, d**. In guttural stems the -s of the case ending in the nominative and vocative unites with the **c** or **g** of the stem, producing **x** ; thus **dux** for **duc-s**, in which the stem is **duc-**, the termination -s ; and **rēx** for **rēg-s**. In labial stems the mute is retained before -s but in dental stems it is dropped.

b. Examples of nouns with mute stems are **prīnceps, rēx, pēs, mīles, virtūs**, and **caput** :

prīnceps (stem **prīncip-**), M., *leader, leading man*

rēx (stem **rēg-**), M., *king*

pēs (stem **ped-**), M., *foot*

	SINGULAR			TERMINATION
Nom.	prīnceps	rēx	pēs	-s
Gen.	prīncipis	rēgis	pedis	-is
Dat.	prīncipī	rēgī	pedī	-ī
Acc.	prīncipem	rēgem	pedem	-em
Voc.	prīnceps	rēx	pēs	-s
Abl.	prīncipe	rēge	pede	-e

prīncēps (stem **rēx** (stem **rēg-**), **pēs** (stem **ped-**),
prīncip-), M., M., *king* M., *foot*
leader, leading man

		PLURAL		TERMINATION
Nom.	prīncipēs	rēgēs	pedēs	-ēs
Gen.	prīncipum	rēgum	pedum	-um
Dat.	prīncipibus	rēgibus	pedibus	-ibus
Acc.	prīncipēs	rēgēs	pedēs	-ēs
Voc.	prīncipēs	rēgēs	pedēs	-ēs
Abl.	prīncipibus	rēgibus	pedibus	-ibus

mīles (stem **virtūs** (stem **caput** (stem
mīlit-) M., **virtūt-**), F., **capit-**),N.,
soldier *valor, virtue* *head*

SINGULAR

Nom.	mīles	virtūs	caput
Gen.	mīlitis	virtūtis	capitis
Dat.	mīlitī	virtūtī	capitī
Acc.	mīlitem	virtūtem	caput
Voc.	mīles	virtūs	caput
Abl.	mīlite	virtūte	capite

PLURAL

Nom.	mīlitēs	virtūtēs	capita
Gen.	mīlitum	virtūtum	capitum
Dat.	mīlitibus	virtūtibus	capitibus
Acc.	mīlitēs	virtūtēs	capita
Voc.	mīlitēs	virtūtēs	capita
Abl.	mīlitibus	virtūtibus	capitibus

c. Like **rēx** are declined **lēx, lēgis,** F., *law,* and in the plural,
Allobrogēs, Allobrogum; also **dux, ducis,** M., *leader,* **pāx, pācis,** F.,
peace, and **vōx, vōcis,** F., *voice, utterance.*

d. Like **mīles** in declension are **eques, equitis,** M., *horseman,
knight,* **comes, comitis,** M., *companion,* and **hospes, hospitis,** M., *guest.*

e. **Quiēs,** F., *repose,* is declined **quiēs, quiētis, quiētī,** etc. ; but
seges, F., *grainfield,* has **ětis** in the genitive and is declined **segēs,
segetis, segetī, segetem,** etc., and **pariēs,** F., *house wall,* is declined
pariēs, -ětis, etc.

f. Like **virtūs** are **salūs, salūtis, F.**, in singular only, *safety,* **servitūs, servitūtis, F.**, *slavery;* here also belong the feminine nouns whose nominative ends in -tās, as **cīvitās, cīvitātis,** *state,* **aetās, aetātis,** *age.*

g. Other examples of nouns with dental stems are **cūstōs, -tōdis, M.**, *guard,* **nepōs, -pōtis, M.**, *grandson, spendthrift;* and **lac, lactis, N.**, *milk.*

11. *a.* Liquid stems end in -l or -r.

b. Examples of nouns with liquid stems are **cōnsul, victor,** and **pater** :

cōnsul (stem **cōnsul-**), **M.**, **victor** (stem **victōr-**), **M.**, **pater** (stem **patr-**),
  consul *victor* **M.**, *father*

SINGULAR

Nom.	cōnsul	victor	pater
Gen.	cōnsulis	victōris	patris
Dat.	cōnsulī	victōrī	patrī
Acc.	cōnsulem	victōrem	patrem
Voc.	cōnsul	victor	pater
Abl.	cōnsule	victōre	patre

PLURAL

Nom.	cōnsulēs	victōrēs	patrēs
Gen.	cōnsulum	victōrum	patrum
Dat.	cōnsulibus	victōribus	patribus
Acc.	cōnsulēs	victōrēs	patrēs
Voc.	cōnsulēs	victōrēs	patrēs
Abl.	cōnsulibus	victōribus	partribus

c. Like **consul** are **sōl, sōlis, M.**, *sun,* **exsul, exsulis, M.**, *exile;* also some -r stems, as **Caesar, Caesaris, M.**, *Caesar;* **mulier, mulieris, F.**, *woman,* **arbor, arboris, F.**, *tree.*

d. Like **victor** are declined masculine nouns of agency in -tor, as **mercātor, -ōris,** *trader,* **dēprecātor, -ōris,** *intercessor;* and abstract nouns in -or, as **timor, -ōris, M.**, *fear.*

e. Like **pater** are declined **frāter, frātris, M.**, *brother,* and **māter, mātris, F.**, *mother.*

12. *a.* Nasal stems end in -n, except in **hiems, hiemis,** F., *winter,* of which the stem ends in -m.

b. Examples are **sermō, homō,** and **nōmen** :

sermō (stem **sermōn-**), **homō** (stem **homin-**), **nōmen** (stem **nomin-**),
M., *conversation*   M., *man*   N., *name*

SINGULAR

Nom.	sermō	homō	nōmen
Gen.	sermōnis	hominis	nōminis
Dat.	sermōnī	hominī	nōminī
Acc.	sermōnem	hominem	nōmen
Voc.	sermō	homō	nōmen
Abl.	sermōne	homine	nōmine

PLURAL

Nom.	sermōnēs	hominēs	nōmina
Gen.	sermōnum	hominum	nōminum
Dat.	sermōnibus	hominibus	nōminibus
Acc.	sermōnēs	hominēs	nōmina
Voc.	sermōnēs	hominēs	nōmina
Abl.	sermōnibus	hominibus	nōminibus

c. Like **sermō** are declined **latrō, latrōnis,** M., *bandit;* **Mīlo, Milōnis,** M.; and nouns in -iō, as **suspīciō, suspīciōnis,** F., *suspicion,* **coniūrātiō, -ōnis,** F., *conspiracy,* **Cūriō, Cūriōnis,** M., and **Cicero, -ōnis.**

d. Like **homō** are declined **ōrdō, ōrdinis,** M., *order;* **necessitūdō, -inis,** F., *close connection;* **nēmō,** *Dat.* **nēminī,** *Acc.* **nēminem** (the place of the *Gen.* and *Abl.,* and sometimes the *Dat.,* being supplied by *Gen.* **nūllīus,** *Abl.* **nūllō,** *Dat.* **nūllī,** from **nūllus**), M., *no one;* **Apollo, Apollinis,** M.; **sōlitūdo, sōlitūdinis,** F., *wilderness;* and **virgŏ, -inis,** F.

e. Like **nōmen** are declined other neuters in -men, as **flūmen, flūminis,** *river,* and **certāmen, -inis,** *contest.*

13. *a.* The -s of -s stems becomes **r** between vowels in the oblique cases (rhotacism). In **honōs,** -r generally appears also in the nominative; -r is always found in the nominative of **rūmor** and many other nouns of this class.

b. Examples of nouns with -s stems are **mōs, honōs** or **honor,** and **genus** :

mōs (stem mōr-), M., *custom*	honōs, honor (stem honōr-), M., *honor*	genus (stem gener-), N., *race*

SINGULAR

Nom.	mōs	honōs *or* honor	genus
Gen.	mōris	honōris	generis
Dat.	mōrī	honōrī	generī
Acc.	mōrem	honōrem	genus
Voc.	mōs	honor	genus
Abl.	mōre	honōre	genere

PLURAL

Nom.	mōrēs	honōrēs	genera
Gen.	mōrum	honōrum	generum
Dat.	mōribus	honōribus	generibus
Acc.	mōrēs	honōrēs	genera
Voc.	mōrēs	honōrēs	genera
Abl.	mōribus	honōribus	generibus

c. Like mōs is declined flōs, M., *flower*.

d. Like honor are soror, sorōris, F., *sister*, uxor, uxōris, F., *wife*.

e. Like genus are declined the neuters fūnus, fūneris, *funeral;* latus, lateris, *side;* mūnus, mūneris, *gift;* onus, oneris, *burden, load;* opus, operis, *work;* scelus, sceleris, *crime;* vulnus, vulneris, *wound*.

f. Similar in declension to genus, but having a different vowel before the endings of the oblique cases, are the neuters corpus, corporis, *body;* dēdecus, -oris, *disgrace;* facinus, -oris, *evil deed;* frīgus, frīgoris, *cold;* pectus, pectoris, *breast;* tempus, temporis, *time;* and rōbur, rōboris, *strength*.

g. Among other nouns of the third declension with nominative in -s and genitive in -ris are the feminine Cerēs, Cereris, F., *Ceres*, and the neuters iūs, iūris, *Nom.* plural iūra, aes, aeris, *copper, bronze, money*, and ōs, ōris, *mouth, face, Nom.* plural ōra.

h. iūs iūrandum, N., *oath*, is thus declined in the singular : *Nom.* iūs iūrandum, *Gen.* iūris iūrandī, *Dat.* iūrī iūrandō, *Acc.* iūs iūrandum. *Abl.* iūre iūrandō.

14. *a.* The nominative singular of masculine and feminine nouns with -i stems ends ordinarily in -is, the genitive plural in -ium.

b. Examples of masculine and feminine -i stems with nominative singular in -is are turris, ignis, and hostis.

turris (stem **turri-**), F.,   **ignis** (stem **īgni-**),   **hostis** (stem **hosti-**),
       tower   M., *fire*   C., *enemy*

SINGULAR

				TERMINATION
Nom.	turris	ignis	hostis	-is
Gen.	turris	ignis	hostis	-is
Dat.	turrī	ignī	hostī	-ī
Acc.	turrim or -em	ignem	hostem	-im, -em
Voc.	turris	ignis	hostis	-is
Abl.	turrī or -e	ignī or -e	hoste	-e, -ī

PLURAL

Nom.	turrēs	ignēs	hostēs	-ēs
Gen.	turrium	ignium	hostium	-ium
Dat.	turribus	ignibus	hostibus	-ibus
Acc.	turrīs or -ēs	ignīs or -ēs	hostīs or -ēs	-īs, ēs
Voc.	turrēs	ignēs	hostēs	-ēs
Abl.	turribus	ignibus	hostibus	-ibus

c. Like **turris**, in the singular only, is Tiberis, -is, *Acc.* -im, M., *the Tiber;* also **Tamesis**, -is, *Acc.* -im, M., *the Thames.*

15. *a.* The nominative singular of some nouns with -i stems end in -ēs, of a few others in -er. Examples are **caedēs, linter**:

caedēs (stem **caedi-**), F., *slaughter*   **linter** (stem **lintri-**), F., *skiff*

	SINGULAR	PLURAL	SINGULAR	PLURAL
Nom.	caedēs	caedēs	linter	lintrēs
Gen.	caedis	caedium	lintris	lintrium
Dat.	caedī	caedibus	lintrī	lintribus
Acc.	caedem	caedēs or -īs	lintrem	lintrēs, -īs
Voc.	caedēs	caedēs	linter	lintrēs
Abl.	caede	caedibus	lintrī or -e	lintribus

b. Like **caedēs** are declined the feminine nouns, **mōlēs, mōlis,** *mass,* **sēdēs,** -is, *abode;* also **famēs,** -is, *hunger,* which, however, has **famē** in the ablative singular.

c. The Greek name **Achillēs** is thus declined : **Achillēs, Achillis, Achillī, Achillem, Achillēn** or **Achillea, Achillēs** or **Achilles, Achille.**

16. *a.* The nominative singular of neuter nouns with -i stems ends in -e, -al, and -ar ; the ablative singular ends in -ī, the genitive plural in -ium.

b. Examples of neuter nouns with -i stems are **mare** and **animal**.

mare (stem **mari-**), N.,	**animal** (stem **animali-**), N.,
sea	*animal*

	SINGULAR	PLURAL	SINGULAR	PLURAL	TERMINATIONS SINGULAR	PLURAL
Nom.	mare	maria	animal	animālia	-e or wanting	-ia
Gen.	maris	marium	animālis	animālium	-is	-ium
Dat.	marī	maribus	animālī	animālībus	-ī	-ibus
Acc.	mare	maria	animal	animālia	-e or wanting	-ia
Voc.	mare	maria	animal	animālia	-e or wanting	-ia
Abl.	marī	maribus	animālī	animālibus	-ī	-ibus

c. Praeneste, N., is declined thus : *Nom.* **Praeneste,** *Gen.* **Praenestis,** *Dat.* **Praenestī,** *Acc.* **Praeneste,** *Abl.* **Praeneste** ; no plural.

d. Like **animal** is **vectīgal, -ālis.**

17. *a.* The declension of nouns with mixed stems in the singular conforms to that of mute stems, in the plural to that of -i stems.

b. Examples of nouns with mixed stems are **mōns, pars, nox,** and **urbs** :

mōns	**pars**	**nox**	**urbs**
(stem **mont-**),	(stem **part-**),	(stem **noct-**),	(stem **urb-**),
M., *height*	F., *part*	F., *night*	F., *city*

SINGULAR

Nom.	mōns	pars	nox	urbs
Gen.	montis	partis	noctis	urbis
Dat.	montī	partī	noctī	urbī
Acc.	montem	partem	noctem	urbem
Voc.	mōns	pars	nox	urbs
Abl.	monte	parte	nocte	urbe

PLURAL

Nom.	montēs	partēs	noctēs	urbēs
Gen.	montium	partium	noctium	urbium
Dat.	montibus	partibus	noctibus	urbibus
Acc.	montēs, -īs	partēs, -īs	noctēs, -īs	urbēs, -īs
Voc.	montēs	partēs	noctēs	urbēs
Abl.	montibus	partibus	noctibus	urbibus

c. Among nouns with mixed stems used by Cicero are **pōns, pontis,** M., *bridge;* **parēns, -entis,** M. and F., *parent;* **falx, falcis,** F., *sickle, hook;* **fax, facis,** F., *torch;* **fraus. fraudis,** F., *deception;* **frōns,** frontis, F., *forehead;* laus, laudis, F., *praise;* līs, lītis, F., *law suit;* mors, mortis, F., *death;* nix, nivis, F., *snow;* plēbs, plēbis, F., *people;* sors, sortis, F., *lot;* stirps, stirpis, F., *trunk.*

d. Defective is the noun with the stem **spont-**, which has only a genitive, **spontis**, and ablative, **sponte**.

18. *a.* The declension of the nouns **vīs, vōs, carō,** and **Iuppiter,** is exceptional, not conforming to any of the types which have been given :

vīs (stems vi-, vīr-), F., *force*	bōs (stem bov-), C., *ox, cow*	carō (stem carn-), F., *flesh*	Iuppiter (stem iov-, pater in the nom.)**,** M., *Jupiter*

SINGULAR

Nom.	vīs	bōs	carō	Iuppiter
Gen.	——	bovis	carnis	Iovis
Dat.	——	bovī	carnī	Iovī
Acc.	vim	bovem	carnem	Iovem
Voc.	vīs	bōs	carō	Iuppiter
Abl.	vī	bove	carne	Iove

PLURAL

Nom.	vīrēs	bovēs	carnēs
Gen.	vīrium	boum or bovum	carnium
Dat.	vīribus	bōbus or būbus	carnibus
Acc.	vīrēs	bovēs	carnēs
Voc.	vīrēs	bovēs	carnēs
Abl.	vīribus	bōbus or būbus	carnibus

b. **Senex,** M., *old man,* stem **seni-** in oblique cases, is declined thus : senex, senis, senī, senem, senex, sene ; senēs, senum, senibus, senēs, senēs, senibus.

c. **Iter,** *n., journey, route,* has a stem **itiner-** in the oblique cases : iter, itineris, itinerī, iter, iter, itinere ; itinera, itinerum, itineribus, itinera, itinera, itineribus.

NAMES OF THE FIRST, SECOND, AND THIRD DECLENSIONS

19. *a.* Of the second declension are all Roman first names (**prae-nōmina**) used by Cicero, and in reading the text the name should be supplied, in the proper case form, from the abbreviation. The first names are Aulus, *Gen.* Aulī (abbreviaton A.), Appius (Ap.), Gaius (abbreviation C., originally meant G.), Decimus (D.), Gnaeus (Cn.),

Lūcius (L.), Mānius (M'.), Mārcus (M.), Pūblius (P.), Quīntus (Q.), Servius (Ser.), Sextus (Sex.), Spurius (Sp.), Tiberius (Ti.), and Titus (T.).

b. The clan names (nōmina), ending in -ius (as Iūlius, Tullius), are of the second declension.

c. The family names or surnames (cognōmina) are partly of the first declension, as Catilīna (full name, Lūcius Sergius Catilīna) ; of the second, as Flaccus (Mārcus Fulvius Flaccus, Lūcius Valerius Flaccus, etc.) ; and of the third, as Caesar (11. c), the full name being declined thus : Nom. Gaius Iūlius Caesar, Gen. Gaī Iūlī Caesaris or Gaiī Iūliī Caesaris (8. a), Dat. Gaiō Iūliō Caesarī, Acc. Gaium Iūlium Caesarem, Voc. Gaī Iūlī Caesar (8. c), Abl. Gaiō Iūliō Caesare.

d. Of the third declension is the family name Cicerō, the full name of the orator being declined thus : Mārcus Tullius Cicerō, Mārcī Tullī (or Tulliī) Cicerōnis, Mārcō Tulliō Cicerōnī, Mārcum Tullium Cicerōnem, Mārce Tullī (8. c) Cicerō, Mārcō Tulliō Cicerōne.

e. A few names of cities are declined in the plural only. Of the first declension are Athēnae, -ārum, F., Athens and Syracūsae, -ārum, F., Syracuse; of the third, Gādēs, -ium, F., Gades, Sardēs, Sardium, F., Sardis.

f. The names of foreign peoples are ordinarily declined in the plural only. A few are of the first declension, as Belgae, -ārum, M., the Belgians. The rest are of the second declension, as Cimbrī, -ōrum, M., the Cimbri, or of the third, as Allobrogēs -um, M., the Allobroges.

FOURTH DECLENSION

20. a. Nouns of the fourth declension ending in -us are generally masculine, nouns ending in -ū are neuter ; domus, manus, and Idūs (plural) are feminine.

b. Examples of nouns of the fourth declension are frūctus and cornū :

frūctus (stem frūctu-) M., fruit   cornū (stem cornu-), N., horn

	SINGULAR	PLURAL	SINGULAR	PLURAL
Nom.	frūctus	frūctūs	cornū	cornua
Gen.	frūctūs	frūctuum	cornūs	cornuum
Dat.	frūctuī	frūctibus	cornū	cornibus
Acc.	frūctum	frūctūs	cornū	cornua
Voc.	frūctus	frūctūs	cornū	cornua
Abl.	frūctū	frūctibus	cornū	cornibus

c. **Domus** (stem **domu-**), f., *house*, has also a stem **domo-** of the second declension, from which are formed a locative singular, **domī**, *at home*, an ablative singular, **domō**, and an accusative plural, **domōs**.

d. Many nouns of the fourth declension are defective, being used only in the ablative singular, as **iussū** and **nātū**.

FIFTH DECLENSION

21. *a.* Nouns of the fifth declension end in -ēs, and are femi‹ nine except **diēs**, *day*, which is masculine ; but when referring to a certain day **diēs** is usually feminine.

b. Examples of nouns of the fifth declension are :

diēs (stem **diē-**), M., *day*   **rēs** (stem **rē-**), F., *thing*

	SINGULAR	PLURAL		SINGULAR	PLURAL
Nom.	diēs	diēs		rēs	rēs
Gen.	diēī	diērum		reī	rērum
Dat.	diēī	diēbus		reī	rēbus
Acc.	diem	diēs		rem	rēs
Voc.	diēs	diēs		rēs	rēs
Abl.	diē	diēbus		rē	rēbus

c. In the genitive and dative singular -ēī becomes -eī when a consonant precedes, as in **reī**.

ADJECTIVES

22. *a.* In adjectives of the first and second declensions the mas‹ culine is declined like **lēgātus** (**6.** *a*), **puer** (**7.** *a*), or **ager** (**7.** *a*), the feminine like **via** (**3**), and the neuter like **bellum** (**6.** *a*).

b. Declined like **lēgātus**, **via**, **bellum** are many adjectives, as **bonus, bona, bonum,** *good:*

	SINGULAR			PLURAL		
	MASCULINE	FEMININE	NEUTER	MASCULINE	FEMININE	NEUTER
Nom.	bonus	bona	bonum	bonī	bonae	bona
Gen.	bonī	bonae	bonī	bonōrum	bonārum	bonōrum
Dat.	bonō	bonae	bonō	bonīs	bonīs	bonīs
Acc.	bonum	bonam	bonum	bonōs	bonās	bona
Voc.	bone	bona	bonum	bonī	bonae	bona
Abl.	bonō	bonā	bonō	bonīs	bonīs	bonīs .

c. Distributive adjectives are declined like **bonus** except that in the genitive plural they have -**um** instead of -**ōrum**, as **quadrāgēnum**, *of forty each.*

d. A few adjectives are declined like **puer, via, bellum**, as **miser, misera, miserum**, *wretched:*

	SINGULAR			PLURAL		
	MASCULINE	FEMININE	NEUTER	MASCULINE	FEMININE	NEUTER
Nom.	miser	misera	miserum	miserī	miserae	misera
Gen.	miserī	miserae	miserī	miserōrum	miserārum	miserōrum
Dat.	miserō	miserae	miserō	miserīs	miserīs	miserīs
Acc.	miserum	miseram	miserum	miserōs	miserās	misera
Voc.	miser	misera	miserum	miserī	miserae	misera
Abl.	miserō	miserā	miserō	miserīs	miserīs	miserīs

e. Like **miser** are declined **līber**, *free*, and **tener**, *tender.*

f. Declined like **ager, via, bellum** are most adjectives in -**er**, as **aeger, aegra, aegrum**, *sick*, **integer**, etc. :

	SINGULAR			PLURAL		
	MASCULINE	FEMININE	NEUTER	MASCULINE	FEMININE	NEUTER
Nom.	aeger	aegra	aegrum	aegrī	aegrae	aegra
Gen.	aegrī	aegrae	aegrī	aegrōrum	aegrārum	aegrōrum
Dat.	aegrō	aegrae	aegrō	aegrīs	aegrīs	aegrīs
Acc.	aegrum	aegram	aegrum	aegrōs	aegrās	aegra
Voc.	aeger	aegra	aegrum	aegrī	aegrae	aegra
Abl.	aegrō	aegrā	aegrō	aegrīs	aegrīs	aegrīs

23. *a.* Six adjectives in -**us** (**ūnus**, *one ;* **sōlus**, *alone ;* **tōtus**, *whole ;* **alius**, *other ;* **ūllus**, *any ;* **nūllus**, *none*) and three in -**er** (**alter**, *the other ;* **ūter**, *which (of two)* ? and **neuter**, *neither*, have -**īus** (or -**ius**) in the genitive and -**ī** in the dative singular of all genders, and lack the vocative ; the plural is regular. They are thus declined in the singular :

	SINGULAR			SINGULAR		
	MASCULINE	FEMININE	NEUTER	MASCULINE	FEMININE	NEUTER
Nom.	alius	alia	aliud	alter	altera	alterum
Gen.	[alīus	alīus	alīus]	alterius	alterius	alterius
Dat.	aliī	aliī	aliī	alterī	alterī	alterī
Acc.	alium	aliam	aliud	alterum	alteram	alterum
Abl.	aliō	aliā	aliō	alterō	alterā	alterō

	SINGULAR			SINGULAR		
	MASCULINE	FEMININE	NEUTER	MASCULINE	FEMININE	NEUTER
Nom.	tōtus	tōta	tōtum	uter	utra	utrum
Gen.	tōtīus	tōtīus	tōtīus	utrīus	utrīus	utrīus
Dat.	tōtī	tōtī	tōtī	utrī	utrī	utrī
Acc.	tōtum	tōtam	tōtum	utrum	utram	utrum
Abl.	tōtō	tōtā	tōtō	utrō	utrā	utrō

b. The genitive singular of **alter** is generally **alterius**, instead of **alterīus** ; and **alterius** is ordinarily used in place of the genitive **alīus**.

24. Some adjectives of the third declension have three endings in the nominative singular, others two, and others only one. Adjectives with three endings are declined like **ācer, ācris, ācre,** *sharp:*

	SINGULAR			PLURAL		
	MASCULINE	FEMININE	NEUTER	MASCULINE	FEMININE	NEUTER
Nom.	ācer	ācris	ācre	ācrēs	ācrēs	ācria
Gen.	ācris	ācris	ācris	ācrium	ācrium	ācrium
Dat.	ācrī	ācrī	ācrī	ācribus	ācribus	ācribus
Acc.	ācrem	ācrem	ācre	ācrēs, -īs	ācrēs, -īs	ācria
Voc.	ācer	ācris	ācre	ācrēs	ācrēs	ācria
Abl.	ācrī	ācrī	ācrī	ācribus	ācribus	ācribus

25. *a.* Adjectives of the third declension with two endings are in part formed on -i stems, like nouns, and in the positive degree, as **fortis, forte,** *strong;* in part they are comparatives formed on -s stems (**13.** *a*), as **fortior, fortius,** *stronger,* **melior, melius,** *better:*

	SINGULAR		PLURAL	
	MASCULINE AND FEM.	NEUTER	MASCULINE AND FEM.	NEUTER
Nom.	fortis	forte	fortēs	fortia
Gen.	fortis	fortis	fortium	fortium
Dat.	fortī	fortī	fortibus	fortibus
Acc.	fortem	forte	fortēs or -īs	fortia
Voc.	fortis	forte	fortēs	fortia
Abl.	fortī	fortī	fortibus	fortibus

NOTE. — Many adjectives of two endings have also -e in the ablative. This is found chiefly in verse, and rarely in classical prose. However, when these adjectives become proper names, -e is the rule. The genitive plural is rarely -um for -ium.

	SINGULAR		PLURAL	
	MASCULINE AND FEM.	NEUTER	MASCULINE AND FEM.	NEUTER
Nom.	melior	melius	meliōrēs	meliōra
Gen.	meliōris	meliōris	meliōrum	meliōrum
Dat.	meliōrī	meliōrī	meliōribus	meliōribus
Acc.	meliōrem	melius	meliōrēs or -īs	meliōra
Voc.	melior	melius	meliōrēs	meliōra
Abl.	meliōre	meliōre	meliōribus	meliōribus

b. **Plūs,** *more,* is defective, in the singular, having only the neuter forms, *Nom.* **plūs,** *Gen.* **plūris,** *Acc.* **plūs,** *Abl.* **plūre** ; the plural is declined : *Nom.* **plūrēs, plūra,** *Gen.* **plūrium, plūrium,** *Dat.* **plūribus, plūribus,** *Acc.* **plūrēs or plūrīs, plūra,** *Abl.* **plūribus, plūribus.**

26. *a.* With adjectives of the third declension having one ending in the nominative singular are included also present participles. Examples are **duplex,** *double,* **regēns,** *ruling,* and **vetus,** *old :*

	SINGULAR		PLURAL	
	MASCULINE AND FEM.	NEUTER	MASCULINE AND FEM.	NEUTER
Nom.	duplex	duplex	duplicēs	duplicia
Gen.	duplicis	duplicis	duplicium	duplicium
Dat.	duplicī	duplicī	duplicibus	duplicibus
Acc.	duplicem	duplex	duplicēs or -īs	duplicia
Voc.	duplex	duplex	duplicēs	duplicia
Abl.	duplicī	duplicī	duplicibus	duplicibus

	SINGULAR		PLURAL	
	MASCULINE AND FEM.	NEUTER	MASCULINE AND FEM.	NEUTER
Nom.	regēns	regēns	regentēs	regentia
Gen.	regentis	regentis	regentium	regentium
Dat.	regentī	regentī	regentibus	regentibus
Acc.	regentem	regēns	regentēs or -īs	regentia
Voc.	regēns	regēns	regentēs	regentia
Abl.	regente (participle) regentī (adjective)	regente (participle) regentī (adjective)	regentibus	regentibus

	SINGULAR		PLURAL	
	MASCULINE AND FEM.	NEUTER	MASCULINE AND FEM.	NEUTER
Nom.	vetus	vetus	veterēs	vetera
Gen.	veteris	veteris	veterum	veterum
Dat.	veterī	veterī	veteribus	veteribus
Acc.	veterem	vetus	veterēs	vetera
Voc.	vetus	vetus	veterēs	vetera
Abl.	vetere	vetere	veteribus	veteribus

b. The adjective **prīnceps, -cipis** is declined like the noun (**10.** *b*) ; the adjectives **anceps, ancipitis, particeps, -cipis,** and **praeceps, -cipitis** also have an increase in the oblique cases.

COMPARISON OF ADJECTIVES

27. *a.* Examples of the regular comparison of adjectives, and of participles used as adjectives, are :

POSITIVE	COMPARATIVE	SUPERLATIVE
altus, -a, -um, *high*	altior, altius, *higher*	altissimus, -a, -um, *very high, highest*
antīquus, -a, -um, *ancient*	antīquior, -ius	antīquissimus
fortis, -e, *brave*	fortior, fortius	fortissimus
nōbilis, -e, *noble*	nōbilior, nōbilius	nōbilissimus
ferāx, *fertile*	ferācior, ferācius	ferācissimus
potēns, *able*	potentior, potentius	potentissimus
apertus, *open*	apertior, apertius	apertissimus

b. **Novus,** *new,* lacks the comparative, but has a superlative, **novissimus,** *last.*

28. *a.* Examples of adjectives in -**er,** with comparative in -**ior** and superlative in -**rimus,** are :

POSITIVE	COMPARATIVE	SUPERLATIVE
asper, aspera, -rum, *rough*	asperior, -ius	asperrimus, -a, -um
celer, celeris, -ere, *swift*	celerior, -ius	celerrimus
crēber, -bra, -brum, *frequent*	crēbrior, crēbrius	crēberrimus
pulcher, -chra, -chrum, *beautiful*	pulchrior, -ius	pulcherrimus

b. **Vetus,** *Gen.* **veteris,** *old,* sup. **veterrimus,** lacks the comparative.

29. Six adjectives in -**ilis** have -**limus** in the superlative : **facilis, difficilis, gracilis, humilis, similis, dissimilis** :

POSITIVE	COMPARATIVE	SUPERLATIVE
facilis, -e, *easy*	facilior, facilius	facillimus, -a, -um
difficilis, -e, *difficult*	difficilior, -ius	difficillimus
humilis, -e, *low*	humilior, -ius	humillimus
similis, -e, *like*	similior, -ius	simillimus

30. A comparative and superlative are sometimes formed by prefixing **magis,** *more,* and **maximē,** *most,* as **magis dīvīnus,** *more divine,* and **maximē digna,** *most worthy.*

31. The adjectives **dīves** or **dīs**, *rich*, **honōrificus**, *complimentary*, and **magnificus**, *splendid* are thus compared :

POSITIVE	COMPARATIVE	SUPERLATIVE
dīves or dīs	dīvitior or dītior	dīvitissimus or dītissimus
honōrificus	honōrificentior	honorificentissimus
magnificus	magnificentior	magnificentissimus

32. Several common adjectives are irregular in comparison :

POSITIVE	COMPARATIVE	SUPERLATIVE
bonus, -a, -um, *good*	melior, melius, *better*	optimus, -a, -um, *best*
malus, *bad*	peior, peius, *worse*	pessimus, *worst, very bad*
parvus, *small*	minor, minus, *less*	minimus, *least*
magnus, *great*	maior, maius, *greater*	maximus, *greatest*
multus, *much*	plūs, gen. plūris (25, b)	plūrimus, *most*

33. Several adjectives lack the positive, though the stem appears in prepositions and adverbs ; others have a positive only in a limited or special use. Examples are :

POSITIVE	COMPARATIVE	SUPERLATIVE
(citrā, *on this side*)	citerior, citerius, *on this side, hither*	citimus, -a, -um, *nearest*
(ultrā, *beyond*)	ulterior, ulterius, *farther*	ultimus, *farthest*
(intrā, *within*)	interior, interius, *inner*	intimus, *inmost*
(prope, *near*)	propior, propius, *nearer*	proximus, *nearest*
(dē, *down*)	dēterior, dēterius, *inferior*	dēterrimus, *worst*
(prae, prō, *before*)	prior, prius, *former*	prīmus, *first*
posterus, *following*	posterior, *later*	postrēmus, *latest, last*
īnferus, *below*	īnferior, īnferius, *lower*	īnfimus, / īmus, } *lowest*
superus, *above*	superior, superius, *higher*	suprēmus, *last* / summus, *highest*
exterus, *foreign*	exterior, *outer*	extrēmus, *outermost*

ADVERBS

34. *a.* Adverbs regularly formed from adjectives have the positive in -ē (-ĕ in **facile**) or -ter, the comparative in -ius, and the superlative in -ē :

POSITIVE	COMPARATIVE	SUPERLATIVE
amplē (amplus), *fully*	amplius, *more fully*	amplissimē, *most fully*
aegrē (aeger), *ill*	aegrius	aegerrimē
mātūrē (mātūrus), *early*	mātūrius	mātūrrimē
facile (facilis), *easily*	facilius	facillimē
fortiter (fortis), *bravely*	fortius	fortissimē
audācter (audāx), *boldly*	audācius	audācissimē
ācriter (ācer), *fiercely*	ācrius	ācerrimē

b. Some adverbs formed from adjectives end in -ō (-ŏ in **cito**) as **continuō, subitō, prīmō** ; such, with comparative and superlative are :

POSITIVE	COMPARATIVE	SUPERLATIVE
crēbrō (crēber), *frequently*	crēbrius	crēberrimē
tūtō (tūtus), *safely*	tūtius	tūtissimē
cito (citus), *quickly*	citius	citissimē

c. A few adverbs formed from adjectives end in -um (acc. singular neuter), as **multum** (**multus**), *much*, **plūrimum**, *very greatly;* in -tim, as **prīvātim** (**prīvātus**), *privately;* and in -tus, as **dīvīnitus** (**dīvīnus**), *by divine power.*

35. The following adverbs have irregularities in formation or in comparison :

POSITIVE	COMPARATIVE	SUPERLATIVE
bene, *well*	melius, *better*	optimē, *best*
male, *ill*	peius, *worse*	pessimē, *worst*
magnopere, *greatly*	magis, *more*	maximē, *most*
multum, *much*	plūs, *more*	plūrimum, *most*
nōn multum, parum, } *little*	minus, *less*	minimē, *least*
nūper, *recently*	——	nūperrimē, *most recently,* **very** *recently*
diū, *long*	diūtius, *longer*	diūtissimē, *longest*
saepe, *often*	saepius, *oftener*	saepissimē, *most often, oftenest*
prope, *near*	propius, *nearer*	proximē, *nearest, next*
——	potius, *rather*	potissimum, *especially, above all*
satis, *enough*	satius, *better*	——
——	prius, *before*	prīmum, *first*

NUMERALS

36. The Roman notation, and cardinal, ordinal, and distributive adjectives are presented in the following list :

ROMAN NOTATION	CARDINALS	ORDINALS	DISTRIBUTIVES
I	ūnus, ūna, ūnum	prīmus, *first*	singulī, *one by one*
II	duo, duae, duo	secundus, *second*	bīnī, *two each*
III	trēs, tria, *three*	tertius, *third*	ternī, trīnī, *three by three, three each*
IIII or IV	} quattuor, *four*	quārtus, *fourth*	quaternī, *four by four, four each*
V	quīnque, *five*	quīntus, *fifth*	quīnī, *five by five, five each*
VI	sex, *six*	sextus, *sixth*	sēnī, *six by six, six each*
VII	septem, *seven*	septimus, *seventh*	septēnī, *by sevens, seven each*
VIII	octō, *eight*	octāvus, *eighth*	octōnī, *by eights, eight apiece*
VIIII or IX	} novem, *nine*	nōnus, *ninth*	novēnī, *nine each*
X	decem, *ten*	decimus, *tenth*	dēnī, *ten each*
XI	ūndecim, *eleven*	ūndecimus, *eleventh*	ūndēnī, *eleven each*
XII	duodecim, *twelve*	duodecimus, *twelfth*	duodēnī, *twelve each*
XIII	tredecim, *thirteen*	tertius decimus, *thirteenth*	ternī dēnī, *thirteen each*
XIIII or XIV	} quattuordecim, *fourteen*	quārtus decimus, *fourteenth*	quaternī dēnī, *fourteen each*
XV	quīndecim, *fifteen*	quīntus decimus, *fifteenth*	quīnī dēnī, *fifteen each*
XVI	sēdecim, *sixteen*	sextus decimus, *sixteenth*	sēnī dēnī, *sixteen each*
XVII	septendecim, *seventeen*	septimus decimus, *seventeenth*	septēnī dēnī, *seventeen each*
XVIII	duodēvīgintī, *eighteen*	duodēvīcēsimus, *eighteenth*	duodēvīcēnī, *eighteen each*

Roman Notation	Cardinals	Ordinals	Distributives
XVIIII or XIX	ūndēvīgintī, *nineteen*	ūndēvīcēsimus, *nineteenth*	ūndēvīcēnī, *nineteen each*
XX	vīgintī, *twenty*	vīcēsimus, *twentieth*	vīcēnī, *twenty each*
XXI	vīgintī ūnus, ūnus et vīgintī, *twenty-one*	vīcēsimus prīmus ūnus et vīcēsimus, *twenty-first*	vīcēnī singulī, singulī et vīcēnī, *twenty-one each*
XXII	vīgintī duo, duo et vīgintī, *twenty-two*	vīcēsimus secundus, alter et vīcēsimus, *twenty-second*	vīcēnī bīnī, bīnī et vīcēnī, *twenty-two each*
XXX	trīgintā, *thirty*	trīcēsimus, *thirtieth*	trīcēnī, *thirty each*
XXXX or XL	quadrāgintā, *forty*	quadrāgēsimus, *fortieth*	quadrāgēnī, *forty each*
L	quīnquāgintā, *fifty*	quīnquāgēsimus, *fiftieth*	quīnquāgēnī, *fifty each*
LX	sexāgintā, *sixty*	sexāgēsimus	sexāgēnī, *sixty each*
LXX	septuāgintā, *seventy*	septuāgēsimus, *seventieth*	septuāgēnī, *seventy each*
LXXX	octōgintā, *eighty*	octōgēsimus, *eightieth*	octōgēnī, *eighty each*
LXXXX or XC	nōnāgintā, *ninety*	nōnāgēsimus, *nine-tieth*	nōnāgēnī, *ninety each*
C	centum, *one hundred*	centēsimus, *one hundredth*	centēnī, *one hundred each*
CI	centum ūnus, centum et ūnus, *one hundred and one*	centēsimus prīmus, centēsimus et prīmus, *hundred and first*	centēnī singulī, *one hundred and one each*
CC	ducentī, -ae, -a, *two hundred*	ducentēsimus, *two hundredth*	ducēnī, *two hundred each*
CCC	trecentī, -ae, -a, *three hundred*	trecentēsimus, *three hundredth*	trecēnī, *three hundred each*
CCCC	quadringentī, *four hundred*	quadringentēsimus, *four hundredth*	quadringēnī *four hundred each*
D	quīngentī, *five hundred*	quīngentēsimus, *five hundredth*	quīngēnī, *five hundred each*

Roman Notation	Cardinals	Ordinals	Distributives
DC	sescentī, *six hundred*	sescentēsimus, *six hundredth*	sescēnī, *six hundred each*
DCC	septingentī, *seven hundred*	septingentēsimus, *seven hundredth*	septingēnī, *seven hundred each*
DCCC	octingentī, *eight hundred*	octingentēsimus, *eight hundredth*	octingēnī, *eight hundred each*
DCCCC	nōngentī, *nine hundred*	nōngentēsimus, *nine hundredth*	nōngēnī, *nine hundred each*
M	mīlle, *thousand*	mīllēsimus, *thousandth*	singula mīlia, *a thousand each*
MM	duo mīlia, *two thousand*	bis mīllēsimus, *two thousandth*	bīna mīlia, *two thousand each*

37. *a.* **Ūnus** is declined like **tōtus (23.** *a.***)**

b. **Duo** and **trēs** are declined thus :

Nom.	duo	duae	duo	trēs	tria
Gen.	duōrum	duārum	duōrum	trium	trium
Dat.	duōbus	duābus	duōbus	tribus	tribus
Acc.	duōs, duo	duās	duo	trēs, trīs	tria
Abl.	duōbus	duābus	duōbus	tribus	tribus

c. Like **duo** is declined **ambō**, except -ō instead of -o.

d. **Ducentī, -ae, -a** and the other words for *hundreds* to **nōngentī, -ae, -a** are declined like the plural of **bonus**, but the genitive plural generally ends in **-um.**

e. When plural nouns, which generally have a singular meaning are used with a plural meaning, a numeral in agreement must be distributive ; with such nouns **trīnī** is always used instead of **ternī.** Thus, **trīnīs litterīs,** *with three letters.*

38. *a.* **Mīlle** in the singular is ordinarily used as an indeclinable adjective ; sometimes as a substantive, as **hominum mīlle,** a *thousand (of) men.* In the plural it is used as a substantive and thus declined :

Nom. mīlia   *Gen.* mīlium   *Dat.* mīlibus   *Acc.* mīlia   *Abl.* mīlibus

b. The Roman numerical symbols are frequently used in place of ordinal as well as cardinal adjectives. In reading Latin the proper form of the adjective should be supplied ; thus, HS. $\overline{\text{XX}}$CD (or XXCD) should be read as **sēstertia vīcēna et quadringentōs sēstertiōs.**

PRONOUNS

39. *a.* The personal pronouns of the first and second person are declined as follows :

	SINGULAR	PLURAL	SINGULAR	PLURAL
Nom.	ego, *I*	nōs, *we*	tū, *thou*	vōs, *you*
Gen.	meī	nostrum, nostrī	tuī	vestrum, vestrī
Dat.	mihi	nōbīs	tibi	vōbīs
Acc.	mē	nōs	tē	vōs
Voc.	——	——	tū	vōs
Abl.	mē	nōbīs	tē	vōbīs

b. The place of a personal pronoun of the third person is taken by the demonstratives (**160.** *a* and *b*).

40. *a.* In the oblique cases the pronouns of the first and second person may be used in a reflexive sense, as **mē condemnō,** *I condemn myself;* **meī,** may mean *of myself,* **tibi,** *to* or *for thyself, yourself,* etc.

b. The reflexive pronoun of the third person has no separate forms for the three genders, and is declined in singular and plural alike, as follows :

> *Gen.* **suī,** *of himself, of herself, of itself, of themselves*
> *Dat.* **sibi,** *to* or *for himself, herself, itself, themselves*
> *Acc.* **sē** or **sēsē,** *himself, herself, itself, themselves*
> *Abl.* **sē** or **sēsē,** *with,* or *by, himself, herself, itself, themselves*

41. The possessive pronouns are declined like adjectives. They are : **meus, mea, meum,** *my ;* **noster, nostra, nostrum,** *our ;* **tuus tua, tuum,** *thy ;* **vester, vestra, vestrum,** *your ;* and **suus, sua, suum,** *his, her, its, their.* Suus is used only in a reflexive sense.

42. *a.* The demonstrative pronouns are **hīc,** *this, such ;* **iste,** *that of yours, that ;* **ille,** *that, such ;* **is,** *that, he, such,* and **īdem,** *the same.*

b. **Hīc,** *this, such,* is declined thus :

	SINGULAR			PLURAL		
	MASCULINE	FEMININE	NEUTER	MASCULINE	FEMININE	NEUTER
Nom.	hic	haec	hoc	hī	hae	haec
Gen.	huius	huius	huius	hōrum	hārum	hōrum
Dat.	huic	huic	huic	hīs	hīs	hīs
Acc.	hunc	hanc	hoc	hōs	hās	haec
Abl.	hōc	hāc	hōc	hīs	hīs	hīs

43. *a.* The demonstrative pronoun **ille**, *that, such,* is declined as follows :

	SINGULAR			PLURAL		
	MASCULINE	FEMININE	NEUTER	MASCULINE	FEMININE	NEUTER
Nom.	ille	illa	illud	illī	illae	illa
Gen.	illīus	illīus	illīus	illōrum	illārum	illōrum
Dat.	illī	illī	illī	illīs	illīs	illīs
Acc.	illum	illam	illud	illōs	illās	illa
Abl.	illō	illā	illō	illīs	illīs	illīs

b. The demonstrative pronoun **iste, ista, istud**, *that of yours, that,* is declined like **ille**.

44. The determinative pronoun **is**, *that, he, such,* is thus declined :

	SINGULAR			PLURAL		
	MASCULINE	FEMININE	NEUTER	MASCULINE	FEMININE	NEUTER
Nom.	is	ea	id	eī, iī,	eae	ea
Gen.	eius	eius	eius	eōrum	eārum	eōrum
Dat.	eī	eī	eī	eīs, iīs	eīs, iīs	eīs, iīs
Acc.	eum	eam	id	eōs	eās	ea
Abl.	eō	eā	eō	eīs, iīs	eīs, iīs	eīs, iīs

45. The demonstrative pronoun **īdem**, *the same,* is declined as follows :

	SINGULAR			PLURAL		
	MASCULINE	FEMININE	NEUTER	MASCULINE	FEMININE	NEUTER
Nom.	īdem	eadem	idem	eīdem, iīdem, *or* īdem	eaedem	eadem
Gen.	eiusdem	eiusdem	eiusdem	eōrundem	eārundem	eōrundem
Dat.	eīdem	eīdem	eīdem	eīsdem, iīsdem, *or* īsdem	eīsdem, iīsdem, *or* īsdem	eīsdem, iīsdem, *or* īsdem
Acc.	eundem	eandem	idem	eōsdem	eāsdem	eadem
Abl.	eōdem	eādem	eōdem	eīsdem, iīsdem, *or* īsdem	eīsdem, iīsdem, *or* īsdem	eīsdem, iīsdem, *or* īsdem

46. The intensive pronoun **ipse**, *self*, is thus declined :

| | SINGULAR | | | PLURAL | | |
	MASCULINE	FEMININE	NEUTER	MASCULINE	FEMININE	NEUTER
Nom.	ipse	ipsa	ipsum	ipsī	ipsae	ipsa
Gen.	ipsīus	ipsīus	ipsīus	ipsōrum	ipsārum	ipsōrum
Dat.	ipsī	ipsī	ipsī	ipsīs	ipsīs	ipsīs
Acc.	ipsum	ipsam	ipsum	ipsōs	ipsās	ipsa
Abl.	ipsō	ipsā	ipsō	ipsīs	ipsīs	ipsīs

47. The relative pronoun **quī**, *who, which*, is declined as follows :

| | SINGULAR | | | PLURAL | | |
	MASCULINE	FEMININE	NEUTER	MASCULINE	FEMININE	NEUTER
Nom.	quī	quae	quod	quī	quae	quae
Gen.	cuius	cuius	cuius	quōrum	quārum	quōrum
Dat.	cui	cui	cui	quibus	quibus	quibus
Acc.	quem	quam	quod	quōs	quās	quae
Abl.	quō	quā	quō	quibus	quibus	quibus

48. *a.* The substantive interrogative pronoun is **quis, quid**, *who? what?* It is declined as follows :

| | SINGULAR | | PLURAL | | |
	MASC. AND FEM.	NEUTER	MASCULINE	FEMININE	NEUTER
Nom.	quis	quid	quī	quae	quae
Gen.	cuius	cuius	quōrum	quārum	quōrum
Dat.	cui	cui	quibus	quibus	quibus
Acc.	quem	quid	quōs	quās	quae
Abl.	quō	quō	quibus	quibus	quibus

b. The adjective interrogative pronoun is **quī, quae, quod**, *what?* It is declined like the relative pronoun (**47**).

c. Interrogative **quis** and **quī** may be strengthened by -**nam**, as **quemnam**, *whom, then.*

49. *a.* The indefinite pronouns follow the declension of the relative and interrogative pronouns, but only the pronominal part of the compounds is declined. The following indefinite pronouns are used in both substantive and adjective forms :

SUBSTANTIVE FORMS			ADJECTIVE FORMS		
MASC. AND FEM.	NEUT.		MASC.	FEM.	NEUT.
quis *or* qui (Masc.)	quid	{ *anyone,* *anything*	qui *or* quis	quae *or* qua *Nom.* and *Acc.* Pl. Neut., quae *or* qua	quod } *any*
aliquis aliqui	aliquid	{ *someone* *something*	aliqui	aliqua	aliquod } *any*
quispiam	quidpiam	{ *someone,* *some-* *thing*	quispiam	quaepiam	quodpiam } *some*
quisquam	quicquam	{ *anyone,* *anything* *at all*	quisquam		quicquam } *any* (*rare*)
(Plural lacking.)			(Plural lacking.)		
quisque	quidque	{ *each one,* *each thing*	quisque	quaeque	quodque } *each*
quīvīs quaevīs quidvīs *Acc.* quemvīs quam- vīs quidvīs		{ *anyone,* *anything* *you please*	quīvīs *Acc.* quemvīs quodvis	quaevīs quamvīs	quodvīs } *any you please*
quīdam quaedam quiddam *Acc.* quendam quandam quiddam		{ *a cer-* *tain* *person* *or* *thing*	quīdam *Acc.* quendam	quaedam quandam quoddam	quoddam } *a cer-* *tain*

b. The indefinite pronoun **quis, quī,** is used mostly after **sī, nisī, seu, nē,** and **num.** It never begins a clause or a sentence.

50. a. The indefinite relative **quīcumque, quaecumque, quod-cumque,** *whoever, whatever,* the first part **quī-** being declined like the relative **quī,** is used both as an adjective and as a substantive ; **quaecumque fortūna,** *whatsoever fortune,* **ad quōscumque,** *to whomever.*

b. The parts of the indefinite relative **quisquis, quidquid,** or **quicquid,** *whoever, whatever,* are both declined like **quis (48)**, but only **quisquis, quicquid,** and **quōquō** are in common use, as **quicquid est,** *whatever it is* ; **quōquō modō,** *in whatever way.*

51. Cicero uses two compounds of **uter (23.** a) with the force of indefinite pronouns, **uterque, utraque, utrumque (utrīusque,** etc.), *each* of two. Plural *both, the two ;* and **alteruter, alterutra, alterutrum,** *one or the other.*

VERBS[1]

52. The verb **sum** is inflected as follows:

PRINCIPAL PARTS:

PRES. INDICATIVE	PRES. INFINITIVE	PERF. INDICATIVE	FUT. PART. (Perf. Part. lacking)
sum	**esse**	**fuī**	**futūrus**

INDICATIVE MOOD

PRESENT

SINGULAR	PLURAL
sum, *I am*	**sumus**, *we are*
es, *you are*	**estis**, *you are*
est, *he (she, it) is*	**sunt**, *they are*

IMPERFECT

eram, *I was*	**erāmus**, *we were*
erās, *you were*	**erātis**, *you were*
erat, *he was*	**erant**, *they were*

FUTURE

erō, *I shall be*	**erimus**, *we shall be*
eris, *you will be*	**eritis**, *you will be*
erit, *he will be*	**erunt**, *they will be*

PERFECT

fuī, *I have been,* *I was*	**fuimus**, *we have been, we were*
fuistī, *thou hast been, you were*	**fuistis**, *you have been, you were*
fuit, *he has been, he was*	**fuērunt**, **fuēre**, { *they have been, they were* }

PLUPERFECT

fueram, *I had been*	**fuerāmus**, *we had been*
fuerās, *thou hadst, you had, been*	**fuerātis**, *you had been*
fuerat, *he had been*	**fuerant**, *they had been*

SUBJUNCTIVE

PRESENT

SINGULAR	PLURAL
sim	**sīmus**
sīs	**sītis**
sit	**sint**

IMPERFECT

essem	**essēmus**
essēs	**essētis**
esset	**essent**

PERFECT

fuerim	**fuerīmus**
fuerīs	**fuerītis**
fuerit	**fuerint**

PLUPERFECT

fuissem	**fuissēmus**
fuissēs	**fuissētis**
fuisset	**fuissent**

[1] Since the principal parts of all the verbs in the Latin text of this book are given in the vocabulary, it has not been thought necessary to extend this outline by presenting either a list of verbs or a discussion of the stems.

INDICATIVE MOOD

FUTURE PERFECT

fuerō, *I shall have been*   fuerimus, *we shall have been*
fueris, *thou wilt have been*   fueritis, *you will have been*
fuerit, *he will have been*   fuerint, *they will have been*

IMPERATIVE

Pres. es, *be thou*   este, *be ye*
Fut. estō, *thou shalt be*   estōte, *ye shall be*
     estō, *he shall be*   suntō, *they shall be*

INFINITIVE

Pres. esse, *to be*
Perf. fuisse, *to have been*
Fut. futūrus esse, *or* **fore,** *to be about to be*

PARTICIPLE

Fut. futūrus, *about to be*

FIRST CONJUGATION

53. Verbs of the first conjugation are inflected like **amō,** *I love.*

PRINCIPAL PARTS:

PRES. INDICATIVE	PRES. INFINITIVE	PERF. INDICATIVE	PERF. PASS. PARTICIPLE
Active. amō	amāre	amāvī	amātus

PRES. INDICATIVE	PRES. INFINITIVE	PERF. INDICATIVE
Passive. amor	amārī	amātus sum

ACTIVE VOICE

INDICATIVE MOOD

PRESENT

SINGULAR	PLURAL
amō, *I love*	amāmus, *we love*
amās, *you love*	amātis, *you love*
amat, *he loves*	amant, *they love*

PASSIVE VOICE

INDICATIVE MOOD

PRESENT

SINGULAR	PLURAL
I am loved, etc.	
amor	amāmur
amāris	amāminī
or -re	
amātur	amantur

ACTIVE VOICE
INDICATIVE MOOD

IMPERFECT

amābam, *I was loving*   amābāmus, *we were loving*

amābās, *you were loving*   amābātis, *you were loving*

amābat, *he was loving*   amābant, *they were loving*

FUTURE

amābō, *I shall love*   amābimus, *we shall love*

amābis, *thou wilt, you will, love*   amābitis, *you will love*

amābit, *he will love*   amābunt, *they will love*

PERFECT

amāvī, *I have loved, I loved*   amāvimus, *we have loved, we loved*

amāvistī, *you have loved, you loved*   amāvistis, *you have loved, you loved*

amāvit, *he has loved, he loved*   amāvērunt, -ēre, *they have loved, they loved*

PLUPERFECT

amāveram, *I had loved*   amāverāmus, *we had loved*

amāverās, *you had loved*   amāverātis, *you had loved*

amāverat, *he had loved*   amāverant, *they had loved*

FUTURE PERFECT

amāverō, *I shall have loved*   amāverimus, *we shall have loved*

amāveris, *you will have loved*   amāveritis, *you will have loved*

amāverit, *he will have loved*   amāverint, *they will have loved*

PASSIVE VOICE
INDICATIVE MOOD

IMPERFECT

I was loved, etc.

amābar   amābāmur

amābāris   amābāminī

or -re

amābātur   amābantur

FUTURE

I shall, you will, be loved, etc.

amābor   amābimur

amāberis,   amābiminī

or -re   amābuntur

amābitur

PERFECT

I have been loved or I was loved, etc.

amātus (-a, -um) sum   amātī (-ae, -a) sumus

amātus es   amātī estis

amātus est   amātī sunt

PLUPERFECT

I had been loved, etc.

amātus erām   amātī erāmus

amātus erās   amātī erātis

amātus erat   amātī erant

FUTURE PERFECT

I shall, you will have been loved

amātus erō   amātī erimus

amātus eris   amātī eritis

amātus erit   amātī erunt

ACTIVE VOICE		PASSIVE VOICE	
SUBJUNCTIVE		**SUBJUNCTIVE**	
PRESENT		PRESENT	

SINGULAR	PLURAL	SINGULAR	PLURAL
I may love, let us love, etc.		*I may be loved, etc.*	
amem	amēmus	amer	amēmur
amēs	amētis	amēris, *or* -re	amēminī
amet	ament	amētur	amentur

IMPERFECT		IMPERFECT	
I might love		*I might be loved*	
amārem	amārēmus	amārer	amārēmur
amārēs	amārētis	amārēris, *or* -re	amārēminī
amāret	amārent	amārētur	amārentur

PERFECT		PERFECT	
I may have loved		*I may have been loved*	
amāverim	amāverīmus	amātus sim [1]	amātī sīmus
amāverīs	amāverītis	amātus sīs	amātī sītis
amāverit	amāverint	amātus sit	amātī sint

PLUPERFECT		PLUPERFECT	
I might have loved		*I might have been loved*	
amāvissem	amāvissēmus	amātus essem [2]	amātī essēmus
amāvissēs	amāvissētis	amātus essēs	amātī essētis
amāvisset	amāvissent	amātus esset	amātī essent

IMPERATIVE

SINGULAR	PLURAL
Pres. amā, *love thou*	amāte, *love ye*
Fut. amātō, *thou shalt love*	amātōte, *ye shall love*
amātō, *he shall love*	amantō, *they shall love*

IMPERATIVE

SINGULAR

Pres. amāre, *be thou loved*
Fut. amātor, *thou shalt be loved*
amātor, *he shall be loved*

PLURAL

Pres. amāminī, *be ye loved*
Fut. amantor, *they shall be loved*

INFINITIVE

Pres. amāre, *to love*
Perf. amāvisse, *to have loved*
Fut. amātūrus esse, *to be about to love*

INFINITIVE

Pres. amārī, *to be loved*
Perf. amātus esse, *to have been loved*
Fut. amātum īrī, *to be about to be loved*

[1] Here **fuerim, fuerīs, fuissem,** *etc.,* are sometimes used for **sim, essem,** *etc.*

ACTIVE VOICE	PASSIVE VOICE
PARTICIPLE	**PARTICIPLE**

Pres. amāns, *loving (Gen.* amantis)   *Perfect* amātus, -a, -um, *loved having been loved*

Fut. amātūrus, -a, -um, *about to love*   *Gerundive* amandus, -a, -um, *to be loved, worthy to be loved*

GERUND	SUPINE

Gen. amandī, *of loving*   *Acc.* amātum, *to love*
Dat. amandō, *for loving*   *Abl.* amātū, *to love, to be loved*
Acc. amandum, *loving*
Abl. amandō, *by loving*

SECOND CONJUGATION

54. Verbs of the second conjugation are conjugated like **moneō,** *I advise.*

PRINCIPAL PARTS:

PRES. INDICATIVE	PRES. INFINITIVE	PERF. INDICATIVE	PERF. PASS. PARTICIPLE
Active. moneō	monēre	monuī	monitus

PRES. INDICATIVE	PRES. INFINITIVE	PERF. INDICATIVE
Passive. moneor	monērī	monitus sum

ACTIVE VOICE	PASSIVE VOICE
INDICATIVE MOOD	**INDICATIVE MOOD**
PRESENT TENSE	PRESENT TENSE

SINGULAR	PLURAL	SINGULAR	PLURAL
I advise, etc.		*I am advised,* etc.	
moneō	monēmus	moneor	monēmur
monēs	monētis	monēris *or* -re	monēminī
monet	monent	monētur	monentur

ÍMPERFECT	IMPERFECT
I was advising, or *I advised,* etc.	*I was advised,* etc.
monēbam monēbāmus	monēbar monēbāmur
monēbās monēbātis	monēbāris, *or* -re monēbāminī
monēbat monēbant	monēbātur monēbantur

7

ACTIVE VOICE		PASSIVE VOICE	
INDICATIVE MOOD		**INDICATIVE MOOD**	

FUTURE

I shall, you will, advise		*I shall, you will, be advised*	
monēbō	monēbimus	monēbor	monēbimur
monēbis	monēbitis	monēberis, *or* -re	monēbiminī
monēbit	monēbunt	monēbitur	monēbuntur

PERFECT

I have advised, or I advised		*I have been advised, I was advised*	
monuī	monuimus	monitus sum	monitī sumus
monuistī	monuistis	monitus es	monitī estis
monuit	monuērunt, *or* -ēre	monitus est	monitī sunt

PLUPERFECT

I had advised		*I had been advised*	
monueram	monuerāmus	monitus eram	monitī erāmus
monuerās	monuerātis	monitus erās	monitī erātis
monuerat	monuerant	monitus erat	monitī erant

FUTURE PERFECT

I shall, you will, have advised		*I shall, you will, have been advised*	
monuerō	monuerimus	monitus erō	monitī erimus
monueris	monueritis	monitus eris	monitī eritis
monuerit	monuerint	monitus erit	monitī erunt

SUBJUNCTIVE		**SUBJUNCTIVE**	

PRESENT

I may advise, let us advise, etc.		*I may be advised, etc.*	
moneam	moneāmus	monear	moneāmur
moneās	moneātis	moneāris, *or* -re	moneāminī
moneat	moneant	moneātur	moneantur

IMPERFECT

I might advise, you would advise, etc.		*I might be advised, etc.*	
monērem	monērēmus	monērer	monērēmur
monērēs	monērētis	monērēris, *or* -re	monērēminī
monēret	monērent	monērētur	monērentur

ACTIVE VOICE		PASSIVE VOICE	
SUBJUNCTIVE		**SUBJUNCTIVE**	

PERFECT

I may have advised, etc.		
monuerim	monuerīmus	
monuerīs	monuerītis	
monuerit	monuerint	

PERFECT

I may have been advised, etc.	
monitus sim	monitī sīmus
monitus sīs	monitī sītis
monitus sit	monitī sint

PLUPERFECT

I might have advised, you would have advised, etc.

monuissem	monuissēmus
monuissēs	monuissētis
monuisset	monuissent

PLUPERFECT

I might have been advised, etc.

monitus essem	monitī essēmus
monitus essēs	monitī essētis
monitus esset	monitī essent

IMPERATIVE

Pres.	monē, *advise thou*	monēte, *advise ye*
Fut.	monētō, *thou shalt advise*	monētōte, *ye shall advise*
	monētō, *he shall advise*	monentō, *they shall advise*

IMPERATIVE

Pres.	monēre, *be thou advised*	monēminī, *be ye advised*
Fut.	monētor, *thou shalt be advised*	
	monētor, *he shall be advised*	monentor, *they shall be advised*

INFINITIVE   PARTICIPLE

Pres.	monēre, *to advise*	*Pres.*	monēns, *advising* (Gen. monentis)
Perf.	monuisse, *to have advised*		
Fut.	monitūrus esse, *to be about to advise*	*Fut.*	monitūrus, -a, -um, *about to advise*

INFINITIVE   PARTICIPLE

Pres.	monērī, *to be advised*	*Perf.*	monitus, -a, -um *advised, having been advised*
Perf.	monitus esse, *to have been advised*		
Fut.	monitum īrī *to be about to be advised*	*Ger.*	monendus, -a, -um, *to be advised, worthy to be advised*

ACTIVE VOICE

GERUND	SUPINE
Gen. monendī, *of advising*	
Dat. monendō, *for advising*	
Acc. monendum, *advising*	*Acc.* monitum, *to advise*
Abl. monendō, *by advising,*	*Abl.* monitū, *to advise, to be advised*

THIRD CONJUGATION

55. Verbs of the third conjugation are inflected like **regō,** *I rule.*

PRINCIPAL PARTS:

PRES. INDICATIVE	PRES. INFINITIVE	PERF. INDICATIVE	PERF. PASS. PARTIC
Active. regō	regere	rēxī	rēctus

PRES. INDICATIVE	PRES. INFINITIVE	PERF. INDICATIVE
Passive. regor	regī	rēctus sum

ACTIVE VOICE	PASSIVE VOICE
INDICATIVE MOOD	**INDICATIVE MOOD**
PRESENT TENSE	PRESENT TENSE
I rule, etc.	*I am ruled,* etc.

SINGULAR	PLURAL	SINGULAR	PLURAL
regō	regimus	regor	regimur
regis	regitis	regeris *or* -re	regiminī
regit	regunt	regitur	reguntur

IMPERFECT		IMPERFECT	
I was ruling, or *I ruled*		*I was ruled*	
regēbam	regēbāmus	regēbar	regēbāmur
regēbās	regēbātis	regēbāris, *or* -re	regēbāminī
regēbat	regēbant	regēbātur	regēbantur

ACTIVE VOICE		PASSIVE VOICE	
INDICATIVE MOOD		**INDICATIVE MOOD**	
FUTURE		FUTURE	
I shall rule, you will rule, etc.		*I shall, you will, be ruled*	
regam	regēmus	regar	regēmur
regēs	regētis	regēris, *or* -re	regēminī
reget	regent	regētur	regentur

PERFECT		PERFECT	
I have ruled, or I ruled		*I have been ruled, or I was ruled*	
rēxī	rēximus	rēctus sum	rēctī sumus
rēxistī	rēxistis	rēctus es	rēctī estis
rēxit	rēxērunt, *or* -ēre	rēctus est	rēctī sunt

PLUPERFECT		PLUPERFECT	
I had ruled		*I had been ruled*	
rēxeram	rēxerāmus	rēctus eram	rēctī erāmus
rēxerās	rēxerātis	rēctus erās	rēctī erātis
rēxerat	rēxerant	rēctus erat	rēctī erant

FUTURE PERFECT		FUTURE PERFECT	
I shall, you will, have ruled		*I shall, you will, have been ruled*	
rēxerō	rēxerimus	rēctus erō	rēctī erimus
rēxeris	rēxeritis	rēctus eris	rēctī eritis
rēxerit	rēxerint	rēctus erit	rēctī erunt

ACTIVE VOICE		PASSIVE VOICE	
SUBJUNCTIVE		**SUBJUNCTIVE**	
PRESENT		PRESENT	
I may rule, let us rule, etc.		*I may be ruled,* etc.	
SINGULAR	PLURAL	SINGULAR	PLURAL
regam	regāmus	regar	regāmur
regās	regātis	regāris, *or* -re	regāminī
regat	regant	regātur	regantur

IMPERFECT		IMPERFECT	
I might rule, you would rule, etc.		*I might be ruled, you would be ruled*	
regerem	regerēmus	regerer	regerēmur
regerēs	regerētis	regerēris, *or* -re	regerēminī
regeret	regerent	regerētur	regerentur

ACTIVE VOICE		PASSIVE VOICE	
SUBJUNCTIVE		**SUBJUNCTIVE**	

PERFECT

I may have ruled

rēxerim	rēxerīmus
rēxerīs	rēxerītis
rēxerit	rēxerint

PERFECT

I may have been ruled

rēctus sim	rēctī sīmus
rēctus sīs	rēctī sītis
rēctus sit	rēctī sint

PLUPERFECT

*I might have ruled, you would have
ruled*

rēxissem	rēxissēmus
rēxissēs	rēxissētis
rēxisset	rēxissent

PLUPERFECT

*I might have been ruled, you would
have been ruled*

rēctus essem	rectī essēmus
rēctus essēs	rectī essētis
rēctus esset	rectī essent

IMPERATIVE

Pres. rege, *rule*   regite, *rule ye*
thou

Fut. regitō, *thou* regitōte, *ye shall*
shalt rule   rule

regitō, *he*   reguntō, *they*
shall rule   shall rule

IMPERATIVE

Pres. regere, *be*   regiminī, *be ye*
thou ruled   ruled

Fut. regitor, *thou*
shalt be
ruled

regitor, *he*   reguntor, *they*
shall be   shall be ruled
ruled

INFINITIVE   PARTICIPLE

Pres. regere, *to*   *Pres.* regēns,
rule   ruling

Perf. rēxisse, *to*   (*Gen.* re-
have ruled   gentis)

Fut. rēctūrus esse, *Fut.* rēctūrus,
to be about   -a, -um,
to rule   about to
rule

INFINITIVE   PARTICIPLE

Pres. regī, *to be*   *Perfect,* rēctus
ruled   -a, -um, *ruled,*

Perf. rēctus esse,   having   been
to have   ruled
been   *Gerundive*
ruled   regendus, -a

Fut. rēctum īrī, *to*   -um, *to be*
be about to   ruled, deserving
be ruled   to be ruled

ACTIVE VOICE

GERUND	SUPINE

Gen. regendī, *of ruling*
Dat. regendō, *for ruling*
Acc. regendum, *ruling*
Abl. regendō, *by ruling*

Acc. rēctum, *to rule*
Abl. rēctū, *to rule, to be ruled*

56. Verbs in -iō of the third conjugation have in the present system forms in which -i- is followed by a vowel ; these forms are like the corresponding forms of the fourth conjugation. An example is **capiō,** *I take.*

PRINCIPAL PARTS :

PRES. INDICATIVE	PRES. INFINITIVE	PERF. INDICATIVE	PERF. PASS. PARTICIPLE
Active. capiō	capere	cēpī	captus

	PRES. INDICATIVE	PRES. INFINITIVE	PERF. INDICATIVE
Passive.	capior	capī	captus sum

ACTIVE VOICE		PASSIVE VOICE	
INDICATIVE MOOD		**INDICATIVE MOOD**	
PRESENT TENSE		PRESENT TENSE	
SINGULAR	PLURAL	SINGULAR	PLURAL
capiō	capimus	capior	capimur
capis	capitis	caperis, *or* -re	capiminī
capit	capiunt	capitur	capiuntur
IMPERFECT		IMPERFECT	
capiēbam	capiēbāmus	capiēbar	capiēbāmur
capiēbās	capiēbātis	capiēbāris	capiēbāminī
capiēbat	capiēbant	capiēbātur	capiēbantur
FUTURE		FUTURE	
capiam	capiēmus	capiar	capiēmur
capiēs	capiētis	capiēris	capiēminī
capiet	capient	capiētur	capientur
PERFECT		PERFECT	
cēpī	cēpimus	captus sum	captī sumus
cēpistī	cēpistis	captus es	captī estis
cēpit	cēpērunt *or* -ēre	captus est	captī sunt
PLUPERFECT		PLUPERFECT	
cēperam	cēperāmus	captus eram	captī erāmus
cēperās	cēperātis	captus erās	captī erātis
cēperat	cēperant	captus erat	captī erant
FUTURE PERFECT		FUTURE PERFECT	
cēperō	cēperimus	captus erō	captī erimus
cēperis	cēperitis	captus eris	captī eritis
cēperit	cēperint	captus erit	captī erunt

ACTIVE VOICE

SUBJUNCTIVE

PRESENT

SINGULAR	PLURAL
capiam	capiāmus
capiās	capiātis
capiat	capiant

IMPERFECT

caperem	caperēmus
caperēs	caperētis
caperet	caperent

PERFECT

cēperim	cēperīmus
cēperīs	cēperītis
cēperit	cēperint

PLUPERFECT

cēpissem	cēpissēmus
cēpissēs	cēpissētis
cēpisset	cēpissent

IMPERATIVE

Pres.	cape	capite
Fut.	capitō	capitōte
	capitō	capiuntō

PASSIVE VOICE

SUBJUNCTIVE

PRESENT

SINGULAR	PLURAL
capiar	capiāmur
capiāris, *or* -re	capiāminī
capiātur	capiantur

IMPERFECT

caperer	caperēmur
caperēris	caperēminī
caperētur	caperentur

PERFECT

captus sim	captī sīmus
captus sīs	captī sītis
captus sit	captī sint

PLUPERFECT

captus essem	captī essēmus
captus essēs	captī essētis
captus esset	captī essent

IMPERATIVE

Pres.	capere	capiminī
Fut.	capitor	
	capitor	capiuntor

INFINITIVE   PARTICIPLE

Pres. capere	*Pres.* capiēns
Perf. cēpisse	(*Gen.* capientīs)
Fut. captūrus esse	*Fut.* captūrus, -a, -um

INFINITIVE   PARTICIPLE

Pres. capī	
Perf. captus esse	*Perf.* captus, -a, -um
Fut. captum īrī	*Ger.* capiendus, -a, -um

GERUND	SUPINE
Gen. capiendī	
Dat. capiendō	
Acc. capiendum	*Acc.* captum
Abl. capiendō	*Abl.* captū

57. *a.* Inflected like **capiō** are its compounds, **accipiō, concipiō, dēcipiō, excipiō, incipiō, percipiō, praecipiō, recipiō,** and **suscipiō.**

b. The following verbs in -iō, inflected like **capiō,** are among those used by Cicero : **cupiō,** *ardently desire;* **faciō,** *do, make,* and its compounds **afficiō, cōnficiō, dēficiō, efficiō, perficiō, praeficiō, prōficiō, reficiō,** and **sufficiō** ; **fugiō,** *run away,* and its compounds **cōnfugiō, effugiō, prōfugiō,** and **refugiō** ; **iaciō,** *throw,* and its compounds **abiciō, coniciō, dēiciō, ēiciō, iniciō, obiciō, prōiciō, reiciō,** and **subiciō** ; **pariō,** *bring forth ;* compounds of **quatiō,** *shake,* as **percutiō** ; compounds of **rapiō,** *seize,* as **arripiō, corripiō, dīripiō, ēripiō,** and **surripiō** ; **sapiō,** *have sense;* **alliciō,** *attract;* and compounds of **specio,** *look,* **aspiciō, cōnspiciō, dēspiciō, perspiciō, prōspiciō,** and **respiciō.**

c. Similar in inflection to the passive of **capiō** are the following deponent verbs in -ior : **patior,** *suffer* (inflected below, **60**), and its compound **perpetior** ; **morior,** *die ;* and the following compounds of **gradior,** *step,* **aggredior, congredior, ēgredior, ingredior,** and **prōgredior.**

FOURTH CONJUGATION

58. Verbs of the fourth conjugation are inflected like **audiō,** *I hear.*

PRINCIPAL PARTS :

PRES. INDICATIVE	PRES. INFINITIVE	PERF. INDICATIVE	PERF. PASS. PARTICIPLE
Active. audiō	audīre	audīvī	audītus

PRES. INDICATIVE	PRES. INFINITIVE	PERF. INDICATIVE
Passive. audior	audīrī	audītus sum

ACTIVE VOICE	PASSIVE VOICE
INDICATIVE MOOD	**INDICATIVE MOOD**
PRESENT TENSE	PRESENT TENSE
I hear, etc.	*I am heard,* etc.

SINGULAR	PLURAL	SINGULAR	PLURAL
audiō	audīmus	audior	audīmur
audīs	audītis	audīris, *or* -re	audīmini
audit	audiunt	audītur	audiuntur

Active Voice		Passive Voice	
INDICATIVE MOOD		**INDICATIVE MOOD**	
Imperfect		Imperfect	
I was hearing, or *I heard*, etc.		*I was heard.* etc.	
audiēbam	audiēbāmus	audiēbar	audiēbāmur
audiēbās	aubiēbātis	aubiēbāris, *or* -re	aubiēbāminī
aubiēbat	audiēbant	aubiēbātur	audiēbantur

Future		Future	
I shall hear, you will hear, etc.		*I shall, you will be heard*, etc.	
audiam	audiēmus	audiar	audiēmur
audiēs	audiētis	audiēris, *or* -re	audiēminī
audiet	audient	audiētur	audientur

Perfect		Perfect	
I have heard, or *I heard*, etc.		*I have been heard*, or *I was heard*, etc.	
audīvī	audīvimus	audītus sum	audītī sumus
audīvistī	audīvistis	audītus es	audītī estis
audīvit	audīvērunt, *or* -ēre	audītus est	audītī sunt

Pluperfect		Pluperfect	
I had heard, etc.		*I had been heard*, etc.	
audīveram	audīverāmus	audītus eram	audītī erāmus
audīverās	audīverātis	audītus erās	audītī erātis
audīverat	audīverant	audītus erat	audītī erant

Future Perfect		Future Perfect	
I shall, you will, have heard, etc.		*I shall, you will, have been heard*, etc.	
audīverō	audīverimus	audītus erō	audītī erimus
audīveris	audīveritis	audītus eris	audītī eritis
audīverit	audīverint	audītus erit	audītī erunt

SUBJUNCTIVE		**SUBJUNCTIVE**	
Present		Present	
I may hear, let us hear, etc.		*I may be heard, let us be heard*, etc.	
SINGULAR	PLURAL	SINGULAR	PLURAL
audiam	audiāmus	audiar	audiāmur
audiās	audiātis	audiāris, *or* -re	audiāminī
audiat	audiant	audiātur	audiantur

ACTIVE VOICE	PASSIVE VOICE
SUBJUNCTIVE	**SUBJUNCTIVE**

ACTIVE VOICE

SUBJUNCTIVE

IMPERFECT

I might hear, you would hear,
etc.

audīrem	audīrēmus
audīrēs	audīrētis
audīret	audīrent

PERFECT

I may have heard, etc.

audīverim	audīverīmus
audīverīs	audīverītis
audīverit	audīverint

PLUPERFECT

I might have heard, you would
have heard, etc.

audīvissem	audīvissēmus
audīvissēs	audīvissētis
audīvisset	audīvissent

IMPERATIVE

Pres. audī, *hear thou* audīte, *hear ye*

Fut. audītō, *thou*   audītōte, *ye*
      shalt hear   *shall hear*

     audītō, *he*   audiuntō, *they*
      shall hear   *shall hear*

INFINITIVE   PARTICIPLE

Pres. audīre, *to hear*   *Pres.* audiēns,
                         hearing
Perf. audīvisse, *to*   (*Gen.*
     have heard   audien-
                           tis)

PASSIVE VOICE

SUBJUNCTIVE

IMPERFECT

I might be heard, you would be heard,
etc.

audīrer	audīrēmur
audīrēris, *or* -re	audīrēminī
audīrētur	audīrentur

PERFECT

I may have been heard, etc.

audītus sim	audītī sīmus
audītus sīs	audītī sītis
audītus sit	audītī sint

PLUPERFECT

I might have been heard, you
would have been heard, etc.

audītus essem	audītī essēmus
audītus essēs	audītī essētis
audītus esset	audītī essent

IMPERATIVE

Pres. audīre, *be*   audīminī, *be ye*
      thou heard   *heard*

Fut. audītor, *thou*
      shalt be
      heard

     audītor, *he*   audiuntor, *they*
      shall be   *shall be heard*
      heard

INFINITIVE   PARTICIPLE

Pres. audīrī, *to be*   *Perf.* audītus,
     heard   -a, -um,
Perf. audītus esse,   *heard,*
     to have   *having*
     been heard   *been*
                    heard

ACTIVE VOICE

INFINITIVE	PARTICIPLE
Fut. audītūrus esse,	*Fut.* audītūrus,
to be about	-a, -um,
to hear	about to
	hear

PASSIVE VOICE

INFINITIVE	PARTICIPLE
Fut. audītum īrī,	*Ger.* audiendus,
to be about	-a, -um,
to be heard	to be
	heard,
	worthy to
	be heard

GERUND

Gen. audiendī, *of hearing*
Dat. audiendō, *for hearing*
Acc. audiendum, *hearing*
Abl. audiendō, *by hearing*

SUPINE

Acc. audītum, *to hear*
Abl. audītū, *to hear, to be heard*

DEPONENT VERBS

59. *a.* The forms of deponent verbs are generally passive, while the meaning is active.

b. The passive meaning is found in the gerundive of deponent verbs, and sometimes in the perfect participle.

c. Deponent verbs have in the active form a future infinitive, present and future participles, gerund, and supine.

60. Deponent verbs in the four conjugations are inflected as **hortor,** *urge;* **vereor,** *fear;* **sequor,** *follow;* and **patior,** *suffer, allow;* **largior,** *give freely:*

INDICATIVE MOOD

	FIRST CONJUGATION	SECOND CONJUGATION	THIRD CONJUGATION	THIRD CONJ. IN -ior	FOURTH CONJUGATION
Pres.	hortor	vereor	sequor	patior	largior
	hortāris, -re	verēris, -re	sequeris, -re	pateris, -re	largīris, -re
	hortātur	verētur	sequitur	patitur	largītur
	hortāmur	verēmur	sequimur	patimur	largīmur
	hortāminī	verēminī	sequiminī	patiminī	largīminī
	hortantur	verentur	sequuntur	patiuntur	largiuntur
Imp.	hortābar, *etc.*	verēbar, *etc.*	sequēbar, *etc.*	patiēbar, *etc.*	largiēbar, *etc.*

INDICATIVE MOOD

	First Conjugation	Second Conjugation	Third Conjugation	Third Conj. in -ior	Fourth Conjugation
Fut.	hortābor	verēbor	sequar	patiar	largiar
Perf.	hortātus	veritus	secūtus	passus	largītus
	sum	sum	sum	sum	sum
Plup.	hortātus	veritus	secūtus	passus	largītus
	eram	eram	eram	eram	eram
F. P.	hortātus erō	veritus erō	secūtus erō	passus erō	largītus erō

SUBJUNCTIVE

Pres.	horter	verear	sequar	patiar	largiar
Imp.	hortārer	verērer	sequerer	paterer	largīrer
Perf.	hortātus	veritus	secūtus	passus	largītus
	sim	sim	sim	sim	sim
Plup.	hortātus	veritus	secūtus	passus	largītus
	essem	essem	essem	essem	essem

IMPERATIVE

Pres.	hortāre	verēre	sequere	patere	largīre
Fut.	hortātor	verētor	sequitor	patitor	largītor

INFINITIVE

Pres.	hortārī	verērī	sequī	patī	largīrī
Perf.	hortātus	veritus	secūtus	passus	largītus
	esse	esse	esse	esse	esse
Fut.	hortātūrus	veritūrus	secūtūrus	passūrus	largītūrus
	esse	esse	esse	esse	esse

PARTICIPLES

Pres.	hortāns	verēns	sequēns	patiēns	largiēns
Fut.	hortātūrus	veritūrus	secūtūrus	passūrus	largītūrus
Perf.	hortātus	veritus	secūtus	passus	largītus
Ger.	hortandus	verendus	sequendus	patiendus	largiendus

GERUND

Gen.	hortandī	verendī	sequendī	patiendī	largiendī
Dat.	hortandō	verendō	sequendō	patiendō	largiendō
Acc.	hortandum	verendum	sequendum	patiendum	largiendum
Abl.	hortandō	verendō	sequendō	patiendō	largiendō

SUPINE

Acc.	hortātum	veritum	secūtum	passum	largītum
Abl.	hortātū	veritū	secūtū	passū	largītū

61. *a.* Besides the deponent verbs previously mentioned, of the first conjugation, are : **arbitror,** *think,* **cohortor,** *urge on,* **cōnor,** *attempt,* **cōnsōlor,** *console,* **dominor,** *hold sway,* **glōrior,** *boast,* **grātulor,** *congratulate,* **mīror** and **admīror,** *wonder at,* **miseror,** *lament,* **dē-populor,** *completely lay waste,* **recordor,** *recall,* and **speculor,** *spy out.*

b. Of the second conjugation are **fateor,** *acknowledge,* and its compounds, **cōnfiteor** and **profiteor, polliceor,** *promise,* **tueor,** *protect,* **intueor,** *look upon,* and **vereor,** *be afraid.*

c. Of the third conjugation are **complector,** *embrace,* **dēfetīscor,** *become exhausted,* **fruor,** *enjoy,* **lābor,** *slip, fall away,* and **ēlābor,** *escape;* **loquor,** *speak;* **nāscor,** *be born;* **nancīscor,** *obtain;* **nītor,** *strive, rely on;* **oblīvīscor,** *forget;* **proficīscor,** *set out;* **queror,** *complain;* the compounds of **sequor, cōnsequor, exsequor, īnsequor, persequor, prōsequor** ; **reminīscor,** *remember,* **ulcīscor,** *avenge,* and **ūtor,** *use, adopt.*

d. Of the fourth conjugation are **adorior,** *attack;* **experior,** *try;* **largior,** *give freely;* **dīmētior,** *measure off;* **partior,** *divide,* and **potior,** *to obtain possession of.*

62. Semi-deponent verbs have a perfect system passive in form but active in meaning ; they are **audeō, fīdō,** with its compounds, **cōnfīdō** and **diffīdō, gaudeō,** and **soleō:**

> **audeō, audēre, ausus sum,** *dare.*
> **fīdō, fīdere, fīsus sum,** *trust.*
> **gaudeō, gaudēre, gāvīsus sum,** *rejoice.*
> **soleō, solēre, solitus sum,** *be wont.*

PERIPHRASTIC CONJUGATION

63. The periphrastic conjugation has an active and a passive form, made up by combining the future active participle and the future passive participle, or gerundive, with the verb **sum,** thus :

a. ACTIVE PERIPHRASTIC CONJUGATION

INDICATIVE MOOD	SUBJUNCTIVE MOOD
Pres. **amātūrus (-a, -um) sum,** *I am about to love*	*Pres.* **amātūrus sim,** *I may be about to love*
Imp. **amātūrus eram,** *I was about to love*	*Imp.* **amātūrus essem,** *I might be about to love*
Fut. **amātūrus erō,** *I shall be about to love*	*Perf.* **amātūrus fuerim,** *I may have been about to love*

INDICATIVE MOOD	SUBJUNCTIVE MOOD

Perf. **amātūrus fuī,** *I have been, was, about to love*

Plup. **amātūrus fueram,** *I had been about to love*

Fut. P. **amātūrus fuerō,** *I shall have been about to love.*

Plup. **amātūrus fuissem,** *I might have been about to love*

INFINITIVE

Pres. **amātūrus esse,** *to be about to love*
Perf. **amātūrus fuisse,** *to have been about to love*

b. Passive Periphrastic Conjugation

INDICATIVE	SUBJUNCTIVE

Pres. **amandus (-a, -um) sum,** *I am to be loved, I must be loved*

Imp. **amandus eram,** *I had to be loved*

Fut. **amandus erō,** *I shall have to be loved*

Perf. **amandus fuī,** *I have had to be loved, had to be loved*

Plup. **amandus fueram,** *I had deserved to be loved*

Fut. P. **amandus fuerō,** *I shall have had to be loved*

Pres. **amandus sim,** *I may have to be loved*

Imp. **amandus essem,** *I might have to be loved*

Perf. **amandus fuerim,** *I may have had to be loved*

Plup. **amandus fuissem,** *I might have had to be loved*

INFINITIVE

Pres. **amandus esse,** *to have to be loved*
Perf. **amandus fuisse,** *to have had to be loved*

64. Perfects in -āvī, -ēvī, and -īvī, and other tenses formed from the same stems, are sometimes contracted by the loss of -vi- or -ve- before -s- or -r- ; perfects in īvī lose the -v- before -r- but retain the vowel. Examples are : **honestārunt** for **honestāvērunt** ; **cōnsuērunt** for **cōnsuēvērunt** ; **audīstis** for **audīvistis** ; **audīsset** for **audīvisset.**

IRREGULAR VERBS

65. Of the irregular verbs the most frequently used are **sum, dō, eō, ferō, fīō, volō**, and certain compounds.

66. *a.* Of the compounds of **sum** Cicero uses **absum, adsum, dēsum, īnsum, intersum, obsum, possum, praesum, prōsum, subsum**, and **supersum**. These are inflected like **sum (52)**, except **possum** ; but in **prō-sum** (**prōfuisse**) the preposition has the form **prōd-** before vowels, as **prōdest**.

b. **Possum**, *I am able*, is inflected as follows :

PRINCIPAL PARTS :   **possum**   **posse**   **potuī**

	INDICATIVE MOOD		SUBJUNCTIVE MOOD	
	SINGULAR	PLURAL	SINGULAR	PLURAL
Pres.	possum	possumus	*Pres.* possim	possīmus
	potes	potestis	possīs	possītis
	potest	possunt	possit	possint
Imp.	poteram, pote-	poterāmus	*Imp.* possem	possēmus
	rās, *etc.*	-erātis, *etc.*	possēs	possētis
Fut.	poterō, poteris,	poterimus	posset	possent
	etc.		*Perf.* potuerim	potuerīmus
Perf.	potuī, potuistī,	potuimus	potuerīs	potuerītis
	etc.		potuerit	potuerint
Plup.	potueram, po-	potuerāmus	*Plup.* potuissem	potuissēmus
	tuerās, *etc.*		potuissēs	potuissētis
Fut. P.	potuerō, potue-	potuerimus	potuisset	potuissent
	ris, *etc.*			

INFINITIVE	PARTICIPLE
Pres. posse	*Pres.* potēns (*used as an adjective*)
Perf. potuisse	*Gen.* potentis

67. *a.* **Dō, dare**, *give*, has **-a-** instead of **-ā-** in the present system except in the second person of the present indicative and the present imperative. The inflection of the perfect system (**dedī**, *etc.*), is regular.

PRINCIPAL PARTS :   **dō**   **dare**   **dedī**   **datus**

ACTIVE VOICE

INDICATIVE MOOD			SUBJUNCTIVE MOOD		
Pres.	dō	damus	*Pres.*	dem	dēmus
	dās	datis		dēs	dētis
	dat	dant		det	dent
Imp.	dabam, *etc.*	dabāmus	*Imp.*	darem	darēmus
Fut.	dabō, *etc.*	dabimus		darēs	darētis
Perf.	dedī, *etc.*	dedimus		daret	darent
Plup.	dederam, *etc.*	dederāmus	*Perf.*	dederim, *etc.*	dederīmus, *etc.*
Fut. P.	dederō, *etc.*	dederimus	*Plup.*	dedissem, *etc.*	dedissēmus, *etc.*

IMPERATIVE		INFINITIVE	PARTICIPLE
Pres.	dā	date	*Pres.* dare	dāns
Fut.	datō	datōte	*Perf.* dedisse	
	datō	dantō	*Fut.* datūrus esse	datūrus -a, -um

GERUND	SUPINE
dandī, *etc.*	datum, datū

b. The passive of **dō** has -a- instead of -ā-, as **darī, datur, dabar, dabor, darer, datus**, *etc.;* the first person of the present indicative passive is not in use.

c. The compounds of **dō** are of the third conjugation except **circumdō**, which is inflected like **dō**.

68. *a.* **Eō, īre,** *go,* is thus inflected :

PRINCIPAL PARTS : **eō, īre, īvī (iī), itum**

INDICATIVE MOOD			SUBJUNCTIVE MOOD		
Pres.	eō	īmus	*Pres.*	eam	eāmus
	īs	ītis		eās	eātis
	it	eunt		eat	eant
Imp.	ībam, *etc.*	ībāmus	*Imp.*	īrem	īrēmus
Fut.	ībō, *etc.*	ībimus		īrēs	īrētis
Perf.	iī	iimus		īret	īrent
	īstī *or* iistī	īstis *or* iistis	*Perf.*	ierim	ierīmus
	iit	iērunt *or* iēre		ierīs	ierītis
Plup.	ieram, *etc.*	ierāmus		ierit	ierint
Fut. P.	ierō, *etc.*	ierimus	*Plup.*	īssem, *etc.*	īssēmus, *etc.*

ACTIVE VOICE

IMPERATIVE	INFINITIVE	PARTICIPLE	
Pres. ī īte	*Pres.* īre	*Pres.* iēns	*Gen.* euntis
Fut. ītō ītōte	*Perf.* īsse		
ītō euntō	*Fut.* itūrus esse	*Fut.* itūrus,	*Gerundive* eundum
	Pass. īrī	-a, -um	

GERUND	SUPINE
eundī, eundō, *etc.*	itum, itū

b. Cicero uses the compounds **abeō, adeō, anteeō, circumeō, coeō, exeō, ineō, intereō, obeō, pereō, praeeō, praetereō, prōdeō, redeō, subeō,** and **trānseō,** inflected like eō.

c. Transitive compounds of **eō** are used also in the passive, most often in the third person singular, as present indicative -**ītur,** imperfect -**ībātur,** perfect -**itum est** ; present subjunctive -**eātur (subeātur** ; imperfect -**īrētur** ; infinitive -**īrī** ; participles -**itus, -a, -um**) neuter plural **praeterita,** and -**eundus, -a, -um,** as in **ad facinus obeundum** and in the passive periphrastic conjugation, as **subeunda est.**

69. *a.* **Ferō, ferre,** *bear, carry,* is inflected as follows :

PRINCIPAL PARTS :

Active.	**ferō**	**ferre**	**tulī**	**lātus**
Passive.	**feror**	**ferrī**		**lātus sum**

ACTIVE VOICE		PASSIVE VOICE	
INDICATIVE MOOD		INDICATIVE MOOD	
SINGULAR	PLURAL	SINGULAR	PLURAL
Pres. ferō	ferimus	*Pres.* feror	ferimur
fers	fertis	ferris	feriminī
fert	ferunt	fertur	feruntur
Imp. ferēbam, *etc.*	ferēbāmus	*Imp.* ferēbar	ferēbāmur
Fut. feram	ferēmus	*Fut.* ferar	ferēmur
Perf. tulī	tulimus	*Perf.* lātus sum	lātī sumus
Plup. tuleram	tulerāmus	*Plup.* lātus eram	lātī erāmus
Fut. P. tulerō	tulerimus	*Fut. P.* lātus erō	lātī erimus

ACTIVE VOICE		PASSIVE VOICE	
SUBJUNCTIVE MOOD		**SUBJUNCTIVE MOOD**	

Pres.	feram	ferāmus	*Pres.*	ferar	ferāmur
	ferās	ferātis		ferāris, *or* -re	ferāminī
	ferat	ferant		ferātur	ferantur
Imp.	ferrem	ferrēmus	*Imp.*	ferrer	ferrēmur
	ferrēs	ferrētis		ferrēris	ferrēminī
	ferret	ferrent		ferrētur	ferrentur
Perf.	tulerim	tulerīmus	*Perf.*	lātus sim	lāt sīmus
Plup.	tulissem	tulissēmus	*Plup.*	lātus essem	lātī essēmus

IMPERATIVE		IMPERATIVE	

Pres.	fer	ferte	*Pres.*	ferre	feriminī
Fut.	fertō	fertōte	*Fut.*	fertor	
	fertō	feruntō		fertor	feruntor

INFINITIVE	PARTICIPLE	INFINITIVE	PARTICIPLE

Pres. ferre	*Pres.* ferēns	*Pres.* ferrī	
Perf. tulisse	(*Gen.* ferentis)	*Perf.* lātus esse	*Perf.* lātus, -a, -um
Fut. lātūrus esse	*Fut.* lātūrus,	*Fut.* lātum īrī	*Ger.* ferendus,
	-a, -um		-a, -um

GERUND	SUPINE

Gen. ferendī	
Dat. ferendō	
Acc. ferendum	*Acc.* lātum
Abl. ferendō	*Abl.* lātū

b. Cicero uses the compounds, **afferō, anteferō, cōnferō, dēferō, differō, efferō, īnferō, offerō, perferō, praeferō, prōferō,** and **referō,** which are inflected like **ferō.**

70. *a.* **Fīō,** *become,* is used as a passive of **faciō,** with the meaning *be made, be done.* In its conjugation i is long except in fit and when followed by er; as, **fīēbam, fīam,** but **fĭerī, fĭerem.** The perfect passive system of this verb is formed regularly from **faciō.** It is inflected as follows :

PRINCIPAL PARTS :   **fīō   fierī   factus sum**

INDICATIVE MOOD		SUBJUNCTIVE MOOD	
SINGULAR	PLURAL	SINGULAR	PLURAL
Pres. fīō	fīmus	*Pres.* fīam	fīāmus
fīs	fītis	fīās	fīātis
fit	fīunt	fīat	fīant
Imp. fīēbam, *etc.*	fīēbāmus	*Imp.* fierem	fierēmus
Fut. fīam	fīēmus	fierēs	fierētis
Perf. factus sum	factī sumus	fieret	fierent
Plup. factus eram	factī erāmus	*Perf.* factus sim	factī sīmus
Fut. P. factus erō	factī erimus	*Plup.* factus essem	factī essēmus

IMPERATIVE

Pres. fī   fīte

INFINITIVE	PARTICIPLE
Pres. fierī	
Perf. factus esse	*Perf.* factus, -a, -um
Fut. factum īrī	*Ger.* faciendus, -a, -um

b. Compounds of **faciō** with prepositions follow the simple verb in their passive inflections, as, **interficiēre**, future indicative, second person singular, and **interficī**, infinitive.

c. The compound **patefaciō** has an infinitive **patefierī** and a passive participle **patefactus, -a, -um**.

71. Volō, *I wish*, and its compounds, nōlō, *I am unwilling*, and mālō, *I prefer*, are inflected as follows :

PRINCIPAL PARTS :	volō	velle	voluī
	nōlō	nōlle	nōluī
	mālō	mālle	māluī

INDIC.	SUBJ.	INDIC.	SUBJ.	INDIC.	SUBJ.
PRESENT	PRESENT	PRESENT	PRESENT	PRESENT	PRESENT
volō	velim	nōlō	nōlim	mālō	mālim
vīs	velīs	nōn vīs	nōlīs	māvīs	mālīs
vult	velit	nōn vult	nōlit	māvult	mālit
volumus	velīmus	nōlumus	nōlīmus	mālumus	mālīmus
vultis	velītis	nōn vultis	nōlītis	māvultis	mālītis
volunt	velint	nōlunt	nōlint	mālunt	mālint

INDIC.	SUBJ.	INDIC.	SUBJ.	INDIC.	SUBJ.

IMPERFECT		IMPERFECT		IMPERFECT	
volēbam, *etc.*	vellem	nōlēbam	nōllem	mālēbam	māllem

FUTURE		FUTURE		FUTURE	
volam, *etc.*		nōlam		mālam	

PERFECT		PERFECT		PERFECT	
voluī, *etc.*	voluerim	nōluī	nōluerim	māluī	māluerim

PLUPERFECT		PLUPERFECT		PLUPERFECT	
volueram	voluissem	nōlueram	nōluissem	mālueram	māluissem

FUTURE PERFECT		FUTURE PERFECT		FUTURE PERFECT	
voluerō, *etc.*		nōluerō		māluerō	

IMPERATIVE

Pres. nōlī   nōlīte
Fut. nōlītō   nōlītōte
      nōlītō   nōluntō

INFINITIVE	INFINITIVE	INFINITIVE
Pres. velle	nōlle	mālle
Perf. voluisse	nōluisse	māluisse

PARTICIPLE

Pres. volēns   nōlēns   ——

DEFECTIVE VERBS

72. *a.* Cicero uses the following defective verbs : **inquam**, *I say*, **inquis, inquit** ; **coepī**, *I have begun, I began*, which belongs chiefly to the perfect system ; **meminī**, *I remember*, and **ōdī**, *I hate*, which are perfect in form, but present in meaning.

b. **Coepī, meminī**, and **ōdī** are inflected as follows :

INDICATIVE MOOD			SUBJUNCTIVE MOOD		
Perf. coepī, etc.	meminī	ōdī	coeperim	meminerim	ōderim
Plup. coep-	memine-	ōderam	coepissem	meminissem	ōdissem
eram	ram				
Fut. P. coeperō	meminerō	ōderō			

IMPERATIVE	INFINITIVE		
Sing. mementō	*Perf.* coepisse	meminisse	ōdisse
	Fut. coeptūrus		ōsūrus
Plur. mementōte	esse		esse

PARTICIPLE

Perf. coeptus, *begun*	ōsus
Fut. coeptūrus	ōsūrus

c. Passive forms of **coepī** are sometimes used, as **est id coeptum,** *that was begun.*

d. Cicero uses also the defective verb **aiō,** *I say,* inflected thus : **aiō, ais, ait, —, —, aiunt** ; imperfect, **aiēbam,** *etc.*, participle **aiēns.**

IMPERSONAL VERBS

73. *a.* Of the impersonal verbs Cicero oftenest uses **licet,** *it is permitted*, and **oportet,** *it is necessary, it behooves ;* he has also **decet,** *it becomes*, **paenitet,** *it makes sorry*, and **pudet,** *it makes ashamed.*

b. The impersonal **licet** is inflected as follows :

	INDICATIVE		SUBJUNCTIVE
Pres.	licet, *it is permitted*	*Pres.*	liceat, *it may be permitted*
Imp.	licēbat, *it was permitted*	*Imp.*	licēret, *it might be permitted*
Fut.	licēbit, *it will be permitted*	*Perf.*	licuerit, *it may have been permitted*
Perf.	licuit, *it has been permitted* or *it was permitted*	*Plup.*	licuisset, *it might have been permitted*
Plup.	licuerat, *it had been permitted*		
Fut. P.	licuerit, *it will have been permitted*		

INFINITIVE

Pres.	licēre, *to be permitted*	*Perf.*	licuisse, *to have been permitted*

c. The third person singular of a number of verbs is used impersonally, as **accidit,** *it happens, it turns out ;* **cōnstat,** *it is certain;* **interest,** *it is important ;* and **placet,** *it pleases.*

d. Cicero uses impersonally the passive of several intransitive verbs, making prominent the action rather than the doer ; as **pugnā-**

tur, *fighting goes on*, lit. *it is fought;* quōcumque ventum est, *whither-soever (they) came*, lit. *whithersoever it was come*, the *coming* being made prominent.

e. Verbs are often used impersonally in the passive periphrastic conjugation, denoting obligation or necessity (**229.** *c*) ; as, reī frūmentāriae prōspiciendum [esse], *that he should provide for supplies*, lit. *that it ought to be provided for supplies* by him.

WORD FORMATION

74. The following classes of words are derived from verbs :

a. Nouns with the suffix **-tor** denoting the agent, as vic-tor, *victor*, from vincō ; dēfēn-sor (for dēfend-tor as dēfēn-sus for dēfend-tus), *defender*, from dēfendō.

b. Nouns with the suffixes -tiō (-siō), -tus, -tūra, -ium, denoting an action or the result of an action, as coniūrā-tiō, *a swearing together, conspiracy* (coniūrō) ; adven-tus, *arrival* (adveniō) ; exercitus, *army*, conceived as a product of *training* (exerceō) ; imperium, *command, sovereignty* (imperō) ; iūdic-ium, *judgment* (iūdicō).

c. Nouns with the suffix -or, denoting a condition or state, as tim-or, *fear* (timeō).

d. Nouns with the suffixes -men or -mentum, -ulum, -bulum -crum, denoting process, means, or result, as flū-men, *stream, river*, conceived as *a flowing* or *current* (fluō) ; impedī-mentum, *hindrance* (impediō), pl. impedīmenta, *baggage*, conceived as an aggregation of hindrances ; vinc-ulum, *bond, chain*, conceived as a means of binding (vinciō) ; simulā-crum, *image*, conceived as something *made like* something else (simulō, *make like*).

e. Adjectives with the suffix -āx, denoting a quality or tendency, as audāx, *bold* (audeō, *be bold*).

f. Adjectives with the suffixes -ilis and -bilis, denoting passive qualities, or capacity, as fac-ilis, *easy*, i.e. capable of being done or made (faciō) ; incrēdibilis, *incredible* (negative in- + crēdibilis, *capable of being believed*, from crēdō). **212.** *h.*

g. A few adjectives in -tīvus, as fugi-tīvus, *fugitive* (fugiō).

75. The following classes of words are derived from nouns :

a. Diminutive nouns, ending in -lus (fem. -la, neut. -lum), and in -ulus, -olus, -culus, etc., as lect-ulus, *small couch* (lectus) ; articulus, *joint* (artus) ; tabella, *tablet* (tabula).

b. Nouns with the suffix -ātus, denoting an official position or body, as cōnsul-ātus, *consulship* (cōnsul) ; magistrātus, *magistracy, magistrate* (magister); senātus, *senate*, as composed of old men (senex).

c. A few abstract nouns in -tās and -tūs, as cīvi-tās, *citizenship, state* (cīvis) ; vir-tūs, *valor* (vir).

d. Adjectives with the suffix -eus, denoting material, as aureus, *of gold* (aurum) ; ferreus, *of iron* (ferrum).

e. Adjectives with the suffixes -ius, -icus, -cus, -ānus, -īnus, -nus, -ālis, -īlis, -ārius, -āris, -īvus, meaning *connected with, belonging to, from,* etc., as patr-ius, *of a father, ancestral* (pater) ; bell-icus, *of war* (bellum) ; urb-ānus, *of a city, of the city* (urbs) ; Rōm-ānus, *of Rome* (Rōma) ; Lat-īnus, *of Latium, Latin;* nāv-ālis, *naval* (nāvis) ; cōnsul-āris, *of consular rank.*

f. Adjectives with the suffix -ōsus, denoting fullness, as perīculōsus, *full of danger* (perīculum); bellic-ōsus, *warlike* (bellic-us, bellum).

g. Denominative verbs, of the different conjugations, as cūrō, -āre, *care for, take care* (cūra) ; laudō, -āre, *praise* (laus, laudis) ; tribuō, -ere, *assign* (tribus) ; partior, -īrī, *divide* (pars, partis).

76. *a.* Derived from adjectives are abstract nouns with the suffixes -tia, -ia, -tās, and -tūdō, denoting quality or condition, as iusti-tia, *justice* (iustus) ; audāc-ia, *boldness* (audāx) ; grāt-ia, *favor* (grātus) ; cupidi-tās, *desire* (cupidus) ; forti-tūdō, *bravery* (fortis).

b. Derived from adverbs are several adjectives in -urnus, -turnus, -tinus, referring to time, as diū-turnus, *long-continued* (diū).

c. A few adjectives have a diminutive in -ulus ; as tantulus, *so small,* from tantus.

77. Adverbs [1] are sometimes formed from the stem of the perfect passive participle, with the suffix -im, as stat-im, *immediately* (status, stō) ; and from nouns, with the ending -tim (or -im), as fūr-tim, *stealthily,* i.e. like a *thief* (fūr), and part-im, *partly,* which was originally an accusative of pars.

78. Verbs derived from verbs are :

a. Frequentatives, expressing repeated or intensive action ; frequentatives derived from verbs of the first conjugation end in -itō, as clāmitō, *cry out loudly, shout* (clāmō) ; others end in -tō or -sō, as iactō, *toss about, cast* (iaciō), concursō, *rush hither and yon, rush about* (concurrō).

b. Inchoatives, or inceptives, expressing the beginning of an

---

[1] The formation of adverbs from adjectives is treated under adverbs, **34–35.**

action or state, a becoming ; they end in -scō, preceded by -ā-, -ē-, or -ī-, as concupīscō, *desire eagerly* (concupiō).

79. *a.* In the first part of a compound word the final vowel of the stem of a noun or adjective is dropped before a vowel, and becomes -i- before a consonant, while in the case of consonant stems -i- is often inserted ; in the second part vowel changes frequently appear. Thus signi-fer, *standard-bearer* (for signo-fer, signum + fer- in ferō) ; prīn-ceps, *leader*, i.e. *taking foremost place* (for prīmo-cap-s, prīmus + cap- in capiō) ; ampli-ficō, *enlarge* (for amplo-fac-ō, amplus + fac- in faciō).

b. The first part of a compound is often a preposition or other indeclinable word, as per-ficiō, *carry through* (per + faciō) ; in-iussū, *without orders* (negative in- + iussū) ; bi-enn-ium, period of *two years* (for bi-anno-ium, bis + annus + suffix -ium) ; quotannīs, *annually* (quot + ablative of annus).

c. Compounds originating in phrases are sometimes declinable, as prō-cōnsul, *proconsul*, gen. prō-cōnsulis ; sometimes indeclinable, as ob-viam, *in the way.*

d. The following indeclinable prefixes are found only in compound words :

amb-, am- (an-), *about*, as in ambitiō, *canvassing* for office (amb-iō).

com-, co- (old form of cum, *with*), *with*, *together;* see under cum in vocabulary.

dis-, appearing also as dir-, dī-, *apart*, as in dis-cēdō, *go away;* dir-imō, *take apart, break off;* dī-mitto, *dismiss.*

in- = *un-, not*, as in incertus; to be carefully distinguished from the preposition in in composition.

por-, *forth, forward*, as in por-rigō, *reach out, offer.*

re-, red-, *back*, as in re-maneō, *stay behind;* red-eō, *return.*

sē-, sēd-, *apart*, as in sē-parō, *separate*, sēd-itiō, *sedition.*

THE DERIVATION OF ENGLISH WORDS FROM THE LATIN [1]

80. *a.* Very many of the words in the English language in common use are derived, indirectly or directly, from the Latin.

[1] Classes in Latin find it a useful exercise to make, on separate slips or cards, a list of Latin words in each lesson having English derivatives, adding the words derived from them. The Latin words from time to time may be classified, in groups corresponding with the numbered paragraphs **80–85**, the words in each group being arranged in alphabetical order.

The percentage of classical Latin words that have been taken over into English directly, however, is exceedingly small ; the people whose name survives in the word " English " reached Britain too late for any direct contact with classical Latin. But in the Middle Ages a modified Latin was spoken and written by educated men all over Europe ; and classical Latin authors continued to be read, less in the Middle Ages, but extensively after the Revival of Learning. Meanwhile the Latin spoken by the common people in Italy, France, Spain, and other countries conquered by the Romans had developed into the Romance languages, French, Italian, Spanish, and kindred tongues ; and after the Norman Conquest, in the eleventh century, French was both spoken and written in England. Thus it happens that words of Latin origin have come down into the English of today in various ways, some through the writings and speech of those who read classical Latin, a great many through mediæval Latin, but far the greatest number through the Romance languages, particularly French.

b. Some Latin words appear in English in their Latin forms, though they may have passed through other forms and may now have a different meaning ; as " arbor," " census," " color," " senator," " victor," and " omnibus," meaning originally *for all*, from the dative plural masculine of **omnis**.

81. Many Latin words appear in English with slight change of spelling, as " cent " from **centum**; " condition " from **condiciō** through a late spelling **conditiō** ; " difficulty " from **difficultās**; "fort " from **fortis**; " future " from **futūrus**, the future participle associated with **sum** ; " office " from **officium**; " senate " from **senātus**; and " victory " from **victōria** ; " false " from **falsus**; "admire " from **admīror**; " ascend " from **ascendō** ; " accept " from **accipiō** through the frequentative **acceptō**, *accept*, which is formed from **acceptus**, participle of **accipiō**.

82. *a.* Some English words have been formed from Latin words by analogy of Latin or French words already in the language. Examples are " magistracy " and " classical."

b. " Magistracy " goes back to **magistrātus**. From **magistrātus** comes " magistrate," to which the suffix " -cy " was added from analogy to the English nouns of Latin origin ending in " -cy "[1] ; this suffix represents the Latin termination -**tia**, as in " clemency,"

[1] This suffix has no connection with a similar suffix of Greek origin found in " democracy " and a few other English words.

from **clēmentia**. With the addition of the suffix " -cy " the last two letters of " magistrate " disappeared ; hence " magistracy."

c. " Classical " comes from the adjective **classicus**, *first class*, which goes back to **classis**, *class, fleet*, as a class or division of military forces. From **classicus** comes " classic " ; the suffix " -al " was added by analogy with the English words which are derived from the Latin adjectives ending in -**ālis**, as " social " from **sociālis** (ultimately from **socius**, *fellow, ally*), " hospital " from **hospitālis** (ultimately from **hospes**, gen. **hospitis**, *guest*), and " legal " from **lēgālis** (ultimately from **lēx**, **lēgis**, *law*). Similarly, " aural " is derived from **auris**, *ear*, " continual " from **continuus**, and " senatorial " from **senātōrius**, the suffix " -al " replacing the Latin terminations.

83. *a.* Some English words are formed from words of ultimate Latin origin by the addition of a suffix of English origin. Thus " falsehood " comes from " false " (Latin **falsus**), with the suffix " -hood " denoting quality ; " citizenship " from " citizen," which goes back ultimately to Latin **cīvis**, with the suffix " -ship " denoting state or office ; " instantly " from " instant " (Latin **īnstāns**, gen. **īnstantis**, present participle of **īnstō**), and " nobly " from " noble " (Latin **nōbilis**), by addition of the suffix " -ly," which has the same origin as the English word " like."

b. A few English words are formed from Latin words by the addition of an English suffix of Greek origin ; as " jurist " from **iūs**, gen. **iūris**, with the suffix " -ist," which represents a Greek termination denoting the agent ; " Caesarism," " nihilism," " terrorism " from **Caesar**, **nihil**, and **terror**, with the suffix " -ism," also of Greek origin, implying doctrine or practice.

84. Many Latin words, especially those that have come into English through the French, have undergone so great changes that their Latin origin is not at once perceived, though it can always be traced through intermediate forms. Such are " captaincy," from " captain," which is ultimately derived from **caput**, *head*, with the suffix " -cy " (**82.** *b*) ; " city " from **cīvitās** ; " lieutenant " from **locum tenēns** (present participle of **teneō**, *hold*), one holding another's office or place ; " madam," " Madonna," from **mea domina**, feminine corresponding to the masculine **meus dominus** ; " governor " from **gubernātor**, *helmsman;* " peril " from **perīculum**, and " perilous " from **perīculōsus;** " preach " from **praedicō**; and " receive " from **recipiō**.

85. A few common abbreviations represent Latin words; as "no." in "no. 9," in which "no." stands not for "number" but for **numerō**, the Ablative of **numerus**. Also, the symbols for English money, £ s. d., now read as "pounds, shillings, pence," are derived from Latin words : £ = **lībra**, a *pound* in weight, whence **lībrīlis**, *weighing a pound;* s. = **solidus**, a Roman gold coin ; and d. = **dēnārius**, a Roman silver coin, translated *penny*, though its value as silver was originally between fifteen and twenty cents in our currency. **Solidus**, the name of the coin, came from the adjective **solidus**, from which our word "solid" is derived; it survives in our word "soldier" as "one having pay" for military service. **Dēnārius** came from **dēnī**, *ten each*, because it originally contained ten of the monetary units called **as**, and **as** survives in our word "ace."

Our abbreviation "Mr." is for "Master," but "Master" is of Latin origin, being derived from **magister**, *teacher, master*.

86. The value of the contribution which the English language has received from the Latin cannot be measured in percentages of words. The words of English origin which we use are largely concrete, and well fitted to express fundamental ideas ; but we are indebted to the Latin for a very large proportion of the words employed in the arts, sciences, and education, which fit the English language to be the vehicle of expression for a constantly developing civilization.

SYNTAX

SUBJECT AND PREDICATE

All illustrations are to be found in this text.

87. *a.* A noun or pronoun, or an adjective taking the place of a noun, when used as the subject of a finite verb is in the nominative case; as, **Senātus haec intellegit, cōnsul videt; hīc tamen vīvit,** *The senate knows this, the consul sees it; yet this man lives* (In Catilīnam, 1, 1, 13); **quā rē sēcēdant improbī,** *wherefore let the wicked begone* (In Catilīnam 1, 13, 14).

b. A personal pronoun used as a subject is expressed only when there is emphasis or contrast; as, **Ego, sī essent inimīcitiae mihi cum C. Caesar, . . .,** *As for myself, even if I harbored feelings of resentment against Caesar, . . .* (Dē Prōvinciīs Cōnsulāribus, 20, 1).

c. Instead of a noun or other substantive word an infinitive or a clause may be used as the subject of a verb; as, **Difficile est hōc dē omnibus cōnfīrmāre,** *It is difficult to assert this of all of them* (Prō Archiā, 7, 4). Here **cōnfīrmāre** is the subject of **est.**

88. A predicate noun, in the same case as the subject, is used with **sum** and the passives of verbs of *calling, choosing, making, esteeming,* and the like; as, **Etenim cui vīgintī hīs annīs supplicātiō dēcrēta est, ut nōn imperātor appellārētur,** *For to whom within the last twenty years has a thanksgiving been decreed without the title of imperator,* lit. *so that he was not called imperator* (Philippic, 14, 4, 27).

89. *a.* A verb is sometimes omitted when it can easily be supplied from the context; as, **officium** (Dē Prōvinciīs Cōnsulāribus, 20, 15), where **agitur** is to be supplied.

b. Forms of **sum** are often omitted in the compound tenses; as, **discrīmināta** (Livy, 21, 4, 17) for **discrīmināta sunt,** *were apportioned.*

c. In the future active and perfect passive infinitive, and also in the present passive infinitive of the periphrastic conjugation, **esse** is frequently omitted; as, **passūrōs** (Livy, 2, 1, 30) for **passūrōs esse;** **redditum** (Livy, 21, 4, 3) for **redditum esse;** **sūmend·im** (Sallust, 52, 44) for **sūmendum esse.**

90. *a.* In certain connections **est, erat,** etc., may best be translated *there is, there was,* etc., with the subject following; as, **Est enim in nōbīs is animus,** *For there is in me such a disposition* (In Catilīnam, 3, 12, 15).

b. Occasionally the expletive *there* may be used in like manner in translating other verbs than **sum**; as, **occīsus est cum līberīs M. Fulvius cōnsulāris,** *There was slain Marcus Fulvius, an ex-consul, together with his children* (In Catilīnam, 1, 2, 5).

NOUNS

91. *a.* Nouns used as appositives, whether in the nominative or in the oblique cases, agree in case with the nouns to which they belong; as, **Iovem illum, cūstōdem huius urbis,** *yonder Jupiter, the guardian of this city* (In Catilīnam, 3, 12, 42).

b. A noun referring to a part may be in apposition to a noun expressing the whole (partitive apposition); as, **Multī autem, . . . amīcum aliī, pars hospitem aut cōgnātum reperiēbant,** *Many, moreover, found, some a friend, others a guest-friend or kinsman* (Sallust, 61, 16).

92. *a.* A plural noun is often used in Latin where English usage prefers the singular; as, **animōs ac spīritūs capere,** *to endure the arrogance and insolence* (Dē Imperiō Cn. Pompeī, 22, 51).

b. An abstract noun is sometimes used in Latin where English usage expects a concrete plural noun; as, **Quod sī ex tantō latrōciniō iste ūnus tollētur,** *But if that fellow alone is removed from so large a band of brigands* (In Catilīnam, 1, 13, 4).

c. Abstract nouns are sometimes used in the plural to denote different manifestations, occasions, or instances of the quality; as, **lūctūs atque gaudia,** *manifestations of mourning and joy* (Sallust, 61, 20).

Sometimes the pluralizing of abstract nouns makes them concrete; as, **libīdinēs,** *acts of lawlessness* (Dē Imperiō Cn. Pompeī, 22, 28).

Frequently, too, the plural of abstract nouns is regulated by a limiting genitive; thus, **mōtūs animōrum,** *mental activity,* **mōtūs** being plural because there were several minds (Prō Archiā, 8, 8).

d. Proper names in the plural usually mean *men like;* as, **Paulōs, Catōnēs, Gallōs, Scīpiōnēs, Philōs,** *men like Paulus, like Cato, like Gallus, like Scipio, like Philus* (Laelius Dē Amīcitiā, 6, 15). This use is called the generic plural.

e. Diminutives may express affection or contempt; as, **mulierculās,** *dear little women* (In Catilīnam, 2, 10, 35); they may also have a humorous effect; as, **recreandae vōculae,** *of strengthening my poor little voice* (Cicerō, Epistulae, 4, 4).

f. Occasionally Latin uses a concrete noun for an abstract; as, **ex puerīs excessit,** *outgrew his boyhood* (Dē Archiā, 3, 1).

g. A noun in the singular may have a collective meaning; as, **porcō . . . gallīna,** *swine . . . chicken* (Catō Maior Dē Senectūte, 16, 24).

The Vocative Case

93. The vocative case is used only in direct address; as, **M. Tullī, quid agis?** *Marcus Tullius, what are you about?* (In Catilīnam, 1, 11, 7).

The Genitive Case

94. *a.* In the possessive genitive the possessor is emphasized (see **111**); as, **bona cīvium Rōmānōrum,** *the property of Roman citizens* (Dē Imperiō Cn. Pompeī, 7, 3).

b. The possessive genitive is used idiomatically with **causā** and **grātiā**; as, **commūnīs salūtis causā,** *for the common safety* (Dē Imperiō Cn. Pompeī, 16, 42); **D. Brūtī cōnservandī grātiā,** *for the preservation of Decimus Brutus* (Philippic, 14, 2, 4).

c. With **sum** and **fīō** the possessive genitive is used predicatively with the meaning *the business of, belonging to, consisting of, the part of, the duty of,* etc.; as, **Quīntum genus est parricīdārum,** *The fifth class consists of parricides* (In Catilīnam, 2, 10, 15). **Est fideī pietātisque nostrae dēclārāre,** *It is a part of our loyalty and devotion to make manifest* (Philippic, 14, 11, 4).

However, the possessive pronouns must be used instead of the predicate genitive of personal pronouns; as, **vestrum est,** *it is your duty* (In Catilīnam, 3, 12, 5).

95. The subjective genitive designates the person or agent whose act or feeling is expressed in the noun on which the genitive depends; as, **spem Catilīnae,** *the hope of Catiline* (In Catilīnam, 1, 12, 16).

96. *a.* The appositional genitive defines or explains the noun on which it depends; as, **medicīnam cōnsilī atque ōrātiōnis meae,** *the remedy consisting of my words of advice,* hendiadys, lit. *the remedy of my advice and discourse* (In Catilīnam, 2, 8, 10). See **238.** *h.*

b. A genitive may be used in apposition with a possessive pronoun; as, **dē nostrō omnium interitū,** *concerning the destruction of all of us* (In Catilīnam, 1, 4, 13).

97. *a.* The partitive genitive, or genitive of the whole, designates the whole of which a part is expressed in the noun, pronoun, adjective, or numeral on which it depends; as, **partem istam subselliōrum,** *that part of the benches* (*near you*) (In Catilīnam, 1, 7, 12).

b. The part on which the genitive of the whole depends may be indefinitely expressed by the singular neuter of a pronoun or of an adjective, used substantively, or by the adverb **satis** used substantively; as, **quid malī,** *what wrongdoing,* lit. *what of wrongdoing* (In Catilīnam, 2, 4, 13); **quicquam pēnsī,** *any weight,* lit. *anything of weight* (Sallust, 5, 13); **auctōritātis tantum,** *so much authority* (Dē Imperiō Cn. Pompeī, 1, 18); **nihil vērī,** *untruthfulness,* lit. *nothing of truth* (Livy, 21, 4, 26); **satis animī** *sufficient courage* (Dē Imperiō Cn. Pompeī, 24, 5); **quid cōnsilī,** *what plan* (In Catilīnam, 1, 1, 11); **Ubinam gentium,** *Where in the world* (In Catilīnam, 1, 4, 10).

c. In the English phrase *all of these* there is no partitive idea, because *these* and *all* refer to the same whole. Such phrases are not expressed in Latin by the partitive genitive but by words agreeing in case; as, **Haec omnia,** *All of these facts* (In Catilīnam, 1, 4, 27).

d. Instead of the genitive of the whole **ex** or **dē** with the ablative is sometimes used, and regularly so with cardinal numerals (except **mīlia**) and **quīdam;** as, **Ille erat ūnus timendus ex istīs omnibus,** *He alone of all of those men was to be feared* (In Catilīnam 3, 7, 9).

98. *a.* A variety of the genitive of the whole is the genitive of material, which is used to designate the material or units included in the noun on which it depends; as, **multitūdinem gentium illārum,** *the vast population of those nations,* lit. *the multitude* (*made up*) *of those nations* (Dē Prōvinciīs Cōnsulāribus, 13, 36).

b. The material of which anything is made is expressed by the ablative with **ex;** as, **crātēras ex aere pulcherrimās,** *very beautiful mixing-bowls wrought of bronze* (In Verrem, 59, 2).

99. The genitive is used to express origin; as, **Fundānī nostrī fīlia,** *the daughter of my friend Fundanus* (Pliny, 9, 1).

100. *a.* The genitive of quality and the genitive of measure are modified by adjectives or numerals; as, **aureās armillās magnī ponderis,** *golden bracelets of heavy weight* (Livy, 1, 11, 11).

b. The genitive of quality and genitive of measure may be used predicatively; as, **illae omnēs dissēnsiōnēs erant eius modī,** *all those disagreements were such,* lit. *of this kind* (In Catilīnam, 3, 10, 25).

101. The neuter genitives **magnī, tantī,** and some others are used predicatively, without a noun, to express indefinite value; as, **Sed est tantī,** *But it is worth while* (In Catilīnam, 1, 9, 8).

102. The objective genitive is used with nouns to denote the object toward which action or feeling is directed, and with adjectives to limit their application, such as denote *knowledge, memory, fullness, power, guilt, desire, participation,* and sometimes **proprius** and **commūnis;** as, **expertem suī,** *free from its influence* (Laelius Dē Amīcitiā, 23, 18); **huius imperī proprium,** *characteristic of this government* (In Catilīnam, 1, 5, 26).

103. *a.* Verbs of *remembering* and *forgetting* may take the genitive; but with words denoting things they may also take the accusative; as, **oblivīscere caedis atque incendiōrum,** *forget murder and fire* (In Catilīnam, 1, 3, 5); **praeterita meminisse,** *to remember the past* (Dē Imperiō Cn. Pompeī, 16, 30).

With **meminī** the genitive is regular when the object is a personal or reflexive pronoun; with other words the accusative is more common.

Verbs of *reminding* may take a genitive of the thing and an accusative of the person reminded; as, **admonēbat alium egestātis,** *he reminded one of his poverty* (Sallust, 21, 16).

However, a neuter pronoun or adjective is regularly in the accusative case: as, **eōs hōc moneō,** *I give them this advice* (In Catilīnam, 2, 9, 36).

b. A genitive of the charge is used with verbs of accusing and condemning; as, **mē ipse inertiae nēquitiaeque condemnō,** *I accuse myself of inactivity and negligence* (In Catilīnam, 1, 2, 18).

c. The impersonals **paenitet, pudet, miseret, taedet, piget** are used with the accusative of the person affected and the genitive of the object of the feeling; as, **eōs numquam oportēbit consilī suī paenitēre,** *they must never (have cause) to repent of their decision* (Philippic, 14, 11, 15).

d. **Interest** and **rēfert,** *it concerns,* are used with a genitive neuter to express the degree of concern; as, **illud parvī rēfert,** *there is little in the consideration,* lit. *it matters little* (Dē Imperiō Cn. Pompeī, 7, 19).

e. **Rēfert** and **interest,** *it concerns, is for the interest of,* take the genitive of the person concerned, if this is a noun; if a personal pronoun, the ablative singular feminine of the corresponding possessive is used instead; as, **nōn illīus magis interest quam meā,** *it does not concern her* (**illīus**) *more than me* (Pliny, 10, 7). A plausible explanation for this use of the possessive may be found in G. 381, Note 5.

THE DATIVE CASE

104. The dative of the indirect object is used with transitive verbs which have a direct object in the accusative, or an infinitive clause as object, and also with the passive of such verbs; as, **Polliceor hōc vōbīs,** *I promise this to you* (In Catilīnam, 1, 13, 21).

105. The dative of the indirect object is used with many intransitive verbs meaning *persuade, believe, trust, distrust; command, obey, serve, resist; pardon, spare; please, displease, favor, indulge; approach; envy, threaten, rebuke,* and some others; as, **mihi crēde,** *believe me* (In Catilīnam, 1, 3, 5). The Roman point of view in these verbs is somewhat different from that of the English, which with corresponding verbs generally uses a direct object.

106. The special verbs of **105** which take the dative of the indirect object are in the passive used only impersonally and retain the dative; as, **ignōscendum esse,** *that pardon ought to be granted* (In Verrem, 57, 3); **cēterīs auctōritātī parendum esse,** *that all other men must obey the authority* (Dē Imperiō Cn. Pompeī, 22, 15).

107. *a.* The dative of the indirect object may be used with many verbs compounded with the prepositions **ad, ante, com-** (for **cum**), **in, inter, ob, prae, sub,** and **super;** as, **antecellere omnibus,** *to excel all* (Prō Archiā, 3, 12).

b. Transitive verbs compounded with these prepositions may have both a direct and an indirect object, the dative depending not on the preposition but on the compound; as, **huius vītam nōn antepōnat suae,** *he does not prefer the life of this man to his own* (Prō Mārcellō, 7, 12).

108. *a.* The dative is used after adjectives meaning *agreeable, friendly, hurtful, hostile, like, unlike, near, subject, obedient, suitable, appropriate,* and many others of kindred meaning; as, **urbemque Asiae clārissimam nōbīsque amīcissimam,** *a city the most famous of Asia and most friendly to us* (Dē Imperiō Cn. Pompeī, 8, 11).

b. Cicero uses **similis** with the genitive of persons, and the genitive or dative of things; as, **Āiācis similēs,** *like Ajax* (Catō Maior Dē Senectūte, 10, 7).

109. *a.* The dative of reference designates the person or interest affected by the action or state expressed in a verb, or in a clause as a whole; it should be translated by *to, for, of, from, in,* or left untranslated, according to the meaning of the clause in which it appears, and the requirements of English idiom. It is sometimes called the dative of advantage or disadvantage to denote the person or thing for whose benefit or to whose detriment the action is done (**datīvus commodī aut incommodī**) ; as, **Mihi Scīpiō vīvit tamen,** *For me Scipio still lives* (Laelius Dē Amīcitiā, 27, 14) ; **nē . . . inānēs sibi metūs fingeret,** *in order that it might not fashion idle fears for its own undoing* (Pliny, 13, 21).

b. A dative of reference is used with verbs of *taking away*, especially those compounded with **ab, dē,** and **ex** (sometimes called dative of separation) ; as, **cuique nōn auferret,** *from whom it would not take away* (Laelius Dē Amīcitiā, 23, 28).

c. A dative of reference is used with **interdīcō**, which may take also the ablative of the thing ; as, **patribus bonīs interdīcī solet,** *fathers are often prevented from managing their property* (Catō Maior Dē Senectūte, 7, 15).

d. The dative of local standpoint is a special variety of the dative of reference ; as, **dēscendentibus inter duōs lūcōs,** *as you come down between the two groves* (Livy, 1, 8, 8).

110. *a.* The dative is used with the passive periphrastic conjugation to express agency ; as, **certē verendum mihi nōn erat,** *surely I had no cause to fear* (In Catilīnam, 1, 12, 9).

b. The dative may be used with passive verbs to express the agent interested in the action ; as, **ut fīnitimīs oppidīs studia hinc petantur,** *so that the neighboring towns may seek their learning from this place* (Pliny, 7, 39).

111. The dative is used with the verb **sum** to emphasize the fact of possession (see **94.** *a*) ; as, **sī essent inimīcitiae mihi,** *if I had hostile feelings* (Dē Prōvinciīs Cōnsulāribus, 20, 2).

112. *a.* The dative is used with verbs to denote the purpose or tendency of an action ; as, **lūdibriō frātris,** *in mockery of his brother,* lit. *for a mockery* (Livy, 1, 7, 7).

b. **Sum** and several other verbs may have two datives, a dative of purpose or tendency and a dative of reference ; as, **maximō tē mihi ūsuī fore,** *that you will be of very great benefit to me* (Cicero, Epistulae, 1, 13).

The Accusative Case

113. *a.* The direct object of a transitive verb is in the accusative case ; as, **Sēmitam tenēbāmus,** *We were holding a mere path* (Dē Prōvinciīs Cōnsulāribus, 13, 30).

b. Several intransitives compounded with **ad, ante, circum, com-, in, ob, prae, praeter, sub,** and **trāns** are used as transitive verbs, and take the accusative; as, **adiit hērēditātēs,** *he entered on inheritances* (Prō Archiā, 5, 31); **trānsiliet moenia mea,** *will leap across my walls* (Livy, 1, 7, 10).

c. **Animadvertō** and **animum advertō** are regularly used with the accusative of the direct object conceived as the object of the mental action expressed by the compound; as, **ecquid animadvertis hōrum silentium,** *do you at all notice the silence of these men* (In Catilīnam, 1, 8, 29)?

114. *a.* Many transitive verbs compounded with **trāns** or **circum** may unite their two parts so closely as to form a transitive verb of simple meaning; as, **ecquid sēcessūs voluptātēs inoffēnsa trānsmitterēs,** *whether you are bearing without harm the pleasures of the retreat* (Pliny, 11, 7).

b. In the passive construction the accusative becomes the subject, and the nominative case becomes the ablative; as, **(annus) quī sōlstitiālī circumagitur orbe,** *which elapses in a solar year,* lit. *which is driven around by a solar revolution* (Livy, 1, 19, 35).

115. *a.* Verbs of *making, choosing, regarding, giving, sending, having, calling, showing,* and some others, may have two accusatives, one a direct object, the other a predicate accusative; as, **quem Statōrem . . . nōmināmus,** *whom we call the Establisher (Stayer)* (In Catilīnam 1, 13, 31).

b. In the construction of verbs of *making, choosing, calling,* etc., with two accusatives, the predicate accusative may be an adjective; as, **eum simillimum deō iūdicō,** *I judge him (to be) very like unto a god* (Prō Mārcellō, 3, 11).

c. In the passive of verbs of *making, choosing, calling,* etc., the direct object of the active is made the subject and the predicate accusative becomes a predicate nominative; as, **ut . . . id, quod esset ā tē scelerātē susceptum, latrōcinium,** *that your criminal undertaking should be called brigandage* (In Catilīnam, 1, 10, 22).

116. *a.* Verbs of *asking, demanding, teaching* may have two accusatives, one of the person, the other of the thing; as, **Hōs sententiam rogō,** *I ask these men their opinion* (In Catilīnam, 1, 4, 15).

b. With verbs of *asking* and *demanding,* such as **quaerō, petō,** and usually **postulō,** the person is expressed by the ablative with a preposition, the thing asked by an accusative or by a clause; as, **quaesīvit ā**

Gallīs, quid sibi esset cum eīs, *he asked the Gauls what he had to do with them* (In Catilīnam, 3, 5, 30).

c. In the passive construction of these verbs the accusative of the person usually becomes the subject, and the accusative of the thing is retained; as, **omnia docētur,** *he is told everything* (Pliny, 13, 16).

117. *a.* With both intransitive and transitive verbs a neuter pronoun, adjective, or **nihil** is used as an accusative of result produced, to carry forward or qualify the meaning; as, **nihil aliud cōgitet,** *he thinks of nothing else* (Dē Imperiō Cn. Pompeī, 22, 21); **Haec precātus,** *Having uttered this prayer* (Livy, 1, 12, 22).

b. The accusative of result may be a noun of kindred meaning or kindred etymology with the verb (cognate accusative); as, **ipsam victōriam vīcisse vidēris,** *you seem to have conquered victory herself* (Prō Mārcellō, 4, 5).

118. *a.* The accusative is used to express extent and duration; as, **domicilium multōs annōs habēret,** *he had a home for many years* (Prō Archiā, 4, 13).

b. Indefinite extent or degree may be expressed with certain verbs by the neuter accusative of pronouns, or of adjectives used substantively; as, **quicquid increpuerit,** *at every sound,* lit. *whatever resounded* (In Catilīnam, 1, 7, 38).

c. Extent may be expressed by the accusative of **nihil,** a construction often called adverbial accusative; as, **nihil hōrum ōra mōvērunt?** *Have not at all the faces of these men affected you* (In Catilīnam, 1, 1, 6)?

d. **Quod,** singular neuter of the relative **quī,** is used as an adverbial accusative before **sī, nisi,** and **ubi,** where it may be translated *now, moreover, but, and,* or *even,* lit. *as to which;* as, **Quod sī haec vōx . . . fuit,** *But if this voice of mine has been* (Prō Archiā, 1, 1, 13).

e. **Quid,** singular neuter of the interrogative **quis,** is used as an adverbial accusative with the meaning *why?* lit. *as to what thing?* as, **Quid exspectās auctōritātem?** *Why are you waiting for the authority* (In Catilīnam, 1, 8, 31)?

119. *a.* Names of towns or small islands are put in the accusative to express the limit of motion; as, **quōs Faesulās L. Sulla dēdūxit,** *whom Lucius Sulla led forth to Faesulae* (In Catilīnam, 3, 6, 22).

b. In like manner **domum,** the accusative of **domus,** is used to express limit of motion; as, **domum redūxerit,** *conducted me back home* (Philippic, 14, 5, 11). But when **domum** means house it may take the preposition **in**; as, **in M. Laecae domum,** *into the house of Marcus Laeca* (In Catilīnam, 1, 4, 4).

120. The accusative of names of towns is used with **ad** to express *to the vicinity of, in the neighborhood of;* as, **ad Forum Aurēlium praestōlārentur,** *to wait near Forum Aurelium* (In Catilīnam, 1, 9, 29).

121. The subject of the infinitive is in the accusative; as, **tē vīxisse,** *that you have lived* (Prō Mārcellō, 8, 15).

122. *a.* The following prepositions govern the accusative only: **ad,** *to;* **adversus,** *against;* **ante,** *before;* **apud,** *near, with, among;* **circā,** *around;* **circiter,** *about;* **circum,** *around;* **cis,** *on this side of;* **citrā,** *on this side of;* **contrā,** *against;* **ergā,** *towards;* **extrā,** *outside of;* **īnfrā,** *below;* **inter,** *between;* **intrā,** *within;* **iūxtā,** *near;* **ob,** *on account of;* **penes,** *in the possession of;* **per,** *through;* **post,** *after;* **praeter,** *excepting;* **prope,** *near;* **propter,** *on account of;* **secundum,** *along, after, besides, according to;* **suprā,** *above;* **trāns,** *across, on the other side of;* **ultrā,** *beyond;* **versus,** *toward* (regularly follows its noun).

b. Several of these prepositions are used also as adverbs.

123. *a.* With nouns referring to persons, **per** with the accusative is used to express the means through which something is done, as distinguished from direct agency, which is expressed by the ablative with **ā** or **ab**; as, **per Fulviam effēcerat,** *through Fulvia he had brought about* (Sallust, 26, 7).

b. **Propius,** *nearer,* as well as **prope** (**122.** *a*), *near,* may be used with the accusative; as, **prope metum,** *near to fear* (Livy, 1, 25, 50); **propius Albam,** *nearer Alba* (Livy, 1, 25, 56).

c. **Ūsque,** *up to,* is sometimes used with the accusative of the name of a town; it rarely follows the noun; as, **Tarsum ūsque,** *even to Tarsus* (Cicero, Epistulae, 12, 24).

124. *a.* The prepositions **in** and **sub** are used with the accusative to denote motion, with the ablative to denote rest.

b. **Super** is used ordinarily with the accusative, but occasionally with the ablative; as, **super tantā rē,** *on such an important problem* (Pliny, 4, 15).

c. The simple accusative is used in exclamations; as **Ō rēctam sincēramque vītam,** *O real and genuine life* (Pliny, 3, 17).

THE ABLATIVE CASE

125. *a.* The following prepositions are used with the ablative: **ā,** or **ab, abs,** *away from, by;* **cum,** *with;* **dē,** *down from, concerning;*

ex or ē, *out from, out of;* **prae,** *before;* **prō,** *in front of, for, considering, as;* **sine,** *without.*

b. The form **abs** appears only in **abs tē.** Ab and **ex** are regularly used before vowels and **h;** ā and ē, before consonants, but before consonants **ab** and **ex** are also used. See B. 142, 1.

c. With the ablative of the personal, reflexive, and relative pronouns **cum** is ordinarily joined; as, **nōbīscum,** *with us* (Prō Archiā, 7, 28).

126. *a.* Direct agency with the passive is expressed by **ā, ab,** with the ablative; as, **ā mē,** *by me* (In Catilīnam, 1, 2, 26). Compare **123.** *a.*

b. An abstract or collective noun with **ā, ab** is sometimes used to express agency; as, **ā cōnsēnsū cīvitātis,** *by the unanimous consent of the state,* lit. *by the unanimity of the state* (Philippic, 14, 5, 13).

c. **Ā, ab,** and sometimes **ex,** are used to indicate a local relation, where we use *on, in,* or *at;* as, **ab Sabīnīs,** *on the part of the Sabines* (Livy, 1, 12, 9).

127. *a.* An ablative of separation without a preposition is regularly used with many verbs meaning *keep from, refrain from; withdraw from; strip, deprive of; free from; lack, be without;* as, **cūrā līberārent,** *might relieve from anxiety* (In Catilīnam, 1, 4, 24).

b. With several of these verbs the idea of separation may be expressed by a preposition; as, **ā reī pūblicae perīculīs sēiungātur,** *is separated from the dangers of the state* (In Catilīnam, 1, 9, 9).

c. Verbs compounded with **ā, ab, dē, ex** usually require the preposition when the separation is literal or actual; as, **ab eōrum ārīs discēdere,** *to leave their altars* (Philippic, 14, 1, 18).

d. **Egeō** and **indigeō** may also take the genitive; as, **tuī meī indigēbunt,** *my family will need you* (Cicero, Epistulae, 8, 2).

128. A variety of the ablative of separation is the ablative of source, or origin, with **nātus,** participle of **nāscor,** and **ortus,** participle of **orior,** with or without a preposition; as, **nōbilī genere nātus,** *descended from a noble family* (Sallust, 5, 1).

129. The ablative of comparison is used with comparative adjectives and adverbs; as, **Nihil est virtūte amābilius,** *Nothing is more attractive than virtue* (Laelius Dē Amīcitiā, 8, 25); **celerius opīniōne,** *quicker than any one had anticipated* (Cicero, Epistulae, 19, 2).

130. *a.* The place whence is regularly expressed by the ablative with the prepositions **ā, ab, ē, ex,** or **dē;** as, **ex urbe,** *from the city* (In Catilīnam, 1, 5, 31).

b. The names of towns, cities, small islands, **domus**, and **rūs** usually omit the preposition; but it may be used to denote *from the vicinity of;* as, **ut ā Mutinā discēderet**, *that he should withdraw from (the vicinity of) Mutina* (Philippic, 14, 2, 2).

131. *a.* The ablative is used to denote means or instrument; as, **proeliīs frēgit**, *he crushed in war* (Dē Prōvinciīs Cōnsulāribus, 13, 17).

b. The ablative of means may denote persons as well as things; as, **ferentāriīs proelium committi posset**, *the battle could be begun by the light-armed skirmishers* (Sallust, 60, 3).

c. The ablative of means is used with **ūtor, fruor, fungor, vescor,** their compounds, and ordinarily with **potior**; as, **abūtēre patientiā nostrā?** *Will you exhaust our patience* (In Catilīnam, 1, 1, 1)? **potītus imperiō**, *held the supreme power* (Livy, 1, 7, 11).

d. **Potior** may be used also with the genitive, and is regularly so used with **rērum**; as **rērum potīrī volunt**, *wish to become masters of affairs* (In Catilīnam, 2, 9, 2).

e. An ablative of means is used with **frētus**, *relying on*, lit. *supported by;* as, **tē ūnō frētus**, *relying on you alone* (Cicero, Epistulae, 2, 4).

132. *a.* **Opus est**, *there is need*, is used with the ablative of the thing needed; as, **perditā rē pūblicā opus esse**, *needed the ruin of the state* (Sallust, 31, 25).

b. With **opus est** the thing needed may be expressed by a neuter pronoun in the nominative; as, **quod opus erit**, *whatever will be necessary* (Cicero, Epistulae, 17, 1).

133. The ablative of means is used with a few adjectives; as, **omnibus rēbus ōrnātās ac refertās**, *adorned and fitted out with every kind of equipment* (Dē Imperiō Cn. Pompeī, 8, 22).

134. The ablative is sometimes used to express the way by which; as, **Aurēliā viā profectus est**, *he set out by the Aurelian Way* (In Catilīnam, 2, 4, 8).

135. *a.* An ablative denoting cause is used with many verbs and adjectives, particularly those which express *pleasure, pain, trust, distrust, boastfulness*, and the like; as, **neglegentiā plectimur**, *we are chastised for negligence* (Laelius Dē Amīcitiā, 22, 32).

b. In some phrases the force of the ablative of cause has become obscured, as in **causā** and **grātiā**, *for the sake of*, with the genitive, and in **iussū, iniussū**, and the like; as, **glōriae causā**, *for the sake of glory* (Dē Archiā, 10, 13); **iussū senātūs**, *at the senate's order* (In Catilīnam, 3, 4, 2).

136. *a.* Manner (answering the question " How? ") is expressed by **cum** and the ablative; when a limiting adjective is used with the noun, **cum** may be omitted; as, **sī ēmorī aequō animō nōn potes,** *if you cannot die with resignation* (In Catilīnam, 1, 8, 17).

b. The ablative of manner is often used without a preposition, especially in certain stock expressions which are almost equivalent to adverbs, such as **modō, pactō, ratiōne, rītū, vī, iūre, iniūriā, silentiō, voluntāte,** and a few others; as, **id nōn iūre factum esse,** *that this was not done justly* (In Catilīnam, 1, 2, 30); **quī ēgī silentiō,** *who have discussed amid silence,* i.e. *without interruption* (Dē Prōvinciīs Cōnsulāribus, 12, 2).

c. A variety of the ablative of manner denotes that in accordance with which something is done; as, **sententiā meā,** *in accordance with my opinion* (Dē Prōvinciīs Cōnsulāribus, 20, 6).

137. *a.* The ablative is used with **cum** to express accompaniment; as, **stetisse in comitiō cum tēlō,** *that (you) stood in the comitium with a weapon* (In Catilīnam, 1, 6, 26); **cum deā Ēgeriā congressūs,** *meetings with the goddess Egeria* (Livy, 1, 19, 22).

b. An ablative of accompaniment referring to military operations, when qualified by an adjective, may be used with or without **cum;** but if the modifier is a numeral, **cum** is regularly employed; as, **cum tribus Antōnī legiōnibus equitātūque cōnflīxit,** *he fought with the three legions of Antonius and with his cavalry* (Philippic, 14, 10, 9).

c. The use of **cum** with the ablative of accompaniment is much broader than the meaning *together with.* Examples are: **nōn ego eum cum summīs virīs comparō,** *I do not compare him with the most illustrious men* (Prō Mārcellō, 3, 10); **tēcum sīc agit,** *thus pleads with you* (In Catilīnam, 1, 7, 29).

138. An ablative of attendant circumstance is used with an adjective, pronominal adjective, or genitive as modifying word, and without a preposition; as, **magnīs perīculīs parta,** *won at great risk* (Dē Prōvinciīs Cōnsulāribus, 12, 16).

139. The ablative is used with certain verbs meaning *exchange, mix,* and *accustom,* to denote association; **misceō, iungō,** and some of their compounds may be used with or without **cum;** as, **quī tēcum iūnxērunt,** *who united with you* (In Catilīnam, 1, 13, 27).

140. The ablative of degree of difference is used with comparatives, and with adverbs or phrases implying comparison; as, **paulō ante,** *a little before,* lit. *by a little before* (In Catilīnam, 1, 8, 42); **multō mē**

vigilāre ācrius, *that I am watching much more sharply* (In Catilīnam, 1, 4, 2).

This construction sometimes approaches the ablative of cause, as, **Quō impēnsius rogō,** *The more earnestly I request* (Pliny, 11, 13).

The correlatives **quō . . . eō,** and **quantō . . . tantō,** used with comparatives, are ablatives of degree of difference; they are best translated by the pronominal adverb *the . . . the;* as, **Quantō vōs attentius ea agētis, tantō illīs animus īnfīrmior erit,** *The more attention you pay to this, the weaker will be the courage of the conspirators* (Sallust, 52, 35).

141. The ablative of price is used with verbs of buying and selling; as, **minōre sūmptū,** *at less expense* (Pliny, 7, 18).

142. *a.* The ablative of specification, regularly without a preposition (answering the question " In respect to what? "), is used with verbs and adjectives; as, **mente captus,** *fettered in mind,* i.e. *insane* (In Catilīnam, 3, 9, 2). This ablative is very closely related to that of means, cause, and manner; as, **propinquitāte coniūnctōs atque nātūrā,** *closely allied in kinship and nature* (Laelius Dē Amīcitiā, 14, 13).

b. The ablative of specification is used with **dignus** and **indignus;** as, **praemiō dignam,** *worthy of reward* (Prō Archiā, 10, 44).

143. *a.* The descriptive ablative, or ablative of quality or characteristic, is modified by an adjective or, more rarely, by a noun in the genitive; as, **magnā speciē ānulōs,** *rings of great beauty* (Livy, 1, 11, 11).

b. The descriptive ablative may be used predicatively; as, **quantā innocentiā dēbent esse imperātōrēs!** *How great ought to be the integrity of generals,* lit. *of how great integrity* (Dē Imperiō Cn. Pompeī, 13, 7)!

144. *a.* The ablative absolute consists of a noun or pronoun in the ablative with a participle, adjective, or noun in the same case, and is loosely related with the rest of the sentence; the name absolute comes from **absolūtus,** *loosened from* or *free from* the rest of the sentence, grammatically.

b. The ablative absolute may express time, attendant circumstance, cause, condition, concession, means, or manner, and may often be translated by a clause; the literal translation in the form of a nominative absolute in English should generally be avoided; as,

(1) Time: **C. Mariō et L. Valeriō cōnsulibus,** *in the consulship of Gaius Marius and Lucius Valerius* (In Catilīnam, 1, 2, 6).

(2) Attendant Circumstance: **Indiciīs expositīs atque ēditīs,** *After the proofs had been set forth and produced* (In Catilīnam, 3, 6, 1).

(3) Cause: **cōnservātā rē pūblicā,** *because the state has been preserved* (In Catilīnam, 3, 6, 38).

(4) Condition: **quā quidem dētrāctā,** *but if this be taken away* (Prō Archiā, 11, 31).

(5) Concession or Opposition: **nūllō adversāriō,** *although no one opposes them* (Cicero, Epistulae, 4, 11).

(6) Means: **Caesare impulsōre atque adiūtōre,** *by the instigation and assistance of Caesar* (Dē Prōvinciīs Cōnsulāribus, 8, 7).

(7) Manner: **dēmissō vultū,** *with downcast countenance* (Sallust, 31, 20).

145. *a.* The place where is regularly expressed by the ablative with the preposition **in;** as, **in Etrūriae faucibus,** *in the mountain-passes of Etruria* (In Catilīnam, 1, 2, 19).

b. Names of towns, excepting those in the singular of the first and second declensions, are put in the ablative of the place where, without a preposition; as, **Syrācūsīs,** *in Syracuse* (In Verrem, 53, 18).

c. Designations of place like **locō, locīs, parte, castrīs,** and many other words when modified by an adjective, particularly by **tōtus, cūnctus, omnis,** and **medius,** are often used without **in;** as, **tōtā Italiā,** *in entire Italy* (In Catilīnam, 2, 4, 14); **prīmā domūs parte,** *in the front of the house* (Pliny, 13, 18). The phrase **terrā marīque** also belongs here; as, **terrā marīque,** *on land and sea* (Prō Archiā, 9, 17).

d. The ablative with **in** may be used figuratively; as, **magnō in aere aliēnō,** *greatly in debt* (In Catilīnam, 2, 8, 12); **in animīs hominum,** *in the minds of men* (Prō Mārcellō, 7, 17).

146. With names of towns and small islands of the first and second declensions, singular, place where is expressed by the locative; as, **Rōmae,** *at Rome* (In Catilīnam, 2, 4, 29). Similarly, **domī,** *at home* (when **domus** means *house,* it usually stands in the ablative with **in**), **humī,** *on the ground,* **bellī** and **mīlitiae,** *in war,* **rūrī,** *in the country;* as, **domī mīlitiaeque,** *in peace and in war* (Sallust, 29, 11).

The appositive of a locative is put in the ablative case, with or without **in;** as, **Antiochīae, celebrī urbe,** *at Antioch, a populous city* (Prō Archiā, 3, 8).

147. *a.* The time when, and time within which anything happens, may be denoted by the ablative without a preposition; as, **quid**

superiōre nocte ēgerīs, *what you did the night before* (In Catilīnam, 1, 1, 10).

b. Words that have only an indirect reference to time are some-times put in the ablative of time when or within which; as, **comitiīs,** *at the election* (In Catilīnam, 1, 5, 16).

c. Intervals of space and duration of time are sometimes expressed by the ablative, especially when modified by an adjective or genitive; as, **pauculīs adhūc diēbus commorābor,** *I shall linger a few days yet* (Pliny, 7, 3).

ADJECTIVES

148. *a.* Adjectives and participles, whether attributive or predica-tive, agree in gender, number, and case with the noun or pronoun to which they belong.

b. Attributive adjectives and participles stand in direct relation with a noun or pronoun; as, **bellum hāc scelerātā coniūrātiōne excitātum,** *a war stirred up by that impious conspiracy* (Dē Prōvinciīs Cōnsulāribus, 13, 17).

c. Predicate adjectives, and participles in predicate used as ad-jectives, are connected with a noun or pronoun through a verb or participle; as, **Potestne haec lūx esse iūcundus (iūcunda)?** *Can this light be pleasing* (In Catilīnam, 1, 6, 23)?

d. A predicate adjective or participle limiting an infinitive or clause is neuter; as, **facile est bene agere,** *it is easy to deal fairly* (Philippic, 14, 11, 16).

e. A participle forming part of an infinitive may agree with the subject of the principal verb; as, **levāta (esse) rēs pūblica vidētur,** *the state seems to have been relieved* (In Catilīnam, 2, 4, 11).

149. Demonstrative and other pronouns used like adjectives agree with the word to which they belong; as, **hōc tempore,** *at this time* (Dē Prōvinciīs Cōnsulāribus, 20, 2); **cum inimīcō suō,** *with their en-emy* (Dē Prōvinciīs Cōnsulāribus, 20, 21); **per sē ipsum,** *through his own power* (In Catilīnam, 4, 11, 7).

150. *a.* An attributive adjective used with two or more nouns regularly agrees with the nearest; as, **signum et manum suam,** *his seal and hand* (In Catilīnam, 3, 5, 18).

b. A predicate adjective used with two or more nouns is regularly plural; when the nouns are of different genders, the adjective is gen-erally masculine if persons are referred to, neuter if only things or abstract qualities are denoted, though even in this case the agreement may be with the nearer substantive; as, **bella intestīna, caedēs, rapīnae, discordia cīvīlis grāta fuēre,** *civil war, murder, robbery, and political strife were pleasing* (Sallust, 5, 3); in this sentence **grāte** might be construed as neuter plural, or feminine singular agreeing with the nearest noun; **genus, aetās, ēloquentia prope aequālia fuēre**, *their birth, their age, and their eloquence were almost equal* (Sallust, 54, 1).

With two or more feminine abstract nouns a predicate adjective may be neuter plural; as, **(inopiā et cōnscientiā) quae utraque eīs artibus auxerat,** *both of which he had aggravated by those qualities* (Sallust, 5, 15).

c. An adjective or participle may agree with a noun in sense, without regard to grammatical gender or number; see **164.** *d.*

d. A noun, particularly a noun with verbal force, is sometimes modified by a prepositional phrase instead of an objective genitive; in other relations this adjectival use never became common; as, **summō ergā vōs amōre,** *by the deepest love towards you* (In Catilīnam, 3, 1, 5); **adventūs in urbēs,** *arrival in the cities* (Dē Imperiō Cn. Pompeī, 5, 21); **iter in Hispāniam,** *road into Spain* (Dē Imperiō Cn. Pompeī, 11, 16).

151. Adjectives are sometimes used in Latin where in English an adverb or a phrase is required; as, **īdem imprūdēns hostēs iūdicāvit,** *the same man unconsciously pronounced them enemies* (Philippic, 14, 8, 9).

152. *a.* Certain adjectives often designate a part of that to which they refer; the adjectives commonly thus used are **extrēmus**; **īnfimus** or **īmus**; **medius**; **multus**; **novissimus,** in **novissimum agmen,** *the rear of a* marching *column* as the *latest part* of a column to pass a given point; **prīmus** and **summus**; as, **extrēmā hieme,** *at the end of winter* (Dē Imperiō Cn. Pompeī, 12, 53); **mediā aestāte,** *in the middle of summer* (Dē Imperiō Cn. Pompeī, 12, 54).

b. The adjectives **prīnceps, prior, prīmus, ultimus** are sometimes used to designate *the first to* do or experience something; as, **Haec sē prīma (legiō) latrōciniō abrūpit Antōnī,** *This was the first legion to tear itself away from the plundering band of Antony* (Philippic, 14, 12, 5).

c. The adjective **multus** and another adjective agreeing with the same noun are joined by **et** or **-que**; as, **multīs meīs et firmīs praesidiīs oppressus,** *overpowered by my many strong guards* (In Catilīnam, 1, 2, 33).

153. *a.* The comparative and superlative of both adjectives and adverbs sometimes have shades of meaning best expressed in English by *too, rather, fairly, quite, very, exceedingly,* or *highly,* and the like, with the positive; as, **fortissimō virō,** *a very (unusually) brave man* (In Catilīnam, 1, 8, 34).

b. A superlative is sometimes modified by an adverb; as, **longē prīmus,** *by far the first* (Livy, 21, 4, 22); **multō iūcundissimus,** *by far the most pleasing* (Dē Imperiō Cn. Pompeī, 1, 2).

c. The highest possible degree is expressed by **quam** with the superlative; as, **quam frūctuōsissimum,** *as productive as possible* (Pliny, 10, 6).

154. *a.* Adjectives and participles are used as substantives, frequently in the plural, less often in the singular; as, **Veterānī,** *The veteran soldiers* (Sallust, 60, 6); **dē improbīs et audācibus** *(for victory over)* *the wicked and the bold* (Philippic, 14, 3, 16); **omnēs bonī,** *all patriotic men* (In Catilīnam, 1, 2, 25); **plūra,** *more thoughts* (Philippic, 14, 11, 20). For the correct translation of such adjectives see **211.**

b. For the use of the ablative singular feminine of the possessive adjective with **rēfert** and **interest,** such as **meā, tuā, vestrā, nostrā,** see **103.** *e.*

PRONOUNS

155. The genitives **meī, nostrī, tuī,** and **vestrī (39.** *a)* are regularly objective, **nostrum** and **vestrum** being used in other relations; with **omnium, vestrum** and **nostrum** are regularly used; as, **memorem vestrī,** *mindful of you* (In Catilīnam, 4, 9, 25); **cuiusque nostrum,** *of each one of us* (In Catilīnam, 4, 6, 3); **omnium vestrum,** *of all of you* (In Catilīnam, 2, 12, 2).

156. The plural is often used for the singular of the pronoun of the first person, just as in our " editorial we "; as, **nōs in cōnsulātū nostrō gessimus,** *we in our consulship performed* (Prō Archiā, 11, 25).

157. *a.* The possessive pronouns are expressed only when required for the sake of clearness, emphasis, or contrast; in translating they must be supplied in accordance with English idiom.

b. When expressed for clearness, and unemphatic, the possessive pronoun usually follows its noun; as, **auctōritās dēcrētōrum vestrōrum,** *the authority of your decrees* (Dē Prōvinciīs Cōnsulāribus, 20, 11); when used for emphasis or contrast, the possessive pronoun precedes its noun; as, **ego meā sententiā,** *in my opinion* (Dē Prōvinciīs Cōnsulāribus, 8, 1).

c. **Noster** is often used to designate that which is Roman; as, **in nostram diciōnem**, *into our power* (Dē Prōvinciīs Cōnsulāribus, 13, 23).

d. A possessive pronoun and a genitive are sometimes coördinated in construction; as, **neque suō neque amīcōrum iūdiciō,** *neither by his own opinion nor that of his friends* (Prō Archiā, 5, 35).

e. **Suus** may mean *characteristic, well-known, proper, appropriate, favorable, right*; as, **suō tempore,** *at the right time* (Philippic, 14, 6, 14).

158. *a.* The reflexive pronoun of the third person, **sē,** and the corresponding possessive, **suus,** refer to the subject of the verb; in a subordinate clause they may refer to the subject of the principal clause (indirect reflexive); as, **quī sē coniungeret,** *in order that he might join himself* (In Catilīnam, 3, 4, 11); **rogant, ut sē dignōs exīstimētis,** *they ask that you may consider them worthy* (Dē Imperiō Cn. Pompeī, 5, 16); **suus,** however, has a wider range of usage than **sē**; as, **admonēbat alium cupiditātis suae,** *he would remind another of his desire* (Sallust, 21, 17); here **suae** refers to **alium.**

b. In the pronouns of the first and second persons the regular forms are sometimes reflexive; as, **mē condemnō,** *I accuse myself* (In Catilīnam, 1, 2, 18).

c. In translating into Latin, the English possessives "his," "her," "its," "their," when referring to the subject of the verb, must be rendered by forms of the reflexive **suus.**

159. The reciprocal relation may be expressed by (**nōs**) **inter nōs,** (**vōs**) **inter vōs,** occasionally by a combination of an active and a passive verb, and by **inter sē** (lit. *among themselves*), which must be translated in accordance with the requirements of English idiom; Livy, Pliny, and later writers use also the adverb **invicem** for the reciprocal relation; as, **nōs inter nōs,** *us with each other* (Cicero, Epistulae, 2, 13); **inter vōs,** *with one another* (Livy, 13, 8); **inter sē,** *with one another* (Prō Archiā, 1, 23); **amāre et amārī didicērunt,** *they have learned (how) to love one another* (In Catilīnam, 2, 10, 35); **quasi invicem ēlēgerīs,** *as if you chose us for each other* (Pliny, 8, 27).

160. *a.* The demonstrative pronoun **hīc,** *this,* refers to something near the speaker or the subject of thought, and is called the demonstrative of the first person; **iste,** *that of yours,* to something near the person addressed, and is called the demonstrative of the second person; **ille,** *that,* to something more remote, and is called the demonstrative of the third person ; and is, *that*, to something thought of in a less definite relation. Iste frequently refers to one's opponent in debate, and so may imply antagonism and contempt ; as, **hīc tamen vīvit,** *nevertheless this man lives* (In Catilīnam, 1, 1, 14) ; **fūror iste tuus,** *that madness of yours* (In Catilīnam, 1, 1, 2) ; **adventū tuō ista subsellia vacuēfacta sunt,** *at your approach the benches near you were vacated* (In Catilīnam, 1, 7, 9) ; **de istīs, quī sē populārēs habērī volunt,** *of those fellows* (compare the English colloquial *guys*) *who wish themselves to be regarded friends of the people* (In Catilīnam, 4, 5, 14) ; **illōs, quī in urbe remānsērunt,** *those men, who have remained in the city* (In Catilīnam, 2, 12, 1).

b. Is is regularly used where the English has a personal pronoun of the third person ; as, **Amoenitās locōrum eum retinet,** *Attractive surroundings hold him back* (Dē Prōvinciīs Cōnsulāribus, 12, 7).

c. The neuter singular and neuter plural of **hīc, ille,** and is are frequently used with the meaning *this* (*thing*), *that* (*thing*), *it, these* (*things*), *those* (*things*); in translating it is best to supply a noun ; as, **illa nimis antīqua praetereō,** *I pass over those precedents as too remote* (In Catilīnam, 1, 1, 25). See **211.**

d. A demonstrative pronoun is sometimes used in Latin where English usage prefers an article ; as, **sī rēs eae, quās gessimus,** *if the success, which we have achieved* (Prō Archiā, 10, 9) ; **eum cōnsulem quī nōn dubitet,** *a consul who will not hesitate* (In Catilīnam, 4, 11, 5).

e. A demonstrative pronoun used as subject is sometimes attracted into agreement with a noun in the predicate ; as, **Haec prīma lēx amīcitiae sanciātur,** *Let this be ratified as the first law of friendship* (Laelius Dē Amīcitiā, 13, 1).

f. Ille may mean *the famous, the well-known;* as, **Ipse ille C. Marius,** *Even the famous Gaius Marius* (Dē Prōvinciīs Cōnsulāribus, 13, 5).

161. *a.* The demonstratives **hīc** and **ille** sometimes refer to what follows ; **hīc** may also refer to that which has just been mentioned ; as, **Haec habuī dē senectūte quae dīcerem,** *This was what I had to say on old age* (Catō Maior Dē Senectūte, 23, 42) ; **Extrēmum illud est,** *The following is my last word* (Dē Prōvinciīs Cōnsulāribus, 20, 1).

b. Hīc and ille are often used in contrast, with the meaning *the latter* (that last mentioned) and *the former* (that previously mentioned), respectively ; as, **Cōnferte hanc pācem cum illō bellō, huius libīdinēs cum illīus continentiā,** *Compare the present peace with the former war,* *the lust of this man* (Verres) *with the moderation of the former* (Marcellus) (In Verrem, 52, 9–12).

For rhetorical reasons the natural signification is sometimes reversed so that **hīc** is *the former,* and **ille**, *the latter;* as, **At est eō meliōre condiciōne quam adulēscēns, quoniam id, quod ille spērat, hīc consecūtus est: ille vult diū vīvere, hīc diū vīxit,** *But he* (an old man) *is in so much the better situation than a young man, since the former has attained what the young man* (*ille*) *hopes for : the one* (the young man) *wishes for a long life, the other has experienced it* (Catō Maior Dē Senectūte, 19, 24).

162. *a.* The intensive pronoun **ipse** with nouns and pronouns has the meaning *self, very, even, only, own, actual, real, regular, proper, likewise, too, exactly, as such, right, voluntarily, merely, particular, personally,* and the like; as, **ipse Caesar,** *Caesar himself* (Dē Prōvinciīs Cōnsulāribus, 12, 5); **ad ipsam requiem animī et corporis,** *merely for mental and physical relaxation* (Prō Archiā, 6, 28); **quae tamen ipsa efflōrēscit ex amīcitiā,** *and yet this spontaneously blossoms forth from friendship* (like a flower) (Laelius Dē Amīcitiā, 27, 9); **ex rē ipsā,** *from the actual fact* (Cicero, Epistulae, 8, 1); **in ipsō itinere et viā,** *on their journey and actually on the road* (Cicero, Epistulae, 12, 1); **in ipsā viā,** *right on the highway* (Cicero, Epistulae, 12, 4); **collocūtiōne ipsā,** *by the mere act of our talking familiarly* (Cicero, Epistulae, 21, 24); **in ipsā victōriā,** *in the very moment of victory* (Philippic, 14, 12, 9); **in ipsō cursū,** *in the race proper* (Pliny, 15, 10); **huic ipsī,** *to this particular man* (Prō Archiā, 1, 15).

b. Contrasted pronouns are often placed in proximity; as, **ut timōrem eius suā sēcūritāte lēnīret,** *to calm his* (the friend's) *fear by his own unconcern* (Pliny, 12, 53).

163. *a.* A relative pronoun agrees with its antecedent in gender and number, but the case depends upon its construction in the clause to which it belongs; as, **cui adulēscentulō, quem irrētīssēs,** *what youth, whom you had entangled* (In Catilīnam, 1, 6, 9)?

b. A relative referring to two or more antecedents of the same gender and number agrees with them in gender, but in number may agree with the nearest antecedent, or be plural; as, **Dē virtūte et gravitāte Caesaris, quam in summō dolōre adhibuisset,** *Regarding the courage and dignity of Caesar, which* (as you say) *he displayed in his extreme sorrow* (Cicero, Epistulae, 11, 28); Cicero might have used **quās** instead of **quam** with equal correctness.

c. A relative referring to two or more antecedents of different gender or number follows the rule of agreement laid down for a predicate adjective (See **150.** *b*); as, **de gladiīs ac sīcīs, quae erant dēprehēnsa,** *about the swords and daggers which had been discovered* (In Catilīnam, 3, 5, 11); although the antecedents of **quae** are masculine and feminine respectively, the relative is neuter because they denote inanimate objects.

164. *a.* The antecedent of a relative pronoun is sometimes omitted; as, **pepigisse eam quod,** *that she had stipulated for this* (**id** understood) *which* (Livy, 11, 12).

b. A relative sometimes refers to an implied antecedent; as, **nostrā, quī remānsissēmus, caede contentum,** *satisfied with killing us who had stayed behind* (In Catilīnam, 1, 3, 23).

c. A noun in the predicate attracts a relative pronoun standing as subject into agreement with it; as, **quī est amīcitiae fōns,** *which is the source of friendship* (Laelius Dē Amīcitiā, 14, 17).

d. A plural relative may refer for its antecedent to a singular collective noun which suggests plurality; as, **Quārtum genus . . . quī iam prīdem premuntur,** *A fourth class, who have long ago been burdened* (In Catilīnam, 2, 10, 2).

165. *a.* An antecedent is sometimes repeated in a relative clause, and should be translated only once; as, **certō diē, quī diēs,** *on a definite day, which* (In Catilīnam, 1, 3, 10).

b. An appositional antecedent is sometimes incorporated in a relative clause, and should be translated; as, **quae praemia,** *rewards which* (Philippic, 14, 14, 43).

c. An antecedent is often incorporated in a relative clause when the antecedent is an appositive, when the relative clause stands first, and when the antecedent is a superlative; as, **quās novās sēdēs,** *which as new abodes* (Livy, 2, 1, 6).

166. The neuter of a relative or demonstrative pronoun, sometimes both a demonstrative and a relative, may refer to a clause or thought as a whole; as, **Quod exspectāvī, iam sum assecūtus, ut,** etc., *What I have been waiting for, I have now accomplished,* (namely) *that,* etc. (In Catilīnam, 2, 4, 1).

167. A relative is often used in Latin at the beginning of a clause or sentence where English idiom requires a demonstrative, with or without a connective; as, **Quam ob rem,** *And for this reason* (In Catilīnam, 1, 9, 16).

168. Of the indefinite pronouns, **quīdam**, *a certain*, is used in respect to persons or things distinctly thought of but not described; **aliquis**, *some, any, somebody*, of persons or things referred to in a general way; **quis** and **quī**, *any, some*, still more vaguely, with **sī, nisi, seu, nē**, and **ubi**; and **quisquam**, *any at all*, in interrogative or negative clauses or in a clause following a comparative; as, **ad breve quoddam tempus**, *for a certain short time* (In Catilīnam, 1, 13, 5); **quisquam dubitābit?** *Will anyone doubt* (Dē Imperiō Cn. Pompeī, 14, 47)?

Nesciō quis is a compound indefinite pronoun meaning *some one or other;* as, **nesciō quō pactō**, *in some manner or other* (In Catilīnam, 1, 13, 2).

169. The indefinite distributive pronoun **uterque** means *each of two*, and is used in the plural as well as the singular; as, **Quōs utrōsque**, *Both of these classes* (In Catilīnam, 2, 9, 33).

170. *a.* The indefinite distributive pronoun **quisque**, *each*, is often used with a superlative to designate a class, or with a numeral ordinal to indicate a proportion; as, **optimō cuique maximē**, *to each man in proportion to his merit* (Dē Imperiō Cn. Pompeī, 1, 4).

b. **Quisque**, *each*, is often used in close connection with **ūnus, sē**, and **suus** and has a tendency to stand in dependent clauses, particularly in relative clauses; as, **Nostrum ūnus quisque**, *Each one of us* (In Verrem, 57, 8); **quod quisque minus per sē ipse posset, id acciperet**, *each man might receive what he could not have through his own efforts* (Laelius Dē Amīcitiā, 8, 4).

171. *a.* Of the pronominal adjectives, **cēterī** (plural) means *the other, the rest* besides those mentioned; **reliquī**, *the rest* in the sense *those remaining* after some are taken; as, **cēterīque fortissimī cīvēs**, *all of the other very brave citizens* (In Catilīnam, 1, 8, 40); **reliquīs vīvīs**, *if the rest remain alive* (In Catilīnam, 1, 13, 13).

b. **Alter** and **alius** are frequently used in a correlative relation; as, **quōrum alter rēs maximās, alter studium adhibēre posset**, *the one of whom could supply illustrious achievements, the other his interest* (Prō Archiā, 3, 22); **aliīs frūctum libīdinum, aliīs mortem parentum pollicēbātur**, *to some he promised the gratification of their passions, to others the death of their parents* (In Catilīnam, 2, 4, 24).

c. The various combinations of **alius alium, alter alterum** form a very condensed expression; as, **cēterī verbō alius aliī variō assentiēbantur**, *the rest by a single word signified their assent to one or another of the different motions* (Sallust, 52, 2).

VERBS

Agreement, Moods and Tenses, Questions

172. *a.* A finite verb agrees with its subject in number and person; in compound forms of the verb the participle must agree with the subject also in gender; as, **Tū, Iuppiter, quī es cōnstitūtus,** *Thou, O Jupiter, who hast been ordained* (In Catilīnam, 1, 13, 31).

b. When a verb is used with more than one subject, it may agree with the nearest subject, or be plural; as, **Amoenitās eum locōrum, crēdō, urbium pulchritūdō, hominum nātiōnumque illārum hūmānitās et lepōs, victōriae cupiditās, fīnium imperī prōpāgātiō retinet,** *It is the attractive surroundings, I suppose, the beauty of the cities, the culture and charm of those people and nations, a desire for victory, the extension of the boundaries of (our) empire that keep him (there)* (Dē Provinciis Cōnsulāribus, 12, 9).

c. Verbs are sometimes used in the third person plural with an implied indefinite subject, as, **ut aiunt,** *as they say,* i.e. *as the expression goes* (In Catilīnam, 1, 6, 34).

d. A verb in Latin is sometimes used with a personal subject where the English prefers the impersonal construction with " it "; as, **quī sē in illa castra cōnferre dīcuntur,** *who, it is said, went to that camp* (In Catilīnam, 2, 10, 7). Latin prefers the personal subject with the simple tenses (present, imperfect, future), and the impersonal subject with the compound tenses (perfect, pluperfect, future perfect).

e. In Latin intransitive verbs may be used in the passive voice with an impersonal subject; as, **quōcumque ventum sit,** *wherever they* (our armies) *go* (Dē Imperiō Cn. Pompeī, 13, 26). Compare **73.** *d.*

173. *a.* When two subjects express a single idea, the verb may be singular; this is the regular usage with **senātus populusque Rōmānus,** often written S. P. Q. R.; **senātus populusque Rōmānus exstrūxerit,** *the senate and the Roman people have reared* (Philippic, 14, 12, 27); **quae bellum atque libīdō victōrum fert,** *which war and the lust of conquerors bring* (Sallust, 21, 9).

b. A plural verb may be used occasionally with a singular noun, or with an unexpressed subject representing a singular noun, where the sense suggests plurality; as, **pars hospitem aut cognātum reperiēbant,** *others would find a guest-friend or a relative* (Sallust, 61, 19); **nōbilitās invidiā aestuābat, et crēdēbant,** *the nobility burned with jealousy and*

believed (Sallust, 23, 18); in this sentence a singular and a plural verb
are used with the same subject.   See **238.** *o.*

174. A passive verb or participle may occasionally be used in a
reflexive sense; as, **certāmine īrārum ad caedem vertuntur,** *in the heat
of passion they turn to (resort to) bloodshed* (Livy, 1, 7, 6).

175. *a.* The present, imperfect, and future tenses represent an
action as going on in present, past, or future time respectively; as,
ultimus cōnsertō proeliō excēdēbat, *he was usually the last to retire
from a hand-to-hand fight* (Livy, 21, 4, 24).

b. In vivid narration a writer often thinks of past events as in progress and uses the present indicative (historical present).   In translating the historical present a past tense should generally be used;
as, **Petreius tubā signum dat,** *Petreius gave the signal with the trumpet*
(Sallust, 60, 2).

c. The present is used in statements true at all times (universal
present), and statements about customs; as, **Disparēs mōrēs disparia
studia sequuntur,** *Different natures follow different pursuits* (Laelius Dē
Amīcitiā, 20, 32).

d. The imperfect may be used of repeated or customary action;
as, **mē ipse cōnsōlābar,** *I was wont to console myself* (Catō Maior Dē
Senectūte, 23, 27).

e. The imperfect is sometimes used of attempted action (conative
imperfect); as, **cum ex urbe Catilīnam ēiciēbam,** *when I was seeking
to drive Catiline out of the city* (In Catilīnam, 3, 2, 1).

f. The present and imperfect are frequently used with **iam, iam
diū, iam prīdem, iam dūdum,** and similar words to indicate an action
already in progress for a considerable period; the present should be
translated with a progressive perfect, and the imperfect with a progressive pluperfect; as, **quam iam dūdum trāctāmus,** *which we have been
discussing for a long time* (Laelius Dē Amīcitiā, 22, 5); **iam prīdem
studēs,** *you have for a long time been desiring* (In Catilīnam, 1, 8, 44);
quō tē iam prīdem ista tua cupiditās effrēnāta ac furiōsa rapiēbat,
*whither that unbridled and mad desire of yours had been hurrying you
for a long time* (In Catilīnam, 1, 10, 1).

g. In letter writing Latin may use the imperfect or historical perfect
for the present, and the pluperfect for a past tense; in this way the
writer puts himself in the position of the receiver; as, **Etsī erāmus in
cursū,** *Although I am en route* (Cicero, Epistulae, 12, 2); **cum vacuī
temporis nihil habērem,** *as I have no leisure* (Cicero, Epistulae, 4, 4);

herī enim vesperī vēnerat, *for he came yesterday at even-tide* (Cicero, Epistulae, 22, 12).

The word *epistolary* is used to describe the above tenses when so used.

176. *a.* The perfect tense has two uses : the historical perfect and the pure perfect. The historical perfect states a past action as a simple occurrence; as, **Catilīna inter hostium cadāvera repertus est,** *Catiline was found among the corpses of his enemies* (Sallust, 61, 8); the pure perfect, in the sense of the English present perfect, is less common; as, **ut ego fēcī, quī litterās Graecās senex didicī,** *as I have done, who have learned Greek in my old age* (Catō Maior Dē Senectūte, 8, 12).

b. The perfect and pluperfect of **nōscō, cognōscō, cōnsuēscō,** and the defectives **meminī** and **ōdī** express a state resulting from action, and are generally best translated by the present and imperfect; as, **meministīne?** *Do you remember* (In Catilīnam, 1, 3, 9)? **sī tē parentēs odissent tuī,** *if your parents hated you* (In Catilīnam, 1, 7, 23); **eōs mōrēs eamque modestiam virī cognōvī,** *such is the character and such the self-restraint of the gentleman, I am well aware* (Sallust, 51, 14); **quōrum cognōverat promptam audāciam,** *whose ready boldness he knew* (Sallust, 32, 8).

c. The Latin future perfect is used with great precision, where frequently in English a future or present tense might be employed; as, **sī tē interficī iusserō, residēbit reliqua manus,** *if I order you to be killed, the rest of the band will remain behind* (In Catilīnam, 1, 5, 28).

177. *a.* In the sequence of tenses the primary or principal tenses of the indicative are those that denote present or future time, namely, the present, future, or future perfect; the primary or principal tenses of the subjunctive are the present or perfect; the perfect subjunctive, however, may be used as a secondary tense in a result clause. See *b* below.

The secondary tenses of the indicative are those that denote past time, namely, imperfect, perfect, and pluperfect; the secondary or historical tenses of the subjunctive are the imperfect and pluperfect.

The law of sequence requires that primary or principal tenses follow primary or principal tenses; and secondary or historical tenses follow secondary or historical tenses; exceptions to this rule are apparent rather than real; as, **hortāmur ut vītae tuae cōnsulās,** *we urge you that you take thought for your own life* (Prō Mārcellō, 10, 5); **quid**

fierī placēret, ostendī, *I showed what I wanted them to do* (In Catilīnam, 3, 2, 26).

In indirect discourse a future perfect is represented by a perfect subjunctive after primary sequence, and by the pluperfect subjunctive after secondary sequence; as, **sī hīc ōrdō placēre dēcrēverit tē īre in exsilium, obtemperātūrum tē esse dīcis,** *you say that if this body resolves that it is its opinion that you go into exile, you will comply* (In Catilīnam, 1, 8, 22); **sī essent professī,** *if they should enter their names* (Prō Archiā, 4, 12).

b. In clauses of result the present subjunctive may be used after a secondary or historical tense to denote that the action is continuing into the present, and the perfect subjunctive to indicate that the action is finally and permanently disposed of; as, **ita rēgnārunt ut omnēs deinceps conditōrēs numerentur,** *thus they ruled that all are counted as successive founders* (Livy, 2, 1, 7); **Metellus tantā dīligentiā fuit, ut ad iūdicēs vēnerit,** *Metellus was so careful that he came to the judges* (Prō Archiā, 5, 6). But see page 671, footnote.

c. A historical present in the principal clause is sometimes followed by a primary tense, sometimes by a secondary tense, in the subordinate clause; this variation in sequence is termed *repraesentātiō;* as **mandat, quibus rēbus possent, opēs factiōnis cōnfirment,** *he gave instructions that, by what means they could, they should strengthen the resources of the party* (Sallust, 32, 9).

d. A perfect infinitive depending upon a primary verb of saying, etc., is followed regularly by secondary sequence, whenever, if turned into an equivalent indicative, it would be a secondary tense; as, **Satis mihi multa verba fēcisse videor, quā rē esset hōc bellum necessārium,** *I think I have said enough* (to show) *why this war is necessary* (Dē Imperiō Cn. Pompeī, 10, 1).

178. The tenses of the infinitive in indirect discourse express time relative to that of the verbs on which they depend, the present infinitive expressing the same time as the governing verb; the perfect infinitive, time earlier than that of the governing verb; and the future infinitive, time later than that of the governing verb; as, **Patēre tua cōnsilia nōn sentīs?** *Do you not feel that your plans are exposed* (In Catilīnam, 1, 1, 8)? **Dīxī caedem tē contulisse,** *I said that you had fixed the murder* (In Catilīnam, 1, 3, 16); **cūr minōre dolōre, peritūrōs (esse) sē arbitrentur,** *why they think that they will perish with less pain* (In Catilīnam, 2, 10, 13).

179. *a.* Direct questions in Latin are introduced by question words and are of two kinds:

(1) Single questions, introduced by interrogative pronouns and adverbs, or by the enclitic -ne attached to the emphatic word of the question and asking for information, by **nōnne** implying the answer "Yes," or **num** implying the answer "No"; **Quid tandem tē impedit?** *What, pray, hinders you* (In Catilīnam, 1, 11, 15)? **Mōsne maiōrum?** *Is it the custom of our forefathers* (In Catilīnam, 1, 11, 15)? **nōnne mālle dēbēmus?** *Ought we not to prefer* (Prō Archiā, 12, 8)? **Num īnfitiārī potes?** *You cannot deny, can you* (In Catilīnam, 1, 3, 20)?

The enclitic -ne sometimes has its original negative force; as, **Vidētisne ut . . .** *Do you not see how* (Catō Maior Dē Senectūte, 10, 1)?

(2) Double questions, which ordinarily have **utrum** or the enclitic -ne in the first member, and **an,** *or,* or **annōn,** *or not,* in the second; as, **Utrum plūrēs arbitrāminī hostium urbēs an sociōrum cīvitātēs esse dēlētās?** *Do you think that more cities of the enemy or more states of the allies have been destroyed* (Dē Imperiō Cn. Pompeī, 13, 30)? The first member of a double question may be omitted, **an** alone introducing the second; as, **An . . . cavendum est?** *Need you take precautions* (Prō Mārcellō, 7, 13)?

b. Direct questions are either real or rhetorical; real questions expect an answer, but rhetorical questions, being equivalent to an emphatic statement, do not expect an answer. Rhetorical questions may be either in the indicative or in the subjunctive.

The subjunctive in rhetorical questions is either deliberative or potential; as,

(1) Potential, implying a negative opinion on the part of the speaker; as, **Hōc tantum bellum quis arbitrārētur ab ūnō imperātōre cōnficī posse?** *Who would have thought that this great war could be brought to a successful close by one general* (Dē Imperio Cn. Pompeī, 11, 32)?

(2) Deliberative, implying doubt, indignation, surprise, impossibility; as, **cur . . . committāmus?** *Why should we not intrust* (Dē Imperiō Cn. Pompeī, 17, 9)?

c. Exclamatory questions are often expressed by a subjunctive clause, with or without **ut**; as, **Tē ut ūlla rēs frangat?** *You, anything break your resolution* (In Catilīnam, 1, 9, 1)?

180. *a.* The first person plural of the present subjunctive is frequently used to express an exhortation (hortatory subjunctive); as, **videāmus,** *let us see* (Catō Maior Dē Senectūte, 5, 6).

b. The third person singular or plural of the present subjunctive is often used to express a command (jussive subjunctive); as, **exeant,** *let them go forth* (In Catilīnam, 2, 4, 6).

c. A wish capable of realization is expressed by the present subjunctive, often with **utinam**; as, **Utinam tibi istam mentem dī immortālēs duint!** *May the gods grant you such a mind* (In Catilīnam, 1, 9, 4)!

d. A wish incapable of realization is expressed in present time by **utinam** with the imperfect subjunctive and in past time by **utinam** with the pluperfect subjunctive; as, **Utinam cōpiam tantam habērētis,** *Oh, that you had so great an abundance* (Dē Imperiō Cn. Pompeī, 10, 6)!

e. The subjunctive is used to express an action as *possible* or *conceivable;* this use is called the potential subjunctive. In English various modal auxiliaries, like *may, might, can, could, would, should,* are used. The present or, less often, the perfect is used for the potential of the present or future, and the imperfect, commonly in the indefinite second person, the ideal " you," represents the potential of the past. The following varieties should be noted:

(1) Modest affirmations, expressed in the first person singular by such phrases as **haud sciō** (**sciam**) **an, nesciō an,** with the subjunctive. In origin this construction belongs under indirect questions, but by Cicero's time these phrases had become stereotyped expressions, all equivalent to **forsitan** (**fors sit an**) with the potential subjunctive; as, **haud sciō an nūlla beātior possit esse,** *I am inclined to think that none can be happier* (Catō Maior Dē Senectūte, 16, 15); **nesciō an amplius mihi negōtī contrahātur,** *I am inclined to think that a larger measure of difficulty may be in store for me* (In Catilīnam, 4, 5, 6); **forsitan possim,** *perhaps I might be* (Philippic, 7, 18). See **204** (5).

The potential subjunctives **velim, nōlim, mālim** are also used to express softened assertions; as, **velim tabellāriōs īnstituātis certōs,** *I should like you to organize special couriers* (Cicero, Epistulae, 14, 18).

(2) The indefinite or ideal " you "; as, **Ubi intenderīs ingenium,**
When you (one) exert your understanding (Sallust, 51, 5);
haud facile discernerēs, *not easily could you have decid*d*
(Livy, 21, 4, 8).

(3) Possibility and capacity; as, **Ubi enim aut iūcundius morārentur quam in patriā,** *For where could they linger more pleasantly* (Pliny, 7, 16)?

(4) **Vellem, nōllem, māllem** often indicate an action not performed
at the present time; as, **Nōllem (tē id facere),** *I should have
been unwilling for you to do this* (Philippic, 14, 7, 15).

f. The subjunctive may be used in an independent sentence to indicate something as conceded for the sake of argument. The present
expresses present time and the perfect past time; as, **Sed habeat sānē,**
But grant that it has (Catō Maior Dē Senectūte, 23, 10); **Nē sint in
senectūte vīrēs,** *Grant that old age has no physical strength* (Catō Maior
Dē Senectūte, 11, 1).

181. *a.* The imperative mood has two tenses, present and future.
The future imperative is used as follows:

(1) In commands that have a distinct reference to future time; as,
**tum tē, sī volēs, cum patriae, quod dēbēs, solveris, satis diū
vīxisse, dīcitō,** *then, if you wish, when you shall have paid
your debt to your country, you shall say that you have lived
long enough* (Prō Mārcellō, 9, 6).

(2) In the formal language of laws, precepts, wills, maxims, or in
any statements to which an air of impressiveness or formality
is to be imparted; as, **quoniam supplicātiō dēcrēta est, celebrātōte illōs diēs,** *since a thanksgiving has been decreed, celebrate those days* (In Catilīnam, 3, 10, 2).

(3) **Scītō, scītōte, mementō, mementōte,** and **habētōte** (when it
means *consider*) are used regularly in place of the present
imperatives, which these verbs lack; as, **scītō,** *know, be informed* (Cicero, Epistulae, 1, 2); **scītōte,** *know* (In Verrem,
60, 1); **mementō,** *remember* (Pliny, 9, 37); **mementōte,** *remember, be reminded* (Catō Maior Dē Senectūte, 18, 1);
habētōte, *consider* (In Verrem, 58, 23).

b. Besides the regular **nōlī, nōlīte** with the infinitive, **cavē nē** and
vidē nē, vidēte nē may be used to express a negative command (pro-
hibition); as, **nōlī nostrō perīculō esse sapiēns,** *do not be wise at our
expense* (Prō Mārcellō, 8, 13); **vidēte nē, cum velītis, exīre nōn**

liceat, *see to it that you do not lose the privilege of leaving the city when you wish* (Cicero, Epistulae, 14, 14).

c. The future indicative is sometimes used with the force of an imperative; as, **arcēbis,** *do thou keep away* (In Catilīnam, 1, 13, 35).

182. An infinitive in a principal clause may be used in the place of an imperfect or perfect indicative, the subject always being in the nominative. This is called the historical infinitive, and by its use the writer or speaker gives the suggestion of movement or action; sometimes this infinitive intimates dramatic elements, such as feeling, emotion, and excitement; as, **Sabīnae mulierēs ex trānsversō impetū factō dirimere īnfestās aciēs, dirimere īrās,** *the Sabine women, rushing in sideways, separated the hostile lines, separated the raging warriors* (īrās = īrātōs) (Livy, 1, 13, 4); **Ad hōc maledictīs increpābat omnēs bonōs, suōrum ūnum quemque nōmināns laudāre,** *In addition to this he proceeded to revile all loyal subjects, and to praise by name each one of his own followers* (Sallust, 21, 16); **concutī ferrum, vincula movērī,** *the clanking of iron resounded and the rattling noise of chains* (Pliny, 13, 22).

CAUSAL AND TEMPORAL CLAUSES, RELATIVE CLAUSES, CLAUSES OF PURPOSE AND RESULT

183. *a.* In causal clauses introduced by **quod, quia,** and **quoniam** the indicative is used when the reason is that of the writer or speaker, the subjunctive when the reason is presented as some one else's; as, **Magna dīs immortālibus habenda est grātia quod īnfestam pestem effūgimus,** *We ought to feel very grateful to the gods because we have escaped a hostile scourge* (In Catilīnam, 1, 5, 12); **praetōrēs, quod eōrum operā ūsus essem, laudantur,** *the praetors are praised because I employed their services* (In Catilīnam, 3, 6, 10).

Quoniam usually implies an evident reason; as, **Quoniam quidem circumventus ab inimīcīs praeceps agor, incendium meum ruīnā restinguam,** *Seeing plainly that I have been entrapped and am being driven headlong, I shall extinguish my own burning by a general destruction* (Sallust, 31, 30); **Quoniam geminī essent, Palātium Rōmulus, Remus Aventīnum capiunt,** *Since they were twins, Romulus took the Palatine, Remus the Aventine* (Livy, 1, 6, 9).

b. In causal clauses the subjunctive of a verb of saying or thinking is sometimes used to introduce a statement of a reason ascribed to

some one else; as, **cuius cum mōribus et nātūrā congruāmus, quod in
eō quasi lūmen aliquod probitātis et virtūtis perspicere videāmur,**
*with whose habits and nature we are in sympathy, because we seem to
behold in him a lamp of integrity and virtue, so to speak* (Laelius, Dē
Amicītiā, 8, 24); **perspicere videāmur** is merely a modification of
perspiciāmus.

c. The subjunctive introduced by **nōn quod, nōn quia,** *not because,*
or **quam quō** (= **quam eō quod**), *than because,* may be used to express
an alleged or assumed reason, sometimes called also a rejected or
hypothetical reason; with **magis quod, quia . . . quam quō, quod** the
words appear in inverse order; as, **Lībertātis orīginem inde, magis
quia annuum imperium cōnsulāre factum est quam quod dēminūtum
quicquam sit ex rēgiā potestāte numerēs,** *As for the origin of liberty,
you may count it from this point rather because the consul's term of
office was fixed for a year, than because there was any diminution in
power from that of the kings* (Livy, 2, 1, 21).

184. *a.* A causal clause introduced by **cum,** *since,* has its verb in
the subjunctive; as, **cum inimīcitiae fuerint numquam,** *since personal
animosities never have existed* (between Caesar and me) (Dē Prōvinciīs
Cōnsulāribus, 20, 5).

b. The adverb **praesertim,** *especially,* is sometimes used to make
prominent the causal idea in a clause introduced by **cum;** as, **praesertim cum fuerit ascrīptus,** *especially since he was enrolled* (Prō
Archiā, 5, 10).

185. *a.* **Cum** temporal, *when,* referring to the present or future, is
used with the indicative; as, **cum testimōnium datur,** *when public
testimony is given* (Philippic, 14, 5, 13); **cum neque audiēs neque
vidēbis,** *when you will neither hear nor see* (In Catilīnam, 1, 10, 11).

The indicative is also regularly used when the time of the main verb
and that of the temporal clause coincide; this use is sometimes called
the *explicative* **cum;** as, **cum tacent, clāmant,** *when they are silent, they
cry aloud* (In Catilīnam, 1, 8, 37).

b. With **cum** temporal, *when,* referring to past time, the indicative
may be used when the force of **cum** is purely temporal; as, **tum, cum
ex urbe Catilīnam ēiciēbam,** *at that time, when I was seeking to drive
Catiline out of the city* (In Catilīnam, 3, 2, 1); **tum, cum tē ā cōnsulātu
reppulī,** *at the time when I kept you from the consulship* (In Catilīnam,
1, 10, 20).

c. With **cum** temporal, *when,* referring to past time, the subjunctive

is used when an idea of circumstance, condition, or situation is involved, when the time is *described* rather than *dated*. This is the regular
construction in classical Latin, the imperfect subjunctive being used
to express incomplete action and the pluperfect subjunctive completed action; as, **cum advesperāsceret, ad pontem Mulvium pervēnērunt,** *when evening was approaching, they reached the Mulvian
bridge* (In Catilīnam, 3, 2, 29); **Cum ā mē quoque id respōnsum tulissēs, ad praetōrem vēnistī,** *When from me also you had received this
reply, you came to the praetor* (In Catilīnam, 1, 8, 7).

d. When the logical relations of two clauses are inverted, so that
the main clause becomes a cum-temporal clause, and the temporal
clause becomes the main clause, **cum** regularly takes the indicative;
this is called **cum** *inversum;* as, **Iam aliquantum spatiī aufūgerat, cum
respiciēns videt,** *He had already fled a considerable distance, when,
looking back, he saw* (Livy, 1, 25, 31).

186. *a.* **Cum** temporal with the indicative may be used to denote
recurrent or iterative action; as, **Neque, cum aliquid mandārat, cōnfectum putābat,** *And, when he had given a commission, he did not
consider it carried out* (In Catilīnam, 3, 7, 15). See **205.**

Although most of the earliest examples of iterative action are with
cum, any conjunction or relative may be so used; as, **quotiēnscumque
mē petistī, per mē tibi obstitī,** *as often as you sought (to attack) me, I
withstood you by my own efforts* (In Catilīnam, 1, 5, 19); **quamquam
abscesserat imāgō, memoria imāginis oculīs inerrābat,** *although the
ghost had disappeared, its impression kept hovering before their mind's
eye* (Pliny, 13, 9).

In Livy and later writers the subjunctive is also common; as, **ubi
quid fortiter ac strenuē agendum esset,** *whenever some act was to be
performed with bravery and energy* (Livy, 21, 4, 11). See **205.**

b. **Cum** temporal correlatively with the adverb **tum** is used in the
sense *not only . . . but also, but, both . . . and;* as, **cum illa certissima
vīsa sunt argūmenta, tum multō certiōra illa,** *not only did these proofs
seem very strong, but also still stronger the following* (In Catilīnam, 3,
5, 63).

187. *a.* **Cum** adversative or concessive, *although, while, whereas,* is
used with the subjunctive; as, **cum eam servāret M. Tullius,** *while
Marcus Tullius was attempting to save it* (Sallust, 31, 25); **cum
occidissēmus,** *although we had been lost* (Prō Mārcellō, 4, 6).

b. **Quamvīs** with the subjunctive, **quamquam** with the indicative also express concession; as, **quamvīs sīs sapiēns, nōn negābis,** *although you are wise, you will not deny* (Prō Mārcellō, 8, 22); **quamquam amīserat,** *although he had lost* (In Catilīnam, 3, 6, 40).

In the Silver Age (see page 707) the subjunctive is often used with **quamquam**; as, **quamquam acquiēscam,** *although I try to resign myself* (Pliny, 14, 10).

188. *a.* The temporal conjunctions **ubi, ut,** *when,* **postquam,** *after,* **posteā quam** (written as two words) *after that, after,* and **simul atque, simul,** *as soon as,* are used with the indicative, usually in the perfect tense as, **Postquam Catō assēdit,** *After Cato had sat down* (Sallust, 53, 1); **simul atque assēdistī,** *as soon as you took your seat* (In Catilīnam, 1, 7, 11).

The historical present is less often used with the above conjunctions; as, **Postquam videt,** *After he saw* (Sallust, 21, 19); **postquam legō,** *after I have been reading* (Pliny, 3, 11).

b. The conjunction **ut,** *as,* is used with the indicative; as, **ut trāditur,** *according to tradition,* lit. *as it is handed down* (Livy, 1, 16, 21).

c. **Ubi prīmum, ut prīmum,** and **cum prīmum,** *as soon as* (lit. *when first*), are used with the perfect indicative; as, **ut prīmum ex puerīs excessit,** *as soon as he outgrew his boyhood* (Prō Archiā, 3, 1).

d. The pluperfect indicative is used with **postquam** when a definite interval of time is mentioned; as, **Undecimō diē, postquam ā tē discesseram,** *Eleven days after I left you* (Cicero, Epistulae, 21, 1).

189. *a.* **Priusquam** and **antequam,** *until, before,* are used with the indicative to denote an actual occurrence or a fact; the limit is stated as *real;* as, **antequam ego nātus sum,** *before I was born* (Catō Maior Dē Senectūte, 14, 21).

b. **Priusquam** and **antequam,** *sooner than, before, until,* are used with the subjunctive, implying expectancy or purpose in an action; the limit is stated as *ideal;* as, **Priusquam dīmicārent, foedus ictum est,** *Before they could fight, a treaty was struck* (Livy, 1, 24, 10).

190. *a.* **Dum** temporal in the sense of *while* is used with the indicative historical present; in the sense of *so long as, while,* with the indicative present, imperfect, and perfect; as, **dum aedificant,** *while they were building* (In Catilīnam, 2, 9, 26); **tam diū dum urbis moenibus continēbātur,** *only so long as he was confined by the city's walls* (In Catilīnam, 3, 7, 10).

b. **Dum,** *until,* may be used with the subjunctive to denote intention or expectancy; the limit is stated as *ideal;* as, **nē exspectēmus qui-**

dem, dum rogēmur, *that we do not even wait until we should be asked*
(Laelius Dē Amīcītiā, 13, 3).

c. **Quoad** in the temporal sense of *so long as, until,* denoting a fact,
is used with the indicative; in the sense of *until* denoting intention or
expectancy, with the subjunctive; as, **quoad vīvet,** *as long as he shall
live* (In Catilīnam, 4, 11, 7).

d. The subjunctive with **dum, modo, dummodo** is used to express a
proviso; as, **modo permaneat studium et industria,** *provided earnestness and activity remain* (Catō Maior Dē Senectūte, 7, 7). Compare
194. *f.*

191. The adversative conjunctions **etsī, tametsī, etiam sī,** *although,*
follow the uses of **sī** (see **206–208**); as, **quam etsī spērō falsam esse,**
and, although I hope this is unfounded (Prō Mārcellō, 7, 4); **nōnne
impetrāre dēbeat, etiam sī vim adhibēre nōn possit,** *ought it not to
obtain its request, even if it should not be able to apply force* (In Catilīnam, 1, 8, 2)?

192. Relative clauses, introduced by a relative or general relative
pronoun, have their verb in the indicative unless an idea of purpose,
characteristic, cause, result, or condition is involved; as, **cēterī fortissimī cīvēs, quī circumstant senātum,** *the other very brave citizens, who
stand around the senate* (In Catilīnam, 1, 8, 40).

193. *a.* A relative clause of purpose may be introduced by **quī**
(= **ut is,** *in order that he*), or by the relative adverbs, such as **quō**
(= **ut eō**), **quā** (= **ut eā**), **ubi** (= **ut ibi**), **unde** (= **ut inde**), and has
its verb in the subjunctive; as, **C. Sulpicium mīsī, quī ex aedibus
Cethēgī, sī quid tēlōrum esset, efferret,** *I sent Gaius Sulpicius to bring
out of the house of Cethegus whatever weapons were there* (In Catilīnam,
3, 3, 23); **Haec habuī dē amīcitiā quae dīcerem,** *This was what I had
to say on friendship* (Laelius Dē Amīcitiā, 27, 39); **Postquam eō
ventum est, unde ferentāriīs proelium committī posset,** *After they
came to a place from which the battle could be begun by the light-armed
skirmishers* (Sallust, 60, 3).

NOTE. — In the last illustration the idea of characteristic is inter
woven with that of purpose. This often happens when the purpose
clause is introduced by some form of relative. See **194.** *a.*

b. In relative clauses of purpose **quō** is generally used with a comparative; as, **quō plūs vīrium frequentia faceret,** *in order that a large
attendance might produce added strength* (lit. *more of strength*) (Livy,
2, 1, 31).

194. *a.* A relative clause with the subjunctive, introduced by a relative pronoun or relative adverb, may characterize an indefinite antecedent (clause of characteristic); as, **Itinera, quae per hōsce annōs nostrī imperātōrēs fēcerint,** *The marches, which during late years our generals have made* (Dē Imperiō Cn. Pompeī, 13, 29); **Repertī sunt duo equitēs Rōmānī, quī tē istā cūrā līberārent,** *Two Roman knights were found to relieve you of that anxiety* (In Catilīnam, 1, 4, 24); **nihil erat, quod nōn ipse obīret,** *there was nothing, which he did not personally undertake* (In Catilīnam, 3, 7, 16); **ut sē dignōs exīstimētis, quōrum salūtem tālī virō commendētis,** *that you consider them worthy of having their welfare intrusted to such a man* (Dē Imperiō Cn. Pompeī, 5, 17); **Habēs, ubi ostentēs,** *You have an opportunity to display* (In Catilīnam, 1, 10, 17). Compare **193.** *a.*

General expressions like **est, sunt quī, nēmō est quī, quis est quī, nihil est quod, quid est quod, sōlus, ūnus est quī,** and also the adjectives **dignus, indignus, idōneus** are regularly construed with the subjunctive of characteristic; as, **Quid est quod tē dēlectāre possit?** *What is there which can please you* (In Catilīnam, 1, 6, 1)? **ut sē dignōs exīstimētis, quōrum salūtem tālī virō commendētis,** *that you may consider them worthy of having their welfare intrusted to such a man* (Dē Imperiō Cn. Pompeī, 5, 17).

b. Clauses of characteristic have their origin in the potential subjunctive (see **180.** *e*), the idea of possibility easily developing into that of tendency or result; therefore a clause of characteristic is in reality a relative clause of result. But compare **193.** *a.* Note. Thus, *Caesar was the general who conquered Pompey* is an ordinary relative clause stating a fact about one person, and would be in the indicative; but, *Caesar was the sort of, the kind of general who usually conquered* states a characteristic that is true not only of Caesar, but of all others belonging to the same class. In such a sentence **quī = ut** is in a result clause; as, **Sed quam longē vidētur ā carcere abesse dēbēre, quī sē ipse iam dignum cūstōdiā iūdicārit!** *But how far does it seem that a man (of the kind) ought to be from jail who voluntarily (ipse) has already judged himself deserving of custody* (In Catilīnam, 1, 8, 16)!

c. A relative clause of characteristic may have a causal force; the relative is often preceded by **ut, utpote,** or **quippe;** as, **ut quī sē dēdiderit,** *since he has devoted himself* (Pliny, 9, 30).

d. A relative clause of characteristic may have an adversative force; as, **Cethēgus, quī ante respondisset, repente conticuit,** *Although*

Cethegus had previously replied, he suddenly became silent (In Catilīnam, 3, 5, 13).

e. A relative clause with the subjunctive may have a conditional force; as, **cui item exercitus in manū sit,** *if he, like Cicero* (**item**), *should have an army at his disposal* (Sallust, 51, 49).

f. A relative clause of characteristic may express *proviso* or *restriction;* as, **nihil est molestum, quod nōn dēsiderēs,** *nothing is troublesome, which* (provided that) *you do not miss* (Catō Maior Dē Senectūte, 14, 3); **quod quidem sēnserim,** *at least as far as I have noticed* (Laelius Dē Amīcitiā, 27, 25).

195. A relative clause of result may be introduced by **quī** (= **ut is,** *so that he*), or **quīn** (= **quī nōn, quae nōn, quod nōn**), and has its verb in the subjunctive; no exact line can be drawn between relative clauses of characteristic (see **194.** *b*) and relative clauses of result, and it is best to class the two as belonging under the same category; as, **Quis tam esset ferreus, quī eam vītam ferre posset?** *Who would be so iron-hearted as to be able to endure this life* (Laelius Dē Amīcitiā, 23, 29)? **Nēmō vestrum est quīn saepe audierit,** *There is no one of you who has not often heard* (In Verrem, 52, 6).

196. *a.* Clauses of purpose, often called final sentences, are regularly introduced by **ut, utī,** *in order that, that,* or **nē,** *in order that not, lest,* and have their verb in the subjunctive; as, **ut ad tuōs īsse videāris,** *in order that you may seem to have gone to your own friends* (In Catilīnam, 1, 9, 24); **nē quid dē summā rē pūblicā dēminuerētur,** *in order that the welfare of the state might not suffer in any degree* (In Catilīnam, 4, 6, 21).

b. A clause of purpose introduced by **ut** or **nē** is frequently used parenthetically, the verb being easily supplied from the context; the tense is regularly present in classical Latin; as, **ut plūra nōn dīcam,** *to leave more unsaid,* lit. *that I may not say more* (Dē Imperiō Cn. Pompeī, 15, 1); **Ac nē longum sit,** *And, not to be tedious,* lit. *in order that it may not be tedious,* (I say) (In Catilīnam, 3, 5, 1).

c. In clauses of purpose **nē . . . nēve (neu)** is used in the sense of *that not . . . nor,* and **ut (utī) . . . nēve (neu)** in the sense of *that . . . and that not,* with the subjunctive; as, **ut maneās in sententiā nēve cuiusquam vim pertimēscās,** *that you stand fast in your opinion and fear not the violence of anyone* (Dē Imperiō Cn. Pompeī, 24, 4).

197. *a.* Clauses of result, called also consecutive sentences, are most often introduced by **ut** or **utī,** *so that, that* (negative **nōn**), and have their verb in the subjunctive; as, **Neque enim is es, ut tē pudor umquam ā turpitūdine revocārit,** *For you are not such a man that shame has ever recalled you from baseness* (In Catilīnam, 1, 9, 13).

b. Clauses of result are often preceded by a word of measure or quality, **tam, tantus, ita, sīc, adeō,** etc.; as, **quoniam sunt ita multī, ut eōs carcer capere nōn possit,** *since they are so many that a prison cannot hold them* (In Catilīnam, 2, 10, 18).

c. A clause of result with the subjunctive may be introduced by **quam** after a comparative, with or without **ut**; as, **Quid ā tē mihi iūcundius potuit iniungī, quam ut praeceptōrem quaererem?** *What more pleasant task could you have intrusted to me than that I should look for a teacher* (Pliny, 4, 1)?

d. Two result clauses with **ut** sometimes follow the expression **tantum abest, āfuit;** as, **tantum abest, ut aliquam mihi bonam grātiam quaesīsse videar, ut intellegam,** *I am so far from seeming to have courted any popularity that I realize* (Dē Imperiō Cn. Pompeī, 24, 28).

e. Parallel negative expressions used in result and purpose clauses may be grouped as follows:

Result	*Purpose*
ut nōn	nē (ut nē)
ut nēmō	nē quis
ut nūllus	nē ūllus
ut nūsquam	nē ūsquam
ut numquam	nē umquam
ut neque . . . neque	nē aut . . . aut, ut nēve . . . nēve

SUBSTANTIVE CLAUSES

198. *a.* Substantive clauses are used as subject of a verb, as object of a verb, and in other relations similar to those in which nouns are used.

b. A substantive clause introduced by **quod,** meaning *the fact that, that,* has its verb in the indicative, and may stand as subject, or predicate, or object of a verb, or in apposition; as, **illa nimis antīqua praetereō, quod C. Servīlius Ahāla Sp. Maelium occīdit,** *I pass over those* (precedents) *as too remote, the fact that Gaius Servilius Ahala slew Spurius Maelius . . .,* the **quod**-clause being in apposition with **illa** (In Catilīnam, 1, 1, 25).

c. A substantive clause introduced by **quod,** meaning *as to the* *fact that, as regards the fact that,* may have the force of an accusative or ablative of specification; as, **Quod mē īnstitūtum ad illum poēma iubēs perficere,** *As to your bidding me to finish the poem which I had begun in Caesar's honor* (**ad illum,** *i.e.* **ad Caesarem**)(Cicero, Epistulae, 11, 30).

199. *a.* Substantive clauses with the subjunctive introduced by **ut,** or **utī,** *that,* and **nē,** *that not,* are used after verbs of *commanding, urging, reminding, asking, persuading, conceding* and *permitting, deciding, striving,* and the like; the subjunctive may often best be translated by an infinitive; as, **hortātus sum, ut ea, quae scīret, sine timōre indicāret,** *I urged him to disclose his knowledge fearlessly* (In Catilīnam, 3, 4, 2).

Some of the more common verbs and phrases are:

(1) Commanding: **imperō,** *order;* **interdīcō,** *enjoin;* **mandō,** *command;* **negōtium dō,** *assign the task;* **praecipiō,** *enjoin, direct;* **dēnūntiō,** *enjoin;* **praedīcō,** *order in advance.*

(2) Urging: **cohortor,** *encourage;* **hortor,** *urge;* **sollicitō,** *press.*

(3) Reminding: **admoneō,** *admonish;* **moneō,** *warn.*

(4) Asking: **dēprecor,** *beg to escape;* **ōrō,** *beg;* **obsecrō,** *beseech;* **obtestor,** *pray;* **petō,** *ask earnestly;* **postulō,** *demand;* **rogō,** *ask.*

(5) Persuading: **addūcō,** *prevail upon;* **persuādeō,** *persuade;* **impellō,** *incite.*

(6) Conceding and permitting: **concēdō,** *grant;* **patior,** *suffer, allow;* **permittō,** *permit.*

(7) Deciding: **cēnseō,** *decree;* **cōnstituō,** *determine;* **placuit,** *it pleased;* **sanciō,** *bind;* **dēcernō,** *decree.*

(8) Striving: **agō,** *arrange;* **contendō,** *strive;* **dō operam,** *take pains;* **impetrō,** *obtain one's request;* **labōrō,** *put forth effort.*

b. Such verbs are sometimes used impersonally in the passive, the substantive clause taking the place of a subject; as, **ut lēgum poenās pertimēscās, nōn est postulandum,** *that you should fear greatly the penalties of the laws ought not to be expected* (In Catilīnam, 1, 9, 11).

c. With such verbs the substantive clause is sometimes replaced by the infinitive, with or without a subject accusative. When they are used as verbs of saying and thinking (**verba sentiendī et dēclārandī**), the infinitive must be employed according to the principles of indirect discourse (see **213**); as, **Nōnne hunc ad mortem rapī imperābis?** *Will you not order this man to be hurried away to execution* (In Catilīnam, 1, 11, 14)? **rēs monet, cavēre ab illīs,** *the situation suggests that we take precautions against the conspirators* (**illīs**) (Sallust, 52, 8); **cēnseō ob eās rēs senātum exīstimāre,** *I move that for these reasons the senate thinks* (Philippic, 14, 14, 15); but in line 21 of this chapter this same verb (**cēnseō**) governs the subjunctive according to *a.* above.

d. As a negative connective between substantive subjunctive clauses **nēve** (before vowels and **h**) and **neu** (before consonants) are used, with the meaning *and that . . . not, or that . . . not.*

200. *a.* In substantive clauses with **ut** after **admoneō, cōhortor, cōnstituō, dēcernō, imperō, mandō, nūntiō,** *order,* **postulō,** *demand,* **pacīscor** (Pliny, 6, 1), and **rogō,** *ask,* and a few phrases, with **dīc, fac, licet, necesse** the **ut** is sometimes omitted; as, **senātus dēcrēvit, darent operam cōnsulēs,** *the senate decreed that the consuls should see to it* (Sallust, 29, 7); **suādeō, ad nōs quam prīmum recurrās,** *my advice is, hurry back to us as soon as possible* (Cicero, Epistulae, 10, 8); **et licet rideās,** *and you may laugh* (Pliny, 2, 1); **Ipse fac veniās,** *Be sure you come yourself* (Cicero, Epistulae, 9, 8).

b. **Iubeō,** *order, bid,* and **vetō,** *forbid,* are regularly used with the infinitive and subject accusative; **cōnor,** *attempt,* with the infinitive; as, **Exīre ex urbe iubet cōnsul hostem,** *A consul orders a public enemy to depart from the city* (In Catilīnam, 1, 5, 35).

c. With the potential subjunctives, **velim, nōlim, mālim,** etc. the simple subjunctive without **ut** is commonly used; this construction is often equivalent to an optative subjunctive (see **180.** *c, d*); as, **velim tribuās,** *I should like you to attribute* (Cicero, Epistulae, 6, 2).

201. *a.* Substantive clauses with the subjunctive introduced by **nē** (if the main clause is positive), *that not,* **quō minus** (if the main clause is either positive or negative), *that not* (lit. *by which the less*), and **quīn** (if the main clause is negative), *that not,* are used after verbs of *hindering, preventing,* and *refusing;* the conjunction often may best be rendered by *from* with a verbal noun in *-ing;* as, **idem enim tē impedīret, quō minus mēcum esses,** *for the same reason would hinder you from being with me* (Cicerō, Epistulae, 22, 9); **impedītī, nē triumphārent,** *prevented from celebrating a triumph* (Sallust, 30, 10).

The principal verbs belonging to this class are: **dēterreō,** *hold back through fear;* **impediō,** *hinder;* **prohibeō,** *prevent;* **recūsō,** *refuse;* **retineō,** *restrain;* **temperō,** *restrain one's self;* **teneō,** *hold back;* **terreō,** *frighten.*

Impediō occasionally, prohibeō often, takes the infinitive. (See **223.** *a* (3)).

b. Substantive clauses with the subjunctive introduced by **quīn** are used also after general expressions of doubt and negation, **quīn** being translated *that;* as, **nōn dubitat, quīn brevī sit Trōia peritūra,** *he does not doubt that Troy would quickly fall* (Catō Maior Dē Senectūte, 10, 9).

Instead of the simple subjunctive the active periphrastic is often employed, as in the illustration cited above, especially to represent a future tense whose action is subsequent to that of the main verb.

c. After **dubitō,** meaning *doubt,* a substantive clause with **quīn** and the subjunctive is commonly used (see *b* above) ; after **dubitō,** *hesitate,* generally the infinitive, rarely a clause with **quīn;** as, **Num dubitās id facere?** *You do not hesitate to do this, do you* (In Catilīnam, 1, 5, 34)?

202. Substantive clauses with the subjunctive introduced by **ut** and **nē** are used after verbs of fearing; after such verbs **ut** is to be translated *that not,* and **nē,** *that,* or *lest,* because **ut** shows that the positive is wished and the negative is feared; whereas **nē** shows that the negative is wished and the positive is feared; as, **Ōrātor metuō nē languēscat senectūte,** *As for the orator, I fear that he does grow feeble from old age* (Catō Maior Dē Senectūte, 9, 15) ; **nē** here conveys a negative wish, *i.e.* may the orator not grow feeble from old age, but I fear that he will.

Nē nōn is used regularly instead of **ut** if the main clause contains or implies a negative; as, **crēdō, erit verendum mihi, nē nōn potius hōc omnēs bonī sērius ā mē quam quisquam crūdēlius factum esse dīcat,** *I suppose I shall have to fear that patriotic men will say that I have acted too cruelly rather than that I have acted too tardily* (In Catilīnam, 1, 2, 25) ; the force of **erit verendum** is really made negative by the ironical turn imparted to these words by **crēdō;** hence, **nē nōn.**

203. Clauses of result introduced by **ut** or **utī** and **ut nōn** are used as substantive clauses in four ways :

(1) As the subject of impersonal verbs ; as, **restat, ut dē imperātōre dīcendum esse videātur,** *it remains for me, as it seems, to speak regarding the choice of a general* (Dē Imperiō Cn. Pompeī, 10, 3).

The more important impersonal forms thus used are **accēdēbat** [1] **;** **accidit,** *it happened;* **contingit,** *it happens;* **efficitur,** *it follows;*

---

[1] Past verbs of happening are followed only by the imperfect subjunctive, never by the perfect. See **177,** *b.*

ēvenit, *it happens;* fit; fīēbat; factum est; factum esse, fierī; īnstitūtum est, *the custom became fixed;* placuit, *it pleased;* relinquēbātur, *the result was,* lit. *it was left;* reliquum est, *it remains;* restat, *it remains;* and the future infinitive of sum in both forms, futūrum esse and fore; sequitur, *it follows.*

(2) Occasionally as predicate or appositive with cōnsuētūdō est, iūs est, mōs est, animus est, and similar expressions; as, Est in nōbīs is animus, ut nūllīus audāciae cēdāmus, *W̜ (I) have such a disposition that we (I) yield to the boldness of no one* (In Catilīnam, 3, 12, 15).

In classical Latin the infinitive is far more common with this construction; as, quibus vendere mōs erat, *who made a business of selling* (Sallust, 29, 12). See 222. *d.*

This use should be carefully distinguished from a substantive clause of purpose; as, Hīs fīnibus ūtendum arbitror, ut sit inter eōs commūnitās, *These are the limits which I think ought to be adopted,* namely, *that there should be between them a community of interest* (Laelius Dē Amīcitiā, 17, 1).

(3) As object after verbs of action and accomplishment; as, perficiam ut putētis, *I shall cause you to think* (Prō Archiā, 2, 19). The verbs thus used are committō, efficiō, perficiō. [1]

(4) As appositive of a noun or neuter pronoun, like hōc or illud, whose meaning the ut-clause defines; as, Illud perficiam ut ea, quae gessī in cōnsulātū, tuear, *That I shall accomplish,* namely, *that I shall uphold the acts of my consulship* (In Catilīnam, 3, 12, 35).

204. Indirect questions are used as substantive clauses after expressions of inquiry, narration, deliberation, and uncertainty, and have the subjunctive. For the sequence see **201.** *c.* The following types of indirect questions are used:

(1) Introduced by the interrogative particles -ne, num, an (later prose) in single questions; in double questions, by the correlative particles utrum . . an, *whether . . or;* utrum . . necne, *whether . . or not,* necne representing annōn of the direct form; -ne . . an, *whether . . or;* -ne . . an . . an, *whether . . or . . or;* -ne . . -ne, *whether . . or;* and an

---

[1] Verbs of effecting may also take a substantive clause of purpose; as, quī, nē quid tāle in rē pūblicā fierī posset, effēcerit, *who brought it about that no such action could be possible in the state* (Philippic, 14, 5, 27).

alone, **utrum** being omitted, *or;* as, **ut difficile dictū sit, utrum hostēs magis virtūtem an mānsuētūdinem dīlēxerint,** *so that it is difficult to tell whether the enemy feared his valor more or loved his gentleness* (Dē Imperiō Cn. Pompeī, 14, 45); **Interrogāvī ipsōs an essent Chrīstiānī,** *I asked them personally whether they were Christians* (Pliny, 16, 12). See (5) below.

(2) Introduced by an interrogative pronoun; as, **Quid proximā nocte, quem nostrum ignōrāre arbitrāris?** *Who of us, think you, does not know what you did last night* (In Catilīnam, 1, 1, 10)?

(3) Introduced by pronominal adjectives, and adverbs used interrogatively; as, **statuistī, quō quemque proficīscī placēret,** *you decided to which point each man should proceed,* lit. *you decided whither it was your pleasure for each man to set out* (In Catilīnam, 1, 4, 19); **Mīrum est ut animus excitētur,** *It is wonderful how the mind is stimulated* (Pliny, 2, 10).

(4) Introduced by **sī,** *if, whether,* after verbs of effort and expectation, and trial. This use is never common, and no example occurs in this text.

(5) For **haud sciō an, nesciō an, forsitan,** see **180.** *e* (1).

(6) The idiomatic phrase **mīrum quantum,** *wonderfully,* lit. *it is marvelous how much,* is practically equivalent to an adverb, and is usually accompanied by the indicative; as, **Id mīrum quantum prōfuit,** *This helped marvelously* (Livy, 2, 1, 36); but in Livy, 1, 16, 31 the subjunctive is used; as, **Mīrum quantum illī virō nūntiantī haec fidēs fuerit,** *It is wonderful to what extent credence was placed in the report of this man.*

CONDITIONAL SENTENCES

GENERAL (ITERATIVE ACTION) AND PARTICULAR

205. Conditional sentences are either general or particular. A general condition denotes repeated or iterative action, **sī** being almost equivalent to *whenever.*

The indicative mood is the rule for iterative sentences in Ciceronian Latin, but the subjunctive becomes common with Livy and later writers, especially in the secondary tenses. See **186.**

With the ideal second person the subjunctive must be used.

Anyone of the three types of conditional sentences may be general, but in conditional sentences of the first type, called conditions of fact, reality,· or logical conditions, the following classification of tenses should be noted:

(1) Present tense in both protasis and apodosis to denote iterative action in present time, the action of the two clauses being contemporaneous or identical in time; as, **pōma ex ēvelluntur, crūda sī sunt,** *apples are plucked from trees with difficulty if they are unripe* (Catō Maior Dē Senectūte, 19, 51); **memoria minuitur, nisi eam exerceās,** *the memory is impaired unless you exercise it* (Catō Maior Dē Senectūte, 7, 1).

(2) Imperfect tense in both protasis and apodosis to denote iterative action in past time, the action of the two clauses being contemporaneous or identical; as, **sī attenderēs ācrius, strepitus vinculōrum reddēbātur,** *if you listened more attentively, a rattling of chains was heard* (Pliny, 13, 2).

(3) Future tense in both protasis and apodosis, to denote iterative action in future time, the actions of the two clauses being contemporaneous; as, **sī ad mē bonōrum concursum fierī vidēbis, ad tē improbōs invītābis?** *if you see all loyal citizens gathering about me, will you summon the wicked to your side* (Philippic, 14, 7, 14)?

(4) Perfect tense in the protasis, present in the apodosis to denote iterative action in present time when the action of the subordinate clause is prior or antecedent to that of the main clause; as, **sī aquam gelidam bibērunt, prīmō relevārī videntur,** *if they drink cold water, at first they seem to be relieved* (In Catilīnam, 1, 13, 10).

(5) Future perfect tense in the protasis, future in the apodosis to denote iterative action in future time when the action of the subordinate clause is prior to that of the main clause; as, **Quod sī exēmeris ex rērum nātūrā benevolentiae coniūnctiōnem, nec domus ūlla nec urbs stāre poterit,** *But if you take away from nature the bond of good will, neither any house nor city will be able to stand* (Laelius Dē Amīcitiā 7, 9).

(6) Pluperfect tense in the protasis, imperfect in the apodosis to denote iterative action in past time when the action of the subordinate clause is prior to that of the main clause; as, **quem (= sī ūllum) quisque vīvus pugnandō locum cēperat, eum, āmissā animā, corpore tegēbat,** *whatever position a man*

*had taken up in fighting, while still alive, this he was covering
with his body when life was lost* (Sallust, 61, 3).

206. Particular conditions of the first type (conditions of fact or
reality) introduced by **sī**, *if*, or **nisi**, *unless*, have the indicative (any
tense) in the protasis, and the indicative (any tense), imperative, or
hortatory subjunctive in the apodosis; as,

(1) Present indicative in both protasis and apodosis: **sī mē cōnsulis, suādeō**, *if you consult me, I advise it* (In Catilīnam, 1,
5, 36).

(2) Present indicative in the protasis, present imperative in the
apodosis: **sī mihi cōnflāre vīs invidiam, rēctā perge in exsilium**, *if you wish to kindle (a flame of) unpopularity for me,
proceed straightway into exile* (In Catilīnam, 1, 9, 17).

(3) Future indicative in the protasis, jussive subjunctive in the
apodosis: **sī aberunt, praetor urbānus supplicātiōnēs cōnstituat**, *if they are absent, let the city praetor appoint suppli-
catory rites* (Philippic, 14, 14, 23).

(4) Future perfect indicative in the protasis, future indicative in
the apodosis: **Vix feram sermōnēs hominum, sī id fēceris**,
I shall hardly be able to endure the talk of men, if you do this,
lit. *will have done* (In Catilīnam, 1, 9, 19).

(5) Perfect indicative in the protasis, present indicative in the
apodosis; as, **sī hostium fuit ille sanguis, summa (est)
mīlitum pietās**, *If it was the blood of enemies, the loyalty of the
soldiers is supreme* (Philippic, 14, 3, 3).

207. Conditions of the second type (conditions of possible realization, ideal, or less vivid future conditions), introduced by **sī**, *if*, **nisi**,
unless, or **sīn**, *but if*, take the present or perfect subjunctive in the
protasis, and the present, rarely the perfect, subjunctive in the apodosis; the subjunctive in the apodosis is potential (**180.** *e*); as,

(1) Present subjunctive in both protasis and apodosis: **Haec sī
tēcum patria loquātur, nōnne impetrāre dēbeat, etiam sī vim
adhibēre nōn possit?** *If your country should speak thus with
you, ought she not to obtain her request, even if she should not
be able to apply force* (In Catilīnam, 1, 8, 1)?

(2) Perfect subjunctive in the protasis, present subjunctive in the
apodosis: **quod sī adeptī sint, fugitīvō alicui concēdī sit
necesse**, *which, if they should obtain it, must inevitably be given
up to some runaway slave* (In Catilīnam, 2, 9, 17).

(3) The indicative in the apodosis to emphasize the situation as an actual one: **Quod sī sint id adeptī, num illī sē cōnsulēs spērant futūrōs?** *But supposing they should have obtained this, those men do not expect to become consuls, do they* (In Catilīnam, 2, 9, 13)?

208. *a.* Conditions of the third type (conditions contrary to fact, called also unreal or impossible), introduced by **sī,** *if,* or **nisi,** *unless,* take the subjunctive in both protasis and apodosis, the imperfect referring to present time, the pluperfect to past time; as,

(1) Imperfect: **sī mē meīs cīvibus iniūriā vidērem, carēre mē aspectū cīvium māllem,** *if I saw that I was unjustly an object of suspicion to my fellow-citizens, I should prefer to be deprived of the sight of my fellow-citizens* (In Catilīnam, 1, 7, 16).

(2) Pluperfect: **sī (hōc idem) fortissimō virō, M. Mārcellō, dīxissem, iam mihi senātus vim et manūs intulisset,** *if I had made this same statement to that great hero, Marcus Marcellus, ere now the senate would have laid violent hands on me* (In Catilīnam, 1, 8, 33).

b. The indicative is used in the apodosis of conditions contrary to fact when there is present an idea of necessity, propriety, or possibility; so also with the active and passive periphrastic conjugations (see **63**); as, **Quod sī Cn. Pompeius prīvātus esset hōc tempore, tamen is erat dēligendus,** *But if Gnaeus Pompey were at this time a private citizen, yet he would be the one to be chosen* (Dē Imperiō Cn. Pompeī, 17, 1).

But when the possibility is conditioned the subjunctive is used; as, **tanta vīlitās annōnae cōnsecūta est, quantam vix ex summā ūbertāte agrōrum diūturna pāx efficere potuisset,** *such a cheap price of provisions followed, as a prolonged peace could scarcely have produced as a result of the greatest fertility of the fields* (Dē Imperiō Cn. Pompeī, 15, 8); the protasis is implied in **ex summā ūbertāte agrōrum.** See **209.**

c. The imperfect subjunctive, referring to past time, may be used in conditions contrary to fact, if a lasting state of affairs is implied; as, **sī nihil litterīs adiuvārentur, numquam sē ad eārum studium contulissent,** *if they were not at all continually aided by literature, they never would have devoted themselves to its pursuit* (Prō Archiā, 7, 20).

209. In the protasis of a conditional sentence an ablative absolute, a participle, or other form of expression implying a condition, may be used in place of the clause with **sī**; as, **Sulla, crēdō, hunc petentem repudiāsset,** *Sulla, I suppose, would have rejected my client* (**hunc**), *if he had petitioned him* (Prō Archiā, 10, 38). Compare also **144.** *b* (4).

210. *a.* Conditional clauses of comparison are used with the subjunctive introduced by **velut sī, quasi, ac sī, ut sī, tamquam, tamquam sī,** *as if, just as if;* as, **aedificiīs omnibus sīc pepercit, quasi ad ea defendenda vēnisset,** *all buildings he spared thus, as if he had come to defend them* (In Verrem, 54, 7); **velut sī sēnsisset audītās precēs,** *just as if he had perceived an answer to his prayers,* lit. *that his prayers had been heard* (Livy, 1, 12, 22).

b. **Nisi forte, nisi vērō, nisi sī,** *unless perchance, unless indeed, unless to be sure,* introduce an exception with ironical force, and take the indicative; as, **nisi vērō L. Caesar crūdēlior vīsus est,** *unless indeed Lucius Caesar seemed too cruel* (In Catilīnam, 4, 6, 10).

The above particles are regularly used to introduce a **reductiō ad absurdum.** See **239.** *s.*

GENERAL OBSERVATIONS

TRANSLATION, LATIN AND ENGLISH STYLE

211. Latin is not an algebraic equation but a powerful and vigorous language characterized by syntactical fullness, rhetorical dignity, precision, and rhythm. Since the Latin mode of expression is often quite different from that of the English, the following points must be fully appreciated by the student before he can hope to translate correctly and idiomatically:

The Latin word-order is more flexible than that of the English, because it shows its relationships by *inflections*, whereas English must depend in large measure upon the *order* of words. Compare the Latin and the English of the following simple sentence: **C. Caesaris longē aliam videō fuisse ratiōnem,** *Gaius Caesar's reasoning, I see, was widely different* (Dē Prōvinciīs Cōnsulāribus, 13, 20).

Latin prefers *subordination*, English *coördination;* as, **omnia, quae dīlāpsa iam diffluxērunt,** *all* (*bonds*) *which have now become disorganized and disturbed* (Prō Mārcellō, 8, 5).

The prevailing prose style in Latin is *periodic* in its structure, *i.e.* the main thought is kept in suspense, as it were, by the introduction of various associated thoughts, all of which are related to the dominant idea so as to produce a complex whole, characterized by harmony and balance. This arrangement affords the writer or speaker an opportunity to develop contrasts, by the use of libration (**lībra, scale, balance**). However, the student must not conclude that Latin always uses the periodic sentence; indeed, very often the Latin word-order and sentence-structure resemble the English. The first two sentences in chapter one of the Manilian Law, page 153, are a good illustration; also the beginning of the Fourteenth Philippic, page 331.

Latin has a tendency toward *concrete* expression, English towards *abstract;* as, **Caesare impulsōre atque adiūtōre,** *by the instigation and assistance of Caesar* (Dē Prōvinciīs Cōnsulāribus, 8, 7).

Latin is less imaginative than English, and therefore uses its words less freely in a *figurative* or *metaphorical* sense. For instance, we say *a decisive battle;* the Latin would say **maximum proelium.** We say *deep grief,* but the Latin says more simply **magnus maeror.**

Latin is more exacting in *tense relationships* than English; in a complex sentence the actions are subjected to a close analysis, as to whether they are *contemporaneous* or whether one is *prior* to the other. See iterative action, **205.**

In comparison with English ancient Latin has fewer nouns, but a large percentage of these have a general aspect, the specific coloring being imparted by the context. English, with a wealth of synonyms at its disposal, employs a specific noun for each specific concept; as, **Ea rēs,** *This rumor* (Sallust, 23, 16).

Latin also fashions many nouns from masculine and neuter adjectives, particularly the latter. In translating such substantivized words the student should avoid the translation *thing* or *things,* but should color the Latin adjective with a suitable noun; as, **Quōrum dē honōre utinam mihi plūra in mentem,** *O that more thoughts would come to my mind regarding the honoring of these men* (Philippic, 14, 11, 20)! See **154.** *a.*

The emphatic word or thought tends to come first; the translator should therefore center his attack on that point. In English the emphasis gravitates towards the end. Compare the opening sentence of Cicero's oration *Prō Archiā,* page 221.

212. *a.* A frequent substitute for the missing perfect active participle in Latin is an ablative absolute, so placed with reference to the subject as to assume the position of a limiting adjunct or an appositive construction; that is, the subject stands either before, after, or within the ablative absolute; as, **quī, audītā rē, frequentēs ad mē**

convēnerant, *who, having heard the news, had come in throngs to me*
(In Catilīnam, 3, 3, 11); **Hīs rēbus comparātīs Catilīna,** *Catiline,
having made these preparations* (Sallust, 26, 1); **C. Pomptīnus, rē pūblicā līberātā,** *Gaius Pomptinus, having freed the state* (Dē Prōvinciīs
Cōnsulāribus, 13, 20).

b. Latin has a tendency to reënforce meaning by synonymic combination; in Cicero this is not only a device to secure emphasis, but
is also a matter of movement and rhythm, and the reader should avoid
injecting more thought into such duplicate pairs than the writer intended; as, **In animīs vestrīs omnēs triumphōs meōs condī et collocārī,** *It is in your hearts that I wish all my triumphs to be deeply enshrined* (In Catilīnam, 3, 11, 6); such combinations are often set off
by alliteration (see **239.** *a*); **ut prūdēns et sciēns tamquam ad interitum ruerem voluntārium,** *so that I rushed with wide open eyes to voluntary destruction, as it were* (Prō Mārcellō, 5, 9); **nam et sine amōre
et sine cupiditāte et rūrsus sine odiō et sine invidiā iūdicābunt,** *for
they will judge without fear or favor and on the other hand without hatred
or malice* (Prō Mārcellō, 9, 15); **in vēnīs atque vīsceribus reī pūblicae,**
in the flesh and blood of the state (In Catilīnam, 1, 13, 7); **Proinde, cōnsentīte, cōnspīrāte,** *Therefore, unite wholeheartedly* (Pliny, 7, 33).

This trait of Latin style — grouping words and phrases in pairs —
serves in part to explain such figures as chiasmus, hendiadys, hysteron-
proteron, zeugma, and others; see **238** and **239.**

c. The tendency of Latin towards concrete expression is illustrated
by the common use of a perfect participle modifying a concrete noun,
for which English uses an abstract noun followed by a prepositional
phrase; as, **corruptī cīvitātis mōrēs,** *the corruption of public morals*
(Sallust, 5, 17); AB URBE CONDITĀ, *from the founding of the city*
(Livy, title, page 405).

d. Assonance, resemblance of sound, is another characteristic of
Latin style; as, **neque rēs neque spēs,** *neither possession nor prospects* (Sallust, 21, 2).

e. The genitives **animī** and **rērum** are often added to various nouns
to define the extent of their application; as a rule these words should
be omitted in the English translations; as, **rērum nātūra,** *nature,* i.e.
the universe (Laelius Dē Amīcitiā, 7, 10); **convenientia rērum,** *complete harmony* (Laelius Dē Amīcitiā, 27, 3); **animī dolor,** *grief* (Pliny,
9, 42).

f. Latin does not personify the names of countries as readily as does

English but prefers to substitute the names of the respective peoples; as, **hunc et Tarentīnī et Rēgīnī et Neāpolitānī cīvitāte dōnārunt,** *Tarentum, Regium, and Neapolis conferred citizenship upon my client* (Prō Archiā, 3, 22).

g. Pronouns are regularly brought together (iuxtaposition); as, **ut ea ipsa mihi nōta essent,** *that those very points might be known to me* (Catō Maior Dē Senectūte, 8, 14). See **162.** *c.*

h. Adjectives with the suffix **-bilis (74.** *f*), corresponding to the English *-able* and *-ible*, are not common in Latin prose, which more often employs substitutes, such as the perfect participle passive (especially in Livy) and the gerundive; as, **contemptior,** *more despicable* (Catō Maior, Dē Senectūte, 9, 5); **expetendum,** *desirable* (Laelius Dē Amīcitiā, 22, 27); **inviolātī,** *inviolable* (Livy, 2, 1, 12); **optanda,** *desirable* (Catō Maior Dē Senectūte, 19, 6).

i. The genitive, **reī pūblicae,** and the phrase, **in** or **dē rē pūblicā,** are often equivalent to the English word *political, state, national;* as, **difficillimō reī pūblicae tempore,** *in a most difficult political situation* (Philippic, 14, 11, 14); **quid dē rē pūblicā sentiat,** *what his political views are* (In Catilīnam, 1, 13, 20); **scītōte hōc in rē pūblicā sēminārium Catilīnārum futūrum,** *be assured that this will be a state nursery for men like Catiline* (In Catilīnam, 2, 10, 33); **in tantīs reī pūblicae perīculīs,** *in so great a political crisis* (In Catilīnam, 3, 3, 18); **hanc in rē pūblicā viam,** *this political path* (In Catilīnam, 4, 5, 3).

j. A relative clause is often a circumlocution for a noun or substantive expression; as, **eōrum quī nunc sunt,** *of the present generation* (Philippic, 14, 12, 24); **Quod superest,** *As for the rest* (Pliny, 4, 10).

k. Occasionally the perfect participle passive is so used as to be equivalent to the missing present participle passive; as, **turbā fugientium āctus,** *being carried along in the crowd of fugitives* (Livy, 1, 12, 14).

l. Latin verbs sometimes combine two actions into one concentrated expression; as **Respicit,** *He looked around and saw* (Pliny, 13, 33).

m. An affirmative verb in Latin is not infrequently translated by a negative verb in English, and vice versa; as, **mittō,** *I am not saying* (Pliny, 15, 14); **Nec ignōrō,** *I know full well* (Pliny, 4, 18).

n. In translating adjectives from Latin into English there is frequently an interchange between the superlative and positive degree; as, **maximīs proeliīs,** *decisive battles* (Dē Prōvinciīs Cōnsulāribus, 13, 24).

INDIRECT DISCOURSE (ŌRĀTIŌ OBLĪQUA)

213. *a.* Indirect discourse is introduced by a verb or other expression of saying, perceiving, ascertaining, thinking, knowing, or remembering, often referred to as **verba sentiendī et dēclārandī**; as, **dūxit tōtam Galliam (sibi) in nostram diciōnem esse redigendam,** *he considered that he must reduce the whole of Gaul under our sway* (Dē Prōvinciīs Cōnsulāribus, 13, 21).

b. The verb of saying, on which indirect discourse depends, is sometimes not expressed, but implied in the context; as, **Catilīna pollicērī tabulās novās; praetereā, esse in Hispāniā citeriōre Pīsōnem,** *Catiline promised cancellation of debts; furthermore* (he said) *that Piso was in hither Spain* (Sallust, 21, 9); the historical infinitive **pollicērī** suggests the verb of saying on which **esse** depends.

214. *a.* In indirect discourse the principal statements, corresponding with the principal clauses of direct discourse, are expressed by the subject accusative and the infinitive; subordinate clauses have the subjunctive; as, **Erat scrīptum ipsīus manū sēsē, quae eōrum lēgātīs cōnfirmāsset, factūrum esse,** *It had been written with his own hand that he would do what he had assured their ambassadors* (In Catilīnam, 3, 5, 6).

b. A subordinate clause containing an implied quotation may have the subjunctive; as, **sī quis indicāvisset dē coniūrātiōne,** *if anyone should give information regarding the conspiracy* (Sallust, 30, 16), **indicāvisset** representing a future perfect tense of the direct discourse; **Sī quid dīcere vellet, fēcī potestātem,** *In case he wanted to say anything, I gave him an opportunity* (In Catilīnam, 3, 5, 27); **vellet** would have been **vīs** in direct discourse.

c. In indirect discourse a subordinate or parenthetical clause, presenting a statement of fact which is not necessarily a part of the indirect discourse, may have the indicative; as, **Hīc quis potest esse tam mente captus, quī neget haec omnia quae vidēmus deōrum potestāte administrārī,** *Under these circumstances who can be so bereft of reason as to deny that all this which we see is governed by the power of the gods* (In Catilīnam, 3, 9, 3)?

215. The subject accusative in indirect discourse is sometimes omitted when it is easily understood from the context, especially when it refers to the same person as the subject of the verb on which the indirect discourse depends; as, **etsī satis crēdēbat patribus, (eum)**

sublīmen raptum (esse) procellā, *although they readily believed the fathers (senators) (who said) that he had been caught up on high in the blast* (Livy, 1, 16, 9).

216. Commands expressed in direct quotation by the imperative, or by the jussive subjunctive, in indirect discourse have the subjunctive, the negative being **nē**; as, **nē exīstimārent,** *that they should not think* (Sallust, 31, 23); in direct discourse **nōlīte exīstimāre** would have been used.

217. *a.* Ordinary questions in indirect discourse have the subjunctive; for example, **Hodiē quid ēgistī?** *What have you been doing today* (Pliny, 3, 3)? transferred to indirect discourse depending upon **Plīnius dīcit** would become **hodiē quid ēgerit.**

b. Deliberative questions in indirect discourse retain the subjunctive, but the tense is governed by that of the verb on which the indirect discourse depends (**177**); this construction is not essentially different from that of an indirect deliberative subjunctive; thus, **quid agam?** *What am I to do?* after a past tense in indirect discourse becomes **quid ageret;** similarly, **quid scrīberem nōn habēbam,** *I did not know what to write* (Cicerō, Epistulae, 25, 3); in the direct form **scrīberem** would have been **scrībam; est certum, quid respondeam,** *I am decided what to reply* (Prō Archiā, 7, 5). See **204.**

c. Rhetorical questions in indirect discourse have the infinitive (**179.** *b*); for example, **Ubinam gentium sumus?** *Where in the world are we* (In Catilīnam, 1, 4, 10)? would become **ubinam gentium sē esse** in indirect discourse.

218. An apodosis of a conditional sentence containing a statement is expressed in indirect discourse by the accusative and infinitive, containing a command, by the subjunctive; the protasis, containing the condition, has the subjunctive, as follows:

(1) *a.* In the first type (conditions of fact, logical, or real conditions), the tense of the infinitive in indirect discourse corresponds with the tense of the apodosis in the direct form, while the tense of the protasis, introduced by **sī** or **sīn,** is governed by that of the verb on which the indirect discourse depends (**177.** *a*); as, **intellegō, sī iste in Mānliāna castra pervēnerit, nēminem tam stultum fore,** *I know that if that fellow arrives at the camp of Manlius, no one will be so foolish* (In Catilīnam, 1, 12, 22); **pervēnerit** represents a future perfect indicative of direct discourse.

b. If **intellēxī** had been used instead of **intellegō, pervēnisset** would have appeared in the protasis; the apodosis would remain the same in either case.

Therefore, in the protasis of the first type a perfect or pluperfect subjunctive in indirect discourse may represent a future perfect indicative in the direct form, according as the verb of saying is a primary or a secondary tense.

(2) In the second type (less vivid future or ideal conditions, called also conditions of possible realization) the present subjunctive of the apodosis in the direct form becomes regularly the future infinitive in indirect discourse; in the protasis the present subjunctive is used after a primary verb of saying, but imperfect in case the indirect discourse follows a secondary verb. A perfect subjunctive in the protasis remains so after a primary verb of saying, but is changed to a pluperfect tense after a secondary verb of saying; as, **illud est quod ā Archȳtā dīcī solitum nostrōs senēs commemorāre audīvī, sī quis in caelum ascendisset nātūramque mundī et pulchritūdinem sīderum perspēxisset, īnsuāvem illam admīrātiōnem eī fore,** *the following statement is true, which I have heard the older men of our generation mention as an oft-repeated saying of Archytas, that if one should mount up to heaven and survey the nature of the universe and the beauty of the constellations, one's admiration for this sight would be without pleasure for him* (Laelius Dē Amīcitiā, 23, 33); in the direct statement the pluperfects **ascendisset** and **perspēxisset** would be perfect subjunctives, and **fore** would be present subjunctive.

(3) In the third type (conditions contrary to fact or unreal) the protasis in indirect discourse always remains unchanged in tense; the apodosis, if active, whether imperfect or pluperfect in the direct form, becomes the perfect infinitive of the active periphrastic conjugation; if the apodosis is passive or has no supine stem, the periphrastic form **futūrum fuisse** (impersonal) **ut** with the imperfect subjunctive passive must be used; for example, **nisi Īlias exstitisset, īdem tumulus nōmen etiam obruisset,** *if the Iliad had not existed, the same tomb would have also buried his reknown* (Prō Archiā, 10, 25), when made to depend upon **Cicerō dīcit** or **dīxit** would become **nisi Īlias exstitisset, eundem tumulum nōmen etiam ob-**

rutūrum fuisse; again, sī mē meīs cīvibus iniūriā suspectum vidērem, carēre aspectū cīvium māllem, *if I saw that I was unjustly an object of suspicion to my fellow citizens, I should prefer to withdraw from their sight* (In Catilīnam, 1, 7, 16), when made to depend upon **Cicerō dīcit** or **dīxit** would become **sī sē suīs cīvibus iniūriā suspectum vidēret, futūrum fuisse ut carēre aspectū cīvium mallet.**

Indicative apodoses of this type (208. *b*) are turned into the perfect infinitive; as, **perficiam ut, etiam sī nōn esset, putētis ascīscendum fuisse,** *I shall cause you to think that even if he were not (a citizen) he ought to be admitted to citizenship* (Prō Archiā, 2, 19).

219. The apodosis of a conditional sentence is sometimes incorporated in a substantive clause introduced by **ut, nē,** or **quīn**; as, **in tantum aes aliēnum incidērunt, ut, sī salvī esse velint, Sulla sit eīs ab īnferīs excitandus,** *they have incurred such heavy debts that, if they should wish to be saved, they must raise Sulla from the dead* (In Catilīnam, 2, 9, 28); **nōn dubitō, quīn, sī tē mea summa ergā tē studia parum mihi adiūnxerint, rēs pūblica nōs inter nōs conciliātūra coniūnctūraque sit,** *I do not doubt that (even) if my most enthusiastic efforts on your behalf have failed to unite me to you, the interests of the state will bind us closely together to each other* (Cicerō, Epistulae, 2, 14).

When the apodosis of a contrary-to-fact conditional sentence is made to depend upon a construction that requires the subjunctive, the pluperfect active only is changed, this becoming a perfect subjunctive of the active periphrastic conjugation, after either a primary or a secondary tense; as, **Neque ambigitur quīn Brūtus id factūrus fuerit, sī priōrum rēgum alicui rēgnum extorsisset,** *And there is no doubt that Brutus would have done this, if he had wrested the throne from some one of the earlier kings* (Livy, 2, 1, 9). An imperfect tense remains unchanged, and also usually a pluperfect passive.

220. The verb of a clause subordinate to a clause having its verb in the subjunctive, or in the infinitive, is ordinarily put in the subjunctive (subjunctive by attraction); as, **vōbīs erit videndum, Quirītēs, quā condiciōne posthāc eōs esse velītis, quī sē prō salūte vestrā obtulerint invidiae,** *you will have to decide, Quirītēs, in what condition you wish those men to be hereafter, who have exposed themselves to unpopularity* (In Catilīnam, 3, 12, 25); **obtulerint** is attracted into the subjunctive by **velītis.**

THE INFINITIVE

221. *a.* The infinitive is used with many verbs to complete the meaning (complementary infinitive); as, **quid Oceanō longius invenīrī potest?** *What can be found more distant than the Ocean* (Dē Prōvinciīs Cōnsulāribus, 12, 12)?

b. A participle, adjective, or noun in predicate with a complementary infinitive is attracted to the case of the subject of the verb on which the infinitive depends; as, **Potestne tibi huius caelī spīritus esse iūcundus?** *Can the breath of this atmosphere be pleasing to you* (In Catilīnam, 1, 6, 24)?

222. *a.* An infinitive may be the subject or the predicate of an impersonal verb, or of other verbs used impersonally; as, **illīs quiēta movēre magna mercēs vidēbātur,** *although to disturb the public peace seemed to those men a great reward* (Sallust, 21, 3).

b. An infinitive is sometimes used as the subject of an infinitive, especially in indirect discourse; as, **quod eam necesse putās esse in cōnsulis corpore dēfīgere,** *that you think it necessary to plunge it in the body of a consul* (In Catilīnam, 1, 6, 40); **dēfīgere** is the subject of **esse.**

c. An infinitive used as subject may have a subject accusative; as, **quicquid increpuerit, Catilīnam timērī nōn est ferendum,** *that at every sound Catiline is feared, is intolerable* (In Catilīnam, 1, 7, 38); **Catilīnam timērī** is the subject of **ferendum est.**

d. The infinitive as a verbal noun may be in apposition with another noun; as, **Ea potēstās per senātum maxima permittitur, exercitum parāre, bellum gerere,** *This is the greatest power conferred through the agency of the senate,* namely, *the power of getting ready an army, of waging war* (Sallust, 29, 10). Compare **203** (2).

223. *a.* The accusative with the infinitive may be used not only after words of speech and thought (indirect discourse, **213.** *a*), but also after words expressing *will* or *desire, feeling, permission* and *prevention, persuasion, command, training* and *compulsion;* as, **Tūne auctōrem sceleris exīre patiēre?** *Will you permit the author of crime to go forth* (In Catilīnam, 1, 11, 11)? **Cupiō mē esse clementem,** *I desire to be merciful* (In Catilīnam, 1, 2, 17).

Words commonly so used are:

(1) Expressing will or desire: **cupiō,** *desire;* **dēsīderō,** *desire;* **mālō,** *prefer;* **nōlō,** *be unwilling;* **studeō,** *be eager;* **volō,** *wish* (sometimes followed by an **ut**-clause; Livy 1, 16, 27).

(2) Expressing feeling: **admīror**, *be surprised;* **doleō**, *grieve;* **gaudeō**, *rejoice;* **glōrior**, *boast;* **queror**, *complain* (usually followed by a **quod**-clause) ; **magnō dolōre ferō**, *feel deeply chagrined;* **molestē ferō**, *to be annoyed.*

(3) Expressing permission or prevention : **patior**, *suffer*, *allow* (sometimes followed by an **ut**-clause) ; **prohibeō**, *prevent* . . . *from* (also followed by a clause, **201.** *a*).

(4) Expressing command, training, or compulsion : **iubeō**, *order;* **vetō**, *forbid;* **assuēfaciō**, *train;* **cōgō**, *force.*

b. **Cupiō, mālō, nōlō, studeō,** and **volō** frequently have the in-ﬁnitive without a subject accusative (complementary infinitive) ; as, **competitōrēs tuōs interficere voluistī**, *you wished to kill your rivals* (In Catilīnam, 1, 5, 17).

224. *a.* When verbs which, in the active voice, have the accusative and infinitive, are used in the passive, a subject nominative may take the place of the accusative, the infinitive remaining the same ; in translating, the English impersonal construction should often be used. Latin, as a rule, uses a personal subject in the simple tenses (present, future, imperfect), and an impersonal subject in the compound tenses (perfect, pluperfect, future perfect) ; as, **līberae querimōniae dē aliōrum iniūriīs esse dīcuntur**, *it is said that their complaints regarding the injuries received from others are unhindered,* lit. *the complaints are said to be* (Dē Imperiō Cn. Pompeī, 14, 36) ; **Quam multōs scrīptōrēs rērum Alexander sēcum habuisse dīcitur**, *How many historians Alexander is said to have had with him* (Prō Archiā, 10, 17) ; **L. Quīnctiō Cincinnātō nūntiātum est eum dictātōrem esse factum**, *word was brought to Lucius Quinctius Cincinnatus that he had been made dictator* (Catō Maior Dē Senectūte, 16, 8).

b. The accusative and the infinitive may stand as the subject of an impersonal verb, or of other verbs used impersonally ; as, **Ad mortem tē, Catilīna, dūcī iussū cōnsulis iam prīdem oportēbat**, *You ought long ago to have been led to execution* (In Catilīnam, 1, 1, 19), **tē ducī** being the subject of **oportēbat.**

c. The infinitive with a subject accusative may be used to express an exclamation ; in the English translation the phrase *to think that, the idea that,* or a similar expression should be supplied ; the interrogative particle **-ne** is often appended to the emphatic word ; as, **Quemquamne fuisse tam scelerātum!** *To think that anyone should have been so wicked* (Philippic, 14, 5, 31) !

For the exclamatory subjunctive clause with or without **ut** see **179.** *c.*

225. The place of the future infinitive, active or passive, may be taken by **fore** or **futūrum esse** and a clause with **ut** and the subjunctive; this is the regular substitute for supineless verbs and for the future infinitive passive, which only Cicero uses with any degree of frequency; as, **sē spērāre dīxērunt fore ut ea cōnsilia illūstrārentur,** *they said that they hoped that those designs would be brought to light* (In Catilīnam, 3, 8, 32).

PARTICIPLES

226. *a.* The time denoted by a present participle is the same as that of the principal verb; as, **Catilīnam orbem terrae vāstāre cupientem perferēmus?** *Shall we tolerate Catiline, who desires to destroy the whole world* (In Catilīnam, 1, 1, 24)?

b. The time denoted by a perfect participle is prior to that of the principal verb; as, **Ā quō nōn receptus etiam ad mē venīre ausus es,** *And when you were not received by him, you dared to come even to me* (In Catilīnam, 1, 8, 5).

c. Perfect participles of deponent and semi-deponent verbs are often used in Latin where English usage prefers a present participle; Latin is more exact in expressing tense relationships; as, **ratus,** *thinking* (Livy, 1, 19, 5).

d. The perfect participle of some deponents may be passive in sense; as, **perīclitātīs mōribus amīcōrum,** *after testing the character of friends,* lit. *having been tested* (Laelius Dē Amīcitiā, 17, 34).

227. *a.* A participle is often used to express concisely an idea which might have been expanded into a clause, particularly an idea of *cause, condition, opposition, characterization, description,* or *time;* as,

(1) Expressing cause: **(nūbēs) dēstitūta aut etiam pondere suō victa in lātitūdinem vānēscēbat,** *(the cloud), because it was without support or had been overcome even by its own weight, dissipated itself laterally* (Pliny, 11, 24).

(2) Expressing condition: **hīc morbus relevātus vehementius ingravēscet,** *this disease, if relieved, will grow worse and worse* (In Catilīnam, 1, 13, 12).

(3) Expressing concession or opposition: **Multōrum tē oculī et aurēs nōn sentientem cūstōdient,** *The eyes and ears of many will keep guard over you, though you perceive it not* (In Catilīnam, 1, 2, 35).

(4) Expressing characterization or description: **adversārium nōbilitāte, ingeniō, virtūte, praestantem nōn modo extollere iacentem,** *a prostrate foe outstanding in birth, ability, and merit* (Prō Mārcellō, 3, 8).

(5) Expressing time: **volventēs hostilia cadāvera amīcum reperiēbant,** *while rolling over the corpses of the enemy they discovered a friend* (Sallust, 61, 17).

b. A participle may express manner or circumstance; as, **pugnāns cōnfoditur,** *still fighting, he was stabbed to death* (Sallust, 60, 20).

228. *a.* A perfect participle is often used in agreement with the subject or the object of a verb where English usage prefers a coördinate clause; as, **perinde atque ipse cōgitāns sentiō,** *just as I myself think and feel* (Prō Mārcellō, 4, 4).

b. A perfect passive participle in agreement with a noun is sometimes used where the participle has the main idea and is best translated by a noun; as, **corruptī cīvitātis mōrēs,** *the corruption of public morals* (Sallust, 5, 17).

c. A participle in agreement with the object of a verb is sometimes used to depict an action or a situation more vividly, especially with verbs of *seeing, hearing,* and *representing;* as, **urbem ex faucibus fātī ēreptam vidētis,** *you see the city rescued from the jaws of death* (In Catilīnam, 3, 1, 6).

229. *a.* **Habeō** and **teneō** with a perfect passive participle in agreement with the object may be used to express the continued effect of an action; as, **pecūniās magnās collocātās habent,** *they have large sums of money invested* (Dē Imperiō Cn. Pompeī, 7, 15); **ducēs comprehēnsōs tenētis,** *you hold the leaders under arrest* (In Catilīnam, 3, 7, 2).

b. The future passive participle (gerundive) in agreement with the object of certain verbs is used to express purpose or accomplishment; as, **senātuī placēre, ut cōnsulēs monumentum locandum cūrent,** *that the senate does decree that the consuls shall see to the issuing of a contract for a memorial* (Philippic, 14, 14, 39); **attribuit nōs trucīdandōs,** *he assigned us to be massacred* (In Catilīnam, 4, 6, 24).

The verbs commonly thus used are **attribuō,** *assign;* **cūrō,** *arrange, provide;* **dō,** *give;* **locō,** *issue a contract for;* **trādō,** *deliver.*

c. The future passive participle combined with the forms of **sum** in the passive periphrastic conjugation (**63**) is often used to express obligation, necessity, or propriety; as, **prōpāganda (sunt) subolēs,** *the population must be increased* (Prō Mārcellō, 8, 4).

If the verb is intransitive, the subject is regularly impersonal; as, **tamen C. Caesarī succēdendum nōndum putārem**, *nevertheless I should still not favor the proposal to supersede Gaius Caesar*, lit. *that it ought to be succeeded to* (Dē Prōvinciīs Cōnsulāribus, 8, 2). See **110**. *a*.

d. A participle with a negative may be translated by *without* and a verbal noun; as, **Nisi tē salvō et manente**, *Without your being safe and remaining* (Prō Mārcellō, 10, 1).

e. The future active participle, usually with a verb of motion, may express *purpose, destiny,* or *intention;* this construction is not Ciceronian, but becomes more common with Livy and later writers; as, **ascendit ipse, lātūrus auxilium**, *he went on board in person to bear aid* (Pliny, 12, 36).

GERUND AND GERUNDIVE CONSTRUCTION

230. *a*. In place of the gerund with an object, the gerundive construction is often used, with the noun in the case in which the gerund might have been put, and the gerundive agreeing with it. Some of the more common uses of the gerund and of the gerundive construction are as follows:

(1) Genitive after nouns and adjectives, and with **causā** and **grātiā** expressing purpose: **propter dīripiendī cupiditātem**, *on account of their desire for plundering them* (Dē Imperiō Cn. Pompeī, 22, 34); **suī cōnservandī causā**, *for the sake of saving themselves* (In Catilīnam, 1, 3, 18).

(2) Dative after verbs and adjectives of *fitness:* **quisque pugnandō locum cēperat**, *each man had taken a place for fighting* (Sallust, 61, 3).

(3) Accusative after **ad** to express purpose: **vīvis nōn ad dēpōnendam sed ad cōnfīrmandam audāciam**, *you live not to lay aside but to strengthen your boldness* (In Catilīnam, 1, 2, 14).

Livy uses the accusative of the gerund as an appositive: **ad rēs dīversissimās, parendum atque imperandum**, *for (two) widely separated duties, obeying and commanding* (Livy, 21, 4, 7).

(4) Ablative of means or cause without a preposition, and ablative with the prepositions **in, ex,** or **dē**: **nōn modo impellendō, vērum etiam adiuvandō**, *not only by urging but also by assisting them* (In Catilīnam, 2, 4, 26); **industria in agendō**, *energy in action* (Dē Imperiō Cn. Pompeī, 11, 6).

b. The gerundive, as participle or adjective, may mean *capable of being, fit to be, worthy to be,* expressing the idea of our English adjective with the suffix *-able* or *-ible.* See **212.** *h.*

THE SUPINES

231. The supine in **-um** is used, chiefly after verbs of motion, to express purpose; as, **aquam ea extrā moenia petītum ierat,** *she had gone outside of the walls to fetch water* (Livy, 1, 11, 7).

232. The supine in **-ū** is used after a few adjectives to denote in what respect their meaning is to be taken; as, **optimum factū,** *the best thing to do* (Sallust, 32, 4).

CONJUNCTIONS

233. *a.* The copulative conjunctions are **et,** *and,* **et . . . et,** *both . . . and, on the one hand . . . on the other,* to express simple connection; **-que,** *and,* **-que . . . -que,** *both . . . and,* to express a closer connection; **atque** or **ac,** *and also, and indeed, and,* to express a close connection and also make that which follows slightly more prominent; and **neque** or **nec,** *and . . . not,* **neque** (or **nec**) **. . . neque** (or **nec**), *neither . . . nor, not . . . and not;* **et . . . neque,** *both . . . and not;* **neque** or **nec . . . et,** *and not . . . and,* to express a connection with a negative idea.

b. The enclitic conjunction **-que,** *and,* is attached to the word introduced by it, or to the first word of a phrase or clause which it introduces, excepting a prepositional phrase; **-que** introducing a prepositional phrase may be attached to the first word after the preposition.

c. After words expressing similarity, or the opposite, **atque** or **ac** has the force of *than, as;* as, **vōs ea aequē ac priōre nocte dēfendite,** *defend these just the same as you did last night* (In Catilīnam, 3, 12, 45).

d. The conjunctions **et, -que, atque, ac,** and **neque** are used in various combinations, and sometimes join more than two members; as, **et . . . que, -que . . . et, et . . . atque, atque . . . et, atque . . . -que, neque . . . atque, neque . . . et, -que . . . -que . . . -que, ac . . . atque . . . -que, et . . . atque . . . et . . . et . . . et.**

e. Two negatives are equivalent to an affirmative; but when such negatives as **nōn, nēmō, nihil, numquam** are combined with **neque . . . neque, nōn . . . nōn, nōn modo,** or **nē . . . quidem** the negation is merely continued and reëmphasized; as, **numquam hīc neque suō neque amīcōrum iūdiciō revincētur**, *never will my client be convicted either by his own judgment or that of his friends* (Prō Archiā, 5, 34).

234. *a.* When more than two words stand in the same relation, the copulative conjunction may be expressed with all, or omitted with all, or the last two words may be joined by -que; in each case English usage generally prefers " and " between the last two words; as, **labōribus, cōnsiliīs, perīculīs meīs**, *by my labors, counsels, and dangers* (In Catilīnam, 3, 2, 5); **sunt mōrōsī et anxiī et īrācundī et difficilēs senēs**, *old men are fretful, worrisome, choleric, and surly* (Catō Maior Dē Senectūte, 18, 32); **bona, fortūnās, coniugēs līberōsque vestrōs**, *your goods, your fortunes, your wives, and children* (In Catilīnam, 3, 1, 2).

b. Sometimes, especially after a negative expression, Latin uses **et, -que**, and **atque** or **ac**, where English usage prefers *but;* as, **Neque enim ego illa nec ūlla umquam secūtus sum arma cīvīlia, semperque mea cōnsilia pācis et togae socia fuērunt**, *For I, for my part, adopted neither that nor any other cause in civil strife, but my intentions were always associated with peace and the toga* (Prō Mārcellō, 5, 4).

235. *a.* The disjunctive conjunction **aut,** *or*, is used to connect alternatives that cannot, in most cases, both be true at the same time; **vel,** *or*, negative **nēve** or **neu,** *or not, and not*, to connect alternatives between which there might be a choice; and **sīve** or **seu,** *or if*, to connect alternatives involving a condition; as, **aut imberbēs aut bene barbātōs**, *either without a beard or with full beard* (In Catilīnam, 2, 10, 22); **Satis diū vel nātūrae vīxī vel glōriae**, *Long enough have I lived (to satisfy) either nature or glory* (Prō Mārcellō, 8, 8); **sīve amor sīve amīcitia**, *either love or friendship, whatever name you give it* (Laelius Dē Amīcitiā, 27, 6).

b. The disjunctive conjunctions are often used in pairs, as **aut . . . aut,** *either . . . or,* **vel . . . vel,** *either . . . or,* **sīve . . . sīve,** *whether . . . or, either . . . or.* Vel is an old imperative of **volō,** *wish*, and so means literally, *take your choice.*

236. *a.* The adversative conjunction **at,** *but, at any rate*, is used to express contrast or restriction, to introduce an opposing argument or the imaginary objection of an opponent; **autem,** *however, on the other hand, moreover*, to express contrast or addition; **sed,** *but*, to correct or limit a preceding statement; **tamen,** *nevertheless, yet*, to emphasize the importance of something that follows in opposition to a preceding statement; and **vērō, at vērō,** *in fact, but in truth,* to emphasize a contrast with a preceding statement.

b. The adversative conjunctions **autem** and **vērō** are regularly placed after the first word of a clause.

c. The adversative conjunction **tamen** sometimes stands after the first word of a clause.

d. The common correlatives are **nōn sōlum . . . sed etiam,** *not only . . . but also;* **nōn modo . . . sed etiam,** *not only . . . but also;* **nōn modo . . . sed,** *not only . . . but;* **nōn modo nōn . . . sed nē . . . quidem,** *not only not . . . but not even.*

e. In **nōn modo . . . nē . . . quidem** Latin uses **nōn modo** as equivalent to **nōn modo nōn,** when a verb appears only in the second member; as, **Numquam tū nōn modo ōtium, sed nē bellum quidem nisi nefārium concupistī,** *Never have you coveted not only not peace, but not even war except a criminal one* (In Catilīnam, 1, 10, 6). See **233.** *e.*

237. *a.* Conjunctions denoting logical relations in Latin are chiefly **itaque, igitur** (usually post-positive), **ergō,** *accordingly, therefore, then* (lit. *and so*), to introduce a statement of a fact or situation naturally resulting from what preceded; **proinde,** *hence, accordingly,* to introduce a command; **nam, namque, enim** (post-positive), *for,* **etenim,** *for, you see, for, mind you,* to introduce an explanation of a preceding statement; and **quā rē, idcircō,** *wherefore, and therefore,* to introduce a logical consequence, or a command.

b. In presenting a succession of points the writer often uses **prīmum,** *first,* and **deinde,** *then, in the second place;* sometimes, also, **dēnique,** *in fine,* to introduce the conclusion of an argument.

c. In the adverbial phrase **nē . . . quidem,** *not even,* the word or phrase emphasized is placed between the two words; as, **nē bellum quidem,** *not even war* (In Catilīnam, 1, 10, 6).

d. **Quam** in comparative sentences takes the same case after it as before it; as, **dīcam nūllam esse laudem ampliōrem quam eam,** *I maintain that there is no greater glory than this* (Prō Mārcellō, 2, 5).

When the main clause is an infinitive, **quam** is usually followed by the infinitive also, but in Livy and later writers the subjunctive with or without **ut** may also be employed; as, **magis mihi videntur vōta factūrī contrā rem pūblicam quam arma lātūrī,** *they seem to me more likely to entertain desires against the state than likely to bear arms against it* (In Catilīnam, 2, 8, 32); for the subjunctive after **quam** see **197.** *c.*

The indicative, instead of the infinitive or subjunctive, may be used after **quam** if the thought demands a statement of fact; as, **Soleō saepe ante oculōs . . . nec disiūnctissimās terrās citius passibus cuiusquam potuisse peragrārī, quam tuīs nōn dīcam cursibus, sed victōriīs lūstrātae sunt,** *I am wont often to keep before my eyes, that most widely separated countries could not have been traversed by the footsteps of anyone more quickly than they actually have been covered, I will not say, by your marches, but by your victories* (Prō Mārcellō, 2, 14).

FIGURES OF SPEECH

238. The following grammatical figures occur in this text:

a. Anacoluthon (an-ạ-kolū′thon)[1], want of grammatical sequence, occurs when the logical arrangement of a sentence is abandoned; **Nam et . . . Deinde;** et expects a corresponding **et** for line 11, but the original arrangement is abandoned, **Deinde** being substituted for the second et (Dē Imperiō Cn. Pompeī, 7, 6).

b. Anastrophe (a-nas′trō-fē), inversion of the natural order of words; the figure is commonly applied when the preposition follows its case; as, **mēcum** (In Catilīnam, 1, 4, 1).

c. Archaism (är′kā-is′m), the use of ancient, obsolete, or antiquated diction; as, **aerumnārum requiem,** *a surcease of woe* (Sallust, 51, 22), **aerumna** being an archaic word.

d. Asyndeton (a-sin′de-ton), the omission of a conjunction where a connective might have been used; as, **Gabīnī,** (*and*) *of Gabinius* (Prō Archiā, 5, 2).

e. Brachylogy (bra-kil′ọ-ji), a condensed form of expression; as, **melius perībimus,** *'twill be better for us to perish* (Livy, 1, 13, 10).

f. Ellipsis (e-lip′sis), the omission of words essential to the meaning; as, **nisi . . . flexissent** (In Catilīnam, 3, 8, 24) is used without the apodosis, which may be supplied by inserting the words **et ventūra esse,** *and would come upon us unless the gods should change fate itself.*

g. Hellenism (hel′en-iz′m) or *Grecism* (grē′siz′m), a Greek phrase, idiom, or construction; as, **redamāre,** *to love in return* (Laelius Dē Amīcitiā, 14, 7), the Latin word being coined by Cicero to express the Greek ἀντιφιλεῖν.

h. Hendiadys (hen-dī′ạ-dis), the use of two nouns with a connective where a noun with a modifying genitive or adjective might have

---

[1] The key to the pronunciation is given on page 709.

been expected; as, **vīs ac nātūra,** *natural power* (Laelius Dē Amīcitiā, 15, 8).

i. Hypallage (hip-al'ạ-jē), an interchange in the syntactic relation of words; as, **eōrum collēctiō dispersa,** *the collecting of these scattered members* (Dē Imperiō Cn. Pompeī, 9, 7); **dispersa** logically belongs with **eōrum,** hence, it should be translated as if **dispersōrum.**

j. Hysteron proteron (his'tẽr-on prot'ẽr-on), a reversing of the natural order of the sense; as, **vīdī . . . eōs nōbīscum esse et Rōmae remānsisse,** *I saw that they were with us and had remained at Rome* (In Catilīnam, 3, 2, 8).

k. Pleonasm (plē'ọ-naz'm), use of more words than necessary to express the idea; as, **cum prīmō coepisset,** *although at first he had begun* (In Catilīnam, 3, 5, 60).

l. Polysyndeton (pol-ị-sin'dẹ-ton), the use of more conjunctions than the sense requires; as, **Lūcullōs et Drūsum et Octāviōs et Catōnem et tōtam Hortēnsiōrum domum,** *the Luculli, and Drusus, and the Octavii, and Cato, and the entire family of the Hortensii* (Prō Archiā, 3, 39).

m. Prolepsis (prō-lep'sis), or *anticipation,* the use of a noun as object in a clause preceding that in which it naturally belongs as sub-ject; as, **deinde . . . semel** (Laelius Dē Amīcitiā, 12, 15); **deinde** presupposes **semel** which comes after.

n. Syncope (sin'kọ-pē), omission of a letter or syllable from the middle of a word; as, **peragrārunt** for **peragrāvērunt** (Dē Prōvinciīs Cōnsulāribus, 13, 30).

o. Synesis (sin'ẹ-sis), construction according to the sense, without regard to the grammatical form; as, **nōbilitās aestuābat, et . . . crēdēbant** (Sallust, 23, 19); **aestuābat** is singular to agree grammati-cally with the subject, **nōbilitās,** but **crēdēbant** is plural to agree in sense.

p. Tmesis (t'mē'sis or mē'-), separation of parts of a compound word by one or more words; as, **prius dēscendērunt in aequum quam** (Livy, 1, 12, 4).

q. Zeugma (zūg'mạ), the use of a verb or an adjective with two different words to only one of which it is strictly applicable in sense; as, **acervīs corporum et cīvium sanguine redundāvit,** *was choked with heaps of dead bodies and overflowed with the blood of citizens* (In Cati-līnam, 3, 10, 16); **redundāvit** is connected strictly only with **san-guine; beneficiīs, summō ingeniō praeditus,** *favored with kind-*

nesses, endowed with consummate genius (Dē Imperiō Cn. Pompeī, 23, 7).

239. The following rhetorical figures occur in this text:

a. Alliteration (a-lit″ĕr-ā′shun), repetition of the same letter at the beginning of successive words; as, **post Pūnicum prīmum perfectum** (Livy, 1, 19, 9).

b. Anaphora (an-af′ọ-rạ), the repetition of the same word at the beginning of successive phrases or clauses; as, **Nihil . . . nihil . . . nihil** (In Catilīnam, 1, 3, 28).

c. Antithesis (an-tith′ẹ-sis), the juxtaposition of contrasted expressions in like order; as, **Nōn igitur ūtilitātem amīcitia, sed ūtilitās amīcitiam secūta est,** *It is not, therefore, friendship that has followed upon advantage, but advantage upon friendship* (Laelius Dē Amīcitiā, 14, 35).

d. Figūra Etymolōgica (fig-ū′rạ et″i-mọ-loj′i-kạ) combination of words of kindred origin, but of different meanings; as, **invidia . . . invidōs** (In Catilīnam, 3, 12, 37).

e. Chiasmus (kī-as′mus), an arrangement of contrasted words in inverse order; called *chiasmus* from the Greek letter *Chi* (**X**), in which the lines are crossed; as, **accommodātam huic reō, vōbīs . . . nōn molestam,** *suitable to this defendant, to you not disagreeable* (Prō Archiā, 2, 8).

f. Climax (klī′max), an arrangement of words, phrases, or clauses with gradual increase of interest or vigor of expression to the end; as, **Nihil agis, nihil mōlīris, nihil cōgitās,** *You do nothing, you attempt nothing, you plan nothing* (In Catilīnam, 1, 3, 28).

g. Corrēctiō (kọ-rek′sh(y)ō), the recalling of a word in order to use a stronger one in its place; as, **hīc tamen vīvit. Vīvit? Immō vērō etiam in senātum venit,** *yet this fellow lives. "Lives" did I say? Nay, he even comes into the senate* (In Catilīnam, 1, 2, 15).

h. Epanalepsis (ep″an-ạ-lep′sis), repetition of the same word or phrase after other words have intervened; as, **colligerem . . . Collēgī** (Pliny, 1, 2).

i. Euphemism (ū′fẹ-miz′m), the use of a mild expression in order to avoid a word of bad omen; as, **bonōrum ferrāmentōrum,** *good tools* (In Catilīnam, 3, 5, 15); Cicero avoids the use of **tēlōrum** to imply that Catiline was a collector of steel implements in general.

j. Euphony (ū′fọ-ni), pleasing sound produced by words so combined as to appeal to the ear; as, **cum uxōre et fīliola et mellītō Cice-**

rōne cōnsūmitur (Cicerō, Epistulae, 3, 13) ; the combination of liquid (l, r), nasal (m, n) sounds together with the broad vowels and alliteration produce an harmonious effect.

k. Hyperbaton (hī-per′ba̧-ton), the arrangement of words in unusual order, as the separation of words that belong together, such as the insertion of one or more words between the parts of an ablative absolute; as, **huius auctōritātem locī,** *this place of dignity* (Dē Imperiō Cn. Pompeī, 2, 7) ; **Magnō mē metū līberābis,** *You will free me from great fear* (In Catilīnam, 1, 5, 6).

l. Irony, humorous or light sarcasm in which the intended implication is the opposite of the literal meaning of the words ; as, **Amoenitās eum locōrum, crēdō, nātiōnum illārum hūmānitās et lepōs retinet,** *It is the attractive surroundings, I suppose, the culture and charm of those nations that hold him there* (Dē Prōvinciīs Cōnsulāribus, 12, 7).

m. Litotes (lī′to-tēz), the affirmation of an idea through the negative of its opposite ; as, **nequāquam paribus animīs,** *with very different feelings* (Livy, 1, 25, 51).

n. Metonymy (mē-ton′i-mǐ), a figure of speech in which one word is substituted for another that it suggests ; as, **vestrīs vectīgālibus,** *the lands tributary to you* (Dē Imperiō Cn. Pompeī, 2, 17) ; **vectīgālibus,** *taxes,* is put for the regions in which they were raised.

o. Onomatopoeia (on″ō-mat″ō-pē′ya̧), the use of words in which the sound suggests the sense; as, **tempestās cum magnō fragōre tonitribusque,** *a storm with loud peals of thunder* (Livy, 1, 16, 3).

p. Oxymoron (-mō′ron), the use of a contradictory epithet; a paradox; as, **absentēs adsunt** (Laelius Dē Amīcitiā, 7, 5).

q. Paronomasia (par″ǫ-nǫ-mā′zhi-a̧), a play upon words; punning; as, **exsul . . . cōnsul** (In Catilīnam, 1, 10, 20).

r. Praeteritiō (pret-ęr-i′sh(y)ō), from **praeterīre,** *to pass by;* a figure by which a speaker or writer pretends to pass by what at the same time he really mentions; as, **Praetermittō ruīnās fortūnārum tuārum,** *I pass over the downfall of your fortune* (In Catilīnam, 1, 6, 17).

s. Reductiō ad absurdum (rē-duk′sh(y)ō ad ab-sêr′dum), the reducing of a supposition or hypothesis to an absurdity ; as, **Etenim,** etc., *For, mind you, when men in Magna Graecia were wont to bestow citizenship without pay upon many ordinary men endowed with no talents at all or with very moderate ones, I suppose that Regium, Locri, Naples, or Tarentum was unwilling to give to this my client, endowed*

*with consummate genius, what they were in the habit of lavishing upon
stage performers* (Prō Archiā, 5, 11) !

t. Synecdoche (si-nek′dǫ-kē), a figure by which a part is put for the
whole or the reverse; as, **Rhēnum, Oceanum, Nīlum legentēs,** *when
they read of the Rhine* (Germany), *the Ocean* (Britain), *and the Nile*
(Egypt) (Prō Mārcellō, 9, 7).

EXPRESSIONS RELATING TO TIME

240. *a.* The Roman year (**annus**) is usually dated by the consuls
in office, their names being given in the ablative absolute with **cōnsulibus**; as, **Lepidō et Tullō cōnsulibus,** *in the consulship of Lepidus
and Tullus* (In Catilīnam, 6, 25), *i.e.* in 66 B.C.

b. In Cicero's time the year commenced on January 1, and the
months were named (**mēnsis**) **Iānuārius, Februārius, Mārtius** (originally the first month of the year), **Aprīlis, Maius, Iūnius, Quīnctīlis**
(from **quīnque**; named the *fifth* month when the year began with
March), **Sextīlis** (**sex**), **September, Octōber, November, December**
(the *tenth* month, reckoning March as the first). Afterwards **Quīnctīlis** was changed to **Iūlius** (our *July*) in honor of Julius Caesar, and
Sextīlis to **Augustus** (our *August*) in honor of the Emperor Augustus.

241. *a.* Dates in the month were reckoned backward from three
points, the mode of reckoning being similar to that which we use when
we say, " Four days yet before the New Moon." These points
designated by plural feminine nouns, are *the Kalends,* **Kalendae,**
the *first* day of the month; *the Nones,* **Nōnae** (ninth before the
Ides), the *seventh* day of March, May, July, and October, the *fifth* day
of other months; and *the Ides* (**Īdūs**), the *fifteenth* day of March,
May, July, and October, the *thirteenth* of other months.

b. In giving dates the days at the beginning and end of a given
period were both included, and abbreviations were employed. Thus,
a. d. v. Kal. Apr. in full would be **ante diem quīntum Kalendās Aprīlēs,**
which is translated as if it were (**diēs**) **quīntus ante Kalendās Aprīlēs,**
the fifth (day) before the Calends of April; since March had 31 days,
we start from April 1 and count back:

DAY I	DAY II	DAY III	DAY IV	DAY V
April 1	March 31	March 30	March 29	March 28

and so we find the fifth day, which is March 28 according to our
method of writing dates.

c. **Prīdiē** with the accusative may be used in counting backwards; as, **prīdiē Kalendās Iānuāriās,** *the day before the Kalends of January* (In Catilīnam, 1, 5, 26), hence, December 31.

d. In 46 B.C. the Calendar was reformed by Julius Caesar by virtue of his authority as Supreme Pontiff and since that year it has undergone slight change. As the dates of the Gallic War and of the Civil War are prior to 46 B.C., they fall in the period of the Unreformed Calendar, when there was much confusion. Thus, the twenty-eighth day of March of the Unreformed Calendar in 58 B.C. is considered by some to be the same as March 24 of our Calendar; by others, the same as March 25; by others still, as April 16 of our Calendar.

242. *a.* The day from sunrise to sunset was divided into twelve hours, **hōrae,** which varied in length according to the season of the year, and were numbered 1–12; thus, **hōrā septimā,** *the seventh hour.* Since the sixth hour ended at noon, the seventh hour at the equinoxes would correspond exactly with the hour between twelve and one o'clock according to our reckoning; at other times the seventh hour would end after, or before, one o'clock.

b. The method of reducing the Roman hours to our system of reckoning may be illustrated by the following problem:

Question. "What, approximately, is our equivalent of the fourth Roman hour in the last week of August in the region of Dover, England?"

Answer. In the region of Dover in the last week in August the sun rises about 5 o'clock and sets about 7. The length of the day is therefore about 14 hours by our reckoning. Since the Romans divided the full day into 12 equal hours, we divide 14 by 12 and have $1\frac{1}{6}$, that is, the Roman hour in this problem = $1\frac{1}{6}$ of our hours. At the beginning of the fourth Roman hour 3 Roman hours have passed; $3 \times 1\frac{1}{6} = 3\frac{1}{2}$, that is, at the beginning of the fourth Roman hour $3\frac{1}{2}$ of our hours have passed since sunrise. As sunrise is reckoned about 5 o'clock by our time, we add $3\frac{1}{2}$ to 5, making 8.30; that is, 8.30 A.M., by our reckoning from midnight, will approximately represent the beginning of the fourth hour of the day by Roman reckoning under the conditions of the problem.

c. When the sun was not visible, recourse might be had to water clocks.

£XPRESSIONS RELATING TO LENGTH AND DISTANCE

243. *a.* Terms denoting measurement are **digitus,** *finger-breadth;* **pēs,** *foot,* which measured approximately .97 of the English foot; **passus,** *pace;* and **mīlle passūs,** *mile,* plural **mīlia passuum,** *miles.* The **passus** contained two ordinary steps (**gradus**), and measured the distance between the points where the same heel is lifted and touches the ground again.

b. The relations of the units of measurement, and their modern equivalents, are as follows:

			ENGLISH FEET		METERS
	1 digitus	=	.728 inch	=	.0185
16 digitī	= 1 pēs	=	11.65 inches	=	.296
2½ pedēs	= 1 gradus	=	2 feet 5⅛ inches	=	.74
2 gradūs	= 1 passus	=	4 feet 10¼ inches	=	1.48
1000 passūs	= mīlle passūs	=	4854 feet	=	1480.00

Since the Roman foot was approximately .97 of the English foot in length, the Roman mile, 4854 English feet in length, was 426 feet shorter than the English mile of 5280 feet; 12 English miles are a little more than the equivalent of 13 Roman miles.

c. Long distances may be loosely expressed by **iter** (accusative) with the genitive.

CICERO AND THE MODERN WORLD

The sincere student of Cicero will find that his name is synonymous not only with eloquence, as Quintilian says (11, 112), but even with a liberal education. His works abound on every hand with a modernity of thinking and acting, so that the reader, quite unconsciously and indirectly, is brought face to face with dramatic events and momentous problems that have always shaped the destiny of men and nations. Such by-products, of course, are a valuable adjunct to the study of all literature and history, but they are especially conspicuous when the student undertakes to interpret Cicero. In order to stimulate his interest and present a focal point about which the work of each member of the class may converge, let the instructor assign a special topic at the very beginning of the year with the suggestion that any pertinent material in the text read throughout the year be transferred to a special notebook, and that at a specified time before the close of the year this material be expanded into a theme to be read before the class.

Cicero was one of the first Roman statesmen who hailed from the intellectual élite, and his position may be profitably compared with that of Woodrow Wilson. Politically, Cicero was an idealist, who fought hard to keep afloat in the adverse sea of realism in which Roman politicians had been seeking to pilot the ship of state. Woodrow Wilson had similar difficulties to contend with before, during, and after the World War.

Further parallel problems are suggested in a study of the following topics:

Gangsters in Ancient Rome and America of Today

Graft in Government

Honesty and Responsibility of Public Officials

The Problem of the Unemployed

Politics, Business, and War

Provincial Administration

Family Life

The Soldier's Bonus

Humanism and War

Monetary Standards and Stabilization

Criminal Prosecution

Legal Procedure

The Problem of Immigration

Political Parties

Peace and War

Life and Living

The *Summum Bonum* of Life

Success and Achievement

Capital Punishment

Foreign Policies

The Waning Power of the Senate

Racial Hatreds

Patriotism and Loyalty

Military Preparedness

Religion and Skepticism

Racketeering, Then and Now

Ancient and Modern Youth

Culture and Scholarship

In Defense of Catiline

HELPS TO THE STUDY OF CICERO

For references on the writings of Cicero, his public life, and the history of Rome in his time, see Kelsey's *Topical Outline of Latin Literature*, page 15 (revised edition, Boston, 1899).

For a concise account of Cicero's literary activity, with the manuscripts of his various works and the more important editions, special treatises, dictionaries, and articles, see Klotz, *Geschichte der römischen Litteratur*, Bielefeld und Leipzig, 1930; Schanz, *Geschichte der römischen Litteratur*, I, 4th edition (Munich, 1927); Teuffel and Schwabe's *History of Roman Literature*, English Translation of the Fifth German Edition, by Warr, Volume I, (London, 1900).

For editions and literature prior to 1881, see Engelmann's *Bibliothēca scrīptōrum classicōrum*, 8th edition, Part II (Leipzig, 1882).

For ancient oratory, and Cicero as an orator, see Blass, *Die attische Beredsamkeit* (2d edition, 4 volumes, Leipzig, 1887–1898); Cucheval and Berger, *Histoire de l'éloquence latine depuis l'origine de Rome jusqu'à Cicéron* (2d edition, 2 volumes, Paris, 1881); Jebb's *Attic Orators* (2 volumes, London, 1876); Poiret, *Essai sur l'éloquence judiciaire à Rome pendant la république* (Paris, 1886); Westermann, *Geschichte der römischen Beredsamkeit* (Leipzig, 1835); and the introductions to annotated editions of the *Dē Ōrātōre, Brūtus*, and *Ōrātor*.

Useful for the study of Cicero's Latin are Lebreton, *Études sur la langue et la grammaire de Cicéron* (Paris, 1901), and the lexicons by Merguet, *Lexikon zu den Reden des Cicero* (4 volumes, Jena, 1877–1884), and *Lexikon zu den philosophischen Schriften Cicero's* (3 volumes, Jena, 1887–1894).

For Roman constitution and constitutional history, see Abbott, *A History and Description of Roman Political Institutions* (Boston, 1909); Granrud, *Roman Constitutional History* (Boston, 1902); Greenidge, *Roman Public Life*, one of the "Handbooks on Archaeology and Antiquities" (New York, 1901); Greenidge, *Legal Procedure of Cicero's Time* (New York, 1901). For general reference, see Laistner, M. L. W., *A Survey of Ancient History to the Death of Constantine* (New York, 1929).

For pictures illustrating almost every phase of ancient life capable of pictorial illustration, and ancient Rome at various periods, see Fowler, W. W., *Social Life at Rome in the Age of Cicero* (New York, 1913); Hill, *Illustrations of School Classics* (New York, 1903); Huelsen, Christian, *The Forum and the Palatine* (New York, 1928); Johnston, H. W., *The Private Life of the Romans* (Chicago, 1932); McDaniel, W. B., *Roman Private Life and Its Survivals* (Boston, 1924); Platner, *Topography and Monuments of Ancient Rome* (Boston, 1911); Schreiber, *Atlas of Classical Antiquities*, translated by Anderson (New York, 1895); Showerman, Grant, *Rome and the Romans* (New York, 1931). An admirable list of illustrative material for class use (wall pictures, maps, models, photographs, and stereopticon slides) is given in *Classical Archaeology in Schools, with an Appendix containing Lists of Archaeological Apparatus*, by Gardner and Myres (Oxford, Clarendon Press, 1902; sold by Frowde, 91 Fifth Avenue, New York; price, 30 cents).

Lives of Cicero: Aly, *Cicero, sein Leben und seine Schriften* (Berlin, 1891); Boissier, *Cicéron et ses amis* (12th edition, Paris, 1902); English translation by Jones, *Cicero and His Friends, a Study of Roman Society in the Time of Caesar* (New York, 1897); Collins, *Cicero*, in "Ancient Classics for English Readers"; Fausset, W. Y., *The Student's Cicero*, adapted from the German of Dr. Munk's "Geschichte der römischen Litteratur" (London, 1890); Forsyth (2 volumes, London, 1864); modern, by Middleton (2 volumes, London, 1741. New edition, 1848); Peterson, T., *Cicero, a Biography* (Berkeley, 1920); ancient, by Plutarch; Rolfe, John C., *Cicero and His Influence* (New York, 1923); Sihler, E. G., *Marcus Tullius of Arpinum* (New Haven, 1914); Trollope (2 volumes, London and New York, 1880); Strachan-Davidson, J. L., *Cicero and the Fall of the Roman Republic* (New York, 1903).

EDITIONS

TEXT OF COMPLETE WORKS

Baiter and Kayser: *M. Tullii Ciceronis opera quae supersunt omnia.* Leipzig, 1860–1869. *Memorābilia vītae Cicerōnis* in Volume I; *Index nōminum* in Volume XI.

Klotz: *M. Tullii Cicerōnis scrīpta quae mānsērunt omnia.* 5 parts, in 2 volumes. Leipzig, 1863–1871. New revision by C. F. W. Müller, 1893–1898.

Orelli, Baiter, Halm: *M. Tullii Cicerōnis opera quae supersunt omnia.* 8 volumes. Zürich, 1833–1862. Volume 5 contains a collection of the scholiasts on Cicero; Volumes 6–8, the valuable *Onomasticon Tulliānum,* in which are included a chronological view of Cicero's life, the Roman Calendar from 63 to 45 B.C., and a bibliography (Volume 6); a full geographical and historical index (Volume 7); a lexicon of Greek Words, collections of the laws cited and of *formulae,* the *Fāstī cōnsulārēs,* and the Roman triumphs to the reign of Tiberius (Volume 8).

ORATIONS

The following are among the annotated editions:

Benecke: *Ōrātiōnēs in L. Catilīnam.* Leipzig, 1828. *Dē imperiō Cn. Pompeī.* Leipzig, 1834.

Deuerling: *Rede über das Imperium des Cn. Pompeius.* 6th edition. Gotha, 1901.

Gast: *Erste, vierte, und vierzehnte Philippische Rede.* Leipzig, 1891.

Hachtmann: *Reden gegen Catilina.* 8th edition. Gotha, 1906.

Halm: *Die Reden für Roscius aus Ameria und über das Imperium des Cn. Pompeius.* 11th edition, revised by Laubmann. Berlin, 1896. English version of the 8th edition, by A. S. Wilkins. London, 1879; latest reprint, 1889.

Halm: *Die Reden gegen Catilina, und für Archias.* 15th edition, revised by Laubmann. Berlin, 1916. English version of Halm's 7th edition, with some additions, by A. S. Wilkins. London, 1870; latest reprint, 1891.

King: *The Philippic Orations.* 2d edition. Oxford, 1878.

Long: All the orations. 4 volumes. London, 1855–1862.

Pasdera: *Le orazioni Catilinarie.* Turin, 1885.

Reid: *Prō Archiā.* New edition. Cambridge, 1891.

Reis: *Ōrātiōnēs in L. Catilīnam quattuor.* Leipzig, 1927.

Richter and Eberhard: *Catilinarische Reden.* 6th edition. Leipzig, 1897. *Rede über das Imperium des Cn. Pompeius.* 5th edition, 1901. *Rede für den Dichter Archias.* 4th edition, 1894. *Reden für Marcellus, Ligarius, Deiotarus.* 4th edition, 1904.

Thomas: *Prō Archiā*, with French notes. Paris, 1900.

Upcott: *Speeches against Catilina*. Oxford, 1887.

Wolf: *M. Tullī Cicerōnis quae vulgō fertur ōrātiō prō M. Mārcellō.* Berlin, 1802. Compare with this edition, *Ōrātiōnem prō M. Mārcellō, quam Frid. Aug. Wolfius ā M. Tulliō Cicerōne abiūdicāvit, dēnuo dēfendit . . .*, Franciscus Hahne. Dis. inaug Braunschweig, 1876.

Among special works bearing on the orations are:

Beesly: *Catiline, Clodius, and Tiberius*. London, 1878. Contains an erratic but brilliant apology for Catiline.

Hagen: *Untersuchungen über römische Geschichte*. Erster Theil. *Catilina*. Königsberg, 1854.

Hardy, E. G., *The Catilinarian Conspiracy in Its Context*. Oxford, 1924.

Reinach: *Dē Archiā Poētā*. Paris, 1890.

Stern: *Catilina und die Parteikämpfe in Rom der Jahre 66–63*. Dorpat, 1883.

LETTERS

Boot: *Epistolārum ad Atticum librī xvi*. Latin notes, critical and explanatory. 2 volumes. Amsterdam, 1865–1866.

Mendelssohn: *Epistulārum librī sedecim*. Leipzig, 1893.

Schütz: All the letters; Latin notes. 6 volumes. Halle, 1809–1812.

Tyrrell: *The Correspondence of M. Tullius Cicero, arranged according to its chronological order, with a revision of the text, a commentary, and introductory essays*. Dublin and London. Volumes I–VII, 1879–1901. New edition, 1933.

There are numerous annotated collections of selected letters of Cicero. Among them may be mentioned those by Aly, *Briefe Ciceros und seine Zeitgenossen, zur Einführung in das Verständniss des Zeitalters Ciceros* (5th edition. Berlin, 1897); Muirhead (London, 1885); Parry (London, 1867); Pritchard and Bernard (2d edition. London, 1888); Süpfle, 10th edition, revised by Boeckel (Karlsruhe, 1893); Tyrrell (London and New York, 1891); Watson (4th edition. Oxford, 1892).

Books useful in connection with the letters are:

Church: *Roman Life in the Days of Cicero*. London and New York, 1884.

Jeans: *The Life and Letters of Cicero;* a translation of the Letters in Watson's edition. London, 1880.

Merivale: Abeken's *Cicero in His Letters.* London, 1854.

Interesting estimates of Cicero by literary men will be found in the following works:

Adams, J. Q.: *Lectures on Rhetoric and Oratory.* Cambridge, 1810. Volume I, pages 117–138.

De Quincey: *Historical Essays and Researches.* Edited by D. Masson. Edinburgh, 1890. Pages 179–221.

Lamartine: *Memoirs of Celebrated Characters.* New York, 1854. Volume I, pages 335–437.

Newman, J. H.: *Historical Sketches.* London, 1872. Volume II, pages 245–300.

Plasberg: *Cicero in seinen Werken und Briefen.* Leipzig, 1926.

Zielinski: *Cicero im Wandel der Jahrhunderte.* Berlin, 1912.

N. B. — The teacher will find a complete bibliography of the most recent works on Cicero, Sallust, Livy, Pliny, and the other Greek and Roman writers in Marouzeau, *L'Années de Bibliographie Classique* and in Klussman, *Bibliothēca Scrīptōrum Classicōrum.* These works are available in any first-class library.

OUTLINE OF THE HISTORY OF LATIN LITERATURE

The Latin language has had an unbroken development of more than two thousand years, and during this time it has directed and dominated not only the course of the speech but also the civilization of the Western world. This development may be briefly summed up in the following six periods:

1. *The Preliterary Period*, extending from the earliest times (753 B.C.?) to 240 B.C., the time of Livius Andronicus, the earliest Roman author known to us. Our knowledge ot the Latin for this period depends almost entirely upon scanty inscriptions and fragments of laws, hymns, and sacred formulas preserved in the writings of later writers, such as Cato, Livy, Cicero, and others.

2. *The Archaic Period*, extending from Livius Andronicus (240 B.C.) to the date of Cicero's first extant oration (81 B.C.). The following are some of the better known writers of this period:

Livius Andronicus, Naevius, Ennius, Plautus, Pacuvius, Terence, Lucilius, Cato the Elder, and Accius.

3. *The Golden Age*, extending from Cicero (81 B.C.) to the death of the Emperor Augustus (14 A.D.). This is the period of Classical Latin and comprehends most of the authors usually read in high school and college. The following deserve special mention:

Lucretius, Cicero, Caesar, Catullus, Sallust, Nepos, Virgil, Horace, Ovid, Tibullus, Propertius, Livy, and Varro.

4. *The Silver Age*, extending from the death of Augustus (14 A.D.) to the death of the Emperor Marcus Aurelius (180 A.D.). This period is marked by a reaction against the literary excellence of the previous age, in so far as writers sought greater freedom of expression by introducing idioms from the colloquial language, by the use of sententious phrases, and by employing poetical expressions. The following authors may be mentioned:

Celsus, the Senecas, Pliny the Elder, Pliny the Younger, Lucan, Martial, Tacitus, Suetonius, Phaedrus, Quintilian, Juvenal, Persius, Curtius, Velleius Paterculus, Minucius Felix, Valerius Maximus, and Gellius.

5. *The Brass and Iron Ages*, extending from 180 A.D. to the fall of the Western Empire, 476 A.D. This is the period of Late Latin when many radical changes were introduced into the language, and when patristic literature, representing the writings of the Church Fathers, appeared. The following writers may be mentioned:

Tertullian, Lactantius, Ambrose, Augustine, Prudentius, Claudian, Jerome, Cyprian, Ausonius, Eutropius, Macrobius, Justin, Victor, Martianus Capella.

6. *Mediaeval Latin*, extending from 476 A.D. to the eighteenth century and even to much later times. Mediaeval Latin, therefore, though strictly applicable to the Middle Ages, really comprises a period of time far greater in extent. During this period Latin underwent many changes through a progressive development in the various provinces, and eventually crystallized in Italian, Spanish, Portuguese, Provençal (the language spoken in southeastern France), and the Roumanian. It would be impossible, because of lack of space, to give even a partial list of writers of this period.

ENGLISH PRONUNCIATION OF PROPER NAMES

The system below is used in this book to indicate the English pronunciation of proper names. It is intended to be lucid and consistent, and at the same time to present as few points of divergence as possible from the systems found in the best dictionaries. The so-called long vowels have above them a macron or some mark indicative of quality; the short stressed vowels have no mark at all; the obscure unstressed vowels have a dot under them, thus: —

ā as in ‘ fate.’	ẹ as in ‘ hatẹd.’*	ǫ as in ‘ demǫcrat.’*
a “ “ ‘ fat.’	ė “ “ ‘ her.’	ū “ “ ‘ use.’
ạ “ “ ‘ idea.’*	ī “ “ ‘ pine.’	u “ “ ‘ up.’
ä “ “ ‘ arm.’	i “ “ ‘ pin.’	ụ “ “ ‘ singular.’*
â “ “ ‘ all.’	ị “ “ ‘ unịty.’*	ụ “ “ ‘ circụs.’*
ē “ “ ‘ me.’	ō “ “ ‘ no.’	ʊ̄ “ “ ‘ rude.’
e “ “ ‘ met.’	o “ “ ‘ not.’	ʊ “ “ ‘ full.’

The system which has been followed in this book for Anglicising Greek and Latin Proper Names is self-explanatory, but it may be stated that the more important rules are to be found in Rolfe’s edition of Cornelius Nepos (Allyn and Bacon), pages 246 and 247. Helpful hints may also be found in Webster’s dictionary.

The student should remember to accent the first syllable when the word has but two syllables; in words of more than two syllables the penult (next to the last) must be accented if originally long, otherwise the antepenult (third last). To assist the student in remembering this, the long penult has been frequently given an accent both throughout the notes and the vocabulary.

By careful observation and persistent effort the student will soon learn the sounds of the vowels, diphthongs, and consonants, since an attempt has been made to indicate in the notes the pronunciation of every word occurring in the text proper, and many more that do not occur in the text.

---

* The obscure unstressed vowels are in effect very much alike, but they differ slightly according to the character of the adjoining consonants. They are most correctly sounded when one glides over them rapidly and naturally.

IDIOMS AND PHRASES

ā mē ipse nōn dēscīvī, *I did not prove false to myself.*

ab eō vehementissimē dissentiō, *I disagree with him most emphatically.*

ab ineunte aetāte, *from the beginning of (civil) life.*

ab īnferīs, *from the Underworld, from the dead.*

ab occidente, *in the west.*

abest nōn nēmō, *more than one is away, some are away.*

abiectus metū, *prostrated with fear.*

accipere in vestram fidem, *to take into your confidence.*

ad caelum efferre laudibus, *to laud to the skies.*

ad expilandōs sociōs dīripiendāsque prōvinciās, *to rob allies and plunder provinces.*

ad Lepidum habitāre, *to live at the house of Lepidus, to live at Lepidus's.*

ad rem pūblicam adīre, *to engage in the administration of public affairs, to take office.*

adīre hērēditātem, *to enter upon an inheritance, to take possession of an inheritance.*

adnītī dē triumphō, *to make every effort to secure a triumph.*

adversae rēs, *adversity, misfortune.*

aequē cārus ac, *just as dear as.*

aequō animō, *calmly, without anxiety; with resignation.*

aequum est, *it is fair, it is right.*

aere aliēnō premī, *to be heavily in debt.*

aes aliēnum, *debt, indebtedness.*

in tantum aes aliēnum, *so deeply into debt.*

agere cum aliquō, *to treat with anyone, to plead with anyone.*

agere grātiās, *to thank.*

nihil agis, *you accomplish nothing.*

quid agis? *How do you do? How are you?* also, *What are you about? What do you mean?*

agitur dē vectīgālibus, *the revenues are imperiled.*

agitur populī Rōmānī glōria, *the glory of the Roman people is at stake.*

alia omnia, *all things else, everything else.*

aliquā ex parte, *in some measure.*

aliquid amplum cōgitāre, *to entertain some noble sentiment.*

aliquid dē ingeniīs iūdicāre, *to form any judgment of (his) abilities.*

aliquid locī, *some place, some room.*

aliquid respondit, *he made some answer or other.*

aliquid sapientiae, *any degree of prudence, any prudence.*

amābō tē, *will you kindly, please.*

amāns reī pūblicae, *devoted to his country.*

amantissimus reī pūblicae, *very devoted to his country, of the loftiest patriotism.*

amplius negōtī, *a larger measure of difficulty, more trouble.*

amplius negōtī mihi contrahitur, *I am more deeply involved in difficulty.*

anceps contentiō, *a contest on two sides.*

animō cernere, *to see in fancy, to see in imagination.*

quō animō esse dēbētis? *What feeling ought you to have? How ought you to feel?*

quō animō ferre dēbētis? *With what spirit ought you to endure?*

animōs ac spīritus capere, *to endure the arrogance and insolence.*

animōsē et fortiter facere aliquid, *to do something with spirit and bravery.*

animum armātum retinēre, *to retain a spirit of hostility.*

animum indūcere, *to make up one's mind.*

animum vincere, *to conquer one's spirit.*

ante ācta vīta, *past life.*

ante cīvitātem datam, *prior to the granting of citizenship.*

paucīs ante diēbus, *a few days ago.*

paulō ante, *a little while ago.*

ante mē, *before me; before my time.*

apud īnferōs, *in the Underworld.*

apud Laecam, *at Laeca's house, at Laeca's.*

apud Tenedum, *off Tenedos.*

aspicere inter sēsē, *to look at one another.*

auctor gravior, *an adviser of greater weight.*

audītā rē, *having heard of the matter.*

aurēs dare, *to give attention.*

āversus ā Mūsīs, *unfriendly to the Muses.*

āversus ā vērō, *hostile to truth.*

bella legere, *to read about wars.*

bellum in multā varietāte versātum, *a war waged with many vicissitudes.*

bellum apparāre, *to get ready for war.*

bellum cōnficere, *to put an end to a war, to bring a war to a successful termination.*

bellum coniungere, *to unite in waging war.*

bellum excitāre, *to stir up war.*

bellum īnferre, *to make war upon.*

bellum suscipere, *to commence war.*

bene barbātus, *with full beard.*

bene dē rē pūblicā merērī, *to do good service for one's country, to be useful to the state.*

bene dē rē pūblicā spērāre, *to have great hope for the state.*

bene pōtus, *having drunk freely, being quite mellow.*

bonō animō dīcere, *to say with good intention.*

bonō animō esse, *to be of good cheer; to be well disposed.*

meā causā, *on my account, for my sake.*

honōris causā nōminō, *I mention in the way of honor; I mention with due respect.*

vītandae suspīciōnis causā, *in order to avoid suspicion.*

dē certā causā, *for a certain reason.*

causam dīcere, *to state a case, to plead a case.*

certior factus, *having been informed.*

certior fierī, *to be informed.*

certiōrem facere, *to inform.*

cīvitātem alicui dare, *to grant citizenship to anyone, to bestow the franchise on anyone.*

in cīvitātem ascrībere, *to enroll as a citizen.*

eum cīvitāte dōnāre, *to bestow the franchise on him.*

cōgere senātum, *to convene the senate.*

collātīs signīs, *in the shock of battle, in regular engagements.*

colōniās cōnstituere, *to found colonies.*

concēdī alicui necesse est, *it must inevitably be given up to some one.*

cōnsilia inīre, *to form plans.*

cōnsulere alicui, *to look out for the interest of anyone.*

cōnsulere aliquem, *to consult anyone, to ask advice of anyone.*

cōnsulere vōbīs, *to look out for your interest.*

contrā atque, *opposite to what, contrary to what.*

dare operam, *to take pains, to make an effort.*

dē caelō percellī, *to be struck by lightning.*

dētrīmentum accipere, *to suffer loss.*

difficilī reī pūblicae tempore, *at a time of peril for the state, at a critical time for the state.*

diffidēns rēbus suīs, *in a state of despair regarding his own resources.*

dīlēctum habēre, *to raise a levy, to draft.*

domī libenter sum, *I am glad to be at home.*

domī meae, *at my house.*

ē portū ēgredī, *to set sail.*

eadem fortūna quae illōrum, *the same lot as that of those.*

eō magis, *all the more.*

eōs hōc moneō, *I give them this warning.*

eōs praemiīs affēcit, *he bestowed gifts upon them.*

erit verendum mihi, *I shall have to be afraid, I shall have to fear.*

est mihi tantī, *it is well worth while for me, it is well worth my while.*

mihi est invidiōsum, *I find it a source of unpopularity, it is a source of unpopularity to me.*

etiam atque etiam, *again and again.*

ex bellī ōre ac faucibus, *from the open jaws of war.*

ex eō quaeritur, *the question is put to him, inquiry is made of him.*

ex hāc parte, *on this side.*

ex magnā spē dēturbārī, *to be deprived of great hopes.*

ex marmore cōnstitūtus, *fashioned in marble.*

ex mediā morte, *from the midst of death.*

ex pedibus labōrāre, *to have trouble with one's feet, to have the gout.*

ex puerīs, *from childhood.*

ex senātūs cōnsultō, *in accordance with a decree of the senate, in accordance with the senate's decree.*

ex tempore, *off-hand, on the spur of the moment, without preparation.*

ex vestrō iūdiciō, *in consequence of your judgment.*

exercitum cōnficere, *to raise an army.*

extrēmā hieme, *at the end of winter.*

extrēmā pueritiā, *at the end of boyhood.*

fac ut sciam, *let me know.*

fac ut tuam valētūdinem cūrēs, *do take care of your health.*

fac ut valeās, *do keep well.*

facere alicui pergrātum, *to do anyone a great favor.*

facere potestātem dīcendī, *to offer an opportunity to speak, to give an opportunity for saying.*

faciam tē certiōrem, *I will inform you.*

facultās oblāta est, *an opportunity was presented.*

falsō memoriae prōditum, *based upon unfounded tradition.*

familiārissimē vīvere, *to be on the most intimate terms.*

mē fefellit diēs, *I was mistaken in the day.*

num mē fefellit diēs? *I was not mistaken in the day, was I? Was I mistaken in regard to the date?*

vix feram, *I shall find it hard to endure, I shall hardly be able to bear.*

ferenda nōn fuērunt, *they ought not to have been endured.*

ferenda mihi nōn fuērunt, *I ought not to have put up with them.*

ferre molestē, *to be annoyed, to feel grieved.*

ferrō flammāque, *with fire and sword.*

fidem facere, *to convince, to command confidence.*

minōrem fidem facere, *to fail to convince, to fail to command entire confidence.*

fidem pūblicam dare, *to give a pledge of safety in the name of the state.*

fingere sibi, *to imagine.*

fundāmenta iacere, *to lay the foundations.*

grātiam alicuius conciliāre, *to win the favor of some one.*

grātiam habēre, *to feel thankful, to be grateful.*

bonam grātiam quaerere, *to court popularity.*

grātiam referre, *to return a favor, to requite, to recompense.*

grātiās agere, *to give thanks, to thank.*

maximās grātiās agere, *to thank most heartily.*

grātum facere, *to do a favor.*

hieme summā, *in the dead of winter, in the depth of winter.*

hōc praecipiendum est, *this advice ought to be given.*

eīs hōc praecipiendum est, *they ought to be given this piece of advice.*

hodiernō diē māne, *this morning.*

in honōre esse dēbēbit is, *he will deserve to be in honor.*

honōrum gradūs, *the grades of public office, the avenues of official preferment.*

iam diū teneō, *I have long been holding.*

iam dūdum hortor, *I have long been urging.*

iam prīdem studēs, *you have long*

been eagerly desiring, this long time you have been eager.

iam tum, even then, at that very time.

id quod cōnsequī cōnantur, what they are trying to attain, their ends.

id temporis, at that particular time, at just that time.

īdem quī, the same as.

idem sentīre, to have the same feeling or the same opinion.

imperāre obsidēs, to levy hostages, to make a requisition for hostages.

imperāre omnibus gentibus, to rule over all peoples.

in agendō, in action.

in armīs, under arms, in arms; in the pursuit of arms, in war.

in caelum, to the skies.

in cūstōdiam dare, to place in custody, to put under surveillance.

in datō beneficiō, in the granting of a favor.

in diēs, day by day, every day.

in diēs singulōs, each successive day.

in eam partem, ut, to the end that.

in eandem ferē sententiam, to much the same effect, of about the same import.

in malīs, in the midst of evils.

in perditīs rēbus, in profligacy.

in perpetuum, for all time, forever.

in posteritātem, for the future.

in posterum, for the future.

in posterum tempus, for future time, for the future.

in praesēns tempus, for the present.

in quaestū relinquere, to leave on interest.

incumbite in causam, throw yourselves into the cause.

ineunte adulēscentiā, at the beginning of youth.

ineunte vēre, at the opening of spring.

īnferre bellum, to make war upon.

inīre cōnsilium, to form a plan.

īnspectante praetōre, under the eyes of the praetor.

integrīs signīs, with the seals unbroken.

inter sē, with each other, with one another.

īra victōriae, the fury of victory.

istō pactō ut, in such a way as, as.

iūdicium facere, to pass an opinion, to pass judgment.

iūs cīvitātis, the rights of citizenship, citizenship.

lātius opīniōne, more widely than you think, or than one would think.

laudibus in caelum ferre, to praise to the skies.

locō mōtus est, he was forced from his vantage-ground.

locōrum opportūnitās, advantages of position.

magnō in aere aliēnō, deeply in debt.

male ēmere, to purchase at too high a price, to buy too dear.

male gerere negōtium, to manage one's business badly.

maximās grātiās agere, to return most hearty thanks.

maximē ēlabōrandum est, very great effort must be made, all pains must be taken.

mē imperante, at my bidding.

mē quid pudeat? why should I be ashamed?

meā interest, it is for my interest

or *to my advantage; I am concerned.*

mediā aestāte, *at midsummer.*

memoriā tenēre, *to remember, to keep in mind.*

mente captus, *beside himself.*

meō nōmine, *in my name, on my account; in my honor.*

meōrum factōrum paenitēbit, *I shall be sorry for what I did, I shall regret my action.*

mihi crēde, crēdite, *believe me, upon my word.*

mihi in animō est, *it is my intention, I intend.*

mihi in mentem venit, *it occurs to me.*

mihi placet, *I think best, I resolve.*

mihi suādeō, *I am persuaded.*

minus est errātum, *no mistake has been made.*

molestē ferre, *to be annoyed, to feel grieved.*

multum valēre, *to be very powerful; to have great influence, to be very important.*

mūtuē respondēre, *to make adequate return, to make a fair return.*

nē longum sit, *not to be tedious, not to bore you.*

necesse est pervenīre, *must inevitably come, must inevitably fall (to).*

nesciō an, *perhaps I might better say, probably.*

nesciō quid, *something, some.*

nesciō quō modō, *somehow.*

nesciō quō pactō, *somehow.*

nihil aliud nisi dē hoste cōgitāre, *to think of nothing but the enemy,*

to have no thought for anything except the enemy.

nihil dē rē pūblicā cōgitāre, *to give no thought to political matters, to give no thought to public affairs.*

nihil nisi dē parricīdiō cōgitāre, *to think of nothing but murder.*

nihil dēcrētum est, *no decree was passed, no motion was carried.*

nihil mihi nocērī potest, *no harm can be done me.*

nōbīs cōnsulibus, *in our consulship, in my consulship.*

noctēs ac diēs, *day and night.*

nōlī esse, *be not.*

nōlī dēfatīgārī, *be not wearied, do not allow yourself to become weary.*

nōlīte dubitāre, *do not hesitate.*

meō nōmine, *in my name, in my honor.*

suō nōmine, *on his own account.*

novīs rēbus studēre, *to be eager for a revolution, to be desirous of a revolution.*

nūdius tertius, *day before yesterday.*

nūllō impediente, *with no one hindering, with none to hinder.*

nūllō modō, *in no way, by no means.*

occāsiō oblāta est, *an opportunity presented itself.*

omnēs ūnum volunt, *all are of one opinion.*

omnium rērum dēspērātiō, *utter despair.*

operae pretium est, *it is worth while.*

operam dare, *to take pains, to make an effort.*

opīniōne celerius, *sooner than was expected.*

tē oportet dūcī, *you ought to be led.*

tē iam prīdem oportēbat dūcī, *you ought long ago to have been led.*

optimē dē rē pūblicā merērī, *to render most important service to one's country.*

optimō iūre, *with the fairest possible reason.*

opus est, *there is need, it is necessary.*

orbis terrae, orbis terrārum, *the world, the whole world.*

pāce tuā, *with your permission.*

parum comitātus, *with too small a retinue, with too small an escort.*

parvī rēfert, *it matters little.*

pauca dīcere, *to say a few words.*

paulum mihi est morae, *I am suffering a little delay.*

pecūniās collocātās habēre, *to have sums of money invested.*

per causam, *under the pretext.*

per hanc causam, *under this pretext, with this as a pretext.*

per fortūnās vidē, *for heaven's sake see to it* or *take care.*

perinde atque, *just as, exactly as.*

permagnī nostrā interest, *it is of very great importance to us;* or, *it is very important for me.*

permultum valēre, *to be exceedingly powerful, to possess very great influence.*

pingue quiddam sonantēs atque peregrīnum, *offering some stupid and outlandish composition.*

eīs placet, *they think best, they resolve.*

plūrimum posse, *to have the greatest influence, to be most powerful, to be preëminent.*

plūrimum valēre, *to have very great weight, to exert very great influence.*

poenam sceleris sufferre, *to suffer punishment for crime.*

poenam suscipere, *to receive punishment, to undergo punishment.*

poenās expetere ab aliquō, *to inflict punishment on anyone, to visit anyone with retribution.*

post cīvitātem datam, *after the granting of citizenship, after the franchise was granted*

post hominum memoriam, *within the memory of man.*

post urbem conditam, *since the founding of the city, since the city was founded.*

post hanc urbem conditam, *since the founding of this city, since this city was founded.*

praeter opīniōnem omnium, *contrary to the expectation of all.*

praeter spem, *contrary to expectation, beyond one's expectation.*

prīmō quōque tempore, *at the earliest possible moment.*

priōre nocte, *night before last.*

prō eō ac mereor, *in such measure as I deserve, in proportion to my deserts.*

proeliīs secundīs ūtī, *to have successful engagements, to come off victorious in battle.*

prope īnspectantibus vōbīs, *almost under your eyes.*

proximā nocte, *last night.*

quā rē, *wherefore.*

quae cum ita sint, *now since these things are so, and since this is so, under these circumstances.*

quam ob rem, *on what account, wherefore.*

quam plūrimī, *as many as possible.*

quam prīmum, *as soon as possible.*

quantum est situm in nōbīs, *so far as in us lies, so far as in me lies.*

quem ad fīnem? *to what limit? how far?*

quem ad modum? *in what way? how; as.*

quem vēnisse gaudent, *at whose arrival they rejoice.*

quicquid increpuerit, *at every sound.*

quicquid possum, *whatever influence I possess, whatever I can accomplish.*

quicquid studī, *whatever enthusiasm.*

quid cōnsilī? *what scheme? what plan?*

quid illō fierī placet? *What does he want to have done?*

quid interest? *What difference is there?*

quid mihi cum vōbīs est? *What business have I with you? What have I to do with you?*

quid novī? *what news?*

quid novī, *anything new, anything without precedent.*

quid tēlōrum, *any weapons.*

si quid tēlōrum, *whatever weapons.*

quid Tulliā fīet? *What will become of Tullia?*

quiētā rē pūblicā, *when the state is undisturbed, when the state is free from agitation.*

quoad erit integrum, *so long as it shall remain an open question.*

quod reliquum est, *for the rest, for the future.*

ratiō tōtīus bellī, *the plan of the entire campaign,* or *of the entire war.*

referre ad senātum, *to lay before the senate.*

referre grātiam, *to return a favor, to requite, to recompense.*

reliquum est, *it remains.*

rem dēferre ad patrēs cōnscrīptōs, *to report a matter to the senate in session.*

rem gerere, *to manage business.*

rem optimē gerere, *to manage business exceedingly well.*

remōtō Catilīnā, *with Catiline out of the way.*

rērum potīrī, *to get control of the government.*

rēs gestae, *achievements, exploits, deeds.*

rēs sē habet, *the case stands.*

salūtem dīcere, *to send greeting.*

salūtem nūntiāre, *to carry one's regards.*

satis facere reī pūblicae, *to do one's duty by the state.*

satis laudis, *sufficient praise, praise enough.*

scrīptor rērum, *writer of history, historian.*

scrīptor rērum suārum, *chronicler of his achievements, biographer.*

sē praetūrā abdicāre, *to resign the office of praetor.*

sē prō cīve gerere, *to conduct one's self as a citizen.*

secundae rēs, *prosperity.*

ā senātōriō gradū longē abesse,

to be far too young for membership in the senate.

senātuī placuit, the senate voted, the senate passed a resolution.

senātum cōnsulere, to ask the opinion of the senate, to consult the senate.

senātum convocāre, to convoke the senate, call a meeting of the senate.

sententiam ferre, to cast a vote.

sententiam rogāre, to put the question, to call for a vote.

sī cūrae tibi est, if you care about it, if you take interest in it.

sī in eō stat, if he persists in that, if he remains firm in that.

sī vestra voluntās feret, if such be your pleasure.

sī vōbīs placet, if you think best.

simul ac, simul atque, as soon as.

sine contrōversiā, beyond question, indisputably.

sine dubiō, beyond doubt.

sine ūllā morā, at once.

suā sponte, of their own accord.

suī cōnservandī causā, in order to save themselves.

summa rēs pūblica, the highest interest of the state.

summum supplicium, the severest punishment.

summus imperātor, a commander of the first rank.

suō nōmine on his own account.

superiōre nocte, night before last.

supplicium dē aliquō sūmere, to inflict punishment upon anyone.

tandem aliquandō, now at length, then at length.

tantum abest ut . . . videar, ut, so far am I from appearing, . . . that.

tē auctōre, on your advice.

tē oportet, see oportet.

terrā marīque, on land and sea.

tertiā ferē vigiliā exāctā, at about the end of the third watch.

sī trānsāctum est, if all is over.

tuā sponte, of your own accord.

ubinam gentium sumus? Where in the world are we?

ūllō modō, in any way, by any means.

ūnā significātiōne litterārum, by a single written order.

urbī satis praesidī est, the city has a sufficient garrison, the city is amply garrisoned.

ut arbitror, in my judgment.

ut levissimē dīcam, to put the case very mildly, to speak with extreme moderation.

ut prīmum, as soon as.

ūtī aliquō familiāriter, to be on intimate terms with anyone.

vacuī temporis nihil, no leisure time, no leisure.

vadimōnium dēserere, to forsake an obligation to appear in court, to forfeit one's recognizance.

vehementer angī, to be greatly troubled, to be much disturbed.

vehementer cum senātū cōnsociārī, to be thoroughly in accord with the senate.

vehementer errāre, to be very much mistaken.

velim dīspiciās rēs Rōmānās, will you kindly think over matters at Rome.

velim eī mē excūsēs, I should like to have you make excuse for me to him, excuse me to him.

veniam dare, *to pardon.*

ventum est, *they* (or *he*) *came, have come.*

verba facere, *to speak.*

verbīs amplissimīs, *in most distinguished terms, in the handsomest terms, in elaborate terms.*

verendum erat mihi, *I ought to have feared.*

verērī nē, *to fear that.*

verērī ut, *to fear that — not.*

vestrum est prōvidēre, *it is your duty to make provision.*

vī et minīs, *by threats of violence.*

vir optimus, *an exceedingly worthy gentleman, a most excellent man.*

vīs et manūs, *violent hands.*

vītae meae ratiōnēs, *my plan of life.*

vix feram, *I shall find it hard to bear, I shall hardly be able to endure.*

vōculae recreandae causā, *in order to strengthen* (*my*) *poor voice.*

voluptātem capere, *to receive pleasure, take delight.*

THE GREEK ALPHABET

Capital	Small	Latin or English Equivalent	Name
A	α	a	alpha
B	β	b	beta
Γ	γ	g	gamma
Δ	δ	d	delta
E	ε	ĕ	epsilon
Z	ζ	z	zeta
H	η	ē	eta
Θ	θ	th	theta
I	ι	i	iota
K	κ	c or k	kappa
Λ	λ	l	lambda
M	μ	m	mu
N	ν	n	nu
Ξ	ξ	x	xi
O	ο	ŏ	omicron
Π	π	p	pi
P	ρ	r	rho
Σ	σ, s	s	sigma
T	τ	t	tau
Υ	υ	y	upsilon
Φ	φ	ph	phi
X	χ	ch	chi
Ψ	ψ	ps	psi
Ω	ω	ō	omega

The Greek alphabet is the source of the Latin.

The vowel sounds are similar to those of Latin; upsilon is pronounced like French u or German ü; iota subscript in ᾳ, η, ῳ is not pronounced.

A vowel at the beginning of a word has either the rough breathing (ʽ) or the smooth (ʼ) written over it. The rough breathing indicates that *h* is to be sounded before the vowel; the smooth breathing means that the vowel is sounded without *h*.

There are three accents: the acute (ʹ), the circumflex (ˆ), the grave (ˋ). To the Greeks these accents meant a change in pitch; modern students pronounce them as stress accents.

VOCABULARY

ABBREVIATIONS

VOCABULARY

A

A., with proper names = **Aulus**, a Roman *praenōmen*, or forename.

a. d., = **ante diem**.

a. u. c., = **annō urbis conditae**, ' in the year from the founding of the city,' or **ab urbe conditā**, 'after the founding of the city'; used with dates reckoned from the year in which Rome was said to have been founded, 753 B.C.

ā, ab, and **abs**, [cf. ἀπό, Eng. of, off], prep. with abl., originally implying separation, *from, away from, out of;* of place or direction, *from, out of, at,* especially with adverbs of distance, as **longē ā domō, procul ā nōbīs, ab Sabīnīs**, *on the side of the Sabines;* of time, *from, since, after,* as **ab ineunte aetāte, ab adulēscentiā, ab illō tempore, ā senātōriō gradū longē**; of agency, with passive verbs and gerundives, *by, on the part of;* of source, *from, through,* especially with verbs and adj. signifying fearing, hoping, expecting, defending, liquidating; the prep. **ā** with the person is used with **quaerō, quaesō, postulō, petō, poenās expetō**, and **dissentiō**.

abaliēnō, -āre, -āvī, -ātum, [ab + aliēnus], 1, a., *convey away, sell,* *alienate, transfer ownership of; remove; estrange, make hostile.*

abdicō, -āre, -āvī, -ātum, [ab + dicō], 1, a., *abdicate;* reflex., with abl., *resign, lay down, renounce,* used of withdrawal from an office before the expiration of the term of appointment, as **sē praetūrā abdicāvit**, *he resigned his office of praetor.*

abditus, -a, -um, [part. of abdō], adj., *concealed, hidden; secluded, secret.*

abdō, -dere, -didī, -ditum, [ab + dō], 3, a., *put away, remove, conceal;* reflex., **abdere sē**, *to betake one's self to, to devote one's self to, to hide one's self in.*

abeō, -īre, abīvī or **-iī, abitum**, fut. part. **abitūrus**, [ab + eō], irr., n., *go away, depart, leave; pass away, be gone, disappear, vanish.*

abhorreō, -ēre, -uī, ――, [ab + horreō], 2, a. and n., *shrink back from, shudder at; be at variance with, be inconsistent with, be averse to; be not connected with;* often construed with **ā** and the abl.

abiciō, abicere, -iēcī, -iectum, [ab + iaciō], 3, a., *throw away, cast away, throw down; give up, abandon;* reflex., **abicere sē**, *throw one's self down, prostrate one's self, give up in despair.*

I

abiectus, -a, -um, [part. of abiciō], adj., *cast down, overwhelmed, despondent; low, mean, worthless.* **abiectus metū,** *prostrated with fear.*

abnegō, -āre, -āvī, -ātum, [ab + negō], 1, a., *refuse, deny, repudiate.*

abōminor, -ārī, -ātus sum, [ab + ōmen], 1, dep., *deprecate; abhor, detest, execrate.*

abrumpō, -ere, -rūpī, -ruptum, [ab + rumpō], 3, a., *break off, break away; tear, rend, burst.*

abscēdō, -ere, -cessī, -cessum, [abs + cēdō], 3, n., *give way, go off, withdraw, depart; march away; disappear; desist from, abandon, give up; pass away.*

absconditus, -a, -um, [part. of abscondō], adj., *hidden, concealed, secret.*

absēns, -entis, [part. of absum], adj., *absent, away, not present.*

absentia, -ae, [absum], f., *absence.*

absolūtiō, -ōnis, [absolvō, *discharge*], f., *as a legal term, acquittal; completeness.*

absolvō, -ere, -solvī, -solūtum, [ab + solvō], 3, a., *set free, release; acquit, declare innocent, absolve; pay off, satisfy, pay; complete, bring to an end, finish.*

abstergeō, -ēre, -tersī, -tersum, [abs + tergeō], 2, a., *wipe off, wipe away; break off; remove, banish, drive off, expel.*

abstinentia, -ae, [abstinēns], f., *abstinence, starvation; self-restraint, temperance, integrity.*

abstrahō, -ere, abstrāxī, abstrāctum, [abs + trahō], 3, a., *draw away; withdraw, remove; divert, cut off.*

absum, abesse, āfuī, fut. part. **āfutūrus,** [ab + sum], irr., n., *be away from, be absent, be far, be from.* **cuius aetās ā ——— longē abesset,** *whose age was far too young for ———.* **tantum abest ut ——— ut,** *so far from ——— that.*

absūmō, -ere, -sūmpsī, -sūmptum, [ab + sūmō], 3, a., *take away, diminish; exhaust; spend, consume, waste; destroy, ruin, kill.*

absurdus, -a, -um, [ab + surdus, *deaf*], adj., *out of tune, discordant, harsh; incongruous, inconsistent, silly; stupid, absurd, unreasonable.*

abundāns, -antis, [part. of abundō], adj., *overflowing, rich, abounding.*

abundantia, -ae, [abundō], f., *plenty, abundance.*

abundē, [abundus], adv., *in profusion, more than enough, in abundance, abundantly, amply.*

abundō, -āre, -āvī, -ātum, [ab + undō, from unda, *wave*], 1, n., *overflow, abound in, be rich in.*

abūtor, -ūtī, -ūsus sum, [ab + ūtor], 3, dep., *use up; abuse, outrage.*

ac, see atque.

accēdō, -cēdere, -cessī, -cessum, [ad + cēdō], 3, n., *come to, draw near to, draw near, approach;* used often as synonymous with the passive of **addō,** *be added.*

accelerō, -āre, -āvī, -ātum, [ad + celerō, from celer], 1, a. and n., *hasten, quicken; hurry, make haste.*

accendō, -ere, -cenḍī, -cēnsum, 3, a., *kindle, set on fire, light; inflame, excite, arouse; encourage; exasperate, embitter.*

acceptus, -a, -um, comp. acceptior, sup. acceptissimus, [accipiō], adj., *welcome, acceptable, pleasing; popular.*

accersītus, -a, -um, see arcessō.

accidō, -cidere, -cidī, ——, [ad + cadō], 3, n., *fall upon, fall to; reach, come to; come to pass, happen, occur, take place.*

accipiō, -cipere, -cēpī, -ceptum, [ad + capiō], 3, a., *take to one's self, receive, accept; meet with, experience, suffer; take in, hear, learn, understand; undertake, assume.*

Accius, -ī or -iī, m., L. *Accius, an early Roman tragic poet, born 170 B.C. He lived to a great age and wrote many tragedies; also an historical poem and three prose works. Only a few fragments of his writings are extant, but these indicate marked literary power.*

accommodātus, -a, -um, [part. of accommodō], adj., *adapted, suited, fit, suitable, appropriate.*

accommodō, -āre, -āvī, -ātum, [ad + commodō, from commodus], 1, a., *fit, adjust, adapt, accommodate to.*

accubō, -āre, ——, ——, [ad + cubō], 1, n., *lie at, lie near; especially recline at table, in accordance with the Roman custom, the body reclining on a couch, the left arm resting on a cushion, the right arm being left free to take food.*

accūrātē, comp. accūrātius, sup. accūrātissimē, [accūrātus, *carefully wrought*], adv., *carefully, with pains, with painstaking; precisely, exactly.*

accūsātor, -ōris, [accūsō, *accuse*], m., *accuser, prosecutor, plaintiff.*

accūsō, -āre, -āvī, -ātum, [ad, causa], 1, a., *reproach, accuse, blame, find fault with; prosecute, indict.*

ācer, ācris, ācre, comp. ācrior, sup. ācerrimus, adj., *sharp, piercing; harsh, bitter; keen, zealous, spirited; passionate, violent; fierce, severe.*

acerbē, comp. acerbius, sup. acerbissimē, [acerbus], adv., *harshly, cruelly, bitterly; painfully, grievously, severely.*

acerbitās, -ātis, [acerbus], f., *bitterness; harshness, severity; pl., sorrows, anguish, affliction.*

acerbus, -a, -um, [ācer], adj., *sharp to the taste, bitter; harsh, severe, cruel; distressing, rigorous, burdensome.*

acervus, -ī, m., *heap, pile; great quantity, multitude, mass.*

Achāia, -ae, ['Αχαΐα], f., *Achāia, a Roman province, comprising all of Greece except Thessaly.*

Achillēs, -is, ['Αχιλλεύς], m., *Achillēs, son of Peleus and Thetis, famous hero of the Greeks in the Trojan war.* ARCH. 10.

Achradīna, -ae, f., *the Archradine, a part of the city of Syracuse, joined with the other parts of the city by a bridge.*

aciēs, -ēī, f., *sharp point, sharp edge; of an army, line of battle, battle-array; battle, engagement; force, efficiency; sharpness of vision or sight.*

acquiēscō, -ere, -quiēvī, -quiētum, [ad + quiēscō], 3, n., *become quiet, be at rest, have peace, rest, repose; be content, be satisfied; resign one's self to.*

acquīrō, -ere, -quīsīvī, -quīsītum, [ad + quaerō], 3, a., *get in addition, get besides, obtain besides; acquire, gain, add.*

ācriter, comp. **ācrius,** sup. **ācerrimē,** [ācer], adv., *sharply, keenly, cruelly; earnestly, zealously, vigorously, attentively.*

acroāma, -atis, [ἀκρόαμα, from ἀκροάομαι, *listen*], n., lit. *entertainment for the ear; reader, story-teller, musician,* applied especially to those who furnished entertainment at table with stories, jests, or songs.

ācta, -ōrum, [agō], n., pl., *proceedings.*

Actiacus, -a, -um, [Actium], adj., *of or relating to* Actium.

āctiō, -ōnis, [agō], f., *a driving or doing, action; action at law, lawsuit, prosecution, trial;* pl. often *public acts, measures.*

āctum, -ī, [agō], n., *act, deed, proceeding, method of procedure.*

āctus, -ūs, [agō], m., *a driving or doing; act, achievement; the act of a play.*

acūmen, -inis, [acuō], n., *the utmost point or extremity of anything, the tip; acuteness, keenness, sharpness, understanding, intelligence.*

acūtus, -a, -um, [part. of acuō], adj., *sharpened, pointed, sharp, cutting; pungent, shrill, violent; keen, requiring alertness.*

ad, prep. with acc. only, *to; of motion and direction, to, towards, up to;* of place, *in the vicinity of, at, near to, at the house of, in the presence of, among, according to;* of time, *till, to, up to, until;* of purpose, especially with the gerund, *for, in order to, for the purpose of, in;* of other relations, *with regard to, according to, in respect to, in consequence of, as to, in; about, almost, as many as.*

adaequō, -āre, -āvī, -ātum, [ad + aequō], 1, a. and n., *make equal to, make equal with, match; keep up with;* in Cicero usually followed by **cum** with an abl.

addiscō, -ere, -didicī, —, [ad + discō], 3, a., *learn in addition, add to one's knowledge, go on learning; gain knowledge of.*

addō, -dere, -didī, -ditum, [ad + dō], 3, a., *put to, bring to; add, join to, increase, augment; consider also.*

addūcō, -dūcere, -dūxī, -ductum, [ad + dūcō], 3, a., *lead to, bring to, conduct, lead; prompt, induce, incite to, persuade, influence.*

Adelphī, -ōrum, [Ἀδελφοί], m. pl., *the Brothers,* the name of a play by Terence. SEN. 18.

adeō, -īre, -iī or **-īvī, -itum,** [ad + eō], irr., a. and n., *go to, come to, approach; enter upon, undertake; encounter, incur; undergo, submit to.* **ad rem pūblicam adīre,** *to engage in the administration of public affairs.* **hērēditātem adīre,** *to take possession of an inheritance.*

adeō [ad + eō], adv., *to this, thus far, so far, so much; so long, so.* **ūsque adeō,** *even to such a degree, even thus far, even so far.* **atque adeō,** *and even, yet more, still further.*

adeps, -ipis, m. or f., of animals, *fat, lard;* of men, *corpulence, fleshiness, obesity.*

adhaerēscō, -ere, -haesī, -haesum, [adhaereō], 3, inch., *cleave, stick, adhere; cling; be devoted to; correspond to, accord with, fit, suit.*

adhibeō, -ēre, -uī, -itum, [ad + habeō], 2, a., *hold to, bring, apply; furnish, offer, bestow; employ, use, exercise.*

adhortor, -ārī, -ātus sum, [ad + hortor], 1, dep., *encourage, arouse; urge, urge on, exhort.*

adhūc [ad + hūc], adv., *heretofore, hitherto, as yet, up to this time; still, yet.*

adiciō, -ere, -iēcī, -iectum, [ad + iaciō], 3, a., *throw to, cast to, fling at, put, set near; cast, throw; turn, direct, fix; increase, add, superadd; do in addition.* **ūnum adicere,** *to add one thing more.*

adigō, -ere, -ēgī, -āctum, [ad + agō], 3, a., *drive, urge, bring by force, take; drive home, plunge, thrust; bring, force, compel.* **aliquem iūre iūrandō adigere,** *to have some one swear.*

adimō, -ere, adēmī, adēmptum, [ad + emō], 3, a., *take away, remove; deprive of, free from.*

adipīscor, -ipīscī, -eptus sum, [ad + apīscor], 3, dep., *arrive at; obtain, attain, reach; get, gain, secure, win.*

aditus, -ūs, [adeō], m., *a going to, approach, access; way of approach, entrance, avenue, passage; arrival.*

adiūmentum, -ī, [for adiuvāmentum, from adiuvō], n., *help, assistance, aid, support.*

adiungō, -ere, adiūnxī, adiūnctum, [ad + iungō], 3, a., *join to, attach to; join, add, annex, associate, unite to; win, secure; apply.*

adiūtor, -ōris, [adiuvō], m., *helper, assistant, confederate; aid, deputy.*

adiūtrīx, -īcis, [adiūtor], f., *female assistant, helper.*

adiuvō, -iuvāre, -iūvī, -iūtum, [ad + iuvō], 1, a., *help, assist; be of assistance to; aid, support, sustain.*

adminiculum, -ī, [from admaniculum, *that to which I apply my hands; that by which I hold*], n., *prop, support, help.*

administer, -trī, [ad + minister], m., *attendant, assistant, helper; tool, instrument.*

administra, -ae, [administer], f., *female assistant, (female) servant, handmaid.*

administrō, -āre, -āvī, -ātum, [ad + ministrō, from minister], 1, a., *manage, control, handle, administer, regulate; direct, guide, serve.*

admīrābilis, -e, [admīror], adj., *admirable, wonderful, strange, astonishing.*

admīrandus, -a, -um, [part. of admīror], adj., *worthy of admiration, to be admired, wonderful, admirable, strange.*

admīrātiō, -ōnis, [admīror], f., *admiration, wonder; surprise, astonishment.*

admīror, -ārī, -ātus sum, [ad + mīror], 1, dep., *admire, view with wondering approval, wonder at; wonder, be astonished.*

admittō, -ere, admīsī, admissum, [ad + mittō], 3, a., *send to, let go; admit, receive; give access, allow access, grant admittance; permit; commit, perpetrate.* mare nāvem nōn admittit, *the sea does not permit their boat to be launched.*

admodum, [ad + modus], adv., *to the proper limit, to full measure; full, quite, at least, no less than; no more than, just, only; fully, entirely, very; at all, whatever; considerably.* nōn admodum, *not so very much, but moderately.*

admoneō, -ēre, -uī, -itum, [ad + moneō], 2, a., *remind, suggest; advise, urge, warn; bid.* admonitus, -ūs, used only in the abl., [admoneō], m., *reminding, request, suggestion, warning; remonstrance.*

admoveō, -ēre, -mōvī, -mōtum, [ad + moveō], 2, a., *move to, bring up, carry, conduct, drive; apply to, direct.* cōnsōlātiōnēs admovēre, *to proffer comfort.*

admurmurātiō, -ōnis, [admurmurō], f., *murmuring, murmur of a crowd, expressing approval or dissent.*

adnuō, -nuere, -nuī, ——, [ad + nuō], 3, n., *nod to, nod; nod assent, give assent, signify approval.*

adōrnō, -āre, -āvī, -ātum, [ad + ōrnō], 1, a., *provide, furnish, equip, prepare; decorate, embellish, adorn.*

adsum, -esse, -fuī, [ad + sum], irr., n., *be near, be present, be at hand; stand by, assist, support, help; of motion, appear, attend; of time, have come, be at hand, impend.*

adulēscēns, -entis, [part. of adolēscō], adj., *young, youthful.* As subst., m. or f., *youth, young man, young woman.*

adulēscentia, -ae, [adulēscēns], f., *youth, the period of life beyond* pueritia, *and reckoned ordinarily between the ages of 15 and 25 or 30 years; by metonymy,* = adulēscentēs, *young people, youth.*

adulēscentulus, -ī, [adulēscēns], m., dim., *very young man, lad, young fellow.*

adulter, -tera, adj., *adulterous, unchaste.* As subst., *adulter,* -terī, m., *adulterer, seducer, paramour.*

adulterium, -ī or -iī, [adulter], n., *adultery.*

adultus, -a, -um, [adolēscō], adj., *full grown, mature, fully developed, adult.*

advena, -ae, [cf. adveniō], m. and f., *stranger, foreigner, immigrant; visitor, chance comer.*

adveniō, -īre, -vēnī, -ventum, [ad + veniō], 4, n., *come to, reach, arrive at; come, arrive.*

adventīcius, -a, -um, [adveniō], adj., *foreign, imported; strange.*

adventō, -āre, -āvī, -ātum, [adveniō], 1, freq., *come frequently; advance, press forward, march on, approach; arrive.*

adventus, -ūs, [adveniō], m., *coming, approach; arrival; presence.*

adversārius, -a, -um, [adversor], adj., *opposed, opposite; antagonistic, hostile, contrary.* As subst., adversārius, -ī or -iī, m., *opponent, antagonist, enemy, adversary.*

adversor, -ārī, -ātus sum, [adversus], 1, dep., *resist, withstand, oppose.*

adversus, [advertō], adv. and prep., *against:*
(1) As adv., *opposite to, against, to* or *toward a thing,* in a friendly or hostile sense.
(2) As prep., with acc. *only, before, facing; in the presence of, face to face with; to, towards, in answer to; in comparison with; in respect of, against; in opposition to.*

adversus, -a, -um, [advertō], adj., *turned towards, facing, in front; unfavorable, unsuccessful, adverse; opposed, hostile.* adversae rēs, *misfortune, calamity, adversity, trouble, troubles.* adversīs vulneribus, *with their wounds in front.* in adversum subīre, *to go up the face of the hill.*

advesperāscit, -āscere, -āvit, ——, [ad + vesperāscit], 3, n., impers., *evening approaches, it grows dusk, it is twilight.*

advocātiō, -ōnis, [advocō], f., *attendance on a friend when called to assist him with one's counsel or presence; a summoning as counsel; consultation; the advocates, counsel, bar, body of pleaders; a delay for consultation; legal aid, legal support.*

advolō, -āre, -āvī, -ātum, [ad + volō], 1, n., *fly to, hasten to.*

aedēs, see aedis.

aedificātiō, -ōnis, [aedificō], f., *the process of building; a building, structure, edifice; plan, site; building area.*

aedificium, -ī or -iī, [aedificō], n., *building, edifice.*

aedificō, -āre, -āvī, -ātum, [aedis + faciō], 1, a., *erect a building, build, erect; construct.*

aedīlis, -is, [aedēs], m., *aedile, buildings commissioner,* designation of certain magistrates in Rome, who had charge of buildings and public works, had an oversight of public exhibitions and dramatic performances, and were entrusted with the keeping of the decrees of the senate and other public documents.

aedīlitās, -ātis, [aedīlis], f., *office of aedile, aedileship.*

aedis or aedēs, -is, f., *of the gods, temple, sanctuary;* of men, in pl. only, *house, habitation, dwelling.*

aeger, -gra, -grum, adj., *sick, ill, suffering, feeble; afflicted, distressed, troubled.*

aegrē, comp. aegrius, sup. aegerrimē, [aeger], adv., *painfully, with distress; with difficulty, hardly, scarcely; unwillingly, reluctantly.*

aegrōtō, -āre, -āvī, ——, [aegrōtus, sick], 1, n., *be sick, be ill;* properly of the body, but also of the mind, *languish, pine, suffer.*

Aelius, -ī or -iī, with Sex., *Sextus Aelius Paetus,* an early Roman jurist. He was curule aedile 200 B.C., consul 198 B.C., and censor 193 B.C. He left an important work on Roman law, which has perished. SEN. 9.

Aemilius, -a, the name of a Roman gens, greatly distinguished for the illustrious men whom it furnished. See Paulus, Scaurus.

aequālis, -e, [aequō], adj., *equal, like, even, on a par; of the same*

age, equally old. As subst.,
aequālis, -is, m., *contemporary,
fellow, friend of the same age,
match.*

aequātus, -a, -um, [part. of **aequō**],
adj., *made equal to, level, equaled,
even.* **Mārte aequātō,** *on equal
terms.*

aequē [**aequus**], adv., *equally; in
like manner, just as, to the same
extent.* **aequē ac,** *just as, as
much as, as.* **aequē ac tū,** *equally
with you.* **aequē cārus ac,** *just
as dear as.*

aequitās, -ātis, [**aequus**], f., *even-
ness; fairness, equity; calmness,
repose, equanimity, contentment,
equability.*

aequō, -āre, -āvī, -ātum, [**aequus**],
1, a., *make equal, equalize, place
on an equality with, match; make
level, smooth; become equal, equal,
come up to, attain, reach; offset.*

aequus, -a, -um, adj., *even, plain,
level; equal, equitable, reasonable,
fair, just, honorable; calm, patient,
resigned; favorable, kind.* **aequum est,** *it is fair, it is reasonable.*

āēr, āeris, acc. **āera,** [ἀήρ], m., *air,
atmosphere, sky; mist, vapor;
weather.*

aerārium, -ī or **-iī,** [**aerārius**], n.,
*treasury; the public treasure,
finances.* The Roman treasury
was a part of the temple of
Saturn in the Forum, in which
public funds were kept.

aerumna, -ae, f., *hardship, trouble,
tribulation.*

aes, aeris, n., *copper; bronze,* an
alloy of copper and tin ; by metonymy, applied to things made
of copper or bronze, as *bronze*

tablet, money. **aes aliēnum,**
debt. **in tantum aes aliēnum,** *so
deeply in debt.* **aere aliēnō premī,**
to be heavily in debt.

Aesculāpius, -ī or **-iī,** *Aesculāpius,*
son of Apollo, and god of healing
and medicine among the ancients. See illustration, page
211.

aestās, -ātis, f., *summer.* **media
aestās,** *midsummer.*

aestimō, -āre, -āvī, -ātum, 1, a.,
value, estimate, appraise, rate.

aestuō, -āre, -āvī, -ātum, [**aestus**],
1, n., *rage, burn; be warm, burn,
glow; swell, undulate, heave;
be excited, be inflamed; waver,
vacillate, hesitate, be in doubt;
boil, seethe, be in a ferment.*

aestus, -ūs, m., lit. *violent agitation;* of fire or fever, *heat, glow;*
also = **aestās,** *summer;* of water,
surge, swell, tide; of human emotions and actions, *fire, warmth,
ardor; doubt, indecision.*

aetās, -ātis, [for **aevitās,** from
aevum], f., *period of life, age,
lifetime; time, period, generation; old age; an age, epoch.*
ab ineunte aetāte, *from youth
up, from early manhood.*

aeternitās, -ātis, [**aeternus**], f.,
*eternity, immortality; undying
fame, enduring renown.*

aeternus, -a, -um, [for **aeviternus,**
from **aevum**], adj., *lasting, everlasting, eternal, endless; unbroken,
perpetual, immortal, imperishable.*

Aetōlī, -ōrum, [Αἰτωλός], m., pl.,
Aetolians, inhabitants of Aetolia,
a district in Greece north of the
entrance of the Corinthian Gulf,
and east of Acarnania.

aevum, -ī, n., *never-ending time, eternity; period of life, lifetime, life, age; old age; age, generation, period; the age, men of the age; time.* aevō terrāque, *by long lying in the ground.*

affectus, -a, -um, [part. of afficiō], adj., *provided, endowed, gifted; affected, disposed; weakened, impaired; advanced, nearly at an end, in a favorable stage of progression.*

affectus, -ūs, [afficiō], m., *a state, disposition, mood; desire, fondness for, affection.*

afferō, -ferre, attulī, allātum, [ad + ferō], irr., a., *bring to, carry to; convey, bring, introduce; report, announce; produce, contribute, offer.* nihil afferre, *to prove nothing, make no contribution of value.*

afficiō, -ficere, -fēcī, -fectum, [ad + faciō], 3, a., *do something to, treat, use; affect, influence; visit with, afflict; weaken, impair, break down.* eōs praemia affēcit, *he bestowed gifts upon them.*

affīnis, -e, [ad + finis], adj., *adjoining, neighboring; connected with, implicated in, accessory to.*

affīnitās, -ātis, [affīnis], f., *relationship by marriage.*

affīrmō, -āre, -āvī, -ātum, [ad + fīrmō], 1, a., *strengthen; confirm by words, encourage; maintain, assert.*

afflīctō, -āre, -āvī, -ātum, [freq. of afflīgō], 1, a., *break to pieces; crush; distress, torment, harass.* sēsē afflīctāre, *to beat* (their) *breasts.*

afflīctus, -a, -um, comp. afflīctior, [part. of afflīgō], adj., *cast down,*

prostrate; dejected, discouraged, wretched, distressed.

afflīgō, -flīgere, -flīxī, -flīctum, [ad + flīgō], 3, a., *strike at, dash at; shatter; overthrow, ruin, damage, injure, distress.*

affluēns, -entis, [pres. part. of affluō], adj. and part., *generally an adj., abounding, overflowing, abundant.*

Āfrica, -ae, f., *Africa,* referring at first only to that part of the continent under the dominion of the Carthaginians; then, the province *Africa,* comprising territory formerly held by Carthage, and organized after the destruction of the city, 146 B.C.; in the broadest sense, *the African continent, Africa,* as the term is understood today.

Āfricānus, -a, -um, [Āfrica], adj., *of Africa, African.* Used as a surname for the two Scipios who were victorious in Africa, *P. Cornēlius Scīpiō Āfricānus,* who defeated Hannibal at Zama, 202 B.C.; and *P. Cornēlius Scīpiō Aemiliānus Āfricānus,* adoptive grandson of the elder Scipio, who destroyed Carthage, 146 B.C.

Agathoclēs, -is or -ī, m., *Agathoclēs,* tyrant of Syracuse, 317 to 289 B.C., who long waged war against Carthage, and brought the other Greek cities of Sicily under his control.

agellum, -ī, [dim. of ager], n., *a small estate, little field.*

ager, -grī, [cf. English *acre*], m., *land, field, estate,* referring to improved or productive land; *territory, district, domain;* pl.

agrī, sometimes *country, the open country, plain,* as opposed to cities or mountains.

aggredior, -ī, -gressus sum, [ad + gradior, *walk*], 3, dep., *approach, apply to, address; go against, fall upon, attack, assault; advance to fight; undertake, set about, assume, begin; attempt, try.*

aggregō, -āre, -āvī, -ātum, [ad + grex], 1, a., lit. *add to a flock; attach, join; collect, bring together, gather together.*

agitātiō, -ōnis, [agitō], f., *movement, motion, agitation; pursuit, prosecution, activity in; brandishing, quick movement, flourishing, swinging.*

agitātor, -ōris, [agitō], m., *driver of cattle* or *horses; driver, charioteer, competitor in the circus.*

agitō, -āre, -āvī, -ātum, [freq. of agō], 1, a., *drive, set in motion; move to and fro, brandish, wave, agitate; stir up, vex, trouble, distress; consider, deliberate, discuss.* **ferōcius agitāre,** *to behave more wildly.* **plūra agitāre,** *to devise more schemes, increase activity.*

agnōscō, -nōscere, -nōvī, -nitum, [ad + gnōscō], 3, a., *discern, recognize, identify; acknowledge; perceive, know by; perceive the meaning of, understand.*

āgnus, -ī, m., *lamb.*

agō, agere, ēgī, āctum, 3, a. and n., *set in motion, drive, lead; direct, conduct, guide; incite, urge; press forward, chase, pursue; drive off* as plunder, *rob; do, act, transact, perform; manage, carry on, accomplish;* of time, *spend, pass, live;* also, *treat, deal with, confer,* *plead with;* pass. sometimes, *be at stake, be in peril.* Imp. **age** as an interjection, *come now! come! well!* **grātiās agere,** *to give thanks.* **cum populō agere,** *to bring a matter before the people.* **agitur de vectīgālibus,** *the revenues are imperiled.* **nihil agis,** *you accomplish nothing.* **agere cum aliquō,** *to treat with anyone, plead with anyone.* **in agendō,** *in action.* **quid aliud ēgit?** *What other object had he?* **male cum aliquō agitur,** *it goes badly with somebody.* **id agere ut,** *to resolve to.* **āctum (est) praeclārē vōbīscum,** *you have fared most admirably.* **bene agere cum,** *to deal fairly with.* **nihil agere,** *to be* (busy) *doing nothing.* **tēcum agere,** *to make this request of you.* **ācta agimus,** *we are doing what is done, we act too late.* **maximās grātiās agere,** *to give heartiest thanks.* **Quid agis?** colloquially, *How are you?* also, *What are you about?*

agrestis, -e, [ager], adj., *of fields, rural, rustic; rude, coarse, uncultivated, wild.* As subst., **agrestis, -is,** m., usually in pl., *countryman, peasant, boor.*

agricola, -ae, [ager + colō], m., *one that cultivates the fields,* whether by his own hands or by slaves; *husbandman, plowman, farmer, peasant; rustic, clown, boor.*

Ahāla, -ae, m., name of a patrician family of the Servilian gens. **C. Servīlius Ahāla,** cf. **Maelius.**

Āiāx, -ācis, m., *Āiāx,* son of Telamon, grandson of Aeacus. He sailed against Troy in twelve ships, and is represented in the Iliad as second only to Achilles in bravery. In the contest for the armor of Achilles he was conquered by Odysseus, and this, says Homer, was the cause of his death. Later poets relate that his defeat by Odysseus threw him into a state of madness; that he rushed from his tent and slaughtered the sheep of the Greek army, fancying they were his enemies; and that at length he put an end to his own life. SEN. 10; VERR. 60.

aiō (pres. ind. aiō, **aïs, aït, aiunt,** impf. **aiēbam**), 3, def., n., *say yes; assert, say, tell, affirm;* generally used parenthetically.

alacer, -cris, -cre, adj., *lively, quick, active; eager, excited, enthusiastic; cheerful, happy.*

Alba, -ae, [albus, *white*], f., name of two important towns in Italy:

(1) *Alba,* or *Alba Longa,* the mother-city of Rome, situated between Mons Albanus and the Alban Lake, 15 miles southeast of Rome; said to have been built by Ascanius, son of Aeneas, and destroyed at an early period.

(2) *Alba,* or *Alba Fūcentia,* a city and fortress situated on the borders of the Marsian country, about sixty miles northeast of Rome and a short distance northwest of the Fucine Lake.

Albānus, -a, -um, [Alba], adj., *of* or *pertaining to* **Alba Longa.** As subst., **Albānī, -ōrum,** m. plur., *the people of Alba, the Albans.*

āleātor, -ōris, [ālea], m., *player with dice, gambler*

Alexander, -drī, ['Αλέξανδρος] m., *Alexander,* in this book referring only to Alexander III., surnamed the Great, king of Macedonia. He was born 356 B.C., the son of Philip II. of Macedonia and Olympias. He broke the power of Persia, and led an army beyond the Indus. He died at Babylon, 323 B.C.

Alexandrīa, -ae, [Alexander], f., *Alexandria,* the capital city and chief port of Egypt, founded by Alexander.

algor, -ōris, [algeō], m., *cold.*

aliās, [originally acc. plur. f. of alius], adv., *at another time, some other time, at other times; sometimes.* aliās —— aliās, *at one time* —— *at another.* alias —— plērumque, *occasionally* —— *generally.*

alibī, [alius + ibī], adv., *elsewhere, somewhere else, at another place; otherwise, in another matter, in other things, in other respects.* aliī alibī, *some in one place, some in another.* alibī —— alibī, *in one place* —— *in another.*

aliēnus, -a, -um, [alius], adj., *of another, another's; strange, foreign; unsuitable, out of place, ill-adapted; unfriendly, hostile.* As subst., **aliēnus, -ī,** m., *stranger, foreigner.* **aliēnum, -ī,** n., *the property of another.* aliēnus ā rē pūblicā nostrā, *inconsistent with our national policy, foreign to the spirit of our national policy.* dē aliēnō, *of another man's bounty.* aliēnī appetēns, *covetous of the property of others.*

aliquamdiū, [**aliquam**, sc. **partem**,+ **diū**], adv., *for a while, awhile, for some time.*

aliquandō [**alius** + **quandō**], adv., *at some time or other, some time; at any time, ever; at some time in the past, once, formerly; at some time in the future, hereafter; at length, finally, at last.* **tandem aliquandō**, *now at length, then at length.*

aliquantō [**aliquantus**], adv., *in a degree, considerably, somewhat, rather;* usually with comparatives. **post aliquantō**, *some time afterwards.*

aliquantum, -ī, [n. of **aliquantus**] n., *a little, some, a considerable amount, something.* As an adv., *somewhat, in some degree, considerably, not a little.* **aliquantum spatiī**, *for some considerable distance.*

aliquī, aliqua, aliquod, [**alius**+**quī**], indef. pron. adj., *some, any, some one or other, some other.* **in aliquās terrās**, *into some other countries.*

aliquis, aliqua, aliquid, nom. and acc. pl. n. **aliqua**, [**alius** + **quis**], indef. pron., *some one, anyone, anybody;* pl., *some, any.* Neut. **aliquid** as subst., *something, anything.*

aliquō [**aliquī**], adv., *to some place, somewhere; to some other place, elsewhere.*

aliquot [**alius** + **quot**], num. adj., indecl., *some, several, a number.*

aliter [**alius**], adv., *otherwise, differently; in any other way, in another manner, in a contrary way.* **aliter —— aliter**, *otherwise than.*

alius, -a, -ud, gen. **alīus** (very rare, usually supplied by **alterĭus**, genitive of **alter**), dat. **aliī**, adj., *another, some other, other, different, else.* **alius —— alius,** *one —— another, the one —— the other;* pl., **aliī —— aliī**, *some —— others;* often as subst., **alius**, *another,* **aliī**, *others.* **longē alius,** *far different.* **nihil aliud nisi,** *nothing else but.* **nihil aliud nisi dē hoste cōgitāre**, *to think of nothing but the enemy, to have no thought for anything but the enemy.* **alia omnia**, *all things else, everything else.*

alliciō, -licere, -lexī, -lectum, [**ad** + **laciō**, obsol.), 3, a., *entice to, allure; attract, persuade.*

alligō, -āre, -āvī, -ātum, 1, a., *bind to, bind up; fetter, shackle; fasten; hold fast; hinder, detain; bind, oblige, lay under obligation; accuse.*

Allobrogēs, -um, acc., **Allobrogas**, m., pl., *Allobrogēs,* a people of Transalpine Gaul, who lived on the east side of the Rhone, north of the Isara. Their chief city was Geneva. They were brought under the rule of Rome by Q. Fabius Maximus, 121 B.C., and in Cicero's time their territory formed a part of the Roman province in Gaul.

alō, alere, aluī, altum or **alitum**, 3, a., *nourish, sustain, maintain, support; cherish, promote, increase;* in pass., with abl., *be nourished by* (= **vescor**), *feed upon, live on.*

Alpēs, -ium, f., pl., *the Alps.*

altāria, -ium, [**altus**], n., pl., *high altar, altar.* See **āra**.

altē, comp. altius, sup. altissimē, [altus], adv., *high, on high, from above, loftily; deep, deeply, far; profoundly; from afar, remotely, from farther back.*

alter, -tera, -terum, gen. alterīus or alterius, dat. alterī, pron. adj., *one* of two, *the one, the other, another; second, next.* alter —— alter, *the one* —— *the other, the former* —— *the latter.*

altercātiō, -ōnis, [altercor], f., *debate, discussion, alternate discourse; altercation.*

alternus, -a, -um, [alter], adj., *one after the other, by turns, alternate, reciprocal;* of verses, *alternate hexameter and pentameter,* that is, *elegiac.*

alteruter, -utra, -utrum, [alter + uter], adj., *one or the other, one of two, either.* in alterutrō, *in either case, in the case of either.*

altum, -ī, [altus], n., *height; depth; the deep, the sea; the sky.*

altus, -a, -um, comp. altior, sup. altissimus, [alō], adj., lit. *nourished, grown great; high, lofty, elevated; deep, profound.*

alveolus, -ī, [dim. of alveus, hollow], m., *tray, basin; dice-board,* a small board upon which dice were thrown; by metonymy, *gaming, gambling.*

amābilis, -e, comp. amābilior, sup. amābilissimus, [amō], adj., *worthy of love, lovable, amiable, lovely, attractive.*

amāns, -antis, comp. amantior, sup. amantissimus, [part. of amō], adj., *fond, affectionate towards, devoted to;* often followed by the gen. amāns reī pūblicae,

devoted to (his) *country, patriotic.* amantissimus reī pūblicae, *of the loftiest patriotism.*

amanter, comp. amantius, sup. amantissimē, [amāns], adv., *affectionately, amiably.*

ambigō, -ere, ——, ——, [ambi- + agō], 3, n., *to busy one's self with two things at the same time; go about, go around, avoid; hesitate, waver, doubt, be in doubt about; argue, dispute, contend, debate.* neque ambigitur, *and there is no doubt.*

ambitiō, -ōnis, [ambiō, go around], f., *going about; soliciting of votes; striving for favor, flattery,* or *adulation; desire for honor, thirst for popularity.*

ambitiōsus, -a, -um, [ambitiō], adj., *surrounding, encompassing, entwining; ambitious, eager for honor, solicitous of favor; high-sounding, grand.*

ambitus, -ūs, [ambiō], m., *going round, moving about, revolution; circuit, circumference, border; suing for office, canvassing for votes.* ambitū corrumpī, *to be perverted to private ends, be misused with ulterior motives.*

ambō, ambae, ambō, acc. m. ambō or ambōs, num. adj., *both taken together, both.* alter ambōve, *one or both.*

ambulātiō, -ōnis, [ambulō], f., *walking about, walking; walk, promenade.*

ambulō, -āre, -āvī, -ātum, 1, n., *walk, walk about, take a walk.*

ambūrō, -ere, -ussī, -ūstum, [ambi- + ūrō], 3, a., *burn round; scorch, singe; consume; benumb.*

āmēns, -entis, [ab + mēns], adj., *out of one's senses, distracted, frantic, mad; foolish, stupid.*

āmentia, -ae, [āmēns], f., *madness; folly, stupidity*

amīcē, sup. amīcissimē, [amīcus], adv., *in a friendly manner.*

amiciō, -īre, amixī or amicuī, amictum, [am-, for ambi-, + iaciō], 4, a., *throw around, wrap about, wrap around,* used of outer garments; *clothe, cover, surround, enclose.*

amīcitia, -ae, [amīcus], f., *friendship; alliance.*

amīcus, -a, -um, comp. amīcior, sup. amīcissimus, [amō], adj., *loving, friendly, dear; kind, well disposed; pleasing, agreeable.* amīcissimō, *in the case of a dearest friend.*

amīcus, -ī, [adj. amīcus], m., *friend.*

Amīsus, -ī, ['Αμῑσός], f., *Amīsus,* an important city on the southern shore of the Pontus Euxinus southeast of Sinope; now Eski Samsun. IMP. P. 5.

amita, -ae, f., *aunt, father's sister.*

āmittō, -ere, āmīsī, āmissum, [ab + mittō], 3, a., *send away, dismiss, let go; lose, part with.*

amō, -āre, -āvī, -ātum, 1, a., *love, like; be fond of, take pleasure in;* in requests, *I pray, please.*

amoenitās, -ātis, [amoenus, *pleasant*], f., *pleasantness, charm.* amoenitās locōrum, *attractive surroundings.* amoenitās ōrae, *pleasant shore.*

amor, -ōris, [amō], m., *love, affection, devotion; eager desire, passion.*

āmoveō, -ēre, -mōvī, -mōtum, [ā + moveō], 2, a., *move away, take away, remove; abstract, steal; banish; lay aside, set aside; get rid of.* sē āmovēre, *to take oneself off, retire, withdraw.*

amplē, comp. amplius, sup. amplissimē, [amplus], adv., *largely, amply, abundantly; liberally, magnificently.* See amplius.

amplector, -ectī, -exus sum, [ambi- + plectō], 3, dep., *twine about, encircle, embrace; embrace with esteem, love, esteem, cling to.*

amplexor, -ārī, -ātus sum, [amplector], 1, dep., *embrace; be fond of, value, esteem; cling to, cherish.*

amplexus, -ūs, [amplector], m., *act of embracing; loving embrace, caress; encircling, surrounding, circuit; limits, confines.*

amplificō, -āre, -āvī, -ātum, [amplificus, from amplus + faciō], 1, a., *broaden, enlarge, extend; increase, amplify, enhance.*

amplitūdō, -inis, [amplus], f., *breadth, great extent, greatness, size; dignity, grandeur.*

amplius [comp. of amplus and amplē], indecl. adj. and adv., *further, besides, more.* nihil amplius quam, *nothing but.* As subst., amplius, indecl., n., *more, greater amount, larger sum.* amplius negōtī, *larger measure of difficulty, more trouble.*

amplus, -a, -um, comp. amplior, sup. amplissimus, adj., *large, great, spacious, ample, considerable; magnificent, splendid, glorious; renowned, distinguished, honorable.* verbīs amplissimīs, *in the handsomest terms, in elaborate terms.*

an, conj., introducing the second member of a disjunctive question, direct or indirect, *or, or rather, or indeed.* The first member ordinarily has utrum or -ne, but it is sometimes omitted. In direct questions **an** is often not translated; in indirect questions, *whether.* **haud sciō an** = *I am inclined to think, perhaps, probably.*

Anāgnīnus, -a, -um, [Anāgnia], adj., *of* or *pertaining to Anagnia,* a town in Latium. As subst., **Anāgnīnum, -ī,** n., *estate at Anagnia, villa at Anagnia.*

anceps, -cipitis, [ambi- + capiō], adj., *two-headed, double, twofold; wavering, uncertain, doubtful, undecided.* **anceps contentiō,** *contest on two sides.*

ancilla, -ae, [dim. of ancula, *a female attendant*], f., *maidservant, handmaid.*

Andrius, -a, -um, [Andros], adj., *from Andros, Andrian.* **Andria, -ae,** f. sing. as subst., *woman of Andros;* the *Maid of Andros,* a comedy by Terence. Ам. 24.

angō, angere, anxī, ——, 3, a., *draw tight, squeeze, choke; distress, torment, vex.* **vehementer angī,** *to be greatly troubled, be much disturbed.*

angor, -ōris, [angō], m., *(properly) compression of the throat, throttling, whether by disease or accident; strangling, suffocation; anguish, torment, trouble.*

anguis, -is, abl. angue, m. and f., *serpent, snake.* Servius says **anguēs** are properly of the water, **serpentēs** of the earth, and **dracōnēs** of temples; but this distinction is hardly ever observed.

angulus, -ī, m., *angle, corner;* by metonymy, *nook, lurking-place.*

angustiae, -ārum, [angustus, *narrow*], f., *straitness, narrowness; narrow place, defile, strait;* of time, *shortness, brevity; scarcity, want; difficulty, distress.* **ōre et angustiīs,** *narrow mouth, narrow entrance.*

angustus, -a, -um, [angō], adj., *narrow, strait, contracted; short, brief; pinching, stinting; critical, difficult; narrow; base, little, petty.*

anīlis, -e, [anus, *old woman*], adj., *of an old woman; old-womanish, silly.*

anima, -ae, f., *current of air; air, breeze; breath, souǐ, life;* especially in pl., *souls* of the dead, *shades.* See **animus.**

animadversiō, -ōnis, [animadvertō], f., *observation, inquiry; reproach, censure; chastisement, punishment.*

animadvertō, -vertere, -vertī, -versum, [animum + advertō], 3, a., *direct attention to, regard; notice, observe, consider, perceive, see; censure, punish, inflict punishment.* **in aliquem animadvertere,** *to punish somebody.*

animāns, -antis, [animō], adj. and part., *giving life, animating.* As subst., **animāns, -antis,** m. and f., *a living being.*

animus, -ī, m., *soul, life; intellect, mind, reason; imagination; heart, feeling, desire, affection; passion; courage, spirit; temper,* *arrogance, haughtiness; design, resolution.* **animus** refers to the spiritual and emotional part of man's nature as distinguished on the one hand from the body (**corpus**) and on the other from the life-principle, the physical life (**anima**). **animō aequō,** *with resignation, calmly.* **in animum indūcere,** *to resolve.* **quō animō esse dēbētis?** *What feeling ought you to have? How ought you to feel?* **quō animō ferre dēbētis?** *With what spirit ought you to endure?* **bonō animō dīcere,** *to say with good intention.* **mihi in animō est,** *it is my intention, I intend.* **animō bonō esse,** *to be of good cheer.*

annālis, -e, [**annus**], adj., *yearly.* As subst., **annālis, -is,** abl. **annālī,** m., *record of events, chronicles, annals.* The Pontifex Maximus each year used to record public events on tablets, called **Annālēs Maximī;** hence historical works are called **Annālēs.**

annītor, -nītī, -nīxus sum, [**ad** + **nītor**], 3, dep., *lean upon; exert oneself; strive, make an effort.* **annītī dē triumphō,** *to make every effort to secure a triumph.*

Annius, -a, the name of a Roman gens. See **Chīlō, Milō** (2), **Sevērus.**

anniversārius, -a, -um, [**annus** + **vertō**], adj., *returning every year, annual, yearly.*

annōna, -ae, [**annus**], f., *the year's produce, crop; grain, provisions;* by metonymy, *price of grain, market.*

annotō, -āre, -āvī, -ātum, [**ad** + **notō**], 1, a., *observe, remark, write down, make note of.*

annus, -ī, m., *year.*

annuus, -a, -um, [**annus**], adj., *for a year, lasting a year; annual, yearly.*

anquīrō, -ere, -quīsīvī, -quīsītum, [**am-,** for **ambi-** + **quaerō**], 3, a. and n., *seek on all sides, look about for, search for; inquire diligently, examine into; prosecute.*

ante, adv. and prep., *before:*

(1) As adv., of space, *before, in front, ahead;* of time, *before, previously, earlier, ago.* **paulō ante,** *a little while ago.* **antequam,** *sooner than, before.* **paucīs ante diēbus,** *a few days ago.* **multō ante,** *much sooner, much earlier.*

(2) As prep., with acc. only, of space and time, *before, before the time of, previous to, antedating;* in comparisons, *before, superior to, in comparison with.* **ante mē,** *before my time.* **ante cīvitātem datam,** *prior to the granting of citizenship.* **ante sē,** *before (his) eyes.*

anteā [**ante** + **eā**], adv., *before, formerly, previously, hitherto.*

antecapiō, -ere, -cēpī, -ceptum, [**ante** + **capiō**], 3, a., *obtain before, receive before, take prior possession of, preoccupy; anticipate, forestall.*

antecēdō, -ere, -cessī, -cessum, [**ante** + **cēdō**], 3, a. and n., *go before, get the start, precede, have precedence of; excel, surpass, be eminent.*

antecellō, -ere, ——, ——, [ante
+ unused cellō, *rise*], 3, n., *rise
beyond, excel, surpass.*

anteferō, -ferre, -tulī, -lātum,
[ante + ferō], irr., a., *carry before; place before, esteem more
highly, prefer.*

antelūcānus, -a, -um, [ante +
lūx], adj., *before light, before daybreak.* antelūcānae cēnae, *feasts
continuing till morning, all-night
dinners.* officia antelūcāna, *social calls before daylight, early
visits of ceremony, salutations
at daybreak; early morning visitors.*

antepōnō, -pōnere, -posuī, -posi-
tum, [ante + pōnō], 3, a., *set
before; esteem above, prefer.*

antequam, see ante.

antevertō, -ere, -vertī, -versum,
[ante + vertō], 3, a., *take a place
before, go before, precede; anticipate; prefer, place before.*

Antiochīa, -ae, ['Αντιόχεια], f.,
Antioch, name of several cities,
of which the most important was
that in Syria, on the Orontes
river. ARCH. 3.

Antiochus, -ī, ['Αντίοχος], m.,
Antiochus, name of several kings
of Syria, of whom the most famous was Antiochus III., called
the Great. He came to the
throne of Syria 223 B.C.; was
defeated by the Romans at Ther-
mopylae, in Greece, 191 B.C.,
and again the following year in a
battle at the foot of Mt. Sipylus,
in Asia Minor. Two years later
he was forced to accept humiliat-
ing terms of peace, and was
murdered 187 B.C.

antīquitās, -ātis, [antīquus], f.,
antiquity, age; the past.

antīquus, -a, -um, comp. antīquior,
sup. antīquissimus, [ante], adj.,
*old, ancient, aged; primitive,
former, old-fashioned; reverend,
venerable.* As subst., antīquī,
-ōrum, m., pl., *ancients, the
ancients, the men of old.*

Antōnius, -a, name of a Roman
gens of which there were several
distinguished members.

Antōnius, -a, -um, [Antōnius], adj.,
of or pertaining to Antony. As
subst., Antōniī, -ōrum, m., pl.,
*the men of Antony, Antony's
followers.*

Antōnius, -ī, the name of a Roman
gens. Three of the name are
mentioned in this book:

(1) *C. Antōnius Hybrida,* uncle of M. Antonius the triumvir, and colleague of Cicero in
the praetorship and consulship.
SALL. 21; 24.

(2) *Mārcus Antōnius,* the triumvir, a mortal enemy of Cicero,
whom Cicero attacked in the
Philippic orations, conquered by
Octavianus at Actium. PHIL. 1,
et seq.; EP. 24.

(3) *L. Antōnius,* brother of
Marcus, was praetor in Macedo-
donia in 44, fell into the hands
of M. Brutus, and was put to
death by Brutus in 42 to avenge
the death of Cicero. PHIL. 3.

ānulus, -ī, [dim. of ānus, *a round-
ing, a ring*], m., *ring, finger-
ring, seal-ring, signet-ring.*

anxius, -a, -um, [angō], adj., *anxious, troubled, solicitous; troublesome, afflicting; cautious, uneasy.*

Apamēa, -ae, f., *Apamĕa,* a city of Phrygia. Ep. 12.

aper, aprī, m., *wild boar.*

aperiō, -īre, -uī, -tum, 4, a., *uncover, unclose, discover, reveal, open; lay open, open up, render accessible, expose; make known, unfold, explain.*

apertē [apertus], adv., *openly; plainly, clearly, without reserve.*

apertus, -a, -um, [part. of aperiō], adj., *uncovered; unclosed, open; unobstructed, plain, clear, manifest.* As subst., **apertum, -ī,** n., *the open, the open air.* **in apertō,** *in the open.*

Apollō, -inis, m., son of Jupiter and Latona, and twin brother of Diana. He is said to have been the inventor of the art of shooting with the bow, of soothsaying, of the healing art, of music, and of poetry. It was he who presided over the Muses. He was also regarded as the god of the shepherds. In later times, he was confounded with the god of the sun.

apparātus, -a, -um, [part. of apparō], adj., *made ready, ready, furnished; sumptuous, magnificent.* **apparātus, -ūs,** m., *preparing, providing, preparation, getting ready; apparatus, tools, instruments, supplies; splendor, magnificence, pomp, state; display, elaboration.*

appāreō, -ēre, -uī, -itum, [ad + pāreō], 2, n., *appear, come in sight; be evident, be apparent, be visible; appear as servant, attend, serve.*

apparō, -āre, -āvī, -ātum, [ad + parō], 1, a., *prepare, make ready, provide; make ready for; add to.*

appellō, -āre, -āvī, -ātum, [ad + pellō], 1, a., *address, speak to, apply to; name, term, entitle, call; entreat, beg, call upon, appeal to, make overtures to.*

Appennīnus, -ī, m., *the Appennine mountains, the Appennines,* the high mountain-range in Central Italy.

appetēns, -entis, [part. of appetō], adj., *eager for, desirous of; greedy.*

appetō, -petere, -petīvī or **-petiī, -petītum,** [ad + petō], 3, a. and n., *strive for, reach after; attack, assault; long for, desire, seek.*

Appī Forum, -ī, n., *Appī Forum. Forum of Appius,* a small market town on the Appian Way, 43 miles southeast of Rome.

Appius, -ī or **-iī,** m., *Appius,* a Roman forename, common in the Claudian gens. See **Pulcher.**

Appius, -a, -um, adj., *Appian, of Appius.* **Via Appia,** *Appian Way,* the most famous of Roman roads, built by the censor Appius Claudius Caecus about 300 B.C., and extending from Rome to Capua. See illustration, page 390.

applicātiō, -ōnis, [applicō], f., *act of applying; inclination, attaching to.*

applicō, -āre, -āvī, -ātum or **-itum,** [ad + plicō], 1, a., *join, connect, attach to, add to; apply to, direct, turn; bring, put; arrive, put in, land.*

apportō, -āre, -āvī, -ātum, [ad + portō], 1, a., *carry, convey, bring along; bring in, bring (to some place).*

appositus, -a, -um. comp. **appositior**, sup. **appositissimus**, [ap-
pōnō], adj. and part., *contiguous,
neighborly; bordering upon; fit,
proper, suitable, appropriate,
adapted, fitted.*

approbō, -āre, -āvī, -ātum, [ad +
probō], 1, a., *give assent to, approve, favor, sanction.*

appropinquātiō, -ōnis, [appropin-
quō], f., *approach, drawing near,
near approach.*

appropinquō, -āre, -āvī, -ātum,
[ad + propinquō], from **propinquus**], 1, n., *come near to, draw
nigh to, approach.*

aprīnus, -a, -um, [aper], adj., *relating to a wild boar.*

aptō, -āre, -āvī, -ātum, [aptus],
1, a., *adapt, fit, apply, adjust;
make ready, prepare, get ready.*

aptus, -a, -um, [cf. apīscor],
adj., *fitted, joined; suited, suitable, proper, fit, appropriate,
adapted.*

apud, prep. with acc. only, *with,
near, at, by; of persons, before,
in the presence of, to, among, in
the opinion of, in the power of, at
the house of, with, in the time of;*
of place, *at, near to, in, in the
vicinity of, off the coast of.* **apud
Laecam,** *at the house of Laeca,
at Laeca's.* **apud Cicerōnem,** *in
the writings of Cicero.*

Apuleius, -ī, m., *P. Apuleius,* tribune of the plebs. PHIL. 3.

Āpūlia, -ae, f., *Apūlia,* a region in
the southeastern part of Italy,
north of Calabria, east of Lucania and Samnium.

aqua, -ae, f., *water.* **aqua dulcis,**
fresh water.

aquila, -ae, f., *eagle;* by metonymy,
eagle of a standard, the metal
eagle carried on a pole as the
standard of a Roman legion.

āra, -ae, f., *altar.* āra is the general term for *altar,* while **altāria**
refers primarily to an elevation
on the altar to receive burnt
offerings; though the later term
by synecdoche is often used of
the altar as a whole.

arbitrium, -ī or -iī, [arbiter, *judge*],
n., *judgment, decision of an
arbitrator, opinion; dominion,
authority; power, choice; will.*

arbitror, -ārī, -ātus sum, [arbiter],
1, dep., *give one's judgment,
declare a decision; be of the
opinion, believe, think, consider,
judge.* **ut arbitror,** *in my judgment.*

arbor, -oris, [old form **arbōs**], f.,
tree.

arceō, -ēre, -cuī, ——, 2, a., *keep
away, ward off; hinder, prevent.*

accessō, -ere, accessīvī, accessītum,
[intens. of **accēdō, ar-** for ad-], 3,
a., *send for, summon, invite,
fetch.*

Archiās, -ae, ['Αρχίας], m., *A.
Licinius Archiās,* a Greek poet,
in whose defense Cicero delivered one of his most famous
orations. ARCH. 1, *et seq.*

Archimēdēs, -is, m., *Archimēdēs,* a
famous inventor and mathematician of Syracuse, who assisted in defending that city
against the Romans in 212 B.C.
He is said to have invented the
catapults whereby he kept the
enemy at a distance and also to
have used powerful burning-

glasses for setting fire to the Roman ships. He was killed by Roman soldiers at the taking of the city. VERR. 58.

Archȳtās, -ae, m., *Archȳtās,* a distinguished philosopher and statesman of Tarentum. AM. 23; SEN. 12.

ārdēns, -entis, [part. of ārdeō], adj., *glowing, hot; fiery, eager, ardent.*

ārdenter, comp. **ārdentius,** sup. **ārdentissimē,** [ārdēns], adv., *hotly, ardently, vehemently.*

ārdeō, -ēre, ārsī, ārsum, 2, n., *be on fire, burn, glow; flash, shine; be inflamed, be afire.*

ārdor, -ōris, [ārdeō], m., *flame, fire, heat; eagerness, zeal, animation.*

ārea, -ae, [āreō, *to be dry*], f., *area on which corn is beaten; ground* (for a house), *building-site; open space, court, playground.* **ārea domūs,** *courtyard.*

Arethūsa, -ae, f., *Arethūsa,* a celebrated fountain near Syracuse. VERR. 53.

argenteus, -a, -um, [argentum], adj., *of silver, made of silver, silver.*

argentum, -ī, n., *silver;* by metonymy, *silverware, silver money, money.*

Argīlētum, -ī, n., *the Argīlētum,* a part of Rome near the Aventine, where were the shops of booksellers, cobblers, and mechanics. LIV. I, 19. **īnfimum Argīlētum,** *the lowest part of the Argiletum.*

argūmentum, -ī, [arguō], n., *argument, evidence, proof; sign, mark, indication, token; subject.*

arguō, -ere, -uī, -ūtum, 3, a., *make known, show, prove, disclose, betray; accuse, complain of; inform, allege against, blame; find guilty.*

Ariobarzānēs, -is, m., *Ariobarzānēs,* name of three kings of Cappadocia, in Asia Minor. The most important was *Ariobarzānēs Philorhōmaeus,* who came to the throne by election under Roman influence about 93 B.C. He gained his surname (= φίλος + 'Ρωμαῖος) from his intimate relations with the Romans, by whom he was several times restored to his kingdom after having been driven out by Mithridates. He resigned the throne to his son, *Ariobarzānēs Philopatōr,* probably in 63 B.C.

Aristaeus, -ī, m., *Aristaeus,* son of Apollo and Cyrene, regarded by the ancients as the protector of flocks and shepherds, and of vine and olive plantations. He taught men to keep bees, and averted from the fields the burning heat of the sun, and the causes of destruction. VERR. 57.

Aristīdēs, -is, m., *Aristīdēs,* an Athenian, famed for his uprightness, and called " Just " on account of the integrity and purity of his life. SEN. 7.

Aristotelēs, -is, ['Αριστοτέλης], m., *Aristotle,* a famous Greek philosopher, born at Stagīra, in Chalcidice, 384 B.C. He was a pupil of Plato, and the tutor of the Prince Alexander, afterwards called the Great. He was the founder of the so-called Peripatetic school of philosophy. He left numerous writings, some of the most important of which have been preserved. He died 322 B.C. See Companion, page 547.

arma, -ōrum, n., pl., *armor, outfit,* as coat of mail, helmet, shield, greaves; *implements of war, arms, weapons;* by metonymy, *tools, implements.* **in armīs,** *under arms, in arms; in the pursuit of arms, in war.*

armātus, -a, -um, [armō], adj., *armed, equipped, furnished, under arms.* As subst., **armātī, -ōrum,** m. pl., *armed men, soldiers.*

Armenius, -a, -um, adj., *Armenian, of Armenia.* As subst., **Armeniī, -ōrum,** m., pl., *Armenians, inhabitants of Armenia,* a country in the northeastern part of Asia Minor, north of Mesopotamia.

armilla, -ae, [armus, *shoulder*], f., *bracelet* or *ring* worn on the left arm by soldiers who had distinguished themselves in battle, with which they were publicly presented by their general; *bracelet, armlet, arm-ring.*

arō, -āre, -āvī, -ātum, 1, a. and n., *plow, till, cultivate.*

Arpīnās, -ātis, adj., *of Arpīnum,* a town in Latium, about fifty miles southeast of Rome, celebrated as the birthplace of Gaius Marius and Cicero. As subst., **Arpīnās, -ātis,** n., *estate near Arpīnum,* Cicero's favorite country-place; his villa there was surrounded by the waters of the little river Fibrenus.

arripiō, -ere, -ripuī, -reptum, [ad + rapiō], 3, a., *snatch, catch hurriedly, grasp, seize; take, embrace; seize upon, learn with avidity; ridicule, attack.*

ars, artis, f., *skill, art; science, knowledge, learning; trait, practice, virtue, quality.*

arthrīticus, -a, -um, [ἀρθρῑτικός, from ἄρθρον, *joint*], adj., *gouty, having the gout.*

artifex, -icis, [ars, cf. faciō], m. and f., *master of an art, performer, actor, professional; contriver, trickster.*

artificium, -ī or **-iī,** [artifex], n., *profession, trade, employment; workmanship, skillful contrivance, skill, ingenuity; trick, artifice; work of art.*

arx, arcis, f., *citadel, castle, stronghold; bulwark, refuge, protection.*

ascendō, -ere, ascendī, ascēnsum, [ad + scandō], 3, a. and n., *mount, ascend, go up, rise, board ship, go on board, embark.*

ascīscō, -ere, ascīvī, ascītum, [ad + scīscō], 3, a., *receive, accept, adopt; associate with one's self, win over.*

ascrībō, -ere, ascrīpsī, ascrīptum, [ad + scrībō], 3, a., *write in addition, write in a list, enroll, enter, add; appoint, assign; ascribe, impute.* **in cīvitātem ascrībere,** *to enroll as a citizen.*

Asia, -ae, [Ἀσία], f., *Asia,* usually referring to Asia Minor.

Asiāticus, -a, -um, [Asia], adj., *of Asia, Asiatic.*

aspectus, -ūs, [aspiciō], m., *sight, look, glance; view, appearance, aspect, countenance.*

asper, -era, -erum, adj., *adverse, cruel, perilous; harsh, rough, wild, fierce.*

asperitās, -ātis, [asper], f., *unevenness, roughness; harshness, severity; austerity; adversity; difficulty; rudeness; inhumanity.*

āspernor, -ārī, -ātus sum, [ab + spernō], 1, dep., *despise, disdain, reject with contempt.* haud āspernārī, *to consent.*

aspiciō, -icere, -exī, -ectum, [ad + speciō], 3, a. and n., *look upon, behold, look, glance; observe, see, consider.* inter sēsē aspiciēbant, *they glanced at one another.*

asportō, -āre, -āvī, -ātum, [abs + portō], 1, a., *carry away, carry off, transport, remove.*

assēnsus, -ūs, [assentiō], m., *agreement, approval.*

assentātiō, -ōnis, [assentor], f., *act of assenting, approving; adulation, flattery; undue complacency, subservience.*

assentiō, -īre, -sēnsī, -sēnsum, [ad + sentiō], 4, n., also dep., assentior, -īrī, -sēnsus sum, *give assent, approve, agree with, agree to.*

assentor, -ārī, -ātus sum, [freq. assentiō], 1, dep., *agree with constantly, flatter, fawn.*

assequor, -sequī, -secūtus sum, [ad + sequor], 3, dep., *follow up, come up to; accomplish, effect; obtain, gain.*

asservō, -āre, -āvī, -ātum, [ad + servō], 1, a., *watch over, keep, preserve; guard with care, keep under guard.*

assīdō, -sīdere, -sēdī, ——, [ad + sīdō, *sit down*], 3, n., *sit down, take a seat.*

assiduē, [assiduus], adv., *constantly, continually, unceasingly.*

assiduitās, -ātis, [assiduus], f., *constant attendance; unremitting service; devotion; continuance, constancy.*

assiduus, -a, -um, [assideō], *settled, having landed property; constantly present, constantly in attendance; assiduous, persevering, diligent, industrious; frequent, continual, incessant; common, commonplace.*

assistō, -ere, astitī, ——, [ad + sistō], *stand by, take a stand near, attend; station oneself; rise, stand before.*

assuēfaciō, -facere, -fēcī, -factum, [assuētus + faciō], 3, a., *accustom to, habituate;* pass., *become accustomed to, be used to.*

assuēscō, -ere, assuēvī, assuētum, [ad + suēscō], 3, a. and n., *accustom, habituate; become accustomed.* huic reī assuēscitur, *men habituate themselves to this thing.*

assurgō, -ere, -surrēxī, -surrēctum, [ad + surgō], 3, n., *rise up, rise, stand up before; rise in the presence of.*

astō, -stāre, -stitī, ——, [ad + stō], 1, n., *stand by, stand near, stand at; stand up, stand.*

astūtia, -ae, [astūtus, *shrewd, cunning*), f., *adroitness, shrewdness, craft, cunning; dexterity;* often pl., *tricks, cunning, devices.*

asȳlum, -ī, n., *place of refuge, sanctuary, asylum.*

at, conj., *introducing*
  (1) *A contrast, but, but on the other hand, but yet.*

(2) A qualification after a negative and **sī, etsī**, etc., *but yet, nevertheless, however, at least.*
(3) A direct opposition, *but, but on the contrary.*

Athēnae, -ārum, ['Aθῆναι], f., pl., *Athens.*

Athēniēnsis, -e, [Athēnae], adj., *of Athens, Athenian.* As subst., **Athēniēnsis, -is,** m., *man of Athens, Athenian.*

Athēnodōrus, -ī, m., *Athēnodŏrus,* a philosopher at Athens. PLIN. 13.

āthlēta, -ae, m., *wrestler, athlete, combatant in public games.*

Atīlius, -ī or **-iī,** m., *Atīlius Crēscēns,* an intimate friend of the younger Pliny. PLIN. 3.

atque, before consonants **ac,** [ad + que], conj., *copulative and comparative:*
(1) Copulative, *and also, and even, as well as, and, and especially, and so, and too, and yet.* **etiam atque etiam,** *again and again, repeatedly.*
(2) Comparative, *as, than, than as.* **contrā atque,** *contrary to what.* **perinde atque,** *just as.* **prō eō ac,** *according as.*

atquī [at + quī], conj., *and yet, but yet, and nevertheless, however, but somehow, but in any case.*

atrōx, -ōcis, [āter], adj., *fierce, cruel, savage; severe, harsh; horrible, terrible, violent.* **atrōx negōtium,** *critical situation.*

attendō, -ere, attendī, attentum, [ad + tendō], 3, a., *direct to,* used either with or without **animum;** *consider, give heed; listen, pay attention to, listen to.*

attentē, comp. **attentius,** sup. **attentissimē,** [attentus, *attentive*], adv., *carefully, considerately, heedfully, vigorously, attentively.*

attenuō, -āre, -āvī, -ātum, [ad + tenuō], 1, a., *make thin; lessen, diminish, reduce, weaken; make less formidable.*

Attica, -ae, [Atticus], f., *Attica,* a pet name given by Cicero to Caecilia, the little daughter of his friend Atticus. EP. 21.

Atticus, -ī, ['Aττικός], m., *Atticus, Titus Pompōnius Atticus,* an intimate friend of Cicero, to whom he dedicated several of his works and addressed many letters. EP. 1, *et al.*

attingō, -ere, attigī, attāctum, [ad + tangō], 3, a. and n., *touch, touch upon; lay hands on, seize, attack; approach, reach, attain to; relate to, concern; mention, refer to.*

attrahō, -ere, -trāxī, -trāctum, [ad + trahō], 3, a., *draw, pull; attract, draw to; drag before; allure, lead.*

attribuō, -buere, -buī, -būtum, [ad + tribuō], 3, a., *assign, allot, bestow; intrust, give in charge; attribute, ascribe.*

auctiōnārius, -a, -um, [auctiō], adj., *of auction, for auction.*

auctor, -ōris, [augeō], m., *producer; father, progenitor; founder; writer, authority; counselor, adviser, promotor, leader.* **auctōre mē,** *at my suggestion, by my advice, after my example, on the strength of my example.* **sine auctōre,** *anonymously.* **tē auctōre,** *on your advice.* **auctor**

gravior, *an adviser of greater weight.*

auctōritās, -ātis, [auctor], f., *authority, supremacy; decision, resolve, will, opinion; decree, warrant, assurance; influence, dignity, reputation, weight, importance, consequence.*

aucupium, -ī or **-iī, [aucupor, hunt],** n., *bird-catching, fowling.*

aucupor, -ārī, -ātus sum, [auceps, fowler], 1, dep., *chase, hunt; lie in wait for, strive after, catch.*

audācia, -ae, [audāx], f., *daring, boldness, courage, bravery; audacity, impudence, insolence, presumption; deed of boldness, daring deed, effrontery.*

audāx, -ācis, comp. **audācior,** sup. **audācissimus, [audeō],** adj., *daring, bold, courageous; audacious, rash, foolhardy, desperate.*

audeō, audēre, ausus sum, 2, semi-dep., a. and n., *dare, be bold, venture, risk.*

audientia, -ae, [audiō], f., *hearing, attention.* **audientiam facere,** *to procure a hearing.*

audiō, -īre, -īvī or **-iī, -ītum,** 4, a., *hear, hear of; listen to, learn from; assent to, agree to, approve, grant.*

audītōrium, -ī or **-iī, [audītor, hearer],** n., *lecture-room.*

auferō, auferre, abstulī, ablātum, [ab + ferō], irr., a., *take away, remove, withdraw; carry off, snatch away, rob, steal; sweep away, destroy.*

aufugiō, -ere, -fūgī, ——, [ab + fugiō], 3, n., *flee away, run away, escape.*

augeō, augēre, auxī, auctum, 2, a. and n., *increase, enlarge, aug-*

ment; extend, add to, enrich, praise, extol.

augur, -uris, [avis], m. and f., *seer, soothsayer, diviner, augur, a Roman priest who foretold events by the flying, singing, etc., of birds. The college of Augurs was composed only of distinguished men.*

augurium, -ī or **-iī, [augur],** n., *observance of omens, interpretation of omens, divination, augury; omen, sign, event interpreted by augury; prediction, forecast.*

auguror, -ārī, -ātus sum, [augur], 1, dep., *act as augur, predict, foretell; surmise, imagine, conjecture, suppose.*

augustus, -a, -um, [augeō], *venerable, august, sacred, majestic, awful. Augustus,* a title of honor given to Octavius Caesar by the senate in 27 B.C., and subsequently applied to his successors, equivalent to "Imperial Majesty," or "Emperor."

Aulus, -ī, m., *Aulus,* a common Roman forename.

Aurēlium, -ī or **-iī,** see **Forum Aurēlium.**

Aurēlius, -a, -um, adj., *of an Aurelius, Aurelian,* name of a Roman gens. **Aurēlia via,** *Aurelian Way,* the great north coast-road, leading from Rome to Pisa.

aureus, -a, -um, [aurum], adj., *of gold, golden.*

auris, -is, [cf. audiō], f., *ear.* **aurēs adhibēre, aurēs dare,** *to give attention, to listen.*

aurum, -ī, n., *gold.*

auspicium, -ī or **-iī, [auspex, diviner],** n., *augury from birds.*

auspices, divination; sign, omen; guidance, authority.

aut, conj., marking an important difference, *or;* corrective or emphatic, *or at least, or surely, or rather, or else.* **aut —— aut,** *either —— or.*

autem, conj., always postpositive and generally in weak antitheses, sometimes in contrasted conditions, *however, but, on the contrary, and now.*

autumnus, -ī, [cf. **augeō**], m., *autumn.*

auxilium, -ī or **-iī,** [cf. **augeō**], n., *help, aid, assistance, support;* in pl., often *auxiliary troops, auxiliaries.*

avāritia, -ae, [**avārus**], f., *greed, avarice, covetousness.*

avārus, -a, -um, [**aveō**], adj., *eagerly desirous, grasping, covetous, penurious, greedy.*

Aventīnum, -ī, n., *the Aventine,* one of the seven hills of Rome. Liv. 1, 6.

aveō, -ēre, ——, ——, 2, a., *wish for, long after, desire, desire earnestly, crave, be eager for.*

āversus, -a, -um, [part. of **āvertō**], adj., *turned away, turned back; withdrawn; unfavorable, averse, hostile, opposed.* **āversus ā vērō,** *hostile to truth.* **āversus ā Mūsīs,** *unfriendly to the Muses.*

āvertō, -ere, āvertī, āversum, [**ā** + **vertō**], 3, a., *turn away, turn aside; remove, carry off, withdraw; ward off, avert, estrange.*

avidē, comp. **avidius,** sup. **avidissimē,** [**avidus**], adv., *eagerly, greedily, with eagerness, with avidity.*

avidus, -a, -um, [**aveō**], adj., *eager, desirous, coveting; covetous, greedy, avaricious; jealous of.*

avis, -is, abl., **avī** or **ave,** f., *a bird.* **secundīs avibus,** *under or with favorable omens.*

avītus, -a, -um, [**avus**], adj., *of a grandfather; ancestral, hereditary.*

āvocō, -āre, -āvī, -ātum, [**ā** + **vocō**], 1, a., *call away, withdraw; call off, divert, turn aside, turn.*

avunculus, -ī, [dim. of **avus**], m., *uncle, mother's brother.*

avus, -ī, m., *grandfather.*

Axius, -ī or **-iī,** m., *Axius,* a friend of Cicero. Ep. 21.

B

bacchor, -ārī, -ātus sum, [**Bacchus**], 1, dep., *celebrate the festival of Bacchus; revel, hold revelry, rave, exult.*

Balbus, -ī, m., name of several men mentioned in Roman history, of whom the most important is *Lūcius Cornēlius Balbus,* a native of Gades, in Spain. He served under several Roman generals in the war with Sertorius, and was rewarded by Pompey with the Roman citizenship. He afterwards moved to Rome, where he came to possess great influence, through his wealth and his friendship with Caesar, Pompey, and other prominent men. His citizenship was called in question, and defended by Cicero in the oration *Prō Balbō,* which is extant. He was consul 40 B.C., but the time of his death is not known. Ep. 10.

balineum, -ī, n., *a bath, bathing-place*.

barba, -ae, f., *beard*.

barbaria, -ae, [barbarus], f., *foreign country;* = barbarī, *uncivilized people; savagery, barbarism*.

barbarus, -a, -um, [βάρβαρος], adj., *unintelligible; strange, foreign; of foreigners, barbarian; barbarous, cruel, savage, rude, uncivilized*.

barbātus, -a, -um, [barba], adj., *bearded, with a beard*. bene barbātus, *with full beard*.

Basilus, -ī, m., name of a family of the Minucian gens. Prominent among those bearing the name was *L. Minucius Basilus*, who won distinction while serving under Caesar in Gaul. Afterwards, however, he was one of the assassins of Caesar, and his share in the killing of the Dictator drew from Cicero a celebrated letter of congratulation (Ep. 23). The year after Caesar's death Basilus was himself murdered by his slaves, on account of his inhuman treatment of them.

basis, -is, f., *foundation, base, support, pedestal*.

beātus, -a, -um, [beō, *make happy*], adj., *happy, fortunate, prosperous; wealthy, rich, opulent*.

bellē, comp. bellius, sup. bellissimē [bellus, *fine*], adv., *prettily, neatly, well*. bellē sē habēre, *to be in good health*.

bellicōsus, -a, -um, [bellicus], adj., *warlike, martial*.

bellicus, -a, -um, [bellum], adj., *of war, military; warlike*.

bellō, -āre, -āvī, -ātum, [bellum], 1, n., *wage war, carry on war, war; fight, contend*.

bellum, -ī, [for duellum, from duo], n., *war*.

bēlua, -ae, f., *great beast, beast, wild beast, monster*.

bene, comp. melius, sup. optimē, [bonus], adv., *well, successfully, prosperously; very, quite*. Comp., *better*. Sup., *best*.

beneficium, -ī or -iī, [beneficus], n., *kindness, favor, service, benefit; honor, promotion*. in datō beneficiō, *in the granting of a favor*. beneficiō tuō, *thanks to you*.

beneficus, -a, -um, comp. beneficentior, sup. beneficentissimus, [bene + faciō], adj., *generous, liberal, serviceable*.

benevolē, [benevolus, *kind, bountiful*], adv., *kindly, in a friendly manner*.

benevolentia, -ae, [benevolēns], f., *good-will, kindness, friendship*.

benignē, comp. benignius, sup. benignissimē, [benignus, *friendly*], adv., *in a friendly manner, kindly, courteously, cheerfully*.

benignitās, -ātis, [benignus], f., *kindness, courtesy; favor, liberality, bounty*.

bēstia, -ae, f., *beast, animal, brute*.

bibliothēca, -ae [βιβλιοθήκη], f., *library, room for books; collection of books*.

bibō, bibere, bibī, bibitum, 3, a. and n., *drink*.

Bibulus, -ī, m., name of a family of the Calpurnian gens. The best known member is *L. Calpurnius Bibulus*, who was consul with Caesar in the year 59 B.C.

Being in sympathy with the aristocratic party, he opposed Caesar whenever possible, both during the consulship and afterwards. He had a commission under Pompey in the Civil War, but died 48 B.C., just before the battle of Dyrrhachium. Ep. 12.

bīduum, -ī, [bis, cf. diēs], n., *period of two days, two days.*

biennium, -ī or **-iī,** [bis + annus], n., *a period of two years, two years.*

bīnī, -ae, -a, [cf. bis], dist. num. adj., *two each, two by two, two at a time; double.*

bipertītō [bipartītus, from bi for bis + partior], adv., *in two divisions, in two parts, in two parties.*

bis, adv. num., *twice, at two times, on two occasions; doubly, twofold, in two ways.*

Bīthȳnia, -ae, [βιθῡνία], f., *Bīthȳnia,* a province in Asia Minor, bounded on the west by the Propontis and on the north by the Pontus Euxinus.

blanditia, -ae, (blandus, *agreeable, enticing*), f., *caressing, fondness; flattery;* in the pl. *flatteries, blandishments, allurements.*

Bona Dea, -ae, f., *Bona Dea, the Good Goddess,* an Italian divinity, also called *Fauna* and *Maia.* She was supposed to preside over the fructifying powers of the earth, as well as over the chastity and faithfulness of women. She was worshiped at Rome as an austere virgin, men being forbidden to enter her temple. Her rites were celebrated by the Vestal Virgins and by matrons.

bonitās, -ātis, [bonus], f., *goodness, kindness, friendliness; excellence.*

bonus, -a, -um, comp. **melior,** sup. **optimus,** adj., *good, worthy, excellent, kind, loyal, patriotic.* As subst., **bonus, -ī,** m., *good man;* pl. **bonī, -ōrum,** *the good.* **bonum, -ī,** n., *good thing, advantage;* pl. **bona, -ōrum,** *goods, property, possessions, blessings.*

bracchium, -ī or **-iī,** n., *the fore-arm, the lower arm; arm.*

brevis, -e, adj., *short, brief, little.* **brevī** [sc. **tempore**], *in a short time, soon.*

brevitās, -ātis, [brevis], f., *shortness, brevity; conciseness.*

breviter [brevis], adv., *shortly, briefly, concisely, in a few words.*

Britannia, -ae, f., *Britain,* including England and Scotland.

Brundisium, -ī or **-iī,** n., *Brundisium,* an important seaport on the Adriatic, in Calabria. It was the usual port of departure for Greece and the East; now Brindisi.

Brūtus, -ī, m., cognomen of several well-known Romans, of whom four are mentioned in this book :

(1) *L. Iūnius Brūtus,* nephew of Tarquin, and leader in expelling him ; consul in the first year of the republic. Liv. 2, 1.

(2) *Decimus Iūnius Brūtus,* consul 138 B.C. As proconsul of Further Spain he gained important victories, for which he celebrated a splendid triumph, 136 B.C. Arch. 11.

(3) *Decimus Iūnius Brūtus Albīnus,* who served under Caesar in

Gaul and later in the Civil War. Afterwards he joined the conspiracy against Caesar's life, and conducted the Dictator to the Senate-house on the day of the assassination. After Caesar's death he obtained Cisalpine Gaul as a province, and refused to give it up to Antonius. When Octavianus prepared to wreak vengeance on the murderers of Caesar, Brutus attempted to escape into Macedonia, but was betrayed by a Gallic chief and put to death by order of Antonius, 43 B.C. EP. 24; 25.

(4) *Marcus Iunius Brutus,* the friend of Cassius and Cicero, born 85 B.C. In the Civil War he joined the side of Pompey, but was pardoned by Caesar, and was one of the assassins that took Caesar's life. He joined with Cassius in gathering an army against Antonius and Octavianus. In the first engagement at Philippi, 42 B.C., Brutus came off victorious. But three weeks later he suffered a complete defeat and put an end to his life by falling on his sword. EP. 25.

bucca, -ae, f., *cheek; declaimer; trumpeteer.*

bucula, -ae, [dim. of **bos,** *ox, cow*], f., *heifer, young cow.*

bulla, -ae, f., *water-bubble, bubble; boss, knob* (upon a door); *stud* (in a girdle).

bustum, -i, [**buro,** obsol. form of **uro**], n., *place of burning and burying; funeral pyre; mound, tomb, grave.*

Buthrotum, -i, [βουθρωτόν], n., *Buthrotum,* a town on the coast of Epirus, opposite Corcyra.

C

C., see **Gaius.**

cadaver, -eris, [akin to **cado**], n., *dead body, corpse, carcass.*

cado, cadere, cecidi, casum, 3, n., *fall, fall down; fall away, fall dead, die, be slain, perish; fall under, be subject to; fall to the lot of, befall, happen.*

caducus, -a, -um, [**cado**], adj., *inclined to fall, falling; perishable, transitory, frail, fleeting.*

Caecilius, -a, the name of a Roman gens. See **Statius, Plinius.**

caedes, -is, [cf. **caedo**], f., *slaughter, massacre, carnage, murder.*

caedo, -ere, cecidi, caesum, [causative of **cado**], 3, a., *cut, hew, cut down, fell; cut off, cut to pieces; strike upon, knock at, beat, strike, cudgel; kill, murder, slay, slaughter; vanquish, destroy.*

caelestis, -e, [**caelum**], adj., *of heaven, heavenly, celestial.* As subst., **caelestes, -ium,** m., pl., *heaven-dwellers, the gods.* **ordo caelestis,** *order of the heavenly bodies.*

Caelius, -a, the name of a Roman gens. *Caelius Vinicianus,* tribune in 53 B.C., followed Caesar's cause in the Civil War. EP. 11.

caelum, -i, n., *sky, heaven, heavens; the skies; air, atmosphere, climate, weather.* **in caelum,** *to the skies.* **de caelo percelli,** *to be struck by lightning.*

Caeparius, -i or **-ii,** [**caepe,** *onion*], m., *M. Caeparius,* an acquaintance of Cicero; nothing further is known about him. EP. 20.

Caesar, -aris, m., name of a prominent family in the Julian gens, of which four members are mentioned in this book:

(1) *Gaius Iūlius Caesar,* the Dictator, born 100 B.C., assassinated March 15, 44 B.C.

(2) *L. Iūlius Caesar,* consul 64 B.C., uncle of Mark Antony, whose course after the death of the Dictator he opposed. CAT. **4,** 6; EP. 1.

(3) *Gaius Iūlius Caesar Octāviānus,* see **Octāviānus.**

(4) *L. Iūlius Caesar Strabō,* consul with P. Rutilius 90 B.C., censor with P. Crassus the following year; killed by Cinna. ARCH 5.

Caesariānus, -a, -um, [Caesar], adj., *of Caesar, Caesar's.*

Caiēta, -ae, [Καιήτη], f., *Caiēta,* a sea-coast town, with a harbor, in the southwestern part of Latium.

calamitās, -ātis, f., *loss, damage, hurt; calamity, misfortune, ruin, disaster, adversity.*

calamitōsus, -a, -um, [calamitās], adj., *causing loss, ruinous, destructive, disastrous, pernicious, calamitous; suffering loss; unfortunate, miserable, unhappy.*

calidus, comp. **calidior,** [cf. caleō, *be warm*], adj., *warm, hot; fiery, eager, spirited; fierce, impassioned, vehement; hasty, inconsiderate, rash.*

cālīgō, -inis, f., *thick air, mist, vapor, darkness, obscurity; confusion, ignorance; calamity, affliction.*

callidus, -a, -um, [calleō], adj., *skillful, shrewd; crafty, cunning, artful.*

calor, -ōris, [cf. caleō, *be warm*], m., *warmth, heat, glow.*

Calpurnius, -a, the name of a distinguished gens at Rome. Two women of the name are mentioned in this book:

(1) *Calpurnia Hispulla,* aunt of Pliny's wife. PLIN. 8.

(2) *Calpurnia,* wife of the younger Pliny and niece of the preceding. PLIN. 8, 11.

calumnia, -ae, f., *trickery, cunning; pretense, evasion; misrepresentation; false accusation, malicious charge, false prosecution; underhand tactics, intrigues.*

Calvisius, -ī or **-iī,** m., *C. Calvisius Rūfus,* friend and correspondent of the younger Pliny. PLIN. 15.

calx, -cis, f., *heel; limestone, chalk, lime; goal of the race course.*

camera, -ae, f., *vault, arched roof, arch, arched ceiling.*

Campānia, -ae, f., *Campānia,* the coast region south of Latium, with capital at Capua. PLIN. 11.

campus, -ī, m., *plain, level field, open field;* often = **Campus Mārtius,** *the Campus Mārtius,* a grassy open space in the northwestern part of Rome, along the Tiber and outside the Servian Wall, where the people met for reviews and elections by centuries.

candidus, -a, -um, [candeō, *shine, glitter*], adj., *shining, white, clear, bright; splendid, beautiful, comely; clothed in white; pure, guileless; honest, sincere; frank, candid; happy, prosperous.*

canō, canere, cecinī, cantum, [for casnō, from root cas, *sing*], 3, a. and n., *sing, make music, play; sing of, celebrate;* as prophecies were given in verse, *foretell, predict.*

canōrus, -a, -um, [canor, *melody*], adj., *tuneful.*

cantō, -āre, -āvī, -ātum [freq. of canō], 1, a. and n., *sing, play.*

cantus, -ūs, [canō], m., *singing, playing; song, music.*

cānus, -a, -um, adj., *white, hoary, gray; old, venerable.* As subst., cānī [sc. capillī], -ōrum, m. pl., *gray hairs.*

capāx, -ācis, [capiō], adj., *able to hold; containing much, large, spacious, roomy; capacious; capable of, fit for, able, apt.*

capessō, -ere, -īvī or -iī, -ītum, [capiō], 3, a., *seize eagerly, lay hold of; betake oneself to, repair to; take hold of with zeal, take up, undertake; execute, manage.* capessere rem pūblicam, *to take an active part in the government.* capessere fugam, *to take to flight.*

capillus, -ī, [cf. caput], m., *hair of the head, the hair.*

capiō, capere, cēpī, captum, 3, a., *take, lay hold of, seize, grasp; get possession of, master, control; capture, storm, reduce; captivate, win; deceive, betray, catch; harm, deprive of; suffer, experience; receive, entertain; enter upon, undertake; accept, gain, enjoy, reap; take in, comprehend, grasp; hold, be large enough for.*

capitālis, -e, [caput], adj., *of the head, foremost; involving life, capital: deadly, dangerous, bane-ful.* rēs capitālis, *an offense punishable with death.*

Capitōlīnus, -a, -um, adj., *of the Capitol, Capitoline.* collis Capitōlīnus, the Capitol proper, on the summit of the Capitoline hill, on which the temple of Jupiter was built; used also for the whole hill.

Capitōlium, ī or iī, [caput], n., (1) in a narrower sense, *the Capitol,* a temple on Mons Saturnius dedicated by the Tarquinii to Jupiter, Juno, and Minerva, afterwards made the most splendid temple at Rome; very often, (2) *the Capitoline Hill, the Capitoline,* the hill on which the Capitol stood, which contained also the citadel of Rome.

Cappadocia, -ae, [Καππαδοκία], f., *Cappadocia,* an extensive country of Asia Minor lying south of the Euxine Sea, north of Cilicia, and west of the upper course of the Euphrates.

capra, -ae, [caper, *he-goat*], f., *she-goat.* Caprae Palūs, *Goat Swamp,* a marsh near Rome. LIV. 1, 16.

Capua, -ae f., *Capua,* an ancient and luxurious city of Campania, 136 miles southeast of Rome.

caput, -itis, n., *head;* by metonymy, *person, being, life, soul;* of elevation, *top, summit;* of streams, *source, fountain-head;* of plants, *tops, heads;* of civil rights, *citizenship;* of writings. *chapter, passage, point;* of things in general, *chief thing, principal thing.*

Carbō, -ōnis, m., *Carbō*, name of a plebeian family of the Papirian gens; in this book there are mentioned two of the name: (1) *Gaius Papirius Carbō* was born 164 B.C., and died in 119. He was a strong partisan of Tiberius Gracchus, and after the latter's death was nominated one of the three commissioners for carrying out the Sempronian land-law. He was tribune in 131 B.C., and was suspected of being concerned in the death of Scipio. After the death of C. Gracchus he deserted the popular party, and as consul in 120 B.C., undertook the defense of Opimius, the murderer of Gracchus. In 119 he put an end to his own life. AM. 12.

(2) *C. Papirius Carbō Arvīna*, tribune 90 B.C. or 89. He joined with his colleague M. Plautius Silvanus in proposing a law on citizenship, which was afterwards known as the *Lēx Plautia Papiria*. ARCH. 4.

carcer, -eris, m., *prison, dungeon, place of confinement;* by metonymy, of a race-course, usually pl., **carcerēs, -um,** *starting-places, barriers.*

careō, -ēre, -uī, fut. part. **caritūrus,** 2, n., *be without, not have; do without, abstain from, keep from, hold aloof from; want, lack, be deprived of;* usually with abl.

cāritās, -ātis, [**cārus**], f., *dearness, high price; love, affection.*

carmen, -inis, [for **casmen,** from root **cas,** *sing,* found in **ca(s)nō**], n., *song, strain of music; poem,*

verse, hymn; form of prayer, antiphon, liturgy; as oracular responses and incantations were in verse, *response* of an oracle, *prophecy, incantation, charm;* also *metrical inscription, inscription in verse.*

carpō, -ere, carpsī, carptum, 3, a., *pick, pluck, cull, crop, gather; browse, graze on; tear off; gnaw at, tear; censure, carp at, slander, revile; wear away, destroy; harass, inflict injury on; cut to pieces.* **sinistrīs sermōnibus carpere,** *to slander, make insinuating remarks.*

cārus, -a, -um, adj., *dear, precious, valued; esteemed, beloved; affectionate; costly.*

cāseus, -ī, (probably a Celtic word), *cheese.*

Cassius, -a, -um, adj., *of Cassius, Cassian.* **lēx Cassia,** *bill of Cassius;* esp., that carried by L. Cassius in 137 B.C., which extended the ballot to the juries in the criminal courts. AM. 12.

Cassius, -a, name of a prominent Roman gens. Two Cassii are mentioned in this book:

(1) *L. Cassius Longīnus*, a competitor of Cicero for the consulship for 63 B.C.; afterwards prominent in the conspiracy of Catiline, in which he asked to be assigned the burning of Rome as his part. He also conducted negotiations with the Allobroges, but escaped arrest. His fate is unknown. CAT. 3, 4, *et seq.*

(2) *C. Cassius Longīnus Vārus*, consul 73 B.C., proconsul in Cis-

alpine Gaul the following year.
IMP. P. 23.

castē [castus], adv., *without spot, purely, virtuously; piously, religiously.*

castīgātōrius, -a, -um, [castīgātor, *reprover*], adj., *relating to chastisement* or *reproof; implying reproof.*

castitās, -ātis, [castus, *pure*], f., *purity, chastity.*

castrēnsis, -e, [castra], adj., *of camp, in camp;* of a military movement, *with a camp,* i.e. *open,* as opposed to treacherous or secret operations.

castrum, -ī, n., *fortress, castle.* Pl. **castra, -ōrum,** *camp, encampment.*

cāsus, -ūs, [cadō], m., lit. *falling, fall; happening, accident, event, occurrence; chance, emergency; destruction; mishap, misfortune, calamity.*

catēna, -ae, f., *chain, fetter, shackle; constraint, fetter, bond.*

Catīlius, -a, a Roman cognomen. *Catīlius Sevērus,* a young friend of Pliny, later proconsul of Asia and governor of Syria under Hadrian. PLIN. 6.

Catilīna, -ae, m., *L. Sergius Catilīna, Catiline,* originator of a dangerous conspiracy suppressed by Cicero, who pronounced against him the famous Catilinarian orations. CAT. **1, 2, 3, 4**; EP. 1; PHIL. 5; SALL. 5, *et seq.*

Catō, -ōnis, [catus, *shrewd*], m.. *Cato,* name of a noted family of the Porcian gens. Four Catos are mentioned in this book:

(1) *M. Porcius Catō,* known as *Cato the Elder,* or *Cato the Censor;* born 234 B.C. at Tusculum,

14 miles southeast of Rome; dieu 149 B.C. He was eminent as a general, statesman, orator, and writer. He was considered by Romans of later times as the ideal of Roman character. His treatise "On Farming" is extant; only fragments of his other writings are preserved. ARCH. 7, 9; SEN. 1, *et seq.;* AM. 6, *et al.*

(2) *Mārcus Porcius Catō,* son of Cato the Censor by his first wife. He distinguished himself greatly in the battle of Pydna and was highly praised by Aemilius Paulus, whose daughter he afterwards married. He died while filling the office of praetor. SEN. 6, 23.

(3) *Porcius Catō,* a friend of Archias. It is uncertain what Cato this was; but probably it was *M. Porcius Catō,* father of Cato Uticensis. ARCH. 3.

(4) *M. Porcius Catō Uticēnsis,* so named from Utica in Africa, the place of his death; born 95 B.C. In the midst of an active public life he was a consistent adherent of the stoic philosophy. Accepting a commission from Pompey in the war with Caesar, he proved a failure as an officer. Finding himself in straits he preferred suicide to surrender and fell on his sword 46 B.C. ARCH. 9; SALL. 52, *et seq.;* PLIN. 6.

Catulus, -ī, m., name of a family of the Lutatian gens, of which two members are mentioned in this book:

(1) *Q. Lutātius Catulus,* consul with C. Marius 102 B.C., when

the poet Archias came to Rome. ARCH. 3; VERR. 57.

(2) *Q. Lutātius Catulus,* son of the preceding, consul 78 B.C. He was prominent as a leader of the aristocratic party, and was a man of fine character. He opposed the Gabinian and Manilian laws, but supported Cicero warmly against the Catilinarian conspirators. He died 60 B.C. CAT. 3, 10; IMP. P. 22; ARCH. 3.

causa, -ae, f., *cause, reason; pretext, excuse, motive; condition, case, situation; lawsuit, judicial process; side, faction.* **causā** with preceding gen., *for the sake of, on account of.* **causam dīcere,** *to plead a cause.* **per causam,** *under the pretext.* **per hanc causam,** *under this pretext, with this as pretext.* **meā causā,** *on my account, for my sake.* **vītandae suspīciōnis causā,** *in order to avoid suspicion.*

cautiō, -ōnis, [caveō], f., *watchfulness, precaution; safety, security.*

caveō, cavēre, cāvī, cautum, 2, a. and n., *be on one's guard, beware of; take precautions against, guard against, take heed;* as a legal term, *provide, order, decree;* with dat. of person, *protect, take care of.* **id cautum est,** *this precaution was taken.* **cavēre ab illīs,** *to be on guard against those men.*

-ce, an enclitic particle, with demonstrative force (like colloquial English *here, there,* with *this* or *that*) appended to many pronom. words.

cēdō, cēdere, cessī, cessum, 3, a. and n., *go away, retire, retreat; yield, give place to; submit, comply; be inferior to; conform to, concede.*

celeber, -ĕbris, -ĕbre, adj., *frequented, crowded, thronged with;* hence *honored* by the presence of many, *renowned, famous, celebrated, distinguished.*

celebritās, -ātis, [celeber], f., *crowd, throng, multitude; publicity, fame, renown, celebrity.*

celebrō, -āre, -āvī, -ātum, [celeber], 1, a., *crowd, fill, throng, frequent; practice, engage in, repeat; celebrate, solemnize; praise; honor; render famous, make known, publish abroad.*

celeritās, -ātis, [celer], f., *swiftness, speed, quickness.*

celeriter, comp. **celerius,** sup. **celerrimē,** [celer], adv., *swiftly, quickly, speedily; in haste, immediately.*

cella, -ae, [for cērula, dim. from cēra, *cell in a beehive*], f., *place of concealment, store-room, cell, granary.* **cella vīnāria,** *wine cellar.*

cēlō, -āre, -āvī, -ātum, 1, a., *hide from, keep ignorant of, conceal from; elude; hide, cover, keep secret.*

Celsus, -ī, m., *Celsus,* a celebrated Roman writer on medicine, whose full name was *A. Cornēlius Celsus.* He flourished during the first half of the first century, A.D.

cēna, -ae, f., *dinner,* the principal meal of the Romans, in early times taken at noon, afterwards later in the day.

cēnō, -āre, -āvī, -ātum, [cēna], 1,
a. and n., *dine, eat dinner.*

cēnseō, cēnsēre, cēnsuī, cēnsum,
2, a., *assess, rate, estimate; be of
the opinion, propose, vote, urge;
suppose, imagine, think, believe;
decide, determine.* ita cēnseō, *I
make this motion.* cēnseō, *I am
of the opinion.*

cēnsor, -ōris, [cēnseō], m., *censor,*
title of a Roman magistrate. At
Rome there were two censors,
who had charge of the registration lists, the valuation and assessment of property, the farming of certain revenues and the
letting of contracts for public
works. They were chosen every
five years, and served eighteen
months.

cēnsus, -ūs, [cēnseō], m., *registration* of citizens and of property,
enrollment, appraisement, census;
by metonymy, *register of the census, registration list.*

Centō, -ōnis, m., *C. Claudius Centō,*
son of Appius Claudius Caecus
who built the Appian Way,
consul 240 B.C., interrex 217.
SEN. 14.

centum, indecl. num., *a hundred.*

centuria, -ae, [centum], f., *division
of one hundred, century,* a division recognized in the civil as
well as in the military organization of the Romans. The assembly of the people by centuries
was called comitia centuriāta.

centuriātus, -ūs, [centuriō], m.,
*office of centurion, centurion-
ship.*

centuriō, -āre, -āvī, -ātum, [cen-
turia], 1, a., *divide into centuries,*

organize in companies, organize;
used of the organization of infantry.

Cēpārius, -ī or -iī, m., *M. Cēpārius,*
one of the Catilinarian conspirators, from Tarracina. He had
just left Rome in order to stir up
an insurrection among the shepherds of Apulia when he was
arrested and placed in custody.
He was executed with the other
conspirators 63 B.C. CAT. 3, 6;
SALL. 55.

cēra, -ae, f., *wax; writing-tablet,* a
leaf of wood covered with wax;
notebook; seal.

Cerēs, -eris, f., *Cerēs,* the goddess
of grain, identified among the
Romans with the Greek Demeter. *Cerēs* was regarded as
the protectress of agriculture
and of all the fruits of the
earth.

cernō, cernere, crēvī, crētum, 3, a.,
separate in observation, *distinguish, discern, make out; perceive,
see, behold; comprehend, understand;* of judicial or legisla-
tive acts, *decide, decree, resolve.*
animō cernere, *to see in fancy,
see in imagination*

certāmen, -inis, [certō], n., *contest*
to decide a matter, *conflict, struggle, battle, combat, strife; dispute,
dissension; match, trial* of
strength or skill; *rivalry, ambition* to excel, *competition.* certāmine īrārum, *in the heat of
passion.* certāmina serere, *to
sow the seeds of strife.*

certātim, [certō, *vie with*], adv.,
*emulously, zealously, with compe-
tition, earnestly, eagerly.*

certē, comp. certius, [certus], adv.,
surely, certainly, really; at least,
yet surely, yet certainly.

certō [certus], adv., with certainty,
certainly, surely, really, in fact,
positively.

certō, -āre, -āvī, -ātum, [certus],
1, n., vie with, either as an enemy or as a friend; fight, contend, struggle, combat; strive;
rival, compete, emulate.

certus, -a, -um, [old part. of cernō],
adj., certain, fixed, decided, settled; definite, special, particular;
confident, trustworthy, reliable,
sure; unerring, conclusive. illum
certiōrem facere, to inform him.
dē certā causā, for a definite reason. certior factus, having been
informed. certior fierī, to be informed. spēs certissima, most
positive hope. prō certō, for certain, positively. prō certō habēre, to regard as assured. certus
fugae, determined on flight.

cervīcal, -ālis, [cervīx], n., pillow,
cushion.

cervīx, -īcis, f., neck, throat.

cēterum, [acc. n. sing. of cēterus],
adv., for the rest, in other respects,
else, otherwise; besides; but yet,
notwithstanding, still, on the other
hand; but however.

cēterus, -a, -um, nom. sing. m. not
in use, adj., other, the other, rest,
remainder; pl., the rest, all other,
the other. As subst., pl., m.,
cēterī, -ōrum, the others, all the
rest, everyone else; n., cētera,
-ōrum, the rest, all else, everything
else.

Cethēgus, -ī, m., name of a patrician family of the Cornelian

gens. This book has mention of
two members of this family:
(1) M. Cethēgus, censor 209
B.C., consul 204, was distinguished for his eloquence and his
correctness in the use of Latin
words. Cicero calls him the
first Roman orator. SEN. 14.
(2) C. Cornēlius Cethēgus, one
of the boldest and most dangerous of the Catilinarian conspirators. He joined the conspiracy
on account of debts contracted
in profligate living, and was
assigned the task of murdering
the principal senators. He was
arrested, convicted on the evidence of weapons found at his
house and of his letter to the Allobroges, and condemned along
with the other conspirators.
CAT. 3, 3; SALL. 32; 55.

Chīlō, -ōnis, [χίλων], m., Q. Annius
Chīlō, a Roman involved in the
conspiracy of Catiline. No particulars about his life are known.
CAT. 3, 6.

Chīus, -a, -um, [Χῖος], adj., Chian,
of Chios, an island off the west
coast of Asia Minor. As subst.,
Chiī, -ōrum, m., pl., the people of
Chios, the Chians. ARCH. 8.

Chrīstiānus, -a, -um, [Chrīstus],
Christian, relating to Christianity. As subst., Chrīstiānus, -ī,
m., a Christian.

Chrīstus, -ī, m., Christ.

cibus, -ī, m., food, victuals, nutri-
ment; sustenance.

Cicerō, -ōnis, [cicer, chickpea], m.,
name of a family in the Tullian
gens. Three Ciceros are mentioned in this book:

(1) *M. Tullius Cicerō*, the orator and writer. See Companion, page 485.

(2) *Q. Tullius Cicerō*, brother of the orator; born about 102 B.C. He served with distinction under Caesar in Gaul, and held several offices. In the Civil War he went over to the side of Pompey, but after the battle of Pharsalia he quarreled with his brother and came to terms with Caesar. A reconciliation was soon effected, however, and Quintus was put to death in the proscription of the triumvirs, 43 B.C. Ep. 3; 11; 21.

(3) *M. Tullius Cicerō*, son of the orator and Terentia; born 65 B.C. He was not a strong character, but had an eventful life, being finally admitted by Octavianus as a colleague in the consulship, 30 B.C. Ep. 3; 11; 13; 14.

cieō, -ēre, cīvī, citum, 2, a., *cause to go, move, stir, drive; disturb, rouse, summon, call, appeal to, excite, enliven; produce, cause, occasion, beget.* **pugnam ciēre,** *begin the fight, put spirit into a fight.*

Cilicēs, -um, m. pl., *the Cilicians, people of Cilicia.*

Cilicia, -ae, [Κιλικία], f., *Cilicia,* a Roman province in the southern part of Asia Minor.

Cimber, -brī, m., see **Gabinius.**

Cimbricus, -a, -um, [Cimbrī], adj., *of the Cimbri, Cimbrian.*

Cincinnātus, -ī, m., *L. Quīnctius Cincinnātus,* twice dictator (458 and 439 B.C.), and finest type of

the old Roman simplicity and patriotism. He lived on his farm, cultivating the land with his own hands. He was appointed dictator the second time in order to oppose the alleged machinations of Spurius Maelius. Sen. 16.

cingō, -ere, cīnxī, cīnctum, 3, a., *surround, enclose; gird, wreathe, gird on;* of places, *surround, encircle, invest, beset, besiege.*

cinis, -eris, [cf. κόνις, *dust, ashes*], m., *ashes, embers;* of the dead, *ashes,* the remains left after cremation.

Cinna, -ae, m., in this book *L. Cornēlius Cinna,* an unprincipled demagogue who became a leader of the popular party during Sulla's absence in the east, 87–84 B.C., and joined with Marius in the massacre of the aristocracy. He was slain in a mutiny of the forces which he had collected in order to meet Sulla, 84 B.C. Phil. 8.

circā, adv. and prep., *about:*
(1) adv., *around, round about, all around, near.*
(2) prep. with acc. only, of space and time, *about, around, surrounding, encompassing; about, among, through; near to, near by; nearly, almost; on both sides.*

Circēnsis, -e, [Circus], adj., *of or relating to the Circus.* As subst., **Circēnsēs** [sc. **Lūdī**], **-ium,** m. pl., *the Circensian Games* (contests held in the Circus Maximus).

circiter [circus], adv. and prep. with acc., *about, not far from, near.*

circum [acc. of circus, circle], adv. and prep. :

(1) As adv., about, around, round about.

(2) As prep., with acc., around, about, all around; among, through; in the neighborhood of. near, near by.

circumagō, -ere, -ēgī, -āctum, [circum + agō], 3, a., drive in a circle, turn round; turn about, turn, wheel around; with se or pass., pass away, be spent, elapse, revolve.

circumclūdō, -clūdere, -clūsī, -clūsum, [circum + claudō], 3, a., shut in, enclose; hem in, surround.

circumdō, -dare, -dedī, -datum, [circum + dō], 1, a., put around, place about; surround, encircle, besiege.

circumscrībō, -scrībere, -scrīpsī, -scrīptum, [circum + scrībō], 3, a., encircle, limit, bound, circumscribe; cheat; cancel, set aside.

circumscrīptor, -ōris, [circumscrībō], m., defrauder, cheat.

circumspiciō, -spicere, -spexī, -spectum, [circum + speciō], 3, a. and n., look about; survey, observe; be cautious, exercise caution; ponder, consider; look for, seek after.

circumstō, -stāre, -stetī, ——, [circum + stō], 1, a. and n., stand around; surround; be at hand, threaten; as a military term, surround, besiege, beset.

circumveniō, -īre, -vēnī, -ventum, [circum + veniō], 4, a., come around, be around, encircle, surround; beset; oppress; afflict, overthrow; deceive, defraud; en-

snare, entrap, entangle in difficulties, attack.

citerior, -ōris, sup. citimus, [citer from cis], adj., on this side, on the nearer or hither side; nearer, next. citerior Gallia, hither Gaul.

cithara, -ae, f., cithara, cither, guitar, lute. See illustration, page 452.

cito, comp. citius, sup. citissimē, [citus], adv., quickly, speedily, soon.

citrō, [dat. of citer, from cis, on this side], adv., in this direction, to this side, towards the inside; only in the phrase ultrō citrōque, hither and thither, this way and that, here and there, to and fro, backwards and forwards, reciprocally.

cīvīlis, -e, [cīvis], adj., of a citizen, of citizens, civil, civic; political, public.

cīvis, -is, m. or f., citizen, fellow-citizen.

cīvitās, -ātis, [cīvis], f., citizenship; community of citizens, state, commonwealth. cīvitātem alicui dare, to grant citizenship to anyone, bestow the franchise on anyone. post cīvitātem datam, after the granting of citizenship, after the franchise was granted.

clādēs, -is, f., destruction, injury, mishap, harm, misfortune, disaster; slaughter; defeat, overthrow, massacre; calamity. suīs clādibus, at the risk of personal ruin.

clam, adv. and prep., secretly, in secret.

clāmitō, -āre, -āvī, -ātum, [clāmō], 1, a. and n., cry aloud, bawl, *vociferate; proclaim, reveal, betray.*

clāmō, -āre, -āvī, -ātum, 1, a. and n., *cry out, shout, exclaim; call upon, invoke; proclaim, declare.*

clāmor, -ōris, [clāmō], m., *loud cry, outcry, shout; din, uproar; acclamation, applause; war-shout; sound, noise.*

clandestīnus, -a, -um, [clam], adj., *secret, hidden, concealed, clandestine.*

clārē, comp. clārius, sup. clārissimē, [clārus], adv., *brightly; distinctly, plainly, clearly; illustriously, honorably, splendidly; in loud tones, aloud.*

clāritās, -ātis, [clārus], f., *brightness, clearness, fame, splendor.*

clārus, -a, -um, adj., *clear, bright, shining; distinct, manifest, plain; renowned, noble, illustrious, honored, famous.*

classis, -is, f., *fleet.*

Claudius, -a, name of a Roman gens with both patrician and plebeian branches. See **Centō, Mārcellus, Pulcher.**

claudō, claudere, clausī, clausum, 3, a., *shut, shut up, close; bring to a close, finish, end; shut in, invest, besiege.*

clāvus, -ī, m., *nail; rudder, helm, tiller; purple stripe.*

Cleanthēs, -is, m., *Cleanthēs,* a Stoic philosopher (fl. 263 B.C.), pupil and successor of Zeno. SEN. 7.

clēmēns, -entis, adj., *mild, calm; gentle, kind, forbearing.*

clēmenter [clēmēns], adv., *calmly, mildly; gently, kindly, with forbearance.*

clēmentia, -ae, [clēmēns], f., *mildness, forbearance, clemency.*

cliēns, -entis, gen. pl. clientium, m., *personal dependent, client,* a freeman protected by a patron; he received from him an allotment of land or food, and accompanied him in war; *client, retainer, follower; companion, favorite; vassal.*

Clōdius, a form of the name **Claudius**; in this book = *P. Clōdius Pulcher,* a bitter enemy of Cicero. He was killed in a skirmish between his followers and those of Milo near Bovillae, Jan. 20, 52 B.C. EP. 1; 4; PROV. CONS. 20.

Cn., see **Gnaeus.**

Cnidius, -a, -um, [Cnidus], adj., *of* or *pertaining to Cnidus,* a city in Caria; *Cnidian.* As subst., **Cnidiī, -ōrum, m. pl.,** *the people of Cnidus.* VERR. 60.

Cnidus or **Cnidos, -ī, [Κνίδος], f.,** *Cnidus,* a city in Caria, in the extreme southwestern part of Asia Minor.

coāctus, see **cōgō.**

coaedificō, -āre, ――, -ātum, [com- + aedificō], 1, a., *build up, build upon; build together, build and join, join* (in building).

cōdicillī, -ōrum, [dim. of cōdex, *account book, ledger*]**, m. pl.,** *writing tablet, notebook; note, petition, will.*

coëmō, -ere, -ēmī, -ēmptum, [com- + emō], 3, a., *purchase, buy up.*

coëō, -īre, -īvī or -iī, -itum, [com- + eō], irr., n., *go together, come together, meet, assemble, collect; join in battle, encounter; gather,* *unite, combine; agree; ally one-self, conspire.*

coepiō, -ere, coepī, coeptum, pres. not found in classical Latin, def., a. and n., *begin, commence.* Part. **coeptus, -a, -um,** *commenced, begun, undertaken.*

coërceō, -cēre, -cuī, -citum, [com- + arceō], 2, a., *confine* on all sides, *hold together, shut in, encompass; restrain, repress, hold, control, curb.*

coetus, -ūs, [coëō], m., *assembly, company; crowd, meeting.*

cōgitātē [cōgitātus, from cōgitō], adv., *with reflection, thoughtfully.*

cōgitātiō, -ōnis, [cōgitō], f., *reflection, meditation; thought, reasoning, imagination.*

cōgitō, -āre, -āvī, -ātum, [com- + agitō], 1, a., *consider thoroughly, think over, ponder, reflect upon; meditate, design, plan, purpose, plot.* **cōgitat hōc facere,** *he is thinking of doing this.* **aliquid amplum cōgitāre,** *to entertain some noble sentiment.*

cognātiō, -ōnis, [cognātus], f., *kinship, relationship; connection, affinity.*

cognātus, -ī, [com- + nāscor, generated along with], m., *kinsman, blood-relation.*

cognitiō, -ōnis, [cognōscō], f., *a becoming acquainted with, knowledge, acquaintance;* as a legal term, *investigation, inquiry, trial.*

cognitor, -ōris, [cognōscō], m., *attorney, advocate; defender, protector, supporter.*

cognitus, -a, -um, [part. of cognōscō], adj., *known, acknowledged, approved.*

cognōmen, -inis, [cf. cognōscō], n., *family name, surname; name.*

cognōscō, -ere, cognōvī, cognitum, [com- + (g)nōscō], 3, inch. a., *become acquainted with; learn, ascertain, know thoroughly; know; examine, inquire into, investigate; recognize, identify, acknowledge; appreciate.*

cōgō, cōgere, coēgī, coāctum, [com- + agō], 3, a., *drive together; collect, gather together, assemble; urge, oblige, constrain, compel, force.* **cōgere senātum,** *to convene the senate.*

cohaereō, -ēre, cohaesī, cohaesum, [com- + haereō], 2, n., *cling together, be united; be closely connected with.*

cohibeō, -ēre, -uī, -itum, [com- + habeō], 2, a., *hold together, confine, contain; hold in check, restrain, repress, subdue.*

cohors, -hortis, f., *enclosure, yard; crowd, company, throng, multitude;* as a military term, *cohort, battalion,* the tenth part of a legion; also, *staff* of a general, *body-guard, retinue.* **cohors praetōria,** *general's body-guard.*

cohortātiō, -ōnis, [cohortor], f., *an exhorting, inciting, exhortation, encouragement.*

cohortor, -ārī, -ātus sum, [com- + hortor], 1, dep., *encourage, admonish, exhort, urge on, address.*

collātiō, -ōnis, [collātus, from cōnferō], f., *bringing together; hostile meeting, collision; contribution, collection; comparison.*

collēga, -ae, [cf. colligō, unite], m., *associate in office, colleague.*

collēgium, -ī or -iī, [cf. collēga], n., *association in office, colleagueship; association, corporation, society, college.*

colligō, -ere, collēgī, collēctum, [com- + legō], 3, a., *gather, bring together, collect, assemble; acquire, incur; deduce, infer.*

collis, -is, m., *hill, height, elevation.*

collocō, -āre, -āvī, -ātum, [com- + locō], 1, a., *set right, place, set, put, arrange; set up, erect; locate, station;* of money, *invest, lay out.* pecūniās collocātās habēre, *to have sums of money invested.*

collocūtiō, -ōnis, [colloquor, *speak with*], f., *conversation, conference, talk; familiar talk, chat.*

colloquium, -ī or -iī, [colloquor], n., *conversation, discourse, conference.*

collum, -ī, m., *neck.*

colluviō, -ōnis, [colluō, *moisten*], f., *filth* or *dirt* occasioned by a conflux of different impurities; *washings, sweepings, dregs, impurities, offscourings.*

colō, colere, coluī, cultum, 3, a. and n., *till, cultivate; stay at, abide in, dwell in, inhabit; care for, cherish, esteem, love, favor;* of the gods, and the services of religion, *honor, worship, revere, reverence;* of pursuits or virtues, *follow, seek, practice, devote oneself to, adhere to, cherish.*

Colōnēus, -a, -um, adj., *one at* or *from Colonos* (a town near Athens). Oedipus Colōnēus, *Oedipus at Colonos,* the title of a tragedy by Sophocles. SEN. 7.

colōnia, -ae, [colōnus], f., *colony, settlement.*

colōnus, -ī, [colō], m., *husbandman, tiller of the soil;* by metonymy, *colonist, settler.*

Colophōn, -ōnis, [Κολοφών], m., *Colophōn,* a city in the western part of Asia Minor, north of Ephesus.

Colophōnius, -a, -um, [Colophōn]. adj., *of Colophon.* As subst., Colophōniī, -ōrum, m., pl., *the people of Colophon, the Colophonians.*

color, -ōris, m., *color, tint, hue; complexion; appearance, coloring.*

com-, prep., old form of cum ; found only in composition. See cum.

comes, -itis, [com- + eō], m. or f., *companion, associate, comrade, mate; intimate; attendant, retainer, dependant.*

cōmicus, -a, -um, adj., *of comedy, comic, in the comic style; represented in comedy.*

cōmitās, -ātis, [cōmis, *courteous*], f., *courtesy, kindness, affability, gentleness, politeness.*

comitātus, -ūs, [comitor], m., *escort, train, retinue; company, band, crowd.*

comitia, -ōrum, [pl. of comitium], n. pl., *assembly of the people, assembly, election* by the people in assembly. comitia cōnsulāria, *assembly for electing consuls, consular election.*

comitium, -ī or -iī, [com- + eō], n., *place of meeting;* at Rome, *the Comitium,* an open place north of the Forum, where assemblies were held.

commemorātiō, -ōnis, [commemorō], f., *calling to mind, reminding; remembrance, reminder.*

commemorō, -āre, -āvī, -ātum, [com- + memorō], 1, a., *call to mind, keep in mind, remember; bring to mind, recall; relate, recount, mention.*

commendātiō, -ōnis, [commendō], f., *commending, recommendation; that which recommends, excellence, worth.*

commendō, -āre, -āvī, -ātum, [com- + mandō], 1, a., *commit for safe keeping, intrust, confide; commend, recommend, ask favor for.*

commentum, -ī, [comminīscor, contrive], n., *invention, pretense, falsehood; embellishment.*

commercium, -ī or -iī, [com- + merx, wares], n., *commercial intercourse, trade; intercourse, fellowship, communication.* commercium habēre cum aliquō, *have relations with anybody.*

comminus, [com- + manus], adv., *in close contest, hand to hand, at close quarters.*

committō, committere, -mīsī, -missum, [com- + mittō], 3, a., *bring together, combine, put together, unite;* of military engagements, *set together, engage in, fight, carry on, wage; intrust, commit; expose; commit* a crime, *perpetrate, be guilty of, do, practice.*

commodē [commodus], adv., *properly, skillfully; conveniently, suitably, comfortably.* parum commodē, *badly.*

commoditās, -ātis, [commodus, convenient], f., *fitness, convenience; fit occasion; advantage, benefit;* of persons, *complaisance, courtesy, forbearance.*

commodō, -āre, -āvī, -ātum, [commodus], 1, a. and n., *supply, furnish, grant, lend.*

commodum, -ī, [commodus], n., *convenience, opportune moment; advantage, interest, gain; emolument.*

commodus, -a, -um, [com- + modus], adj., *with due measure, complete; suitable, fit; useful, pleasant, obliging; polite, gentle.*

commoror, -ārī, -ātus sum, [com- + moror], 1, dep., *linger, stay, tarry, remain, stay temporarily.*

commoveō, -movēre, -mōvī, -mōtum, [com- + moveō], 2, a., *stir, shake, move,* used especially of violent motion; *trouble, disturb, disquiet; affect, influence.*

commūnicō, -āre, -āvī, -ātum, [commūnis], 1, a., *divide with, share; join, add.*

commūnis, -e, [com- + mūnus], adj., *common, in common; general, public;* of manners, *affable, courteous; sociable.* in commūne, *for the common good.* commūnis valētūdinis, *common to weak health.*

commūnitās, -ātis, [commūnis], f., *sharing in common; society, fellowship; friendly intercourse; courtesy, condescension, affability.*

commūniter [commūnis], adv., *in common, generally, together.*

commūtō, -āre, -āvī, -ātum, [com- + mūtō], 1, a., *change throughout, change entirely; exchange, substitute, change.*

compāgēs, -is, [compingō, join together], f., *joining together; joint, structure.*

comparō, -āre, -āvī, -ātum, [com-
+ parō], 1, a., *make ready, provide, prepare; get together, get,
collect, obtain; levy.* comparan-
dus, -a, -um, *comparable.*

comparō, -āre, -āvī, -ātum, [com-
+ pār, *equal to*], 1, a., *match, join;
count as equal; compare.*

compellō, -ere, compulī, compul-
sum, [com- + pellō], 3, a., *drive
together; drive, impel, force; incite, urge, constrain.*

compēnsō, -āre, -āvī, -ātum, [com-
+ pēnsō, *weigh together*], *balance,
make good; compensate, make up,
counterbalance.*

comperiō, -īre, comperī, compertum, 4, a., *find out, learn, ascertain.* compertum habēre, *to
have discovered, have information
about.*

compēs, -pedis, usually pl., [com-
+ pēs]. f., *fetter, shackle; bonds,
chains.*

competītor, -ōris, [competō], m.,
competitor, rival, opponent.

complector, -plectī, -plexus sum,
[com- + plectō, *braid*], 3, dep.,
*embrace, clasp; encircle, enclose,
seize; comprehend, understand;
explain, describe, sum up.*

compleō, -ēre, -ēvī, -ētum, [com-
+ pleō, *fill*], 2, a., *fill up, fill;
complete, fulfill, accomplish, finish; live through, pass.*

complexus, -ūs, [complector], m.,
embracing, embrace.

complicō, -āre, -āvī, -ātum, [com-
+ plicō, *fold*], 1, a., *fold together,
fold up, fold, roll up.*

complūrēs, -a or -ia, gen. complūrium, [com- + plūrēs], adj.,
pl., *several, a number, many.*

compōnō, -ere, composuī, composi-
tum, [com- + pōnō], 3, a., *put
together, collect, unite; compare,
contrast; compose, write; construct, build; set in order, arrange,
prepare; lay at rest, bury.*

compositē, comp. compositius,
[compōnō], adv., *in an orderly
manner, properly; in polished* or
studied language.

comprehendō, -hendere, -hendī,
-hēnsum, [com- + prehendō], 3,
a., *take hold of, seize, catch; lay
hold of, arrest, capture; grasp,
comprehend; recount, set forth.*

comprimō, -primere, -pressī, -pres-
sum, [com- + premō], 3, a., *press
together, compress; check, repress,
restrain; subdue, suppress, keep
under.*

comprobō, -āre, -āvī, -ātum, [com-
+ probō], 1, a., *approve, sanction,
assent to; attest, establish, prove.*

cōnātus, -ūs, [cōnor], m., *attempt,
endeavor, effort, undertaking.*

concēdō, -ere, concessī, concessum, [com- + cēdō], 3, a. and
n., *withdraw, depart; yield, give
place to, submit; grant, concede,
allow; admit, acknowledge; give
up, forgive, pardon.* concēdente
collēgā, *with the consent of his
colleague.*

concerpō, -ere, -cerpsī, -cerptum,
[com- + carpō], 3, a., *tear in
pieces, rend; gather, pluck.*

concertō, -āre, -āvī, -ātum, [com-
+ certō], 1, n., *contend with,
strive with; dispute, debate with.*

concidō, -cidere, -cidī, ——, [com-
+ cadō], 3, n., *fall down, collapse;
fall dead, fall; decline, fail, be
destroyed.*

concīdō, -ere, -cīdī, -cīsum, [com-
+ caedō], 3, a., *cut up, cut to
pieces, ruin, destroy; kill; beat
soundly; strike down, prostrate;
annul.*

concíliō, -āre, -avī, -ātum, [con-
cilium], 1, a., *obtain, procure,
win, gain; win over, win the favor
of, conciliate.*

concilium, -ī or -iī, [concieō, *bring
together*], n., *meeting, assembly;
assembly for consultation, council.*

conciō or concieō, -īre or -ēre, -cīvī,
-cītum, [com- + cieō], 2 or 4, a.,
*bring together, call together, collect;
move violently, shake; attract;
rouse, excite, provoke, instigate.*

concipiō, -cipere, -cēpī, -ceptum,
[com- + capiō], 3, a., *take up, receive; imagine, conceive of; understand; harbor, entertain, plan.*
concipere ex, *spring from.*

concitō, -āre, -āvī, -ātum, [freq. of
conciō], 1, a., *stir up, arouse, excite; urge, move, instigate.*

conclāmō, -āre, -āvī, -ātum, [com-
+ clāmō], 1, a. and n., *cry out
together, shout; cry for help; cry
violently, shout loudly, exlaim.*

conclūdō, -ere, -clūsī, -clūsum,
[com- + claudō], 3, a., *shut up,
enclose; limit, restrain; close,
conclude; demonstrate, argue.*

concordia, -ae, [concors], f., *harmony, union, concord.* Personified, Concordia, -ae, f., *goddess
of Union, Concord,* in whose
honor several temples were
erected at Rome.

concupīscō, -īscere, -īvī, -ītum,
[com- + cupiō], 3, inch., *greatly
desire, long for, eagerly desire,
covet.*

concurrō, -ere, -currī or -cucurrī,
-cursum, [com- + currō], 3, n.,
*run together, assemble; meet,
clash, come together in fight, join
battle; make haste, run for help;
meet, coincide; happen.*

concursus, -ūs, [concurrō], m.,
*running together; concourse,
throng, assembly; assault, attack;
meeting, collision.*

concutiō, -ere, -cussī, -cussum,
[com- + quatiō, *shake*], 3, a.,
*shake, strike together, confound;
agitate, shock; search out, examine; terrify, alarm, trouble.*

condemnō, -āre, -āvī, -ātum, [com-
+ damnō], 1, a., *sentence, find
guilty, convict, condemn.*

condiciō, -ōnis, [condīcō], f., *agreement, condition, compact, terms;
position, rank, lot, circumstances.*

condīmentum, -ī, [condiō, *season*],
n., *spice, seasoning, flavoring,
sauce.*

conditor, -ōris, [condō], m., *maker,
builder, establisher, founder, author.*

condītus, -a, -um, [part. of con-
diō, *season*], adj., *well-seasoned.*
condītiōrem facere aliquam rem,
add a zest to anything.

condō, condere, condidī, conditum,
[com- + dō], 3, a., *put together,
found, build; compose, write;
lay aside, store up; preserve; lay
in the tomb, bury; hide, conceal.*
post hanc urbem conditam, *since
the founding of this city, since this
city was founded.*

condūcō, -ere, -dūxī, -ductum,
[com- + dūcō], 3, a., *draw together, assemble, unite; hire, rent,
employ; be of use, be profitable.*

cōnfectiō, -ōnis, [cōnficiō], f., *finishing, preparing; ending, completion.*

cōnfectus, -a, -um, [part. of cōnficiō], adj., *impaired, weakened, overcome, consumed, exhausted.* bellum cōnfectum, *a war brought to a successful conclusion.*

cōnferō, -ferre, -tulī, collātum, [com- + ferō], irr., a., *bring together, collect, gather, join; match against, oppose; compare, contrast; consult, confer, consider; carry, bring; employ, devote, apply; bestow, lend, grant; refer, assign; put off, postpone; ascribe, throw blame upon, lay charge to; transfer.* sē cōnferre, *to betake himself, to turn, to go; to devote himself.* iter cōnferre, *to direct one's course.*

cōnfertus, -a, -um, [part. of cōnferciō, cram together], adj., *crowded, dense; compact, close; crammed, filled; gorged.* hostēs cōnfertissimī, *the thick of the foe.*

cōnfessiō, -ōnis, [cōnfiteor], f., *confession, acknowledgment.*

cōnfestim [com-, cf. festīnus], adv., *immediately, speedily, forthwith, suddenly.*

cōnficiō, -ficere, -fēcī, -fectum, [com- + faciō], 3, a., *accomplish, execute, complete; do, make, bring about, draw up; bring together, procure, provide, prepare; wear out, consume, subdue, overcome, exhaust; kill, destroy, despatch.* bellum cōnficere, *to put an end to a war, bring a war to a successful conclusion.* valētūdinēs mē cōnfēcērunt, [their] *ill health has worried me greatly.*

cōnfīdō, -fīdere, -fīsus sum, [com- + fīdō], 3, semi-dep., n., *trust, rely on, confide, believe; be confident, be assured.*

cōnfīrmō, -āre, -āvī, -ātum, [com- + fīrmō], 1, a., *make firm, make strong, strengthen, reinforce; encourage, cheer; confirm, establish; assert, affirm, assure, prove.*

cōnfiteor, -fitērī, -fessus sum, [com- + fateor], 2, dep., *confess, acknowledge, admit; allow, grant, concede; disclose, show.*

cōnflagrō, -āre, -āvī, -ātum, [com- + flagrō], 1, a. and n., *burn, be on fire, be consumed, burn up; be destroyed* by fire.

cōnflīgō, -ere, cōnflīxī, cōnflīctum, [com- + flīgō], 3, a. and n., *dash together; be in conflict, contend, fight; be at war, be at variance.*

cōnflō, -āre, -āvī, -ātum, [com- + flō], 1, a., *blow up, kindle, inflame; get together, bring together, raise, compose; cause, produce, bring about.*

cōnfluō, -ere, -flūxī, ——, [com- + fluō, flow], 3, n., *flow together, run together; crowd, throng; assemble, be gathered.*

cōnfodiō, -ere, -fōdī, -fossum, [com- + fodiō, dig], 3, a., *dig up; stab, pierce, pierce through; assassinate.*

cōnfōrmātiō, -ōnis, [cōnfōrmō], f., *shaping, molding, form, fashion; training, culture.*

cōnfōrmō, -āre, -āvī, -ātum, [com- + fōrmō], 1, a., *shape, mold, form, fashion; train, educate, cultivate.*

congerō, -ere, congessī, congestum, [com- + gerō], 3, a., *bring together, collect, heap up, accumulate; build, construct.*

congredior, -gredī, -gressus sum, [com- + gradior], 3, dep., *come together, meet; meet in strife, contend, fight.*

congregō, -āre, -āvī, -ātum, [com- + grex], 1, a., lit. *gather into a flock; assemble, gather together, collect; associate, unite.*

congressus, -ūs, [congredior], m., *meeting together, assembly; conversation, interview; joining battle, encounter, fight.*

congruō, -gruere, -gruī, ——, 3, n., *agree, coincide; harmonize, correspond, accord.*

coniciō, -icere, -iēcī, -iectum, [com- + iaciō], 3, a., *cast together, unite; drive, throw, cast, hurl, direct, aim; urge, force; place, put; conjecture, guess; forecast, foretell.*

coniectūra, -ae, [coniciō], f., *conjecture, inference, guess.*

coniūnctiō, -ōnis, [coniungō], f., *union, agreement; intimacy, close friendship.*

coniūnctus, -a, -um, comp. **coniūnctior,** sup. **coniūnctissimus,** [part. of coniungō], adj., *united, allied, connected; intimate, accordant.*

coniungō, -ere, coniūnxī, coniūnctum, [com- + iungō], 3, a., *unite, connect, join; associate, combine in, wage in common.* **bellum coniungere,** *to unite in waging war.*

coniūnx, -ugis, [cf. coniungō], m. and f., *married person, consort, spouse,* whether *husband* or *wife.*

coniūrātī, -ōrum, [coniūrātus, from coniūrō], m., pl., *conspirators.*

coniūrātiō, -ōnis, [coniūrō], f., *association under oath, conspiracy, confederacy.*

cōnīveō, -ēre, cōnīvī or **cōnixī, ——,** [com- + nīveō], 2, n., *shut the eyes; overlook, connive, wink at.*

cōnor, -ārī, -ātus sum, 1, dep., *undertake, endeavor, attempt, try; make an effort, seek, aim.*

conquiēscō, -iēscere, -iēvī, conquiētum, [com- + quiēscō], 3, n., *rest, repose; stop, cease; find rest, be at rest, enjoy peace.*

conquīrō, -ere, -quīsīvī, -quīsītum, [com- + quaerō], 3, a., *seek for, go in quest of; bring together, collect.*

cōnsalūtō, -āre, -āvī, -ātum, [com- + salūtō], 1, a., *greet in unison, salute cordially, greet.*

cōnsanguineus, -a, -um, [com- + sanguineus], adj., *related by blood, kindred.* As subst., **cōnsanguineus, -ī,** m., *kinsman, relative.*

cōnscelerātus, -a, -um, [cōnscelerō], adj., *stained with guilt, wicked, criminal, depraved, villanous.*

cōnscientia, -ae, [cōnsciō], f., *knowledge shared by others, common knowledge;* of the individual, *feeling, sense, consciousness, knowledge; sense of right, conscience; sense of guilt.*

cōnscīscō, -ēre, -scīvī, -scītum, [com- + scīscō, *vote*], 3, a., *vote together; approve of, decree, resolve; adjudge; inflict on oneself.*

46   VOCABULARY

cōnscius, -a, -um, [com- + sciō], adj., *knowing in common, conscious with, participant, accessory, witness.* As subst., cōnscius, -ī or -iī, m., *partaker, accessory, accomplice, confidant, witness.*

cōnscrībō, -ere, -scrīpsī, -scrīptum, [com- + scrībō], 3, a., *write together, write in a roll, enroll; enlist, levy; draw up, compose, write, write over.* cōnscrīptus, -ī, [part. of cōnscrībō], m., *one enrolled;* used especially in addressing the Roman Senate in the designation patrēs cōnscrīptī, *fathers elect, chosen fathers,* senators, for patrēs et cōnscrīpti, *fathers and elect.* Liv. 2, 1, 35.

cōnsecrō, -āre, -āvī, -ātum, [com- + sacrō], 1, a., *offer as sacred, dedicate, consecrate; devote, deify, immortalize.*

cōnsenēscō, -nēscere, -nuī, ——, [com- + senēscō, *grow old*], 3, inch., *grow old together, become old, grow gray.*

cōnsēnsiō, -ōnis, [cōnsentiō], f., *agreeing together, agreement, unanimity.*

cōnsēnsus, -ūs, [cōnsentiō], m., *agreement, unanimity, concord.*

cōnsentiō, -īre, cōnsēnsī, cōnsēnsum, [com- + sentiō], 4, n., *agree together, agree, be in accord; determine in common, resolve together, decree; conspire, plot.*

cōnsequor, -sequī, -secūtus sum, [com- + sequor], 3, dep., *follow after, follow up, press upon, pursue; overtake, reach; arrive at, get, attain, secure; copy after, imitate, adopt; result, ensue;* *achieve, fulfill.* id quod cōnsequī cōnantur, *what they are trying to obtain, their ends.*

cōnserō, -ere, -seruī, -sertum, [com- + serō, *entwine*], 3, a., *connect together, entwine, tie, join, unite.* manibus cōnsertīs, *in a hand-to-hand encounter.* proeliō cōnsertō, [*from*] *a hand-to-hand encounter.*

cōn-servātiō, -ōnis, [cōnservō], f., *keeping, preserving.*

cōnservō, -āre, -āvī, -ātum, [com- + servō], 1, a., *preserve, keep safe, keep, maintain, save; keep intact, observe, guard.* suī cōnservandī causā, *in order to save themselves.*

cōnsessus, -ūs, [cōnsīdō], m., *assembly, convention.*

cōnsīderō, -āre, -āvī, -ātum, 1, a., *look at closely, examine; reflect upon, consider, contemplate.*

cōnsīdō, -sīdere, -sēdī, -sessum, [com- + sīdō], 3, n., *sit down, seat oneself, be seated, sit; settle, sink down.*

cōnsilium, -ī or -iī, [cf. cōnsulō], n., *body of counselors, deliberative body, council; deliberation, consultation; plan, design, measure, purpose, determination, resolution; advice, counsel; understanding, judgment, prudence, wisdom; decision.* cōnsilia inīre, *to adopt plans.* prīvātō cōnsiliō, [*by*] *personal precautions.* in cōnsilium, *for advice.* quid cōnsilī? *what scheme, what plan?*

cōnsistō, -ere, cōnstitī, ——, [com- + sistō, *place*], 3, n., *stand still, stop; stay, remain; stand, be firm, find a foothold; exist, stand* forth; consist of, consist in, depend on.

cōnsociō, -āre, -āvī, -ātum, [com- + sociō], 1, a., *associate, ally oneself, join, unite; agree upon.* vehementer cum senātū cōnsociāre, *to be thoroughly in accord with the senate.*

cōnsōlātiō, -ōnis, [cōnsōlor], f., *comforting, comfort, consolation.*

cōnsōlor, -ārī, -ātus sum, [com- + sōlor, comfort], 1, dep., *encourage, comfort, cheer, console.*

cōnspectus, -ūs, [cōnspiciō], m., *sight, look, view; presence.*

cōnspiciō, -spicere, -spexī, cōnspectum, [com- + speciō], 3, a. and n., *observe, see, catch sight of, perceive, gaze upon; face towards;* pass., *be conspicuous, be distinguished.* unde maximē cōnspicī poterat, *from where the best view of it was to be had.*

cōnspicuus, -a, -um, [cōnspiciō], adj., *visible, apparent; conspicuous, distinguished, eminent.*

cōnspīrō, -āre, -āvī, -ātum, [com- + spīrō, breathe], 1, a., *blow together, sound in unison; harmonize, accord, unite; plot, conspire.*

cōnstāns, -antis, [cōnstō], adj., *firm, immovable, steady, constant; trustworthy, steadfast; faithful, unchanging.*

cōnstanter [cōnstāns], adv., *with firmness, firmly, resolutely; with consistency, consistently, evenly.*

cōnstantia, -ae, [cōnstāns], f., *firmness, steadiness, steadfastness; consistency, harmony; constancy, self-possession.*

cōnstituō, -ere, cōnstituī, cōnstitūtum, [com- + statuō], 3, a.,

put, place, set, set up; *draw up, station, cause to halt; establish, constitute, prepare, construct, erect, found; designate, appoint; set in order, regulate, administer; arrange, decide, determine, decree, resolve.* ad cōnstitūtum, *to the place agreed upon.*

cōnstō, -āre, cōnstitī, cōnstātum, [com- + stō], 1, n., *be consistent, agree, be correct; be established, be settled, remain firm, stand firm; be certain, be known, be clear; consist of; be dependent, depend.* modus cōnstet, *let a limit be set, let moderation characterize.* Impers., cōnstat, cōnstāre, *it is clear, it is agreed, it is proved.*

cōnstringō, -ere, cōnstrinxī, cōnstrictum, [com- + stringō], 3, a., *bind, fetter; curb, restrain, hold firmly.*

cōnsuēscō, -ere, -suēvī, -suētum, [com- + suēscō, become used], 3, inch., a. and n., *accustom oneself, habituate, accustom, form a habit;* perf., cōnsuēvī, *I am accustomed, I am wont, I have a habit.*

cōnsuētūdō, -inis, [cōnsuētus], f., *custom, habit, usage, practice; intimacy, companionship, close friendship.* stuprī vetus cōnsuētūdō, *an intrigue of long standing.*

cōnsul, -ulis, [cf. cōnsulō], m., *consul,* title of the two chief magistrates of Rome, who were chosen annually. cōnsul dēsīgnātus, *consul-elect,* one who has been elected consul, but has not yet entered upon the discharge of

official duties. **prō cōnsule**, pl.
prō cōnsulibus, used as an indecl.
noun, *deputy consul, proconsul.*
nōbīs cōnsulibus, *in our consulship, in my consulship.*
cōnsulāris, -e, [cōnsul], adj., *of a
consul, consular; of consular
rank, who has been consul.* As
subst., **cōnsulāris, -is**, m., *exconsul, man of consular rank.*
cōnsulātus, -ūs, [cōnsul], m., *office
of consul, consulship, consulate.*
cōnsulō, -ere, cōnsuluī, cōnsultum,
3, a. and n., *deliberate, take counsel; decide, resolve;* with acc.,
*consult, refer to, ask advice of,
counsel with;* with dat., *consult
for, look out for the interests of,
take thought for.* **cōnsulere timōrī**, *have regard for* [*our*] *fear.*
cōnsultātiō, -ōnis, [cōnsultō], f.,
*mature deliberation, consultation;
an asking of advice, inquiry.*
cōnsultō, -āre, -āvī, -ātum, [freq.
of cōnsulō], 1, a. and n., *reflect, consult, take counsel; advise
with; have a care for;* with dat.,
deliberate for the good of.
cōnsultum, -ī, [cōnsultus, from
cōnsulō], n., *deliberation; decree,
resolution, decision.* **ex senātūs
cōnsultō**, *in accordance with a
decree of the senate, in accordance
with the senate's decree.*
cōnsūmō, -ere, cōnsūmpsī, cōnsūmptum, [com- + sūmō], 3, a.,
*use up, devour; destroy, consume; waste, exhaust, weaken,
waste away, wear away;* of time
or divisions of time, *spend, pass,
consume.*
cōnsurgō, -ere, -surrēxī, -surrēctum, [com- + surgō, *rise*], 3, n.,

*rise together, stand up, start up,
rise in a body; arise, originate.*
contāgiō, -ōnis, [contingō], f., *a
touching, contact; contagion, infection; pollution, vicious companionship, contamination.*
contāminō, -āre, -āvī, -ātum, 1, a.,
mingle, blend; pollute, stain, defile.
contegō, -tegere, -tēxī, -tēctum,
[com- + tegō], 3, a., *cover up,
cover; bury; conceal, hide.*
contemnō, -ere, contempsī, contemptum, [com- + temnō], 3, a.,
*esteem lightly, despise, disdain,
contemn; disparage, speak of with
contempt; disregard, defy; slight,
neglect.*
contemplor, -ārī, -ātus sum, [perhaps from com- + templum, *a
place from which there is a free
prospect on all sides*], 1, dep.,
*gaze at, view attentively; behold,
observe, consider, regard.*
contemptus, -a, -um, comp. **contemptior**, sup. **contemptissimus**,
[contemnō], adj., *despised, despicable, contemptible, vile, abject.*
contendō, -ere, contendī, contentum, [com- + tendō], 3, a. and
n., *stretch tight, strain; aim,
hurl; press, hasten; contend, vie,
strive, fight; dispute; compare,
contrast; maintain, assert, affirm,
protest.*
contentiō, -ōnis, [contendō], f.,
*straining, strain, struggle, effort,
exertion; strife, contention, contest; dispute, controversy; comparison, contrast.*
contentus, -a, -um, [contineō],
adj., *satisfied, pleased, happy,
contented, content.*

conterŏ, -ere, -trīvī, -trītum, [com-
+ terō, *rub*], 3, a., *grind, pound,
wear away;* of time, *consume,
waste, use,* and, passively, *employ; exhaust, expend; destroy,
annihilate.*

conterreō, -ēre, -uī, -itum, [com- +
terreō], 2, a., *terrify, frighten,
subdue by terror, alarm.*

conticēscō, -ere, conticuī, ——,
[cŏm- + taceō], 3, inch., *become
silent, be still, cease speaking; be
hushed, cease, stop.*

continēns, -entis, [contineō], adj.,
*bordering, adjacent; connected,
consecutive, continual;* of character, *self-restrained, of self-control, temperate.*

continentia, -ae, [continēns], f.,
*restraint, self-restraint, self-con-
trol; self-mastery, temperance.*

contineō, -ēre, continuī, contentum, [com- + teneō], 2, a. and
n., *hold together, enclose, bound,
comprise, contain; shut in, restrain, repress, hold, check, curb;
include, comprehend, involve.*

contingō, -tingere, -tigī, -tāctum,
[com- + tangō], 3, a. and n.,
*touch, take hold of; extend to,
reach to; affect; reach, arrive at,
come to; happen, turn out, come
to pass, occur.*

continuō [continuus], adv., *immediately, directly, without delay;
necessarily, of course.*

cōntiō, -ōnis, [for conventiō, from
conveniō], f., *gathering, assembly,
convocation; address, discourse,
harangue.*

cōntiōnātor, -ōris, [cōntiōnor, *harangue*], m., *haranguer, agitator,
demagogue.*

contrā, adv. and prep.:
  (1) As adv., *opposite, in front
of; face to face, in opposition, on
the other side; on the contrary;
in answer, in reply.* contrā atque, contrā ac, *otherwise than,
different from what, contrary to.*
  (2) As prep., with acc. only,
*against, before, opposite to, facing,
over against, contrary to; in reply to; in hostility to, to the disadvantage of, in spite of.* quod
contrā, *whereas on the contrary,
while on the contrary, opposite
to what, contrary to what.*

contrāctus, -a, -um, [contrahō],
adj., *drawn together, short, narrow, restricted; shrunken,
pinched, drawn.*

contrahō, -ere, contrāxī, contrāc-
tum, [com- + trahō], 3, a., *draw
together, collect, assemble; draw
in, contract, shorten, diminish,
lessen; accomplish, bring about,
execute;* of a debt, *contract.*
amplius negōtī mihi contrahitur,
*I am more deeply involved in diffi-
culty.* contrahere frontem, *to
frown.*

contrārius, -a, -um, [contrā], adj.,
*opposite, lying over against; con-
trary, opposed, conflicting; uncon-
genial.*

contrōversia, -ae, [contrōversus],
f., *quarrel, dispute, controversy,
contention.*

contubernium, -ī or -iī, [com- +
taberna, *cabin*], n., *companionship in a tent, dwelling together
of a number of persons in the same
tent; relation of a general and his
personal follower; constant intercourse, company.*

contumēlia, -ae, [com-, cf. tumeō], f., *reproach, insult, invective, abuse.*

cōnūbium, -ī or -iī, [com- + nūbō, marry], n., *marriage, wedlock; right of intermarriage.*

convalēscō, -ere, convaluī, ——, [com- + valeō], 3, inch., *grow strong, gain strength; recover, regain health.*

convenae, -ārum, [conveniō], m. and f. pl., *persons who come together; assembled strangers, refugees, vagabonds.*

convenientia, -ae, [conveniō], f., *harmony, agreement.* **convenientia rērum,** *complete agreement, harmony in everything.*

conveniō, -īre, convēnī, conventum, [com- + veniō], 4, a. and n., *come together, meet together, meet, assemble; be agreed upon, be settled; be fit, be suitable to, be appropriate to.* Impers. **convenit, -īre, convēnit,** *it is agreed, it is settled, it is fit, it is suitable, it is appropriate, it is consistent, it is right.* **tempus et locus convenit,** *the time and place are agreed upon* or *are suitable.*

conventus, -ūs, [conveniō], m., *assembly, meeting, throng; corporation; court.*

convertō, -ere, convertī, conversum, [com- + vertō], 3, a. and n., *turn around, turn about, reverse, invert, throw back; turn, direct; change, alter, transform; undergo change, be changed.*

convīcium, -ī or -iī, [com-, cf. vōx], n., *outcry, cry, utterance; din, noise; wrangling, altercation, reproach, insult, abuse.*

convincō, -ere, convīcī, convictum, [com- + vincō], 3, a., *overcome, convict, refute; prove beyond question, show clearly.*

convīvium, -ī or -iī, [com- + vīvō], n., *banquet, feasting together, social meal, feast.*

convocō, -āre, -āvī, -ātum, [com- + vocō], 1, a., *call together, summon together, convoke, summon.*

cooperiō, -īre, -peruī, -pertum, [com- + operiō, *cover*], 4, a., *cover, overwhelm, hide, bury.*

coopertus, -a, -um, adj., *buried, involved, covered.*

coorior, -īrī, -ortus sum, [com- + orior], 3 and 4, dep., *come forth, stand up, appear; rise with force, break forth; break out, begin; rise in opposition, stand up in hostility.*

Cōos, -ī, f., *Cos,* an island in the Aegean Sea, southwest of Asia Minor, the birthplace of Hippocrates the physician, and of Apelles, the painter.

cōpia, -ae, [co-opia, from com- + ops], f., *abundance, ample supply, plenty; multitude, number, throng; fullness, copiousness; ability, power, facility, fluency;* mostly in pl., *wealth, resources, riches, prosperity; forces, troops.* **facere cōpiam,** *offer the opportunity to* or *of.*

cōpiōsus, -a, -um, [cōpia], adj., *well supplied, rich, abounding in; copious, eloquent.*

coquō, -ere, coxī, coctum, 3, a., *cook, bake, heat; burn, parch, dry up; ripen, make mature; think out, mature, plan; vex, harass, disturb.*

coctus, -a, -um, adj., *ripe.*

coquus, -ī, [coquō], m., *cook.*

cōram [com-, cf. ōs], adv. and prep., *before:*
(1) As adv., *before the eyes, face to face; present, in person.*
(2) As prep., with abl. only, *before, in the face of, in the presence of.*

Corcȳra, -ae, [Κέρκυρα], f., *Corcȳra,* an island in the Adriatic Sea, off Epirus; now *Corfu.*

Corduba, -ae, [Κορδύβη], f., *Corduba,* a city on the Baetis River, in the southern part of Spain; now *Cordova.*

Corinthius, -a, -um, [Corinthus], adj., *of Corinth, Corinthian.* As subst., Corinthiī, -ōrum, m., pl., *the people of Corinth, the Corinthians.* Corinthium signum, *a statue of Corinthian bronze.*

Corinthus, -ī, [Κόρινθος], f., *Corinth,* a city on the Isthmus of Corinth. The name survives in the village *Corinto,* which stands near the ancient site.

Coriolānus, -ī, m., *C. Mārcius Coriolānus,* an old Roman hero, unjustly exiled. Allying himself with the Volscians, enemies of Rome, he had come within striking distance of the city when he was moved by the entreaties of his wife to spare his fatherland. AM. 12.

Cornēlius, -a, name of a Roman gens which included a number of prominent families, both patrician and plebeian. The *Cornēliī* mentioned in this book are described under their family names; see Balbus, Cethēgus,

Cinna, Dolābella, Lentulus, Scīpiō, Sulla, Tacitus, Verrēs.

Cornūtus, -ī, m., *M. Cornūtus, praetor urbānus.* PHIL. 6, 14.

corpus, -oris, n., *body; living body, flesh; dead body, trunk, corpse; substance, reality; person, individual; frame, structure, system, mass.*

corpusculum, -ī, [dim. of corpus], n., *puny body, tiny body; flesh.*

corrēctiō, -ōnis, [corrigō], f., *amendment, improvement, correction; a being put right.*

corrigō, -rigere, -rēxī, -rēctum, [com- + regō], 3, a., *straighten out, make straight; amend, correct, change for the better; improve, reform, make good.*

corrōborō, -āre, -āvī, -ātum, [com- + rōborō, from rōbur], 1, a., *strengthen, encourage; fortify, confirm.*

corrumpō, -ere, corrūpī, corruptum, [com- + rumpō], 3, a., *destroy, spoil, ruin, waste; bribe, corrupt, buy over; falsify, pervert, tamper with.* corrumpere . . . ut, *to induce by bribes to.*

corruō, -ere, corruī, ——, [com- + ruō], 3, a. and n., *fall together, fall down, sink down; fall in a heap, fall lifeless; collapse; fail.*

corruptēla, -ae, [corruptus], f., *seduction, corruption.*

corruptor, -ōris, [corruptus], m., *seducer, corruptor, briber.*

corruptus, -a, -um, [part. of corrumpō], adj., *spoiled; bad, profligate, corrupt.* corruptī cīvitātis mōrēs, *the corruption of public morals.* As subst., quis

corruptus, *what reprobate, what profligate.*

Coruncānius, -a, a Roman gentile name. Tiberius Coruncānius, consul 280 B.C., Pontifex Maximus in 252, the first plebeian so honored, was also the first person at Rome who gave regular instruction in law. He was himself a distinguished jurist. SEN. 6.

cotīdiānus, -a, -um, [cotīdiē], adj., *of every day, of each day, daily.*

cotīdiē [quot + diēs], adv., *every day, daily.*

Cotta, -ae, m., *Cotta.* Two of the name are mentioned in this book : (1) *L. Aurēlius Cotta,* praetor 70 B.C. and consul, with L. Manlius Torquatus, 65 B.C. After the Catilinarian conspiracy was crushed Cotta proposed a public thanksgiving for Cicero, whose firm friend he remained in the troubled times that followed. CAT. **3,** 8. (2) *M. Aurēlius Cotta,* partisan of Pompey in the Civil War. EP. 11.

Cōus, -a, -um, [Cōos], adj., *of or belonging to Cos.* As subst., **Cōī, -ōrum,** m. pl., *the natives of Cos, the Coans.*

crās, adv., *tomorrow.*

crassus, -a, -um, comp, **crassior,** perhaps from **crēscō**], adj., *solid. gross, stout, heavy; stolid, stupid.*

Crassus, -ī, m., name of a prominent family in the Licinian gens. Four of the family are mentioned in this book : (1) *P. Licinius Crassus,* consul in 205 B.C. with the elder

Africanus; Pontifex Maximus from 212 to his death in 183. He was famed both as a lawyer and a statesman. SEN. 9, 14. (2) *L. Licinius Crassus,* born 140 B.C., consul 95 B.C. He was the most distinguished orator of his time. He died 91 B.C. ARCH. 3; VERR. 59; PHIL. 6. (3) *P. Licinius Crassus Dīves,* who was consul 97 B.C. Afterwards for several years he commanded in Spain, and was awarded a triumph in 93 B.C. He was censor with L. Julius Caesar in 89 B.C. Being a partisan of the aristocracy, he killed himself to escape proscription when Cinna and Marius gained possession of Rome. ARCH. 5. (4) *M. Licinius Crassus Dīves,* born about 105 B.C. He had an inordinate desire for wealth, and amassed a large fortune. He conquered Spartacus in the Servile War, 71 B.C., and was consul with Pompey in the following year. He united with Pompey and Caesar in the first triumvirate. He set out upon an expedition against the Parthians, in which he was defeated with great loss and slain, 53 B.C.

crātēra, -ae, f., *mixing-bowl, wine-bowl; bowl, jar.*

crēber, -bra, -brum, adj., *thick, close, frequent, numerous; crowded, abundant, abounding; repeated.*

crēbrēscō, -ere, -bruī, ——, [crēber], 3, inch., n., *become frequent, increase; spread abroad.*

crēbrō, comp. **crēbrius,** sup. **crēberrimē,** [crēber], adv., *in quick* *succession, frequently, repeatedly, often.*

crēdibilis, -e, [crēdō], adj., *to be believed, worthy of belief, likely, credible.*

crēdō, crēdere, crēdidī, crēditum, 3, a. and n., *lend; intrust, commit, consign; trust, confide in, believe in; believe, think, suppose, imagine;* often used parenthetically = *I dare say, likely enough, perhaps, of course.* **mihi crēde,** *believe me, upon my word.* **crēdō,** *of course, presumably.* **satis crēdere,** *to trust fully.* **oculīs crēdere,** *to see for oneself.*

crēdulus, -a, -um, [crēdō], adj., *that easily believes, credulous, confiding, unsuspecting; simple.*

cremō, -āre, -āvī, -ātum, 1, a., *burn, consume by fire.*

creō, -āre, -āvī, -ātum, 1, a., *bring forth, create, give origin to; cause, occasion; make, choose, elect, appoint.*

crēscō, crēscere, crēvī, crētum, 3, inch., *spring up; grow, increase, swell, enlarge; grow strong, be strengthened.*

Crētēnsis, -e, [Crēta], adj., *of Crete, Cretan.* As subst., **Crētēnsēs, -ium,** m., pl., *the inhabitants of Crete, the Cretans.*

crīmen, -inis, [cernō], n., *judgment, accusation; reproach; criminal accusation; crime, offense.*

crīminātiō, -ōnis, [crīminor, *accuse of crime*], f., *charge against somebody, complaint; calumny.*

crīminor, -ārī, -ātus sum, [crīmen], 1, dep., *accuse of crime; charge with, denounce, charge.*

crīnis, -is, m., *hair, hair of the head.*

Crispus, -ī, m., *Crispus,* a Roman surname. See **Sallustius** (2).

Crotōniātēs, -ae, [Crotōn], m., *a man of Crotona,* a Greek city in southern Italy. SEN. 9.

cruciātus, -ūs, [cruciō, *torture*], m., *torture, torment; anguish, agony.*

crūdēlis, -e, [crūdus, *unfeeling*], adj., *unfeeling, cruel, merciless, hard-hearted;* of things, *pitiless, harsh, bitter.*

crūdēlitās, -ātis, [crūdēlis], f., *harshness, cruelty, severity.*

crūdēliter, comp. **crūdēlius,** sup. **crūdēlissimē,** [crūdēlis], adv., *harshly, cruelly, with cruelty.*

crūditās, -ātis, [crūdus], f., *overloading of the stomach, indigestion.*

crūdus, -a, -um, [for cruidus, from **cruor,** *blood*], adj., *bloody, trickling with blood; with full stomach, stuffed with food; fresh, vigorous; immature, raw, rough, cruel, merciless.*

crūs, -ūris, n., *leg, shank, shin.*

cubiculum, -ī, [cubō, *lie down*], n., *room for reclining, bedchamber.*

culpa, -ae, f., *fault, error, ground of reproach, blame; crime, offense, reproach.*

cultiō, -ōnis, [colō], f., *cultivation, preparation.* **agrī cultiō,** *tilling of the field, agriculture.*

cultūra, -ae, [colō], f., *tillage, cultivation, care; training, education, culture; refinement, style; reverence, adoration.*

cultus, -ūs, [colō], m., *labor, care, cultivation, culture; training, education; style, care, way of life;*

civilization, refinement; honoring, reverence, adoration, veneration; attire, dress, garb, clothing.

cum, prep. with ablative only, *with;* of association, *with, along with, in the company of, together with;* of comparison, *with, as over against, compared with;* of time, *at, at the time of, together with, at the same time with;* of manner and circumstance, *with, under, amid, to, at.* With the personal pronouns and with **quī cum** is enclitic; as, **mēcum, nōbīscum, quōcum. cum . . . tum**, *granting that . . . then.* **cum . . . tum maxime**, *not only . . . but especially.* **cumque**, *and not only.*

In composition the earlier form **com-** is used, which remains unchanged before **b, p, m**, but is changed to **col-** or **con-** before **l, cor-** or **con-** before **r, con-** before other consonants, and **co-** before vowels and **h**.

cum, conj., *when;* of definite time, *at the time when, when. while, as long as, after;* of indefinite time or repeated action, *whenever, as often as, at times when;* of relative time, descriptive or circumstantial, *when, while, after, on the occasion that, under the circumstances that, at thẽ moment when;* of cause or concession, with subj., *since, inasmuch as, although, notwithstanding.* **tum — cum**, *then — when* or *while.* **cum — tum**, *both — and, not only — but also, while — especially.* **cum prīmum**, *as soon as.* **cum prae-**

sertim, *especially since.* **cum quippe**, *since of course.*

Cūmānus, -a, -um, [Cūmae], adj., *Cumaean, of Cumae*, an ancient city on the coast of Campania, west of Naples. As subst., **Cūmānum, -ī**, (properly sc. **praedium**), n., *estate near Cumae, Cumaean estate*, where Cicero had a villa. EP. 20.

cumulātē, comp. **cumulātius**, sup., **cumulātissimē**, [cumulātus], adv., *in rich abundance, copiously, with abundant interest.*

cumulō, -āre, -āvī, -ātum, [cumulus], 1, a., *heap up; pile up; increase, augment, accumulate; overload, overwhelm, crown.* **cumulātus studiōsē**, *with the most careful usury.*

cūnae, -ārum, f., *cradle, nest.*

cunctātiō, -ōnis, [cunctor], f., *delaying, tarrying, delay; hesitation, doubt.*

cunctor, -ārī, -ātus sum, 1, dep., *to delay action, find reasons for delay;* hence, *delay; loiter; hesitate, doubt.*

cūnctus, -a, -um, [for **co-iūnctus, com- + iūnctus**], adj., *all together, all, whole, entire.*

cupiditās, -ātis, [cupidus], f., *desire, eagerness, passion; greed, covetousness, cupidity, lust.*

cupīdō, -inis, [cupiō], f., *desire, wish, longing, eagerness; passion, ambition; excessive desire, greed; love, desire, lust.* As subst., **Cupīdō, -inis**, m., *Cupid* son of Venus, and god of desire.

cupidus, -a, -um, [cupiō], adj., *eagerly desirous, desirous, eager;*

fond, loving; passionate, lustful; greedy, avaricious.

cupiō, cupere, cupīvī or **-iī, cupītum,** 3, a., *long for, wish, desire; be well disposed, wish well, favor; be devoted to, be zealous for.*

cūr [older **quŏr,** from early dat. **quoi + reī**], adv., *why? for what purpose? wherefore? for what reason?* rel., *why, wherefore.*

cūra, -ae, f., *care, attention, pains; pursuit, business, office;* arising from love, *love, affection;* arising from mental disturbances, *anxiety, solicitude, concern, trouble, sorrow, grief.*

cūrātē, comp. **cūrātius, [cūrātus,** *anxious),* adv., *carefully, diligently.*

Çurēs, -ium, m. and f. pl., *Curēs,* a Sabine town. LIV. I, 13.

cūria, -ae, f., *cūria, association,* one of the ten divisions into which each of the three primitive Roman tribes were divided; by metonymy, *senate-house,* the place where the Roman senate sat; *the senate.* In Cicero's time there were at Rome two senate-houses:

(1) *The senate-house* proper, known as the **Cūria Hostīlia,** named from Tullus Hostilius, situated north of the Forum. It was enlarged, destroyed by fire in 52 B.C., rebuilt by Faustus Sulla, son of the Dictator, and called **Cūria Cornēlia;** but Sulla's structure was soon afterwards torn down by Julius Caesar. Caesar commenced a new senate-house, which was finished in magnificent style

after his death by Augustus, and called **Cūria Iūlia.**

(2) *The senate-house of Pompey, Pompey's senate-house,* **Cūria Pompeia,** in the same edifice with the Portico erected by Pompey in the Campus Martius. Here Caesar was assassinated; after that the senate-house of Pompey was closed.

Curiātius, -a, an Alban name. **Curiātiī, -ōrum,** m. pl. as subst., *the Curiātiī,* the Alban champions in Rome's fight with Alba Longa.

Cūriō, -ōnis, [**cūriō,** *priest of a cūria*], m., name of a family in the Scribonian gens.

C. Scrībōnius Cūriō, was consul 76 B.C., and celebrated a triumph over the Dardanians in 71 B.C. He was an intimate friend of Cicero, whom he supported in the defense of the Manilian bill and in the execution of the Catilinarian conspirators. He died 53 B.C. IMP. P. 23.

Cūrius, -a, the name of a Roman gens. Two by the name are mentioned in this book:

(1) *M. Cūrius Dentātus,* a favorite hero of the Roman republic, celebrated in later times as a noble specimen of old Roman frugality and virtue. He was consul in 290 B.C., and in 275 he defeated Pyrrhus so completely that the king was obliged to quit Italy. He spent the closing years of his life on a small farm in the country of the Sabines. SEN. 16.

(2) Q. *Cūrius*, through whose declarations to Fulvia first word of the conspiracy of Catiline was brought to Cicero. SALL. 23.

cūrō, -āre, -āvī, -ātum, [cūra], 1, a., *care for, look after, see to, attend to; preside over, govern; pay, settle.* **tē cūrante,** *under your care.*

curriculum, -ī, [dim. of currus], n., *small chariot; race, racecourse; course, career; exerciseground.* **dē spatiō curriculōque,** *from its old course and track.*

currō, currere, cucurrī, cursum, 3, n., *run, hasten;* of motion over water or through the air. *move quickly, sail, fly;* of water, *run, flow, roll, spread.*

currus, -ūs, [cf. currō], m., *chariot, car, wagon; triumphal chariot.*

cursō, -āre, ——, ——, [freq. of currō], 1, n., *run hither and thither, run constantly.*

cursus, -ūs, [currō], m., *running; course, passage, way, march, journey, voyage; speed, race; career, progress.* **in cursū,** *on the road, in progress, en route.* **ad cursūs lūnae,** *according to the revolutions of the moon.*

Curtius, -ī or **-iī,** m., *Mettius Curtius,* Sabine chief and hero. LIV. I, 12.

curvō, -āre, -āvī, -ātum, [curvus, *curved*], 1, a., *bend, curve; make yield, move.*

cūstōdia, -ae, [cūstōs], f., *guarding; guard, watch, care, protection; confinement, custody; guardhouse, prison.* **in cūstōdiam dare,** *to place in custody, to put under surveillance.*

cūstōdiō, -īre, -īvī, -ītum, [cūstōs], 4, a., *guard, watch, protect, keep; hold back, restrain; keep in custody, hold captive.*

cūstōdītē, comp. **cūstōdītius,** [cūstōditus,** from cūstōdiō], adv., *cautiously, carefully.*

cūstōs, -ōdis, m. and f., *guard, watch, keeper, overseer; guardian, protector.*

Cȳzicēnī, -ōrum, m., pl., *inhabitants of Cȳzicus.*

Cȳzicus, or **Cȳzicum, -ī,** [Κόζικος], n., *Cȳzicus, Cȳzicum,* an important city of Asia Minor on the south shore of the Propontis.

D

D., see **Decimus.**

damnātiō, -ōnis, [damnō], f., *conviction, condemnation.*

damnō, -āre, -āvī, -ātum, [damnum], 1, a., lit., *inflict loss upon; find guilty, convict, condemn.* **damnātus sōlitūdine,** *condemned to vacancy.*

damnum, -ī, [damnō], n., *harm, damage, loss; penalty, financial loss.*

dē, prep. with abl., denoting separation, *from;* of place and motion, *from, away from, out of;* of time, *away from, after, during, in the course of, in;* of source, *of, from, out of, proceeding from, sprung from;* of the whole, partitively, *of, out of, from among;* of material, *made of, out of, from;* of cause, *on account of, for, through, by;* of relation, *concerning, about, in respect to, of, in the matter of, for victory over.*

dē imprōvīsō, *unexpectedly.* dē industriā, *intentionally.*

dea, -ae, [deus], f., *goddess.*

dēbeō, dēbēre, dēbuī, dēbitum, [for dēhibeō, dē + habeō], 2, a., *withhold, keep back; owe, be indebted, be in debt to, be under obligations; ought, must, should.*

dēbilis, -e, [dē + habilis, *easily handled*], adj., *weak, frail, feeble; crippled, disabled, helpless.*

dēbilitō, -āre, -āvī, -ātum, [dēbilis], 1, a., *make weak, weaken, cripple, disable; dishearten, crush.*

dēbitus, -a, -um, [part. of dēbeō], adj., *due, appropriate, fitting, becoming, meet; doomed, fated.*

dēcēdō, -ere, dēcessī, dēcessum, [dē + cēdō], 3, n., *go away, withdraw, depart; retreat, retire, leave; give precedence to.*

decem, indecl. num. adj., *ten.*

Decemb., see December.

December, -bris, -bre, [decem], adj., *of the tenth; of the tenth month, of December,* so named because the tenth month counting from March, which was reckoned by the early Romans the beginning of the year.

decempeda, -ae, [decem + pēs], f., *ten-foot pole, measuring rod.*

dēcernō, -ere, dēcrēvī, dēcrētum, [de + cernō], 3, a. and n., *decide, determine, resolve, vote, decree; decide by combat, fight, contend.* nihil dēcrētum est, *no decree was passed, no motion was carried.*

dēcertō, -āre, -āvī, -ātum, [dē + certō], 1, n., *go through a contest, fight a contest out; contend, dispute, vie.*

decet, decēre, decuit, 2, impers., a. and n., *be becoming, be meet, be fitting, be proper;* with acc. as obj., *befit, be seemly for, be becoming to, be appropriate to.* quod contrā decuit, *whereas on the contrary.*

dēcidō, -ere, dēcidī, ——, [dē + cadō], 3, n., *fall down, fall away; fall, perish.*

decimus, -a, -um, [decem], adj., *tenth.*

Decimus, -ī, abbreviated D., [decimus], m., *Decimus,* a common Roman forename.

dēclārō, -āre, -āvī, -ātum, [dē + clārō], 1, a., *make clear, disclose; show, prove; declare, proclaim, announce.*

dēclīnātiō, -ōnis, [dēclīnō], f., *bending aside, movement to one side; slight deviation, avoidance.*

dēclīnō, -āre, -āvī, -ātum, 1, a. and n., *bend aside, swerve; lower, let sink; turn aside, deviate, digress; avoid, shun.*

decorō, -āre, -āvī, -ātum, [decus], 1, a., *adorn, embellish, beautify; honor, distinguish.*

decŏrus, -a, -um, [cf. decet], adj., *becoming, seemly, suitable; adorned, beautiful, handsome.*

dēcrēscō, -ere, -crēvī, -crētum, [dē + crēscō], 3, inch. n., *grow less, become fewer; diminish, wane, shrink.*

dēcrētum, -ī, [dēcernō], n., *decree, decision, resolution, vote.*

dēcurrō, -ere, -cucurrī or -currī, -cursum, [de + currō], 3, a., *run down, hasten down; run over, run through, traverse; march, move, maneuver; come, come away;* pass., *pass through;* with reflex., *betake oneself, have recourse to.* **dēcursō spatiō,** *when I have run my race.*

decus, -oris, [cf. decet], n., *grace, glory, honor; decoration, adornment; moral dignity, worth, propriety.*

dēdecus, -oris, [dē + decus], n., *disgrace, shame, infamy, dishonor; cause of shame, reproach.*

dēdicō, -āre, -āvī, -ātum, [dē + dicō], 1, a., *dedicate, consecrate, set apart* as sacred.

dēditiō, -ōnis, [dēdō], f., *giving up, surrendering; surrender, capitulation.*

dēditus, -a, -um, [part. of dēdō], adj., *given up, devoted to, addicted to.*

dēdō, -dere, -didī, -ditum, [dē + dō], 3, a., *give up, surrender, yield, deliver up; devote, consign, submit, abandon.*

dēdūcō, -dūcere, -dūxī, -ductum, [dē + dūcō], 3, a., *lead down, bring down, draw out; draw off, take off, remove; bring out, withdraw, lead off* or *away; derive, deduce;* of colonists, *lead forth, conduct;* of a ship, *draw out from the dock, draw down, launch; accompany to work.*

dēfatīgātiō, -ōnis, [dēfatīgō], f., *wearying, tiring out; weariness, fatigue, exhaustion.*

dēfatīgō, -āre, -āvī, -ātum, [dē + fatīgō, tire], 1, a., *tire out, exhaust; wear out, make weary.*

dēfectiō, -ōnis, [dēficiō], f., *failure, lack, disappearance; desertion, rebellion.* **dēfectiō sōlis,** *eclipse of the sun.*

dēfendō, -ere, dēfendī, dēfēnsum, [dē + obsolete fendō], 3, a., *ward off, repel, keep off; defend, guard, protect; maintain* in defense, *allege.*

dēfēnsiō, -ōnis, [dēfendō], f., *defense.*

dēferō, -ferre, -tulī, -lātum, [dē + ferō], irr., a., *bear away, bring down; carry off, bear, carry; grant, allot, give; take, transfer, deliver; report, give account of, announce, state; bring before, lay before, refer to; enter for registration, register, return; denounce, charge.* **rem dēferre ad patrēs cōnscrīptōs,** *to report a matter to the senate in session.*

dēfessus, -a, -um, [part. of dēfetīscor, *become weary*], adj., *tired out, weary, worn out, exhausted.*

dēficiō, -ficere, -fēcī, -fectum, [dē + faciō], 3, a. and n., *withdraw, fall off, revolt; fail, cease, be wanting, run out; faint, sink, become exhausted; forsake, abandon, desert, leave.*

dēfīgō, -fīgere, -fīxī, -fīxum, [dē + fīgō], 3, a., *fasten, fix; drive, thrust; set up, plant; direct, turn; fix down, plunge.*

dēfīniō, -īre, -īvī, -ītum, [dē + fīniō], 4, a., *bound, limit; fix, determine, establish.*

dēflagrō, -āre, -āvī, -ātum, [dē + flagrō], 1, a. and n., *burn down, be destroyed by fire, be consumed by fire.*

dēflectō, -ere, -flexī, -flexum, [dē + flectō], 3, a., *bend aside, divert, lead astray, swerve; digress.*

dēfleō, -ēre, -ēvī, -ētum, [dē + fleō, *weep*], 2, a., *weep over, lament, deplore, wail.*

dēfōrmō, -āre, -āvī, -ātum, [dē + fōrma], 1, a., *bring out of shape, disfigure, mar; deteriorate; disgrace, dishonor.*

dēfungor, -ī, -fūnctus sum, [dē + fungor], 3, dep., *have done with, acquit oneself of, discharge, perform, fulfill.*

dēgō, -ere, dēgī, ——, [dē + agō], 3, a. and n., *spend, pass.*

dēiciō, -icere, -iēcī, -iectum, [dē + iaciō], 3, a., *throw down, hurl down; strike down, kill, slay, destroy; turn aside, avert; deprive of, rob;* of the eyes or face, *cast down.*

dein, see deinde.

deinceps [dein, for deinde, + capiō], adv., *one after another, in order; next, next in order, next successively.*

deinde [dē + inde], adv., *from that time, thereafter, thence; afterwards, then, next; besides, still.*

dēlābor, -lābī, -lāpsus sum, [dē + lābor], 3, dep., *glide down, slip down, descend; come down, sink, fall.*

dēlectātiō, -ōnis, [dēlectō], f., *delight, pleasure, gratification, enjoyment.*

dēlectō, -āre, -āvī, -ātum, [freq., dē, root lac in obsolete laciō, *entice*], 1, a., *delight, please, charm, entertain;* in the pass., *take pleasure in.*

dēlēctus, -a, -um, [part. of dēligō], adj., *chosen, elect, choice, select, picked.*

dēleō, -ēre, -ēvī, -ētum, 2, a.,

erase, efface, obliterate; blot out, destroy utterly, overthrow, extinguish.

dēlīberātiō, -ōnis, [dēlīberō], f., *deliberation, consideration; ground of deliberation.*

dēlīberō, -āre, -āvī, -ātum, [dē + lībrō, from lībra, *balance*], 1, a. and n., *weigh well, consider, deliberate, take counsel; consult; resolve.*

dēlicātus, -a, -um, [cf. dēliciae], adj., *delightful, charming; given to pleasure, voluptuous, effeminate; fastidious.*

dēliciae, -ārum, [dēlectō], f., *pleasure, delight, charm; luxury; frivolity.*

dēlīctum, -ī, [dēlinquō], n., *fault, misdoing, offense; crime, wrong.*

dēligō, -ligere, -lēgī, -lēctum, [dē + legō], 3, a., *choose, select, pick out, designate.*

dēlīrātiō, -ōnis, [dēlīrō, *be crazy*], f., *going out of the furrow in plowing; silliness, folly, dotage.*

Delphicus, -a, -um, [Delphī], adj., *of* or *pertaining to Delphī,* the seat of the most famous worship of Apollo. **Delphica mēnsa,** *a table made in the form of a tripod.*

dēlūbrum, -ī, [dē, luō, *cleanse*], n., lit., *place of cleansing* or *expiation; shrine, sanctuary, temple.*

dēmēns, -entis, [dē + mēns], adj., *out of one's mind, distracted, mad, insane; foolish, rash, blind.*

dēmenter [dēmēns], adv., *recklessly, foolishly, blindly.*

dēmergō, -ere, -mersī, -mersum, [dē + mergō, *dip*], 3, a., *sink, submerge, dip, bury; plunge, overwhelm; cause to sink.*

dēmetō, -ere, -messuī, -messum, [dē + metō, *reap*], 3, a., *mow, reap, gather, harvest, pluck.*

dēmigrō, -āre, -āvī, -ātum, [dē + migrō], 1, n., *migrate, remove; go off, go away, depart.*

dēminuō, -uere, -uī, -ūtum, [dē + minuō], 3, a., *make smaller, diminish; take away, reduce, impair, curtail.*

dēminūtiō, -ōnis, [dēminuō], f., *lessening, diminution, decrease, loss.*

dēmissus, -a, -um, [dēmittō], adj., *lowered, sunken, drooping, hanging low; of low rank, humble; downcast, dejected; unassuming, shy.*

dēmō, -ere, dēmpsī, dēmptum, [dē + emō], 3, a., *take away, remove, withdraw; count out, except.*

Dēmocritus, -ī, m., *Dēmócritus,* a celebrated Greek philosopher, born at Abdera in Thrace about 460 B.C. He died in 361, at a most advanced age, after spending a large inheritance on travels into distant lands in pursuit of knowledge. His knowledge was most extensive, embracing not only the natural sciences, mathematics, mechanics, grammar, music, and philosophy, but various other useful arts. Because of his cheerfulness of spirit he is often referred to as the laughing philosopher. He was the founder of the atomic theory.

dēmōnstrātiō, -ōnis, [dēmōnstrō], f., *showing, pointing out; exposition, explanation; manner of showing.*

dēmōnstrō, -āre, -āvī, -ātum, [dē + mōnstrō], 1, a., *point out, show, indicate; prove, establish.*

dēmum [dē], adv., *at length, at last, then, just, only; in fact, in truth, certainly.* **tum dēmum,** *then at length, then indeed, not till then.*

dēnegō, -āre, -āvī, -ātum, [dē + negō], 1, a., *reject, refuse, deny.*

dēnique, adv., *at last, at length, finally; besides, and thereafter; in a word, in short, briefly.* **nunc dēnique,** *now at length, only now, not till now.* **tum dēnique,** *then at last, not until then, then only.*

dēnsus, -a, -um, adj., *compact, dense, crowded; thick, close, full.*

dēnūntiō, -āre, -āvī, -ātum, [dē + nūntiō], 1, a., *announce, declare, proclaim; intimate, warn, threaten, denounce; order.*

dēpellō, -pellere, -pulī, -pulsum, [dē + pellō], 3, a., *drive out, drive away, expel; turn aside, ward off, avert, thwart; dissuade, drive, force.*

dēpendō, -ere, dēpendī, dēpēnsum, [dē + pendō], 3, a. and n., *pay, render.*

dēplōrō, -āre, -āvī, -ātum, [dē + plōrō], 1, a. and n., *weep bitterly, wail, lament; bewail, deplore; abandon, give up for lost.*

dēpōnō, -ere, dēposuī, dēpositum, [dē + pōnō], 3, a., *lay down, set down, set, place; lay aside, put off, put away; commit, intrust; give up, resign.*

dēportō, -āre, -āvī, -ātum, [dē + portō], 1, a., *carry down, take away, carry off; of movement*

from the provinces to Rome,
bring home, bring back, bring
away.

dēposcō, -poscere, -poposcī, ——,
[dē + poscō], 3, a., *demand, re-*
quest earnestly, call for; request,
claim.

dēpositum, -ī, [dēpōnō], n., *thing*
deposited; deposit, trust.

dēprāvō, -āre, -āvī, -ātum, [dē +
prāvus], 1, a., *distort, pervert;*
corrupt, seduce, spoil, deprave.

dēprecātor, -ōris, [dēprecor], m.,
averter; advocate, intercessor.

dēprecor, -ārī, -ātus sum, [dē +
precor], 1, dep., *pray to avert,*
seek to avert by prayer, plead
against; plead for, intercede for.

dēprehendō, -hendere, -hendī,
-hēnsum, [dē + prehendō], 3, a.,
take away; seize upon, seize,
catch, capture; overtake, surprise,
discover, detect, find out; compre-
hend, understand.

dēprimō, -ere, dēpressī, dēpres-
sum, [dē + premō], 3, a., *press*
down; sink; overwhelm. dēpressus, -a, -um, adj., *brought*
low. humī dēpressus, *sunk in*
the ground.

dēprōmō, -prōmere, -prōmpsī,
-prōmptum, [dē + prōmō], 3, a.,
draw out, bring forth, fetch; de-
rive, obtain.

dērēctō, [dērēctus, *straight*], adv.,
directly, straight.

dērelinquō, -linquere, -līquī, -līc-
tum, [dē + relinquō], 3, a., *for-*
sake entirely, leave altogether,
abandon.

dēscendō, -ere, dēscendī, dēscēn-
sum, [dē + scandō, *rise*], 3, n.,
climb down, come down, descend;

fall, sink; go down, go down hill,
come down, march down; pene-
trate; lower oneself, yield, agree
to; condescend.

dēscrībō, -scrībere, -scrīpsī,
-scrīptum, [dē + scrībō], 3, a.,
copy off, transcribe, write off;
draw, describe; define, fix, assign,
designate; map out, arrange,
draw up.

dēserō, -serere, -seruī, -sertum,
[dē + serō, *join*], 3, a., *leave, for-*
sake, desert, abandon; leave in
the lurch; forfeit.

dēsertus, -a, -um, [dēserō], adj.,
deserted, solitary; lonely, waste.

dēsīderātiō, -ōnis, [dēsīderō], f., *a*
desiring, longing, a feeling of
regret.

dēsīderium, -ī or -iī, [dēsīderō], n.,
longing for, ardent desire, want,
wish; regret, grief.

dēsīderō, -āre, -āvī, -ātum, [cf.
cōnsīderō], 1, a., *long for, desire*
ardently, want, wish for; call for,
demand, desire, expect; miss, lack,
feel the want of.

dēsīdō, -ere, -sēdī, ——, [dē +
sīdō, *sink*], 3, n., *sink, settle, fall,*
deteriorate; waste time.

dēsignātiō, -ōnis, [dēsignō], f.,
marking out, specification; desig-
nation to office; arrangement.

dēsignātus, -a, -um, [part. of
dēsignō], adj., *elect, chosen,* applied to public officers elected
but not yet installed. cōnsul
dēsignātus, *consul-elect.*

dēsignō, -āre, -āvī, -ātum, [dē +
signō], 1, a., *mark out, point out,*
designate; choose, elect.

dēsinō, -sinere, dēsiī, dēsitum,
[dē + sinō], 3, a. and n., *leave off,*

cease, quit, desist; come to an end, stop, close.

dēsipiēns, -entis, [part. of **dēsipiō,** *be void of understanding*], adj., *foolish, silly, out of one's mind.*

dēsistō, -sistere, -stitī, -stitum, [dē + sistō], 3, n., *leave off, cease, desist from.*

dēsōlō, -āre, -āvī, -ātum, I, a., *leave alone, forsake, abandon, desert.*

dēspērō, -āre, -āvī, -ātum, [dē + spērō], I, a. and n., *lose all hope of, despair of; be hopeless, give up hope, give up.*

dēspiciō, -spicere, -spexī, -spectum, [dē + speciō], 3, a. and n., *look down upon; despise, disdain.*

dēstinō, -āre, -āvī, -ātum, I, a., *make fast, make firm, bind, fix, stay; determine, resolve, design, assign, appoint.* **dēstinātus, -a, -um,** adj., *fixed, determined; destined, inevitable; betrothed.*

dēstituō, -ere, -stituī, -stitūtum, [dē + statuō, *fix*], 3, a., *set down, put away; leave alone, abandon, desert, betray.*

dēstringō, -stringere, -strīnxī, -strictum, [dē + stringō], 3, a., *strip off;* of a sword, *unsheathe, draw.*

dēsuētūdō, -inis, [dēsuētus, *out of use*], f., *disuse, want of use* or *practice.*

dēsum, -esse, -fuī, [dē + sum], irr., n., *be away, be absent; be wanting, be lacking, be missing, fail; be neglectful, be not at hand, be at fault; be inadequate.*

dētestor, -ārī, -ātus sum, [dē + testor], I, dep., *curse; call down upon, denounce; ward off, avert.*

dēterreō, -ēre, -terruī, -territum, [dē + terreō], 2, a., *frighten off, discourage; prevent, hinder; repress, control.*

dētestābilis, -e, [dētestor], adj., *execrable, abominable, detestable.*

dētrahō, -ere, dētrāxī, dētrāctum, [dē + trahō], 3, a., *draw off, pull down, pull off; take from, take away; remove, withdraw, deprive, rob; disparage.*

dētrīmentum, -ī, [dēterō, *rub away*], n., *loss, damage, hurt, harm.*

dēturbō, -āre, -āvī, -ātum, [dē + turbō], I, a., *thrust down, strike down, expel; dispossess, deprive of.* **ex magnā spē dēturbārī,** *to be deprived of great hopes.*

deus, -ī, m., *god, deity, divinity.* **deus ex māchinā,** *a god from a machine,* — referring to an artificial stage device of the ancient Greek drama, whereby a god was let down upon the stage to disentangle the plot. The expression has become proverbial.

dēvinciō, -īre, dēvīnxī, dēvinctum, [dē + vinciō], 4, a., *bind fast, fetter; attach closely, lay under obligation, oblige.*

dēvincō, -ere, dēvīcī, dēvictum, [dē + vincō], 3, a., *conquer completely, subdue; overpower, supersede.*

dēvocō, -āre, -āvī, -ātum, [dē + vocō], I, a., *call away, recall; call off, draw away from.*

dēvoveō, -vovēre, -vōvī, -vōtum, [dē + voveō], 2, a., *vow, offer, devote, consecrate.*

dextera, or **dextra, -ae,** [properly **dextera manus**], f., *right hand.*

di-, see **dis-.**

diaeta, -ae, [δίαιτα, from ξάω, *to live*], f., *regular mode of living, diet; apartment.*

Diāna, -ae, f., a divinity of the Romans entirely identified with the Greek Artemis, goddess of the chase and patroness of celibacy. Her worship was introduced at Rome by Servius Tullius, who dedicated a temple to her on the Aventine.

diciō, -ōnis, nom. sing. and pl. not used, [dīcō], f., *dominion, rule, sway, authority, jurisdiction.* aliquem diciōnis aliēnae facere, *to make anyone subject to foreign sway.*

dīcō, dīcere, dīxī, dictum, 3, a. and n., *say, tell, utter, speak; relate, declare, affirm, assert, maintain; name, call; appoint, fix upon, settle, fix.*

dictātor, -ōris, [dictō], m., *dictator,* a Roman magistrate of unlimited power, at first appointed only in great emergencies.

dictātūra, -ae, [dictātor], f., *dictatorship, office of dictator.*

dictiō, -ōnis, [dīcō], f., *speaking, delivery, pleading; diction, conversation.* iūris dictiō, *the administration of justice.*

dictitō, -āre, -āvī, -ātum, [intens. of dictō], 1, a., *say frequently, keep saying; declare, maintain, assert; allege, pretend.*

dictō, -āre, -āvī, -ātum, [freq. of dīcō], 1, a., *say for another, suggest;* of dictation to an amanuensis, *dictate.*

diēs, -ēī, m. and f., f. usually of a period of time, *day; daylight; set day, appointed time; time,* space of time, interval, period. in diēs, *day by day.*

differō, -ferre, distulī, dīlātum, [dis + ferō], irr., a. and n., *bear apart, disperse; put off, defer, postpone; be different from, differ,* vary. cognitiōnem differre, *suspend court.*

difficilis, -e, comp. difficilior, sup. difficillimus, [dis- + facilis], adj., *not easy, hard, difficult; troublesome, perilous; hard to manage, obstinate; hard to suit, ill-tempered.*

difficiliter, comp. difficilius, sup. difficillimē, [difficilis], adv., *with difficulty.* difficillimē, *with the greatest difficulty.*

difficultās, -ātis, [difficilis], f., *trouble, difficulty, embarrassment, distress.*

diffīdō, -fīdere, -fīsus sum, [dis- + fīdō], 3, semi-dep., *distrust, lack confidence in, be distrustful of, despair of.* diffīdēns rēbus suīs, *in a state of despair regarding his own resources.*

diffluō, -fluere, -flūxī, ——, [dis- + fluō], 3, n., *flow in different directions, flow away; be dissolved, become lax, go to ruin.*

diffundō, -ere, -fūdī, -fūsum, [dis- + fundō], 3, a., *spread by pouring, pour forth; spread, scatter, diffuse, extend; gladden, exhilarate.*

digitus, -i, m., *finger.*

dignitās, -ātis, [dignus], f., *worth, desert, merit; distinction, eminence, reputation; greatness, majesty, dignity; self-respect, honor.*

dignus, -a, -um, adj., *worthy, deserving, suitable; fit, becoming, proper.* **nōn nisi dignus,** *only a worthy man.*

dīgressus, -ūs, [dīgredior, *go apart*], m., *parting, separation, departure.*

dīiūdicō, -āre, -āvī, -ātum, [dī- + iūdicō], 1, a. and n., *distinguish, discern; decide, determine, settle, adjust.*

dīiūnctus, -a, -um, [dīiungō], adj., see **disiūnctus.**

dīlābor, -lābī, -lāpsus sum, [dī- + lābor], 3, dep., *fall apart, fall to pieces; scatter, disperse, go to ruin, perish.*

dīlātiō, -ōnis, [dī- + lātiō, *bearing*], f., *putting off, postponement, adjournment, delay.*

dīlēctus, -ūs, [dīligō], m., *choosing, selection, choice;* especially as a military term, *levy, recruiting, draft, conscription.*

dīligēns, -entis, comp. **dīligentior,** sup. **dīligentissimus,** [part. of **dīligō],** adj., *painstaking, careful, attentive, diligent; scrupulous, faithful, watchful.*

dīligenter, comp. **dīligentius,** sup. **dīligentissimē,** [**dīligēns**], adv., *with painstaking, carefully, diligently, attentively; faithfully.*

dīligentia, -ae, [dīligēns], f., *carefulness, attentiveness, watchfulness, diligence, care; faithfulness; painstaking.*

dīligō, -ere, dīlēxī, dīlēctum, [dī- + legō], 3, a., *select out, single out; choose* above all others, *esteem, prize, love, cherish; be content with, appreciate.*

dīlūcēscō, -ere, dīlūxī, ——, [dīlūceō, *be clear*], 3, inch., *grow light, dawn.*

dīmētior, dīmētīrī, dīmēnsus sum, [dis- + mētior, *measure*], 4, dep. and pass., *measure out bit by bit, lay out;* in the pass., *be measured, planned, adapted.*

dīmicātiō, -ōnis, [dīmicō], f., *combat, fight, struggle; contest, rivalry.*

dīmicō, -āre, -āvī, -ātum, [dī- + micō, *flash*], 1, n., *contend, fight, struggle; be in conflict, be in peril, be in danger, run risk.*

dīmittō, -ere, dīmīsī, dīmissum, [dī- + mittō], 3, a., *send in different directions, send out, send away, send forth; dismiss, break up; let go, discharge, release; forsake, leave, renounce, abandon.*

dīnumerō, -āre, -āvī, -ātum, [dī- + numerō], 1, a., *count, number, reckon, compute.*

Diogenēs, -is, m., *Diogenēs,* a Stoic philosopher, was a pupil of Chrysippus, and succeeded Zeno of Tarsus as the head of the Stoic school at Athens. He was one of the three ambassadors sent by the Athenians to Rome in 155 B.C. SEN. 7.

dīreptiō, -ōnis, [dīripiō], f., *plundering, pillaging.*

dīreptor, -ōris, [dīripiō], m., *plunderer, pillager, marauder.*

dirimō, -ere, -ēmī, -ēmptum, [dis- + emō], 3, a., *take apart, divide, cut off; interrupt, delay; separate, break off; destroy, bring to naught.*

dīripiō, -ere, dīripuī, dīreptum, [dī- + rapiō], 3, a., *tear asunder, tear in pieces; lay waste, pillage, plunder, rob, ravage.*

dīritās, -ātis, [dīrus], f., *mischief, misfortune, calamity; fierceness,* *cruelty, harshness; harshness of temper.*

dīrumpō, -ere, -rūpī, -ruptum, [dis- + **rumpō**], 3, a., *break to pieces, shatter; sunder, sever.*

dīrus, -a, -um, adj., *ill-omened, dire, producing fear,* particularly in a religious sense; *ominous, portentous; fearful, awful, dread; dreadful, cruel, fierce, relentless.*

dis- or **dī-,** inseparable prep., used only as a prefix with other words, adding the force of *apart, asunder, in different directions; between, among; not, un-; utterly, entirely.* **dis-** is found before **c, p, q, s,** and **t,** but becomes **dif-** before **f,** and **dir-** before vowels. **dī-** is found before **d, g, l, m, n, r,** and **v.**

discēdō, -ere, discessī, discessum, [dis- + **cēdō**], 3, n., *go apart, withdraw; go away, depart, leave, retire; come off, be left, remain,* as the result of a battle or struggle.

discernō, -ere, -crēvī, -crētum, [dis- + **cernō**], 3, a., *separate, set apart, divide; distinguish, discern.* **discrēta vēlō,** *shut off by a curtain.*

discerpō, -ere, -cerpsī, -cerptum, [dis- + **carpō**], 3, a., *tear in pieces, rend, mangle, mutilate.*

discessiō, -ōnis, [discēdō], f., *separation, division; formal vote.* **discessiōnem facere in sententiam alicuius,** *to divide the senate on the measure of anyone.*

discessus, -ūs, [discēdō], m., *parting, separation; going away, departure, removal.*

dīscidium, -ī or **-iī,** [dīscindō, *tear asunder*], n., *dissension, parting, discord, alienation.*

disciplīna, -ae, [for discipulīna, from **discipulus**], f., *training, instruction, education; learning, science, discipline; study, culture.*

discō, discere, didicī, ——, 3, a. and n., *learn, learn to know; become acquainted with; learn how.*

discordia, -ae, [discors, *inharmonious*], f., *disunion, dissension, variance, quarrel.*

discrībō, -ere, discrīpsī, discrīptum, [dis- + **scrībō**], 3, a., *assign by parts, apportion, divide off.*

discrīmen, -inis, [discernō], n., *intervening space, interval; separation, division; distinction, difference; turning point, decisive moment, crisis; peril, danger, hazard.* **discrīmen facere,** *to make a distinction.* **pōnere in discrīmine,** *to regard as important.*

discrīminō, -āre, -āvī, -ātum, [discrīmen], 1, a., *divide, part, separate, apportion.*

discursus, -ūs, [discurrō, *run different ways*], m., *running to and fro; running about; straggling, bustle.*

disertus, -a, -um, [disserō, *discuss*], adj., *skillful, clever; wellspoken, eloquent.*

disiciō, -ere, -iēcī, -iectum, [dis- + **iaciō**], 3, a., *throw asunder, scatter, break up, tear to pieces; rout, disperse; ruin, destroy; overthrow, frustrate, bring to naught.*

disiūnctus, -a, -um, [part. of **disiungō**], adj., *separated, parted, apart; remote, distant.*

dispār, -aris, [dis- + **pār**], adj., *unlike, unequal, unmatched.*

dispēnsō, -āre, -āvī, -ātum, 1, a., *weigh out to several persons, pay out; distribute, share; manage, regulate.*

dispergō, -ere, dispersī, dispersum, [dis- + **spargō**], 3, a., *scatter, strew here and there, disperse.*

dispersē, [**dispersus,** from **dispergō,** *scatter*], adv., *here and there; occasionally; in different places; separately.*

dispersus, -a, -um, [part. of **dispergō**], adj., *scattered, dispersed.*

displiceō, -ēre, -uī, -itum, [dis- + **placeō**], 2, n., *displease.* **mihi displicet,** *I dislike.*

dispōnō, -ere, -posuī, -positum, [dis- + **pōnō**], 3, a., *place here and there, array, distribute; set in order, arrange, dispose; place at different points; draw up, post, assign.*

disputātiō, -ōnis, [**disputō**], f., *reckoning, computing, considering; an argument, discussion, debate, dispute.*

disputō, -āre, -āvī, -ātum, [dis- + **putō**], 1, a. and n., *investigate, discuss, treat; argue, maintain; dispute, controvert.*

dissēminō, -āre, -āvī, -ātum, [dis- + **sēminō,** *sow seed*], 1, a., *spread abroad, scatter abroad, disseminate.*

dissēnsiō, -ōnis, [**dissentiō**], f., *difference of opinion, disagreement; strife, discord.*

dissentiō, -īre, dissēnsī, dissēnsum, [dis- + **sentiō**], 4, n., *differ in opinion, disagree, dissent.*

disserō, -ere, -seruī, -sertum, [dis- + **serō**], 3, n., *examine, argue about, discuss, speak, treat; explain, state.*

dissimilitūdō, -inis, [**dissimilis**], f., *unlikeness, difference, dissimilarity.*

dissimulātor, -ōris, [**dissimulō**], m., *dissembler, one who conceals a fact.*

dissimulō, -āre, -āvī, -ātum, [dis- + **simulō**], 1, a. and n., *keep secret, conceal; dissemble, disguise.*

dissipō, -āre, -āvī, -ātum, [dis- + unused **supō,** *throw*], 1, a., *scatter, strew, disperse, spread abroad.*

dissociō, -āre, -āvī, -ātum, [dis- + **sociō,** *unite*], 1, a., *break fellowship with, put out of union, disunite; separate in sentiment, set at variance, estrange.*

dissolūtiō, -ōnis, [**dissolvō**], f., *dissolving, destroying, breaking up, destruction, abolition; looseness; effeminacy.*

dissolūtus, -a, -um, [part. of **dissolvō**], adj., *loose; negligent, remiss, careless; abandoned, dissolute.*

dissolvō, -ere, dissolvī, dissolūtum, [dis- + **solvō**], 3, a., *take apart, unloose, separate; dissolve, destroy; free from debt.*

distantia, -ae, [**distō**], f., *remoteness, diversity, divergence, unlikeness, difference.*

distentus, -a, -um, [part. of **distineō**], adj., *engaged, busy, occupied.*

distineō, -ēre, distinuī, distentum, [dis- + **teneō**], 2, a., *hold apart; keep back, detain, occupy, engage.*

distō, -āre, ——, ——, [dis- + **stō**], 1, n., *stand apart, be separate, be distant; be distinct.*

distribuō, -ere, distribuī, distribū-tum, [dis- + tribuō], 3, a., *apportion, distribute, divide off.*

diū, comp. **diūtius,** sup. **diūtissimē,** [cf. **diēs**], adv., *for a long time, a long time, long, too long.* **quam diū,** *how long; as long as.* **satis diū,** *long enough.* **tam diū,** *so long.*

dīus, -a, -um, [for **dīvus**], adj., *divine, godlike.* As subst., **dīus, -ī,** m., *god, divinity.* **dīum, [dīvum], -ī,** [**dīus,** *divine*], n., *sky.* **sub dīō,** *under the sky, in the open.* **mē dīus Fidius,** see **Fidius.**

diūturnus, -a, -um, [diū], adj., *of long duration, long, lasting, protracted, prolonged.*

dīvellō, -ere, dīvellī, dīvulsum or **-volsum,** [dī- + vellō], 3, a., *rend asunder, tear apart, tear in pieces; separate, remove, destroy.*

dīversē, comp. **dīversius,** [dīver-sus], adv., *in different directions, in different ways, hither and thither.* **paulō dīversius,** *a little less closely together.*

dīversōrium, -ī or **-iī,** [dīvertō, *turn aside*], n., *inn, lodging-house, halting-place.*

dīversus, -a, -um, [part. of dīvertō], adj., lit., *turned different ways; opposite, contrary, conflicting; separate, apart, remote, far distant; different, unlike, diverse.* **dīversa inter sē mala,** *evils mutually opposed.* **dīversus ā,** *contrary to.*

dīves, -itis, adj., *rich, opulent, wealthy; costly, sumptuous.*

Dīves, -itis, [dīves], m., *a name in the Crassus family; see* **Crassus.**

dīvidō, -ere, dīvīsī, dīvīsum, 3, a., *divide, part, separate; divide up, distribute, apportion, share; scatter, spread, extend; separate.*

dīvīnitus, [dīvīnus], adv., *divinely, by inspiration; marvelously, admirably.*

dīvīnus, -a, -um, [dīvus], adj., *of a god, of a divinity, divine; godlike, superhuman; religious, sacred; inspired* by divine influence, *prophetic.*

dīvīsus, -a, -um, [part. of dīvidō], adj., *divided, separated, spread.*

dīvitiae, -ārum, [dīves], f., pl., *riches, wealth, treasures.*

dō, dare, dedī, datum, 1, a., *give, deliver; grant, present, confer, bestow, offer; afford, furnish; surrender, give up, yield, concede; resign, abandon; spare, forgive; place, put, cause, produce, inflict; excite, awaken; announce, report.* **operam dare,** *to give heed, to make an effort, to take pains, take care.*

doceō, docēre, docuī, doctum, 2, a., *teach, instruct, inform, train; explain, show, set forth, tell.* **fābulam docēre,** *to stage, bring out, produce* a play.

doctrīna, -ae, [doceō], f., *teaching, instruction; learning, science.*

doctus, -a, -um, [part. of doceō], adj., *trained, learned, taught, experienced; skilled, cultured.* As subst., **doctī, -ōrum,** m. pl., *wise men, learned men, scholars.*

Dolābella, -ae, m., in this book P. Cornēlius Dolābella, a profligate man, who nevertheless gained the hand of Cicero's daughter Tullia. They were married 50 B.C., and divorced four years later. Dolabella joined the party of Caesar, after whose death he secured the consulship by unfair means. He obtained Syria, as a province, where he conducted himself with such injustice and brutality that he was declared a public enemy. To escape capture he ordered a soldier to kill him, 43 B.C. EP. 14; PHIL. 3.

doleō, dolēre, doluī, ——, 2, a. and n., *suffer, be in pain; feel pain, grieve, lament; feel pained, feel hurt, be sorry, be annoyed; cause pain, hurt.*

dolor, -ōris, [doleō], m., *pain, suffering, pang; grief, sorrow, affliction, trouble, woe, anguish; anger, resentment; indignation, chagrin, mortification.* **dolōre afficī,** *to be grieved, to suffer grief.*

dolus, -ī, m., *device, contrivance; treachery, deception, cunning, stratagem.* **dolus malus,** *bad faith.*

domesticus, -a, -um, [domus], adj., *of the house; domestic, private, personal;* as opposed to that which is foreign, *internal, intestine, civil.*

domicilium, -ī or -iī, [domus], n., *habitation, dwelling, abode; dwelling-place, home.*

dominātiō, -ōnis, [dominor, from dominus], f., *mastery, rule, dominion, supremacy.*

dominor, -ārī, -ātus sum, [dominus], 1, n., dep., *be lord, be in power, have dominion, bear rule; rule, be supreme, prevail, extend; govern, reign, tyrannize.*

dominus, -ī, m., *master, lord, possessor, owner; ruler, chief.*

Domitius, -ī or -iī, m., Cn. Domitius Calvīnus, praetor 56 B.C. EP. 11.

domō, -āre, -uī, -itum, 1, a., *tame, break in, train; master, subdue, vanquish, conquer, reduce.*

domus, -ūs, loc. domī, f., *house, dwelling, abode, home; household, family.* **domī,** *at home.* **domī meae,** *at my house.*

dōnō, -āre, -āvī, -ātum, [dōnum], 1, a., *give, present, grant* as a gift; *forgive, pardon.* **eum cīvitāte dōnāre,** *to bestow citizenship on him.*

dōnum, -ī, [dō], n., *gift, present;* of an offering to a deity, *offering, sacrifice.*

dormiō, -īre, -īvī, -ītum, 4, n., *sleep; be at ease.*

Drūsus, -ī, m., in this book *M. Līvius Drūsus,* a Roman prominent as a political leader at the beginning of the first century B.C. He at first sided with the aristocracy, but afterwards won over the people by carrying measures in their interest. Having finally organized a conspiracy, he was murdered in his own house, 91 B.C. ARCH. 3.

dubitātiō, -ōnis, [dubitō], f., *doubt, hesitation; uncertainty, perplexity.*

dubitō, -āre, -āvī, -ātum, [dubius], 1, a. and n., *doubt, call in question, question; be uncertain, waver; deliberate, consider; hesitate, delay, be irresolute.*

dubius, -a, -um, adj., *doubtful, wavering, uncertain, undecided, dubious; precarious, critical.* **nōn dubium est quīn,** *there is no* *doubt that.* **sine dubiō,** *beyond doubt, undoubtedly, certainly.* **in dubiō esse,** *to be at stake.*

ducentī, -ae, -a, or **CC,** gen. **-tum,** [**duo + centum**], num. adj., *two hundred.*

dūcō, dūcere, dūxī, ductum, 3, a., *lead, guide, conduct, direct; lead forth, draw forth; derive, deduce; take in, inhale; calculate, consider, esteem, reckon.* **in mātrimōnium dūcere,** *to marry.* **dūcī** [sc. **ad supplicium**], *to be executed.*

dūdum [**diū + dum**], adv., *a little while ago, but now; before, formerly.* See **iam.**

dulcēdō, -inis, [**dulcis**], f., *sweetness; agreeableness, pleasantness, charm.*

dulcis, -e, adj., *sweet; agreeable, pleasant, charming; dear.*

dum, conj., *while, whilst, all the time that, as long as, until, till, to the time when; provided that, if only.* **dum modo,** *if so be that, provided that, if only.*

dumtaxat [**dum + taxō,** *examine*], adv., lit., *while one examines; to this extent, so far; simply, merely, only; if only, if but.*

duo, -ae, -o, num. adj., *two, the two.*

duodecim, or **XII,** [**duo + decem**], num. adj., *twelve.*

duodecimus, -a, -um, [**duodecim**], num. adj., *twelfth.*

duplex, -icis, [**duo + plicō,** *fold*], adj., *twofold, double; twice as long, twice as great; two, a choice of two; double-tongued, deceitful.*

duplicō, -āre, -āvī, -ātum, [**duplex**], 1, a., *double, multiply by two, enlarge, increase; double up, bend.*

dūrō, -āre, -āvī, -ātum, [**dūrus**], 1, a., *make hard, harden, solidify; harden with use, make hardy; make dull, blunt; grow hard; be patient, wait, persevere, endure; hold out, continue, last, remain.*

dūrus, -a, -um, adj., *hard; rough, rude, uncultivated; unfeeling, pitiless, stern, cruel, inexorable; hard to bear, burdensome.*

dux, ducis, [cf. **dūcō**], m. and f., *leader, guide; master, counselor; commander, general; ruler, head, chief, leading man.*

Dyrrachium, -ī, [Δυρράχιον], n., *Dyrrachium,* formerly called *Epidamnus,* a city on the seacoast of Illyria, nearly opposite Brundisium.

E

ē, see **ex.**

ēbrius, -a, -um, [perhaps **bria,** *a cup*], adj., *full, sated* [*with drink*]; *drunk, intoxicated.*

ebur, -oris, n., *ivory.*

ecquī, ecquae or **ecqua, ecquod,** gen. wanting, [**ec + quī**], inter. adj., in direct questions, *is there any? any?* in indirect questions, *whether any.*

ecquid [**ecquis**], inter. adv., in direct questions, *at all?* giving merely an emphatic turn to the question, and often not translated in words; in indirect questions, *if at all, whether.*

edāx, -ācis, [**edō**], adj., *greedy, voracious, gluttonous.*

ēdictum, -ī, [**ēdīcō**], n., *proclamation, edict, order.*

ēdiscō, -ere, ēdidicī, ——, [**ē + discō**], 3, a., *learₐ thoroughly,* *learn by heart, commit to memory; learn, study.*

ēdō, ēdere, ēdidī, ēditum, [ē + dō], 3, a., *give out, put forth; bring forth, beget, produce; relate, tell, utter; publish, declare, disclose, give account of.*

ēducō, -āre, -āvī, -ātum, [ē + ducō], 1, a., *bring up, train, educate; support, raise.*

ēdūcō, -ere, ēdūxī, ēductum, [ē + dūcō], 3, a., *lead forth, lead out; draw out, draw forth; bring up, rear;* of a sword, *draw.*

efferō, -āre, -āvī, -ātum, [efferus, *savage*], 1, a., *make wild, make savage, barbarize; uncivilize, brutalize.*

efferō, efferre, extulī, ēlātum, [ex + ferō], irr., a., *carry forth, bring out, remove; carry out* for burial, *bear* to the grave; *bring forth, bear, produce; lift up, raise, elevate, extol; set forth, spread abroad, publish, proclaim;* pass., of emotions, *be carried away, be puffed up, be inspired.* **ad caelum efferre laudibus,** *to laud to the skies.*

efficāx, -ācis, comp. **efficācior,** sup. **efficācissimus,** [efficiō], adj., *powerful, efficient, effective.*

efficiō, -ere, effēcī, effectum, [ex + faciō], 3, a., *bring about, bring to pass, cause, accomplish, make; produce, yield, bear; make out, show, prove.*

effigiēs, -ēī, [cf. **effingō**], f., *copy, representation, image, likeness; ideal, symbol.*

effingō, -ere, effīnxī, effīctum, [ex + fingō], 3, a., *stroke; wipe clean; form, fashion, mold; represent, portray.*

efflōrēscō, -ere, -flōruī, ——, [inch. of **flōrēscō,** *begin to blossom*], 3, n., *bloom, flourish, abound, blossom.*

effodiō, -ere, -fōdī, -fossum, [ex + fodiō, *dig*], 3, a., *dig out, dig up, mine, excavate.*

effrēnātē, comp. **effrēnātius,** [effrēnātus], adv., *without bridle, without check, violently, unrestrainedly.*

effrēnātus, -a, -um, [ex + frēnātus, *bridled*], adj., *unbridled, unrestrained, uncontrolled.*

effugiō, -ere, effūgī, ——, [ex + fugiō], 3, a. and n., *flee away, slip out of; flee from, avoid, shun; escape, get away.*

effundō, -ere, -fūdī, -fūsum, [ex + fundō], 3, a., *pour out, pour forth, shed, spread abroad: drive out, cast out, send forth; hurl headlong, throw down, prostrate; produce abundantly; lavish, squander, waste; empty, exhaust, discharge; expend; give up, let go, abandon, resign.*

egēns, -entis, [part. of **egeō**], adj., *needy, lacking; in want, destitute.*

egeō, egēre, eguī, ——, 2, n., *be in want of, be lacking; need, lack, want, be without, be destitute of.*

Ēgeria, -ae, f., *nymph, wife and adviser of Numa.* LIV. 1, 19.

egestās, -ātis, [egēns], f., *want, need, poverty, indigence.* **ad egestātēs explendās,** *to satiate the indigence.*

ego, meī, pl. **nōs,** gen. **nostrum** and **nostrī,** [cf. ἐγώ], pers. pron., *I, we.*

egomet [ego + -met, *self*], strengthened form of **ego,** *I myself.*

ēgredior, ēgredī, ēgressus sum, [ē + gradior], 3, dep., *go out, go forth, come forth; depart, go out; go up, ascend;* of an army, *march out;* from a ship, *disembark, land.* ē portū ēgredī, *to set sail.*

ēgregiē, comp. ēgregius, [ēgregius], adv., *above others, excellently, splendidly, finely, exceedingly well.*

ēgregius, -a, -um, [ē + grex], adj., *extraordinary, remarkable, distinguished; excellent, fine, noble.*

ēiciō, ēicere, ēiēcī, ēiectum, [ē + iaciō], 3, a., *cast out, cast forth, hurl forth; thrust out, drive away, expel; banish, drive into exile; wreck.* sē ēicere, *to rush out, to break forth.* ēicere vīcīnōs, *to trespass.*

ēlābor, ēlābī, ēlāpsus sum, [ē + lābor], 3, dep., *slip away, slip off, escape, drop.*

ēlabōrātus, -a, -um, [ēlabōrō], adj., *highly wrought, finished, labored.*

ēlabōrō, -āre, -āvī, -ātum, [ē + labōrō], 1, a. and n., *labor, struggle, make an effort; take pains, work out, elaborate.* in aliquā rē ēlabōrāre, *to accomplish something in anything.* maximē ēlabōrandum est, *special pains must be taken.*

ēlegāns, -antis, [for ēligēns, part. of ēligō], adj., *fastidious, nice, accustomed to select; dainty, delicate; select, choice, neat, finished, tasteful, elegant; fine.*

elephantus, -ī, m., *elephant.*

ēlevō, -āre, ——, -ātum, [ē + levō], 1, a., *lift up, raise; lighten, alleviate; make light of, dimin-*

ish; impair; disparage, detract from.

ēligō, -ere, -lēgī, -lēctum, [ē + legō, *choose*], 3, a., *pluck out, pick out, choose, single out.*

ēloquentia, -ae, [ēloquēns, *eloquent*], f., *eloquence, the faculty of speaking to the purpose.*

ēlūceō, -ēre, -lūxī, ——, [ē + lūceō, *shine*], 2, n., *shine out, gleam; be conspicuous; appear, be manifest.*

ēlūdō, ēlūdere, ēlūsī, ēlūsum, [ē + lūdō], 3, a. and n., *quit playing; parry, avoid, evade, elude, escape; delude, deceive; trifle with, make sport of, mock.*

ēmendō, -āre, -āvī, -ātum, [ē + mendum, *fault*], 1, a., *free from faults, correct, emend, improve; revise; atone for, compensate for; make wholly good.*

ēmentior, -īrī, -ītus sum, [ē + mentior, *lie*], 4, dep., *speak falsely, falsify, pretend, falsely assert, lie.*

ēmereō, -ēre, -uī, -itum, [ē + mereō], 2, a., *obtain by service, earn, merit, deserve; serve out, complete.* hominēs ēmeritīs stīpendiīs, *discharged veterans.*

ēmergō, -ere, ēmersī, ēmersum, [ē + mergō], 3, a. and n., *bring to light, raise up; come forth, come up out of, emerge, rise up, as from water; free oneself, get clear, escape.*

ēmissus, see ēmittō.

ēmittō, -ere, ēmīsī, ēmissum, [ē + mittō], 3, a., *send forth, send out, drive out, expel; hurl, discharge; send out, publish; set free, let go, let slip; utter, give utterance to.*

emō, emere, ēmī, ēmptum, 3, a., *buy, purchase.*

ēmorior, ēmorī, ——, [ē + morior], 3, dep., *die off. die.*

ēmoveō, -ēre, -mōvī, -mōtum, [ē + moveō], 2, a., *move out, move away, remove, expel, dislodge.*

ēmptiō, -ōnis, [emō], f., *a buying, purchase.*

ēmptor, -ōris, [emō], m., *buyer, purchaser.*

ēnārrō, -āre, -āvī, -ātum, [ē + nārrō], 1, a., *set forth in detail, recount, describe.*

enim, conj., *postpositive, for, because; for instance, now really, in fact; indeed, of course, really, certainly; no doubt, to be sure.*

ēnitēscō, -ere, -nituī, ——, [inch. from ēniteō, *shine forth*], 3, n., *begin to shine forth, shine out, gleam, brighten; be eminent, be distinguished; be displayed.*

Ennius, -ī or **-iī,** m., *Quintus Ennius,* the most eminent among the early Roman poets; born at Rudiae, in Calabria, 239 B.C., died at Rome, 169 B.C. He wrote epic, dramatic, and miscellaneous poetry, none of which is now extant except in fragments. His *Annālēs,* treating of the history of Rome from the beginning to his own times, was the first Latin poem in hexameter verse. ARCH. 9; 11; SEN. 14; AM. 6, 17.

ēnotō, -āre, -āvī, -ātum, [ē + notō], 1, a., *make notes, mark down, note down, write.*

eō, īre, īvī or **iī, itum,** irr., n., *go, come; go forth, depart; move on,* *sail, fly, march, advance, enter; concur in; pass, prosper, turn out.*

eō [cf. **is**], adv., *there, in that place; for that reason, on that account; to that place, thither; to that degree, so far.*

eōdem [idem], adv., *in the same place; to the same place, thither; to the same point, to the same purpose; thereto, besides.*

Ephesius, -a, -um, [Ephesus], adj., *of Ephesus, Ephesian.* As subst., **Ephesiī, -ōrum,** m., pl., *the natives of Ephesus, Ephesians.*

Ephesus, -ī, [Ἔφεσος], f., *Ephesus,* a celebrated Greek city on the west coast of Asia Minor.

epigramma, -atis, [ἐπίγραμμα], n., *inscription; epigram.*

epistula, -ae, [ἐπιστολή], f., *letter, epistle.*

epulae, -ārum, [perhaps from edō, *eat*], f., pl., *viands, dishes, meats; feast, banquet, entertainment.*

eques, -itis, [equus], m., *horseman, rider; cavalryman, trooper; knight, member of the equestrian order.* In the early days of Rome the poorer citizens served in the army as infantry, the wealthier as cavalry. As the state grew the class of cavalrymen increased in importance and influence, and gained special privileges. In Cicero's time the Roman knights (**equitēs Rōmānī**) formed a distinct and powerful order, between the senate and the plebs. They were engaged especially in farming the revenues.

equester, -tris, -tre, [eques], adj., *of a horseman, equestrian, of* cavalry; of the knights of the equestrian order, knightly.

equidem [interj. e + quidem], adv., *indeed, truly, certainly, at all events, at least, surely; for my part, in my case; by all means, of course, to be sure.*

equitātus, -ūs, [equitō, from **equus**], m., *cavalry; equestrian order.*

equus, -ī, m., *horse.*

ērēctus, -a, -um, comp. **ērēctior.** [part. of **ērigō**], adj., *directed upwards, upright, high; lofty, noble; arrogant, haughty; intent, eager, on the alert.*

ergā, prep. with acc., *towards, to, in respect to.*

ergō, adv., *therefore, then, accordingly;* often used, like **causā** and **grātiā,** with preceding gen., *on account of, because of, for the sake of.*

ērigō, ērigere, ērēxī, ērēctum, [ē + **regō**], 3, a., *raise up, set up, erect, elevate; stir up, arouse, animate, cheer, encourage.*

ēripiō, ēripere, ēripuī, ēreptum, [ē + **rapiō**], 3, a., *snatch away, tear away, take away; rescue, save, deliver, set free, free.*

ērogō, -āre, -āvī, -ātum, [ē + **rogō**], 1, a., *take out, appropriate, pay, expend.*

errō, -āre, -āvī, -ātum, 1, a. and n., *wander, go astray, roam about, stray; be in error, err, go wrong; go astray, mistake.* **vehementer errāre,** *to be greatly mistaken.*

error, -ōris, [errō], m., *wandering, straying, missing the way; doubt, uncertainty, ambiguity; going wrong, mistake, error, delusion.*

ērubēscō, -ere, -buī, ——, [ē + rubēscō, *grow red*], 3, inch., n.,

grow red, blush with shame, feel ashamed.

ērudiō, -īre, -īvī, -ītum, [ē + **rudis**], 4, a., *teach, instruct; educate, polish.*

ērudītē, comp. **ērudītius,** sup. **ēruditissimē,** [**ērudītus**], adv., *learnedly, with erudition.*

ērudītus, -a, -um, [part. of ērudiō], adj., *learned, educated; skilled, accomplished, cultured.*

ērumpō, -ere, ērūpī, ēruptum, [ē + **rumpō**], 3, a. and n., *break out, burst forth, sally forth; cause to burst forth, hurl forth.*

essedum, -ī, n., *two-wheeled war-chariot, car,* of the early Britons.

et, adv. and conj.:
(1) As adv., *also, too, besides, moreover, even.*
(2) As conj., *and;* introducing a contrasted thought or question, *and yet, but still, but; though; and in fact.* **et — et,** *both — and, as well — as, on the one hand — on the other.* **et — neque,** *both — and not.* **neque — et,** *both not — and.*

etenim [et + enim], conj., *for truly, and really, and indeed, because, since.*

etiam [et + iam], adv. and conj., *and also, and furthermore, now too, even yet, also, even, likewise; certainly, by all means; as the answer to a question, "Yes."* **etiam atque etiam,** *again and again, repeatedly, persistently.* **etiam nunc,** *yet still, even now, even till now.* **etiam sī,** *even if, although.*

Etrūria, -ae, f., *Etrūria,* a country in Italy, west of the Tiber and south of the valley of the Po.

etsī [et + sī], conj., *although, though, even if, and yet.*

Eurōpa, -ae, f., *Eurōpa,* daughter of Agenor, king of Phoenicia, and sister of Cadmus. Her beauty charmed Zeus, who assumed the form of a bull and mingled with the herd as Eurōpa and her maidens were sporting on the seashore. Encouraged by the tameness of the animal, Eurōpa ventured to mount his back; whereupon the god rushed into the sea, and swam with her to Crete.

ēvādō, ēvādere, ēvāsī, ēvāsum, [ē + vādō], 3, a. and n., *go forth, come forth, come out; get away, escape; turn out, prove to be, result; turn out to be.*

ēvehō, -ere, -vexī, -vectum, [ē + vehō], 3, a., *carry out, bring forth, convey out, lead forth; spread abroad, carry away; lift up, raise, elevate;* in the pass., *be borne forth, move forth, proceed, sail, advance.* **spīritū ēvectus,** *shot upward by the blast.*

ēvellō, -ere, -vellī, -volsum or **-vulsum,** [ē + vellō, *tear away*], 3, a., *tear out, pluck out, eradicate; pull off, tear off.*

ēveniō, -īre, ēvēnī, ēventum, [ē + veniō], 4, n., *come out; come to pass, happen, turn out.*

ēventum, -ī, [n. part. of ēveniō], n., *an issue, occurrence, event; result, effect.*

ēventus, -ūs, [ēveniō], m., *outcome, issue, result; occurrence, event.*

ēversiō, -ōnis, [ēvertō], f., *turning out, overthrowing, overthrow, ruin.*

ēvertō, -ere, ēvertī, ēversum, [ē + vertō], 3, a., *overturn, overthrow, upturn; throw down, hurl down, ruin, destroy.*

ēvidēns, comp. **ēvidentior,** sup. **ēvidentissimus,** [ē + videō]. adj., *looking out; obvious, apparent, evident, plainly to be seen.*

ēvītō, -āre, -āvī, -ātum, [ē + vītō], 1, a., *shun, avoid.*

ēvocātor, -ōris, [ēvocō], m., lit., *one who calls forth* to arms; *recruiter, summoner.*

ēvomō, -ere, ēvomuī, ēvomitum, [ē + vomō], 3, a., *vomit forth; cast out, expel.*

ex, often before consonants **ē,** prep. with abl. only, *out of, out from;* of place, *from, out of, down from;* of time, *from, since, after;* of source and material, *from, of;* of partition, *of, out of, from among;* of transition, *from, out of;* of cause, *from, by reason of, by, in consequence of;* of measure and correspondence, *according to, with, in, by, on.* **aliquā ex parte,** *in some measure.*

exaequō, -āre, -āvī, -ātum, [ex + aequō], 1, a., *make equal, place on an equal footing; equal, attain equality with.* **sē exaequāre,** *to bring oneself down to the level of.*

exaggerō, -āre, -āvī, -ātum, [ex + aggerō, from agger], 1, a., *heap up, pile up, accumulate; magnify, exaggerate.*

exagitō, -āre, -āvī, -ātum, [ex + agitō], 1, a., *drive out, drive* *away;* rouse, keep in motion, *disquiet* greatly, harass, persecute, disturb, torment, vex; stir *up,* irritate, rouse, excite, incite; *provoke* (man), embroil (the state).

exanimis, -e, [ex + anima], adj., *breathless; lifeless, dead; dismayed, terrified.*

exārdēscō, -ere, exārsī, exārsum, [ex + ārdēscō], 3, inch., *blaze out, blaze up; take fire, be inflamed, kindle, glow; become aroused.*

exarō, -āre, -āvī, -ātum, [ex + arō, *plow*], 1, a., *plow out, dig up, harvest; write, set down, scrawl.*

exaudiō, -īre, -īvī, -ītum, [ex + audiō], 4, a., *hear from without; hear clearly; perceive; listen to, obey.*

excēdō, -ere, excessī, excessum, [ex + cēdō], 3, a. and n., *go forth, depart, withdraw, leave; go beyond, exceed, pass beyond; pass, tower above.*

excellēns, -entis, [part. of excellō], adj., *eminent, preëminent; superior, surpassing, distinguished.*

excellō, -ere, excelluī, excelsum, 3, a. and n., *be eminent; be superior, excel, surpass.*

excelsus, -a, -um, [part. of excellō], adj., *elevated, high, lofty.* As subst., excelsum, -ī, n., *elevation, height.*

exceptiō, -ōnis, [excipiō], f., *exception, restriction, limitation; protest, objection.*

excerpō, -ere, -cerpsī, -cerptum, [ex + carpō], 3, a., *pick out,* *choose, select; take out, except, omit.*

excidō, -ere, excidī, ——, [ex + cadō], 3, n., *fall from, fall away; slip away, escape; pass away, perish.*

excipiō, -ere, excēpī, exceptum, [ex + capiō], 3, a., *take out, withdraw; except, make an exception of; take up, receive, welcome; catch, capture; intercept; follow, succeed; listen to.*

excitō, -āre, -āvī, -ātum, [freq. of exciō], 1, a., *call out, rouse, summon; call up, raise; build, construct; stimulate, inspire, awaken; stir up, kindle, excite.*

exclūdō, -ere, exclūsī, exclūsum, [ex + claudō], 3, a., *shut out, exclude, cut off; prevent, hinder.*

excolō, -ere, excoluī, excultum, [ex + colō], 3, a., *cultivate, improve, refine.*

excubiae, -ārum, [cf. excubō, *watch*], f., pl., *watching; watchmen, sentinels, guards.*

excurrō, -ere, -cucurrī or -currī, -cursum, [ex + currō], 3, n., *run out, hasten forwards; make an incursion; run, extend, spread; display oneself.*

excūsātiō, -ōnis, [excūsō], f., *excusing, excuse; mode of defending oneself.*

excutiō, -ere, -cussī, -cussum, [ex + quatiō, *shake*], 3, a., *shake out, shake forth, cast out, drive out, send forth; project, throw; search, investigate; force away discard, remove, wrest, extort.*

exedō, -ere, -ēdī, -ēsum, [ex + edō, *eat*], 3, a., *eat up, consume, devour; prey upon, destroy; corrode.*

exemplar, -āris, [exemplum], n., *copy, image, likeness; pattern, model, example.*

exemplum, -ī, [eximō, lit. *that which is taken out],* n., *specimen, sample; pattern, model; precedent, warning, example, lesson; penalty; way, manner;* of writing, *transcript, copy; illustration.* **crūdēlissimīs exemplīs,** *with all manner of cruelties, with every circumstance of cruelty.* **hōc exemplō,** *in accordance with this precedent.*

exeō, -īre, -iī, -itum, [ex + eō], irr., n., *go out, come forth; go away, depart, withdraw; turn out, result;* of time, *run out, end, expire.*

exerceō, -cēre, -cuī, -citum, [ex + arceō], 2, a., *keep busy, keep active, keep at work; train, discipline; employ, exercise, practice, administer; disturb, plague, vex; pass.* **exercēre grātiam, inimīcitiās,** *feel partiality, cherish enmity.*

exercitātiō, -ōnis, [exercitō, freq. of **exerceō],** f., *exercise, practice; training, experience.*

exercitus, -ūs, [exerceō], m., *army.*

exhauriō, -īre, exhausī, exhaustum, [ex + hauriō], 4, a., *draw off,* as liquid from a vessel; *draw out, take out; take away, remove; empty, exhaust, bring to an end; fulfill.*

exigō, -ere, exēgī, exāctum, [ex + agō], 3, a., *drive out, thrust out; thrust, drive; exact, demand, require, collect; pass, spend; examine, consider.* **tertiā ferē vigiliā exāctā,** *at about the end of the third watch.*

exiguus, -a, -um, [cf. **exigō],** adj., *small, little, scanty; poor, mean, paltry.*

exīlis, -e, adj., *narrow, slender, meager, lean; cheerless, comfortless; worthless, insincere; dry, inadequate.*

eximiē [eximius], adv., *exceedingly, very much.*

eximius, -a, -um, [eximō, take out], adj., *choice, fine, excellent; uncommon, extraordinary, remarkable.*

eximō, -ere, -ēmī, -ēmptum, [ex + emō], 3, a., *take away, remove; release, deliver; make an exception of;* of time, *consume, waste, lose.*

exīstimō, -āre, -āvī, -ātum, [ex + aestimō], 1, a. and n., *reckon, estimate; esteem, consider; think, suppose.*

exitiōsus, -a, -um, [exitium], adj., *destructive, deadly, pernicious.*

exitium, -ī or -iī, [exeō], n., *destruction, ruin, mischief, death.*

exitus, -ūs, [exeō], m., *going forth, departure, exit; outlet, passage; way out, end, conclusion; end of life, death; outcome, result, issue.*

exoptō, -āre, -āvī, -ātum, [ex + optō], 1, a., *wish earnestly, desire greatly, long for.*

exōrdior, -īrī, -ōrsus sum, [ex + ōrdior], 4, dep., *prepare to weave; commence, make a beginning.*

exorior, -īrī, -ortus sum, [ex + orior], 3 and 4, dep., *come forth, rise, appear; begin, take origin, be caused, be produced; recover oneself, take courage.*

exōrnō, -āre, -āvī, -ātum, [ex + ōrnō], 1, a., *equip, furnish, sup-*

ply, provide; deck out, embellish, adorn.

expeditus, -a, -um, [part. of **expedio,** *set free*], adj., *unfettered, free, without a burden; ready, prompt, easy; unembarrassed; convenient, ready at hand.* **cēna expedīta,** *plain and simple meal, meal easily dispatched.* As subst., **expedītī, -orum,** m. pl., *foot soldiers unencumbered with baggage; light troops.*

expellō, -ere, expulī, expulsum, [ex + pellō], 3, a., *drive out, thrust forth, cast forth, expel.*

expergīscor, -gīscī, experrēctus sum, [expergō, *arouse*], 3, dep., *wake up, awake; be alert.*

experior, -īrī, expertus sum, 4, dep., *try, prove, test, find out* by a test; *make trial of, undertake; undergo, experience.* **experīrī rē,** *gain knowledge from experience.*

expers, -tis, [ex + pars], adj., lit., *having no part in; destitute of, devoid of, without.* **expers esse alicuius,** *to free from the influence of anyone.*

expetō, -ere, expetīvī, expetītum, [ex + petō], 3, a., *seek after, strive for, aim at; ask, demand, request; desire, wish.* **poenās expetere ab aliquō,** *to inflict punishment on anyone.*

expleō, -ēre, -ēvī, -ētum, [ex + -pleō], 2, a., *fill up, fill full; complete, finish; satisfy, appease; discharge, perform, do.*

explicō, -āre, -āvī and **-uī, -ātum** and **-itum,** [ex + plicō]. 1, a., *unfold, unroll; spread out, display; set free, release; set in order, adjust, set forth, explain.*

explōrātus, -a, -um, [part. of **explōrō**], adj., *ascertained, established, certain, sure.*

explōrō, -āre, -āvī, -ātum, [ex + plōrō], 1, a., *search out, investigate; spy out, examine; reconnoiter.*

expōnō, -ere, exposuī, expositum, [ex + pōnō], 3, a., *put forth, exhibit; put on shore, disembark; set forth, relate, explain.*

exposcō, -ere, -poposcī, ——, [ex + poscō], 3, a., *ask earnestly for, pray for, beg, entreat; demand, require surrender of, claim.*

expressus, -a, -um, [part. of **exprimō**], adj., *standing out, prominent, bold, realistic.*

exprimō, -ere, expressī, expressum, [ex + premō], 3, a., *press out, squeeze forth; extort, wrest from; represent, copy, imitate; portray, express, describe.*

exprobō, -āre, -āvī, -ātum, [ex + probrum], 1, a. and n., *reproach with, blame for, find fault; cast up against, throw in the teeth of.*

exprōmō, -ere, exprōmpsī, exprōmptum, [ex + prōmō], 3, a., *show forth, exhibit, display; utter, state.*

expugnātiō, -ōnis, [expugnō], f., *taking by storm, storming.*

expūrgō, -āre, -āvī, -ātum, [ex + pūrgō], 1, a., *cleanse, purify; vindicate, justify;* with reflex., *clear oneself of a charge.*

exscrībō, -ere, -scrīpsī, -scrīptum, [ex + scrībō], 3, a., *write out, write off, copy; resemble.*

exsequor, -i, -secūtus sum, [ex + sequor], 3, dep., *follow to the grave; follow after, accompany; go after, pursue; prosecute, carry* *out, enforce; obtain; perform, execute, accomplish, fulfill; investigate, examine; relate, describe; punish, avenge.*

exsilium, -ī or -iī, [exsul], n., *exile, banishment; place of exile, retreat.*

exsistō, -ere, **exstitī, exstitum,** [ex + sistō], 3, n., *come forth, come out, appear; spring up, arise, become; be manifest, be, exist.*

exspectātiō, -ōnis, [exspectō], f., *awaiting for, expecting, expectation; longing for; reputation.*

exspectātus, -a, -um, [part. of exspectō], adj., *longed for, welcome.*

exspectō, -āre, -āvī, -ātum, [ex + spectō], 1, a. and n., *look out for, wait for, await; long for, desire, expect; apprehend, dread.*

exspīrō, -āre, -āvī, -ātum, [ex + spīrō, *breathe*], 1, a. and n., *breathe out, give forth; breathe one's last, perish, come to an end.*

exspoliō, -āre, -āvī, -ātum, [ex + spoliō], 1, a., *spoil utterly; pillage, plunder; deprive, rob.*

exstinguō, -ere, **exstīnxī, exstīnctum,** [ex + stinguō, *quench*], 3, a., *quench, put out, extinguish; deprive of life, kill; blot out, destroy utterly, annihilate.*

exstō, -āre, ——, ——, [ex + stō], 1, n., *stand out, stand forth, project; appear, exist, be found.*

exstrūctiō, -ōnis, [exstruō], f., *building up, erecting; structure, building.*

exstruō, -ere, -strūxī, -strūctum, [ex + struō, *heap up*], 3, a., *heap up, pile, accumulate; load, heap full; build up, raise, rear, erect, construct; depict.* **mēnsae exstrūctae,** *heaped up tables.*

exsul, -ulis, m. and f., *exile, outlaw, wanderer.*

exsultō, -āre, -āvī, -ātum, [freq. of **exsiliō**], 1, n., *leap up, bound up; revel, exult, delight in.*

extenuō, -āre, -āvī, -ātum, [ex + tenuō], 1, a., *make thin; lessen, diminish, detract from, minimize.*

exter or **exterus,** -a, -um, adj., *outward, outer; foreign, strange.* Comp. **exterior,** -us, *outer, exterior.* Sup. **extrēmus,** -a, -um, *outermost, utmost; last, remotest, extreme.* As subst., **extrēmum,** -ī, n., *end; border.* **extrēma persequī,** *to follow up to the last.* **ūsque ad extrēmum,** *to the very end.*

exterminō, -āre, -āvī, -ātum, [ex + terminus], 1, a., *drive out, expel, banish, remove.*

externus, -a, -um, [exter], adj., *outward, external; foreign, strange.*

exterreō, -ēre, -terruī, -territum, [ex + terreō], 2, a., *frighten out of, strike with terror, frighten.*

extollō, -ere, ——, ——, [ex + tollō], 3, a., *lift up, raise, elevate; extol, praise highly.*

extorqueō, -ēre, **extorsī, extortum,** [ex + torqueō], 2, a., *wrench from, wrest away; obtain by force, extort.*

extrā [exter; for exterā, sc. parte], adv. and prep. :
　(1) As adv., *on the outside, without.*
　(2) As prep., *outside of, beyond, aside from, except.*

extrēmus, -a, -um, see **exter.**

exūrō, -ere, **exussī, exūstum,** [ex + ūrō], 3, a., *burn up, consume.*

F

F., see **fīlius.**

Fabius, -a, name of an ancient and distinguished patrician gens. See **Maximus.**

Fābricius, -a, name of a Roman gens. Esp., *C. Fābricius Luscinus,* consul 282 B.C., censor in 275, leader of the Roman forces against Pyrrhus. SEN. 6.

fābula, -ae, [from **fārī,** *speak*], f., *narration, account; fable, legend; myth; affair, matter; play, drama; plot, action.*

facētē, comp. **facētius,** sup. **facētissimē,** [**facētus,** *witty*], adv., *finely, gracefully, pleasantly, wittily.*

faciēs, -ēī, [**faciō**], f., *kind, class; appearance, form, shape, countenance, look, appearance, aspect.*

facile, comp. **facilius,** sup. **facillimē,** [**facilis**], adv., *easily, without trouble; readily, willingly, promptly.* **haud facile,** *with difficulty.*

facilis, -e, comp. **facilior,** sup. **facillimus,** [**faciō**], adj., *easy, not difficult; accessible, approachable, affable, courteous, kindly.*

facilitās, -ātis, [**facilis**], f., *ease, readiness, facility; affability, courtesy.*

facinerōsus, -a, -um, [**facinus**], adj., *criminal, vicious.* As subst., **facinerōsus, -ī,** m., *criminal, felon, malefactor.*

facinus, -oris, [cf. **faciō**], n., *deed, act, action; evil deed, misdeed; outrage, crime, villainy.*

faciō, facere, fēcī, factum, 3, a. and n., *make, fashion, construct; compose; do, perform, execute;* *bring about, cause, produce; conduct, represent; choose, appoint; render, grant; value, esteem.* **fac ut tuam valētūdinem cūrēs,** *do take care of your health.* **fac ut valeās,** *do keep well.* **plūris facere,** *to value more highly.* **satis facere,** *to give satisfaction, to satisfy; to make amends, to excuse.* See **fīō.**

factiō, -ōnis, [**faciō**], f., *making, preparing; taking sides, partisanship, intrigue; association, order, sect, party.*

factiōsus, -a, -um, [**factiō**], adj., *heading a party, attaching persons to oneself for the sake of forming a party or faction; partisan, factious, seditious, revolutionary; intriguing, guilty of treason.* As subst., **factiōsus, -ī,** n., *an intriguer.*

factum, -ī, [**factus, faciō**], n., *deed, act, exploit, achievement; event; outcome.*

facultās, -ātis, [**facilis**], f., *capability, ability, power; possibility, opportunity, means; supply, stock, property;* especially in pl., *resources, goods, riches.*

faenum, -ī, n., *hay.*

faenus, -oris, n., *profit of capital, interest, gain, profit, advantage.*

Faesulae, -ārum, f., pl., *Faesulae,* an ancient city in the northern part of Etruria; now *Fiesole,* near Florence.

Faesulānus, -a, -um, adj., *of Faesulae, Faesulan.* As subst., **Faesulānus, -ī,** m., *man from Faesulae.* SALL. 60.

falcārius, -ī or **-iī,** [**falx**], m., *scythe-maker, sickle-maker.*

fallō, fallere, fefellī, falsum, 3, a. and n., *deceive, cheat, betray; disappoint; escape the notice of, escape notice, be unobserved;* pass. often *be mistaken, deceive oneself, be wrong, be deceived.* **mē fefellit diēs,** *I was mistaken in the day.*

falsō, [falsus], adv., *falsely, untruly, erroneously.*

falsus, -a, -um, [part. of **fallō**], adj., *deceptive, false, delusive; groundless, unfounded, misleading.*

fāma, -ae, [for, *speak*], f., *report, rumor, saying, tradition; public opinion, repute, renown, fame, reputation.*

famēs, -is, f., *hunger, starvation; want, famine.*

familia, -ae, [famulus, *servant*], f., *body of servants, household, domestics; family, kindred; estate.* **pater familiās,** *master of a house, head of a family.* **māter familiās,** *mistress of a house, matron.* **familiae gladiātōriae,** *gladiatorial schools* or *troops.*

familiāris, -e, [familia], adj., *belonging to a household, private; intimate, friendly, familiar.* As subst., **familiāris, -is,** m., *intimate friend, friend, companion.*

familiāritās, -ātis, [familiāris], f., *familiarity, intimacy, familiar intercourse, intimate acquaintance.*

familiāriter, comp. **familiārius,** sup. **familiārissimē,** [familiāris], adv., *intimately, on intimate terms.*

Fannius, -a, name of a Roman gens. *C. Fannius Strabō,* son-in-law of Laelius, was born in 160 B.C. He was author of a history of his own times, no part of which has come down to us. Cicero introduces him as the speaker in his *Dē Rēpūblicā,* and in his Laelius. Aм. 4, *et seq.*

fānum, -ī, [for], n., *shrine, sanctuary.*

fās, only nom. and acc. in use, [for, *speak*], n., *right according to divine law; divine law, justice.* **fās est,** *it is right, it is allowable, it is proper, it is permitted.*

fascis, -is, m., *bundle, packet;* in pl., *the fasces,* the bundle of rods tied about an ax, carried before the highest magistrates of Rome as a symbol of authority.

fāstus, -a, -um, [fās], adj., *on which it is allowed to speak;* hence, with **diēs,** a day on which the praetor's court was open, *judicial day.* These **diēs fāstī** were marked in a book or calendar, and published. Hence, **Fāstī,** *the days marked in the calendar.* See Companion, page 697.

fātālis, -e, [fātum], adj., *of fate, ordained by fate, destined; fateful, destructive, dangerous.*

fateor, fatērī, fassus sum, [for], 2, dep., *confess, admit, own, acknowledge; show, indicate.*

fatīgō, -āre, -āvī, -ātum, 1, a., *weary, fatigue; vex, harass, importune; lay siege to.*

fātum, -ī, [for], n., *prophetic utterance, prediction, oracle; destiny, fate; ill fate, calamity, ruin, destruction; death.*

faucēs, -ium, f., pl., *pharynx, throat, jaws; entrance, defile,* pass. **ex bellī ōre ac faucibus,** *from the open jaws of war.*

faventēs, -ium, [subst. from part. of **faveō**], m. pl., *supporters, backers.*

faveō, favēre, fāvī, fautum, 2, n., *be kind to, be well disposed toward, favor; befriend, protect, promote.*

favor, -ōris, [faveō], m., *favor, good-will; inclination, partiality; praise, approval, applause, popularity; acclamation, encouragement, moral support; encouraging shouts.*

fax, facis, [cf. **faciō**], f., *torch, fire-brand;* by metonymy, *fire-ball, meteor, comet; fire, flame.*

febrīcula, -ae, [dim. of **febris**], f., *slight fever, slight attack of fever.*

febris, -is, f., *fever.*

fēlīcitās, -ātis, [fēlīx], f., *good fortune, good luck, success.* As subst., **Fēlīcitas, -ātis,** f., *goddess of good fortune, Good Fortune,* worshiped as a divinity by the Romans. VERR. 57.

fēlīciter, comp. **fēlīcius,** sup. **fēlīcissimē,** [fēlīx, *fruitful*], adv., *fruitfully, abundantly; auspiciously, favorably; luckily, successfully.*

fēmina, -ae, f., *female, woman.*

fera, -ae, [ferus, *wild*], f., *wild beast, wild animal.*

ferē, adv., *almost, nearly, about; usually, generally, for the most part.* **non ferē,** *scarcely ever.*

ferentārius, -ī or **-iī,** [ferō], m., *light armed soldier, skirmisher;* in the pl., *light armed troops, light armed infantry.* SALL. 55.

feriō, -īre, ——, ——, [ferō], 4, a., *strike, smite, hit; kill by striking, slay; impress.*

fermē, [for a conjectured **ferimē,** sup. of **ferē**], adv., *almost; quite, entirely, fully, altogether, just; in general, usually, commonly; nearly, well-nigh, about;* with a neg., *hardly, scarcely.*

ferō, ferre, tulī, lātum, irr., a. and n., *bear, carry, bring; lead, conduct, drive; bring forth, produce; yield; endure, put up with, suffer, tolerate; report, tell, celebrate; allow, permit, require.* **prae sē ferre,** *to profess, to show, to manifest.* **sententiam ferre,** *to cast a vote.* **vix feram,** *I shall find it hard to endure, I shall hardly be able to bear.* **levissimē ferre,** *not to be greatly concerned.*

ferōcia, -ae, [ferōx], f., *wildness, fierceness; high spirit, savage courage, bravery; barbarity, ferocity.*

ferōciter, comp. **ferōcius,** sup. **ferōcissimē,** [ferōx], adv., *courageously, bravely; fiercely, savagely; insolently, haughtily.*

ferōx, -ōcis, [ferus, *wild*], adj., *wild, bold, courageous, valiant; warlike, spirited, brave, fierce; in high spirits; savage, headstrong; insolent, cruel; emboldened, impetuous.*

ferrāmentum, -ī, [ferrum], n., *iron tool, tool; ax, hatchet.*

ferreus, -a, -um, [ferrum], adj., *of iron, iron; hard-hearted, unfeeling, cruel.*

ferrum, -ī, n., *iron;* by metonymy, *iron tool, sword.* **flamma atque ferrum,** *fire and sword.* **sonus ferrī,** *the clanking of iron.*

ferus, -a, -um, adj., *wild, savage, barbarous, cruel.*

fessus, -a, -um, adj., *wearied, exhausted, worn out; weak, feeble, infirm.*

festīnātiō, -ōnis, [festīnō], f., *hastening, hurry, speed; eagerness, precipitation.* **nē quid festīnātiōnī [meae] pereat,** *to satisfy my impatience.*

fēstīvus, -a, -um, comp. **fēstīvior,** sup. **fēstīvissimus, [fēstus],** adj., *agreeable, pleasing; jovial, humorous, witty, lively; elegant, handsome.*

fēstus, -a, -um, adj., *festal.*

fictum, -ī, [fingō], n., *falsehood, fiction.*

fidēlis, -e, [fidēs], adj., *faithful, trustworthy, trusty; safe, reliable.*

fidēlitās, -ātis, [fidēlis], f., *faithfulness, trustworthiness, fidelity.*

fidēs, -ē or **-eī, [fidō],** f., *confidence, trust, reliance, faith, credence; good-faith, trustworthiness, fidelity, honor; credibility; assurance, promise, pledge of safety;* in business relations, *credit; protection; corroboration; plighted faith; security.* **fidem facere,** *to convince.* **minōrem fidem facere,** *to fail to convince.* **fidem pūblicam dare,** *to give a pledge of safety in the name of the state.* **accipere in vestram fidem,** *to take into your confidence.* **factā fidē immortālitātis,** *now that they were assured of his immortality.* **fidem fallere,** *to violate or break a promise.*

fidēs, -ium, f., *stringed instrument; lyre, lute, cithern.*

Fidius, -ī or **-iī, [fidēs],** m., *All-faithful,* an epithet of Jupiter as protector of oaths and defender of good faith. **mē dīus Fidius, = ita mē dīus Fidius iuvet,** *so help me the All-faithful! by the god of Truth! most certainly!* EP. 9.

fīdō, -ere, fīsus sum, 3, semi-dep., n., *trust to, put confidence in, rely upon.* **ingeniō fīdere,** *to have confidence in the powers of (one's) intellect.*

fīdūcia, -ae, [fīdus], f., *trust, confidence, reliance; self-confidence, presumption; pledge, security.*

fīdus, -a, -um, [fīdō], adj., *trusty, faithful; trustworthy, credible.*

fīgō, fīgere, fīxī, fixum, 3, a., *fix, set, place, fasten, attach; set up, post up.*

Figulus, -ī, m., *C. Mārcius Figulus,* consul 64 B.C. EP. 1.

figūra, -ae, [cf. **fingō**], f., *form, shape, figure, beauty; quality, kind, form; style, nature, manner; phase.*

fīlia, -ae, [fīlius], f., *daughter.*

fīliola, -ae, [dim. of **fīlia**], f., *little daughter.*

fīliolus, -ī, [fīlius], m., *little son.*

fīlius, -ī or **-iī,** sometimes abbreviated F., f., m., *son.*

fingō, fingere, fīnxī, fictum, 3, a., *touch gently; mold, fashion; compose; instruct, teach; imagine, think; invent, contrive, feign.*

fīnis, -is, [cf. **findō**], m., *limit, border, boundary, end;* in pl., *borders,* hence *territory, land, country.* **quem ad fīnem?** *to what limit? how far?*

fīniō, -īre, -īvī, -ītum, [fīnis], 4, a., *confine in limits, bound; restrain, check; prescribe, determine, fix* *appoint, assign; put an end to, finish, terminate; make an end, come to an end, cease.*

fīnitimus, -a, -um, [fīnis], adj., *bordering on, neighboring, adjoining.*

fīō, fierī, factus sum, irr., n., used as pass. of faciō, *be made, be done; become, happen, come to pass.* fierī potest, *it may happen.* quid Tulliā fiet? *what will become of Tullia?*

firmāmentum, -ī, [fīrmō], n., *means of strengthening; support, stay, prop.*

firmō, -āre, -āvī, -ātum, [fīrmus, *steadfast*], 1, a., *make firm, strengthen, fortify, secure; encourage, animate; confirm, establish, declare.*

firmus, -a, -um, adj., *steadfast, strong, powerful; firm, fast, trusty, faithful.*

Flaccus, -ī, [flaccus, *flabby, flap-eared*], m., *Roman surname especially common in the Fulvian and Valerian gentes.* Three of the name are mentioned in this book:

(1) *M. Fulvius Flaccus,* a friend of the Gracchi, and consul, 125 B.C. In the disturbances attending the attempt of C. Gracchus to carry out reforms, Flaccus organized an armed band. He came into conflict with the forces of the senatorial party, and was routed and slain, 121 B.C. CAT. I, 2; 12.

(2) *L. Valerius Flaccus,* consul with Marius, 100 B.C. In this year the reckless measures and violent deeds of Saturninus

and Glaucia led to a decree of the senate that the consuls should maintain the dignity of the State. As Marius was in sympathy with the revolutionary party, Valerius Flaccus was instrumental in putting Saturninus and Glaucia to death. He was Master of the Horse under Sulla, 82 B.C. He is often confused with another Flaccus of the same name; Mommsen, Vol. III, N. on p. 394. CAT. I, 2.

(3) *L. Valerius Flaccus,* son of the preceding. He was praetor 63 B.C., and assisted Cicero in obtaining evidence of the Catilinarian conspiracy. The following year he had Asia as his province. In 59 B.C. he was accused of extortion in his administration of the province, and defended by Cicero in an oration which is still extant. Though no doubt guilty, he was acquitted. CAT. 3, 2; 3; 6.

flāgitiōsē, sup. flāgitiōsissimē, [flāgitiōsus], adv., *shamefully, basely.*

flāgitiōsus, -a, -um, [flāgitium], adj., *shameful, base, disgraceful; profligate, dissolute.*

flāgitium, -ī or -iī, [cf. flāgitō], n., lit., *importunity; shameful act, outrage; burning shame, shame, disgrace.*

flāgitō, -āre, -āvī, -ātum, 1, a., *ask urgently, demand, require; press earnestly, importune.*

flagrō, -āre, -āvī, -ātum, 1, n., *burn, blaze, flame, glow; burn with desire for anything, be on fire, be stirred.*

Flāminīnus, -ī, m., Roman family name. Esp., *T. Quinctius Flāminīnus,* who defeated Philip of Macedon at Cynoscephalae, 197 B.C. VERR. 58.

flamma, -ae, f., *blaze, flame, fire; warmth, passion; glow, rage, wrath; spurt of flame.*

flectō, flectere, flexī, flexum, 3, a. and n., *bend, turn, direct; sway, change; move, persuade, influence; prevail upon, soften, appease.*

flētus, -ūs, [fleō], m., *weeping, crying.*

flōrēns, -entis, [flōreō], adj., *in bloom, flowering, blooming; flourishing, prosperous.*

flōreō, -ēre, -uī, ——, [flōs], 2, n., *bloom, blossom; flourish, prosper; be eminent.*

flōs, flōris, m., *flower, blossom, bloom; period of bloom, prime, promise; ornament, best part.*

fluctus, -ūs, [fluō, flow], m., *flowing; flood, tide, billow, sea-water; commotion, disturbance.*

flūmen, -inis, [fluō], n., *stream, flood, river; flow, fluency.*

fluō, -ere, flūxī, flūxum, 3, n., *flow, run; overflow, run down; pour, throng; fall away, fall off, vanish; spring, arise, come forth; go, proceed; roll, move, spread; perish.*

focus, -ī, m., *fireplace, hearth; home.*

foederātus, -a, -um, [part. of foederō], adj., *leagued, allied, confederate.*

foedus, -a, -um, adj., *foul, filthy, ugly; vile, base, shameful.*

foedus, -eris, [cf. fīdō], n., *treaty, compact, league, alliance; cove-*

nant, agreement, contract. **foedus faciō,** *I make a treaty.*

folium, -ī or **-iī, n.,** *leaf (of a tree).*

fōns, fontis, m., *spring, fountain, well; source, origin, cause.*

fore, see **sum.**

forēnsis, -e, [forum], adj., *of the market, of the forum; public, forensic.*

foret, old form of **sum,** equivalent to **esset.**

forīs [foris], adv. of place, *out of doors, without, abroad.*

fōrma, -ae, f., *form, figure, shape, appearance, looks, beauty; image, model, plan; nature, kind.* **certa fōrma,** *definite pattern, fixed standard.*

Formiae, -ārum, f., pl., *Formiae,* a coast city in the southern part of Latium, on the Appian Way. Cicero had an estate and a favorite villa in the vicinity.

formīdō, -inis, f., *dread, fear, terror;* of religious emotions, *awe, reverence.*

formīdolōsus, -a, -um, [formīdō], adj., *dreadful, fearful, terrible.*

fōrmō, -āre, -āvī, -ātum, [fōrma], 1, a., *form, fashion, build; direct, train, influence.* **citharā fōrmāre,** *to accompany on the cithara.*

fornix, -icis, m., *arch, vault, cellar.*

fors, fortis, [cf. ferō], f., *chance, luck, accident.*

forsitan [= fors sit an], adv., *perhaps, perchance, it may be.*

fortasse [for fortassis, = forte an sī vīs], adv., *perhaps, possibly, perchance.*

forte [abl. of fors], adv., *by chance, by accident, accidentally; per-*

haps, perchance; fortunately. sī
forte, *if by any chance, in the hope that.*

fortis, -e, adj., *strong, mighty; sturdy, brave, manly, bold, fearless; spirited, impetuous; well.* **nimis fortis,** *excessively strenuous.* **fortiter,** comp. **fortius,** sup. **fortissimē,** [fortis], adv., *strongly, steadily; boldly, bravely, manfully.*

fortitūdō, -inis, [fortis], f., *strength; firmness, courage, bravery, fortitude.*

fortūna, -ae, [fors], f., *chance, luck, fate, fortune; condition, lot, circumstances; prosperity, success; misfortune, adversity;* by metonymy, *possessions, property;* personified, *Goddess of Fortune, Fortune.* **per fortūnās,** *for heaven's sake!*

fortūnātus, -a, -um, [part. of fortūnō], adj., *prosperous, fortunate, lucky, happy.*

forum, -ī, n., *public square, public place; market-place, exchange, forum; tribunal;* at Rome, often for **Forum Rōmānum,** *the Roman Forum, the Forum,* an open space between the Palatine and Capitoline hills, surrounded by public buildings and shops, where the political and commercial life of the Roman world centered. **forum agere,** *to hold court.*

Forum Aurēlium, -ī, n., *Forum Aurēlium,* or *Forum Aurēlī,* a town on the coast of Etruria and the Via Aurelia, about 75 miles north of Rome.

forus, -ī, m., *gangway of ship; row of seats in the Circus, separated by passages; cell of bees.* **per forōs,** *over the deck.*

foveō, fovēre, fōvī, fōtum, 2, a., *warm, keep warm; cherish, foster; encourage; nurse.*

fragilis, -is, [frangō], adj., *easily broken, brittle; weak, frail, fickle.*

fragor, -ōris, [frangō], n., *breaking;* to indicate the noise that is heard when anything is broken, *crash, din; peal of thunder.*

frangō, frangere, frēgī, frāctum, 3, a., *break, shatter, dash to pieces, crush; break down, weaken, subdue, overcome.*

frāter, -tris, m., *brother.*

fraus, fraudis, f., *cheating, deceit, fraud; offense, crime; delusion, error, mistake; injury, harm, wrong.* **fraudē,** *treacherously.*

frequēns, -entis, adj., *regular, repeated; frequent, common, usual; in great numbers, crowded; thronged, in crowds.*

frequenter, comp. **frequentius,** sup. **frequentissimē,** [frequēns], adv., *often, frequently: in great numbers, by many.*

frequentia, -ae, [frequēns], f., *assembling in great numbers, thronging together, concourse; multitude, great numbers, crowd, throng.*

frequentō, -āre, -āvī, -ātum, [frequēns], 1, a., *visit often; visit in great numbers, throng, frequent; attend; gather in throngs, crowd together; inhabit.*

frētus, -a, -um, adj., *sustained by, relying on; depending, trusting,* *confident;* usually followed by an abl.

frīgeō, -ēre, ——, ——, 2, n., *be cold, freeze; be inactive, droop; be slighted, be coldly received.*

frīgidus, -a, -um, [frīgeō], adj., *cold, cool, chill; indifferent, remiss, feeble; without force, flat, insipid, dull; trivial, frigid, vain.* **frīgidae rēs,** *trifles.* **frīgida** [sc. aqua], *cold plunge.*

frīgus, -oris, n., *cold, chilliness.*

frōns, frontis, f., *brow, forehead; countenance, face; front, forepart; looks, appearance.*

frūctuōsus, -a, -um, sup. **frūctuōsissimus,** [frūctus], adj., *abounding in fruit, profitable, advantageous, gainful.*

frūctus, -ūs, [fruor], m., *enjoyment, delight, pleasure; fruit, produce; income, yield, profit; reward, return, recompense.*

frūgālitās, -tātis, [frūgālis, *thrifty*], f., *economy, thriftiness; self-control, temperance.*

frūmentārius, -a, -um, [frūmentum], adj., *of grain, of provisions, grain.*

fruor, fruī, frūctus sum, 3, dep., *enjoy, delight in, take pleasure in, rejoice in.*

frūstrā, [fraus], adv., *in a deceitful manner, in deception, in error; without effect, to no purpose, in vain, for nothing; without reason, groundlessly.*

frūx, frūgis, [cf. fruor], f., *fruit, produce; result, success, value.*

fūcōsus, -a, -um, [fūcus, *red dye*], adj., *painted, colorful; spurious, counterfeit, fair-seeming.*

fuga, -ae, [cf. fugiō], f., *flight,*

escape; exile, banishment; avoidance, shunning.

fugiō, -ere, fūgī, fugitum, 3, a. and n., *flee, fly, run away; become a fugitive, go into exile; vanish, disappear; avoid, shun; escape the notice of, escape; omit, forbear.*

fugitīvus, -a, -um, [fugiō], adj., *that has run away, fugitive.* As subst., **fugitīvus, -ī,** m., *runaway, deserter.*

fulgeō, fulgēre, fulsī, ——, 2, n., *flash, lighten; gleam, glisten, shine, glitter.*

fulgor, -ōris, [fulgeō], m., *flash of lightning, lightning; brightness, splendor, glory, renown.*

fulmen, -inis, [fulgeō], n., *flash of lightning, stroke of lightning, thunderbolt; destructive power.*

fultūra, -ae, [fulciō, *prop up*], f., *prop, support.*

Fulvia, -ae, f., *Fulvia.* Through her aid information concerning the conspiracy of Catiline first reached Cicero. She is otherwise unknown. SALL. 23.

Fulvius, -a, name of a prominent plebeian gens, which removed to Rome at an early date from Tusculum; pl. **Fulviī, -ōrum,** m., *the Fulvii,* meaning the eminent men of the gens who had done good service for the state. For the Fulviī mentioned in this book see the family names, **Flaccus, Nōbilior.**

fundāmentum, -ī, [fundō], n., *foundation, basis, support.*

Fundānus, -a, -um, adj., *of or belonging to* **Fundī,** sea-coast town of Latium. See **Minicius.**

funditus [fundus], adv., *from the bottom; utterly, entirely.*

fundō, -ere, fūdī, fūsum, 3, a., *pour, pour out, shed; scatter, diffuse; bring forth, bear; overthrow, vanquish, rout.*

fundō, -āre, -āvī, -ātum, [fundus], 1, a., *found, establish.*

fūnestus, -a, -um, [fūnus], adj., *deadly, fatal, destructive; associated with death, mournful, sad.*

fungor, fungī, fūnctus, sum, 3, dep., *be engaged in, perform; fulfill, discharge, execute, do.*

fūnus, -eris, n., *corpse, dead body; funeral procession, funeral rites, burial, funeral; death, murder; destruction, ruin, fall, disaster.*

furēns, -entis, [part. of furō], adj., *raving, raging, mad, furious.*

furia, -ae, [furō], f., *madness; fury, scourge, curse;* in pl., *violent passion, rage, fury.* Personified, **Furiae, -ārum,** f. pl., *the Furies, three goddesses of vengeance; avenging spirits, tormenting spirits.*

furibundus, -a, -um, [furiō, *drive mad*], adj., *mad, wild with fury, raging.*

furiōsus, -a, -um, [furia], adj., *full of raging, mad, furious.*

Furius, -a, name of an ancient patrician gens. Two of the name are mentioned in this book :

(1) *P. Furius,* one of the Catilinarian conspirators, from Faesulae. CAT. **3,** 6.

(2) *L. Furius Philus,* consul 136 B.C. Receiving Spain as his province, he took thither two of his bitterest enemies as quaestors, that they might be forced

to attest to the uprightness of his administration. He was a man of unusual culture for the times. ARCH. 7.

furō, -ere, furuī, ——, 3, n., *rave, rage, be mad, be furious.*

furor, -ōris, [furō], m., *frenzy, rage, fury, madness; prophetic frenzy, inspiration.*

fūrtim [fūrtum], adv., *by stealth, secretly, furtively.*

fūrtum, -ī, n., *theft, robbery; thing stolen; artifice, craft.*

futūrus, -a, -um, see **sum.** As subst., **futūrum, -ī,** n., *future.*

G

Gabīnius, -a, name of a plebeian gens. In this book three of the name are mentioned :

(1) *A. Gabīnius,* tribune of the people, 66 B.C. He proposed a bill the result of which was to put the entire command of the war against the pirates into the hands of Pompey, with almost unlimited power. He was praetor 61 B.C. In 58 B.C. he was consul with Clodius, whom he assisted in procuring the exile of Cicero. As proconsul he governed the province of Syria so unlawfully that on his return to Rome he was sent into exile, his property being confiscated. He died 48 B.C. PROV. CONS. 8; PHIL. 8.

(2) *P. Gabīnius Capitō,* praetor 89 B.C. ARCH. 5.

(3) *P. Gabīnius Cimber,* one of the worst of the Catilinarian conspirators. CAT. **3,** 3, *et al.*; SALL. 55.

Gabīnius, -a, -um, adj., *of Gabīnius.*
lēx Gabīnia, *bill of Gabīnius.*
Two such bills are mentioned in this book :
(1) That of 67 B.C., proposed by A. Gabinius to give Pompey absolute jurisdiction for three years over all the Mediterranean coast for fifty miles inland. IMP. P. 1, *et seq.*
(2) That introduced by A. Gabinius, tribune of the plebs in 139 B.C., regarding proposed changes in the ballot law. AM. 12.

Gaius, -ī or **-iī,** abbreviated **C.,** m., *Gaius,* Roman forename. See *19, a.*

Gallī, -ōrum, m., pl., *natives of Gaul, Gauls.*

Gallia, -ae, f., *Gaul,* including
(1) **Gallia Cisalpīna,** or **Gallia citerior,** *Cisalpine Gaul,* south of the Alps and north of the Apennines.
(2) **Gallia Trānsalpīna,** or **Gallia ulterior,** *Transalpine Gaul,* covering the regions now included in France, Belgium, Holland, the western parts of Germany and Switzerland.

Gallicus, -a, -um, adj., *of the Gauls, of Gaul, Gallic.*

gallīna, -ae, [gallus, *cock*], f., *hen, fowl.*

gallīnārius, -a, -um, [gallīna], adj., *of hens, of poultry.* **silva Gallīnāria,** *Gallinarian Wood, Hen Forest,* an extensive forest on the coast of Campania, north of Cumae. It was on the road to Cumae, and a favorite resort of bandits. EP. 20.

Gallus, -i, m., *Roman surname in* the Sulpician gens. See **Sulpicius** (1).

gāneō, -ōnis, [gānea, *eating-house*], m., *glutton, debauchee.*

garriō, -īre, ——, ——, 4, a., *chat- ter, prattle, babble.*

gaudeō, -ēre, gāvīsus sum, 2, semi-dep., n., *rejoice, be glad, delight in.* **quem vēnisse gaudent,** *at whose arrival they rejoice.*

gaudium, -ī or **-iī,** [gaudeō], n., *joy, gladness, delight, enjoyment.* **gaudiō afficī,** *to be filled with joy.*

gelidus, -a, -um, [gelū], adj., *very cold, ice-cold, cold.*

geminō, -āre, -āvī, -ātum, [geminus], 1, a., *double; couple, join, unite.*

geminus, -a, -um, adj., *born together, twin-born; paired, double, two-fold; both, two; resembling, similar, like.* As subst., **geminī, -ōrum,** m., pl., *twins.*

gemitus, -ūs, [gemō, *groan*], m., *sighing, groan, lamentation; pain, sorrow.*

gemma, -ae, f., *bud, eye; precious stone, jewel, gem.*

gemmātus, -a, -um, [part. of gemmō, *bud, gem*], adj., *gemmed, set with jewels, jeweled.*

gener, -erī, m., *daughter's husband, son-in-law.*

gēns, gentis, [cf. **genō,** *bear*], f., *clan, house,* used of a group of families tracing descent from a common ancestor, having a common name, and participating in the same religious rites; hence, *species, breed, brood; people, nation, race.*

genus, -eris, [cf. **genō,** *bear*], n., *birth, descent, family; sort, kind;*

race, breed, stock; class, order, description. **ūnō in genere,** in the same category.

Germānus, -a, -um, [Germānia], adj., of or pertaining to Germany, German. As subst., **Germānī, -ōrum,** m. pl., German.

gerō, -ere, gessī, gestum, 3, a., bear, carry, have; cherish, entertain; perform, do; manage, conduct, transact, accomplish; of war, carry on, wage. **sē gerere,** to conduct oneself, to behave, to act. **rēs gestae,** exploits, deeds, achievements. **male gerere negōtium,** to manage one's business badly. **rem gerere,** to manage business. **rem optimē gerere,** to manage business exceedingly well. **sē prō cīve gerere,** to conduct oneself as a citizen. **rēs geritur,** they fight.

gestiō, -īre, -īvī, -ītum, [gestus, n., leap with joy, skip; desire eagerly, earnestly desire, long.

gignō, -ere, genuī, genitum, 3, a., give birth to, bring forth; occasion, give rise to.

Glabriō, -ōnis, m., M' Acīlius Glabrio, consul with C. Calpurnius Piso, 67 B.C. The following year he was proconsul of Cicilia, and succeeded Lucullus in the direction of the war against Mithridates. He proved a failure as a general and was succeeded by Pompey. At the trial of the Catilinarian conspirators he spoke in favor of the death penalty. IMP. P. 4.

gladiātor, -ōris, [gladius], m., swordsman, fighter in the public games, gladiator, gangster.

gladiātōrius, -a, -um, [gladiātor], adj., of gladiators, gladiatorial.

gladius, -ī or **-iī,** m., sword.

Glaucia, -ae, m., C. Servīlius Glaucia, praetor 100 B.C. He united with Saturninus in opposition to the senatorial party, was declared an outlaw, and perished with Saturnius at the hands of a mob. CAT. 1, 2; 3, 6.

glōria, -ae, f., glory, fame, praise; pride, vanity, ambition.

glōrior, -ārī, -ātus sum, [glōria], 1, dep., boast, brag, vaunt, pride oneself.

glōriōsus, -a, -um, [glōria], adj., full of glory, glorious, renowned; haughty, ostentatious, boastful.

glūtinātor, -ōris, [glūten, glue], m., gluer, bookbinder.

Gnaeus, -ī, abbreviated **Cn.,** m., Gnaeus, Roman forename. See 19, a.

gnāvus, -a, -um, adj., busy, active, diligent.

Gorgiās, -ae, m., Gorgiās, Greek rhetorician and sophist in Sicily. A dialogue of Plato bears his name. He was born about 480 B.C., and lived upwards of a hundred years. SEN. 7.

Gorgōn, -onis, f., Gorgon, one of the three frightful daughters of Phorcus, esp., Medūsa, who alone of the sisters was mortal. She was at first a beautiful maiden, but her hair was changed into serpents by Athena. Her head now became so fearful that every one who looked at it was changed into stone. She was killed by Perseus. VERR. 56.

Gracchus, -ī, m., name of a family

of the Sempronian gens. The two most distinguished members, often together called **Gracchī**, gen. -**ōrum**, *the Gracchi*, were : (1) *Tiberius Semprōnius Gracchus*, quaestor in Spain 137 B.C., where he distinguished himself. He was tribune of the people 133 B.C., and inaugurated salutary reforms looking toward an equable distribution of the public lands. Standing for re-election for the next year, he was slain in a tumult stirred up by the aristocracy. CAT. I, 1 ; AM. 12. (2) *C. Semprōnius Gracchus*, brother of Tiberius. He entered upon the tribuneship 123 B.C., followed in the footsteps of his brother as a reformer, and met a violent death 121 B.C. CAT. I, 2 ; AM. 12.

gradus, -ūs, m., *step, pace, walk; position, base; stairs; approach, advance; degree, grade, rank; interval.*

Graecia, -ae, f., *Greece;* sometimes = **Magna Graecia,** *Magna Graecia,* name applied to Lower Italy on account of the number of Greek cities there.

Graeculus, -ī, [contemptuous dim. of **Graecus**], m., *affected Greek, petty Greek, Greekling.*

Graecus, -a, -um, [Γραϊκός], adj., *of the Greeks, Grecian, Greek.* As subst., **Graecī, -ōrum,** m., pl., *Greeks.* **Graeca, -ōrum,** n., pl., *Greek writing, Greek.*

grāmineus, -a, -um, [**grāmen,** *grass*], adj., *of grass, covered with grass, grassy.* **hastae grāmineae,** *poles of grass, bamboo poles.*

grandis, -e, adj., *full-grown, large, great, full, abundant; grown-up, tall; advanced in years, aged, old, heavy with years; great, strong, powerful; weighty, severe.*

grātia, -ae, [**grātus**], f., *favor, esteem, regard, love; kindness, courtesy; gratitude; grace; return of courtesy, thanks, return, recompense; influence.* **grātiā,** with gen., *for the sake of, on account of.* **grātiās habēre,** *to be grateful, to feel grateful.* **grātiam referre,** *to make grateful return, to recompense.* **grātiam habēre, to feel grateful. bonam grātiam quaerere, to court popularity. reditus in grātiam, reconciliation.*

Grātius, -ī or **-iī,** m., *Grātius,* the opponent of the poet Archias. ARCH. 4, 6.

grātuītō [**grātuītus,** *without pay*], adv., *without pay, without recompense, for nothing, gratuitously.*

grātulātiō, -ōnis, [**grātulor**], f., *showing joy, rejoicing, congratulation; joyful festival, public thanksgiving.*

grātulor, -ārī, -ātus sum, [**grātus**], 1, dep., *show joy, rejoice; congratulate.*

grātus, -a, -um, adj., *pleasing, agreeable, acceptable, dear; thankful, grateful, deserving.* **grātum facere,** *to do a favor.*

gravis, -e, adj., *heavy, of weight; loaded, laden; oppressive, offensive, severe, difficult; hard to bear, burdensome; weighty, important; eminent, venerable; great, of authority.*

gravitās, -ātis, [**gravis**], f., *weight, heaviness; oppressiveness, sever-*

ity; importance, dignity, gravity, influence.

graviter, comp. gravius, sup. gravissimē, [gravis], adv., weightily; vehemently, violently, severely, strongly; deeply, sadly.

gravor, -ārī, -ātus sum, [pass. of gravō, from gravis], 1, dep., be burdened; be reluctant, hesitate.

grex, gregis, m., flock, herd; band, company, clique, gang.

gubernāculum, -ī, [gubernō], n., helm, rudder; guidance, control, government. rēcta gubernācula tenēre, to steer a straight course.

gubernātiō, -ōnis, [gubernō], f., piloting, guidance; direction, management.

gubernātor, -ōris, [gubernō], m., helmsman, pilot; ruler, governor.

gubernō, -āre, -āvī, -ātum, [cf. κυβερνάω], 1, a., steer, act as pilot; direct, guide, control.

gula, -ae, f., gullet, throat, maw; appetite.

gustō, -āre, -āvī, -ātum, [gustus], 1, a., taste, partake of; enjoy; lunch.

gymnasium, -ī or -iī, n., place of exercise (Greek school for gymnastic training); gymnasium; Greek school, high school, college.

H

habeō, -ēre, -uī, -itum, 2, a., have, hold, possess; carry, wear; retain, keep, detain, contain; occupy, inhabit; be master of, own, rule; treat, use; pronounce, utter; have in mind, entertain; purpose, intend; think, believe, esteem; exercise, practice; receive, accept; reserve, conceal. rēs sē habet,

the case stands. hōc habēbis, take that! id quod rēs habet, as indeed is the case.

habilis, -e, comp. habilior, [habeō], adj., easily handled; fit, proper; nimble, swift.

habitātiō, -ōnis, [habitō], f., inhabiting; dwelling, habitation; lodgings, rooms.

habitō, -āre, -āvī, -ātum, [freq. of habeō], 1, a. and n., occupy continually, inhabit; dwell, reside, live.

habitus, -ūs, [habeō], m., condition, appearance; attire, dress; nature, character, quality. habitus ōris, mien.

haedus, -ī, m., young goat, kid.

haereō, -ēre, haesī, haesum, 2, n., stick, hang, cleave, cling; hold fast, be fixed; be perplexed, hesitate, be at a loss.

haesitō, -āre, -āvī, -ātum, [freq. of haereō], 1, n., stick fast; be at a loss, hesitate; be perplexed, doubt.

Hamilcar, -aris, m., Hamilcar Barca, father of Hannibal.

Hannibal, -alis, m., Hannibal, the famous general of the Carthaginians in the second Punic War. When only twenty-nine years of age he led an army from Spain and over the Alps into Italy, where he sustained himself for fifteen years. His campaigns cost the Romans not less than 300,000 men. He was finally forced to withdraw to Africa, where he was defeated at Zama, 202 B.C. He led the life of a fugitive for twenty years afterwards, and perished, it is said

by poison, in Bithynia. LIV. 21,
4; PHIL. 4.

haruspex, -icis, m., *soothsayer,
diviner.*

Hasdrubal, -alis, m., *Hasdrubal,*
Carthaginian general, son-in-law
of Hamilcar Barca, on whose
death, in 229 B.C., he succeeded
to the command in Spain. He
was assassinated by a slave,
and was succeeded in 221 B.C. by
Hannibal.

hasta, -ae, f., *staff, pole; spear,
lance.*

haud, adv., *not at all, by no
means.*

haudquāquam, adv., *by no means
whatever, not at all.*

hauriō, -īre, hausī, haustum, 4,
a., *draw off, drain, empty; pierce,
penetrate; drink in, imbibe, take
in, receive.*

hebēscō, -ere, ——, ——, [hebeō],
be dull], 3, inch., *grow blunt, become dull.*

Helvētiī, -ōrum, m., pl., *the Helvētiī,*
a Celtic tribe which invaded
Gaul.

Hēraclīa, -ae, [Ἡράκλεια], f.,
Heraclea, a Greek city in
Lucrania, near the shore of
the Gulf of Tarentum, below
Metapontum.

Hēraclīēnsēs, -ium, [**Hēraclīa**], m.,
pl., *people of Heraclea, Hera-
cleans;* sing. **Hēraclīēnsis, -is,**
m., *man of Heraclea, Heraclean.*

herba, -ae, f., *herb, grass; blade of
grass; plant.*

hercule [voc. of **Herculēs**], interj.,
by Hercules! assuredly! **mē
hercule,** *in Hercules' name!
most assuredly!*

hērēditās, -ātis, [hērēs], f., *heir-
ship, inheritance.*

herī, adv., *yesterday.*

Hēsiodus, -ī, m., *Hesiod,* a Greek
poet who lived in the age of
Homer, and wrote a poem on
agriculture, Works and Days,
and another on the origin of the
world and the birth of the Gods,
his Theogony. SEN. 7.

hesternus, -a, -um, [herī], adj., *of
yesterday, yesterday's.* **hesternō
diē,** *yesterday.*

hetaeria, -ae, f., *fraternity, brother-
hood, secret association.*

**hībernō, -āre, -āvī, -ātum, [hīber-
nus],** 1, n., *pass the winter, winter,
be in winter quarters, have winter
quarters.*

hībernus, -a, -um, [hiems], adj.,
of winter, in the winter, winter-.
As subst., **hīberna, -ōrum,** (properly sc. **castra**), n., pl., *winter
quarters.*

hīc, haec, hŏc, gen. **huius,** dem.
pron., *this, this — here,* used with
reference to the speaker; *the
present, the actual; the following,
the one,* referring to that which
follows; *he, she, it.* **ille — hīc,**
the former — the latter.

hīc, [hīc], adv., *here, in this place;
herein, in this, on this point;
now, at this time, then.*

hīce, haece, hŏce, gen. **huiusce,**
emphatic form of **hīc,** *this.*

hiems, -emis, f., *winter, winter
time; wintry weather, storm, tempest.* **extrēmā hieme,** *at the end
of winter.* **hieme summā,** *in the
dead of winter.*

Hierō, -ōnis, m., *Hierō,* name of
several kings of Syracuse; esp.,

Hierō II., tyrant of Syracuse in the third century B.C., just previous to the Second Punic War. VERR. 53.

hilaris, -e, adj., *of good cheer, lively, gay, joyful.*

hinc [hīc], adv., *hence, from this place, from this.* hinc — illinc, *on the one side — on the other, on this side — on that, here — there.* iam hinc, *henceforward.* hinc — hinc, *on one side — on the other side.*

Hirrus, -i, m., *Hirrus,* tribune in 53 B.C., and opponent of Cicero's triumph. EP. 11.

Hīrtius, -a, name of a Roman gens; esp., *A. Hīrtius,* consul in 43 B.C., with Pansa, probable author of the eighth book of Caesar's Gallic War. *Hīrtius* and his colleague fell at the battle of Mutina, fighting against Antony. PHIL. 2.

Hispānī, -ōrum, m., pl., *Spaniards.*

Hispānia, -ae, f., *Spain.*

Hispāniēnsis, -e, adj., *of Spain, Spanish, in Spain.*

Hīspulla, -ae, f., a woman's name. See Calpurnia (1).

historia, -ae, f., *history, narrative of past events; narrative, account, report.*

histriō, -ōnis, [from the Tuscan word, hister], m., *stage-player, actor, play-actor, player.*

hodiē [hōc, diē], adv., *today; at this time, now; to this day.*

hodiernus, -a, -um, [hodiē], adj., *of today, today's.* hodiernus diēs, *this day, today.*

Homērus, -ī, ['Ομηρος], m., *Homer.* SEN. 7, 10.

homō, -inis, m. and f., *human being, man; race of man, mankind, human race.*

honestās, -ātis, [honōs], f., *honor* bestowed by others, *reputation; uprightness, integrity.*

honestē [honestus], adv., *honorably, creditably, virtuously.*

honestō, -āre, -āvī, -ātum, [honestus], 1, a., *cover with honor, dignify, honor, adorn.*

honestus, -a, -um, [honōs], adj., *honored, respected; worthy of respect, honorable; noble, worthy.*

honōrābilis, -e, [honōrō, *honor*], adj., *that procures honor, worthy of honor, estimable, honorable.*

honōrātus, -a, -um, comp. honōrātior, sup honōrātissimus, [part. of honōrō, *honor*], adj., *honored, respected; honorable, respectable; distinguished with public office.*

honōrificus, -a, -um, comp. honōrificentior, sup. honōrificentissimus, [honor + faciō], adj., *that does honor, honorable, causing or bringing honor.*

honōs, or honor, -ōris, m., *honor, esteem, repute; praise, glory, renown; public honor, dignity, office, election to office.* Personified, Honor, -ōris, m., *Honor.*

honōrēs, -um, *official titles.* in honōre esse dēbēbit, *he will deserve to be in honor.* honōrum gradus, *grades of public office, avenues of official preferment.*

hōra, -ae, [cf. ὥρα], f., *hour,* which among the Romans was properly a twelfth part of the time from sunrise to sunset.

Horātius, -ī, m., name of the Roman champion in the Alban

War. As subst., **Horātiī, -orum,** m., pl., the *Horātiī.* The *Horātiī* belonged to one of the most ancient patrician gentes at Rome. Liv. i, 24.

horrēns, -entis, [part. of **horreō**], adj., *bristly, shaggy, rough.*

horreō, -ēre, horruī, ——, 2, a. and n., *stand on end, stand erect, bristle, be erect; shake, tremble, quiver, shiver; shudder, shudder at, tremble at, be afraid of, dread; be frightful, be desolate.*

horribilis, -e, [horreō], adj., *fearful, dreadful, terrible, horrible.*

horror, -ōris, [horreō], m., *shuddering, trembling, chill; quaking, terror, horror; dread, veneration, religious awe.*

hortātus, -ūs, found only in the abl., [hortor], m., *encouragement, incitement.*

Hortēnsius, -a, name of a plebeian gens. Three of the name, the orator, his father, and his brother, are spoken of by Cicero together as **Hortensiī,** gen. **-ōrum.** *Q. Hortēnsius,* the orator, was born 114 B.C. He became eminent as an advocate at an early age. He was consul 69 B.C. In 66 B.C. he spoke in opposition to the Manilian bill, which Cicero defended. Afterwards he was viewed by Cicero with jealousy as a rival, though sometimes they were both retained upon the same side of a case. He died 50 B.C. IMP. P. 22.

hortor, -ārī, -ātus sum, 1, dep., *urge, encourage, exhort, incite.*

hortus, -ī, m., *any place sur-*rounded by a fence or an enclosure; hence, *garden, pleasuregarden, park; kitchen-garden, fruit-garden.*

hospes, -itis, m., *entertainer, host; one entertained, guest, visitor; one bound by the ties of hospitality.*

hospitium, -ī or -iī, [hospes], n., *entertainment, reception* as a guest; *tie of hospitality, hospitality, friendship; guest-chamber, inn.*

hostīlis, -e, [hostis], adj., *of an enemy, enemy's; hostile, inimical.*

Hostīlius, -a, the name of a Roman gens. *Tullus Hostīlius,* a Roman leader in the Sabine War. Liv. i, 12.

hostis, -is, m. and f., *stranger, foreigner; public enemy, enemy, foe.*

hūc [hīc], adv., *hither, to this place, to this point, so far.* **nunc hūc — nunc illūc,** *now in this direction — now in that.*

hūmānitās, -ātis, [hūmānus], f., *human nature, humanity; kindness, good nature, politeness; culture, refinement.*

hūmāniter, [hūmānus], adv., *after the manner of men; like a man, as becomes a man; humanely, courteously, kindly.*

hūmānus, -a, -um, [homō], adj., *of man, human; humane, kind, courteous, polite; cultured, refined; gentle.*

humilis, -e, [humus], adj., *low; slight, small; base, mean, obscure, insignificant.*

humus, -ī, f., *ground, soil, earth; land, country;* locative **humī,** *on the ground, to the ground.*

I

Iacchus, -ī, m., the name of Bacchus in the Eleusinian mysteries.

iaceō, -ēre, -uī, ——, [cf. iaciō], 2, n., *lie, lie prostrate, be prostrate; lie dead, have fallen; be level; be cast down, be dejected; be despised.*

iaciō, iacere, iēcī, iactum, 3, a., *throw, cast, hurl; lay, establish; build, construct; throw up, charge; throw out, mention, declare, utter.*

iactō, -āre, -āvī, -ātum, [freq. of iaciō], 1, a., *throw, fling, hurl; toss, toss about; shake, brandish; emit, utter, say.* **sē iactāre,** *to boast, show off, make a display.*

iactūra, -ae, [iaciō], f., *throwing away; loss, damage; outlay, expense, sacrifice.*

iactus, -ūs, [iaciō], m., *throwing, casting, throw, cast, stroke.*

Iālysus, -ī, m., *Iālysus,* grandson of Phoebus, subject of a celebrated painting by Protogenes. VERR. 60.

iam, adv., *now, at this time, just now; already, ere now, so soon; forthwith, straightway, immediately, presently; then, then surely, no doubt, precisely, indeed, even; besides, again, moreover;* with comp., *from time to time, gradually.* **iam dūdum,** *long before, for a long time, this long time.* **iam prīdem,** *long since, long ago.* **iam tum,** *even then, at that very time.* **iam prīdem studēs,** *you have long been eagerly desiring, this long time you have been eager.* **iam dūdum hortor,** *I have long been urging.* **iam diū teneō,** *I have long been holding.* **tē iam prīdem oportēbat dūcī,** *you ought long ago to have been led.* **iam nunc,** *right now, directly.* **iam inde,** *ever since.* **iam in fīne,** *when the end is already in view.*

Iānuārius, -a, -um, [Iānus], adj., *of January.* As subst., **Iānuārius, -ī** or **-iī, m.,** *January.*

Iānus, -ī, m., *Jānus,* a two-faced Roman god and his temple. He was represented with two faces, looking in opposite directions, and had a temple in the Roman Forum with two doors, shut in time of peace, open in time of war. Only three times in Roman history were these gates closed. LIV. 19.

ibī or **ibi, adv.,** *there, in that place; then, thereupon; in that case, on that occasion.*

īcō, -ere, īcī, ictum, 3, a., *strike, hit, smite, stab.* **ictus, -a, -um,** adj., *stricken.* **foedus īcere,** *to make a solemn treaty or compact.*

Īd., see **Īdus.**

idcircō [id + circus], adv., *therefore, on that account, for this reason.*

īdem, eadem, idem, gen. **eiusdem, [is],** dem. pron., *the same;* often with the force of an adv., *also, besides, too, likewise, furthermore;* followed by **et, -que,** or **atque,** *the same as, identical with.* **idem sentīre,** *to have the same feelings, the same opinion.* **īdem quī,** *the same as.*

identidem [perhaps idem + et + idem], adv., *again and again, repeatedly, often, now and then, at intervals, ever and anon; continually, constantly, habitually.*

ideō [id + eō], adv., *for that reason, on this account, therefore.*

īdōlon, -i, n., *image, apparition, idol; phantom, ghost.*

idōneus, -a, -um, adj., *fit, suitable, proper; capable, sufficient.*

Īdūs, Īduum, abbreviated **Īd.,** f., pl., *the Ides, the middle of the month,* one of the three days to which dates were reckoned in the Roman Calendar. In March, May, July, and October the Ides came on the 15th; in other months, on the 13th.

iēiūnus, -a, -um, adj., *fasting, hungry; barren, unproductive; insignificant, trifling; mean, low.*

igitur, conj., *then, therefore, accordingly;* in summing up, *I say then, you see, in short.*

ignārus, -a, -um, [in- + gnārus], adj., *unfamiliar with, not knowing, unacquainted with, ignorant; unskilled in, inexperienced.*

ignāvus, -a, -um, [in + gnāvus], adj., *inactive, lazy, slothful, idle; sluggish, listless, without spirit; cowardly, dastardly.*

igniculus, -ī, [dim. of ignis], m., *a little fire, a spark; fire, vehemence.*

ignis, -is, m., *fire.*

ignōminia, -ae, [in-+nōmen], f., *disgrace, dishonor, infamy, ignominy; degradation.*

ignōrantia, -ae, [ignōrō], f., *want of knowledge, ignorance, unacquaintance.*

ignōrō, -āre, -āvī, -ātum, [cf. ignārus], 1, a. and n., *not know, be unacquainted with, be ignorant.*

ignōscō, -ere, ignōvī, ignōtum, [in- + (g)nōscō], 3, a., *pardon, forgive, excuse, overlook.*

ignōtus, -a, -um, [in- + (g)nōtus], adj., *unknown, unrecognized, unfamiliar, strange; without repute, obscure, mean.*

Īlias, -ados, ['Ιλιάς], f., *the Iliad.*

illacrimō, -āre, -āvī, -ātum, [in + lacrimō, *weep*], 1, n., or **illacrimor, -ārī, -ātus, sum** 1, dep., *shed tears, weep over, lament.*

illaesus, -a, -um, [in + laesus, from laedō], adj., *unhurt, unharmed, unmutilated.*

ille, illa, illud, gen. **illīus,** dem. pron., *that,* referring to that which is remote; *he, she, it;* referring to that which is familiar, *the well-known, the famous; the following.* **ille — hīc,** *the former — the latter.* **ille — ille — ille,** *one — another — a third, so and so — such a one — a third.*

illecebra, -ae, [in + laciō, *entice*], f., *enticement, allurement, charm, seduction.*

illīc [illī + -ce], adv., *in that place, yonder, there; in that matter, therein.*

illō [properly the old dative of ille], adv., *to that place, thither.*

illūc [ille], adv., *to that place, thither; to that point, to that end; to such a pitch.*

illūdō, -ere, illūsī, illūsum, [in + lūdō], 3, a. and n., *play at; make sport; ridicule, jeer at, mock.*

illūstris, -e, [in, cf. lūstrō, *make bright*], adj., *bright, shining, brilliant; clear, manifest, plain; famous, distinguished, noble.*

illūstrō, -āre, -āvī, -ātum, [in + lūstrō, *make bright*], 1, a., *make* *light; make clear, clear up, disclose, explain; make famous, make renowned.*

Illyricum, -ī, n., *Illyria, a country on the east side of the Adriatic Sea, north of Epirus.*

Illyricus, -a, -um, adj., *of the Illyrians, of Illyria, Illyrian.*

imāginor, -ārī, -ātus sum, [imāgō], 1, dep., *picture to oneself, imagine, fancy.*

imāgō, -inis, [cf. imitor], f., *copy, likeness, form, image; statue, bust; phantom, ghost; conception, thought; semblance, shadow.*

imbēcillitās, -ātis, [imbēcillus, *feeble*], f., *feebleness, weakness, helplessness, powerlessness.* **imbēcillitās valētūdinis,** *ill-health.*

imbēcillus, -a, -um, comp. **imbēcillior,** [in + vacillō, *totter*], adj., *weak, feeble.*

imberbis, -e, [in- + barba], adj., *beardless, without a beard.*

imbuō, -ere, -uī, -ūtum, 3, a., *fill, especially with moisture, moisten, stain, taint, infect; color, tinge.*

imitātiō, -ōnis, [imitor], f., *copying, imitation.*

imitor, -ārī, -ātus sum, 1, dep., *imitate, copy after; copy, portray.*

immānis, -e, adj., *monstrous, huge; fierce, cruel, wild, inhuman.*

immānitās, -ātis, [immānis], f., *hugeness, enormity; monstrosity, heinousness, savageness, cruelty.*

immātūrus, -a, -um, [in- + mātūrus], adj., *unripe; untimely, premature.*

immemor, -oris, [in + memor], adj., *unmindful, not thinking, negligent, heedless.*

immeritō [immeritus, *undeserving*], adv., *undeservedly, unjustly, without cause.*

immineō, -ēre, ——, ——, [in, cf. **minor],** 2, n., *overhang; be near, be at hand, impend; threaten, menace; be eager for, long for.*

imminuō, -ere, -uī, -ūtum, [in + minuō], 3, a., *lessen, diminish; encroach upon, infringe upon, reduce.*

immittō, -ere, immīsī, immissum, [in + mittō], 3, a., *send in, let in, admit, introduce; send against, set on; discharge, hurl.*

immō, adv., *nay indeed, nay, on the contrary, no indeed.* **immō vērō,** *nay rather, nay more.*

immoderātus, -a, -um, [in + moderātus], adj., *boundless, immeasurable; unrestrained, excessive, extravagant.*

immodicus, -a, -um, [in + modicus, *in proper measure*], adj., *beyond bounds, enormous; excessive, unrestrained, extravagant.*

immortālis, -e, [in- + mortālis], adj., *undying, immortal; endless, eternal, imperishable.*

immortālitās, -ātis, [immortālis], f., *immortality, endless life; undying renown, imperishable fame.*

immūnis, -e, [in + mūnus], adj., *free* or *exempt from a public office* or *charge; not bound, disengaged; making no return; unburdened, untaxed; free from, devoid of; selfish, unserviceable; uncommunicative.*

immūtātus, -a, -um, [part. from immūtō, *change*], adj., *changed, altered, revolutionized.*

Imp., see **imperator.**

impediō, -īre, -īvī, -ītum, [in, cf. **pēs, ped-is],** 4, a., *entangle; hinder, embarrass; obstruct, impede, check, prevent.*

impellō, -ere, impulī, impulsum, [in + **pellō],** 3, a., *strike against, strike; move, impel; urge, incite, persuade.*

impendeō, -ēre, ——, ——, [in + **pendeō],** 2, a. and n., *overhang; be near, be at hand, be imminent; impend, threaten.*

impendium, -ī or **-iī,** [impendō], n., *money laid out for anything, cost, expense; interest, usury.*

impendō, -ere, -pendī, -pēnsum, [in + **pendō,** *weigh*], 3, a., *weigh out, expend; employ, apply, use.*

impēnsē, comp. **impēnsius,** [impēnsus,** *ample*], adv., *exceedingly, greatly; eagerly, zealously.* **quō impēnsius,** *wherefore the more urgently.*

imperātor, -ōris, [imperō], m., *commander-in-chief, general; commander, leader, director.* **summus imperātor,** *a commander of the first rank.*

imperātōrius, -a, -um, [imperātor], adj., *of a commander, of a general.*

imperitō, -āre, -āvī, -ātum, [freq. of **imperō**], 1, a. and n., *command, govern, rule, be supreme.*

imperītus, -a, -um, [in- + **perītus**], adj., *inexperienced, unskilled, unacquainted with.*

imperium, -ī or **-iī,** [imperō], n., *command, order; authority, control; sovereignty, dominion, empire, supremacy, sway.*

imperō, -āre, -āvī, -ātum, [in + **parō**], 1, a. and n., *command,* *order; control, be master of; rule, govern; make requisition for, require, levy.* **mē imperante,** *at my bidding.*

impertiō, -īre, -īvī, -ītum, [in + **partiō,** from **pars**], 4, a., *share with, bestow upon, bestow, impart; assign, give.*

impetrō, -āre, -āvī, -ātum, [in + **patrō,** *perform*], 1, a., *gain one's end, accomplish, get, obtain, procure, by request or by means of influence.*

impetus, -ūs, [impetō], m., *onset, attack, assault; impulse, rapid motion, rush; violence, fury.*

impietās, -ātis, [impius], f., *ungodliness, impiety; disloyalty, treason; unnatural conduct.*

impius, -a, -um, [in- + **pius**], adj., *undutiful, irreverent, ungodly; wicked, impious, shameless.* As subst., **impiī, -ōrum,** m., pl., *the wicked.*

impleō, -ēre, -ēvī, -ētum, [in + obsolete **pleō,** *fill*], 2, a., *fill up, satiate; complete, finish, end; fulfill, execute; satisfy, content.* **nōndum quattuordecim annōs implēverat,** [she] *had not yet completed her fourteenth year.*

implicō, -āre, -āvī or **-uī, -ātum** or **-itum,** [in + **plicō**], 1, a., *entangle, involve, encircle, clasp; connect intimately, unite, join.*

implōrō, -āre, -āvī, -ātum, [in + **plōrō**], 1, a. and n., *beseech, entreat, implore.*

impōnō, -ere, -posuī, -positum, [in + **pōnō**], 3, a., *place upon; establish, introduce; set over; put on board, embark; set up, raise high; inflict; assign, apply;*

assess, exact; impose upon, deceive.

importūnus, -a, -um, adj., *unsuitable; harsh, rude, hard, cruel, savage.*

improbitās, -ātis, [**improbus**], f., *wickedness, badness, depravity.*

improbō, -āre, -āvī, -ātum, [**in- + probō**], 1, a., *disapprove of, censure, condemn, blame.*

improbus, -a, -um, [**in- + probus**], adj., *wicked, bad, depraved, base; shameless, outrageous.*

imprūdēns, -entis, [**in + prūdēns**], adj., *not foreseeing, not expecting; unaware, unsuspecting, ignorant; inconsiderate, heedless.*

impūbēs, -eris, [**in- + pūbēs**], adj., *under age, youthful, beardless.*

impudēns, -entis, [**in- + pudēns**], adj., *without sense of shame, shameless, indecent, impudent.*

impudenter, [**impudēns**], adv., *shamelessly, indecently, impudently.*

impudentia, -ae, [**impudēns**], f., *shamelessness, impudence.*

impudīcus, -a, -um, [**in- + pudīcus**], adj., *shameless, immodest, unchaste.* As subst., **impudīcī, -ōrum,** m., pl., *the unchaste.*

impulsor, -ōris, [**impellō**], m., *one who incites, an inciter, an instigator.*

impūnē, comp. **impūnius,** [**impūnis, in + poena**], adv., *without punishment, with impunity; unharmed, without danger.*

impūnitās, -ātis, [**impūnis**], f., *exemption from punishment; safety, impunity; rashness, inconsiderateness; free pardon.*

impūnītus, -a, -um, [**in- + pūnītus**], adj., *unpunished, without restraint, unrestrained, secure.*

impūrus, -a, -um, [**in- + pūrus**], adj., *unclean, filthy; defiled, abandoned, vile.* As subst., **impūrī, -ōrum,** m., pl., *the filthy.*

in, prep. with acc. and abl.:

(1) With the acc.: of place, after verbs implying motion, *into, to, up to, towards, against;* of time, *into, till, to, unto, for;* of purpose, *for, with a view to;* of result, *to, unto;* of other relations, *to, in, respecting, concerning, according to, after.*

(2) With the abl. of place, *in, within, on, upon, among, over, under;* of time, *in, in the course of, within, during, while;* of other relations, *involved in, under the influence of, in case of, in relation to, on the condition, respecting.*

In composition **in** retains its form before the vowels and most of the consonants; is often changed to **il-** before **l, ir-** before **r**; usually becomes **im-** before **m, b, p.**

in-, inseperable prefix, = **un-,** *not,* as in **inaudītus,** *unheard;* **incertus,** *uncertain.*

inanimus, -a, -um, [**in + anima**], adj., *lifeless, inanimate.*

inānis, -e, adj., *empty, vacant, unoccupied; useless, profitless, worthless, vain.*

inaudītus, -a, -um, [**in- + audītus**], adj., *unheard-of, unusual, strange.*

inaugurō, -āre, -āvī, -ātum, [**in + augurō,** *act as augur*], 1, a. and n., *to consult the birds; take omens from the flight of birds, practice augury, divine; consecrate, install, inaugurate.* ad inaugurandum, *for taking the auspices.*

inaurātus, -a, -um, [part. of inaurō, *gild*], adj., *gilded, golden.*

incēdō, -ere, -cessī, -cessum, [in + cēdō], 3, n., *go along, advance, proceed, move; attack; approach; occur, ensue.*

incendium, -ī or -iī, [incendō], n., *fire, conflagration;* of the feelings, *heat, flame, vehemence, passion.*

incendō, -ere, incendī, incēnsum, 3, a., *set fire to, kindle, burn;* of the feelings, *inflame, arouse, incite, irritate, enrage.*

incēnsiō, -ōnis, [incendō], f., *burning.*

inceptum, -ī, [incipiō], n., *beginning, undertaking; attempt.*

incertus, -a, -um, [in- + certus], adj., *unsettled, not • determined, uncertain, unascertained, doubtful;* of persons or character, *wavering, irresolute, at a loss.* incertum [sc. erat] procul intuentibus, *it was difficult to tell for those who saw it from a distance.*

incidō, -ere, incidī, incāsum, [in + cadō], 3, n., *fall in, strike; light upon, fall in with; fall into, become involved; fall out, happen, occur.* As subst., incidentia, -ium, n., pl., *falling objects.*

incīdō, -ere, incīdī, incīsum, [in + caedō], 3, a., *cut into, cut open, cut through; carve, engrave; break off, interrupt.*

incipiō, -cipere, -cēpī, -ceptum, [in + capiō], 3, a. and n., *take hold of; begin, commence, begin to speak; begin to be* or *to appear.*

incitāmentum, -ī, [incitō], n., *incentive, inducement.*

incitō, -āre, -āvī, -ātum, [in + citō, hasten], 1, a., *hasten, quicken; urge on, spur on, rouse, stir.*

inclāmō, -āre, -āvī, -ātum, [in + clāmō], 1, a. and n., *call upon with a loud voice; give a cry, make a call; appeal, invoke; exclaim against, cry in remonstrance, rebuke; cry.*

inclīnātus, -a, -um, [part. of inclīnō], adj., *wavering; inclined, disposed; depressed, fallen, deteriorated.*

inclīnō, -āre, -āvī, -ātum, 1, a. and n., *bend, turn; incline; be inclined, be favorably disposed.*

inclūdō, -ere, inclūsī, inclūsum, [in + claudō], 3, a., *shut in, inclose, confine, shut up in; obstruct, hinder; include, comprehend.*

incognitus, -a, -um, [in- + cognitus], adj., *not examined, untried, unknown.*

incohō, -āre, -āvī, -ātum, 1, a. and n., *begin, commence;* of a subject, *take in hand, begin to discuss, propose, undertake to treat.*

incola, -ae, [incolō, *inhabit*], m., *inhabitant, resident; foreign resident, immigrant.*

incolumis, -e, [in- + columis], adj., *unharmed, uninjured, safe, sound, whole.*

incommodum, -ī, [incommodus], n., *inconvenience, disadvantage, trouble; misfortune, loss, defeat.*

incōnstantia, -ae, [incōnstāns,

fickle], f., *inconstancy, change-ableness, fickleness.*

incorruptē, comp. **incorruptius,** [incorruptus], adv., *uncorruptly, fairly, justly.*

incrēbrēscō, -ere, -crebuī, —— [in + crēbrēscō, *increase*], 3, inch., n., *become strong, grow, increase, rise, spread.*

incrēdibilis, -e, [in- + crēdibilis], adj., *beyond belief, incredible, extraordinary, unparalleled.*

incrēdibiliter [incrēdibilis], adv., *incredibly, extraordinarily.*

increpitō, -āre, -āvī, -ātum, [freq. of increpō], 1, a., *cry* or *call out to anyone;* hence, *blame, chide, scold, speak angrily.* **verbīs increpitāns,** *with loud rebukes.*

increpō, -āre, -uī, -itum, [in + crepō], 1, a. and n., *make a noise, resound, crash; occur, be noised abroad; cause to resound; upbraid, scold.* **quicquid increpuerit,** *at every sound.*

incruentus, -a, -um, [in + cruentus, *bloody*], adj., *bloodless, without bloodshed.*

incultus, -a, -um, [in + cultus], adj., *untilled, uncultivated; wild, abandoned, savage.*

incultus, -ūs, [in + cultus], m., *omitting* or *neglecting to take care of a thing; want of cultivation, neglect; desolation; filth.*

incumbō, -ere, incubuī, incubitum, [in + obsolete **cumbō,** *lie*], 3, n., *lie upon, lean, rest, recline; press upon, oppress; exert oneself, make an effort, apply oneself; be inclined, lean towards.* **incumbite in causam,** *throw yourself into the cause.*

incūria, -ae, [in + cūra], f., *want of care, negligence, neglect.*

incurrō, -ere, -cucurrī or **-currī, -cursum,** [in + currō], 3, a., *run into, run upon, rush at, make an attack; run against, incur, meet; strike against, offend; stumble; happen, occur to.*

inde, adv., *from that place, thence, from that point; therefrom, from that; from that time, thereafter, after that; in consequence, therefore.* **iam inde ā prīncipiō,** *even from the very beginning.* **iam inde ā cōnsulātū meō,** *ever since my consulship.*

index, -icis, [cf. indicō], m. and f., *discloser, informer, witness; sign, mark; inscription, title, label for a title; forefinger.*

indicium, -ī or **-iī,** [indicō], n., *disclosure, information; mark, sign, proof; testimony, evidence.*

indicō, -āre, -āvī, -ātum, [index], 1, a., *point out, make known, disclose, reveal, designate; accuse, charge.*

indigentia, -ae, [indigēns, from indigeō], f., *need, want, indigence; a feeling of need.*

indigeō, -ēre, -uī, ——, [indu, old form of in + egeō], 2, n., *need, want, lack; stand in need of, require.*

indignus, -a, -um, [in- + dignus], adj., *unworthy, undeserving, unbecoming, not fit; shameful, outrageous.* As subst., **indignum, -ī,** n., *outrage, shame.*

indolēs, -is, f., *an inborn quality, natural quality; nature, character, genius, disposition, capacity.*

indūcō, -ere, indūxī, inductum, [in + dūcō], 3, a., *lead in, in-*

troduce, bring forward, conduct; spread over, overspread, overlay; move, persuade, induce. animum indūcere, to make up one's mind, to bring oneself to, to resolve.

indulgēns, -entis, [part. of indulgeō, indulge], adj., indulgent, kind, tender, fond.

induō, -ere, -uī, -ūtum, 3, a., put on, assume, dress in; clothe, cover; entangle, pierce, involve.

industria, -ae, [industrius], f., activity, diligence, zeal, industry.

industrius, -a, -um, adj., active, diligent, zealous, industrious.

inedia, -ae, [in + edō], f., abstaining from food, fasting, privation.

ineō, -īre, -īvī or -iī, -itum, [in + eō], irr., a. and n., go into, enter; come in, come on, begin; undertake, engage in, adopt.

ineptia, -ae, [ineptus], f., folly, absurdity, foolishness; pl., trifles, notions, absurdities.

ineptus, -a, -um, [in + aptus], adj., unsuitable to the time, place, or circumstance; absurd, awkward, silly, inept, impertinent; unsuitable, unfit.

inerrō, -āre, ——, ——, [in + errō], I, n., wander, err. inerrābat [īdōlon] oculīs, the phantom swam before their eyes, kept hovering before their mind's eye.

iners, -ertis, [in- + ars], adj., unskillful, awkward; idle, indolent, inactive, sluggish, worthless.

inertia, -ae, [iners], f., unskillfulness, want of skill; idleness, indolence, inactivity.

inexercitātus, -a, -um, [in + exercitātus, trained], adj., un-

trained, unexercised, unskillful, without experience.

inexpiābilis, -e, [in + expiābilis, from expiō, make amends for], adj., not to be atoned for, inexpiable; implacable, irreconcilable; obstinate.

īnfāmis, -e, [in + fāma], adj., disreputable, notorious, infamous.

īnfantia, -ae, [īnfāns, without speech], f., inability to speak, want of eloquence; childhood, childishness.

īnfēlīx, -īcis, [in + fēlīx, fruitful], adj., unfruitful, not fertile, barren; unfortunate, ill-fated, unhappy, unlucky, calamitous.

īnfēnsus, -a, -um, adj., hostile, inimical; enraged.

īnferior, -ius, [comp. of īnferus], adj., lower, inferior. As subst., īnferiōrēs, -um, m., pl., inferiors, those who are inferior.

īnferō, -ferre, intulī, illātum, [in + ferō], irr., a., carry in, bring in, introduce; bring to, carry into, convey, bring; bring against, wage, direct; bring forward, produce; excite, cause, inflict. sē īnferre, to present oneself, to repair, to enter. bellum īnferre, to make war upon.

īnferus, -a, -um, comp. īnferior, sup. īnfimus or īmus, [cf. īnfrā], adj., below, underneath, lower, underground; of the Underworld. As subst., īnferī, -ōrum, m., pl., folk of the Underworld, inhabitants of the Lower World; the dead, the shades. ad īnferōs, among the dead, in the shades below. apud īnferōs, in the Underworld. ab īnferīs, from the dead.

īnfēstus, -a, -um, adj., *unsafe, disturbed, molested; hostile, troublesome, dangerous.* **cum īnfēstīs signīs,** *in bitter combat.*

īnfīdus, -a, -um, [in + fīdus], adj., *not to be trusted; treacherous, false.*

īnfimus, -a, -um, [sup. of īnferus], adj., *lowest, last; meanest, most degraded, basest.*

īnfīnītus, -a, -um, [in- + fīnītus], adj., *boundless, unlimited; endless, infinite.*

īnfīrmitās, -ātis, [īnfirmus], f., *want of strength, weakness, infirmity; sickness, illness; inconstancy.*

īnfīrmō, -āre, -āvī, -ātum, [īnfirmus], 1, a. and n., *weaken; refute, disprove.*

īnfīrmus, -a, -um, [in- + fīrmus], adj., *not strong, weak, infirm, feeble, unhealthy; inconstant, superstitious; of no account, trivial, invalid.*

īnfitiātor, -ōris, [īnfitior], m., *denier, repudiator.* **lentus īnfitiātor,** *bad debtor.*

īnfitior, -ārī, -ātus sum, [in- + fateor], 1, dep., *not acknowledge, deny, disown; repudiate.*

īnflammō, -āre, -āvī, -ātum, [in + flammō], 1, a., *set on fire, light up, kindle; inflame, excite, arouse, stir.*

īnflexibilis, -e, [in + flexibilis, *pliant*], adj., *that cannot be bent; inflexible; unchangeable, unyielding.*

īnflō, -āre, -āvī, -ātum, [in + flō], 1, a., *blow into, breathe upon; inspire; puff up, elate.*

īnfluō, -ere, -flūxī, -flūxum, [in + fluō], 3, n., *flow into; stream in, throng in; invade; make way gently, pour in.*

īnfōrmō, -āre, -āvī, -ātum, [in + fōrmō], 1, a., *shape, mold; instruct, educate; describe.*

īnfrāctus, -a, -um, [part. of īnfringō, *break*], adj., *broken; exhausted, weakened; subdued.*

īnfundō, -ere, -fūdī, -fūsum, [in + fundō, *pour*], 3, a., *pour in, pour upon; administer; throw in; press in, crowd in; impart; mix, mingle.*

ingenium, -ī or -iī, [in, cf. gignō], n., *innate quality, nature; disposition, character, temper; ability, capacity, talent, genius, mental power; natural bent.*

ingēns, -entis, adj., *beyond natural size, huge, enormous; great, remarkable.*

ingenuus, -a, -um, [in, cf. gignō], adj., *native; free-born, of free parents; noble, upright, ingenuous, frank.* As subst., **ingenuī, -ōrum,** m., pl., *the free-born,* meaning the better classes of Roman citizens.

ingrātus, -a, -um, [in- + grātus], adj., *unacceptable, unpleasant; ungrateful, thankless.*

ingravēscō, -ere, ——, ——, [ingravō], 3, inch., *grow burdensome; grow worse, be aggravated, increase.*

ingredior, -gredī, -gressus sum, [in + gradior], 3, dep., *advance, go forward, proceed; go into, enter; enter upon, engage in, undertake, begin.*

inhabitō, -āre, -āvī, -ātum, [in + habitō], 1, a., *inhabit, dwell in.*

inhabitantēs, -ium, m., pl. of part. as subst., *inhabitants.*

inhaereō, -ēre, -haesī, -haesum, [in + haereō], 2, n., *stick fast,* cling, inhere; engage deeply, be closely connected.

inhiō, -āre, -āvī, -ātum, [in + hiō], 1, a. and n., gape, open the mouth to; gape with amazement, be amazed; gaze eagerly.

inhonestus, -a, -um, [in + honestus], adj., dishonorable, disgraceful, shameful.

inhūmānus, -a, -um, [in + hūmānus], adj., rude, brutal, inhuman; ill-bred, coarse, uncultivated; unkind, unkindly.

inhumātus, -a, -um, [in + humātus, buried], adj., unburied.

inibi [in + ibi], adv., therein, in that place, there. inibi esse, be at the point of being achieved, be near at hand.

iniciō, -icere, -iēcī, -iectum, [in + iaciō], 3, a., cast into, throw in; hurl upon, cast upon; heap up, build; put on, throw around; lay hands upon, take possession of; inspire in, cause.

inimīcitia, -ae, [inimīcus], f., hostility, enmity, personal animosity.

inimīcus, -a, -um, [in- + amīcus], adj., unfriendly, hostile, inimical; hurtful, injurious. As subst., inimīcus, -ī, personal enemy, enemy.

inīquus, -a, -um, [in- + aequus], adj., uneven, sloping, steep; ill-matched, unequal; unfavorable, disadvantageous; unfair, unjust; adverse, hostile.

initiō, -āre, -āvī, -ātum, [initium], 1, a., initiate, consecrate; used especially of initiation into the sacred mysteries.

initium, -ī or iī, [ineō], n., entrance; beginning, commencement. initiō, at the start.

iniūcundus, -a, -um, [in- + iūcundus], adj., unpleasant, displeasing, disagreeable.

iniungō, -ere, -iūnxī, -iūnctum, [in + iungō], 3, a., join into, join; impose, enjoin, occasion, bring upon; impose a commission on.

iniūria, -ae, [iniūrius, from in- + iūs], f., outrage, wrong, injury, injustice; insult; abl. iniūriā, often with the force of an adv., unjustly, undeservedly, wrongfully.

iniussus, -ūs, found only in abl., [in + iussus], m., without command, without bidding or orders.

innītor, -ī, -nīxus sum, [in + nītor, bear upon], 3, dep., lean upon, support oneself by.

innocēns, -entis, [in- + nocēns], adj., harmless, inoffensive; blameless, innocent, upright, incorruptible.

innocentia, -ae, [innocēns], f., blamelessness, innocence; uprightness, integrity.

innoxius, -a, -um, [in + noxius, harmful], adj., harmless; not guilty, blameless; unharmed.

innumerābilis, -e, [in + numerābilis], adj., countless, innumerable.

innuō, -ere, -uī, —— [in + nuō, nod], 3, n., nod, hint, beckon.

inoffēnsus, -a, -um, [in + offēnsus], adj., that at which one does not stumble; unhindered, uninterrupted; without injury, without misfortune.

inopia, -ae, [inops], f., want, lack; need, scarcity, poverty.

in prīmīs, see prior.

inquam, inquis, inquit, def., n., postpositive, *say;* used only to cite a direct statement.

inquiētō, -āre, ——, ——, [inquiētus, *disturbed*], 1, a., *disturb.*

inquilīnus, -a, -um, [for incolīnus, from incolō], adj., *inhabiting a place which is not one's own property; of foreign birth.* As subst., **inquilīnus, -ī,** m., *sojourner, lodger, immigrant, lodger, resident alien.*

īnsatiābiliter, [īnsatiābilis, *not to be satisfied*], adv., *insatiably.*

īnscrībō, -ere, īnscrīpsī, īnscrīptum, [in + scrībō], 3, a., *write upon, inscribe; assign, appropriate; mark.*

īnsequor, -ī, -secūtus sum, [in + sequor], 3, dep., *follow, follow after; succeed; pursue, strive after; overtake; censure, reproach.*

īnserō, -ere, -seruī, -sertum, [in + serō], 3, a., *put in, insert, introduce; associate, join, enroll; mingle with.*

īnsideō, -ēre, īnsēdī, īnsessum, [in + sedeō], 2, a. and n., *sit upon; settle, be inherent in, inhere; take possession of, hold.*

īnsidiae, -ārum, [cf. īnsideō], f., pl., *ambush, ambuscade; snare, trap, plot, artifice, device.*

īnsidiātor, -ōris, [īnsidior], m., *lurker, waylayer, highwayman.*

īnsidior, -ārī, -ātus sum, [īnsidiae], 1, dep., *lie in wait for, watch for, plot against.*

īnsigne, -is [īnsignis], n., *mark, sign, token; indication, proof; badge, decoration, distinction.*

īnsignis, -e, [in + signum], adj., *distinguished by a mark; remark-able, distinguished, prominent, conspicuous.* **īnsigne odium,** *an object of extraordinary hatred.*

īnsimulō, -āre, -āvī, -ātum, [in + simulō], 1, a., *charge, bring as a charge; accuse, blame.*

īnsipienter [īnsipiēns, *foolish*], adv., *unwisely, foolishly.*

īnsistō, -ere, -stitī, ——, [in + sistō], 3, a. and n., *step towards; set foot, take a stand, stand on, step on, tread on; make a stand, halt, pause; enter on, pursue, follow; press on; persist, insist, press vigorously, apply oneself; be busy about; urge.*

īnsolēns, -entis, [in- + solēns], adj., *unusual; immoderate, arrogant, haughty, insolent; odd, strange, in bad taste.*

īnsolenter, comp. **īnsolentius,** [īnsolēns], adv., *unusually; immoderately, haughtily, insolently.*

īnsolentia, -ae, [īnsolēns], f., *novelty, strangeness; haughtiness, arrogance, insolence; strange behavior.*

īnsolitus, -a, -um, [in- + solitus], adj., *unaccustomed, unwonted, unusual; uncommon, strange.*

īnsomnia, -ae, [īnsomnis, *without sleep*], f., *sleeplessness; want of sleep, watching; dream.*

īnsonō, -āre, -uī, ——, [in + sonō], 1, n., *make a noise in; resound, sound, clank.*

īnspectō, -āre, -āvī, -ātum, only pres. part. found in classical Latin, [freq. of īnspiciō], 1, a. and n., *look at, observe, view.* **īnspectante praetōre,** *under the eyes of the praetor.* **prope īnspectantibus vōbīs,** *almost under your eyes.*

īnspērāns, -antis, [in- + spērāns, spērō], adj., *not hoping, beyond hope, not expecting.*

īnspērātus, -a, -um, [in- + spērātus, spērō], adj., *unhoped for, unexpected, unforeseen.* **ex īnspērātō,** *at an unexpected success, unexpectedly.*

īnstaurō, -āre, -āvī, -ātum, 1, a., *renew, repeat, resume; refresh.*

īnstillō, -āre, -āvī, -ātum, [in + stillō, *make drops*], 1, a., *pour in by drops, instill; drop upon, fall on; infuse; drop into.*

īnstituō, -ere, īnstituī, īnstitūtum, [in + statuō], 3, a. and n., *put in place, plant; found, establish; arrange, draw up; build, construct; provide, prepare; undertake, begin; appoint, designate; purpose, resolve, decide, propose; teach, instruct, train up.* **vītam īnstituere,** *to order one's life.*

īnstitūtum, -ī, [īnstituō], n., *purpose, design, plan; custom, usage, practice, precedent; institution, regulation.*

īnstō, -stāre, -stitī, -stātum, [in + stō], 1, n., *stand upon, be near at hand, approach, draw nigh; press upon, press on to fight, pursue, harass; menace, threaten; insist upon, urge.*

īnstrūctus, -a, -um, [part. of īnstruō], adj., *furnished, provided, equipped; arranged; versed.*

īnstruō, -ere, īnstrūxī, īnstrūctum, [in + struō], 3, a., *build in; make ready, furnish, provide, prepare, equip;* of troops, *draw up, set in array, array; inform, enlighten.*

īnsuāvis, -e, [in + suāvis], adj., *unpleasant, disagreeable, without pleasure.*

īnsula, -ae, f., *island, isle.* Esp., **Īnsula,** *the Island,* a part of the city of Syracuse. VERR. 52.

īnsum, inesse, īnfuī, [in + sum], irr., n., *be in, be on; exist in, belong to.*

īnsuper [in + super], adv., *upon, above, on the top, overhead; from above; over and above; moreover, besides.*

intāctus, -a, -um, [in + tāctus, *touched*], adj., *untouched, uninjured, intact; untried, fresh; undefiled.*

integer, -gra, -grum, comp. integrior, sup. integerrimus, [in, cf. **tangō**], adj., *untouched, whole, entire; unimpaired, unhurt, sound, fresh, vigorous; undecided, undetermined; impartial; blameless, spotless, pure;* of a seal, *unbroken.* **quoad erit integrum,** *as long as it shall remain an open question.* **dē integrō,** *anew, afresh.*

integrē [integer], adv., *faultlessly; blamelessly, irreproachably, without prejudice.*

integritās, -ātis, [integer], f., *completeness, soundness; blamelessness, integrity, uprightness.*

intellegenter [intellegēns], adv., *intelligently, intelligibly, appreciatively.*

intellegō, -ere, intellēxī, intellēctum, [inter + legō], 3, a., *see into, perceive, gather; understand, discern, comprehend.*

intemperātus, -a, -um, [in + temperātus, *restrained*], adj., *exces-*

sive, unrestrained, immoderate, intemperate.

intempestīvus, -a, -um, [in + **tempestīvus,** *timely*], adj., *untimely, unseasonable; inopportune, out of place, ill-timed.*

intempestus, -a, -um, [in + **tempus**], adj., *unseasonable, dark, unpropitious; unwholesome, unhealthy.* **intempesta nox,** *the dead of night.*

intendō, -ere, intendī, intentum or **-sum,** [in + **tendō**], 3, a. and n., *stretch out, extend; stretch, fasten; direct, aim; bend, strain, turn; urge; purpose, intend.* **ingenium intendere,** *exert the intellect.* **animō intendī,** *to concentrate attention.*

intentiō, -ōnis, [**intendō**], f., a *stretching, straining; exertion, effort, application; intention, purpose; ardor, concentration; mental tension.*

intentus, -a, -um, [**intendō**], adj., *intent upon, attentive, eager; on the watch, vigilant;* with dat., *devoted to, bent on.*

inter, prep., with acc. only, *among; of position and relation, between, among, amid, surrounded by, into the midst of; of time, between, during, in the course of, through, while, in, within.* **inter sē,** *with one another, with each other.*

intercalārius, -a, -um, adj., *inserted between, for insertion; intercalary.*

intercēdō, -ere, intercessī, intercessum, [inter + **cēdō**], 3, n., *come between, intervene, pass; come to pass, occur; interpose; oppose, withstand.*

intercessor, -ōris, [**intercēdō**], m.,

he who opposes or protests against; the one who vetoes; mediator, surety; interferer, protester, adversary, preventer.

interdīcō, -ere, -dīxī, -dictum, [inter + **dīcō**], 3, a., *interpose by speaking; forbid, prohibit, interdict; enjoin, command.*

interdiū [inter + **diū**], adv., *during the day, in the daytime, by day.*

interdum [inter + **dum**], adv., *now and then, sometimes, at times.* **interdum — interdum,** *by times — at other times.*

intereā [inter + **eā**], adv., *meanwhile, in the meantime.*

intereō, -īre, -iī, -itum, [inter + **eō**], irr., n., *go among; be lost among, hence, go to ruin, decay, perish, die.*

interficiō, -ficere, -fēcī, -fectum, [inter + **faciō**], 3, a., *destroy; slay, kill, murder.*

interim, adv., *meanwhile, in the meantime; nevertheless.*

interimō, -ere, interēmī, interēmptum, [inter + **emō**], 3, a., *do away with, destroy; slay, kill.*

interior, -ius, gen. **-ōris,** sup. **intimus,** adj., *inner, interior; nearer, deeper;* sup., *inmost, innermost, deepest; intimate, close.*

interitus, -ūs, [**intereō**], m., *overthrow, ruin; destruction, death.*

intermittō, -ere, -mīsī, -missum, [inter + **mittō**], 3, a., *give over for a time, interrupt; leave an interval, pause; suffer to elapse; leave off, cease.*

interneciō, -ōnis, [inter, cf. **nex**], f., *massacre, slaughter, utter destruction, destruction.*

internecīvus, -a, -um, [interneciō,
massacre], adj., *murderous, de-*
structive.

interpellātiō, -ōnis, [interpellō], f.,
interrupting in speaking; speak-
ing between, interruption.

interpellō, -āre, -āvī, -ātum, [in-
ter + unused pellō], 1, a., *in-*
terrupt; hinder, obstruct, prevent.

interpōnō, -ere, -posuī, -positum,
[inter + pōnō], 3, a., *put between,*
place among, interpose; insert,
introduce, make insertions in.

interpretor, -ārī, -ātus sum, [in-
terpres], 1, dep., *explain, inter-*
pret; understand, comprehend,
make out; conclude, decide.

interrēgnum, -i, [inter + rēgnum],
n., *interval between two reigns,*
interregnum, a vacancy in the
consulate, between the death or
departure of the consuls and the
choice of their successors.

interrogō, -āre, -āvī, -ātum, [in-
ter + rogō], 1, a., *ask, inquire of,*
question.

interrumpō, -ere, -rūpī, -ruptum,
[inter + rumpō], 3, a., *break*
apart, break off, interrupt; break
to pieces, break up.

intersum, -esse, -fuī, [inter +
sum], irr., n., *be between, lie be-*
tween; intervene, elapse; be dif-
ferent, differ; be present, take
part in. Impers., **interest,** *it*
concerns, it is important, it makes
a difference. **quid interest?** *What*
difference is there? **meā interest,**
it is for my interest, to my advan-
tage; I am concerned.

intervāllum, -ī, [inter + vāllum],
n., lit., *room between (two) pali-*
sades; hence, *intermediate dis-*

tance, distance, interval; intermis-
sion.

interveniō, -īre, -vēnī, -ventum,
[inter + veniō], 4, n., *come be-*
tween, intervene, interrupt; hap-
pen, occur; hinder, prevent; ap-
pear.

interventus, -ūs, [interveniō],
m., *coming between, coming in;*
intervention, appearance.

intestīnus, -a, -um, [intus], adj.,
internal, intestine.

intimus, -a, -um, see **interior.**

intrā [cf. interior], prep. with acc.
only, *within, inside of; into;*
during, in the course of. **intrā**
domum, *within our own household.*

intrō, -āre, -āvī, -ātum, [cf. intrā], 1,
a., *go into, enter: penetrate, force a*
way in; reach, attain.

intrōdūcō, -ere, intrōdūxī, in-
trōductum, [intrō + dūcō], 3, a.,
lead in, bring in, introduce.

introitus, -ūs, [intrō, *to the inside,*
+ eō], m., *going in, entrance;*
way of entrance, approach, door,
opening; beginning, introduc-
tion. **Pontī introitus,** *the mouth*
of the Pontus, the entrance to the
Pontus.

intueor, -ērī, intuitus sum, [in +
tueor], 2, dep., *look upon, gaze*
at; contemplate, consider; ad-
mire, wonder at.

inūrō, -ere, inussī, inūstum, [in
+ ūrō], 3, a., *burn in; brand*
upon, brand, imprint.

inūsitātus, -a, -um, [in- + ūsitā-
tus], adj., *unusual, uncommon,*
rare.

inūtilis, -e, [in- + ūtilis], adj., *use-*
less, unprofitable, unserviceable;
inexpedient, unavailing, hurtful.

invādō, -ere, -vāsī, -vāsum, [in + vādō, *go*], 3, a. and n., *go into, enter; move against, rush upon, fall upon, assail; seize, take possession of, usurp; lay hold of, attack, befall; undertake, attempt; accost.*

invalidus, -a, -um, [in + validus, *able*], adj., *not strong, infirm, feeble; inadequate, unsuitable.*

invehō, -ere, -vexī, -vectum, [in + vehō], 3, a., *bring* or *carry in* or *into a place; bring to, carry against, introduce; ride on, drive up, be carried by, drive over; fall upon, assail, make an assault;* pass., as dep., invehor, -ī, -vectus sum, *be borne, ride, sail in; inveigh, assail.*

inveniō, -īre, invēnī, inventum, [in + veniō], 4, a., *come upon, find, meet; discover, invent, contrive, devise; find out, learn.*

inventor, -ōris, [inveniō], m., *one who finds out* or *contrives something new; contriver, author, discoverer, inventor, founder, originator.*

invēstīgō, -āre, -āvī, -ātum, [in + vēstīgō], 1, a., *track; trace out, search into, investigate, find out.*

inveterāscō, -ere, inveterāvī, ——, [in + veterāscō], 3, inch., *grow old; become fixed, be established, become rooted.*

invicem [in + vices], adv., *by turns, in turn, one after another, alternately; one another, each other, mutually, reciprocally; for each other.* sēcum invicem, *to each other in turn; for each other.*

invictus, -a, -um, sup. invictissimus, [in- + victus], adj., *unconquered; unconquerable, invincible.*

invidia, -ae, [invidus], f., *envy, jealousy; dislike, hatred, grudge; odium, unpopularity.*

invidus, -a, -um, [invideō], adj., *envious, jealous.* As subst., invidus, -ī, m., *envious person,* pl., *the envious.*

invigilō, -āre, -āvī, -ātum, [in + vigilō], 1, n., *watch over, be devoted, be intent.*

inviolātus, -a, -um, [in + violātus, *injured*], adj., *unhurt, inviolate, inviolable.*

invīsus, -a, -um, [part. of invideō], adj., *hated, detested, odious, hostile.*

invītō, -āre, -āvī, -ātum, 1, a., *invite, ask, urge; attract, allure; entertain, feast.*

invītus, -a, -um, adj., *unwilling, reluctant, against the will.*

iocor, -ārī, -ātus sum, [iocus, *joke*], 1, dep., *jest, joke, say in jest.* inter sē iocābantur, *they were joking with one another.*

ipse, -a, -um, gen. ipsīus, dem. pron., *self; himself, herself, itself;* often emphatic, *he;* often best rendered freely, as *very, precisely, likewise, in person.* See Companion, *162, a.*

īra, -ae, f., *anger, wrath; rage, passion, indignation, fury.* īra victōriae, *the fury of victory.*

īrācundia, -ae, [īrācundus], f., *proneness to anger; anger, rage, passion, violence.*

īrācundus, -a, -um, [īra], adj., *prone to anger, irritable; passionate, wrathful, angry.*

īrāscor, -āscī, -ātus sum, [īra], 3, dep., *be in anger, get angry; fly into a passion, rave, be furious.*

īrātus, -a, -um, [part. of īrāscor], adj., *angered, angry, furious, violent.*

irrēpō, -ere, irrēpsī, irrēptum, [in + rēpō, *creep*], 3, n., *creep into, steal in, be stealthily inserted.*

irrētiō, -īre, -īvī, -ītum, [in + rēte], 4, a., *catch in a net, ensnare, entangle, involve.*

irrīdeō, -ēre, -rīsī, -rīsum, [in + rīdeō], 2, a. and n., *laugh at, joke, jeer, mock, ridicule.*

irrumpō, -ere, -rūpī, -ruptum, [in + rumpō], 3, n., *break in violently; break in, force way in, burst into, invade; interrupt.*

is, ea, id, gen. eius, determinative pron., *he, she, it; that, this, the, the one;* before ut = tālis, *such;* with comparatives abl. eō = *the, all the,* as eō magis, *all the more;* after et, -que, atque, *and that too, and in fact.*

Īsocratēs, -is, m., *Isocrates,* a Greek rhetorician and orator. He was an ardent lover of his country, and, accordingly, when the battle of Chaeronea had destroyed the last hopes of freedom, he put an end to his life in 338 B.C., at the age of 98. SEN. 7.

iste, ista, istud, gen. istīus, dem. pron., *referring to the person addressed, sometimes ironically, that, that of yours; he, she, it; this; such.*

istim, adv., *thence, from thence.*

istō [iste], adv., *to you, thither, to where you are; in that matter.*

istūc [iste], adv., *thither, to you, to where you are; in that direction; to that thing, to that subject; in your direction; your wish.*

ita, adv., *thus, so, in this way, as follows; such, of this kind; to such a degree, so far; in that case; with this in view.* quae cum ita sint, *and since this is so, and accordingly.* ut ita dīcam, *so to speak.* sī ita vultis, *if you please.* ita ut, *only in so far.* ita tamen ut, *and yet with the proviso that.*

Italia, -ae, [Ἰταλός], f., *Italy.*

Italicus, -a, -um, adj., *of Italy, Italic, Italian.*

itaque [ita + -que], conj., *and so, and thus, accordingly; consequently, therefore.*

item, adv., *likewise, also, besides, moreover, too.*

iter, itineris, [cf. eō], n., *going; way, journey, march; road, path, passage, course.* in itinere, *on the march.*

iterō, -āre, -āvī, -ātum, [iterum], 1, a., *do a second time, repeat, renew.*

iterum, adv., *a second time, again, once more, in turn.* iterum et saepius, *again and again.*

iubeō, -ēre, iussī, iussum, 2, a., *order, bid, give orders, command, direct; exhort, entreat; decree, ratify, approve.*

iūcundē, comp. iūcundius, [iūcundus], adv., *agreeably, delightfully, pleasantly.*

iūcunditās, -ātis, [iūcundus], f., *pleasantness; delight, enjoyment.*

iūcundus, -a, -um, adj., *pleasant, agreeable, pleasing, delightful.*

iūdex, -icis, [iūs, cf. dīcō], m. and f., *judge; juror; decider, umpire.*

iūdiciālis, -e, [iūdicium], adj., *of a court, of the courts, judicial.*

iūdicium, -ī or -iī, [iūdex], n., *trial,*

court; judgment, sentence; decision, opinion, conviction. **iūdicium facere**, pass an opinion,
pass judgment. **ex vestrō iūdiciō**, in consequence of your judgment. **imperium atque iūdicium**,
military and judicial authority.
vocārī in iūdicium, be summoned
before the magistrate.

iūdicō, -āre, -āvī, -ātum, [iūdex],
1, a., judge, pass judgment, decide; pronounce judgment upon,
judge of; declare, proclaim.
aliquid de ingeniō iūdicāre, to
form any judgment of (his) abilities.

iugulum, -ī, [dim. of iugum], n.,
collar-bone; throat, neck.

Iugurtha, -ae, m., Jugurtha, king
of Numidia, who came to the
throne on the death of Micipsa,
118 B.C. Through his treatment
of the sons of Micipsa he became
involved in a war with Rome,
and was captured by Marius,
106 B.C. After adorning the triumph of Marius, 104 B.C., he was
thrown into the lower chamber of
the Mamertine prison, and there
starved to death. IMP. P. 20.

Iūlius, -a, name of a celebrated
patrician gens, of which the Caesar family formed a part. See
Caesar Proculus.

Iūlius, -a, -um, adj., Julian. **lēx
Iūlia**, the name of a bill proposed
by C. Caesar in 59 B.C., directed
against extortionate practices in
the provinces. EP. 12.

iungō, iungere, iūnxī, iūnctum,
[cf. iugum], 3, a., join, unite, connect; yoke, attach; bring together,
associate, ally.

Iūnius, -a, -um, adj., of June. As
subst., **Iūnius, -ī** or **-iī**, m., June.

Iūnius, -a, name of prominent plebeian gens, to which the Brutus
family belonged. See **Brūtus
Mauricus**.

Iuppiter, Iovis, m., Jupiter, son
of Saturn, chief of the gods; by
metonymy, heaven, sky, air.

iūrgium, -ī or **-iī**, [iūrgō, quarrel],
n., quarrel, strife, dispute; taunt.

iūs, iūris, n., right, law, duty; justice, equity; prerogative, authority, power; court of justice; abl.
iūre often with adverbial force,
by right, rightfully, justly. **prō
iūre nostrae amīcitiae**, in the
name of our friendship.

iūs iūrandum, iūris iūrandī, n.,
oath.

iussus, -ūs, only abl. in use, [iubeō],
m., order, command, decree.

iūstē [iūstus], adv., rightly, justly;
fairly, uprightly.

iūstitia, -ae, [iūstus], f., justice,
equity, uprightness; clemency,
compassion.

iūstus, -a, -um, [iūs], adj., just,
upright; fair, lawful, proper,
equitable; right, suitable, sufficient,
complete. **parum iūstus**, far from
reasonable, unfair.

iuvenis, -e, comp. **iūnior**, adj., young,
youthful. As subst., [iuvenis, -is],
m. or f., one in the flower of age, a
young person, youth (i.e. one between twenty and forty years);
warrior.

iuventūs, -ūtis, [iuvenis], f., age
of youth, youth, reckoned ordinarily from the twentieth to the
fortieth year; by metonymy,
young people, young folk, youth.

iuvō, -āre, iūvī, iūtum, 1, a. and
n., *help, aid, assist, support;
gratify, please, delight.*
iūxtā, [for iunxtā, from iungō], adv.
and prep., *near:*
(1) As adv., *near to, nigh, near
at hand, close at hand, close to,
by the side of; in like manner,
equally, alike, on a par.* iūxtā
mēcum, *as well as I do.* iūxtā
ac, *equally as much as.*
(2) As prep., with acc., *very
near, close to, near to; next to,
immediately after; beside, on a
par with; near, approaching to,
like, almost the same as; along
with, together with; in consequence of, in accordance with.*

K

K., Kal., Kalend. = Kalendae.
Kalendae, -ārum, abbreviated
Kal., [cf. calō, *convoke*], f., pl.,
the Kalends, the first day of the
month. Kalendae Maiae, *the
first of May.*
Karthāginiēnsis, -e, [Karthāgō],
adj., *of Carthage, Carthaginian.*
As subst., Karthāginiēnsēs,
-ium, m., pl., *people of Carthage,
Carthaginians.*
Karthāgō, -inis, f., *Carthage.*

L

L., = Lūcius.
labefactō, -āre, -āvī, -ātum, [freq.
of labefaciō], 1, a., *cause to totter,
shake, disturb; weaken, under-
mine; overthrow, ruin, destroy.*
lābēs, -is, [lābor], f., *sinking in,
settling; spot, blemish, stain, disgrace.*

Labiēnus, -ī, m., *T. Labiēnus,*
tribune of the plebs in 63 B.C.,
was a friend and partisan of
Caesar and his chief legatus in
his wars against the Gauls; but
on the breaking out of the Civil
War in 49 B.C., he went over
to Pompey. He was slain at
the battle of Munda, 45 B.C.
EP. 11.
lābor, lābī, lāpsus sum, 3, dep.,
*glide, slip, sink, fall; go to ruin,
perish; fall into error, err, go
astray.*
labor, -ōris, m., *labor, toil, effort,
exertion, care; hardship, trouble.*
labōriōsus, -a, -um, [labor], adj.,
*laborious, toilsome, wearisome;
troubled.*
labōrō, -āre, -āvī, -ātum, [labor],
1, a. and n., *toil, labor; be in
distress, be in trouble, suffer pain,
suffer; totter, threaten to give way.*
lac, lactis, n., *milk.*
Lacedaemōn, -onis, f., *Sparta.*
SEN. 18.
Lacedaemonius, -a, -um, adj.,
Spartan, Lacedaemonian. SEN.
18.
lacertus, -ī, m., *muscular part of
the arm* from the shoulder to the
elbow, *upper arm; muscle.*
lacessō, -ere, lacessīvī, lacessītum,
[laciō, *entice*], 3, a., *excite,
provoke; irritate, harass, defy.*
lacrima, -ae, f., *tear.*
lactēns, -entis, [part. of unused
lacteō, from lac], adj., *taking
milk, suckling.*
Laeca, -ae, m., *M. Porcius Laeca,*
a senator who took a prominent
part in the conspiracy of Catiline. CAT. 1, 4.

laedō, -ere, laesī, laesum, 3, a.,
hurt, wound, injure; offend,
grieve, pain, vex; betray, violate.

Laelius, -a, name of a Roman gens.
Two of the names are mentioned
in this book :
  (1) C. Laelius, called the Elder,
was the friend of Scipio Africanus
the elder and fought in almost all
of his campaigns with him. He
was consul 190 B.C. SEN. 21.
  (2) Gaius Laelius Sapiēns,
whose friendship with the
younger Scipio Africanus was
proverbial, and is celebrated in
Cicero's Dē Amīcitiā. He was
born about 186 B.C., performed
heroic exploits in the third
Punic War, and was consul
140 B.C. He is Cicero's typical
example of the best results of
cultivation acting on a character
which exhibited in their fullest
extent the ideal Roman virtues.
ARCH. 7; EP. 2; SEN. 9, et al.;
AM. 4, et seq.

laetitia, -ae, [laetus], f., joy, rejoicing; delight, gladness, pleasure.

lactor, -ārī, -ātus sum, [cf. laetus],
1, dep., rejoice, be joyful, be glad.

laetus, -a, -um, adj., joyful, cheerful, glad; happy, pleased, delighted.

laevus, -a, -um, adj., left, on the
left side; of ill omen, unfavorable;
inconvenient, unfortunate, unlucky; bad, pernicious. As
subst., laeva, -ae, f., the left
hand. ad laevam, to the left.

laguncula, -ae, f., small bottle;
wine-flask.

lancea, -ae, f., Spanish lance, light
spear, lance.

langueō, -ēre, ——, ——, 2, n.,
languish, be faint, be weary, be
languid; be dull, sink, be heavy,
be listless, be without energy;
hesitate.

languēscō, -ere, languī, ——,
[langueō],3,inch., n., become faint,
grow weak, become listless; become feeble.

languidus, -a, -um, adj., weak,
sluggish, languid; feeble, inactive, listless.

Lāodicēa, -ae, f., Lāodicĕa, a city
in Phrygia.

lapideus, -a, -um, [lapis], adj., of
stone, consisting of stone.

lapis, -idis, m., stone; landmark;
statue.

laqueus, -ī, m., noose, snare;
halter; trap.

Lār, Laris, m., protecting deity;
hearth, house, dwelling, household,
family, abode. Pl., Larēs, -um,
household gods, the Lares, guardi-
ans of the house.

largior, -īrī, -ītus sum, [largus],
4, dep., lavish, dispense, distribute, bestow; give largesses, bribe.

largīrī ut, grant the favor of.

largītiō, -ōnis, [largior], f., lavish
giving, dispensing, bestowing, distribution; bribery.

largītor, -ōris, [largior], m., lavish
giver, dispenser, spendthrift, prodigal; giver of bribes, briber.

lascīvia, -ae, [lascīvus, sportive], f.,
sportiveness, playfulness; jollity;
wantonness, licentiousness.

lātē [lātus], adv., broadly, widely;
extensively, far and wide.

latebra, -ae, [lateō], f., hiding-place,
lurking-place, recess, retreat; pretense, excuse.

lateō, -ēre, -uī, ——, 2, n., *lie hid, be hidden, lurk; be concealed, escape notice.*

Latīnus, -a, -um, adj., *of Latium, Latin; Roman.* As subst., Latīnī, -ōrum, m., pl., *inhabitants of Latium, the Latins.*

lātiō, -ōnis, [cf. lātus, tollō], f., *bringing forward;* of a law, *proposal.*

lātitūdō, -inis, [lātus], f., *breadth, width; extent, size, compass.* in lātitūdinem, *sideways.*

Latium, -ī or -iī, n., *Latium,* the country in which Rome was situated, on the west side of Italy, between Etruria and Campania.

lātor, -ōris, [cf. lātus, tollō], m., *bringer;* of a law, *proposer, mover.*

latrō, -ōnis, m., *originally mercenary soldier;* hence, *highwayman, bandit, brigand.*

latrōcinium, -ī or -iī, [latrōcinor], n., *highway robbery, brigandage, robbery; band of robbers.*

latrōcinor, -ārī, -ātus sum, [latrō], 1, dep., *originally, be a hired soldier;* hence, *practice highway robbery, plunder, rob along the highways.*

lātus, -a, -um, adj., *broad, wide, extensive; in breadth, extending.*

latus, -eris, n., *side, flank.* latera, *lungs;* by metonymy, *body, person, life.* ex lateribus, *on their flanks.*

laudābilis, -e, [laudō], adj., *praiseworthy, commendable, laudable.*

laudō, -āre, -āvī, -ātum, [laus], 1, a., *praise, commend, extol, eulogize; deliver a funeral oration.*

laurea, -ae, f., *laurel tree; laurel garland, crown of laurel.*

Laurentīnus, -a, -um, adj., *of or pertaining to Laurentum,* a coast town of Latium. As subst., Laurentīnum, -ī, n., *estate or villa at Laurentum.*

laus, laudis, f., *praise, commendation; glory, fame, renown; credit, merit.*

Lāvīnium, -ī or -iī, n., *Lāvīnium,* a city of Latium founded by Aeneas, and called after his wife Lavinia.

lavō, -āre or -ere, lavāvī or lāvī, lavātum or lautum or lōtum, 1 and 3, *wash, bathe; wet, moisten.*

laxō, -āre, -āvī, -ātum, [laxus, wide], 1, a., *extend, make wide, enlarge; undo, unloose, release; slacken, relax, unbend; lighten, relieve, recreate; mitigate, moderate, weaken; lessen, abate, reduce.*

lēctitō, -āre, -āvī, -ātum, [freq. of legō], 1, a., *read often, read again and again, peruse.*

lectulus, -ī, [dim. of lectus], m., *small couch, (little) bed.*

lēctus, -a, -um, [part. of legō], adj., *chosen, picked, selected; choice, excellent.*

lectus, -ī, m., *couch, bed, lounge.*

lēgātus, -ī, [legō], m., *ambassador, envoy, legate; lieutenant.*

legiō, -ōnis, [cf. legō], f., *legion,* a body of soldiers containing ten cohorts of infantry, and accompanied ordinarily by three hundred cavalrymen.

lēgitimus, -a, -um, [lēx], adj., *legal, lawful, legitimate; just, proper.*

legō, -ere, lēgī, lēctum, 3, a., *bring together, collect; select,* choose; coast along; elect, appoint; read, peruse. **bella legere,** to read about wars. **legendus,** worth reading about.

lēniō, -īre, -īvī, -ītum, [lēnis], 4, a., soften, mollify, calm, soothe; appease, mitigate, pacify.

lēnis, -e, adj., soft, gentle, mild, smooth, calm; kind, moderate.

lēnitās, -ātis, [lēnis], f., softness, gentleness, mildness, tenderness.

Lentulus, -ī, [lēns, lentil], m., name of one of the proudest families of the Cornelian gens. Of the eighteen Lentuli mentioned by Cicero the following are referred to in this book :

(1) *P. Cornēlius Lentulus,* consul 162 B.C., afterwards princeps senatus. He was wounded in the riot in which C. Gracchus was slain, 121 B.C., and died soon afterwards. He was grandfather of the Lentulus associated with Catiline. CAT. **4,** 6.

(2) *L. Cornēlius Lentulus,* praetor 89 B.C. ARCH. 5.

(3) *Cn. Cornēlius Lentulus Clōdiānus,* consul in 72, censor 70 B.C., and one of the lieutenants of Pompey in the campaign against the pirates. IMP. P. 23.

(4) *P. Cornēlius Lentulus Sura,* an important member of the Catilinarian conspiracy. He was consul 71 B.C., but was expelled from the senate the following year on account of his infamous morals. He expected, from his high rank, to become a leader in the conspiracy, but he lacked the resolution requisite for success.

He was executed along with the other conspirators, Dec. 5, 63 B.C. CAT. **3,** 2, *et seq.*; SALL. 32, 52, 55.

lentus, -a, -um, [cf. lēnis], adj., pliant, yielding, tough; slow, backward; easy, unconcerned. **lentō gradū,** at a slow pace.

lepidus, -a, -um, [cf. lepōs], adj., pleasant, agreeable, fine; nice, pretty.

Lepidus, -ī, [lepidus], m., name of a distinguished family of the Aemilian gens. The following members are mentioned in this book :

(1) *M. Aemilius Lepidus,* consul 78 B.C. He attempted to overthrow the constitution established by Sulla, was opposed by Catulus, his colleague in the consulship, and unsuccessful. The following year he took up arms against his opponents, was defeated in a battle in the Campus Martius, fled from Italy, and died shortly after. CAT. **3,** 10.

(2) *M'. Aemilius Lepidus,* consul 66 B.C. He was a member of the aristocratic party, but when the war broke out between Caesar and Pompey, he went into retirement. CAT. **1,** 6 ; 8.

lepōs, -ōris, m., pleasantness, charm, grace, politeness; pleasantry, wit, humor.

levāmen, -inis, [levō], n., consolation, solace.

levis, -e, adj., light; airy, flitting, swift, nimble; slight, trifling, trivial, easy; capricious, inconstant, fickle, untrustworthy; moderate.

levitās, -ātis, [levis], f., *lightness; light-mindedness, fickleness, inconstancy.*

leviter, comp. levius, sup. levissimē, [levis], adv., *lightly; slightly, somewhat; easily.* ut levissimē dīcam, *to put the case very mildly, to speak with extreme moderation.* levissimē, *without great difficulty.*

levō, -āre, -āvī, -ātum, [levis], 1, a., *lift up, raise; lighten, make lighter, relieve; remove; take away, take down; console, refresh; mitigate, alleviate, lessen; release, discharge, free.*

lēx, lēgis, f., *law, enactment, statute; rule, regulation; manner; agreement; condition, stipulation, terms.*

libellus, -ī, [dim. of liber], m., *little book, pamphlet; memorial, notice, indictment; placard, handbill; accusation, information, complaint.*

libenter [libēns], adv., *willingly, cheerfully; gladly, with pleasure.* quō libentius, *all the more gladly.*

līber, -era, -erum, [cf. libet], adj., *free; unrestrained, unrestricted; unimpeded, loose.*

Līber, -erī, m., *Līber,* an ancient Italian deity who presided over the cultivation of the vine and the fertility of the fields. He was later identified with Bacchus, god of wine. VERR. 57.

liber, -brī, m., *book.*

Lībera, -ae, f., *Lībera,* an Italian goddess, protectress of the vine, identified with Proserpina. VERR. 53.

līberālis, -e, [līber], adj., *of freedom; worthy of a freeman, noble,* honorable, dignified, ingenuous; kind, gracious; generous, liberal.

līberāliter [līberālis], adv., *nobly, kindly; generously, liberally; properly; respectably.*

līberātor, -ōris, [līberō], m., *freer, deliverer, liberator.*

līberē, comp. līberius, [līber], adv., *freely; frankly, openly, boldly.*

līberī, -ōrum or līberum, [līber], m., properly, *free persons;* hence, *children of a family, children.*

līberō, -āre, -āvī, -ātum, [līber], 1, a., *set free, make free, free, liberate; release, extricate, deliver; acquit, absolve.*

lībertās, -ātis, [līber], f., *freedom, liberty, independence.*

lībertīnus, -a, -um, [lībertus], adj., *of a freedman.* lībertīnus homō, *freedman.* As subst., lībertīnus, -ī, m., *freedman.*

libet, -ēre, libuit and libitum est, 2, n., impers., *it pleases, it is pleasing, it is agreeable.*

libīdō, -inis, [libet], f., *desire, longing, inclination; passion, sensuality, wantonness, lust; pleasure, desire, passion.*

librāriolus, -ī, [dim. of librārius], m., *copyist, transcriber, scribe; library slave.*

librārius, -a, -um, [liber], adj., *of books, belonging to books.* As subst., librārius, -ī or -iī, m., *copyist, scribe, secretary.*

Liburnicus, -a, -um, adj., *belonging to Liburnia, Liburnian.* Liburnica [sc. navis], -ae, f., *light and swift vessel, brigantine, galley,* named from the barks of the Liburnian pirates of Dalmatia.

licentia, -ae, [licet], f., *freedom, liberty, license, leave; boldness, presumption, unrestrained liberty, lawlessness; dissoluteness, wantonness; insolence.*

licet, -ēre, licuit and **licitum est,** 2, n., impers., *it is allowed, it is lawful, it is permitted;* used to introduce a concessive subj., *passing over into a conjunction, granted that, even if, conceding that, notwithstanding.*

Licinius, -a, name of a plebeian gens, to which belonged several prominent families and many distinguished members. See **Archiās, Crassus, Lūcullus, Sura.**

lignum, -ī, n., *gathered wood, firewood; timber, wood; piece of wood.*

līmen, -inis, [perhaps from **līmus,** *aslant*], n., *cross-piece, threshold; door; entrance; house, dwelling, abode.* **in līmine,** *at the door.* **intrā līmen,** *inside the room.*

līneāmentum, -ī, [**līnea,** *line*], n., *line drawn with the pen, chalk, etc.; line, stroke, mark; feature, lineament.*

lingua, -ae, f., *tongue;* by metonymy, *language, utterance; speech, dialect; garrulity, boastful speech.*

linteum, -ī, [**linteus,** *of linen*], n., *linen cloth; kerchief; napkin; sail, sail-cloth.*

līnum, -ī, [λίνον], n., *flax;* by metonymy, *flaxen thread, thread, cord; rope, cable; linen cloth, net.*

liquefaciō, -facere, -fēcī, -factum, pass. **liquefīō, -fierī, -factus sum,** [**liqueō + faciō,**] 3, a., *make liquid, dissolve, melt.*

liquidō [**liquidus,** *transparent*], adv., *clearly, plainly; with certainty, with truth; with a clear conscience.*

līs, lītis, f., *strike, dispute, quarrel; law-suit, action, process, litigation, controversy.* **lītēs urbānae,** *law-suits carried on in the city.*

littera, -ae, f., *letter, written character;* usually pl., *writing, document, inscription; letter, epistle; literature, letters.*

litterātus, -a, -um, [**littera**], adj., *of letters; learned, liberally educated.*

litterula, -ae, [**littera**], f., *little letter,* of the alphabet; in the pl., *short letter, note; literary learning.* **hōc litterulārum,** *these few lines, this little note.*

litūra, -ae, [**linō,** *smear*], f., *smearing, erasure,* especially of wax on a writing-tablet in order to make an erasure; hence, *blotting out, correction.*

lītus, -oris, n., *sea-shore, sea-side, beach, strand; river-bank.*

Līvius, -a, name of a Roman gens. Two of the names are mentioned in this book:

(1) *Līvius Andronīcus,* the earliest Roman poet, who wrote both tragedies and comedies, and translated the Odyssey into rude Saturnian verses. SEN. 14.

(2) *T. Līvius,* the Roman historian, born at Patavinium, in the north of Italy, 59 B.C. His literary talents secured the patronage of Augustus, and it was during the latter's reign that Livy composed the chief part of his great History of Rome. See Companion, page 562.

locō, -āre, -āvī, -ātum, [locus], 1, a., *put, place; arrange, dispose; rank; place by contract, let a contract, let out.*

Locrēnsēs, -ium, m., pl., *Locrians,* inhabitants of Locri Epizephyrii, in the southwestern part of Italy.

locuplēs, -ētis, [locus, cf. -pleō], adj., *rich in lands, opulent, wealthy; richly stored, well supplied; trustworthy.*

locus, -ī, m., pl. **locī, -ōrum,** when referring to single places; **loca, -ōrum,** when referring to places connected, as a region, *place, spot; post, station, position; location, region, country; topic, subject* under discussion or cited, *passage; commonplace; opportunity; room.* **locō mōtus est,** *he was forced from his vantageground.* **aliquid locī,** *some place, some room.* **locum habēre,** *to have standing.* **eō locō,** *in such a position.*

longē, comp. **longius,** sup. **longissimē,** [longus], adv., *far, far off, at a distance; for a long time, long; greatly, much, by far.*

longinquitās, -ātis, [longinquus], f., *distance, remoteness;* of time, *length, duration.*

longinquus, -a, -um, [longus], adj., *far removed, remote, distant; prolonged, lasting.* As subst., **longinqua, -ōrum,** n., pl., *far-off events, remote events.* IMP. P. 12.

longiusculus, -a, -um, [longior], adj., *rather long, quite long.*

longus, -a, -um, adj., *long, extended, far-reaching, expanded; of long duration, prolonged, tedious; distant, remote.* **nē**

longum sit, *not to be tedious, to speak briefly.*

loquāx, -ācis, [loquor], adj., *talkative, loquacious, full of words.*

loquor, loquī, locūtus sum, 3, dep., *speak, say, talk; tell, mention, declare; show, indicate, testify.*

Lūcius, -ī or **-iī,** abbreviated L., m., *Lūcius,* a Roman forename.

lūctuōsus, -a, -um, [lūctus], adj., *full of sorrow, lamentable, sorrowful, mournful.*

lūctus, -ūs, [lūgeō, *mourn*], m., *mourning, grief, sorrow, lamentation; distress, affliction.*

lūculentus, -a, -um, [lūx], adj., *full of light, bright, splendid; distinguished, excellent, brilliant.*

Lūcullus, -ī, m., name of a family in the Licinian gens. Three members of it, L. Licinius Lucullus and his sons Lucius and Marcus, are mentioned together by Cicero as **Lūcullī,** gen. -ōrum. ARCH. 3, *et al.:*

(1) *L. Licinius Lūcullus,* consul 74 B.C. He distinguished himself as quaestor of Sulla in Greece and Asia, and afterwards by his successes in the war with Mithridates. As he failed to bring this to a successful termination, he was recalled, and afterwards resigned himself to a life of luxury. IMP. P. 2, *et al.*

(2) *M. Licinius Lūcullus,* brother of (1), consul 73 B.C. Having obtained Macedonia as his province, he defeated the barbarous tribes along the northern frontier in numerous engagements, and captured several seditious Greek cities on the

Euxine Sea. He was honored with a triumph, 71 B.C. ARCH. 4.

lūcus, -ī, m., *wood* or *thicket* of trees consecrated to some deity; *sacred grove, consecrated wood; the park* surrounding a temple; *wood, grove.*

lūdibrium, -ī or -iī, [lūdus], n., *mockery, derision, wantonness; object of mockery, laughing-stock, butt, jest, sport; dishonoring; sport, joke.* lūdibriō, *in mockery.*

lūdō, -ere, lūsī, lūsum, 3, a. and n., *play; appear in a public game; play, sport, frolic; make game of, ridicule.*

lūdus, -ī, [cf. lūdō], m., *play, game, sport, pastime; joke, fun;* pl., often *public games, spectacles.*

lūgeō, -ēre, lūxī, lūctum, 2, a. and n., *mourn, lament, bewail, deplore.*

lūmen, -inis, [cf. lūceō], n., *light;* by metonymy, *source of light,* as *lamp, torch; light of the eye, eye; brightness, glory.*

lūna, -ae, [for lūcīna, from lūceō], f., *moon.*

luō, -ere, luī, ——, 3, a., *loose, pay, pay off; atone for, expiate.* poenās luere, *to pay the penalty of.*

lupīnus, -a, -um, [lupus], adj., *of a wolf, wolf's.*

Lupus, -ī, m., *Lupus,* a friend of Cicero and of D. Brutus, EP. 25.

lūstrō, -āre, -āvī, -ātum, [lūstrum], 1, a., *make light, light up; wander over, traverse;* of religious services, *make pure by expiatory offerings, purify, lustrate.*

lūx, lūcis, [cf. lūceō], f., *light, brightness;* by metonymy, *daylight, day; light of life, life; eyesight, eye; public view, the public; help, succor.* ante lūcem, *before dawn.*

lūxuria, -ae, [lūxus], f., *extravagance, riotous living, excess, luxury, sensuality.*

lūxuriō, -āre, -āvī, -ātum, [lūxuria], 1, n., *vegetate excessively; be rank; be luxuriant, abound to excess; abound in; swell, enlarge, grow rapidly; be self-indulgent, be wanton, run riot, be dissolute.*

Lycomēdēs, -is, m., *Lycomēdēs,* king of Scyros. At his court Achilles was reared as a girl, after being sent to Scyros by his mother Thetis to prevent his going to the Trojan War. AM. 20.

Lȳsander, -rī, m., *Lysander,* one of the most distinguished of the Spartan generals and diplomatists. It was he who, in 405 B.C. by his defeat of the Athenian fleet off Aegospotami, brought the Peloponnesian War to a conclusion. He was killed in battle under the walls of Haliartus, 395 B.C.

Lȳsimachus, -ī, *Lysimachus,* father of Aristides. SEN. 7.

M

M., = *Mārcus,* a common Roman forename (praenōmen).

M'., = *Mānius,* a Roman forename (praenōmen).

Macedonia, -ae, [Μακεδονία], f., *Macedonia, Macedon.*

Macedonicus, -a, -um, adj., *Macedonian.*

māchinātor, -ōris, [māchinor], m., *contriver, designer, deviser, inventor.*

māchinor, -ārī, -ātus sum, [māchina], 1, dep., *contrive, design, devise, invent; scheme, plot.*

maciēs, -ēī, f., *leanness, thinness, meagerness; poverty.*

mactō, -āre, -āvī, -ātum, [mactus, glorified], 1, a., *glorify, extol; sacrifice, devote* in honor of the gods; *kill, put to death; afflict, visit* with punishment, *punish.*

maculō, -āre, -āvī, -ātum, [macula, stain], 1, a., *stain, defile, pollute; dishonor.*

maculōsus, -a, -um, [macula, stain], adj., *spotted, speckled, mottled; stained, defiled; polluted, filthy.*

madefaciō, -ere, -fēcī, -factum, [madeō, be wet, + faciō], 3, a., *make wet, moisten; dye deep.*

Maelius, -ī or -iī, m., with Sp., *Spurius Maelius,* a wealthy plebeian who, in a time of great famine at Rome, 440 B.C., bought up grain in Etruria and either distributed it among the poor gratuitously or sold it at a very low price. In the following year he was accused of aiming at the supreme power and slain by Servilius Ahala, the master of the horse, while attempting to escape arrest. CAT. I, 1; SEN. 16.

maeror, -ōris, [maereō], m., *mourning, sadness, grief, sorrow.*

maestus, -a, -um, [maereō, grieve], adj., *full of sadness, sorrowful, melancholy; severe.*

magis [root mag in magnus], adv., *more, in a greater measure; in a higher degree, far more, rather, in preference; in a higher degree.* **eō magis,** *all the more on that account.* **tantō magis,** *so much the more.* **quō magis,** *all the more for that reason; that — the better.* **multō magis,** *much the more.*

magister, -trī, [cf. magnus], m., *master, leader, director; instructor, teacher; guide, guardian.*

magistrātus, -ūs, [magister], m., *office of magistrate, civil office, magistracy;* by metonymy, *magistrate, public officer.*

magnificē, comp. magnificentius, sup. magnificentissimē, [magnificus], adv., *nobly, grandly, gloriously; splendidly, magnificently.*

magnificentia, -ae, [magnificus], f., *grandeur, nobleness, highmindedness; magnificence; splendor, sumptuousness; display, boastfulness.*

magnificus, -a, -um, comp. magnificentior, sup, magnificentissimus, [magnus + faciō], adj., *that has performed anything by which he appears or becomes great; great, elevated, noble, distinguished, eminent, august; splendid, rich, fine, costly, sumptuous, magnificent.*

magnitūdō, -inis, [magnus], f., *greatness, size, magnitude; quantity, abundance, extent.*

magnopere, see opus.

magnus, -a, -um, comp. maior, sup. maximus, adj., *great, vast, wide, large, tall; abundant, considerable; grand, noble, mighty; stately, lofty; eminent, powerful; old, aged; proud, boastful. As* subst., comp. **maiōrēs, -um,** m., pl., *fathers, ancestors.*

Magnus, -ī, m., surname of Pompey. See **Pompeius** (1).

maior, see **magnus.**

Maius, -a, -um, adj., *of May.* As subst., **Maius, -ī,** m., *May.*

male [malus], comp. **peius,** sup. **pessimē,** adv., *ill, badly, wretchedly, awkwardly; maliciously, evilly, wickedly; unfortunately; unsuccessfully; excessively, greatly;* sometimes with adj., *scarcely, not at all.*

maledīcō, -ere, -dīxī, -dictum, [male + dīcō], 3, a., *speak ill of, abuse, revile, slander, curse.*

maledictum, -ī, n., *reproach, foul saying, abusive word, expression of blame.*

maleficium, -ī or **-iī,** [maleficus], n., *evil deed, offense, wickedness; mischief, hurt, wrong.*

malleolus, -ī, [dim. of **malleus,** *hammer*], m., *small hammer;* by metonymy, *fire-dart, fire-brand.*

mālō, mālle, māluī, [magis + volō], irr., a., *wish rather, choose rather, prefer.*

malum, -ī, [malus], n., *evil, misfortune, calamity; hurt, punishment; wrong-doing, crime.*

malus, -a, -um, comp. **peior,** sup. **pessimus,** adj., *bad; wicked, depraved, evil, impious; pernicious, hostile, injurious, destructive.*

mālus, -ī, m., *upright pole, beam, mast, staff.*

mandātum, -ī, [mandō], n., *charge, commission; command, order, instruction.*

mandō, -āre, -āvī, -ātum, [manus + dō], 1, a., *put in hand, commit;*

deliver over, confide, intrust; enjoin, order, command.

māne, adv., *in the morning, early in the morning.* **hodiernō diē māne,** *this morning.*

maneō, -ēre, mānsī, mānsum, 2, a. and n., *stay, remain, tarry; continue, last, persist, endure; await, wait for, expect; fall to one's lot, be destined to.* **mānsūrus,** *destined to live.*

Mānēs, -ium, m., *Mānēs.* The *Mānēs* [*the Good*] was the name which the Romans gave to the souls of the departed, who were worshiped as gods. LIV. 1, 24.

manicātus, -a, -um, [manica, *sleeve*], adj., *with long sleeves, long-sleeved.*

manifestō [manifestus], adv., *clearly, plainly, manifestly.*

manifestus, -a, -um, [manus, cf. unused fendō], adj., *clear, plain; evident, manifest, exposed; convicted* from direct evidence, *caught in the act.* **manifestum facere,** *prove.* **sīcutī dē manifestīs rērum capitālium,** *as in the case of those caught in the common mission of a capital crime.*

Mānīlius, -a, name of a plebeian gens. *C. Mānīlius,* tribune of the people 66 B.C. He brought forward the bill placing Pompey in command of the war with Mithridates. After the expiration of his term of office he was brought to trial and condemned. The nature of his offense is not understood. IMP. P. 24.

Mānius, -ī or **-iī,** abbreviated **M'.,** [māne], m., *Mānius,* a Roman forename (praenōmen).

Mānliānus, -a, -um, adj., *of Manlius, Manlian.*

Mānlius, -a, name of a patrician gens. Three of the name are mentioned in this book :
(1) *T. Mānlius Torquātus,* consul 235 B.C., censor 231, and consul a second time in 224. He was dictator in 210. In 235 B.C. he opposed in the senate the ransom of those Romans who had been taken prisoners after the battle of Cannae. LIV. 1, 19.
(2) *C. Mānlius,* an important member of the Catilinarian conspiracy. Having served with distinction as a centurion under Sulla, he was placed by Catiline in charge of the troops at Faesulae. In the final battle with Antony, Manlius commanded the right wing and was killed. CAT. 1, 3, *et al.;* SALL. 24; 60.
(3) *L. Mānlius Torquātus,* consul with L. Aurelius Cotta, 65 B.C. He was active in helping to suppress the Catilinarian conspiracy. CAT. 3, 8.

mānō, -āre, -āvī, -ātum, 1, a. and n., *drip, trickle, flow; spread abroad, be diffused.*

mānsuētē [mānsuētus], adv., *gently, mildly, calmly.*

mānsuētūdō, -inis, [mānsuētus], f., *gentleness, mildness, clemency.*

manubiae, -ārum, [manus], f., pl., *booty* taken in war, *spoils;* proceeds from the sale of booty, *booty-money, prize-money.*

manūmittō, -ere, -mīsī, -missum, [manus + mittō], 3, a., *release, set at liberty; enfranchise, manumit, emancipate; make free.*

manus, -ūs, f., *hand; handwriting, style; band, force, company, forces, troops.* **vīs et manus,** *violent hands.* **in manibus habēre,** *have at hand, in possession; be busy upon.* **alicui in manū esse,** *be in the power of anyone, be in the grasp of anyone.* **in manūs venīre,** *to come to hand.*

Mārcellīnus, -ī, m., *Mārcellīnus,* a friend and correspondent of Pliny. PLIN. 9.

Mārcellus, -ī, [Mārcus], m., name of a plebeian family in the Claudian gens. Prominent members are together referred to as **Mārcellī,** gen. **-ōrum** (ARCH. 9). Two are mentioned in this book :
(1) *M. Claudius Mārcellus,* the most illustrious of the family, five times consul. When consul the third time, 214 B.C., he went to Sicily, and after a siege of two years' duration took Syracuse, though it was defended by the engines of Archimedes. He also rendered other important services to the state. IMP. P. 16; VERR. 52, *et al.*
(2) *M. Claudius Mārcellus,* consul 51 B.C. and subject of the oration *Prō Mārcellō.* CAT. 1, 8.

Mārcius, -a, the name of a Roman gens. See **Coriolānus, Figulus, Philippus, Rēx.**

Mārcus, -ī, abbreviated **M.,** m., *Mārcus,* a common Roman forename (praenōmen) ; our *Mark.*

mare, -is, abl. **marī,** sometime mare, n., *sea.*

margarītum, -ī, n., *pearl.*

maritimus, -a, -um, [mare], adj.,
of the sea, marine, maritime.

marītus, -ī, [cf. mās, *male*], m.,
married man, husband.

Marius, -ā, name of a plebeian
gens. The most distinguished
person bearing the name was
C. Marius, famous as the conqueror of the Teutones and
Cimbri, and as a leader of the
popular party; born 157 B.C.,
near Arpinum. He served with
distinction under Scipio in Spain,
being present at the siege of Numantia. He put an end to the
war with Jugurtha, 106 B.C. He
annihilated the Teutones near
Aix, in France, 102 B.C., and the
Cimbri the following year near
Vercelli, in Italy. His opposition to the aristocratic party led
to a merciless Civil War. He
was seven times consul, and died
86 B.C. CAT. 1, 2; *et al.;* PROV.
CONS. 13.

marmor, -oris, [= μάρμαρος], n.,
marble, block of marble; by metonymy, *marble monument, statue.*

marmoreus, -a, -um, [marmor],
adj., *made of marble, marble-
like.*

Mārs, Mārtis, m., *Mārs,* the Roman god of war, identified with
the Greek Ares; by metonymy,
war, battle; conflict, contest.

Mārtius, -a, -um, [Mārs], adj.,
*of Mars, sacred to Mars; of the
month of March, of March.*
Mārtia legiō, *the Mars legion.*

māter, -tris, f., *mother; parent,
nurse; origin, source.*

mātrōnālis, -e, [mātrōna, *a married
woman*], adj., *of* or *belonging to*

*a married woman; of a matron;
womanly, matronly.*

mātūrē, comp. mātūrius, sup.
mātūrissimē, [mātūrus], adv.,
*seasonably, opportunely; early,
soon, speedily.*

mātūritās, -ātis, [mātūrus], f.,
ripeness, maturity.

mātūrō, -āre, -āvī, -ātum, [mā-
tūrus], 1, a. and n., *make ripe,
bring to maturity, ripen; hasten,
accelerate.*

mātūrus, -a, -um, adj., *ripe, mature; fit, proper; of mature
years; early, speedy.*

mātūtīnus, -a, -um, [Mātūta, *the
goddess of dawn*], adj., *of the
morning, early.* tempore mātūtīnō, *early morning.*

Maurētānia, -ae, f., *Maurētānia,* a
country of northern Africa.
SALL. 21.

Mauricus, -i, m., *Iūnius Mauricus,*
brother of Arulenus Rusticus,
and a friend of the younger
Pliny, was banished by Domitian, but restored by Nerva.
PLIN. 4.

maximē [maximus], adv., *in the
highest degree, especially, particularly; exceedingly, very.*

Maximī, -ōrum, pl. of Maximus,
m., *men like Maximus,* referring
to Q. Fabius Maximus; *Maximī.*
ARCH. 9.

maximus, see magnus.

Maximus, -ī, *Maximus,* m., name
of a family of the Fabian gens.
The most famous was Q. Fabius
Maximus, whose policy of avoiding open battle wore out Hannibal, and won for him the epithet
Cunctātor. IMP. 16; SEN. 6; 12.

meātus, -ūs, [meō, go], m., going, passing, motion; way, path, passage.

Mēdēa, -ae, [Μήδεια], f., Mēdēa, a mythical sorceress, said to have been a daughter of Aeëtes, king of Colchis, and to have been married to Jason, leader of the Argonauts, by whom she was afterwards deserted. VERR. 60.

medeor, -ērī, ――, 2, dep., heal, cure; relieve, remedy, correct, restore. M. pl. of pres. part. used as subst., medentēs, -ium, doctors, surgeons.

medicīna, -ae, [medicus], f., the healing art, medicine; remedy, antidote.

medicus, -ī, m., physician, doctor.

mediocris, -e, [medius], adj., middling, moderate, ordinary; mean, poor, inferior, indifferent; unimportant.

mediocriter [mediocris], adv., moderately, ordinarily; somewhat, slightly. nec mediocriter, to a marked extent.

Mediōlānum, -ī, n., Milan, a city of northern Italy.

meditor, -ārī, -ātus sum, 1, dep., reflect upon, think of, consider; meditate, plan, devise; study, exercise, practice, prepare.

medius, -a, -um, adj., middle, in the middle, in the midst; midway, intervening, between, among. mediā aestāte, at midsummer. ex mediā morte, from the midst of death.

medulla, -ae, [akin to medius], f., marrow, of the bones; kernel, center, heart, inmost part.

mel, mellis, n., honey; sweetness, pleasantness.

melior, see bonus.

Melita, -ae, f., Malta, an island in the Mediterranean between Sicily and Africa. EP. 6.

mellītus, -a, -um, [mel], adj., of honey, sweet with honey; honey-sweet, darling.

membrānula, -ae, [dim. of membrāna, skin, membrane], f., little membrane; parchment, piece of parchment.

membrum, -ī, n., limb, member; part, branch, portion, division.

meminī, -isse, ――, def., a. and n., remember, recollect; be mindful, bear in mind.

Memmius, -ī or -iī, m., Memmius, tribune of the plebs, 54 B.C. EP. 11.

memor, -oris, [cf. meminī], adj., mindful, remembering, heedful.

memorābilis, -e, [memorō], adj., worthy of being mentioned; worth repeating, memorable, remarkable, worthy of remembrance.

memoria, -ae, [memor], f., memory, remembrance, recollection; narration, tradition. memoriā tenēre, to remember, keep in mind. post hominum memoriam, within the memory of man.

memoriola, -ae, [dim. of memoria], f., memory.

memorō, -āre, -āvī, -ātum, [memor], 1, a., bring to remembrance, mention, recount, tell, describe; name, call.

mendācium, -ī or -iī, [mendāx, given to lying], n., lie, falsehood, fiction.

mendīcitās, -ātis, [mendīcus, beggarly], f., beggary, indigence, extreme poverty.

mēns, mentis, f., *mind, intellect,
soul; feeling, disposition, heart,
spirit; plan, purpose, design,
intent; boldness, courage.* **captus mente,** *beside himself.* **mihi
in mentem venit,** *it occurs to
me.*

mēnsa, -ae, [from mēnsus, part. of
mētior, *measure*], f., *properly,
surveying-board; table; meal,
course; sacrificial altar.*

mēnsis, -is, m., *month.*

mentiō, -ōnis, f., *mention.*

mercātor, -ōris, [mercor, *trade*],
m., *trader, merchant, dealer.*

mercēs, -ēdis, f., *price, pay, wages;
reward, recompense; salary.*

mereō, -ēre, -uī, -itum, 2, a. and
n., *deserve, merit, be entitled to,
be worthy of; earn, acquire, gain,
win, obtain; buy, purchase; serve
for pay, serve as a soldier; confer
a favor, render a service.* **merēre
velle,** *be willing to take.*

mereor, -ērī, -itus sum, 2, dep.,
*deserve, be entitled to, merit;
merit recompense, behave.* **optimē dē rē pūblicā merērī,**
*to render most important service to
one's country.* **bene dē rē pūblicā merērī,** *to do good service for
one's country, to be useful to the
state.* **merērī dē,** *deserve.*

meretrīcius, -a, -um, [meretrīx,
courtesan], adj., *of prostitutes;
meretricious.*

meritō [meritum], adv., *deservedly,
justly.*

meritum, -ī, [meritus], n., *merit,
service, kindness, favor.*

meritus, -a, -um, [part. of mereō],
adj. *deserving; deserved, just, due,
proper.*

merus, -a, -um, adj., *pure, un-
adulterated; naked, uncovered;
only, mere; true, genuine; strong,
excessive.*

Messalla, -ae, m., *M. Valerius
Messalla,* consul 53 B.C., and
friend of Caesar. EP. 11.

-met, enclitic suffix used with most
of the personal pronouns, adding
an intensive force.

mēta, -ae, [akin to mētior], f.,
*anything in the form of a cone;
cone, pyramid; conical column
at the end of the Circus; hence,
turning-post, goal; winning-post,
mark; end, extremity, boundary,
limit.*

mētātor, -ōris, [mētor, *measure*],
m., *one who marks off, fixer of
boundaries, surveyor.*

Metellus, -ī, m., *name of a prominent plebeian family of the Cae-
cilian gens.* The Metelli mentioned in this book are:

(1) *Q. Caecilius Metellus Numidicus,* consul 109 B.C. For
two years, first as consul, then
as proconsul, he conducted the
war against Jugurtha, with such
success that, although superseded in command by Marius,
he was honored with a triumph
on his return to Rome 107 B.C.,
and received the honorary surname *Numidicus.* Having incurred the enmity of the leaders
of the popular party, he was
driven into exile, 100 B.C., but
was recalled the following year.
ARCH. 3.

(2) *Q. Caecilius Metellus Pius,*
son of the preceding, praetor
89 B.C., consul 80 B.C. He re-

ceived the surname *Pius* (' Devoted') because of his activity in procuring the recall of his father from exile. He was a successful general under Sulla in the war against the Marian party. Like his father he was a patron of literature and the arts. ARCH. 3, *et al.*

(3) *Q. Caecilius Metellus Crēticus*, tribune of the people 75 B.C.; legatus the following year, and consul 69 B.C. He gained his honorary surname from his conquest of Crete, which he completed in two years, returning to Rome 66 B.C. SALL. 30.

(4) *Q. Caecilius Metellus Celer*, praetor 63 B.C., consul 60 B.C. He rendered valuable assistance to Cicero in suppressing the conspiracy of Catiline, and was an ardent supporter of the aristocratic party. He died 59 B.C. CAT. **1**, 8; **2**, 12; EP. 3, SALL. 30.

(5) *M. Metellus*, an associate of Catiline, about whom nothing further is known. CAT. **1**, 8.

mētior, -īrī, mēnsus sum, 4, dep., *measure; measure out, distribute; pass over, traverse; estimate, judge, value.*

metuō, -ere, -uī, -ūtum, [metus], 3, a. and n., *fear, be afraid, dread; be apprehensive of, avoid.*

metus, -ūs, m., *fear, dread, apprehension, anxiety.* **per metum,** *in fear.*

meus, -a, -um, [mē], poss. pron., adj., *of me, mine, my, my own.* As subst., **meī, -ōrum,** m., *my kindred, my friends.*

mī, voc. of **meus.**

micāns, -antis, [part. of **micō,** *shine*], adj., *twinkling, gleaming, flashing, glowing.*

mīles, mīlitis, m. and f., *soldier, common soldier; foot-soldier, infantry;* by metonymy, *soldiery, army.*

mīlitāris, -e, [mīles], adj., *of a soldier, of war, warlike, military.* **rēs mīlitāris,** *art of war.* **signa mīlitāria,** *military standards.*

mīlitia, -ae, [mīles], f., *military service, warfare, service, war;* by metonymy, *soldiery.* **domī mīlitiaeque,** *at home and in the field.*

mīlle, pl. **mīlia** or **mīllia,** num. adj., *thousand.* **mīlle passūs,** *mile.* **mīlia passuum,** *miles.*

Milō, -ōnis, *Milo,* the name of two persons mentioned in this book :

(1) *Milō,* a famous Greek athlete, victorious six times in wrestling at the Olympic games, and as often at the Pythian. SEN. 9.

(2) *T. Annius Papiniānus Milō,* tribune of the plebs in 57 B.C., took an active part in obtaining the recall of Cicero from exile. Thenceforward he carried on a fierce contest with P. Clodius, who was slain in an encounter between the followers of the two men near Bovillae. Cicero defended Milo on this occasion, but Milo was condemned and exiled. EP. 11.

minae, -ārum, f., pl., *of a wall, projecting points, pinnacles; threats, menaces.* **vī et minīs,** *by threats of violence.*

Minerva, -ae, f., *Minerva, the goddess of wisdom and intelligence, and patroness of all the arts and trades among the Romans.* She was also identified with Pallas Athene, and so more or less associated with war. VERR. 53.

Minicius, -a, name of a Roman gens, with both patrician and plebeian branches. *C. Minicius Fundānus,* a friend of Pliny, and probably proconsul in Asia under Hadrian. PLIN. 3, 9.

minimē, see **parum.**

minimus, -a, -um, see **parvus.**

ministra, -ae, [minister], f., *female attendant, handmaid, maid-servant; deaconess.*

minitor, -ārī, -ātus sum, [freq. of **minor], 1, dep.,** *keep threatening, threaten, menace.*

minor, -ārī, -ātus sum, [minae], 1, dep., *project; threaten, menace.*

minor, see **parvus.**

minuō, -ere, minuī, minūtum, [cf. minor], 3, a. and n., *make small, lessen, diminish; reduce, lower, weaken.*

minus, see **parvus** and **parum.**

minūtus, -a, -um, [minuō], adj., *little, small, minute; petty, insignificant.*

mīrābilis, -e, [mīror], adj., *marvelous, wonderful, admirable; extraordinary, strange, singular.*

mīrāculum, -ī, [mīror], n., *strangeness; marvelous thing, wonder, miracle; wonderful appearance.* **commentō mīrāculī,** *by the invention of a wonderful occurrence.*

mīrandus, -a, -um, [mīror], adj., *wonderful, strange, singular;* *marvelous.* **mīrandum in modum,** *in wondrous wise.*

mīrificē [mīrificus], adv., *wonderfully, exceedingly.*

mīrificus, -a, -um, [mīrus + faciō], adj., *causing wonder, causing admiration, wonderful, marvelous, extraordinary, strange.*

mīror, -ārī, -ātus sum, [mīrus], 1, dep., *wonder at, marvel; be astonished, be amazed; admire, esteem, regard.*

mīrus, -a, -um, adj., *wonderful, marvelous, strange, amazing, extraordinary.* **nec mīrum,** *and no wonder, and it is not strange.* **mīrum quantum,** *wonderfully.* **mīrum [sc. est],** *it is remarkable.*

misceō, -ēre, miscuī, mixtum, 2, a., *mix, mingle, blend; unite, join, associate, assemble; stir up, disturb, embroil.*

Mīsēnum, -ī, [Μίσηνόν], n., *Mīsēnum,* a promontory and town on the coast of Campania, west of Neapolis (Naples); now **Capo Miseno, Miseno.**

miser, -era, -erum, adj., *wretched, miserable, unhappy, pitiable; sad, distressing; poor, worthless, vile.* **mē miserum!** *ah, unhappy me! woe me!*

miserābilis, -e, [miseror], adj., *pitiable, to be pitied, deplorable, lamentable; sad, wretched.*

miserandus, -a, -um, [part. of miseror], adj., *to be pitied, pitiable, deplorable; wretched, touching.*

miseria, -ae, [miser], f., *wretchedness, affliction, misery, distress.*

misericordia, -ae, [misericors], f., *tender-heartedness, compassion, mercy, pity.*

misericors, -cordis, [misereor + cor], adj., *tender-hearted, compassionate; merciful, pitiful.*

miseror, -ārī, -ātus sum, [miser], 1, dep., *lament, deplore, commiserate; feel compassion, pity; express pity over.*

Mithridātēs, -is, [Μιθριδάτης, name of Persian origin, *given to Mithras, gift to the Sun*], m., *Mithridātēs,* name of several kings of Pontus, of whom the best known is *Mithridātēs Eupatōr,* also called *the Great.* He waged war with Rome for many years. He committed suicide, 63 B.C. IMP. P. 8, *et al.*

Mithridāticus, -a, -um, [Mithridātēs], adj., *of Mithridates.* **Mithridāticum bellum** *the war with Mithridates.* ARCH. 9.

mītigō, -āre, -āvī, -ātum, [mītis + agō], 1, a., *make mild, make tender; ripen, mellow; tame, make gentle; pacify, soothe, calm, appease, mitigate.*

mītis, -e, adj., *mild, mellow, ripe; soft, gentle, kind.*

mittō, -ere, mīsī, missum, 3, a., *send, dispatch; announce, report, suggest; furnish, produce; dismiss, let go; forget, cease; release; put forth, send forth; hurl, cast, throw; omit, pass over the fact that, fail to say.*

mixtus, -a, -um, [part. of misceō], adj., *mixed, confused.*

moderātē [moderātus], adv., *with moderation, with self-control, moderately.*

moderātiō, -ōnis, [moderor], f., *keeping within bounds, regulation; self-restraint, self-control, moderation, temperance.*

moderātus, -a, -um, [part. of moderor], adj., *kept within bounds, restrained; self-restrained, moderate.*

moderor, -ārī, -ātus sum, [modus], 1, dep., *to keep within bounds, limit, regulate; control, restrain, govern.*

modestē, sup. **modestissimē,** [modestus], adv., *with moderation, temperately, moderately; discreetly.*

modestia, -ae, [modestus], f., *moderation; unassuming conduct, modesty; discretion, sobriety; shame, sense of honor, dignity; correctness of conduct; self-restraint, temperance.*

modestus, -a, -um, [modus], adj., *keeping within bounds; gentle, forbearing, modest, discreet.*

modicus, -a, -um, [modus], adj., *having or keeping a proper measure; moderate, modest, temperate; middling, mean, ordinary, scanty, small.*

modo [modus], adv. and conj.: (1) As adv., *only, merely, simply, but; just now, lately, a little while ago, recently; more recently.* **nōn modo — sed,** *not only — but.* See **dum.** (2) As conj., *if only, on condition that, provided that.* **modo nē,** *provided that not.*

modus, -ī, m., *measure, extent; rhythm, melody; proper measure, moderation; limit, bound; way, manner, fashion, method.* **huiusce modī,** *of this sort, of such a kind.* **ūllō modō,** *in any way, by any means.* **nūllō modō,** *in no way, by no means.* **quem ad modum,** *in what way? how: as.*

quōdam modō, *in a fashion, in
some way.* incrēdibilem in modum, *in a remarkable manner.*
nesciō quō modō, *somehow or
other.* istō modō, *on that principle.* aliō quōdam modō, *in a
somewhat different way.*

moenia, -ium, n., pl., *walls* for
defense, *city walls, fortifications;*
by metonymy, *walled town, city.*

mōlēs, -is, f., *mass, bulk; massive
structure, dam, dyke, foundation;
weight, greatness, strength, quantity; difficulty, labor.*

molestē [molestus], adv., *with
difficulty, with vexation.* molestē
ferre, *to bear with vexation, to be
annoyed.*

molestia, -ae, [molestus], f., *trouble,
annoyance, vexation, distress.*

molestus, -a, -um, [mōlēs], adj.,
*troublesome, annoying, irksome,
grievous.* quibus erat molestum,
who were annoyed.

mōlior, -īrī, -ītus sum, [mōlēs],
4, dep., *endeavor, strive, toil; set
in motion, labor upon; direct,
continue; undertake, attempt;
build, construct.*

mollis, -e, adj., *supple, pliant;
tender, delicate, soft; mild, easy,
agreeable; effeminate, weak.*

mōmentum, -ī, [for movimentum,
from moveō], n., lit., *that which
puts anything in motion; that
which is put into one of two evenly
balanced scales and gives it the
turn;* hence, *that which gives a
turn to, decides anything; weight,
turn, decision, influence, motive.*
minimum mōmentum, *the least
important factor.* mōmentum
facere, *to exert influence.*

moneō, -ēre, -uī, -itum, 2, a., *remind, admonish, warn; instruct,
teach; foretell, announce.* eōs
hōc moneō, *I give them this
warning.*

monitiō, -ōnis, [moneō], f., *warning,
admonition, advice.*

monitum, -ī, [moneō], n., *admonition, advice, counsel, suggestion;
oracle.*

monitus, -ūs, [moneō], m., *reminding, warning, admonition; advice; admonition by the gods,
omen.*

mōns, montis, m., *mountain, range
of mountains; heap, mass.*

mōnstrum, -ī, [moneō], n., *omen,
portent, miracle; prodigy, monster, monstrosity, abomination.*

monumentum, -ī, [moneō], n.,
lit., *means of reminding; memorial, monument; chronicle, record.*

mora, -ae, f., *delay, pause; cause
of delay, hindrance, obstacle.*

mōrātus, -a, -um, [mōs], adj.,
*mannered, endowed with good
(or bad) morals.*

morbus, -ī, [morior], m., *sickness,
disease, ailment, disorder.*

morior, morī and morīrī, mortuus
sum, 3 and 4, dep., *die, expire;
wither, decay, pass away.*

moror, -ārī, -ātus sum, [mora],
1, dep., *delay, stay, wait, remain,
linger; retard, detain, cause to
wait, hinder.*

mōrōsitās, -ātis, [mōrōsus], f.,
*peevishness, fretfulness, morose-
ness, ill-temper.*

mōrōsus, -a, -um, [mōs], adj.,
*difficult to please, wayward, peev-
ish, fretful; capricious; ill-
tempered.*

mors, mortis, f., *death;* by metonymy, *dead body, corpse.*

mortālis, -e, [mors], adj., *subject to death, mortal; of a mortal, human, transitory.* As subst., mortālēs, -ium, m., pl., *mortals, mortal men, men, mankind.*

mortuus, -a, -um, [part. of morior], adj., *dead; decayed.* As subst., mortuī, -ōrum, m., pl., *the dead.*

mōs, mōris, m., *manner, habit, custom, way, humor; usage, practice, fashion;* pl., mōrēs, -um, *manners, morals,* often *character.*

mōtus, -ūs, [moveō], m., *motion, movement; graceful movement, gesticulation; emotion, affection, impulse, agitation; disturbance, tumult, commotion.* terrae mōtus, *earthquake.*

moveō, -ēre, mōvī, mōtum, 2, a. and n., *move, set in motion, disturb, remove; excite, affect, stir up; produce, promote; change, transform.* quiēta movēre, *to disturb the public peace.* senātū movēre, *to expel from the senate.*

mox, adv., *soon, presently; afterwards; thereupon, then, in the next place.*

Mūcius, -a, the name of a Roman gens. See Scaevola.

mūcrō, -ōnis, m., *point, edge,* especially of a sword; by metonymy, *sword; sharpness, edge.*

muliebris, -e, [mulier], adj., *of a woman, womanly; effeminate, unmanly.*

mulier, -eris, f., *woman, female; wife.*

muliercula, -ae, [dim. of mulier], f., *little woman, girl.*

multiplex, -icis, [multus + plicō, fold], adj., *with many folds, much-winding; manifold, many times as great, far more; of many parts, changeable, versatile; deceitful; intricate, tortuous; repeated many times.*

multitūdō, -inis, [multus], f., *great number, multitude, crowd, throng.* multitūdō aquae, *great quantity of water.*

multō, -āre, -āvī, -ātum, [multa, fine], 1, a., *punish.*

multō [abl. n. of multus], adv., *by much, much; far, by far, very, greatly.*

multum [multus], adv., *much, greatly, far; often, frequently.*

multus, -a, -um, comp. plūs, sup. plūrimus, adj., *much,* pl. *many, in large numbers; abundant, considerable;* often used as subst. in m. and n., pos., comp., and sup.

Mulvius, adj., *Mulvian.* Mulvius pōns, *the Mulvian bridge,* which crossed the Tiber two miles north of Rome; now Ponte Molle. It was built by M. Aemilius Scaurus, the censor, 109 B.C. CAT. 3, 2.

mundus, -ī, m., *toilet ornament, decoration, dress* (of women); *the universe, world, earth; mankind.*

mūniceps, -ipis, [mūnia, *official duties,* capiō], m. and f., *inhabitant of a free town, citizen, burgher; fellow citizen.*

mūnicipium, -ī or -iī, [mūniceps], n., *free city, free town, municipality,* a city which had lost its independence and submitted to

Rome, but which was permitted to retain self-government in local affairs, its citizens becoming Roman plebeians.

mūnificentia, -ae, [**mūnificus,** *bountiful*], f., *benevolence, liberality, generosity, munificence.*

mūnimentum, -ī, [**mūniō**], n., *anything by which a person protects himself; place of defense, fortification, intrenchment, rampart, bulwark, protection; defense, shelter.*

mūniō, -īre, -īvī, -ītum, [**moenia**], 4, a., *defend with a wall, wall; fortify, defend, protect; secure, guard, strengthen, build structures; surround.*

mūnītiō, -ōnis, [**mūniō**], f., *defending, fortifying; defenses, rampart, bulwark; work of engineering.*

mūnītus, -a, -um, [part. of **mūniō**], adj., *fortified, defended; secure, safe.*

mūnus, -eris, n., *service, office, employment, function, duty; favor, kindness: present, gift; spectacle, show, contest, exhibition.* **deōrum munere,** *by favor of the gods.*

mūnusculum [dim. of **mūnus**], n., *small gift, trifling present.*

mūrus, -ī, m., *wall*, especially of a city, *city wall.*

Mūsa, -ae, [Μοῦσα], f., *Muse, one of the nine Muses,* goddesses of music, poetry, and the sciences.

mūsculus, -ī, [**mūs,** *mouse*], m., *little mouse;* hence, from the resemblance, *muscle of the body.*

Mutina, -ae, f., *Mutina,* a city of northern Italy, where Brutus was shut up by Antony. PHIL. I.

mūtō, -āre, -āvī, -ātum, [freq. of **moveō**], I, a. and n., *move, remove; change, alter, transform; interchange, exchange.*

mūtuē [**mūtuus**], adv., *in return, mutually.* **mūtuē respondēre,** *to make an adequate return, make a fair return.*

mūtus, -a, -um, adj., *dumb, without speech, speechless, voiceless; silent, mute, still.*

mūtuus, -a, -um, [**mūtō**], adj., *borrowed, lent; in return, in exchange, reciprocal, mutual.*

myoparō, -ōnis, m., kind of light vessel used by pirates; *small warship, privateer.*

Myrōn, -ōnis, m., *Myrōn,* a Greek sculptor of the fifth century B.C. The most celebrated of his works was the *Discobolus.*

mystagōgus, -ī, m., kind of priest who showed strangers the remarkable things of a temple; *guide to mysteries; custodian of sacred things.*

Mytilēnaeus, -a, -um, [**Mytilēnē**], adj., *of Mytilēnē,* a city on the island of Lesbos; now **Mytilini.**

N

Naevius, -ī or **-iī,** m., *Cn. Naevius,* an early Roman poet. Naevius wrote the first national Roman epic, a poem about the first Punic War. SEN. 14.

nam, conj., explanatory and causal. *for, for instance; for, seeing that, because, inasmuch as.*

namque [**nam** + **que**], conj., a strengthened **nam,** introducing a reason or explanation in close connection with what precedes;

for, and in fact, seeing that, inasmuch as.

nancīscor, -ī, nactus and **nanctus sum,** 3, dep., *obtain, secure, get, receive; meet with, fall in with, find, reach; incur.* **aurēs nancīscī,** *gain attention.*

nārrō, -āre, -āvī, -ātum, 1, a., *make known, tell, relate, narrate, set forth; say, speak, tell, mention, describe.*

nāscēns, -entis, [part. of **nāscor**], adj., *rising, young, newly fledged.*

nāscor, nāscī, nātus sum, 3, dep., *be born, be produced; spring up, grow, start; arise, begin.* **nātālis, -e,** [**nātus**], adj., *of birth, birth-, natal.*

nātiō, -ōnis, [**nāscor, nātus**], f., *birth; breed, stock, kind; nation, people.*

nātūra, -ae, [**nāscor**], f., *birth; innate quality, disposition; inclination, temper, character; law of nature, course of things, nature, world.* **vīs ac nātūra,** *the natural force.* **propinquitāte atque nātūrā,** *as if by a natural relationship.* **nātūrā,** *naturally.*

nātūrālis, -e, [**nātūra**], adj., *by birth, one's own; of the nature of things, produced by nature, according to nature, natural.*

nātus, -a, -um, [part. of **nāscor**], adj., *born, produced, sprung from; designed by nature, constituted by nature.* As subst., **nātus, -ī,** m., *son.*

nātus, -ūs, only in the abl. sing., **nātū,** [**nāscor**], m., *birth, age, years.* **grandis nātū,** *very old.* **maior nātū,** *older.* **maximus nātū,** *oldest.* **minimus nātū,** *youngest.* **maiōrēs nātū,** *elders.*

naufragus, -a, -um, [**nāvis + frangō**], adj., *shipwrecked, wrecked; ruined.* As subst., **naufragī, -ōrum,** m., pl., *castaways; ruined men, bankrupts.*

nāvālis, -e, [**nāvis**], adj., *of ships, ship-, naval, nautical.*

nāvigātiō, -ōnis, [**nāvigō**], f., *sailing, navigation, voyage.*

nāvigō, -āre, -āvī, -ātum, [**nāvis + agō**], 1, a. and n., *sail, set sail, cruise; sail over, navigate.*

nāvis, -is, f., *ship.* **nāvis longa,** *ship of war, warship.*

nē, adverb and conj. :

(1) As adv., *not.* **nē — quidem,** *not — even.*

(2) As conj., *in order that not, that not, lest, for fear that, granted that not.*

nē, [= ναί, νή], interj., *truly, indeed, verily, really.*

-ne, enclitic adv. and conj. :

(1) As adv., *purely interrogative and marking a direct question,* untranslatable except in the inflection of the voice.

(2) As conj., *introducing an indirect question, whether.* **-ne — an, -ne — -ne,** *whether — or.*

Neāpolis, -is, f., *New City,* a part of Syracuse.

Neāpolitānī, -ōrum, m., pl., *Neapolitans, inhabitants of Neapolis,* now **Napoli,** *Naples.*

nec, neque, [**nē + -que**], adv. and conj., *and not, also not, nor, nor yet, nor however.* **nec — nec,** *neither — nor.* **nec — et, nec — -que,** *on the one hand not — on the other, not only not — but also.* **nec nōn,** *and certainly,*

and indeed. **neque enim,** *for
— not, and yet — not.*

necessārius, -a, -um, [necesse],
adj., *unavoidable, inevitable,
pressing, needful.* As subst., **necessārius, -ī** or **-iī,** m., *kinsman,
man, relative, friend, client.*

necesse, adj., n., indecl., *unavoidable, inevitable, necessary.* **necesse est,** *it is inevitable, it is
necessary, one must.* **concēdī
alicui necesse est,** *it must inevitably be given up to some one.*

necessitās, -ātis, [necesse], f.,
*unavoidableness, necessity, exi-
gency; need, want; connection,
relationship, friendship.*

necessitūdō, -inis, [necesse], f.,
*inevitableness, necessity; intimate
relation, relationship, intimacy,
friendship; distress, difficulty.*

necne [nec + -ne], conj., *found in
the second part of a double question, usually indirect, or not.*

necō, -āre, -āvī, -ātum, [nex], 1,
a., *kill, slay, put to death, destroy.*

nefandus, -a, -um, [nē + fandus,
from for], adj., *not to be mentioned, unutterable; wicked, impious, heinous, abominable.*

nefārius, -a, -um, [nefās], adj.,
*impious, heinous, abominable,
nefarious; wicked, dastardly.*

nefāstus, -a, -um, [nē + fāstus],
adj., *not right, contrary to religion,
irreligious, impious; unhallowed,
unpropitious.* **diēs nefāstī,** *days
on which courts or public assemblies must not sit.* **nefāstī diēs
fastīque,** *holidays and work-days.*

neglegēns, -entis, [neglegō], adj.,
*heedless, careless, unconcerned, ne-
glectful; improvident.*

neglegenter, comp. **neglegentius,**
[neglegēns], adv., *carelessly,
negligently, heedlessly.*

neglegentia, -ae, [neglegēns], f.,
*carelessness, negligence, heedless-
ness, neglect.*

neglegō, -ere, neglēxī, neglēctum,
[nec + legō], 3, a., *disregard,
neglect, not attend to, not heed,
slight; despise, contemn, treat
with indifference.*

negō, -āre, -āvī, -ātum, 1, a. and
n., *say no; deny, refuse, decline.*

negōtior, -ārī, -ātus sum, [negō-
tium], 1, dep., *do business, carry
on business, trade, traffic.*

negōtium, -ī or **-iī,** [nec + ōtium],
n., *business, employment, occupation; difficulty, trouble; matter,
affair.*

nēmō, pl. and gen. and abl. sing.
replaced by forms from **nūllus,**
[nē + homō], m. and f., *no one,
nobody.* **nōn nēmō,** *many a
one, somebody.* **abest nōn nēmō,**
*more than one is away, some are
away.*

Neoptolemus, -ī, m., *Neoptolemus,*
son of Achilles, Pyrrhus. He
was one of the heroes concealed
in the wooden horse; and at the
capture of Troy killed Priam, and
received as his spoil Andromache,
widow of Hector.

nepōs, -ōtis, m., *grandson; spendthrift, prodigal.*

nēquāquam, adv., *in no wise, by no
means, not at all.*

neque, see **nec.**

nequedum, adv., *and not yet, nor
yet.*

nequeō, -īre, -quīvī, -quitum, irr.,
n., *not to be able, cannot, be unable.*

nēquitia, -ae, [**nēquam**], f., *worthlessness, inefficiency; wickedness, vileness.*

Nerviī, -ōrum, the *Nerviī,* a Gallic people.

nervus, -ī, m., *sinew, muscle, tendon;* by metonymy, *string of a bow, bow-string;* of a musical instrument, *string, chord.*

nesciō, -īre, -īvī or **-iī, -ītum,** [**nē + sciō**], 4, a., *not know, be ignorant;* often used in parenthetical phrases expressing uncertainty. **nesciō an,** *I know not whether = perhaps, probably.* **nesciō quid, nesciō quod,** *I know not what = something, some, certain.* **nesciō quō modō,** *I know not how = somehow.*

Nestōr, -oris, *Nestōr,* king of Pylos, noted for his age and wisdom, the old man eloquent in Homer.

neu, see **nēve.**

neuter, -tra, -trum, gen., **-trīus,** dat. **-trī,** [**nē + uter**], pronom. adj., *neither the one nor the other, neither* (of two).

nēve, or **neu,** [**nē + -ve**], conj., *and not, nor; and that not, and lest, and in order that not.*

nex, necis, f., *death* by violence, *murder, slaughter.*

nī, [**nisi** by apocope], adv. and conj., *if not, unless.*

niger, -gra, -grum, adj., *black, dark, dusky; gloomy, ill-omened; wicked.*

nihil, or **nīl,** [**nē + hilum,** *trifle*], n., indecl., *nothing;* acc. often with adverbial force, *not at all, in no respect, by no means.*

nihilum, -ī, n., *not a shred, nothing.* **prō nihilō putāre,** *regard as* valueless. **nihilō minus,** *none the less.*

Nīlus, -ī, [Νεῖλος], m., *Nile,* the great river of Egypt. MAR. 9.

nimbus, -ī, n., *a rain-storm, a pouring of rain, a black rain-cloud; cloud; throng.*

nīmīrum [**nī + mīrum**], adv., *doubtless, without doubt, certainly; to be sure, truly.*

nimis, adv., *too, too much, beyond measure, excessively; to any great extent.*

nimium [**nimius**], adv., *too much, too; very, greatly, exceedingly.*

nimius, -a, .**-um,** [**nimis**], adj., *excessive, beyond measure, too great, too much.* As subst., **nimium, -ī** or **-iī,** n., *too much, excess.*

nisi [**nē + sī**], conj., *if not, unless, except, save only.* **nisi vērō,** ironical, *unless perchance, unless perhaps.* **nisi quod,** *except that.* **nisi ut,** *without.*

nitidus, -a, -um, [cf. **niteō**], adj., *shining, bright, glittering; sleek, spruce, trim, blooming.*

nix, nivis, f., *snow.*

Nōbilior, ōris, [**nōbilis**], m., name of a family of the Fulvian gens. The most distinguished member was *M. Fulvius Nōbilior,* who was curule aedile 195 B.C., and praetor two years later. When consul, 189 B.C., he set out against the Aetolians, taking the poet Ennius with him. Having been successful in his expedition, he returned to Rome 187 B.C., and celebrated the most magnificent triumph and games witnessed up to that time. He was a patron of the liberal arts, and left many public works. ARCH. 11.

nōbilis, -e, [cf. nōscō], adj., *well-known, famous, renowned, illustrious; high-born, of noble descent; noble, excellent, fine.*

nōbilitās, -ātis, [nōbilis], f., *celebrity, fame; high birth, noble origin; aristocracy, nobles; nobility, excellence, superiority.*

nōbilitō, -āre, -āvī, -ātum, [nōbilis], 1, a., *make known, make renowned; make notorious.*

noceō, -ēre, -uī, -itum, 2, a. and n., *harm, hurt, injure; inflict injury, do mischief.* nihil mihi nocērī potest, *no harm can be done me.*

noctū [old abl. of noctus, for nox], adv., *in the night, at night, by night.*

noctuābundus, -a, -um, [nox], adj., *traveling by night, after traveling all night long; in the night-time, by night.*

nocturnus, -a, -um, [nox], adj., *of night, by night, nocturnal.*

nōdus, -ī, m., *a knot; a band, bond.*

nōlō, nōlle, nōluī, ——, [nē + volō], irr., n., *wish not, will not, not wish, not will, be unwilling.* nōlī esse, *be not.* nōlī dēfatīgārī, *be not wearied, do not allow yourself to become wearied.* nōlīte dubitāre, *do not hesitate.*

nōmen, -inis, [cf. nōscō], n., *name, appellation, designation; fame, renown, repute.* meō nōmine, *in my name, on my account; in my honor.* in hōc nōmine, *in regard to this item.*

nōminātim [nōminō], adv., *by name; expressly, in particular, especially.*

nōminō, -āre, -āvī, -ātum, [nōmen], 1, a., *call by name, name; render famous, make renowned; nominate, designate; mention, report; accuse, charge.* honōris causā nōminō, *I mention in the way of honor; I mention with due respect.*

nōn [old noenum, from nē + oenum = ūnum], adv., *not, not at all, by no means.* nōn modo — sed, *not only — but.* nōn nisi, *only.* nōn tam, *not particularly, not so very.*

Nōnae, -ārum, abbreviated Nōn., [nōnus], f., *the Nones,* one of the days of the month to which dates were reckoned in the Roman calendar. It was the ninth day before the Ides, and hence came on the fifth day of the month, except in March, May, July, and October, when it fell on the seventh. See Īdūs, Kalendae.

nōndum [nōn + dum], adv., *not yet.*

nōnne [nōn + -ne], inter. adv., expecting an affirmative answer in a dir. question, *not;* in an indir. question, *if not, whether not.*

nōnus, -a, -um, [novem], num. adj., *ninth.*

nōs, nostrum, see ego.

nōscitō, -āre, ——, ——, [freq. of nōscō], 1, a., *know, recognize.*

nōscō, -ere, nōvī, nōtum, 3, a., *become acquainted with, get knowledge of, learn;* in tenses from pf. stem, *have learned,* hence, *know, be familiar with, understand.*

noster, -tra, -trum, [nōs], poss. pron. adj., *our, ours, our own, of us.* **dē nostrō omnium interitū,** *about the destruction of us all.* CAT. 1, 4.

nota, -ae, [cf. **nōscō**}, f., *mark, sign; stamp, spot; letter; nod, token; mark* of ignominy, *disgrace.*

notō, -āre, -āvī, -ātum, [nota], 1, a., *mark, stamp; note, observe; single out, designate; censure, reprimand.*

nōtus, -a, -um, [part. of nōscō], adj., *known, familiar; well-known, famous, notorious; of ill repute, ill-reputed.*

novem or **VIIII., IX.,** num. adj., *nine.*

November, -bris, -bre, [novem], adj., lit., *of the ninth; of November,* the ninth month reckoning from March, which the early Romans considered the first month of the year.

novissimē, sup. adv., *very recently, of late, lastly.*

novō, -āre, -āvī, -ātum, [novus], 1, a., *introduce as new, make new, renew, renovate; invent; change, alter; make a change, effect a revolution.* **nē quid novārētur** *that no revolutionary movement should be made.* **novandī spēs,** *hopes of effecting a revolution.*

novus, -a, -um, adj., *new, recent, fresh, young; unfamiliar, strange; last, latest, extreme.* **rēs novae,** *new things;* in a political sense, *innovations, revolution.* **tabulae novae,** *new accounts, a new account,* meaning the canceling or abolition of debts. **homō novus,** a technical term for one who was the first of his family to hold

curule office, *an upstart, a parvenu.* **quid novī?** *what news?* **nihil novī,** *no news.* [ali] **quid novī,** *anything new, anything without precedent.* **nihil novum,** *no novelty.*

nox, noctis, f., *night;* by metonymy, *darkness, obscurity.* **superiōre nocte,** *the night before last.* **noctēs ac diēs,** *day and night.* **priōre nocte,** *the night before last.* **proximā nocte,** *last night.*

nūbēs, -is, f., *cloud, mist, vapor; dense mass, swarm.*

Nūcerīnus, -a, -um, adj., *of Nuceria,* in Campania.

nūdius [for **nunc diēs,** sc. **est**], adv., used only with an ordinal number in phrases expressing time, *it is now the — day since.* **nūdius tertius,** *it is now the third day* or *day before yesterday.*

nūdus, -a, -um, adj., *naked, bare, uncovered;* often, *without an outer garment* or *without a shield, lightly clad, exposed; vacant, destitute, without; mere, only.*

nūgātor, -ōris, [nūgor, *jest*], m., *jester, joker, trifler, braggart.*

nūllus, -a, -um, gen. **nūllīus,** [nē + ullus], adj., *not any, none, no.* As subst., **nūllus, -īus,** m., *nobody, no one, no man.* **nōn nūllus,** *some one,* pl. *some.* **nūllus nōn,** *every, all.*

num, inter. adv., usually expecting a negative answer, in a direct question, *now, then,* or, following a negative translation of the question, *— not so, — is it?* in an indirect question, *whether, if.*

Numa, -ae, m., *Numa Pompilius,* second king of Rome. He was renowned for his wisdom and piety. His chief care was the establishment of religion among his subjects. LIV. I, 19.

nūmen, -inis, [nuō], n., *nod; will, command; divine will, divine power, divinity, deity; divine favor, favor of the gods.*

numerō, -āre, -āvī, -ātum, [numerus], I, a., *count, reckon, number, count out, pay.*

numerus, -ī, m., *number; large number, multitude, quantity, body; rank, position, place; measure of music or poetry, rhythm, time, numbers.*

Numidicus, -a, -um, [Numidia], adj., *Numidian, of Numidia,* a country in northern Africa between Mauritania and the territory of Carthage; modern Algiers. See **Metellus** (I).

Numitor, -ōris, m., *Numitor,* last king of Alba, and grandfather of Romulus. LIV. I, 6.

nummus, -ī, gen. pl., usually **nummum,** m., *coin, money;* referring to the Roman silver coin of account, *sestertius, sesterce; penny, farthing, trifle.*

numquam [nē + umquam], adv., *never, at no time; by no means.* **nōn numquam,** *sometimes.*

nunc [num + -ce], adv., *now, at this time, at present, at the present time; under these circumstances, as it is, as matters are, as a matter of fact.*

nūntiō, -āre, -āvī, -ātum, [nūntius], I, a., *announce, declare; report, communicate.*

nūntius, -a, -um, adj., *that brings tidings, announcing, informing.*

As subst., **nūntius, -ī** or **-iī,** m., *newscarrier, messenger, reporter; news, message, tidings.*

nūper, sup. **nūperrimē,** [novus + per], adv., *lately, recently, not long since.*

nūptiae, -ārum, [nūpta, bride], f., pl., *marriage, wedding, nuptials.*

nūsquam, [nē + ūsquam], adv., *nowhere, in no place; on no occasion; to no place, to no purpose.*

nūtō, -āre, -āvī, -ātum, [freq. of nuō, nod], I, n., *nod; totter, waver, falter; doubt, hesitate.*

nūtriō, -īre, -īvī, -ītum, 4, a., *suckle, nourish, feed, nurse, foster, bring up, rear; support, maintain; take care of, attend; cherish, cultivate, sustain.*

nūtrīx, -īcis, [nūtriō], f., *nurse, wet-nurse.*

nūtus, abl. **-ū,** found only in nom., acc., and abl. sing., acc. and abl. pl., [nuō], m., *nod; compliance, assent; will, command.*

O

Ō, interj., *O! oh!*

ob, prep. with acc., *to, towards, for, on account of, by reason of.* **quam ob rem,** *wherefore, hence.*

In composition **ob** is usually assimilated before **c, f, g, p,** but remains unchanged before other letters. It adds the meaning *towards, at, before, against.*

obeō, -īre, -īvī or **-iī, -itum,** [ob + eō], irr., a. and n., *go to meet; come up to, reach; go over, traverse, visit; engage in, undertake, enter upon; perform, discharge, execute, accomplish; of a crime, commit.*

obiciō, -icere, -iēcī, -iectum, [ob + iaciō], 3, a., *throw before; offer, present, expose; upbraid, reproach with, taint.*

obiūrgātiō, -ōnis, [obiūrgō], f., *chiding, reproof, rebuke.*

obiūrgō, -āre, -āvī, -ātum, [ob + iūrgō], 1, a., *chide, rebuke, reprove; urge, adjure.*

oblectāmentum, -ī, [oblectō], n., *that which delights* or *pleases; delight, pleasure, amusement; source of pleasure, diversion, enjoyment.*

oblectātiō, -ōnis, [oblectō], f., *delight, charm.*

oblectō, -āre, -āvī, -ātum, [ob + lactō, *allure*], 1, a., *delight, amuse, entertain, divert, interest.*

oblinō, -ere, oblēvī, oblitum, [ob + linō], 3, a., *besmear, smear, stain, daub; cover with, defile.*

oblitus, see **oblinō.**

oblītus, -a, -um, [part. of oblīvīscor], adj., *forgetful, unmindful, regardless.*

oblīviō, -ōnis, [oblīvīscor], f., *forgetfulness, oblivion.*

oblīviōsus, -a, -um, [oblīviō], adj., *forgetting easily* or *soon; that easily forgets; forgetful, oblivious.*

oblīvīscor, -vīscī, oblītus sum, 3, dep., *forget, be forgetful; disregard, neglect, omit.*

obmūtēscō, -ere, -mūtuī, ——, 3, n., *become dumb, be silent; cease, become silent.*

obnoxius, -a, -um, [ob + noxius, *harmful*], adj., *liable, addicted to, guilty; submissive, complying, complaisant, servile; weak, timid; in the power of, a slave to.*

oboediō, -īre, -īvī, -ītum, [ob + audiō], 4, n., *hearken. listen; give heed to, obey, yield obedience, be subject.*

obruō, -ere, obruī, obrutum, [ob + ruō], 3, a., *overwhelm, cover, bury; overthrow, destroy.*

obscūrē [obscūrus], adv., *darkly, indistinctly, obscurely, covertly.*

obscūrō, -āre, -āvī, -ātum, [obscūrus], 1, a., *make dark, darken, obscure; hide, conceal; keep hidden, suppress.*

obscūrus, -a, -um, adj., *dark, dusky, dim, obscure; not known, unfamiliar; indistinct, unintelligible, hard to understand; ignoble, mean, low.*

obsecrō, -āre, -āvī, -ātum, [ob + sacrō], 1, a., *beseech, implore, entreat.*

obsecundō, -āre, -āvī, -ātum, [ob + secundō], 1, n., *be favorable, comply with, humor, accommodate.*

obsequium, -ī or **iī,** [obsequor], n., *deference to another's wishes; compliance, complaisance, obedience; flattery.* in obsequiō, *in the payment of deference.*

obsequor, -ī, -secūtus sum, [ob + sequor], 3, dep., *comply with; yield, gratify, humor, submit, be accommodating; yield, give up, indulge; obey, follow directions of.*

observō, -āre, -āvī, -ātum, [ob + servō], 1, a., *watch, heed, observe, take notice of; guard, keep; treat with respect, pay attention to, regard, honor.*

obses, -idis, [ob, cf. sedeō], m. and f., *hostage; security, pledge, surety, assurance.*

obsideō, -ēre, obsēdī, obsessum, [ob + sedeō], 2, a. and n., *stay,* remain; beset, invest, besiege; lie in wait for, look out for.

obsidiō, -ōnis, [obsideō], f., *siege, blockade.*

obstinātiō, -ōnis, [obstinō, resolve], f., *firmness, steadfastness; stubbornness, obstinacy.*

obstipēscō, -ere, obstipuī, ——, 3, inch., *be astounded, stand amazed, be amazed; become senseless, be stupefied.*

obstō, -āre, obstitī, obstātum, [ob + stō], 1, n., *stand before; be in the way; withstand, oppose, hinder, thwart, restrain.*

obstrepō, -ere, -uī, -itum, [ob + strepō], 3, a. and n., *roar at, resound, make a noise; outbawl, drown out* by cries.

obstringō, -ere, -strīnxī, -strictum, [ob + stringō, bind tight], 3, a., *tie fast; confine; bind, fetter; lay under obligation.*

obstruō, -ere, -strūxī, -strūctum, [ob + struō, heap up], 3, a., *build against; block, make impassable; impede, obstruct.*

obsum, -esse, -fuī, [ob + sum], irr., n., *be against; injure, hurt, be prejudicial to.*

obsurdēscō, -ere, -surduī, ——, [ob + surdus, deaf], 3, n., *become deaf; turn a deaf ear to; be dull of apprehension.*

obtegō, -ere, -tēxī, -tēctum, [ob + tegō], 3, a., *cover over, protect; conceal, keep secret.*

obtemperō, -āre, -āvī, -ātum, [ob + temperō], 1, n., *comply, conform, submit, obey.*

obtineō, -ēre, obtinuī, obtentum, [ob + teneō], 2, a. and n., *hold fast, keep, maintain; assert, prove, show.*

obtingō, -ere, obtigī, ——, [ob + tangō], 3, a. and n., *fall to one's lot, befall; happen, occur.*

obtrectō, -āre, -āvī, -ātum, [ob + tractō], 1, a. and n., *disparage, underrate, decry; raise objections to, be opposed to, thwart.*

obturbō, -āre, -āvī, -ātum, [ob + turbō], 1, a., *stir up, trouble; confuse, disturb, distract.*

obveniō, -īre, -vēnī, -ventum, [ob + veniō], 4, n., *meet* or *come in the way, go to meet; befall, occur; fall to the lot of, be allotted.*

obversor, -ārī, -ātus sum, [ob + versor], 1, dep., *move to and fro before something; make an appearance, show oneself; hover before; turn in the face of, present.*

obviam [ob + viam], adv., *in the way, against, in face of, to meet.* **mihi obviam vēnit,** *he came to meet me.*

obvius, -a, -um, [ob + via], adj., *in the way, across the path; so as to meet, meeting, to meet; against, to encounter; open, exposed, liable, subject.* **obvius fierī,** *to encounter.* **obvius esse,** *meet.*

occāsiō, -ōnis, [ob, cf. cāsus, cadō], f., *opportunity, suitable time, favorable moment, occasion; pretext, excuse.*

occāsus, -ūs, [ob + cāsus, from cadō], m., *of the heavenly bodies, going down, setting; by metonymy, sunset, west; downfall, destruction, ruin, death.*

occidēns, -entis, pl. wanting, [part. of occidō], m., *sunset, west.* **ab occidente,** *in the west.*

occīdiō, -ōnis, [occīdō], f., *massacre, utter destruction, extermination.*

occīdō, -ere, occīdī, occīsum, [ob + caedō], 3, a., *strike down; cut down, kill, slay, murder.*

occidō, -ere, occidī, occāsum, [ob + cadō], 3, n., *fall down, fall; die, perish, be slain;* of heavenly bodies, *go down, set.*

occultē [occultus], adv., *secretly, privately; in concealment, in secret.*

occultō, -āre, -āvī, -ātum, [freq. of occulō, *cover*], 1, a., *conceal, hide, secrete.*

occultus, -a, um, [part. of occulō, *cover*], adj., *concealed, covered up; hidden, secret.* haud occultum habēre, *not to keep secret.*

occupātiō, -ōnis, [occupō], f., *taking possession, seizure; business, employment, business obligations.*

occupō, -āre, -āvī, -ātum, [ob, cf. capiō], 1, a., *take possession of, seize, gain; fall upon, surprise, attack; anticipate, outstrip; take up, employ.*

occurrō, -ere, occurrī, occursum, [ob + currō], 3, n., *run to, run to meet, meet, fall in with; rush upon, attack; oppose, resist; present* itself or oneself, *occur, suggest itself, be thought of.*

Ōceanus, -ī, ['Ὠκεανός], m., *the great sea* that encompasses the land, *outer sea, ocean.*

Octāviānus, -a, -um, adj., *Octavian,* of or *relating to Octāvius.* bellum Octāviānum, *the war of Cn. Octāvius with Cinna.*

Octāviānus, -ī, [Octāvius], m., *Octavian,* usually called *Augustus;* born 63 B.C., son of C. Octavius and Atia, daughter of Julia, sister of Julius Caesar. His name was at first the same as that of his father, C. Octāvius. He was adopted by Julius Caesar, and his name became, according to the rule in such cases, C. Iūlius Caesar Octāviānus. The title *Augustus* was added 27 B.C., when the supremacy of Octavian as emperor was formally recognized. His reign lasted till his death, 14 A.D. EP. 24; LIV. I, 19; PHIL. 2, *et al.*

Octāvius, -a, [octāvus], name of a plebeian gens, raised to patrician standing by Julius Caesar. Cn. Octāvius, consul 76 B.C., L. Octāvius, consul 75, and perhaps other members of the family are mentioned together by Cicero as Octāvii, gen. -ōrum. ARCH. 3. The father of L. Octavius was Cn. Octāvius, a partisan of Sulla, consul with Cinna 87 B.C. As Cinna endeavored to bring back the party of Marius to power, Octavius opposed him with force. In the violent conflict that ensued he was murdered. CAT. 3, 10.

octāvus, -a, -um, or VIII, [octō], num. adj., *eighth.*

oculus, -ī, m., *eye.*

ōdī, ōdisse, fut. part. ōsūrus, def., a., *hate; dislike, be displeased with.*

odiōsus, -a, -um, [odium], adj., *hateful, offensive; unpleasant, disagreeable.*

odium, -ī or -iī, [cf. ōdī], n., *hatred, grudge, ill-will, enmity; offense, aversion, abomination, nuisance; disgust, dissatisfaction.*

odor, -ōris, m., *smell, scent, odor, stench; pleasant odor, perfume, essences, spices; disagreeable smell, stench; inkling, hint, presentiment, suggestion.*

Oedipūs, -podis, m., *Oedipus,* a king of Thebes, solver of the riddle of the sphinx. Also: *the name of a tragedy by Sophocles.* SEN. 7.

offendō, -ere, offendī, offēnsum, [ob + unused fendō], 3, a. and n., *strike against, stumble; hit upon, find; commit a fault, offend, be offensive; vex, displease.*

offēnsa, -ae, [offendō], f., *disfavor, offense, hatred, enmity; injury, affront.*

offēnsiō, -ōnis, [offendō], f., *stumbling; aversion, dislike, disgust, hatred; mishap, misfortune, defeat.* **offēnsiōnem habēre,** *to involve unpopularity.*

offēnsus, -a, -um, [part. of offendō], adj., *offended, vexed, embittered; offensive, odious.*

offerō, -ferre, obtulī, oblātum, [ob + ferō], irr., a., *present, offer, exhibit; bring forward, adduce; bestow, confer.*

officiō, -ere, -fēcī, -fectum, [ob + faciō], 3, n., *do* or *act contrary to; come in the way of, hinder, oppose, thwart, obstruct, be an obstacle to; hurt, be detrimental; obstruct the view.*

officiōsē, comp. **officiōsius,** [officiōsus,** *courteous*], adv., *courteously, obligingly, kindly.*

officium, -ī or **-iī,** [for opificium, opus + faciō], n., *service, kindness, favor, courtesy; duty, obligation; office, function, employ-*ment. **officiō togae virīlis,** *at a coming of age.*

offīrmō, -āre, -āvī, -ātum, [ob + fīrmo], 1, a. and n., *make firm; hold fast, persevere; persist, be obstinate.*

oleārius, -a, -um, [oleum], adj., *of oil, for oil.*

oleum, -ī, n., *oil, olive-oil.*

ōlim [cf. **ollus,** old form of **ille**], adv., *at that time, formerly, once, long since, erstwhile; ever; some time, some day, hereafter.*

Olympius, -a, -um, adj., *of* or *relating to Olympia, Olympian.* **Juppiter Olympius,** *Olympian Jove,* so called because of a famous temple and statue in Olympia.

ōmen, -inis, n., *omen, sign, token, harbinger.*

ōminor, -ārī, -ātus sum, [ōmen], 1, dep., *forbode, augur, interpret, predict, prophesy.*

omittō, -ere, omīsī, omissum, [ob + mittō], 3, a., *let go, let loose; lay aside, give up, dismiss, neglect; throw aside; pass by, pass over, omit.*

omnīnō [omnis], adv., *altogether, wholly, at all, by all means, certainly; as a general rule; to be sure, no doubt;* with numerals, *in all, just.*

omnis, -e, adj., *all, every, entire; all sorts of.* As subst., pl., **omnēs, -ium,** m. and f., *all men; all;* **omnia, -ium,** n., *everything, all things.*

opera, -ae, [opus], f., *effort, exertion, work, labor; service.*

operārius, -a, -um, [opera], adj., *of labor.* As subst., **operārius, -ī**

or -iī, m., *laborer, workman, artisan.*

operiō, -īre, -peruī, -pertum, 4, a., *close, cover, conceal; burden.*

opertus, -a, -um, adj., *hidden; overwhelmed.*

operōsus, -a, -um, [opera], adj., *full of labor, painstaking; active, busy, industrious, laborious; troublesome, tiresome; difficult, elaborate.*

Opīmius, -ī or -iī, m., *L. Opīmius,* consul 121 B.C. He was an ardent and unscrupulous adherent of the aristocratic party, and was responsible for the death of C. Gracchus. CAT. I, 2.

opīniō, -ōnis, [opīnor], f., *opinion, supposition, conjecture, expectation.* praeter opīniōnem, *contrary to expectation.* opīniōne celerius, *sooner than was expected.* lātius opīniōne, *more widely than you think, than one would think.*

opīnor, -ārī, -ātus sum, 1, dep., *be of the opinion, suppose; conjecture, imagine, think, judge.*

opitulor, -ārī, -ātus sum, [ops, cf. tulī], 1, dep., *bear aid, aid, help, assist, succor.*

oportet, -ēre, oportuit, 2, impers., *it is necessary, it behooves.* mē oportet, *I ought, I must.* tē oportet dūcī, *you ought to be led.*

oppetō, -ere, -īvī, -ītum, [ob + petō], 3, a., *go to meet, encounter.*

oppidum, -ī, n., *town, city.*

oppleō, -ēre, -ēvī, -ētum, [ob + pleō, *fill*], 2, a., *fill completely, fill, fill up; occupy.*

oppōnō, -ere, opposuī, oppositum, [ob + pōnō], 3, a., *place*
opposite, set before, oppose; bring forward, present, adduce.

opportūnē, sup., opportūnissimē, [opportūnus], adv., *conveniently, fitly, seasonably, opportunely.*

opportūnitās, -ātis, [opportūnus], f., *suitableness, fitness, advantage, opportuneness.* locōrum opportūnitās, *advantages of position.*

opportūnus, -a, -um, [ob + portō], adj., *suitable, fit, convenient; meet, advantageous, useful.*

oppositus, -ūs, used only in abl. sing. and acc. pl., [oppōnō], m., *placing against, opposition, interposition.*

oppressus, see opprimō.

opprimō, -ere, oppressī, oppressum [ob + premō], 3, a., *press against, press upon; oppress, weigh down, overwhelm, cover; put down, suppress; overthrow, crush, subdue; surprise; of a fleet, sink.*

oppugnō, -āre, -āvī, -ātum, [ob + pugnō], 1, a., *attack, assail; assault, storm, besiege.*

ops, opis, nom. and dat. sing. not in use, f., *aid, assistance, help, support; power, ability; often in pl., property, riches, means, resources, treasure, wealth.* prō cuiusque opibus, *in proportion to the resources of each.*

optābilis, -e, [optō], adj., *to be wished, desirable.*

optātus, -a, -um, comp. optātior, sup. optātissime, (part. of optō), adj., *wished, desired, longed for, desirable, pleasing.*

optimās, -ātis, [optimus], adj., *of the best, aristocratic.* As subst., optimās, -ātis, m., *adherent of the nobility, aristocrat.*

optimē, see **bene.**

optimus, see **bonus.**

optō, -āre, -āvī, -ātum, 1, a., *choose, select, prefer; wish, desire, wish for, long for.*

opus, -eris, n., *work, task, labor, toil; structure, building; work of art, book; deed, action, effect;* in phrases with **esse,** *necessity;* as **opus est,** *it is necessary, there is need of,* with the dative of the person in need, and the ablative of the thing needed. **magnō opere,** *very much, exceedingly, greatly; earnestly, vehemently, urgently.* **tantō opere,** *so much, so very, in so great a measure.* **nimiō opere,** *too much.*

opusculum, -ī, [dim. of **opus**], n., *little work, trifling task.*

ōra, -ae, f., *edge, border; boundary, limit; coast, sea-coast;* by metonymy, *territory, region, country.*

ōrātiō, -ōnis, [ōrō], f., *speaking, speech, discourse; diction, style; set speech, harangue, oration; subject, theme; oratorical power, eloquence.*

ōrātor, -ōris, [ōrō], m., *speaker, orator; ambassador, legate.*

orbis, -is, m., *ring, circle; orb, disk;* by metonymy, *wheel; region, country, territory; round, circuit.* **orbis terrae** or **terrārum,** *earth, world, universe.*

orbitās, -ātis, [orbus], f., *destitution, bereavement; childlessness; orphanhood.*

orbō, -āre, -āvī, -ātum, [orbus], 1, a., *deprive, strip, rob; make destitute; bereave,* of children or parents.

orbus, -a, -um, adj., *deprived, bereft, destitute; bereaved, parentless, orphaned, fatherless, childless.*

ōrdior, -īre, ōrsus sum, 4, dep., *begin, commence; set about, undertake, set out.*

ōrdō, -inis, m., *row, line; order, rank; series, array.*

oriēns, -ientis, [part. of **orior**], m., *rising sun, morning sun;* by metonymy, *east, Orient.*

orīgō, -inis, [orior], f., *beginning, commencement, source, start, descent, lineage, birth, origin; race, stock, family; ancestor, founder;* in the pl., **orīginēs,** *-um, early history.*

orior, orīrī, ortus sum, 4, dep., *arise, rise, become visible; spring, descend, begin, originate; be born, be descended.* **ortus, -a, -um,** adj., *sprung from, arising from, descended from.*

ōrnāmentum, -ī, [ōrnō], n., *outfit, equipment, apparatus; mark of honor, decoration; distinction, ornament.*

ōrnātus, -a, -um, [part. of ōrnō], adj., *fitted out, equipped, provided; furnished, decorated, adorned; eminent, illustrious.*

ōrnātus, -ūs, [ōrnō], m., *splendid dress, apparel; adornment, decoration; furniture, equipment; honor, source of dignity.*

ōrnō, -āre, -āvī, -ātum, 1, a., *fit out, equip, prepare; adorn, embellish, decorate; honor, distinguish.*

ōrō, -āre, -āvī, -ātum, [ōs, *mouth*], 1, a. and n., *speak; argue, plead, entreat, implore, beseech.*

ortus, -ūs, [orior], m., *rising, rise; beginning, origin, source.* ortus sōlis, *sunrise;* by metonymy, *east.*

ōs, ōris, n., *mouth;* by metonymy, *face, look, countenance, features; orifice, aperture.* ūnō ōre, *unanimously.*

os, ossis, gen. pl., ossium, n., *bone; marrow; bones, outlines.*

ōsculum, -ī, [ōs], n., *little mouth; kiss.*

ostendō, -ere, ostendī, ostentum, [obs, old form of ob, + tendō], 3, a., *stretch out, spread before; show, disclose, manifest, point out; make known, tell, declare; give promise of; parade.*

ostentātiō, -ōnis, [ostentō], f., *exhibition, display; vain display, pomp, ostentation, boasting.*

ostentō, -āre, -āvī, -ātum, [freq. of ostendō], 1, a., *show, exhibit; show off, display, parade, boast.*

Ōstiēnsis, -e, [ōstium], adj., *of Ostia,* the seaport of Rome at the mouth of the Tiber. Ōstiēnse incommodum, *the disaster at Ostia.* IMP. 12.

ōstium, -ī or -iī, [ōs], n., *door;* by metonymy, *mouth, entrance.* Ōceanī ōstium, *the mouth of the Ocean,* i.e., the Straits of Gibraltar.

ōtiōsus, -a, -um, [ōtium], adj., *at leisure, unoccupied, disengaged; indifferent, neutral; calm, quiet, peaceful.* As subst., ōtiōsī, -ōrum, m., pl., *the idle, the neutral, the peaceable.*

ōtium, -ī or -iī, n., *leisure, ease, idleness; repose, rest; quiet, peace.*

ovis, -is, f., *sheep.*

ovō, -āre, -āvī, -ātum, 1, n., *exult, rejoice; receive an ovation, triumph; triumph in the ovation, or lesser triumph.* ovāns, *in an ovation.*

P

P., see Pūblius.

pābulum, -ī, [pāscō, *feed*], n., *food for cattle, fodder; nourishment, sustenance.*

pacīscor, pacīscī, pactus sum, 3, dep., *agree, agree upon; contract, covenant, stipulate.*

pācō, -āre, -āvī, -ātum, [pāx], 1, a., *make peaceful, pacify, subdue.*

pactiō, -ōnis, [pacīscor], f., *agreement, covenant, contract, stipulation.*

pactum, -ī, [pactus], n., *agreement, compact, manner, way, means.* nūllō pactō, *by no means.* istō pactō ut, *in such a way as.* nesciō quō pactō, *in some fashion or other.* ūllō pactō, *in any way.* ex pactō tradendī, *by virtue of the compact to give up.*

pactus, -a, -um, [part. of pacīscor], adj., *agreed, settled, stipulated.*

Paeān, -ānis, m., *Paeān, the Healer,* a name of Apollo, as god of healing.

paedagōgus, -ī, m., *slave to guide and attend children; tutor; pedagogue.*

paene, adv., *almost, nearly.*

paenitentia, -ae, [paeniteō], f., *repentance, penitence.*

paeniteō, -ēre, -uī, ——, 2, a., *make sorry; be sorry, repent.* Impers., paenitet, -ēre, paenituit, *it makes sorry, it repents, it grieves, it displeases, it dissat-isfies, it offends.* **mē numquam paenitēbit,** *I shall never regret.* **meōrum factōrum paenitēbit,** *I shall be sorry for what I did, I shall regret my action.* **haud paenitēre,** *be not dissatisfied with, be content with.*

Paetus, -ī, m., *L. Papīrius Paetus,* a friend of Cicero, who had a residence near Naples. EP. 20. See also **Aelius.**

pāgella, -ae, [dim., cf. **pāgina**], f., *small page, little page, sheet* of writing material.

palam, adv., *openly, plainly, pub-licly.*

Palātīnus, -a, -um, [**Palātium**], adj., *of the Palatine hill, Palatine.*

Palātium, -ī or **-iī,** [**Palēs,** an ancient divinity of shepherds], n., *Palatine,* one of the seven hills of Rome, southeast of the Forum.

palūs, -ūdis, f., *marsh.*

Pamphȳlia, -ae, [Παμφυλια], f., *Pamphȳlia,* a narrow country on the south coast of Asia Minor, bounded on the east by Cilicia, on the north by Pisidia, and on the west by Lycia.

pānārium, -ī or **-iī,** [**pānis,** *bread*], n., *bin* or *pantry to keep bread in; bread-basket; provision-hamper.*

pandō, -ere, pandī, passum, 3, a., *spread out, extend, unfold, expand; throw open, lay open, open, spread; unfold, make known, reveal, explain; dishevel,* of the hair.

pangō, -ere, pepigī and **pēgī, pāctum,** 3, a., *fasten, fix; determine, agree upon; contract, bargain for; betroth.*

pannus, -ī, m., *piece of cloth, garment of cloth; rag, patch.*

Pānsa, -ae, m., *C. Vibius Pānsa,* consul with A. Hirtius 43 B.C. He was a partisan of Caesar. Both Pansa and Hirtius set out against Antony, and fell before Mutina. EP. 24; PHIL. 2, *et al.*

papilla, -ae, [dim. of **papula,** *pimple*], f., *nipple, teat, breast.*

Papīrius, -a, the name of a Roman gens. See **Carbō, Paetus.**

Pāpius, -a, -um, adj., *of a Papius.* **lēx Pāpia,** *the law of Papius,* a law proposed by C. Papius concerning the expulsion of foreigners from Rome. ARCH. 5.

pār, paris, adj., *equal; as large as, like; well-matched; suitable.* **pār est,** *it is the fair thing; it is right, fair.* **nēquāquam paribus animīs,** *with very different feelings.*

Paralus, -ī, m., *Paralus,* an ancient Athenian hero. His likeness was painted by Protogenes. VERR. 60.

parātus, -a, -um, [part. of **parō**], adj., *prepared, ready; furnished, provided; versed, skilled.*

parcē, comp. **parcius,** [**parcus**], adv., *sparingly, frugally, thriftily; parsimoniously, stingily.*

parcō, -ere, pepercī and **parsī, parsum,** 3, n., *spare; treat with forbearance, use carefully, be indulgent; abstain, cease, refrain, stop; let alone, omit.*

parcus, -a, -um, adj., *sparing, frugal, thrifty, economical; niggardly, stingy, penurious, parsimonious; chary, moderate; spare, scanty, little, small, slight.*

parēns, -entis, [pariō], m. and f., *parent, father, mother; ancestor, progenitor.*

pāreō, -ēre, -uī, -itum, 2, n., *appear, be visible; obey, submit, comply; gratify, yield.*

pariēs, -etis, m., *wall, house wall.*

Parīlis, -e, [Palēs], adj., *of Pales, an ancient Italian divinity of flocks and shepherds.* As subst., Parīlia, -ium, n., pl., *Parīlia, festival of Pales,* celebrated annually on April 21.

pariō, parere, peperī, partum, fut. part. paritūrus, 3, a., *bring forth, give birth to, produce; acquire, obtain, secure; procure, get, gain.*

Parma, -ae, f., *Parma,* a city in northern Italy. PHIL. 4.

Parmēnsis, -e, [Parma], adj., *of Parma.* As subst., Parmēnsēs, -ium, m. pl., *inhabitants of Parma.* PHIL. 3.

parō, -āre, -āvī, -ātum, 1, a. and n., *make ready, prepare, provide, furnish, arrange; intend, purpose, design; procure, acquire, get.*

parricīda, -ae, [pater + caedō], m., *murderer of a parent, parricide; murderer, assassin; murderous criminal, outlaw.*

parricīdium, -ī or -iī, [parricīda], n., *murder of a parent, parricide; murder, assassination; horrible crime, treason.* nihil nisi dē parricīdiō cōgitāre, *to think of nothing but murder.*

pars, partis, f., *part, portion, share, division; several, some; party, side; office, function; rôle, character; region, country: direction, end.* ex hāc parte, *on this side.* in eam partem ut, *to the end that.*

aliquā ex parte, *in some measure.* ex alterā parte — ex alterā, *on the one side — on the other.* aliquā parte, *to some extent.*

Parthus, -a, -um, adj., *of or pertaining to Parthia,* a country east of the Euphrates. As subst., Parthus, -ī, m., *a Parthian, the Parthian.* EP. 12.

particeps, -cipis, [pars + capiō], adj., *sharing, partaking.* As subst., particeps, -cipis, m., *sharer, partner, comrade, colleague.*

partim [pars], adv., *partly, in part.*

partior, -īrī, -ītus sum, [pars], 4, a., *share, apportion, divide; take one's share in.*

partītiō, -ōnis, [partior], f., *sharing, division, distribution.*

partus, -ūs, [pariō], m., *bearing, bringing forth, birth, delivery; motherhood; young, offspring.*

parum, comp. minus, sup. minimē, [cf. parvus], adv., *too little, not enough, insufficiently;* comp., *less, too little;* sup., *least, in the smallest degree, very little, not at all, not in the least.*

parvus, -a, -um, adj., *little, small; inconsiderable, insignificant.* As subst., parvum, -ī, n., *a little.* parvī, *of little value, of slight moment, of small account.* parvī rēfert, *it matters little, it makes little difference.*

passus, -ūs, [cf. pandō], m., *step, pace, footstep; track, trace.*

pāstor, -ōris, [pāscō], m., *shepherd, herdsman.*

pāstus, -ūs, [pāscō, feed], m., *feeding; pasture, fodder; food.*

patefaciō, -facere, -fēcī, patefactum, [pateō + faciō], 3, a., *open up, lay open, throw open; disclose, bring to light.*

pateō, -ēre, -uī, ——, 2, n., *lie open, be open, stand open; be accessible, be exposed; extend; be evident, be clear, be well known.*

pater, -tris, m., *father;* pl., *fathers, forefathers, ancestors; elders, senators.* pater in sē, *the resemblance to his father.* See cōnscrīptus.

paternus, -a, -um, [pater], adj., *of a father, father's, paternal; of one's native country, of the fatherland.*

Paternus, -ī, m., *Plīnius Paternus,* a correspondent of the younger Pliny. He is otherwise unknown. PLIN. 14.

patiēns, -entis, [part. of patior], adj., *bearing, supporting, enduring, permitting, able to endure* or *bear* (with gen.).

patientia, -ae, [patiēns], f., *long-suffering, endurance, submission, patience; forbearance, indulgence, lenity.*

patior, patī, passus sum, 3, dep., *suffer, bear, endure, undergo, meet with; allow, permit, let.*

patria, -ae, [patrius], f., *fatherland, native country, native place; dwelling-place, home.*

patricius, -a, -um, [pater], adj., *of fatherly dignity; patrician, noble.* As subst., patriciī, -ōrum, m., pl., *patricians, nobility.*

patrius, -a, -um, [pater], adj., *of a father, father's, fatherly; of one's fathers, ancestral.*

patruus, -ī, [pater], m., *father's brother, uncle on the father's side.*

pauculus, -a, -um, [dim. of paucus], adj., *very few, very little.* pauculīs adhuc diēbus, *for the next few days yet.*

paucus, -a, -um, adj., *few, small, little.* As subst., pl., paucī, -ōrum, m., *few, a few;* pauca, -ōrum, n., *a few things, little, a few words, few words.* ad paucōs diēs, *only for a few days.*

paulātim, [paulum], adv., *little by little, by degrees, gradually.* paulātim incēdere, *to advance slowly.*

paulisper [paulum + per], adv., *for a little while, for a short time.*

paulō [abl. of paulum], adv., *by a little, a little, somewhat.* paulō ante, *a little while ago, shortly before.*

paululum, [paululus, *very little*], adv., *a little, a very little, somewhat.* paululum modo, *but for a moment.*

paulus, -a, -um, adj., *little, small. slight.* As subst., paulum, -ī, n., *a little, trifle.* paulum mihī est morae, *I am suffering a little delay.*

Paulus, -a, [paulus], m., *the name of a celebrated patrician family in the Aemilia gens.* Two members are mentioned in this book: (1) L. *Aemilius Paulus,* named also *Macedonicus* after his victory over Perseus, born 230 or 229 B.C.; consul 182 and 168 B.C. When consul the first time he subdued the ῙIngauni, a piratic people of Liguria, and was honored with a triumph. In 168 B.C. he took command of the war with Perseus, king of Macedonia, whom he completely defeated at the battle of Pydna. He celebrated a splendid triumph the following year, and died 160 B.C. SEN. 6; 14; 21; AM. 6. (2) *L. Aemilius Paulus*, consul 50 B.C., brother of M. Aemilius Lepidus the triumvir. SALL. 31.

paveō, -ēre, pāvī, ——, 2, a. and n., *be struck with fear, be in terror, tremble, quake with fear, be afraid, be terrified.*

pavor, -ōris, [paveō], m., *trembling, shaking, anxiety, fear, dread, alarm.*

pāx, pācis, f., *peace; treaty, agreement, reconciliation; concord, harmony; tranquillity, rest, quiet, grace.* **pāce tuā,** *by your leave, with your permission.* **cum bonā pāce,** *in peace and quiet; with full acquiescence.* MAR. 2.

peccātum, -ī, [peccō], n., *fault, transgression, sin.*

peccō, -āre, -āvī, -ātum, 1, a. and n., *make a mistake, transgress, offend; commit a fault, sin, do wrong.*

pectō, -ere, pexī, pexum, 3, a., *comb, comb out.*

pecūnia, -ae, [pecus], f., lit., *wealth in cattle;* hence, *property, wealth; money.*

pecus, -udis, f., *a head of cattle,* meaning one of a number; *brute, animal, beast;* especially, *a sheep.*

pedes, -itis, [pēs], m., *foot-traveler, walker; foot-soldier;* collectively, *infantry;* in the pl., **peditēs, -um,** *infantry.*

pedester, -tris, -tre, [pēs], adj.,

on foot, pedestrian; on land. **pedestrēs cōpiae,** *forces of infantry.*

peior, see **malus.**

Peliās, -ae, m., *Peliās,* an aged king of Iolcos, in Thessaly, who sent Jason to Colchis to fetch the golden fleece. SEN. 23.

pellō, -ere, pepulī, pulsum, 3, a., *strike, push; drive away, force back, banish, rout; remove, dispel;* of a musical instrument, *strike, touch, play.*

penārius, -a, -um, adj., *of or relating to provisions, for provisions.*

Penātēs, -ium, [penus, *provision*], m., pl., *household gods, guardian deities of the house, Penātēs;* by metonymy, *hearth, home.*

pendeō, -ēre, pependī, ——, [pendō], 2, n., *hang, hang down; be suspended, overhang, float; rest, be dependent; be in suspense, be undecided, hesitate.*

penetrō, -āre, -āvī, -ātum, 1, a. and n., *enter, penetrate; make way to, reach.*

penitus, adv., *inwardly, deeply, far within; thoroughly, utterly, through and through.*

pēnsum, -ī, [part. n. of pendō], n., *wool weighed out to a slave for a day's spinning; allotment of wool; charge, duty, office; weight, consideration, importance.* **neque quicquam pēnsī habēbat,** *nor did he regard it as of any importance.*

pēnūria, -ae, f., *want, need, destitution, poverty, penury.*

per, prep. with acc. only, *through;* of space, *through, across, along, over, among;* of time, *through, during, in the course of, at the* *time of;* of agency, means, and manner, *through, by, by the hands of, by means of, under pretense of, for the sake of;* in oaths, *in the name of, by.* per sē, *on his own responsibility, authority; by his own resources; by his own efforts.* In composition per adds the force of *through, thoroughly, perfectly, completely, very much, very.*

perāctiō, -ōnis, [peragō], f., *completion.* aetātis perāctiō, *the last act of life's drama.*

peragō, -ere, -ēgī, -āctum, [per + agō], 3, a., *drive through, pierce through, thrust through, transfix; pass through, traverse; disturb, trouble, agitate; carry out, execute, finish, accomplish, complete; follow to the end; go over, set forth, relate, describe, detail, treat in detail.*

peragrō, -āre, -āvī, -ātum, [per + ager], 1, a., *wander through, pass over, traverse.*

perbellē [per + bellē, *finely*], adv., *very well, very prettily, very finely.*

percellō, -ere, perculī, perculsum, 3, a., *beat down, strike down, smite; overthrow, destroy; deject, dishearten.*

percipiō, -cipere, -cēpī, -ceptum, [per + capiō], 3, a., *take wholly, seize; perceive, observe; learn, know, understand; gather.*

perculsus, see percellō.

percunctor or percontor, -ārī, -ātus sum, 1, dep., *ask particularly, question strictly, inquire, investigate.*

percutiō, -cutere, percussī, percussum, [per + quatiō, *shake*], 3, a., *strike through, thrust through,*

pierce, transfix; strike hard, smite, hit, kill, slay. dē caelō percussus, *struck by lightning.*

perditus, -a, -um, [part. of perdō], adj., *lost, hopeless, ruined, desperate; corrupt, profligate, incorrigible.* in perditīs rēbus, *in profligacy.*

perdō, -ere, perdidī, perditum, [per + dō], 3, a., *make away with, waste, destroy, ruin; squander, dissipate, lose utterly.*

perdūcō, -ere, perdūxī, perductum, [per + dūcō], 3, a., *lead through, conduct, guide; lengthen, prolong; win over, gain over, induce.*

peregrē [per + ager], adv., *abroad, away from home, out of the country; from abroad, from foreign parts; abroad, to foreign parts.*

peregrīnātiō, -ōnis, [peregrīnor], f., *sojourning abroad, traveling, wandering, travel.*

peregrīnor, -ārī, -ātus sum, [peregrīnus], 1, dep., *sojourn abroad, travel, wander, roam.*

peregrīnus, -a, -um, [per + ager], adj., *strange, foreign, alien.* As subst., peregrīnus, -ī, m., *foreigner, stranger.*

pereō, -īre, -iī or -īvī, -ītum, [per + eō], irr., n., *pass away, vanish, disappear; perish, be destroyed, die; be wasted, fail, be lost.*

perfectiō, -ōnis, [perficiō], f., *finishing, completion, perfecting, accomplishment.*

perfectus, -a, -um, [part. of perficiō], adj., *finished, complete, perfect, excellent, faultless.*

perferō, -ferre, -tulī, -lātum, [per + ferō], irr., a., *bear through; bring, convey; carry news, an-*

nounce, *report;* carry through, *accomplish,* bring about; *put up* with, *bear, suffer, endure.*

perficiō, -ficere, -fēcī, -fectum, fut. part. perfectūrus, [per + faciō], 3, a., *carry through, complete, accomplish;* bring about, cause, *effect.*

perfidia, -ae, [perfidus, *faithless*], f., *faithlessness, treachery, perfidy.*

perfringō, -ere, perfrēgī, perfrāctum, [per + frangō], 3, a., *break through, break in pieces, shatter, fracture;* of laws, *violate, break.*

perfruor, -fruī, -frūctus sum, [per + fruor], 3, dep., *enjoy fully, be greatly delighted.*

perfugiō, -ere, -fūgī, ——, [per + fugiō], 3, n., *flee for refuge, escape, flee;* go over, *desert;* take refuge.

perfugium, -ī or -iī, [perfugiō], n., *refuge, shelter, asylum.*

perfundō, -ere, -fūdī, -fūsum, [per + fundō], 3, a., *pour over, wet, moisten, drench, bathe;* steep, *dye;* scatter over, *bestrew;* imbue, *inspire, fill.* horrōre perfūsus, *paralyzed with fear.*

perfungor, -fungī, -fūnctus sum, [per + fungor], 3, dep., *perform, discharge;* go through with, *undergo,* get rid of, *pass through.*

pergō, -ere, perrēxī, perrēctum, [per + regō], 3, a. and n., *go on, proceed, advance, march;* hasten, *make haste.*

pergrātus, -a, -um, [per + grātus], adj., *very agreeable, exceedingly pleasant.* As subst., pergrātum, -ī, n., *great favor,* as fēcistī mihi pergrātum, *you have done me a great favor.*

perīclitor, -ārī, -ātus sum, [perī-

culum], 1, dep., *try, test, make trial of;* imperil, *risk, endanger;* be in danger. perīclitāntēs, -ium, m. pl. of pres. part. as subst., *defendants.*

perīculōsus, -a, -um, [perīculum] adj., *full of danger, dangerous, perilous.*

perīculum, -ī, n., *trial, attempt;* risk, *hazard, danger, peril;* legal action, *lawsuit, suit.* in perīculum vocārī, *to be imperiled.* in perīcula venīre, *to be endangered.*

perimō, -ere, -ēmī, -emptum, [per + emō], 3, a., *take away entirely, annihilate, extinguish, destroy;* hinder, *prevent;* kill, *slay.*

perinde [per + inde], adv., *in the same manner, just so, equally, in like manner.* perinde ac, or atque, *just as.*

perinīquus, -a, -um, [per + inīquus], adj., *very unfair, exceed-ingly unjust.*

perītus, -a, -um, adj., *experienced, practiced, trained, skillful, expert.*

perlūctuōsus, -a, -um, [per + lūctuōsus], adj., *very mournful*

permagnus, -a, -um, [per + magnus], adj., *very great, very extensive, exceedingly important.* As subst., permagnum, -ī, n., *very great thing.* permagnī interest, *it is of very great importance.*

permaneō, -ēre, permānsī, permānsum, [per + maneō], 2, n., *remain, stay;* hold out, *continue, persist.*

permittō, -ere, permīsī, permissum, [per + mittō], 3, a., *let go; commit, surrender, intrust, put in charge of;* allow, *suffer, permit, grant.*

permolestē, [permolestus, very troublesome], adv., with much trouble, with much displeasure.

permoveō, -ēre, permōvī, permōtum, [per + moveō], 2, a., move deeply; arouse, agitate, influence, prevail upon.

permultum [permultus], adv., very much, very far.

permultus, -a, -um, [per + multus], adj., very much; pl., very many, in great numbers. As subst., permultum, -ī, n., a great deal, very much.

perniciēs, -ēī, [per + nex], f., destruction, ruin, overthrow, disaster.

perniciōsus, -a, -um, [perniciēs], adj., destructive, ruinous, baleful, pernicious.

pernōbilis, -e, [per + nōbilis], adj., very famous; very noble, most *oble.

pernoctō, -āre, -āvī, fut. part. pernoctātūrus, [per + noctō], 1, n., remain all night, stay all night, pass the night.

perobscūrus, -a, -um, [per + obscūrus], adj., very obscure.

perpellō, -ere, -pulī, ——, [per + pellō], 3, a., drive, force, compel, prevail upon; impress deeply, induce.

perpetuitās, -ātis, [perpetuus], f., uninterrupted duration, continuous succession, continuity, perpetuity; unending endurance.

perpetuus, -a, -um, [per, cf. petō], adj., continuous, uninterrupted, constant, perpetual; whole, entire. As subst., n., in the phrase in perpetuum, for all time, forever.

perquam [per + quam], adv., as much as possible, very, very much, extremely, exceedingly.

persaepe [per + saepe], adv., very often, very frequently.

perscrībō, -ere, perscrīpsī, perscrīptum, [per + scrībō], 3, a., write in full, write out; describe fully in writing, recount, detail; of public documents, put on record, record.

persequor, -sequī, -secūtus sum, [per + sequor], 3, dep., follow persistently, follow after, pursue; prosecute, avenge; perform, accomplish; set forth, relate; go through.

persevērantia, -ae, [persevērō], f., steadfastness, persistency, perseverance.

persevērō, -āre, -āvī, -ātum, [per + sevērus], 1, a. and n., continue steadfastly, persist, persevere.

Persicus, -a, -um, adj., of or pertaining to Persia, Persian.

persolvō, -ere, -solvī, -solūtum, [per + solvō], 3, a., unravel, solve, explain; pay, pay out, pay over; give, show, render, suffer; fulfill; bestow on, render, inflict.

persōna, -ae, [per, cf. sonus], f., mask, part, character, rôle; personage, person.

perspiciō, -spicere, -spexī, perspectum, [per + speciō], 3, a., look through, look into; inspect, examine; perceive clearly, see plainly, observe, discern, note.

perstringō, -ere, -strīnxī, -strictum, [per + stringō], 3, a., bind closely, touch closely, affect deeply; wound, move, touch, thrill.

persuādeō, -ēre, persuāsī, persuāsum, [per + suādeō], 2, a.

and n., *convince, persuade; induce, prevail upon.*

perterreō, -ēre, perterruī, perterritum, [per + terreō], 2, a., *frighten greatly, terrify.*

pertimēscō, -ere, pertimuī, ——, [per + timēscō], 3, inch., *be greatly alarmed, be much frightened; fear greatly, be much afraid of.*

pertinācia, -ae, [pertināx], f., *persistency, obstinacy, stubbornness.*

pertineō, -ēre, -uī, ——, [per + teneō], 2, n., *reach, extend; belong, pertain, concern, refer; tend, lead, be conducive, conduce.* pertinēre ad aliquam rem, *to concern anything.*

perturbātus, -a, -um, [part. of perturbō], adj., *disturbed, agitated, embarrassed, unsettled.*

perturbō, -āre, -āvī, -ātum, [per + turbō], 1, a., *greatly disturb, throw into disorder; disturb, confuse, unsettle.*

pervagātus, -a, -um, [part. of pervagor], adj., *widespread, well-known.*

pervagor, -ārī, -ātus sum, [per + vagor, *ramble*], 1, dep., *wander over, rove about, extend; be known, spread through, pervade.*

perveniō, -īre, pervēnī, perventum, [per + veniō], 4, n., *come through, come up, arrive, reach; attain, come to; come, fall.* necesse est pervenīre, *must inevitably come, must inevitably fall* (to).

perversē [perversus, *distorted*], adv., *the wrong way, awry, wrongly, ill, perversely.*

pervigilō, -āre, -āvī, -ātum, [per + vigilō], 1, n., *watch through, watch all night, remain awake, watch.*

pervulgātus, -a, -um, [part. of pervulgō, *make common*], adj., *very common, widely known.*

pēs, pedis, m., *foot.* ex pedibus labōrāre, *to have trouble with one's feet, to have gout.*

pessimē, see male.

pessimus, see malus.

pessimum, -ī, [pessimus], n., *the worst, the worst thing* or *part; a very great evil.* pessimō pūblicō, *with the greatest detriment to the state.*

pestifer, -era, -erum, [pestis + ferō], adj., *destructive, pernicious, noxious, baleful.*

pestilēns, -entis, [pestis], adj., *pestilential, infected; unhealthy, unwholesome; pernicious, noxious, destructive.*

pestis, -is, f., *plague, pest, pestilence; bane, curse; ruin, destruction, death.*

petītiō, -ōnis, [petō], f., *in fencing or fighting, thrust, blow, aim, attack; canvass for votes, candidacy; claim, suit.*

petō, -ere, petīvī and -iī, petītum, 3, a., *strive for, aim at, seek; rush at, attack, assail; demand, require; beg, beseech, entreat; woo, court; pursue; wrest, draw from.* petere cōnsulātum, *to be a candidate for the consulship.* studia petere, *to seek instruction.*

Petreius, -a, the name of a Roman gens. *Marcus Petreius,* a man of military experience, served as legate to C. Antonius in 62 B.C. and defeated the army of Catiline. In 55 he was sent to Spain as legate of Pompey. He fought against Caesar in Africa and died after the battle of Thapsus. SALL. 60.

petulantia, -ae, [petulāns, *pert*], f., *pertness, sauciness, impudence; waywardness.*

pexus, -a, -um, see pectō.

Phārnacēs, -is, m., *Phárnacēs*, king of Pontus, and son of Mithridates. In the Civil War between Caesar and Pompey, Pharnaces seized the opportunity to reinstate himself in his father's dominions; but he was decisively defeated by Caesar, near Zela, 47 B.C. PHIL. 8.

Pharsālius, -a, -um, adj., *in, from,* or *belonging to, Pharsalia.* pugna Pharsālia, *the battle of Pharsalia,* in which Pompey's power was overthrown by Caesar.

Philippus, -ī, [Φίλιππος], m., *L. Mārcius Philippus,* pro-praetor in Syria 59 B.C., consul 56 B.C. He was the stepfather of C. Octavius. During the civil wars, however, he remained neutral, and lived to see his stepson the emperor Augustus. EP. 22; PROV. CONS. 8.

Philippicus, -a, -um, adj., *Philippian, Philippic,* pertaining to Philip of Macedon. ōrātiōnēs Philippicae, the orations of Demosthenes against Philip, from which Cicero called his own against Antony *Philippicae.*

philosophus, -a, -um, [φιλόσοφος] adj., *philosophical.* As subst., philosophus, -ī, m., *philosopher.*

Philotīmus, -ī, [Φιλότιμος], m., *Philotimus,* a freedman of Cicero or of Terentia. EP. 14.

Philus, -i, m., a Roman surname.

L. Furius Philus, consul 136 B.C. AM. 6.

Pīcēnum, -ī, n., *Pīcēnum,* a district on the east coast of Italy, lying northeast from Rome and east of Umbria.

Pīcēnus, -a, -um, adj., *of Picenum, Picene.*

pictor, -ōris, [pingō], m., *painter.*

pictūra, -ae, [pictus, from pingō], f., *painting, picture; painting, the art of painting.*

pietās, -ātis, [pius], f., *dutiful conduct, dutifulness, sense of duty; religiousness; faithfulness* in discharge of duty, particularly toward kindred; *duty, fealty, affection, gratitude, loyalty, devotion; dutiful affection;* toward one's country, *patriotism.*

piget, -ēre, piguit and pigitum est, 2, a., impers., *it annoys, it troubles, it disgusts; it causes to repent, it makes sorry.* nec mē piget, *and I am not sorry.*

pigneror, -ārī, -ātus sum, [pignus], 1, dep., *take as a pledge; lay claim to, appropriate, select.*

pignus, -oris and -eris, n., *pledge, gage, pawn, security, guaranty; hostage; wager, stake.*

pila, -ae, f., *ball;* by metonymy, *ball-playing, game of ball.*

Pilia, -ae, f., *Pilia,* wife of Cicero's friend Atticus, to whom she was married 56 B.C. EP. 9, 21.

pīlum, -ī, n., *heavy javelin, pilum.*

pingō, -ere, pīnxī, pictum, 3, a., *paint, depict, portray; stain, color; adorn, decorate.*

pinguis, -e, adj., *fat, rich, fertile; dull, stupid.* pingue quiddam sonantēs atque peregrīnum, *of-*

fering some stupid and outlandish composition.

pīnus, -ūs, f., *pine, pine-tree; fir, fir-tree; ship of pine.*

piscis, -is, m., *a fish, fish.*

Pīso, -ōnis, m., *Cn. Pīso,* a profligate young noble, who had dissipated his fortune and joined Catiline. He was murdered in Spain, to which he had been sent by the senate. SALL. 21.

pius, -a, -um, adj., *dutiful, conscientious, devout, religious; devoted,* especially to kindred; *faithful, loving, filial.*

Pius, -ī or **-iī,** [pius], m., *Pius,* honorary surname of *Q. Caecilius Metellus.* See **Metellus,** (2).

pl., see **plēbs.**

placeō, -ēre, -uī or **-itus sum,** 2, n., *please, be pleasing; give pleasure, meet with approval; secure approval, suit, satisfy;* often impers., **placet, -ēre, -itum est,** *it pleases, it is agreed, it seems right, it is resolved, it is decided.* **placuit senātuī,** *the senate voted, the senate passed a resolution.* **quid illī fierī placet?** *What does he want to have done?* **sī vōbīs placet,** *if you think best.* **eīs placet,** *they think best, they resolve.* **mihi placet,** *I think best, I resolve; it is my opinion; I like.*

plācō, -āre, -āvī, -ātum, [cf. **placeō**], 1, a., *quiet, soothe, calm; appease, conciliate, reconcile.*

Plancus, -ī, m., *L. Munātius Plancus,* consul 42 B.C. He was a lieutenant of Caesar in Gaul (Caes. Bel. Gal. v. 24, 25), and afterwards a partisan of the Dictator. After the death of Caesar

he was active in political affairs until the establishment of the Empire. EP. 25.

plānē [plānus], adv., *plainly, clearly, distinctly; wholly, quite.*

Platō, -ōnis, [Πλάτων], m., *Plato,* a Greek philosopher, pupil of Socrates, teacher of Aristotle, and founder of the Academic School. He was born in 428 B.C. and died in 347 B.C. SEN. 7.

plaudō, -ere, plausī, plausum, 3, a. and n., *clap, strike, beat; applaud, express approbation, praise.*

plausus, -ūs, [plaudō], m., *clapping, expression of approbation, applause.*

Plautius, -a, -um, adj., *of* or *pertaining to a Plautius.* **lēx Plautia dē vī,** probably passed by *M. Plautius Silvānus,* tribune of the plebs, and directed against breaches of the peace. SALL. 31.

Plautus, -ī, m., *T. Maccius Plautus,* the most celebrated Roman comic writer. SEN. 14.

plēbs, plēbis, and **plēbēs, -ēī** or **-ī,** often abbreviated **pl.,** plural wanting, f., *common people, commons, common folk, populace; mass, throng, multitude.*

plectō, -ere, ——, ——, only passive, 3, a., *be punished, suffer punishment, be beaten; be blamed, incur censure.*

plēnus, -a, -um, [cf. **-pleō**], adj., *full, filled; complete, whole; abounding, rich.*

plērumque [plērusque], adv., *for the most part, generally, commonly, very often.*

plērusque, -raque, -rumque, [plērus], adj., *a very great part,* *the majority, most.* As subst., **plērīque, -ōrumque,** m., pl., *the greater part, the majority, about all.*

Plīnius, -a, name of a Roman gens. Two by the name are mentioned in this book:

(1) *Gaius Plīnius Secundus,* called the Elder, was born in the middle of the reign of Tiberius and perished, a martyr to scientific curiosity, in the great eruption of Vesuvius 79 A.D. Although he was the most learned and prolific writer of his day, the bulk of his voluminous works is lost, with the exception of his Natural History, in thirty-seven books. PLIN. 12.

(2) *Gaius Plīnius Caecilius Secundus,* nephew and adopted son of the preceding, was born 62 A.D. at Novum Comum. Trained in rhetoric under Quintilian, he began his public career as an advocate in the nineteenth year of his age. He served in Syria as military tribune, and was later the emperor's quaestor, a tribune of the people, and praetor. Under Trajan he was consul in 100 A.D., and about 112 governed the province of Bithynia as imperial legate. He died about 114 A.D. PLIN. 1, *et seq.*

plōrātus, -ūs, [plōrō, *cry*], m., *wailing, weeping, lamenting.*

Plōtius, -ī or **-iī,** m., *L. Plōtius Gallus,* a native of Cisalpine Gaul, and a rhetorician. He opened a school for the study of Latin and rhetoric at Rome about 88 B.C. ARCH. 9.

plūrimum [plūrimus], adv., *very much, very greatly; for the most part, commonly.*

plūrimus, -a, -um, see **multus.**

plūs, plūris, see **multus.**

Plutarchus, -ī, m., *Plutarch,* Greek writer of biographies and other works, who flourished during the second half of the first century A.D. His fame rests mainly on the *Parallel Lives,* frequently quoted in this text.

pōculum, -ī, [cf. pōtō, *drink*], n., *drinking-vessel, cup, goblet, bowl, beaker; drink, draught, potion.*

poēma, -atis, n., *composition in verse, poem, poetry.*

poena, -ae, [ποινή], f., *compensation, recompense; penalty, punishment, retribution, vengeance.*

poēta, -ae, [ποιητής], m., *poet.*

poliō, -īre, -īvī, -ītum, 4, a., *smooth, polish; adorn, decorate, embellish.*

polliceor, -ērī, -itus sum, [por, for prō, + liceor], 2, dep., *offer, promise.*

polluō, -ere, polluī, pollūtum, 3, a., *soil, stain, pollute; contaminate, dishonor, disgrace.*

Pompeius, -a, name of a plebeian gens. Two bearing the name are mentioned in this book:

(1) *Cn. Pompeius Magnus,* born Sept. 30, 106 B.C. He was victorious over the pirates and over Mithridates, was a member of the first triumvirate, and was killed in Egypt, whither he had fled for refuge, after the battle of Pharsalia, Sept. 29, 48 B.C.

Imp. P. 1, *et seq.;* Ep. 2; 11; 16.

(2) *Q. Pompeius Rūfus,* tribune of the plebs, 52 B.C., friend of Pompey and Cicero. In 61 he obtained the province of Africa with the title of proconsul. During the years of Catiline's conspiracy, he was in service in Capua and Apulia. Sall. 30.

Pompōniānus, -ī, m., *Pompōniānus,* owner of a villa near Vesuvius. Plin. 12.

Pompōnius, -a, name of a plebeian gens. The best known member is *T. Pompōnius Atticus.* See Atticus.

Pomptīnus, -ī, m., *C. Pomptīnus,* praetor when Cicero was consul, 63 B.C. He rendered important service in crushing the Catilinarian conspiracy. In 51 B.C. he was legatus to Cicero in Cilicia. Cat. 3, 2; 3; 6; Prov. Cons. 13.

pomum, -ī, n., the fruit of any tree fit for eating; *fruit; orchard-fruit; apple.*

pondus, -eris, [cf. pendō, *weigh*], n., *weight; mass, load, burden; importance, influence, authority.*

pōnō, -ere, posuī, positum, 3, a., *set down, place, set, put; lay, fix, station; lay aside, take off; allay, quiet; spend, employ; count, reckon, consider; assert, allege; maintain; propose, offer; put away, dismiss;* of arms, *lay down.*

pōns, pontis, m., *bridge.*

pontifex, -icis, [pōns, cf. faciō], m., *high-priest, pontiff, pontifex.* Pontifex Maximus, *supreme pontiff, chief of the priests, the*

chief of the guild of *pontiscēs,* or pontiffs, who had the supervision of all sacred observances at Rome.

pontificius, -a, -um, [pontifex], adj., *of* or *belonging to the pontifex, pontifical.*

Pontus, -ī, [Πόντος], m., *Pontus,* a large country in the northeastern part of Asia Minor, south of the Pontus Euxinus, from which it received its name; the ancient name of the Black Sea.

popīna, -ae, f., *eating-house, cook-shop.*

populāris, -e, [populus], adj., *of the people; devoted to the people, democratic, political; acceptable to the people, popular.* As subst., populāris, -is, m., *associate, fellow.* In the plural, the *people's party,* the *democrats.*

populus, -ī, m., *people, nation; multitude; host, throng.* populus Rōmānus, *the Roman people,* meaning *the whole body of citizens* taken together, as distinguished from foreign peoples or from the classes and factions at Rome.

Porcius, -a, -um, adj., *of* or *belonging to a Porcius.* lēx Porcia, passed *circa* 199 B.C., reënacted the earlier lēgēs Valeriae providing that no magistrate should scourge or put to death a Roman citizen without appeal to the people. Sall. 51.

Porcius, -ī or -iī, m., the name of a Roman gens. See Catō.

porcus, -ī, m., *swine, hog, pig.*

porrō, adv., *forward, onward, farther on; to a distance, at a distance; afar off, far; of old, aforetime,* formerly; henceforth, afterwards, in future; again, in turn; then, next, furthermore, moreover; then again, further.

porta, -ae, f., *gate of a city, city-gate, gate; passage, outlet.*

portentum, -ī, [portendō], n., *omen, sign, portent; monster, monstrosity.*

porticus, -ūs, [porta], f., *covered walk between columns, colonnade, arcade, porch, portico.*

portō, -āre, -āvī, -ātum, 1, a., *bear, carry, take, bring.*

portus, -ūs, m., *harbor, port; haven, refuge.* **ex portū vectīgal**, *revenue from customs.*

poscō, -ere, poposcī, ——, 3, a., *ask urgently, beg, demand; require, need, call for.*

positus, -a, -um, [part. of pōnō], adj., *placed, situated, lying; resting on, dependent upon.*

possessiō, -ōnis, [por, for prō, + sedeō], f., *taking possession, seizure; occupation, possession;* especially in pl., *property, estates, possessions.*

possideō, -sidēre, -sēdī, -sessum, [por, for prō, + sedeō], 2, a., *possess, be master of, own; hold possession of, occupy.*

possum, posse, potuī, [potis + sum], irr., n., *be able, can, have power; have influence, avail.* **quicquid possum**, *whatever influence I possess, whatever I can accomplish.* **plūrimum posse**, *to have very great influence, to be most powerful, to be preëminent.* **plūs posse**, *to be stronger, more powerful.* **quantum possum**, *as far as I can.*

post, adv., *of place, behind, back, backwards;* of time, *afterwards, after, later, next.* **post fuēre**, *were secondary considerations, fell into the background.*

post, prep. with acc., *after;* of place, *behind;* of time, *after, since;* of other relations, *after, inferior to, beneath, next to.*

posteā [post + eā], adv., *after that, thereafter, later; then, afterwards.* **posteā quam**, followed by a clause, *after, after that.*

posteritās, -ātis, [posterus], f., *future time, the future; future generations, posterity.* **in posteritātem**, *for the future.*

posterius [posterus], adv. comp., *after, later, at a later day.*

posterus, -a, -um, nom. sing. m. not found, comp. **posterior**, sup. **postrēmus**, [post], adj., *following, coming after, subsequent, future.* Comp., **posterior, -us**, *later, inferior, less important.* Sup., **postrēmus, -a, -um**, *last, hindmost; lowest, worst.* As subst., **posterī, -ōrum**, m., pl., *men of the future, descendants, posterity;* also, n. sing. in the phrase **in posterum = in posterum tempus**, *for the future.*

posthāc [post + hāc], adv., *after this, henceforth, hereafter, in the future.*

postmodum [post + modus], adv., *after a while, a little later, afterwards, presently.*

postquam or **post quam** or **posteā quam**, conj., *after that, after, as soon as, when; since, because, as.*

postrēmō [postrēmus], adv., *at last, finally, lastly.*

postrēmus, see posterus.

postulō, -āre, -āvī, -ātum, 1, a., *ask, request; demand, require, claim, desire, have a claim to.*

potēns, -entis, [part. of possum], adj., *able, strong, powerful, mighty; potent, influential.*

potentia, -ae, [potēns], f., *might, force, power; political power; authority, influence.*

potestās, -ātis, [potis], f., *ability, power, capacity; authority, sovereignty; magistracy, office; opportunity, privilege.* facere potestātem dīcendī, *to offer an opportunity to speak, to give an opportunity for saying.*

pōtiō, -ōnis, [pōtō, drink], f., *act of drinking, drinking, draught, potion.*

potior, -īrī, -ītus sum, [potis], 4, dep., *become master of, take possession of, obtain, acquire; be master of, hold, possess.* rērum potīrī, *to get control of the government.*

potis or pote, comp. potior, sup. potissimus, pos. indecl., adj., *able, capable.* Comp., *better, preferable, superior, more important.* Sup., *chief, principal, most prominent.*

potissimum [potissimus], adv., *chiefly, principally; especially, above all, most of all.* hīc potissimum, *here rather than anywhere else.*

potius [potis], adv., comp., *rather, more.*

pr., see prīdiē.

prae, prep. with abl., *before, in front of; in comparison with, compared with, in view of; by*

reason of, on account of, because of; before, compared with, under the influence of.* In composition, *before, very.* prae sē ferre, *show, exhibit, assert.*

praebeō, -ēre, -uī, -itum, [prae + habeō], 2, a., *hold forth, offer; give, furnish, supply, grant; present, show.*

praeceps, -cipitis, [prae + caput], adj., *headlong, head foremost, in haste; steep, precipitous, abrupt; rash, hasty, inconsiderate.*

praeceptor, -ōris, [praecipiō], m., *one who anticipates or takes beforehand; teacher, instructor, preceptor; public teacher of rhetoric, professor of rhetoric.*

praeceptum, -ī, [praecipiō], n., *maxim, precept, teaching; injunction, direction, order.*

praecipiō, -cipere, -cēpī, praeceptum, [prae + capiō], 3, a., *take beforehand, anticipate; advise, admonish, instruct, enjoin, bid; give precepts.* eīs hōc praecipiendum est, *they ought to be given this piece of advice.* hōc praecipiendum est, *this advice ought to be given.* tempore praeceptō, *by priority, by precedence in time.*

praecipuē [praecipuus], adv., *especially, chiefly, eminently.*

praeclārē [praeclārus], adv., *very clearly, very plainly; excellently, admirably.*

praeclārus, -a, -um, [prae + clārus], adj., *very bright; splendid, admirable, excellent; distinguished, famous, illustrious, renowned.*

praeoō, -ōnis, [prae + vocō], m.,

crier, herald; auctioneer; eulogist.

praecōnium, -ī or **-iī, [praecōnius,** from praecō], n., *proclaiming, heralding; commendation, eulogy.*

praecurrō, -ere, praecucurrī, ——, [prae + currō], 1, a. and n., *run before, hasten on before; outstrip, surpass, excel; forestall.*

praecursōrius, -a, -um, [praecursor, forerunner], adj., *that which runs before, running before.*

praeda, -ae, f., *booty, plunder, spoil;* by metonymy, *gain, profit.*

praedātor, -ōris, [praedor], m., *plunderer, pillager.*

praedicātiō, -ōnis, [praedicō], f., *proclaiming, proclamation; commendation, praise.*

praedicō, -āre, -āvī, -ātum, [prae + dicō], 1, a. and n., *proclaim, announce; relate, declare openly, assert; praise, boast.* **ut praedicās,** *as you assert.*

praedīcō, -dīcere, -dīxī, -dictum, [prae + dīcō], 3, a., *tell beforehand, foretell, predict; advise, warn, admonish.*

praeditus, -a, -um, [prae + datus], adj., *gifted, endowed, provided.*

praedium, -ī or **-iī,** n., *farm, estate.*

praedō, -ōnis, [praeda], m., *plunderer, robber.*

praeeō, -īre, -īvī or **-iī, -itum,** [prae + eō], irr., n., *go before, lead the way, precede; dictate, prescribe.* **praeeunte mē,** *at my dictation, repeating the words after me.*

praefectūra, -ae, [praefectus], f., *overseership, office of prefect, prefectship; prefecture,* a subject community governed by a prefect sent from Rome.

praeferō, -ferre, -tulī, -lātum, [prae + ferō], irr., a., *carry in front of, bear before, bear forward; place before, set before, prefer; manifest, reveal.*

praeficiō, -ficere, -fēcī, praefectum, [prae + faciō], 3, a., *set over, put in charge; appoint to command, place at the head.*

praelūceō, -ēre, -lūxī, ——, [prae + lūceō, shine], 2, n., *shine before, shed light upon, light up; outshine, surpass.*

praemittō, -ere, praemīsī, praemissum, [prae + mittō], 3, a., *send forward, dispatch in advance.*

praemium, -ī or **-iī, [prae,** cf. emō], n., *advantage, favor; reward, recompense, prize, booty.*

Praeneste, -is, n., *Praeneste,* an ancient city of Latium, 23 miles east of Rome; now Palestrina. CAT. 1, 3.

praenūntius, -ī or **-iī, [prae +** nūntius], m., *foreteller, harbinger, omen.*

praepōnō, -ere, praeposuī, praepositum, [prae + pōnō], 3, a., *place before; set over, put in charge, place in command, appoint; set before, prefer.*

praeposterus, -a, -um, [prae + posterus], adj., *having that first which ought to be last; in reverse order, in disorder; inverted, perverted, absurd; preposterous, unseasonable; perverse, unreasonable.*

praeripiō, -ere, -ripuī, -reptum, [prae + rapiō], 3, a., *take away* *anything before another receives it; snatch away, carry off; seize prematurely; forestall, anticipate.*

praescrībō, -ere, praescrīpsī, praescrīptum, [prae + scrībō], 3, a., *write before; determine beforehand, order, prescribe, give directions; set forth.*

praesēns, -entis, [part. of praesum], adj., *at hand, present, in person; prompt, instant, impending; powerful, influential; favoring, propitious; gracious.* in **praesēns tempus,** *for the present.* **perīculum praesēns,** *an immediate* or *personal danger.*

praesentia, -ae, [praesēns], f., *presence; present time.*

praesentiō, -īre, praesēnsī, praesēnsum, [prae + sentiō], 4, a., *perceive in advance, presage, divine.*

praesertim [prae, cf. serō], adv., *especially, chiefly; particularly, principally.*

praesideō, -ēre, praesēdī, ——, [prae + sedeō], 2, a. and n., lit., *sit before;* hence, *watch over, guard, protect; preside over, direct, manage.*

praesidium, -ī or **-iī,** [praeses], n., *defense, protection; guard, garrison; post, intrenchment, fortification; aid, help, assistance.*

praestābilis, -e, comp. **praestābilior,** [praestō], adj., *preëminent, distinguished, excellent, choice-worthy.* **praestābilior, -ius,** *preferable.*

praestāns, -antis, [part. of praestō], adj., *preëminent, excellent, superior, distinguished.*

praestō, adv., *at hand, present, here.*

praestō, -āre, -stitī, -stātum or **-stitum,** [prae + stō], 1, a. and n., *stand before; stand out, excel, be preëminent, be excellent; vouch for, be responsible for, answer for; fulfill, perform, discharge; maintain, keep, preserve; be superior to.* **praestat,** *it is better, preferable.*

praestōlor, -ārī, -ātus sum, 1, dep., *stand ready for, wait for.*

praestringō, -ere, -strīnxī, -strictum, [prae + stringō, *touch*], 3, a., *draw together, bind fast, compress; make dull, blunt, dim, dazzle; blind; confuse, overwhelm, baffle.*

praesum, -esse, -fuī, [prae + sum], irr., n., *be set over, have charge of, rule, command.*

praetendō, -ere, -tendī, -tentum, [prae + tendō], 3, a., *stretch forth, extend, spread before, draw over; hold out as an excuse, offer as a pretext, allege, simulate.*

praeter [prae], prep. with acc., *past, by, before, in front of, along; contrary to, against; except, besides, apart from.* In composition, *past, by, beyond, besides.*

praevtereā [praeter + eā], adv., *besides, moreover, further.*

praetereō, -īre, -īvī or **-iī, -itum,** [praeter + eō], irr., a. and n., *go by, go past, pass by; pass over, disregard, omit.*

praeteritus, -a, -um, [part. of praetereō], adj., *gone by, past.* As subst., **praeterita, -ōrum,** n., pl., *the past, bygones.* in **praeteritum,** *in the past.*

praetermittō, -mittere, -mīsī, -missum, [praeter + mittō], 3, a., *let pass; omit, leave undone, neglect; pass over, overlook.*

praeterquam [praeter + quam], adv., *except, besides, save.*

praetextātus, -a, -um, [praetexta], adj., *wearing the toga praetexta; juvenile.*

praetextus, -a, -um, [part. of **praetexō,** *border*], adj., *bordered, edged.* **toga praetexta,** or, as subst., **praetexta, -ae,** f., *bordered toga, toga praetexta, the praetexta,* a toga having a purple border, worn as the official robe of the higher magistrates, and by the children of Roman citizens until they became of age.

praetor, -ōris, sometimes abbreviated **P. R.,** [for unused **praeitor,** from **praeeō**], m., *chief magistrate, commander;* as an officer of Rome, *praetor,* a magistrate intrusted with the administration of justice.

praetōrius, -a, -um, [praetor], adj., *of a praetor, of praetors, praetorian; of a general, of a commander.*

praetūra, -ae, [praeeō], f., *office of praetor, praetorship.*

prāvus, -a, -um, adj., *crooked, distorted, wrong, vicious, bad; depraved, debased; absurd.*

precor, -ārī, -ātus sum, [cf. **prex**], 1, dep., *entreat, pray, supplicate, beg, beseech; call upon, invoke.*

premō, -ere, pressī, pressum, 3, a., *press; press hard, pursue closely, crowd; cover, crown, adorn; press down, cause to sink;* *load, burden, oppress; overwhelm, crush, restrain, check; urge.*

pretium, -ī or **-iī,** n., *price, value, worth; reward, recompense, return.* **operae pretium est,** *it is worth the effort, it is worth while.*

prex, precis, nom. and gen. sing. not found, [cf. **precor**], f., *prayer, petition, entreaty; imprecation, curse.*

prīd., see **prīdiē.**

prīdem, adv., *long ago, long since.* **iam prīdem,** *this long time.*

prīdiē, in dates often abbreviated **pr., prīd.,** [root **pri** in **prior,** + **diē**], adv., *on the day before, the previous day.*

prīmārius, -a, -um, [prīmus], adj., *first in rank, eminent, distinguished, of the highest standing.* As subst., **prīmāriī, -ōrum,** m., pl., *the chief men, those in the van, the leaders.*

prīmō [prīmus], adv., *at first, first, in the first place.*

prīmōris, -e, [prīmus], adj., *first, foremost.* As subst., **prīmōrēs, -um,** m., pl., *those of the first rank, chieftains.* **ad prīmōrēs,** *to the front, to the front of the battle.*

prīmum [prīmus], adv., *at first, in the first place, first; for the first time.* **ut prīmum,** *as soon as.* **quam prīmum,** *as soon as possible.* **omnium prīmum,** *first of all.*

prīmus, see **prior.**

prīnceps, -ipis, [prīmus, cf. **capiō**], adj., *first, foremost, chief.* As subst., **prīnceps, -ipis,** m., *chief, leader, head; founder, originator, contriver.*

prīncipātus, -us, [prīnceps], m., *be-*

ginning, origin; first place, chief part, supremacy, leadership; chief command over, reign, empire, dominion, sovereignty. **prīncipā-tus sententiae,** precedence in debate, the right of speaking and voting first.

prīncipium, -ī or **-iī,** [prīnceps], n., beginning, commencement, origin, principle. **prīncipiō,** abl., in the beginning, at first, in the first place.

prior, -us, gen. **-ōris,** adj. in the comp. degree, sup. **prīmus,** former, previous, prior, first. Sup. **prīmus, -a, -um,** first, foremost; chief; first in excellence, noble, eminent, distinguished. As subst., n., pl., in the phrase in **prīmīs,** among the first, especially, chiefly, principally. **prīmō statim concursū,** the very moment of their charge. **prīmō statim adventū,** at the very first moment of arrival.

prīstinus, -a, -um, [prius], adj., former, early, original.

prius [prior], adv., in the comp. degree, sooner, before; previously.

priusquam or **prius quam,** sooner than, earlier than, before, before that.

prīvātus, -a, -um, [part. of prīvō], adj., personal, individual, private, retired. **prīvātō cōnsiliō,** on his own authority, by his private or personal efforts. As subst., **prīvātus, -ī,** m., private citizen, private person, as opposed to one holding office.

prīvō, -āre, -āvī, -ātum, [prīvus, one's own], 1, a., deprive, strip, rob; free, release, deliver.

prō, prep. with abl., before, in front of, in the presence of; for, in be-

half of; instead of, in place of, in return for, for; in view of, considering, in the name of; in comparison with, according to, because of, on account of. **prō eō atque,** just the same as, just as, even as. In composition, before, forwards, for.

prō, interj., O! ah! alas!

proavus, -ī, [prō + avus], m., great-grandfather; forefather, ancestor.

probē, sup. probissimē, [probus], adv., rightly, properly, correctly, fitly, thoroughly. **probē discere,** to learn in a good environment, amid wholesome influences.

probitās, -ātis, [probus, good], f., goodness, uprightness, worth.

probō, -āre, -āvī, -ātum, [probus, good], 1, a., approve, commend, esteem, recommend; make credible, show, prove, demonstrate; make good, convince, induce to approve.

probrum, -ī, n., shameful act, crime, base deed; immodesty, unchastity; shame, dishonor, infamy; insult, reproach. **probrī grātiā,** on account of his disgraceful life.

probus, -a, -um, adj., that is as it ought to be; estimable, good, excellent, upright, honest, honorable.

prōcēdō, -ere, prōcessī, prōcessum, [prō + cēdō], 3, n., go before, go forward, proceed, advance; appear, arise; make progress; succeed, prosper, go well.

procella, -ae, f., violent wind, storm, tempest; by metonymy, violence, commotion.

prōcessiō, -ōnis, [prōcēdō], f., marching forward, advance.

prōclīnō, -āre, -āvī, -ātum, [prō +

clīnō, *bend*], 1, a., *bend forward,
bend, incline.* **iam rē prōclīnātā,**
now at the crisis; since now (his)
fortune is wavering.

prōclīvis, -e, comp. **prōclīvior,** [prō
+ **clīvus,** *ascent*], adj., *sloping,
steep, going down-hill; descend-
ing, declining; inclined, disposed,
liable, prone; subject, ready,
willing.*

prōcōnsul, -is, m., *proconsul,* one
who, after being consul, was
govèrnor of a province.

prōcos., see **prōcōnsul.**

prōcreō, -āre, -āvī, -ātum, [prō +
creō], 1, a., *bring forth, procreate,
produce; make, cause.*

procul, adv., *afar off, at a distance,
far away; from afar.*

Proculus, -ī, m., *Iūlius Proculus,*
Roman senator. LIV. 1, 16.

prōcūrātiō, -ōnis, [prōcūrō], f.,
*charge, management, administra-
tion.*

prōdeō, -īre, -iī or **-īvī, -itum,**
[prōd- + eō], irr., n., *go forth,
come forth; stand out, appear;
advance, proceed.*

prōdigium, -ī or **-iī,** n., *omen, sign,
portent; prodigy, monster.*

prōdigus, -a, -um, adj., *lavish,
wasteful, prodigal.* As subst.,
prōdigus, -ī, m., *spendthrift,
prodigal.*

prōditiō, -ōnis, [prōdō], f., *discovery;
betrayal, treason, treachery.*

prōditor, -ōris, [prōdō], m., *betrayer,
traitor.*

prōdō, -ere, prōdidī, prōditum,
[prō + dō], 3, a., *put forth, exhibit; relate, report, hand down,
transmit; make known, disclose,
betray.* **falsō memoriae prōdi-**

tum, *based upon unfounded tradition.* **exemplum prōdere,** *to set
an example.* **prōditum est
memoriae,** *for the recollection of
posterity.*

proelium, -ī or **-iī,** n., *battle, strife,
contest, combat.*

profānus, -a, -um, [pro + fānum,
shrine], adj., *out of the temple;
not sacred, profane, secular;
wicked, impious.*

profectiō, -ōnis, [profectus, from
proficīscor], f., *setting out, departure.*

profectō [prō + factō], adv., *actually, indeed, in fact, really, by
all means.*

prōferō, -ferre, -tulī, -lātum, [prō
+ ferō], irr., a., *carry out, bring
out, bring forth, produce; put
forth, stretch out, extend; make
known, reveal, show.*

professiō, -ōnis, [profiteor], f.,
*acknowledgment, declaration, pro-
fession, promise.*

prōficiō, -ficere, -fēcī, -fectum,
[prō + faciō], 3, a. and n., *make
progress, advance, succeed; accomplish, effect, bring about, gain;
help, avail, be serviceable.*

proficīscor, -ficīscī, -fectus sum,
[prōficiō], 3, dep., *set out, go
forward, start, go, depart, proceed; begin, commence.*

profiteor, -fitērī, -fessus sum, [prō
+ fateor], 2, dep., *declare publicly, make a declaration; acknowledge, own, profess; avow
oneself, profess to be; promise;
teach publicly.*

prōflīgātus, -a, -um, [part. of
prōflīgō], adj., *abandoned, vile,
dissolute, profligate.*

prōflīgō, -āre, -āvī, -ātum, 1, a.,
strike to the ground, overthrow,
overcome; destroy, crush, ruin.

profugiō, -fugere, -fūgī, ——, [prō
+ fugiō], 3, a. and n., flee, run
away, escape; flee for refuge, take
refuge.

profundō, -ere, profūdī, profūsum,
[prō + fundō], 3, a., pour out,
pour forth; spend freely, lavish;
squander, dissipate, waste.

profūsus, -a, -um, [profundō], adj.,
hanging down; immoderate, unrestrained, extravagant, wasteful,
lavish, prodigal. suī profūsus,
lavish with his own property.

prōgeniēs, -ēī, [prō + gignō], f.,
descent, race, family; descendants, posterity; offspring, child.

prōgredior, -gredī, -gressus sum,
[prō + gradior], 3, dep., go forth,
go forward, proceed, advance.

prohibeō, -ēre, -uī, -itum, [prō +
habeō], 2, a., hold before; hold
back, hold, restrain, check, repress;
hinder, prevent; keep, protect,
defend, preserve.

prōiciō, -icere, -iēcī, -iectum, [prō
+ iaciō], 3, a., throw forth, cast
out, expel, banish; hold forth,
extend; throw away, give up,
resign.

proinde [prō + inde], adv., hence,
accordingly, then; just so, in like
manner, equally, even; according
as.

prōlātō, -āre, -āvī, -ātum, [prōlātus,
from prōferō], 1, a., extend, enlarge; put off, postpone, defer,
delay.

prōlēs, -is, f., growth, offshoot; children, descendants, race, posterity;
child, son, offspring, descendant.

prōmiscuus, -a, -um, [prōmisceō,
mix], adj., mixed, without distinction; common, usual, ordinary.

prōmissum, -ī, [prōmittō], n., thing
promised, promise.

prōmissus, -a, -um, [prōmittō], adj.,
suffered to grow, growing long,
hanging down long.

prōmittō, -ere, prōmīsī, prōmissum,
[prō + mittō], 3, a., put forth;
foretell; promise, assure; hold
out, give hope of, cause to expect.

prōmptus, -a, -um, [part. of prōmō,
give forth], adj., set forth, brought
forward; disclosed, exposed, manifest.

prōpāgātiō, -ōnis, [prōpāgō, off-
shoot], f., propagating; extension,
enlargement; perpetuation, honoring.

prōpāgō, -āre, -āvī, -ātum, 1, a.,
extend, enlarge, increase; gener-
ate, propagate; prolong, continue,
preserve.

prope, comp. propius, sup. proximē,
adv., near, near by, nigh; nearly,
almost; often having the force
of a preposition and followed by
the acc., near, near to, almost to,
in the vicinity of. Comp., propius, nearer. Sup., proximē, next,
most nearly, very near, nearest.
ab aliquā rē propius absum, the
nearer I am to anything.

propediem or prope diem, adv.,
within a few days, shortly, after a
while.

properō, -āre, -āvī, -ātum, [pro-
perus, quick], 1, a. and n., make
haste, hasten, hurry; quicken, accelerate, do quickly.

propinquitās, -ātis, [propinquus], f.,

nearness, relationship, affinity, kindred. quasi **propinquitās,** *sort of relationship.*

propinquus, -a, -um, [prope], adj., *near, neighboring, near at hand; kindred, related.* As subst., **propinquus, -ī,** m., *relative, kinsman.*

propior, -us, gen. **-ōris,** adj. in comp. degree, sup. **proximus,** *nearer, closer, nigher; later, more recent; of more concern, of greater importance.* Sup. **proximus, -a, -um,** *nearest, next, closest; latest, last, most recent; most important.*

propitius, -a, -um, [prō + petō], adj., *appeased, well-disposed, gracious, propitious.*

propius, see **prope.**

prōpōnō, -ere, prōposuī, prōpositum, [prō + pōnō], 3, a., *put forth, set before, display; propose, resolve, intend; point out, declare; determine upon, settle, determine; publish, make known; display, expose to view.*

prōpraetor, -ōris, [prō + praetor], m., *ex-praetor, made governor of a province without military command; propraetor.*

proprius, -a, -um, adj., *own, individual, peculiar; personal, characteristic; exact, appropriate; lasting, enduring.*

propter [prope], adv. and prep., *near:*
(1) As adv., *near, at hand, hard by, near by.*
(2) As prep., with acc., *near, next to, close to; on account of, by reason of, for, because of, for the sake of.*

propterea [propter + eā], adv., *therefore, for this reason, on that*

account. **propterea quod,** *because.*

propudium, -ī or **-iī,** [prō + pudet], n., *shameful act; vile wretch.*

prōpugnāculum, -ī, [prōpugnō], n., *bulwark, rampart, place of defense; defense, protection.*

prōripiō, -ere, -ripuī, -reptum, [prō + rapiō], 3, a., *drag forth, drive out, impel;* with reflex., *fling oneself forth* or *from.*

prōrsus, adv., *forward, right onward; by all means, certainly, utterly, absolutely, entirely, plainly; in short, in a word, in fact.*

prōscrībō, -ere, -scrīpsī, -scrīptum, [prō + scrībō], 3, a., *make public by writing; publish, proclaim, announce; post up, offer for sale, proclaim, advertise; punish with confiscation, deprive of property; outlaw, proscribe, proclaim beyond the protection of law.*

prōscrīptiō, -ōnis, [prōscrībō], f., *public notice of sale; confiscation, proscription.*

prōsequor, -sequī, -secūtus sum, [prō + sequor], 3, dep., *follow, attend, accompany, escort; follow up, pursue; honor, distinguish.*

prōsperus, -a, -um, [prō + spēs], adj., *according to hope, as desired; favorable, fortunate, prosperous.* **rēs prōsperae,** *prosperity, easy circumstances.*

prōspiciō, -spicere, -spexī, prōspectum, [prō + speciō], 3, a. and n., *look forward, look out; behold; look out for, provide for, take care of.*

prōsternō, -ere, prōstrāvī, prōstrātum, [prō + sternō], 3, a., *spread* *out; cast down, overthrow, prostrate; throw to the ground, ruin, destroy.*

prōstrātus, see **prōsternō.**

prōsum, prōdesse, prōfuī, [prō + sum], irr., n., *be of use, profit, serve, help.*

prōtinus, [prō + tenus, *as far as*], adv., *before oneself, onward; directly, without pause, uninterruptedly; immediately, at once.*

prout, [prō + ut], conj., *according as, in proportion as, accordingly, proportionately, just as, as, depending on whether.*

prōvehō, -ere, -vexī, -vectum, [prō + vehō], 3, a., *carry forth, convey;* in pass., *advance, move forward, drive; make progress, elevate; prolong, remain.*

prōverbium, -ī or **-iī,** [prō + verbum], n., *old saying, adage, proverb.*

prōvidentia, -ae, [prōvidēns], f., *foresight; forethought, precaution.*

prōvideō, -ēre, prōvīdī, prōvīsum, [prō + videō], 2, a. and n., *see beforehand, see in advance, foresee, discern; see to, take care, look after, provide, be careful.*

prōvincia, -ae, f., *office, duty; public office, command; province,* territory governed by a magistrate sent out from Rome; *administration of a province, provincial government.*

prōvolō, -āre, -āvī, ——, [prō + volō], 1, n., *fly forth, fly forward, hurry forth, rush out.*

proximē, *lately; most closely.*

proximum, -i, [proximus], n., *neighborhood, vicinity, nearest place.*

proximus, -a, -um, see **propior.**

prūdēns, -entis, [for **prōvidēns**], adj., *foreseeing; knowing, experienced, versed; with knowledge, deliberate; discreet, wise, prudent, circumspect.*

prūdenter, comp. **prūdentius,** [for **prōvidenter,** from **provideō**], adv., *wisely, prudently, cautiously.*

prūdentia, -ae, [prūdēns], f., *foresight; knowledge, acquaintance, skill; sagacity, discretion, practical wisdom, good sense; knowledge of law.*

pruīna, -ae, f., *hoar-frost, frost, rime.*

prytanēum, -ī, n., *public building in Greek towns; city-hall, hall of the prytanes* (magistrates), *state dining-hall.*

Pseudolus, -ī, m., *the Liar,* title of a comedy by Plautus. SEN. 14.

-pte, pronominal suffix appended to adjective and, more rarely, to substantive personal pronouns, esp. in the ablative; the Eng. *self* or *own.*

pūbēs, -is, f., *grown-up males, youth able to bear arms; youth, young men;* collectively, *youth, throng, people.*

pūblicānus, -a, -um, [pūblicus], adj., *of the public revenue.* As subst., **pūblicānus, -ī,** m., *farmer of the public revenue, revenue farmer, publican.*

pūblicātiō, -ōnis, [pūblicō], f., *seizure for the state, confiscation.*

pūblicē [pūblicus], adv., *for the state, in the name of the state, publicly, officially; by the state; at public expense.*

pūblicō, -āre, -āvī, -ātum, [pūblicus], 1, a., *seize for the state, confiscate: publish.*

pūblicus, -a, -um, [for populicus, from populus], adj., *of the people, public; common, general; usual, ordinary.* rēs pūblica, *commonwealth, state, republic.*

Pūblius, -ī or -iī, abbreviated P., m., *Pūblius,* Roman forename.

pudeō, -ēre, -uī, and puditum est, 2, a. and n., *be ashamed, make ashamed, put to shame.* Commonly impers., pudet, -ēre, puditum est, *it makes ashamed.* mē pudet, *I am ashamed.* mē quid pudeat? *Why should I be ashamed?*

pudīcē, comp. pudīcius, [pudīcus, *modest*], adv., *shamefacedly; modestly, chastely, virtuously.*

pudor, -ōris, [pudeō], m., *shame, sense of shame; sense of right, conscientiousness; feeling of decency, modesty, propriety; cause for shame, ignominy, disgrace.*

puella, -ae, [dim. of puer], f., *female child, girl, maiden; young woman, young wife.*

puellāris, -e, [puella], adj., *of a girl, girlish, maidenly, youthful.*

puer, -erī, m., *boy, lad, youth,* properly used of boys and young men till they reached the seventeenth year. ex puerīs, *from childhood.*

puerīlis, -e, [puer], adj., *boyish, childish, youthful; puerile, trivial.* aetās puerīlis, *the age of childhood.*

puerīliter [puerīlis], adv., *boyishly, like a child; childishly, foolishly.*

pueritia, -ae, [puer], f., *boyhood, childhood, youth.* extrēma pueritia, *at the end of boyhood.* ā pueritiā statim, *from* [my] *early years.*

pugillāris, -e, [pugillus, *handful*], adj., *that can be held in a fist, as large as the clenched hand.* As subst., pugillārēs, -ium, m., pl., [sc. libellī], *writing-tablets.*

pugna, -ae, f., *fight, battle, engagement, contest.*

pugnō, -āre, -āvī, -ātum, [pugna], 1, a. and n., *fight, give battle; contend, engage in strife, dispute; struggle, strive, endeavor.*

pulcher, -chra, -chrum, comp. pulchrior, sup. pulcherrimus, adj., *beautiful, handsome, lovely, fair; fine, excellent; noble, honorable; illustrious, glorious.*

Pulcher, -chrī, m., surname in Claudian gens. Two of the name are mentioned in this book:

(1) *Appius Claudius Pulcher,* praetor 89 B.C. ARCH. 5.

(2) *Appius Claudius Pulcher,* brother of Clodius, proconsul in Cilicia 52 B.C. EP. 12.

(3) *C. Claudius Pulcher,* aedile 99 B.C. VERR. 59.

pulchrē, sup. pulcherrimē, [pulcher], adv., *beautifully, excellently, finely, nobly, very honorably, successfully.* rē pūblicā pulcherrimē gestā, *after a brilliant conduct of public affairs.*

pulchritūdō, -inis, [pulcher], f., *beauty, excellence, attractiveness.*

pulvīnar, -āris, [pulvīnus, *bolster*], n., *couch of the gods,* placed before a statue of a deity at the time of a religious festival; by metonymy, *shrine, temple; altar.*

pūmex, -icis, m., *pumice-stone; rock with cavities, porous rock; lava bed; calcined stone; lava.*

Pūnicus, -a, -um, [Poenī], adj.,
Punic, Carthaginian.

pūniō, -īre, -īvī, -ītum, [poena], 4,
a., *punish, chastise.*

puppis, -is, acc. **puppim,** abl. **puppī,**
f., *hinder part of a ship, stern of
ship, poop; ship.*

pūrgō, -āre, -āvī, -ātum, [for **pūrigō,**
pūrus + agō], 1, a., *make clean,
cleanse, purify; justify, vindicate.*

pūrus, -a, -um, adj., *free from dirt,
free from mixture, clean, pure,
unstained, unspotted ; naked,
unadorned; chaste, undefiled, un-
polluted; faultless, free from flaw;
honest, unselfish.*

putō, -āre, -avī, -ātum, 1, a.,
*cleanse; reckon, estimate, esteem,
value, deem, regard; think, judge,
consider, suspect, believe, suppose.*

putrefaciō, -ere, -fēcī, -factum,
[**puter,** *rotten,* **+ faciō**], 3, a.,
*make rotten, cause to rot, putrefy,
soften.*

Pȳthagorās, -ae, m., *Pȳthágorās,*
Greek philosopher of the sixth
century B.C., head of the Italian
school. SEN. 7.

Q

Q., see **Quīntus.**

quā [abl. fem. of **quī**], adv., *on
which side, at what place, by what
way, where.*

quadrīduum, -ī, [**quattuor + diēs**],
n., *period of four days.*

quadringentī, -ae, -a, [**quattuor +
centum**], num. adj., *four hundred.*

quadrirēmis, -is, [**quattuor + rēmus,** *oar*], adi., *with four banks of
oars.* As subst., **quadrirēmis**
[sc. **nāvis**], **-is,** f., *quadrireme.*

quaerō, -ere, quaesīvī, quaesītum,
3, a., *seek, look for, strive to
obtain; save, acquire, get, gain;
miss, lack; demand, require;
make inquiry, investigate; aim at,
plan.* **ex eō quaeritur,** *question
is put to him, inquiry is made
of him.* **quid quaeris?** *in short,
in a word.*

quaesītor, -ōris, [**quaerō**], m., *in-
vestigator, prosecuting officer.*

quaesō, -ere, ——, ——, [cf.
quaerō], def., a. and n., *beg, pray,
beseech, entreat;* often parenthetical, **quaesō,** *I pray, please.*

quaestiō, -ōnis, [**quaerō**], f., *examination, inquiry, investigation;
judicial investigation, trial, court;
subject of investigation, question,
case.*

quaestor, -ōris, [for **quaesītor,** from
quaerō], m., *quaestor,* an officer
charged with public duties which
varied according to the period
and circumstances. At first
there were but two quaestors,
but the number was increased
from time to time until it reached
forty under Caesar's administration, 45 B.C. At that time
the quaestors were engaged in
the care of public moneys and
of military stores, partly at Rome
and partly in the provinces,
which were assigned by lot.
They were chosen annually, at
the **comitia tribūta.**

quaestus, -ūs, [**quaerō**], m., *gain,
acquisition; profit, advantage, interest; business, employment, occupation.* **in quaestū relinquere,**
to leave on interest.

quālis, -e, [cf. **quī**], pron. adj.,
inter. and rel., *of what sort? wha*

kind of? of such a kind, such.
tālis — quālis, *such — as.*

quāliscumque, quālecumque, adj.,
*of what quality whatsoever, of
whatever kind; of any kind whatever, any without distinction.*

quam [quī], adv., *in what manner?
how, how much, as, just as, even
as;* after comparatives, *than.*
quam diū, *as long as, how long?*
quam prīmum, *as soon as possible.* quam plūrimī, *as many as
possible.* tam — quam, *so — as.*

quamlibet, [quam + libet], adv., *at
pleasure, as much as one will,
however much, to any extent, in
any degree.*

quam ob rem, see ob.

quamquam [quam + quam], conj.,
*though, although, notwithstanding
that; and yet, however.*

quamque = -que + quam.

quamvīs [quam + vīs, from volō],
adv. and conj.:
(1) As adv., *as you will, as
much as you will, however much.*
(2) As conj., *however much, although, albeit, no matter how much
or many.*

quandō [quam], adv. and conj.,
when:
(1) As adv., *when, at what
time;* inter., *when? at what
time?* after nē, nisi, num, or sī,
some time, at any time, ever.
(2) As conj., *when, at the time
that; since, because, seeing that,
inasmuch as.*

quandōque, adv., *at what time soever, whenever, whensoever, as
often as; since, inasmuch as; at
some time, at one time or another.*

quandōquidem or quandō quidem,

conj., *since indeed, since, seeing
that.*

quantulus, -a, -um, [dim. of quan-
tus], adj., *how little, how small,
how much* (of a trifle). quantulum est, *what a small matter it
would be.*

quantum [quantus], adv., rel.,
so much as, so far as, as far as;
inter., *how much? how far?*

quantus, -a, -um, adj., inter., *how
great? how much?* rel., *as great
as, as much as.* quantī, *how
valuable, of how great import.*
tantus — quantus, *as great as,
as much as.*

quantuscumque, -tacumque, -tum-
cumque, [quantus + -cumque],
rel. adj., *of whatsoever size, however great, no matter how great;
however small, however trifling.*

quāpropter [quā + propter], adv.,
inter., *wherefore? for what reason? why?* rel., *wherefore, and
on this account.*

quā rē, adverbial phrase, inter.,
*by what means? whereby? how?
on what account? wherefore?
why?* rel., *wherefore, and for
that reason, therefore; by reason
of which, so that.*

quārtus, -a, -um, or IV., [quattuor],
num. adj., *fourth.*

quasi [qua + sī], adv. and conj.,
*as if, just as if, as though, as it
were, as one might say.* quasi
. . . sīc, *just as . . . so.*

quātenus, [properly quā tenus
parte], adv., *to what point, how
far; as far as, to the distance
that; till when, how long; how
far, to what extent; in so far as,
inasmuch as.* est enim quāte-

nus, *for there is a certain point to which.*

quatiō, -ere, ——, quassum, 3, a., *shake, brandish, cause to tremble; strike, crush, shatter; move, affect; vex, weary.*

quattuor, or **IIII., IV.,** num. adj., indecl., *four.*

quattuordecim, XIIII., or **XIV.,** [quattuor + decem], num. adj., indecl., *fourteen.*

-que, enclitic conj., *and, and so;* adversatively, usually after a negative, *but.* **-que —— -que, -que —— et** or **atque,** *both —— and, as well —— as.*

quem ad modum, adverbial phrase, inter., *in what way? how?* rel., *in what way, how, just as, as.*

queō, quīre, quīvī or **quiī, quitum,** irr., n., *be able, can.*

querella, -ae, [queror], f., *complaining, complaint, lament, lamentation, plaint.*

querimōnia, -ae, [queror], f., *complaining, lamentation; complaint, accusation, charge, reproach.*

queror, querī, questus sum, 3, dep., *complain, lament; bewail, bemoan; make complaint.*

quī, quae, quod, gen. **cuius,** inter. adj. pron., *which? what? what sort of a?*

quī, quae, quod, gen. **cuius,** rel. pron., *who, which, what, that;* at the beginning of a clause often best rendered by a personal or demonstrative pron., *with* or *without and* or *but.*

quī, quae, quod, gen. **cuius,** indef. adj. pron., used after **sī, nisi, nē,** and **num,** *any.*

quī [old abl. of rel. **quī**], adv., inter.,

how? in what way? by what means? rel., *whereby, wherewith.*

quia, conj., *because, since.*

quīcum [old abl. of rel. and inter. **quī + cum**] = **cum quō** or **cum quā,** *with whom, together with whom.*

quīcumque, quaecumque, quodcumque, [quī + -cumque], indef. rel. pron., *whoever, whatever, whichever; whosoever, whatsoever; any whatever, every, all that.*

quid, see **quis.**

quīdam, quaedam, quiddam, and, as adj., **quoddam,** [quī], indef. pron., *certain one, certain; certain man, one, somebody, something;* pl., *some, certain, certain ones.* **ad quoddam tempus,** *for some time, for a short time.* **est quiddam,** *it is worth something.*

quidem [quī], adv., *indeed, in fact, certainly; at least, yet.* **nē —— quidem,** setting off an emphatic word, *not —— even.*

quiēs, -ētis, f., *rest, repose, quiet; sleep.*

quiēscō, -ere, quiēvī, quiētum, [quiēs], 3, n., *rest, repose, be at rest, keep quiet; sleep, be silent.*

quiētus, -a, -um, [part. of **quiēscō**], adj., *at rest, undisturbed, quiet, at peace.* **quiētā rē pūblicā,** *when the state is undisturbed, when the state is free from agitation.*

quīn [quī + ne], adv. and conj., *why not? wherefore not? but indeed, in fact, nay indeed;* in dependent clauses, *so that not, but that, but, without;* after words of doubting, *that;* after words of hindering translate by *from* with a verbal noun. **quīn etiam,** *more-*

over, nay more. **quīn** = **quī nōn,** *who — not, but.*

Quīnctīl., see **Quīnctīlis.**

Quīnctīlis, -e, [quīntus], adj., *of the fifth month,* i.e. *of July.* The name of the month was changed to *Iūlius* (July) in honor of Julius Caesar.

Quīnctius, -a, the name of a patrician gens at Rome. See **Cincinnātus, Flāminīnus.**

quīndecim, or **XV.,** [quīnque + decem], num. adj., indecl., *fifteen.*

quīnquāgintā, num., *fifty.*

quīnque, or **V.,** num. adj., indecl., *five.*

quīntus, -a, -um, or **V.,** [quīnque], num. adj., *fifth.*

Quīntus, -ī, abbreviated **Q.,** [quīntus], m., *Quīntus,* common Roman forename. See especially **Cicerō** (2).

quippe, adv. and conj., *of course, obviously, naturally, by all means; certainly, indeed; since, for, for in fact, for obviously; seeing that.* **quippe cum,** *inasmuch as.*

Quirītēs, -ium, [**Curēs,** ancient town of the Sabines], m., pl., originally *people of Cures;* after the union of the Sabines with the Romans, *Roman citizens, Quirītēs;* sometimes in sing., **Quirīs, -ītis,** *Roman citizen, Quirite.* LIV. I, 13.

quis, quae, quid, inter. pron., *who? which? what?* acc. n. **quid,** often with an adverbial force, *why?* **quid mihi cum vōbīs est?** *What business have I with you? What have I to do with you?* **quid?** *what! tell me, moreover,*

and again, then again. **quid est quod,** *why is it that?* **quid, quod?** *what of the fact that? and furthermore.*

quis, qua, quid, indef. pron., often found after **sī, nisi, nē,** and **num,** *anyone, any, anything.*

quisnam, quaenam, quidnam, [quis + nam], inter. pron., *who then? which, what, pray? who in the world?*

quispiam, quaepiam, quidpiam, and, as adj., **quodpiam,** indef. pron., *anyone, anybody, anything; some one, something, some, any.*

quisquam, quaequam, quicquam or **quidquam,** indef. adj. pron., *any;* often as subst., *anyone, anybody, anything.* **neque quisquam,** *and no one, and none.* **neque quisquam omnium,** *and no man in all the world.*

quisque, quaeque, quidque, and, as adj., **quodque,** indef. pron., *each, every, everyone, everything, all.*

quisquis, ——, quicquid or **quidquid,** and, as adj., **quodquod,** indef. rel. pron., *whoever, whatever, whatsoever, everyone who, everything which.* **quidquid est,** *as far as it goes, call it what you will.*

quīvīs, quaevīs, quidvīs, and, as adj., **quodvīs,** [quī + vīs, from volō], indef. pron., *whom you please, what you please, any you please; any at all, anyone, anything.*

quō, for **aliquō** in clauses introduced by **sī, nisi, nē,** and **num.**

quō [old dat. and abl. of quī], adv. and conj.:

(1) As adv., inter., *whither?*
*to what place? to what end?
wherefore? why?* rel., *whither,
where, at what time, when;* of degree of difference, *by what, by as
much as;* of result, *by reason of
which, wherefore, whereby, and so.*
(2) As conj., *that, in order
that, that thereby.* quōminus or
quō minus, *that not,* usually best
translated by *from* with a verbal
noun.

quoad [quō + ad], adv., *as far as,
till, until; as long as, while.*

quōcircā [quō + circā], conj., *for
which reason, wherefore, and
therefore.*

quōcumque [quō + -cumque], adv.,
whithersoever, to whatever place.

quod [acc. neut. of quī], conj., *that,
in that, the fact that; because,
since, inasmuch as; in view of
the fact that, as regards the fact
that, wherein; so far as, to the
extent that.* nōn est quod, nihil
est quod, *there is no reason why.*
nihil est quod respondeam, *I
have no reply to make.*

quodsī or quod sī, conj., *but if.*

quondam [quom, old form of cum,
+ -dam], adv., *once on a time,
at one time, once, formerly; at
times, sometimes, once in a while.*

quoniam [quom, old form of cum,
+ iam], conj., *since, seeing that,
whereas, because.*

quoque, conj., placed after the
emphatic word, *also, too, even.*

quōquō [old dative of quisquis],
adv., *to whatever place, whither-
soever.*

quōrsum or quōrsus [quō + ver-
sus], adv., *to what place, whither,*

*to what end, why; to what pur-
pose, with what view, for what.*

quot, indecl. adj., *how many?*

quotiēns [quot], adv., *how often?
as often as, as many as, as.*

quotiēnscumque [quotiēns + -cum-
que], adv., *just as often as, as often
as.*

quō ūsque, adverbial phrase, *till what
time? how long?*

R

rāmus, -ī, m., *branch, bough, twig.*

rapāx, -ācis, comp. rapācior,
[rapiō], adj., *tearing, greedy,
rapacious; prone to snatch* or *to
appropriate.*

rapīna, -ae, [rapiō], f., *robbery,
plundering; pillage, plunder.*

rapiō, rapere, rapuī, raptum, 3,
a., *seize, snatch, tear away, carry
off; snatch away, hurry along,
impel; rob, ravage, plunder, lay
waste.*

rārus, -a, -um, [the opposite of
dēnsus], adj., *of loose texture,
thin, rare; with large intervals,
here and there, scanty, thin,
scattered, far apart;* of soldiers,
*in open order, scattered, dis-
persed, straggling, single; infre-
quent, scarce; uncommon, rare,
extraordinary, remarkable.* rārī
et cēdentēs capillī, *hair thin
and receding from the forehead.*

ratiō, -ōnis, [reor], f., *reckoning,
calculation, account; transac-
tion, business, matter, affair;
respect, regard, consideration; relation, condition; manner, way,
mode, plan, kind, style; judgment, reason, understanding;
propriety, order, rule: theory,*

doctrine, science, knowledge; motive. **ratiō totīus bellī,** *the plan of the entire campaign, of the entire war.* **vītae meae ratiōnēs,** *my plan of life.* **officiī ratiō,** *the requirements, claims, of* [*my*] *office.* **ratiōnem habēre alicuius reī,** *to have consideration for a thing, to pay attention to a thing.* **ratiō cōnstat,** *the account is good, is correct.* **ratiō bellī,** *military policy.* **ratiōnem habēre cum aliquō,** *to have a reckoning with anyone.* **ratiō nōn nūlla,** (there would be) *some grounds* (for it). **in ratiōne petītiōnis,** *in the matter of my suit.*

ratus, see **reor.**

re- or **red-,** inseparable prefix, *again, back, anew, against.*

Reātīnus, -a, -um, [**Reāte**], adj., *of Reate,* an important town in the Sabine country, 48 miles northeast of Rome. In Cicero's time it was governed as a prefecture. Cf. **praefectūra.**

recēdō, -ere, -cessī, -cessum, [**re- + cēdō**], 3, n., *go back, give ground, withdraw; vanish, disappear.* **venter recessit,** [*his*] *belly sagged.*

recēns, -entis, adj., *fresh, young, recent, new; vigorous.*

recēnseō, -ēre, -cēnsuī, -cēnsum, [**re- + cēnseō**], 2, a., *count, number, reckon; examine, review, hold a review of; enroll; go over, reckon up, recount.*

receptus, see **recipiō.**

recessus, -ūs, [**recēdō**], m., *retreat, withdrawal, departure;* by metonymy, *retired spot, recess, nook, corner, retired place.*

recipiō, -ere, recēpī, receptum, [**rē- + capiō**], 3, a., *take back, receive back, regain, recover; admit, receive, welcome; acquire, gain; promise.* **sē recipere,** *to withdraw, to retire.* **sessum recipere,** *to admit to a seat.*

recitō, -āre, -āvī, -ātum, [**re- + citō**], 1, a., *read aloud, declaim, rehearse.*

reclāmō, -āre, -āvī, -ātum, [**re- + clāmō**], 1, a. and n., *cry out against, exclaim against, protest.*

recognōscō, -gnōscere, -gnōvī, -gnitum, [**re- + cognōscō**], 3, a., *recall to mind, recollect, recall; review, examine, look over.*

recolō, -ere, recoluī, recultum, [**re- + colō**], 3, a., *cultivate again; practice again, resume, renew.*

reconciliātiō, -ōnis, [**reconciliō**], f., *restoration, renewal.*

recondō, -ere, recondidī, reconditum, [**re- + condō**], 3, a., *put back; put away, shut up, hide, conceal, cover.*

recoquō, -ere, -coxī, -coctum, [**re- + coquō**], 3, a., *boil again, renew by boiling; restore youth.*

recordātiō, -ōnis, [**recordor**], f., *recollection, remembrance.*

recordor, -ārī, -ātus sum, [**re- + cor**], 1, dep., *call to mind, recall, remember, recollect.*

recreō, -āre, -āvī, -ātum, [**re- + creō**], 1, a., *recreate; renew, restore, revive, invigorate.* **vōculae recreandae causā,** *in order to strengthen* (my) *poor voice.*

rēctā [abl. of **rēctus,** sc. **viā**], adv., *straightway, directly, straight.*

rēctē [**rēctus**], adv., *in a straight line; rightly, correctly, properly;*

suitably, well, duly, appropriately.

Rēctīna, -ae, f., *Rēctīna,* wife of Tascus. PLIN. 12.

rēctus, -a, -um, [part. of regō], adj., *straight; upright; correct, proper, befitting; just, virtuous.*

recubō, -āre, ——, ——, [re- + cubō, *lie down*], 1, n., *lie upon the back, lie down; lie back, recline.*

recuperō or **reciperō, -āre, -āvī, -ātum,** 1, a., *get back, regain, recover.*

recurrō, -ere, recurrī, ——, [re- + currō], 3, n., *run back, hasten back; return, revert, recur.*

recūsātiō, -ōnis, [recūsō], f., *declining, refusal, protest.*

recūsō, -āre, -āvī, -ātum, [re- + causa], 1, a. and n., *raise objections to, decline, refuse, reject; protest.*

red-, see **re-.**

redāctus, see **redigō.**

redamō, -āre, ——, ——, [re-+ amō], 1, n., *return love for love.*

reddō, -ere, reddidī, redditum, [red- + dō], 3, a., *give back, return, restore; pay back, requite; render, make; give, grant; surrender, resign; report, declare.* **sonus reddēbātur,** *a sound was heard.* **bene reddita vīta,** *a well-spent life.*

redeō, -īre, -iī, -itum, [red- + eō], irr., n., *go back, return, come back; be brought back, be restored.*

redigō, -ere, redēgī, redāctum, [red- + agō], 3, a., *drive back, lead back, bring back; bring under, reduce, subdue.*

redimō, -ere, redēmī, redēmptum,

[red- + emō], 3, a., *buy back, redeem, ransom; buy up, take by contract, farm; gain, acquire, secure.*

reditus, -ūs, [redeō], m., *going back, returning, return; income, revenue.*

redūcō, -ere, -dūxī, -ductum, [re- + dūcō], 3, a., *lead back, bring back, escort back, accompany; draw off, cause to retreat; restore, replace.*

redundō, -āre, -āvī, -ātum, [red- + undō, from unda], 1, n., *run over, overflow; swim, reek; remain, be left, be in excess, abound.*

referō, -ferre, rettulī, relātum, [re- + ferō], irr., a., *bring back, lead back, carry back; give back, restore, repay; reply, answer; repeat; report, announce, relate; consider, refer; recall, reproduce.* **ad senātum referre,** *lay before the senate, submit to the senate for consideration.* **sē referre,** *to go back, to return.* Cf. **grātia.**

rēfert, rēferre, rētulit, [rē, from rēs, + ferō], impers., *it is of advantage, it profits; it is of importance, it matters; it concerns.*

refertus, -a, -um, [part. of referciō], adj., *crowded full, stuffed, filled; thronged, replete.*

reficiō, -ficere, refēcī, refectum, [re- + faciō], 3, a., *make over, reconstruct, restore; renew, refresh, reinvigorate, recruit.*

reformīdō, -āre, ——, -ātum, [re- + formīdō], 1, a., *dread greatly, shrink from, shudder at, be afraid of.*

refrīgēscō, -ere, -frīxī, ——, [re- + frīgēscō, *grow cold*], 3, n., *grow cold, be chilled, lose fire or warmth; become remiss, lose force, abate, fail, flag.*

refugiō, -fugere, refūgī, ——, [re- + fugiō], 3, a. and n., *flee back, take refuge, flee; turn away, avoid, shun.* **refugit animus,** *the mind shudders.*

refūtō, -āre, -āvī, -ātum, 1, a., *repel, resist, oppose, withstand; disprove, rebut, refute.*

rēgālis, -e, [rēx], adj., *kingly, royal.* **nōmen rēgāle,** *the name of king.*

rēgiē [rēgius], adv., *after the manner of a king, despotically.*

Rēgīnus, -a, -um, [Rēgium], adj., *of Regium,* a city in Italy, on the Sicilian strait : now **Reggio.** As subst., **Rēgīnī, -ōrum,** m., pl., *people of Regium.*

regiō, -ōnis, [regō], f., *direction, line;* by metonymy, *boundary line, limit; region, territory, country; tract, quarter.*

rēgius, -a, -um, [rēx], adj., *of a king, like a king, kingly, royal, regal.* **bellum rēgium,** *war with the king.*

rēgnō, -āre, -āvī, -ātum, [rēgnum], 1, a. and n., *be king, rule, reign; hold sway, prevail.*

rēgnum, -ī, [regō], n., *kingship; dominion, rule, government, power, authority; realm, kingdom.*

regō, regere, rēxī, rēctum, 3, a., *keep straight, lead straight; direct, lead, guide; control, regulate; rule, govern, be master of.*

reiciō, -icere, reiēcī, reiectum, [re- + iaciō], 3, a., *throw back, force back; cast off, repel, reject; refuse, disdain.*

relaxō, -āre, -āvī, -ātum, [re- + laxō], 1, a., *make wide, loosen, open; relieve, ease, cheer, lighten.*

relevō, -āre, -āvī, -ātum, [re- + levō, lift up], 1, a., *lift up; mak, light, lighten; relieve, free, ease; soothe, alleviate, mitigate, console.*

religiō, -ōnis, f., *conscientiousness, sense of right; devoutness, piety, reverence, devotion; religious scruple, fear of the gods, religious obligation; worship of the gods, religion, faith, cult; sacredness, holiness.*

religiōsus, -a, -um, [religiō], adj., *conscientious, scrupulous, devout, pious; sacred, consecrated, holy, venerable.*

relincunt, see **relinquō.**

relinquō, -ere, relīquī, relīctum, [re- + linquō], 3, a., *leave behind, leave, abandon; forsake, desert; relinquish, dismiss, give up; bequeath, transmit.*

reliquiae, -ārum, [reliquus], f., pl., *what is left, remainder, leavings, remains, relics, remnant, rest; fragments; ashes.*

reliquus, -a, -um, [cf. relinquō], adj., *left, remaining; future, subsequent; other, rest.* As subst., **reliquum, -ī,** n., *the rest, the future;* also, **reliqua, -ōrum,** n., pl., *the balance, the future.* **reliquum est ut,** *it remains that, it only remains to.* **quod reliquum est,** *for the rest, for the future.* **nihil reliquī facere,** *to leave no remnant, leave nothing remaining.*

relūceō, -ēre, -lūxī, ——, [re- + lūceō, shine], 2, n., *shine back, shine out, blaze, shine, glow.*

remaneō, -ēre, remānsī, ——, [re- + maneō], 2, n., *stay behind, remain, be left; continue, last, abide, endure.*

remedium, -ī or -iī, [re- + medior], n., *that which restores health, a cure, remedy, antidote, medicine.* in remedium formīdinis, *to allay their fear.*

rēmex, -igis, [rēmus + agō], m., *rower, oarsman.*

remissiō, -ōnis, [remittō], f., *sending back; easing, relaxing, abatement; relaxation, recreation.*

remissus, -a, -um, [part. of remittō], adj., *relaxed; mild, gentle, indulgent; negligent, slack, remiss; light, merry.*

remittō, -ere, remīsī, remissum, [re- + mittō], 3, a. and n., *send back, cause to return; loosen, slacken, relax; give back, return, restore; give up, grant, pardon.*

remoror, -ārī, -ātus sum, [re- + moror], 1, dep., *hold back, delay, detain, hinder.*

removeō, -ēre, remōvī, remōtum, [re- + moveō], 2, a., *move back; remove, take away; withdraw, set aside; abolish, deprive of.* remōtō Catilīnā, *with Catiline out of the way.*

remūnerātiō, -ōnis, [remūneror, repay], f., *recompense, reward, return, repayment.*

Remus, -ī, m., *Remus,* brother of Romulus. LIV. 1, 6.

renovō, -āre, -āvī, -ātum, [re- + novō], 1, a., *renew, restore, revive.*

renūntiō, -āre, -āvī, -ātum, [re- + nūntiō], 1, a., *bring back word, report; give notice, announce,*

declare, proclaim; with two acc., *declare elected, proclaim as chosen.*

reor, rērī, ratus sum, 2, dep., *reckon, think, suppose, imagine, judge, believe.*

reparō, -āre, -āvī, -ātum, [re- + parō], 1, a., *get again, recover; restore, renew; purchase, obtain; refresh, revive; take in exchange.*

repellō, -ere, reppulī, repulsum, [re- + pellō], 3, a., *drive back, thrust back, repel; keep back, ward off, repulse, reject.*

repente [repēns], adv., *suddenly, unexpectedly.*

repentīnus, -a, -um, [repēns], adj., *sudden, unexpected, unlooked for, hasty.*

reperiō, -īre, repperī, repertum, 4, a., *find again, find, meet with; find out, discover, learn; invent, devise.*

repetō, -ere, repetīvī, repetītum, [re- + petō], 3, a., *seek again; attack anew, fall upon again; demand anew, demand back, claim; repeat, undertake again, renew; recall, recollect, say again, write again; revive.* repetere altius, *to recount more in detail.*

reportō, -āre, -āvī, -ātum, [re- + portō], 1, a., *carry back; carry off, obtain, get, gain.*

repraesentātiō, -ōnis, [repraesentō, *to bring before one*], f., *bringing before one, representation;* technical word of syntax to indicate the use of primary sequence in indirect discourse depending on a secondary tense, i.e. *the act of imagining past events vividly as going on before one's eyes.*

repraesentō, -āre, -āvī, -ātum, [re- + praesentō, *make present*],

1, a., *make present again; set in
view, exhibit, display; manifest,
depict, represent; pay down, pay
in cash; perform immediately,
realize, do now, accomplish instantly; hasten.*

reprehendō, -ere, reprehendī, re-
prehēnsum, [re- + prehendō], 3,
a., *hold back, hold fast, seize;
restrain, check; blame, censure,
rebuke, reprove.*

reprimō, -ere, repressī, repres-
sum, [re- + premō], 3, a., *press
back; check, restrain, confine,
curb, repress.*

repudiō, -āre, -āvī, -ātum, [repu-
dium, *casting off*], 1, a., *cast off,
put away; reject, refuse, repudiate, scorn, disdain.*

repuerāscō, -ere, ——, ——, [re-
+ puerāscō, *become a boy*],
3, inch., n., *become a boy* or *child
again, renew childhood; frolic
childishly.*

repugnō, -āre, -āvī, -ātum, [re- +
pugnō], 1, n., *oppose, resist, struggle, contend against.* repugnante vestrā auctōritāte, *in
spite of your authority.*

reputō, -āre, -āvī, -ātum, [re- +
putō], 1, a., *count over, reckon,
compute; think over, ponder,
meditate, reflect upon, reflect.*

requiēs, -ētis, acc. requiētem or
requiem, [re- + quiēs], f., *rest,
pause; repose, recreation; res-
pite, relief.*

requīrō, -ere, requīsīvī or -iī,
requīsītum, [re- + quaerō], 3, a.,
*seek again, search for; ask, in-
quire, demand; miss, lack, feel
the want of.*

rēs, reī, f., *thing, object, matter,*
*affair; occurrence, event, case;
condition, circumstance; reality,
fact; effects, property, possessions, estate; profit, advantage,
interest; cause, reason, ground,
account; business, suit, action;
battle, campaign; state, commonwealth, government.* rēs gestae,
exploits, achievements. rēs
secundae, *prosperity.* rērum
potīrī, *to obtain the sovereignty.* summa rēs pūblica,
highest interest of the state. rēs
Rōmāna, *the Roman state.* male
rem gerere, *to mismanage property, to fail.* rēs familiāris,
property. ad rem pūblicam sē
cōnferre, *to enter upon a political
career, adopt politics.* rem pūblicam gerere, *to consult the good
of the state, to serve the state.* rē
ipsā, rē vērā, *actually, in real
truth.* rē, *in real fact, in reality.*
in tantā rē, *in so serious a crisis.*
bonae rēs, *prosperity.* rēs
monet, *the situation suggests.*
rēs hūmānae, *human possessions.*
rēs novae, *a change of fortune,
a revolution.* rēs atque perīcula
nostra, *our dangerous situation.*
magnae rēs, *occasions of great
weight, important problems.* ā
rēbus gerendīs, *from active duties.*
rēs pūblica quaedam, *a sort of
state.* quā dē rē, *wherefore,
therefore, for this reason.* rē
verbō, *in effect, in express terms.*

rescrībō, -ere, rescrīpsī, rescrīp-
tum, [re- + scrībō], 3, a., *write
back, reply in writing.*

reservō, -āre, -āvī, -ātum, [re- +
servō], 1, a., *keep back, save up,
reserve, retain.*

**resideō, -ēre, resēdī, ——, [re- +
sedeō],** 2, a. and n., *remain sitting; remain, stay, reside; remain behind, be left, stay.*

**resīdō, -ere, -sēdī, ——, [re +
sīdō,** *settle*], 3, n., *sit down,
settle, sink, subside; abate, grow
calm, fall.*

**resignō, -āre, -āvī, -ātum, [re- +
signō],** 1, a., *unseal, open; annul, cancel, destroy.*

**resistō, -ere, restitī, ——, [re- +
sistō],** 3, n., *stand back; remain
behind, stay, be left; withstand,
oppose, resist.*

**resolvō, -ere, -solvī, -solūtum,
[re- + solvō],** 3, a., *untie again
that which was tied; unfasten,
release, open; relax, enfeeble;
cancel, make void.*

respectō, -āre, -āvī, -ātum, [respiciō], 1, a. and n., *look back
upon, gaze about; gaze at, look
upon; await, expect; have an
eye to, regard, care for.*

**respergō, -ere, -spersī, -spersum,
[re- + spargō,** *strew*], 3, a.,
sprinkle over, besprinkle, bestrew; defile.

**respiciō, -ere, respexī, respectum,
[re- + speciō,** *look*], 3, a. and n.,
*look back, look behind; look back
upon, gaze upon; look out for,
have a care for, be mindful of,
consider.*

respondeō, -ēre, respondī, responsum, [re- + spondeō], 2, a.
and n., *answer, reply; give answer, respond; be a match for;
accord, agree.* **aliquid respondit,**
he made a reply.

respōnsum, -ī, [respondeō], n.,
answer, reply, response.

rēs pūblica, reī pūblicae, f., see
pūblicus.

restinguō, -ere, restīnxī, restīnctum, [re- + stinguō], 3, a., *put
out, extinguish, quench; annihilate, destroy.*

**restituō, -ere, restituī, restitūtum,
[re- + statuō],** 3, a., *replace, restore; revive, renew, reinstate.*

**restō, restāre, restitī, ——, [re- +
stō],** 1, n., *withstand, resist,
oppose; be left, remain.* Impers.,
restat, *it remains.*

**resūmō, -ere, -sūmpsī, -sūmptum,
[re- + sūmō],** 3, a., *take up
again, take back, resume.*

**retardō, -āre, -āvī, -ātum, [re- +
tardō,** *impede*], 1, a. and n., *keep
back, hinder, impede; delay,
tarry.*

rēte, rētis, n., *net, toil, snare.*

**retegō, -ere, -tēxī, -tēctum, [re-
+ tegō],** 3, a., *uncover, bare,
open; disclose, discover, reveal.*

reticentia, -ae, [reticeō], f., *keeping
silent, silence, reticence.*

**reticeō, -ēre, reticuī, ——, [re- +
taceō],** 2, a. and n., *be silent,
keep silent; keep secret, conceal.*

**retineō, -ēre, retinuī, retentum,
[re- + teneō],** 2, a., *hold back,
hold fast; detain, restrain, check,
repress; keep, preserve, maintain.*

retrāctātiō, -ōnis, [retrahō], f.,
*drawing back, refusal, objection,
shrinking.*

**retrahō, -ere, -trāxī, -trāctum,
[re- + trahō],** 3, a., *draw back,
withdraw, bring back; remove,
divert, turn; make known again.*

retrō, adv., *of motion, backward,
back, to the rear; of rest, behind,*

on the back side, in the rear; of time, back, in past times, before, formerly; in thought, back, behind, in return, on the contrary, on the other hand, vice versa.

retundō, -ere, rettudī, retūsum or retūnsum, [re- + tundō], 3, a., beat back, blunt, dull; check, restrain.

reus, -ī, [rēs], m., defendant in a legal action, the accused, prisoner.

revellō, -ere, -vellī, -volsum or -vulsum, [re- + vellō], 3, a., pluck away, pull away, tear out, tear off; abolish, do away with; pull off.

revertor, revertī, reversus sum or revertī, [re- + vertor], 3, dep., turn back, return, go back.

revincō, -ere, revīcī, revictum, [re- + vincō], 3, a., conquer; convict, refute.

revīvīscō, -ere, -vīxī, ——, [re- + vīvō], 3, n., come to life again. be restored to life, live again, be revived; recover, gather strength, renew vigor.

revocō, -āre, -āvī, -ātum, [re- + vocō], 1, a., call back, call again, recall, bring back; withdraw, turn aside, divert; restore; recover.

rēx, rēgis, [cf. regō], m., king, chief, ruler, monarch, despot.

Rēx, Rēgis, m., surname in the gens Mārcia. Esp., Q. Mārcius Rēx, brother-in-law of Clodius, consul in 68 B.C., governor of Cilicia as proconsul in 67. Being refused a triumph on his return to Rome, he remained outside the city till the Catilinarian conspiracy broke out in

63 B.C., when the senate sent him to Faesulae, to watch the movements of Manlius, Catiline's general. SALL. 30.

Rhēnus, -ī, m., the Rhine. MAR. 9.

Rhodius, -a, -um, [Rhodus, 'Ρόδος], adj., Rhodian, of Rhodes, an important island near the southwestern coast of Asia Minor. As subst., Rhodiī, -ōrum, m., pl., people of Rhodes, Rhodians.

rīdeō, -ēre, rīsī, rīsum, 2, a. and n., laugh; laugh at, ridicule, deride.

rīdiculus, -a, -um, [rīdeō], adj., laughable, amusing; absurd, ridiculous, contemptible.

rīte, adv., in due form, with proper ceremony. conditīs rīte mānibus, after the performance of funeral rites, when the ghost had been properly laid.

rīvālis, -is, [rīvus, brook], m., of or belonging to a rivulet, having a brook in a field in common with another; neighbor, competitor, rival, suitor.

rōbur, -oris, n., hard wood; oak tree, oak; strength, power, vigor, force; best part, pith, kernel.

rōbustus, -a, -um, [rōbur], adj., of oak-wood; strong, hardy, firm, robust.

rogātiō, -ōnis, [rogō], f., question, asking, entreaty, prayer, request; an inquiry after the people's will upon a proposed law, reference to popular vote; proposed law, resolution, bill. ante diem rogātiōnis, before the passage of the bill.

rogātus, -ūs, found only in the abl., [rogō], m., request, entreaty.

rogitō, -āre, ——, ——, [freq. of rogō], 1, a., *ask eagerly, inquire persistently, keep asking, ask.*

rogō, -āre, -āvī, -ātum, 1, a., *ask, question, inquire; request, implore, beg for;* of a bill or resolution, *bring forward for approval, propose, introduce.* sententiam rogō, *ask an opinion, call upon to vote.*

Rōma, -ae, f., *Rome.*

Rōmānus, -a, -um, [Rōma], adj., *of Rome, Roman, Latin.* As subst., Rōmānus, -ī, m., *Roman.*

Rōmulus, -ī, m., *Rōmulus,* mythical founder and first king of Rome; said to have been the son of Mars and Rhea Silvia. Liv. 1, 6.

Rōscius, -ī or -iī, m., *Q. Rōscius,* the most famous comic actor at Rome. He was an intimate friend of Cicero. He died 62 B.C. ARCH. 8.

rōstrum, -ī, [rōdō, *gnaw*], n., *that with which one gnaws, a beak, bill, mouth; a ship's beak;* pl., Rōstra, -ōrum, *Rostra,* platform for speakers in the Forum, adorned with the beaks of the ships taken from the Antians, 338 B.C.; *stage, orator's pulpit, platform.*

Rudīnus, -a, -um, [Rudiae], adj., *of Rudiae,* a town in Calabria, celebrated as the birthplace of Ennius. ARCH. 10.

rudis, -e, adj., *unwrought, wild, coarse; rude, uncultivated, rough, unpolished; unskilled, ignorant.*

Rūfus, -ī, [rūfus, *red, red-haired*], m., a family name common to several gentes. See Sulpicius, Pompeius, Calvisius.

rūga, -ae, f., *crease in .he face, wrinkle.*

ruīna, -ae, [ruō], f., *tumbling down, falling down; downfall, fall, ruin, destruction, overthrow, calamity;* pl., *ruins.*

rūmor, -ōris, m., *report, rumor, common talk; current opinion, reputation.*

ruō, -ere, ruī, rutum, 3, a. and n., *fall with violence, tumble down, fall in ruins, go to ruin; hasten, hurry, dash along, run.*

Rupilius, -a, name of a Roman gens. Two of the family are mentioned in this book : (1) *Pūblius Rupilius,* consul in 132 B.C. As consul, and afterwards as proconsul, he brought the Servile War to an end. He had been identified with the party opposing Tiberius Gracchus, and in 123 B.C., when Gaius Gracchus became tribune, he was condemned on account of his illegal and cruel acts in the prosecution of the friends of Tiberius. AM. 20. (2) *Lūcius Rupilius,* younger brother of the preceding, friend of Scipio Africanus the younger. Nothing is known of him save that he failed to obtain the consulship. AM. 20.

rūrsus or rūrsum [for reversus, reversum, from revertō], adv., *on the contrary, on the other hand, in turn; again, once more, anew.*

rūsticātiō, -ōnis, [rūsticor], f., *sojourn in the country; country life.*

rūsticor, -ārī, -ātus sum, [rūsticus], 1, dep., *sojourn in the country, stay in the country, rusticate.*

rūsticus, -a, -um, [rūs, *country*], adj., *of the country, rural, rustic; rough, coarse, plain, simple.* As subst., rūsticus, -ī, m., *rustic, peasant, countryman.*

S

S. D. = salūtem dīcit, *sends greeting.*

S. D. PLŪR. = salūtem dīcit plūrimam, *sends heartiest greeting.*

S. T. E. Q. V. B. E. = sī tū exercitusque valētis, bene est.

S. V. B. E. = sī valēs, bene est.

S. V. B. E. V. = sī valēs, bene est; valeō.

Sabīnus, -a, -um, adj., *Sabine, of the Sabines.* As subst., Sabīnī, -ōrum, m., pl., *the Sabines*, one of the most ancient and powerful of the peoples of central Italy. They were a people of simple and virtuous habits, faithful to their word, and imbued with deep religious feeling. Hence, we find frequent mention of omens and prodigies in their country. With the exception of the Sabines in Lucania and Campania, they never attained any high degree of civilization or mental culture; but they were always distinguished by their love of freedom, which they maintained with the greatest bravery. The Sabines formed one of the elements of which the Roman people was composed.

sacer, -ra, -rum, [sanciō], adj., *dedicated, consecrated, devoted, sacred; accursed, execrable, detestable, horrible, infamous.*

sacerdōs, -ōtis, [sacer, cf. dō], m. and f., *priest, priestess.*

sacerdōtium, -ī or -iī, [sacerdōs], n., *priesthood, office of a priest, priestly office.*

sacrārium, -ī or -iī, [sacrum], n., *shrine, sanctuary, chapel.*

sacrāmentum, -ī, [sacrō, *consecrate*], *that by which a person binds himself or another to do something; hence, a sum deposited by a party in a civil process as security for a future judgment; forfeit money, guaranty; an oath, military oath of allegiance.*

sacrificium, -ī or -iī, [sacrificus, *for sacrificing*], n., *sacrifice.*

sacrōsānctus, -a, -um, [sacer + sānctus], adj., *revered as sacred, inviolable.*

sacrum, -ī, [sacer], n., *sacred thing, sacred place, sanctuary; act of worship, sacred rite, rite, sacrifice, worship.*

saeculum, or, by syncope, saeclum, -ī, n., *race, breed; generation, lifetime, age; century, hundred years.*

Saenius, -ī or -iī, m., *L. Saenius*, praetor, took an active part in the first disclosures of Catiline's conspiracy, but is otherwise unknown. SALL. 30.

saepe, comp. saepius, sup. saepissimē, adv., *often, frequently, many times.* iterum et saepius, *over and over again.*

saepiō, -īre, saepsī, saeptum, [saepēs, *hedge*], 4, a., *hedge in, inclose, surround; fortify, protect, guard.*

sagātus, -a, -um, [sagum], adj., *clothed in a sagum, wearing a military cloak.* **sagātī,** *clad in the garb of war.*

sagāx, -ācis, adj., *of acute senses, keen-scented; sagacious, keen, quick, shrewd.*

sagulum, -ī, [dim. of **sagum**], n., *small military cloak; traveling cloak.*

sagum, -ī, n., *coarse woolen blanket, rough mantle; military cloak.* **ad saga īre,** *to fight.* **ad saga sūmenda,** *to assume the garb of war.*

SAL., see **salūs.**

SAL. D. = **salūtem dīcit.**

Salamīnius, -a, -um, [Salamīs], adj., *of Salamis,* island southwest of Attica; also, *of the city Salamis* on the island of Cyprus. As subst., **Salamīniī, -ōrum,** m., pl., *people of Salamis.*

Sallustius, -ī or **-iī,** m., *Sallust,* Roman name. Two by the name are mentioned in this book:
(1) *Cn. Sallustius,* client or friend of Cicero's, and a man of some literary taste. Ep. 18.
(2) *C. Sallustius Crispus,* born 86 b.c. of a plebeian family, quaestor 59, while tribune of the plebs in 52 joined the popular party and actively opposed Milo. In 50 he was expelled from the Senate, probably because he belonged to Caesar's party. He followed Caesar in the Civil War. He accompanied Caesar in his African War, and was left as governor of Numidia. Returning from Africa,

he spent the years before his death, 34 b.c., in writing his historical works. See Companion, page 527.

saltem, adv., *save, at least, at the least, at all events, anyhow;* with neg., *not — at least, not even, nor even.*

saltō, -āre, -āvī, -ātum, [freq. of **saliō**], 1, a. and n., *dance.*

salūs, -ūtis, in addresses of letters abbreviated **Sal., S.,** f., *health, vigor; welfare, prosperity, safety, deliverance; greeting, salutation.* **salūtem dīcere,** *to send greeting.* **salūtem nūntiāre,** *to carry one's regards.*

salūtāris, -e, [salūs], adj., *of well-being, healthful, health-giving, wholesome, salutary.*

salūtō, -āre, -āvī, -ātum, [salūs], 1, a., *greet, salute, hail; wish health to, visit, call upon.*

salveō, -ēre, ——, ——, [salvus], 2, n., *be well, be in good health,* **salvēre iubēre,** *to salute, to offer greetings to.*

salvus, -a, -um, adj., *well, sound, safe; unharmed, uninjured, in good condition, in good health,* **salvā Terentiā,** *Terentia is doing well.*

Samos or **Samus, -ī, [Σάμος],** f., *Samos,* an island in the Aegean Sea, near Ephesus.

Sampsiceramus, -ī, m., *Sampsiceramus,* a nickname of Pompey.

sanciō, -īre, sānxī, sānctum, 4, a., *make sacred, consecrate; establish, decree, ordain, enact; approve, ratify.*

sānctus, -a, -um, [part. of **sanciō**], adj., *consecrated, inviolable, sacred; venerable, holy, divine; pure, upright, conscientious, just* sānē [sānus], adv., *sensibly, reasonably, discreetly; indeed, by all means, truly, very.*

sanguis, -inis, m., *blood;* by metonymy, *bloodshed, slaughter; stock, family; vigor, force.*

sānō, -āre, -āvī, -ātum, [sānus], 1, a., *make sound, heal, cure; restore, repair, allay.*

sapiēns, -entis, [part. of sapiō], adj., *wise, discreet, sensible, prudent.* As subst., sapientēs, -ium, m., pl., *wise, wise men.*

sapienter [sapiēns], adv., *wisely, discreetly, prudently.*

sapientia, -ae, [sapiēns], f., *good sense, discernment, discretion, prudence; wisdom, philosophy; science.* aliquid sapientiae, *any degree of prudence, any wisdom.*

sapiō, sapere, sapīvī, ——, 3, a. and n., *taste; have taste, have discernment, discern; be wise, be discreet.* perquam exiguum sapere, *to have very limited knowledge.* quantum sapiō, *so far as my taste goes, as far as I can judge.* quī sapiat, *one of good sense.*

Sapphō, -ūs, f., *Sapphō,* famous Greek poetess of Mytilene, or famous bronze statue of her at Syracuse, stolen by Verres. VERR. 57.

sarcina, -ae, [sarciō, *mend*], f., *package, bundle, load, pack;* in pl., *packs, luggage, baggage.*

Sardinia, -ae, f., *Sardinia,* an island west of Italy.

sat, see satis.

satelles, -itis, m. and f., *attendant, follower; assistant in crime, accomplice, abettor, tool.*

satietās, -ātis, [satis], f., *sufficiency, fullness, satiety; weariness, loathing, disgust.*

satiō, -āre, -āvī, -ātum, [satis], 1, a., *satisfy, sate, satiate; appease, glut, fill; cloy, disgust.*

satis, or sat, adj., indecl. subst., and adv. :
(1) As adj., *enough, sufficient, ample.*
(2) As subst., *enough, sufficiency, plenty.* satis laudis, *sufficient praise, praise enough.*
(3) As adv., *sufficiently, enough, adequately, amply.*

satis faciō, facere, fēcī, factum, 3, n., *satisfy, give satisfaction; do enough for, do one's duty by.*

satius [comp. of satis], adj., n., *more satisfying, more serviceable, fitter, preferable.*

saturitās, -ātis, [satur, *sated*], f., *fullness, superabundance, abundance.*

Sāturnālia, -ōrum, abl. -ibus, [Sāturnus,] n., *festival of Saturn, the Saturnalia,* which commenced on the 17th of December, and at different periods lasted three, four, five, or seven days.

Sāturnīnus, -ī, m., *L. Appulēius Sāturnīnus,* a leader of the democratic party, tribune for the second time 100 B.C. Resorting to violent measures in order to carry out his plans, he was declared a public enemy by the Senate, and was slain by a mob in the Curia Hostilia. CAT. I, 2; 12.

Satyrus, -ī, m., *Satyr,* kind of semi-deity, attendant of the god Dionysus; having two goat's feet, snub nose, pointed ears, and two small horns growing out of the forehead; living in woods, fields, and on mountains, and a frequent subject in art. VERR. 60.

saucius, -a, -um, adj., *wounded, hurt; injured, weakened, smitten.*

Saxa, -ae, m., Roman surname. L. *Decidius Saxa*, native of Celtiberia in Spain, and originally one of Caesar's common soldiers. He eventually accompanied Antony to the East, and was made by him governor of Syria. Here he was defeated by the younger Labienus and the Parthians, and was slain in the flight after the battle, 40 B.C. PHIL. 4.

saxum, -ī, n., *large stone, rock.*

scaena, -ae, [σκηνή], f., *stage, scene.* **in scaenā,** *on the stage.*

scaenicus, -a, -um, [scaena], adj., *scenic, dramatic, theatrical.* **scaenicī artificēs,** *actors.*

Scaevola, -ae, m., frequent surname in the Mucian gens.

(1) *P. Mūcius Scaevola*, one of the most eminent of the early Roman jurists, consul 133 B.C.

(2) *Quintus Mūcius Scaevola*, generally called the Augur, to distinguish him from Scaevola the Pontifex Maximus, was consul in 117 B.C. He married the daughter of Laelius, the friend of Scipio Africanus the younger. He was tribune of the plebs in 128 B.C., plebeian aedile in 125, and as praetor was governor of the province of Asia in 121. He was consul in

117. He was much distinguished for his knowledge of the law, but none of his writings are recorded. He is one of the speakers in the *Dē Ōrātōre*, in the *Laelius*, and in the *Dē Rēpūblicā*.

(3) *Quīntus Mūcius Scaevola*, son of the preceding, was tribune in 106 B.C., consul in 95, and subsequently proconsul in Asia. He was afterwards Pontifex Maximus, and was killed in 82 B.C., during the proscriptions carried out by the Marian party. AM. 4.

scando, -ere, ——, ——, 3, a. and n., *rise, climb, mount, get up, ascend.*

Scaurus, -a, m., frequent surname in the Aemilian gens. Two of this name are mentioned in this book:

(1) *Mārcus Aemilius Scaurus,* Roman statesman of the time of the Jugurthine War. He was born 163 B.C., consul 115 with M. Caecilius Metellus; censor 109. He was a warm supporter of the aristocratic party. He died 90 B.C. ARCH. 3.

(2) *Mārcus Aemilius Scaurus,* stepson of the dictator Sulla, served with Pompey as quaestor in the third Mithridatic War. Praetor in 56 B.C., in the following year he governed the province of Sardinia, which he plundered without mercy. Brought to trial on his return to Rome, he was defended by Cicero, Hortensius, and others, and was acquitted, but was

condemned when accused again in 52 B.C. Ep. 11.

scelerāte [scelerātus], adv., *impiously, wickedly, scandalously.*

scelerātus, -a, -um, [part. of scelerō, *pollute*], adj., *polluted, defiled, profaned; wicked, impious, accursed; sacrilegious, infamous, scandalous.* As subst., **scelerātus, -ī,** m., *scoundrel, rogue.*

scelestus, -a, -um, [scelus], adj., *impious, wicked, infamous, accursed; knavish; abandoned, stained with crime.*

scelus, -eris, n., *wicked deed, crime; sin, wickedness.*

schola, -ae, f., *intermission of work, leisure for learning; learned conversation, debate; a meeting place for teachers and pupils; a school.*

sciēns, -entis, [part. of sciō], adj., *knowing, intelligent, skilled, expert, versed;* often used where the English idiom prefers an adv., *knowingly, intentionally.*

scientia, -ae, [sciēns], f., *knowledge, acquaintance, science, skill, art.*

scīlicet [scīre licet], adv., *you may know, certainly, obviously, of course; no doubt, forsooth, likely.*

scindō, -ere, ——, scissum, 3, a., *cut, tear, force apart, split, cleave, divide; part, separate.*

sciō, scīre, scīvī, scītum, 4, a., *know, understand; perceive, have knowledge of, be assured.* **scītō,** *be informed, be assured; let me inform you.*

Scīpiō, -ōnis, [scīpiō, *staff*], m., *Scīpio,* name of a celebrated fam-

ily of the Cornelian gens; pl., **Scīpiōnēs, -um,** *the Scipios, the Scipio family.* Four Scipios are mentioned in this book:

(1) *P. Cornēlius Scīpiō Āfricānus,* also called *Maior* to distinguish him from (2), born about 234 B.C. After several years of successful generalship in Spain, he was consul 205 B.C. In the following year he conveyed an army to Africa, where he was uniformly successful against the Carthaginians, finally defeating Hannibal near Zama, 202 B.C. He was honored with a triumph, 201 B.C. The year of his death is uncertain. Arch. 9.

(2) *P. Cornēlius Scīpiō Aemiliānus Africānus,* often called *Minor* to distinguish him from (1), born about 185 B.C. He was the son of L. Aemilius Paulus, the conqueror of Macedonia (see **Paulus**), and was adopted by Scipio Africanus. He was elected consul for 147 B.C., and took charge of the war against Carthage then in progress, capturing and destroying the city the following year. In 134 B.C. he was again made consul, and took command of the war in Spain. He captured and razed Numantia in 133 B.C. Returning to Rome, he violently opposed the measures of Ti. Gracchus. He died 129 B.C. Arch. 7; Imp. P. 16; Ep. 2; Sen. 9, *et seq.;* Am. 6, *et al.*

(3) *P. Cornēlius Scīpiō Nāsīca Corculum,* son-in-law of Scipio

Africanus the elder, consul in 162 B.C., and elected Pontifex Maximus in 150, was renowned for his knowledge of pontifical and civil law. SEN. 14.

(4) *P. Cornēlius Scīpiō Nasīca Serāpio*, consul 138 B.C., and pontifex maximus. He also opposed Ti. Gracchus, and was the leader of the mob which slew Gracchus. CAT. I, I; AM. 12.

scīscitor, -ārī, -ātus sum, [scīscō, *enact*], 1, dep., *inform oneself, seek to know, ask, inquire, question.*

scītus, -a, -um, [part. of scīscō], adj., *knowing; fit, proper, sensible; witty, clever; skillful, adroit, shrewd.* scītum est, *it is a witty saying.*

scortum, -ī, n., *hide; harlot, prostitute.*

scrībō, -ere, scrīpsī, scrīptum, 3, a., *scratch, engrave; write, write out; compose; levy.* scrībendus, -a, -um, adj., *worthy of being written about, deserving of record.*

scrīptiō, -ōnis, [scrībō], f., *writing; composing in writing, composition.*

scrīptor, -ōris, [scrībō], m., *writer, scribe; author, composer, reporter, narrator.* rērum scrīptor, *writer of history, historian.* scrīptor rērum suārum, *chronicler of his achievements, biographer.*

scrīptum, -ī, [part. n. of scrībō], n., *something written, a writing.*

scūtum, -ī, n., *shield, infantry shield, buckler,* of two boards, joined, covered with linen and hide, and edged with iron; *de-*

fense, protection, shelter, safeguard.

sē, see suī.

sē or sēd, old prep. with abl., *apart from, without;* used especially in composition.

sēcēdō, -ere, sēcessī, sēcessum, [sē + cēdō], 3, n., *go apart, separate; withdraw, go away; withdraw to the country.*

sēcernō, -ere, sēcrēvī, sēcrētum, [sē + cernō], 3, a., *separate, part, sever, divide; set apart.*

sēcessus, -ūs, [sēcēdō], m., *going away, separation, retirement, solitude; hiding-place, retreat.*

sēcrētus, -a, -um, [part. of sēcernō], adj., *severed, separated, apart; retired, remote, lonely, secret; hidden, private.*

secundum [secundus], prep. with acc., *following, after, next to; according to, in accordance with.*

secundus, -a, -um, [sequor], adj., *following, next, second; secondary, inferior; favorable, fair, prosperous; fortunate, propitious.* secundum proelium facere, *to fight a successful battle.* secundissimus ventus, *favoring wind.* proeliīs secundīs ūtī, *to have successful engagements, to come off victorious in battle.*

Secundus, -ī, m., Roman proper name. See Plīnius.

secūris, -is, abl., secūrī, [secō], f., *ax, battle-ax.*

sēcūritās, -ātis, [sēcūrus], f., *freedom from alarm, composure, freedom from anxiety; freedom from danger, security, safety.*

sēcūrus, -a, -um, comp. sēcūrior, [sē + cūra], adj., *free from care, unconcerned, untroubled; tranquil, cheerful, free from danger, safe, secure.*

sēd, see **sē.**

sed, conj., *but, but also, on the contrary; however, yet.* **nōn sōlum — sed etiam,** *not only — but also.* **sed iam,** *now however.* **sed vērō,** *but actually.*

sedeō, -ēre, sēdī, sessum, 2, n., *sit; sit idle, be inactive; be settled, remain fast.*

sēdēs, -is, [cf. **sedeō**], f., *seat, chair; abode, dwelling-place, habitation; place, site, foundation.*

sēditiō, -ōnis, [**sēd** + **itiō,** from **eō**], f., *dissension, discord; insurrection, mutiny, sedition.*

sēdō, -āre, -āvī, -ātum, [cf. **sedeō**], 1, a. and n., *bring to rest; calm, quiet, check, stop; allay, appease.*

sēdulitās, -ātis, [**sēdulus**], f., *assiduity, persistency, earnestness.*

sēgregō, -āre, -āvī, -ātum, [**sē** + **grex**], 1, a., lit., *separate from the flock; separate, set apart, remove.*

sēiungō, -ere, sēiūnxī, sēiūnctum, [**sē** + **iungō**], 3, a., *disjoin, disunite, part, separate; keep apart, disconnect.*

sēlēctus, -a, -um, [part. of **sēligō**], adj., *chosen, selected, select.*

semel, adv., *once, a single time; once for all, but once; finally.* **semel et saepius,** *more than once.*

sēmen, -inis, [cf. **serō,** *sow*], n., *seed;* by metonymy, *race; source, origin, essence, principle.*

sēminārium, -ī or **-iī,** [**sēmen**], n., *nursery, school; hot-bed.*

sēmita, -ae, [**sē** + **meō,** *go*], f., *narrow way, side-way, path, footpath, lane, by-way.*

semper, adv., *always, ever; at all times, perpetually, forever.*

sempiternus, -a, -um, [**semper**], adj., *everlasting, eternal, perpetual, imperishable.*

Semprōnius, -a, name of a Roman gens with both patrician and plebeian branches. See **Gracchus, Tuditānus.** As adj., *of a Sempronius, Sempronian.*

senātor, -ōris, [cf. **senex**], m., *senator, member of the senate.*

senātus, -ūs or **-ī,** [**senex**], m., *council of elders, senate.* **senātūs cōnsultum, senātī dēcrētum,** *decree of the senate.*

senectūs, -ūtis, [**senex**], f., *old age, advanced years;* collectively, *old men.*

senēscō, -ere, senuī, ——, [inch. of **seneō,** *be old*], 3, n., *grow old, become old; decay, lose strength, grow weak; be enfeebled, waste away, decline; fall off, be diminished, be impaired.*

senex, senis, comp. **senior,** adj., *old, aged.* As subst., **senex, -is,** m., *old man;* **senior, -ōris,** m., *elder, older person.*

senīlis, -e, [**senex**], adj., *of an old man, of old people, of old age, senile.*

sēnsim [**sentiō**], adv., *just perceptibly, gradually, by degrees, little by little, slowly.*

sēnsus, -ūs, [**sentiō**], m., *perception, sense, consciousness; sensation, emotion, feeling, sentiment; impulse.*

sententia, -ae, [**sentiō**], f., *opinion,*

judgment, notion; motion, proposal, measure; decision, will; resolution, determination, sentence. **in eandem ferē sententiam**, to much the same effect, of about the same import. **sententiam tollere**, remove a measure. **sententiā complectī**, to sum it up finally in a formal motion. **in sententiam discēdere**, to divide in favor of a proposal. **meā sententiā**, in my opinion.

sentīna, -ae, f., bilge water; off-scourings, dregs, refuse.

sentiō, -īre, sēnsī, sēnsum, 4, a., feel, hear, see, perceive; experience, discern, observe; think, believe, suppose, judge; decide, declare. **optimē sentīre dē rē pūblicā**, to harbor loyal feelings towards the state. **contrā rem pūblicam sentīre**, to entertain designs against the state. **male sentīre**, to harbor ill feelings, to have anti-public feelings. **ūnum atque idem sentīre dē**, to have one feeling about. **quod quidem sēnserim**, as far, at least, as I could observe.

sepeliō, -īre, sepelīvī or **-iī, sepultum**, 4, a., bury, inter; overwhelm, ruin, destroy.

septem or **VII.**, num. adj., indecl., seven.

September, -bris, [septem], adj., of the seventh; of the seventh month, reckoning March as the first month of the year, of September.

septemdecim, or **XVII.**, [septem + decem], num. adj., indecl., seventeen.

Septicius, -ī or **-iī**, m., C. Septicius

Clārus, friend of the younger Pliny. PLIN. I.

septimus, -a, -um, or **VII.**, [septem], adj., seventh.

sepulchrum, -ī, [cf. sepeliō], n., grave, tomb, sepulcher.

sepultūra, -ae, [cf. sepeliō], f., burial, interment, funeral obsequies.

sepultus, see sepeliō.

sequor, sequī, secūtus sum, 3, dep., follow, attend, accompany; come after, come next; seek, be destined for; chase, pursue; result, ensue; conform to, comply with; strive after, aim at. **quid sequitur**, the future.

serēnus, -a, -um, adj., clear, fair, bright, serene; cheerful, joyous, tranquil.

sērius, see sērō.

sermō, -ōnis, [serō, weave, compose], m., conversation, talk, discourse, speech; manner of speaking; report, rumor, common talk.

sērō, comp. **sērius**, sup. **sērissimē**, [sērus], adv., late, at a late hour, at a late period. Comp., **sērius**, later, often too late.

serō, -ere, ——, sertum, 3, a., sow, plant; cultivate; beget, bring forth; found, establish, produce, cause, excite; scatter, spread, disseminate. **serere certāmina**, to sow the seeds of strife.

serpō, -ere, serpsī, serptum, 3, n., creep, crawl, glide; come imperceptibly, extend gradually, spread abroad stealthily, increase; penetrate.

Serrānus, -ī, m., Roman surname. *Serrānus Domesticus*, who delivered the funeral oration for his son in a speech composed by Cicero, is otherwise unknown. Ep. 11.

Sertōriānus, -a, -um, adj., *of Sertorius, Sertorian, from Sertorius,* referring to Q. Sertorius, a Roman general of the party of Marius. He carried on war in Spain for ten years against the party of Sulla until he was murdered, 72 B.C.

servīlis, -e, [servus], adj., *slavish, servile, of a slave.* **servīle bellum,** *rebellion of slaves.*

Servīlius, -a, name of a Roman gens, at first patrician, afterwards including plebeian families also. The following *Servīlii* are mentioned in this book:

(1) *C. Servīlius Ahāla,* cf. **Maelius.** Sen. 16.

(2) *C. Servīlius Glaucia,* see **Glaucia.**

(3) *P. Servīlius Vatia,* see **Vatia.**

serviō, -īre, -īvī, -ītum, [servus], n., *be a servant, serve; be devoted to, aim at, labor for, have regard to; gratify, court.*

servitium, -ī or **-iī,** [servus], n., *servitude, slavery; body of slaves.*

servitūs, -ūtis, [servus], f., *slavery, service, serfdom.*

servō, -āre, -āvī, -ātum, 1, a., *save, preserve, keep, protect, guard; store away, maintain; give heed, watch, observe; preserve the memory of.*

servulus, -ī, [dim. of servus], m., *young slave, young man-servant, boy.*

servus, -ī, m., *slave, servant.*

sēsē, see **suī.**

sēstertius, -a, -um, [for semis

tertius, *three less one half*], or **H S** [for **II + semis**], num. adj., *two and a half.* As subst., **sēstertius, -ī,** gen. pl. **sēstertium,** [originally sc. **nummus**], m., *sesterce,* small silver coin, originally 2½ *asses,* = about 4¹⁄₁₀ cents.

Sēstius, -ī or **-iī,** m., *P. Sēstius,* quaestor of C. Antonius, Cicero's colleague in the consulship 63 B.C. He was tribune 57 B.C., and was active in procuring Cicero's recall from banishment. The following year he was brought to trial for the use of violence, and was defended by Cicero in an oration which is still extant. In the Civil War he at first joined the side of Pompey, but afterwards went over to Caesar. Cat. 1, 8.

seu, see **sīve.**

sevērē [sevērus], adv., *gravely, seriously; with severity, severely.*

sevēritās, -ātis, [sevērus], f., *gravity, seriousness; sternness, severity, austerity.*

sevērus, -a, -um, adj., *grave, serious; stern, strict, severe, rigid.*

Sevērus, -ī, m., Roman proper name. *Annius Sevērus,* of whom nothing is known apart from the correspondence of Pliny the younger with him. Plin. 5. See also **Catilius.**

Sex., see **Sextus.**

sex, or **VI.,** num. adj., indecl., *six.*

sexāgintā, or **LX.,** num. adj., indecl., *sixty.*

Sext., see **Sextīlis.**

Sextīlis, -e, in dates often abbreviated **Sext.,** [sextus], adj., *sixth;*

of the sixth month, reckoning from March, *of August.* The name of the month *Sextīlis* was changed to *Augustus* in honor of the emperor, 8 B.C.

sextus, -a, -um, or **VI.,** [sex], num. adj., *sixth.*

Sextus, -ī, abbreviated **Sex.,** [sextus], m., *Sextus,* Roman forename. See **Aelius.**

sexus, -ūs, only sing. gen. and abl., m., *sex.*

sī, conj., *if; if indeed, inasmuch as, since; when; even if, though, although;* in indir. questions, *whether;* in purpose clauses, *to see if, to try whether.* **sī quidem,** *if only, if indeed.*

Sibyllīnus, -a, -um, [Sibylla], adj., *of a Sibyl, Sibylline.*

sīc [sī + -ce], adv., *thus, in this way; so, in such a manner; just so, in the same way.* **sīc — ut,** *thus — so, just as — so.* **ut — sīc,** *while — yet, though — still.*

sīca, -ae, f., *dagger, poniard.*

sīcārius, -ī or **-iī,** [sīca], m., *assassin, murderer.*

Sicca, -ae, m., *Sicca,* an intimate friend of Cicero. He had an estate at Vibo, in the southwestern part of Italy, where Cicero took refuge from his enemies for a time in 58 B.C., and again in 44 B.C. EP. 6.

Sicilia, -ae, [Σικελία], f., *Sicily.*

Siculus, -a, -um, adj., *of Sicily, Sicilian.* As subst., **Siculī, -ōrum,** m., pl., *Sicilians.*

sīcut, or **sīcutī,** [sīc + ut], adv., *just as, so as, as; as indeed, as it were, as if.*

sīdus, -eris, n., *group of stars, constellation, heavenly body, star; sky, heaven.*

Sīgēum, -ī, [Σίγειον], n., *Sīgēum,* promontory of Troas, at the entrance of the Hellespont. Near it there was a town of the same name.

significātiō, -ōnis, [significō], f., *expression, indication, sign, token.* **ūnā significātiōne litterārum,** *by a single written order.*

significō, -āre, -āvī, -ātum, [signum + faciō], I, a., *make signs, show, point out; make known, indicate, notify; signify, mean, portend.* **manū significāre,** *to indicate with a wave of the hand.* **hōs significāre,** *to mean by these.*

signō, -āre, -āvī, -ātum, [signum], I, a., *set a mark upon, mark, designate; seal, seal up; adorn, decorate; point out, indicate; note; execute a will.*

signum, -ī, n., *sign, mark, token, indication; ensign, standard; omen, prognostication; image, figure, statue;* of a letter, *seal, signet.* **signum dare,** *to give the signal.* **collātīs signīs,** *in the shock of battle.* **ad prīma signa sustinēre,** *to keep under control.* **integrīs signīs,** *with the seals unbroken.* **ad prīma signa,** *in the front.* **signum locō,** *to mark the spot, as a marker for the spot.*

Silanion, -ōnis, m., *Silanion,* noted Greek sculptor of the time of Alexander the Great. VERR. 57.

Sīlānus, -ī, m., *D. Iūnius Sīlānus.* He distinguished himself by the magnificent games which he gave in his aedileship, about 70 B.C. He was consul 62 B.C. SALL. 51.

silentium, -ī or **-iī, [silēns], n.,** *silence, quiet, stillness.* **silentiō, in silence.** **per silentium noctis,** *in the silence of the night.*

sileō, -ēre, -uī, ——, 2, a. and n., *be silent, keep silence, be still; pass over in silence, suppress.*

silva, -ae, f., *forest, wood, grove.*

Silvānus, -ī, [silva], m., M. Plautius Silvânus, tribune of the people 89 B.C., at the same time with C. Papirius Carbo. ARCH. 4.

silvestris, -e, [silva], adj., *of a forest, wooded, woody.*

similis, -e, comp. **similior,** sup. **simillimus, adj.,** *like, similar, resembling.* Sup., *very like, closely resembling.*

similitūdō, -inis, [similis], f., *likeness, similarity, resemblance.*

Simōnidēs, -is, m., Simônidēs, Greek lyric poet (6th century B.C.) of Ceos, an island of the Cyclades. SEN. 7.

simplex, -icis, [sim-, as in **simul,** + **plex,** cf. **plicō,** *fold*], adj., *simple, unmixed; frank, straightforward, sincere.*

simpliciter [simplex], adv., *simply, plainly; frankly, artlessly.*

simul, adv., *at the same time, at once, simultaneously, together; and also.* **simul — simul,** *partly — partly, not only — but at the same time.* **simul ac,** or **simul atque,** *as soon as.* **simul et,** *as soon as.* **simul — simul,** *at once — and.*

simulācrum, -ī, [simulō], n., *likeness, image, form, figure; appearance, semblance, pretense; apparition.*

simulātiō, -ōnis, [simulō], f., *feigning, pretense, simulation, deceit.*

simulātor, -ōris, [simulō], m., *copier, imitator; one who feigns what is not, pretender, simulator.*

simulō, -āre, -āvī, -ātum, [similis], 1, a., *make like, imitate, copy, reproduce, represent; feign, simulate. pretend, pretend that which is not so.*

simultās, -ātis, [simul], f., *hostile encounter; grudge, jealousy, enmity, hatred, animosity.*

sīn [sī + nē], conj., *if however, but if.*

sincērus, -a, -um, adj., *clean, pure, whole, entire; genuine, candid, truthful.*

sine, prep. with abl., *without.*

singulāris, -e, [singulī], adj., *one by one, alone, single, solitary; singular, matchless, extraordinary, unique, remarkable.*

singulī, -ae, -a, adj., pl., *one at a time, single, individual; one to each, separate.* **in diēs singulōs,** *each successive day, day by day.*

sinister, -tra, -trum, adj., *left, on the left hand, at the left side; favorable, auspicious; fortunate; unlucky, unfavorable, inauspicious; wrong, improper; adverse, bad.*

sinō, -ere, sīvī, situm, 3, a., *let down, place, situate, give leave, permit, allow, suffer, let.*

Sinōpē, -ēs, [Σινώπη], f., Sinôpē, a prosperous commercial Greek city on the southern shore of the Pontus Euxinus, about half way between Trapezus and Heraclea; originally a colony from Miletus.

sinus, -ūs, m., *fold, curve, hollow,*

coil; fold of a garment; by metonymy, bosom, lap; bay, gulf; hollow, valley.

sī quandō [for sī aliquandō], if at any time, whenever.

sī quī [for sī aliquī], if any.

sīquidem or sī quidem, conj., if only, if indeed; since indeed, since.

sī quis [for sī aliquis], if anyone.

sistō, -ere, stitī, statum, [stō], 3, a. and n., cause to stand, set up, place; lead, send, bring; establish, confirm; stop, halt, check; with reflex., betake oneself, present oneself, come.

sitis, -is, acc. -im, pl. wanting, f., thirst; eager desire, eagerness.

Sittius, -a, the name of a Roman gens. P. Sittius, of Nuceria, was connected with Catiline, and went to Spain in 64 B.C. From this country he crossed over into Mauretania in the following year. He joined Caesar when the latter came to Africa in 46, and was of great service to Caesar in the war waged by the latter against Pompey. The war over, he was rewarded by Caesar with the western part of Numidia, where he settled. On Caesar's death, he was killed by Arabio, son of Masinissa. SALL. 21.

situs, -a, -um, [part. of sinō], adj., placed, situated, lying; buried, laid at rest. quantum est situm in nōbīs, so far as in us lies, as far as in me lies.

situs, -ūs, [sinō], m., situation, site, position, location, station.

sīve or seu [sī + -ve], conj., or

if, or. sīve — sīve, whether — or, be it that — or that, either — or, if — or if.

Smyrnaeī, -ōrum, [Smyrna], m., pl., people of Smyrna.

socer, -erī, m., father-in-law.

societās, -ātis, [socius], f., fellowship, association, union, society; league, alliance.

socius, -a, -um, [cf. sequor], adj., sharing, partaking, associated, allied. As subst., socius, -ī or -iī, m., fellow, partner, sharer; companion, associate, friend; ally, helper.

Sōcratēs, -is, m., Sōcratēs, Greek philosopher. SEN. 8.

Sōcraticus, -a, -um, adj., of or pertaining to Sōcratēs; Socratic.

sodālis, -is, adj., companionable, sociable, friendly. As subst., m. and f., companion, associate, intimate friend, comrade.

sōl, sōlis, m., sun; by metonymy, sunshine, sun's heat. sōle ūtī, to take a sun-bath.

sōlācium, -ī or -iī, n., comfort, solace, consolation.

solea, -ae, f., sole of the foot; sandal.

soleō, -ēre, solitus sum, 2, semidep., be accustomed, be wont, be used. ut fierī solet, as generally happens.

solidus, -a, -um, adj., undivided, entire; massive, dense, substantial, solid; sound, trustworthy, genuine.

sōlitārius, -a, -um, [sōlus], adj., alone, isolated, separate, lonely, solitary.

sōlitūdō, -inis, [sōlus], f., being alone, loneliness; lonely place, solitude, wilderness. **per sōlitūdinem**, *by themselves.*

sollemnis, -e, adj., *celebrated every year, annual, stated, established, appointed; religiously fixed, sacred, consecrated, festive, solemn; regular, wonted, common, usual, customary, habitual, ordinary.* As subst., **sollemne, -is,** n., *religious rite, sacrifice; festival, ceremony; custom, practice, habit.*

sollicitātiō, -ōnis, [sollicitō], f., *vexing, harassing, vexation; inciting, instigation, solicitation.*

sollicitō, -āre, -āvī, -ātum, [sollicitus], 1, a., *stir, agitate, move; trouble, harass; urge, incite, instigate, tempt, solicit; interest.*

sollicitūdō, -inis, [sollicitus], f., *apprehension, anxiety, solicitude.* **sollicitūdine afficī,** *to be distressed with anxiety.*

sollicitus, -a, -um, [unused **sollus,** = tōtus, + citus], adj., *agitated, disturbed; troubled, worried, anxious, alarmed; causing anxiety, alarming, distressing; uneasy, restless.* **sollicitum [-am] habēre,** *to keep in a state of anxiety.*

Solōn, -ōnis, m., *Solōn, Athenian lawgiver.* Sen. 8.

sōlor, -ārī, -ātus sum, 1, dep., *comfort, console, solace; soothe, lighten, lessen; relieve, mitigate.*

sōlstitiālis, -e, [sōlstitium, *stopping of the sun*], adj., *of the summer solstice, solstitial; of the sun, solar.* **sōlstitiālis orbs,** *a solar revolution.*

solum, -ī, n., *bottom, base, foundation; ground, soil, floor; by metonymy, country, region, place.*

sōlum [sōlus], adv., *only, merely.* **nōn sōlum,** *not only, not merely.*

sōlus, -a, -um, gen. **sōlīus,** dat. **sōlī,** adj., *alone, only, single; lonely, solitary, deserted, unfrequented.*

solūtus, -a, -um, [part. of solvō], adj., *unbound, free, loose; lax, negligent, careless, remiss.*

solvō, -ere, solvī, solūtum, [sē + luō], 3, a., *loose, unbind, release, disengage, free; break up, dismiss; relax, overcome; annul, make void, end; perform, keep, fulfill; pay, pay off; accomplish, complete; pay, discharge.*

somniculōsus, -a, -um, [somnīculus, dim. of **somnus**], adj., *inclined to sleep, drowsy, sleepy, sluggish.*

somnus, -ī, m., *sleep, slumber.*

sonāns, -antis, comp. **sonantior,** [part. of sonō], adj., *sounding, resounding, resonant.*

sonō, -āre, -uī, -itum, [sonus], 1, a. and n., *sound, resound; sing, celebrate; speak, utter, express.*

sonus, -ī, m., *sound, noise.*

Sophoclēs, -is, m., *Sophocles,* the Greek tragic writer (5th century B.C.). Sen. 7.

sordidus, -a, -um, [sordēs, *dirt*], adj., *dirty, unclean, foul, sordid; base, mean, humble; small, paltry; abject, vile, despicable, disgraceful; mean, niggardly, penurious.*

soror, -ōris, f., *sister.*

sortītus, -ūs, [sortior, *cast lots*], m., *casting of lots, drawing of lots.* **sortītū,** *by lot.*

sōspitō, -āre, ——, ——, [sōspēs, *safe*], 1, a., *save, keep safe, preserve, protect; prosper.*

Sp., see **Spurius.**

spargō, -ere, sparsī, sparsum, 3, a., *strew, scatter; casi, hurl; spread abroad, disperse, disseminate.*

spatiōsus, -a, -um, [spatium], adj., *at long intervals; roomy, spacious, extensive; long-continuing, prolonged.*

spatium, -ī or **-iī,** n., *space, distance, interval; room, extent; path, track; period, time.* **aliquid spatī,** *moment.* **spatium valētūdinis,** *long-continued sickness.*

speciēs, -ēī, [speciō], f., *aspect, sight, appearance; vision, apparition; beauty, splendor, show.* **plūrēs speciēs,** *variety of charges* (have been brought).

spectāculum, -ī, [spectō], n., *place from which one sees anything; spectator's seat, place in the theater; show, sight, spectacle.*

spectō, -āre, -āvī, -ātum, [freq. of **speciō,** *look*], 1, a., *look on, behold, observe; gaze at, inspect; face, lie, be situated; try, test, prove;* of games, *attend.* As subst., **spectantēs, -ium,** m., pl., *onlookers, observers.*

speculātor, -ōris, [speculor], m., *spy, scout, explorer.*

speculor, -ārī, -ātus sum, [specula, *watch-tower*], 1, dep., *spy out, watch, examine, explore.*

spērō, -āre, -āvī, -ātum, [spēs], 1, a., *hope, hope for, look for, expect; believe, trust.* **bene dē rē pūblicā spērāre,** *to have great hope for the state.*

spēs, speī, f., *hope, expectation; trust, promise; anticipation, prospect.* **in spem,** *in anticipation.*

omnia in spē habēre, *to have everything good in prospect.* **spem facere,** *to give grounds to expect.*

spīritus, -ūs, [spīrō, *breathe*], m., *breath, breathing;* by metonymy, *breeze, air; breath of a god, inspiration; breath of life, life, spirit; courage, haughtiness, pride.*

spīrō, -āre, -āvī, -ātum, 1, a. and n., *breathe, draw breath; breathe out, exhale, emit; live, be alive; be full of, be inspired with, aim at.* **ut spīrantis,** *as of a living man.*

splendēscō, -ere, ——, ——, [inch. of **splendeō,** *shine*], 3, n., *become bright, begin to shine; derive luster, shine.*

splendidē [splendidus], adv., *brightly, magnificently, splendidly, nobly, brilliantly.*

splendidus, -a, -um, comp. **splendidior,** sup. **splendidissimus,** [splendeō, *shine*], adj., *bright, glittering; brilliant, splendid, magnificent, illustrious, distinguished.*

splendor, -ōris, [cf. **splendeō**], m., *brightness, brilliancy; splendor, dignity, eminence, honor.*

spoliātiō, -ōnis, [spoliō], f., *pillaging, robbing, plundering; despoiling; unlawful deprivation.*

spoliō, -āre, -āvī, -ātum, [spolium], 1, a., *strip, uncover; rob, plunder, despoil, deprive.*

spolium, -ī or **-iī,** n., *skin, hide;* by metonymy, *arms* stripped from an enemy, *spoils, booty, prey.*

spondeō, -ēre, spopondī, spōnsum, 2, a. and n., *promise to contribute, promise sacredly, vow, give as-*

surance; stipulate, agree; engage, betroth; forebode.

spōns, found only in the abl. **sponte,** [cf. **spondeō**], f., *free will, accord.* **suā sponte,** *of one's own accord, of their own accord, freely, voluntarily.*

spōnsālia, -ium, [pl. adj. n. from **spōnsus**], n., pl., *betrothal, espousal, wedding.*

Spurius, -ī or -iī, abbreviated **Sp.,** [**spurius,** *illegitimate*], m., *Spurius,* Roman forename.

squālor, -ōris, [**squāleō,** *be rigid*], m., *roughness, dirtiness, filthiness, foulness, squalor; neglected raiment, filthy garments; mourning.*

Stabiae, -ārum, f., pl., *Stabiae,* town of Campania, near Pompeii. See Map following page 6.

stabiliō, -īre, -īvī, -ītum, [**stabilis**], 4, a., *make firm, stay, support; fix, establish, secure.*

stabilis, -e, [**stō**], adj., *firm, steadfast, stable, fixed; lasting, enduring, secure.*

stabilitās, -ātis, [**stabilis**], f., *steadfastness, stability, durability, security.*

Statilius, -ī or -iī, m., *L. Statilius,* a man of equestrian rank who joined the conspiracy of Catiline. He was arrested and executed along with the other conspirators in December, 63 B.C. CAT. 3, 3, *et seq.;* SALL. 55.

statim [**stō**], adv., *steadily, regularly; forthwith, straightway, instantly, immediately, at once.*

statiō, -ōnis, [**stō**], f., *act of standing; standing place, post, position; guard, sentinels, outposts; harbor, bay, inlet.*

Stātius, -ī or -iī, m., *Caecilius Stātius,* Roman comic poet. SEN. 11.

stator, -ōris, [cf. **sistō, stō**], m., *stay, supporter, protector;* used as an epithet of Jupiter, *Iuppiter Stator.* LIV. 1, 12.

statua, -ae, [**stō**], f., *image, statue.*

statuō, -ere, statuī, statūtum, [**status**], 3, a., *set up, erect, construct, make; establish, fix; resolve, determine, decide, settle.*

status, -ūs, [**stō**], m., *standing, posture; position, attitude; state, situation, condition, constitution.*

sternō, -ere, strāvī, strātum, 3, a., *spread out, extend; strew, scatter; prepare, arrange; lay low, throw to the ground, prostrate; raze, level; cast down.* **sternī iubet sibi,** *he orders a couch to be prepared.*

Stēsichorus, -ī, m., *Stēsichorus,* Greek lyric poet (*circa* 608 B.C.) of Sicily.

stilus, -ī, m., *column, pillar; pointed stake, pointed instrument; iron pen, stylus, pencil.*

stimulō, -āre, -āvī, -ātum, [**stimulus**], 1, a., *goad, rouse, incite, stimulate; torment, vex, disturb.*

stimulus, -ī, m., *goad, prick; spur, incentive, encouragement; torment, pain.*

stīpendiārius, -a, -um, [**stīpendium**], adj., *of tribute, liable to tribute, tributary; receiving tribute, receiving pay, serving for pay, mercenary.* As subst., **stīpendiārius,** -ī or -iī, m., *tributary.*

stīpendium, -ī or -iī, [**stips,** *gift,* cf. **pendō**], n., *tax, tribute; income,* *pay, bounty; military service, campaigning.*

stīpō, -āre, -āvī, -ātum, 1, a., *stuff, fill full; crowd together, pack, throng; accompany.*

stirps, stirpis, f., *trunk, stem, stalk; race, family; offspring, descendant; source, origin, beginning.*

stō, stāre, stetī, statum, 1, n., *stand; stand up, be upright; stand firm, abide, endure, continue; stand still, delay, linger; remain, be fixed, be determined.* sī in eō stat, *if he persists in this, if he remains firm in this.*

Stōicus, -a, -um, adj., *of or pertaining to the Stoics, Stoic, Stoical.* As subst., Stōicus, -ī, m., *Stoic, the Stoic.* See Companion, page 547.

stomachus, -ī, m., *oesophagus by which food is conveyed to the stomach; gullet, stomach, windpipe; taste, liking; temper, bile, displeasure; irritation, vexation, chagrin, anger.*

strāgēs, -is, [cf. sternō], f., *throwing or striking down; overthrow, ruin, slaughter, massacre; disordered mass, wreck.*

strātum, -ī, [n. part. of sternō], n., *covering, horse-cloth; bed-covering, quilt, pillow; bed, couch.*

strēnuē [strēnuus], adv., *briskly, promptly, actively, strenuously.*

strēnuus, -a, -um, adj., *brisk, active, vigorous, strenuous, ready for work; brave.*

strepitus, -ūs, [strepō], m., *noise, din, clash, crash, murmur, rattling.*

struō, -ere, strūxī, strūctum, 3, a., *place together, join together, heap up; build, erect, construct; set*

in order, arrange; draw up; cause, occasion, contrive, instigate; order, dispose, regulate.

studeō, -ēre, -uī, ——, 2, a. and n., *be eager, be zealous, be devoted; strive after, desire, wish; study, go to school.* novīs rēbus studēre, *to be eager for a revolution, to be desirous of a revolution.*

studiōsē [studiōsus], adv., *eagerly, zealously, devotedly, studiously, carefully.*

studiōsus, -a, -um, [studium], adj., *eager, zealous, assiduous, devoted, studious; friendly, favorable.* As subst., studiōsī, -ōrum, m., pl., *students, scholars, those interested in* or *devoted to study.*

studium, -ī or -iī, [studeō], n., *zeal, desire, inclination, enthusiasm, endeavor; pursuit, inquiry, study, research; good-will, devotion, attachment; interest;* in plural, studia, *learning.* quicquid studī, *whatever enthusiasm.* studium litterārum, *an interest in literature.* studium reī pūblicae, *patriotism.*

stultē, comp. stultius, sup. stultissimē, [stultus], adv., *foolishly, stupidly.*

stultitia, -ae, [stultus], f., *folly, foolishness, simplicity, silliness, fatuity.*

stultus, -a, -um, adj., *foolish, simple; stupid, dull, silly.*

stuprum, -ī, n., *defilement, disgrace, outrage; debauchery, lewdness.* stuprī vetus cōnsuētūdō, *liaison of long standing.*

Suāda, -ae, f., *Suāda, goddess of persuasion.* Suādae medulla, *the very marrow of eloquence.*

suādeō, -ēre, suāsī, suāsum, 2, a. and n., *advise, recommend; exhort, urge, impel, persuade.* mihi suādeō, *I am persuaded.*

suāvis, -e, adj., *sweet, agreeable, grateful, pleasant.*

suāvitās, -ātis, [suāvis], f., *sweetness, pleasantness; agreeableness, attractiveness; suavity.*

sub, prep. with acc. and abl., *under:*

(1) With acc., after verbs of motion, *under, below, near to, to, up to, towards, down into; until, about, just before; following, after, just after.*

(2) With abl., of place, *under, beneath, below, behind, at the foot of, by, near;* of time, *during, in, within, at, by, in the time of;* of other relations, *under, in the power of, subject to; by reason of, in consequence of.*

In composition, sub is often assimilated before m, r, and usually before c, f, g, p. It adds the force of *under, beneath; somewhat, a little; secretly, by stealth.*

subdolus, -a, -um, [sub + dolus, trick], adj., *somewhat crafty, cunning, sly, deceptive, deceitful.*

subeō, -īre, -īvī or -iī, -itum, [sub + eō], irr., a. and n., *go under, enter; advance, draw near; come after, succeed; come up, occur, suggest itself; undergo, submit to, be subject to, endure, suffer.*

subiaceō, -ēre, -iacuī, ——, [sub + iaceō], 2, n., *lie below* or *near.*

subiciō, -icere, -iēcī, -iectum, [sub + iaciō], 3, a., *throw under, place under; submit, present,*

give; subordinate; subjoin, append; forge, counterfeit.

subiector, -ōris, [subiciō], m., *forger.*

subigō, -ere, subēgī, subāctum, [sub + agō], 3, a., *bring under; subdue, conquer, subjugate, reduce.*

subitō [subitus], adv., *suddenly, unexpectedly.*

subitus, -a, -um, [subeō], adj., *sudden, unexpected, surprising.*

sublevō, -āre, -āvī, -ātum, [sub + levō], 1, a., *lift from beneath, raise up, support; lighten, alleviate, assuage; encourage, console, relieve, help.*

sublīmis, -e, adj., *uplifted, high, exalted; aloft, in a high position; eminent, distinguished.*

subolēs, -is, f., *sprout, shoot; offspring, posterity, stock, race.*

subsellium, -ī or -iī, [sub + sella], n., *low bench, seat, form; court, tribunal.*

subsequor, -ī, -cūtus sum, [sub + sequor], 3, dep., *follow after, follow up; follow, adhere to, comply with, conform to; imitate.*

subsidium, -ī or -iī, [sub + sedeō], n., *reserve force; aid, help, assistance, support, protection.*

subsīdō, -ere, -sēdī, -sessum, [sub + sīdō], 3, n., *sit down; settle down, sink down, subside; remain, abide, stay; lie in wait, lie in ambush.*

subsistō, -ere, -stitī, ——, [sub + sistō], 3, n., *cause to stop; take a stand, remain standing, halt; remain, stay; stand firm, hold out, resist; end, pause, cease.*

subsum, -esse, ——, ——, [sub + sum], irr., n., *be under; be near at hand, be near; impend, approach; be concealed, lurk in, be in reserve.*

subtīliter, comp. **subtīlius,** sup. **subtīlissimē,** [**subtīlis,** *precise*], adv., *acutely, minutely, accurately, in detail; plainly, simply, without adornment.* **subtīliter iūdicāre,** *to be a shrewd judge.*

suburbānus, -a, -um, [**sub** + **urbānus**], adj., *near the city, near Rome, suburban.* As subst., **suburbānum** [sc. **praedium**], **-ī,** n., *an estate near Rome, suburban villa.*

subveniō, -īre, -vēnī, -ventum, [**sub** + **veniō**], 4, n., *come to the help of, aid, assist, obviate, remedy, cure.*

succēdō, -ere, successī, successum, [**sub** + **cēdō**], 3, a. and n., *come under, enter; approach, draw near, come to; follow, succeed, take the place of; be successful, prosper.*

succīdia, -ae, [**succīdō,** *cut from under*], f., *leg of pork, flitch of bacon.* **succīdia altera,** *second meat-supply.*

succurrō, -ere, -currī, -cursum, [**sub** + **currō**], 3, n., *run to, run under, run to help; help, relieve; come to mind, suggest itself.*

Suētōnius, -iī, m., *C. Suētōnius Tranquillus,* biographer of the first twelve Roman emperors, friend of the younger Pliny. He flourished in the first half of the first century A.D.

sufferō, -ferre, sustulī, sublātum, [**sub** + **ferō**], irr., a., *undergo, endure, suffer.*

sufficiō, -ere, -fēcī, -fectum, [**sub**

+ **faciō**], 3, a. and n., *substitute, put under, lay the foundation for; dip, dye, tinge; choose as a substitute; give, yield, afford, supply; be sufficient, suffice, avail, be adequate, satisfy.*

suī, sibī, sē or **sēsē,** reflex. pron., *himself, herself, itself, themselves; him, her, it,* etc. **inter sē,** *mutually, reciprocally, one another, each other.*

Sulla, -ae, m., *Sulla,* name of a patrician family of the Cornelian gens. The most distinguished member was *L. Cornēlius Sulla,* the dictator, born 138 B.C. He served with distinction under Marius, first in the Jugurthine War, afterwards, 104–101 B.C., in the campaigns against the Teutones and Cimbri. He became a leader of the aristocratic party, defeated his enemies, and in 82 B.C. was made dictator. After two years of absolute government, in which he introduced many reforms, he retired from the dictatorship, and died the following year, 78 B.C. CAT. 2, 9, *et al.;* SALL. 5; PHIL. 8.

Sullānus, -a, -um, adj., *relating to Sulla, of Sulla, Sullan.*

Sulpicius, -a, name of a Roman gens, at first patrician, afterwards including plebeian families also. Three of the name are mentioned in this book :

(1) *C. Sulpicius Gallus,* consul in 166 B.C. He was an accomplished orator and man of letters and a student of Greek literature. He was likewise deeply versed in astrology. In

168 B.C. he served as tribune of the soldiers under Aemilius Paulus in Macedonia, and during this campaign predicted the eclipse of the moon. Sen. 14.

(2) *C. Sulpicius,* praetor 63 B.C. Cat. **3, 3.**

(3) *P. Sulpicius Rūfus,* born 124 B.C., tribune of the people 88 B.C. At first he supported the aristocratic party. Afterwards he joined Marius, with whom he fled on the approach of Sulla, but was captured and murdered. Cat. **3,** 10.

sulpur, -uris, n., *brimstone, sulphur.*

sum, esse, fui, fut. part. futūrus, irr., n., *be, exist; stay; fall;* with gen., *belong to, be the part* or *duty of, be possessed of, be valued at, cost;* with dative, *be for, serve for, belong to, possess, have.* id quod tum hominum erat, *existing population.* eī quī nunc sunt, *present generation.* est fideī, *it is a part of (our) good faith.* erat centum mīlium nummum, *it was worth a hundred thousand sesterces.* hominis est *it is the part of a real man.*

summa, -ae, [properly f. of summus, sc. rēs], f., *chief place, highest rank, leadership; sum, aggregate, whole; main thing, chief reason; sum total.* ad trecentōrum summam, *to the total of three hundred.*

summātim [summa], adv., *summarily, briefly, in brief; generally.*

summittō, -ere, -mīsī, -missum, [sub + mittō], 3, a., *let down, lower, sink, drop; reduce, moderate;*

bring down, humble, surrender. sē summittere, *to condescend, to be modest.*

summus, -a, -um, see superus.

sūmō, -ere, sūmpsī, sūmptum, [sub + emō], 3, a., *take, lay hold of; assume, take on; consume, spend; enter upon, begin; exact; obtain, acquire; select, choose.* mūtuus sūmptus, *obtained as a loan, borrowed, lent.*

sūmptuōsē [sūmptuōsus], adv., *expensively, sumptuously.*

sūmptuōsus, -a, -um, [sūmptus], adj., *expensive, costly, sumptuous; wasteful, extravagant.*

sūmptus, -ūs, [sūmō], m., *expenditure, expense, cost, outlay.* sūmptum facere, *to be at an expense, to make an expenditure.*

suōpte, strengthened form of suō, suā. See -pte.

super, adv. and prep., *above, over.*

(1) Adv., *above, over; besides, moreover, thereupon; in addition, more.*

(2) Prep., with acc. or abl., *over, upon, on; concerning.*

superbia, -ae, [superbus], f., *haughtiness, pride, arrogance, insolence; conceit, vanity; rudeness, discourtesy; high spirit.*

superbus, -a, -um, [super], adj., *haughty, proud, arrogant, domineering.*

superior, see superus.

supernē [supernus, *that is above*], adv., *from above, above, upwards; over the top of the shield.*

superō, -āre, -āvī, -ātum, [superus], 1, a. and n., *rise above, overtop, surmount, transcend; exceed, be abundant; surpass, outstrip;*

overcome, subdue, defeat, suppress, conquer.

superstitiō, -ōnis, [**superstes,** *standing by*], f., *dread of the supernatural, credulous wonder, anxious credulity, superstition; superstitious rite; object of dread.*

supersum, -esse, -fuī, [**super +** **sum**], irr., n., *be left, remain over* or *from, remain; live after, survive, outlive, be still alive.* **quod superest,** *as for the rest; the future.* **superest ut,** *it remains that.*

superus, -a, -um, comp. **superior,** sup. **suprēmus** or **summus,** [**super**], adj., *above, upper, higher.* **superior, -ius,** *higher, upper; former, previous, preceding; past, earlier; superior.* Sup., **suprēmus, -a, -um,** *highest, loftiest, topmost; last, final; extreme, utmost, outermost;* sup. **summus,** *highest, topmost; greatest, best, utmost, extreme;* often used of a part, as **summus mōns,** *the top of the mountain.* **ad summam senectūtem,** *in extreme old age.* Comp. as subst., **superiōrēs, -um,** m., pl., *men of the older time, elders;* **superiōrēs,** *those in a superior position.*

supervacāneus, -a, -um, [**super +** **vacuus**], adj., *over and above, needless, superfluous, redundant.*

suppeditō, -āre, -āvī, -ātum, [**sub +** **pēs**], 1, a. and n., *furnish, provide, supply freely; abound, be in store, be at hand.*

suppetō, -ere, -īvī or **-iī, -ītum,** [**sub + petō**], 3, n., *be at hand, be in store, be available; be sufficient for, be equal to.*

supplex, -icis, [**sub,** cf. **plicō**], adj. *bending the knee, begging, entreating; submissive, suppliant.* As subst., m., *suppliant, petitioner.*

supplicātiō, -ōnis, [**supplicō**], f., *public supplication, public thanksgiving, day of prayer.*

supplicium, -ī, or **-iī,** [**supplex**], n., *entreaty, supplication; kneeling* for punishment, *punishment, penalty, torture, torment.* **summum supplicium,** *severest punishment.* **supplicium dē aliquō sūmere,** *to inflict punishment on anyone.*

supplicō, -āre, -āvī, -ātum, [**supplex**], 1, n., *kneel down before anyone; humble oneself, pray humbly, beseech, implore, supplicate.*

supprimō, -ere, -pressī, -pressum, [**sub + premō**], 3, a., *press down; sink, send to bottom; keep back, withhold; check, restrain; conceal, suppress.*

suprā [for **superā,** abl. f. of **superus,** properly sc. **parte**], adv. and prep.

(1) As adv., *above, on top, over.*

(2) As prep., with acc., *over, above, beyond, more than.* **suprā quam,** *more than.*

suprēmus, see **superus.**

Sura, -ae, m., *L. Licinius Sura,* intimate friend of Trajan, and three times consul, in 92, 102, and 107 A.D. On his death Trajan honored him with a public funeral. He was responsible in great part for the success of Trajan's Dacian campaigns. PLIN. 13.

surgō, -ere, surrēxī, surrēctum,

[sub + regō], 3, a. and n., *rise, get up, stand up.*

surripiō, -ere, -ripuī, -reptum, [sub + rapiō], 3, a., *snatch away, take secretly, steal; take by treachery, take by surprise.*

succēnseō, -ēre, -uī, ——, [succēnsus, from succendō], 2, n., *be angry, be provoked.*

suscipiō, -cipere, -cēpī, susceptum, [subs, old form of sub, + capiō], 3, a., *take up; undertake, begin, enter upon; incur, undergo, submit to, suffer, bear.* bellum suscipere, *to commence war.*

suspectus, -a, -um, [part. of suspiciō], adj., *mistrusted, suspected, subject to suspicion.*

suspēnsus, -a, -um, [part. of suspendō, hang up], adj., *raised, elevated; uncertain, doubtful, hesitating, in suspense, anxious.* suspēnsum et anxium, *cause of suspense and anxiety.*

suspīciō, -ōnis, [suspiciō], f., *mistrust, suspicion, distrust.*

suspīciōsus, -a, -um, [suspīciō, suspicion], adj., *full of suspicion, mistrustful, ready to suspect, suspicious; causing mistrust, arousing suspicion.*

suspicor, -ārī, -ātus sum, [sub, cf. speciō], 1, dep., *mistrust, distrust, suspect; surmise, suppose.*

suspīrō, -āre, -āvī, -ātum, [sub + spīrō], 1, a. and n., *exhale, draw a deep breath; heave a sigh, sigh for, long for.*

sustentō, -āre, -āvī, -ātum, [freq. of sustineō], 1, a., *hold up, sustain; hold out, endure, suffer, bear; put off, defer, delay.*

sustineō, -ēre, sustinuī, sustentum, [subs, old form of sub, + teneō], 2, a., *hold up, bear up, support, sustain; hold in, control, check; bear, undergo, endure, hold out.*

suus, -a, -um, [cf. suī], poss. pron. adj., *his, her, its, their, his own, their own; own, peculiar, just, suitable, favorable; dear, beloved; self-possessed, composed.* As subst., suī, -ōrum, m., pl., *one's people, friends, relatives, party.* sua, -ōrum, n., pl., *one's possessions, one's property.*

Synnas, -adis, f., *Synnas, Phrygian city.*

Syrācūsae, -ārum, f., pl., *Syracuse, famous city in Sicily.*

Syrācūsānus, -a, -um, adj., *of Syracuse, Syracusan.* As subst., Syrācūsānus, -ī, m., *man of Syracuse, Syracusan.*

Syria, -ae, [Συρία], f., *Syria, a country lying east of the Mediterranean Sea, between Cilicia and Palestine; organized into a Roman province 64 B.C.*

T

T., see Titus.

tabella, -ae, [dim. of tabula], f., *tablet; writing-tablet, juror's tablet, vote;* pl. often *writing, letter, dispatch.*

tabellārius, -a, -um, [tabella], adj., *of a tablet.* As subst., tabellārius, -ī or -iī, m., *letter-carrier, messenger, courier.*

tabernāculum, -ī, [taberna, hut], n., *tent.* in tabernāculō, *under canvas.*

tābēscō, -ere, tābuī, ——, [tābeō,

waste away], 3, inch., *melt, decay, decompose; pine away, languish, waste away.*

tabula, -ae, f., *board, plank; tablet, writing-tablet; writing, record, memorandum, account; picture, painting.* **tabulae pūblicae,** *public records.*

tabulārium, -ī or **-iī,** [tabula], n., *depository of records, archives.*

taceō, -ēre, -uī, -itum, 2, a. and n., *be silent, keep silence; pass over in silence, leave unsaid.*

tacitē [tacitus], adv., *silently, in silence.*

taciturnitās, -ātis, [taciturnus], f., *keeping silent, silence.*

tacitus, -a, -um, [part. of taceō], adj., *silent, passed in silence; concealed, hidden, secret; still, mute, noiseless.*

Tacitus, -ī, m., *Roman proper name*; esp., *Cornēlius Tacitus.* He was born early in Nero's reign, and began his official career, as quaestor, not later than 79 A.D. Praetor under Domitian, Tacitus rose to the consulship as Nerva's colleague, 97 A.D. In the following year he published the biography of Agricola, his father-in-law. Then followed the works that have made him famous, the Histories and Annals, presenting the history of the Roman Empire from the death of Augustus down to that of Domitian. It is most probable that Tacitus died about 115 A.D.

taedet, -ēre, taeduit, taesum est, 2, a., *it excites loathing, disgusts,* *offends, wearies.* **mē taedet,** *I am disgusted.*

taeter, -tra, -trum, comp. **taetrior,** sup. **taeterrimus,** adj., *offensive, loathsome, foul; repulsive, shameful, abominable, base.*

tālāris, -e, [tālus, *ankle*], adj., *of the ankles, reaching to the ankles.*

tālis, -e, pron. adj., *such, of such a kind; such as this, as follows; of so especial a kind, so distinguished.* **tālis — quālis,** *such — as.* **nē quid tāle,** *that no such thing.*

tam, adv., *so much, to such a degree, so, so very.* **tam — quam,** *so — as, as much — as.*

tamen, adv., *notwithstanding, nevertheless, be this as it may, for all that; however, yet, still.* **quī tamen,** *although he.*

tametsī [for tamen etsī], conj., *although, though, notwithstanding that; and yet.*

tamquam [tam + quam], adv., *just as, as if; as it were, just as if, as much as.*

tandem [tam + -dem], adv., *at length, at last, finally; in questions, pray now, now, I pray.*

tangō, -ere, tetigī, tāctum, 3, a., *touch; border on, adjoin; arrive at, come to; move, affect, impress;* of lightning, *strike.*

tantō opere, see **opus.**

tantum [tantus], adv., *so much, so greatly, to such a degree; only so much, only, merely.*

tantum modo, adv., *only, merely.*

tantus, -a, -um, adj., *of such size, so great, such; so very great, so important; only so much, so trivial, so small.* As subst., **tan-**

cum, -ī, n., *so much.* tantī, gen. of price, *of such a price, of so great value; of so little account, of so slight importance.* est mihi tantī, *it is well worth while for me, it is well worth my while.* tantō, abl. of degree of difference, *by so much, so much.* tantus — quantus, *so much — as, so great — as.*

tardē, comp. tardius, sup. tardissimē, [tardus], adv., *slowly, late.* Sup., *latest, very late.*

tarditās, -ātis, [tardus], f., *slowness, tardiness.*

tardō, -āre, -āvī, -ātum, [tardus], 1, a. and n., *make slow, hinder, delay, retard; linger, tarry.*

tardus, -a, -um, comp. tardior, sup., tardissimus, adj., *slow, sluggish; late, delaying; dull, heavy, stupid.* tardior, *unusually dull.*

Tarentīnus, -a, -um, [Tarentum], adj., *Tarentine, of Tarentum,* important Greek city on the Gulf of Tarentum. As subst., Tarentīnī, -ōrum, m., pl., *people of Tarentum.*

Tarentum, -ī, n., *Tarentum,* important city in southern Italy, now Taranto.

Tarpeia, -ae, f., *Tarpeia,* betrayer of the arx at Rome. LIV. 1, 11.

Tarpeius, -ī, m., *Spurius Tarpeius,* Roman officer, commander of the citadel. LIV. 1, 11.

Tarquinius, -ī or -iī, m., *L. Tarquinius,* last king of Rome, who won for himself the surname of *Superbus* because of his cruelty and tyrany. LIV. 2, 1.

Tarsus, -ī, f., *Tarsus,* chief city of Cilicia, birthplace of the Apostle Paul.

Tascus, -ī, m., *Tascus,* husband of Rectina, imperiled by the eruption of Vesuvius. PLIN. 12.

Tatius, -ī or -iī, m., *Titus Tatius,* Sabine king, later colleague of Romulus. LIV. 1, 10.

taurus, -ī, m., *bull, bullock, steer.*

tēctum, -ī, [tegō], n., *covered place, shelter; house, dwelling; covering, roof.*

tegō, -ere, tēxī, tēctum, 3, a., *cover; hide, conceal, shelter; cloak, veil; protect, guard.*

tēlum, -ī, n., *missile, spear, dart, javelin, arrow;* by metonymy, *sword, ax, dagger, weapon.* quid tēlōrum, *any weapons.* sī quid tēlōrum, *whatever weapons.*

Temenītēs, -is, m., epithet of Apollo at Syracuse, derived from Temenos, name of a place near the city, where there was a statue of him.

temere, adv., *by chance, at random, without design; rashly, heedlessly, thoughtlessly, recklessly.*

temeritās, -ātis, [temere], f., *chance, accident; rashness, recklessness, indiscretion, foolhardiness.*

temperantia, -ae, [temperāns], f., *moderation, discretion, self-control, temperance.*

temperō, -āre, -āvī, -ātum, [tempus], 1, a. and n., *be moderate, control oneself, forbear, be temperate; control, rule, govern, regulate, restrain.*

tempestās, -ātis, [tempus], f., *period, time, season; weather, bad weather, storm, tempest; calamity, misfortune.*

tempestīvus, -a, -um, [tempestās], adj., *seasonable, opportune, timely; appropriate, fitting, suitable; in good season, early.*

templum, -ī, n., *consecrated place, sacred inclosure, sanctuary; temple, shrine, fane.* templa, -ōrum, sometimes *spaces* marked out *for the taking of auspices.*

temptō, -āre, -āvī, -ātum, [intensive of tendō], 1, a., *handle, touch, feel; try, attempt, essay; attack, assail.*

tempus, -oris, n., *period of time, time, season, point of time; right time, opportunity, occasion; condition, times, circumstances; time of need, exigency, emergency.* id temporis, *at that time.* ex tempore, *offhand, without preparation.* temporis causā, *to serve the interests of the moment, for interested motives, to suit the occasion.* suō tempore, *at the right time.* difficillimō tempore, *at a most critical period.* prō tempore atque perīculō, *suited to the present crisis and peril.* prīmō quōque tempore, *at the earliest possible moment.*

tendō, -ere, tetendī, tentum and tēnsum, 3, a. and n., *stretch out, stretch, extend; hold a course, direct one's course, go, proceed; aim at, strive, endeavor; bend one's course.* magnā vī tendere, *to exert oneself vigorously.*

tenebrae, -ārum, f., pl., *darkness, gloom; darkness of night, night.*

Tenedos or Tenedus, -ī, [Τένεδος], f., *Tenedos,* island in the Aegean Sea, near the coast of

Troas. ARCH. 9. apud Tenedum, *off Tenedos.*

teneō, -ēre, -uī, tentum, 2, a. and n., *hold, have, keep; possess, be master of, occupy; grasp firmly, hold fast, fetter, bind; restrain, check, guard, preserve, defend.*

tener, -a, -um, adj., *soft, delicate, tender.* As subst., tenerī, -ōrum, m., pl., *the young, boys, youths.* quamlibet tenerī, *the very young, the exceedingly young.*

tenuis, -e, adj., *thin, fine; narrow, slight, insignificant; mean, poor, weak.*

ter [cf. trēs], num. adv., *thrice, three times.*

Terentia, -ae, f., *Terentia,* wife of Cicero, to whom she was married about 80 B.C. She was a woman of strong character, and had a large property. Cicero divorced her in 46 B.C. She is said to have married again and to have lived to be over a hundred years old. EP. 1; 3; 14; 17; 18; 19.

Terentiānus, -a, -um, adj., *of Terence, Terentian, occurring in Terence.* verbum Terentiānum, *the saying in Terence.* AM. 24.

Terentius, -ī or -iī, m., *P. Terentius Afer,* Roman writer of comedy, friend of Laelius and Scipio. AM. 24.

tergum, -ī, n., *back, back part, reverse, rear; skin, hide, leather.* ā tergō, *from the rear, from behind, in the rear.*

terminō, -āre, -āvī, -ātum, [terminus], 1, a., *bound, limit; set limits to, circumscribe; close, end, finish, terminate.*

ternī, -ae, -a, [ter], adj. num. distr., *three each, three, triple.*

terra, -ae, f., *land,* as opposed to the water; *soil, ground, region, country; earth.* **orbis terrae** or **terrārum,** *the world, the whole world.* **terrā marīque,** *by land and sea.*

terrestris, -e, [terra], adj., *of the earth, on earth, on land, terrestrial; earthly.*

terribilis, -e, [terreō], adj., *frightful, dreadful, terrible.*

terror, -ōris, [cf. terreō], m., *fright, alarm, terror, overwhelming fear;* by metonymy, *cause of fright, dread; terrible news.*

tertiō [tertius], adv., *for the third time.* **iterum ac tertiō,** *twice again, twice more.*

tertius, -a, -um, or **III.,** [ter], num. adj., *third.*

Testa, -ae, m., *C. Trebātius Testa,* eminent jurist, a friend of Cicero and of Caesar. He wrote on legal subjects, but his writings have perished. EP. 10.

testāmentum, -ī, [testor], n., *will, testament.*

testimōnium, -ī or **-iī,** [testis], n., *evidence, attestation, testimony, proof.*

testis, -is, m. and f., *witness.*

testor, -ārī, -ātus sum, [testis], 1, *cause to serve as a witness, call to witness, appeal to, invoke; declare.*

theātrum, -ī, n., *play-house, theater; parade-ground; audience; stage.*

Themistoclēs, -ī or **-is,** [Θεμιστο-κλῆς], m., *Themistoclēs,* the great leader of the Athenians and of

Greece in the wars with Persia. SEN. 7; AM. 12.

Theophanēs, -is, [Θεοφάνης], m., *Cn. Pompeius Theóphanēs,* a learned Greek, native of Mytilene. He became an intimate friend of Pompey, whose name he took. He accompanied Pompey, who considered his advice of much weight, in a number of campaigns. After the battle of Pharsalia he returned to Italy, and was pardoned by Caesar. He appears to have outlived both Caesar and Cicero. ARCH. 10.

Thespiae, -ārum, f., pl., *Thespiae,* a town of Boeotia, at the foot of Mt. Helicon.

Thespiēnsis, -e, [Thespiae], adj., *in* or *from Thespiae.* As subst., **Thespiēnsēs, -ium,** m., pl., *the people of Thespiae.*

Thrēcēs, -um, m., pl., *Thracians.*

Ti., see Tiberius.

Tib., see Tiberius.

Tiberīnus, -a, -um, [Tiberis], adj., *of the Tiber.*

Tiberis, -is, m., *Tiber,* the great river of western Italy, on which Rome is situated; now **Tevere.**

Tiberius, -ī or **-iī,** abbreviated **Ti.** or **Tib.,** m., *Tiberius,* Roman forename.

Tigrānēs, -is, [Τιγράνης], m., *Tigrănēs,* king of Armenia and neighboring regions, and son-in-law of Mithridates, whom he assisted in the wars with Rome. He surrendered to Pompey 66 B.C., who left him the government of Armenia proper and the title of king. IMP. P. 2, *et al.*

timeō, -ēre, -uī, ——, 2, a. and n.,

be afraid, be fearful; be apprehensive, be anxious; dread, fear.
alicui timēre, to fear for the safety of anyone.

timidē [timidus], adv., fearfully, timidly.

timidus, -a, -um, [timeō], adj., afraid, fearful, timid, cowardly.

Tīmōn, -ōnis, m., Tīmōn, famous misanthrope (hater of mankind) of Athens. Tīmōnem nesciō quem, a certain Timon. Am. 23.

timor, -ōris, [cf. timeō], m., fear, dread, apprehension, alarm, timidity; awe, reverence.

tīrō, -ōnis, m., newly levied soldier, young soldier, recruit; beginner, tiro.

Tīrō, -ōnis, [tīrō, recruit], m., Tīrō, at first a slave of Cicero, then set free and given the name M. Tullius Tīrō. Being a man of ability and culture, he became the confidential secretary and literary assistant of the orator. He also wrote works of his own. He is said to have collected and published Cicero's letters. A system of short-hand was credited to him as inventor. Ep. 13.

tīrunculus, -ī, [dim. of tīrō], m., young beginner, mere beginner, young recruit; novice.

tītillātio, -ōnis, [tītillō, tickle], f., tickling, titillation; relish.

titulus, -ī, n., superscription, inscription; label, title; placard, notice.

Titus, -ī, abbreviated T., m., Titus, Roman forename, said to be of Sabine origin.

toga, -ae, [tegō], f., toga, gown, an outer robe of white woolen stuff, worn by Roman citizens when not engaged in military pursuits; hence, peace. ad togās redīre, to return to the garb of peace.

togātus, -a, -um, [toga], adj., wearing the toga, clad in the toga; in the garb of peace, in civil life, as a civilian.

tolerābilis, -e, [tolerō], adj., bearable, endurable, tolerable.

tolerō, -āre, -āvī, -ātum, [cf. tollō], 1, a., bear, endure, sustain, suffer.

tollō, -ere, sustulī, sublātum, 3, a., lift, lift up, raise, elevate; bring up, educate; make away with, remove, dispose of; ruin, destroy. sublātō auctōre, suppressing the name of (one's) authority.

tonitrus, -ūs, [tonō, thunder], m., thunder. fragor et tonitrus, peals of thunder.

tormentum, -ī, [torqueō], n., engine for hurling stones; missile, shot; instrument of torture, rack; torture, anguish, pain, torment.

torpeō, -ēre, ——, ——, 2, n., be stiff, be numb, be inactive; be stupid, be dull; be paralyzed, be suspended.

Torquātus, -i, m., a Roman surname. See Mānlius (1) and (3).

tortuōsus, -a, -um, [tortus, twisted], adj., full of turns, winding; intricate, involved, complicated, confused; tortuous, wily.

tot, num. adj., indecl., so many, in such numbers.

totidem [tot + -dem], adj. num., just so many, just as many, the same number of.

totiēns [tot], num. adv., *so often, as often, so many times.*

tōtus, -a, -um, gen. **tōtīus,** adj., *all, the whole, total, entire, all;* used where the English idiom prefers an adv., *altogether, wholly, entirely, fully.*

trāctātus, -ūs, [trāctō], m., *handling, management, treatment.* **ipsō trāctātū,** *from the mere handling of the matter.*

trāctō, -āre, -āvī, -ātum, [freq. of trahō], 1, a., *draw, pull; touch, handle; manage, practice, conduct, control; treat.*

trādō, -ere, trādidī, trāditum, [trāns + dō], 3, a., *deliver, surrender, hand over; commit, intrust, confide; give over, betray; transmit, relate.* **sē trādere,** *to give oneself up to, surrender, devote oneself to.*

tragoedia, -ae, [τραγῳδία, *goat song*], f., *tragedy; art of tragedy.*

trahō, -ere, trāxī, trāctum, 3, a., *draw, drag; draw in, take on, assume; lead on, attract, influence; get, obtain, derive; protract, extend.*

Traiānus, -ī, m., *M. Traiānus Ulpius,* Roman emperor, 98 to 117 A.D., of Spanish birth, served with distinction in the East and in Germany. Consul in 91, at the close of 97 he was adopted by the emperor Nerva. In the following year Trajan succeeded to the empire. He died in 117 A.D. after successful military operations in Dacia and against the Armenians and Parthians. Plin. 16, 17.

tranquillitās, -ātis, [tranquillus], f., *quietness, stillness, calmness; tranquillity, serenity.*

tranquillus, -a, -um, adj., *quiet, still, calm, tranquil; peaceful, undisturbed, serene.*

trāns, prep. with acc., *across, over, beyond.* In composition **trāns** stands as **trān-,** rarely **trāns-,** before **s**; **trāns-,** or **trā-,** before **i, d, l, m, n**; **trāns-,** rarely **trā-,** before **f, v**; and remains unchanged before the other letters.

Trānsalpīnus, -a, -um, [trāns + Alpīnus], adj., *beyond the Alps, Transalpine.* Cf. **Gallia.**

trānscendō, -ere, trānscendī, trānscēnsum, [trāns + scandō], 3, a. and n., *climb over, pass over, surmount; overstep, transgress.*

trānseō, -īre, -iī, -ītum, [trāns + eō], irr., a. and n., *go across, cross over, pass over, go through; pass by, disregard; pass, spend; go beyond, transgress; endure.*

trānsferō, -ferre, -tulī, -lātum, [trāns + ferō], irr., a., *bear across, convey over, transport, transfer, turn.*

trānsfuga, -ae, [trānsfugiō, *desert*], m. and f., *one who joins the enemy, deserter.*

trānsigō, -ere, trānsēgī, trānsāctum, [trāns + agō], 3, a., *pierce through; carry through, bring to an end, conclude, perform, accomplish, transact; settle, agree, make a settlement.*

trānsiliō, -īre, -uī or **-īvī, ——,** [trāns + saliō, *leap*], 4, a. and n., *leap across, spring over, overleap; pass by, neglect, omit; go beyond.*

trānsmittō, -ere, trānsmīsī, trāns-

missum, [trāns + mittō], 3, a. and n., *send across, carry over, bring across, transmit; pass over, cross over, traverse; hand over, intrust, commit, devote; pass, spend; bear, enjoy.*

trānsversus, -a, -um, adj., *turned across, lying across, athwart, cross-wise; at cross purposes, inopportune.* **ex trānversō,** *across, from one side, sideways.* **trānsversae** [sc. **viae**], *cross streets.*

Trebātius, -ī, see **Testa.**

trecentī, -ae, -a, [trēs + centum], num. adj., *three hundred.*

tredecim, or **XIII,** [trēs + decem], num. adj., indecl., *thirteen.*

tremō, -ere, -uī, ——, 3, a. and n., *shake, quake, tremble; tremble at, shudder at.*

tremor, -ōris, [tremō], m., *any tremulous motion; shaking, trembling, tremor; earthquake.*

trepidātiō, -ōnis, [trepidō], f., *confused hurry, alarm, agitation, confusion, consternation, trepidation.*

trepidō, -āre, -āvī, -ātum, [trepidus, *agitated*], 1, n., *hurry with alarm, be in confusion; be agitated; tremble at, be afraid of; waver, hesitate, be in a state of anxiety; flicker, palpitate.*

tribūnal, -ālis, [tribūnus], n., *judgment-seat, tribunal, a raised platform on which were the seats of magistrates.*

tribūnātus, -ūs, [tribūnus], m., *the office of a tribune, tribuneship.*

tribūnīcius, -a, -um, [tribūnus], adj., *of a tribune, tribunitial;*

begun by a tribune, arising from the tribunes.

tribūnus, -ī, [tribus], m., *representative of a tribe, tribune.* **tribūnus plēbis** or **plēbeī,** or simply **tribūnus,** *tribune of the people,* i.e. of the common people or commons, a magistrate whose duty it was to protect the plebeians against the patricians.

tribuō, -ere, tribuī, tribūtum, [tribus], 3, a., *assign, bestow, confer, grant, give; concede, allow; spend, devote; ascribe, attribute; give proper due to.* **alicui nihil tribuere,** *to give a man no preference.* **tantum tribuitur,** *so much respect is paid.*

trīcēnī, -ae, -a, [trīgintā], num. distr. adj., *thirty at a time, thirty each, thirty.*

trīduum, -ī, [trēs + diēs], n., *three days' time, space of three days, three days.*

triennium, -ī or **-iī,** [trēs + annus, sc. **spatium**], n., *three years' time, three years.*

trigeminus, -a, -um, [trēs + geminus], adj., *born three at a time; triple.* As subst., **trigeminī** [sc. **frātrēs**], -ōrum, m., pl., *three brothers, triplet brothers.*

trīste, comp. **trīstius,** [trīstis], adv., *sadly, sorrowfully; harshly, severely; with difficulty.* **trīstius,** *with more difficulty.*

trīstis, -e, adj., *sad, sorrowful, dejected, melancholy, downcast; morose, sullen, peevish, ill-humored; harsh, stern, severe; saddening, dismal, gloomy.*

trīstitia, -ae, [trīstis], f., *sadness,*

sorrow, grief, dejection; disagreeableness, sternness of temper.

triumphō, -āre, -āvī, -ātum, [triumphus], 1, a. and n., *celebrate a triumph, triumph; exult, greatly rejoice.*

triumphus, -ī, m., *triumphal procession, triumph,* the ceremonial entrance of a commander into Rome in celebration of an important victory; *celebration of victory.* **triumphum agere,** *to celebrate a triumph.*

triumvir, -virī, [trēs + vir], m., *one of three associates in office, member of a board of three.* **triumvirī** or **tresvirī capitālēs,** magistrates elected annually by the people and representing our police officials. They had to apprehend and commit to prison criminals, and with the aediles to preserve the public peace; they had the care of public prisons and of executions and could inflict summary punishment on slaves and persons of low rank not citizens. SALL. 55.

Trōia, -ae, f., *Troy.*

tropaeum, -ī, [τρόπαιον], n., *memorial of victory, trophy.*

trucīdō, -āre, -āvī, -ātum, [trux + caedō], 1, a., *slaughter, massacre, butcher.*

truculentus, -a, -um, adj., *fierce, savage, fearful, grim; clownish, rude, rustic.* Esp., **Truculentus, -ī,** m., *The Churl,* the title of a play by Plautus. SEN. 14.

truncus, -ī, m., *stem, stock, trunk.*

tū, tuī, pl., **vōs,** pers. pron., *thou, you.*

tuba, -ae, f., *trumpet, war-trumpet.*

Tuditānus, -ī, m., *M. Semprōnius Tuditānus,* consul 240 B.C. SEN. 14.

tueor, -ērī, tuitus sum, 2, dep., *look at, gaze upon, consider; care for, preserve, guard, uphold, defend, keep, maintain.*

Tullia, -ae, f., *Tullia,* daughter of Cicero and Terentia, born probably 79 or 78 B.C. She was married in 63 B.C. to C. Calpurnius Piso, but was left a widow 57 B.C. The following year she became the wife of Furius Crassipes, a young man of wealth and high position, but was soon divorced. In 50 B.C. she was married to P. Cornelius Dolabella. She died 45 B.C. Though her life was far from fortunate, she appears to have possessed a lofty nature, and was the idol of her father, who was brokenhearted over her death. See **Dolābella.** EP. 3; 9; 14; 18; 21.

Tulliānus, -a, -um, adj., *of or belonging to, named after or proceeding from, Tūllius.* As subst., **Tulliānum, -ī,** n., *the Tulliānum,* a part of the prison in Rome, so called from Servius Tullius, who built it.

Tulliola, -ae, [dim. of **Tullia**], f., *Tulliola,* Cicero's pet name for his daughter Tullia. EP. 8; 9.

Tullius, -a, name of a Roman gens, to which the Cicero family belonged. See **Cicerō.**

Tullus, -ī, m., *L. Volcātius Tullus,* consul 66 B.C. with M'. Aemilius Lepidus. CAT. 1, 6.

tum, adv., *then, at that time; there-*

upon, moreover. **cum — tum,** often *both — and, not only — but also.* **tum vērō,** *then indeed, just then.* **tum — tum — tum,** *sometimes — sometimes — at other times.* **tum — sī,** *then only — if.* **tum quoque,** *even then.*

tumultus, -ūs, [tumeō], m., *commotion, disturbance, tumult, uproar; insurrection, mutiny.*

tumulus, -ī, [tumeō], m., *mound, hillock, hill; grave, sepulchral mound.*

tunc, adv., *then, at that time, just then, thereupon.*

tunica, -ae, f., *undergarment, tunic, shirt.*

turba, -ae, f., *turmoil, uproar, disorder; disorderly multitude, mob; the common crowd, mass.*

turbidus, -a, -um, [turba], adj., *full of confusion, wild, disordered; troubled, disturbed, turbulent.* **turbidus diēs,** *a period of confusion.*

turbulentus, -a, -um, [turba], adj., *disturbed, boisterous, stormy; restless, disordered, troublesome.*

turpis, -e, adj., *ugly, unsightly, repulsive; shameful, base, disgraceful, dishonorable.*

turpiter, comp. **turpius,** sup. **turpissimē,** [turpis], adv., *in an unsightly manner, repulsively; shamefully, basely, disgracefully, dishonorably.*

turpitūdō, -inis, [turpis], f., *unsightliness, repulsiveness; shamefulness, baseness, disgrace, dishonor.*

tūs, tūris, n., *incense, frankincense.*

Tusculānus, -a, -um, [Tusculum],

adj., *Tusculan, of Tusculum,* a town on a spur of the Alban mountains, 15 miles southeast of Rome. As subst., **Tusculānum, -ī,** n., *estate at Tusculum, Tusculan villa,* a favorite villa of Cicero's.

tūtēla, -ae, [tueor], f., *watching, defense, protection; guardianship, wardship; charge, care, trust; preservation, regency.*

tūtō, sup. **tūtissimō,** [tūtus], adv., *safely, securely, in safety.* Sup., *in the greatest safety, most safe.*

tūtor, -ārī, -ātus sum, [tueor], 1, dep., *watch, guard, defend, protect.*

tūtus, -a, -um, [part. of **tueor**], adj., *guarded, safe, secure, out of danger; watchful, cautious.*

tuus, -a, -um, [tū], poss. pron. adj., *thy, thine, your, yours; your own.* As subst., pl., **tuī, -ōrum,** m., *your kinsmen, your friends;* **tua, -ōrum,** n., *your property, your possessions.*

Tycha, -ae, f., *Tycha,* a part of the city of Syracuse. VERR. 53.

Tyranniō, -ōnis, m., *Tyranniōn,* a native of Amisus, in Pontus, taken captive by Lucullus in 72 B.C. and brought to Rome, where he was later manumitted. At Rome *Tyrannion* occupied himself in teaching; but found employment also in arranging the library of Apellicon, which Sulla brought to Rome. Cicero speaks in the highest terms of his learning and ability. EP. 9.

tyrannus, -ī, [τύραννος], m., *ruler, monarch, sovereign, king; despot, tyrant.*

U

über, -eris, n., *udder, breast.*

übertās, -ātis, [**über**], f., *richness, fertility, fruitfulness, productiveness.*

ubi or **ubī,** adv., *of place, where, wheresoever, in what place;* of time, *when, whenever, as soon as;* used in place of a relative pron., *wherewith, by which, with whom, by whom; how.*

ubinam [**ubi** + **nam**], adv., inter., *where? where on earth?* **ubinam gentium sumus?** *Where in the world are we?*

ubīque [**ubī** + **-que**], adv., *anywhere, in any place; in every place, everywhere; in any place whatsoever.*

ulcīscor, ulcīscī, ultus sum, 3, dep., *take vengeance on, punish; avenge, require.*

ūllus, -a, -um, gen. **ūllīus,** adj., *any.* As subst., **ūllus, ūllīus,** m., *anyone, anybody.*

ulterior, -ius, gen. **-ōris,** sup. **ultimus,** [cf. **ultrā**], adj. in the comp. degree, *farther, beyond, more distant, more remote.* Neut. **ulterius,** often as adv., *beyond, farther on, further, more, longer, to a greater degree.* Sup. **ultimus, -a, -um,** *farthest, most distant, uttermost, extreme, last.* **in ultimam prōvinciam,** *to the farthest part of the province.*

ultimus, -a, -um, see **ulterior.**

ultrā [sc. **parte,** from **ulter**], adv. and prep.

(1) Adv., *on the other side, beyond, farther, over, more, besides, in addition.*

(2) Prep. with acc. only, *on the farther side of, beyond, past, over, across; above, exceeding, more than.*

ultrō [cf. **ultrā**], adv., *beyond, on the other side; besides, moreover, of one's own accord, voluntarily.*

Umbrēnus, -ī, m., *P. Umbrēnus,* a freedman, one of the Catilinarian conspirators. Having been engaged in the business of money-lending in Gaul, he was employed to try to win the support of the Allobroges to the conspiracy. CAT. **3,** 6.

umquam, adv., *at any time, ever.*

ūnā [**ūnus**], adv., *together, at once, at the same time.*

unde, adv., *whence, from which place; from which, from whom.*

ūndecim, or **XI.,** [**ūnus** + **decem**], num. adj., indecl., *eleven.*

ūndecimus, -a, -um, or **XI.,** [**ūndecim**], num. adj., *eleventh.*

ūndēquīnquāgēsimus, -a, -um, [**ūndēquīnquāgintā**], num. adj., *forty-ninth.*

undique [**unde** + **-que**], adv., *from all sides, on all sides, all around, everywhere.*

unguentum, -ī, [**unguō**], n., *ointment, perfume.*

ūnicē [**ūnicus**]. adv., *singularly. uniquely, above all others.*

ūniversus, -a, -um, [**ūnus** + **versus**], adj., *all together, whole, entire; general, universal.* **in ūniversum,** *in general, generally; taken in the whole; as a general rule.* As subst., **ūniversī, -ōrum,** m., pl., *the whole body of men, all men.*

ūnus, -a, -um, gen. ūnīus, sometimes in poetry, ūnius, num. adj., one, one only, a single one; alone, sole, single; one and the same. omnēs ad ūnum, (they) to a man.

urbānus, -a, -um, in titles sometimes abbreviated urb., [urbs], adj., of the city; in city fashion, polite, refined, courteous. As subst., urbāna, -ōrum, n., pl., the affairs of the city.

urbs, urbis, f., city; especially the city, Rome.

urgeō, -ēre, ūrsī, ——, 2, a. and n., press, press on, push, impel, urge; press hard, weigh down, oppress; urge on, drive.

urget, see urgeō.

Urios, -us, acc. Urion, m., lit., giver of fair winds (to sailors). Iuppiter Urios, God of Fair Winds. VERR. 57.

ūsitātus, -a, -um, [part. of ūsitor; freq. of ūtor], adj., usual, wonted, customary; common, ordinary; familiar.

ūspiam, adv., at any place, anywhere, somewhere.

ūsquam, adv., anywhere, at any place, in any place, to any place.

ūsque, adv., even to, even, as far as; all the way, continuously, as long as.

ūsūra, -ae, [ūtor], f., use, enjoyment; interest on money, usury.

ūsūrpō, -āre, -āvī, -ātum, [ūsus, cf. rapiō], 1, a., lit., seize for use; make use of, use, employ; practice, adopt; speak of, talk of; resort to.

ūsus, -ūs, [ūtor], m., use, employment, enjoyment; practice, experience, skill; intercourse, familiarity; benefit, profit, advantage, service, need; intimacy. esse ūsuī alicui, to be of benefit to anyone.

ut or utī, adv., of place, where; of time, as, as soon as, just as; of manner, interrogative, how? in what way? in what manner? relative, as, as for instance, seeing that, as if, on the supposition that. ut prīmum, as soon as. ut — ita, so — as, while — still.

ut or utī, conj. with subj., of result, that, so that; of purpose, in order that, that; of concession, though, although.

uter, -tra, -trum, gen. utrīus, pron. adj., which of two, whichever, either of two.

uterque, utraque, utrumque, gen. utrīusque, [uter + -que], adj., each, either; one and the other, both; pl. as subst., each party, each side, both. utrāque in rē, in either case.

ūtilis, -e, [ūtor], adj., useful, serviceable; profitable, expedient, advantageous; fit, suitable.

ūtilitās, -ātis, [ūtilis], f., utility, use; profit, benefit, advantage, expediency.

utinam [utī + nam], adv., oh that! if only! would that!

utique [utī + que], adv., in any case, by all means; with a neg., not by any means, not at all; in particular, especially, at least.

ūtor, ūtī, ūsus sum, 3, dep., use, employ, make use of; exercise, practice, perform; serve oneself with, enjoy, indulge in; find to be, find.

utrimque [uterque], adv., *on both sides, on either hand, from both sides.*

utrōque [uterque], adv., *in either direction, to both places.* **auctōrēs [mē] trahunt utrōque,** *the authorities lead me in both directions,* i.e. *they are divided.*

utrum [uter], adv., in direct questions indicated only by the inflection of the voice in translating; in indirect questions, *whether.* utrum — an, *whether — or.*

uxor, -ōris, f., *wife.*

V

vacillō, -āre, -āvī, -ātum, 1, n., *sway to and fro, stagger, totter; waver, hesitate, vacillate, falter.*

vacō, -āre, -āvī, -ātum, 1, n., *be empty, be vacant; be without; be idle, be at leisure, have time.* **corporī vacāre,** *to be free to attend to one's physical needs.*

vacuēfaciō, -facere, -fēcī, -factum, [vacuus + faciō], 3, a., *make empty, make vacant, clear, free.*

vacuus, -a, -um, [vacō], adj., *empty, void, vacant, free, without; idle, unemployed, unengaged, at leisure; free from care.* **vacuī temporis nihil,** *no leisure time, no leisure.*

vadimōnium, -ī or -iī, [vas, *bail*], n., *guarantee* of an appearance before a tribunal at a given time by bail; *bail-bond, bail, security.* **vadimōnium dēserere,** *to forfeit one's bail.*

vādō, -ere, ——, ——, 3, n., *go,* especially *go in haste, rush, proceed rapidly.*

vadum, -ī, [cf. vādō, *go*], n., *shallow place, shoal, ford, shallow crossing; body of water, sea.*

vāgīna, -ae, f., *scabbard, sheath.*

vāgiō, -īre, -iī, ——, 4, n., *squeal, cry, squall, scream.*

vagor, -ārī, -ātus sum, [vagus], 1, dep., *stroll about, wander, roam, rove; be spread, extend, spread abroad, diffuse itself.*

valdē, comp. valdius, [for valide from validus], adv., *strongly, exceedingly; very much. very; certainly.*

valeō, -ēre, -uī, -itum, 2, n., *be strong, be vigorous, be healthy; have power, avail, prevail, succeed; be able, be capable.* **plūrimum valēre,** *to have very great weight, to exert very great influence.* **permultum valēre,** *to be exceedingly powerful, to possess very great influence.* **multum valēre,** *to be very powerful, to have great influence, be very important.* **nihil valēre,** *to be powerless.* **cūrā ut valeās,** *do take care of yourself.* Imp. **valē,** as a greeting, *farewell, good-by.*

Valerius, see Flaccus, (2) and (3); Messalla.

valētūdō, -inis, [valeō], f., *health, state of health; ill health, sickness, feebleness, weakness.*

vallēs, -is, f., *valley, vale, hollow.*

vāllō, -āre, -āvī, -ātum, [vāllum], 1, a., *fortify with a rampart: fortify, protect, defend.*

valvae, -ārum, f., pl., *pair of door-leaves, folding doors.*

vānēscō, -ere, ——, ——, [vāneō, from vānus], 3, n., *pass away, disappear, vanish; get thinner.*

vānitās, -ātis, [vānus], f., *emptiness,*

aimlessness, absence of purpose;
deceit, untruth, fickleness; vanity,
vain-glory.

vānus, -a, -um, adj., *containing*
nothing, void, vacant; ground-
less, unmeaning, fruitless; osten-
tatious, boastful, vain; deceptive,
delusive, untrustworthy; to no
purpose, for naught.

variē [**varius**], adv., *variously,*
changeably, differently, in vari-
ous ways; with varying for-
tune.

varietās, -ātis, [**varius**], f., *diver-*
sity, variety; difference, disagree-
ment, dissension; change, vicis-
situde. **bellum in multā vari-**
etāte versātum, *a war waged*
with many vicissitudes.

varius, -a, -um, adj., *diversified,*
varying, changeable, various,
manifold, versatile; diverse, dif-
ferent.

Varrō, -ōnis, m., *M.* Terentius
Varrō, " the most learned of the
Romans," born 116 B.C. In the
Civil War he held a command
under Pompey, but was pardoned
by Caesar, and afterwards devoted himself exclusively to
literary pursuits. He wrote
voluminously, on a great variety
of subjects. He was an intimate
friend of Cicero. He died 28
B.C. EP. 24.

vās, vāsis, pl. **vāsa, vāsōrum,** n.,
vessel, dish, utensil.

vāstātiō, -ōnis, [**vāstō**], f., *laying*
waste, devastating, devastation.

vāstitās, -ātis, [**vāstus**], f., *waste,*
desert; desolation, ruin, destruc-
tion.

vāstō, -āre, -āvī, -ātum, [**vāstus**],

1, a., *make desert, lay waste, make*
desolate, devastate, destroy.

vāstus, -a, -um, adj., *waste, desert;*
empty, vast. **vāstus animus,** *an*
insatiable spirit, a restless spirit.

Vatia, -ae, m., [**vatius,** *bow-legged*],
m., name of a family of the Ser-
vilian gens. Two members are
mentioned in this book :

(1) *P. Servīlius Vatia,* grandson of Q. Metellus Macedonicus,
consul 79 B.C. In 78 B.C. he was
proconsul of Cilicia, and went
against the pirates that infested
the southern coast of Asia Minor.
He was successful, receiving the
honorary surname *Isauricus* for
the reduction of the Isauri. He
was honored with a triumph,
74 B.C. He died 44 B.C. IMP.
P. 23.

(2) *P. Servīlius Vatia,* praetor
in 54 B.C., belonged originally
to the aristocratic party, but
espoused Caesar's cause on the
breaking out of Civil War, and
was consul with Caesar in 48 B.C.
After the death of Caesar in 44,
he supported Cicero and the
rest of the autocratic party in
opposition to Antony, but became reconciled to Antony and
was again consul in 41 B.C.
PHIL. 4; 8.

-ve, enclitic conj., [**vel**], *or, or if*
you please, or also; after a negative, *and.*

vectīgal, -ālis, [**vehō**], n., *revenue*
of the state, tax, impost, duty,
tribute.

vectīgālis, -is, [**vectīgal**], m., *payer*
of tribute, tributary.

vehemēns, -entis, adj., *eager, ar-*

dent, impetuous, vehement; strong, forcible, vigorous, effective.

vehementer, comp. **vehementius,** sup. **vehementissimē,** [**vehemēns**], adv., *eagerly, impetuously, vehemently; strongly, exceedingly, very much, extremely.*

vel [old imp. of **volō**], conj., *or, or if you will, or even.* **vel — vel,** *either — or, whether — or.* **vel potius,** *or rather.*

vel [**volō**], adv., *or even, or indeed, assuredly, certainly; perhaps, it may be; very, utmost.* **vel maximē,** *in the very highest degree, most of all.*

vēlōcitās, -ātis, [**vēlōx,** *swift*], f., *swiftness, speed, fleetness, rapidity, velocity.*

vēlum, -ī, n., *sail;* by metonymy, *awning, curtain, veil.*

velut [**vel** + **ut**], adv., *even as, just as, like as, like; as, for instance, for example.* **velut sī** or **velutsī,** *just as if, just as though, as if, as though.*

vēna, -ae, f., *blood-vessel, vein, artery;* pl., *veins, heart.*

vēnābulum, -ī, [**vēnor**], n., *hunting-spear.*

vēnātiō, -ōnis, [**vēnor**], f., *hunting, the chase; a hunt, combat of wild beasts; game.*

vēnditātiō, -ōnis, [**vēnditō**], f., *offering for sale; specious display; vaunting, boasting, puffing.*

vēnditō, -āre, -āvī, -ātum, [freq. of **vēndō**], 1, a., *keep offering for sale, try to sell; offer for sale; deal in, sell; give for a bribe; recommend.*

vēndō, -ere, vēndidī, vēnditum,

[**vēnum,** *sale* + **dō**], 3, a., *sell; sell for a bribe, give for pay, betray.*

venēficus, -ī, [**venēnum,** cf. **faciō**], m., *poisoner.*

venēnum, -ī, n., *poison, venom;* by metonymy, *magical potion, charm.*

vēneō, -īre, -īvī or **-iī, -ĭtum,** [**vēnum,** *sale,* + **eō**], irr., n., *go to sale, be sold.*

venerābilis, -e, [**veneror**], adj., *worthy of respect, reverend, venerable.*

venerābundus, -a, -um, [**veneror**], adj., *venerating, reverential, with respect; full of awe.*

veneror, -ārī, -ātus sum, 1, dep., *reverence, worship, adore; venerate, do homage to; beseech.*

venia, -ae, f., *indulgence, favor, kindness; permission, pardon, forgiveness.*

veniō, -īre, vēnī, ventum, 4, n., *come; come into, enter; approach; spring; result, occur.* **ventum est,** *they* (or *he*) *came, have come.* **fac veniās,** *be sure to come.*

vēnor, -ārī, -ātus sum, 1, dep., *hunt, chase.*

venter, -tris, m., *belly, paunch.*

Ventidius, -ī or **-iī,** m., *P. Ventidius Bassus,* a celebrated Roman general, and an aid of Caesar's in Gaul and in the Civil War. After Caesar's death, Ventidius sided with Antony. In 39 B.C. Antony sent Ventidius into Asia, where he defeated the Parthians and Labienus.

ventus, -ī, m., *wind.*

Venus, -eris, f., *Venus,* goddess of

love, identified with the Greek Aphrodite. VERR. 55; 60.

venustās, -ātis, [venus, *charm*], f., *comeliness, attractiveness, beauty; artistic grace, taste, art.*

vēr, vēris, n., *spring, spring-time.* ineunte vēre, *at the opening of spring.*

verber, -eris, n., *lash, whip, scourge;* by metonymy, *blow, stroke, scourging, flogging.*

verberō, -āre, -āvī, -ātum, [verber], I, a., *beat, lash, scourge, flog; attack, chastise, plague, torment.*

verbum, -ī, n., *word.* verba facere, *to speak.*

vērē [vērus], adv., *really, truly, in fact; properly, rightly.* ut vērē dīcam, *to tell the truth.* quō vērius, *that with greater accuracy.*

verēcundia, -ae, [verēcundus], f., *coyness, shyness, modesty, sense of shame, bashfulness; respect.*

vereor, -ērī, -itus sum, 2, dep., *reverence, stand in awe of, revere; fear, be afraid, dread, apprehend; respect.* verērī nē, *to fear that.* verērī ut, *to fear that — not.*

vēritās, -ātis, [vērus], f., *truth, truthfulness; sincerity, straightforwardness; reality, fact.*

vērnus, -a, -um, [vēr], adj., *of spring, spring.*

vērō [vērus], adv., *truly, certainly, in truth; but in fact, however, but.* immō vērō, *no indeed, nay rather.*

Verrēs, -is, m., a Roman family name. *C. Cornēlius Verrēs,* propraetor in Sicily in 73 B.C., and later accused by Cicero in the

famous speeches against him. He was condemned and forced to retire to Marseilles. He was proscribed by M. Antony in 43. VERR. 52, *et seq.*

versō, -āre, -āvī, -ātum, [freq. of vertō], I, a., *turn often, keep turning, turn over, turn; manage, direct; revolve, consider.* Pass., versor, -ārī, -ātus sum, *move about, dwell, remain, stay; be situated, be associated, be; be engaged in, be busy, be employed.*

versus [part. of vertō], adv. and prep. with acc., *turned in the direction of, towards, facing.*

versus, -ūs, [vertō], m., *line, verse.*

vertō, -ere, vertī, versum, 3, a. and n., *turn, turn back, move; ply, drive.*

vērum, -ī, [vērus], n., *truth, fact, reality.*

vērum [vērus], adv., *truly; but in truth, but notwithstanding, but, however, still.* nōn modo — vērum, *not only — but.* nōn modo — vērum etiam, *not only — but also.*

vērus, -a, -um, adj., *true, real, genuine, well founded; proper, reasonable, just; truthful, veracious.*

Vērus, -ī, m., *Vērus,* who, apart from the fact that he seems to have been a tenant who leased the farm mentioned in PLIN. 10, is otherwise unknown.

vesper, -erī or -eris, m., *evening-star;* by metonymy, *evening, eve.* Loc. vesperī, *in the evening.* ad vesperum, *at eventide.*

vespera, -ae, f., *evening.*

Vesta, -ae, [cf. Ἑστία], f., *Vesta,* a Roman divinity, daughter of Saturn and Ops; in her service were the Vestal Virgins, who kept a fire always burning on her altar.

Vestālis, -e, [Vesta], adj., *of Vesta, Vestal.* **virgō Vestālis,** *Vestal virgin.*

vester, -tra, -trum, [vōs], poss. pron. adj., *your, yours.* **vestrum est prōvidēre,** *it is your duty to make provision.*

vēstīgium, -ī or **-iī,** n., *sole of the foot;* by metonymy, *foot, step, foot-print, track; trace, sign, vestige.* **ē vēstīgiō,** *immediately.*

vestiō, -īre, -īvī, -ītum, [vestis], 4, a., *cover with a garment, provide with clothing, clothe; array, adorn;* in pass., *clothe oneself with, wear.*

vestis, -is, f., *garment, covering for the body; clothes, clothing, robe;* in pl., **vestēs, -ium,** f., *trousseau.*

vestītus, -ūs, [vestiō], m., *clothing, dress, apparel, attire.* **vestītum mūtāre,** *to put on mourning.*

Vesuvius, -ī or **-iī,** m., *Vesuvius,* a volcano near Naples.

veterānus, -a, -um, [vetus], adj., *old, veteran.* As subst., **veterānī, -ōrum,** m., pl., *veteran soldiers, veterans.*

vetō, -āre, vetuī, vetitum, 1, a., *will that something shall not be; oppose, forbid, prohibit.*

vetus, -eris, sup. **veterrimus,** adj., *old, aged; of long standing; of a former time, former, earlier, ancient.*

vetustās, -ātis, [vetus], f., *old age, age; long duration, long standing; great age, antiquity, ancient times.*

vexātiō, -ōnis, [vexō], f., *disturbing, harassing; distress, hardship, trouble.*

vexō, -āre, -āvī, -ātum, [freq. of vehō], 1, a., *shake, jolt; disturb, harass, trouble, waste, aggravate.*

via, -ae, f., *way, road, street, highway;* by metonymy, *passage, march, journey; mode, manner.*

viāticum, -ī, [viāticus, from via], n., *traveling-money, traveling expenses, viaticum.*

viātor, -ōris, [via], m., *wayfarer, traveler; court-officer, magistrate's attendant, summoner.*

Vibō, -ōnis, f., *Vibō,* a city in the southwestern part of Italy, on the west coast of Bruttium. It was originally a Greek settlement with the name *Hippōnium* (Ἱππώνιον), but it received a Roman colony 192 B.C. In Cicero's time it was a flourishing municipal town. EP. 5; 6.

vibrō, -āre, -āvī, -ātum, 1, a. and n., *brandish, shake, hurl, throw; quiver, gleam, flash.*

vīcēsimus, -a, -um, [vīgintī], num. adj., *twentieth.*

vīcīnus, -a, -um, [vīcus, street, quarter], adj., *of the neighborhood, neighboring, near, adjacent.* As subst., **vīcīnus, -ī,** m., *neighbor.*

(vicis), gen. **vicis,** acc. **vicem,** abl. **vice,** pl. nom. **vicēs,** acc. **vicēs** or **vicīs,** dat. and abl. **vicibus,** f., *change, interchange; remuneration; lot, condition; post, office, duty.* **vicem,** acc. used

as adverb, *to the extent of.*
vicem meam, *to the extent of my own turn, on my own account.*
in vicem, *mutually, in turn.*
vice ūnīus exanimēs, *in mortal fear for their single representative.*
vicissim [vicis], adv., *on the other hand, on the contrary, again, in turn, back; mutually, in turns.*
vicissitūdō, -inis, [vicis], f., *change from one thing to another; interchange, alternation, vicissitude.*
victima, -ae, f., *beast for sacrifice, sacrificial victim; victim sacrificed to the gods after some successful event or victory; victim.*
victor, -ōris, [vincō], m., *conqueror, victor;* often in apposition with the force of an adj., *victorious, conquering.*
victōria, -ae, [victor], f., *victory; success, triumph.*
victrīx, -īcis, [victor], f., *conqueress, victress; she that is victorious.*
vīctus, -ūs, [vīvō], m., *that which sustains life, means of living; nourishment, provisions, food; way of life, mode of living.*
vīcus, -ī, m., properly *abode;* hence, *street, quarter,* of a city; *village, hamlet; country-seat, villa.*
dēlicet [for vidēre licet], adv., *it is evident, clearly, plainly, obviously, evidently; of course, you see, forsooth, to wit, namely;* often used ironically.
videō, -ēre, vīdī, vīsum, 2, a., *see, discern, perceive; look at, observe; understand, comprehend; see to, care for, provide.* Pass., videor, vidērī, vīsus sum, *be seen, appear, seem, be regarded;*

impers., vidētur, *it seems right, it seems best.*
viduus, -a, -um, adj., *deprived, destitute, widowed, bereaved; unmarried.*
vigeō, -ēre, -uī, ——, 2, n., *be vigorous, be strong, thrive, flourish, bloom.*
vigilāns, -antis, [part. of vigilō], adj., *watchful, vigilant, anxious, careful.*
vigilia, -ae, [vigil], f., *watching, wakefulness, staying awake; watch, guard; watchfulness, vigilance;* pl., *watchmen, sentinels.*
vigilō, -āre, -āvī, -ātum, [vigil], 1, a. and n., *keep awake, be wakeful, spend* (time) *awake or watching; be watchful, keep watch, be vigilant, watch.*
vīgintī or XX., num. adj., indecl., *twenty.*
vigor, -ōris, [vigeō], m., *liveliness, activity; force, vigor.*
vīlis, -e, adj., *of small price, of little value, cheap; poor, mean, worthless, base, vile.*
vīlitās, -ātis, [vīlis], f., *cheapness.*
vīlla, -ae, f., *country-seat, farm-dwelling, villa, farm.*
vīnārius, -a, -um, [vīnum], adj., *of wine, for wine.* cella vīnāria, *wine cellar.*
vinciō, -īre, vinxī, vinctum, 4, a., *bind, fetter, tie; fasten, restrain, confine.*
vincō, -ere, vīcī, victum, 3, a. and n., *conquer, overcome, defeat, subdue; be superior, excel, surpass; convince, get the better of, demonstrate.*
vinculum, or in shorter form vin-

clum, -ī, [vinciō], n., *band, fetter, rope, cord; bond, tie, relation.*

vindex, -icis, m. and f., *defender, protector; avenger, punisher, champion.* vindicēs rērum capitālium, *public executioners.*

vindicō, -āre, -āvī, -ātum, [vindex], 1, a., *lay claim to, claim, assume; protect, defend, liberate, deliver; avenge, punish, take vengeance; excuse.*

Viniciānus, -ī, m., *Caelius Viniciānus.* See Caelius.

vīnulentia, -ae, [vīnulentus, *full of wine*), f., *wine-bibbing, intoxication from wine; propensity to immoderate wine-bibbing.*

vīnum, -ī, n., *wine.*

violō, -āre, -āvī, -ātum, [cf. vīs], 1, a., *treat with violence, injure, outrage; profane, desecrate.*

vir, virī, m., *man, husband; man of courage, hero.*

virginalis, -e, [virgō], adj., *of a maiden, maidenly.*

virgō, -inis, [cf. vireō], f., *maid, maiden, girl, virgin.* fīlia virgō, *a maiden daughter.*

viriditās, -ātis, [viridis, *green*], f., *green color, greenness, verdure; freshness, briskness, vigor.*

virīlis, -e, [vir], adj., *of a man, like a man, manly; full-grown, mature; bold, spirited, noble.*

virtūs, -ūtis, [vir], f., *manliness; courage, fortitude, bravery; moral worth, goodness, virtue, merit; prowess;* in pl., virtūtēs, *acts of bravery.* virtūs animī, *moral courage.* Personified, Virtūs, -ūtis, *goddess of Valor, Virtūs.*

vīrus, -ī, n., *potent juice, medicinal liquid, poison, venom, virus.*

vīs, acc. vim, abl. vī, pl. vīrēs, -ium, f., *force, strength, energy, power; violence, compulsion; quantity, number;* pl. often *military forces, forces, troops.* vīs fortūnae, *the bounty of fortune.* vīs et nātūra, *natural power.* vīs amīcitiae, *the essence of friendship.* per vim, *violently, by violence.*

vīscus, -eris, often in pl., vīscera, -um, n., *internal organs, vitals, inwards, viscera; inmost part, bowels, center, heart.*

vīsō, vīsere, vīsī, vīsum, [freq. of videō], 3, a., *look at attentively, view, behold; go to see, visit.*

vīta, -ae, [vīvō], f., *life, existence; mode of life, course of life; career.*

vītālis, -e, [vīta], adj., *of life, vital; lively.*

vitiōsus, -a, -um, comp. vitiōsior, sup. vitiōsissimus, [vitium], adj., *full of faults, defective; wicked, depraved, vicious, evil.*

vitium, -ī or -iī, n., *fault, blemish, defect; failing, offense, vice, crime; defect, deficiency; evil.*

vītō, -āre, -āvī, -ātum, 1, a. and n., *shun, avoid, evade.*

vituperātiō, -ōnis, [vituperō], f., *blaming, blame, censure, reproach, charge.*

vituperō, -āre, -āvī, ——, [vitium], 1, a., *injure; find fault with, blame, reproach, disparage.* vituperāre senectūtis, *to charge against old age.*

vīvō, vīvere, vīxī, vīctum, 3, n., *live, be alive; pass the time, reside, dwell; support life, sustain life; live at ease; last, endure.*

vīvus, -a, -um, [cf. vīvō], adj.,

alive, living, having life; green, vigorous. As subst., **vīvī, -ōrum,** m., pl., the living, those who are alive.

vix, adv., hardly, with difficulty, scarcely, barely.

vixdum [vix + dum], adv., scarcely yet, hardly, but just.

vocō, -āre, -āvī, -ātum, [vōx], 1, a. and n., call, summon, invoke; call together, convoke; call by name, name, designate.

vōcula, -ae, [dim. of vōx], f., weak voice, small voice, poor voice.

volēns, -entis, [volō, wish], adj., willing, glad, eager; well-wishing, favorable, kindly, propitious, gracious.

volō, velle, voluī, irr., a., will, wish, desire; intend, purpose, mean; claim, assume, assert. **omnēs ūnum volunt,** all have the same opinion.

volō, -āre, -āvī, -ātūrus, 1, n., fly; move swiftly, speed, hasten.

Volturcius, -ī or **-iī,** m., T. Volturcius, a native of Croton, one of the Catilinarian conspirators. After his arrest at the Mulvian Bridge he turned state's evidence, was pardoned, and was rewarded for the information he gave. CAT. 3, ei seq.; SALL. 52.

voluntārius, -a, -um, [voluntās], adj., of one's free will, willing; willful, intentional, voluntary.

voluntās, -ātis, [volō, wish], f., will, wish, inclination, desire; purpose, aim; good-will, favor. **sī vestra voluntās feret,** if such be your pleasure. **summā voluntāte alicuius,** with the free consent

of anyone. **ex voluntāte,** in accordance with the wishes of.

voluptās, -ātis, [cf. volō], f., pleasure, delight, enjoyment; gratification, satisfaction. **voluptātem capere,** to take delight, to receive pleasure.

volvō, -ere, volvī, volūtum, 3, a., cause to revolve, roll, turn over; ponder, think over, reflect on, consider. **volvere sēcum,** to ponder in one's mind.

vōs, see tū.

vōsmet [vōs + -met], strengthened form of vōs.

vōtum, -ī, [voveō], n., vow, pledge; wish, desire, prayer.

voveō, -ēre, vōvī, vōtum, 2, a., make a vow, promise solemnly, pledge, dedicate, consecrate; wish, desire, wish for.

vōx, vōcis, [cf. vocō], f., voice, sound; call, cry, speech, word, utterance, saying. **ūnā vōce,** with unanimity.

vulgāris, -e, [vulgus], adj., of the multitude, common; commonplace, low, mean, vulgar, ordinary.

vulgātus, -a, -um, comp. vulgātior, [part. of vulgō, to make common], adj., common, public; commonly known, notorious; usual.

vulgus, -ī, n., the common people, public, crowd, throng, mob, rabble, populace.

vulnerō, -āre, -āvī, -ātum, [vulnus], 1, a., wound, hurt, injure, harm, pain.

vulnus, -eris, n., wound, injury; blow, stroke; disaster, misfortune, calamity.

vultur, -uris, [according to some from volō, to fly], m., vulture.

vultus, -ūs, m., *look, expression; features, face, countenance, visage.*

X

Xenocratēs, -is, m., *Xenócratēs,* an academic philosopher. He died in 314 B.C., at the age of 82. SEN. 7.

Z

Zēnō, -ōnis, m., *Zēnō,* the founder of the Stoic school of philosophy. He is said to have presided over his school for 58 years, and to have died at the age of 98. SEN. 7. See Companion, page 547.

INDEX TO GRAMMAR AND SYNTAX

INDEX TO GRAMMAR AND SYNTAX

References are to sections.

223

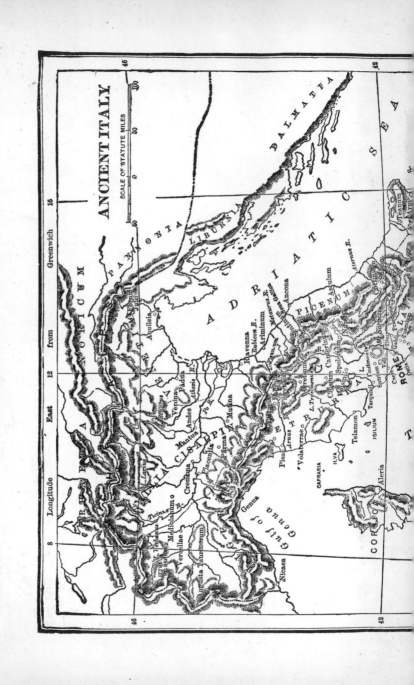